Fourth Edition

EVERYTHING'S AN argument

with readings

Andrea A. Lunsford
STANFORD UNIVERSITY

John J. Ruszkiewicz
UNIVERSITY OF TEXAS AT AUSTIN

Keith Walters
PORTLAND STATE UNIVERSITY

BEDFORD / ST. MARTIN'S
BOSTON ◆ NEW YORK

For Bedford/St. Martin's

Developmental Editors: John Elliott, Genevieve Hamilton
Associate Editor: Laura King
Senior Production Editors: Shuli Traub, Karen Baart, Rosemary Jaffe
Senior Production Supervisor: Nancy Myers
Marketing Manager: Karita dos Santos
Editorial Assistant: Katherine Paarlberg
Production Assistants: Sarah Ulicny, Blake Royer, Kristen Merrill
Copyeditor: Alice Vigliani
Photo Research: Robin Raffer
Text Design: Anna Palchik
Cover Design: Donna Lee Dennison
Cover Photos: (clockwise from top) Copyright © Royalty-Free/Corbis; Copyright © Andersen Ross/Jupiter Images; Copyright © Bob Sacha/Corbis; Copyright © Ryan Red Corn from Red Hand Media; Copyright © Webstream/Alamy; Copyright © StockTrek/Getty Images; Copyright © Joseph Sohm, Chromo-Sohm, Inc./Corbis
Composition: Pine Tree Composition, Inc.
Printing and Binding: R.R. Donnelley & Sons Company

President: Joan E. Feinberg
Editorial Director: Denise B. Wydra
Editor in Chief: Karen S. Henry
Director of Marketing: Karen Melton Soeltz
Director of Editing, Design, and Production: Marcia Cohen
Managing Editor: Elizabeth M. Schaaf

Library of Congress Control Number: 2006925050

Manufactured in the United States of America.

1 0 9 8 7
f e d c

For information, write: Bedford/St. Martin's, 75 Arlington Street, Boston, MA 02116 (617-399-4000)

ISBN 10: 0–312–44750–7
ISBN 13: 978–0–312–44750–2

Acknowledgments

Acknowledgments and copyrights appear at the back of the book on pages 1092–1102, which constitute an extension of the copyright page. It is a violation of the law to reproduce these selections by any means whatsoever without the written permission of the copyright holder.

PREFACE

Everything's an Argument with Readings remains a labor of love for us, a lively introduction to rhetoric drawn directly from our experiences teaching persuasive writing. The chapters still practically write themselves, and we take special pleasure in discovering fresh and provocative everyday arguments that illuminate the ways we all use language—both verbal and visual—to assert our presence in the world. Apparently, the book continues to strike a chord with many students and instructors who have made *Everything's an Argument with Readings* a best-seller in its field since its debut. We offer now a fourth edition, thoroughly revised to reach even more writers and instructors and to account for changes we see in the way arguments are framed and circulated throughout the world.

The purposefully controversial title of this text sums up three key assumptions we share. First, language provides the most powerful means of understanding the world and of using that understanding to help shape lives. Second, arguments seldom if ever have only two sides: rather, they present a dizzying array of perspectives, often with as many "takes" on a subject as there are arguers. Understanding arguments, then, calls for carefully considering a full range of perspectives before coming to judgment. Third, and most important, all language—including the language of sound and images or of symbol systems other than writing—is in some way argumentative or persuasive, pointing in a direction and asking for response. From the latest blog entry to the presidential seal, from the American flag to the Toyota Prius green-leaf logo, from the latest hip-hop hit to the brand identity of Nike, texts everywhere beckon for response. People walk, talk, and breathe persuasion very much as they breathe the air: *everything* is a potential argument.

So our purpose in *Everything's an Argument with Readings* is to present argument as something that's as natural and everyday as an old pair of sneakers, as something we do almost from the moment we are born (in fact, an infant's first cry is as poignant a claim as we can imagine), and as something that's worthy of careful attention and practice. In pursuing this goal, we try to use ordinary language whenever possible and to keep our use of specialized terminology to a minimum. But we also see argument, and want students to see it, as a craft both delicate and powerful. So we have designed *Everything's an Argument with Readings* to be itself an argument for argument, with a voice that aims to appeal to readers cordially but that doesn't hesitate to make demands on them when appropriate. To emphasize this point, we've added a new boxed activity in every rhetorical chapter of the new edition: "If Everything's an Argument . . ." asks students to think critically about this book as itself an argument and to analyze rhetorical choices made by the authors and editors in such areas as cover images, examples and illustrations throughout the text, and the structure of chapters.

We also aim to balance attention to the critical *reading* of arguments (analysis) with attention to the *writing* of arguments (production). Moreover, we have tried to demonstrate both activities with lively—and realistic—examples, on the principle that the best way to appreciate an argument may be to see it in action. Indeed, we continue to work hard to try to enhance the power of the examples, expand the range of texts we present, and include works oriented toward the concerns of college students in all their diversity. In this edition, the six new full-length arguments in the rhetorical text (out of the ten such models) include a student newspaper article on why *Napoleon Dynamite* became a cult film among young people and a student's detailed formal proposal to improve wheelchair access on her campus.

In the last two editions, we tried to broaden the use of visual media throughout. We've intensified that effort in this latest edition, with every chapter presenting new images and fresh argumentative situations. The new full-color design of the fourth edition allows us to integrate coverage of visual argument more thoroughly throughout each chapter and to include a new boxed visual analysis activity called "Not Just Words" in every rhetorical chapter.

This fourth edition also features a reorganization and streamlining of the early chapters to focus more clearly and emphatically on *pathos*, *ethos*, and *logos*, giving students a firmer grounding in these central Aristotelian concepts before they begin to study and practice specific kinds of arguments. In particular, we have integrated much of the information from the former "Arguments Based on Values" chapter into the three chapters on these key concepts.

Based on advice from reviewers, we've added two new chapters to the rhetoric. Chapter 5, "Thinking Rhetorically," helps students put into practice what they've learned in Chapters 1–4; it models the skills of analysis and close reading of arguments and ends with a Guide to Writing a Rhetorical Analysis that provides students with detailed guidelines for carrying out rhetorical analyses of their own. Chapter 7, "Arguments of Fact," guides students in analyzing the kinds of factual assertions made by journalists, scientists, politicians, and others, and in writing their own compelling arguments based on factual claims. Throughout, we have tried to encourage students to be more critical in their evaluation of factual sources; and given the problems that reviewers of the book tell us students are having in judging potential source materials, we have added two "source maps" modeling evaluations of print and electronic sources in Chapter 19, "Evaluating and Using Sources."

We have paid particular attention in this revision to issues of style and presentation. The former chapter on figurative language and argument, retitled "Style in Arguments," now includes discussion of more basic elements of style such as syntax and punctuation. In addition, the former chapter on spoken arguments has been expanded into a new chapter called "Presenting Arguments," which discusses print and multimedia formats, such as blogs and Webcasts, as well as oral presentations.

In selecting arguments for the anthology, we've tried to choose topics of interest and concern to the students we teach just as we have sought to finds texts and issues worth arguing about. In choosing new selections, we have sought readings that will challenge students to consider new perspectives on topics they may feel they already understand and, in particular, to contextualize themselves in a world characterized by increasing globalization. We have retained several of the topics that have worked especially well in earlier editions—body image, media stereotypes, sports and politics, bilingualism in America, language and identity, and religion in public life. In revising these chapters we have tried to find a balance between including texts that students and teachers reported finding useful and instructive and adding new ones that treat contemporary issues while leading us to think about argumentation and about our world in novel ways. For example, how and why are humorous approaches to ethnic stereotypes simultaneously as potent and dangerous as they are? How does the rising importance of religion in American public life compare to the changing role of religion in other countries? How does such knowledge help us understand ourselves and others and debates in different societies?

In addition to including many new selections in the chapters on body image, media stereotypes, sports and politics, and religion in public life, we have added two new chapters treating timely topics: the competing efforts to define, create, and sometimes mandate diversity on college and university campuses ("What Should 'Diversity on Campus' Mean?") and the gap between the ways Americans see themselves and the ways they are often seen by citizens of other countries, an issue of continuing importance since the events of September 11, 2001 ("Why Do They Love Us? Why Do They Hate Us?").

The anthology in this edition is organized into chapters, rather than clusters within chapters, as were the second and third editions. We trust this way of arranging the material will better assist teachers as they help students interact with the arguments presented here.

Finally, in response to requests from instructors who've used earlier editions, we've included longer, more complex arguments even as we have sought to include a broader range of arguments, including book reviews, research-based writing, and research writing itself. We continue to reproduce the arguments we include as they originally appeared to the greatest extent possible because appearance is such a crucial component of any written, visual, or electronic argument. As Demosthenes contended, the three most important parts of any message remain "delivery, delivery, and delivery."

Here is a summary of the key features that continue to characterize *Everything's an Argument with Readings* and of the major new features in this edition:

Key Features

Two books in one, neatly linked. Up front is a brief guide to argument; in back is a thematically organized anthology of readings. The two parts of the book are linked by cross-references in the margins, leading students from the argument chapters to specific examples in the readings and from the readings to appropriate rhetorical instruction.

A uniquely wide-ranging scope that supports the argument made by the book's title. Seeing that arguments are *everywhere*—poems and ads, email and Web sites, essays and speeches—helps students understand why they need to learn to analyze and write them.

Fresh and important topics that encourage students to take up complex positions. Readings on topics such as *How Does the Media Stereotype You?*, *Is Sports Just a Proxy for Politics?*, and *What Role Should Religion Play in Public Life?* demand that students explore the many sides of an issue, not just pro or con.

A real-world design, with readings presented in the style of the original publication. Different formats for newspaper articles, magazine articles, essays, writing from the Web, and other media help students recognize and think about the effect design and visuals have on written arguments.

The most student-friendly argument text available. Chapters open with and frequently illustrate their points with everyday, real-life examples. Abstract terminology is kept to a minimum and explained clearly and simply where it is necessary, making this book especially easy for students to understand.

Unique chapters on arguments of fact, humorous arguments, and intellectual property help students question and defend factual claims, analyze and write comic genres like parody and satire, and understand and avoid plagiarism.

New to This Edition

Current, provocative new chapter topics have been added to topics retained from the previous edition. Among the new chapters are "What Should 'Diversity on Campus' Mean?" and "Why Do They Love Us? Why Do They Hate Us?"

Seventy new selections on timely topics raise provocative political, academic, and religious topics. A sampling:

- "Who's a Looter?: In Storm's Aftermath, Pictures Kick Up a Different Kind of Tempest"—a reporter asks hard questions about racial bias in the Hurricane Katrina media coverage.
- In an excerpt from the book *God on the Quad: How Religious Colleges and the Missionary Generation Are Changing America*, author Naomi Schaefer Riley offers a firsthand look at the growing influence of religious colleges.

- In a *New York Times* opinion piece Samuel G. Freedman argues that, in some cases, it's Latino parents who most object to bilingual education.
- A statement from the National Collegiate Athletic Association on the use of Native American mascots, names, and imagery at NCAA championships is paired with a Jim Shore essay condoning the use of Native American imagery in sports.

Six new full-length arguments in the earlier chapters—on topics ranging from why *Napoleon Dynamite* became a cult film to why literature matters to how the jobs of prison guards affect them—also help provide a diverse and provocative range of engaging new readings for students. In response to instructor feedback from around the country, more student essays and more readings citing sources have been added.

A new full-color design and integrated coverage of visual argument throughout the book help students see much more clearly how arguments are made and must be examined in visual as well as verbal texts. Each chapter before the anthology now includes a boxed visual analysis activity, "Not Just Words," that focuses on the chapter topic.

A reorganization and streamlining of the early chapters to focus more strongly on pathos, ethos, and logos, gives students a firmer grounding in these three central concepts before they begin to study specific kinds of arguments in detail.

A unique new chapter on "Arguments of Fact" helps students question the kinds of factual assertions made by journalists, scientists, politicians, and others—as well as to write their own convincing arguments based on factual claims.

A new chapter on "Thinking Rhetorically" models for students the skills of analyzing arguments and ends with a new Guide to Writing a Rhetorical Analysis that provides detailed guidelines for rhetorically analyzing a text.

A new boxed activity in each chapter of the rhetoric, "If Everything's an Argument. . . ," helps students recognize the relevance and value of the "everything's an argument" claim by encouraging them to think critically about the book itself as an argumentative text, asking them to analyze rhetorical choices made by the authors and editors in such areas as the cover images, the examples and images throughout the text, and the structure of chapters.

Acknowledgments

We owe a debt of gratitude to many people for making *Everything's an Argument* possible. Our first thanks must go to the students we have taught in our writing courses for nearly three decades, particularly first-year students at The Ohio State University, Stanford University, and the University of Texas at Austin, and to the six students whose fine argumentative essays appear in our chapters. Almost every chapter in this book has been informed by a classroom encounter with a student whose shrewd observation or perceptive question sent an ambitious lesson plan spiraling to the ground. (Anyone who has tried to teach claims and warrants on the fly to skeptical first-year students will surely appreciate why we have qualified our claims in the Toulmin chapter so carefully.) But students have also provided the motive for writing this book. More than ever, students need to know how to read and write arguments effectively if they are to secure a place in a world growing ever smaller and more rhetorically challenging.

We are grateful to our editors at Bedford/St. Martin's who contributed their talents to our book, beginning with Joan Feinberg and Nancy Perry, who have enthusiastically supported the project and provided us with the resources and feedback needed to keep us on track. Most of the day-to-day work on the project has been handled by the remarkably patient and perceptive and good-humored John Elliott. He prevented more than a few lapses of judgment yet understands the spirit of this book—which involves, occasionally, taking risks to make a memorable point. We have appreciated, too, his meticulous line editing as well as his ability to find just the right example when we were struggling to do so. Genevieve Hamilton provided amazing advice and support in putting together the readings in the anthology. Her eye for visual argument, her ability to think simultaneously about issues of rhetorical theory, presentation, and pedagogy, and her willingness to take risks made the task of revising earlier chapters and constructing new ones great fun despite the hard work. Joanna Lee, Genevieve's assistant, provided support time and time again and helped manage the daunting task of turning a manuscript into the book you now hold.

We are similarly grateful to others at Bedford/St. Martin's who contributed their talents to our book: Shuli Traub, Karen Baart, and Rosemary Jaffe, who were superb project editors; Anna Palchik, who completely reworked her design of our book to accommodate color; Alice Vigliani, who meticulously copyedited this fourth edition; Laura King, who was indispensable in coordinating the entire art program for our book, researching images and writing captions throughout; Robin Raffer, who was our art researcher par excellence; Katie Paarlberg, the editorial assistant we could not have done without; Nancy Myers, who ably coordinated all our work with the printer; and Karita dos Santos, who served as our outstanding marketing manager.

We'd also like to thank the astute instructors and students who reviewed the third edition, among them Eileen Baland, Graduate Arts and Humanities, University of Texas, Dallas; Mary R. Bowman, English Department, University of Wisconsin-Stevens Point; Carl Eugene Bledsoe, English Department, Kennesaw State University and Georgia Virtual High School; Karen Burge, English Department, Wichita State University; April Cooper, English Department, University of Tennessee; Jim Coppoc, English Department, Iowa State University; Judith Cortelloni, Department of Humanities and Social Sciences, Lincoln College; Sarah Eichelman, English Department, Walters State Community College; Kellye Freeman, English Department, Mississippi State University; Phyllis Frus, English Department, Hawaii Pacific University; Lynée L. Gaillet, English Department, Georgia State University; Gregory Giberson, English Department, Salisbury University; Rachel Greil, English Department, Kennesaw State University; Richard Heppner, Jr., English Department, Slippery Rock University; Beth Huber, English Department, Western Carolina University; Elizabeth A. Kelly, English Department, Western Carolina University; Melissa McCool, English Department, Mississippi State University; Robbi Muckenfuss, Developmental Studies, Durham Technical Community College; Dennis H. Sigmon, English, Theatre, and Languages Department, University of North Carolina, Pembroke; Marti Singer, English Department, Georgia State University; Kristin M. Smith, Developmental Studies Department, Durham Technical Community College; Julie Sorge, English Department, University of Kansas; Sarah Spring, English Department, Texas A & M University; Elizabeth Angela Titus, English Department, Northern Illinois University; Mark Tjarks, English Department, Hawaii Pacific University; Kathleen Turner, Department of English, Northern Illinois University; Julie Wheeler, English Department, University of Colorado at Denver.

Taryne Hallett contributed in important ways to the selection of new readings for the anthology and the Web site for this book and Taryne and John Kinkade ably prepared the instructor's guides for this fourth edition, building on the earlier wonderful work of Jodi Egerton, Michal Brody, and Ben Feigert. We thank all of them for their contributions to this and earlier editions of *Everything's an Argument with Readings*.

We hope that *Everything's an Argument with Readings* responds to what students and instructors have said they want and need. And we hope readers of this text will let us know how we've done: please share your opinions and suggestions with us at <bedfordstmartins.com/everythingsanargument>.

Andrea A. Lunsford
John J. Ruszkiewicz
Keith Walters

CONTENTS

Coca-Cola
abc
Disney
intel inside
IBM
EXXON
Lilly
She's Disabled

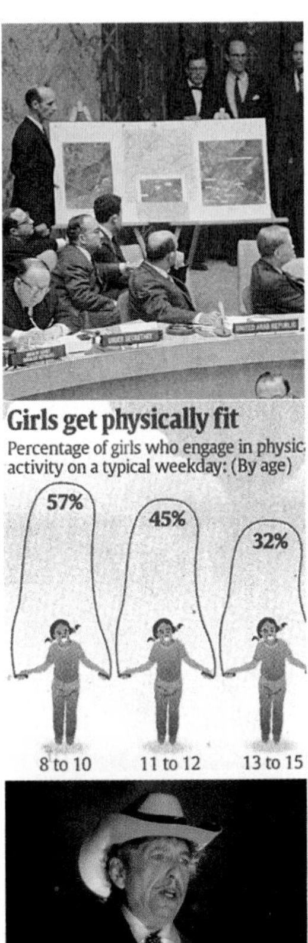
Girls get physically fit
Percentage of girls who engage in physic
activity on a typical weekday: (By age)
57%
45%
32%
8 to 10
11 to 12
13 to 15

Part 2: Writing Arguments 137

David B.
Epileptic

I AM THE

NIGHT OF THE LIVING DEAD
They keep coming back in a bloodthirsty lust for HUMAN FLESH!...
Pits the dead against the living in a struggle for survival!
FFICER
EW

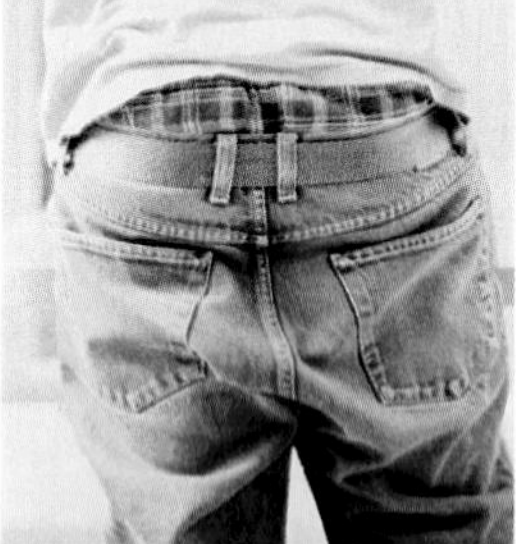

USDA RURAL LOUISIANA
DEVELOPMENT
2004 ANNUAL REPORT
Committed to the future of rural communities.

Part 4: Conventions of Argument 467

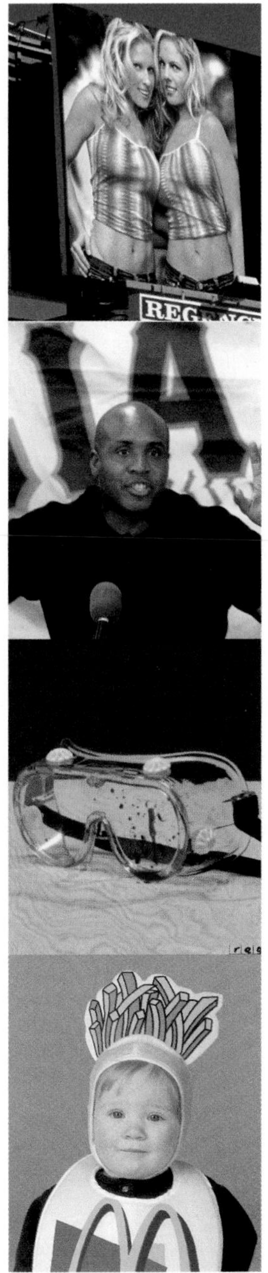

MLA Handbook
for Writers of
Research Papers

Part 5: Arguments 583

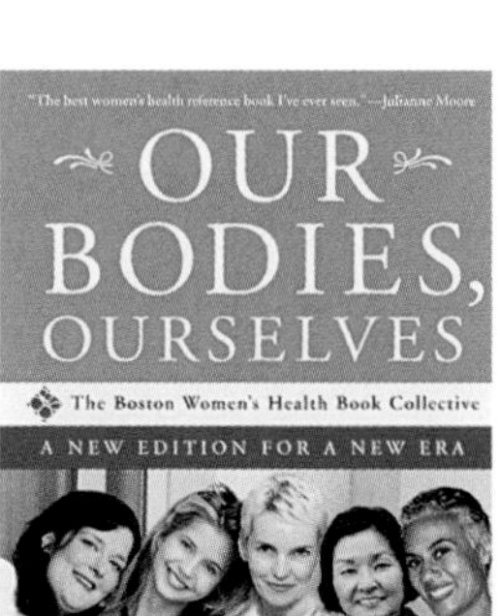

Labeled:

He might dump me.
He'll think I'm judging him.
But I care about him.
You scan me:
I'm just another
wrong.
last time
was in kickboxing.
My decision.
i am
MY ANTI-DRUG.

ANTI-SEMITISM
IS ANTI-ME
diversity is...
deeper than skin deep
confidence
perspective

"LIVES WOVEN TOGETHER"

TOM CRUISE
M:i:III
LA MISSION COMMENCE LE 03.05.06

PART 1

READING arguments

1
Everything Is an Argument

"Movie of the year!" blares the headline of an online ad for *Star Wars: Episode III–Revenge of the Sith*.

A professor interrupts a lecture to urge her students to spend less time on Instant Messaging and more in the company of thick, old books.

A senator tries to tell an irate C-SPAN caller that the Homeland Security Bill does not reduce citizens' constitutional rights or their privacy.

A nurse assures a youngster eyeing an approaching needle, "This won't hurt one bit."

A sports columnist blasts a football coach for passing on fourth down and two in a close game—even though the play produces a touchdown.

"Please let me make it through this chem exam!" a student silently prays.

• • •

These visual and verbal messages all contain arguments. From the clothes you wear to the foods you choose to eat to the groups you decide to join—all of these everyday activities make nuanced, sometimes implicit, arguments about who you are and what you value. Thus an argument can be any text—whether written, spoken, or visual—that expresses a point of view. Sometimes arguments can be aggressive, composed deliberately to change what people believe, think, or do. At other times your goals may be more subtle, and your writing may be designed to convince yourself or others that specific facts are reliable or that certain views should be considered or at least tolerated.

In fact, some theorists claim that language is itself inherently persuasive (even when you say "hi, how's it going?" for instance, in one sense you're arguing that your hello deserves a response) and hence *every* text is also an argument, designed to influence readers. For example, a poem that observes what little girls do in church may indirectly critique the role religion plays in women's lives, for good or ill:

> I worry for the girls.
> I once had braids,
> and wore lace that made me suffer.
> I had not yet done the things
> that would need forgiving.
>
> –Kathleen Norris, "Little Girls in Church"

To take another example, observations about family life among the poor in India may suddenly illuminate the writer's life and the reader's experience, forcing comparisons that quietly argue for change:

> **I have learned from Jagat and his family a kind of commitment, a form of friendship that is not always available in the West, where we have become cynical and instrumental in so many of our relationships to others.**
>
> **–Jeremy Seabrook, "Family Values"**

Even humor makes an argument when it causes readers to become aware—through bursts of laughter or just a faint smile—of the way things are and how they might be different. Take a look, for example, at an excerpt from the introduction to *Dave Barry Hits Below the Beltway,* along with its cover, which also makes a humorous argument:

> **To do even a halfway decent book on a subject as complex as the United States government, you have to spend a lot of time in Washington, D.C. So the first thing I decided, when I was getting ready to write this book, was that it would not be even halfway decent.**
>
> **–Dave Barry, *Dave Barry Hits below the Beltway***

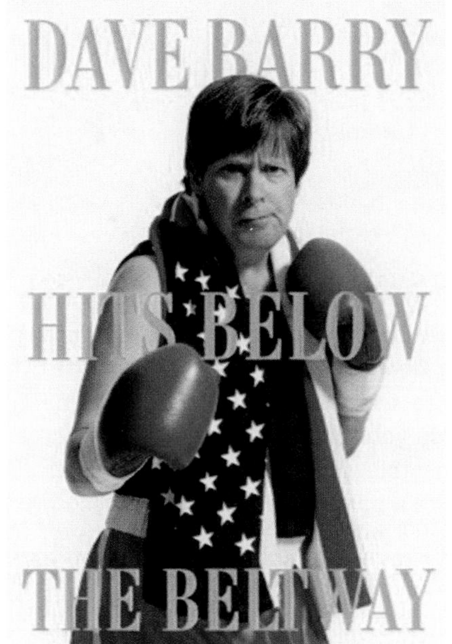

Dave Barry's humorous argument begins on his book's cover.

Not Just Words

Take a look at the two bumper stickers above. Each one makes a visual argument about President George W. Bush and about his relationship to the country and to the world. Spend some time working with one other student in your class to analyze these visual arguments. As simply as possible, state the claim you think each argument makes. Then write a paragraph that elaborates on that claim.

More obvious as arguments are those that make a claim and present evidence to support it. Such writing often moves readers to recognize problems and to consider solutions. Suasion of this kind is usually easy to recognize:

> **Discrimination against Hispanics, or any other group, should be fought and there are laws and a massive apparatus to do so. But the way to eliminate such discrimination is not to classify all Hispanics as victims.**
>
> **–Linda Chavez, "Towards a New Politics of Hispanic Assimilation"**

> **[W]omen unhappy in their marriages often enter full-time employment as an escape. But although a woman's entrance into the workplace does tend to increase the stability of her marriage, it does not increase her happiness.**
>
> **–The Popular Research Institute, Penn State University**

> **Resistance to science is born of fear. Fear, in turn, is bred by ignorance. And it is ignorance that is our deepest malady.**
>
> **–J. Michael Bishop, "Enemies of Promise"**

Purposes of Argument

If in some ways all language has an argumentative edge that aims to make a point, not all language use aims to win out over others. In contrast to the traditional Western concept of argument as being about fighting or combat, communication theorists such as Sonja Foss, Cindy Griffin, and Josina Makau describe an *invitational* argument, the kind that aims not to win over another person or group but to invite others to enter a space of mutual regard and exploration. In fact, as you'll see, writers and speakers have as many purposes for arguing as for using language, including—in addition to winning—to inform, to convince, to explore, to make decisions, even to meditate or pray.

Of course, many arguments *are* aimed at winning. Such is the traditional purpose of much writing and speaking in the political arena, in the business world, and in the law courts. Two candidates for office, for example, try to win out over each other in appealing for votes; the makers of one soft drink try to outsell their competitors by appealing to public tastes; and two lawyers try to defeat each other in pleading to a judge and jury. In your college writing, you may also be called on to make an argument that appeals to a "judge" and/or "jury" (your instructor and classmates). You might, for instance, argue that peer-to-peer file-sharing is legal because of the established legal precedent of fair use. In doing so, you may need to defeat your unseen opponents—those who oppose such file-sharing.

At this point, it may be helpful to acknowledge a common academic distinction between argument and persuasion. In this view, the point of *argument* is to discover some version of the truth, using evidence and reasons. Argument of this sort leads audiences toward conviction, an agreement that a claim is true or reasonable, or that a course of action is desirable. The aim of *persuasion* is to change a point of view or to move others from conviction to action. In other words, writers or speakers argue to discover some truth; they persuade when they think they already know it.

Argument (discover a truth) ⟶ conviction
Persuasion (know a truth) ⟶ action

In practice, this distinction between argument and persuasion can be hard to sustain. It's unnatural for writers or readers to imagine their minds divided between a part that pursues truth and a part that seeks to persuade. And yet, you may want to reserve the term *persuasion* for writing that's aggressively designed to change opinions through the use of both reason and other appropriate techniques. For writing that sets out to persuade at all costs, abandoning reason, fairness, and truth altogether, the term *propaganda,* with all its negative connotations, seems to fit. Some would suggest that *advertising* often works just as well.

But, as we've already suggested, arguing isn't always about winning or even about changing others' views. In addition to invitational argument, another school of argument—called Rogerian argument, after the psychotherapist Carl Rogers—is based on finding common ground and establishing trust among those who disagree about issues, and on approaching audiences in nonthreatening ways. Writers who follow Rogerian approaches seek to understand the perspectives of those with whom they disagree, looking for "both/and" or "win/win" solutions (rather than "either/or" or "win/lose" ones) whenever possible. Much successful argument today follows such principles, consciously or not.

Some other purposes or goals of argument are worth considering in more detail.

Arguments to Inform

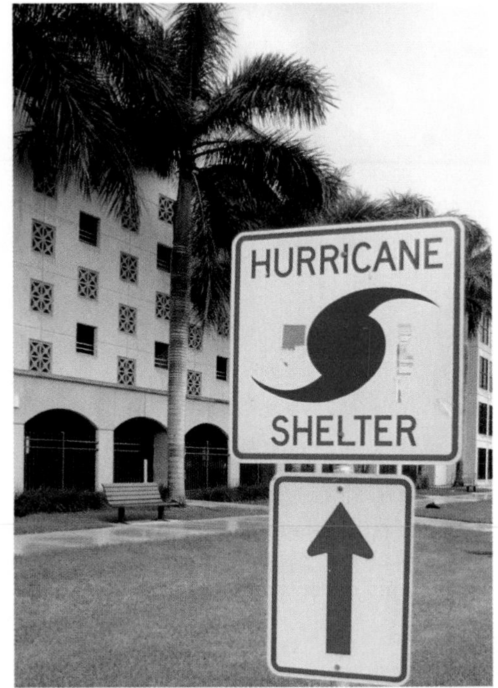

A visual argument to inform in Key West, Florida

Many arguments, from street signs to notices of meetings to newspaper headlines, may not seem especially "argumentative" because their main purpose is just to inform members of an audience about something they didn't know. Other informative arguments are more obviously intended to persuade. For example, an essential step in selling anything, especially something new, is to inform or remind the customer that it exists, as in advertisements like the one for *Star Wars* mentioned at the very beginning of this chapter. Political campaigns use arguments to inform extensively, as well. Think of all the posters you've seen with names and smiling faces of candidates and the offices they're seeking: "Rice in 2008," "Lujan for Mayor." Of course, these verbal or visual texts are often aimed at winning out over an unnamed opponent, just as many ads are aimed at unnamed competing products. But on the surface, at least, they serve simply to give a candidate "name recognition" by informing voters that he or she is running for office.

Arguments to inform can be also more subtle than ads or signs. Consider how Joan Didion uses argument to inform readers about the artist Georgia O'Keeffe:

> **This is a woman who in 1939 could advise her admirers that they were missing her point, that their appreciation of her famous flowers was merely sentimental. "When I paint a red hill," she observed coolly**

Georgia O'Keeffe, *Rust Red Hills* (1930)

By citing examples from various media, including personal ads, W. Charisse Goodman creates a strong argument to convince readers that the media is prejudiced against "large" women.

LINK TO P. 605

> **in the catalogue for an exhibition that year, "you say it is too bad that I don't always paint flowers. A flower touches almost everyone's heart. A red hill doesn't touch everyone's heart."**
>
> **–Joan Didion, "Georgia O'Keeffe"**

By giving specific information about O'Keeffe and her own ideas about her art, Didion in this passage argues that readers should pay closer attention to *all* the work of this artist.

Arguments to Convince

If you were writing a report that attempted to identify the causes of changes in global temperatures, you would likely be trying not to conquer opponents but to satisfy readers that you had thoroughly examined those causes and that they merit serious attention. As a form of writing, reports typically aim to persuade readers rather than win out over opponents. Yet the presence of those who might disagree is always implied, and it shapes a writer's strategies. In the following passage, for example, Paul Osterman argues to convince readers of the urgency surrounding jobs for all citizens:

> **Among employed 19- to 31-year-old high school graduates who did not go to college, more than 30 percent had not been in their position for even a year. Another 12 percent had only one year of tenure. The pattern was much the same for women who had remained in the**

President George W. Bush was arguing to convince on May 1, 2003, when he landed on the USS *Abraham Lincoln* flight deck and announced "Mission Accomplished" in Iraq. Such pictures were later used against Bush, however, when it became clear that the announcement was, at best, premature.

> **labor force for the four years prior to the survey. These are adults who, for a variety of reasons—a lack of skills, training, or disposition—have not managed to secure "adult" jobs.**
>
> **–Paul Osterman, "Getting Started"**

Osterman uses facts to report a seemingly objective conclusion about the stability of employment among certain groups, but he's also arguing against those who find that the current job situation is tolerable and not worthy of concern or action.

Arguments to Explore

Many important subjects call for arguments that take the form of exploration, either on your own or with others. If there's an "opponent" in such a situation at all (often there is not), it's likely the status quo or a current trend that—for one reason or another—is puzzling. Exploratory arguments may be deeply personal, such as E. B. White's often-reprinted essay "Once More to the Lake," in which the author's return with his young son to a vacation spot from his own childhood leads him to reflect

Meghan Daum makes use of an exploration argument when she invites readers to consider what it is about Dove's ads using real women that makes so many people uncomfortable.

LINK TO P. 618

on time, memory, and mortality. Or the exploration may be aimed at addressing serious problems in society. James Fallows explores what he sees as "America's coming economic crisis" by projecting himself forward to the election of 2016—and then looking back to speculate on what might happen between 2005 and 2016. Along the way, he considers changes that may occur in education:

> . . . we could have shored up our universities. True, the big change came as early as 2002, in the wake of 9/11, when tighter visa rules . . . cut off the flow of foreign talent that American universities had channeled to American ends. In the summer of 2007 China applied the name "twenty Harvards" to its ambition, announced in the early 2000s, to build major research institutions that would attract international talent. It seemed preposterous (too much political control, too great a language barrier), but no one is laughing now. . . . The Historic Campus of our best-known university, Harvard, is still prestigious worldwide. But its role is increasingly that of the theme park, like Oxford or Heidelberg, while the most ambitious students compete for fellowships at the Har-Bai and Har-Bei campuses in Mumbai and Beijing.
>
> –James Fallows, "Countdown to a Meltdown"

Perhaps the essential argument in any such piece is the writer's assertion that a problem exists (in this case, the damage that tighter visa rules do to American economic competitiveness) and that the writer or reader needs to solve it. Some exploratory pieces present and defend solutions. Paul Goldberger, for example, takes on the question of how best to rebuild Ground Zero, exploring the false starts and what he argues is a massive "failure of imagination" that led to an unnecessarily elaborate plan for the Freedom Tower, a 2.6 million square foot office building. After exploring several possibilities, Goldberger concludes that a much smaller (but still very tall) memorial tower would solve the problem of how to commemorate the site by integrating the structure fully into housing and extensive cultural space:

> A great tower by Calatrava or another architect equally adept at turning engineering into poetic form would give New York the defiantly proud icon it has craved since the towers fell. And it wouldn't require anybody to live or work a hundred stories above the street. Most important, it would be a way of transcending the false divide between commemoration and renewal. A soaring tower can be made to coexist with apartments and museums. The planners at Ground Zero have

A digital rendering of the Freedom Tower designed by architects Michael Arad and Peter Walker

treated the sacred and the everyday as two distinct spheres. The answer isn't to split the site into a memorial sector and a business sector but, rather, to find ways to honor the dead while rejuvenating the city, to acknowledge the past while looking toward the future. Ground Zero is the first great urban-design challenge of the twenty-first century, and the noblest way to honor what happened here is to rebuild the site with the complexity and vitality that characterizes the best of Manhattan.

–Paul Goldberger, "Eyes on the Prize"

Arguments to Make Decisions

Closely allied to argument that explores is that which aims at making good, sound decisions. In fact, the result of many exploratory arguments may be to argue for a particular decision, whether that decision relates to the best computer for you to buy or the "right" person to choose as your life partner. For college students, choosing a major is a momentous decision, and one way to go about making that decision is to argue your way through several alternatives in your own mind as well as with friends, colleagues, maybe even your parents. By the time you've examined the pros and cons of each alternative, you should be at least a little closer to a good decision. In the following paragraphs, college student Jessica Cohen reasons her way toward another momentous decision, asking should she, or should she not, become an egg donor for a wealthy couple:

> Early in the spring of last year a classified ad ran for two weeks in the *Yale Daily News*: "EGG DONOR NEEDED." The couple [Michelle and David] that placed the ad was picky, and for that reason was offering $25,000 for an egg from the right donor. . . . I kept dreaming about all the things I could do with $25,000. I had gone into the correspondence [with David and Michelle] on a whim. But soon, despite David's casual tone and the optimistic attitude of all the classifieds and information I read, I decided that this process was something I didn't want to be part of. I understand the desire for a child who will resemble and fit in with the family. But once a couple starts choosing a few characteristics, shooting for perfection is too easy—especially if they can afford it. The money might have changed my life for a while, but it would have led to the creation of a child encumbered with too many expectations.
>
> –Jessica Cohen, "Grade A: The Market for a Yale Woman's Eggs"

"I told my parents that if grades were so important they should have paid for a smarter egg donor."

Arguments to Meditate or Pray

Sometimes arguments can take the form of intense meditations on a theme, or of prayer. In such cases, the writer or speaker is most often hoping to transform something in him- or herself or to reach a state of equilibrium or peace of mind. If you know a familiar prayer or mantra, think for a moment of what it "argues" for and how it uses quiet meditation to accomplish that goal. Such meditations don't have to be formal prayers, however. Look, for example, at an excerpt from Michael Lassell's poem "How to Watch Your Brother Die." This poem, which evokes the confusing emotions of a man during the death of his gay brother, uses a kind of meditative language that allows the reader to reach an understanding of the speaker and to evoke meditative thought in others:

> **Feel how it feels to hold a man in your arms**
> **whose arms are used to holding men.**
> **Offer God anything to bring your brother back.**
> **Know you have nothing God could possibly want.**
> **Curse God, but do not**
> **abandon Him.**
>
> **–Michael Lassell, "How to Watch Your Brother Die"**

Another sort of meditative argument can be found in the stained-glass windows of churches and other public buildings. Dazzled by a spectacle of light, people pause to consider a window's message longer than they might were the same idea conveyed on paper. The window engages viewers with a power not unlike that of poetry (see p. 16).

As these examples suggest, the effectiveness of argument depends not only on the purposes of the writer but also on the context surrounding the plea and the people it seeks most directly to reach. Though we'll examine arguments of all types in this book, we'll focus chiefly on the kinds made in professional and academic situations.

Occasions for Argument

Another way of thinking about arguments is to consider the public occasions that call for them. In an ancient textbook of rhetoric, or the art of persuasion, the philosopher Aristotle provides an elegant scheme for classifying the purposes of arguments, one based on issues of time—past, future, and present. His formula is easy to remember and helpful

Rose and lancet windows in France's Chartres Cathedral

in suggesting strategies for making convincing cases. But because all classifications overlap with others to a certain extent, don't be surprised to encounter many arguments that span more than one category—arguments about the past with implications for the future, arguments about the future with bearings on the present, and so on.

Arguments about the Past

Debates about what has happened in the past are called forensic arguments; such controversies are common in business, government, and academia. For example, in many criminal and civil cases, lawyers interrogate witnesses to establish exactly what happened at an earlier time: *Did the defendant sexually harass her employee? Did the company deliberately ignore evidence that its product was deficient? Was the contract properly enforced?* The contentious nature of some forensic arguments is evident in this excerpt from a letter to the editor of *The Atlantic Monthly*:

> **Robert Bryce's article on the U.S. military's gas consumption in Iraq ("Gas Pains," May *Atlantic*) is factually inaccurate, tactically misguided, and a classic case of a red herring.**
>
> **–Captain David J. Morris**

In replying to this letter, the author of the article, Robert Bryce, disputes Morris's statements, introducing more evidence in support of his original claim. Obviously, then, forensic arguments rely on evidence and testimony to re-create what can be known about events that have already occurred.

Forensic arguments also rely heavily on precedents—actions or decisions in the past that influence policies or decisions in the present—and on analyses of cause and effect. Consider the ongoing controversy over Christopher Columbus: Are his expeditions to the Americas events worth celebrating, or are they unhappy chapters in human history—or a mixture of both? No simple exchange of evidence will suffice to still this debate; the effects of Columbus's actions beginning in 1492 may be studied and debated for the next five hundred years. As you might suspect from this example, arguments about history are typically forensic.

Forensic cases may also be arguments about character, such as when someone's reputation is studied in a historical context to enrich current perspectives on the person. Allusions to the past can make present arguments more vivid, as in the following text about Ward Connerly, head of an organization that aims to dismantle affirmative action programs:

> **Despite the fact that Connerly's message seems clearly opposed to the Civil Rights Movement, some people are fond of pointing out that the man is black. But as far as politics goes, that is irrelevant. Before black suffrage, there were African Americans who publicly argued against their own right to vote.**
>
> **–Carl Villarreal, "Connerly Is an Enemy of Civil Rights"**

Such writing can be exploratory and open-ended, the point of argument being to enhance and sharpen knowledge, not just to generate heat or score points.

Theodor de Bry's 1594 engraving tells one version of the Christopher Columbus story.

Arguments about the Future

Debates about what will or should happen in the future are called deliberative arguments. Legislatures, congresses, and parliaments are called deliberative bodies because they establish policies for the future: *Should two people of the same sex be allowed to marry? Should the United States build a defense against ballistic missiles?* Because what has happened in the past influences the future, deliberative judgments often rely on prior forensic arguments. Thus deliberative arguments often draw on evidence and testimony, as in this passage:

> The labor market is sending a clear signal. While the American way of moving youngsters from high school to the labor market may be imperfect, the chief problem is that, for many, even getting a job no longer guarantees a decent standard of living. More than ever, getting ahead, or even keeping up, means staying in school longer.
>
> –Paul Osterman, "Getting Started"

But since no one has a blueprint for what's to come, deliberative arguments also advance by means of projections, extrapolations, and reasoned guesses—*If X is true, Y may be true; if X happens, so may Y; if X continues, then Y may occur:*

> **In 2000, according to a World Health Organization assessment, 1.1 billion people worldwide had no regular access to safe drinking water, and 2.4 billion had no regular access to sanitation systems. Lack of access to clean water leads to four billion cases of diarrhea each year. Peter Gleick, an expert on global freshwater resources, reveals that even if we reach the United Nations' stated goal of halving the number of people without access to safe drinking water by 2015, as many as 76 million people will die from water-borne diseases before 2020.**
>
> **–Pacific Institute for Studies in Development, Environment, and Security**

Arguments about the Present

Arguments about the present are often arguments about contemporary values—the ethical premises and assumptions that are widely held (or contested) within a society. Sometimes called epideictic arguments or ceremonial arguments because they tend to be heard at public occasions, they include inaugural addresses, sermons, eulogies, graduation speeches, and civic remarks of all kinds. Ceremonial arguments can be passionate and eloquent, rich in anecdotes and examples. Martin Luther King Jr. was a master of ceremonial discourse, and he was particularly adept at finding affirmation in the depths of despair:

> **Three nights later, our home was bombed. Strangely enough, I accepted the word of the bombing calmly. My experience with God had given me a new strength and trust. I know now that God is able to give us the interior resources to face the storms and problems of life.**
>
> **–Martin Luther King Jr., "Our God Is Able"**

King argues here that the arbiter of good and evil in society is, ultimately, God. But not all ceremonial arguments reach quite so far.

More typical are values arguments that explore contemporary culture, praising what's admirable and blaming what's not. In the following argument, student Latisha Chisholm looks at rap after Tupac Shakur—and doesn't like what she sees:

> **When I think about how rap music has changed, I generally associate the demise of my appreciation for the industry with the death of**

> Tupac. With his death, not only did one of the most intriguing rap rivalries of all time die, but the motivation for rapping seems to have changed. Where money had always been a plus, now it is obviously more important than wanting to express the hardships of Black communities. With current rappers, the positive power that came from the desire to represent Black people is lost. One of the biggest rappers now got his big break while talking about sneakers. Others announce retirement without really having done much for the soul or for Black people's morale. I equate new rappers to NFL players that don't love the game anymore. They're *only* in it for the money. . . . It looks like the voice of a people has lost its heart.
>
> –Latisha Chisholm, "Has Rap Lost Its Soul?"

As in many ceremonial arguments, Chisholm here reinforces common values such as representing one's community honorably and fairly.

Kinds of Argument

Yet another way of categorizing arguments is to consider their status or stasis—that is, the kinds of issues they address. This categorization system is called stasis theory. In ancient Greek and Roman civilizations, rhetoricians defined a series of questions by which to examine legal cases. The questions would be posed in sequence, because each depended on the question(s) preceding it. Together, the questions helped determine the point of contention in an argument, the place where disputants could focus their energy and hence what kind of an argument they should make. A modern version of those questions might look like the following:

- Did something happen?
- What is its nature?
- What is its quality?
- What actions should be taken?

Here's how the questions might be used to explore a "crime."

DID SOMETHING HAPPEN?

> Yes. A young man kissed a young woman against her will. The act was witnessed by a teacher and friends and acquaintances of both parties. The facts suggest clearly that something happened. If you were going

CULTURAL CONTEXTS FOR ARGUMENT

Considering What's "Normal"

If you want to communicate effectively with people across cultures, then you need to try to learn something about the norms in those cultures—and to be aware of the norms guiding your own behavior.

- Be aware of the assumptions that guide your own customary ways of arguing a point. Remember that most of us tend to see our own way as the "normal" or "right" way to do things. Such assumptions guide your thinking and your judgments about what counts—and what "works"—in an argument. Nevertheless, just because it seems "normal" to take a very aggressive stance in an argument, don't forget that others may find that aggression startling or even alarming.
- Keep in mind that if your own ways seem inherently right, then even without thinking about it you may assume that other ways are somehow less than right. It's "right" to drive on the right side of the road in the United States but on the left in England and Australia; arguing that one way is the only really right way would not get you very far. Such thinking makes it hard to communicate effectively across cultures.
- Remember that ways of arguing are influenced by cultural contexts and that they differ widely across cultures. Pay attention to the ways people from cultures other than your own argue, and be flexible and open to the many ways of thinking you'll no doubt encounter.
- Respect the differences among individuals within a given culture; don't expect that every member of a community behaves—or argues—in just the same way.

The best advice, then, might be *don't assume*. Just because you think wearing a navy blazer and a knee-length skirt "argues" that you should be taken seriously as a job candidate at a multinational corporation, such dress may be perceived differently in other settings. And if you're conducting an interview where a candidate doesn't look you in the eye, don't assume that this reflects any lack of confidence or respect; he or she may intend it as a sign of politeness.

Sexual harassment?

to write an argument about this event, this first stasis question proves not very helpful, since there's no debate about whether the act occurred. If the event were debatable, however, you could develop an argument of fact.

WHAT IS THE NATURE OF THE THING?

Is Ebonics a separate language, a dialect of English, or something else? John Rickford's "Suite for Ebony *and* Phonics" and David D. Troutt's "Defining Who We Are in Society" offer slightly different answers, basing their claims on different kinds of evidence.

LINK TO PP. 810 AND 818

The act might be construed as "sexual harassment," defined as the imposition of unwanted or unsolicited sexual attention or activity on a person. The young man kissed the young woman on the lips. Kissing people who aren't relatives on the lips is generally considered a sexual activity. The young woman did not want to be kissed and complained to her teacher. The young man's act meets the definition of "sexual harassment." Careful analysis of this stasis question could lead to an argument of definition.

WHAT IS THE QUALITY OF THE THING?

Both the young man and young woman involved in the action are six years old. They were playing in a schoolyard. The boy didn't realize that kissing girls against their will was a violation of school policy;

school sexual harassment policies had not in the past been enforced against first-graders. Most people don't regard six-year-olds as sexually culpable. Moreover, the girl wants to play with the boy again and apparently doesn't resent his action. Were you to decide on this focus, you would be developing an argument of evaluation.

WHAT ACTIONS SHOULD BE TAKEN?

The case has raised a ruckus among parents, the general public, and some feminists and anti-feminists. The consensus seems to be that the school overreacted in seeking to brand the boy as a sexual harasser. Yet it is important that the issue of sexual harassment not be dismissed as trivial. Consequently, the boy should be warned not to kiss girls against their will. The teachers should be warned not to make federal cases out of schoolyard spats. With this stasis question as your focus, you would be developing a proposal argument.

As you can see, each of the stasis questions explores different aspects of a problem and uses different evidence or techniques to reach conclusions. You can use stasis theory to explore the aspects of any topic you're considering. In addition, studying the results of your exploration of the stasis questions can help you determine the major point you want to make and thus identify the type of argument that will be most effective.

Arguments of Fact—Did Something Happen?

An argument of fact usually involves a statement that can be proved or disproved with specific evidence or testimony. Although relatively simple to define, such arguments are often quite subtle, involving layers of complexity not apparent when the question is initially posed.

For example, the question of pollution of the oceans—*Is it really occurring?*—would seem relatively easy to settle. Either scientific data prove that the oceans are being polluted as a result of human activity, or they don't. But to settle the matter, writers and readers would first have to agree on a number of points, each of which would have to be examined and debated: *What constitutes pollution? How will such pollution be measured? Over what period of time? Are any current deviations in water quality unprecedented? How can one be certain that deviations are attributable to human action?* Nevertheless, questions of this sort can be disputed primarily on the facts, complicated and contentious as they may be. But should you choose to develop an argument of fact, be aware of how difficult it can sometimes be to establish "facts." (For more on arguments based on facts, see Chapter 4.)

Arguments of Definition—What Is the Nature of the Thing?

Just as contentious as arguments based on facts are questions of definition. An argument of definition often involves determining whether one known object or action belongs in a second—and more highly contested—category. One of the most hotly debated issues in American life today involves a question of definition: *Is a human fetus a human being?* If one argues that it is, then a second issue of definition arises: *Is abortion murder?* As you can see, issues of definition can have mighty consequences—and decades of debate may leave the matter unresolved.

Writer Christopher Hitchens defines a word familiar to almost everyone—then gives it a twist:

> **On its own, the word "cowboy" is not particularly opprobrious. It means a ranch hand or cattle driver, almost by definition a mounted one, herding the steers in the general direction of Cheyenne and thus providing protein on the hoof. The job calls for toughness that has little appeal to the sentimental. A typical cowboy would be laconic, patient, somewhat fatalistic, and prone to spend his wages on brawling and loose gallantry. His first duty is to cattle, and he has to have an eye for weather. Unpolished, but in his way invaluable. A rough job but someone's got to do it. And so forth. . . .**
>
> **[But today] the word "cowboy" has a special relationship with the state of Texas, its "lone star" logo, and the name of its Dallas football team. . . . President Bush has played to this strength, if it is a strength, at least three times. . . .**
>
> **Boiled down, the use of the word "cowboy" expresses a fixed attitude and an expectation, on the part of non-Texans, about people from Texas. It's a competition between a clichéd mentality . . . and a cliché itself. How well—apart from some "with us or with the terrorists" rhetoric—does the president fit the stereotype?**
>
> **–Christopher Hitchens, "Cowboy"**

Bob Costas, eulogizing Mickey Mantle, a great baseball player who had many universally human faults, advances his assessment by means of an important definitional distinction:

> **In the last year, Mickey Mantle, always so hard upon himself, finally came to accept and appreciate the distinction between a role model and a hero. The first he often was not, the second he always will be.**
>
> **–Bob Costas, "Eulogy for Mickey Mantle"**

But arguments of definition can be less weighty than these, though still hotly contested: *Is video game playing a sport? Is Lil' Kim an artist? Is the Subaru Outback an SUV?* To argue such cases, one would first have to put forth definitions, and then those definitions would have to become the foci of debates themselves. (For more about arguments of definition, see Chapter 8.)

An artist—or not? Lil' Kim arriving at the 2005 MTV Video Music Awards

Arguments of Evaluation—What Is the Quality of the Thing?

Arguments of definition lead naturally into arguments of quality—that is, to questions about quality. Most auto enthusiasts, for example, wouldn't be content merely to inquire whether the Corvette is a sports car. They'd prefer to argue whether it's a *good* sports car or a better sports car than, say, the Viper. Or they might want to assert that it's the best sports car in the world, perhaps qualifying their claim with the caveat *for the price*.

Arguments of evaluation are so common that writers sometimes take them for granted, ignoring their complexity and importance in establishing people's values and priorities. For instance, the stasis question "What is the quality of the thing?" is at the heart of attempts to understand the nuclear capability of North Korea. Strategists working to develop U.S. policy toward North Korea need to use this stasis question to develop a compelling argument of evaluation.

Consider how Rosa Parks assesses Martin Luther King Jr. in the following passage. Though she seems to be defining the concept of "leader," she's actually measuring King against criteria she has set for "*true* leader," an important distinction:

> Dr. King was a true leader. I never sensed fear in him. I just felt he knew what had to be done and took the leading role without regard to consequences. I knew he was destined to do great things. He had an elegance about him and a speaking style that let you know where you stood and inspired you to do the best you could. He truly is a role model for us all. The sacrifice of his life should never be forgotten, and his dream must live on.
>
> –Rosa Parks, "Role Models"

Parks's comments represent a type of informal evaluation that's common in ceremonial arguments; because King is so well known, she doesn't have to burnish every claim with specific evidence. (See p. 19 for more on ceremonial arguments.) In contrast, Molly Ivins in praising Barbara Jordan makes quite explicit the connections between her claim and the evidence:

> Barbara Jordan, whose name was so often preceded by the words "the first black woman to . . ." that they seemed like a permanent title, died Wednesday in Austin. A great spirit is gone. The first black woman to serve in the Texas Senate, the first black woman in Congress (she and Yvonne Brathwaite Burke of California were both elected in 1972, but Jordan had no Republican opposition), the first black elected to

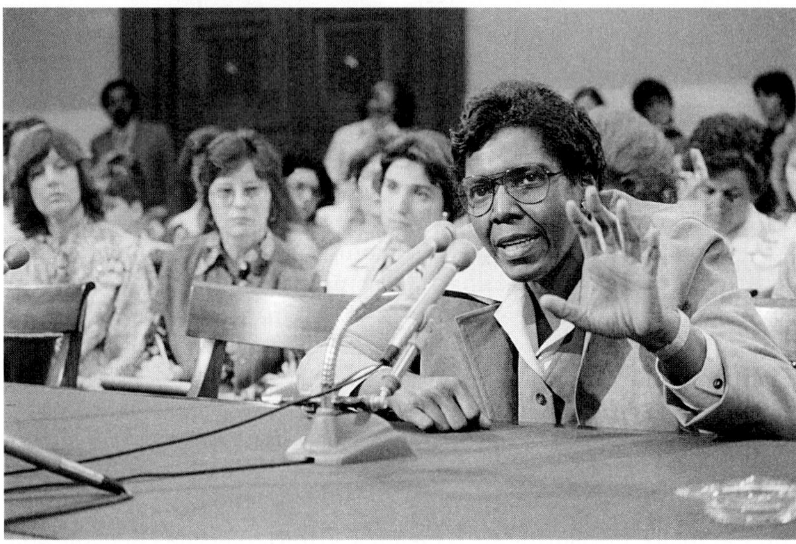

Barbara Jordan addressing fellow members of Congress in 1978

> **Congress from the South since Reconstruction, the first black woman to sit on major corporate boards, and so on. Were it not for the disease that slowly crippled her, she probably would have been the first black woman on the Supreme Court—it is known that Jimmy Carter had her on his short list.**
>
> **And long before she became "the first and only black woman to . . ." there was that astounding string of achievements going back to high school valedictorian, honors at Texas Southern University, law degree from Boston University. Both her famous diction and her enormous dignity were present from the beginning, her high school teachers recalled. Her precise enunciation was a legacy from her father, a Baptist minister, and characteristic of educated blacks of his day. Her great baritone voice was so impressive that her colleagues in the Legislature used to joke that if Hollywood ever needed someone to be the voice of the Lord Almighty, only Jordan would do.**
>
> **–Molly Ivins, "Barbara Jordan: A Great Spirit"**

An argument of evaluation advances by presenting criteria and then measuring individual people, ideas, or things against those standards. Both the standards and the measurement can be explored argumentatively. And that's an important way to think of arguments—as ways to expand what's known, not just to settle differences. (For more about arguments of evaluation, see Chapter 9.)

Proposal Arguments—What Actions Should Be Taken?

In arguments that propose action, writers first have to succeed in presenting a problem in such a compelling way that readers ask: *What can we do?* A proposal argument often begins with the presentation of research to document existing conditions. Thus if you're developing an argument about rising tuition costs at your college, you could use all of the stasis questions to explore the issue and to establish that costs are indeed rising. But the last question—"What actions should be taken?"—will probably be the most important, since it will lead you to develop concrete proposals to address the rise in fees. Knowing and explaining the status quo enable writers to explore appropriate and viable alternatives and then to recommend one preferable course of action. In examining a nationwide move to eliminate remedial education in four-year colleges, John Cloud considers one possible proposal to avoid such action:

> **Students age 22 and over account for 43% of those in remedial classrooms, according to the National Center for Developmental Education.**

> [. . . But] 55% of those needing remediation must take just one course. Is it too much to ask them to pay extra for that class or take it at a community college?
>
> –John Cloud, "Who's Ready for College?"

Where a need is already obvious, writers may spend most of their energies describing and defending the solution. U.S. senators Barack Obama and Richard Lugar, for example, assume that one great threat to national security comes from the next flu pandemic. Here they detail the steps necessary to solve this problem:

> We recommend that this administration work with Congress, public health officials, the pharmaceutical industry, foreign governments and international organizations to create a permanent framework for curtailing the spread of future infectious diseases. Among the parts of that framework could be these: Increasing international disease surveillance, response capacity and public education, especially in Southeast Asia; Stockpiling enough antiviral doses to cover high-risk populations and essential workers; Ensuring that, here at home, Health and Human Services and state governments put in place plans that address issues of surveillance, medical care, drug and vaccine distribution, communication, protection of the work force, and main-

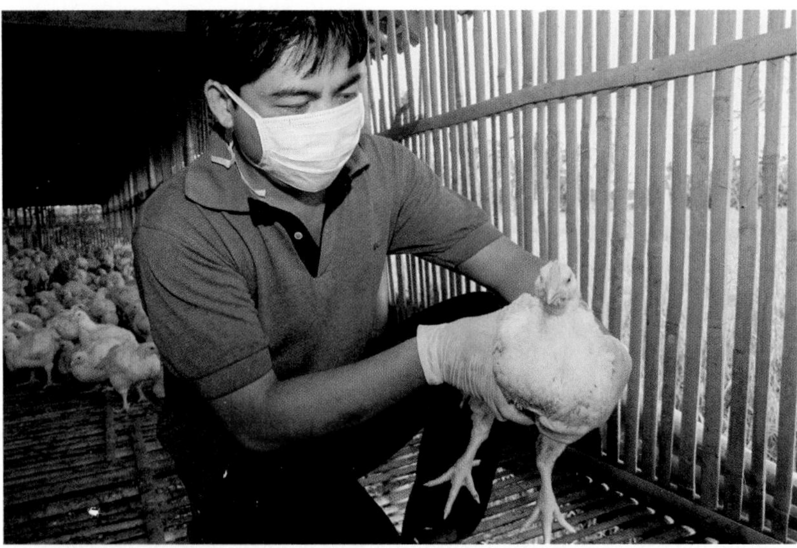

Veterinarian holding chicken to be tested for avian flu

> **tenance of core public functions in case of a pandemic; Accelerating research into avian flu vaccines and antiviral drugs; Establishing incentives to encourage nations to report flu outbreaks quickly and fully. So far, [avian flu] has not been found in the United States. But in an age when you can board planes in Bangkok or Hong Kong and arrive in Chicago, Indianapolis, or New York in hours, we must face the reality that these exotic killer diseases are not isolated health problems half a world away, but direct and immediate threats to security and prosperity here at home.**
>
> **–Barack Obama and Richard Lugar, "Grounding a Pandemic"**

Americans in particular tend to see the world in terms of problems and solutions; indeed, many expect that almost any difficulty can be overcome by the proper infusion of technology and money. So proposal arguments seem especially appealing to Americans, even though quick-fix attitudes may themselves constitute a problem. (For more about proposal arguments, see Chapter 11.)

STASIS QUESTIONS AT WORK

Suppose you have an opportunity to speak at a student conference on the issue of global warming. The Campus Young Republicans are sponsoring the conference, but they've made a point of inviting students with varying perspectives to speak. You are concerned about global warming and are tentatively in favor of strengthening industrial pollution standards aimed at reducing global warming trends. You decide that you'd like to learn a lot more by investigating the issue more fully and preparing to speak on it. You use the stasis questions to get started.

- **Did something happen?** Does global warming exist? Many in the oil and gas industry and some scientists who've studied the issue insist that global warming isn't a worldwide phenomenon, or that it essentially doesn't exist, or that the evidence is still inconclusive. The Bush administration, which had previously expressed skepticism, appeared to accept the phenomenon as real in 2005, though it still refused to sign an international agreement aimed at reducing global warming. Most scientists who've studied the issue and most other governments, on the other hand, argue that the phenomenon

(continued)

(continued)

A glacier in Central Asia turning into a lake. Are human causes responsible?

does indeed exist and that it has reached very serious proportions. In coming to your own conclusion about global warming, you'll weigh the factual evidence very carefully, making sure that you can support your answer to the question "Does it exist?" and that you can point out problems associated with opposing arguments.

- **What is the nature of the thing?** Looking for definitions of global warming also reveals great disagreement. To the extent that the Bush administration and the oil and gas industry acknowledge the phenomenon as real, they tend to define it as largely a matter of naturally occurring events (periodic long-term fluctuations in climate), while most scientists and other governments base their definition mostly on human causes (emissions of carbon dioxide and methane). Thus you begin to consider questions of cause and effect and competing definitions very carefully: *How do the definitions these groups choose to use foster the goals of each group? What's at stake*

(continued)

Washington, D.C., turning into a lake. Even in proposal arguments, humor can help.

"Gentlemen, it's time we gave some serious thought to the effects of global warming."

for the administration and the industry in promoting their definition of global warming? What's at stake for the scientists and governments who put forth the opposing definition? Exploring this stasis question will help you understand how the context of an argument shapes the claims that the argument makes.

- **What is the quality of the thing?** This question will lead you to examine claims that global warming is—or is not—harming our environment. Again, you quickly find that these charges are hotly contested, as the energy industry and the Bush administration largely dismiss the claims by most scientists and governments that the phenomenon is causing great environmental harm. Exploring these arguments will allow you to ask who or what entities are providing evidence in support of their claim and who stands to gain in this analysis. *Where does evidence for the dangers of global warming*

(continued)

(continued)

come from? Who stands to gain if the dangers are accepted as real and present, and who stands to gain if they aren't?

- **What actions should be taken?** In this case as well, you find wide disagreement. If global warming is a naturally occurring phenomenon, or may not be causing serious harm, then it's at least arguable that nothing needs to be done, that the problem will correct itself in time. Or perhaps those in the administration who have made these arguments ought to sponsor a new study of global warming, in an effort to prove once and for all that their understanding of global warming and its effects is the correct one. If, on the other hand, global warming is caused mainly by human activity and poses a clear threat to the quality of the environment, then the administration is bound to recommend implementing appropriate and effective responses to such danger (although not everyone agrees on precisely what such responses should be). You quickly discover that the definitions and assessment of harm being used directly shape the actions (or lack of action) that each side recommends. As you investigate the proposals being made and the reasons that underlie them, you come closer and closer to developing your own argument.

Using the stasis questions as a way to get into the topic of global warming adds up to a crash course on the subject. As you sort through the claims and counterclaims associated with each of the questions, you move toward identifying your own stance on global warming—and toward the claim you want to make about it for the student conference. You come to the conclusion that global warming does exist and that it does present a serious danger. Yet given the audience for the conference, you know that you still have quite a bit of work to do. Since many conference attendees will not agree with your conclusion, you begin to gather the most fair and evenhanded research available to make your case, and you begin working to establish your own credibility and to consider how best you can present your case to your specific audience.

Audiences for Arguments

No argument, of course, even one that engages stasis questions thoroughly, can be effective unless it speaks compellingly to others. Audiences for argument exist across a range of possibilities—from the flesh-and-blood person sitting right across the table from you, to the "virtual" participants in an online conversation, to the imagined ideal readers a written text invites.

The figure below may help you think about your own wide range of possible readers or audiences.

Readers and writers in context

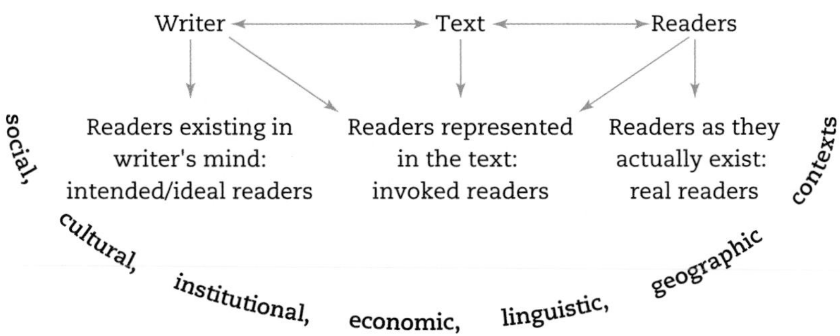

As a writer, you'll almost always be addressing an intended reader, one who exists in your own mind. As we write this textbook, we're certainly thinking of those who will read it: you are our intended reader, and ideally you know something about and are interested in the subject of this book. Though we don't know you personally, a version of you exists very much in us as writers, for we are *intending* to write for you. In the same way, the editors of student-produced *Soul Sistah* call out the audience they hope to address:

> ***Soul Sistah* is a seasonal magazine dedicated to creatively exploring spirituality as it connects to black identity, womanhood, music, culture, and sexuality. Aiming to reach a multicultural readership and writership, *Soul Sistah* is addressed to everyone interested in understanding black women's experience as well as those seeking to explore their own spirituality. . . . By giving people a forum to express themselves honestly, *Soul Sistah* creates intimacy among readers, writers, and editors.**
>
> –Editors of *Soul Sistah*

This passage reflects the editors' intention of talking to a certain group of people. But if texts—including visual texts—have intended readers (those the writer consciously intends to address), they also have invoked

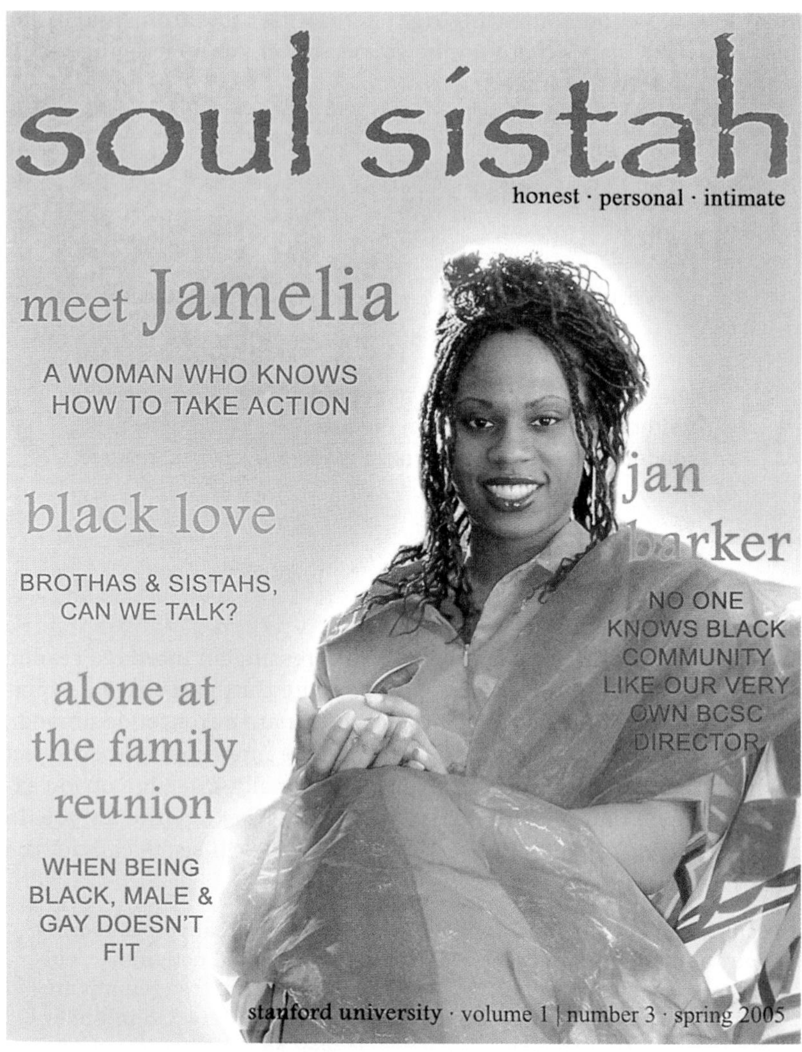

Soul Sistah, a campus magazine

readers (those who can be seen represented in the text). Later in this chapter, for example, "you" (our audience) are invoked as one who recognizes the importance of respecting readers. For another example, look at the first paragraph of this chapter; it invokes readers who are interested in the goals of argument, whether those goals are overt or subtle. And the editors of *Soul Sistah* also invoke particular readers—those interested in honest self-expression and spirituality.

Note that in spite of invoking a particular audience, the editors don't use the pronouns *we* or *us* but instead rely on *everyone*. Although the use of personal pronouns can often help make readers feel a connection to the writer, it can also be dangerous: if readers don't fit into the *us*, they can easily feel excluded from a text, and thus disaffected from it. Such is the risk that writer bell hooks takes in the passage below:

> **The most powerful resource any of us can have as we study and teach in university settings is full understanding and appreciation of the richness, beauty, and primacy of our familial and community backgrounds.**
>
> **–bell hooks, "Keeping Close to Home: Class and Education"**

This sentence reflects hooks's intention of talking to a certain *us*—"we [who] study and teach in university settings." Readers who don't fit into such an *us* may feel excluded from this group and thus from hooks's essay. And even those for whom this isn't an issue may feel alienated by hooks's celebration of "the richness, beauty, and primacy of our familial and community backgrounds." Readers who see their own backgrounds as lacking in richness or beauty—or those who came to college precisely to get away from the "primacy" of their families or communities—may well not read beyond the "our" to see how hooks develops this argument.

In addition to intended readers and the readers invoked by the text of the argument, any argument will have "real" readers—and these real people may not be the ones intended or even the ones that the text calls forth. You may pick up a letter written to someone else, for instance, and read it even though it's not intended for you. Even more likely, you may read email not sent to you but rather forwarded (sometimes unwittingly) from someone else. Or you may read a legal brief prepared for a lawyer and struggle to understand it, since you're neither the intended reader nor the knowledgeable legal expert invoked in the text. As these examples suggest, writers can't always (or even usually) control who the real readers of any argument will be. As a writer, then, you want to think carefully about these real readers and to summon up what you do know about them, even if that knowledge is limited.

When Julia Carlisle wrote an op-ed article for the *New York Times* about being "young, urban, professional, and unemployed," she intended to address readers who would sympathize with her plight; her piece invokes such readers through the use of the pronoun *we* and examples meant to suggest that she and those like her want very much to work at jobs that aren't "absurd." But Carlisle ran into many readers who felt not only excluded from her text but highly offended by it. One reader, Florence Hoff, made clear in a letter to the editor that she didn't sympathize with Carlisle at all. In fact, she saw Carlisle as self-indulgent, as feeling entitled to one kind of job while rejecting others—the jobs that Hoff and others like her are only too glad to hold. In this instance, Carlisle needed to think not only of her intended readers or of the readers her text invited in, but also of all the various "real" readers who were likely to encounter her article in the *Times*.

Considering Contexts

No consideration of readers can be complete without setting those readers in context. In fact, reading always takes place in what you might think of as a series of contexts—concentric circles that move outward from the most immediate context (the specific place and time in which the reading occurs) to broader and broader contexts, including local and community contexts, institutional contexts (such as school, church, or business) and cultural and linguistic contexts. Julia Carlisle's article, for instance, was written at a specific time and place (New York City in 1991), under certain economic conditions (increasing unemployment), and from the point of view of a white, college-educated, and fairly privileged person addressing an audience made up mostly of the same kind of people.

If Everything's an Argument . . .

Work with one or two members of your class to examine the front and back covers of this textbook. What arguments do you find being made there? How do these arguments shape your understanding of this text's purposes? What use do the covers make of emotional, ethical, and/or logical appeals? What other kinds of images or words might have been used to achieve this purpose more effectively? What audience do these covers seem to address—and how do they do so?

Thinking carefully about the context of an argument will almost always raise questions of value. Such is the case with Julia Carlisle's letter and the response it evoked: here we can see a clear clash of values, with Carlisle implicitly valuing and privileging white-collar jobs while Hoff's response calls Carlisle on her values and suggests that Hoff holds a different set of values that gives respect to blue-collar work as well. In fact, beliefs and values are often implicit rather than spelled out explicitly in arguments. But sometimes it's important to be very specific. Such was the case with Sharon Clahchischilliage, a Navajo woman who wanted to run for Secretary of State in New Mexico, even though doing so would require her to resist some of the values of her own culture. As a report in the *Washington Times* explains,

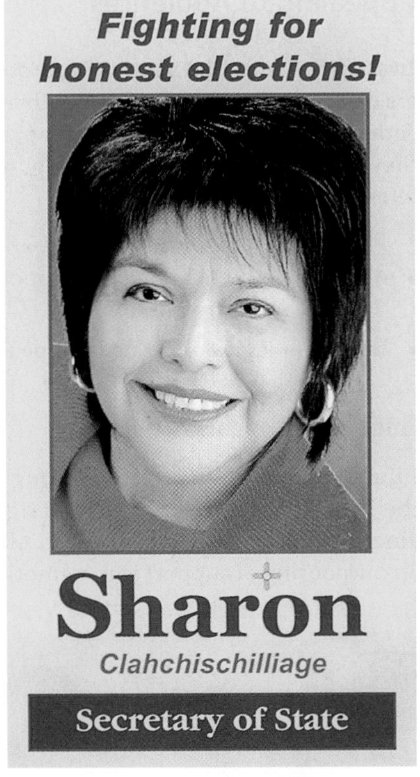

Sharon Clahchischilliage's campaign flyer

> **By placing her face on billboards around the state and publicizing her justcallmesharon.com Web site, she is bucking tribal customs. Navajos as a rule do not stare people in the eyes, nor ask for money or boast about their capabilities.**
>
> **"I'm going against the norms of my culture," she admits, "just by being a candidate."**
>
> **–Julia Duin, "Navajo Woman Vies for Political Distinction"**

As we have seen, such broader contexts and the values they entail always affect both you as a writer of arguments and those who will read and respond to your arguments. As such, they deserve your careful investigation. As you compose arguments of your own, you need to think carefully about the contexts that surround your readers—and to put your topic in context as well.

Appealing to Audiences

Twenty-five hundred years ago, Aristotle identified three key ways writers can appeal to their audiences in arguments; he labeled these appeals *pathos*, *ethos*, and *logos*. These general appeals are as effective today as they were in Aristotle's time, though we usually think of them in slightly different terms:

- pathos — emotional appeals or appeals to the heart
- ethos — ethical appeals or appeals based on the writer's authority and credibility
- logos — logical appeals or appeals to reason

Emotional Appeals

Human beings often respond strongly to emotional appeals that tug at the heartstrings. While facts and figures (or logical appeals) may convince us that the AIDS epidemic in Africa is real and serious, what elicits an outpouring of support is the emotional power of televised images and

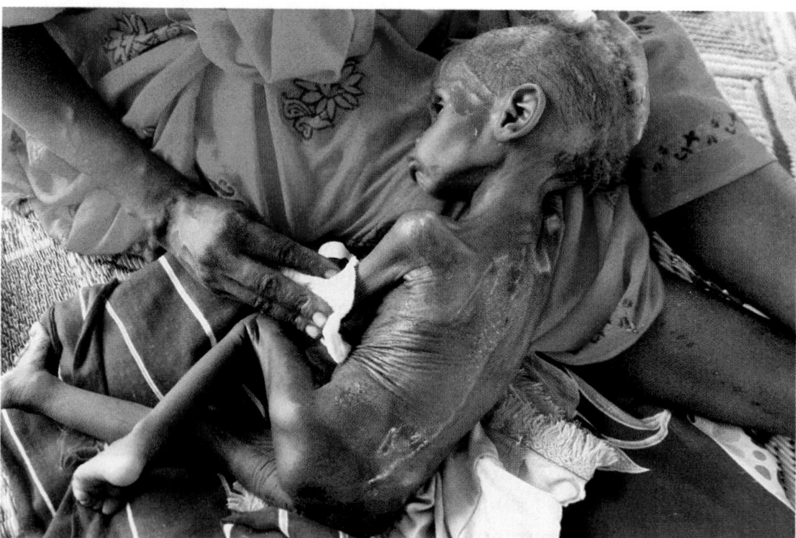

A starkly visual emotional appeal: a mother holds her ill daughter at a Doctors Without Borders clinic in Sudan, where violence and disease are killing tens of thousands.

newspaper accounts of suffering people. Concrete and descriptive language can paint pictures in readers' minds, thus building in emotional appeal, as in the following example from a student argument about providing better campus access for those using wheelchairs: "Marie inched her heavy wheelchair up the narrow, steep entrance ramp to the library, her arms straining to pull up the last twenty feet, her face pinched with the sheer effort of it." In addition, figurative language—metaphors, similes, analogies, and so on—can capture attention and appeal to emotions. In a scathing review of *Star Wars: Episode III,* reviewer Anthony Lane of the *New Yorker* uses a metaphor to stir an emotion in his readers—in this case, derision at how bad the movie is: "We already know the outcome—Anakin will indeed drop the killer-monk Jedi look and become Darth Vader, the hockey goalkeeper from hell." And, as we've already noted, visuals can make very powerful appeals to emotion. (For more about emotional appeals, see Chapter 2.)

Ethical Appeals

Equally important to an argument's success is the writer's ethos, or presentation of self. Audiences respond well to writers or speakers who seem authoritative or trustworthy. You can thus make ethical appeals to any audience by demonstrating that you're knowledgeable—you know what you're talking about and can make your case. In a researched article about the cost of protection against terrorism, for example, writer William Finnegan introduces a series of facts to support the argument that New York is having to protect itself with little help from the federal government: "In fiscal year 2004, Wyoming received $37.74 [in Homeland Security funds] per capita, and North Dakota $30.82, while New York got $5.41." Another good way to project authority is to mention your qualifications, though not in a boastful way: "My three-month observation of the communications procedures in a highly successful software firm demonstrates that. . . ."

In addition, you can build credibility in various other ways: by highlighting values that you and your audience share, by demonstrating that you're fair and evenhanded, and by showing that you respect your audience. A writer of an argument urging smokers to support a ban on smoking in restaurants might begin, for example, by saying, "For ten years I was a serious smoker, and I know how serious the addiction can be," thus demonstrating shared experiences and empathy for the audience. One final important aspect of establishing both your authority and your

A homepage that makes an ethical appeal

credibility is acknowledging opposing views and, if necessary, their strengths and the limitations of your own argument: "This proposal won't solve all the problems with the project, but it will at least put it on a more solid financial basis."

Visuals can make ethical appeals as well. For example, the banner on the homepage of the U.S. Environmental Protection Agency (above) aims to establish its credibility. The title emphasizes that this page has the authority of a U.S. government agency behind it. Underneath the title of the sponsoring agency are three pictures—of rows of healthy crops, a beautiful coastline, and a clean-looking city, each chosen to illustrate values Americans hold in common. The caption echoes the goal of protecting human health and the environment, thus making a strong ethical appeal in a very small space. (For more about ethical appeals, see Chapter 3.)

Logical Appeals

Appeals to logic are often given most prominence and authority in U.S. culture: "just the facts, ma'am," a famous early television detective used to say. Indeed, audiences respond well to the use of logic—to facts, statistics, credible testimony, cogent examples, even a narrative or story that embodies a good sound reason in support of an argument. Traditionally, logical arguments are identified as using either inductive or deductive reasoning, but in practice the two almost always work together. *Inductive reasoning* is the process of drawing a generalization on the basis of a number of specific examples: if you become sick on several occasions after eating shellfish, for instance, you'll likely draw the inductive conclusion that you're allergic to such food. *Deductive reasoning*, on the other hand, reaches a conclusion by assuming a general principle (called the major premise) and then applying that principle to a specific case (called the minor premise). The inductive generalization "Shellfish makes me ill," for example, could serve as the major premise

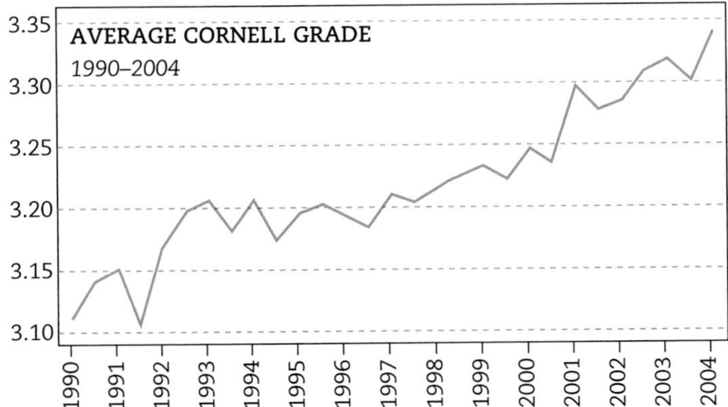

Grade inflation at Cornell. *Source:* "Society: Gut Check," *Atlantic Monthly,* June 2005, p. 44.

for a deductive chain of reasoning: "Since all shellfish makes me ill, I shouldn't eat the shrimp on this buffet." If you can draw sound inductive or deductive conclusions, and present them clearly in either words or images, they can exert strong appeals to your audience. The figure above shows a visual that makes a logical appeal about the existence of grade inflation at Cornell University. (For more about logical appeals, see Chapter 4.)

Arguments and Their Rhetorical Situations

In this chapter, we've been examining elements of argument one at a time, moving from purposes and kinds of arguments to identifying the crux of any argument (its stasis) and to ways to formulate arguments in ways that appeal to audiences. This discussion has emphasized the social nature of argument, the fact that even if we're arguing with ourselves there's some give-and-take involved, and that the argument exists in a particular context of some kind that influences how it can be shaped and how others will receive it. *The rhetorical situation* is a shorthand phrase for this entire set of concerns, and it can be depicted as a simple triangle. (See the figure on p. 42.)

It's important to think about your rhetorical situation as dynamic, since each element of it has the potential to affect all the other elements. A change of audience, for example, can lead you to reconsider all of your appeals. If you begin to think in this dynamic way, you'll be

The rhetorical triangle

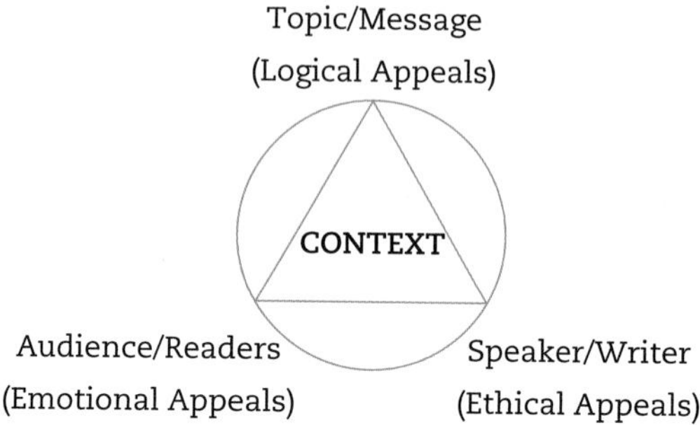

developing a rhetorical turn of mind: you'll find yourself viewing any topic from a number of perspectives (*what might a different audience think of this?*) and hence develop greater critical engagement with the issues and ideas most important to you. Such a rhetorical frame of mind might even lead you to challenge the title of this textbook: *Is everything really an argument?*

RESPOND •

1. Can an argument really be any text that expresses a point of view? What kinds of arguments—if any—might be made by the following items?

    the embossed leather cover of a prayer book

    a Boston Red Sox cap

    a Livestrong bracelet

    the label on a best-selling rap CD

    the health warning on a package of cigarettes

    a belated birthday card

    the nutrition label on a can of soup

    the cover of a science fiction novel

    a colored ribbon pinned to a shirt lapel

    a Rolex watch

2. Write short paragraphs describing times in the recent past when you've used language to inform, to convince, to explore, to make decisions, and to meditate or pray. Be sure to write at least one paragraph

for each of these purposes. Then decide whether each paragraph describes an act of argument, persuasion, or both, and offer some reasons in defense of your decisions. In class, trade paragraphs with a partner, and decide whether his or her descriptions accurately fit the categories to which they've been assigned. If they don't, then work with your partner to figure out why. Is the problem with the descriptions? The categories? Both? Neither?

3. In a recent newspaper or periodical, find three editorials—one that makes a ceremonial argument, one a deliberative argument, and one a forensic argument. Analyze the arguments by asking these questions: *Who is arguing? What purposes are the writers trying to achieve? To whom are they directing their arguments?* Then consider whether the arguments' purposes have been achieved in each case. If they have, offer some reasons for the arguments' success.

4. What common experiences—if any—do the following objects, brand names, and symbols evoke, and for what audiences in particular?

   a USDA organic label

   the Nike swoosh

   the golden arches

   the Sean John label as seen on its Web site

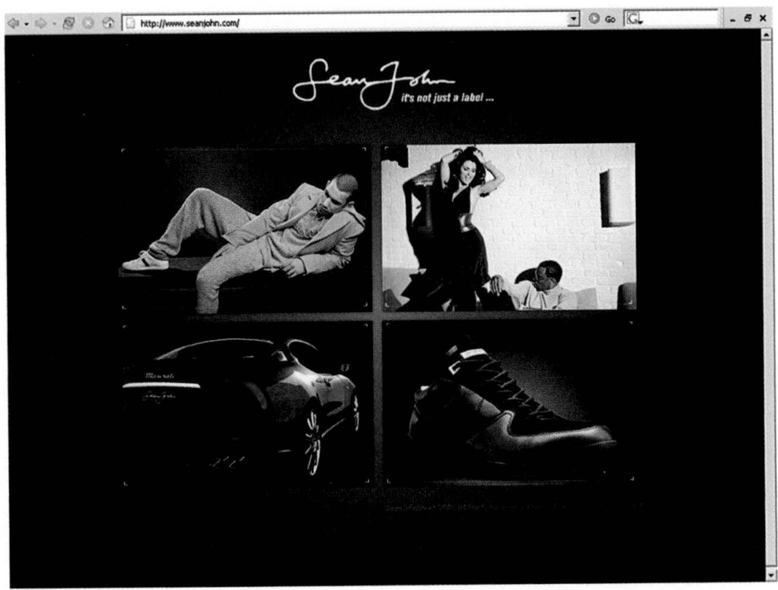

a can of Coca-Cola

Sleeping Beauty's castle on the Disney logo

Oprah Winfrey

the Vietnam Veterans Memorial

Ground Zero

a dollar bill

5. Read the main editorial in your campus newspaper for three or four days. Then choose the most interesting one, and consider how the editor creates credibility, or ethos, in the editorial.
6. Take a look at the bumper sticker below, and then analyze it. What is its purpose? What kind of argument is it? Which of the stasis questions does it most appropriately respond to? What appeals does it make to its readers, and how?

2
Arguments from the Heart—*Pathos*

What makes you glance at a magazine ad long enough to notice a product? These days, it's probably an image or boldfaced words promising pleasure (a Caribbean beach), excitement (extreme diving on Maui), beauty (a model in low-rise jeans), security (a strong firefighter), or good health (more models). In the blink of an eye, ads can appeal to your emotions, intrigue you, perhaps even seduce you. Look closer, and you might find good logical reasons given for buying a product or service. But would you have even gotten there without an emotional tug to pull you into the page?

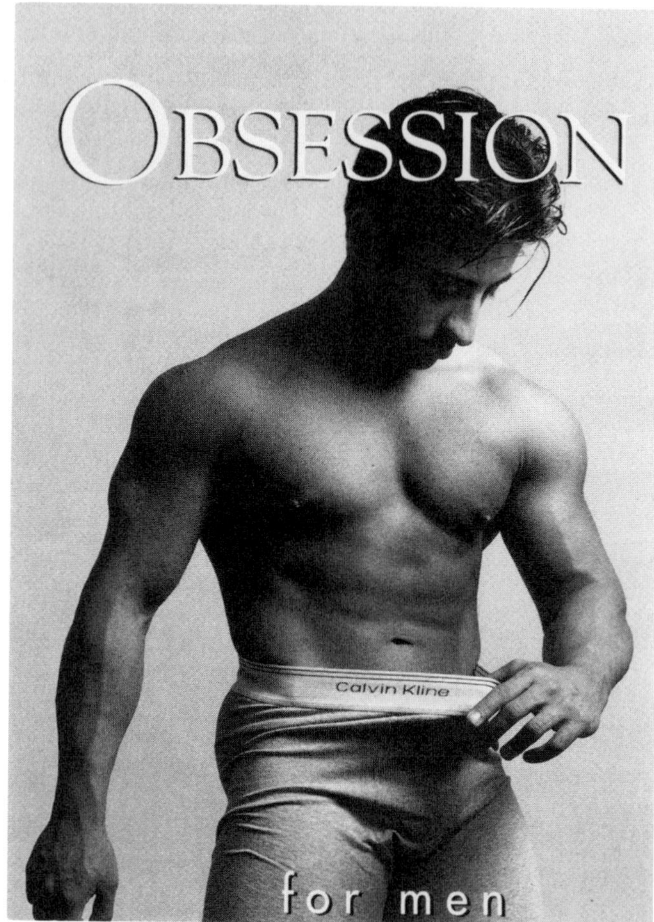

This image parodies ads that exploit one of the most powerful of emotional appeals.

Emotional appeals (sometimes called appeals to *pathos*) are powerful tools for influencing what people think and believe. We all make decisions—even important ones—based on our feelings. We rent funky apartments or buy zonked-out cars because we fall in love with some small detail. On impulse, we collect whole racks of shirts or shoes we're later too embarrassed to wear. We date, maybe even marry, people everyone else seemed to know are wrong for us—and sometimes it works out just fine.

That may be because we're not computers that use cost/benefit analyses to choose our friends or make our political decisions. Feelings belong in our lives. There's a powerful moment in Shakespeare's *Macbeth* when the soldier Macduff learns that his wife and children have been executed by the power-mad king. A well-meaning friend urges Macduff to "dispute it like a man." Macduff responds gruffly, "But I must also feel it as a man" (*Macbeth*, 4.3.219–21). As a writer, you must learn like Macduff to appreciate legitimate emotions, particularly when you want to influence the public. When you hear that formal or academic arguments should rely solely on facts, remember that facts alone often won't carry the day, even for a worthy cause. The civil rights struggle of the 1960s is a particularly good example of a movement that persuaded people equally by means of the reasonableness and the passion of its claims.

Of course, you don't have to look hard for less noble campaigns fueled with emotions such as hatred, envy, and greed. Democracies suffer when people use emotional arguments (and related fallacies such as personal attacks and name-calling) to drive wedges between groups, making them fearful and hateful. For that reason, writers can't use emotional appeals casually. (For more about emotional fallacies, see Chapter 17.)

Understanding How Emotional Arguments Work

You already know that words, images, and sounds can arouse emotions. In fact, the stirrings they generate are often physical. You've likely had the clichéd "chill down the spine" or felt something in the "pit of the stomach" when a speaker (or photograph or event) hits precisely the right note. On such occasions, it's likely that the speaker has you and people like you very purposefully in mind. At Stanford's Black Graduation ceremony in June 2005, graduating senior Efundunke Hughes was elected by her classmates to address the convocation of graduates, their parents, and friends. Speaking directly to them, Hughes called on all the students there to think not of their own achievements but rather of their ancestors, their grandparents, and especially their parents to whom they owed their success: "Stand with me today to acknowledge

Not Just Words

Take a look at this image, at first glance the familiar stars and stripes of the American flag. But a second glance reveals corporate logos rather than stars. Now look carefully at the picture, and then write for two or three minutes about the emotions that the image arouses in you. Do you respond first to the flag and then to the logos? What clash of emotional appeals do you see here, and how do you feel about that conflict? Try your hand at creating one or two possible titles or captions for this image.

and honor *them*, those who have loved and supported and nurtured us: only by standing on *their* strong shoulders have we been able to reach our dreams and goals. So stand now and begin to thank them." The audience at this commencement ceremony rose to their feet with long applause and loud cheers—for all those who had helped the students there.

Sometimes speakers are called upon to address not a particular group (such as a graduation gathering) but an entire nation, even the entire world. Such was the case during World War II when Prime Minister Winston Churchill spoke to the British House of Commons on June 4, 1940, seeking to raise British spirits and strengthen their resolve in resisting the German attacks:

> **We shall not flag or fail. We shall go on to the end. We shall fight in France, we shall fight on the seas and oceans, we shall fight with growing confidence and growing strength in the air, we shall defend our island, whatever the cost may be, we shall fight on the beaches, we shall fight on the landing grounds, we shall fight in the fields and in the streets, we shall fight in the hills. We shall never surrender.**
>
> **–Winston Churchill, "We Shall Fight on the Beaches"**

When writers and speakers can find the words and images to evoke certain emotions in people, they might also move their audiences to sympathize with ideas they connect to those feelings, and even to act on them. Make people aware of how much they owe to others, and they'll acknowledge that debt; make people hate an enemy, and they'll rally against him; help people to imagine suffering, and they'll strive to relieve it; make people feel secure or happy (or insecure or unhappy), and they'll buy products that promise such good feelings.

Arguments from the heart probably count more when you're persuading than when you're arguing. When arguing, you might use reasons and evidence to convince readers something is true—for instance, that preserving wetlands is a worthy environmental goal. When persuading, however, you want people to take action—to join an environmental boycott, contribute money to an organization dedicated to wetlands protection, or write a well-researched op-ed piece for the local paper about a local marsh threatened by development.

Argument (discover a truth) ——→ conviction
Persuasion (know a truth) ——→ action

He Ain't Heavy, We're All Brothers.

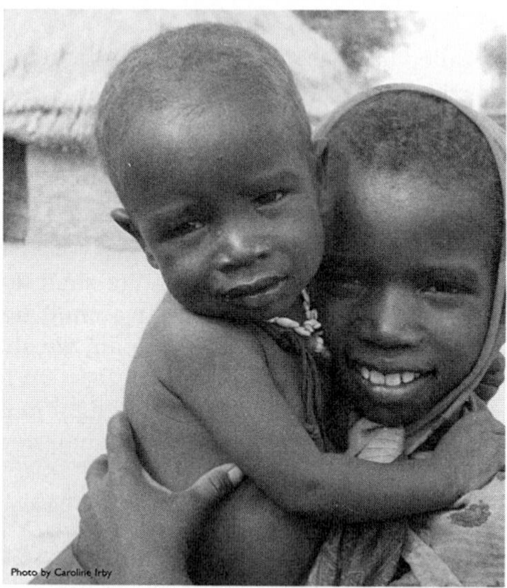

In Sudan, where civil war has ravaged and emptied thousands of villages, we are bringing food, water, health care and protection to 350,000 children and families in 44 camps. Save the Children is the leading independent organization creating lasting change for children in need in the U.S. and around the world.

To learn more about our work, contact Fiona Hodgson
203-221-4002 fiona@savechildren.org 54 Wilton Road, Westport, CT 06880
www.savethechildren.org

Save the Children motivates contributors with a touching image and an inspiring story.

The practical differences between being convinced and acting on a conviction can be enormous. Your readers may agree that contributing to charity is a noble act, but that conviction may not be enough to persuade them to part with their spare change. You need a spur sharper than logic, and that's when emotion might kick in. You can embarrass readers into contributing to a good cause ("Change a child's life for the price of a pizza") or make them feel the impact of their gift ("Imagine the smile on that little child's face") or tell them a moving story ("In a tiny village in Central America . . ."). Doubtless, you've seen such techniques work.

Using Emotions to Build Bridges

You may sometimes want to use emotions to connect with readers, to assure them that you understand their experiences or, to use a famous political line, "feel their pain." Such a bridge is especially important when you're writing about matters that readers regard as sensitive. Before they'll trust you, they'll want assurances that you understand the issues in depth. If you strike the right emotional note, you'll establish an important connection.

That's what Apple founder Steve Jobs does in a 2005 commencement address, in which he tells the audience that he doesn't have a fancy speech, just three stories from his life:

> **My second story is about love and loss. I was lucky. I found what I loved to do early in life. Woz and I started Apple in my parents' garage when I was twenty. We worked hard and in ten years, Apple had grown from just the two of us in a garage into a $2 billion company with over 4,000 employees. We'd just released our finest creation, the Macintosh, a year earlier, and I'd just turned thirty, and then I got fired. How can you get fired from a company you started? Well, as Apple grew, we hired someone who I thought was very talented to run the company with me, and for the first year or so, things went well. But then our visions of the future began to diverge, and eventually we had a falling out. When we did, our board of directors sided with him, and so at thirty, I was out, and very publicly out. . . .**
>
> **I didn't see it then, but it turned out that getting fired from Apple was the best thing that could have ever happened to me. The heaviness of being successful was replaced by the lightness of being a beginner again, less sure about everything. It freed me to enter one of the most creative periods in my life. During the next five years I started a company named NeXT, another company named Pixar and fell in love with an amazing woman who would become my wife. Pixar went on to create the world's first computer-animated feature**

Myriam Marquez connects emotionally with readers in her essay "Why and When We Speak Spanish in Public" describing the respect and comfort she creates for her parents by speaking Spanish with them, even in public. Marquez broaches this controversial topic by acknowledging that people don't like her decision and connecting her choice to a common value, family.

LINK TO P. 754

> film, "Toy Story," and is now the most successful animation studio in the world.
>
> –Steve Jobs, "You've Got to Find What You Love, Jobs Says"

In no obvious way is Jobs's recollection a formal argument. But it prepares his audience to accept the advice he'll give later in his speech, at least partly because he's speaking from deep personal experiences of his own.

A more obvious way to build an emotional tie is simply to help readers identify with your experiences. If, like Georgina Kleege, you were blind and wanted to argue for more sensible attitudes toward blind people, you might ask readers in the very first paragraph of your argument to confront their prejudices. Here Kleege, a writer and college instructor, makes an emotional point by telling a story:

> I tell the class, "I am legally blind." There is a pause, a collective intake of breath. I feel them look away uncertainly and then look back. After all, I just said I couldn't see. Or did I? I had managed to get there on my own—no cane, no dog, none of the usual trappings of blindness. Eyeing me askance now, they might detect that my gaze is not quite focused. . . . They watch me glance down, or towards the door where someone's coming in late. I'm just like anyone else.
>
> –Georgina Kleege, "Call It Blindness"

Given the way she narrates the first day of class, readers are as likely to identify with the students as with Kleege, imagining themselves sitting in a classroom, facing a sightless instructor, confronting their own prejudices about the blind. Kleege wants to put them on edge emotionally.

Let's consider another rhetorical situation: how do you win over an audience when the logical claims you're making are likely to go against what many in the audience believe? Once again, a slightly risky appeal to emotions on a personal level may work. That's the tack Michael Pollan takes in bringing readers to consider that "the great moral struggle of our time will be for the rights of animals." In introducing his lengthy exploratory argument, Pollan uses personal experience to appeal to his audience:

> The first time I opened Peter Singer's *Animal Liberation*, I was dining alone at the Palm, trying to enjoy a rib-eye steak cooked medium-rare. If this sounds like a good recipe for cognitive dissonance (if not indigestion), that was sort of the idea. Preposterous as it might seem to

A visual version of Michael Pollan's rhetorical situation

THE BIRTH OF A VEGETARIAN

> **supporters of animal rights, what I was doing was tantamount to reading *Uncle Tom's Cabin* on a plantation in the Deep South in 1852.**
>
> **–Michael Pollan, "An Animal's Place"**

In creating a vivid image of his first encounter with Singer's book, Pollan's opening builds a bridge between himself as a person trying to enter into the animal rights debate in a fair and open-minded, if still skeptical, way and readers who will surely be passionate about either side of this argument.

If Everything's an Argument . . .

Look at the opening pages of this chapter, and note the words and images that give, as the first paragraph puts it, an "emotional tug to pull you into the page." Given that these pages are trying to impress on college students the importance of emotional appeals in arguments, how well do they accomplish that goal? Are there other things the authors and editors might have done to make these pages even more emotionally appealing to this audience?

Using Emotions to Sustain an Argument

Mukhtaran Bibi in September 2004

You can also use emotional appeals to make logical claims stronger or more memorable. That is, in fact, the way photographs and other images add power to arguments. In a TV attack ad, the scowling black-and-white photograph of a political opponent may do as much damage as the claim that his bank laundered drug money. Or the attractive skier in a spot for lip balm may make us yearn for brisk, snowy winter days. The technique is tricky, however. Lay on too much emotion—especially those like outrage, pity, or shame, which make people uncomfortable—and you may offend the very audiences you hoped to convince. But sometimes a strong emotion such as anger adds energy to a passage, as it does when columnist Nicholas Kristof berates the Pakistani government for imprisoning Mukhtaran Bibi—a woman who had done nothing except speak out against gang rape and the U.S. government for its refusal to condemn such actions—and accompanies his column with a picture of the woman he is trying to help. As you read the excerpt from Kristof's editorial, ask yourself why that particular picture was chosen to accompany the text. What does it add to the emotional pull of the argument? (Consider the positioning of the woman and her expression and gesture, as well as the use of color.)

> **Excuse me, but Ms. Mukhtaran, a symbol of courage and altruism, is the best hope for Pakistan's image. The threat to Pakistan's image comes from President Musharraf for all this thuggish behavior.**
>
> **I've been sympathetic to Mr. Musharraf till now, despite his nuclear negligence. . . . So even when Mr. Musharraf denied me visas all this year, to block me from visiting Ms. Mukhtaran again and writing a follow-up column, I bit my tongue.**
>
> **But now President Musharraf has gone nuts.**
>
> **"This is all because they think they have the support of the U.S. and can get away with murder," Ms. Jahangir said. Indeed, on Friday, just as all this was happening, President Bush received Pakistan's foreign minister in the White House and praised President Musharraf's "bold leadership."**

> **So, Mr. Bush, how about asking Mr. Musharraf to focus on finding Osama, instead of kidnapping rape victims who speak out? And invite Ms. Mukhtaran to the Oval Office—to show that Americans stand not only with generals who seize power, but also with ordinary people of extraordinary courage.**
>
> **–Nicholas Kristof, "Raped, Kidnapped, and Silenced"**

Here the challenge in Kristof's sarcasm becomes part of the argument: *If you act in the way President Musharraf has done, you open yourself to such a powerful response.*

In the same way, writers can generate emotions by presenting logical arguments in their starkest terms, stripped of qualifications or subtleties. Readers or listeners are confronted with core issues or important choices and asked to consider the consequences. It's hard to imagine an argument more serious than a debate about life and death, or one more likely to raise powerful feelings. Here is Andrew Sullivan on his blog in June 2005, commenting on the report that autopsy results on Terri Schiavo, the Florida woman whose family had fought bitterly over whether or not to

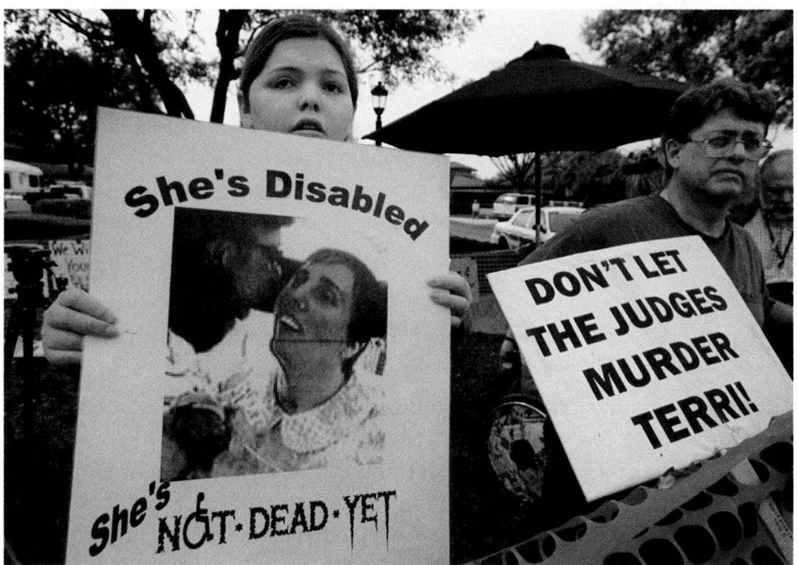

Demonstrators and politicians used highly charged language and images in their unsuccessful efforts to prevent Terri Schiavo's husband from removing her life support systems.

stop the life support systems that had been keeping her alive for over a decade, showed that she would never have been able to recover:

> **1:09 P.M. June 15, 2005. In her final days, Terri Schiavo was blind and her brain was about half its expected size. She wasn't in a PVS [Persistent Vegetative State]? Please. Bill Frist needs to acknowledge his reckless political opportunism at the time. The attempts of the fringe, theocon right to allege that her husband abused her have also been exposed as malicious falsehoods. Remember the lies that were told, the junk science that the theocons came up with, the endless slanders and misrepresentations? It's rare that we get an objective resolution of a fiercely disputed matter. We have now. And it ain't pretty.**
>
> **–Andrew Sullivan, "They Lied"**

You might imagine how an opponent of suspending life support might respond: *Nothing can ever justify such an action.* Would a less in-your-face approach appeal more successfully to such an audience, or is Sullivan right to take the emotional issue head on—and with his own emotions clearly on display?

As you can see, it's difficult to gauge how much emotion will work in a given argument. Some issues—such as racism, date rape, abortion, gun control—provoke strong feelings and, as a result, are often argued on emotional terms. But even issues that seem deadly dull—such as funding for Medicare and Social Security—can be argued in emotional terms when proposed changes in these programs are set in human terms: *Cut benefits and Grandma will have to eat cat food; don't cut benefits and the whole health care system will go broke, leaving nothing for aging baby boomers.* Both alternatives might scare people into paying enough attention to take political action.

Using Humor

Arguments of humor are a mainstay of the online weekly publication *The Onion.* Their article about anthropomorphic recyclables pokes fun at our often hypersensitivity to race and ethnicity.

LINK TO P. 673

Humor has always played an important role in argument, sometimes as the sugar that makes the medicine go down. You can certainly slip humor into an argument to put readers at ease, thereby making them more open to a proposal you have to offer. It's hard to say "no" when you're laughing. Humor also makes otherwise sober people suspend their judgment and even their prejudices, perhaps because the surprise and naughtiness of wit are combustive: they provoke laughter or smiles, not reflection. That may be why TV sitcoms like *Sex and the City* or *Will & Grace* have become popular with mainstream audiences, despite their sometimes controversial subjects. Similarly, it's possible to make a point through humor that might not work at all in more sober writing. Consider the gross stereotypes about men that humorist Dave Barry presents here, tongue in cheek, explaining why people don't read the instructions that come with the products they buy:

> **The third reason why consumers don't read manuals is that many consumers are men, and we men would no more read a manual than we would ask directions, because this would be an admission that the person who wrote the manual has a bigger . . . OK, a bigger grasp of technology than we do. We men would rather hook up our new DVD player in such a way that it ignites the DVDs and shoots them across the room—like small flaming UFOs—than admit that the manual-writer possesses a more manly technological manhood than we do.**
>
> **–Dave Barry, "Owners' manual Step No. 1: Bang head against the wall"**

Our laughter testifies to a kernel of truth in Barry's observations and makes us more likely to agree with his conclusions.

A writer or speaker can use humor to deal with especially sensitive issues. For example, sports commentator Bob Costas, given the honor of eulogizing the great baseball player Mickey Mantle, couldn't ignore well-known flaws in Mantle's character. So he argues for Mantle's greatness by admitting the man's weaknesses indirectly through humor:

> **It brings to mind a story Mickey liked to tell on himself and maybe some of you have heard it. He pictured himself at the pearly gates, met by St. Peter who shook his head and said "Mick, we checked the record. We know some of what went on. Sorry, we can't let you in. But before you go, God wants to know if you'd sign these six dozen baseballs."**
>
> **–Bob Costas, "Eulogy for Mickey Mantle"**

Similarly, politicians use humor to admit problems or mistakes they couldn't acknowledge in any other way. Here, for example, is President Bush at the 2004 Radio & TV Correspondents Dinner discussing his much-mocked intellect:

> **Those stories about my intellectual capacity do get under my skin. You know, for a while I even thought my staff believed it. There on my schedule first thing every morning it said, "Intelligence briefing."**
>
> **–George W. Bush**

Not all humor is well intentioned. In fact, among the most powerful forms of emotional argument is ridicule—humor aimed at a particular target. Eighteenth-century poet and critic Samuel Johnson was known

A VILLAGE IN TEXAS IS MISSING ITS IDIOT

STAMPANDSHOUT.COM

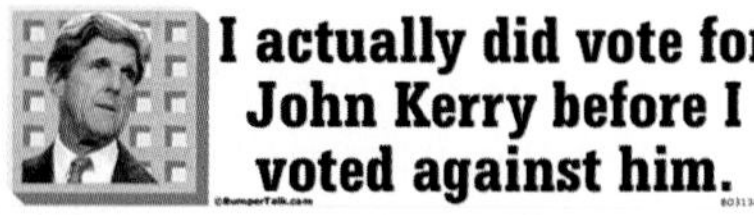

for his stinging and humorous putdowns, such as this comment to an aspiring writer: “Your manuscript is both good and original, but the part that is good is not original and the part that is original is not good.” Today, even bumper stickers can be vehicles for succinct arguments (see the ones above).

But ridicule is a two-edged sword that requires a deft hand to wield it. Humor that reflects bad taste discredits a writer completely, as does ridicule that misses its mark. Unless your target deserves assault and you can be very funny, it’s usually better to steer clear of humor. (For more on humorous arguments, see Chapter 13.)

Using Arguments from the Heart

The creators of the National Youth Anti-Drug Media Campaign chose to use stereotyped photos of youth who looked like they might use drugs with a written message that challenged that perception. This kind of emotional appeal probably impacts readers more strongly than a picture of drugs or even of an all-American clean-cut youth with a straightforward anti-drug message.

LINK TO P. 822

You don’t want to play puppetmaster with people’s emotions when you write arguments, but it’s a good idea to spend some time early in your writing or designing process thinking about how you want readers to feel as they consider your persuasive claims. For example, would readers of your editorial about campus traffic policies be more inclined to agree with you if you made them envy faculty privileges, or would arousing their sense of fairness work better? What emotional appeals might persuade meat eaters to consider a vegan diet—or vice versa? Would sketches of stage props on a Web site persuade people to buy a season ticket to the theater, or would you spark more interest by featuring pictures of costumed performers?

Consider, too, the impact that telling a story can have on readers. Writers and journalists routinely use what are called human interest stories to give presence to issues or arguments. You can do the same, using a particular incident to evoke sympathy, understanding, outrage, or amusement. Take care, though, to tell an honest story.

RESPOND•

1. To what specific emotions do the following slogans, sales pitches, and maxims appeal?

   “Just do it.” (ad for Nike)

   “Think different.” (ad for Apple Computers)

"Reach out and touch someone." (ad for AT&T)

"In your heart, you know he's right." (1964 campaign slogan for U.S. presidential candidate Barry Goldwater, a conservative)

"It's the economy, stupid!" (1992 campaign theme for U.S. presidential candidate Bill Clinton)

"By any means necessary." (rallying cry from Malcolm X)

"Have it your way." (slogan for Burger King)

"You can trust your car to the man who wears the star." (slogan for Texaco)

"It's everywhere you want to be." (slogan for Visa)

"Know what comes between me and my Calvins? Nothing!" (tag line for Calvin Klein jeans)

"Don't mess with Texas!" (antilitter campaign slogan)

2. Bring a magazine to class, and analyze the emotional appeals in as many full-page ads as you can. Then classify those ads by types of emotional appeal, and see whether you can connect the appeals to the subject or target audience of the magazine. Compare your results with those of your classmates, and discuss your findings. For instance, do the ads in newsmagazines like *Time* and *Newsweek* appeal to different emotions and desires from the ads in publications such as *Cosmopolitan, Rolling Stone, Sports Illustrated, Automobile,* and *National Geographic?*

3. How do arguments from the heart work in different media? Are such arguments more or less effective in books, articles, television (both news and entertainment shows), films, brochures, magazines, email, Web sites, the theater, street protests, and so on? You might focus on a single medium, exploring how it handles emotional appeals, or compare different media. For example, why do Internet news groups seem to encourage angry outbursts? Are newspapers an emotionally colder source of information than television news programs? If so, why?

4. Spend some time looking for arguments that use ridicule or humor to make their point—check out your favorite Web sites; watch for bumper stickers, posters, or advertisements; and listen to popular lyrics. Bring one or two examples to class, and be ready to explain how the humor makes an emotional appeal and whether it's effective or not.

3
Arguments Based on Character—*Ethos*

It was a memorable moment—Massachusetts senator John Kerry walking up to the podium at the Democratic National Convention in 2004 to accept his party's nomination for president and beginning his speech with a smart military salute and these words:

"I'm John Kerry, and I'm reporting for duty."

It made a fine image too, suggesting powerfully that the Democratic Party had chosen a presidential candidate with real credentials to serve as commander-in-chief in time of war, unlike incumbent President George W. Bush, whose Air National Guard record during the

John Kerry at the Democratic National Convention, July 29, 2004

Vietnam era was regularly (if sometimes inaccurately) called into question by mainstream media. Kerry, in contrast, had actually fought in Vietnam and received three Purple Hearts. By his salute, Kerry affirmed that having served his country once, he was ready to do so again. He was making an argument based on character, or *ethos*—the presentation of self that a writer or speaker brings to an argument.

Audiences clearly pay attention to ethos. Before we'll listen to others, we usually must respect their authority, admire their integrity and motives, or at least acknowledge what they stand for. "Others," of course, can be a person, such as presidential candidate John Kerry; a group or organization, like the American Civil Liberties Union or Students for Academic Freedom; or an institution, such as a corporation, newspaper, or college. We observe people, groups, or institutions making and defending claims all the time and ask ourselves: *Should we pay attention to them? Can we trust them?* Establishing a persuasive ethos, however, is not simply a matter of seeming honest or likable but also of affirming an identity and sharing values with one's intended audiences.

Touch the photo to see which Swift officers support John Kerry, or click it to read more.

The purpose of this photo is to correct the misleading use of our images—against our will—to further John Kerry's campaign.

Not Just Words

A group called Swift Vets and POWs for Truth used a number of visual arguments in an attempt to undermine Senator John Kerry's ethos during the presidential campaign of 2004. One argument involved a photograph the group claimed the Kerry campaign had used without authorization to suggest that all soldiers who fought with him in Vietnam supported his presidential bid. The group took advantage of the graphic capabilities of the Web to make its point.

- Do some research to explore the facts surrounding the use of the "Band of Brothers" photograph. How well does the visual

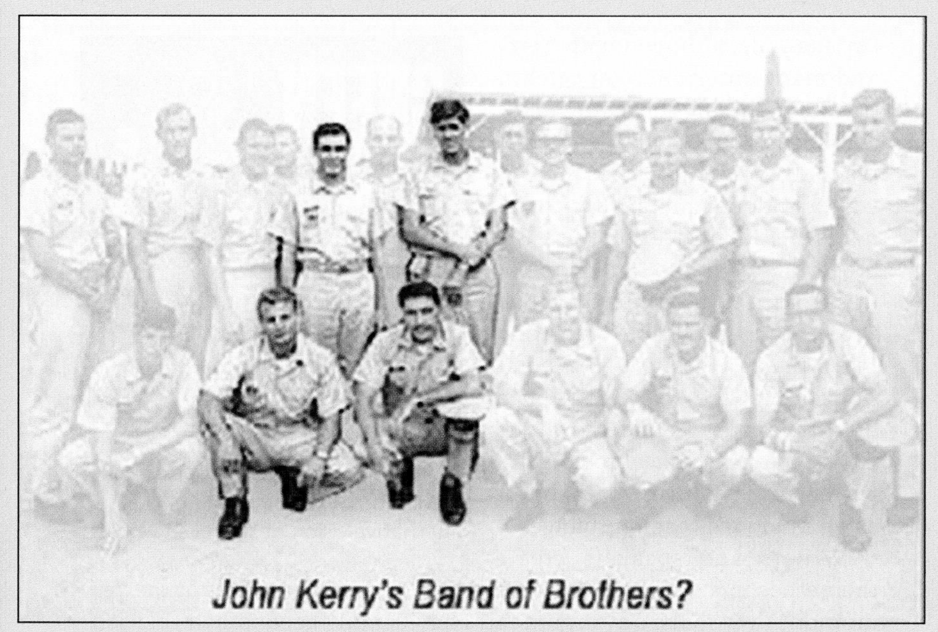

John Kerry's Band of Brothers?

presentation alone convey the complexities of the situation? You might explore campaign Web sites (many of which are archived) or coverage in newspapers and magazines, using such resources as LexisNexis and EBSCO.

- What issues of ethos does this visual argument raise? What questions does it raise about Kerry? What questions might it raise about the Swift Vets and POWs for Truth?
- Working in a group, imagine arguments that might use a similar technique, especially on issues of value or character. Choose one of the ideas, and create a full mock-up of the argument, either on paper or on the Web.

For example, although both Kerry and many entertainment celebrities were singing the same political tune in 2004, they attempted to reach different audiences. Kerry's very traditional military salute signaled his identification with the broad middle of the American political spectrum, while the band Green Day used a different and more charged, gesture—a revolutionary's raised fist clutching a heart-shaped grenade—on its 2004 CD *American Idiot* to connect with mainly younger voters interested in more sweeping change.

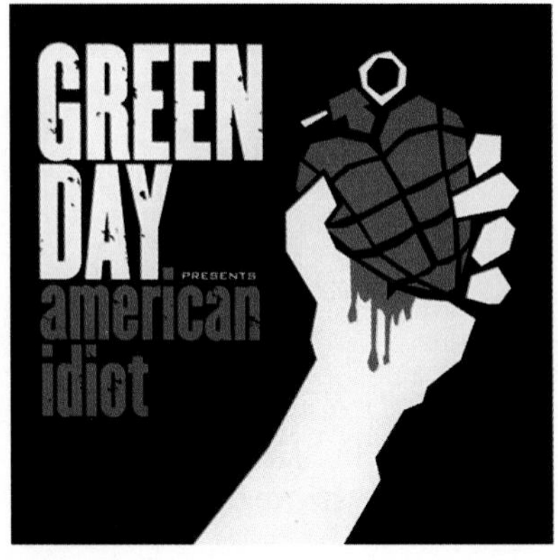

For the cover of its 2004 rock opera, Green Day used a traditional revolutionary gesture to support an alternative vision of American values.

Writers and speakers create their ethos in at least two ways. First, they shape themselves at the very moment they make any argument. They usually accomplish this self-fashioning through the language they use, the evidence they offer, the respect they show those with whom they disagree, and the way they tender themselves to an audience physically—through gestures, posture, eye contact, and tone of voice (or their equivalents in writing or imagery). Kerry's salute was just such a character-defining moment, crafted to affirm his stature and proclaim his values before a cheering convention and millions of TV viewers, a great many of whom may have not known much about him prior to his acceptance speech. Arguments of character frequently merge with issues of value in just this way because audiences tend to trust people with whom they can identify.

But writers and speakers also bring their previous lives, work, and reputations to the table when they make an argument. If they are well known, liked, and respected, that reputation will contribute to their persuasive power. If their character is problematic in any respect, they may have to use the speech to reshape an audience's perception. Some people in Kerry's audience were aware and worried that he was involved in Vietnam-era antiwar protests. The salute was possibly designed to reassure them that Kerry would be a trustworthy steward of the country's interests—one who respected the role of the military enough to begin his new role as an official presidential candidate by evoking its traditions and values.

Understanding How Arguments Based on Character Work

Because life is complicated, we often need shortcuts to help us make choices; we can't weigh every claim to its last milligram or trace every fragment of evidence to its original source. And we have to make such decisions daily: *Which college or university should I attend? Whom should I vote for in the next election? Which reviewers of Peter Jackson's* King Kong *will I believe? What are the real risks in taking prescription painkillers?* To answer the more serious questions, people typically turn to professionals for wise, well-informed, and frank advice: a doctor, lawyer, teacher, pastor. But people look to equally knowledgeable individuals to guide them in less momentous matters as well: a coach, a friend, maybe even a waiter (*Is the fish really fresh?*). Depending on the subject, an *expert* can be anyone with knowledge and experience, from a professor of nuclear physics at an Ivy League college to a short-order cook at the local diner.

Readers give people (or institutions) they know a hearing they might not automatically grant to a stranger or to someone who hasn't earned their respect or affection. That trust indicates the power of arguments based on ethos/character and accounts for why people will take the word of the "car guy" in their neighborhood more seriously than the reviews in *Consumer Reports*. And they'll believe *Consumer Reports* more readily than the SUV ads in *People*. Appeals or arguments about character often turn on claims such as the following:

- A person (or group) does or does not have the authority to speak to this issue.
- A person is or is not trustworthy or credible on this issue.
- A person does or does not have good motives for addressing this subject.

"Wearing a Head Scarf Is My Choice as a Muslim; Please Respect It" is an essay by Mariam Rahmani in which she defends her religious tradition. As a Muslim woman who wants to wear a scarf, Rahami is able to present herself as an authority on the issue. She does not claim to speak for all Muslim women but uses her position to argue for a choice.

LINK TO P. 897

Claiming Authority

When you read an argument, especially one that makes an aggressive claim, you have every right to wonder about the writer's authority: *What does he know about the subject? What experiences does she have that make her especially knowledgeable? Why should I pay attention to this writer?*

When you offer an argument yourself, you have to anticipate pointed questions exactly like these and be able to answer them, directly or indirectly. Sometimes the claim of authority will be bold and personal, as it is when *Wall Street Journal* political writer Peggy Noonan responds to complaints by columnist Anna Quindlen that her political views provoke hate mail. What gives Noonan special expertise to speak on this subject? She too has taken the heat from those who dislike what she puts in her own columns:

> She [Anna Quindlen] said, as she has in the past—she says it a lot, actually—that she gets a lot of hate mail because of the views she holds. I don't doubt it. But when she speaks of it she always seems to be suggesting she has a lot of courage to write what she writes. *See what I have to put up with, and see how I persevere.* There's an air of indignation. *Do you believe what a nice liberal has to put up with from these right-wing primitives?*

Noonan dents Quindlen's ethos by suggesting that the columnist's complaints are a chronic form of heroic posturing.

Anna Quindlen

Peggy Noonan

Well Anna, . . . I have never written of this or even spoken of it, but let me tell you something.

My political philosophy is conservative. I am pro-life. I live in New York City, surrounded by modern people. They are mostly left-wing, they are all pro-choice, many of them passionately and even furiously so. I have written books saying Ronald Reagan is a great man and Hillary Clinton is a bad woman. I know something about being a target, and I know something about hate mail. I have received not hundreds but thousands of the most personal and obscene denunciations; I have received death threats; I have been threatened with blackmail; I have been informed that I do not deserve to live; I have received a three page typed double spaced letter with perfect grammar and syntax the first sentence of which was "Dr. Ms. Noonan, Let me explain to you why you are a . . ." and here I cannot suggest the word used. But damned if he didn't make a good case. I used to hear regularly from a woman who'd tell me she hopes I have a brain hemorrhage.

Deliberately both comparing and contrasting herself with Quindlen, Noonan claims that she too has taken heat from readers, but in her case, without making an issue of it. Addressing her target directly by first name and with "Let me tell you something" creates an aggressively challenging ethos, one that risks arrogance but suits her point about harsh personal attacks.

The note of humor here probably enhances Noonan's credibility with readers.

I have never talked about this because I would consider speaking of it both self-pitying and self-aggrandizing. But there's another reason. I'm a grownup. I know you pay a price for the stands you take.

Noonan claims the ethos of a responsible adult.

It's a disputatious world. Rocks get thrown. I could make myself safer by changing my views, but why would I abandon what I think is true so that people I think are wrong will like me? That doesn't make sense. So I stand where I stand and pay. And you know what? Too bad. Tough. That's life. Nothing is free. If you hold a controversial position you will draw controversy and

Even the sentence fragments here reinforce the toughness of the ethos Noonan creates.

> **its cousins: denunciation, dislike, etc. It's the price you pay.**
>
> **–Peggy Noonan, "Stand Up and Take It Like an American"**

Noonan is unusually blunt in the way she establishes her ethos in this column.

Ariel Dorfman speaks of his personal experiences living in English- and Spanish-speaking countries when he explains why he believes everyone should learn a second language. By sharing his own progression from militant monolingual to thankful bilingual, Dorfman establishes an ethos of experience and a base from which to speak authoritatively.

LINK TO P. 797

Writers typically establish their authority in other and less striking ways. We may not have lords and dukes in the United States, but many of us, it seems, have a job title that confers some clout. When writers attach such titles to their names, they're saying, "This is how I've earned the right to be heard"—they are medical doctors or have law degrees or have been board certified to work as psychotherapists. Similarly, writers can assert authority by mentioning who employs them—their institutional affiliations—and how long they've worked in a given field.

Bureaucrats often identify themselves with their agencies, and professors with their schools. As a reader, you'll likely pay more attention to an argument about global warming if it's offered by someone who identifies herself as a professor of atmospheric and oceanic science at the University of Wisconsin, Madison, than by your Uncle Sid who sells tools at Sears. But you'll prefer your uncle to the professor when you need advice about a reliable rotary saw.

When your readers are apt to be skeptical of both you and your claim—as is usually the case when your subject is controversial—you may have to be even more specific about your credentials. That's exactly the strategy Richard Bernstein uses to establish his right to speak on the delicate subject of teaching multiculturalism in American colleges and universities. At one point in a lengthy argument, he challenges those who make simplistic pronouncements about non-Western cultures, specifically "Asian culture." But what gives a New York writer named Bernstein the authority to write about Asian peoples? Bernstein tells us in a sparkling example of an argument based on character:

> **The Asian culture, as it happens, is something I know a bit about, having spent five years at Harvard striving for a Ph.D. in a joint program called History and East Asian Languages and, after that, living either as a student (for one year) or a journalist (six years) in China and Southeast Asia. At least I know enough to know there is no such thing as the "Asian culture."**
>
> **–Richard Bernstein, *Dictatorship of Virtue***

Clearly, Bernstein understates the case when he says he knows "a bit" about Asian culture and then mentions a Ph.D. program at Harvard and years of living in Asia. But the false modesty may be part of his argumentative strategy, too.

When you write for readers who trust you and your work, you may not have to make an open claim to authority. But you should know that making this type of appeal is always an option. A second lesson is that it certainly helps to know your subject when you're making a claim.

Even if an author doesn't make an explicit effort to assert it, authority can be conveyed through tiny signals that readers may pick up almost subconsciously. Sometimes it comes just from a style of writing that presents ideas with robust confidence. For example, years ago when Allan Bloom wrote a controversial book about problems in American education, he used tough, self-assured prose to argue for what needed to be done. We've italicized the words that convey his confident ethos:

> **_Of course,_ the only _serious_ solution [to the problems of higher education] is the one that is almost universally rejected: the _good old_ Great Books approach. . . . I am _perfectly aware_ of, and actually agree with, the objections to the Great Books Cult. . . . But _one thing is certain:_ wherever the Great Books make up a central part of the curriculum, the students are excited and satisfied.**
>
> **–Allan Bloom, _The Closing of the American Mind_ (emphasis added)**

Establishing Credibility

Whereas authority is a measure of how much command someone has over a subject, credibility speaks to a writer's honesty and respect for the audience. The simplest way of establishing your credibility with an audience that doesn't know you is to make reasonable claims and then to back them up with evidence and documentation—or, in electronic environments, to link your claims to sites with reliable information. That is, authority is itself a good way to build credibility.

In "Bad as They Wanna Be," Thad Williamson establishes his credibility by beginning the essay with a declaration of his devotion to collegiate sports. This pronouncement positions him in allegiance with the same institutions that he criticizes, lending him an air of evenhandedness.

LINK TO P. 716

But there's a lot more to it than that. Consider that a number of studies over the years have shown that tall, thin, good-looking people have an advantage in getting a job or getting a raise. Apparently, employers make assumptions about such people's competence based on nothing more than good looks. You probably act the same way in some circumstances, even if you resent the practice. (A more recent study shows that good-looking instructors score significantly higher in teaching evaluations than their more unsightly colleagues.)

You might recall these studies when you make an argument, knowing that like it or not, readers and audiences are going to respond to how you

CULTURAL CONTEXTS FOR ARGUMENT

Ethos

In the United States, students writing arguments are often asked to establish authority by drawing on certain kinds of personal experience, by reporting on research they or others have conducted, and by taking a position for which they can offer strong evidence and support. But this expectation about student authority is by no means universal.

Indeed, some cultures regard student writers as novices who can most effectively make arguments by reflecting on what they've learned from their teachers and elders—those who are believed to hold the most important knowledge, wisdom, and, hence, authority. Whenever you're arguing a point with people from cultures other than your own, therefore, you need to think about what kind of authority you're expected to have:

- Whom are you addressing, and what is your relationship with that person?
- What knowledge are you expected to have? Is it appropriate or expected for you to demonstrate that knowledge—and if so, how?
- What tone is appropriate? If in doubt, always show respect: politeness is rarely if ever inappropriate.

present yourself as a person. In other words, be sure that your writing *visually* conveys your message as effectively as possible. Choose a medium that shows you at your best. Some writers love the written text, garnished with quotations, footnotes, charts, graphs, and bibliography. Others can make a better case online or in some purely visual form. Design arguments that assure readers they can trust you. And remember that even correct spelling counts.

You can also establish credibility by connecting your own beliefs and values to core principles that are well established and widely respected. This strategy is particularly effective when your position seems to be—at first glance, at least—a threat to traditional values. For example, when author Andrew Sullivan argues in favor of legalizing same-sex marriages, he does so in language that echoes the themes of family-values conservatives:

> **Legalizing gay marriage would offer homosexuals the same deal society now offers heterosexuals: general social approval and specific**

> **legal advantages in exchange for a deeper and harder-to-extract-yourself-from commitment to another human being. Like straight marriage, it would foster social cohesion, emotional security, and economic prudence. Since there's no reason gays should not be allowed to adopt or be foster parents, it could also help nurture children. And its introduction would not be some sort of radical break with social custom. As it has become more acceptable for gay people to acknowledge their loves publicly, more and more have committed themselves to one another for life in full view of their families and their friends. A law institutionalizing gay marriage would merely reinforce a healthy social trend. It would also, in the wake of AIDS, qualify as a genuine public health measure. Those conservatives who deplore promiscuity among some homosexuals should be among the first to support it.**
>
> **–Andrew Sullivan, "Here Comes the Groom"**

Yet another way to affirm your credibility as a writer is to use language that shows your respect for readers, addressing them neither above nor below their capabilities. Citing trustworthy sources and acknowledging them properly prove too that you've done your homework (another sign of respect) and suggests that you know your subject. So does presenting ideas clearly and fairly. Details matter: helpful graphs, tables, charts, or illustrations may carry weight with readers, as will the visual attractiveness of your work (or your Web site, for that matter). Again, even correct spelling counts.

Writers who establish their credibility this way seem trustworthy. But sometimes, to be credible, you have to admit limitations, too: *This is what I know; I won't pretend to understand more.* It's a tactic used by people as respected in their fields as was the late biologist Lewis Thomas, who in this example ponders whether scientists have overstepped their bounds in exploring the limits of DNA research:

> **Should we stop short of learning some things, for fear of what we, or someone, will do with the knowledge? My own answer is a flat no, but I must confess that this is an intuitive response and I am neither inclined nor trained to reason my way through it.**
>
> **–Lewis Thomas, "The Hazards of Science"**

When making an argument, many people would be reluctant to write "I suppose" or "I must confess," but those are the very concessions that might increase a reader's confidence in Lewis Thomas.

In fact, a very powerful technique for building credibility is to acknowledge outright any exceptions, qualifications, or even weaknesses

A classic "It's ugly, *but* . . ." campaign. Conceding your weaknesses can give a strong boost to your credibility.

Ugly is only skin-deep.

It may not be much to look at. But beneath that humble exterior beats an air-cooled engine. It won't boil over and ruin your piston rings. It won't freeze over and ruin your life. It's in the back of the car for better traction in snow and sand. And it will give you about 29 miles to a gallon of gas.

After a while you get to like so much about the VW, you even get to like what it looks like.

You find that there's enough legroom for almost anybody's legs. Enough head-room for almost anybody's head. With a hat on it. Snug-fitting bucket seats. Doors that close so well you can hardly close them. (They're so airtight, it's better to open the window a crack first.)

Those plain, unglamorous wheels are each suspended independently. So when a bump makes one wheel bounce, the bounce doesn't make the other wheel bump. It's things like that you pay the $1585* for, when you buy a VW. The ugliness doesn't add a thing to the cost of the car.

That's the beauty of it.

©Volkswagen of America, Inc. *Suggested Retail Price, East Coast P.O.E. ($1663 West Coast P.O.E.), Local Taxes and Other Dealer Delivery Charges, if Any, Additional.

in your argument. Making such concessions to objections that readers might raise, called *conditions of rebuttal*, sends a strong signal to the audience that you've scrutinized your own position and can therefore be trusted when you turn to arguing its merits. Speaking to readers directly, using *I* or *you*, for instance, also enables you to come closer to them when that strategy is appropriate. Using contractions will have the same effect because they make prose sound more colloquial. Consider how linguist Robert D. King uses such techniques (as well as an admission that he might be wrong) to add a personal note to the conclusion of a serious essay arguing against the notion that language diversity is endangering the United States:

> **_If I'm wrong_, then the great American experiment will fail—not because of language but because it no longer means anything to be an American; because we have forfeited that "willingness of the heart" that F. Scott Fitzgerald wrote was America; because we are no longer joined by Lincoln's "mystic chords of memory." We are not even close to the danger point. _I suggest_ that we relax and luxuriate in our linguistic richness and our traditional tolerance of language differences. Language does not threaten American unity. Benign neglect is a good policy for any country when it comes to language, and _it's a good policy_ for America.**
>
> **–Robert D. King, "Should English Be the Law?" (emphasis added)**

In some situations, however, you may find that a more formal tone gives your claims greater authority. Choices like these are yours to make as you search for the ethos that best represents you in a given argument.

Coming Clean about Motives

When people are trying to sell us anything, whether it be a political idea or a trip to Cancun, it's only natural to question their motives. *Whose interests are they serving? How will they profit from their proposal?* Such suspicions go right to the heart of ethical arguments. It's not an accident that Jonathan Swift ends his satirical *A Modest Proposal* with his narrator claiming he will benefit in no way from what he suggests—that the people of eighteenth-century Ireland end their poverty by selling their infant children as the *other* white meat:

> **I profess, in the sincerity of my heart, that I have not the least personal interest in endeavoring to promote this necessary work, having**

> no other motive than the public good of my country, by advancing our trade, providing for infants, relieving the poor, and giving some pleasure to the rich. I have no children by which I can propose to get a single penny; the youngest being nine years old, and my wife past child-bearing.
>
> –Jonathan Swift, *A Modest Proposal*

Even this monster of a narrator appreciates that his idea will gain no traction if his motives are suspect in the least.

He's also smart enough to discuss his potential conflicts of interest (his own children, his wife)—always a sensible strategy whenever your motives for offering an idea might seem driven by its potential advantage to yourself, or by your attachment to a particular class, gender, faction, or other group. Here, for example, in taking on the Bush administration's push to make the programming of public radio and TV less liberal, Michael Winship frankly admits that he has a long personal involvement with and stake in the issue:

> As the *New York Times* led in its May 2 edition, "the Republican chairman of the Corporation for Public Broadcasting [Ken Tomlinson] is aggressively pressing public television to correct what he and other conservatives consider liberal bias, prompting some public broadcasting leaders—including the chief executive of PBS—to object that his actions pose a threat to editorial independence."
>
> In the interest of full disclosure, for more than thirty years, off and on, I have toiled in the vineyards of public broadcasting, sometimes more fruitfully than others.
>
> . . . One of Tomlinson's primary targets is PBS' Bill Moyers, of whom he has a "very vehement dislike," according to a former CPB employee, for his liberal point of view. (In the interest of even fuller disclosure, for that aforementioned thirty years and more, I have been, off and on, a colleague and/or employee of Bill's.)
>
> –Michael Winship, "Speaking as a Public Broadcasting Stooge and Tool"

Note that even though Winship is writing for the Common Dreams News Center, a Web site that bills itself as "Breaking News and Views for the Progressive Community," he doesn't assume that just because most of his readers are likely to share his views he needn't mention these personal connections. Especially in online venues, writers have to expect that many of their readers will hold very different views and will be quick to point out unmentioned affiliations as serious drawbacks to credibility. In fact, attacks on such loyalties are common in political circles, where it's almost a sport to assume the worst about an opponent's motives and associations. But we all have connections and interests that, to use less pejorative language, represent the ties that bind us to other human beings. It makes sense that a woman might be concerned with women's issues or that investors might look out for their investments. So it can be good strategy to let your audiences know where your loyalties lie when such information does, in fact, shape your work.

There are other ways, too, to invite readers to regard you as trustworthy. Nancy Mairs, in an essay entitled "On Being a Cripple," wins the attention and probably the respect of her readers by facing her situation with a riveting directness:

> **First, the matter of semantics. I am a cripple. I choose this word to name me. I choose from among several possibilities, the most common of which are "handicapped" and "disabled." I made the choice a number of years ago, without thinking, unaware of my motives for doing so. Even now, I am not sure what those motives are, but I recognize that they are complex and not entirely flattering. People—crippled or not—wince at the word "cripple," as they do not at "handicapped" or "disabled." Perhaps I want them to wince. I want them to see me as a tough customer, one to whom the fates/gods/viruses have not been kind, but who can face the brutal truth of her existence squarely. As a cripple, I swagger.**
>
> **–Nancy Mairs, "On Being a Cripple"**

The paragraph takes some risks because the writer is expressing feelings that may make readers unsure how to react. Indeed, Mairs herself

If Everything's an Argument . . .

Analyze the ethos of the authors and editors of *Everything's an Argument* as they reveal themselves in this particular chapter. Look carefully at such elements as the language the authors use (formal? informal? condescending? chummy?), the examples and images they draw on (predictable? PC? fresh and imaginative? out-of-touch?), or the political and cultural attitudes they convey. Does the chapter suggest a coherent ethos, or do you find inconsistencies that surprise or confuse you? Write a page describing the ethos and the appeal it does or doesn't have for you, being sure to offer specific evidence for your claims.

admits that she doesn't completely understand her own feelings and motives. Yet the very admission of uncertainty helps her to build a bridge to readers.

RESPOND.

1. Consider the ethos of each of the following public figures. Then describe one or two public arguments, campaigns, or products that might benefit from their endorsements as well as several that would not.

   Oprah Winfrey—TV celebrity

   Ellen DeGeneres—comedian and talk-show host

   Dick Cheney—vice president

   Katie Holmes—actress

   Colin Powell—former secretary of state in the Bush administration

   Al Sharpton—civil rights activist and politician

   Queen Latifah—actress and rap artist

   Dave Chappelle—humorist and columnist

   Jeff Gordon—NASCAR champion

   Barbara Boxer—senator from California

   Bill O'Reilly—TV news commentator

   Marge Simpson—sensible wife and mother on *The Simpsons*

2 Voice is a choice. That is, writers modify the tone and style of their language depending on whom they want to seem to be. In the excerpts from this chapter, Allan Bloom wants to appear poised and confident; his language aims to convince us of his expertise. Peggy Noonan wants to appear mature, strong, and perhaps *personally* offended by the opinions offered by Anna Quindlen. In different situations, even when writing about the same topics, Bloom and Noonan would likely adopt different voices. Rethink and then rewrite the Noonan passage on p. 66, taking on the voice—the character—of someone who uses the pronoun "I" much less frequently than Noonan does, perhaps not at all. You may also need to change the way you claim authority, establish credibility, and demonstrate competence as you try to present a different and less personal ethos.

3. Opponents of Richard Nixon, the thirty-seventh president of the United States, once raised doubts about his integrity by asking a single ruinous question: *Would you buy a used car from this man?* Create

Public figures try to control their images for obvious reasons. Would you buy a used car from any of these distinguished men and women?

your own version of the argument of character. Begin by choosing an intriguing or controversial person or group and finding an image online. Download the image into a word-processing file. Create a caption for the photo modeled after the question asked about Nixon: *Would you give this woman your email password? Would you share a campsite with this couple? Would you eat lasagna this guy prepared?* Finally, write a serious 300-word argument that explores the character flaws or strengths of your subject(s).

4. A well-known television advertisement from the 1980s featured a soap-opera actor promoting a pain relief medication. "I'm not a doctor," he said, "but I play one on TV." Today, many celebrities, from athletes like Tiger Woods to actresses like Susan Sarandon, use their fame in pitches for products or political causes. One way or another, each case of celebrity endorsement relies on arguments based on character. Develop a one-page print advertisement for a product, service, or political position you use often—anything from soap to auto repair to cell phone service. There's one catch: Your advertisement should rely on arguments based on character, and you should choose as a spokesperson someone who would seem the least likely to use or endorse your product or service. The challenge is to turn an apparent disadvantage into an advantage by exploiting character.

4
Arguments Based on Facts and Reason—*Logos*

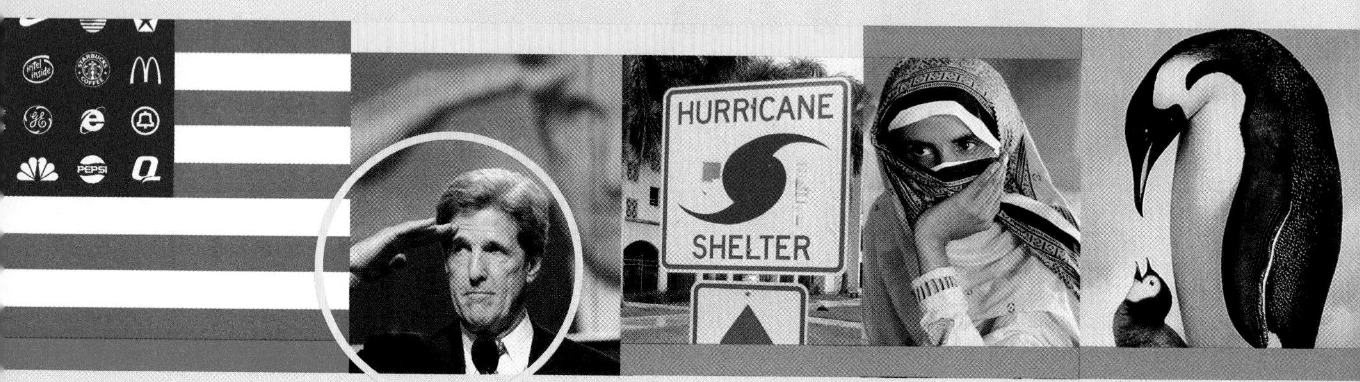

SPOCK: "Logic and practical information do not seem to apply here."

MCCOY: "You admit that?"

SPOCK: "To deny the facts would be illogical, Doctor."

–from *Star Trek* episode, "A Piece of the Action"

When writers need to persuade, they usually try their best to provide readers with good reasons to believe them. When the choice is between logic and emotion, many of us will side with *Star Trek*'s Dr. McCoy rather than the stern Spock. Most of us respect appeals to

Adlai Stevenson presents the American case at the United Nations during the Cuban Missile Crisis.

logos—arguments based on facts, evidence, and reason—but, like the good doctor, we're inclined to test the facts against our feelings and against the ethos of those making the appeal. Aristotle, among the first philosophers to write about persuasion, gives us a place to begin. He divided proofs based on facts and reason into two kinds: those derived from what we'd call *hard evidence* (Aristotle described these as *inartistic appeals*—facts, clues, statistics, testimonies, witnesses), and those based upon *reason and common sense* (what Aristotle termed *artistic appeals*). Though these categories overlap and leak (what, after all, is *common sense?*), they remain useful even today.

The differences can be observed in arguments presented forty years apart at the United Nations when American representatives charged other nations with harboring weapons of mass destruction. "Do you, Ambassador Zorin, deny that the U.S.S.R. has placed and is placing medium and intermediate range missiles and sites in Cuba?" American UN ambassador Adlai Stevenson famously asked on October 25, 1962, knowing that he had the hard evidence of spy photographs to prove his claim. The images showed the alleged construction beyond a reasonable doubt in an

LIBERATING
IRAQI CHILDREN
FROM TYRANNY

IT'S CO$TING
TOO MUCH!

www.protestwarrior.com

Not Just Words

Sometimes the difference between appeals isn't self-evident. What one person considers an appeal to reason may look like an emotional or ethical argument to another. Add in the element of irony or parody, and the categories scramble even more. Study the "Liberating Iraqi Children" poster on this page from the <ProtestWarrior.com> Web site. What kind of arguments does it make, and how exactly does it make them? You might answer this question first by listing all the claims you can take from it, both those that seem straightforward and any others that may be ironic or parodic. Then describe what you think the poster's point is. How does it make that point? Who is the target of the poster? Who is its audience? Finally, working within a group, discuss whether and why the poster does or doesn't represent an appeal to logic and reason.

era when doctoring photographs was no easy process. Ambassador Stevenson had more than a smoking gun: he had real missiles.

In contrast, Secretary of State Colin Powell did not have the same kind of open-and-shut case when he argued to the same Security Council on February 5, 2003, that Iraq was harboring weapons of mass destruction in contravention to UN resolutions. Instead, he had to assure his worldwide audience that "What you will see is an accumulation of facts and disturbing patterns of behavior." None of his materials—including some photographs—had the immediacy or transparency of the 1962 Cuban Missile Crisis images. So Powell had to hope that the pattern and weight of evidence offered in a lengthy presentation would make his claim seem compelling: "that Saddam Hussein and his regime are concealing their efforts to produce more weapons of mass destruction." Since no such weapons or weapon stockpiles were subsequently found in Iraq following a second Iraq War, one might infer (logically) that hard evidence is superior to reasoning aided by less-than-compelling inferences and probabilities. But hard evidence won't always be available, nor will it always be as overwhelming as the photographs Stevenson had to display. And yet decisions and choices have to be made.

Providing Hard Evidence

As the Stevenson/Powell examples suggest, people today usually prefer arguments based on facts and testimony to those grounded in reason. In a courtroom as well as in the popular media, for example, lawyers or reporters look for the "smoking gun"—the piece of hard evidence that ties a defendant or politician to a crime. It might be an audiotape, a fingerprint, a stained dress, or, increasingly, DNA evidence. Popular crime shows such as *CSI: Crime Scene Investigation* focus intensely on gathering this sort of "scientific" support for a prosecution. Less dramatically, the factual evidence in an argument might be columns of data carefully collected over time to prove a point about climate change or racial profiling or the effects of Title IX on collegiate sports. After decades of exposure to science and the wonders of technology, audiences today have more faith in claims that can be counted, measured, photographed, or analyzed than in those that are merely defended with words. If you live in a state where you can be ticketed after a camera catches you running a red light, you know what hard evidence means.

David Carr's argument that minorities are not represented enough in magazines is bolstered by his presentation of statistics—hard evidence—which reflect his survey of 741 magazine covers from 2002.

LINK TO P. 649

Factual evidence, however, takes many forms. Which ones you use will depend on the kind of argument you're writing. In fact, providing appropriate evidence ought to become a habit whenever you write an argument. The evidence makes your case plausible; it may also supply the details that make writing interesting. Consider Aristotle's claim that all arguments can be reduced to just two components:

Statement + Proof

Here's another way of naming those parts:

Claim + Supporting Evidence

In a scholarly article, you can actually see this connection between statements and proof in the text and the notes. As an example, we reprint a single page from a much-cited review of Michael Bellesiles's *Arming America: The Making of America's Gun Culture* by James Lindgren published in the *Yale Law Review* (see p. 83). Bellesiles had used evidence gathered from eighteenth-century documents to argue that gun ownership in frontier America was much rarer than advocates of the right to bear arms believed. Upon publication, *Arming America* was hailed by gun critics for weakening the claim of gun advocates today that the ownership of weapons has always been a part of American culture. But Lindgren, as well as many other critics and historians, found so many evidentiary flaws in Bellesiles's arguments that questions were soon raised about his scholastic integrity. Lindgren's review of *Arming America* runs for more than 50 meticulous pages (including an appendix of errors in Bellesiles's work) and contains 212 footnotes. You can see a factual argument in action just by looking at how Lindgren handles evidence on a single page. You may never write an argument as detailed as Lindgren's review, but you should develop the same respect for evidence.

Facts

"Facts," said John Adams, "are stubborn things," and so they make strong arguments, especially when readers believe they come from honest sources. Gathering such information and transmitting it faithfully practically define what we mean by professional journalism in one realm and scholarship in another. We'll even listen to people we don't agree with when they overwhelm us with evidence. On p. 84, for example, a reviewer for the conservative journal *National Review* praises the work of William Julius Wilson, a liberal sociologist, because of how well he presents his case.

This selection from James Lindgren's review of Michael Bellesiles's *Arming America* first appeared in the *Yale Law Review*, vol. 111 (2002).

B. *How Common Was Gun Ownership?*

The most contested portions of *Arming America* involve the book's most surprising claim, that guns were infrequently owned before the mid-1800s. As I show below, the claim that colonial America did not have a gun culture is questionable on the evidence of gun ownership alone. Compared to the seventeenth and eighteenth centuries, it appears that guns are not as commonly owned today. Whereas individual gun ownership in every published (and unpublished) study of early probate records that I have located (except Bellesiles's) ranges from 40% to 79%; only 32.5% of households today own a gun.[44] This appears to be a much smaller percentage than in early America—in part because the mean household size in the late eighteenth century was six people,[45] while today it is just under two people.[46] The prevailing estimate of 40% to 79% ownership differs markedly from Bellesiles's claim that only about 15% owned guns.[47] In the remainder of this Section, I explain why.

1. *The Gun Censuses*

Bellesiles bases his claims of low gun ownership primarily on probate records and counts of guns at militia musters.[48] He also discusses censuses of all guns in private and public hands, but on closer examination, none of these turns out to be a general census of all guns.

The trend is set in Bellesiles's first count of guns in an American community—the 1630 count of all the guns in the Massachusetts Bay Colony of about 1000 people. Bellesiles's account is quite specific: "In 1630 the Massachusetts Bay Company reported in their possession: '80 bastard musketts, . . . [10] Fowlinge peeces, . . . 10 Full musketts . . . .' There were thus exactly one hundred firearms for use among seven towns

44. This results from my analysis of the March 2001 release of the National Opinion Research Center's *General Social Survey, 2000* [hereinafter 2000 NORC GSS]. The data are also available at Nat'l Opinion Research Ctr., General Social Survey, *at* http://www.icpsr.umich.edu/GSS/ (last visited Apr. 8, 2002). According to the survey, 32.5% of households owned any gun, 19.7% owned a rifle, 18.6% owned a shotgun, and 19.7% owned a pistol or revolver. 2000 NORC GSS, *supra*. Only 1.2% of respondents refused to respond to the question. *Id.*

45. Inter-Univ. Consortium for Political & Soc. Research (ICPSR), Census Data for the Year 1790, http://fisher.lib.virginia.edu/cgi-local/censusbin/census/cen.pl?year=790 (last visited Aug. 10, 2001).

46. 2000 NORC GSS, *supra* note 44.

47. BELLESILES, *supra* note 3, at 445 tbl.1.

> **In his eagerly awaited new book, Wilson argues that ghetto blacks are worse off than ever, victimized by a near-total loss of low-skill jobs in and around inner-city neighborhoods. In support of this thesis, he *musters mountains of data, plus excerpts from some of the thousands of surveys and face-to-face interviews that he and his research team conducted among inner-city Chicagoans.* It is a book that deserves a wide audience among thinking conservatives.**
>
> –John J. Dilulio Jr., "When Decency Disappears" (emphasis added)

In this instance, the facts are respected even above differences in political thinking or ideology.

When your facts are compelling, they may stand on their own in a low-stakes argument, supported by little more than a tag that gives the source of your information. Consider the power of phrases such as "reported by the *New York Times*," "according to CNN," or "in a book published by Oxford University Press." Such sources gain credibility if they have, in readers' experience, reported facts accurately and reliably over time. In fact, one reason you document the sources you use in an argument is to let the credibility of those sources reflect positively on you—a good reason to find the best, most reliable material to support your claims.

But arguing with facts also sometimes involves challenging the biases of reputable sources if they lead to unfair or selective reporting. You don't have to search hard to find critics of the *Times* or CNN these days. In recent years, bloggers and other online critics in particular have enjoyed pointing out the biases or factual mistakes of mainstream media (MSM) outlets. Conservative columnist Peggy Noonan explores the consequences of this critical *new media:*

> **Now anyone can take to the parapet and announce the news. This will make for a certain amount of confusion. But better that than one-party rule and one-party thought. Only 20 years ago, when you were enraged at what you felt was the unfairness of a story, or a bias on the part of the storyteller, you could do this about it: nothing. You could write a letter.**
>
> **When I worked at CBS a generation ago I used to receive those letters. Sometimes we read them, and sometimes we answered them, but not always. Now if you see such a report and are enraged you can do something about it: You can argue in public on a blog or on TV, you can put forth information that counters the information in the report. You can have a voice. You can change the story. You can bring down a news division. Is this improvement? Oh yes it is.**
>
> –Peggy Noonan, "MSM Requiem"

In an ideal world, good information would always drive out bad. But you'll soon learn that such is not always the case. Sometimes bad information gets repeated in an echo chamber that amplifies the errors. Here is Colin Powell explaining subsequently how his UN presentation on Iraqi weapons of mass destruction could have been so far off the mark:

> **When I made that presentation in February 2003, it was based on the best information that the Central Intelligence Agency made available to me. We studied it carefully; we looked at the sourcing in the case of the mobile trucks and trains. There was multiple sourcing for that. Unfortunately, that multiple sourcing over time has turned out to be not accurate. And so I'm deeply disappointed. But I'm also comfortable that at the time that I made the presentation, it reflected the collective judgment, the sound judgment of the intelligence community. But it turned out that the sourcing was inaccurate and wrong and in some cases, deliberately misleading. And for that, I am disappointed and I regret it.**
>
> —Colin Powell, *Meet the Press*

Obviously, as a reader and researcher, you should look beyond headlines, bylines, and reputations, scrutinizing any facts you collect before passing them on yourself. Test their reliability, and admit any problems right at the start.

Statistics

Let's deal with a cliché right up front: *Figures lie and liars figure.* Like most clichés, it contains a grain of truth. It's possible to lie with numbers, even those that are accurate, because numbers rarely speak for themselves. They need to be interpreted by writers. And writers almost always have agendas that shape the interpretations.

For example, you might want to herald the good news that unemployment in the United States stands at just a little over 5 percent. That means 95 percent of Americans have jobs, an employment rate much higher than that of most other industrial nations. But let's spin the figure another way. In a country as populous as the United States, unemployment at 5 percent means that millions of Americans don't earn a daily wage. Indeed, *one out of every twenty adults* who wants work can't find it. Suddenly that's a sobering number. And, as you can see, the same statistic can be cited as a cause for celebration or shame.

We don't mean to suggest that numbers are meaningless or that you have license to use them in any way that serves your purposes. Quite the contrary. But you do have to understand the role you play in giving numbers a voice and a presence. Consider the way Armen Keteyian, writing for the *Sporting News*, raises serious questions about the safety of aluminum bats in high school and college sports, despite the insistence by many sports officials that they're safe. Keteyian makes his case by focusing on statistics and numbers—which we've highlighted—suggesting otherwise:

> Bat companies point to the NCAA's *annual injury report* ranking baseball as one of the safest collegiate sports. The report also shows "there is *no . . . significant increase in batted ball injuries*." But last December, after *an 18-month study*, the U.S. Consumer Product Safety Commission released a report that called *the NCAA's injury statistics "inconclusive* . . . and not complete enough" to determine whether current aluminum bats are more dangerous than wood.
>
> "Let's be honest," says Anderson. "Bat manufacturers have been wonderful for college baseball. So you get caught up in that, the free product, the fact it's saving you money. But all of a sudden I see my young man lying on the ground, and I'm going, 'Is this the right thing?' "
>
> Birk [a college baseball player injured by a ball coming fast off of an aluminum bat] and many others were struck—and in some cases nearly killed—by balls hit off aluminum bats certified by the NCAA and the national high school federation. To be approved, an aluminum bat must not cause *a batted ball to travel any faster than the best wood bat does*. But there's a catch: Bats are tested in a laboratory on a machine *set at a 70 mph pitch speed and a 66 mph swing speed*. Why not test at far more realistic numbers, say, *85 mph pitches and 80 mph swings?*
>
> Simple, says MacKay: "It would scare people to death."
>
> Why? Reaction time. Experts say *the fastest batted ball a pitcher can defend against is about 97 mph*. Translation: *Less than four-tenths of a second.*
>
> *Ninety-seven mph also is the fastest a ball can be hit by a certified bat in the lab test*. Sounds safe, right? But what about on the field? Well, it turns out nobody officially tests balls hit by aluminum bats under game conditions.
>
> "We've seen some things on our radar gun—*108 miles per hour, 110 at different times*," says Anderson. "*I've witnessed 114 myself*. Makes you question whether we are doing the right thing."
>
> I wanted to ask the NCAA about this and more but it refused comment.
>
> –Armen Keteyian, "Bats Should Crack, Not Skulls" (emphasis added)

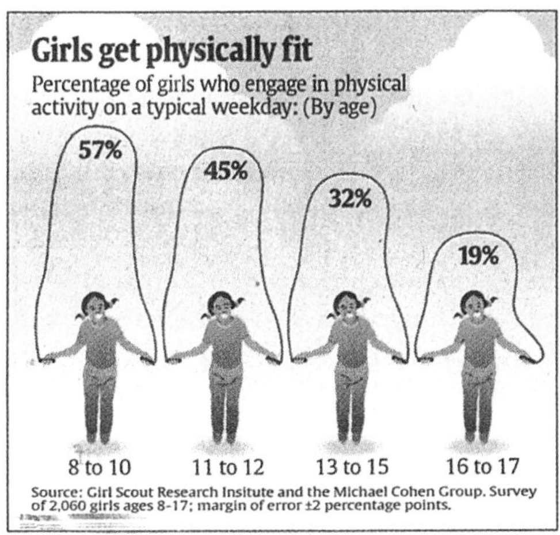

By Cindy Clark and Alejandro Gonzalez, USA TODAY

USA Today is famous for the tables, pie charts, and graphs it creates to present statistics and poll results. What claims might the evidence in this graph support? How does the design of the item influence your reading of it?

This is hardly the last word on aluminum bats. Proponents might cite different numbers and studies or argue that aluminum bats have advantages that outweigh exaggerated (to them, at least) safety concerns. The controversy is not likely to end anytime soon—unless the spike in injuries becomes more painfully obvious.

Surveys and Polls

Some of the most influential forms of statistics are those produced by surveys and polls. These measures play so large a role in people's political and social lives that writers, whether interpreting them or fashioning surveys themselves, need to give them special attention.

When they verify the popularity of an idea or proposal, surveys and polls provide persuasive appeals because, in a democracy, majority opinion offers a compelling warrant: *A government should do what most people want*. Polls come as close to expressing the will of the people as anything short of an election—the most decisive poll of all. (For more on warrants, see Chapter 6, p. 152.) However, surveys and polls can do much more than help politicians make decisions. They can also provide persuasive reasons for action or intervention. When surveys show, for example, that most American sixth-graders can't locate France or Wyoming on the map, that's an appeal for better instruction in

The Pew Global Attitudes Project used survey data to bolster the claims presented in their report on the importance of religion in the lives of people around the world. The authors were able to correlate survey responses with data on nations and respective wealth, providing strong evidence that the United States is unusual in its combination of wealth and religion.

LINK TO P. 851

geography. When polls suggest that consumer confidence is declining, businesses may have reason to worry about their bulging inventories.

It always makes sense, though, to push back against any poll numbers reported—especially, in fact, when they support your own point of view. Ask who commissioned the poll, who is publishing its outcome, who was surveyed (and in what proportions), and what stakes these parties might have in its outcome.

Are we being too suspicious? No. In fact, this sort of scrutiny is exactly what you should anticipate from your readers whenever you do surveys of your own to explore an issue. You should be confident that you've surveyed enough people to be accurate, that the people you chose for the study were representative of the selected population as a whole, and that you chose them randomly—not selecting those most likely to say what you hoped to hear.

The meaning of polls and surveys is also affected by the way questions are asked. Professional pollsters generally understand that their reputations depend on making their questions as neutral or unbiased as possible. But the exact wording of a poll or survey question can make a difference (as can the order and format of the questions). How much? Some would say a great deal. A group favoring school vouchers, for example, claims that poll results on the issue of providing tax-funded vouchers to parents for their children's education can vary more than twenty points, depending on how the question is asked (see the figure on p. 89). Of course, you should read this group's report with the same skepticism we're recommending that you approach any survey or poll with.

You must also read beyond the headlines to be sure you understand how the results of a poll are being interpreted. For instance, in late June 2005, *USA Today* chose the headline "Poll shows Americans 'generally in a funk'" for a story reporting on changing attitudes about terrorism and war. The poll asked questions such as the following:

- **Do you approve or disapprove of the way George W. Bush is handling his job as president?**
- **How worried are you that you or someone in your family will become a victim of terrorism—very worried, somewhat worried, not too worried, or not worried at all?**
- **How likely is it that there will be further acts of terrorism in the United States over the next several weeks—very likely, somewhat likely, not too likely, or not at all likely?**

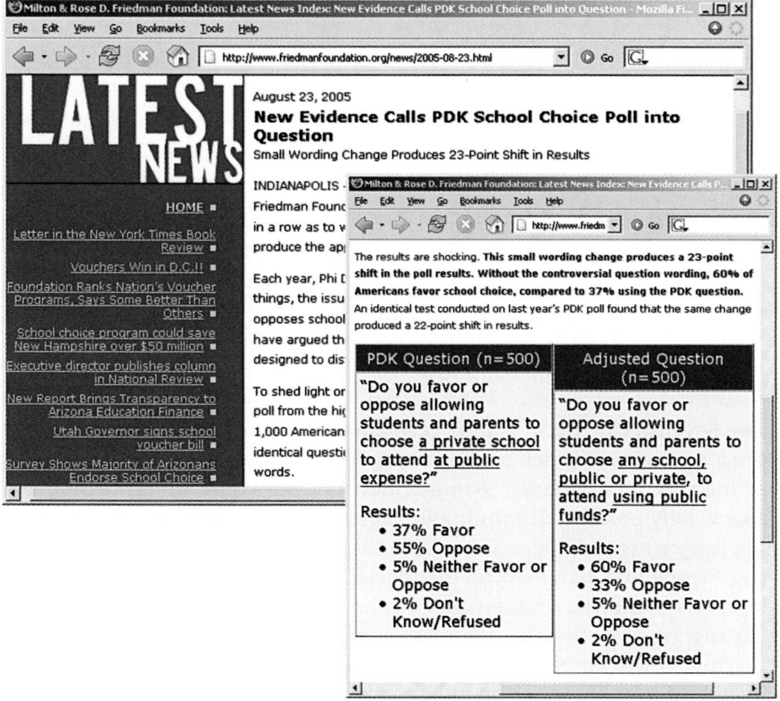

The Friedman Foundation finds that changing a poll's words changes its result.

- **In general, do you approve or disapprove of the way the United States is treating the prisoners being held at Guantánamo Bay in Cuba?**

The quotation marks around "generally in a funk" prove to be important. Why? Because the Americans responding to the *USA Today*/CNN/Gallup poll weren't actually queried about their general attitudes or overall mood. Instead, the headline reflects an *interpretation* of the poll numbers by Stephen Wayne, a professor of political science at George-town University, whose political leanings are not recorded. "Funk" is Wayne's term; another expert might have described the poll outcomes very differently since, for example, while public support for President Bush was declining slightly, so was fear of terrorism. A more neutral (and potentially accurate) headline might simply have noted contradictory attitudes.

Testimonies, Narratives, and Interviews

We don't want to give the impression that numbers and statistics make the only good evidence. Indeed, writers support arguments with all kinds of human experiences, particularly those they or others have undergone or reported. The testimony of reliable witnesses counts in almost any situation in which a writer seeks to make a case for action, change, or sympathetic understanding.

In a court, for example, decisions are often based on detailed descriptions of what happened. Following is a reporter's account of a court case in which a panel of judges decided, based on the testimony presented, that a man had been sexually harassed by another man. The narrative, in this case, supplies the evidence:

> The Seventh Circuit, in a 1997 case known as Doe v. City of Belleville, drew a sweeping conclusion allowing for same-sex harassment cases of many kinds. Title VII was sex-neutral, the court ruled; it didn't specifically prohibit discrimination against men or women. Moreover, the judges argued, there was such a thing as gender stereotyping, and if someone was harassed on that basis, it was unlawful. This case, for example, centered on teenage twin brothers working a summer job cutting grass in the city cemetery of Belleville, Ill. One boy wore an earring, which caused him no end of grief that particular summer—including a lot of menacing talk among his co-workers about sexually assaulting him in the woods and sending him "back to San Francisco." One of his harassers, identified in court documents as a large former marine, culminated a verbal campaign by backing the earring-wearer against a wall and grabbing him by the testicles to see "if he was a girl or a guy." The teenager had been "singled out for this abuse," the court ruled, "because the way in which he projected the sexual aspect of his personality"—meaning his gender—"did not conform to his co-workers' view of appropriate masculine behavior."
>
> –Margaret Talbot, "Men Behaving Badly"

Personal experience carefully reported can also support a claim convincingly, especially if a writer has earned the trust of readers. In the following excerpt, Christian Zawodniak describes his experiences as a student in a first-year college writing course. Not impressed by his instructor's performance, Zawodniak provides specific evidence of the instructor's failings:

> My most vivid memory of Jeff's rigidness was the day he responded to our criticisms of the class. Students were given a chance anonymously

> to write our biggest criticisms one Monday, and the following Wednesday Jeff responded, staunchly answering all criticisms of his teaching: "Some of you complained that I didn't come to class prepared. It took me five years to learn all this." Then he pointed to the blackboard on which he had written all the concepts we had discussed that quarter. His responses didn't seem genuine or aimed at improving his teaching or helping students to understand him. He thought he was always right. Jeff's position gave him responsibilities that he officially met. But he didn't take responsibility in all the ways he had led us to expect.
>
> –Christian Zawodniak, "Teacher Power, Student Pedagogy"

This portrait of a defensive instructor gives readers details by which to assess the argument. If readers believe Zawodniak, they learn something about teaching. (For more on establishing credibility with readers, see Chapter 3.)

Personal revelations made in interviews can similarly provide the stuff of argument—the technique is a staple of some news shows such as *60 Minutes*. Following is an excerpt from a printed interview published in the *San Francisco Examiner* between writer Gregory Dictum and convicted arsonist Jeff Luers. Sentenced to serve twenty-two years and six months in the Oregon State Penitentiary for setting fire to three SUVs at an auto dealership, Luers uses the session with Dictum to justify what to him was an environmental protest:

> DID YOU CONSIDER YOURSELF ENGAGED IN TERRORISM WHEN YOU SET FIRE TO THOSE SUVS?
>
> No. Really, when you look at the use of the word today, terrorism is nothing more than a way to define armed struggles that you disagree with.
>
> We were trying to draw attention to the use of resources in America that are contributing to climate change and global warming. Obviously, during an act of property destruction, objects are smashed, burned or demolished. That happens. But what makes an individual act of sabotage more heinous than crimes committed by governments and transnational corporations? If we're going to look at the definition of terrorism or the definition of violence, then we need to put it in its proper perspective. We certainly ought to open the definition up to corporate destruction of rivers, forests, oceans and all ecosystems, because those certainly aren't acts of love.
>
> THE SUV CAPER WASN'T YOUR FIRST ATTEMPT TO BRING ATTENTION TO ENVIRONMENTAL ISSUES. WHAT OTHER EFFORTS HAD YOU BEEN INVOLVED IN PRIOR TO THAT ACTION?

I had been involved in civil-disobedience direct action. I spent a year and a half in an endangered old-growth forest outside of Eugene. I've done tree sits, roadblocks, lockdowns and some more confrontational things. I've been involved in street protests. I've met with and lobbied members of Congress. I've debated with timber-industry officials.

WAS BURNING THE SUVS THE MOST EXTREME THING YOU'D DONE?

Yeah, I'd say it was.

WERE YOU CONSCIOUS OF IT BEING A STEP IN A NEW DIRECTION FOR YOU?

I was trying to move into the realm of more radical actions. If you compare arson actions that have happened in the U.S., the majority of them were quite major. That's the goal that I was working toward—to be more of an underground guerrilla activist. The SUVs were kind of a baby step.

EVEN SO, THE JUDGE THREW THE BOOK AT YOU. WAS THIS AN EFFORT TO MAKE AN EXAMPLE OF YOU, OR WAS IT JUST THE START OF TOUGHER SENTENCING IN GENERAL?

About six months ago, there was a man from Springfield who took his case to trial—he didn't take a plea bargain. He was accused of multiple counts of arson in the City of Springfield [Oregon] for lighting apartment buildings on fire. And in every single one of his fires, people actually had to be evacuated. The fire department had to do door-to-door searches to ensure that no one was in the buildings. He very, very clearly put people in danger, and he was sentenced to 15 years—seven years less than me.

I'm obviously biased, but I have to say that my sentence is out of the norm. The only official explanation that has ever been given came from Kent Mortimore, chief deputy D.A. in Lane County [the county in which Eugene is located], who says, basically, bottom line, I'm a terrorist and I got what I deserved.

AT THE SAME TIME, THE SENTENCE HAS INCREASED YOUR PLATFORM AND YOUR NOTORIETY. I WOULDN'T BE TALKING TO YOU IF IT HADN'T BEEN SO UNUSUAL, FOR ONE THING.

Yeah, I think their idea backfired. I think the goal was to make me serve as a deterrent to anyone else that wanted to be involved in radical actions and dissent. And I think that they failed to understand that all they did was galvanize my position.

With the growing trend toward ecotage in this country, I think that they looked upon me as representing that as a whole. But I didn't back down. I didn't plea out, and I didn't make apologies.

Luers is obviously defending his actions as an activist, resisting the label of eco-terrorist, and encouraging supporters who are protesting his lengthy prison sentence. And what about the interviewer? Does he play the role of neutral observer in presenting this story, or does he tip his hand? The interview, even in this brief excerpt, offers readers sensitive to nuances any number of pieces of evidence useful for arguments.

Using Reason and Common Sense

In the absence of hard facts, claims may be supported with other kinds of compelling reasons. The formal study of principles of reasoning is called *logic*, but few people—except perhaps mathematicians and philosophers—use formal logic to present their arguments. Many people might recognize the most famous of all syllogisms (a vehicle of deductive reasoning), but that's about the extent of what they know about formal logic:

All human beings are mortal.

Socrates is a human being.

Therefore, Socrates is mortal.

Yet even as gifted a logician as Aristotle recognized that most people argue very well using informal logic (some might say *common sense*). Consciously or not, people are constantly stating claims, drawing conclusions, and making and questioning assumptions whenever they read or write. Mostly, people rely on the habits of mind and cultural assumptions they share with their readers or listeners.

In Chapter 6, we describe a system of informal logic you may find useful in shaping credible arguments—Toulmin argument. Here, we want briefly to examine some ways people use informal logic in their daily lives.

Once again, we begin with Aristotle, who used the term *enthymeme* to describe a very ordinary kind of sentence, one that includes both a claim and a reason:

Enthymeme = Claim + Reason

Enthymemes are the sort of logical statements everyone manufactures almost effortlessly. The following sentences are all enthymemes:

Forecast at a Glance

TODAY	TONIGHT	THURSDAY
Scattered Showers	Scattered Showers	Scattered Showers
Hi: 76°F	Lo: 62°F	Hi: 78°F
Pop: 40%	Pop: 40%	Pop: 40%

A day for a picnic?

> **We'd better cancel the picnic because it's going to rain.**
>
> **Flat taxes are fair because they treat everyone the same.**
>
> **I'll buy a PC laptop instead of a Mac because it's cheaper.**
>
> **NCAA football needs a real playoff to crown a real national champion.**

On their own, enthymemes can be persuasive statements when most readers agree with the assumptions on which they're based. Sometimes the statements seem so obvious that readers don't realize they're drawing inferences when they agree with them.

Consider the first example:

> **We'd better cancel the picnic because it's going to rain.**

When a person casually makes such a claim, it's usually based on more specific information, so let's expand the enthymeme a bit to say more of what the speaker may mean:

> **We'd better cancel the picnic this afternoon because the weather bureau is predicting a 70 percent chance of rain for the remainder of the day.**

Embedded in this brief argument are all sorts of assumptions and fragments of cultural information that help make it persuasive:

> **Picnics are ordinarily held outdoors.**
>
> **When the weather is bad, it's best to cancel picnics.**
>
> **Rain is bad weather for picnics.**
>
> **A 70 percent chance of rain means that rain is more likely to occur than not.**

When rain is more likely to occur than not, it makes sense to cancel picnics.

The weather bureau's predictions are reliable enough to warrant action.

You'd sound ridiculous if you drew out all these inferences just to suggest that a picnic should be canceled. For most people, the original statement carries all this information on its own; it's a compressed argument, based on what audiences know and will accept. But sometimes your enthymemes aren't self-evident:

Be wary of environmentalism because it's religion disguised as science.

iPods are undermining civil society by making us even more focused on ourselves.

It's time to make all public toilets unisex because to do otherwise is discriminatory.

In those cases, you'll have to work much harder to defend both the claim and the assumptions it's based on, drawing out the sort of inferences that seem self-evident in other enthymemes. And you'll likely also have to supply credible evidence. A simple declaration of fact won't suffice.

Cultural Assumptions and Values

Some of the assumptions in an argument will be based on shared values derived from culture and history. In the United States, for example, few arguments work better than those based on principles of fairness and equity. Most Americans will at least say that they believe all people should be treated the same way, no matter who they are or where they come from. That principle is announced in the Declaration of Independence.

Because fairness is culturally endorsed, in American politics and media enthymemes based on equity ordinarily need less support than those that challenge it. That's why, for example, both sides in debates over affirmative action programs seek the high ground of fairness: Proponents claim that affirmative action is needed to correct enduring inequities from the past; opponents suggest that the preferential policies should be overturned because they cause inequity today. Here's Linda Chavez drawing deeply on the equity principle:

> **Ultimately, entitlements based on their status as "victims" rob Hispanics of real power. The history of American ethnic groups is one of overcoming disadvantage, of competing with those who were already here and proving themselves as competent as any who came before. Their fight was always to be treated the same as other Americans, never to be treated as special, certainly not to turn the temporary disadvantages they suffered into permanent entitlement. Anyone who thinks this fight was easier in the earlier part of this century when it was waged by other ethnic groups does not know history.**
>
> **–Linda Chavez, "Towards a New Politics of Hispanic Assimilation"**

Chavez expects Hispanics to accept her claims because she believes they don't wish to be treated differently from other ethnic groups in the society.

Naturally, societies in other times and places have operated from very different premises—they may have privileged a particular race, gender, religion, or aristocratic birth. Such powerful culturally based assumptions may operate within smaller groups, especially those with long traditions. Indeed, *tradition* itself may be one such value. No doubt you've heard ideas or actions defended on the grounds that *we have always done it that way*. Understanding such core cultural assumptions is a key both to making successful arguments and to challenging the status quo.

Providing Logical Structures for Argument

Some types of argument are less tightly bound to cultural assumptions. Instead, they provide structures that can support very different, and sometimes even opposing, claims. In the second part of this book, we examine some of these patterns and strategies: *arguments of fact, arguments of definition, evaluations, causal arguments,* and *proposals*. Although we present them individually, you'll routinely blur their boundaries. Arguments should be consistent, but they needn't follow a single pattern.

In fact, there are many types of logical structures to build on—arguments that your readers will understand without the need for much explanation. In the following pages, we identify just a few.

Degree

Arguments based on degree—in all their endless permutations—are so common that people barely notice them. Nor do people pay much attention to how they work because they seem self-evident. Most audiences will readily accept that *more of a good thing or less of a bad thing is good*. In the novel *The Fountainhead*, novelist Ayn Rand asks: "If physical slavery is repulsive, how much more repulsive is the concept of servility of the spirit?" Most readers immediately comprehend the point Rand intends to make about slavery of the spirit because they already know that physical slavery is cruel and would reject any forms of slavery that were crueler still on the principle that *more of a bad thing is bad*. Rand may still have to offer evidence that "servility of the spirit" is, in fact, worse than bodily servitude, but she has begun with a structure readers can grasp. Here are other arguments that work similarly:

If I can get a ten-year warranty on a humble Kia, shouldn't I get the same or better warranty from Lexus?

The health benefits from using stem cells in research will surely outweigh the ethical risks.

Better a conventional war now than a nuclear confrontation later.

Analogies

Analogies usually involve explaining one idea or concept by comparing it to something else. People understand comparisons intuitively. Indeed, people habitually think in comparative terms, through similes and metaphors: *Life is like a box of chocolates; war is hell*. An analogy is typically a complex or extended comparison. Following is an extended analogy that supports a controversial claim made in the very first sentence:

Today, one of the most powerful religions in the Western World is environmentalism. Environmentalism seems to be the religion of choice for urban atheists. Why do I say it's a religion? Well, just look at the beliefs. If you look carefully, you see that environmentalism is in fact a perfect 21st century remapping of traditional Judeo-Christian beliefs and myths.

There's an initial Eden, a paradise, a state of grace and unity with nature, there's a fall from grace into a state of pollution as a result of eating from the tree of knowledge, and as a result of our actions there is a judgment day coming for us all. We are all energy sinners, doomed to die, unless we seek salvation, which is now called sustainability.

The sounds of foreign languages are compared to exotic spice in Firoozeh Dumas's essay about ethnic names, "The 'F' word, *Funny in Farsi*." The use of analogy allows Dumas to invite readers to pronounce foreign names just as one would try an exotic delicacy.

LINK TO P. 787

> Sustainability is salvation in the church of the environment. Just as organic food is its communion, that pesticide-free wafer that the right people with the right beliefs, imbibe.
>
> Eden, the fall of man, the loss of grace, the coming doomsday—these are deeply held mythic structures. They are profoundly conservative beliefs. They may even be hard-wired in the brain, for all I know. I certainly don't want to talk anybody out of them, as I don't want to talk anybody out of a belief that Jesus Christ is the son of God who rose from the dead. But the reason I don't want to talk anybody out of these beliefs is that I know that I can't talk anybody out of them. These are not facts that can be argued. These are issues of faith.
>
> And so it is, sadly, with environmentalism. Increasingly it seems facts aren't necessary, because the tenets of environmentalism are all about belief.
>
> –Michael Crichton, "Remarks to the Commonwealth Club"

Needless to say, environmentalists (a very large and diverse group) would resist such a categorization and challenge the details of the analogy. And analogies of argument *are* routinely abused, so much so that *faulty analogy* (see p. 511) is one of the most familiar fallacies of argument.

Precedent

Arguments from precedent are related to arguments of analogy in that they both involve comparisons. Sometimes an argument of precedent focuses on comparable institutions. Consider an assertion like the following:

> If motorists in most other states can pump their own gas safely, surely the state of New Jersey can trust its own drivers to be as capable. It's time for New Jersey to permit self-service gas stations.

You could pull a lot of inferences out of this claim to explain its reasonableness: People in New Jersey are about as capable as people in other states; people with equivalent capabilities can do the same thing; pumping gas is not hard, and so forth. But you don't have to because most readers would *get* the argument simply because of the way it is put together.

Here's an excerpt from a more extended argument by a Yale law professor on the rather odd topic of single-sex toilets. It uses several arguments of precedent:

If Everything's an Argument . . .

Examine the examples cited in this chapter of *Everything's an Argument*, looking for patterns, tendencies, biases, habits, and so on, and then use those findings to support a factual claim about the chapter or its authors and editors. For example, do the examples habitually come from certain types of sources (academic more than popular), or do the authors favor some genres (Web pages) over others (blogs)? Do you detect political, cultural, racial, or gender biases in the examples? Or perhaps you find the authors and editors trying too hard to seem open-minded and inclusive. Are there kinds of examples you think *should* be included in a chapter on facts and reason that you do not find here? Do the examples seem dated or eccentric to you, perhaps suggesting that the authors and editors come from a specific generation (boomers, Generation Xers)? It's okay to reach a little beyond this chapter for your evidence: perhaps "Arguments Based on Facts and Reason" confirms a tendency you've already detected elsewhere in the book. Write a page or so defending your claim with the evidence you've gathered.

We don't have single-sex toilets at home, and we don't need them at the office. Then there's also the small question of efficiency. I see my male colleagues waiting in line to use the men's room, when the women's toilet is unoccupied. Which is precisely why Delta Airlines doesn't label those two bathrooms at the back of the plane as being solely for men and women. It just wouldn't fly.

The University of Chicago just got the 10 single-use restrooms on campus designated gender neutral. It's time Yale followed suit. And this is not just an academic problem. There are tens of thousands of single-use toilets at workplaces and public spaces throughout the nation that are wrong-headedly designated for a single-sex. All these single-use toilets should stop discriminating. They should be open to all on a first-come, first-lock basis. This is not just good sense. It's the law.

–Ian Ayres, "Looking Out for No. 2"

Other precedents deal with issues of time:

What was done in the past is a good/bad model for what we should do now.

For instance, every military action by the United States since the early 1970s has been ominously branded, at some moment and for persuasive reasons, as "another Vietnam." Cases in court are also routinely argued on precedents. What courts have decided in the past often determines how courts will rule on a similar or related issue. Even parents use precedents in dealing with their children:

We never let your older sister have a car while she was in high school, so we're not about to let you have one either.

It should be easy to appreciate the appeal in overturning precedents, particularly in a society as fond of rebellious stances as American culture. But there's no denying that you can support a claim effectively by showing that it's consistent with previous policies, actions, or beliefs.

You'll encounter additional kinds of logical structures as you create your own arguments. You'll find some of them in Chapter 6 on Toulmin argument and still more in Chapter 17, "Fallacies of Argument."

RESPOND •

1. Discuss whether the following statements are examples of hard evidence or rational appeals. Not all cases are clear-cut.

    "The bigger they are, the harder they fall."

    Drunk drivers are involved in more than 50 percent of traffic deaths.

    DNA tests of skin found under the victim's fingernails suggest that the defendant was responsible for the assault.

    Polls suggest that a large majority of Americans favor a constitutional amendment to ban flag burning.

    A psychologist testified that teenage violence could not be blamed on computer games.

    Honey attracts more flies than vinegar.

    History proves that cutting tax rates increases government revenues because people work harder when they can keep more of what they earn.

"We have nothing to fear but fear itself."

Air bags ought to be removed from vehicles because they can kill young children and small-framed adults.

2. We suggest in this chapter that statistical evidence becomes useful only when responsible authors interpret the data fairly and reasonably. As an exercise, go to the *USA Today* Web site or to the newspaper itself and look for the daily graph, chart, or table called the *USA Today* snapshot. (On the Web site, you'll have a series of these items to choose from.) Pick a snapshot, and use the information in it to support at least three different claims. See if you can get at least two of the claims to make opposing or very different points. Share your claims with classmates. (We don't mean to suggest that you learn to use data dishonestly, but it's important that you see firsthand how the same statistics can serve a variety of arguments.)
3. Testimony can be just as suspect as statistics. For example, check out the newspaper ads for some recent movies. How lengthy are the quotes from reviewers? A reviewer's stinging indictment of a shoot-'em-up film—"this blockbuster may prove to be a great success at the box office, but it stinks as filmmaking"—could be reduced to "A great success." Bring to class a full review of a recent film that you enjoyed. (If you haven't enjoyed any films lately, select a review of one you hated.) Using testimony from that review, write a brief argument to your classmates explaining why they should see that movie (or why they should avoid it). Be sure to use the evidence from the review fairly and reasonably, as support for a claim that you're making.

   Then exchange arguments with a classmate, and decide whether the evidence in your peer's argument helps convince you about the movie. What's convincing about the evidence? If it doesn't convince you, why not?
4. Choose an issue of some consequence, locally or nationally, and then create a series of questions designed to poll public opinion on the issue. But design the questions to evoke a range of responses. See if you can design a reasonable question that would make people strongly inclined to favor or approve an issue, a second question that would lead them to oppose the same proposition just as intensely, a third that tries to be more neutral, and additional questions that provoke different degrees of approval or disapproval. If possible, try out your questions on your classmates.

5 Thinking Rhetorically

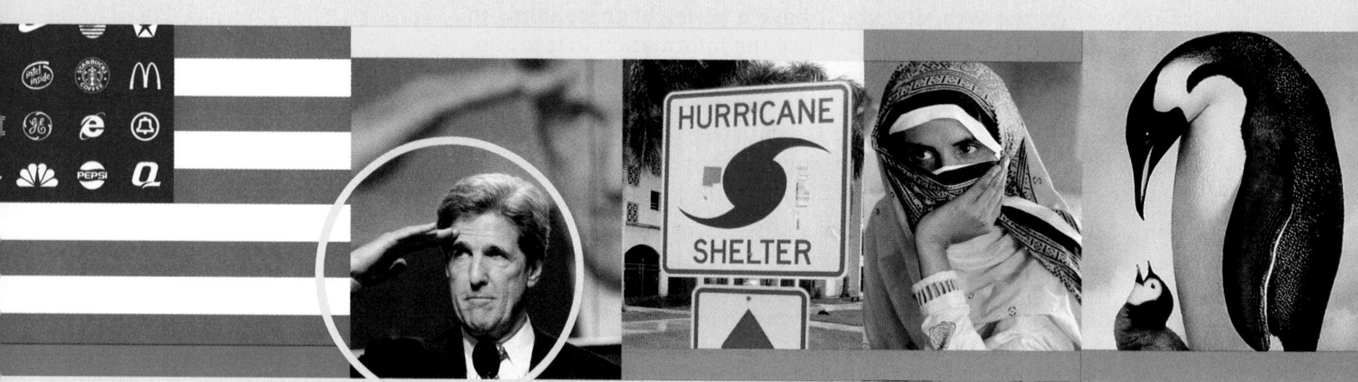

When the thirty-second spot first aired in late March 2004, many viewers reacted with disbelief: *What the . . . ?! The guy with the mustache . . . and a sexy underwear model . . . it couldn't be . . .* could *it?*

But it was—counterculture folk legend, pop icon, and 1997 Kennedy Center honoree Bob Dylan crooning "Love Sick" in a TV ad for Victoria's Secret, a purveyor of sexy women's underclothes. Dylan, who had never before pitched a product other than his own recordings, now looked like a cross between Snidely Whiplash and

Salvador Dali as he traded glances with a winged vixen in high heels. The bard who'd penned "The Times They Are A-Changin'" and "Blowin' in the Wind" had sold his birthright, disillusioned critics charged, for—yikes—a bra and blue panties.

Media critic Seth Stevenson, writing in *Slate,* devoted a full column to analyzing the pitch, trying first to figure out why an artist of Dylan's stature would do a commercial—Money? Whimsy? Exposure? But then he turns to a question just as intriguing, especially if—thinking rhetorically—one is curious about how ads work their persuasive magic:

> Why would a brand that's about sexiness, youth, and glamour want any connection at all with a decrepit, sixtysomething folksinger? The answer, my friend, is totally unclear. The answer is totally unclear.
>
> Even if Victoria's Secret hopes to bring in more boomer women, do those women want their underwear to exude the spirit and essence of Bob Dylan? Or, conversely, is Bob Dylan the sort of man they're hoping to attract? Even if you're of the belief that men frequently shop at VS for their ladies, I still don't see the appeal of this ad. I, for instance, am a man, and I can assure you that Bob Dylan is not what I'm looking for in a woman's undergarment. (And if I found him there—man, would that be disturbing.)
>
> Victoria's Secret wouldn't return my calls, but media reports say the idea of putting Dylan's face in the ad (they'd been using his song—"Love Sick"—in ads for the past year or so) came straight from corporate chief Les Wexner. To the company's surprise, Dylan

Bob Dylan and the products he pitches

> **accepted their offer. It's at this point that someone at Victoria's Secret should have stopped the madness. Just because you can hire Bob Dylan as the figurehead for your lingerie line, doesn't mean you should. Perhaps no one was willing to say no to the big boss, or perhaps they fully expected Dylan to say no. Joke's on them.**
>
> **–Seth Stevenson, "Tangled Up in Boobs"**

To pose the sort of questions Stevenson asks here is to perform (on a small scale) what's called a *rhetorical analysis,* a close reading of a text to find how and whether it works to persuade. In just these few paragraphs from a longer piece, Stevenson considers some of the basic strategies of argument explored in this book's preceding chapters. He first identifies the ethos of the company making the appeal (sexiness, youth, glamour) and finds it hard to reconcile with the ethos of the celebrity in the ad (decrepit, sixtysomething). He considers the emotional pull the TV commercial might have, maybe enticing dirty old men to buy expensive underwear for their ladies, but then rejects the logic of that approach: even men who shop for underwear at Victoria's Secret certainly don't want to think about Dylan when they do. Then Stevenson takes a step beyond the ad itself to consider the rhetorical world in which it might have been created—one in which it would seem so cool to have a superstar spokesperson like Bob Dylan that you don't think about the messages you might be sending. Stevenson's conclusion? "Joke's on them."

Whenever you encounter a similarly puzzling, troubling, or even successful appeal, try subjecting it to a rhetorical analysis of your own, asking yourself what strategies the piece employs to move your heart, win your trust, and change your mind—and why it does or doesn't do so. Here's how.

Randy Cohen inspired much discussion when he answered a reader's question about how to deal with a realtor who, because of religious reasons, would not shake her hand. The varying responses to Cohen's column evaluate his arguments of *ethos* and challenge his arguments of *logos.* The sixth response offers a comparison of rhetorical strategy.

LINK TO P. 894

Composing a Rhetorical Analysis

Arguments have many strategies. But exactly how does a Bose ad make you want to buy new speakers or an op-ed piece in the *Washington Post* suddenly change your thinking about school vouchers? A rhetorical analysis might help you understand. You perform a rhetorical analysis by analyzing how well the components of an argument work together to persuade or move an audience. You can study arguments of any kind—advertisements, as we've seen, or editorials, political cartoons, perhaps even movies or photographs. (If everything really is an argument, then just about any communication can be opened up rhetorically.)

Because arguments have many aspects, you may need to focus a rhetorical analysis on elements that stand out or make the piece intriguing or problematic. You could begin by exploring issues such as the following:

- What is the purpose of this argument? What does it hope to achieve?
- Who is the audience for this argument?
- What appeals or techniques does the argument use—emotional, logical, ethical?
- Who is making the argument? What ethos does it create, and what values does it assume?
- How does it try to make the writer or creator seem trustworthy?
- What authorities does the argument rely on or appeal to?
- What facts are used in the argument? What logic? What evidence? How is the evidence arranged and presented?
- What claims are advanced in the argument? What issues are raised, and which ones are ignored or, perhaps, evaded?
- What are the contexts—social, political, historical, cultural—for this argument? Whose interests does it serve? Who gains or loses by it?
- What shape does the argument take? How is the argument presented or arranged? What media do the argument use?
- How does the language or style of the argument work to persuade an audience?

Questions like these should get you thinking. But don't just describe techniques and strategies in a rhetorical analysis. Instead, show how the key devices in an argument actually make it succeed or fail. Quote language freely from a written piece, or describe the elements in a visual argument. (Annotating a visual text is one option.) Show readers where and why an argument makes sense and where it seems to fall apart (just as Stevenson does in the Victoria's Secret ad). If you believe that an argument startles audiences or challenges them, insults them, or lulls them into complacency, explain precisely why that's so and provide evidence. Don't be surprised when your rhetorical analysis itself becomes an argument. That's what it should be.

Understanding the Purpose of an Argument

To understand how well any argument works, ask what its purpose might be: To sell shoes? To advocate Social Security reform? To push a political agenda? In many cases, that purpose may be obvious, or at least seem so. A conservative newspaper will likely advance a right-wing agenda on its editorial page; ads from a baby food company will show happy infants delighted with stewed prunes and squash. But some projects may be coy about their persuasive intentions or blur the lines between types of argument. Perhaps you've responded to a mail survey or telephone poll only to discover that the questions are leading you to switch your cell phone service. Does such a stealthy argument succeed? That may depend on whether you're more intrigued by the promise of cheaper phone rates than offended by the bait-and-switch. The deception could provide material for a thoughtful rhetorical analysis in which you measure the strengths, risks, and ethics of such strategies.

Genre can be important in determining how to assess an argument. You probably know the difference between different types (or *genres*) of arguments—say, between an op-ed column and a bumper sticker. You'd have every right to challenge an argument in an editorial if it lacked sufficient evidence; you'd look foolish making the same complaint about a bumper sticker. But you could still expect that a bumper sticker meet the expectations of *its* genre: compressed, attention-getting, sometimes clever or sarcastic argument.

Funny, offensive, or both?

Understanding Who Makes an Argument

Knowing *who* is claiming *what* is key to any analysis. That's why you'll usually find the name of a person or an institution attached to an argument or persuasive appeal. Remember the statements included in TV ads during the last federal election campaign: "Hello, I'm Jane Doe and I approved this ad"? Federal law requires such statements so that viewers can tell the difference between ads actually endorsed by candidates and those sponsored by special interest groups not always affiliated with the campaigns. Their interests and motives might be very different.

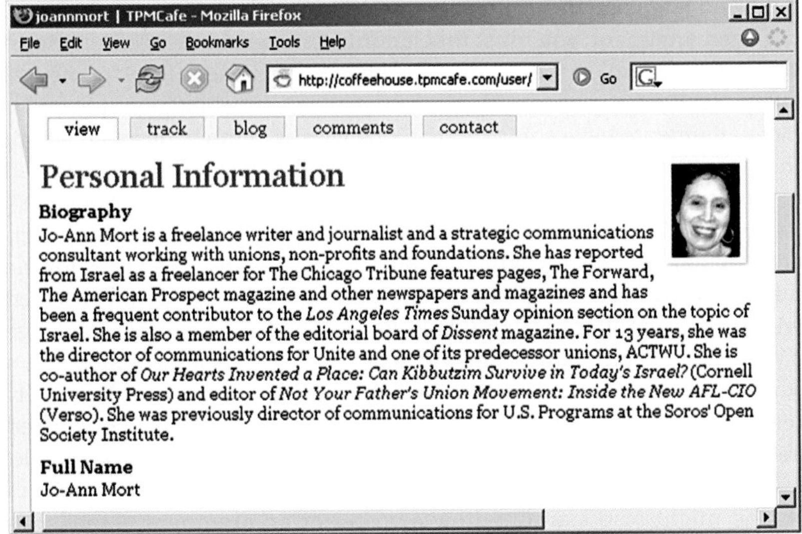
joannmort | TPMCafe - Mozilla Firefox

File Edit View Go Bookmarks Tools Help

http://coffeehouse.tpmcafe.com/user/

view track blog comments contact

Personal Information

Biography

Jo-Ann Mort is a freelance writer and journalist and a strategic communications consultant working with unions, non-profits and foundations. She has reported from Israel as a freelancer for The Chicago Tribune features pages, The Forward, The American Prospect magazine and other newspapers and magazines and has been a frequent contributor to the *Los Angeles Times* Sunday opinion section on the topic of Israel. She is also a member of the editorial board of *Dissent* magazine. For 13 years, she was the director of communications for Unite and one of its predecessor unions, ACTWU. She is co-author of *Our Hearts Invented a Place: Can Kibbutzim Survive in Today's Israel?* (Cornell University Press) and editor of *Not Your Father's Union Movement: Inside the New AFL-CIO* (Verso). She was previously director of communications for U.S. Programs at the Soros' Open Society Institute.

Full Name

Jo-Ann Mort

The blogger bio: required reading for rhetorical analysis

Of course, knowing an author's name is just a starting place for a serious analysis. You need to dig deeper whenever you don't recognize the author of an argument or the institution sponsoring it—and sometimes even when you do. You could do worse than to google the Internet to discover more about such people or groups. What else have they produced? By whom have they been published—the *Wall Street Journal*, the blog DailyKos, or, perhaps, *Spin?* Big difference. If a group has a Web site, what can you learn about its goals, policies, contributors, and, very important, funding? These days, you can't afford to be naïve about who's asking for your ear. Nor do you have an excuse for ignoring the biases, special interests, and conflicts of interest in people competing for your attention. The information is out there for you to find.

Identifying and Appealing to Audiences

Audience is the third person of the rhetorical Trinity, after author and purpose. Most arguments are composed with specific audiences in mind, and their success depends, in part, on how well their strategies, content, tone, and language meet the expectations of readers or viewers. In analyzing an argument, you must first identify its target audience(s), remembering how complex that notion can be (see "Audiences for Arguments" on pp. 32–37). But you can usually make an educated judgment because most arguments have contexts that, one way or another, describe whom they intend to reach and in what ways. Both a photocopied sheet stapled to a bulletin board in a college dorm ("Why You Should Be a Socialist") and a forty-foot billboard for Bud Lite might be aimed at the same general population—college students. But each will adjust its appeals for the different moods of that group in different moments. The political screed will likely be deliberately simple in layout and full of earnest language ("We live in a world of obscene inequality . . .") to appeal to students in a serious vein, while the liquor ad will be visually stunning and virtually text-free to connect with students when they aren't quite so worried about uniting the workers of the world. Your rhetorical analysis might make a case for the success or failure of such audience-based strategies.

You might also examine how a writer or an argument establishes credibility with an audience. One very effective means of building credibility, you will discover, comes through a seven-letter word made famous by Aretha Franklin: *respect*. Respect is crucial in arguments that invoke audiences who don't agree on critical issues or who may not have thought carefully about the issues presented. In introducing an article on problems facing African American women in the workplace, editor-in-chief of *Essence* Diane Weathers considers the problems she faced with respecting *all* her potential readers:

> **We spent more than a minute agonizing over the provocative cover line for our feature "White Women at Work." The countless stories we had heard from women across the country told us that this was a workplace issue we had to address. From my own experience at several major magazines, it was painfully obvious to me that Black and White women are not on the same track. Sure, we might all start out in the same place. But early in the game, most sisters I know become stuck—and the reasons have little to do with intelligence or drive. At some point we bump our heads against that ceiling. And while White women may complain of a glass ceiling, for us, the ceiling is concrete.**
>
> **So how do we tell this story without sounding whiny and paranoid, or turning off our White-female readers, staff members, advertisers and girlfriends? Our solution: Bring together real women (several of them highly successful senior corporate executives), put them in a room, promise them anonymity and let them speak their truth.**
>
> **–Diane Weathers, "Speaking Our Truth"**

Both paragraphs affirm Weathers's determination to treat audiences fairly *and* to deal honestly with a difficult subject. The strategy would merit attention in any rhetorical analysis.

Look, too, for signals that writers share values with readers or at least understand an audience. In the following passage, writer Jack Solomon is very clear about one value he hopes readers have in common—a preference for "straight talk":

> **There are some signs in the advertising world that Americans are getting fed up with fantasy advertisements and want to hear some straight talk. Weary of extravagant product claims and irrelevant associations, consumers trained by years of advertising to distrust what they hear seem to be developing an immunity to commercials.**
>
> **–Jack Solomon, "Masters of Desire: The Culture of American Advertising"**

It's a pretty safe assumption, isn't it? Who favors doubletalk or duplicity? But writers or advertisers can manage even more complex appeals to values, talking the talk to target specific groups and their experiences, values, and perceptions. Here's media critic Seth Stevenson again, first summarizing ads in a new anti-smoking campaign directed specifically at teens:

> **The spots:** ***They appear to be episodes of a sitcom called "Fair Enough." In this series of 30-second segments, a team of tobacco executives brainstorms new ways to market to teens. Among their ideas: fruit-flavored chewing tobacco, tobacco in the form of a gum ball, and an effort to win influence with the "hipster" crowd by giving them free packs of smokes.***
>
> **–Seth Stevenson, "How to Get Teens Not to Smoke"**

Then he does a rhetorical analysis, explaining why the particular TV spot will resonate with its target audience. The creators of the ad clearly knew what might motivate teens to give up cigarettes—insecurity:

> **In fact, the ultimate adolescent nightmare is to appear in any way unsavvy—like an out-of-it rookie who doesn't know the score. These "Fair Enough" ads isolate and prey on that insecurity, and they do a great job. With a dead-on, rerun sitcom parody (jumpy establishing shot; upbeat horn-section theme song ending on a slightly unresolved note; three-wall, two-camera set; canned laugh track), the ads first establish their own savvy, knowing coolness before inviting us to join them in ridiculing big tobacco's schemes. The spots are darkly comic, just the way teens like it. And rather than serving up yet more boring evidence that smoking is deadly (something that all teens, including**

If Everything's an Argument . . .

Choose another chapter in this textbook, and read it with a special eye for how it addresses its readers. Do the authors follow the guidelines offered here—that is, do they demonstrate knowledge and respect their readers? How do they use pronouns to establish a relationship between themselves and their readers? What other strategies for connecting with readers can you identify? Write a page summarizing your observations.

the ones who smoke, already know) the ads move on to the far more satisfying step: kicking big tobacco in the groin.

Examining Arguments from the Heart: *Pathos*

Arguments from the heart appeal to readers' emotions and feelings. Some emotional appeals are, in fact, just ploys to win readers over with a pretty face, figurative or real. You've seen ads promising an exciting life and attractive friends if only you drink the right beer or wear designer clothes. Are you fooled by such claims? Probably not, if you pause to think about them. But that's the strategy, isn't it—to distract you from thought just long enough to make a bad choice. It's a move worth commenting upon in a rhetorical analysis. Yet you might also want to applaud illogical appeals that nonetheless work brilliantly. Consider the stylish iPod TV spots, just silhouettes of people dancing to the tunes from their white ear buds. How do these spots make their case, and is the emotional spike they create suited to the product?

Emotions can add real muscle to arguments, too. For example, persuading people not to drink and drive by making them fear death, injury, or arrest seems like a fair use of an emotional appeal. That's exactly what the Texas Department of Transportation did in 2002 when it created a memorable ad campaign (see the figure on p. 111) featuring the image of a formerly beautiful young woman horribly scarred in a fiery accident caused by a driver who'd had too much to drink. In an analysis, you might note the impact of the headline right above the gut-wrenching image: "Not everyone who gets hit by a drunk driver dies."

In analyzing emotional appeals, judge whether the emotions raised—be they anger, sympathy, fear, envy, joy, or love—advance the claims

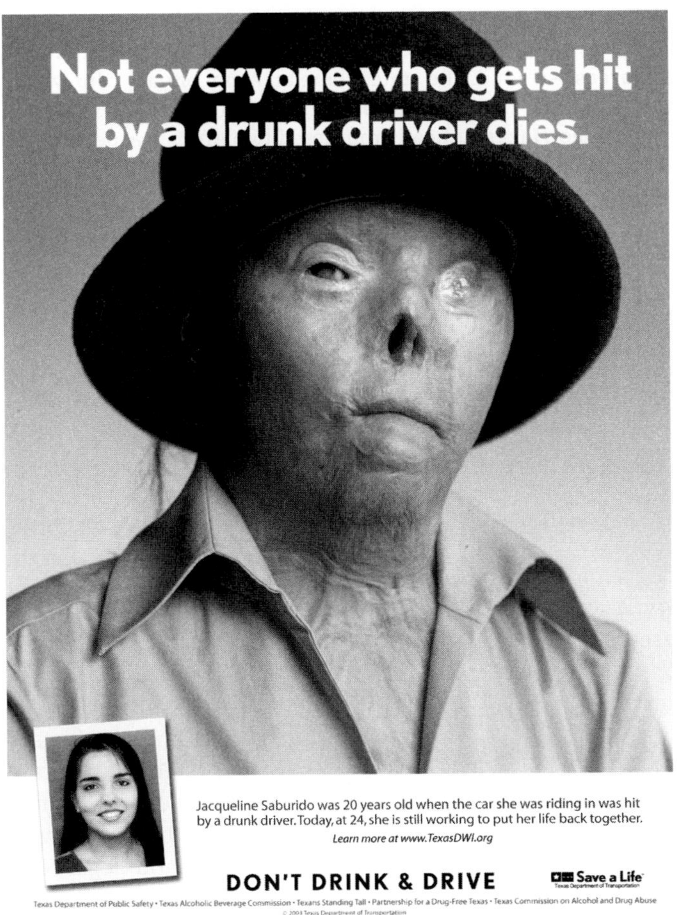

Not everyone who gets hit by a drunk driver dies.
Jacqueline Saburido was 20 years old when the car she was riding in was hit by a drunk driver. Today, at 24, she is still working to put her life back together.
Learn more at www.TexasDWI.org
DON'T DRINK & DRIVE
Save a Life
Texas Department of Transportation
Texas Department of Public Safety • Texas Alcoholic Beverage Commission • Texans Standing Tall • Partnership for a Drug-Free Texas • Texas Commission on Alcohol and Drug Abuse
© 2003 Texas Department of Transportation

Images and words combine to create an unforgettable emotional appeal.

offered. Consider how Paul Begala, a media commentator and former advisor to President Clinton, uses graphic language (*lynch-dragged; crucified; bludgeoned*) and deliberate repetition (*it's red*) to provoke revulsion against states that had just voted Republican in a recent presidential election:

> You see the state where James Byrd was lynch-dragged behind a pickup truck until his body came apart—it's red. You see the state where Matthew Shepard was crucified on a split-rail fence for the

> crime of being gay—it's red. You see the state where right-wing extremists blew up a federal office building and murdered scores of federal employees—it's red. The state where an Army private who was thought to be gay was bludgeoned to death with a baseball bat, and the state where neo-Nazi skinheads murdered two African-Americans because of their skin color, and the state where Bob Jones University spews its anti-Catholic bigotry: they're all red too.
>
> –Paul Begala, "Banana Republicans"

Does the passion here move you, or does it suggest an argument out of control, damaging its own case? Your task in a rhetorical analysis would be to study an author's words, the emotions they evoke, and the claims they support, and then to make such a judgment.

The argument presented by the Commercial Closet Association is one based on character. The group establishes their credibility with respect to presenting best practices by including persons who are gay, lesbian, bisexual, or transgender (GLBT) in corporate advertising, mentioning the establishment and focus of their organization, presenting statistical data, and offering a wealth of examples.

LINK TO P. 654

Examining Arguments Based on Character: *Ethos*

It should come as no surprise: readers believe writers who seem honest, wise, and trustworthy. So in examining the effectiveness of an argument, look for evidence of these traits. Does the writer have the experience or authority to write on this subject? Are all claims qualified reasonably? Is evidence presented in full, not tailored to the writer's agenda? Are important objections to the author's position acknowledged and addressed? Are sources documented? Above all, does the writer sound trustworthy? Here, in a paragraph from a lengthy argument about church/state conflicts in the United States, Professor Noah Feldman of the New York University School of Law hits just the right notes to sound concerned, thoughtful, and above all, evenhanded in balancing the rights of both "values evangelicals" who see a role for religion in the political arena and "legal secularists" who would rather keep religion out of public deliberations.

> The solution I have in mind rests on the basic principle of protecting the liberty of conscience. So long as all citizens have the same right to speak and act free of coercion, no adult should feel threatened or excluded by the symbolic or political speech of others, however much he may disagree with it. If many congressmen say that their faith requires intervening to save Terri Schiavo, that is not a violation of the rules of political debate. The secular congresswoman who thinks

Feldman offers a personal proposal based on a principle both sides will likely accept.

He insists that political debate must allow for people of faith to base their arguments on their deeply held principles.

> **Schiavo should have the right to die in peace can express her contrary view and explain why it is that she believes a rational and legal analysis of the situation requires it. She may lose the vote, but she is not excluded from the process or from the body that votes against her, any more than a Republican would be "excluded" from a committee controlled by Democrats.**
>
> **–Noah Feldman, "A Church-State Solution"**

Then he applies the same principle to secularists, treating both sides with fairness and respect.

In performing such an analysis, pay attention to the details, right down to the choice of words or, in a visual argument, the shapes and colors. The modest, tentative tone of "[t]he solution I have in mind," in Feldman's argument, is an example of the kind of choice that can shape an audience's perception of ethos. But these details need your interpretation. Language that's hot and extreme can mark a writer as either passionate or loony. Work that's sober and carefully organized might suggest that an institution is either competent or anal. Technical terms and abstract phrases can make a writer seem either knowledgeable or pompous.

Examining Arguments Based on Facts and Reason: *Logos*

In judging most arguments, you'll have to decide whether an argument makes a plausible claim and offers good reasons for you to believe it.

Not all arguments you read will package such claims in a single neat sentence, or *thesis*—nor should they. A writer may tell a story from which you have to infer the claim; think of the way many films make a social or political statement by dramatizing an issue, whether it be political corruption, government censorship, or economic injustice. Visual arguments may work the same way: viewers have to assemble the parts and draw inferences before they get the point.

In some conventional arguments, the sort you might find on an editorial page, arguments may be perfectly obvious. Writers stake out a claim and then offer the reasons you should consider; or they work in the opposite direction, laying out a case that leads you toward a conclusion. Consider the following examples. The first is a provocative opening paragraph by economist Paul Krugman previewing the contents of his

What argument does this editorial cartoon by Antonio Neri Licon, "Nerilicon," make? What elements come together to constitute the claim? It may be helpful to look at the Not Just Words box on p. 116 along with the cartoon, which originally appeared in *El Economista,* Mexico City, on March 29, 2005.

column in the *New York Times;* the second occurs nearer the conclusion of a lengthy article defending the car against its many snobbish critics:

> **Fifteen years ago, when Japanese companies were busily buying up chunks of corporate America, I was one of those urging Americans not to panic. You might therefore expect me to offer similar soothing words now that the Chinese are doing the same thing. But the Chinese challenge—highlighted by the bids for Maytag and Unocal—looks a lot more serious than the Japanese challenge ever did.**
>
> **–Paul Krugman, "The Chinese Challenge"**

> **But even if we do all the things that can be done to limit the social costs of cars, the campaign against them will not stop. It will not stop because so many of the critics dislike everything the car stands for and everything society constructs to serve the needs of its occupants.**
>
> **–James Q. Wilson, "Cars and Their Enemies"**

Think of claims like these as vortices of energy in an argument. You need to identify any such statements and then examine a text carefully to see how (sometimes *whether*) they're supported by good reasons and reliable evidence. A lengthy essay may, in fact, contain a series of claims, each developed to support an even larger point. Indeed, every paragraph in an argument may develop a specific and related idea. In a rhetorical analysis, you need to track down all these separate propositions and examine the relationships among them. Are they solidly linked? Are there inconsistencies that the writer should acknowledge? Does the end of the piece support what the writer said (and promised) at the beginning?

Since many logical appeals rely heavily on data and information from sources, you'll also need to examine the quality of the information presented in an argument, assessing how accurately such information is reported, how conveniently it's displayed (in charts or graphs, for example), and how well the sources cited represent a range of *respected* opinion on a topic.

David Bositis makes an appeal to logic in his article about the missampling of minorities in U.S. opinion polls. Bositis bolsters his argument with facts and statistics that support his hypothesis.

LINK TO P. 663

Knowing how to judge the quality of sources is more important now than ever because the electronic pathways, where increasing numbers of writers find their information, are clogged with junk. The computer terminal may have become the equivalent of a library reference room in certain ways, but the sources available online vary much more widely in quality. As a consequence, both readers and writers of arguments today must know the difference between reliable, firsthand, or fully documented sources and those that don't meet such standards. (For more on using and documenting sources, see Chapters 19 and 20.)

Examining the Shape and Media of Arguments

Arguments have a structure. Aristotle carved the structure of logical argument to its bare bones when he observed that it had only two parts:

- statement
- proof

You could do worse, in examining an argument, than just to make sure that every claim a writer makes is backed by sufficient evidence.

Most arguments you read and write, however, will be more than mere statements followed by proofs. Some writers will lay their cards on the table immediately; others may lead you carefully through a chain of claims toward a conclusion. Writers may even interrupt their arguments to offer background information or cultural contexts for readers. Sometimes they'll tell stories or provide anecdotes that make an argumentative point. They'll qualify the arguments they make, too, so they don't bite off more than they can chew. Smart writers may even pause to admit that other points of view are plausible, though they might also spend time undercutting such contrary opinions or evidence. In other words, there are no formulas or acceptable patterns that fit all successful

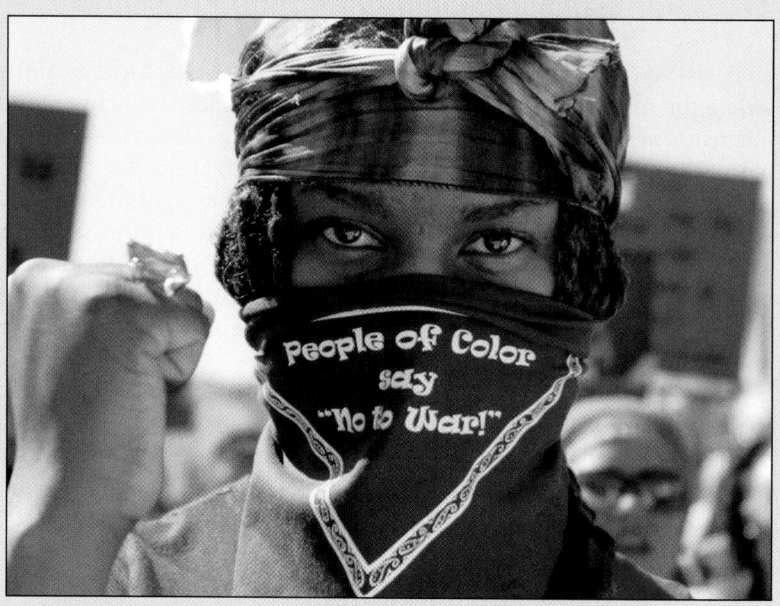

Not Just Words

New media such as Web sites and blogs have practically made a sport out of analyzing the stories and arguments offered by traditional mainstream media (MSM) such as newspapers, TV network news, and print publishers. It's no surprise that the MSM have pushed back, providing readers with uncharacteristically lively examples of rhetorical analyses as part of the daily news.

In September 2005, the *San Francisco Chronicle,* usually regarded as a liberal news source, included in its coverage of an anti–Iraq War demonstration a memorable close-up photograph of a youth at the protest, with the following caption: "Jasmine Williams, 17, a student with the leadership group Youth Together, joins the Iraq war protest in San Francisco."

The image provoked the ire of a presumably more conservative blogger at <zombietime.com.> Zombie, who had also photographed the event and even the same girl, but at a wider angle, found the *Chronicle*'s shot disingenuous, omitting details such as Palestinian flags in the background. Here are some of Zombie's photographs and commentary:

Now we can see that the girl is just one of several teenagers, all wearing terrorist-style bandannas covering their faces. But, as you'll notice, the bandannas are all printed with the same design. Was this a grassroots protest statement the teenagers had come up with all by themselves? To find out, let's take a look at another photo in the series, taken at the same time:

Oops—it looks like they're actually being stage-managed by an adult, who is giving them directions and guiding them toward the front of the march. But who is she? The last picture in the series reveals all. It turns out that the woman giving directions belongs to one of the Communist groups organizing the rally—if her t-shirt is to be believed, since it depicts the flag of Communist Vietnam, which has been frequently displayed by such groups at protest rallies in the U.S. for decades. The *San Francisco Chronicle* featured the original photograph on its front Web page in order to convey a positive message about the rally—perhaps that even politically aware teenagers were inspired to show up and rally for peace, sporting the message, "People of Color say 'No to War!'" And that served the *Chronicle*'s agenda. But this simple analysis reveals the very subtle but insidious type of bias that occurs in the media all the time. The *Chronicle* did not print an inaccuracy, nor did it doctor a photograph to misrepresent the facts. Instead, the *Chronicle* committed the sin of omission: it told you the truth, but it didn't tell you the *whole* truth.

As you might expect, shortly after Zombie's photos and observations made their way around the Web, the *Chronicle* offered a rebuttal. Here's a brief portion of that newspaper's rhetorical analysis of the situation, offered by "readers' representative" Dick Rogers:

> So the *Chronicle* photo didn't exactly shout "Middle America." It was far more dramatic and displayed the protester in far more detail. If the newspaper was setting out to "de-radicalize" the scene, it did a pretty

lame job. If the paper wants to sanitize a protest, it should forget tight shots of radicals in disguise and go for pictures of suburban moms with young children. Now that's centrist.

The accompanying story, by the way, noted the Palestinian angle, the arrests of members of an anarchist group and the presence of counter-demonstrators, one of whom called for "patriotism instead of a socialist revolution."

Readers should ponder what they don't see in pictures, just as they should critically judge what they do see. Photographs are representations of reality, and small slices of it at that.

But a wide-angle view isn't necessarily a bigger slice of reality. It's true that, in some cases, a story is told in more detail by stepping back. In other cases, an image is more powerful and vivid by coming in close.

–Dick Rogers, "Picturing the Debate"

Study the photographs and the contrary rhetorical analyses here. Do you have a problem with the original photograph published in the *Chronicle*, or might one of Zombie's images more accurately represent the protest? Can you make such a judgment without more information? How could you find out more about this controversy?

Apply what you learn from this exercise to your own analysis of several news photographs selected from current newspapers, news magazines, or Web sites. Do the images you've chosen provide the facts you need to make a judgment about a story, or do you suspect something may have been left out of them? Do the images provoke strong emotional responses because of their careful composition, or do they manipulate your feelings? Do you have reason to trust the source offering the images, or might the ethos of that source be suspect? Select one or two of the images, and present your rhetorical analysis of them to your class.

arguments. Many are written on the fly in the heat of a moment. In writing a rhetorical analysis, you'll have to assess the organization of a persuasive text on its own merits.

It's fair, however, to complain about what may be *absent* from an argument. Most arguments of proposal (see Chapter 11), for example, include a section that defends the feasibility of a new idea, explaining how it might be funded or managed. In a rhetorical analysis, you might fault an editorial that supports a new stadium for a city without addressing feasibility issues. Similarly, analyzing a movie review that reads like off-the-top-of-the-head opinion, you might legitimately ask what criteria of evaluation are in play (see Chapter 9).

You also may find that an argument benefits from strong transitions, helpful headings, or a confident voice that makes navigating the claims easy. Don't take such an accomplishment for granted. Nor should you ignore the way a writer or institution uses media in an argument. Would an argument originally made in an editorial, for instance, work better as a cartoon (or vice versa)? Would a lengthy paper have more power if it included more images? Or do you find that images distract from a written argument, diminishing its substance? These are important issues you might comment on or connect to other aspects of an argument, such as its style.

Finally, be open to the possibility of new or nontraditional structures of arguments. The visual arguments you analyze may defy conventional principles of logic or arrangement—for example, making juxtapositions rather than logical transitions between elements; or using quick cuts, fades, or other devices to link ideas. Quite often, these nontraditional structures will also resist the neatness of a thesis, leaving it up to readers to construct at least a part of the argument in their heads. Advertisers are growing quite fond of these sorts of soft-sell multimedia productions that can seem more like games or entertainments than what they really are—product pitches. We're asked not just to buy a product but also to live its lifestyle. Is that a reasonable or workable strategy for an argument? Your analysis might entertain such possibilities.

Looking at Style

Jane Stern's review of the book *Fat Girl* focuses on author Judith Moore's style. Stern approves of Moore's unapologetic stance regarding her weight and her blunt, humorous approach.

LINK TO P. 601

Even a coherent argument flush with evidence may not connect with readers if it's dull, off-key, or offensive. Readers naturally judge the credibility of arguments in part by how stylishly the case is made—even when they don't know exactly what *style* is. Consider how these simple, blunt sentences from the opening of an argument shape your image of the author and probably determine whether you're willing to continue to read the whole piece:

> **We are young, urban and professional. We are literate, respectable, intelligent and charming. But foremost and above all, we know what it's like to be unemployed.**
>
> **–Julia Carlisle, "Young, Privileged and Unemployed"**

Now consider how you'd approach an argument that begins like the following, responding to a botched primary election in Florida following the electoral disaster of 2000:

> **The question you're asking yourself is: Does South Florida contain the highest concentration of morons in the entire world? Or just in the United States? The reason you're asking this, of course, is South Florida's performance in Tuesday's election. This election was critical to our image, because of our performance in the 2000 presidential election—the one that ended up with the entire rest of the nation watching, impatiently, as clumps of sleep-deprived South Florida election officials squinted at cardboard ballots, trying to figure out what the hell the voters were thinking when they apparently voted for two presidents, or no presidents, or part of a president, or, in some cases, simply drooled on the ballot.**
>
> **–Dave Barry, "How to Vote in 1 Easy Step"**

Both styles probably work, but they signal that the writers are about to make very different kinds of cases. Style alone tells readers what to expect.

Manipulating style also enables writers to shape readers' responses to their ideas. Devices as simple as repetition and parallelism can give sentences remarkable power. Consider this sentence from Andrew Sullivan, who argues for greater tolerance of homosexuals in American culture:

> **Growing up homosexual was to grow up normally but displaced; to experience romantic love, but with the wrong person; to entertain grand ambitions, but of the unacceptable sort; to seek a gradual self-awakening, but in secret, not in public.**
>
> **–Andrew Sullivan, "What Are Homosexuals For?"**

The balanced style of this sentence asks readers to pay attention and perhaps to sympathize. But the entire argument can't be presented in this key without exhausting readers—and it isn't. Style has to be modulated almost like music to keep readers tuned in.

In a rhetorical analysis, you can explore many stylistic choices. Why does a formal style work for discussing one type of subject matter, but

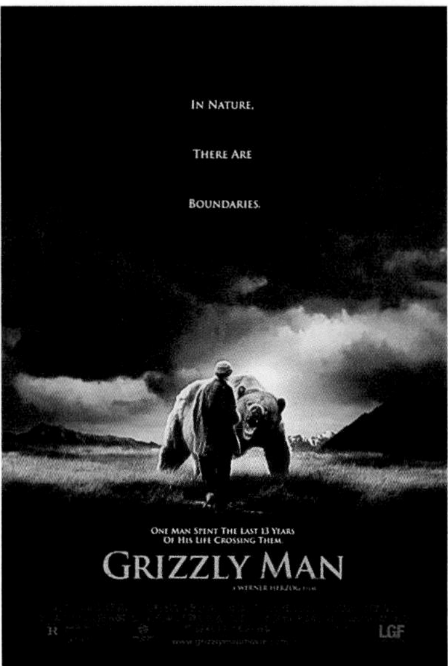

How does *look* support *message* in these documentary film posters?

not another? How does a writer use humor or irony to underscore an important point or to manage a difficult concession? Do stylistic choices, even something as simple as the use of contractions, bring readers comfortably close to a writer, or do a highly technical vocabulary and impersonal voice signal that an argument is for experts only?

To describe the stylistic effects of visual arguments, you may use a different vocabulary, talking about colors, camera angles, editing, balance, proportion, fonts, perspective, and so on. But the basic principle is this: the look of an item—whether it be a poster, an editorial cartoon, or a film documentary—can support the message it carries, undermine it, or muddle it. In some cases, the look will *be* the message. In a rhetorical analysis, you can't ignore style.

Examining a Rhetorical Analysis

Following is an argument in defense of free speech by Derek Bok, a distinguished scholar and past president of Harvard University—credentials that certainly add to his ethos. Responding to it with a detailed analysis is Milena Ateya, a college student who reveals in her piece that she, too, brings unique credentials to this case.

Protecting Freedom of Expression at Harvard

DEREK BOK

March 25, 1991

For several years, universities have been struggling with the problem of trying to reconcile the rights of free speech with the desire to avoid racial tension. In recent weeks, such a controversy has sprung up at Harvard. Two students hung Confederate flags in public view, upsetting students who equate the Confederacy with slavery. A third student tried to protest the flags by displaying a swastika.

These incidents have provoked much discussion and disagreement. Some students have urged that Harvard require the removal of symbols that offend many members of the community. Others reply that such symbols are a form of free speech and should be protected.

Different universities have resolved similar conflicts in different ways. Some have enacted codes to protect their communities from forms of speech that are deemed to be insensitive to the feelings of other groups. Some have refused to impose such restrictions.

It is important to distinguish between the appropriateness of such communications and their status under the First Amendment. The fact that speech is protected by the First Amendment does not necessarily mean that it is right, proper, or civil. I am sure that the vast majority of Harvard students believe that hanging a Confederate flag in public view—or displaying a swastika in response—is insensitive and unwise because any satisfaction it gives to the students who display these symbols is far outweighed by the discomfort it causes to many others.

I share this view and regret that the students involved saw fit to behave in this fashion. Whether or not they merely wished to manifest their pride in the South—or to demonstrate the insensitivity of hanging Confederate flags, by mounting another offensive symbol in return—they must have known that they would upset many fellow students and ignore the decent regard for the feelings of others so essential to building and preserving a strong and harmonious community.

To disapprove of a particular form of communication, however, is not enough to justify prohibiting it. We are faced with a clear example of the conflict between our commitment to free speech and our desire to foster a community founded on mutual respect. Our society has wrestled with this problem for many years. Interpreting the First Amendment, the Supreme Court has clearly struck the balance in favor of free speech.

While communities do have the right to regulate speech in order to uphold aesthetic standards (avoiding defacement of buildings) or to protect the public from disturbing noise, rules of this kind must be applied across the board and cannot be enforced selectively to prohibit certain kinds of messages but not others.

Under the Supreme Court's rulings, as I read them, the display of swastikas or Confederate flags clearly falls within the protection of the free speech clause of the First Amendment and cannot be forbidden simply because it offends the feelings of many members of the community. These rulings apply to all agencies of government, including public universities.

Although it is unclear to what extent the First Amendment is enforceable against private institutions, I have difficulty understanding why a university such as Harvard should have less free speech than the surrounding society—or than a public university.

One reason why the power of censorship is so dangerous is that it is extremely difficult to decide when a particular communication is offensive enough to warrant prohibition or to weigh the degree of offensiveness against the potential value of the communication. If we begin to forbid flags, it is only a short step to prohibiting offensive speakers.

I suspect that no community will become humane and caring by restricting what its members can say. The worst offenders will simply find other ways to irritate and insult.

In addition, once we start to declare certain things "offensive," with all the excitement and attention that will follow, I fear that much ingenuity will be exerted trying to test the limits, much time will be expended trying to draw tenuous distinctions, and the resulting publicity will eventually attract more attention to the offensive material than would ever have occurred otherwise.

Rather than prohibit such communications, with all the resulting risks, it would be better to ignore them, since students would then have little reason to create such displays and would soon abandon them. If this response is not possible—and one can understand why—the wisest course is to speak with those who perform insensitive acts and try to help them understand the effects of their actions on others.

Appropriate officials and faculty members should take the lead, as the Harvard House Masters have already done in this case. In talking with students, they should seek to educate and persuade, rather than resort to ridicule or intimidation, recognizing that only persuasion is likely to produce a lasting, beneficial effect. Through such effects, I believe that we act in the manner most consistent with our ideals as an educational institution and most calculated to help us create a truly understanding, supportive community.

A Curse and a Blessing

MILENA ATEYA

In 1991, when Derek Bok's essay "Protecting Freedom of Expression at Harvard" was first published in the Boston Globe, I had just come to America to escape the oppressive Communist regime in Bulgaria. Perhaps my background explains why I support Bok's argument that we should not put arbitrary limits on freedom of expression. Bok wrote the essay in response to a public display of Confederate flags and a swastika at Harvard, a situation that created a heated controversy among the students. As Bok notes, universities have struggled to achieve a balance between maintaining students' right of free speech and avoiding racist attacks. When choices must be made, however, Bok argues for preserving freedom of expression.

Connects article to personal experience to create ethical appeal.

Provides brief overview of Bok's argument.

States Bok's central claim.

In order to support his claim and bridge the controversy, Bok uses a variety of rhetorical strategies. The author first immerses the reader in the controversy by vividly describing the incident: two Harvard students had hung Confederate flags in public view, thereby "upsetting students who equate the Confederacy with slavery" (51). Another student, protesting the flags, decided to display an even more offensive symbol—the swastika. These actions provoked heated discussions among students. Some students believed that school officials should remove the offensive symbols, whereas others suggested that the symbols "are a form of free speech and should be protected" (51). Bok establishes common ground between the factions: he regrets the actions of the offenders but does not believe we should prohibit such actions just because we disagree with them.

Transition sentence.

Examines the emotional appeal the author establishes through description.

The author earns the reader's respect because of his knowledge and through his logical presentation of the issue. In partial support of his position, Bok refers to U.S.

Links author's credibility to use of logical appeals.

Supreme Court rulings, which remind us that "the display of swastikas or Confederate flags clearly falls within the protection of the free speech clause of the First Amendment" (52). The author also emphasizes the danger of the slippery slope of censorship when he warns the reader, "If we begin to forbid flags, it is only a short step to prohibiting offensive speakers" (52). Overall, however, Bok's work lacks the kinds of evidence that statistics, interviews with students, and other representative examples of controversial conduct could provide. Thus, his essay may not be strong enough to persuade all readers to make the leap from this specific situation to his general conclusion.

Reference to First Amendment serves as warrant for Bok's claim.

Comments critically on author's evidence.

Throughout, Bok's personal feelings are implied but not stated directly. As a lawyer who was president of Harvard for twenty years, Bok knows how to present his opinions respectfully without offending the feelings of the students. However, qualifying phrases like "I suspect that," and "Under the Supreme Court's rulings, as I read them" could weaken the effectiveness of his position. Furthermore, Bok's attempt to be fair to all seems to dilute the strength of his proposed solution. He suggests that one should either ignore the insensitive deeds in the hope that students might change their behavior, or talk to the offending students to help them comprehend how their behavior is affecting other students.

Examines how Bok establishes ethical appeal.

Identifies qualifying phrases that may weaken claim.

Analyzes author's solution.

Nevertheless, although Bok's proposed solution to the controversy does not appear at first reading to be very strong, it may ultimately be effective. There is enough flexibility in his approach to withstand various tests, and Bok's solution is general enough that it can change with the times and adapt to community standards.

Raises points that suggest Bok's solution may work.

In writing this essay, Bok faced a challenging task: to write a short response to a specific situation that represents a very broad and controversial issue. Some people may find that freedom of expression is both a curse and a blessing because of the difficulties it creates. As one who has lived under a regime that permitted very limited,

Returns to personal experience in conclusion.

censored expression, I am all too aware that I could not have written this response in 1991 in Bulgaria. As a result, I feel, like Derek Bok, that freedom of expression is a blessing, in spite of any temporary problems associated with it.

Work Cited

Bok, Derek. "Protecting Freedom of Expression on the Campus." Current Issues and Enduring Questions. Eds. Sylvan Barnet and Hugo Bedau. 6th ed. Boston: Bedford, 2002. 51–52. Rpt. of "Protecting Freedom of Expression at Harvard." Boston Globe 25 May 1991.

GUIDE to writing a rhetorical analysis

Finding a Topic

A rhetorical analysis is usually assigned work: you're asked to describe how an argument works or to assess its effectiveness. When that's the case and you're free to choose your own subject for analysis, look for one or more of the following qualities:

- a verbal or visual argument that challenges you—or rankles, excites, amazes, impresses
- a verbal or visual argument rich enough to give you stuff to analyze
- a text that raises current or enduring issues of substance
- a text that you believe should be taken more seriously

Look for arguments of all kinds. Obvious places for public arguments are the editorial/op-ed pages of any newspaper, political magazines such as *The Nation* or *The New Republic*, Web sites of organizations and interest groups, political blogs such as <DailyKos.com> or <Powerline.com>, corporate Web sites that post their TV ad spots, and so on.

Researching Your Topic

Once you've selected a text to analyze, you should find out all you can about it. Use the library or resources of the Web to explore:

- who the author(s) is/are and what credentials they have (or claim)
- if the author is an institution, what it does; what its sources of funding are; who belongs; and so on
- who is publishing or sponsoring the piece, and what they typically publish
- what the leanings or biases of authors and publishers might be
- what the context of the argument is—what preceded or provoked it; how others responded to it

Formulating a Claim

Begin a rhetorical analysis with a hypothesis in mind. A full thesis might not become evident until after you've looked at the document closely. Your final thesis should reflect the complexity of the piece you're studying, not just state that "the editorial has good pathos and ethos, but lousy logos." In developing a thesis, consider questions such as the following:

- How can I describe what this argument achieves?
- Does the argument have a clear purpose, and does it accomplish it?
- Does the argument have a clear intended audience?
- For what audiences does it work/not work?
- Which of its rhetorical features will likely influence readers most? Audience connections? Emotional appeals? Style?
- Do some aspects of the argument work better than others?
- How do the rhetorical elements interact?

You don't actually have to address these questions in your thesis. Rather, they're offered to take you inside the argument you're studying. Once you're in and you begin to deal with the issues it raises, you'll likely discover the point you need to make.

Here's the hardest part for most writers of rhetorical analyses: whether you agree or disagree with an argument doesn't matter in a rhetorical analysis. You've got to stay out of the fray and pay attention only to how well the argument—even one you dislike—works. That's tough to do. Keep your distance as you write a rhetorical analysis.

Examples of Possible Claims for a Rhetorical Analysis

- Many people today who admire the inspiring language and elevated style of John F. Kennedy's inaugural address might be uneasy with the claims he actually makes.
- Today's editorial in the *Daily Collegian* about campus crimes may scare first-year students, but its anecdotal reporting doesn't get down to hard numbers—and for a good reason. Those statistics don't back the position taken by the editors.
- Powerline has become an influential blog because its admittedly partisan authors show great respect for the intelligence of readers. In particular, they check sources meticulously and immediately acknowledge and correct any errors.
- VW's "Think Small" spot may be the finest print ad of all time, not because it sold a product well (which it did) but because it actually invoked an audience that wasn't there yet: consumers who weren't comfortable with excessive consumption.

- The original design of New York's Freedom Tower, with its torqued surfaces and evocative spire, made a stronger argument about American values than will its last-minute replacement, a fortress-like skyscraper stripped of imagination and unable to make any statement except "I'm 1,776 feet tall."

Preparing a Proposal

If your instructor asks you to prepare a proposal for your project, here's a format you might use:

- Provide a copy of the work you intend to analyze, whether it's a printed text or available in some other medium. (You might have to furnish a photograph, digital image, or URL, for instance.)
- Offer a working hypothesis or tentative thesis.
- Indicate which rhetorical components seem, at the outset of the study, especially compelling and worthy of detailed study. Also note where you see potential connections between elements. For example, does the piece seem to emphasize facts and logic so much that it becomes disconnected from potential audiences? If so, hint at that possibility in your proposal.
- Indicate what background information—about the author, institution, and contexts (political, economic, social, religious) of the argument—you intend to research.
- Define the audience you imagine for the analysis. If you're responding to an assignment, you may be writing primarily for a teacher and classmates. But they make up a complex audience in themselves. If you can do so, within the spirit of the assignment, imagine that your analysis will be published in a local newspaper, on a Web site, or in a blog.
- Suggest the media that you might use in your analysis. Will a traditional paper work? Could you use highlighting or other word-processing tools to focus attention on stylistic details? Would it be possible to use balloons or other callouts to annotate a visual argument?
- Conclude by briefly discussing the key challenges you anticipate in preparing your analysis.

Thinking about Content and Organization

Your rhetorical analysis may take various forms, but it's likely to include elements such as the following:

- facts about the text you're analyzing: author; title or name of the work; where published, located, or seen; date of publication or viewing.
- contexts for the argument. Readers need to know what the text is doing, to what it may be responding, in what controversies it might be embroiled, and so on. Don't assume writers can infer the important contextual elements.
- a synopsis of the text you're analyzing. If you can't actually attach the argument, you must summarize it in enough detail so that a reader can imagine it. Even if you do attach a copy of the piece, the analysis should include a summary.
- some claim(s) about the rhetorical effectiveness of the work. It might be a straightforward evaluative claim or something more complex. The claim can come early in the paper, or you might work toward it steadily, providing the evidence that leads toward the conclusion you've reached.
- a detailed analysis of the argument. Although you'll analyze various rhetorical components and dimensions separately, don't let your analysis become a dull roster of emotional, ethical, and logical appeals. Your rhetorical analysis should be an argument itself that supports a claim; a simple list of rhetorical appeals won't make much of a point.
- evidence for every part of the analysis.
- an assessment of alternative views and counterarguments to your own analysis.

Getting and Giving Response

If you have access to a writing center, discuss the text you intend to analyze with a consultant there before you write the paper. Try to find people who both agree with the argument and others who disagree, and take note of their observations. Your instructor may assign you to a peer group for the purpose of reading and responding to each other's drafts; if not, share your draft with someone on your own. You can use the following questions to evaluate a draft. If you're evaluating someone else's draft, be sure to illustrate your points with examples. Specific comments are always more helpful than general observations.

The Claim

- Does the claim address the rhetorical effectiveness of the argument itself, not the opinion or position it takes?

- Is the claim significant enough to interest readers?
- Does the claim indicate important relationships between various rhetorical components, not just list them?
- Would the claim be one that the author or creator of the piece might regard as serious criticism?

Evidence for the Claim

- Is enough evidence furnished to explain or support all claims you make? If not, what kind of additional evidence is needed?
- Is the evidence in support of the claim simply announced, or are its significance and appropriateness analyzed? Is a more detailed discussion needed?
- Do you use the right kind of evidence, drawn either from the argument itself or from other materials?
- Are any objections readers might have to the claim, criteria, or evidence, or to the way the analysis is conducted, adequately addressed?
- What kinds of sources might you use to explain the context of the argument? Do you need to use sources to check factual claims made in the argument?
- Are all quotations introduced with appropriate signal phrases (such as "As Peggy Noonan points out"), and do they merge smoothly into your sentences?

Organization and Style

- How are the parts of the argument organized? Is this organization effective, or would some other structure work better?
- Will readers understand the relationships among the original text you're analyzing, the claim(s) you're making, your supporting reasons, and the evidence you've gathered—both from the text you're analyzing and any other sources you've used? If not, what could be done to make those connections clearer? Are more transitional words and phrases needed? Would headings or graphic devices help?
- Are the transitions or links from point to point, paragraph to paragraph, and sentence to sentence clear and effective? If not, how could they be improved?
- Is the style suited to the subject and appropriate to your audience? Is it too formal? Too casual? Too technical? Too bland?

- Which sentences seem particularly effective? Which ones seem weakest, and how could they be improved? Should some short sentences be combined, or should any long ones be separated into two or more sentences?
- How effective are the paragraphs? Do any seem too skimpy or too long? Do they break the analysis at strategic points?
- Which words or phrases seem particularly effective, accurate, and powerful? Do any seem dull, vague, unclear, or inappropriate for the audience or your purpose? Are definitions provided for technical or other terms that readers might not know?

Spelling, Punctuation, Mechanics, Documentation, Format

- Check the spelling of the author's name, and make sure the name of any institution involved with the work is correct. Note that the names of many corporations and institutions use distinctive spelling and punctuation.
- Get the name of the text you're analyzing right.
- Are there any errors in spelling, punctuation, capitalization, and the like?
- Does the assignment require a specific format? Check the original assignment sheet to be sure.

RESPOND•

1. Describe a persuasive moment you can recall from a speech, an article, an editorial, an advertisement, or your personal experience. Alternatively, research one of the following famous moments of persuasion and then describe the circumstances of the appeal: what the historical situation was, what issues were at stake, what the purpose of the address was, and what made the particular speech memorable.

   Abraham Lincoln's "Gettysburg Address" (1863)

   Elizabeth Cady Stanton's draft of the "Declaration of Sentiments" for the Seneca Falls Convention (1848)

   Franklin Roosevelt's inaugural address (1933)

   Winston Churchill's addresses to the British people during the early stages of World War II (1940)

   Martin Luther King Jr.'s "Letter from Birmingham Jail" (1963)

   Ronald Reagan's tribute to the *Challenger* astronauts (1986)

   Toni Morrison's speech accepting the Nobel Prize (1993)

   George Bush's speech to Congress following the 9/11 terrorist attack (2001)

2. Find a written argument on the editorial page or op-ed section in a recent newspaper. Analyze this argument rhetorically, drawing upon the principles discussed in this chapter. Analyze the elements of the argument that best explain why it succeeds, fails, or does something else entirely. Perhaps you can show that the author is unusually successful in connecting with readers, but then has nothing to say. Or perhaps you discover that the strong logical appeal is undercut by a contradictory emotional argument. Upon finishing your analysis, readers should feel that they've learned something about the essay you've taken as your subject. Be sure that the analysis does include a summary of the essay and provided basic publication information: written by whom, published where, by whom?

3. Browse a magazine, newspaper, or Web site to find an example of a powerful emotional argument that's made visually, either alone or using words as well. Then, in a paragraph, defend a claim about how the argument works. For example, does an image itself make a claim, or does it draw you in to consider a verbal claim? What emotion does the argument generate? How does that emotion work to persuade you?

4. Find a recent example of a visual argument, either in print or on the Internet. Analyze this argument rhetorically. Even though you may

have a copy of the image, describe the argument carefully in your paper on the assumption that your description is all readers may have to go on. Then make a judgment about the effectiveness of the visual argument, supporting your claim with clear evidence from the "text."

5. Make one of the other chapters in *Everything's an Argument* the subject of a full-blown rhetorical analysis. Follow the advice in this chapter, particularly in the Guide to Writing on pp. 129–134. Pay particular attention to the ethos the authors try to project and the audiences intended and evoked in the chapter you select for study. Your biggest challenge may be to identify what *argument(s)* the chapter makes.

PART 2

WRITING arguments

6
Structuring Arguments

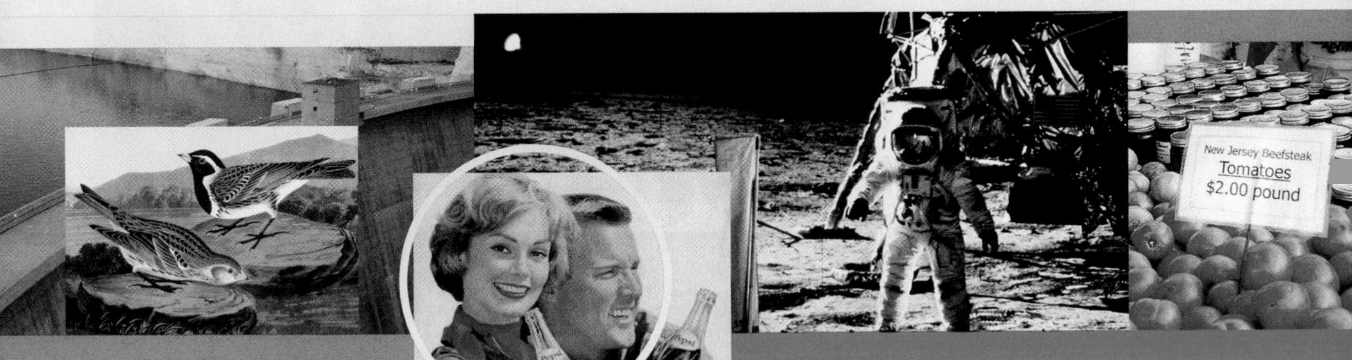

"Don't put the cart before the horse."

"Get your ducks in a row."

"Stop beating around the bush!"

"And your point is?"

• • •

These familiar idiomatic sayings all suggest the importance of getting things in the right order, or structuring them in the best way, to make a clear, persuasive point.

Pepsi-Cola advertisements, 1954 and 2005

"Don't put the cart before the horse" is particularly good advice for writers of arguments—as long as it's clear which part of the argument is the cart and which the horse. Advertisements usually put the cart before the horse by featuring the product in the foreground and linking it to reasons we should purchase. Take a look at the two advertisements for Pepsi-Cola, one from 1954, the other from 2005: note the way each is structured and designed, what the focal point of the image is, and what reasons are provided or implied in support of the argument the advertisements make.

If arguments are carefully structured in advertisements, and they are, then more traditional arguments also pay very careful attention to the design or structure of their cases. You no doubt recognize the words of the 1776 Declaration of Independence proclaiming the sovereignty of the United States:

> **When in the Course of human events, it becomes necessary for one people to dissolve the political bands which have connected them with another, and to assume among the powers of the earth, the separate and equal station to which the Laws of Nature and of Nature's God entitle them, a decent respect to the opinions of mankind requires that they should declare the causes which impel them to the separation.**
>
> **We hold these truths to be self-evident, that all men are created equal, that they are endowed by their Creator with certain unalienable Rights, that among these are Life, Liberty, and the pursuit of**

> **Happiness—that to secure these rights, Governments are instituted among Men, deriving their just powers from the consent of the governed—That whenever any Form of Government becomes destructive to these ends, it is the Right of the People to alter or to abolish it and to institute new Government, laying its Foundation on such principles and organizing its powers in such form, as to them shall seem most likely to effect their Safety and Happiness. Prudence, indeed, will dictate that Governments long established should not be changed for light and transient causes; and accordingly all experience hath shewn that mankind are more disposed to suffer, while evils are sufferable, than to right themselves by abolishing the forms to which they are accustomed. But when a long train of abuses and usurpations, pursuing invariably the same Object evinces a design to reduce them under absolute Despotism, it is their right, it is their duty, to throw off such Government and to provide new Guards for their future security. —Such has been the patient sufferance of these Colonies; and such is now the necessity which constrains them to alter their former Systems of Government. The history of the present King of Great Britain is a history of repeated injuries and usurpations, all having in direct object the establishment of an absolute Tyranny over these States. To prove this, let Facts be submitted to a candid world.**
>
> **–Declaration of Independence, July 4, 1776**

The Declaration then lists the "long train of abuses and usurpations" by King George III, details the colonists' unsuccessful attempts at reconciliation with the British, and ends by asserting the central claim: "That these United Colonies are, and of Right ought to be FREE AND INDEPENDENT STATES."

The authors might have organized this argument in a different way—for example, by beginning with the last two sentences of the excerpt and then listing the facts intended to prove the king's abuse and tyranny. But by choosing first to explain the purpose and "self-evident" assumptions behind their argument and only then moving on to demonstrate how these "truths" have been denied by the British, the authors forge an immediate connection with readers and build to a more memorable and compelling conclusion.

A little over seventy years after the Declaration of Independence, Elizabeth Cady Stanton and Lucretia Mott gathered a group of people together to issue a new Declaration, one that—with great irony—followed the precise structure of the framing document to make a strong argument about women's rights:

> **When, in the course of human events, it becomes necessary for one portion of the family of man to assume among the people of the earth**

> a position different from that which they have hitherto occupied, but one to which the laws of nature and of nature's God entitle them, a decent respect to the opinions of mankind requires that they should declare the causes that impel them to such a course.
>
> We hold these truths to be self-evident: that all men and women are created equal; that they are endowed by their Creator with certain inalienable rights; that among these are life, liberty, and the pursuit of happiness; that to secure these rights governments are instituted, deriving their just powers from the consent of the governed. Whenever any form of government becomes destructive of these ends, it is the right of those who suffer from it to refuse allegiance to it, and to insist upon the institution of a new government, laying its foundation on such principles, and organizing its powers in such form, as to them shall seem most likely to effect their safety and happiness. Prudence, indeed, will dictate that governments long established should not be changed for light and transient causes; and accordingly all experience hath shown that mankind are more disposed to suffer while evils are sufferable, than to right themselves by abolishing the forms to which they are accustomed. But when a long train of abuses and usurpations, pursuing invariably the same object, evinces a design to reduce them under absolute despotism, it is their duty to throw off such government, and to provide new guards for their future security. Such has been the patient sufferance of the women under this government, and such is now the necessity which constrains them to demand the equal station to which they are entitled. The history of mankind is a history of repeated injuries and usurpations on the part of man toward woman, having in direct object the establishment of an absolute tyranny over her. To prove this, let facts be submitted to a candid world.
>
> –"The Declaration of Sentiments: Seneca Falls Conference, 1848"

Such beautifully structured point/counterpoint arguments abound in American history, a part of the fabric of free speech and democracy. Consider celebrations of the Declaration, for instance, which from the very beginning included patriotic proclamations that were an important part of political and social commentary of the day. For example, the Not Just Words box on p. 143 shows the title page of such a speech given by John Quincy Adams in 1793, part of a genre that began right after 1776 and continues to the present day.

Most Fourth of July speeches follow a pattern of praising the Revolutionary heroes and emphasizing freedom, democracy, and liberty. Sometimes, however, orators have sounded a different note. Frederick Douglass certainly had this tradition of celebratory speeches in mind when, in 1852, he delivered his own Fourth of July oration. Note his use

AN

ORATION,

PRONOUNCED

JULY 4th, 1793,

AT THE

REQUEST OF THE INHABITANTS

OF THE

TOWN OF *BOSTON*;

IN COMMEMORATION

OF THE

ANNIVERSARY OF

AMERICAN INDEPENDENCE.

BY JOHN QUINCY ADAMS.

O NOMEN DULCE LIBERTATIS! Cic.

YE shades of ancient heroes! Ye who toil'd,
Through long successive ages to build up
A labouring plan of state; behold at once
The wonder done! THOMSON.

[THE SECOND EDITION.]

BOSTON:

PRINTED by BENJAMIN EDES & SON, in *Kilby-Street*.

M,DCC,XCIII.

Not Just Words

Take a close look at the page above, announcing a Fourth of July celebratory oration. Note how it is designed and structured. If you were revising it to announce a speech in celebration of July 4 in the twenty-first century, what changes would you make to the design, layout, and so on?

of questions to structure what follows and to secure the close attention of his (white) audience:

> Fellow-citizens, pardon me, allow me to ask, why am I called upon to speak here today? What have I, or those I represent, to do with your national independence? Are the great principles of political freedom and natural justice, embodied in the Declaration of Independence, extended to us? And am I, therefore, called upon to bring our humble offering to the national altar, and to confess the benefits and express devout gratitude for the blessings resulting from your independence to us?. . . I say it with a sad sense of the disparity between us. I am not included within the pale of this glorious anniversary! Your high independence only reveals the immeasurable distance between us. The blessings in which you, this day, rejoice, are not enjoyed in common. The rich inheritance of justice, liberty, prosperity and independence, bequeathed by your fathers, is shared by you, not by me. The sunlight that brought life and healing to you, has brought stripes and death to me. This Fourth of July is yours, not mine. You may rejoice, I must mourn.
>
> –Frederick Douglass, "What to the Slave Is the Fourth of July?"

Just eleven years later, President Abraham Lincoln issued the Emancipation Proclamation, a document intended to respond in some ways to Douglass's and other abolitionists' arguments for full rights for all citizens (see the figure on p. 145). Unlike the documents you've seen in previous pages, this one is handwritten in a flowing and formal script. Its title, "By the President of the United States of America, a Proclamation," announces its power and authority and calls all Americans to attention. Yet this famous statement—one of the most important documents in U.S. history—actually provided quite limited freedom for slaves, since it applied only to the states that had seceded from the Union and even exempted parts of them. As a result, the Proclamation itself underscores the deep irony that infused Douglass's earlier speech.

Speaking at the foot of the Lincoln Memorial in Washington, D.C., one hundred years later, on August 28, 1963, Martin Luther King Jr. clearly had both Douglass's address and the Emancipation Proclamation in mind in the opening of his "I Have a Dream" speech:

> Five score years ago, a great American, in whose symbolic shadow we stand today, signed the Emancipation Proclamation. This momentous decree came as a great beacon light of hope to millions of Negro slaves who had been seared in the flames of withering injustice. It came as a joyous daybreak to end the long night of their captivity.

By the President of the United States of America:

A Proclamation.

Whereas, on the twenty-second day of September, in the year of our Lord one thousand eight hundred and sixty-two, a proclamation was issued by the President of the United States, containing, among other things, the following, to wit:

"That on the first day of January, in the "year of our Lord one thousand eight hundred "and sixty-three, all persons held as slaves within "any State or designated part of a State, the people "whereof shall then be in rebellion against the "United States, shall be then, thenceforward, and "forever free; and the Executive Government of the "United States, including the military and naval "authority thereof, will recognize and maintain "the freedom of such persons, and will do no act "or acts to repress such persons, or any of them, "in any efforts they may make for their actual "freedom.

"That the Executive will, on the first day

Emancipation Proclamation, January 1, 1863

> **But one hundred years later, the Negro still is not free. One hundred years later, the life of the Negro is still sadly crippled by the manacles of segregation and the chains of discrimination. One hundred years later, the Negro lives on a lonely island of poverty in the midst of a vast ocean of material prosperity. One hundred years later, the Negro is still languished in the corners of American society and finds himself an exile in his own land.**
>
> **–Martin Luther King Jr., "I Have a Dream"**

King went on to delineate in detail the many injustices still characteristic of U.S. society—and then in one of the most brilliant perorations in the history of speechmaking, he invoked his dream of a future in which the United States would live up to its highest ideals, such as those articulated in the Declaration of Independence. Once this happened, King said, the following would be the outcome:

> **. . . when we allow freedom to ring, when we let it ring from every village and every hamlet, from every state and every city, we will be able to speed up that day when *all* of God's children, black men and white men, Jews and Gentiles, Protestants and Catholics, will be able to join hands and sing in the words of the old Negro spiritual: "Free at last! Free at last! Thank God Almighty, we are free at last!"**
>
> **–Martin Luther King Jr., "I Have a Dream"**

Martin Luther King Jr. on the steps of the Lincoln Memorial

These examples all illustrate the deep complexity and layered quality of most important national arguments, which, as you've seen, can span hundreds of years. In recognition of this complexity, we won't pretend that learning how to make (or analyze) an argument is easy. Nor will we offer any foolproof guidelines for structuring persuasive arguments, because such arguments are as complicated and different as the people who make them. Five-step plans for changing minds or scoring big on *The Daily Show* won't work.

But making effective arguments isn't a mystery either. As you'll see shortly, you already understand, almost intuitively, most of the basic moves in arguing successfully. But it helps to give them names and to appreciate how they work. When you can recognize a reasonable claim, you can make one of your own. When you know that claims need to be supported with sound reasons and reliable evidence, you'll expect to see both in what you read and what you write yourself. You'll also see that all arguments rest on assumptions, some far more controversial than others. And when you do, you'll be prepared to air your differences with a considerable degree of confidence.

Toulmin Argument

To look at argument, we'll borrow some of the key terms and strategies introduced by British philosopher Stephen Toulmin in *The Uses of Argument* (1958). Toulmin was looking for a method that accurately described the way people make convincing and reasonable arguments. Because Toulmin argument takes into account the complications in life—all those situations when people have to qualify their thoughts with words such as *sometimes, often, presumably, unless,* and *almost*—his method isn't as airtight as formal logic, the kind that uses syllogisms (see Chapter 4, p. 93). But for exactly that reason, Toulmin logic has become a powerful and, for the most part, practical tool for understanding and shaping argument in the real world.

You'll find Toulmin argument especially helpful as a way to come up with ideas and test them. Moreover, it will help you understand what goes where in many kinds of arguments. Perhaps most important, you'll acquire good critical thinking habits when you think in Toulmin's terms.

Making Claims

In the Toulmin model, arguments begin with *claims,* which are debatable and controversial statements or assertions you hope to prove. Notice that in this model the arguments depend on conditions set by others—your audience or readers. *It's raining* might be an innocent statement of fact in one situation; in another, it might provoke a debate: *No, it's not. That's sleet.* And so an argument begins, involving a question of definition.

Claims worth arguing tend to be controversial; there's no point worrying about points on which most people agree. For example, there are assertions in the statements *Twelve inches make a foot* and *Earth is the third planet from the sun.* But except in unusual circumstances, such claims aren't worth the time it takes to argue over them.

Claims should also be debatable; they can be demonstrated using logic or evidence, the raw material for building arguments. Sometimes the line between what's debatable and what isn't can be thin. You push back your chair from the table in a restaurant and declare, *That was delicious!* A debatable point? Not really. If you thought the meal was out of sight, who can challenge your taste, particularly when your verdict affects no one but yourself?

But now imagine you're a restaurant critic working for the local newspaper, leaning back from the same table and making the same observation. Because of your job, your claim about the restaurant's cannelloni would have different status and wider implications. People's jobs—including your own—might be at stake. *That was delicious!* suddenly becomes a claim you have to support, bite by bite.

Many writers stumble when it comes to making claims because facing issues squarely takes thought and guts. A claim answers the question *So what's your point?* Some writers would rather ignore the question and avoid taking a stand. But when you make a claim worth writing about, you step slightly apart from the crowd and ask that it notice you.

Is there a danger that you might oversimplify an issue by making too bold a claim? Of course. But making that sweeping claim is a logical first step toward eventually saying something more reasonable and subtle. Here are some fairly simple, undeveloped claims:

> **The filibuster system has outlived its usefulness.**
>
> **It's time to legalize medical use of marijuana.**
>
> **NASA should launch a human expedition to Mars.**
>
> **Vegetarianism is the best choice of diet.**
>
> **Same sex unions deserve the same protections as those granted to marriage between a man and a woman.**

Note that these claims are statements, not questions. There's nothing wrong with questions per se; in fact, they're what you ask to reach a claim:

Questions	**What should NASA's next goal be? Should the space agency establish a permanent moon base? Should NASA launch more robotic interstellar probes? Should NASA send people to Mars or Venus?**
Statement	**NASA should launch a human expedition to Mars.**

Don't mistake one for the other.

Good claims often spring from personal experience. Almost all of us know enough about something to merit the label *expert*—though we don't always realize it. If you're a typical first-year college student, for example, you're probably an expert about high school. You could make trustworthy claims (or complaints) about a range of consequential issues, from competency testing to the administration of athletic programs. And if you aren't a typical college student, what makes you different—perhaps your experiences at work, in the military, or with a family—could make claims fairly leap to mind. Whether you're a typical or nontypical college student, you might also know a lot about music or urban living or retail merchandising, or inequities in government services and so on—all of them fertile ground for authoritative, debatable, and personally relevant claims.

Justice Antonin Scalia presents a definitional argument to make his claim in "God's Justice and Ours" that the Constitution is an enduring rather than a living, evolving document.

LINK TO P. 887

CULTURAL CONTEXTS FOR ARGUMENT

Being Explicit

In the United States, many people (especially those in the academic and business worlds) expect a writer to "get to the point" as directly as possible and to articulate that point efficiently and unambiguously. Student writers are typically expected to make their claims explicit, leaving little unspoken. Such claims usually appear early on in an argument, often in the first paragraph. But not all cultures take such an approach. Some prefer that the claim or thesis be introduced subtly and indirectly, expecting that readers "read between the lines" to understand what's being said. Some even save the thesis until the very end of a written argument. Here are a couple of questions that might help you think about how explicitly you should (or shouldn't) make your points:

- What general knowledge does your audience have about your topic? What information do they expect or need you to provide?
- Do members of your audience tend to be very direct, saying explicitly what they mean? Or are they more subtle, less likely to call a spade a spade? Look for cues to determine how much responsibility you have as the writer and how you can most successfully argue your points.

Offering Evidence and Good Reasons

A claim is just a lonely statement hanging out there in the wind—until it teams up with some evidence and good reasons. You can begin developing a claim simply by drawing up a list of reasons to support it or finding evidence that backs up the point. In doing so, you'll likely generate still more claims in need of more support; that's the way arguments work.

One student writer, for instance, wanted to gather good reasons in support of an assertion that his college campus needed more officially designated spaces for parking bicycles. He had been doing some research—gathering statistics about parking space allocation, numbers of people using particular designated slots, and numbers of bicycles registered on campus. Before he went any further with this argument, however, he decided to list the primary reasons he had identified for more bicycle parking:

- *Personal experience:* At least twice a week for two terms, he had been unable to find a designated parking space for his bike.
- *Anecdotes:* Several of his friends told similar stories; one had even sold her bike as a result.
- *Facts:* He had found out that the ratio of car to bike parking spaces was 100 to 1, whereas the ratio of cars to bikes registered on campus was 25 to 1.
- *Authorities:* The campus police chief had indicated in an interview with the college newspaper that she believed a problem existed for students trying to park bicycles legally.

On the basis of his preliminary listing of possible reasons in support of the claim, this student decided that his subject was worth still more research. He was on the way to amassing a set of good reasons sufficient to support his claim.

In some arguments you read, claims might be widely separated from the reasons offered to support them. In shaping your own arguments, try putting claims and reasons together early in the writing process to create what Aristotle called *enthymemes*, or arguments in brief. Think of these enthymemes as test cases or even as topic sentences:

> **Bicycle parking spaces should be expanded because the number of bikes on campus far exceeds the available spots.**
>
> **It's time to lower the drinking age because I've been drinking since I was fourteen and it hasn't hurt me.**
>
> **Legalization of the medical use of marijuana is long overdue since it has been proven an effective treatment for symptoms associated with cancer.**
>
> **Violent video games should be carefully evaluated and their use monitored by the industry, the government, and parents because these games cause addiction and psychological harm to players.**

As you can see, attaching a reason to a claim often spells out the major terms of an argument. In rare cases, the full statement is all the argument you'll need:

> **Don't eat that mushroom—it's poisonous.**
>
> **We'd better stop for gas because the gauge has been reading empty for more than thirty miles.**

Anticipate challenges to your claims.

"I know your type, you're the type who'll make me prove every claim I make."

More often, your work is just beginning when you've put a claim together with its supporting reasons and evidence. If your readers are capable—and you should always assume they are—they'll then begin to question your statement. They might ask whether the reasons and evidence you're offering really do support the claim: *Should the drinking age be changed simply because you've managed to drink since you were fourteen? Should the whole state base its laws on what's worked for you?* They might ask pointed questions about your evidence: *Exactly how do you know the number of bikes on campus far exceeds the number of spaces available?* Eventually, you've got to address both issues: quality of assumptions and quality of evidence. The connection between claim and reason(s) is a concern at the next level in Toulmin argument. (For more on enthymemes, see Chapter 4, p. 93.)

Determining Warrants

Crucial to Toulmin argument is appreciating that there must be a logical and persuasive connection between a claim and the reasons and data supporting it. Toulmin calls this connection the *warrant;* it answers the question *How exactly do I get from the claim to the data?* Like the warrant in legal situations (a search warrant, for example), a sound warrant in an argument gives you authority to proceed with your case.

The warrant tells readers what your (often unstated) assumptions are—for example, that any practice that causes serious disease should be banned by the government. If readers accept your warrant, you can then present specific evidence to develop your claim. But if readers dispute your warrant, you'll have to defend it before you can move on to the claim itself.

When you state a warrant accurately, you sometimes expose a fatal flaw in an argument. However, stating warrants can be tricky because they can be phrased in various ways. What you're looking for is the general principle that enables you to justify the move from a reason to a specific claim, the bridge connecting them. The warrant is the assumption that makes the claim seem plausible. It's often a value or principle you share with your readers. Let's demonstrate this logical movement with an easy example:

Don't eat that mushroom—it's poisonous.

The warrant supporting this enthymeme can be stated in several ways, always moving from the reason (*It's poisonous*) to the claim (*Don't eat that mushroom*):

That which is poisonous shouldn't be eaten.

If something is poisonous, it's dangerous to eat.

Here's the relationship, diagrammed:

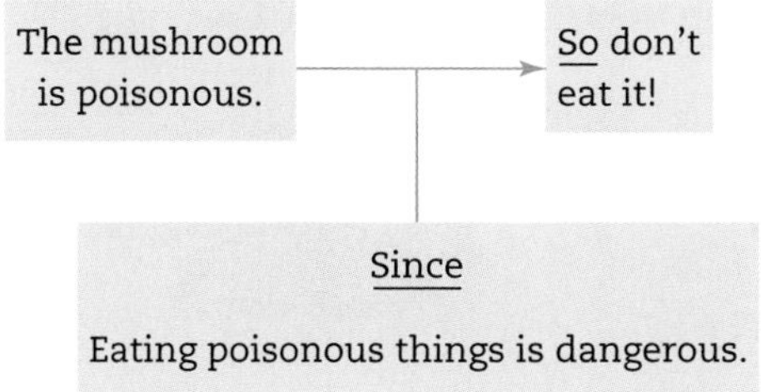

Perfectly obvious, you say? Exactly—and that's why the statement is so convincing. If the mushroom in question is indeed a death cap or destroying angel (and you might still need expert testimony to prove that's what it is), the warrant does the rest of the work, making the claim it supports seem logical and persuasive.

Let's look at a similar example, beginning with the argument in its basic form:

We'd better stop for gas because the gauge has been reading empty for more than thirty miles.

In this case, you have evidence so clear (a gas gauge reading empty) that the reason for getting gas doesn't even have to be stated: the tank is

POCKET NATURALIST™

MUSHROOMS

AN INTRODUCTION TO FAMILIAR NORTH AMERICAN SPECIES

Fly Agaric
Amanita muscaria
To 7 in. (18 cm)
Cap: Yellow to red-orange cap has white warts
Stalk: Whitish, frilled collar
Gills: Free, white to yellow
Spore Print: White
Habitat: Oak and coniferous forests. Was once used, mixed with milk, to poison house flies.

Destroying Angel
Amanita virosa
To 10 in. (25 cm)
Cap: White, smooth
Stalk: Basal bulb, collar
Gills: Free
Spore Print: White
Habitat: Mixed forests. Young caps resemble edible *Agaricus* mushrooms.

Death Cap
Amanita phalloides
To 5 in. (13 cm)
Cap: Smooth, greenish-yellow
Stalk: Widest at base, collar near top
Gills: Free
Spore Print: White
Habitat: All woods, especially under oaks and conifers.

In a pocket field guide, a simple icon—a skull and crossbones—makes a visual argument that implies a claim, a reason, and a warrant.

almost empty. The warrant connecting the evidence to the claim is also compelling and pretty obvious:

If the fuel gauge of a car has been reading empty for more than thirty miles, that car is about to run out of gas.

Since most readers would accept this warrant as reasonable, they would also likely accept the statement the warrant supports.

Naturally, factual information might undermine the whole argument—the fuel gauge might be broken, or the driver might know from previous experience that the car will go another fifty miles even though the fuel gauge reads empty. But in most cases, readers would accept the warrant.

Let's look at a third easy case, one in which stating the warrant confirms the weakness of an enthymeme that doesn't seem convincing on its own merits:

Grades in college should be abolished because I don't like them!

Moving from stated reason to claim, we see that the warrant is a silly and selfish principle:

What I don't like should be abolished.

Most readers won't accept this assumption as a principle worth applying generally. It would produce a chaotic or arbitrary world, like that of the Queen of Hearts in *Alice's Adventures in Wonderland* ("Off with the heads of anyone I don't like!"). So far, so good. But how does understanding warrants make you better at writing arguments? The answer is simple: warrants tell you what arguments you have to make and at what level you have to make them. If your warrant isn't controversial, you can immediately begin to defend your claim. But if your warrant is controversial, you must first defend the warrant—or modify it or look for better assumptions on which to support the claim. Building an argument on a weak warrant is like building a house on a questionable foundation. Sooner or later, the structure will crack.

Let's consider how stating and then examining a warrant can help you determine the grounds on which you want to make a case. Here's a political enthymeme of a familiar sort:

Flat taxes are fairer than progressive taxes because they treat all taxpayers in the same way.

Examples of Claims, Reasons, and Warrants

Smoking causes serious diseases in smokers and endangers nonsmokers as well. → So the federal government should ban smoking.

Since

The Constitution was established to "promote the general welfare," and citizens are thus entitled to protection from harmful actions by others.

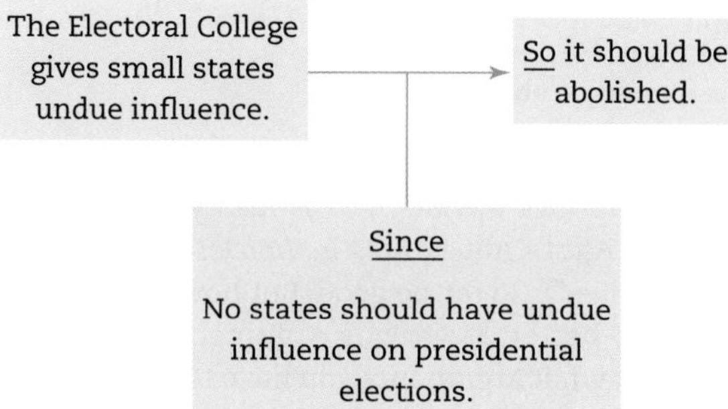

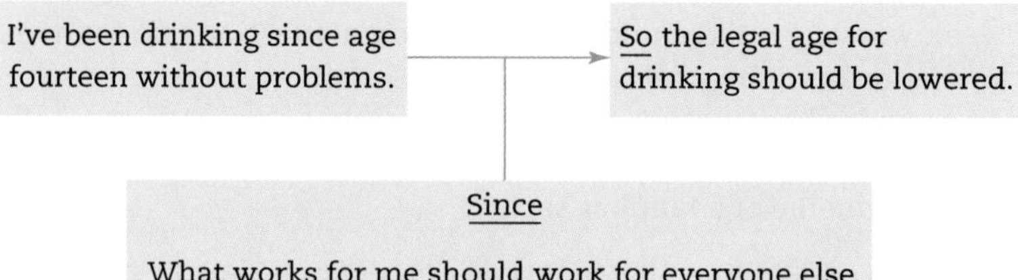

The Electoral College gives small states undue influence.

I've been drinking since age fourteen without problems.
So the legal age for drinking should be lowered.
Since
What works for me should work for everyone else.

Warrants that follow from this enthymeme have power because they appeal to a core American value—equal treatment under the law:

> **Treating people equitably is the American way.**
>
> **All people should be treated in the same way.**

You certainly could make an argument on these grounds. But stating the warrant should also raise a flag if you know anything about tax policy. If the principle is so obvious and universal, why are federal and many state income taxes progressive, requiring people at higher levels of income to pay at higher tax rates than people at lower income levels? Could it be that the warrant isn't as universally popular as it might seem at first glance? To explore the argument further, try stating the contrary claim and warrants:

> **Progressive taxes are fairer than flat taxes because people with more income can afford to pay more, benefit more from government, and can shelter more of their income from taxes.**
>
> **People should be taxed according to their ability to pay.**
>
> **People who benefit more from government and can shelter more of their income from taxes should be taxed at higher rates.**

Now you see how different the assumptions behind opposing positions really are. In a small way, we've stated one basic difference between political right and political left, between Republicans and Democrats. If you decided to argue in favor of flat taxes, you'd be smart to recognize that some members of your audience might have fundamental reservations about your position. Or you might even decide to shift your entire argument to an alternative rationale for flat taxes:

> **Flat taxes are preferable to progressive taxes because they simplify the tax code and reduce the likelihood of fraud.**

Here you have two stated reasons, supported by two new warrants:

> **Taxes that simplify the tax code are desirable.**
>
> **Taxes that reduce the likelihood of fraud are preferable.**

Whenever possible, you'll choose your warrant knowing your audience, the context of your argument, and your own feelings. Moreover, understanding how to state a warrant and how to assess its potential makes subsequent choices better informed.

Be careful, though—especially if you're citing more than one reason for your claim—that you don't give your audience the impression you're just appealing to whatever warrant(s) you think might work with them. This was one difficulty the Bush administration ran into when it began offering reasons for its invasion and occupation of Iraq after some of the original ones proved unsupported by evidence. Switching arguments—from the dangers of weapons of mass destruction, to Saddam Hussein's supposed connection with Al Qaeda, to spreading democracy and women's rights in the Middle East, to the need to "stay the course" in order to retroactively justify the invasion—left many Americans confused about what the reason or reasons for this war actually were. Likewise, if your readers suspect that the warrant of your argument for flat taxes amounts merely to *My own taxes would be lower than they are under progressive taxes,* your credibility may suffer a fatal blow.

Offering Evidence: Backing

As you might guess, claims and warrants provide only the skeleton of an argument. The bulk of a writer's work—the richest, most interesting part—remains to be done after the argument has been outlined. Claims and warrants clearly stated do suggest the scope of the evidence you have yet to assemble.

An example will illustrate the point. Here's an argument in brief—suitably debatable and controversial, if somewhat abstract:

> **NASA should launch a human expedition to Mars because Americans need a unifying national goal.**

Here's the warrant that supports the enthymeme, at least one version of it:

> **What unifies the nation ought to be a national priority.**

To run with this claim and warrant, a writer needs, first, to place both in context because most points worth arguing have a rich history. Entering an argument can be like walking into a conversation already in progress. In the case of the politics of space exploration, the conversation has been a lively one, debated with varying intensity since the launch in 1957 of the Soviet Union's *Sputnik* satellite (the first man-made object to orbit the earth) and sparked again after the 1986 death of all seven crew members in the *Challenger* disaster and, more recently, after the *Columbia* shuttle broke up on reentry in 2003, killing all aboard. A writer stumbling into this dialogue without a sense of history won't get far. Acquiring background knowledge (through reading, conversation, inquiry of all kinds) is the price you have to pay to write on the subject. Without a minimum amount of information on this—or any comparable subject—all the moves of Toulmin argument won't do you much good. You've got to do the legwork before you're ready to make a case. (See Chapter 3 for more on gaining authority.)

If you want examples of premature argument, just listen to talk radio or C-SPAN phone-ins for a day or two. You'll soon learn that the better callers can hold a conversation with the host or guests, fleshing out their basic claims with facts, personal experience, and evidence. The weaker callers usually offer a claim supported by a morsel of data. Then such callers begin to repeat themselves, as if saying over and over again that "Republicans are fascists" or "Democrats are traitors" will make the statement true.

As noted earlier, there's no point defending any claim until you've satisfied readers that any questionable warrants (like those about Republicans and Democrats above) the claim is based on are, in fact, defensible. In Toulmin argument, evidence you offer to support a warrant is called *backing*.

Jim Shore contends that Florida State University's use of the Seminole Indian mascot is a positive thing for his tribal community. What's his enthymeme? His warrants? His backing and grounds?

LINK TO P. 709

WARRANT

What unifies the nation ought to be a national priority.

BACKING

On a personal level, Americans want to be part of something bigger than themselves. (Emotional appeal as evidence)

In a country as regionally, racially, and culturally diverse as the United States, common purposes and values help make the nation stronger. (Ethical appeal as evidence)

In the past, enterprises such as westward expansion, World War II, and the Apollo moon program enabled many—though not all—Americans to work toward common goals. (Logical appeal as evidence)

In addition to evidence necessary to support your warrant (backing), you'll need evidence to support your claim.

ARGUMENT IN BRIEF (ENTHYMEME / CLAIM)

NASA should launch a human expedition to Mars because Americans need a unifying national goal.

EVIDENCE

> **The American people are politically divided along lines of race, ethnicity, religion, gender, and class. (Fact as evidence)**
>
> **A common challenge or problem often unites people to accomplish great things. (Emotional appeal as evidence)**
>
> **Successfully managing a Mars mission would require the cooperation of the entire nation—financially, logistically, and scientifically. (Logical appeal as evidence)**
>
> **A human expedition to Mars would be a valuable scientific project for the nation to pursue. (Appeal to values as evidence)**

As these examples show, you can draw from the full range of argumentative appeals to provide support for your claims. Appeals to values and emotions might be just as appropriate as appeals to logic and facts, and all such claims will be stronger if a writer presents a convincing ethos. Although it's possible to study such appeals separately, they work together in arguments, reinforcing each other. (See Chapter 3 for more on ethos.)

Finally, understand that arguments can quickly shift downward from an original set of claims and warrants to deeper, more basic claims and reasons. In a philosophy course, for example, you might dig many layers deep to reach what seem to be first principles. In general, however, you need to pursue an argument only as far as your audience demands, always presenting readers with adequate warrants and convincing evidence. There comes a point, as Toulmin himself acknowledges, at which readers have to agree to some basic principles or else the argument becomes pointless.

Using Qualifiers

What makes Toulmin's system work so well in the real world is that it acknowledges that *qualifiers*—words and phrases that place limits on claims, such as *usually, sometimes, in many cases*—play an essential role in arguments. By contrast, formal logic requires universal premises: *All humans are mortal*, for example. Unfortunately, life doesn't lend itself well to many such sturdy truths. If we could argue only about these types of sweeping claims, we'd be silent most of the time.

Check out what kind of effects Laurie Goodstein creates in her article about the rise of religious practice around the world when she uses phrases like "most scholars," "most Protestants," or "some liberal commentators."

LINK TO P. 844

Toulmin logic, in fact, encourages you to limit your responsibilities in an argument through the effective use of qualifiers. You can save time if you qualify a claim early in the writing process. But you might not figure out how to limit a claim effectively until after you've explored your subject or discussed it with others.

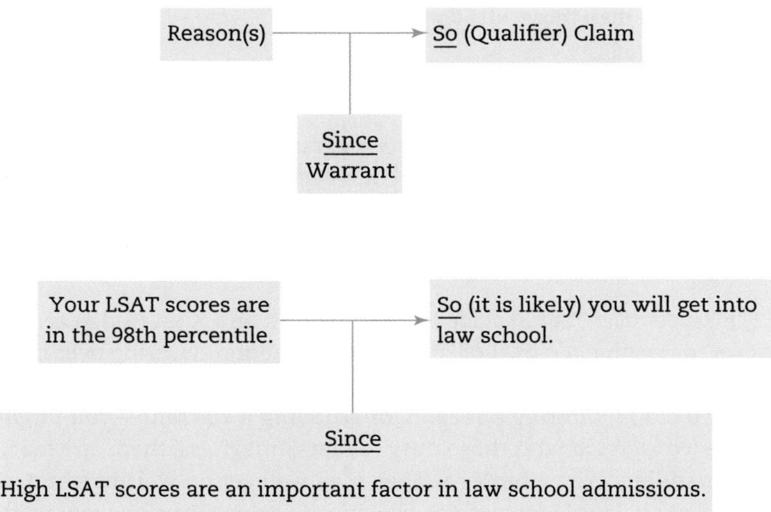
Reason(s)
So (Qualifier) Claim
Since
Warrant
Your LSAT scores are in the 98th percentile.
So (it is likely) you will get into law school.
Since
High LSAT scores are an important factor in law school admissions.

Experienced writers cherish qualifying expressions because they make writing more precise and honest.

Qualifiers

few	more or less	often
it is possible	in some cases	perhaps
rarely	many	under these conditions
it seems	in the main	possibly
some	routinely	for the most part
it may be	most	if it were so
sometimes	one might argue	

Never assume that readers understand the limits you have in mind. By spelling out the terms of the claim as precisely as possible, you'll have less work to do, and your argument will seem more reasonable. In the following examples, the first claim in each pair would be much harder to argue convincingly and responsibly—and tougher to research—than the second claim. (Notice that the second qualified claim above doesn't use terms from the list above but instead specifies and limits the actions proposed.)

Unqualified Claim	**People who don't go to college earn less than those who do.**
Qualified Claim	***In most cases,* people who don't go to college earn less than those who do.**

Unqualified Claim	**Welfare programs should be cut.**
Qualified Claim	***Ineffective federal* welfare programs should be *identified, modified,* and, *if necessary, eliminated.***

Understanding Conditions of Rebuttal

In the conclusion of her study on television's impact on the body image of young Fijian women, Anne E. Becker concedes that "sweeping economic and social changes" have also affected eating attitudes and behaviors.

LINK TO P. 592

In *The Reader over Your Shoulder,* Robert Graves and Alan Hodge advise writers to imagine a crowd of "prospective readers" hovering over their shoulders, asking hard questions. At every stage in Toulmin argument—making a claim, offering a reason, or studying a warrant—you might consider conversing with those nosy readers, imagining them as skeptical, demanding, even a bit testy. They may well get on your nerves. But they'll likely help you foresee the objections and reservations real readers will have regarding your arguments.

In the Toulmin system, potential objections to an argument are called *conditions of rebuttal*. Understanding and reacting to these conditions are essential not only to buttress your own claims where they're weak, but also to understand the reasonable objections of people who see the world differently. For example, you may be a big fan of the Public Broadcasting Service (PBS) and the National Endowment for the Arts (NEA) and prefer that federal tax dollars be spent on these programs. So you offer the following claim:

Claim	**The federal government should support the arts.**

Of course, you need reasons to support this thesis, so you decide to present the issue as a matter of values:

Argument in Brief	**The federal government should support the arts because it also supports the military.**

Now you've got an enthymeme and can test the warrant, or the premises of your claim:

Warrant	**If the federal government can support the military, it can also support other programs.**

But the warrant seems frail—something's missing to make a convincing case. Over your shoulder you hear your skeptical friends wondering what wouldn't be fundable according to your very broad principle. They restate your warrant in their own mocking fashion: *Because we pay for a military, we should pay for everything!* You could deal with their objection in the body of your paper, but revising your claim might be a better way to parry the objections. You give it a try:

Revised Argument	**If the federal government can spend huge amounts of money on the military, it can afford to spend moderate amounts on arts programs.**

Now you've got a new warrant, too:

Revised Warrant	**A country that can fund expensive programs can also afford less expensive programs.**

This is a premise you feel more able to defend, believing strongly that the arts are just as essential to the well-being of the country as a strong military. (In fact, you believe the arts are more important; but remembering those readers over your shoulder, you decide not to complicate your case by overstating it.) To provide backing for this new and more defensible warrant, you plan to illustrate the huge size of the federal budget and the proportion of it that goes to various programs.

Although the warrant seems solid, you still have to offer strong grounds to support your specific and controversial claim. Once again you cite statistics from reputable sources, this time comparing the federal budgets for the military and the arts; you break them down in ways readers can visualize, demonstrating that much less than a penny of every tax dollar goes to support the arts.

But once more you hear those voices over your shoulder, pointing out that the "common defense" is a federal mandate; the government is constitutionally obligated to support a military. Support for public television or local dance troupes is hardly in the same league. And the nation still has a huge federal debt.

Hmmm. You'd better spend a paragraph explaining all the benefits the arts provide for the very few dollars spent, and maybe you should also suggest that such funding falls under the constitutional mandate to "promote the general welfare." Though not all readers will accept these grounds, they'll at least see that you haven't ignored their point of view. You gain credibility and authority by anticipating a reasonable objection.

As you can see, dealing with conditions of rebuttal is a natural part of argument. But it's important to understand rebuttal as more than mere opposition. Anticipating objections broadens your horizons and likely makes you more open to change. One of the best exercises for you or for any writer is to learn to state the views of others in your own favorable words. If you can do that, you're more apt to grasp the warrants at issue and the commonalities you may share with others, despite differences.

Fortunately, today's wired world is making it harder to argue in isolation. Newsgroups and blogs on the Internet provide quick and potent responses to positions offered by participants in discussions. Email and Instant Messaging make cross-country connections feel almost like face-to-face conversations. Even the links on Web sites encourage people to think of communication as a network, infinitely variable, open to many voices and different perspectives. Within the Toulmin system, conditions of rebuttal—the voices over the shoulder—remind us that we're part of this bigger world. (For more on arguments in electronic environments, see Chapters 14 and 15.)

Outline of a Toulmin Argument

Consider the claim mentioned earlier:

Claim	**The federal government should ban smoking.**
Qualifier	**The ban would be limited to public spaces.**
Good Reasons	**Smoking causes serious diseases in smokers.** **Nonsmokers are endangered by second-hand smoke.**
Warrants	**The Constitution promises to "promote the general welfare."** **Citizens are entitled to protection from harmful actions by others.**
Backing	**The United States is based on a political system that is supposed to serve the basic needs of its people, including their health.**
Evidence	**Numbers of deaths attributed to second-hand smoke** **Lawsuits recently won against large tobacco companies, citing the need for reparation for smoking-related health care costs** **Examples of bans already imposed in many public places**

Authority	Cite the surgeon general.
Conditions of Rebuttal	Smokers have rights too. Smoking laws should be left to the states. Such a ban could not be enforced.
Response	The ban applies to public places; smokers can smoke in private. The power of the federal government to impose other restrictions on smoking, such as warning labels on cigarettes and bans on cigarette advertisements on television, has survived legal challenges. The experience of New York City, which has imposed such a ban, suggests that enforcement would not be a significant problem.

A Toulmin Analysis

You might wonder how Toulmin's method holds up when applied to an argument longer than a few sentences. Do such arguments really work the way Toulmin predicts? After all, knowledgeable readers often won't agree even on what the core claim in a piece is, let alone on what its warrants are. Yet such an analysis can be rewarding because it can't help raising basic questions about purpose, structure, quality of evidence, and rhetorical strategy. The following short argument by Alan Dershowitz, a professor at Harvard Law School, is responding to a proposal by the school in late 2002 to impose a speech code on its students. Dershowitz's piece, originally published in the *Boston Globe* newspaper, is followed by an analysis of it in Toulmin's terms. Keep in mind what you've learned about analyzing arguments as you read this article.

If Everything's an Argument . . .

Perform a Toulmin analysis of either the introduction to this chapter (pp. 139–147) or the section "Understanding Conditions of Rebuttal" (pp. 162–165). What central claim are the authors making, and what reasons and evidence do they provide? Do they use any qualifiers? What warrants and backing are involved? Write a page or two summarizing your analysis.

Testing Speech Codes

ALAN M. DERSHOWITZ

We need not resort to hypothetical cases in testing the limits of a proposed speech code or harassment policy of the kind that some students and faculty members of Harvard Law School are proposing. We are currently experiencing two perfect test cases.

The first involves Harvard's invitation to Tom Paulin to deliver a distinguished lecture for which it is paying him an honorarium. Paulin believes that poetry cannot be separated from politics, and his politics is hateful and bigoted.

He has urged that American Jews who make aliya to the Jewish homeland and move into the ancient Jewish quarters of Jerusalem or Hebron "should be shot dead." He has called these Jews "Nazis" and has expressed "hatred" toward "them." "Them" is many of our students and graduates who currently live on land captured by Israel during the defensive war in 1967 or who plan to move there after graduation.

The Jewish quarters of Jerusalem and Hebron have been populated by Jews since well before the birth of Jesus. The only period in which they were Judenrein was between 1948 and 1967, when it was under Jordanian control, and the Jordanian government destroyed all the synagogues and ethnically cleansed the entire Jewish populations.

Though I (along with a majority of Israelis) oppose the building of Jewish settlements in Arab areas of the West Bank and Gaza, the existence of these settlements—which Israel has offered to end as part of an overall peace—does not justify the murder of those who believe they have a religious right to live in traditional Jewish towns such as Hebron.

Paulin's advocacy of murder of innocent civilians, even if it falls short of incitement, is a paradigm of hate speech. It would certainly make me uncomfortable to sit in a classroom or lecture hall listening to him spew his murderous hatred. Yet I would not want to empower Harvard to censor his speech or include it within a speech code or harassment policy.

Or consider the case of the anti-Semitic poet Amiri Baraka, who claims that "neo-fascist" Israel had advance knowledge of the terrorist attack on the World Trade Center and warned Israelis to stay away. This lie received a standing ovation, according to *The Boston Globe*, from "black students" at

Wellesley last week. Baraka had been invited to deliver his hate speech by Nubian, a black student organization, and [was] paid an honorarium with funds provided by several black organizations. Would those who are advocating restrictions on speech include these hateful and offensive lies in their prohibitions? If not, would they seek to distinguish them from other words that should be prohibited?

These are fair questions that need to be answered before anyone goes further down the dangerous road to selective censorship based on perceived offensiveness. Clever people can always come up with distinctions that put their cases on the permitted side of the line and other people's cases on the prohibited side of the line.

For example, Paulin's and Baraka's speeches were political, whereas the use of the "N-word" is simply racist. But much of what generated controversy at Harvard Law School last spring can also be deemed political. After all, racism is a political issue, and the attitudes of bigots toward a particular race is a political issue. Paulin's and Baraka's poetry purports to be "art," but the "N-word" and other equally offensive expressions can also be dressed up as art.

The real problem is that offensiveness is often in the eyes and experiences of the beholder. To many African Americans, there is nothing more offensive than the "N-word." To many Jews, there is nothing more offensive than comparing Jews to Nazis. (Ever notice that bigots never compare Sharon to Pinochet, Mussolini, or even Stalin, only to Hitler!)

It would be wrong for a great university to get into the business of comparing historic grievances or experiences. If speech that is deeply offensive to many African Americans is prohibited, then speech that is deeply offensive to many Jews, gays, women, Asians, Muslims, Christians, atheists, etc. must also be prohibited. Result-oriented distinctions will not suffice in an area so dominated by passion and historical experience.

Unless Paulin's and Baraka's statements were to be banned at Harvard—which they should not be—we should stay out of the business of trying to pick and choose among types and degrees of offensive, harassing, or discriminatory speech. Nor can we remain silent in the face of such hate speech. Every decent person should go out of his or her way to condemn what Tom Paulin and Amiri Baraka have said, just as we should condemn racist statements made last spring at Harvard Law School.

The proper response to offensive speech is to criticize and answer it, not to censor it.

ANALYSIS

Alan M. Dershowitz presents a complete Toulmin argument that the United States should adopt a national ID card program.

LINK TO P. 166

Dershowitz uses an inverted structure for his argument, beginning with his evidence—two extended examples—and then extracting lessons from it. Indeed, his basic claim occurs, arguably, in the final sentence of the piece, and it's supported by three major reasons—although the third reason might be seen as an extension of the second:

> **The proper response to offensive speech is to criticize and answer it, not to censor it, [because]**
>
> - **Clever people can always come up with distinctions that put their cases on the permitted side of the line and other people's cases on the prohibited side of the line.**
> - **It would be wrong for a great university to get into the business of comparing historic grievances or experiences.**
> - **[W]e should stay out of the business of trying to pick and choose among types and degrees of offensive, harassing, or discriminatory speech.**

As Dershowitz presents them, the cases of Tom Paulin and Amiri Baraka suggest that smart people can always find reasons for defending the legitimacy of their offensive speech.

The closest Dershowitz gets to stating a warrant for his argument may be in the following sentence:

> **The real problem is that offensiveness is often in the eyes and experiences of the beholder.**

He doesn't want individuals dictating the limits of free speech because if they did, freedom would likely be restrained by the "eyes and experiences" of specific people and groups, not protected by an absolute and unwavering principle. Dershowitz doesn't actually offer such a warrant, perhaps because he assumes that most readers will understand that protecting free speech is a primary value in American society.

Dershowitz establishes his ethos by making it clear that although he's powerfully offended by the speech of both Paulin and Baraka, he wouldn't censor them—even though Paulin especially says things offensive to him. An implicit ethical appeal is that if Dershowitz himself is willing to experience such hate speech on his own campus, surely the law school should be able to show such tolerance toward its students.

What Toulmin Teaches

Just as few arguments you read are expressed in perfectly sequenced claims or clearly agreed-upon warrants, you might not think of Toulmin's terms yourself as you build arguments. Once you're into your subject, you'll be too eager to make a point to worry about whether you're qualifying a claim or finessing a warrant. That's not a problem if you appreciate Toulmin argument for what it teaches:

- *Claims should be stated clearly and qualified carefully.* Arguments in magazines or newspapers often develop a single point, but to make that point they may run through a complex series of claims. They may open with an anecdote, use the story to raise the issue that concerns them, examine alternative perspectives on the subject, and then make a half-dozen related claims only as they move toward a conclusion. You have the same freedom to develop your own arguments, as long as you make sure that your claims are clear and reasonable.
- *Claims should be supported with evidence and good reasons.* Remember that a Toulmin structure provides just the framework of an argument. Most successful arguments are thick with ideas and different kinds of evidence. You may not think of photographs or graphs as evidence, but they can serve that purpose. So can stories, even those that go on for many paragraphs or pages. Once you acquire the habit of looking for reasons and evidence, you'll be able to separate real supportive evidence from filler, even in arguments offered by professional writers. When you write arguments, you'll discover that it's far easier to make claims than to back them up.
- *Claims and reasons should be based on assumptions readers will likely accept.* Toulmin's focus on warrants confuses a lot of people, but that's because it forces readers and writers to think about their assumptions— something they would often just as soon skip. It's tough for a writer, particularly in a lengthy argument, to stay consistent about warrants. At one point a writer might offer a claim based on the warrant that makes "free speech" an absolute principle. But later he might rail against those who criticize the president in wartime, making national morale a higher value than free speech. Because most people read at the surface, they may not consciously detect the discrepancy—although they may nonetheless sense at some level that something's wrong with the argument. Toulmin pushes you to probe into the values that support any argument and to think of those values as

belonging to particular audiences. You can't go wrong if you're both thoughtful and aware of your readers when you craft an argument.

- *Effective arguments respectfully anticipate objections readers might offer.* In the United States, public argument seems more partisan than ever today. Yet there's still plenty of respect for people who can make a powerful, even passionate, case for what they believe without dismissing the objections of others as absurd or idiotic. They're also willing to admit the limits of their own knowledge. Toulmin argument appreciates that any claim can crumble under certain conditions, so it encourages a complex view of argument, one that doesn't demand absolute or unqualified positions. It's a principle that works for many kinds of successful and responsible arguments.

It takes considerable experience to write arguments that meet all these conditions. Using Toulmin's framework brings them into play automatically; if you learn it well enough, constructing good arguments can become a habit.

Beyond Toulmin

Useful as it is, Toulmin's system isn't the only way to go about developing and constructing an argument. For thousands of years, writers and speakers have depended on a system developed by ancient Greek and Roman orators. This so-called *classical system* provides one way to go beyond Toulmin in terms of structuring an argument. Here's an outline of how arguments are organized in the classical system:

1. Introduction
   - Gains readers' attention and interest
   - Establishes your qualifications to write about your topic
   - Establishes some common ground with your audience
   - Demonstrates that you're fair and evenhanded
   - States your claim
2. Background
   - Presents any necessary information, including personal narrative, that's important to your argument
3. Lines of argument
   - Presents good reasons, including logical and emotional appeals, in support of your claim

4. Alternative arguments
    - Examines alternative points of view / opposing arguments
    - Notes advantages and disadvantages of these views
    - Explains why your view is better than others
5. Conclusion
    - Summarizes the argument
    - Elaborates on the implications of your claim
    - Makes clear what you want the audience to think or do
    - Reinforces your credibility

CULTURAL CONTEXTS FOR ARGUMENT

Organization

As you think about how to organize your writing, remember that cultural factors are at work: the patterns that you find satisfying and persuasive are probably ones that are deeply embedded in your culture. The organizational patterns favored by U.S. engineers in their writing, for example, hold many similarities to the system recommended by Cicero some two thousand years ago. It's a highly explicit pattern, leaving little or nothing unexplained: introduction and thesis, background, overview of the parts that follow, evidence, other viewpoints, and conclusion. If a piece of writing follows this pattern, Anglo-American readers ordinarily find it "well organized."

In contrast, writers who are accustomed to different organizational patterns may not. Those accustomed to writing that's more elaborate or that sometimes digresses from the main point may find the U.S. engineers' writing overly simple, even childish. Those from cultures that value subtlety and indirectness tend to favor patterns of organization that display these values instead.

When arguing across cultures, think about how you can organize material to convey your message effectively. Here are a couple of points to consider:

- Determine when to state your thesis: At the beginning? At the end? Somewhere else? Not at all?
- Consider whether digressions are a good idea, a requirement, or an element that's best avoided.

RESPOND.

1. Following is a claim followed by five possible supporting reasons. State the warrant that would support each of the arguments in brief. Which of the warrants would need to be defended? Which one would a college audience likely accept without significant backing?

   We should amend the Constitution to abolish the Electoral College

   — because a true democracy is based on the popular vote, not the votes of the usually unknown electors.

   — because under the Electoral College system the votes of people who have minority opinions in some states end up not counting.

   — because then Al Gore would have won the 2000 election.

   — because the Electoral College is an outdated relic of an age when the political leaders didn't trust the people.

   — because the Electoral College skews power toward small and mid-size states for no good reason.

2. Claims aren't always easy to find; sometimes they're buried deep within an argument, and sometimes they're not present at all. An important skill in reading and writing arguments is the ability to identify claims, even when they aren't obvious.

   Collect a sample of eight to ten letters to the editor of a daily newspaper (or a similar number of argumentative postings from a political blog). Read each item, and then identify every claim the writer makes. When you've compiled your list of claims, look carefully at the words the writer or writers use when stating their positions. Is there a common vocabulary? Can you find words or phrases that signal an impending claim? Which of these seem most effective? Which ones seem least effective? Why?

3. At their simplest, warrants can be stated as *X is good* or *X is bad*. Return to the letters to the editor or blog postings that you analyzed in exercise 2, this time looking for the warrant behind each claim. As a way to start, ask yourself these questions: *If I find myself agreeing with the letter writer, what assumptions about the subject matter do I share with the letter writer? If I disagree, what assumptions are at the heart of that disagreement?* The list of warrants you generate will likely come from these assumptions.

4. Using a paper you're writing for this class—it doesn't matter how far along you are in the process—do a Toulmin analysis of the argument. At first, you may struggle to identify the key elements, and you might not find all the categories easy to fill. When you're done, see which elements of the Toulmin scheme are represented. Are you short of evi-

dence to support the warrant? Have you considered the conditions of rebuttal? Next, write a brief revision plan: How will you buttress the argument in the places where it is weakest? What additional evidence will you offer for the warrant? How can you qualify your claim to meet the conditions of rebuttal? Having a clearer sense of the logical structure of your argument will help you revise more efficiently.

It might be instructive to show your paper to a classmate and have him or her do a Toulmin analysis, too. A new reader will probably see your argument in a very different way and suggest revisions that may not have occurred to you.

5. Take a look at the General Electric advertisement below, which was featured in a number of magazines during summer 2005. Do a Toulmin analysis of this advertisement, trying to identify as many claims, reasons, warrants, evidence, and qualifiers as possible. What, if anything, do the Toulmin terms leave out of the argument made by the advertisement?

General Electric's "Lapland Longspur and Freight Train: Choo-Choo Tweetus Tweetus" ad. The text at the bottom reads "The Evolution is the cleanest GE locomotive ever made. Just one way ecoimagination is creating a better world," followed by the GE logo and the slogan "Imagination at work."

7
Arguments of Fact

A varsity wrestler stops his teammate from ordering the grilled chicken sandwich at a fast food restaurant. "It's more fattening than the burgers," he warns. Could that possibly be true?

For the umpteenth time, the *Times* is carrying a feature story about the *real* authorship of Shakespeare's plays. All the familiar claimants are mentioned: Francis Bacon, Christopher Marlowe, Ben Jonson, even Edward de Vere, seventeenth Earl of Oxford. But isn't it more likely that the author of *Hamlet, Macbeth,* and *Twelfth*

Night was the person that audiences who first saw those plays thought wrote them—William Shakespeare of Stratford-upon-Avon?

Members of the faculty council are outraged to learn that the Athletic Department aims to raise $100 million to build an addition to the football stadium. The chair of the council complains in an editorial in the campus paper that the professionalization of college sports—football in particular—is not consistent with the educational mission of the university as stated in its charter.

When an instructor announces a tough new attendance policy for her course, a student objects on the grounds that there is no evidence that students who regularly attend their lecture classes perform any better than those who do not. The instructor begs to differ.

A nutritionist notes that many people think that taking Vitamin E daily will prevent colon cancer, heart attacks, cataracts, impotence in men, and wrinkles. The evidence available in many scientific studies suggests they are probably wrong.

• • •

Understanding Arguments of Fact

Given the pressure on natural environments throughout the world, it's a triumph whenever a threatened plant or animal, such as the American alligator, the Peregrine falcon, or, soon, the gray wolf, recovers enough to be removed from the endangered species list. Far more typically, species depart the list because they have become extinct. So imagine the excitement in April 2005 when an article in *Science* magazine carried the good news that the ivory-billed woodpecker, a strikingly handsome bird not seen for more than sixty years in American forests, had been spotted in Arkansas. The *Science* article staked its claim on the evidence of at least seven sightings by searchers and a brief, blurry videotape of a bird resembling the ivory-billed woodpecker flying away from a naturalist's canoe (see the video image on p. 176).

(Top) The ivory-billed woodpecker by J. J. Audubon, American naturalist and painter (1785–1851). (Bottom) Frame from a videotape that may show the bird in flight.

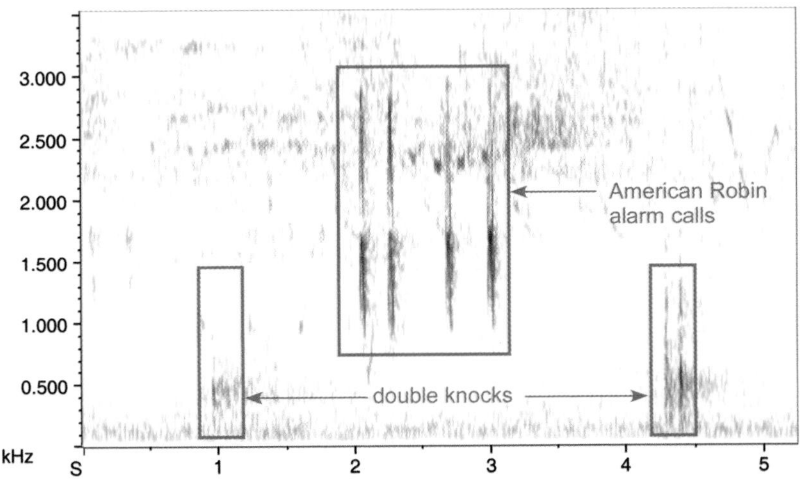

Ornithologists carefully analyzed what may have been the characteristic sounds of the ivory-billed woodpecker, recorded in an Arkansas wood. Like the videotape on the facing page, the evidence was made available for public scrutiny on the Web site of the Cornell Lab of Ornithology.

Was the argument sound? At least a few ornithologists remained doubtful, worried that too-eager colleagues may actually have mistaken a pileated woodpecker, a common bird with similar markings, for the extinct species.

Some of these skeptics withdrew their objections to the claim after hearing audiotapes recorded in an Arkansas bottomland forest carrying the distinctive call and double-rap sound of the ivory-bill (see the figure above). But blue jays or nuthatches might have made the noises, experts also admitted.

What would it take to seal the deal, to assure scientists and birders alike that the ivory-billed woodpecker really did survive in the wilds of Arkansas? As in the heyday of species collection during the eighteenth and nineteenth centuries, a specimen of the bird, dead and mounted, could confirm its existence. But that practice wouldn't be acceptable today, especially with an endangered animal whose numbers might be down to just a few breeding pairs. "What we need, what we need is a photo," said Russell Chariff of the Cornell Lab of Ornithology to the *New York Times*, discussing the burden of proof as it existed in late 2005. True, a photograph might be faked, especially a digital image. But a clear shot of the woodpecker by a reputable researcher could indeed be the clincher—given all the other tantalizing but not quite conclusive evidence in this case.

Ornithologists and amateurs will doubtless continue to scour the Arkansas woods hoping to bring this argument to a conclusion by confirming the bird's existence. Their dilemma will be like that of anyone trying to make a factual argument: to find sufficient evidence for a claim to satisfy a reasonably skeptical audience, in this case of scientists, naturalists, and birders.

Guy Trebay concludes in a *New York Times* article that men's underwear styles and advertising has become more risqué. Consider what he presents as fact and whether or not he has met the burden of proof.

LINK TO P. 622

Factual arguments come in many varieties with different standards of proof. What they have in common is an attempt to establish whether something is or is not so—that is, whether a thing exists (*the ivory-bill*) or whether claims made about something are true (*The poverty rate is higher in New Mexico than in Texas*). At first glance, you might object that these aren't arguments at all, but just a matter of looking things up and writing a report. And you'd be right to an extent: people don't ordinarily argue factual matters that are settled or agreed upon (*The earth orbits the sun*) or that might be decided with simple research (*Manuel Deodoro da Fonseca was the first president of Brazil*) or the equivalent of a rule (*One foot equals 0.3048 meters*).

Transmitting facts, it would seem, should be a dispassionate activity, free of the pressures and biases of argument. Yet facts become arguments when they're controversial in themselves or when they're used to educate people, challenging or changing their beliefs. A factual argument about the existence of a woodpecker has a kind of clean scientific logic to it, but there's passion in the debate if only because so many researchers *want* the bird to survive. And so there's resistance too among those who don't want to rush to judgment until the evidence is definitive—as it could be in this case.

Arguments of fact do much of the heavy lifting in our world. Some of them do the important task of reporting on what has been recently discovered or become known. Such arguments may also explore the implications of that new information and the conflicts that may follow from it. In recent years, for instance, we've seen plenty of contrary medical reports that raise questions about the safety or efficacy of prescription drugs, vitamin regimens, or surgical procedures. Such news has become so routine that the public is asking increasingly sophisticated questions about the studies, such as who sponsored them, who or what exactly was studied, over how many years, and among which populations. Healthy skepticism is the common attitude now, rather than simple acceptance of what the scientific community reports.

Some factual arguments make the public aware of information that's already available to anyone willing to do the work of finding it and studying its implications. Malcolm Gladwell, author of *The Tipping Point* and *Blink*, has become the go-to author for using research to expose patterns in our cultural behavior that seem obvious once he's pointed them out. *Blink*, for example, highlights the important fact that people routinely use gut feelings to make sound (as well as dubious) judgments, an argument with important repercussions for business, education, even the military—if Gladwell is right.

But serious factual arguments almost always have consequences, especially those that touch on public issues. *Can we rely on hydrogen to solve our energy needs? Will the Social Security trust fund really go broke? (Does such a fund even exist?) Does your school have the resources to open a new program in nursing?* Various publics, national or local, need well-reasoned factual arguments on subjects of this kind in order to make well-informed decisions. Such arguments educate audiences.

For the same reason, we need arguments that correct or challenge beliefs and assumptions held widely within a society on the basis of inadequate or incomplete information. Corrective arguments appear daily in the national media, often based on more detailed studies by scientists, researchers, or thinkers that the public may not encounter. Many people, for example, believe that talking on a cell phone while driving is no different from listening to the radio. But that's an intuition not based on hard information: what more and more scientific studies suggest is that using a cell phone in a car is comparable to driving under the influence of alcohol—something the public clearly needs to know.

Factual arguments also routinely address broader questions about the history or myths societies want to believe about themselves. For example, are the accounts we have of the American founding, or the Civil War and slavery, or the heroics of the revolutionary Che Guevara, indeed accurate? Or do the facts we believe in reflect the perspectives and prejudices of earlier times or ideologies? Scholars and historians frequently claim to be completing the historical record or looking both for new information and for new ways of interpreting evidence. Such revisionist history is almost always controversial and rarely settled: The British and Americans will always tell different versions of what happened in North

You've worn the T-shirt, but do you know the man? Writer Alvaro Vargas Llosa argues that Che Guevara doesn't deserve the adulation he receives in some circles, describing him as a megalomaniac in "The Killing Machine," an article in *The New Republic,* July 11, 2005.

America in 1776; Anglos and Latinos will write different histories of the Rio Grande border regions.

It's especially important to have factual arguments that flesh out or correct what's narrowly or mistakenly reported—whether by various news media, corporations, or branches of government. If there has been any growth in factual arguments in the last decade, it may have been in this area because readers on Web sites and blogs can find (or dredge up) obscure facts and information on just about any subject, correcting or expanding the coverage in the mainstream media or elsewhere. For good or ill, the words of public figures and the actions of institutions, from churches to news organizations, are now always *on record* and searchable. When, for example, the *New York Times* criticized federal officials for cutting money for flood control measures in the Mississippi Delta prior to the New Orleans hurricane of 2005, critics of the *Times* quickly located editorials from the same paper in 1993 and 1997 criticizing spending proposals for flood control. Corrective arguments can sometimes play like a game of "Gotcha!" but they broaden readers' perspectives and help them make judgments on the basis of better information. (They also suggest that our institutions are often just as inconsistent, fallible, and petty as the rest of us.)

As you probably suspect, factual arguments have a way of adding interest and complexity to our lives, taking what at one time seems simple and adding new dimensions to it. In many situations, they're the precursors to other forms of analysis, especially causal and proposal arguments. Before we can explore causes or solve problems, we need to know the facts on the ground.

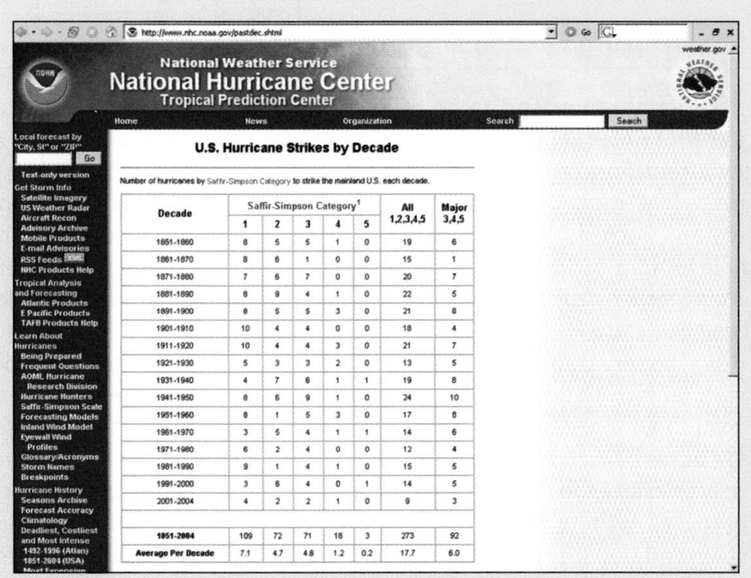

National Weather Service
National Hurricane Center
Tropical Prediction Center

U.S. Hurricane Strikes by Decade

Number of hurricanes by Saffir-Simpson Category to strike the mainland U.S. each decade.

Decade	Saffir-Simpson Category[1]					All 1,2,3,4,5	Major 3,4,5
	1	2	3	4	5		
1851-1860	8	5	5	1	0	19	6
1861-1870	8	6	1	0	0	15	1
1871-1880	7	6	7	0	0	20	7
1881-1890	8	9	4	1	0	22	5
1891-1900	8	5	5	3	0	21	8
1901-1910	10	4	4	0	0	18	4
1911-1920	10	4	4	3	0	21	7
1921-1930	5	3	3	2	0	13	5
1931-1940	4	7	6	1	1	19	8
1941-1950	8	6	9	1	0	24	10
1951-1960	8	1	5	3	0	17	8
1961-1970	3	5	4	1	1	14	6
1971-1980	6	2	4	0	0	12	4
1981-1990	9	1	4	1	0	15	5
1991-2000	3	6	4	0	1	14	5
2001-2004	4	2	2	1	0	9	3
1851-2004	109	72	71	18	3	273	92
Average Per Decade	7.1	4.7	4.8	1.2	0.2	17.7	6.0

Not Just Words

Above is a table on the Web site of the National Hurricane Center that received much attention following the destruction caused by Hurricane Katrina along the American Gulf Coast in summer 2005. Study the table closely, and then try to offer several different factual claims that might be supported by the data you find there. Or locate a statistical study on a subject, and then offer a variety of claims. You can find an enormous variety of statistical information—including many similar tables—by beginning your search at <http://www. fedstats.gov> or <http://www.census.gov/statab/www/>.

Characterizing Factual Arguments

Factual arguments tend to be driven by perceptions and evidence. A writer first notes something new or different or mistaken and wants to draw attention to that fact. Or researchers notice a pattern that leads them to look more closely at some phenomenon or behavior, exploring questions such as *What if?* or *How come?* They're also motivated by simple human curiosity or suspicion: *If being fat is so unhealthy, why aren't mortality rates rising? Just how different are the attitudes of people in so-called red and blue states?*

Such observations can lead quickly toward hypotheses, that is, toward tentative and plausible statements of fact whose merits need to be examined more closely. *Maybe being a little overweight isn't so bad for people as we've been told? Maybe the differences between blue and red staters have been exaggerated by media types looking for a story?* To support such hypotheses, writers would then have to uncover evidence that reaches well beyond the observations (often quite casual or accidental) that triggered the initial interest—like a news reporter motivated to see whether there's a verifiable story behind a source's tip. For instance, the authors of *Freakonomics*, Stephen J. Dubner and Steven Levitt, were intrigued by the National Highway Traffic Safety Administration's claim that car seats for children were 54 percent effective in preventing deaths in auto crashes for children below the age of four. In a *New York Times* op-ed column entitled "The Seat Belt Solution," they posed an important question about that factual claim:

> **But 54 percent effective compared with what? The answer, it turns out, is this: Compared with a child's riding completely unrestrained.**

Their initial question about that claim would lead them to a more focused inquiry, then to a database on auto crashes, and then to a surprising conclusion: For kids above age 24 months, those in car seats might be statistically safer than those without any protection, but they apparently weren't any safer than those confined by much simpler, cheaper, and more readily available devices—seat belts. Looking at the statistics every which way, the authors wonder if children that age wouldn't be just as well off physically—and their parents less stressed and better off financially—if the government mandated seat belts rather than car seats for them.

Safer than a seat belt?

Truth be told, a great many factual arguments begin with people actively looking for a problem or working within a framework that will turn one up. Such factual arguments come close to representing what's been called spin, in which the only arguments offered are favorable to one's own side and evidence is either made to conform to this predetermined claim or wholly ignored when it doesn't suit the party line. For instance, you wouldn't look to the Web site of the Republican National Committee for facts about how well the economy is doing during a Democratic administration (or vice versa); instead, you could be fairly confident of finding statistical analyses and anecdotal evidence all putting the most negative spin on the national situation. PR people on someone's payroll might get away with selective reporting of this kind, but no reputable writer wants to be known for using facts or evidence incorrectly in arguments.

Just what kinds of evidence typically appear in sound factual arguments? The simple answer might be "all sorts," but a case can be made that factual arguments rely on "hard evidence" more than on logic and reason (see Chapter 4). Even so, some pieces of evidence will be harder and more convincing than others. Very early in the twentieth century, for example, astronomer Percival Lowell suspected that there might be a ninth planet wandering out there beyond the orbit of Neptune. Why? Oddities in the orbits of the outer planets Uranus and Neptune, Lowell surmised, could be explained by the gravity of yet another orbital body pulling on these objects. Yet while these orbital irregularities were sufficient to persuade astronomers to hypothesize about an undiscovered Planet X, the argument wasn't closed until twenty-four-year-old astronomer Clyde Tombaugh actually spotted Pluto in 1930. His photographic evidence for the new planet was more direct than Lowell's inferences from orbital paths—the difference between hearing what *might* be the call of an ivory-billed woodpecker and actually capturing the bird's image compellingly on film. (Oddly enough, it turned out that Pluto had nothing to do with the anomalies in the orbits of Uranus and Neptune.)

Does the Pluto example mean that you can't make a factual argument without hard evidence? Of course not. In fact, in many factual arguments, no single piece of evidence will function as a clincher. For example, what *single* piece of evidence would prove that global warming is actually occurring or that students today are less conscientious readers than those in the recent past? In both cases, you might point to lots of evidence drawn from various sources, but no one item would close the case. Instead, you'd be arguing from the preponderance of evidence that you are probably, not certainly, correct. But *probably* right is good enough in many everyday situations and all the assurance readers will be able to expect in many circumstances.

Developing a Factual Argument

Factual arguments on the same subject can bubble with outrage and anger or speak with the dispassionate drone of science. Here are two claims that circulated in the media shortly after Hurricane Katrina struck the Gulf Coast; they suggest the range of factual argument in both substance and style. The first, by Ross Gelbspan, shows the sweeping claims and pithy style of fact-based editorial commentary. It's angry and speculative:

> The hurricane that struck Louisiana and Mississippi on Monday was nicknamed Katrina by the National Weather Service. Its real name is global warming. . . .

> Although Katrina began as a relatively small hurricane that glanced off southern Florida, it was supercharged with extraordinary intensity by the high sea surface temperatures in the Gulf of Mexico.
>
> The consequences are as heartbreaking as they are terrifying.
>
> Unfortunately, few people in America know the real name of Hurricane Katrina because the coal and oil industries have spent millions of dollars to keep the public in doubt about the issue.
>
> The reason is simple: To allow the climate to stabilize requires humanity to cut its use of coal and oil by 70 percent. That, of course, threatens the survival of one of the largest commercial enterprises in history.
>
> –Ross Gelbspan, "Hurricane Katrina's Real Name"

The second claim, by William M. Gray and Philip J. Klotzback, writing for the Department of Atmospheric Science at Colorado State University, addresses much the same issue but provides its answers in a different style:

> Many individuals have queried whether the unprecedented landfall of four destructive hurricanes in a seven-week period during August–September 2004 and the landfall of two more major hurricanes in the early part of the 2005 season is related in any way to human-induced climate changes. There is no evidence that this is the case. If global warming were the cause of the increase in United States hurricane landfalls in 2004 and 2005 and the overall increase in Atlantic basin major hurricane activity of the past eleven years (1995–2005), one would expect to see an increase in tropical cyclone activity in the other storm basins as well (i.e., West Pacific, East Pacific, Indian Ocean, etc.). This has not occurred. When tropical cyclones worldwide are summed, there has actually been a slight decrease since 1995. In addition, it has been well documented that the measured global warming during the 25-year period of 1970–1994 was accompanied by a downturn in Atlantic basin major hurricane activity over what was experienced during the 1930s through the 1960s.
>
> –William M. Gray and Philip J. Klotzback, "Forecast of Atlantic Hurricane Activity for September and October 2005 and Seasonal Update through August"

Clearly, the shape of any factual argument you might compose, from how you state your claim to how you present evidence and the language you use, will be shaped by the occasion for the argument and the audiences you intend to reach. But we can offer some general advice to get you started.

Identifying an Issue

Before you can offer a factual argument, you need to identify an issue or problem that may already have the attention of potential readers or, in your opinion, should have their attention. Or look for anomalies in local or national communities, that is, situations or phenomena out of the ordinary in the expected order of things. You might note, for example, the rapid increase in Native American–owned gambling casinos and resorts in your state. What's going on, and is it important? Or you might notice that many people you know are deciding not to attend college. How widespread is this change, and who are the people making this choice? Or you might explore questions that many people have already formulated but haven't found the time to examine in detail—such as whether cell phones are really as safe as claimed, or whether we'll discover twenty years from now that a generation of Americans has slow-cooked its gray matter.

Whole books get written when authors decide to pursue factual questions, even those that have been explored before. But you do want to be careful not to argue matters that pose no challenge to you or your audiences. You've got nothing new to offer if you try to persuade readers that smoking is harmful to their health. But could you uncover information about smoking on your campus that might provoke thoughtful examinations of the issue? Perhaps you suspect that smoking is correlated in interesting ways to academic majors, sexual orientation, or ethnic identity. Would it be important to recognize these facts—if indeed you could prove them?

Some quick preliminary research and reading might make it possible for you to move from an intuition, hunch, or mere interest to a *hypothesis*, a tentative statement of your claim: *Women in the liberal arts are the heaviest smokers on campus*. A hypothesis like this might seem frivolous at first, or it may provoke enough controversy and resistance to merit the research necessary to support it. Where might such a claim lead if you could find evidence to support it? As noted earlier, factual arguments often provoke other kinds of analysis. Here, you might find yourself moving irresistibly toward arguments about the cause of the phenomenon, but not until you had established its basis in fact.

On the other hand, you might discover, from the sheer number of butts on the ground outside the business school, that your hypothesis is questionable. It may be that men in accounting and marketing blacken their lungs as thoroughly as do women in philosophy. What do you do now? Abandon your hypothesis or modify it. That's what hypotheses are for. They are works in progress.

New details about a subject often lead to new ways to support or refute a claim about it. Conspiracy theorists point to the absence of visible stars in photographs of the moon landing as evidence that it was staged, but photographers know that the camera exposure needed to capture the foreground—astronauts in their bright space suits—would have made the stars in the background too dim to see.

> **one who had been born in Africa and was brought across the Middle Passage. An African-American voice wouldn't have done it."**
>
> **–Jennifer Howard, "Unraveling the Narrative"**

Thus Carretta asks readers to see that the new facts he has discovered about *The Interesting Narrative* do not diminish the work's historical significance. If anything, his work has added new dimensions to its meaning and interpretation.

Deciding Which Evidence to Use

In this chapter, we've been blurring the distinction somewhat between factual arguments aimed at scientific and technical audiences and those offered for more public consumption in media such as editorials, magazines, and Web sites. In the former, you might find exhaustive appendices of information, including charts, graphs, and full databases. Scientific claims themselves are usually stated with great economy and precision, followed by a thorough account of methods and results. The article reporting the discovery of the ivory-billed woodpecker makes its point in two sentences: "The ivory-billed woodpecker (*Campephilus principalis*), long suspected to be extinct, has been rediscovered in the Big Woods region of eastern Arkansas. Visual encounters during 2004 and 2005, and analysis of a video clip from April 2004, confirm the existence of at least one male." The evidence then follows.

Less scientific factual arguments—claims about our society, institutions, behaviors, habits, and so on—are seldom this clean and could draw on evidence from a great many different sources. For example, when the National Endowment for the Arts (NEA) published a study entitled "Reading at Risk" in June 2004 to report "the declining importance of literature to our populace," it drew its conclusion by studying a variety of phenomena in a large population:

> **This survey investigated the percentage and number of adults, age 18 and over, who attended artistic performances, visited museums, watched broadcasts of arts programs, or read literature. The survey sample numbered more than 17,000 individuals, which makes it one of the most comprehensive polls of art and literature consumption ever conducted.**
>
> **–National Endowment for the Arts**

Still, you could imagine other ways to measure an interest in literature, some of which might include nontraditional (graphic novels, for instance) or electronic forms not examined in the NEA study. A phenomenon as broad as "literature" is difficult to define factually because few people can agree on its dimensions. So any study would have to make choices about what evidence to draw from and be prepared to defend those choices.

By contrast, a factual argument about a specific literary work (rather than the larger phenomenon of reading) might be a significantly easier task to manage because you could find much of your evidence in the poem, play, or novel itself, supplemented by historical and biographical information on the life and times of the author. For instance, is *Frankenstein* (1831) really a story about the growing impact of science and industrialism on Europe? To answer the question, you could refer to passages in Mary Shelley's novel itself and to information from histories of the period during which it was written showing a society experiencing rapid technological change.

Quite often, you may have only so many words or pages to make a factual argument. What do you do then? Obviously, you need to present your best evidence as powerfully as possible. But that's not as difficult a task as it may seem. It has been widely noticed that you can make a persuasive factual case with just a few examples—three or four often suffice to make a point. Indeed, going on too long or presenting even good data in a way that makes it seem uninteresting or pointless can undermine a claim.

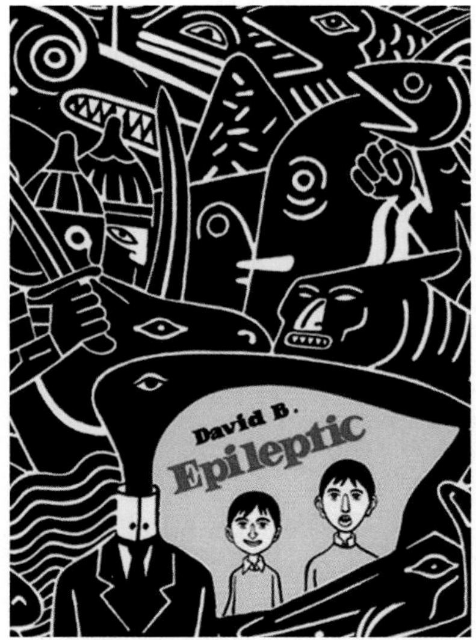

David B.'s *Epileptic* is a graphic novel written, according to *Publisher's Weekly,* with "wrenching psychological depth." Is it literature?

Presenting Your Evidence

In *Hard Times* (1854), British author Charles Dickens poked fun at a pedagogue he named Thomas Gradgrind, who preferred hard facts before all things human or humane: "A man of realities. A man of fact and calculations. A man who proceeds upon the principle that two and two are four, and nothing over, and who is not to be talked into allowing for anything over." When poor Sissy Jupe (designated "girl number twenty" in his classroom) is unable at his command to define a horse, Gradgrind turns to his star pupil:

> "Bitzer," said Thomas Gradgrind. "Your definition of a horse."
>
> "Quadruped. Graminivorous. Forty teeth, namely twenty-four grinders, four eyeteeth, and twelve incisive. Sheds coat in the spring; in marshy countries, sheds hoofs, too. Hoofs hard, but requiring to be shod with iron. Age known by marks in mouth." Thus (and much more) Bitzer.
>
> "Now girl number twenty," said Mr. Gradgrind. "You know what a horse is."
>
> –Charles Dickens, *Hard Times*

But does Bitzer? Rattling off facts about a subject isn't quite the same thing as knowing it, especially when your goal is, as it will be in an argument of fact, to educate and persuade audiences. So you must take care how you present your evidence.

Factual arguments, like any others, do take many forms. They can be as simple and pithy as a letter to the editor (or Bitzer's definition of a

American and other backgrounds increased between 1982 and 2002. In contrast, the number of white Americans reading literature fell by more than 6 million between 1982 and 2002. In summary, because of the changing demographics of the U.S., there was an increase in the number of literary readers from all ethnic and racial groups *except* white Americans.

These changes in the number of literary readers are highlighted in Table 22. White Americans represented 80 percent of literary readers in 2002, down from 87 percent in 1982. African Americans constituted 9 percent of literary readers in 2002, a slight increase from 8 percent in 1982. Hispanic Americans comprised 6 percent of literary readers in 2002, up from 4 percent in 1982. Finally, Americans from other ethnic and racial groups represented 4 percent of literary readers in 2002, an increase from 2 percent in 1982.

Education

Figure 7 illustrates that the literary reading rate decreased significantly for people with all levels of educational attainment. In fact, the literary reading rate decreased by 15 percentage points or more for those in all except the lowest education group (grade school only).

Table 23
Literary Reading by Education, 1982, 1992, and 2002
(Millions of U.S. Adults)

	1982	1992	2002	Change	% change
Grade school	4.2	2.4	1.6	-2.5	-60.9 %
Some high school	9.9	7.6	4.7	-5.2	-52.6
High school graduate	33.1	32.6	24	-9.1	-27.5
Some college	26.1	27.2	30	4	15.2
College graduate / Graduate school	23.5	31.1	35.6	12.2	52.0

The gap between the literary reading rates of college graduates and high school graduates remained large but stable between 1982 and 2002. In 1982, the difference between the reading rates of college graduates (82 percent) and high school graduates (54 percent) was about 28 percentage points. By 2002, after a significant drop in the literary reading rates of both groups, the gap was 29 percentage points.

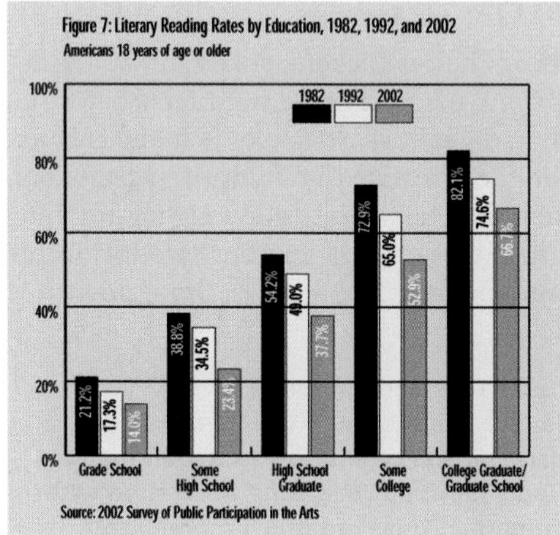

Despite the sharp decreases in literary reading at all education levels, rising levels of education in American society led to an increase in the number of literary readers who had some college education or a college degree. Table 23 shows that the number of readers with a college degree or graduate education increased by about 12 million. The number of literary readers with some college education increased by about 4 million. There were decreases in the number of literary readers at the three other education levels. In particular, the number of literary readers with a high school education decreased by 9 million.

National Endowment for the Arts 25 Reading at Risk

This page from the National Endowment for the Arts report "Reading at Risk" illustrates its use of tables and charts to make information accessible.

Examine the graphic *Reshaping America* from the *New York Times*. Consider how the author's use of two different visuals, numeric percentage and different sized circles, adds to the credibility of the argument.

LINK TO P. 612

horse) or as comprehensive and formal as a senior thesis or even a dissertation. The National Endowment for the Arts 2004 report on literary reading, for example, has all the trappings of a formal scientific report, with no fewer than twenty-five tables and eight figures that present all its numerical findings in a form readers can process easily. Like many studies, it includes a title page, a table of contents, a preface, an executive summary, several chapters of analysis (including a conclusion), and three appendices. All these elements also have the function of supporting the ethos of the work, making it seem serious and credible, well conceived and thorough.

Considering Design and Visuals

Precisely because factual arguments so often rely on evidence that can be measured, counted, computed, or illustrated, they benefit from thoughtful, even artful, presentation of data. So when you prepare a factual argument, consider how its design can enhance the evidence you have to offer. If you have an argument that can be translated into a table, chart, or graph (see Chapter 14), try it. If you have lots of examples, you might present them in a list (bulleted or otherwise) and keep the language in each item roughly parallel. That's what Thomas Jefferson and his coauthors did almost 250 years ago in enumerating factual charges against King George III in the American Declaration of Independence (1776).

Artist Rolando Briseño uses a painting to depict his argument about communication and community. As you look at the painting, think about the impact of the message in *Bicultural Tablesetting* and how it would be different if presented in prose.

LINK TO P. 752

Photos and images have many uses in factual arguments, from technical illustration to imaginative re-creation. We know, of course, that

HE has refuſed his Aſſent to Laws, the moſt wholeſome and neceſſary for the public Good.

HE has forbidden his Governors to paſs Laws of immediate and preſſing Importance, unleſs ſuſpended in their Operation till his Aſſent ſhould be obtained; and when ſo ſuſpended, he has utterly neglected to attend to them.

HE has refuſed to paſs other Laws for the Accommodation of large Diſtricts of People, unleſs thoſe People would relinquiſh the Right of Repreſentation in the Legiſlature, a Right ineſtimable to them, and formidable to Tyrants only.

HE has called together Legiſlative Bodies at Places unuſual, uncomfortable, and diſtant from the Depoſitory of their public Records, for the ſole Purpoſe of fatiguing them into Compliance with his Meaſures.

HE has diſſolved Repreſentative Houſes repeatedly, for oppoſing with manly Firmneſs his Invaſions on the Rights of the People.

HE has refuſed for a long Time, after ſuch Diſſolutions, to cauſe others to be elected; whereby the Legiſlative Powers, incapable of Annihilation, have returned to the People at large for their exerciſe; the State remaining, in the mean Time, expoſed to all the Dangers of Invaſion from without, and Convulſions within.

An early printed version of the Declaration of Independence uses paragraph breaks to highlight the list of grievances against King George III.

even amateurs can manipulate digital images today the way only spy agencies could in the not-so-distant past, erasing people from photographs. But images retain their power to illustrate precisely what readers might otherwise have to imagine—whether it be actual conditions of drought, poverty, or disaster in some part of the world today, or the dimensions of the Roman forum as it existed in the time of Julius Caesar. These days, readers will expect the arguments they read to include visual elements, and there's little reason not to offer this assistance.

Finally, consider how your opportunities for presenting information increase when you take an argument to the Web or use presentation software such as PowerPoint or Keynote. Not only can you use still images and illustrations, but you have access to video and audio resources as well. Readers interested in the ivory-billed woodpecker controversy, for example, could download both the video that purported to show the bird in flight and the audios of its call and knock.

Key Features of Factual Arguments

In drafting a factual argument, make sure you do the following:

- Describe a situation that leads you to raise questions about what the facts in a given situation might be.
- Make a claim that addresses the status of the facts as they're known. You'll usually be establishing, challenging, or correcting them. Your claim can be presented tentatively as a hypothesis, or more boldly as a thesis.
- Offer substantial and authoritative evidence to support your claims.

In academic situations, a claim typically comes first, with the evidence trailing after. But it's not unusual for arguments of fact to present evidence first and then build toward a claim or thesis. Such a structure invites readers to participate in the process by which a factual claim is made (or challenged). The argument unfolds with the narrative drive of a mystery story, with readers eager to know what point the evidence is leading to.

GUIDE to writing an argument of fact

Finding a Topic

You're entering an argument of fact when you:

- make a claim about fact or existence that's controversial or surprising: *Global warming is threatening Arctic species, especially polar bears.*
- correct an error of fact: *The overall abortion rate is not increasing in the United States, though rates are increasing in some states.*
- challenge societal myths: *Many Mexicans fought alongside Anglos in battles that won Texas its independence from Mexico.*

Researching Your Topic

Solid research is the basis for most factual arguments. Use both a library and the Web to locate the information you need. One of your most valuable resources may be a research librarian. Take advantage of other human resources, too: don't hesitate to call experts or talk with eyewitnesses who may have special knowledge. For many factual arguments, you can begin research by consulting the following types of sources:

- newspapers, magazines, reviews, and journals (online and print)
- online databases
- government documents and reports
- Web sites, blogs, and listservs or newsgroups
- books
- experts in the field, some of whom might be right on your campus

In addition, your topic may require field research: a survey, a poll, systematic observation.

Formulating a Hypothesis

Don't rush into a thesis when developing a factual argument. Instead, begin with a hypothesis that expresses your beliefs at the beginning of the project, but that may change as your work proceeds. You might even begin with a question to which you don't have an answer, or with a broad, general interest in a subject:

- **Question:** Have higher admissions standards at BSU reduced the numbers of entering first-year students from small, rural high schools?
- **Hypothesis:** Higher admissions standards at BSU are reducing the number of students admitted from rural high schools, which tend to be smaller and less well funded than those in suburban and urban areas.
- **Question:** Have the iPod and the convenience of its iTunes and comparable music sites reduced the amount of illegal downloading of music?
- **Hypothesis:** The iPod and its iTunes Web site may have done more than lawsuits by record companies to discourage illegal downloads of music.
- **Question:** How are prison guards who work on death row affected by their jobs?
- **Hypothesis:** A death-row assignment will desensitize prison guards to the prisoners held there.

Examples of Arguable Factual Claims

- The fact that a campus survey shows that far more students have read *Harry Potter and the Prisoner of Azkaban* than *Hamlet* indicates that our current core curriculum lacks depth.
- Evidence suggests that the European conquest of the Americas may have had more to do with infectious diseases than any superiority in technology or even weaponry.
- In the long run, dieting may be more harmful than moderate overeating.

Preparing a Proposal

If your instructor asks you to prepare a proposal for your project, here's a format that may help:

State your thesis completely. If you are having trouble doing so, try outlining it in Toulmin terms:

Claim:

Reason(s):

Warrant(s):

- **Explain why the issue you're examining is important, and provide the context for raising the issue. Are you introducing new information, making available information better known, correcting what has been reported incorrectly, or complicating what has been understood more simply?**
- **Identify and describe those readers you most hope to reach with your proposal. Why is this group of readers most appropriate for your proposal? What are their interests in the subject?**
- **Discuss the kinds of evidence you expect to use in the project and the research the paper will require.**
- **Briefly identify the major difficulties you foresee in researching your argument.**
- **Describe the format or genre you expect to use: An academic essay? A formal report? A Web site? A wiki? Will you need charts, tables, graphs, other illustrations?**

Thinking about Organization

Factual arguments can be arranged many different ways. The simplest structure is to make a claim and then prove it. But even so basic an approach will likely need an introductory section that provides a context for the claim and a concluding section that assesses the implications of the argument. A factual argument that corrects an error or provides an alternative view of some familiar concept or historical event will also need a section early on explaining what the error or the common belief is. Don't be stingy with details: be sure your opening answers the *who, what, where, when, how,* and (maybe) *why* questions readers will bring to the case.

Some factual arguments offered in academic fields follow formulas and templates. For example, a typical paper in psychology will include an abstract, a review of literature, a discussion of method, an analysis, and a references list. You may be expected to follow a pre-existing pattern for factual arguments or reports in many fields.

When you have more flexibility in the structure of your argument, pay particular attention to the arrangement of evidence and the transitions between key points. In many cases, it makes sense to lead with a strong piece of evidence or striking example to get readers interested in your subject and then to conclude with your strongest evidence.

Even if your argument isn't correcting an error or challenging a common belief, anticipate objections to it and find a place for them in the body of your argument. Ordinarily, you wouldn't want to end a factual argument in a public venue—in an op-ed piece or letter to the editor, for example—with your concessions and/or refutations. Such a strategy leaves readers thinking about the potential problems with your claim at the point they should be impressed with its strengths instead. But an acknowledgment earlier in an argument of any problems in your analysis will usually enhance your ethos.

Getting and Giving Response

All arguments benefit from the scrutiny of others. Your instructor may assign you to a peer group for the purpose of reading and responding to each other's drafts; if not, get some response on your own from serious readers or consultants at a writing center. You can use the following questions to evaluate a draft. If you're evaluating someone else's draft, be sure to illustrate your points with examples. Specific comments are always more helpful than general observations.

The Claim

- Does the claim clearly raise a serious and arguable factual issue?
- Is the claim as clear and specific as possible?
- Is the claim qualified? If so, how?

Evidence for the Claim

- Is enough evidence provided to get the audience to believe the claim? If not, what kind of additional evidence is needed? Does any of the evidence provided seem inappropriate or otherwise ineffective? Why?
- Is the evidence in support of the claim simply announced, or are its significance and appropriateness analyzed? Is a more detailed discussion needed?
- Are any objections readers might have to the claim or evidence adequately addressed?
- What kinds of sources are cited? How credible and persuasive will they be to readers? What other kinds of sources might be more credible and persuasive?
- Are all quotations introduced with appropriate signal phrases (such as "As Ehrenreich argues,") and blended smoothly into the writer's sentences?
- Are all visuals titled and labeled appropriately? Have you introduced them and commented on their significance?

Organization and Style

- How are the parts of the argument organized? Is this organization effective, or would some other structure work better?
- Will readers understand the relationships among the claims, supporting reasons, warrants, and evidence? If not, what could be done to make those connections clearer? Are more transitional words and phrases needed? Would headings or graphic devices help?
- How might you use visual design elements to make your proposal more effective?
- Are the transitions or links from point to point, paragraph to paragraph, and sentence to sentence clear and effective? If not, how could they be improved?
- Is the style suited to the subject? Is it too formal? Too casual? Too technical? Too bland? How can it be improved?
- Which sentences seem particularly effective? Which ones seem weakest, and how could they be improved? Should some short sentences be combined, or should any long ones be separated into two or more sentences?
- How effective are the paragraphs? Do any seem too skimpy or too long? How can they be improved?
- Which words or phrases seem particularly effective, vivid, and memorable? Do any seem dull, vague, unclear, or inappropriate for the audience or the writer's purpose? Are definitions provided for technical or other terms that readers might not know?

Spelling, Punctuation, Mechanics, Documentation, Format

- Are there any errors in spelling, punctuation, capitalization, and the like?
- Is an appropriate and consistent style of documentation used for parenthetical citations and the list of works cited or references? (See Chapter 20.)
- Does the paper or project follow an appropriate format? Is it appropriately designed and attractively presented? How could it be improved? If it's a Web site, do all the links work?

RESPOND •

1. For each topic in the following list, decide whether the claim is worth arguing to a college audience and explain why or why not:

   Hurricanes are increasing in number and ferocity.

   Many people die annually of cancer.

   Fewer people would die of heart disease each year if more of them paid attention to their diets.

   Japan might have come to terms more readily in 1945 if the Allies hadn't demanded unconditional surrender.

   Boys would do better in school if there were more men teaching in elementary and secondary classrooms.

   The ever-increasing number of minorities in higher education is evidence that racial problems have just about ended in the United States.

   There aren't enough high-paying jobs for college graduates these days.

   Hydrogen may never be a viable alternative to fossil fuels because it takes too much energy to change hydrogen into a useable form.

   Only one of the first forty-three presidents of the United States was a Catholic.

   Political activists have grossly exaggerated the effects of the USA Patriot Act on free expression.

2. Working with a group of colleagues, generate a list of favorite "mysteries" explored on cable TV shows or in dorm-room bull sessions or tabloid newspapers. Aim for twenty. Here are three to get you started: the alien crash landing at Roswell, the existence of Atlantis, the uses of Area 51. Then decide which—if any—of these mysteries might be resolved or explained in a reasonable factual argument and which ones remain eternally mysterious and improbable. Why are people attracted to such topics?

3. The Annenberg Public Policy Center at the University of Pennsylvania hosts <FactCheck.org>, a Web site dedicated to separating facts from opinion or falsehood in the area of politics. It claims to be politically neutral. Analyze one of its cases, either a recent controversial item listed on its homepage or another from its archives. Carefully study the FactCheck case you've chosen. Pay particular attention to the devices FactCheck uses to suggest or ensure objectivity and how it handles facts and statistics. Then offer your own brief factual argument about the site's objectivity. A full case from <FactCheck.org> appears at the end of this chapter as a sample reading.

4. Because digital and electronic technologies have made still and video cameras cheap, small, and durable, they're being increasingly used in many situations to provide factual evidence. Security cameras survey more and more public spaces, from convenience stores to subway stations, to deter assaults or catch criminals in the act. Video recorders on police cars routinely tape encounters between officers and the public, putting both groups under scrutiny. Even responsible citizens can occasionally get tickets in some states from cameras that catch them speeding or entering intersections after traffic lights have turned red. And, of course, the National Football League and some college leagues rely on instant replay to check calls by the officials that are disputed or questionable.

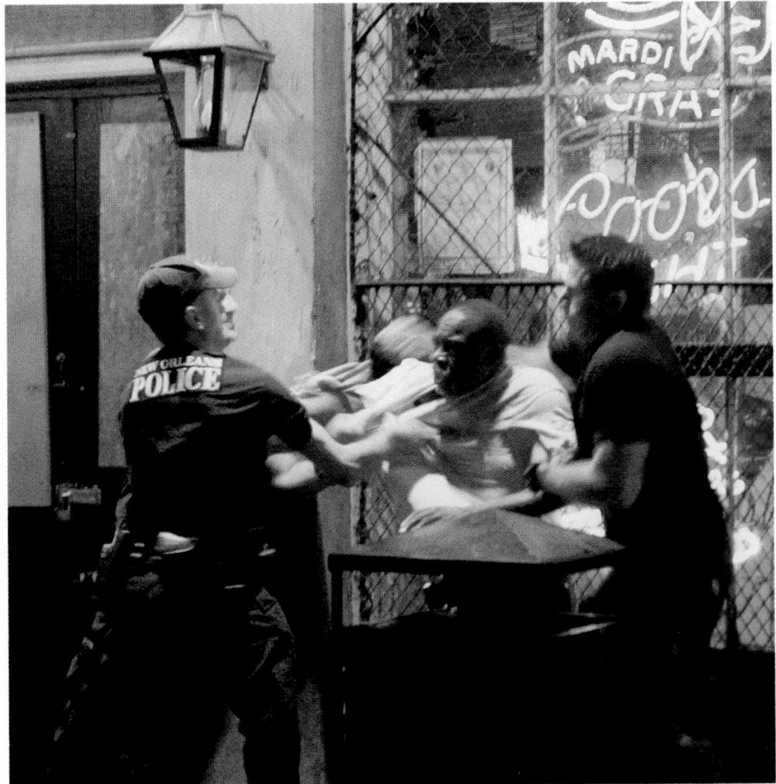

Police in New Orleans were videotaped arresting and beating a man they accused of being disorderly and drunk, a charge the former teacher strongly disputed. The police were subsequently charged with battery.

In all these circumstances, the cameras record what individuals on their own may not see or not remember well, presumably providing a better—though far from perfect—account of an event. (Overturning a call in a Big 10 football game, for example, requires "indisputable video evidence"; otherwise, the call by the referee stands.)

Does all this surveillance enhance our society or undermine it in some ways? Study just one type of surveillance, including any others you think of not mentioned here (baby monitors? cameras on cell phones?). Read up on the subject in the library or on the Web, and then make a factual argument based on what you uncover. For example, you might show whether and how people benefit from the technology, how it's being abused, or both.

The Psychological Experience of Security Officers Who Work with Executions

MICHAEL OSOFSKY

The Louisiana and Alabama "Execution Teams" were interviewed in order to understand the roles, experiences, and effects of carrying out the death penalty. One hundred twenty out of a possible one hundred twenty-four correctional officers were interviewed. Of those questioned, one hundred fifteen completed mental health inventories. The subjects were grouped based on their roles in order to gain a broader picture of the steps and their impact in carrying out the death penalty. Our results show that participants in the execution process stress "caring professionalism." There is an overwhelming emphasis on carrying out one's job at a high level. At the same time, officers are neither dehumanized nor callous, describing acting with respect and decency toward all involved. While their job is their prima facie duty, they experience stress and emotional reactions, frequently having a hard time carrying out society's "ultimate punishment."

An abstract summarizes Osofsky's research. Abstracts are usually required in journal articles.

Working with Professor Philip G. Zimbardo, Michael Osofsky wrote "The Psychological Experience of Security Officers Who Work with Executions" while he was a junior at Stanford University. His essay was published in the Spring 2002 edition of the *Stanford Undergraduate Research Journal*. The paper provides an example of a factual argument with an indirect thesis: the study produces surprising insights into the lives and attitudes of officers who work with prisoners on death row. But it doesn't open with a thesis or even a hypothesis about the security officers. If the piece has a point of view to defend, it may lie in its opening account of arguments for and against the death penalty. Osofsky offers one rationale and a single sentence for the majority position in favor of the death penalty; he provides four arguments and a full paragraph to explicating the position of those who oppose the death penalty. Note that the documentation style in the paper does not conform to conventional MLA or APA styles.

The research essay opens by briefly examining arguments for and against the death penalty—setting the context for Osofsky's study of correctional officers involved in executions.

The topic of state-ordered executions invokes strong emotions from many people throughout the United States and around the world. In the past decade alone, dozens of countries have either placed a moratorium on executions or abolished the death penalty altogether.[1] Simultaneously, ambivalence is the term that best describes the overall attitude towards the death penalty.[2] On the one hand, the majority of the American public believes that serious offenders should be punished to the extent that they inflicted pain and suffering, namely retributive justice or the biblical concept of "an eye for an eye."[3]

Alternatively, a growing minority is horrified by the idea of state-ordered killing, regardless of the heinous nature of the crimes committed. In fact, an ABC Poll conducted in early 2001 found that public support for the death penalty had declined to 63%, a drop from 77% in 1996.[4] Many question whether the death penalty has any positive deterrent effect, citing evidence comparing states with and without capital punishment.[5] Others worry about the economic discrimination against the poor and even racist tendencies associated with the death penalty.[6] Additional opponents of capital punishment feel the punishment to be appalling, arguing that innocent individuals can be put to death.[7] Finally, many individuals question the lengthy appeals process that allows inmates to be executed years after their convictions. Over the course of ten, fifteen, or even twenty years on death row, inmates can be rehabilitated, the family of the victim(s) receive no closure, and prison guards can form a relationship with the inmate.[8–9]

A great deal of intrigue surrounds the members of an execution team. From stereotypes of a hooded executioner to the notion of multiple executioners with only one possessing the deadly bullet, little knowledge exists about the actual nature of how executions are carried out.[10–11]

Our interviews of execution team members at the Louisiana State Penitentiary at Angola and Holman State Prison in Alabama utilize an unprecedented number of subjects through full and uninhibited access to the staff involved. The current study was undertaken in order to gain more understanding about the unusual responsibilities and experiences of those who are directly involved with the legal termination of the lives of others.

The point of the study is explicit: "to gain more understanding" of death row guards and the work they do.

One hundred and twenty correctional officers at the Louisiana State Penitentiary at Angola and Holman State Prison in Alabama were interviewed anonymously in order to understand broad areas of the execution process. The one to two hour interviews were conducted over the summers of 2000 and 2001. During 2000, interviews were conducted of fifty of fifty-two members of the Louisiana execution team. During 2001, fifty interviews were conducted of security officers who either work on Death Row or are a part of the execution process in Louisiana. An additional twenty interviews were carried out involving correctional officers who have worked with executions in Alabama. In addition to gathering demographic and background information, a number of questions were asked about the following topics: (1) The execution experience, including roles, reactions, preparation, emotions experienced, and changes over time; (2) Stresses related to their job and methods to cope with stress; (3) Support network and influence of work on relationships; (4) Aftermath of execution experience for the officer. Based on our interviews, we were able to recreate the step-by-step process of carrying out an execution. The process was largely similar in the two states, but differed due to both situational factors with the two facilities as well as the mode of execution employed in each state. (Louisiana uses lethal injection while Alabama is one of two remaining states still employing the electric chair as its sole means of execution.)

The research methodology is described in detail.

Questions posed to death row officers examine their reactions to the "execution process." Osofsky seems to anticipate emotional reactions and stress.

The security officers were asked to complete three separate measures. During 2000, subjects completed the Beck Depression Inventory (BDI) and the first page of a Clinician Administered Post Traumatic Stress Disorder Scale (CAPS 1) for the DSM-IV, a life events checklist. The reported results from these two measures are primarily descriptive due to our desire to understand the execution process and psychological impacts of carrying out the death penalty. During 2001, we asked the officers to complete a questionnaire pertaining to issues of moral disengagement employed throughout the process. Interviews were tape recorded (without their names on the tapes) in order to guarantee that quotes, reactions, and attributed material were accurate.

After completing the interviews, we classified subjects into one of twelve roles: Wardens, classifications personnel, death row guards, death house/front gate security, liaisons to the press, mental health professionals, spiritual advisors, officers who sit with the victim's family, officers who sit with the inmate's family, the strapdown team, emergency medical technicians, and the Executioner.

Responses to the interviews suggest that guards reflect majority opinion about the death penalty in the United States.

Interview responses conveyed an interesting perspective on the death penalty relative to the existing literature on the subject. Consistent with current national polls, approximately two-thirds of officers indicate general support for the death penalty, stressing the heinous nature of the inmates' crimes and the impact on the victims and their families.

All but three do not believe the death penalty is racially motivated. However, an equal number raised concerns that social class and poverty play major roles in determining who is executed.

Officers do question the equity of the punishment.

"I've never seen a rich man executed," Death Row guard Willie W. asserted. The inmates on Death Row tend to come from poor, underprivileged backgrounds in which they had little access to basic necessities.

Sarah S., the deputy warden, pointed out, "If they had educational opportunities, they wouldn't be here."

The execution team also noted that certain districts within the state are more likely to hand down a death sentence. This variation by district is a function of the District Attorneys, judges, and juries—standards that vary by city and state. A considerable number of the officers discussed their concern that many "lifers" have committed crimes that are as horrific as those committed by the inmates on Death Row. For this reason alone, several members of the execution team argued that either the sentences of those on Death Row should be commuted to life in prison or others should be on Death Row.

Osofsky gives ample attention to a critical view of the death penalty expressed by "several" execution team members.

Further, we repeatedly heard that the death penalty simply takes too long to be carried out. Some described their identification with the inmates' pain in living and awaiting execution. Others discussed the high monetary cost to the state of the lengthy appeals process. Some worried that the victims cannot receive closure until the inmate is dead.

Study is not specific here about numbers. No charts or graphs summarize responses to interview questions.

Ultimately, nearly every person we interviewed echoed two main components of the execution process. On the one hand, and most importantly, the security officers stressed their professionalism. Their duty is to carry out the laws of the United States, whatever those may be. They believe in their jobs, and try to do them as well as they possibly can. On the other hand, they act with decency and humanity toward the inmates. In their efforts to adjust and function successfully, they struggle internally. Although most attempt to suppress painful feelings, they state that if it ever becomes easy to participate in an execution, they would worry about themselves and their loss of humanity. Some deal with their stress by disassociative mechanisms. Some overtly exhibit their distress through transient or persistent stress, guilt, and even depression. Although many officers view Death Row

Factual results here might furnish material for subsequent arguments: guards support implementation of the law yet struggle with the nature of their work.

inmates as the "worst of the worst," all describe treating the inmates with decency. Death Row guard Charles S. said, "I treat them as I would want to be treated. I help them when I can and when my job permits." Strapdown team member Robert A. concurred, "They are people and deserve to be treated as such." While some prisoners do not repent or do so only superficially, the officers describe how many change, becoming cooperative in the process.

Osofsky finds that most officials do, indeed, approach their stressful work with death row inmates humanely and reflectively.

Certainly there are exceptions to the almost universal decency of the officers in this study; wrongful emotional and physical abuse can occur in a maximum-security penitentiary. Some guards have inappropriate motives for working at a prison. From our discussions it appears that most voluntarily leave or are weeded out over time. However, the officers we interviewed did not display hostility toward the inmates, but were concerned with maximizing humanity and dignity. Within the constraints needed to maintain security, they describe being kind to the inmates. Some describe feeling good about a number of inmates who shortly before their execution thank them for their compassion. If anything, after being involved on the death team, correctional officers become more reflective and take their job more seriously than ever.

Works Cited

Osofsky provides notes keyed to the text rather than the alphabetical bibliography more typical of a works cited page.

1. Prokosch E. *Human Rights v. The Death Penalty: Abolition and Restriction in Law and Practice*. Amnesty International, 1998.
2. Finckenauer JO. Public Support for the Death Penalty: Retribution as Just Deserts or Retribution as Revenge? *Justice Quarterly* 1988; 5:81–100.
3. Gale ME. Retribution, Punishment and Death. *UC Davis Law Review* 1985; 18:973–1035.
4. Ellsworth P, Ross L. Public Opinion and Capital Punishment: A Close Examination of the Views of Abolitionists and Retentionists. *Crime and Delinquency* 1983; 29:116–169.

5. Reiman JH. *The Rich Get Richer and the Poor Get Prison*, 4th ed. Boston: Allyn and Bacon, 1985.
6. Jackson J. *Legal Lynching: Racism, Injustice and the Death Penalty*. New York: Marlowe, 1996.
7. Radelet ML, Bedau HA, Putnam CE. *In Spite of Innocence: Erroneous Convictions in Capital Cases*. Boston: Northeastern University Press, 1992.
8. Radelet ML, Vandiver M, Berardo F. Families, Prisons, and Men with Death Sentences: The Human Impact of Structured Uncertainty. *J of Family Issues* 1983; 4:595–596.
9. Goldhammer GE. *Dead End*. Brunswick: Biddle Publishing Company, 1994.
10. Mailer N. *The Executioner's Song*. Boston: Little, Brown, 1979.
11. Elliot RG. *Agent of Death: The Memoirs of an Executioner*. New York: Dutton, 1940.

Abortion Distortions: Senators from both sides make false claims about *Roe v. Wade.*

Summary

July 18, 2005

As President Bush considers exactly whom to nominate to succeed Justice Sandra Day O'Connor on the Supreme Court, Senators Barbara Boxer and Rick Santorum both have distorted some facts about the effect of *Roe v. Wade*.

Boxer, a Democrat, claimed that repeal of *Roe* "means a minimum of 5,000 women a year will die" from illegal abortions. But that's a 69-year-old figure dating to a time before penicillin and the birth-control pill. Experts say nowhere near that many women were dying from abortion complications even in the years just before *Roe* made abortions legal nationwide.

On the other side of the abortion debate, Republican Santorum says that suicides by women, and also crime, "got worse, much worse" after *Roe*. But in fact, the female suicide rate is one-third lower now than in 1973. And the Justice Department's annual survey on crime victimization shows a 69 percent drop in property crime and a 53 percent drop in violent crime since *Roe*.

Analysis

Boxer's False Statistic

On July 5, Sen. Boxer claimed that overturning *Roe v. Wade* would cost the lives of more than 5,000 pregnant women a year. That <u>might</u> have been true before the invention of penicillin and the birth control pill, but it's

---

"Abortion Distortions" is from the Web site <FactCheck.org>, which provides this statement of its mission: "We are a nonpartisan, nonprofit, 'consumer advocate' for voters that aims to reduce the level of deception and confusion in U.S. politics. We monitor the factual accuracy of what is said by major U.S. political players in the form of TV ads, debates, speeches, interviews, and news releases. Our goal is to apply the best practices of both journalism and scholarship, and to increase public knowledge and understanding." The site is sponsored by the Annenberg Public Policy Center at the University of Pennsylvania. Note that this article does include a list of sources, but they are not listed or cited within the text in any conventional way, such as MLA or APA style.

not true now. The best evidence indicates that the annual deaths from illegal abortions would number in the hundreds, not thousands.

Boxer made the claim to support her position that the repeal of *Roe* would be the sort of "extraordinary circumstance" that could justify use of the filibuster to stop the confirmation of a nominee to the Supreme Court. The *Associated Press* quoted her this way:

> Boxer: It means a minimum of 5,000 women a year will die.

So all options are on the table.

But Boxer was just wrong. The figure comes from a 1936 study by Dr. Frederick Taussig who estimated that abortion claimed the lives of 5,000 to 10,000 women a year. It is impossible to know if his figures are accurate, given that no reliable records exist on the total number of illegal abortions that occurred, much less the number of deaths. Taussig extrapolated the data from trends in New York City and Germany.

His estimate is at least plausible. Women had few means to prevent unwanted pregnancies, and illegal abortions were often performed in less than sanitary settings. Furthermore, penicillin wasn't in use until World War II, and not widely available to the civilian population until after the war ended in 1945. And Enovid, the first oral contraceptive, wasn't available until 1957. But whether Taussig's estimate was accurate or not, the conditions of the 1930s don't apply today.

From the 1940s through the 1960s, in fact, the best available evidence shows a dramatic decline in abortion-related deaths occurring even <u>before</u> the first states liberalized abortion laws in 1967. The *Journal of the American Medical Association* quotes official estimates from the National Center for Health Statistics showing an 89 percent decrease in abortion-related deaths by 1966. That is based on counting the number of death certificates that listed complications from abortion as the cause of death. The numbers reported for any given year are assuredly low since doctors could easily misstate the cause of death to protect the family. Still, these are the only figures that allow comparisons over time. There's no reason to think that the rate of under-reporting would vary from one year to another, and so little reason to doubt that a steep downward trend took place long before *Roe* was decided.

Christopher Tietze, one of the leading experts on abortion trends, wrote in 1969 that it was plausible that 5,000 women a year died from abortion in the 1930s, but concluded that it cannot be anywhere near the true rate now. He said that, although the 235 formally listed on death certificates in 1965 was too low, "in all likelihood it (the actual number) was under 1,000." An abortion statistics expert at the Guttmacher Institute, Stanley Henshaw, is studying abortion rates during the first part of the century. Though his data collection is unfinished, Henshaw concurred that Tietze's estimate of fewer than 1,000 deaths is "reasonable."

Boxer would have been correct to say that some increase in deaths of pregnant women would result should abortions be made illegal. But the number is much lower than she claimed. In 1972, the last year before *Roe v. Wade* legalized abortion nationwide, CDC counted only 39 deaths from illegal abortions based on surveys of health care providers, medical examiners' reports, state and national records, and news reports. However, Henshaw said it's difficult to quantify the number of deaths that could result today if *Roe* were overturned. For one thing, it is not clear how many states would actually make abortions illegal again. And Henshaw noted it is unlikely that the numbers of deaths would be as high as they were before 1973 due to medical advances and emergency services available today. In any case, Boxer's 5,000 figure was nearly 70 years out of date, and clearly wrong.

Santorum's Overreaching

Republican Senator Rick Santorum of Pennsylvania claims in a new book that a number of social ills got "much worse" after *Roe* was decided in 1973. He's clearly right about some, but wrong on at least one, female suicide, and possibly on another, crime.

The book is *It Takes a Family: Conservatism and the Common Good,* released on July 4. It devotes several chapters to abortion, and one of them includes this argument:

> **Santorum, p. 250:** Back before 1973, there were all sorts of claims in favor of legal abortion. Legal abortion would lead to less domestic violence, since young women would not be forced into unhealthy and inappropriate marriages. Fewer desperate women would commit suicide. There would be fewer out-of-wedlock births. There would be fewer divorces. There would be fewer children in poverty, less crime, and less child abuse, since all children would be wanted and grow up in stable families. **None of this happened. Not a single social ill improved as a result of legal abortion: in fact, they all got worse, much worse.**

Santorum is right on some things: The percentage of children living in poverty is up, according to the Census Bureau. It was 14.4 percent in 1973 and 17.6 percent in 2003, the most recent year on record. The birth rate among unmarried women aged 15–44 has increased as well. It went from 24.5 per 1,000 unmarried women in 1973 to about 44 most recently, according to the Center for Disease Control's National Center for Health Statistics. And Santorum has a strong case regarding divorce: the number of divorced persons has risen from 3 percent of the adult population before *Roe* to 10 percent most recently. The divorce rate (per 1,000 population) rose for several years after *Roe* and didn't dip back below pre-*Roe* levels until 1999, according to Census Bureau figures.

Santorum may also be right about child abuse and domestic violence. We could find no reliable statistics on either that allow comparisons with 1973, and Santorum's Senate staff did not respond to several requests from us to say where he is getting his information. As things stand, we consider those claims unverified.

But not all the social problems Santorum cited have gotten worse since the Supreme Court decided *Roe v. Wade*. And at least one has actually gotten better.

Suicide Rates

Santorum says suicides by "desperate women" got "much worse" since 1973. Actually, the suicide rate for women has dropped by one-third since *Roe* was decided. According to the Center for Disease Control, the rate was 6.5 per every 100,000 women in 1973, and had fallen to 4.06 by 2001, the most recent year on record.

As seen in this chart, it is true that the female suicide rate went up after *Roe*, but only slightly—by 0.4 percent. It peaked in 1977 before plunging.

And those numbers refer only to the raw rate of suicides per 100,000 women. The National Center for Health Statistics also publishes an "age-adjusted" suicide rate. Statistics show that women in their 40's are more than twice as likely to commit suicide as women in their 20's, and the age-adjusted rates attempt to cancel out changes in the overall rate that might be due simply to a greater concentration of women in the population who have reached a suicide-prone age. The age-adjusted figure offers even less support for Santorum, however. It shows an even more dramatic decrease

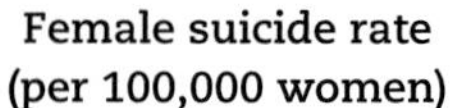

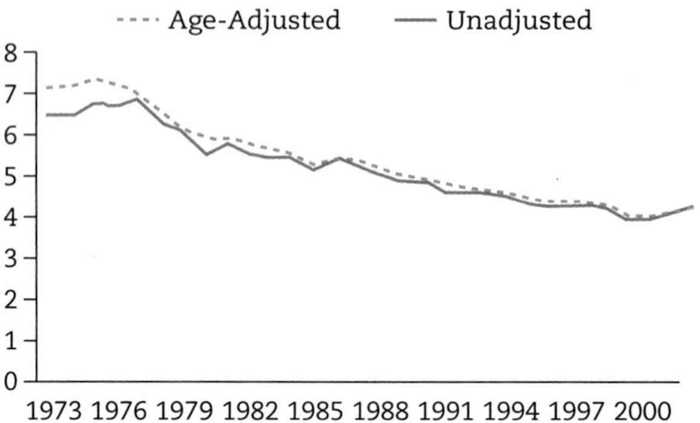

since *Roe*—a decline of 41 percent, compared to a decline of 34 percent for the unadjusted rate. Either way, Santorum was way off.

Crime

Santorum's claim that crime has gotten worse since *Roe* is also doubtful, though here the picture is a bit muddled.

According to the FBI's Uniform Crime Reporting (UCR) Program the overall rate of crimes reported to police is actually 2 percent lower now, though it rose after *Roe* and is still higher for some categories of crime. But according to an annual survey conducted by the Department of Justice, the number of people saying they were crime victims has shown a huge and steady drop since 1973. The survey may be the more accurate, since it attempts to capture the large number of crimes that go unreported to police.

Santorum would be correct to say that the FBI's crime rate rose in the first years after *Roe,* continuing a trend that had been evident for more than a decade. But it plunged starting in 1992 and was about 2 percent below the 1973 level in 2003, the most recent year on record. And it is true that violent crimes reported to police are still 14 percent higher than in 1973, although reported crimes against property are down 3 percent, according to the FBI's statistics.

By another official measure, crime decreased dramatically since 1973 in both categories. The Bureau of Justice Statistics (BJS) National Crime Victimization Survey shows that **crime rates in 2003 are at the lowest levels recorded since the survey's inception,** which coincidentally was the year *Roe* was decided. According to this annual survey, the number of people saying they were victims of property crime dropped steadily after *Roe* to, most recently, about 69 percent below 1973 levels. Meanwhile, the number of people who say they were victimized by violent crime has decreased by 53 percent since 1973. Furthermore, by this measure the rate of violent crime was actually stable between 1973 and 1977, the first several years following *Roe*.

How can the FBI's statistics show an increase in violent crime while the Bureau of Justice Statistics survey shows it dropping by half? There's reason to believe that persons are simply more likely now than in 1973 to report certain crimes to police.

The survey collects responses from a statistical sample of the population, and is not an actual count of crime reports. It attempts to measure the large number of crimes that were never reported to police, as well as those that were. Even now, half of all violent crime goes unreported. Furthermore, the increase in the FBI's violent crime rate is due entirely to big jumps in the numbers of reported rapes and aggravated assaults, which may simply reflect that women are less likely to keep silent about such crimes than they were 30 years ago. The FBI's murder rate, meanwhile, has dropped more than 39 percent since 1973. That's one category of violent crime that is almost always reported, since a dead body is hard to ignore.

In any case, even using the FBI's crime statistics, there is less crime today overall than there was in 1973, contrary to Santorum's claim.

Santorum would have been correct to say that many of the arguments for legalizing abortion proved to be unfounded. But he doesn't have the facts to include female suicide and crime among his examples.

These false claims by Boxer and Santorum show that whoever is named to the current Supreme Court vacancy, truth is already a casualty in the confirmation fight.

—*by Jennifer L. Ernst and Matthew Barge*

Correction, Aug. 22, 2005: In our original article we said the poverty rate for children was 15.1 percent in 1973. Actually, it was 14.4 percent. So the rise in child poverty after *Roe* has been even more pronounced than we originally stated.

Footnote, Aug 22, 2005: Many of our visitors have written to fault us for failing to observe that changes in such things as suicide rates or child poverty rates don't constitute evidence that *Roe* was or was not the cause of those changes. We agree entirely. However, Santorum didn't claim *Roe* was the cause, he said the other side did. We have no quarrel with his logic, only some of his facts.

Sources

Justin M. Norton, "Boxer: Filibuster to Block Anti-abortion Supreme Court Candidate," *The Associated Press,* 5 July 2005.

Christopher Tietze and Sarah Lewit, "Abortion," *Scientific American:* January 1969, 220(1).

Frederick J. Taussig, M.D., F.A.C.S., *Abortion: Spontaneous and Induced* (St. Louis: C.V. Mosby Co., 1936) 25–28.

"Induced Termination of Pregnancy before and after Roe v. Wade," *Journal of the American Medical Association,* 268 (Dec. 1992): 3231–3239.

Suzanne White Junod, Ph.D., "*FDA's Approval of the First Oral Contraceptive,* Enovid," *Update,* Food and Drug Law Institute: (July–August 1998).

Ricki Lewis, Ph.D., "*The Rise of Antibiotic-Resistant Infections,*" *FDA Consumer Magazine,* September 1995.

"Abortion Surveillance—United States, 2001," *Morbidity and Mortality Weekly Report,* Center for Disease Control: 26 Dec. 2004.

"Criminal Victimization, 2003," National Crime Victimization Survey, Bureau of Justice Statistics, September 2004.

"Criminal Victimization, 1973–1995," National Crime Victimization Survey, Bureau of Justice Statistics, April 1997.

"National Crime Victimization Survey Violent Crime Trends, 1973–2003," Bureau of Justice Statistics, website, 12 September 2004.

"National Crime Victimization Survey Property Crime Trends, 1973–2003," Bureau of Justice Statistics, website, 12 September 2004.

"Crime in the United States," Federal Bureau of Investigation, website, undated.

Michael R. Rand and Callie M. Rennison, "True Crime Stories? Accounting for Differences in Our National Crime Indicators," *Chance* Vol. 15, No. 1, 2002.

"Reducing Suicide: A National Imperative," Institute of Medicine, 2002.

"Leading Causes of Death 1900–1998," Center for Disease Control, website, undated.

"*Age-Adjusted Rates for 69 Selected Causes by Race and Sex Using Year 2000 Standard Population: United States, 1968–78,*" National Vital Statistics System, Center for Disease Control/National Center for Health Statistics, undated.

"*Age-Adjusted Death Rates for 72 Selected Causes by Race and Sex Using Year 2000 Standard Population: United States, 1979–98,*" National Vital Statistics System, Center for Disease Control/National Center for Health Statistics, 2002.

Center for Disease Control, Web-based Injury Statistics Query and Reporting System, website, accessed July 2005.

8
Arguments of Definition

A traffic committee must define what a small car is in order to enforce parking restrictions in a campus lot where certain spaces are marked “Small Car Only!” Owners of compact luxury vehicles, light trucks, and motorcycles have complained that their vehicles are being unfairly ticketed.

A panel of judges must decide whether computer-enhanced images will be eligible in a contest for landscape photography. At what point is an electronically manipulated image no longer a photograph?

A scholarship committee must decide whether the daughter of two European American diplomats, born while her parents were assigned to the U.S. embassy in Nigeria, will be eligible to apply for grants designated specifically for "African American students."

A young man hears a classmate describe hunting as a "blood sport." He disagrees and argues that hunting for sport has little in common with "genuine blood sports" such as cockfighting.

A committee of the student union is accused of bias by a conservative student group, which claims that the committee has brought a disproportionate share of left-wing speakers to campus. The committee defends its program by challenging the definition of "left wing" used to classify its speakers.

In a book, an eminent historian distinguishes between *patriotism* and *nationalism:* "Patriotism is the love of a particular land with its particular traditions; nationalism is the love of something less tangible, of the myth of a 'people,' and is often a political and ideological substitute for religion."

• • •

Understanding Arguments of Definition

In the wake of devastating Hurricane Katrina in 2005, thousands of New Orleans residents fled their homes to try to find shelter. As the crisis deepened and the failures of the Federal Emergency Management Authority became evident, the media were full of reports about those who had retreated from the storm's horrors. But what to call these people? In some early reports, those who had left New Orleans were labeled *refugees*. But that term rankled many of them (and others) who were native-born American citizens and were, after all, still in their home country. How, they asked, could they be *refugees,* the term commonly used for people legally admitted to the United States from other countries?

In his article "Cheerleaders: What to Do about Them?" Bryan Curtis traces the definition of *cheerleader* from the 50's through the present time.

LINK TO P. 729

As the media hastened to change its terminology to *evacuees,* however, some foreign refugees began voicing their own feelings of being insulted by the implication that *refugees* was a derogatory term. The matter got even more complicated when some reporters pointed out that any legally designated foreign refugees who had been affected by the hurricane would be eligible for many benefits not available to other Katrina victims. In this case, the definition of one word could mean a great deal for thousands of displaced people. While the debate raged on, some "refugee" agencies leapt into action, sending their services to New Orleans.

In a class on Contemporary Issues of Identity, a student group in charge of the day's discussion arrived early to try an experiment: all around the room, on white boards or on posters on the wall, they displayed racial and sexual labels, most of them slurs, and made sure that there were chairs placed under each one. When members of the class arrived, the student group asked them to choose a seat under a label that was close to something they had been called—or had used to label someone else. The students complied at first, but as they took seats they were visibly uncomfortable: they found that sitting under a label *defined* them in ways they found offensive and hurtful. Instead of discussing the impact of such stereotyping slurs on identity formation, class members found themselves silently but intently removing every word from the walls and white boards. Only when the room was completely free of them did they begin to discuss the strong effect this experience had had on them. Among other things, they learned that labels and stereotypes can make for very bad definitions. In short, what you call something matters. That's what arguments of definition are all about.

In many creation stories, the world and its inhabitants are called into being as a result of being named. In the Jewish and Christian bible, for example, when Adam names the animals he gains authority over them because to name things is, partly, to control them. That's why arguments of definition are so important and so very contentious. They can wield the power to say what someone or something is or can be. As such, they can also be arguments that include or exclude: A *creature is an endangered species or it isn't; an act was harassment or it wasn't; a person deserves official refugee status or doesn't*. Another way of approaching definitional arguments, however, is to think of what comes between *is* and *is not*. In fact, the most productive definitional arguments probably occur in this murky realm.

Consider the controversy over how to define human intelligence. Some might argue that human intelligence is a capacity measured by tests of verbal and mathematical reasoning. In other words, it's defined by IQ and SAT scores. Others might define intelligence as the ability to perform specific practical tasks. Still others might interpret intelligence in emotional terms, as a competence in relating to other people. Any of

Not Just Words

Take a look at the images on this page and the facing one. What definition of *patriotism* can you induce from each one?

©04 MUSLIM OBSERVER
UNCLE SAM GAS
$2.85 PER GALLON
WELCOME
DEATH TO AMERICA
OSAMA GAS
ONLY $2 A GALLON
USA #1
PATRIOTISM IS A RELATIVE THING..

these positions could be defended reasonably, but perhaps the wisest approach would be to construct a definition of intelligence rich enough to incorporate all these perspectives—and maybe more. In fact, one well-known theorist has posited a theory of "multiple intelligences," arguing that human intelligence is too varied and protean to be marked by any one standard.

Actually, it's important to realize that many political, social, and scientific definitions are constantly "under construction," reargued and reshaped whenever they need to be updated for the times. After horrifying photographs of U.S. soldiers holding Iraqi prisoners on leashes and otherwise abusing and humiliating them became public, and reports indicated that other detainees in Iraq and elsewhere had endured even harsher treatment, a fierce debate over what constituted torture broke out. Amnesty International defines torture as "the deliberate infliction of severe pain or suffering by state agents, or similar acts by private individuals for which the state bears responsibility through consent, acquiescence or inaction. We also use the term *torture* to refer to deliberate pain or suffering inflicted by members of armed political groups." Under this definition, many of the abuses at Abu Ghraib and elsewhere would be deemed torture. Others, however, argued for a different definition, saying that these acts were primarily "the use of traditionally unconventional methods of interrogation."

Attempts to redefine words go on all around us. Just a few weeks after the attacks of 9/11, for example, Peter Ferrara, a law professor at George Mason University, thought it was appropriate to refine the meaning of the word *American* in response to a call in Pakistan to kill all people of that nationality. Here are the opening and conclusion of what proved to be an "extended definition" of the term—a lengthy exploration of the many dimensions of the word, some of which people might have not considered earlier:

> **You probably missed it in the rush of news last week, but there was actually a report that someone in Pakistan had published in a newspaper there an offer of a reward to anyone who killed an American, any American.**
>
> **So I just thought I would write to let them know what an American is, so they would know when they found one.**
>
> **An American is English . . . or French, or Italian, Irish, German, Spanish, Polish, Russian or Greek. An American may also be African, Indian, Chinese, Japanese, Australian, Iranian, Asian, or Arab, or Pakistani, or Afghan.**

> **An American is Christian, or he could be Jewish, or Buddhist, or Muslim. In fact, there are more Muslims in America than in Afghanistan. The only difference is that in America they are free to worship as each of them chooses.**
>
> **An American is also free to believe in no religion. For that he will answer only to God, not to the government, or to armed thugs claiming to speak for the government and for God. . . .**
>
> **So you can try to kill an American if you must. Hitler did. So did General Tojo and Stalin and Mao Tse-Tung, and every bloodthirsty tyrant in the history of the world. But in doing so you would just be killing yourself. Because Americans are not a particular people from a particular place. They are the embodiment of the human spirit of freedom.**
>
> **Everyone who holds to that spirit, everywhere, is an American.**
>
> **–Peter Ferrara, "What Is an American?"**

Clearly, Ferrara's definition is in fact an argument in favor of American values and principles. The definition makes an unabashed political point.

In case you're wondering, you usually can't resolve important arguments of definition by consulting dictionaries. (Ferrara certainly wouldn't have found any of his definitions of an American in *Webster's*.) Dictionaries themselves just reflect the way particular groups of people used words at a specified time and place. And, like any form of writing, these reference books mirror the prejudices of their makers—as shown, perhaps most famously, in the entries of lexicographer Samuel Johnson (1709–1784), who gave the English language its first great dictionary. Johnson, no friend of the Scots, defined *oats* as "a grain which in England is generally given to horses, but in Scotland supports the people." (To be fair, he also defined *lexicographer* as "a writer of dictionaries, a harmless drudge.") Thus it's quite possible to disagree with dictionary definitions or to regard them merely as starting points for arguments.

Kinds of Definition

Because there are different kinds of definitions, there are also different ways to make a definition argument. Fortunately, identifying a particular type of definition is less important than appreciating when an issue of definition is at stake. Let's explore some common definitional issues.

Formal Definitions

Formal definitions are what you find in dictionaries. Such definitions involve placing a term in its proper genus and species—that is, first determining the larger class to which it belongs and then identifying the features that distinguish it from other members of that class. That sounds complicated, but a definition will help you see the principle. A *hybrid car* might first be identified by placing it among its peers—vehicles that combine two or more sources of power. Then the formal definition would go on to identify the features necessary to distinguish hybrid cars from other multiply powered vehicles such as mopeds or locomotives—four wheels, a mixture of gasoline and electricity, energy efficient, five-passenger capacity, family-friendly interior, and so on.

Is the 2006 Ford Escape a real hybrid?

People can make arguments from either part of a formal definition, from the genus or the species, so to speak. Does a category of objects or ideas (the "species" of hybrid cars) really belong to the larger class (the "genus" of multiply powered vehicles) to which it could be assigned? *Are all hybrids really powered by two sources, or are some of them just gussied-up versions of the regular gasoline car?* That's the genus argument. Or maybe a particular object or idea doesn't have all the features required to meet the species definition. *Is the new Ford Escape Hybrid efficient enough to count as a genuine hybrid?* That's the species argument.

Questions Related to Genus

- Is tobacco a drug or a crop?
- Do tabloids report the news or sensationalize it?
- Is hate speech a right protected by the First Amendment?

Questions Related to Species

- Is tobacco a harmless drug? A dangerously addictive one? Something in between?
- Is *On the Record with Greta Van Susteren* a news program? A tabloid? Both?
- Is using a racial epithet always an instance of hate speech?

John Rickford's essay "Suite for Ebony *and* Phonics" is a good example of a definitional argument of species, considering the question of whether Ebonics is a dialect of English.

LINK TO P. 810

Before downloading a video clip from *On the Record,* visitors to the Fox News Web site can browse the catalog of photogenic murder victims, missing persons, and suspects featured on the show. Is it a news program, a tabloid, or something in between?

Operational Definitions

Operational definitions identify an object or idea not by what it is so much as by what it does or by the conditions that create it. In an article called "Moms Know . . . All about Operational Definitions," Kathy Parker gives this example: "From the age of six on, I knew the essence of an operational definition, even if the term itself was not known to me. I knew that chores were not considered 'complete' until I had taken the linens off my bed and put them in the laundry hamper, picked up toys and vacuumed my room. I also knew that there would be consequences, if I ignored the definition of 'complete.'" Here's another operational definition used by the American Psychological Association: "Sexual Abuse is any incident of sexual contact involving a child that is inflicted or allowed to be inflicted by the person responsible for the child's care." You'll get arguments that arise from operational definitions when people debate what the conditions are that define something or whether these conditions have been met. (See also the discussion of stasis theory in Chapter 1, p. 20.)

Questions Related to Conditions

- Must sexual imposition be both unwanted and unsolicited to be considered harassment?
- Can institutional racism occur in the absence of individual acts of racism?
- Is a volunteer who is paid still a volunteer?
- Does someone who uses steroids to enhance home-run-hitting performance deserve the title Hall of Famer?

Questions Related to Fulfillment of Conditions

- Was the act really sexual harassment if the accused believed the interest was mutual?
- Has the institution supported traditions or policies that have led to racial inequities?
- Was the compensation given to the volunteer really "pay" or just "reimbursement" for expenses?
- Should Player X, who used steroids prescribed for a medical reason, be ineligible for the Hall of Fame?

Definitions by Example

Resembling operational definitions are definitions by example, which define a class by listing its individual members. For example, one might define *planets* by listing all nine major bodies in orbit around the sun, or *heirloom tomatoes* by listing all those available at the local farmer's market.

Arguments of this sort focus on who or what may be included in a list that defines a category: *great movies, worst natural disasters, groundbreaking painters*. Such arguments often involve comparisons and contrasts with the items most readers would agree from the start belong in this

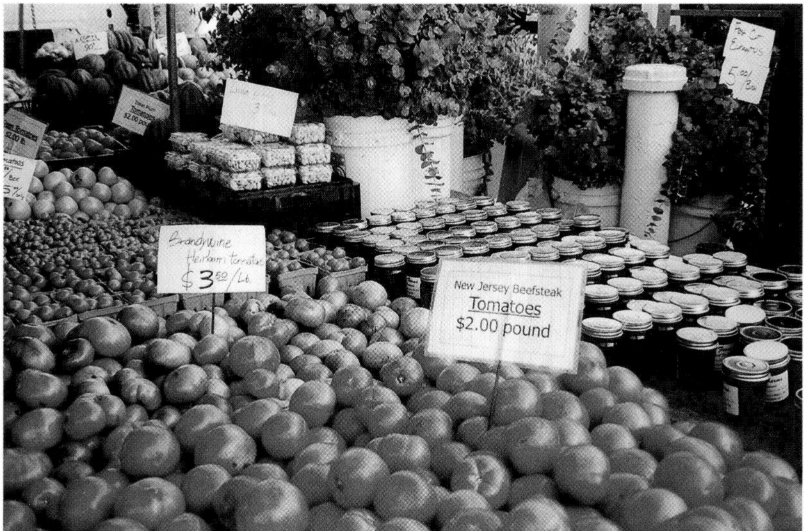

A definition of *heirloom tomatoes* would include the Brandywine but not the New Jersey Beefsteak.

list. One might, for example, wonder why planet status is denied to asteroids, when both planets and asteroids are bodies in orbit around the sun. A comparison between planets and asteroids might suggest that size is one essential feature of the nine recognized planets that asteroids don't meet.

Questions Related to Membership in a Named Class

- Is any pop artist today in a class with Chuck Berry, Elvis Presley, the Beatles, or Aretha Franklin?
- Are comic books, now sometimes called graphic novels, literature?
- Who are the Madame Curies or Albert Einsteins of the current generation?
- Does Washington, D.C., deserve the status of a state?

Other Issues of Definition

Many issues of definition cross the line among the types described here and some other forms of argument. For example, if you decided to explore whether banning pornography on the Internet violates First

Amendment guarantees of free speech, you'd first have to establish definitions of pornography and free speech—either legal ones already settled on by, let's say, the Supreme Court, or other definitions closer to your own beliefs. Then you'd have to argue that types of pornography on the Internet are (or are not) in the same class or share (or do not share) the same characteristics as types of speech that you're arguing are protected by the First Amendment. In doing so, you'd certainly find yourself slipping into an evaluative mode because matters of definition are often also questions of value. (See Chapter 9.)

When exploring or developing an idea, you shouldn't worry about such slippage—it's a natural part of the process of writing. But do try to focus an argument on a central issue or question, and appreciate the fact that any definition you care to defend must be examined honestly and rigorously. Be prepared to explore every issue of definition with an open mind and with an acute sense of what will be persuasive to your readers.

Developing a Definitional Argument

Definitional arguments don't just appear out of the blue; they evolve out of the occasions and conversations of daily life, both public and private. You might get into an argument over the definition of *ordinary wear and tear* when you return a rental car with some battered upholstery. Or you might be asked to write a job description for a new position to be created in your office: you have to define the position in a way that doesn't step on anyone else's turf on the job. Or maybe employees on your cam-

If Everything's an Argument . . .

This chapter itself defines three different kinds of definitions: formal definitions, operational definitions, and definitions by example. Which kind(s)—formal, operational, or examples—have the authors used in defining the three kinds and distinguishing among them? How well do you think they've made their argument? Are there ways they could have made the individual definitions clearer or more distinct from one another? Are there any kinds of definitions you can think of that don't fit into one of these categories?

pus object to being defined as *temporary workers* when they've held their same jobs for years. Or someone derides one of your best friends as *just a nerd*. In a dozen ways every day, you encounter situations that turn out to be issues of definition. They're so frequent and indispensable that you barely notice them for what they are.

Formulating Claims

In addressing matters of definition, you'll likely formulate tentative claims—declarative statements that represent your first response to such situations. Note that these initial claims usually don't follow a single definitional formula.

Claims of Definition

- A person paid to do public service is not a volunteer.
- Institutional racism can exist—maybe even thrive—in the absence of overt civil rights violations.
- Torture has clearly been used by the U.S. military at Guantánamo Bay.
- A municipal fee is often the same darn thing as a tax.
- *Napoleon Dynamite* is one of the latest independent film to achieve cult status.

None of the claims listed here could stand on its own. Such claims often reflect first impressions and gut reactions. That's because stating a claim of definition is typically a starting point, a moment of bravura that doesn't last much beyond the first serious rebuttal or challenge. Statements of this sort aren't arguments until they're attached to reasons, data, warrants, and evidence. (See Chapter 6.)

Finding good reasons to support a claim of definition usually requires formulating a general definition by which to explore the subject. To be persuasive, the definition must be broad and not tailored to the specific controversy:

- A volunteer is . . .
- Institutional racism is . . .
- Torture is . . .
- A tax is . . .
- A cult film is . . .

Now consider how the following claims might be expanded with a general definition in order to become full-fledged definitional arguments:

Arguments of Definition

- Someone paid to do public service is not a volunteer because volunteers are people who . . .
- Institutional racism can exist even in the absence of overt violations of civil rights because, by definition, institutional racism is . . .
- Harsh treatment of detainees becomes torture when . . .
- A municipal fee is the same darn thing as a tax. Both fees and taxes are . . .
- *Napoleon Dynamite* has achieved all the criteria of cult status: . . .

Notice, too, that some of the issues can involve comparisons between things—such as taxes and fees.

Crafting Definitions

Imagine that you decide to tackle the concept of *paid volunteer* in the following way:

> **Participants in the federal AmeriCorps program are not really volunteers because they are paid for their public service. Volunteers are people who work for a cause without compensation.**

In Toulmin terms, the argument looks like this:

Claim	**Participants in AmeriCorps aren't volunteers . . .**
Reason	**. . . because they are paid for their service.**
Warrant	**People who are compensated for their services are, ordinarily, employees.**

As you can see, the definition of *volunteers* will be crucial to the shape of the argument. In fact, you might think you've settled the matter with this tight little formulation. But now it's time to listen to the readers over your shoulder (see Chapter 6) pushing you further. Do the terms of your definition account for all pertinent cases of volunteerism—in particular, any related to the types of public service AmeriCorps volunteers might be involved in? Consider, too, the word *cause* in your original statement of the definition:

> **Volunteers are people who work for a cause without compensation.**

Cause has political connotations that you may or may not intend. You'd better clarify what you mean by *cause* when you discuss its definition in your paper. Might a phrase such as *the public good* be a more comprehensive or appropriate substitute for *a cause?* And then there's the matter of compensation in the second half of your definition:

Volunteers are people who work for a cause without compensation.

Aren't people who volunteer to serve on boards, committees, and commissions sometimes paid, especially for their expenses? What about members of the so-called all-volunteer military? They're financially compensated for their years of service, and they enjoy substantial benefits after they complete their tour of duty.

As you can see, you can't just offer up a definition as part of your argument and assume that readers will understand or accept it. Every part of the definition has to be weighed, critiqued, and defended. That means you'll want to investigate your subject in the library, on the Internet, and in conversation with others, including experts on your term. You might then be able to present your definition in a single paragraph, or you may have to spend several pages coming to terms with the complexity of the core issue.

After conducting research of this kind, you might be in a position to write an extended definition well enough informed to explain to your readers what you believe makes a volunteer a volunteer, a tax a tax, and so on. At the end of this chapter, writer Lynn Peril provides just such a definition of the mind-set she claims is imposed on women in this country, what she calls "Pink Think."

Matching Claims to Definitions

Once you've formulated a definition readers will accept—a demanding task in itself—you might need to look at your particular subject to see if it fits that general definition, providing evidence to show that:

- it is a clear example of the class defined,
- it clearly falls outside the defined class,
- it falls between two closely related classes or fulfills some conditions of the defined class but not others, *or*
- it defies existing classes and categories and requires an entirely new definition.

It's possible that you might have to change your original claim at this point if the evidence you've gathered suggests that qualifications are necessary. It's amazing how often seemingly cut-and-dry issues of definition become blurry—and open to compromise and accommodation—

when you learn more about them. That has proved to be the case as various campuses across the country have tried to define *hate speech* or *sexual harassment*—very tricky matters. And even the Supreme Court has never quite been able to say what *pornography* is. Just when matters seem settled, new legal twists develop. Should virtual child pornography created with software be as illegal as the real thing? Is a virtual image—even a lewd one—an artistic expression, protected like other works of art by the First Amendment?

Considering Design and Visuals

In thinking about how to present your argument of definition, don't forget that design issues—such as boldface and italics, headings, or links in online text—can make a powerful contribution to (or detract seriously from) how credible and persuasive it is. Remember, too, that visuals like photographs, drawings, and graphs can also help make your case. A graph or chart, for example, might help you show visually the hierarchy of a "genus" and "species" relationship in a formal definition. Or photographs might help demonstrate that the conditions for a definition have been met. If you're working with a definitional claim about torture, for example, your choice to introduce an Abu Ghraib prison photograph that circulated widely on the Web might become a focal point of emphasis in your definition, especially if you argue that the photograph perfectly represents your definition of *torture*.

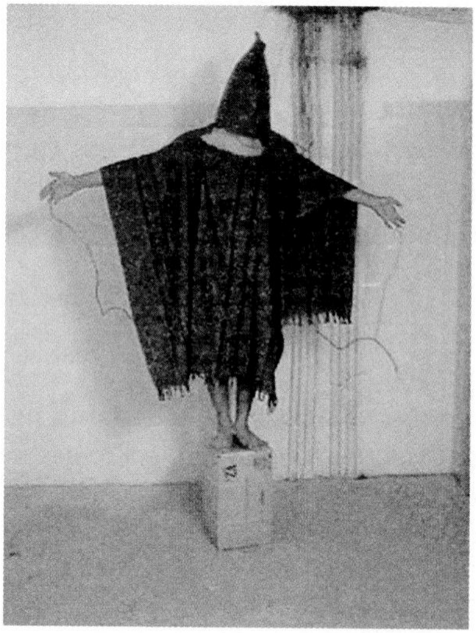

Hooded and wired prisoner at Abu Ghraib

A collection of public service campaign posters in Chapter 26 is presented as a series of tools to challenge people's definitions of different religious groups. Consider how the use of photos enhances the creators' arguments.

LINK TO P. 903

Key Features of Definitional Arguments

In writing an argument of definition of your own, consider that it's likely to include the following parts:

- a claim involving a question of definition
- a general definition of some key concept
- a careful look at your subject in terms of that general definition
- evidence for every part of the argument, including visual evidence if appropriate
- a consideration of alternative views and counterarguments
- a conclusion, drawing out the implications of the argument

It's impossible, however, to predict what emphasis each of those parts might receive or what the ultimate shape of an argument of definition will be.

Whatever form your definitional argument takes, be sure to share your draft with others who can examine its claims, evidence, and connections. It's remarkably easy for a writer in isolation to think narrowly—and not to imagine that others might define *volunteer* or *institutional racism* in a completely different way. Thus it's important to keep a mind open to criticism and suggestions. Look very carefully at the terms of any definitions you offer. Do they really help readers distinguish one concept from another? Are the conditions offered sufficient or essential? Have you mistaken accidental features of a concept or object for more important features?

Amy Tan explores her mastery of different kinds of English in her essay "Mother Tongue." Note her rejection of terms like *broken, fractured,* and *limited* in favor of *simple* when describing the English she uses with her mother.

LINK TO P. 804

Don't hesitate to look to other sources for comparisons with your definitions. You can't depend on dictionaries to offer the last word about any disputed term, but you can at least begin with them. Check the meaning of terms in encyclopedias and other reference works. And search the Web intelligently to find how your key terms are presented there. (In searching for the definition of *wetland,* for example, you could type *wetland definition* into a search engine like Google and get a limited number of useful hits.)

Finally, be prepared for surprises in writing arguments of definition. That's part of the delight in expanding the way you see the world. "I'm not a pig, I'm a sheep dog," thinks Babe in the 1995 film by the same name. Babe then goes right on to win a sheep dog competition. Such is the power of definition.

GUIDE to writing an argument of definition

Finding a Topic

You're entering an argument of definition when you:

- formulate a controversial or provocative definition: *Today, the American Dream means a McMansion in a gated community with a deferential maid, gardener, and personal chef.*
- challenge a definition: *For most Americans today, the American Dream involves not luxury but the secure pensions, health insurance, and vacations that workers in the 1950s and 1960s enjoyed.*
- try to determine whether something fits an existing definition: *Expanding opportunity is (or is not) central to the American Dream.*

Look for issues of definition in your everyday affairs—for instance, in the way jobs are classified at work; in the way key terms are described in your academic major; in the way politicians characterize the social issues that concern you; in the way you define yourself or others try to define you. Be especially alert to definitional arguments that may arise whenever you or others deploy adjectives such as *true, real, actual,* or *genuine: a true Texan; real environmental degradation; actual budget projections; genuine rap music.*

Researching Your Topic

You can research issues of definition by using the following sources:

- college dictionaries and encyclopedias
- unabridged dictionaries
- specialized reference works and handbooks, such as legal and medical dictionaries
- your textbooks (check their glossaries)
- newsgroups and listservs that focus on particular topics

Be sure to browse in your library reference room. Also, use the search tools of electronic indexes and databases to determine whether or how often controversial phrases or expressions are occurring in influential materials: major online newspapers, journals, and Web sites.

Formulating a Claim

After exploring your subject, begin to formulate a full and specific claim, a thesis that lets readers know where you stand and what issues are at stake. In moving toward this thesis, begin with the following types of questions of definition:

- questions related to genus: *Is assisting in suicide a crime?*
- questions related to species: *Is marijuana a harmful addictive drug or a useful medical treatment?*
- questions related to conditions: *Must the imposition of sexual attention be both unwanted and unsolicited to be considered sexual harassment?*
- questions related to fulfillment of conditions: *Has our college kept in place traditions or policies that might constitute racial discrimination?*
- questions related to membership in a named class: *Is any pop artist today in a class with Bob Dylan, the Beatles, Aretha Franklin, or the Rolling Stones?*

Your thesis should be a complete statement. In one sentence, you need to make a claim of definition and state the reasons that support your claim. In your paper or project itself, you may later decide to separate the claim from the reasons supporting it. But your working thesis should be a fully expressed thought. That means spelling out the details and the qualifications: *Who? What? Where? When? How many? How regularly? How completely?* Don't expect readers to fill in the blanks for you.

Examples of Definitional Claims

- Assisting a gravely ill person to commit suicide should not be considered murder when the motive behind the act is to ease a person's suffering, not to do harm or to benefit from the death.
- Although marijuana is somewhat addictive, it should not be classified as a dangerous drug because its immediate effects are far less damaging to the individual and society than those of heroin or cocaine and because it is effective in helping people with life-threatening diseases.
- Flirting with the waitstaff in a restaurant should be considered sexual harassment when the activity is repeated, unsolicited, and obviously unappreciated.

- Giving college admission preference to children of alumni is an example of class discrimination because most such policies privilege families that are rich and already advantaged.

Preparing a Proposal

If your instructor asks you to prepare a proposal for your project, here's a format that may help:

State your thesis completely. If you're having trouble doing so, try outlining it in Toulmin terms:

Claim:

Reason(s):

Warrant(s):

- **Explain why this argument of definition deserves attention. What's at stake? Why is it important for your readers to consider?**
- **Specify whom you hope to reach through your argument and why this group of readers would be interested in it.**
- **Briefly discuss the key challenges you anticipate in preparing your argument: Defining a key term? Establishing the essential and sufficient elements of your definition? Demonstrating that your subject will meet those conditions?**
- **Determine what strategies you'll use in researching your definitional argument. What sources do you expect to consult: Dictionaries? Encyclopedias? Periodicals? The Internet?**
- **Determine what visuals you will include in your definitional argument. How will each one be used?**
- **Consider what format you expect to use for your project: A conventional research essay? A letter to the editor? A Web page?**

Thinking about Organization

Your argument of definition may take various forms, but it's likely to include elements such as the following:

- a claim involving a matter of definition: *Labeling Al Qaeda and similar groups as representatives of "Islamic fascism" is understandable but misleading.*

- an attempt to establish a definition of a key term: *Genuine fascism is a mass movement within a nation resulting from democracy gone wrong.*
- an explanation or defense of the terms of the definition: *Scholars agree that fascism is a modern mass movement distinguished by the primacy of the nation over the individual, the elimination of dissent, the creation of a single-party state, and the glorification of violence on behalf of a national cause.*
- an examination of the claim in terms of the definition and all its criteria: *Fascism is highly nationalistic, but Islam is hostile to nationalism; Islam is a religious movement, but fascism is a secular movement that is usually quite hostile to religion.*
- a consideration of alternative views and counterarguments: *It is true that Osama bin Laden appeals to violence on behalf of his cause of restoring the medieval Islamic empire and that some fascist regimes (like Franco's Spain) were closely allied to religious authorities. . . .*

Getting and Giving Response

All arguments benefit from the scrutiny of others. Your instructor may assign you to a peer group for the purpose of reading and responding to each other's drafts; if not, get some response on your own from serious readers or consultants at a writing center. You can use the following questions to evaluate a draft. If you're evaluating someone else's draft, be sure to illustrate your points with examples. Specific comments are always more helpful than general observations.

The Claim

- Is the claim clearly an issue of definition?
- Is the claim significant enough to interest readers?
- Are clear and specific criteria established for the concept being defined? Do the criteria define the term adequately? Using this definition, could most readers identify what's being defined and distinguish it from other related concepts?

Evidence for the Claim

- Is enough evidence furnished to explain or support the definition? If not, what kind of additional evidence is needed?

- Is the evidence in support of the claim simply announced, or are its significance and appropriateness analyzed? Is a more detailed discussion needed?
- Are all the conditions of the definition met in the concept being examined?
- Are any objections readers might have to the claim, criteria, or evidence, or to the way the definition is formulated, adequately addressed?
- What kinds of sources, including visual sources, are cited? How credible and persuasive will they be to readers? What other kinds of sources might be more credible and persuasive?
- Are all quotations introduced with appropriate signal phrases (such as "As Himmelfarb argues,") and blended smoothly into the writer's sentences?

Organization and Style

- How are the parts of the argument organized? Is this organization effective, or would some other structure work better?
- Will readers understand the relationships among the claims, supporting reasons, warrants, and evidence? If not, what could be done to make those connections clearer? Is the function of every visual clear? Have you related each visual to a particular point in your essay and explained its significance? Are more transitional words and phrases needed? Would headings or graphic devices help?
- Are the transitions or links from point to point, paragraph to paragraph, and sentence to sentence clear and effective? If not, how could they be improved?
- Is the style suited to the subject? Is it too formal? Too casual? Too technical? Too bland? How can it be improved?
- Which sentences seem particularly effective? Which ones seem weakest, and how could they be improved? Should some short sentences be combined, or should any long ones be separated into two or more sentences?
- How effective are the paragraphs? Do any seem too skimpy or too long? How can they be improved?
- Which words or phrases seem particularly effective, vivid, and memorable? Do any seem dull, vague, unclear, or inappropriate for the audience or the writer's purpose? Are definitions provided for technical or other terms that readers might not know?

Spelling, Punctuation, Mechanics, Documentation, Format

- Are there any errors in spelling, punctuation, capitalization, and the like?
- Is an appropriate and consistent style of documentation used for parenthetical citations and the list of works cited or references? (See Chapter 20.)
- Does the paper or project follow an appropriate format? Is it appropriately designed and attractively presented? How could it be improved? If it's a Web site, do all the links work?

RESPOND •

1. Briefly discuss the criteria you might use to define the italicized terms in the following controversial claims of definition. Compare your definitions of the terms with those of your classmates.

   Graphic novels are *serious literature.*

   Burning a nation's flag is a *hate crime.*

   The Bushes have become America's *royal family.*

   Matt Drudge and Larry Flynt are legitimate *journalists.*

   College sports programs have become *big businesses.*

   Plagiarism can be an act of *civil disobedience.*

   Satanism is a *religion* properly protected by the First Amendment.

   Campaign contributions are acts of *free speech.*

   The District of Columbia should have all the privileges of an American *state.*

   Committed gay and lesbian couples should have the legal privileges of *marriage.*

2. This chapter opens with sketches of six rhetorical situations that center on definitional issues. Select one of these situations, and write definitional criteria using the strategy of formal definition. For example, identify the features of a photograph that make it part of a larger class (art, communication method, journalistic technique). Next, identify the features of a photograph that make it distinct from other members of that larger class. Then use the strategy of operational definition to establish criteria for the same object: what does it do? Remember to ask questions related to conditions (*Is a computer-scanned photograph still a photograph?*) and questions related to fulfillment of conditions (*Does a good photocopy of a photograph achieve the same effect as the photograph itself?*).

3. In an essay at the end of this chapter entitled "Pink Think," Lynn Peril makes a variety of claims about a concept she identifies as *pink think,* which she defines in part as "a set of ideas and attitudes about what constitutes proper female behavior." After reading this selection carefully, consider whether Peril has actually defined a concept that operates today. If you think "pink think" still exists, prove it by showing how some activities, behaviors, products, or institutions meet the definition of the concept. Write, too, about the power this concept has to define behavior.

   Alternatively, define a concept of your own that applies to a similar kind of stereotypical behavior—for example, *chick think* or *surfer think* or *geek think*. Then argue that your newly defined concept does, in fact, influence people today. Be sure to provide clear and compelling examples of the concept in action as it shapes the way people think and behave.

The Offbeat Allure of Cult Films

SAYOH MANSARAY

Opening paragraph includes a parodic definition of "great skills."

On a Saturday afternoon in February junior Clare Marshall and her family sit in her living room watching a film that Marshall is an avid fan of: *Napoleon Dynamite*. Marshall and her family say quotes along with the movie and laugh aloud at the hilarious parts. "Girls only want boyfriends who have great skills," Clare says, imitating Napoleon's trademark throaty drawl. "You know, like nun chuck skills, bow hunting skills . . . computer hacking skills."

Marshall is not the only teenager who likes films that are completely different from most movies in theaters. The teen followings of nonmainstream films like *Napoleon Dynamite* and *Donnie Darko* show that today's teens are looking for films that are "off the beaten path," according to English and Literature as Film teacher Mike Horne. Teens are gravitating toward these quirky movies, raising some of them to a cult-like status.

A tentative definition of "cult film" is offered.

The consensus among Blazers is that a cult movie is a quirky, different film that did not do well in theaters but has since gained a strong and faithful following on DVD or video. In recent years the definition of cult films has begun to evolve and broaden to include films that did not actually flop in theaters. Regardless of the specific definition, recent cult films are attracting teen fans.

Sayoh Mansaray wrote this article for *Silver Chips Online*, the online newspaper of Montgomery Blair High School in Silver Spring, Maryland, where she served as public relations co-director and factcheck supervisor. *Silver Chips Online*, which has won a number of awards, is all student-run and is partially sponsored by the *Washington Post*. Note that the article, like most pieces published in newspapers, does not document sources in any formal way.

A still from *Napoleon Dynamite,* starring Jon Heder (center)

"It Feels Real"

As Marshall continues to watch the film, a scene plays in which Napoleon talks to a girl on the phone. The girl has been forced by her mother to thank Napoleon for a picture he drew of her in hopes of getting a date. "It took me like three hours to finish the shading on your upper lip," Napoleon says to the girl, as Marshall quotes along with him.

Another characteristic of cult films is offered: They are "not formulaic" and they "require thought."

Many teens, Marshall included, like cult films because they differ from other films in theaters. Horne says that teens gravitate to cult movies because they are not formulaic. "They are a little bit different, and they require some thought or interpretation," he says.

Reasons for the popularity of cult films are given.

Junior Katrina Jabonete likes *Donnie Darko,* a film about a teen who is teetering on the edge of schizophrenia, because it is so beautifully twisted and darkly weird that the film opens itself to a thousand different interpretations. She believes that teens are drawn to cult movies because they aren't as clean or processed as mainstream flicks and because cult films are less likely to offer a concrete conclusion. Basically, they are more like real life. "[They] deal with problems and emotions in a different, real way," she explains. "Teens relate to [these movies] because it feels real to them."

Time Warp

While recent movies are gaining cult status, some students remain exclusively faithful to the classics, becoming part of groups that view their cult favorites over and over again.

Example of a classic cult film is provided.

Junior Linda Dye fits into this category. She thinks a cult movie is a film that is "so bad it's good." Take her favorite cult film, *The Rocky Horror Picture Show*, a 1975 musical about a group of gender-bending, quasi-alien, quasi-vampire, raving-lunatics-in-drag. "Ever since I first saw it, I've been completely in love with it," she gushes.

Dye is drawn to the film partially because the close-knit following allows her to interact with people she might never have known before. When Dye attended the annual *Rocky Horror* screening at the University of Maryland, she dressed up as one of the film's characters. In a bustier, a feather boa, and heels, Dye, along with the rest of the audience, yelled dialogue to the screen and made up her own lines as the movie played.

For Dye, this energy is what keeps her love for the film and its following alive. "You're sitting with these people you've never met, [but] by the end of the movie there's an energy—you're a community," she says.

"If I Had a Tumor, I'd Name It Marla"

Regardless of whether a movie is a classic or a recent hit, movie fans often display their love of films by quoting them. On snowy days, senior Robin Weiss likes to write one-liners from *Fight Club* like, "If I had a tumor, I'd name it Marla" and "We are a generation of men raised by women" on the icy windshields of random cars.

Marshall likes to answer questions with *Napoleon Dynamite* quotes. If a friend asks, "What are you doing today, Clare?" she might respond with a Napoleon line: "Whatever I feel like doing—gosh!"

Quotable dialogue is a defining characteristic of a cult film.

Horne says that a major component of cult films is quotable dialogue. "Half the fun is reliving it with your friends," he says, smiling. Some fans can quote most of a movie, he adds. Senior Walker Davis, for example, knows most of the lines from *The Big Lebowski*.

Low-budget aspect of cult films, first mentioned in third paragraph, is reiterated here.

According to Davis, cult films are never big budget productions, and no movie studio ever sets out to create a cult film—it just happens.

Many teens, like Marshall, just can't get enough of these films. Horne says that cult films are often bizarre, random, and edgy, which adds to their appeal. He says that people who watch cult films may have different motives than other moviegoers. "Many people look to film as an escape, [but] others are looking to find different thoughts," he says.

Pink Think

LYNN PERIL

From the moment she's wrapped in a pink blanket, long past the traumatic birthday when she realizes her age is greater than her bust measurement, the human female is bombarded with advice on how to wield those feminine wiles. This advice ranges from rather vague proscriptions along the lines of "nice girls don't chew gum/swear/wear pants/fill-in-the-blank," to obsessively elaborate instructions for daily living. How many women's lives, for example, were enriched by former Miss America Jacque Mercer's positively baroque description of the proper way to put on a bathing suit, as it appeared in her guide *How to Win a Beauty Contest* (1960)?

> [F]irst, roll it as you would a girdle. Pull the suit over the hips to the waist, then, holding the top away from your body, bend over from the waist. Ease the suit up to the bustline and with one hand, lift one breast up and in and ease the suit bra over it. Repeat on the other side. Stand up and fasten the straps.

Instructions like these made me bristle. I formed an early aversion to all things pink and girly. It didn't take me long to figure out that many things young girls were supposed to enjoy, not to mention ways they were supposed to behave, left me feeling funny—as if I was expected to pound my square peg self into the round hole of designated girliness. I didn't know it at the time, but the butterflies in my tummy meant I had crested the first of many hills on the roller coaster ride of femininity—or, as I soon referred to it, the other f-word. Before I knew what was happening, I was hurtling down its track, seemingly out of control, and screaming at the top of my lungs.

After all, look what I was up against. The following factoids of femininity date from the year of my birth (hey, it wasn't *that* long ago):

- In May of 1961, Betsy Martin McKinney told readers of *Ladies' Home Journal* that, for women, sexual activity commenced with intercourse

---

Lynn Peril is the publisher of the 'zine *Mystery Date*. This essay is excerpted from the introduction to *Pink Think*, a book that examines the influence of the feminine ideal.

and was completed with pregnancy and childbirth. Therefore, a woman who used contraceptives denied "her own creativity, her own sexual role, her very femininity." Furthermore, McKinney asserted that "one of the most stimulating predisposers to orgasm in a woman may be childbirth followed by several months of lactation." (Mmm, yes, must be the combination of episiotomy and sleep deprivation that does it.) Politely avoiding personal examples, she neglected to mention how many little McKinneys there were.

- During the competition for the title of Miss America 1961, five finalists were given two questions to answer. First they were asked what they would do if "you were walking down the runway in the swimsuit competition, and a heel came off one of your shoes?" The second question, however, was a bit more esoteric: "Are American women usurping males in the world, and are they too dominant?" Eighteen-year-old Nancy Fleming, of Montague, Michigan, agreed that "there are too many women working in the world. A woman's place is in the home with her husband and children." This, along with her pragmatic answer to the first question ("I would kick off both shoes and walk barefooted") and her twenty-three-inch waist (tied for the smallest in pageant history), helped Nancy win the crown.
- In 1961, toymaker Transogram introduced a new game for girls called Miss Popularity ("The True American Teen"), in which players competed to see who could accrue the most votes from four pageant judges—three of whom were male. Points were awarded for such attributes as nice legs, and if the judges liked a contestant's figure, voice, and "type." The prize? A special "loving" cup, of course! Who, after all, could love an unpopular girl?

These are all prime examples of "pink think." Pink think is a set of ideas and attitudes about what constitutes proper female behavior; a groupthink that was consciously or not adhered to by advice writers, manufacturers of toys and other consumer products, experts in many walks of life, and the public at large, particularly during the years spanning the mid-twentieth century—but enduring even into the twenty-first century. Pink think assumes there is a standard of behavior to which all women, no matter their age, race, or body type, must aspire. "Femininity" is sometimes used as a code word for this mythical standard, which suggests that women and girls are always gentle, soft, delicate, nurturing beings made of "sugar and spice and everything nice." But pink think is more than a stereotyped vision of girls and women as poor drivers who are afraid of mice and snakes, adore babies and small dogs, talk incessantly on the phone, and are incapable of keeping secrets. Integral to pink think is the belief that one's success as a woman is grounded in one's allegiance to such behavior. For example, a woman who fears mice isn't necessarily following the dictates of pink think. On the other hand, a woman who isn't afraid of mice but pretends to be because she thinks such helplessness adds to her appearance of femininity is toeing the pink think party line. When you hear the words "charm" or "personality" in the context of successful womanhood, you can almost always be sure you're in the presence of pink think.

While various self-styled "experts" have been advising women on their "proper" conduct since the invention of the printing press, the phenomenon defined here as pink think was particularly pervasive from the 1940s to the 1970s. These were fertile years for pink think, a cultural mindset and consumer behavior rooted in New Deal prosperity yet culminating with the birth of women's liberation. During this time, pink think permeated popular books and magazines aimed at adult women, while little girls absorbed rules of feminine behavior while playing games like the aforementioned Miss Popularity. Meanwhile, prescriptions for ladylike dress, deportment, and mindset seeped into child-rearing manuals, high school home economics textbooks, and guides for bride, homemaker, and career girl alike.

It was almost as if the men and women who wrote such books viewed proper feminine behavior as a panacea for the ills of a rapidly changing modern world. For example, myriad articles in the popular press devoted to the joys of housewifery helped coerce Rosie the Riveter back into the kitchen when her hubby came home from the war and expected his factory job back. During the early cold war years, some home economics texts seemed to suggest that knowing how to make hospital corners and a good tuna casserole were the only things between Our Way of Life and communist incursion. It was patriotic to be an exemplary housewife. And pink-thinking experts of the sixties and seventies, trying to maintain this ideal, churned out reams of pages that countered the onrushing tide of both the sexual revolution and the women's movement. If only all women behaved like our Ideal Woman, the experts seemed to say through the years, then everything would be fine.

You might even say that the "problem with no name" that Betty Friedan wrote about in *The Feminine Mystique* (1963) was a virulent strain of pink-thinkitis. After all, according to Friedan, "the problem" was in part engendered by the experts' insistence that women "could desire no greater destiny than to glory in their own femininity"—a pink think credo.

The pink think of the 1940s to 1970s held that femininity was necessary for catching and marrying a man, which was in turn a prerequisite for childbearing—the ultimate feminine fulfillment. This resulted in little girls playing games like Mystery Date long before they were ever interested in boys. It made home economics a high school course and college major, and suggested a teen girl's focus should be on dating and getting a boyfriend. It made beauty, charm, and submissive behavior of mandatory importance to women of all ages in order to win a man's attention and hold his interest after marriage. It promoted motherhood and housewifery as women's only meaningful career, and made sure that women who worked outside the home brought "feminine charm" to their workplaces lest a career make them too masculine.

Not that pink think resides exclusively alongside antimacassars and 14.4 modems in the graveyard of outdated popular culture: Shoes, clothing, and movie stars may go in and out of style with astounding rapidity, but attitudes have an unnerving way of hanging around long after they've outlived their usefulness—even if they never had any use to begin with.

9 Evaluations

"We don't want to go *there* for Tex-Mex. Their tortillas aren't fresh, their quesadillas are mush, and they get their salsa from New York City!"

The campus Labor Action Committee has been co-chaired for four years by three students whose leadership has led to significant improvements in the way the university treats its workers. Now they're all graduating at once, leaving a leadership vacuum; so the group calls a special meeting to talk about what qualities it needs in its next leaders.

A senior is frustrated by the "C" she received on an essay written for a history class, so she makes an appointment to talk with the teaching assistant who graded the paper. "Be sure to review the assignment sheet first," the TA warns. The student notices that the sheet, on its back side, includes a checklist of requirements for the paper; she hadn't turned it over before.

"We have a lousy homepage," a sales representative observes at a district meeting. "What's wrong with it?" the marketing manager asks. "Everything," the sales rep replies, then quickly changes the subject when she notices the manager's furrowed brow. But the manager decides to investigate the issue. Who knows what an effective Web site looks like these days?

You've just seen *Citizen Kane* for the first time and want to share the experience with your roommate. Orson Welles's masterpiece is playing at the Student Union for only one more night, but *The War of the Worlds* is featured across the street in THX sound. Guess which movie your roomie wants to see? You intend to set him straight.

• • •

Understanding Evaluations

Kristin Cole has a problem. The holiday break is approaching, she's headed out of town, and she still hasn't found a pet-sitter for Baldrick, her lovable cockatiel. When her first email appeal to colleagues in a large academic department fails to turn up a volunteer, she tries a second, this one more aggressively singing the praises of her companion:

> **Apologies for all the duplications, folks! Since nobody's stepped forward to birdsit for me from 15–30 or 31 December, I must repeat my plea.**
>
> **Please take my bird for this time. I'll pay. If you have other pets, all I ask is that your little darlings can't get at my little darling.**
>
> **And let me repeat that Baldrick could be the poster child for birds: he's quiet, loves people, and couldn't be happier than to sit on your shoulder while you go about your day. He'll whistle and make kissy noises in your ear, since he's a huge flirt. I must admit that he loves to chew paper and pens, but that's controllable. And he loves feet—that can be positive, negative, or neutral, depending on you.**

> **He's much easier than a cat or dog—no litter boxes, walks, or poop in the yard. And his food smells like candy. He's pretty much allergy-free, and the mess he makes is easily vacuumable with the dustbuster I'll lend you. He just needs contact with people and a fair amount of supervised out-of-cage time per day.**
>
> **Please do let me know if you can help me out. He's a great pet—he converted me, who had always thought a proper pet needed fur and four legs!**

In just a few lines, Kristin offers about a half-dozen reasons for birdsitting Baldrick, many of them based on the evaluative claim "he's a great pet." The claim deploys several different lines of argument, including appeals to the heart ("he's a huge flirt"), the head ("He's much easier than a cat or dog"), and even credibility ("he converted me, who had always thought a proper pet needed fur and four legs"). About the only potential device Kristin misses is a visual argument—for example, a photo of Baldrick, which she might have attached to the email easily enough.

Kristin makes Baldrick seem lovable and charming for a reason: to persuade someone to board the cockatiel over the holidays. In this

Baldrick: the poster child for birds

respect, her strategy is typical of many arguments of evaluation. They're written to clarify or support other decisions in our lives: what to read, who to hire, what to buy, which movies to see, who to vote for. (In case you're wondering, Kristin's email worked.)

Evaluations are everyday arguments. By the time you leave home in the morning, you've likely made a dozen informal evaluations. You've selected dressy clothes because you have a job interview in the afternoon with a law firm; you've chosen low-fat yogurt and shredded wheat over the pancakes, butter, and syrup you really love; you've queued up just the perfect play list on your iPod for your hike to campus. In each case, you've applied criteria to a particular problem and then made a decision.

Some professional evaluations require much more elaborate standards, evidence, and paperwork (imagine what an aircraft manufacturer has to do to certify a new jet for passenger service), but such work doesn't differ structurally from the simpler choices that people make routinely. And, of course, people do love to voice their opinions, and they always have: a whole mode of ancient rhetoric—called the ceremonial, or epideictic—was devoted entirely to speeches of praise and blame. (See Chapter 1.)

The famously fashionable Gwyneth Paltrow frequently tops best-dressed lists.

Today, rituals of praise and blame are a significant part of American life. Adults who'd choke at the very notion of debating causal or definitional claims will happily spend hours appraising the Tampa Bay Buccaneers or the Boston Red Sox or the Detroit Pistons. Other evaluative spectacles in our culture include awards shows, beauty pageants, most-valuable-player presentations, lists of best-dressed or worst-dressed celebrities, "sexiest people" magazine covers, literary prizes, political opinion polls, consumer product magazines, and—the ultimate formal public gesture of evaluation—elections. Indeed, making evaluations is a form of entertainment in America—one that generates big audiences (think of *American Idol*) and revenues.

Criteria of Evaluation

Whether arguments of evaluation produce simple rankings and winners or lead to more profound decisions about our lives, they involve standards. The particular standards we establish for judging anything—whether an idea, a work of art, a person, or a product—are called *criteria of evaluation*. Sometimes criteria are pretty self-evident. You probably know that a truck that gets ten miles per gallon is a gas hog or that a piece of fish that's served charred and rubbery should be returned. But criteria are often more complex when a potential subject is more abstract: *What makes a judge or a teacher effective? What features make a film a classic? What constitutes a living wage? How do we measure a successful foreign policy or college education?* Struggling to identify such difficult criteria of evaluation can lead to important insights into your values, motives, and preferences.

Why make such a big deal about criteria when many acts of evaluation seem almost effortless? Because we should be most suspicious of our judgments precisely when we start making them carelessly. It's a cop-out simply to think that everyone's entitled to an opinion, however stupid and uninformed it might be. Evaluations always require reflection. And when we look deeply into our judgments, we sometimes discover important "why" questions that typically go unasked:

- You may find yourself willing to challenge the grade you received in a course, but not the practice of grading itself.
- You argue that Miss Alabama would have been a better Miss America than the contestant from New York, but perhaps you don't wonder loudly enough whether such competitions make sense at all.
- You argue passionately that a Republican Congress is better for America than a Democratic alternative, but you fail to ask why voters get only two choices.
- You can't believe people take Britney Spears seriously as a singer, but you never consider what her impact on young girls might be.

Push an argument of evaluation hard enough, and even simple judgments become challenging and intriguing.

William Sea's opinion piece on male gender stereotypes asserts that a double standard now exists for making men out to be macho meatheads or buffoons while advertisers would not dare portray women in similarly offensive roles. Sea questions what anyone gains by stooping to stereotypes in advertising.

LINK TO P. 667

In fact, for many writers, grappling with criteria is the toughest step in producing an evaluation. They've got an opinion about a movie or book or city policy, but they also think that their point is self-evident and widely shared by others. So they don't do the necessary work to specify the criteria for their judgments. If you know a subject well enough to evaluate it, your readers should learn something from you when you offer an opinion. Do you think, for instance, that you could explain what (if anything) makes a veggie burger *good?* The following criteria offered on the *Cooks Illustrated* Web site show that they've given the question quite a bit of thought:

> **Store-bought veggie burgers border on inedible, but most homemade renditions are a lot of work. Could we develop a recipe that was really worth the effort? We wanted to create veggie burgers that even meat eaters would love. We didn't want them to taste like hamburgers, but we did want them to act like hamburgers, having a modicum of chew, a harmonious blend of savory ingredients, and the ability to go from grill to bun without falling apart.**
>
> –*Cooks Illustrated*

After a lot of experimenting, *Cooks Illustrated* came up with a recipe that met these criteria.

Though many people have eaten veggie burgers, they probably haven't thought about them this carefully. But to evaluate them convincingly, it's not enough to claim merely that a good veggie burger is juicy or tasty. Such a claim is also not very interesting.

Criteria of evaluation aren't static either. They differ according to time and audience. Much market research, for example, is designed to find out what particular consumers want now and in the future—what their criteria for buying a product are. Consider what the researchers at Honda discovered when they asked Y-generation men—a targeted demographic of consumers who generally don't consider Honda products—what they wanted in a new car. The answer, reported in the *New York Times,* was surprising:

> **The Honda group found that young adults wanted a basic, no-nonsense vehicle with lots of space—and they didn't seem to care much about the exterior style. "We found that vehicles, in this generation, were not the top priority," Mr. Benner said. "They're the means, not the end. The car is a tool." . . . What distinguishes younger buyers, all car companies seem to agree, is that they don't seem to care as**

Young people think a car should be a tool. Does this Honda Element meet that criterion?

> **much about cars as young people used to—putting more stock in the style of their cellphones or P.D.A.'s than in the style of what they drive.**
> **–Phil Patton, "Young Man, Would You Like That in a Box?"**

Such an evaluation of criteria actually led Honda to build the Element, a boxy—some would say homely—truck with swing-out side doors and an easily reconfigurable interior designed to be a "place" more than a vehicle. The Element did win fans, but less from among the X-generation Honda originally targeted than from their baby boomer parents!

Characterizing Evaluation

One way of understanding evaluative arguments is to consider the types of evidence they use. A distinction we explored in Chapter 4 between hard evidence and arguments based on reason is helpful here. You may recall that we defined hard evidence as facts, statistics, testimony, and other kinds of arguments that can be measured, recorded, or even found—the so-called smoking gun in a criminal investigation. Arguments based on reason are those shaped by language, using various kinds of logic.

We can study arguments of evaluation the same way, looking at some as *quantitative* and others as *qualitative*. Quantitative arguments of evaluation rely on criteria that can be measured, counted, or demonstrated in some mechanical fashion—something is taller, faster, smoother, quieter, more powerful than something else. In contrast, qualitative arguments rely on criteria that must be explained through words, relying on such matters as values, traditions, and even emotions: something is more ethical, more beneficial, more handsome, more noble. Needless to say, a claim of evaluation might be supported by arguments of both sorts. We separate them below merely to present them more clearly.

Quantitative Evaluations

At first glance, quantitative evaluations would seem to hold all the cards, especially in a society as enamored of science and technology as our own. Once you've defined a quantitative standard, making judgments should be as easy as measuring and counting—and in a few cases, that's the way things work out. *Who's the tallest or heaviest or loudest person in your class?* If your colleagues allow themselves to be measured, you could find out easily enough, using the right equipment and internationally sanctioned standards of measurement: the meter, the kilo, or the decibel.

But what if you were to ask, *Who's the smartest person in class?* You could answer this more complex question quantitatively too, using IQ tests or college entrance examinations that report results numerically. In fact, almost all college-bound students in the United States submit to this kind of evaluation, taking either the SAT or ACT to demonstrate their verbal and mathematical prowess. Such measures are widely accepted by educators and institutions, but they are also vigorously challenged. What do they actually measure? They predict likely success in college, which isn't the same thing as intelligence.

Like any standards of evaluation, quantitative criteria must be scrutinized carefully to make sure that what they measure relates to what's being evaluated. For example, in evaluating a car, you might use 0–60 mph times as a measure of acceleration, 60–0 mph distances as a measure of braking capability, skidpad numbers (0.85) as a measure of handling ability, and coefficient of drag (0.29) as a test of aerodynamic efficiency. But all these numbers are subject to error. And even when the numbers are gathered accurately and then compared, one vehicle with another, they may not tell the whole story because some cars generate great test numbers and yet still feel less competent than vehicles with lower scores. The same disparity between numbers and feel occurs with other items—compact disc recordings, for example. CDs can produce

MILITARY FATALITIES: BY TIME PERIOD

Military Fatalities

Period	*US*	*UK*	*Other**	*Total*	*Avg*	*Days*
5	159	5	0	164	1.82	90
4	715	13	18	746	2.35	318
3	579	25	27	631	2.92	216
2	718	27	58	803	1.89	424
1	140	33	0	173	4.02	43
Total	2311	103	103	2517	2.31	1091

Iraq Coalition Casuality Count

Time Periods:

Period 5: December 15, 2005 (the day after Iraq general elections) through today's date.

Period 4: January 31, 2005 (the day after Iraq Elections) through December 14, 2005.

Period 3: June 29, 2004 (the day after the official turnover of sovereignty to Iraq) through January 30, 2005 (Iraq Elections).

Period 2: May 2, 2003, through June 28, 2004 (the day of the official turnover of sovereignty to Iraq).

Period 1: March 20, 2003, through May 1, 2003 (the end of major combat).

Not Just Words

Even what looks like totally objective counting can make a powerful evaluative argument. Look at this simple chart kept by the group Iraq Coalition Casualty Count. It offers a measure of U.S. and British military fatalities in Iraq from March 20, 2003, when counting began, to March 15, 2006, when this chart was downloaded. What arguments of evaluation could be made based on these purely quantitative data?

awesome sonic accuracy numbers, but some listeners feel the music they produce may lack aural qualities important to listening pleasure. Educators, too, acknowledge that some students test better than others, which doesn't necessarily indicate greater intelligence.

We don't mean to belittle quantitative measures of evaluation, only to offer a caveat: even the most objective measures have limits. They've been devised by fallible people looking at the world from their own inevitably limited perspectives.

Qualitative Evaluations

Many issues of evaluation closest to people's hearts simply aren't subject to quantification. *What makes a movie great?* If you suggested a quantitative measure like length, your friends would probably hoot "Get serious!" But what about box office receipts, especially if they could be adjusted to reflect inflation? Would films that made the most money—an easily quantifiable measure—really be the "best pictures"? In that select group would be movies such as *Star Wars*, *The Sound of Music*, *Gone with the Wind*, *Titanic*, and *Harry Potter and the Sorcerer's Stone*. An interesting group of films—but the best?

Tom Sorensen uses a qualitative analysis to evaluate the NBA dress code. What criteria does he use to arrive at his conclusion?

LINK TO P. 723

Or you might go for the "quotability factor," determining which movies are the most quoted of all time. Based on a member survey, the American Film Institute lists the following as the top five most quotable movies:

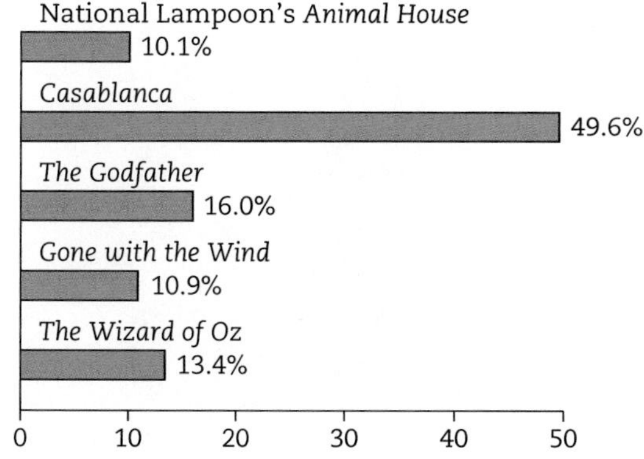

Most quotable movies

To argue for box office revenue and quotability as criteria of film greatness, though, you'd have to defend the criteria vigorously because many people in the audience would express serious doubts about them. More likely, then, in defining the criteria for "great movie," you'd look for standards to account for the merit of films widely respected among serious critics. You might consider the qualities common to such respected movies, exploring such elements as their societal impact, cinematic technique, dramatic structures, casting, and so on. Most of these markers of quality could be defined with some precision, but not measured or counted. Lacking hard numbers, you'd have to convince the audience to accept your standards and make your case rhetorically. As you might guess, a writer using qualitative measures could spend as much time defending criteria of evaluation as providing evidence that these standards are present in the film under scrutiny.

But establishing subtle criteria is what can make arguments of evaluation so interesting. They require you, time and again, to challenge conventional wisdom. Look at the way Nick Gillespie in Reasononline reviews the last *Star Wars* movie, *Revenge of the Sith:*

> **What might be called the continuing cultural hegemony of *Star Wars* is no small matter. With the possible exception of *The Lord of the Rings,***

Star Wars may be "craptacular" when judged by the usual criteria, but it's also a cultural phenomenon. Here, a still from the first episode (1977).

> no other franchise has maintained a similar hold on the public imagination for so long a period of time. In a curious way, the first two installments in *The Godfather* saga did (as evidenced by the appropriation of its themes and motifs in everything from countless lesser mob movies to standup comedy to rap music). But it's undeniable that *Star Wars* is in the warp and woof of American culture, ranging from politics to toys to, of course, movies, novels, and comic books. It very much provides a backdrop, a framework, a system of reference for the ways we talk about things, whether we're talking about missile defense systems, visions of the future and technology, good vs. evil, you name it.
>
> This is all the more stunning given the generally acknowledged mediocrity of the *Star Wars* movies themselves. Indeed, it's a given that if *Star Wars* didn't start to go downhill sometime during the "Cantina Band" sequence in the very first flick, then the series actively started to suck wind harder than Billy Dee Williams in an action sequence by the start of the third release, *Return of the Jedi*, a film so bad that it may well be the space opera equivalent of *The Day the Clown Cried*. (Personally, I lay in with those who peg the beginning of the end, if not the actual end of the end—or perhaps the high point—of the whole series to 1978's little-remembered yet still nightmare-inducing *The Star Wars Holiday Special*, which comes as close to the death-inducing video in *The Ring* as anything ever shown on non-premium cable.)
>
> And yet, despite the craptacular nature of at least four out of six *Star Wars* movies, there's little doubt that no film event has been more anticipated than *Revenge of the Sith* (with the possible exception—and in France only—of the next *Asterix et Obelix* extravaganza).
>
> –Nick Gillespie, "Star Wars, Nothing but Star Wars"

As Gillespie acknowledges, the *Star Wars* saga is full of flaws, some of them of a "craptacular" nature. And yet he goes on to make a much more subtle argument:

> The enormous *Star Wars* industry—the movies, the cartoons, the toys, the pop-cult references—still generates interest, excitement, pleasure (this last is something that most critics, whether liberal or conservative find absolutely terrifying), and, most important, a cultural conversation worth having. The series may well be crap—and a grave disappointment to critics who know so much better than the rest of us—but surely that's the least interesting thing about it.

Gillespie certainly knows that not everyone will agree with his assessment of the *Star Wars* saga, but his lengthy review makes clear to readers why he has come to the qualitative decision that the movies have nurtured "a cultural conversation worth having."

Developing an Evaluative Argument

Developing an argument of evaluation can seem like a simple process, especially if you already know what your claim is likely to be:

> ***Citizen Kane* is the finest film ever made by an American director.**

Having established a claim, you would then explore the implications of your belief, drawing out the reasons, warrants, and evidence that might support it:

Claim	***Citizen Kane* is the finest film ever made by an American director . . .**
Reason	**. . . because it revolutionizes the way we see the world.**
Warrant	**Great films change viewers in fundamental ways.**
Evidence	**Shot after shot, *Citizen Kane* presents the life of its protagonist through cinematic images that viewers can never forget.**

The warrant here is, in effect, a statement of criteria—in this case, the quality that defines "great film" for the writer.

In developing an evaluative argument, you'll want to pay special attention to criteria, claims, and evidence.

Formulating Criteria

Personal ads present evaluation criteria distilled and condensed. W. Charisse Goodman quotes the following ad in her essay about weight prejudice in the United States: "Be any race, be yourself, but be beautiful."

LINK TO P. 605

Most often neglected in evaluations is the discussion of criteria. Although even thoughtless evaluations (*The band stinks!*) might be traced to reasonable criteria, most people don't bother defending their positions until they are challenged (*Oh yeah?*). Yet when writers address audiences whom they understand well or with whom they share core values, they don't defend most of their criteria in detail. One wouldn't expect a film critic like Roger Ebert to restate all his principles every time he writes a movie review. Ebert assumes his readers will—over time—come to appreciate his standards.

Still, the criteria can make or break a piece. In an essay from *Salon.com*'s series of evaluative arguments called "Masterpieces," writer Stephanie Zacharek can barely contain her enthusiasm for the Chrysler Building in midtown Manhattan:

> **Architects, who have both intuition and training on their side, have some very good reasons for loving the Chrysler Building. The rest of**

us love it beyond reason, for its streamlined majesty and its inherent sense of optimism and promise for the future, but mostly for its shimmery, welcoming beauty — a beauty that speaks of humor and elegance in equal measures, like a Noel Coward play.

How can a mere building make so many people so happy — particularly so many ornery New Yorkers, who often pretend, as part of their act, not to like anything? There may be New Yorkers who dislike the Chrysler Building, but they rarely step forward in public. To do so would only invite derision and disbelief.

–Stephanie Zacharek, "The Chrysler Building"

Certainly, it may seem odd to suggest that one measure of a great building is that it makes people happy. And so the writer has a lot to prove. She's got to provide evidence that a building can, in fact, be delightful. And she seems to do precisely that later in the same essay when she gives life even to the windows in the skyscraper:

> **Looking at the Chrysler Building now, though, it's hard to argue against its stylish ebullience, or its special brand of sophisticated cheerfulness. . . . Particularly at night, the crown's triangular windows — lit up, fanned out and stacked high into the sky — suggest a sense of movement that has more in common with dance than with architecture: Those rows of windows are as joyous and seductive as a chorus line of Jazz Age cuties, a bit of sexy night life rising up boldly from an otherwise businesslike skyline.**

The criteria Zacharek uses lead to an inventive and memorable evaluation, one that perhaps teaches readers to look at buildings in a whole new way.

Why does this building make people happy?

Sandra Cisneros and Marjorie Agosín, both U.S. residents and writers of Spanish literature, each formulate their own criteria for preferring Spanish over English when expressing themselves. Consider what criteria they share.

LINK TO PP. 756 AND 758

The Audiovox SMT 5600

So don't take criteria of evaluation for granted. If you offer vague, dull, or unsupportable principles, expect to be challenged. You're most likely to be vague about your beliefs when you haven't thought enough about your subject. So push yourself at least as far as you imagine the readers will. Imagine the readers looking over your shoulder, asking difficult questions. Say, for example, that you intend to argue that any person who wants to stay on the cutting edge of personal technology will obviously prefer Cingular's Audiovox SMT 5600. What standards would such people apply? That it's not only a great phone but a great PDA? But what does that mean? What makes it "great"? Perhaps that it gives access to email, the wireless Web, and PIM data and that it seamlessly integrates with Windows Media Player provide some criteria you could defend. But should you get more—or less—technical? Do you need to assert very sophisticated criteria to establish your authority to write about the subject? These are appropriate questions to ask.

Making Claims

Claims can be stated directly or, in rare instances, strongly implied. For most writers, the direct evaluative claim probably works better, with the statement carefully qualified. Consider the differences between the following claims and how much less the burden of proof would be for the second and third ones:

Jon Stewart is the most important entertainer of this decade.

Jon Stewart is one of the three or four most important TV entertainers of this decade.

Jon Stewart may come to be regarded as one of the three or four most important TV comedians of this decade.

The point of qualifying a statement isn't to make evaluative claims bland, but to make them responsible and manageable. Consider how sensitively Christopher Caldwell frames his claim in the eulogy he writes for former Beatle George Harrison (a eulogy is a very important kind of evaluative argument):

> **Leaving aside the screaming Beatlemaniacs in thrall to the idiosyncrasies of sex appeal, there were never any George People or Ringo People. But George Harrison's death from cancer Thursday at the age of 58 reminds us that there ought to have been. If any of the four could be called "typical" of the group, the most Beatley Beatle, the heart of the Fab Four, the means of bridging Paul's appeal and John's, and thus the glue that held the band together, it was George.**
>
> **–Christopher Caldwell, "All Things Must Pass"**

Caldwell will have to prove this claim, offering evidence that George contributed in important ways to a musical group dominated by John Lennon and Paul McCartney. But he doesn't have to show that George was the most important Beatle, just the group's binding element. And that's a much more manageable task.

Presenting Evidence

The more evidence the better in an evaluation, provided that the evidence is relevant. For example, in evaluating the performance of two computers, the speed of their processors would certainly be important, but the quality of their keyboards or the availability of service might be less crucial, perhaps irrelevant.

Just as important as relevance in selecting evidence is presentation. Not all pieces of evidence are equally convincing, nor should they be treated as such. Select evidence most likely to impress your readers, and arrange the argument to build toward your best material. In most cases, that best material will be evidence that's specific, detailed, and derived from credible sources. Look at the details in these paragraphs by David

Plotz evaluating rapper, producer, and entertainer P. Diddy—at the time still known as Sean "Puffy" Combs:

> **Combs is a Renaissance man, but only by the standards of a P.T. Barnum world. Rarely has someone become so famous by being so mediocre at so many things—a boy wonder without any wonder. Puffy is a famous rapper who can't rap, and he's becoming a movie actor who can't act. He's a restaurateur who serves ho-hum food; a magazine publisher whose magazine was immediately forgettable (*Notorious*—see, you've forgotten already); a music producer whose only talents are stealing old songs and recycling the work of his dead friend the Notorious B.I.G.**
>
> **Combs can be seen as the inverse of the past century's great Renaissance man, Paul Robeson, a truly wonderful singer, actor, athlete, and political activist. Puffy has none of that talent, but unlike the Communist Robeson, he has a profound understanding of capitalism. Puffy has thrived because he has achieved his mediocrity with immense panache, with bling-bling hoopla and PR genius. Puffy is the Sam Glick of hip-hop—a man without wit, talent, charm, or convictions, but so full of drive that he made $230 million anyway.**
>
> **–David Plotz, "Sean Combs: Why Is Puffy Deflating?"**

The details are rich enough to make the case that Sean Combs lacks the talent of a real artist or genius. But notice that Plotz admits what's obvious to anyone aware of the man's fame: he's a success by contemporary standards. Combs's income can't be ignored in this argument.

However, don't be afraid to concede such a point when evidence goes contrary to the overall claim you wish to make. If you're really skillful, you can even turn a problem into an argumentative asset, as Bob Costas does in acknowledging the flaws of baseball great Mickey Mantle in the process of praising him:

> **None of us, Mickey included, would want to be held to account for every moment of our lives. But how many of us could say that our best moments were as magnificent as his?**
>
> **–Bob Costas, "Eulogy for Mickey Mantle"**

Three editorial cartoons taken from the Web site *American Indian Sports Team Mascots Web* employ visual argument to evaluate the use of Indian images as team mascots. Note the succinct argument that can be captured in one frame.

LINK TO P. 712

Considering Design and Visuals

In thinking about how to present your evidence, don't forget to consider the visual aspects of doing so. Design features such as headings for the different criteria you're using or, in online evaluations, links to material related to your subject can enhance your authority and credibility and thus make your evaluation more persuasive. Think, too, about how you

might use visual evidence to good effect. For example, you might use a bar graph, as the American Film Institute did for the most quotable movies (see p. 259), to show how your subject measures up to a similar one. Or in the passage on Combs, Plotz could have included photos of both Combs and Robeson, choosing ones that drew a stark distinction between the two men. Here, for instance, is a photo of Combs, wearing a cut-off T-shirt and lots of bling; compare that photo to the one of Robeson as a serious and well-dressed young man.

If Everything's an Argument . . .

From your standpoint as a student, how would you evaluate this chapter on evaluations? How well does the chapter use examples, explanations, and visuals to establish what an evaluation argument does? How helpful is it in preparing you to write an evaluation argument? Finally, judged by the corresponding criteria, how does this chapter stack up against the two preceding chapters—on arguments of fact and arguments of definition? Think about these questions, and then write a one-page evaluation of this chapter.

Key Features of Evaluations

In drafting an evaluation, you should consider three basic elements:

- an evaluative claim that makes a judgment about a person, idea, or object
- the criterion or criteria by which you'll measure your subject
- evidence that the particular subject meets or falls short of the stated criteria

All these elements will be present in one way or another in arguments of evaluation, but they won't follow a specific order. In addition, you'll often need an opening paragraph to explain what you're evaluating and why. Tell readers why they should care about your subject and take your opinion seriously.

Nothing adds more depth to an opinion than letting others challenge it. When you can, use the resources of the Internet or more local online networks to get responses to your opinions. It can be eye-opening to realize how strongly people react to ideas or points of view that you regard as perfectly normal. When you're ready, share your draft with colleagues, asking them to identify places where your ideas need additional support, either in the discussion of criteria or in the presentation of evidence.

GUIDE to writing an evaluation

Finding a Topic

You're entering an argument of evaluation when you:

- make a judgment about quality: Citizen Kane is *probably the finest film ever made by an American director.*
- challenge such a judgment: Citizen Kane is *vastly overrated by most film critics.*
- construct a ranking or comparison: Citizen Kane is *a more intellectually challenging movie than* Casablanca.

Issues of evaluation arise daily—in the judgments you make about public figures or policies; in the choices you make about instructors and courses; in the recommendations you make about books, films, or television programs; in the preferences you exercise in choosing products, activities, or charities. Be alert to evaluative arguments whenever you read or use terms that indicate value or rank: *good/bad, effective/ineffective, best/worst, competent/incompetent, successful/unsuccessful*. Finally, be aware of your own areas of expertise. Write about subjects or topics about which others regularly ask your opinion or advice.

Researching Your Topic

You can research issues of evaluation by using the following sources:

- journals, reviews, and magazines (for current political and social issues)
- books (for assessing judgments about history, policy, etc.)
- biographies (for assessing people)
- research reports and scientific studies
- books, magazines, and Web sites for consumers
- periodicals and Web sites that cover entertainment and sports
- blogs for exploring current affairs

Surveys and polls can be useful in uncovering public attitudes: *What books are people reading? Who are the most admired people in the country? What activities or businesses are thriving or waning?* You'll discover that Web sites, newsgroups, and blogs thrive on evaluation. Browse these public forums for ideas, and, when possible, explore your own topic ideas there.

Formulating a Claim

After exploring your subject, begin to formulate a full and specific claim, a thesis that lets readers know where you stand and on what criteria you'll base your judgments. Look for a thesis that's challenging enough to attract readers' attention, not one that merely repeats views already widely held. In moving toward this thesis, you might begin with questions of this kind:

- What exactly is my opinion? Where do I stand?
- Can I make my judgment more specific?
- Do I need to qualify my claim?
- According to what standards am I making my judgment?
- Will readers accept my criteria, or will I have to defend them, too?
- What major reasons can I offer in support of my evaluation?

Your thesis should be a complete statement. In one sentence, you need to make a claim of evaluation and state the reasons that support your claim. Be sure your claim is specific enough. Anticipate the questions readers might have: *Who? What? Where? Under what conditions? With what exceptions? In all cases?* Don't expect readers to guess where you stand.

Examples of Evaluative Claims

- Though they may never receive Oscars for their work, Sandra Bullock and Keanu Reeves deserve credit as actors who have succeeded in a wider range of film roles than most of their contemporaries.
- Many computer users are discovering that Mac OS X is a more intuitive, stable, robust, and elegant operating system than anything currently available on PC platforms.
- Jimmy Carter has been highly praised for his work as a former president of the United States, but history may show that even his much-derided term in office laid the groundwork for the foreign policy and economic successes now attributed to later administrations.
- Because knowledge changes so quickly and people switch careers so often, an effective education today is one that trains people *how to learn* more than it teaches them *what to know*.

Preparing a Proposal

If your instructor asks you to prepare a proposal for your project, here's a format that may help:

State your thesis completely. If you're having trouble doing so, try outlining it in Toulmin terms:

Claim:

Reason(s):

Warrant(s):

- **Explain why this issue deserves attention. What's at stake?**
- **Specify whom you hope to reach through your argument and why this group of readers would be interested in it.**
- **Briefly discuss the key challenges you anticipate: Defining criteria? Defending them? Finding quantitative evidence to support your claim? Developing qualitative arguments to bolster your judgment?**
- **Determine what research strategies you'll use. What sources do you expect to consult?**
- **Consider what format you expect to use for your project: A conventional research essay? A letter to the editor? A Web page?**

Thinking about Organization

Your evaluation may take various forms, but it's likely to include elements such as the following:

- a specific claim: *Most trucks are unsuitable for the kind of driving most Americans do.*
- an explanation or defense of the criteria (if necessary): *The overcrowding and pollution of American cities and suburbs might be relieved if more Americans drove small, fuel-efficient cars. Cars do less damage in accidents than heavy trucks and are also less likely to roll over.*
- an examination of the claim in terms of the stated criteria: *Most trucks are unsuitable for the kind of driving Americans do because they are not designed for contemporary urban driving conditions.*

- evidence for every part of the argument: *Trucks get very poor gas mileage; they are statistically more likely than cars to roll over in accidents; . . .*
- consideration of alternative views and counterarguments: *It is true, perhaps, that trucks make drivers feel safer on the roads and give them a better view of traffic conditions. . . .*

Getting and Giving Response

All arguments benefit from the scrutiny of others. Your instructor may assign you to a peer group for the purpose of reading and responding to each other's drafts; if not, get some response on your own from some serious readers or consultants at a writing center. You can use the following questions to evaluate a draft. If you're evaluating someone else's draft, be sure to illustrate your points with examples. Specific comments are always more helpful than general observations.

The Claim

- Is the claim clearly an argument of evaluation? Does it make a judgment about something?
- Does the claim establish clearly what's being evaluated?
- Is the claim too sweeping? Does it need to be qualified?
- Will the criteria used in the evaluation be clear to readers? Do the criteria need to be defined more explicitly or precisely?
- Are the criteria appropriate ones to use for this evaluation? Are they controversial? Does evidence of their validity need to be added?

Evidence for the Claim

- Is enough evidence furnished to ensure that what's being evaluated meets the criteria established for the evaluation? If not, what kind of additional evidence is needed?
- Is the evidence in support of the claim simply announced, or are its significance and appropriateness analyzed? Is a more detailed discussion needed?
- Are any objections readers might have to the claim, criteria, or evidence adequately addressed?
- What kinds of sources, including visual sources, are cited? How credible and persuasive will they be to readers? What other kinds of sources might be more credible and persuasive?

- Are all quotations introduced with appropriate signal phrases (such as "As Will argues,") and blended smoothly into the writer's sentences?

Organization and Style

- How are the parts of the argument organized? Is this organization effective, or would some other structure work better?
- Will readers understand the relationships among the claims, supporting reasons, warrants, and evidence? If not, what could be done to make those connections clearer? Are more transitional words and phrases needed? Would headings or graphic devices help?
- Are the transitions or links from point to point, paragraph to paragraph, and sentence to sentence clear and effective? If not, how could they be improved?
- Are all visuals carefully integrated into the text? Is each visual introduced and commented on to point out its significance? Is each visual labeled as a figure or a table and given a caption as well as a citation?
- Is the style suited to the subject? Is it too formal? Too casual? Too technical? Too bland? How can it be improved?
- Which sentences seem particularly effective? Which ones seem weakest, and how could they be improved? Should some short sentences be combined, or should any long ones be separated into two or more sentences?
- How effective are the paragraphs? Do any seem too skimpy or too long? How can they be improved?
- Which words or phrases seem particularly effective, vivid, and memorable? Do any seem dull, vague, unclear, or inappropriate for the audience or the writer's purpose? Are definitions provided for technical or other terms that readers might not know?

Spelling, Punctuation, Mechanics, Documentation, Format

- Are there any errors in spelling, punctuation, capitalization, and the like?
- Is an appropriate and consistent style of documentation used for parenthetical citations and the list of works cited or references? (See Chapter 20.)
- Does the paper or project follow an appropriate format? Is it appropriately designed and attractively presented? How could it be improved? If it's a Web site, do all the links work?

RESPOND.

1. Choose one item from the following list that you understand well enough to evaluate. Develop several criteria of evaluation you could defend to distinguish excellence from mediocrity in the area. Then choose another item from the list, this time one you don't know much about at all, and explain the research you might do to discover reasonable criteria of evaluation for it.

    fashion designers
    Navajo rugs
    musicals
    spoken word poetry
    UN secretary generals
    NFL quarterbacks
    contemporary painters
    TV journalists
    TV sitcoms
    health food
    animated films

2. Review Kristin Cole's appeal for a pet-sitter for Baldrick (see pp. 251–252), and then write an email of your own in which you try to persuade friends to care for someone or something while you're away. Be sure that the argument includes strong elements of evaluation. Why should friends be eager to pamper your pit bull Killer, care for your fragile collection of tropical orchids, or babysit your ten-year-old twin siblings Bonnie and Clyde?

3. In the last ten years, there has been a proliferation of awards programs for movies, musicians, sports figures, and other categories. For example, before the Oscars are handed out, a half-dozen other organizations have given prizes to the annual crop of films. Write a short opinion piece assessing the merits of a particular awards show or a feature such as *People*'s annual "sexiest man" issue. What should a proper event of this kind accomplish? Does the event you're reviewing do so?

4. Local news-and-entertainment magazines often publish "best of" issues or articles that list readers' and editors' favorites in such categories as "best place to go on a first date," "best ice cream sundae," and "best dentist." Sometimes the categories are very specific: "best places to say 'I was retro before retro was cool'" or "best movie theater seats." Imagine that you're the editor of your own local magazine and

that you want to put out a "best of" issue tailored to your hometown. Develop ten categories for evaluation. For each category, list the evaluative criteria you would use to make your judgment. Next, consider that because your criteria are warrants, they're especially tied to audience. (The criteria for "best dentist," for example, might be tailored to people whose major concern is avoiding pain, to those whose children will be regular clients, or to those who want the cheapest possible dental care.) For several of the evaluative categories, imagine that you have to justify your judgments to a completely different audience. Write a new set of criteria for that audience.

5. Develop an argument using (or challenging) one of the criteria of evaluation presented in this chapter. Among the criteria you might explore are the following:

   A car should be a tool.

   Good TV quotes are those that impress themselves in people's memories.

   Great films change viewers in fundamental ways.

   Good pets need not have fur and four legs.

   Great veggie burgers need just the right shape and texture.

6. For examples of powerful evaluation arguments, search the Web or library for obituaries of famous, recently deceased individuals. Try to locate at least one such item, and analyze the types of claims it makes about the deceased. What criteria of evaluation are employed? What kinds of evidence does it present?

Why I Hate Britney

NISEY WILLIAMS

I'm afraid of having children. Not because of labor pains, but because of the odds that I may actually have a girl. Today, efficiently raising a daughter is almost impossible because of pop culture's persistent emphasis on sex. It's rare to watch MTV or BET and not be bombarded with images of women's bare midriffs, protruding cleavage, and round rumps. Bellies, breasts, and booties. I can't imagine how much more difficult it will be to protect my daughter from this in fifteen years when she'd be approaching puberty.

The thesis is stated clearly and emphatically.

And for my fear of motherhood, I blame Britney Spears.

Well, in all fairness, Britney's not the only one to influence our youth. There is a growing group of sexualized, so-called entertainers who seem to be multiplying like roaches: Britney Spears, Destiny's Child, Christina Aguilera, 3LW, Mariah Carey, Shakira, Jessica Simpson, Pink, J.Lo, etc. — hereafter known as Britney et al. Daily, these destructive divas serve young girls with an earful and eyeful of sex, tempting children to mimic their musical heroes. So much so that the media has coined such phrases as "Baby Britneys," "Teeny Christinees," and "Junior J.Los." Still, while there are other female artists who also discourage the healthy development of our

---

When she wrote this paper, Nisey Williams was a senior at the University of Texas, Austin, an African American Studies and Cultural Anthropology major who plans on teaching honors English to high school students. Although she enjoys all realms of creative writing, her passion is poetry. She hopes to publish poetry and short stories.

"Why I Hate Britney" is her response to an assignment that asked for an argument with a personal voice suitable for publication in a newspaper or magazine. Sources were to be documented in the paper itself, not through formal documentation.

youth—most recently J.Lo with her serial marrying/divorcing practices—Britney remains the most culpable.

A *Dallas Morning News* reporter claims it's "always convenient to blame the sinister influence of Britney" but it's much more than "convenient"—it's practical. Forbes magazine voted Britney as the most powerful celebrity of 2002, beating such influential personalities as Steven Spielberg and Oprah Winfrey. With such recognition comes responsibilities. It's undeniable that Britney is at the forefront of this sex-crazed phenomenon and I, like many others, hold her accountable. On a website called *Pax Vobiscum*, one concerned father of two teenage daughters refers to Britney as "the chief apostlette for the sexualization of our little girls" with her "revealing clothing and 'come-hither' image." This couldn't be more accurate.

Evidence suggests that Spears is responsible for influencing young women.

While she says she hopes to save her virginity for marriage, she also wears see-through outfits and dances like a stripper on the MTV Video Music Awards. Actions speak louder than words; her chastity claim falls short beside her sleazy image. Britney's marketing management is pimping her and she's without the dignity or strength to step off the street corner and hail a cab from Lolita Lane to Respectable Road.

Several other female artists don't sell their bodies in order to sell their music. Among them is Avril Lavigne, one of Arista's latest signers, who openly criticizes Britney for her confusing and contradictory image. In a recent interview with *Chart Attack*, Avril explains that: "The clothes I wear onstage are the clothes I would wear to school or to go shopping. Britney Spears goes up onstage and dresses like a showgirl. She's not being herself. I mean, the way she dresses . . . would you walk around the street in a bra? It's definitely not what I'm going to do." And so far, Avril hasn't had to compromise herself to be a success. Her first album, Let Go, debuted at No. 8 on the Billboard charts and has since gone double platinum. She was also awarded Best New Artist at the 2002 MTV Video Music Awards. Avril

An alternative to Spears's approach to success is offered.

is known as the "Anti-Britney" because, as AskMen.com explained, she "stands out in the current sea of female teen vocalists as a distinctly unmanufactured artist whose success can be directly linked to her musical talent." Can't say the same for Miss Spears.

It's amazing how Britney ignores her influence on children. In *Rolling Stone,* her response to critics judging her clothing style was a reference to her younger days of playing dress-up in her mother's closet—within the confines of her home. She explained: "We put on our mom's clothes and we dressed up. It was our time to daydream and fantasize." Does she seriously think wearing Mom's clothes is the same as having your own and flaunting them at the mall or in the classroom?

Spears does not live up to criteria for responsible behavior—given her role as a model for young girls.

Then in an *In Style* interview, she says she has no patience for those who criticize her skin-baring. In her words: "I mean, I'm a girl! Why not?" Great message for the kiddies, Brit: if you got it, flaunt it. And what about those girls who don't "got it"? Britney basically tells girls that body image is of primary importance—a difficult problem for many young females. Some girls who feel this constant pressure to attain unrealistic goals end up with destructive behaviors such as eating disorders and low self-esteem. Many girls who strive to be Britney look-alikes do not realize they lack her resources, such as makeup artists, silicone enhancements, and millions of dollars.

An alternative perspective is explored and rejected.

The main argument against those like me who bash Britney is that it's up to parents—not celebrities—to teach their children morals and appropriate behavior. While I agree with elements of that claim, there is only so much a parent can do. Sexual material is so intertwined in pop culture that even cautious parents have a hard time keeping their children away from it. In the *Milwaukee Journal Sentinel,* one psychiatrist explains that parents "often don't even think about it [keeping children away from pop culture] because it's an overwhelming task," while another equated "trying to insulate a child from sexual material" with "fighting a tornado."

During the crucial years of adolescence, popular opinion sometimes overrides that of parents. In the same Milwaukee article, one mother reports that her daughter threw a fit in the department store when she refused to buy her thongs. The mother was completely baffled by her child's reaction until the twelve-year-old admitted that the other girls in the locker room teased her for wearing bikini underwear instead of thongs. Many kids will do anything to fit in because peer approval is so necessary to a child learning her place in school.

Numerous examples enforce the claim that children are being sexualized too early by "Britney et al."

Experts are torn on the long-term effects our sex-heavy pop culture may have on children, but many agree that there are likely negative consequences. According to Diane Levin, an education professor who has studied the effects of media on children's development for over twenty years, our sex-saturated culture will rub off on children in the most undesired ways. On *ABCNews.com,* Levin explains that "the kind of increased sexual images that children are seeing parallel with when they get a little older. They start becoming sexually active earlier." Currently, the Alan Guttmacher Institute reports that two out of ten girls and three out of ten boys have had sexual intercourse by age fifteen, while there are also several widespread reports of increased sexual activity—including oral sex—among middle-school students. How much worse will these statistics be by the time my daughter reaches the age of fifteen?

Although there is no documented evidence of how pop culture's over-sexualization affects children, an August 14th taping of *Good Morning, America,* entitled "From Oshkosh to Oh My Gosh," revealed some startling reactions. The show divided the children by sex and then interviewed the two groups separately about issues surrounding pop culture. The result was a roomful of shocked parents who had no idea the word *sexy* was such a frequent and familiar part of their children's vocabulary. When the girls' group watched a Jennifer Lopez video, the relationship between the mature concept of sexiness and popular music became obvious. After one young girl predicted the video's ending was J.Lo removing her shirt, another girl explained that J.Lo did this "to look sexy."

Being sexy is the latest fad for girls of all ages and with the current fashions available, their dreams can become a reality. Clothing designers work side by side with the entertainment industry. There is at least a $90 billion market targeting "tweens"—children between the ages of eight and twelve who are in the in between stages of adolescence and teenagehood. It is this up-and-coming group who fuel pop culture. They listen to the music, worship the singers, and crave their clothing. From Wal-Mart to the Limited Too, stores are fully aware of what their young consumers want and promote their merchandise accordingly.

As a consequence of Spears's influence, parents are finding it more difficult to raise children, underscoring the initial claim in the argument.

Modest girls' clothing is hard to find among the racks of grown-up fashions like low-riding hip huggers, tight midriff-revealing shirts, high-heeled platforms, and miniskirts. One of my co-workers said she had such a difficult time school shopping for her thirteen-year-old daughter that she ended up taking her to Academy for wind suits, free-flowing T-shirts, and soccer shorts. Sporting stores will soon be the last option for frustrated parents, as more retailers prey on the tween market.

However, my beef is not with these merchants. The clothing is harmless by itself. It would sit untouched and undesired if it weren't for Britney et al. flaunting revealing fashions in music videos, posters, magazine covers, and award shows. As *FashionFollower.com* revealed: "Queen Britney single-handedly made the bare midriff a staple of 15-year-old wardrobes across the globe. Now that's something every mother should be proud of."

Pop culture seems to be in downward spiral, continually going from bad to worse. It's bad enough to have to endure countless images of exposed female bodies on every music channel, but it's so much worse to see those same "barely there" outfits on children. Hopefully, there will come a day when it's no longer trendy to be so overtly sexual and pop culture will replace Britney et al. with more respectable female icons.

The Case against Coldplay

JON PARELES

June 5, 2005

There's nothing wrong with self-pity. As a spur to songwriting, it's right up there with lust, anger and greed, and probably better than the remaining deadly sins. There's nothing wrong, either, with striving for musical grandeur, using every bit of skill and studio illusion to create a sound large enough to get lost in. Male sensitivity, a quality that's under siege in a pop culture full of unrepentant bullying and machismo, shouldn't be dismissed out of hand, no matter how risible it can be in practice. And building a sound on the lessons of past bands is virtually unavoidable.

But put them all together and they add up to Coldplay, the most insufferable band of the decade.

This week Coldplay releases its painstakingly recorded third album, "X&Y" (Capitol), a virtually surefire blockbuster that has corporate for-

---

Jon Pareles is the pop music critic of the *New York Times*.

tunes riding on it. (The stock price plunged for EMI Group, Capitol's parent company, when Coldplay announced that the album's release date would be moved from February to June, as it continued to rework the songs.)

"X&Y" is the work of a band that's acutely conscious of the worldwide popularity it cemented with its 2002 album, "A Rush of Blood to the Head," which has sold three million copies in the United States alone. Along with its 2000 debut album, "Parachutes," Coldplay claims sales of 20 million albums worldwide. "X&Y" makes no secret of grand ambition.

Clearly, Coldplay is beloved: by moony high school girls and their solace-seeking parents, by hip-hop producers who sample its rich instrumental sounds and by emo rockers who admire Chris Martin's heart-on-sleeve lyrics. The band emanates good intentions, from Mr. Martin's political statements to lyrics insisting on its own benevolence. Coldplay is admired by everyone—everyone except me.

It's not for lack of skill. The band proffers melodies as imposing as Romanesque architecture, solid and symmetrical. Mr. Martin on keyboards, Jonny Buckland on guitar, Guy Berryman on bass and Will Champion on drums have mastered all the mechanics of pop songwriting, from the instrumental hook that announces nearly every song they've recorded to the reassurance of a chorus to the revitalizing contrast of a bridge. Their arrangements ascend and surge, measuring out the song's yearning and tension, cresting and easing back and then moving toward a chiming resolution. Coldplay is meticulously unified, and its songs have been rigorously cleared of anything that distracts from the musical drama.

Unfortunately, all that sonic splendor orchestrates Mr. Martin's voice and lyrics. He places his melodies near the top of his range to sound more fragile, so the tunes straddle the break between his radiant tenor voice and his falsetto. As he hops between them—in what may be Coldplay's most annoying tic—he makes a sound somewhere between a yodel and a hiccup. And the lyrics can make me wish I didn't understand English. Coldplay's countless fans seem to take comfort when Mr. Martin sings lines like, "Is there anybody out there who / Is lost and hurt and lonely too," while a strummed acoustic guitar telegraphs his aching sincerity. Me, I hear a passive-aggressive blowhard, immoderately proud as he flaunts humility. "I feel low," he announces in the chorus of "Low," belied by the peak of a crescendo that couldn't be more triumphant about it.

In its early days, Coldplay could easily be summed up as Radiohead minus Radiohead's beat, dissonance or arty subterfuge. Both bands looked to the overarching melodies of 1970's British rock and to the guitar dynamics of U2, and Mr. Martin had clearly heard both Bono's delivery and the way Radiohead's Thom Yorke stretched his voice to the creaking point.

Unlike Radiohead, though, Coldplay had no interest in being oblique or barbed. From the beginning, Coldplay's songs topped majesty with moping: "We're sinking like stones," Mr. Martin proclaimed. Hardly alone among British rock bands as the 1990's ended, Coldplay could have been singing not only about private sorrows but also about the final sunset on the British empire: the old opulence meeting newly shrunken horizons. Coldplay's songs wallowed happily in their unhappiness.

"Am I a part of the cure / Or am I part of the disease," Mr. Martin pondered in "Clocks" on "A Rush of Blood to the Head." Actually, he's contagious. Particularly in its native England, Coldplay has spawned a generation of one-word bands — Athlete, Embrace, Keane, Starsailor, Travis and Aqualung among them — that are more than eager to follow through on Coldplay's tremulous, ringing anthems of insecurity. The emulation is spreading overseas to bands like the Perishers from Sweden and the American band Blue Merle, which tries to be Coldplay unplugged.

A band shouldn't necessarily be blamed for its imitators — ask the Cure or the Grateful Dead. But Coldplay follow-throughs are redundant; from the beginning, Coldplay has verged on self-parody. When he moans his verses, Mr. Martin can sound so sorry for himself that there's hardly room to sympathize for him, and when he's not mixing metaphors, he fearlessly slings clichés. "Are you lost or incomplete," Mr. Martin sings in "Talk," which won't be cited in any rhyming dictionaries. "Do you feel like a puzzle / you can't find your missing piece."

Coldplay reached its musical zenith with the widely sampled piano arpeggios that open "Clocks": a passage that rings gladly and, as it descends the scale and switches from major to minor chords, turns incipiently mournful. Of course, it's followed by plaints: "Tides that I tried to swim against / Brought me down upon my knees."

On "X&Y," Coldplay strives to carry the beauty of "Clocks" across an entire album — not least in its first single, "Speed of Sound," which isn't the only song on the album to borrow the "Clocks" drumbeat. The album is faultless to a fault, with instrumental tracks purged of any glimmer of human frailty. There is not an unconsidered or misplaced note on "X&Y," and every song (except the obligatory acoustic "hidden track" at the end, which is still by no means casual) takes place on a monumental soundstage.

As Coldplay's recording budgets have grown, so have its reverberation times. On "X&Y," it plays as if it can already hear the songs echoing across the world. "Square One," which opens the album, actually begins with guitar notes hinting at the cosmic fanfare of "Also Sprach Zarathustra" (and "2001: A Space Odyssey"). Then Mr. Martin, never someone to evade the obvious, sings about "the space in which we're traveling."

As a blockbuster band, Coldplay is now looking over its shoulder at titanic predecessors like U2, Pink Floyd and the Beatles, pilfering freely from all of them. It also looks to an older legacy; in many songs, organ chords resonate in the spaces around Mr. Martin's voice, insisting on churchly reverence.

As Coldplay's music has grown more colossal, its lyrics have quietly made a shift on "X&Y." On previous albums, Mr. Martin sang mostly in the first person, confessing to private vulnerabilities. This time, he sings a lot about "you": a lover, a brother, a random acquaintance. He has a lot of pronouncements and advice for all of them: "You just want somebody listening to what you say," and "Every step that you take could be your biggest mistake," and "Maybe you'll get what you wanted, maybe you'll stumble upon it" and "You don't have to be alone." It's supposed to be compassionate, empathetic, magnanimous, inspirational. But when the music swells up once more with tremolo guitars and chiming keyboards, and Mr. Martin's voice breaks for the umpteenth time, it sounds like hokum to me.

10
Causal Arguments

Concerned that middle-school students are consuming too much junk food and soda pop at lunch, a principal considers banning vending machines on her campus. But then she discovers how much revenue those machines generate for her school, and she quickly has second thoughts.

A scientist questions the widespread assumption that glaciers are receding largely because of global warming caused by human behavior. He offers controversial evidence that glaciers have grown and receded in the Alps and elsewhere several times during the last ten thousand years—even before humans were capable of changing the climate.

Researchers in Marin County, California, discover that the occurrence of breast cancer cases is significantly higher there than in any other urban area in California. They immediately begin work to investigate possible causes.

A large clothing manufacturer wants to increase its worldwide market share among teenage buyers of blue jeans. Its executives know that another company has been the overwhelming market leader for years—and they set out to learn exactly why.

Convinced that there is a strong and compelling causal link between secondhand smoke and lung cancer, the City of New York institutes a total ban of smoking in public indoor spaces.

A state legislator notes that gasoline prices are consistently between twenty-five and fifty cents higher in one large city in the state than elsewhere. After some preliminary investigation, the legislator decides to bring a class action lawsuit on behalf of the people of this city, arguing that price fixing and insider deals are responsible for the price difference.

• • •

The eye-catching title image of a *National Geographic* story from August 2004 poses a simple question: "Why Are We So Fat?" You're probably smart enough to suspect that simple questions like this rarely have simple answers. But in this case the author, Cathy Newman, argues that there are no real surprises:

> **. . . in one sense, the obesity crisis is the result of simple math. It's a calories in, calories out calculation. The First Law of Fat says that anything you eat beyond your immediate need for energy, from avocados to ziti, converts to fat. . . . The Second Law of Fat: The line between being in and out of energy balance is slight. Suppose you consume a mere 5 percent over a 2,000-calorie-a-day average. "That's just one hundred calories; it's a glass of apple juice," says Rudolph Leibel, head of molecular genetics at Columbia University College of Physicians and Surgeons. "But those few extra calories can mean a**

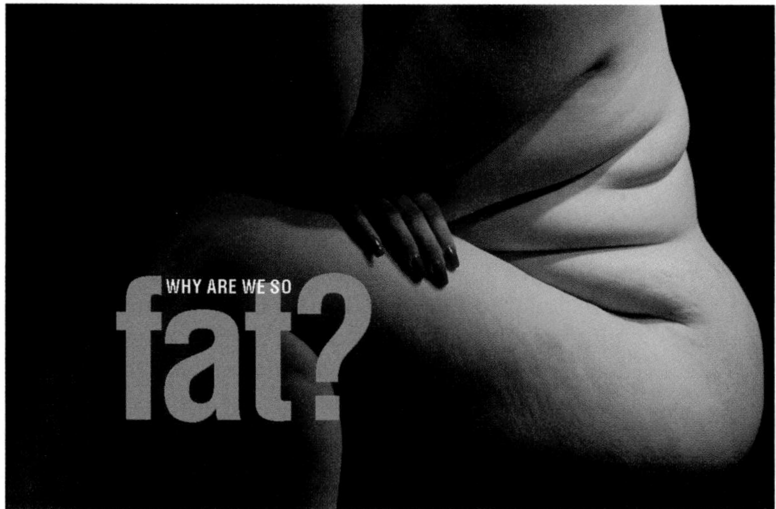

And the answer is . . .?

> **huge weight gain." Since one pound of body weight is roughly equivalent to 3,500 calories, that glass of juice adds up to an extra 10 pounds over a year.**
>
> **–Cathy Newman, "Why Are We So Fat?"**

And yet you know that there's more to it than that—as Newman's full story reveals. "Calories in, calories out" may explain the physics of weight gain. But why in recent years have we so drastically shifted the equation from *out* to *in?* Because food is more readily available and cheaper, and humans instinctually crave fatty foods? Because we've grown addicted to fast food? Because we walk less? Because we've become Internet (or GameBoy) addicts? Whatever the reasons for our increased tonnage, the consequences can be measured by everything from the width of airliner seats to the rise of diabetes in the general population. Many explanations will be offered by scientists, social critics, and health gurus, and just as many will likely be refuted. Figuring out what's going on will be an importance exercise in cause-and-effect argument for years to come.

Understanding Causal Arguments

Causal arguments are at the heart of many major policy decisions, both national and international—from the consequences of poverty in Africa to the causes of terrorism around the globe. But arguments about causes and effects also inform many choices people make every day. Suppose that you need to petition for a grade change because you were unable to turn in a final project on time. You'd probably enumerate the reasons for your failure—the death of your cat, followed by an attack of the hives, followed by a crash of your computer—hoping that a committee reading the petition might see these explanations as tragic enough to change your grade. In identifying the *causes* of the situation, you're implicitly arguing that the *effect*—your failure to submit the project on time—should be considered in a new light. Unfortunately, the committee might accuse you of *faulty causality* (see pp. 506–508), judging that your failure to complete the project is really due more to procrastination and partying than to the reasons you offer.

Causal arguments exist in many forms and frequently appear as part of other arguments (such as evaluations or proposals).

It may help focus your work on causal arguments to separate them into three major categories:

- arguments that state a cause and then examine its effect(s)

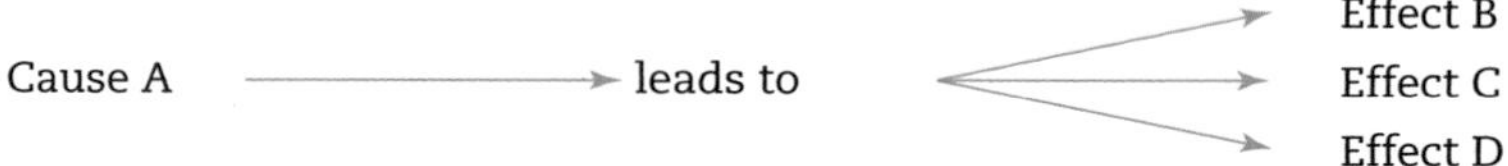

- arguments that state an effect and then trace the effect back to its cause(s)

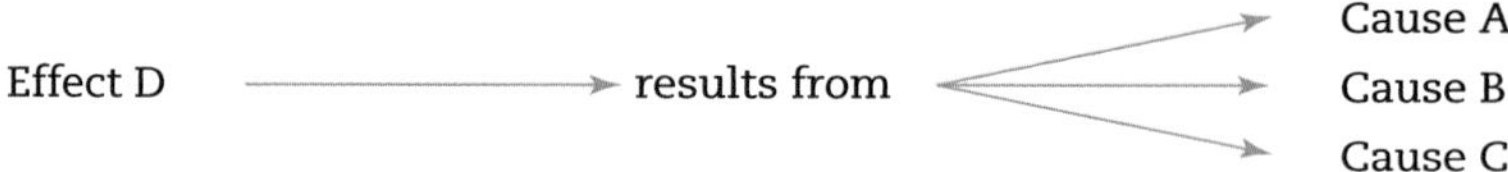

- arguments that move through a series of links: A causes B, which leads to C and perhaps to D

Cause A → leads to Cause B → leads to Cause C → leads to Effect D

ARGUMENTS THAT STATE A CAUSE AND THEN EXAMINE ONE OR MORE OF ITS EFFECTS

What would happen if openly homosexual men and women were allowed to join (or stay in) the American military? That would be a "cause" whose possible effects could be examined in detail and argued powerfully. You could imagine the very different cases (and consequences) presented by people on contrary sides of this hot button issue. In such an argument, you'd be successful if you could show compellingly that the cause would indeed lead to the effects you describe. Or you could challenge the causal assumptions made by people you don't agree with. Take a look at the opening of an article from the Reuters news service reporting on the Live 8 concerts held in July 2005. One might have expected an event such as Live 8 to move the consciences of world leaders or heighten people's awareness about conditions in regions of Africa. But there was another consequence as well:

> **LONDON (Reuters)—They came out of charity. They left with booming record sales.**
>
> **The galaxy of rock stars who took part in Live 8 concerts on Saturday to help beat the curse of poverty have seen their discs fly off the shelves in British music stores—a case of bank balances as well as consciences winning out.**
>
> **–Mike Collett-White, "Stars See Album Sales Soar after Live 8 Gigs"**

But were audiences, in fact, rewarding the artists not so much for their good deeds as for their good performances? One detail in the story suggests the latter—and suggests how absorbing the details of causal arguments can be:

> **The only Live 8 performer to have clocked a drop in sales was Pete Doherty. His former group the Libertines saw sales of their "Up the Bracket" album drop by 35 percent.**
>
> **Doherty's performance was singled out by the British media as one of the worst of the nine-hour Hyde Park music marathon. . . . people at the gig said he struggled with the words of "Children of the Revolution" and looked unsteady on his feet.**

ARGUMENTS THAT BEGIN WITH AN EFFECT AND THEN TRACE THE EFFECT BACK TO ONE OR MORE CAUSES

This type of argument might begin with a certain effect—for example, Hollywood experiencing a record-breaking slump in movie-going in 2005—and then trace the effect (or set of effects) to the most likely

Cartoonist Mark Alan Stamaty portrays an effect and three of its causes.

causes: a rise in DVD sales; the growing popularity of large-screen home theaters and HDTV; noisy, cell phone–using audiences; lousy movies; unimaginative remakes; red-state backlash against liberal Hollywood films or activism in the 2004 elections. Or you might examine the reasons Hollywood executives offer for their industry's dip and decide whether their causal analyses pass muster.

Like other kinds of causal arguments, those tracing effects to a cause can have far-reaching significance. For example, in 1962 the scientist Rachel Carson seized the attention of millions with a famous causal argument about the effects that the overuse of chemical pesticides might have on the environment. Here's an excerpt from the beginning of her book-length study of this subject. Note how she begins with the *effects* before saying she'll go on to explore the causes:

> **[A] strange blight crept over the area and everything began to change. Some evil spell had settled on the community: mysterious maladies**

> **swept the flocks of chickens; the cattle and sheep sickened and died. Everywhere was a shadow of death. The farmers spoke of much illness among their families. . . . There had been several sudden and unexplained deaths, not only among adults but even among children, who would be stricken suddenly while at play and die within a few hours. . . . The roadsides, once so attractive, were now lined with browned and withered vegetation as though swept by fire. These, too, were silent, deserted by all living things. Even the streams were now lifeless. Anglers no longer visited them, for all the fish had died.**
>
> **In the gutters under the eaves and between the shingles of the roofs, a white granular powder still showed a few patches; some weeks before it had fallen like snow upon the roofs and the lawns, the fields and streams. No witchcraft, no enemy action had silenced the rebirth of new life in this stricken world. The people had done it themselves. . . . What has already silenced the voices of spring in countless towns in America? This book is an attempt to explain.**
>
> **–Rachel Carson, *Silent Spring***

Today, one could easily write a casual argument of the first type about *Silent Spring* and the environmental movement it spawned.

ARGUMENTS THAT MOVE THROUGH A SERIES OF LINKS: CAUSE A LEADS TO B, WHICH LEADS TO C AND POSSIBLY TO D

In an environmental science class, for example, you might decide to argue that a national law regulating smokestack emissions from utility plants is needed because of the following reasons:

1. emissions from utility plants in the Midwest cause acid rain,
2. acid rain causes the death of trees and other vegetation in eastern forests,
3. powerful lobbyists have prevented midwestern states from passing strict laws to control emissions from these plants, and
4. as a result, acid rain will destroy most eastern forests by 2020.

In this case, the first link is that emissions cause acid rain; the second, that acid rain causes destruction in eastern forests; and the third, that states have not acted to break the cause-effect relationship established by the first two points. These links set the scene for the fourth link, which ties the previous points together to argue from effect: unless X, then Y.

Characterizing Causal Arguments

Causal arguments tend to share several characteristics.

THEY ARE OFTEN PART OF OTHER ARGUMENTS.

Many causal arguments do stand alone and address questions fundamental to our well-being: *Why are juvenile asthma and diabetes increasing so dramatically in the United States? What are the causes of global warming, and can we do anything to counter them? What will happen to Europe if its birth rate continues to decline?* But causal analyses often work to further other arguments—especially proposals. For example, a proposal to limit the time children spend playing video games might first draw on a causal analysis to establish that playing video games can have bad results—such as violent behavior, short attention spans, and decreased social skills. The causal analysis provides a rationale that motivates the proposal. In this way, causal analyses can be useful in establishing good reasons for arguments in general.

In his article urging changes in the rules and organization of college basketball, Thad Williamson argues about the consequences of commercialism in the game.

LINK TO P. 716

THEY ARE ALMOST ALWAYS COMPLEX.

The complexity of most causal relationships makes establishing causes and effects extremely difficult. For example, scientists and politicians continue to disagree over the extent to which acid rain is actually responsible for the so-called dieback of many eastern forests. Or consider the complexity of analyzing election results. If you compare articles explaining why George W. Bush *won* the presidency in 2004 with those that ask why John Kerry *lost*, you might as well be in different universes.

But when you can show that X *definitely* causes Y, you'll have a powerful argument at your disposal if for no other reason than that causal arguments must take into account an enormous number of factors, conditions, and alternative possibilities. That's why, for example, so much effort went into establishing an indisputable link between smoking and lung cancer. Once proven, decisive legal action could finally be taken to protect—or at least warn—smokers.

THEY ARE OFTEN DEFINITION BASED.

One reason causal arguments are so complex is that they often depend on extremely careful definitions. Recent figures from the U.S. Department of Education, for example, show that the number of high school dropouts is rising and that this rise has caused an increase in youth unemployment. But exactly how does the study define *dropout?* A closer look may suggest that some students (perhaps a lot) who drop out actually "drop back in" later and go on to complete high school. Further, how does the study define *employment?* Until you can provide explicit definitions that answer such questions, you should proceed cautiously with a causal argument like this one.

THEY USUALLY YIELD PROBABLE RATHER THAN ABSOLUTE CONCLUSIONS.

Because causal relationships are almost always extremely complex, they seldom yield more than a high degree of probability and are almost always subject to critique or charges of false causality. (We all know smokers who defy the odds to live long, cancer-free lives.) Scientists in particular are wary of making causal claims—that environmental factors cause infertility, for example, because it's highly unlikely that a condition as variable as infertility could be linked to any one cause.

Even *after* an event, proving what caused it can be hard. No one would disagree that the Japanese bombing of Pearl Harbor took place on December 7, 1941, or that the United States entered World War II shortly thereafter. But what are the causal connections? Did the bombing "cause" the U.S. entry into the war? Even if you're convinced that the bombing was the most immediate cause, what about other related causes: the unstable and often hostile relationship between the U.S. and Japanese governments in the years leading up to the bombing; Japanese imperial ambitions; common U.S. stereotypes of "Oriental" peoples; U.S. objections to the Japanese invasion of China; and so on?

As another example, during the campus riots of the late 1960s, a special commission was charged with determining the "causes" of riots on a particular campus. After two years of work—and almost a thousand pages of evidence and reports—the commission was unable to pinpoint anything but a broad network of contributing causes and related conditions. Thus to demonstrate that A caused B, you must find the strongest possible evidence and subject it to the toughest scrutiny. But understand that a causal argument doesn't fail just because you can't find a single compelling cause. In fact, causal arguments are often most effective when they help readers appreciate how tangled our lives and landscapes really are.

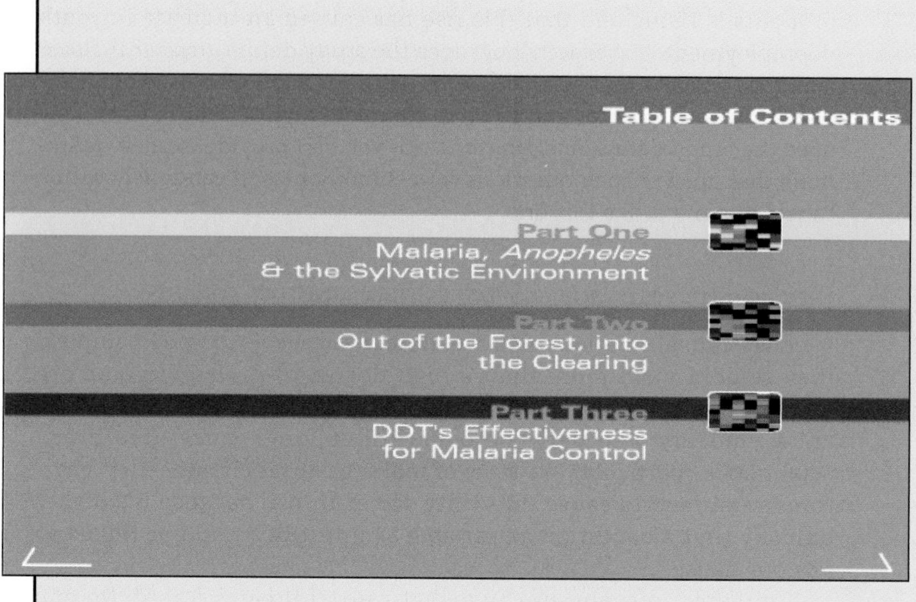

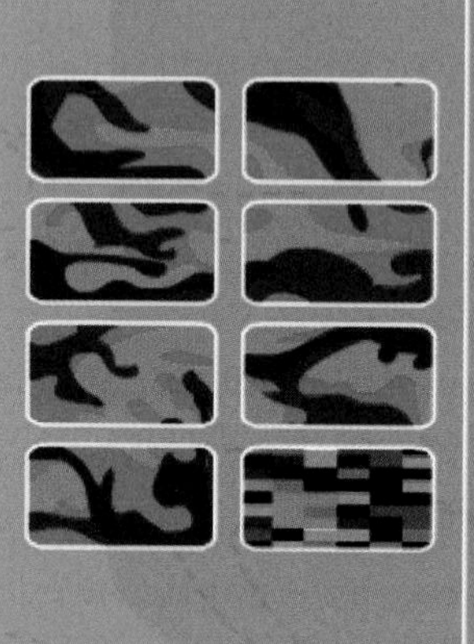

Female *Anopheles* mosquitoes which enter dwellings and bite indoors really have only one choice for a host — a human.

This is why things which keep mosquitoes out of houses (screens, air conditioners, etc.) are so effective in reducing malaria.

However, the countries where malaria is especially severe are also some of the world's poorest nations, and dwellings tend to be quite primitive and open-air.

While there are a few options to combat mosquitoes and the spread of malaria, nothing has been as long-acting, cost-effective and powerful as DDT.

Not Just Words

When Rachel Carson wrote *Silent Spring* to warn of the environmental dangers of pesticides (see p. 290), one of her targets was the widespread use of DDT in American agriculture. DDT was an effective pesticide, but used indiscriminately it had long-term side effects and harmed animals, especially birds. Environmentalists succeeded in virtually banning the use of DDT in the rich industrialized countries. But now there's an interest in some third world nations in restoring its use. Why? Because DDT kills or repels the mosquitoes responsible for malaria, one of the most insidious diseases in some African and Asian countries. One group called Africa Fighting Malaria <http://fightingmalaria.org/> makes a case for "the limited use of DDT for spraying homes and hospitals" in a

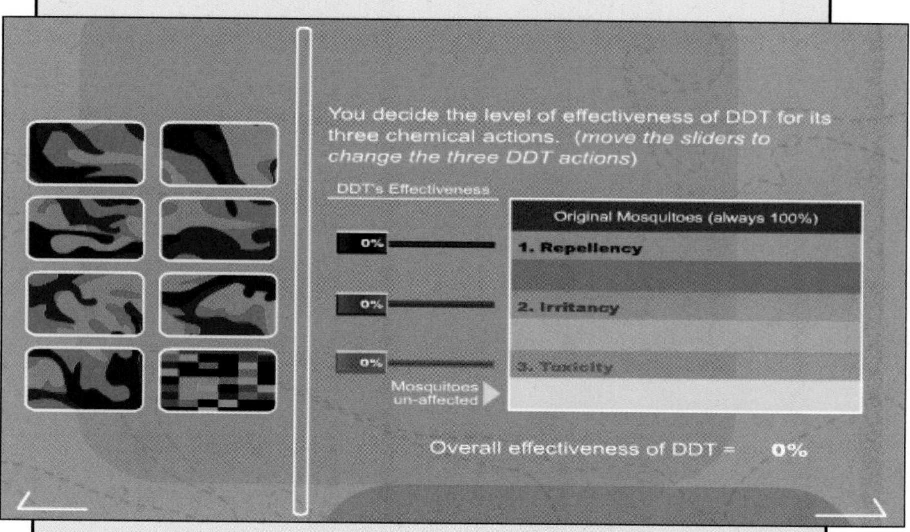

Flash presentation on its Web site. One screen, for example, uses clickable numbers to explain how mosquitoes cause malaria. Another demonstrates how selective spraying of DDT reduces the risk of getting infected by disease-carrying insects. We reproduce several of the screens here. Study them, or check to see if the full Flash presentation is available on the Web site. Then discuss either in class or in a short paper how well a complex causal argument might be made in multimedia environments like the Web and for which audiences they might prove most effective.

Developing Causal Arguments

Formulating a Claim

Of course, you might decide to write a wildly exaggerated or parodic causal argument for humorous purposes. Humorist Dave Barry does precisely this when he tries to explain the causes of El Niño and other weather phenomena: "So we see that the true cause of bad weather, contrary to what they have been claiming all these years, is TV weather forecasters, who have also single-handedly destroyed the ozone layer via overuse of hair spray." Most of the causal reasoning you do, however, will take a more serious approach to subjects you, your family, and friends care about. To begin creating a strong causal claim, try listing some of the effects—events or phenomena—you'd like to know the causes of:

- *What are the biological causes of aging in animals and humans?*
- *What's really responsible for the latest tuition hike?*
- *What has led to warnings of "contamination" along your favorite creek?*
- *Why has the divorce rate leveled off in recent decades?*
- *Why do so few Americans vote, even in major elections?*

For more than a century, mysterious lights have been observed in the night skies near the small west Texas town of Marfa. Numerous *causes* have been advanced, from Indian campfires to swamp gas, some more probable than others. Such unexplained phenomena often have the *effect* of attracting tourists.

Or try moving in the opposite direction, listing some phenomena or causes you're interested in and then hypothesizing what kinds of effects they may produce:

- *What will happen if your campus institutes (or abolishes) an honor code?*
- *What will be the effects of a total crackdown on peer-to-peer file sharing?*
- *What will happen if more conservative (or liberal) judges are appointed to the Supreme Court?*
- *What will happen when China and India become thriving first-world nations?*

Read a little about the causal issues that interest you most, and then try them out on friends and colleagues. Can they suggest ways to refocus or clarify what you want to do? Can they offer leads to finding information about your subject? If you've already asserted some cause-and-effect relationships, can they offer counterexamples or refutations? Finally, map out a rough statement about the causal relationship you want to explore:

A might cause (or might be caused by) B for the following reasons:

1.
2.
3.

Such a statement should be tentative because writing a causal argument will often be a research exercise in which you uncover the facts, not assume them to be true. Often, your early assumptions (*Tuition was raised to renovate the stadium*) might be undermined by the facts you later discover (*Tuition doesn't fund the construction or maintenance of campus buildings*).

Developing the Argument

Once you've drafted a claim, you can explore the cause-effect relationship(s), drawing out the reasons, warrants, and evidence that can support the claim most effectively:

Claim	**Losing seasons caused the football coach to lose his job.**
Reason	**The team lost more than half its games for three seasons in a row.**
Warrant	**Winning is the key to success for major-team college coaches.**
Evidence	**For the last ten years, coaches with more than two losing seasons in a row have lost their jobs.**

Claim	**Certain career patterns cause women to be paid less than men.**
Reason	**Women's career patterns differ from men's, and in spite of changes in the relative pay of other groups, women's pay still lags behind that of men.**
Warrant	**Successful careers are made during the period between ages twenty-five and thirty-five.**
Evidence	**Women often drop out of or reduce work during the decade between ages twenty-five and thirty-five in order to raise families.**

In further developing a causal argument, you can draw on many strategies we've already touched on. In the article the following passage is excerpted from, for instance, Stephen King uses dozens of examples—from *The Texas Chainsaw Massacre, The Gory Ones,* and *Invasion of the Body Snatchers* to *Night of the Living Dead, Psycho, The Amityville Horror,* and *The Thing*—in answering a causal question: Why do people love horror movies?

The mythic horror movie, like the sick joke, has a dirty job to do. It deliberately appeals to all that is worst in us. It is morbidity unchained, our most base instincts let free, our nastiest fantasies realized . . . and it all happens, fittingly enough, in the dark. For those reasons, good liberals often shy away from horror films. For myself, I like to see the most aggressive of them—*Dawn of the Dead,* for instance—as lifting a trap door in the civilized forebrain and throwing a basket of raw meat to the hungry alligators swimming around in that subterranean river beneath.

Why bother? Because it keeps them from getting out, man. It keeps them down there and me up here. It was Lennon and McCartney who said that all you need is love, and I would agree with that.

As long as you keep the gators fed.

–Stephen King, "Why We Crave Horror Movies"

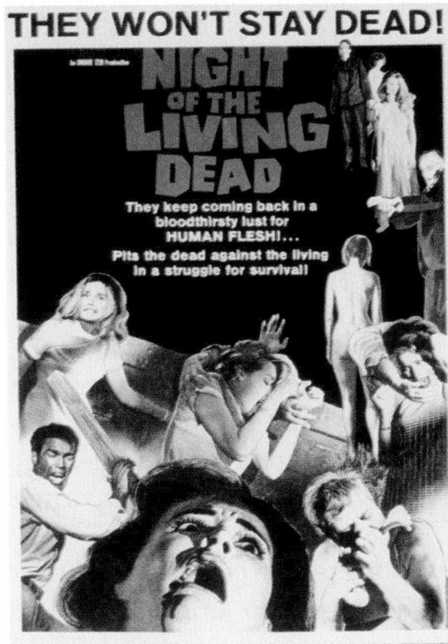

Night of the Living Dead—satisfying uncivilized cravings since 1968

Another way to support (or undermine) a causal argument is through the use of analogies. In such an argument, the strength will lie in how closely you can relate the two phenomena being compared. In exploring why women consistently earn less pay than men even when they're performing the same jobs, Sarah Banda Purvis draws an analogy between working women and sports:

> **An analogy I use when describing my experiences as a female manager in corporate America is that I was allowed to sit on the bench but never given a chance to get on the field and play in the game.**
>
> **–Sarah Banda Purvis, "What Do Working Women Want in the 21st Century?"**

She goes on to trace the effects that constantly being relegated to the "bench" has on earning power. If you find this analogy unsatisfactory, you might suggest that it falsely portrays the causal relationship of women and promotion. After all, benchwarmers are usually players who don't perform as well as those on the field. Surely Purvis doesn't want to suggest that women aren't moving up in the business world because they don't play the game as well as men.

Establishing causes for physical effects—like diseases—often calls for another means of support: testing hypotheses, or theories about possible causes. This kind of reasoning, often highly technical, helped to identify a mystery disease that, years ago, struck some fifty people in Quebec City. Puzzled by cases all involving the same effects (nausea, shortness of breath, cough, stomach pain, weight loss, and a marked blue-gray coloration), doctors at first hypothesized that the common cause was severe vitamin deficiency. But too many cases in too short a time made this explanation unlikely; after all, sudden epidemics of vitamin deficiency are rare. In addition, postmortem examinations of the twenty people who died revealed severe damage to the heart muscle and the liver, features inconsistent with the vitamin-deficiency hypothesis. So the doctors sought a clue to the mysterious disease in something the victims shared: all fifty had been beer lovers and had, in fact, drunk a particular brew.

It seemed possible that the illness was somehow connected to that brand, brewed in both Quebec City and Montreal. But Montreal had no outbreak of the disease. The hypothesis, then, was further refined: Could the brewing processes be different in the two cities? Bingo. The Quebec brewery had added a cobalt compound to its product to enhance the beer's foaminess; the Montreal brewery had not. Furthermore, the compound had been added only a month before the first victims became ill.

Yet doctors in this case were still cautious about the causal connection because the cobalt hadn't been present in sufficient quantities to kill a normal person. Yet twenty had died. After persistent scientific analysis, the doctors decided that this fact must be related to the victims' drinking habits, which in some way reduced their resistance to the chemical. For those twenty people, a normally nonlethal dose of cobalt had, unfortunately, proven fatal.

Not all the evidence in compelling causal arguments needs to be so strictly scientific. Many causal arguments rely on ethnographic observations—that is, on the systematic study of ordinary people in their daily routines. How would you explain, for example, why, when people meet head-on, some step aside and some do not? In an argument that attempts to account for such behavior, investigators Frank Willis, Joseph Gier, and David Smith observed "1,038 displacements involving 3,141 persons" at a Kansas City shopping mall. In results that surprised the investigators, "gallantry" seemed to play a significant role in causing people to step aside for one another—more so than other causes the investigators had anticipated (such as deferring to someone who's physically stronger or higher in status). Doubtless you've read of other such studies—perhaps in psychology courses.

Chong-suk Han explores a variety of circumstances that may lead gay Asian American men to not feel accepted by gay or Asian communities. He supports his argument with examples from books, magazines, surveys, and social discourse.

LINK TO P. 644

Yet another method of supporting a causal argument is to provide evidence for significant correlations. In such an argument, you try to show that if A occurs, B is also likely to occur—for example, if students come from families with high incomes, they're also likely to do well on standardized tests. (That's a correlation that has been repeatedly established.) And as we noted in an earlier chapter, there also seems to be a positive correlation between the attractiveness of college instructors and the teaching evaluations they receive. You may be most familiar with correlations from statistical procedures that enable you to predict, within a degree of certainty, how likely it is that two elements or events will occur together. Recent advances in the human genome project, for example, have identified "clusters" of genes that, when found in correlation with one another, strongly predict the occurrence of certain cancers.

Using a correlation as evidence of causation can be an especially complex task, though. In many cases, B proves to be the cause of A rather than the other way around, or the correlation turns out to be a coincidence, or A and B are both found to be effects of some other cause, rather than one of them causing the other. For example, it was once thought that when an elderly woman falls and her leg or hip is found to be broken, the break is caused by the fall, whereas medical experts now believe that the causal relationship usually runs the other way: the snapping of bones thinned by osteoporosis causes the fall. As you might guess, arguments about correlations keep researchers busy.

Finally, you may want to consider using personal experience in support of a causal argument. Indeed, people's experiences generally lead them to seek out or to avoid various causes and effects. If you're consistently praised for your writing ability, chances are that you'll look for opportunities to produce that pleasant effect. If three times in a row you get sick after eating shrimp, you'll almost certainly identify the shellfish as the cause of your difficulties and stop eating it. Personal experience can also help build your credibility as a writer, gain the empathy of your listeners, and thus support your causal claim. Although one person's experiences cannot ordinarily be universalized, they can still argue eloquently for causal relationships. Leslie Marmon Silko uses personal experience to explain her shift from studying to become a lawyer to becoming a writer/photographer/activist, arguing that the best way to seek justice isn't through the law but through the power of stories:

> When I was a sophomore in high school I decided law school was the place to seek justice. . . . I should have paid more attention to the lesson of the Laguna Pueblo land claims lawsuit from my childhood: The lawsuit was not settled until I was in law school. The U.S. Court of Indian Claims found in favor of the Pueblo of Laguna, but the Indian Claims Court never gives back land wrongfully taken; the court only pays tribes for the land. . . . The Laguna people wanted the land they cherished; instead, they got twenty-five cents for each of the six million acres stolen by the state. The lawsuit had lasted twenty years, so the lawyers' fees amounted to nearly $2 million.
>
> I completed three semesters in the American Indian Law School Fellowship Program before I realized that injustice is built into the Anglo-American legal system. . . . But I continued in law school until our criminal law class read an appeal to the U.S. Supreme Court to stop the execution of a retarded black man convicted of strangling a white librarian in Washington, D.C., in 1949. The majority on the Court refused to stop the execution, though it was clear that the man was so retarded that he had no comprehension of his crime. That case was the breaking point for me. I wanted nothing to do with such a barbaric legal system.
>
> My time in law school was not wasted: I had gained invaluable insights into the power structure of mainstream society, and I continue

> **to follow developments in the law to calculate prevailing political winds. It seems to me there is no better way to uncover the deepest values of a culture than to observe the operation of that culture's system of justice.**
>
> **[But] I decided the only way to seek justice was through the power of stories.**
>
> **–Leslie Marmon Silko, *Yellow Woman and a Beauty of Spirit: Essays on Native American Life Today***

All these strategies—the use of examples, analogies, testing hypotheses, experimental evidence, correlations, and personal experience—can help you support a causal argument or undermine a causal claim you regard as faulty. However, you may still have to convince readers that the reasons you offer are indeed compelling. In terms of causal arguments, that may mean distinguishing among *immediate, necessary,* and *sufficient* reasons. In the case of the mysterious illness in Quebec City, the immediate reasons for illness were the symptoms themselves: nausea, shortness of breath, and so on. But they weren't the root causes of the disease. Drinking the particular beer in question served as a necessary reason: without the tainted beer, the illness wouldn't have occurred. However, the researchers had to search much harder for the sufficient reason—the reason that will cause the effect (the illness) if it's present. In the case of the Quebec City beer, that reason turned out to be the addition of cobalt.

Myriam Marquez shares her analysis of the necessary and sufficient reasons why she and her family speak Spanish in public places.

LINK TO P. 754

If Everything's an Argument . . .

Choose any one or two of the examples or figures in this chapter, and make a stab at explaining why it might have been chosen for the book—over and above the obvious fact that it illustrates a point about causal arguments. For example, do you suspect that the "Why Are We So Fat?" figure leads off the chapter mainly because it would get your attention? Wasn't there a risk that it might repel or offend you? What other considerations might have been behind the decision to use it? Did the fact that the image originally appeared in *National Geographic* make it a plausible choice for a college text? Write at least a paragraph of causal analysis on the item(s) you've selected.

Even everyday causal analysis can draw on this distinction among reasons as well. What caused you, for instance, to pursue a college education? Immediate reasons might be that you needed to prepare for a career of some kind or that you had planned to do so for years. But what are the necessary reasons, the ones without which your pursuit of higher education couldn't occur? Adequate funds? Good test scores and academic record? The expectations of your family? You might even explore possible sufficient reasons, those that—if present—will guarantee the effect of your pursuing higher education. In such a case, you may be the only person with enough information to determine what the sufficient reasons might be.

Considering Design and Visuals

Don't forget the importance of design decisions—fonts, headings, links in online arguments—when composing causal arguments. Not infrequently, you may find that the best way to illustrate a causal relation-

The National Institute of Mental Health uses a visual presentation coupled with text to argue that male Latino immigrants often do not seek help for depression because of cultural taboos about mental illness. Consider how this advertisement would grab someone's attention over a purely text-based version.

LINK TO P. 781

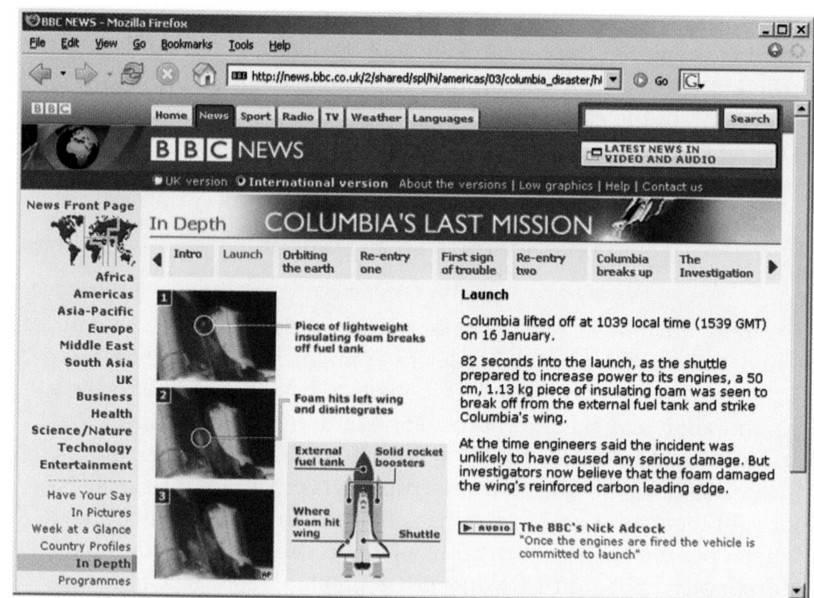

The BBC News provided this graphic to supplement its coverage of a NASA report detailing the cause of the breakup of the Space Shuttle *Columbia* in 2003. Note how the simple words and illustrations make a complex chain of events comprehensible to the general public.

Why have programs of financial aid failed to bring relief to many impoverished countries? Cartoonists Cox & Forkum offer one explanation.

ship is to present it visually. Consider the way even a simple graphic—one that combines words and images—helps readers grasp how or why something happened (see the figure on the facing page).

Or you might study the intriguing ways that editorial cartoonists embed causal relationships in some of their pieces, inviting readers to find causal connections as they interpret the images. You could write a book—and some scholars have—on the political relationships and historical circumstances summarized in the causal argument in the figure above.

Key Features of Causal Arguments

In drafting your own causal argument, you'll need to do the following:

- Thoroughly question every cause-and-effect relationship in the argument, both those you suggest yourself and others already in play.
- Show that the causes and effects you've suggested are highly probable and backed by evidence, or show what's wrong with faulty causal reasoning you may be critiquing.

- Assess any links between causal relationships (*what* leads to, or follows from, *what*).
- Show that your explanations of any causal chains are accurate, or show where links in a causal chain break down.
- Show that plausible cause-effect explanations haven't been ignored or that the possibility of multiple causes or effects has been given due consideration.

In developing a causal argument fully, you'll address many of these items, though their order may vary. You may want to open an essay dramatically by describing an effect and then "flash back" to its multiple causes. Or you might decide to open with a well-known phenomenon, identify it as a cause, and then trace its effects. Or you might begin by suggesting what plausible explanations for an event have been ignored, for one reason or another. In any case, you should sketch an organizational plan and get reactions to it from your instructor, writing center consultants, and colleagues before proceeding to a full draft. When the draft is complete, you should again look for critical readers willing to test the strength of your causal argument.

GUIDE to writing a causal argument

Finding a Topic

Chances are that a little time spent brainstorming—either with friends or other students, or on paper—will turn up some good possibilities for causal arguments of several kinds, including those that grow out of your personal experience. *Just exactly what did lead to my much higher GPA last term?* Beyond your own personal concerns, you may find a good number of public issues that lend themselves to causal analysis and argument: *What factors have led to the near bankruptcy of the nation's major airlines? What will happen if the United States continues to refuse to sign the Kyoto Protocol aimed at reducing greenhouse gas emissions? What effects have been caused by the move to pay professional athletes astronomical sums of money?* As you're brainstorming possibilities for a causal argument of your own, don't ignore important current campus issues: *What have been the effects of recent increases in tuition* (or *What factors caused the increases*)*? What are the likely outcomes of shifting the academic calendar from a quarter to a semester system? If, as some argue, there has been a significant increase of racism and homophobia on campus, what has caused that increase? What are its consequences?*

Finally, remember that it's fair game to question existing assumptions about causality for being inaccurate or not probing deeply enough into the reasons for a phenomenon. You can raise doubts about the facts or assumptions that others have made and, perhaps, offer a better causal connection. For example, some writers have argued that violent video games will lead the teenagers obsessed with them into antisocial behavior. Others, however, have challenged that causal argument, pointing out that juvenile delinquency is, in fact, declining. Why? Maybe teens are too busy playing Resident Evil 4.

Researching Your Topic

Causal arguments will lead you to many different resources:

- current news media—especially magazines and newspapers (online or in print)
- online databases
- scholarly journals

- books written on your subject (here you can do a keyword search, either in your library or online)
- blogs, Web sites, listservs, or newsgroups devoted to your subject

In addition, why not carry out some field research of your own? Conduct interviews with appropriate authorities on your subject, or create a questionnaire aimed at establishing a range of opinion on your subject. The information you get from interviews or from analyzing responses to a questionnaire can provide evidence to back up your claim(s).

Formulating a Claim

First, identify the kind of causal argument you expect to make—one moving from cause(s) to effect(s); one moving from effect(s) to cause(s); or one involving a series of links, with Cause A leading to B, which then leads to C. (See pp. 288–291 for a review of these kinds of arguments.) Or it may be that you'll be debunking an existing cause-effect claim.

Your next move may be to explore your own relationship to your subject. What do you know about the subject and its causes and effects? Why do you favor (or disagree with) the claim? What significant reasons can you offer in support of your position? In short, you should end this process of exploration by formulating a brief claim or thesis about a particular causal relationship. It should include *a statement that says, in effect, A causes (or does not cause, or is caused by) B, and a summary of the reasons supporting this causal relationship.* Remember to make sure that your thesis is as specific as possible and that it's sufficiently controversial or interesting to hold your readers' interest. Recognize, too, than any such claim is tentative—subject to change as your project develops and you learn more about your subject.

Examples of Causal Claims

- Right-to-carry gun laws are, in part, responsible for decreased rates of violent crimes in states that have approved such legislation.
- Newer Web-based techniques for campaign fund-raising will ultimately weaken the power of the national political parties and increase the clout of small, special interest groups.
- The proliferation of images in film, television, and computer-generated texts is changing literacy.
- The many extensions to the copyright terms have led to a serious imbalance between the necessary incentive to creators and the right of the

public to information, thereby closing off the public commons; doing away, in effect, with the fair use doctrine; and adding billions of dollars to the coffers of Disney and other huge entertainment conglomerates.

- Removing pluses and minuses from our school's grading system will have no effect on student grade point averages or grade inflation.

Preparing a Proposal

If your instructor asks you to prepare a proposal for your project, here's a format that may help:

State the thesis of your argument completely. If you're having trouble doing so, try outlining it in Toulmin terms:

Claim:

Reason(s):

Warrant(s):

- **Explain why this argument deserves attention. Why is it important for your readers to consider?**
- **Specify whom you hope to reach through your argument and why this group of readers is an appropriate audience. What interest or investment do they have in the issue? Why will they (or should they) be concerned?**
- **Briefly identify and explore the major challenges you expect to face in supporting your argument. Will demonstrating a clear causal link between A and B be particularly difficult? Will the data you need to support the claim be hard to obtain?**
- **List the strategies you expect to use in researching your argument. Will you be interviewing? Surveying opinion? Conducting library and online searches? Other?**
- **Briefly identify and explore the major counterarguments you might expect in response to your argument.**
- **Consider what format, genre, or media will work best for your argument. Will you be preparing a Web site? A press release? An editorial for the local newspaper? A report for an organization you belong to?**

Thinking about Organization

Whatever genre or format you decide to use, your causal argument should address the following elements:

- a specific causal claim somewhere in the paper: *Devastating flash floods associated with El Niño were responsible for the dramatic loss of homes in central California in early 2003.*
- an explanation of the claim's significance or importance: *Claims for damage from flooding put some big insurance companies out of business; as a result, homeowners couldn't get coverage and many who lost their homes had to declare bankruptcy.*
- supporting evidence sufficient to support each cause or effect—or, in an argument based on a series of causal links, evidence to support the relationships among the links: *The amount of rain that fell in central California in early 2003 was 50 percent above normal, leading inexorably to rapidly rising rivers and creeks.*
- consideration of alternative causes and effects, and evidence that you understand these alternatives and have thought carefully about them before rejecting them: *Although some say that excessive and sloppy logging and poor building codes were responsible for the loss of homes, the evidence supporting these alternative causes is not convincing.*

Getting and Giving Response

All arguments can benefit from the scrutiny of others. Your instructor may assign you to a peer group for the purpose of reading and responding to each other's drafts; if not, get some response on your own from some serious readers or consultants at a writing center. You can use the following questions to evaluate a draft. If you're evaluating someone else's draft, be sure to illustrate your points with examples. Specific comments are always more helpful than general observations.

The Claim

- What's most effective about the claim? What are its strengths?
- Is the claim sufficiently qualified?
- Is the claim specific enough to be clear? How could it be narrowed and focused?
- How strong is the relationship between the claim and the reasons given to support it? How could that relationship be made more explicit?
- Is it immediately evident why the claim is important? How could it be rephrased in a way that more forcefully and clearly suggests its significance?

- Does the claim reveal a causal connection? How could it be revised to make the causal links clearer?

Evidence for the Claim

- What's the strongest evidence offered for the claim? What, if any, evidence needs to be strengthened?
- Is enough evidence offered that these particular causes are responsible for the effect that has been identified, that these particular effects result from the identified cause, or that a series of causes and effects are linked? If not, what kind of additional evidence is needed? What kinds of sources might provide this evidence?
- How credible and persuasive will the sources likely be to potential readers? What other kinds of sources might be more credible and persuasive?
- Is the evidence in support of the claim simply announced, or are its appropriateness and significance analyzed? Is a more detailed discussion needed?
- Have all the major alternative causes and effects as well as objections to the claim been considered? What support is offered for rejecting these alternatives? Where is additional support needed?

Organization and Style

- How are the parts of the argument organized? Is this organization effective, or would some other structure work better?
- Will readers understand the relationships among the claims, supporting reasons, warrants, and evidence? If not, what could be done to make those connections clearer? Are more transitional words and phrases needed? Would headings or graphic devices (diagrams, flowcharts, illustrations) help?
- Are the transitions or links from point to point, paragraph to paragraph, and sentence to sentence clear and effective? If not, how could they be improved?
- Is the style suited to the subject? Is it too formal? Too casual? Too technical? Too bland? Too geeky? How can it be improved?
- Which sentences seem particularly effective? Which ones seem weakest, and how could they be improved? Should some short sentences be combined, or should any long ones be separated into two or more sentences?
- How effective are the paragraphs? Do any seem too skimpy or too long? How can they be improved?

- Which words or phrases seem particularly effective, vivid, and memorable? Do any seem dull, unclear, or inappropriate for the audience or the writer's purpose? Are definitions provided for technical or other terms that readers might not know?

Spelling, Punctuation, Mechanics, Documentation, Format

- Are there any errors in spelling, punctuation, capitalization, and the like?
- Is an appropriate and consistent style of documentation used for parenthetical citations and the list of works cited or references? (See Chapter 20.)
- Does the paper or project follow an appropriate format? Is it appropriately designed and attractively presented? How could it be improved? If it's a Web site, do all the links work?

RESPOND•

1. The causes of some of the following events and phenomena are quite well known and frequently discussed. But do you understand them well enough yourself to spell out the causes to someone else? Working in a group, see how well (and in how much detail) you can explain each of the following events or phenomena. Which explanations are relatively clear-cut, and which seem more open to debate?

   tornadoes

   the Burning Man festival

   the collapse of communism in Eastern Europe in 1989

   earthquakes

   the common cold

   the popularity of the *Harry Potter* films

   the itching caused by a mosquito bite

   the economic recovery of 2004–2005

   a skid in your car on a slippery road

   the destruction of the Space Shuttle *Columbia*

   the rise in cases of autism

2. One of the fallacies of argument discussed in Chapter 17 is the *post hoc, ergo propter hoc* fallacy: "after this, therefore because of this." Causal arguments are particularly prone to this kind of fallacious reasoning, in which a writer asserts a causal relationship between two entirely unconnected events. After Elvis Presley's death, for instance, oil prices in the United States rose precipitously—but it would be a real stretch to argue that the King's passing caused gas prices to skyrocket.

   Because causal arguments can easily fall prey to this fallacy, you might find it useful to try your hand at creating and defending an absurd connection of this kind. Begin by asserting a causal link between two events or phenomena that likely have no relationship: *The enormous popularity of the iPod is partially due to global warming.* Then spend a page or so spinning out an imaginative argument to defend the claim: *A generation terrified by the prospects of drastic weather change try to drown out their fears in earsplitting music.* . . . It's OK to have fun with this exercise, but see how convincing you can be at generating plausible arguments.

3. Working with a group, write a big "Why?" on a sheet of paper or computer screen, and then generate a list of *why* questions. Don't be too critical of the initial list:

   Why?

   — *do people grow old?*

   — *do dogs and cats live such short lives?*

   — *do college students binge drink?*

   — *do teenage boys drive so fast?*

   — *do people cry?*

   Generate as long a list as you can in fifteen minutes or so. Then decide which of the questions might make plausible starting points for intriguing causal arguments.

4. Here's a schematic causal analysis of one event, exploring the difference among immediate, necessary, and sufficient causes. Critique and revise the analysis as you see fit. Then create another of your own, beginning with a different event, phenomenon, incident, fad, or effect.

   Event: Traffic fatality at an intersection

   Immediate Cause: SUV runs a red light and totals a Miata, killing its driver

   Necessary Cause: Two drivers navigating Friday rush-hour traffic (if no driving, then no accident)

   Sufficient Cause: SUV driver distracted by a cell phone conversation

What Makes a Serial Killer?

LA DONNA BEATY

Jeffrey Dahmer, John Wayne Gacy, Mark Allen Smith, Richard Chase, Ted Bundy—the list goes on and on. These five men alone have been responsible for at least ninety deaths, and many suspect that their victims may total twice that number. They are serial killers, the most feared and hated of criminals. What deep, hidden secret makes them lust for blood? What can possibly motivate a person to kill over and over again with no guilt, no remorse, no hint of human compassion? What makes a serial killer?

The cause-effect relationship is raised in a question: What (the causes) makes a serial killer (the effect)?

Serial killings are not a new phenomenon. In 1798, for example, Micajah and Wiley Harpe traveled the backwoods of Kentucky and Tennessee in a violent, year-long killing spree that left at least twenty—and possibly as many as thirty-eight—men, women, and children dead. Their crimes were especially chilling as they seemed particularly to enjoy grabbing small children by the ankles and smashing their heads against trees (Holmes and DeBurger 28). In modern society, however, serial killings have grown to near epidemic proportions. Ann Rule, a respected author and expert on serial murders, stated in a seminar at the University of Louisville on serial murder that between 3,500 and 5,000 people become victims of serial murder each year in the United States alone (qtd. in Holmes and DeBurger 21). Many others estimate that there are close to 350 serial killers currently at large in our society (Holmes and DeBurger 22).

An important term *(serial killer)* is defined through examples.

Authority is cited to emphasize the importance of the causal question.

La Donna Beaty wrote this essay while she was a student at Sinclair Community College in Dayton, Ohio. In the essay, she explores the complex web of possible causes—cultural, psychological, genetic, and others—that may help to produce a serial killer. The essay follows MLA style.

Fascination with murder and murderers is not new, but researchers in recent years have made great strides in determining the characteristics of criminals. Looking back, we can see how naive early experts were in their evaluations: in 1911, for example, Italian criminologist Cesare Lombrosco concluded that "murderers as a group [are] biologically degenerate [with] bloodshot eyes, aquiline noses, curly black hair, strong jaws, big ears, thin lips, and menacing grins" (qtd. in Lunde 84). Today, however, we don't expect killers to have fangs that drip human blood, and many realize that the boy-next-door may be doing more than woodworking in his basement. While there are no specific physical characteristics shared by all serial killers, they are almost always male and 92 percent are white. Most are between the ages of twenty-five and thirty-five and often physically attractive. While they may hold a job, many switch employment frequently as they become easily frustrated when advancement does not come as quickly as expected. They tend to believe that they are entitled to whatever they desire but feel that they should have to exert no effort to attain their goals (Samenow 88, 96). What could possibly turn attractive, ambitious human beings into cold-blooded monsters?

Evidence about general characteristics of serial killers is presented.

One popular theory suggests that many murderers are the product of our violent society. Our culture tends to approve of violence and find it acceptable, even preferable, in many circumstances (Holmes and DeBurger 27). According to research done in 1970, one out of every four men and one out of every six women believed that it was appropriate for a husband to hit his wife under certain conditions (Holmes and DeBurger 33). This emphasis on violence is especially prevalent in television programs. Violence occurs in 80 percent of all prime-time shows, while cartoons, presumably made for children, average eighteen violent acts per hour. It is estimated that by the age of eighteen, the average child will have viewed more than 16,000 television murders (Holmes and

One possible cause is explored: violence in society.

Evidence, including statistics and authority, is offered to support the first cause.

DeBurger 34). Some experts feel that children demonstrate increasingly aggressive behavior with each violent act they view (Lunde 15) and become so accustomed to violence that these acts seem normal (35). In fact, most serial killers do begin to show patterns of aggressive behavior at a young age. It is, therefore, possible that after viewing increasing amounts of violence, such children determine that this is acceptable behavior; when they are then punished for similar actions, they may become confused and angry and eventually lash out by committing horrible, violent acts.

Another theory concentrates on the family atmosphere into which the serial killer is born. Most killers state that they experienced psychological abuse as children and never established good relationships with the male figures in their lives (Ressler, Burgess, and Douglas 19). As children, they were often rejected by their parents and received little nurturing (Lunde 94; Holmes and DeBurger 64–70). It has also been established that the families of serial killers often move repeatedly, never allowing the child to feel a sense of stability; in many cases, they are also forced to live outside the family home before reaching the age of eighteen (Ressler, Burgess, and Douglas 19–20). Our culture's tolerance for violence may overlap with such family dynamics: with 79 percent of the population believing that slapping a twelve-year-old is either necessary, normal, or good, it is no wonder that serial killers relate tales of physical abuse (Holmes and DeBurger 30; Ressler, Burgess, and Douglas 19–20) and view themselves as the "black sheep" of the family. They may even, perhaps unconsciously, assume this same role in society.

A second possible cause is introduced: family context.

Evidence is offered in support of the second cause.

While the foregoing analysis portrays the serial killer as a lost, lonely, abused, little child, another theory, based on the same information, gives an entirely different view. In this analysis, the killer is indeed rejected by his family but only after being repeatedly defiant, sneaky, and threatening. As verbal lies and destructiveness

An alternative analysis of the evidence in support of the second cause is explored.

increase, the parents give the child the distance he seems to want in order to maintain a small amount of domestic peace (Samenow 13). This interpretation suggests that the killer shapes his parents much more than his parents shape him. It also denies that the media can influence a child's mind and turn him into something that he doesn't already long to be. Since most children view similar amounts of violence, the argument goes, a responsible child filters what he sees and will not resort to criminal activity no matter how acceptable it seems to be (Samenow 15–18). In 1930, the noted psychologist Alfred Adler seemed to find this true of any criminal. As he put it, "With criminals it is different: they have a private logic, a private intelligence. They are suffering from a wrong outlook upon the world, a wrong estimate of their own importance and the importance of other people" (qtd. in Samenow 20).

A third possible cause is introduced: mental instability.

Evidence in support of the third cause, including a series of examples, is offered.

Most people agree that Jeffrey Dahmer or Ted Bundy had to be "crazy" to commit horrendous multiple murders, and scientists have long maintained that serial killers are indeed mentally disturbed (Lunde 48). While the percentage of murders committed by mental hospital patients is much lower than that among the general population (35), it cannot be ignored that the rise in serial killings happened at almost the same time as the deinstitutionalization movement in the mental health care system during the 1960s (Markman and Bosco 266). While reform was greatly needed in the mental health care system, it has now become nearly impossible to hospitalize those with severe problems. In the United States, people have a constitutional right to remain mentally ill. Involuntary commitment can only be accomplished if the person is deemed dangerous to self, dangerous to others, or gravely disabled. However, in the words of Ronald Markman, "According to the way that the law is interpreted, if you can go to the mailbox to pick up your Social Security check, you're not gravely disabled even if you think you're living on Mars"; even if a patient is thought to be dangerous, he or she cannot be held longer than ninety days unless it can be proved that the patient actually committed dangerous acts while in the hospital (Markman and Bosco 267). Many of the most heinous criminals have had long histories of mental illness but could not be hospitalized due to these stringent requirements. Richard Chase, the notorious Vampire of Sacramento, believed that he needed blood in order to survive, and while in the care of a psychiatric hospital, he often killed birds and other small animals in order to quench this desire. When he was released, he went on to kill eight people, one of them an eighteen-month-old baby (Biondi and Hecox 206). Edmund Kemper was equally insane. At the age of fifteen, he killed both of his grandparents and spent five years in a psychiatric facility. Doctors determined that he was "cured" and released him into an unsuspecting society. He killed eight women, including his own mother (Lunde 53–56). In another case, the world was soon to be disturbed by a cataclysmic earthquake, and Herbert Mullin knew that he had been appointed by God to prevent the catastrophe. The fervor of his religious delusion resulted in a death toll of thirteen (Lunde 63–81). All of these men had been treated for their mental disorders, and all were released by doctors who did not have enough proof to hold them against their will.

Recently, studies have given increasing consideration to the genetic makeup of serial killers. The connection between biology and behavior is strengthened by research in which scientists have been able to develop a violently aggressive strain of mice simply through selective inbreeding (Taylor 23). These studies have caused scientists to become increasingly interested in the limbic system of the brain, which houses the amygdala, an almond-shaped structure located in the front of the temporal lobe. It has long been known that surgically altering that portion of the brain, in an operation known as a lobotomy, is one way of controlling behavior. This

A fourth possible cause is introduced: genetic makeup.

surgery was used frequently in the 1960s but has since been discontinued as it also erases most of a person's personality. More recent developments, however, have shown that temporal lobe epilepsy causes electrical impulses to be discharged directly into the amygdala. When this electronic stimulation is re-created in the laboratory, it causes violent behavior in lab animals. Additionally, other forms of epilepsy do not cause abnormalities in behavior, except during seizure activity. Temporal lobe epilepsy is linked with a wide range of antisocial behavior, including anger, paranoia, and aggression. It is also interesting to note that this form of epilepsy produces extremely unusual brain waves. These waves have been found in only 10 to 15 percent of the general population, but over 79 percent of known serial killers test positive for these waves (Taylor 28–33).

Statistical evidence in support of the fourth cause is offered.

The look at biological factors that control human behavior is by no means limited to brain waves or other brain abnormalities. Much work is also being done with neurotransmitters, levels of testosterone, and patterns of trace minerals. While none of these studies is conclusive, they all show a high correlation between antisocial behavior and chemical interactions within the body (Taylor 63–69).

A fifth possible cause—heavy use of alcohol—is introduced and immediately qualified.

One of the most common traits that all researchers have noted among serial killers is heavy use of alcohol. Whether this correlation is brought about by external factors or whether alcohol is an actual stimulus that causes certain behavior is still unclear, but the idea deserves consideration. Lunde found that the majority of those who commit murder had been drinking beforehand and commonly had a urine alcohol level of between .20 and .29, nearly twice the legal level of intoxication (31–32). Additionally, 70 percent of the families that reared serial killers had verifiable records of alcohol abuse (Ressler, Burgess, and Douglas 17). Jeffrey

Dahmer had been arrested in 1981 on charges of drunkenness and, before his release from prison on sexual assault charges, his father had written a heartbreaking letter which pleaded that Jeffrey be forced to undergo treatment for alcoholism, a plea that, if heeded, might have changed the course of future events (Davis 70, 103). Whether alcoholism is a learned behavior or an inherited predisposition is still hotly debated, but a 1979 report issued by Harvard Medical School stated that "[a]lcoholism in the biological parent appears to be a more reliable predictor of alcoholism in the children than any other environmental factor examined" (qtd. in Taylor 117). While alcohol was once thought to alleviate anxiety and depression, we now know that it can aggravate and intensify such moods (Taylor 110), which may lead to irrational feelings of powerlessness that are brought under control only when the killer proves he has the ultimate power to control life and death.

The complexity of causal relationships is emphasized: one cannot say with certainty what produces a particular serial killer.

"Man's inhumanity to man" began when Cain killed Abel, but this legacy has grown to frightening proportions, as evidenced by the vast number of books that line the shelves of modern bookstores—row after row of titles dealing with death, anger, and blood. We may never know what causes a serial killer to exact his revenge on an unsuspecting society. But we need to continue to probe the interior of the human brain to discover the delicate balance of chemicals that controls behavior. We need to be able to fix what goes wrong. We must also work harder to protect our children. Their cries must not go unheard. Their pain must not become so intense that it demands bloody revenge. As today becomes tomorrow, we must remember the words of Ted Bundy, one of the most ruthless serial killers of our time: "Most serial killers are people who kill for the pure pleasure of killing and cannot be rehabilitated. Some of the killers themselves would even say so" (qtd. in Holmes and DeBurger 150).

The conclusion looks toward the future: the web of causes examined here suggests that much more work needs to be done to understand, predict, and ultimately control the behavior of potential serial killers.

Works Cited

Biondi, Ray, and Walt Hecox. The Dracula Killer. New York: Simon, 1992.

Davis, Ron. The Milwaukee Murders. New York: St. Martin's, 1991.

Holmes, Ronald M., and James DeBurger. Serial Murder. Newbury Park, CA: Sage, 1988.

Lunde, Donald T. Murder and Madness. San Francisco: San Francisco Book, 1976.

Markman, Ronald, and Dominick Bosco. Alone with the Devil. New York: Doubleday, 1989.

Ressler, Robert K., Ann W. Burgess, and John E. Douglas. Sexual Homicide—Patterns and Motives. Lexington, MA: Heath, 1988.

Samenow, Stanton E. Inside the Criminal Mind. New York: Times, 1984.

Taylor, Lawrence. Born to Crime. Westport, CT: Greenwood, 1984.

Why Literature Matters

DANA GIOIA

April 10, 2005

In 1780, Massachusetts patriot John Adams wrote to his wife, Abigail, outlining his vision of how American culture might evolve. "I must study politics and war," he prophesied, so "that our sons may have liberty to study mathematics and philosophy." They will add to their studies geography, navigation, commerce, and agriculture, he continued, so that their children may enjoy the "right to study painting, poetry, music."

Adams's bold prophecy proved correct. By the mid 20th century, America boasted internationally preeminent traditions in literature, art, music, dance, theater, and cinema.

But a strange thing has happened in the American arts during the past quarter century. While income rose to unforeseen levels, college attendance ballooned, and access to information increased enormously, the interest young Americans showed in the arts—and especially literature—actually diminished.

According to the 2002 Survey of Public Participation in the Arts, a population study designed and commissioned by the National Endowment for the Arts (and executed by the US Bureau of the Census), arts participation by Americans has declined for eight of the nine major forms that are measured. (Only jazz has shown a tiny increase—thank you, Ken Burns.) The declines have been most severe among younger adults (ages 18–24). The most worrisome finding in the 2002 study, however, is the declining percentage of Americans, especially young adults, reading literature.

That individuals at a time of crucial intellectual and emotional development bypass the joys and challenges of literature is a troubling trend. If it were true that they substituted histories, biographies, or political works for literature, one might not worry. But book reading of any kind is falling as well.

That such a longstanding and fundamental cultural activity should slip so swiftly, especially among young adults, signifies deep transformation in

---

Dana Gioia, a poet and businessman, is chair of the National Endowment for the Arts.

contemporary life. To call attention to the trend, the Arts Endowment issued the reading portion of the Survey as a separate report, "Reading at Risk: A Survey of Literary Reading in America."

The decline in reading has consequences that go beyond literature. The significance of reading has become a persistent theme in the business world. The February issue of *Wired* magazine, for example, sketches a new set of mental skills and habits proper to the 21st century, aptitudes decidedly literary in character: not "linear, logical, analytical talents," author Daniel Pink states, but "the ability to create artistic and emotional beauty, to detect patterns and opportunities, to craft a satisfying narrative." When asked what kind of talents they like to see in management positions, business leaders consistently set imagination, creativity, and higher-order thinking at the top.

Ironically, the value of reading and the intellectual faculties that it inculcates appear most clearly as active and engaged literacy declines. There is now a growing awareness of the consequences of nonreading to the workplace. In 2001 the National Association of Manufacturers polled its members on skill deficiencies among employees. Among hourly workers, poor reading skills ranked second, and 38 percent of employers complained that local schools inadequately taught reading comprehension.

Corporate America makes similar complaints about a skill intimately related to reading—writing. Last year, the College Board reported that corporations spend some $3.1 billion a year on remedial writing instruction for employees, adding that they "express a fair degree of dissatisfaction with the writing of recent college graduates." If the 21st-century American economy requires innovation and creativity, solid reading skills and the imaginative growth fostered by literary reading are central elements in that program.

The decline of reading is also taking its toll in the civic sphere. In a 2000 survey of college seniors from the top 55 colleges, the Roper Organization found that 81 percent could not earn a grade of C on a high school–level history test. A 2003 study of 15- to 26-year-olds' civic knowledge by the National Conference of State Legislatures concluded, "Young people do not understand the ideals of citizenship . . . and their appreciation and support of American democracy is limited."

It is probably no surprise that declining rates of literary reading coincide with declining levels of historical and political awareness among young people. One of the surprising findings of "Reading at Risk" was that literary readers are markedly more civically engaged than nonreaders, scoring two to four times more likely to perform charity work, visit a museum, or attend a sporting event. One reason for their higher social and cultural interactions may lie in the kind of civic and historical knowledge that comes with literary reading.

Unlike the passive activities of watching television and DVDs or surfing the Web, reading is actually a highly active enterprise. Reading requires sustained and focused attention as well as active use of memory and imagination. Literary reading also enhances and enlarges our humility by helping us imagine and understand lives quite different from our own.

Indeed, we sometimes underestimate how large a role literature has played in the evolution of our national identity, especially in that literature often has served to introduce young people to events from the past and principles of civil society and governance. Just as more ancient Greeks learned about moral and political conduct from the epics of Homer than from the dialogues of Plato, so the most important work in the abolitionist movement was the novel "Uncle Tom's Cabin."

Likewise our notions of American populism come more from Walt Whitman's poetic vision than from any political tracts. Today when people recall the Depression, the images that most come to mind are of the travails of John Steinbeck's Joad family from "The Grapes of Wrath." Without a literary inheritance, the historical past is impoverished.

In focusing on the social advantages of a literary education, however, we should not overlook the personal impact. Every day authors receive letters from readers that say, "Your book changed my life." History reveals case after case of famous people whose lives were transformed by literature. When the great Victorian thinker John Stuart Mill suffered a crippling depression in late-adolescence, the poetry of Wordsworth restored his optimism and self-confidence — a "medicine for my state of mind," he called it.

A few decades later, W.E.B. DuBois found a different tonic in literature, an escape from the indignities of Jim Crow into a world of equality. "I sit with Shakespeare and he winces not," DuBois observed. "Across the color line I move arm in arm with Balzac and Dumas, where smiling men and welcoming women glide in gilded halls." Literature is a catalyst for education and culture.

The evidence of literature's importance to civic, personal, and economic health is too strong to ignore. The decline of literary reading foreshadows serious long-term social and economic problems, and it is time to bring literature and the other arts into discussions of public policy. Libraries, schools, and public agencies do noble work, but addressing the reading issue will require the leadership of politicians and the business community as well.

Literature now competes with an enormous array of electronic media. While no single activity is responsible for the decline in reading, the cumulative presence and availability of electronic alternatives increasingly have drawn Americans away from reading.

Reading is not a timeless, universal capability. Advanced literacy is a specific intellectual skill and social habit that depends on a great many educational, cultural, and economic factors. As more Americans lose this capability, our nation becomes less informed, active, and independent-minded. These are not the qualities that a free, innovative, or productive society can afford to lose.

11 Proposals

A student looking forward to a much-needed vacation emails three friends proposing that they pool their resources and rent a cottage at a nearby surfing beach since, working together, they can afford better digs closer to the surf.

The members of a club for business majors begin to talk about their common need to create informative, appealing—and easily scannable—résumés. After much talk, three members suggest that the club develop a Web site that will guide members in building such résumés and provide links to other resources.

A project team at a large architectural firm works for three months developing a proposal in response to an RFP (request for proposal) to convert a university library into a digital learning center.

Members of a youth activist organization propose to start an after-school program for neighborhood kids, using the organization's meeting place and volunteering their time as tutors and mentors.

The undergraduate student organization at a large state university asks the administration for information about how long it takes to complete a degree in each academic major. After analyzing this information, the group recommends a reduction in the number of hours needed to graduate.

• • •

Understanding and Categorizing Proposals

Think big and be patient. You might be amazed by what you accomplish. Executive director of the Sierra Club Foundation and renowned environmentalist David Brower (1912–2000) had long blamed himself for not standing firm against the Glen Canyon Dam project in northern Arizona—which in 1963 began holding back the waters of the Colorado River, flooding some of the most wild and beautiful canyons in the world to create a reservoir more than 100 miles long, Lake Powell. "I have worn sackcloth and ashes ever since, convinced that I could have saved the place if I had simply got off my duff," he wrote.

But he did more than penance. In a 1997 article entitled "Let the River Run through It," Brower made a blunt proposal:

> **But as surely as we made a mistake years ago, we can reverse it now. We can drain Lake Powell and let the Colorado River run through the dam that created it, bringing Glen Canyon and the wonder of its side canyons back to life. We can let the river do what it needs to do downstream in the Grand Canyon itself.**
>
> **We don't need to tear the dam down, however much some people would like to see it go. Together the dam's two diversion tunnels can send 200,000 cubic feet of water per second downstream, twice as much as the Colorado's highest flows. Once again Grand Canyon would make its own sounds and, if you listened carefully, you would hear it sighing with relief. The dam itself would be left as a tourist attraction, like the Pyramids, with passers-by wondering how humanity ever built it, and why.**
>
> **–David Brower, "Let the River Run through It"**

Three photos showing the Glen Canyon Dam and the landscapes it inundated—newly revealed as Lake Powell has receded during a recent prolonged drought.

Though drought in the West has shrunk Lake Powell dramatically in the past decade, the concrete arch of Glen Canyon Dam still holds fast against the Colorado River. But in that time, the logic of Brower's proposal and the notion of dam removal in general have gained remarkable traction. Hundreds of smaller dams have already been removed across rivers throughout the country in response to environmental concerns, allowing rivers to return to their natural state, restoring native landscapes, and enabling endangered species of fish to thrive once again. What once may have seemed unthinkable now seems plausible, thanks to Brower's audacious proposal and others like it—buttressed by carefully reasoned arguments showing that some dams did more harm than good, not only environmentally but economically too. Here's Brower, for example, explaining how much water is lost due to the dam and the lake it creates:

> In 1996, the Bureau [of Reclamation] found that almost a million acre-feet, or 8 percent of the river's flow, disappeared between the stations recording the reservoir's inflow and outflow. Almost 600,000 acre-feet were presumed lost to evaporation. Nobody knows for sure about the rest. The Bureau said some of the loss was a gain being stored in the banks of the reservoir but it has no idea how much of that gain it will ever get back. Some bank storage is recoverable, but all too likely the region's downward-slanting geological strata are leading some of Powell's waters into the dark unknown. It takes only one drain to empty a bathtub, and we don't know where, when, or how the Powell tub leaks.

Brower waxes poetic, too, in asking readers to imagine a better future—which is what proposals are all about:

> The sooner we begin, the sooner lost paradises will begin to recover Cathedral in the Desert, Music Temple, Hidden Passage, Dove Canyon, Little Arch, Dungeon, and a hundred others. Glen Canyon itself can probably lose its ugly white sidewalls in two or three decades. The tapestries can re-emerge, along with the desert varnish, the exiled species of plants and animals, the pictographs and other mementos of people long gone. The canyon's music will be known again, and "the sudden poetry of springs," Wallace Stegner's beautiful phrase, will be revealed again below the sculptured walls of Navajo sandstone. The phrase, "as long as the rivers shall run and the grasses grow," will regain its meaning.

Not all proposals are as dramatic as Brower's, but such arguments, whether casual or formal, are important in all of our lives. How many proposals do you make or respond to just in one day? Chances are, more than a few: Your roommate suggests you both skip breakfast in order to get in an extra hour of exercise; you and a colleague decide to collaborate on a project rather than go it alone; you call your best friend to propose checking out a new movie; you decide to approach your boss about implementing an idea you've just had. In each case, the proposal implies that some action should take place and suggests that there are sound reasons why it should.

In their simplest form, proposal arguments look something like this:

A should do B because of C.

A / **B**

Our student government should endorse the Academic Bill of Rights

C

because students should not be punished in their courses for their reasonable political views.

Because proposals come at us so routinely, it's no surprise that they cover a dizzyingly wide range of possibilities, from very local and concrete practices (*A student should switch dorms immediately; A company should switch from one supplier of paper to another*) to very broad matters of policy (*The U.S. Congress should repeal the Homeland Security Act*). So it may help to think of proposal arguments as divided roughly into two kinds—those that focus on practices, and those that focus on policies.

Here are several examples:

David Bositis presents a proposal about practices in his article on polling minorities. He argues that polls and surveys must be more inclusive of minorities if a true and full picture is to be made and stereotypes combatted.

LINK TO P. 663

Proposals about Practices

- The city should use brighter light bulbs in employee parking garages.
- The college should allow students to pay tuition on a month-by-month basis.
- The NCAA should implement a playoff system to determine its Division I football champion.

Proposals about Policies

- The college should adopt a policy guaranteeing a "living wage" to all campus workers.
- The state should repeal all English Only legislation.
- The Supreme Court should pay greater attention to the Tenth Amendment, which restricts the role of the federal government to powers enumerated in the Constitution.

Characterizing Proposals

Proposals have three main characteristics:

- They call for action or response, often in response to a problem.
- They focus on the future.
- They center on the audience.

Proposals always call for some kind of action. They aim at getting something done—understanding that sometimes what needs to be done is nothing. Proposals marshal evidence and arguments to persuade people to choose a course of action: *Let's build a stadium; Let's oppose the latest Supreme Court ruling; Let's create a campus organization for transfer students.* But you know the old saying, "You can lead a horse to water, but you can't make it drink." It's usually easier to *convince* audiences what a good course of action is than to *persuade* them to take it (or pay for it). You can present a proposal as cogently as possible—but most of the time you can't *make* any audience take the action you propose.

Thus proposal arguments must appeal to more than good sense—as David Brower does. Imagination and a little poetry might sometimes carry the day. Ethos matters too. It helps if a writer carries a certain *gravitas*—as Brower did as one of the grand old men of the environmental movement. (He was in his mid-eighties when he made his appeal to drain Lake Powell.) If your word, experience, and judgment are all credible, an audience is more likely to carry out the action you propose.

In addition, proposal arguments focus on the future: what people, institutions, or governments should do over the upcoming weeks, months, or even decades. This orientation toward the future presents special challenges, since few of us have crystal balls. Proposal arguments must therefore offer the best evidence available to suggest that actions we recommend will achieve what they promise.

Finally, proposals have to focus on particular audiences, especially on people who can get something done. Sometimes, proposal arguments are written to general audiences. You can find these arguments, for example, in newspaper editorials and letters to the editor. And such appeals to a broad group make sense when a proposal—say, to finance new toll roads or build an art museum—must surf on waves of community support and financing. But even such grand proposals also need to influence individuals with the power to make change actually happen,

THERE'S NOT ENOUGH ART IN OUR SCHOOLS.

NO WONDER PEOPLE THINK

CARAVAGGIO

IS A GUY ON THE SOPRANOS.

ART. ASK FOR MORE.

For more information about the importance of arts education, please contact www.AmericansForTheArts.org.

AMERICANS for the ARTS

This advertisement by Americans for the Arts makes a clear proposal that targets parents or concerned citizens.

such as financiers, developers, public officials, and legislators. On your own campus, for example, a plan to alter admissions policies might be directed both to students in general and (perhaps in a different form) to the university president, members of the faculty council, and admissions officers. Identifying who all your potential audiences might be is critical to the success of any proposal.

For example, in 2005, many citizens were angered by a Supreme Court decision allowing communities to use the power of eminent domain to seize private property for projects that contributed not, as had been traditional, to the public good (such as roads or schools) but to private economic development (such as hotels and commercial ventures). To send a clear oppositional message, Logan Darrow Clements, a political figure in California, proposed that investors support the development of the "Lost Liberty Hotel" on the 4.8 acres of land in Weare, New Hampshire, that Justice David Souter calls home. Justice Souter is one of the judges who supported this broadening of government authority over personal property. Clements claimed (in a press release) that "This is not a prank. . . . The Towne of Weare has five people on the Board of Selectmen. If three of them vote to use the power of eminent domain to take this land from Mr. Souter we can begin our hotel development." Clements clearly had two audiences in mind: the general public aroused by the expanded scope of eminent domain, as well as the members of Weare's Board of Selectmen. It's unlikely that Souter will ever lose his property, but this proposal argument suggests that he could.

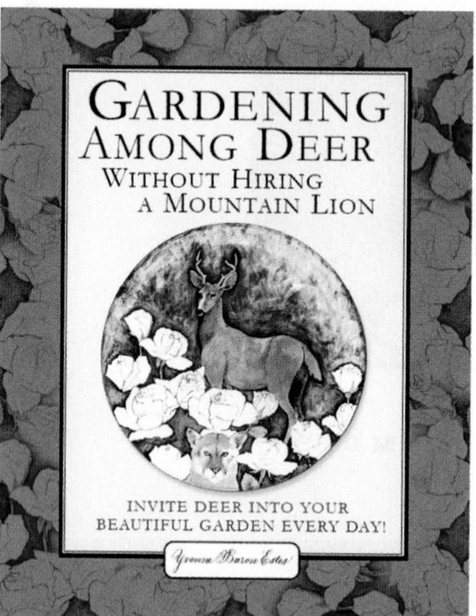

An alternative to open season?

An effective proposal also has to be compatible with the values of the audience. Some ideas may make good sense but cannot be enacted. For example, many American towns and cities have a problem with expanding deer populations. Without natural predators, the animals are moving closer to human homes, dining on gardens and shrubbery, and endangering traffic. Yet one obvious and entirely feasible solution to the problem—culling the herds through hunting or shooting—is usually not acceptable to the communities most plagued by the problem. Too many people still remember *Bambi*.

Developing Proposals

How do you develop an effective proposal? Start by showing that there's a problem that needs a solution or that there's some need that's not being met. Then make a proposal that addresses the problem or meets the need. Explain in detail why adopting your proposal will address the need or problem better than other solutions; finally, show that the proposal is both feasible and acceptable. Sounds easy, but you'll discover that writing a proposal argument can be a process of discovery: at the outset, you think you know exactly what ought to be done; by the end, you may see (and even recommend) other options.

Defining a Need or Problem

You typically make a proposal to solve a problem or prevent one. Thus establishing that a need or problem exists is job one for the writer of a proposal argument.

You'll typically describe the problem you intend to address at the beginning of your project—as a way of leading up to a specific claim. But in some cases you could put the need or problem right *after* your claim as the major reason for adopting the proposal: *Let's ban cell phones on campus now. Why? Because we've become a school of walking zombies. No one speaks or even acknowledges the people they meet or pass on campus. Half of our students are too busy chattering to people they can't see to participate in the community around them.*

Regardless of the practical choices about organization, the task of establishing a need or problem calls on you to:

- paint a picture of the need or problem in concrete and memorable ways
- show how the need or problem affects the audience for the argument as well as the larger society
- explain why the need or problem is significant
- explain why other attempts to address the issue may have failed

Deborah Tannen begins an essay on mother and daughter communication by illustrating various conflicts that arise between women in these relationships. By analyzing what causes the conflicts, Tannen encourages women to pay attention to the differences between the messages and the meta-messages that they send and receive.

LINK TO P. 830

In proposing that a state board of higher education require community service from students enrolled in state colleges, for example, you might begin by painting a picture of a self-absorbed "me first and only" society that values instant gratification. After evoking such a dismal scene, you might trace the consequences of such behavior for your campus and community, arguing, for instance, that it fosters hyper-competition, leaves many of society's most vulnerable members without helping hands, and puts the responsibility of assisting people solely in the hands of government—thereby adding to its size and cost, raising taxes for all. You might have to cite some authorities and statistics to prove that the problem you're diagnosing is real and that it touches everyone likely to read your argument. Once you do, readers will be ready to hear your proposal.

Look at how Craig R. Dean, a lawyer and executive director of the Equal Marriage Rights Fund, prepares his claim—that the United States should legalize same sex marriage—by explaining the significant problems that the existing ban on gay marriages creates:

> In November 1990, my lover, Patrick Gill, and I were denied a marriage license because we are gay. In a memorandum explaining the District's decision, the clerk of the court wrote that "the sections of the District of Columbia code governing marriage do not authorize marriage between persons of the same sex." By refusing to give us the same legal recognition that is given to heterosexual couples, the District has degraded our relationship as well as that of every other gay and lesbian couple.
>
> At one time, interracial couples were not allowed to marry. Gays and lesbians are still denied this basic civil right in the U.S.—and around the world. Can you imagine the outcry if any other minority group was denied the right to legally marry today? Marriage is more than a piece of paper. It gives societal recognition and legal protection to a relationship. It confers numerous benefits to spouses; in the District alone, there are more than 100 automatic marriage-based rights. In every state in the nation, married couples have the right to be on each other's health, disability, life insurance and pension plans. Married couples receive special tax exemptions, deductions and refunds. Spouses may automatically inherit property and have rights of survivorship that avoid inheritance tax. Though unmarried couples—both gay and heterosexual—are entitled to some of these rights, they are by no means guaranteed.
>
> For married couples, the spouse is legally the next of kin in case of death, medical emergency or mental incapacity. In stark contrast, the family is generally the next of kin for same-sex couples. In the shadow of AIDS, the denial of marriage rights can be even more ominous. . . .

> Some argue that gay marriage is too radical for society. We disagree. According to a 1989 study by the American Bar Association, eight to 10 million children are currently being reared in three million gay households. Therefore, approximately 6 percent of the U.S. population is made up of gay and lesbian families with children. Why should these families be denied the protection granted to other families? Allowing gay marriage would strengthen society by increasing tolerance. It is paradoxical that mainstream America perceives gays and lesbians as unable to maintain long-term relationships while at the same time denying them the very institutions that stabilize such relationships.
>
> –Craig R. Dean, "Legalize Gay Marriage"

Notice, too, that Dean makes it clear that the problems facing gays seeking to marry have consequences for all members of the potential audience—who might face problems of their own stemming from intolerance. Though homosexuals might benefit most directly from solving the problem he describes, ultimately everyone in society gains.

Personalizing an abstract problem—such as the legal benefits of marriage that are unavailable to gay and lesbian partners—can help make an argument for a solution. Dying of lung cancer, police lieutenant Laurel Hester (center) spent the last year of her life fighting to persuade Ocean County, New Jersey, officials to transfer her pension benefits to her partner, Stacie Andree (right), after Hester's death.

In describing the problem your proposal argument intends to solve, you may also need to review other earlier and failed attempts to address it. Many issues have a long history you can't afford to ignore. For example, were you to argue for a college football playoff, you might point out that the current Bowl Championship series itself represents an attempt—largely unsuccessful—to crown a more widely recognized national champion. Then there are those problems that seem to grow worse every time someone tinkers with them. Considering how the current system of financing political campaigns in federal elections developed might give you pause about proposing any additional attempt at reform—since every previous reform, one might argue, has resulted in more bureaucracy, more restrictions on political expression, and more unregulated money flowing into the system. *Enough is enough* is a potent argument in light of such a mess.

Making a Strong and Clear Claim

Once you've described and analyzed a problem or state of affairs, you're prepared to make a claim. Begin with your *claim* (a proposal of what X or Y should do) followed by the *reason(s)* why X or Y should act and the *effects* of adopting the proposal:

Claim	**Communities should encourage the development of charter schools.**
Reason	**Charter schools are not burdened by the bureaucracy associated with most public schooling.**
Effects	**Instituting such schools will bring more effective educational progress to communities and offer an incentive to the public schools to improve their programs as well.**

Having established a claim, you can explore its implications by drawing out the reasons, warrants, and evidence that can support it most effectively:

Claim	**In light of a recent Supreme Court decision upholding federal drug laws, Congress should immediately pass a bill allowing states to legalize the use of marijuana for medical purposes.**
Reason	**Medical marijuana relieves nausea for millions of patients being treated for cancer and AIDS.**
Warrant	**The relief of nausea is desirable.**

Evidence **Nine states have already approved the use of cannabis for medical purposes, and referendums are planned in other states. Evidence gathered in large double-blind studies demonstrates that marijuana relieves nausea associated with cancer and AIDS treatments.**

In this proposal argument, the *reason* sets up the need for the proposal, whereas the *warrant* and *evidence* demonstrate that the proposal is just and could meet its objective. Your actual argument, of course, would develop each point in more detail.

Showing That the Proposal Addresses the Need or Problem

An important but tricky part of making a successful proposal lies in relating the claim to the need or problem it addresses. Everyone you know may agree that rising tuition costs at your college constitute a major problem. But will your spur-of-the-moment letter to the college newspaper proposing to reduce the size of the faculty and eliminate all campus bus services really address the problem? Would anyone even take such a proposal seriously? Chances are, you would have a tough time making this connection. On the other hand, proposing that the student government—aided by students in accounting and financing—examine the school's use of its discretionary funds just might kick-start some action on tuition, especially if you can suggest areas where the institution has been notably wasteful. It makes sense that students shouldn't have to pay more to support activities or projects not directly related to their educations.

Addressing his college peers through the campus newspaper, John Zwier proposes that it is not prudent to boycott or otherwise interrupt the impending commencement address from George W. Bush. Zwier acknowledges the frustration of many students and presents what he sees as a better way to approach the situation.

LINK TO P. 884

Of course, sometimes you have to ask audiences to dream a little, explaining to them how a proposal you're making fulfills a need or solves a problem they might not immediately recognize. That's a strategy taken by President John F. Kennedy in a famous speech given on September 12, 1962, explaining his proposal that the United States land a man on the moon by the end of the 1960s. Here are two paragraphs from his speech at Rice University, explaining why:

> **We set sail on this new sea because there is new knowledge to be gained, and new rights to be won, and they must be won and used for the progress of all people. For space science, like nuclear science and all technology, has no conscience of its own. Whether it will become a force for good or ill depends on man, and only if the United States occupies a position of pre-eminence can we help decide whether this new ocean will be a sea of peace or a new terrifying theater of war. I do not say that we should or will go unprotected against the hostile**

misuse of space any more that we go unprotected against the hostile use of land or sea, but I do say that space can be explored and mastered without feeding the fires of war, without repeating the mistakes that man has made in extending his writ around this globe of ours.

There is no strife, no prejudice, no national conflict in outer space as yet. Its hazards are hostile to us all. Its conquest deserves the best of all mankind, and its opportunity for peaceful cooperation may never come again. But why, some say, the moon? Why choose this as our goal? And they may well ask why climb the highest mountain? Why, 35 years ago, fly the Atlantic? Why does Rice play Texas?

We choose to go to the moon. We choose to go to the moon in this decade and do the other things, not because they are easy, but because they are hard, because that goal will serve to organize and measure the best of our energies and skills, because that challenge is one that we are willing to accept, one we are unwilling to postpone, and one which we intend to win, and the others, too.

–John F. Kennedy

Showing That the Proposal Is Feasible

To be effective, proposals must be *feasible:* that is, the action proposed can be carried out in a reasonable way. Demonstrating feasibility calls on you to present evidence—from similar cases, from personal experience, from observational data, from interview or survey data, from Internet research, or from any other sources—showing that what you propose can indeed be done with the resources available. "Resources available" is key: if the proposal calls for funds, personnel, or skills beyond reach or reason, your audience is unlikely to accept it. When that's

If Everything's an Argument . . .

This chapter proposes implicitly that you should follow its advice in order to learn how to write effective proposals. How persuasive do you find this argument? Write your own proposal about how this chapter could be improved for its intended audience of college students, considering such elements as the topics covered, the examples, the visuals, and the organization. What, if anything, strikes you as confusing, outdated, skimpy, overemphasized, biased, unnecessary, or missing? How could these problems be addressed? Consider the authors and editors your audience.

the case, it's time to reassess and modify your proposal, and to test any new ideas against these same criteria. This is also the point to reconsider proposals that others might suggest are better, more effective, or more workable than yours. There's no shame in admitting you may have been wrong. When drafting a proposal, it even makes sense to ask friends to think of counterproposals. If your own proposal can stand up to such challenges, it's likely a strong one.

Using Personal Experience

If your own experience demonstrates the need or problem your proposal aims to address, or backs up your claim, consider using it to develop your proposal (as Craig R. Dean does in the opening of his proposal to legalize gay marriage). Consider the following questions in deciding when to include your own experiences in making a proposal:

- Is your experience directly related to the need or problem you seek to address, or to your proposal about it?
- Will your experience be appropriate and speak convincingly to the audience? Will the audience immediately understand its significance, or will it require explanation?
- Does your personal experience fit logically with the other reasons you're using to support your claim?

Be careful. If a proposal seems crafted to serve mainly your own interests, you won't get far.

Considering Design and Visuals

Because proposals often address very specific audiences, they can take any number of forms: a letter or memo, a Web page, a feasibility report, a brochure, a prospectus. Each form has different design requirements; indeed, the design may add powerfully to—or detract significantly from—the effectiveness of the proposal. Even in a college essay written on a computer, the use of white space and margins, headings and subheadings, and variations in type (such as boldface or italics) can guide readers through the proposal and enhance its persuasiveness. So before you produce a final copy of any proposal, make a careful plan for its design.

A related issue to consider is whether a graphic might help readers understand key elements of the proposal—what the challenge is, why it demands action, what exactly you're suggesting—and help make the

Not Just Words

Enterprises, both private and public, frequently offer proposals for the approval of the citizens or investors who, one way or another, will wind up paying for them. Such proposals are typically packaged to give substance to what may be little more than a dream.

Examine the proposals below, which we've annotated to highlight just a few persuasive strategies. Look for similar examples online or, perhaps, in a magazine or newspaper. (Is your school or community considering a new museum, auditorium, or park, or maybe a local developer plans to turn a warehouse district into a shopping mall? Collect the brochures, ads, or public relations materials for these projects.)

After studying the techniques in such presentations, particularly their visual elements, create a mock-up for a proposal you—and perhaps several of your classmates—might like to offer to your school or community. Choose the medium you think would

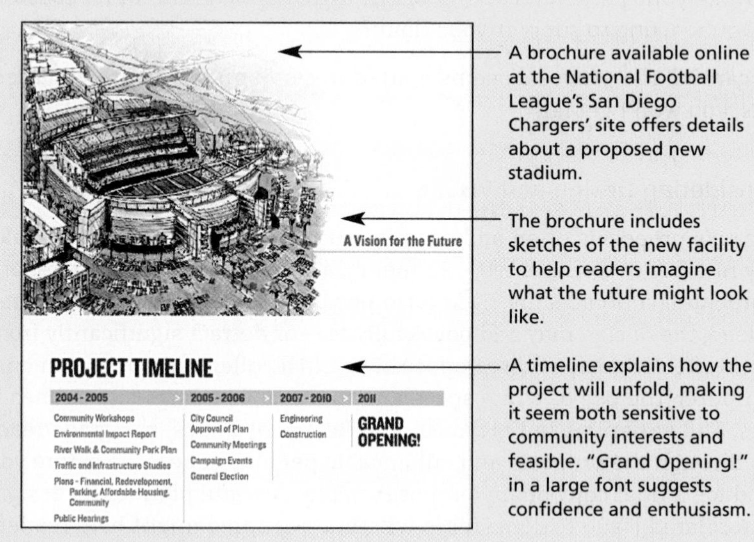

A brochure available online at the National Football League's San Diego Chargers' site offers details about a proposed new stadium.

The brochure includes sketches of the new facility to help readers imagine what the future might look like.

A timeline explains how the project will unfold, making it seem both sensitive to community interests and feasible. "Grand Opening!" in a large font suggests confidence and enthusiasm.

best reach your intended audience: pamphlet, brochure, poster, Web site, position paper, and so on. Be creative in your graphics, remembering that design involves more than just images and photos.

Alternatively, use your project to raise questions about an existing proposal. For instance, does an enhanced public transit system with a costly light-rail line really make sense in your town? How might you raise questions about its potential problems and costs in a pamphlet or print ad?

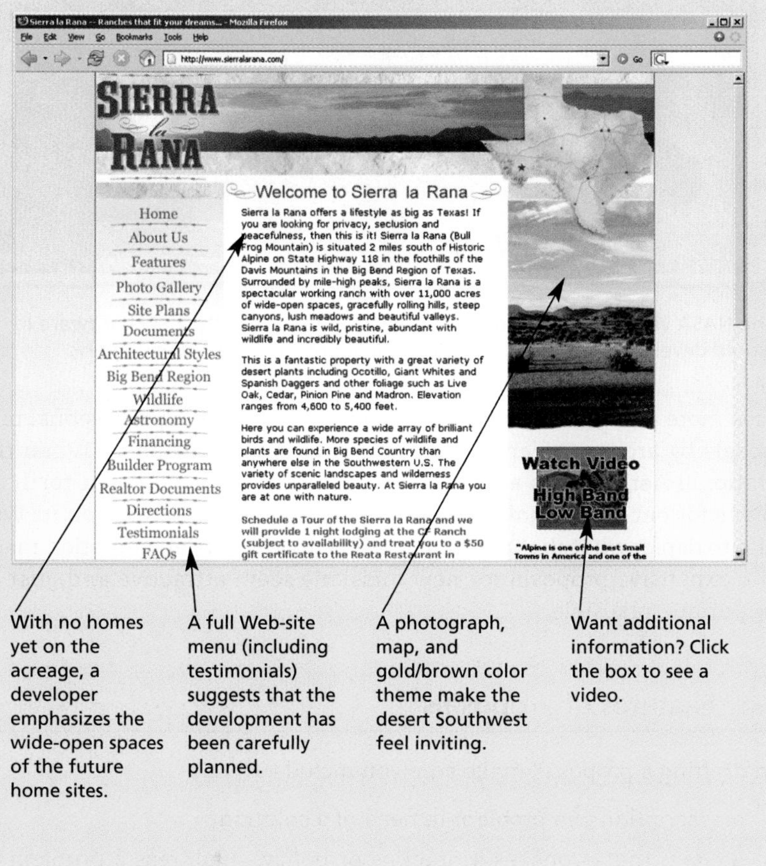

The NASA video used high-quality animation to display the new hardware it would develop to once again explore the moon. See <http://nasa.gov>.

idea more attractive. That's a strategy routinely used in professional proposals by architects, engineers, and government agencies. When the National Aeronautics and Space Administration (NASA) put forth its plans for once again going to the moon, it presented a video on its Web site to depict what those flights might be like. The brief animation made the expensive proposal for new missions seem attractive and, just as important, plausible.

Key Features of Proposals

In drafting a proposal, make sure you include:

- a description of a problem in need of a solution
- a claim that proposes a practice or policy to address a problem or need and that's oriented toward action, directed at the future, and appropriate to your audience

- statements that clearly relate the claim to the problem or need
- evidence that the proposal will effectively address the need or solve the problem, and that it's workable

Fully developing your proposal will call for addressing all these elements, though you may choose to arrange them in several ways. A proposal might open with a vivid description of a problem—even an actual image that represents it (such as photographs of beautiful canyons destroyed by the Glen Canyon Dam). Or it might open with your proposal itself, perhaps stunning or unexpected in its directness.

In any case, organize your proposal carefully and get responses to your organizational plan from your instructor and classmates.

GUIDE to writing a proposal

Finding a Topic/Identifying a Problem

Your everyday experience calls on you to consider problems and to make proposals all the time: for example, to change your academic major for some very important reasons, to add to the family income by starting a home-based business, or to oppose new scholarships restricted to specific student groups. In addition, your work or your job may require you to solve problems or make proposals—to a boss, a board of directors, the local school board, someone you want to impress—the list could go on and on. Of course, you also have many opportunities to make proposals to online groups; with email one click away, the whole world could be the audience for your proposal. In all these cases, you'll be aiming to call for action or to critique action, so why not make an informal list of proposals you'd like to explore in a number of different areas? Or do some freewriting on a subject of great interest to you and see if it leads to a proposal? Either method of exploration is likely to turn up several possibilities for a good proposal argument.

Researching Your Topic

Proposals often call for some research. Even a simple one like *Let's all paint the house this weekend* would raise questions that require some investigation: *Who has the time for the job? What sort of paint will be the best? How much will the job cost?* A proposal that your school board adopt block scheduling would call for careful research into evidence supporting the use of such a system. *Where has it been effective, and why?* And for proposals about social issues (for example, that information on the Internet be freely accessible to everyone, even youngsters), extensive research would be necessary to provide adequate support.

For many proposals, you can begin your research by consulting the following types of sources:

- newspapers, magazines, reviews, and journals (online and print)
- online databases
- government documents and reports
- Web sites, blogs, and listservs or newsgroups
- books
- experts in the field, some of whom might be right on your campus

In addition, you might decide to carry out some field research: a survey of student opinion on Internet accessibility, for example, or interviews with people who are well informed about your subject.

Formulating a Claim

As you think about and explore your topic, begin formulating a claim about it. To do so, come up with a clear and complete thesis that makes a proposal and states the reasons why this proposal should be followed. To get started on formulating a claim, explore and respond to the following questions:

- What do I know about the proposal I'm making?
- What reasons can I offer to support my proposal?
- What evidence do I have that implementing my proposal will lead to the results I want?

Examples of Proposal Claims

- Because Condoleezza Rice is highly principled, is a proven leader, and has a powerful political story to tell, the Republican Party should consider choosing her as its first woman presidential nominee.
- Hospitals, state and local security agencies, and even citizens should stockpile surgical masks that could help prevent the rapid spread of plague pneumonia.
- Congress should repeal the Copyright Extension Act, since it disrupts the balance between incentives for creators and the right of the public to information set forth in the U.S. Constitution.
- The Environmental Protection Agency must move to approve additional oil drilling in Alaska to lessen American dependence on foreign supplies of fuel.

Preparing a Proposal

If your instructor asks you to prepare a proposal for your project, here's a format that may help:

State the thesis of your proposal completely. If you're having trouble doing so, try outlining it in Toulmin terms:

Claim:

Reason(s):

Warrant(s):

- **Explain the problem you intend to address and why your proposal is important. What's at stake in taking, or not taking, the action you propose?**
- **Identify and describe those readers you most hope to reach with your proposal. Why is this group of readers most appropriate for your proposal? What are their interests in the subject?**
- **Briefly discuss the major difficulties you foresee in preparing your argument: Demonstrating that the action you propose is necessary? Demonstrating that it's workable? Moving the audience beyond agreement to action? Something else?**
- **List the research you need to do. What kinds of sources do you need to consult?**
- **Note down the format or genre you expect to use: An academic essay? A formal report? A Web site?**

Thinking about Organization

Proposals, which can take many different forms, generally include the following elements:

- a description of the problem you intend to address or the state of affairs that leads you to propose the action: *Our neighborhood has recently experienced a rash of break-ins and burglaries. Neighbors feel like captives in their homes, and property values are threatened.*
- a clear and strong proposal, including the reasons for taking the action proposed and the effects that taking this action will have: *Our neighborhood should establish a Block Watch program that will help reduce break-ins and vandalism, and involve our kids in building neighborhood pride.*
- a clear connection between the proposal and a significant need or problem: *Break-ins and vandalism have been on the rise in our neighborhood for the last three years in part because neighbors have lost contact with each other.*
- a demonstration of ways in which the proposal addresses the need: *A Block Watch program establishes a rotating monitor system for the streets in a neighborhood and a voluntary plan to watch out for others' homes.*
- evidence that the proposal will achieve the desired outcome: *Block Watch programs in three other local areas have significantly reduced break-ins and vandalism.*
- consideration of alternative ways to achieve the desired outcome, and a discussion of why these are not preferable: *We could ask for additional police presence, but funding would be hard to get.*

- a demonstration that the proposal is workable and practical: *Because Block Watch is voluntary, our own determination and commitment are all we need to make it work.*

Getting and Giving Response

All arguments can benefit from the scrutiny of others. Your instructor may assign you to a peer group for the purpose of reading and responding to each other's drafts; if not, get some response on your own from some serious readers or consultants at a writing center. You can use the following questions to evaluate a draft. If you're evaluating someone else's draft, be sure to illustrate your points with examples. Specific comments are always more helpful than general observations.

The Claim

- Does the claim clearly call for action? Is the proposal as clear and specific as possible?
- Is the proposal too sweeping? Does it need to be qualified? If so, how?
- Does the proposal clearly address the problem it intends to solve? If not, how could the connection be strengthened?
- Is the claim likely to get the audience to act rather than just to agree? If not, how could it be revised to do so?

Evidence for the Claim

- Is enough evidence furnished to get the audience to support the proposal? If not, what kind of additional evidence is needed? Does any of the evidence provided seem inappropriate or otherwise ineffective? Why?
- Is the evidence in support of the claim simply announced, or are its significance and appropriateness analyzed? Is a more detailed discussion needed?
- Are any objections readers might have to the claim or evidence adequately addressed?
- What kinds of sources are cited? How credible and persuasive will they be to readers? What other kinds of sources might be more credible and persuasive?
- Are all quotations introduced with appropriate signal phrases (such as "As Ehrenreich argues,") and blended smoothly into the writer's sentences?
- Are all visuals titled and labeled appropriately? Have you introduced them and commented on their significance?

Organization and Style

- How are the parts of the argument organized? Is this organization effective, or would some other structure work better?
- Will readers understand the relationships among the claims, supporting reasons, warrants, and evidence? If not, what could be done to make those connections clearer? Are more transitional words and phrases needed? Would headings or graphic devices help?
- How have you used visual design elements to make your proposal more effective?
- Are the transitions or links from point to point, paragraph to paragraph, and sentence to sentence clear and effective? If not, how could they be improved?
- Is the style suited to the subject? Is it too formal? Too casual? Too technical? Too bland? How can it be improved?
- Which sentences seem particularly effective? Which ones seem weakest, and how could they be improved? Should some short sentences be combined, or should any long ones be separated into two or more sentences?
- How effective are the paragraphs? Do any seem too skimpy or too long? How can they be improved?
- Which words or phrases seem particularly effective, vivid, and memorable? Do any seem dull, vague, unclear, or inappropriate for the audience or the writer's purpose? Are definitions provided for technical or other terms that readers might not know?

Spelling, Punctuation, Mechanics, Documentation, Format

- Are there any errors in spelling, punctuation, capitalization, and the like?
- Is an appropriate and consistent style of documentation used for parenthetical citations and the list of works cited or references? (See Chapter 20.)
- Does the paper or project follow an appropriate format? Is it appropriately designed and attractively presented? How could it be improved? If it's a Web site, do all the links work?

RESPOND•

1. For each problem and solution, make a list of readers' likely objections to the off-the-wall solution offered. Then propose a more defensible solution of your own, and explain why you think it's more workable.

   Problem Future bankruptcy of the Social Security system
   Solution Raise the age of retirement to eighty.

   Problem Traffic gridlock in major cities
   Solution Allow only men to drive on Mondays, Wednesdays, and Fridays and only women on Tuesdays, Thursdays, and Saturdays. Everyone can drive on Sunday.

   Problem Increasing rates of obesity in the general population
   Solution Ban the sale of high-fat items in fast food restaurants

   Problem Increasing school violence
   Solution Authorize teachers and students to carry handguns.

   Problem Excessive drinking on campus
   Solution Establish an 8:00 P.M. curfew on weekends.

2. People write proposal arguments to solve problems, to change the way things are. But problems aren't always obvious; what troubles some people might be no big deal to others. To get an idea of the range of problems people face on your campus—some of which you may not even have thought of as problems—divide into groups and brainstorm about things that annoy you on and around campus, including everything from bad food in the cafeterias to 8:00 A.M. classes to long lines for football or concert tickets. Ask each group to aim for at least twenty gripes. Then choose one problem and, as a group, discuss how you'd go about writing a proposal to deal with it. Remember that you'll need to (a) make a strong and clear claim, (b) show that the proposal meets a clear need or solves a significant problem, (c) present good reasons why adopting the proposal will effectively address the need or problem, and (d) show that the proposal is workable and should be adopted.

3. In the essay "Mass Transit Hysteria" (see p. 364), P. J. O'Rourke playfully proposes turning public transportation systems into thrill rides to increase their use by the public. Using the Toulmin model discussed in Chapter 6, analyze the proposal's structure. What claim(s) does O'Rourke make, and what reasons does he give to support the claim? What warrants connect the reasons to the claim? What evidence does he provide? Alternatively, make up a rough outline of O'Rourke's proposal and track the good reasons he presents to support his claim.

A Call to Improve Campus Accessibility for the Mobility Impaired

MANASI DESHPANDE

Introduction

Wes Holloway, a sophomore at the University of Texas at Austin, never considered the issue of campus accessibility during his first year on campus. But when an injury his freshman year left him wheelchair-bound, he was astonished to realize that he faced an unexpected challenge: maneuvering around the UT campus. Hills that he had effortlessly traversed became mountains; doors that he had easily opened became anvils; and streets that he had mindlessly crossed became treacherous terrain. Says Wes: "I didn't think about accessibility until I had to deal with it, and I think most people are the same way."

The paper opens with a personal example and dramatizes the issue of campus accessibility.

For the ambulatory individual, access for the mobility impaired on the UT campus is easy to overlook. Automatic door entrances and bathrooms with the universal handicapped symbol make the campus seem sufficiently accessible. But for many students and faculty at UT, including me, maneuvering the UT campus in a wheelchair is a daily experience of stress and frustration. Although the University has made a concerted and continuing effort to improve access, students and faculty with physical disabilities still suffer from discriminatory hardship, unequal opportunity to succeed, and lack of independence. The

---

Manasi Deshpande wrote this formidable essay for a course preparing her to work as a consultant in the Writing Center at the University of Texas at Austin. Note in particular how she reaches out to a general audience to make an argument that might seem to have a narrower constituency. She also makes good use of headings to guide readers through the complexities of her proposal. This essay is documented using MLA style.

University must make campus accessibility a higher priority and take more seriously the hardship that the campus at present imposes on people with mobility impairments. Administrators should devote more resources to creating a user-friendly campus rather than simply conforming to legal requirements for accessibility. The University should also enhance the transparency and approachability of its services for members with mobility impairments. Individuals with permanent physical disabilities would undoubtedly benefit from a stronger resolve to improve campus accessibility. Better accessibility would also benefit the more numerous students and faculty with temporary disabilities and help the University recruit a more diverse body of students and faculty.

Both problem and solution are previewed here, with more details to come in subsequent sections of the paper.

Assessment of Current Efforts

The current state of campus accessibility leaves substantial room for improvement. There are approximately 150 academic and administrative buildings on campus (Grant). Eduardo Gardea, intern architect at the Physical Plant, estimates that only about nineteen buildings fully comply with the Americans with Disabilities Act (ADA). According to Penny Seay, Ph.D., director of the Center for Disability Studies at UT Austin, the ADA in theory "requires every building on campus to be accessible." However, as Bill Throop, associate director of the Physical Plant, explains, there is "no legal deadline to make the entire campus accessible"; neither the ADA nor any other law mandates that certain buildings be made compliant by a certain time. Though not bound by specific legal obligation, the University should strive to fulfill the spirit of the law and recognize campus accessibility as a pressing moral obligation.

This section examines the bureaucratic dimensions of the campus accessibility problem. The author's fieldwork (mainly interviews) enhances her authority and credibility.

While the University has made substantial progress in accessibility improvements, it has failed to make campus accessibility a priority. For example, the Campus Master Plan, published in 1999 by the University, does not include improvements in campus accessibility as one of its major goals for the design and architecture of the University. It mentions accessibility only once to recommend that signs for wayfinding comply with the ADA. The signs should provide "direction to accessible building entrances and routes" and "clear identification of special facilities" (Gleeson et al. 90). Nowhere does the Master Plan discuss the need to design these accessible building entrances, routes, and special facilities or how to fit accessibility improvements into the larger renovation of the campus.

The paper uses several layers of headings to organize its diverse materials.

The Benefits of Change

Benefits for People with Permanent Mobility Impairments

The author outlines the challenges faced by a student with mobility impairment.

Improving campus accessibility would significantly enhance the quality of life of students and faculty with mobility impairments. The campus at present poses discriminatory hardship on these individuals by making daily activities such as getting to class and using the bathroom unreasonably difficult. Before Wes Holloway leaves home, he must plan his route carefully so as to avoid hills, use ramps that are easy to maneuver, and enter the side of the building with the accessible entrance. As he goes to class, Wes must go out of his way to avoid poorly paved sidewalks and roads. Sometimes he cannot avoid them and must take an uncomfortable and bumpy ride across potholes and uneven pavement. If his destination does not have an automatic door, he must wait for someone to open the door for him because it is too heavy for him to open himself. To get into Burdine Hall, he has to ask a stranger to push him through the heavy narrow doors because his fingers would get crushed if he pushed himself. Once in the classroom, Wes must find a suitable place to sit, often far away from his classmates because stairs block him from the center of the room.

Other members of the UT community with mobility impairments suffer the same daily hardships as Wes.

According to Mike Gerhardt, student affairs administrator of Services for Students with Disabilities (SSD), approximately eighty students with physical disabilities, including twenty to twenty-five students using wheelchairs, are registered with SSD. However, the actual number of students with mobility impairments is probably higher because some students choose not to seek services from SSD. The current state of campus accessibility discriminates against all individuals with physical disabilities in the unnecessary hardship it imposes.

Beyond inflicting daily stress on people with mobility impairments, the poor accessibility on campus denies these individuals their independence. Students with physical disabilities must often ask for help from others, especially in opening doors without functional automatic door entrances. Bathrooms without access also deny these individuals their independence. Once when I needed to use a bathroom in Burdine Hall, I found that none of the stalls was accessible. To be able to use the bathroom in privacy, I had to ask a stranger to stand outside the bathroom and make sure no one entered.

Accessibility problems are given a human face in a section providing numerous examples of the problems mobility-impaired people face on campus.

The state of campus accessibility also denies people with physical disabilities an equal opportunity to succeed. In the summer of 2004, I registered for CH 204, a chemistry lab, because I planned to be a Human Biology major. The major requires students to take four labs. When I got to the lab on the first day of class, I found that I could not perform any tasks independently. The supposedly accessible lab bench was just as high as the other benches, so I could not write, take proper measurements, or handle equipment on the bench. I could not reach the sink. The lab was so cramped that I could hardly fit through the aisles, and I wheeled around in fear of bumping into someone carrying glass equipment. Services for Students with Disabilities informed me that it would not be able to provide me with an assistant. Though I was fully capable of performing the labs myself, the lack of accessibility made me unable to complete even the simplest tasks.

The author offers her personal perspective on the subject, a factual appeal with an emotional dimension.

Even with an assistant, I would have lacked independence and felt unequal to my classmates. After this experience, I dropped both the class and the major.

Benefits for People with Temporary Mobility Impairments

The author broadens the appeal of her proposal by showing how improved accessibility will benefit everyone on campus.

In addition to helping the few members of the UT campus with permanent mobility impairments, a faster rate of accessibility improvement would also benefit the much larger population of people with temporary physical disabilities. Many students and faculty will become temporarily disabled from injury at some point during their time at the University. Sprained ankles, torn ACLs, and fractured legs all require use of crutches or a wheelchair. Judy Lu, a second-year Business Honors Program/Plan II/Pre-med major, used crutches for two weeks when she sprained her ankle playing volleyball. She encountered difficulties similar to those facing people with permanent disabilities, including finding accessible entrances, opening doors without automatic entrances, and finding convenient classroom seating. Getting around campus on crutches "was not convenient at all," and her temporary disability required her to "plan ahead a whole lot more" to find accessible routes and entrances.

All members of the UT community face the risk of enduring an injury that could leave them with a temporary physical disability. According to Dr. Jennifer Maedgen, assistant dean of students and director of SSD, about 5 to 10% of the approximately 1,000 students registered with SSD at any given time have temporary disabilities. The number of students with temporary physical disabilities is largely underreported because many students do not know about SSD or do not feel the need for temporary academic accommodations. By improving campus accessibility, the University would reach out not only to its few members with permanent physical disabilities but in fact to all of its members, even those who have never considered the possibility of mobility impairment or the state of campus accessibility.

Numbers provide hard evidence for an important claim.

Benefits for the University

Better accessibility would also benefit the University as a whole by increasing recruitment of handicapped individuals and thus promoting a more diverse campus. When prospective students and faculty with disabilities visit the University, they might decide not to join the UT community because of poor access. On average, about 1,000 students, or 2% of the student population, are registered with SSD. Mike Gerhardt reports that SSD would have about 1,500 to 3,000 registered students if the University reflected the community at large with respect to disability. These numbers suggest that the University can recruit more students with disabilities by taking steps to ensure that they have an equal opportunity to succeed. Improving accessibility is one way to achieve a more diverse campus.

The author offers a new but related argument: enhanced accessibility could bolster recruitment efforts.

COUNTERARGUMENTS

Arguments against devoting more effort and resources to campus accessibility have some validity but ultimately prove inadequate. Some argue that accelerating the rate of accessibility improvements and creating more efficient services require too much spending on too few people. However, this spending actually enhances the expected quality of life of all UT community members rather than just the few with permanent physical disabilities. Unforeseen injury can leave anyone with a permanent or temporary disability at any time. In making decisions about campus accessibility, administrators must realize that having a disability is not a choice and that bad luck does not discriminate well. They should consider how their decisions would affect their campus experience if they became disabled. Despite the additional cost, the University should make accessibility a priority and accommodate more accessibility projects in its budget.

Others argue that more money would not accelerate change because the physical constraints of the campus

The paper examines and refutes two specific objections to the proposal.

limit the amount of construction that can take place. Mr. Gerhardt, for example, argues that "more money wouldn't make a difference" because ADA projects must be spaced over the long term so as to minimize disruption from construction. Other administrators, architects, and engineers, however, feel that money does play a significant role in the rate of ADA improvements. Although Mr. Throop of the Physical Plant acknowledges that the campus only has the capacity to absorb a certain amount of construction, he nonetheless feels that the Physical Plant "could do more if [it] had more monetary resources" and argues that the University "should fund [the Plant] more." Dr. Maedgen of SSD agrees, saying that the main constraint to making the campus more accessible more quickly is "mostly money." Even though there is "a real desire to do it," the problem "tends to be fiscally oriented in nature."

Recommendations

Foster Empathy and Understanding for Long-Term Planning

Having established a case for enhanced campus accessibility, the author offers several suggestions for action.

The University should make campus accessibility a higher priority and work toward a campus that not only fulfills legal requirements but also provides a user-friendly environment for the mobility impaired. Increased effort and resources must be accompanied by a sincere desire to understand and improve the campus experience of people with mobility impairments. It is difficult for the ambulatory person to empathize with the difficulties faced by these individuals. Recognizing this problem, the University should require the administrators who allocate money to ADA projects to use wheelchairs around the campus once a year. This program would help them understand the needs of people using wheelchairs. It would also allow them to assess the progress of campus accessibility as afforded by their allocation of resources. Administrators must realize that people with physical disabilities are not a small, distant, irrelevant group; anyone can join their ranks at any time. Administrators should ask themselves if they would find the current state of campus accessibility acceptable if an injury forced them to use a wheelchair on a permanent basis.

In addition, the University should actively seek student input for long-term improvements to accessibility. The University is in the process of creating the ADA Accessibility Committee, which, according to the Dean of Students' Web site, will "address institution-wide, systemic issues that fall under the scope of the Americans with Disabilities Act." This committee will replace the larger President's Committee on Students with Disabilities. Linda Millstone, the University's ADA coordinator, reports that the three student representatives on the President's Committee "were not engaged" and that even now she is "not hearing a groundswell of interest from students." The University should not take this apparent lack of interest to mean that its members with mobility impairments face no problems. According to Ms. Millstone, a survey done about two years ago indicated that students were "clueless" that the President's Committee even existed. This ignorance is not the fault of students but rather a failure of the University to make its accessibility efforts open and transparent. Students should play a prominent and powerful role in the new ADA Accessibility Committee. Since students with mobility impairments traverse the campus more frequently than most administrators, they understand the structural problems of the campus. The Committee should select its student representatives carefully to make sure that they are driven individuals committed to working for progress and representing the interests of students with disabilities. The University should consider making Committee positions paid so that student representatives can devote sufficient time to their responsibilities.

Improve Services for the Mobility Impaired

The University should also work toward creating more useful, transparent, and approachable services for its members with physical disabilities by making better use of online technology and helping students take control of their own experiences. Usefulness of services would decrease the dependence of people with physical disabilities on others and mitigate the stress of using a wheelchair on campus. Approachability would help these individuals take control of their campus experience by allowing more freedom of expression and encouraging self-advocacy. Transparency would allow people with mobility impairments to understand and appreciate the University's efforts at improving campus accessibility.

First, SSD can make its Web site more useful by updating it frequently with detailed information on construction sites that will affect accessible routes. The site should delineate alternative accessible routes and approximate the extra time required to use the detour. This information would help people with mobility impairments to plan ahead and avoid delays, mitigating the stress of maneuvering around construction sites.

The detail in these proposals makes them seem plausible and feasible.

The University should also develop software for an interactive campus map. The software would work like Mapquest or Google Maps but would provide detailed descriptions of accessible routes on campus from one building to another. It would be updated frequently with new ADA improvements and information on construction sites that impede accessible routes. In addition, the interactive map would rate building features such as entrances, bathrooms, and elevators on their level of accessibility. It would also report complaints received by SSD and the Physical Plant regarding access around and inside buildings. The software would undoubtedly ease the frustration of finding accessible routes to and from buildings.

Since usefulness and approachability of services are most important for students during their first encounters with the campus, SSD should hold formal one-on-one orientations for new students with mobility impairments. SSD should inform students in both oral and written format of their rights and responsibilities and make them aware of problems that they will encounter on the campus. For example, counselors should advise students to look at their classrooms well in advance and assess potential problems such as poor building access, the need for an elevator key, and the design of the classroom. Beyond making services more useful, these orientations would give students the impression of University services as open and responsive, encouraging students to report problems that they encounter and assume the responsibility of self-advocacy.

As a continuing resource for people with physical disabilities, the SSD Web site should include an anonymous forum for both general questions and specific complaints and needs. The forum should be restricted by the University of Texas Electronic Identification (UTEID) to students registered with SSD. Obviously, if a student has an urgent problem, he or she should visit or call SSD as soon as possible. However, for less pressing problems such as a nonfunctional automatic door button or the need for a curb cut, an anonymous forum would allow for an easy way to let administrators know of a problem. By looking at the forum, administrators and the Physical Plant can get a good idea of the most pressing accessibility issues on campus and notify students of when they will fix the reported problems. Many times, students notice problems but do not report them because they find visiting or calling SSD time-consuming or because they do not wish to be a burden. The anonymity and immediate feedback provided by the forum would allow for more freedom of expression and provide students an easier way to solve the problems they face.

The level of detail bolsters the author's personal ethos: she has given careful thought to these ideas and has earned a serious hearing.

Services for the mobility impaired should also increase their transparency by actively advertising current accessibility projects on their Web sites. My research has given me the strong impression that the administrators, architects, and engineers on the front lines of ADA improvements are devoted and hard-working. To a person with a mobility impairment, however, improvements to campus accessibility seem sluggish at best. In addition to actually devoting more resources to accessibility, then, the University should give its members with mobility impairments a clearer idea of its ongoing efforts to improve campus accessibility. Detailed online descriptions of ADA projects, including the cost of each project, would affirm its resolve to create a better environment for its members with physical disabilities.

Conclusion

The conclusion summarizes the argument and rallies support for its proposals.

Although the University has made good progress in accessibility improvements on an old campus, it must take bold steps to improve the experience of its members with mobility impairments. At present, people with permanent mobility impairments face unreasonable hardship, unequal opportunity to succeed, and lack of independence. The larger number of people with temporary disabilities faces similar hardships, and the University as a whole suffers from lack of diversity with respect to disability. To enhance the quality of life of all of its members and increase recruitment of disabled individuals, the University should focus its resources on increasing the rate of accessibility improvements and improving the quality of its services for the mobility impaired. Administrators must learn not to view people with disabilities as a "them" distinct from "us," instead recognizing that the threat of mobility impairment faces everyone. As a public institution, the University has an obligation to make the campus more inclusive and serve as an example for disability rights. With careful planning and a genuine desire to respond to special needs, practical and cost-effective changes to the University campus can significantly improve the quality of life of many of its members and prove beneficial to the future of the University as a whole.

WORKS CITED

"ADA Student Forum." Office of the Dean of Students. 6 Apr. 2005. 23 Apr. 2005 <http://deanofstudents.utexas.edu/events/ssd_forum.php>.

Gardea, Eduardo. Personal interview. 24 Mar. 2005.

Gerhardt, Michael. Personal interview. 8 Apr. 2005.

Gleeson, Austin, et al. *The University of Texas at Austin Campus Master Plan*. Austin: U of Texas, 1999.

Grant, Angela. "Making Campus More Accessible." *Daily Texan Online*. 14 Oct. 2003. 1 Mar. 2005 <http://www.dailytexanonline.com/news/2003/10/14/TopStories/Making.Campus.More.Accessible-527606.shtml>.

Holloway, Wesley Reed. Personal interview. 5 Mar. 2005.

Lu, Judy Yien. Personal interview. 5 Mar. 2005.

Maedgen, Jennifer. Personal interview. 25 Mar. 2005.

Seay, Penny. Personal interview. 11 Mar. 2005.

Throop, William. Personal interview. 6 Apr. 2005.

Mass Transit Hysteria

P. J. O'ROURKE

Wednesday, March 16, 2005

The new transportation bill, currently working its way through Congress, will provide more than $52 billion for mass transit. Mass transit is a wonderful thing, all right-thinking people agree. It stops pollution "in its tracks" (a little ecology-conscious light-rail advocacy joke). Mass transit doesn't burn climate-warming, Iraq-war-causing hydrocarbons. Mass transit can operate with nonpolluting sustainable energy sources such as electricity. Electricity can be produced by solar panels, and geothermal generators. Electricity can be produced by right-thinking people themselves, if they talk about it enough near wind farms.

Mass transit helps preserve nature in places like Yellowstone Park, the Everglades and the Arctic wilderness, because mass transit doesn't go there. Mass transit curtails urban sprawl. When you get to the end of the trolley tracks, you may want to move farther out into the suburbs, but you're going to need a lot of rails and ties and Irishmen with pickaxes. Plus there's something romantic about mass transit. Think Tony Bennett singing "Where little cable cars / Climb halfway to the stars." (And people say mass transit doesn't provide flexibility in travel plans!) Or the Kingston Trio and their impassioned protest of the five-cent Boston "T" fare increase, "The Man Who Never Returned." No doubt some lovely songs will be written about the Washington County, Ore., Wilsonville-to-Beaverton commuter rail line to be funded by the new transportation bill.

There are just two problems with mass transit. Nobody uses it, and it costs like hell. Only 4% of Americans take public transportation to work. Even in cities they don't do it. Less than 25% of commuters in the New York metropolitan area use public transportation. Elsewhere it's far less—9.5% in San Francisco–Oakland–San Jose, 1.8% in Dallas–Fort Worth. As for total travel in urban parts of America—all the comings and goings for work, school, shopping, etc.—1.7% of those trips are made on mass transit.

P. J. O'Rourke is a humorist whose books include *Eat the Rich* (1999) and *Peace Kills* (2005).

Then there is the cost, which is—obviously—$52 billion. Less obviously, there's all the money spent locally keeping local mass transit systems operating. The Heritage Foundation says, "There isn't a single light rail transit system in America in which fares paid by the passengers cover the cost of their own rides." Heritage cites the Minneapolis "Hiawatha" light rail line, soon to be completed with $107 million from the transportation bill. Heritage estimates that the total expense for each ride on the Hiawatha will be $19. Commuting to work will cost $8,550 a year. If the commuter is earning minimum wage, this leaves about $1,000 a year for food, shelter and clothing. Or, if the city picks up the tab, it could have leased a BMW X-5 SUV for the commuter at about the same price.

We don't want minimum-wage workers driving BMW X-5s. That's unfair. They're already poor, and now they're enemies of the environment? So we must find a way to save mass transit—get people to ride it, be eager to pay for it, no matter what the cold-blooded free-market types at Heritage say. We must do it for the sake of future generations, for our children.

That's it! The children. The solution to the problems of mass transit is staring us in the face. Or, in the case of my rather short children, staring us in the sternum. All over America men and women, at the behest of their children, are getting on board various light-rail systems that don't even go anywhere. And these trips—if you factor in the price of cotton candy, snow cones and trademarked plush toys—cost considerably more than $19. Yet we're willing to stand in line for ages to utilize this type of mass transit. All we have to do is equip Hiawatha with a slow climb, a steep, sudden plunge, several sharply banked curves, and maybe a loop-the-loop over by St. Paul.

The new mass transit can harness clean, renewable resources. "Unplug the Prius, honey! I'm taking the waterslide to work!" And it need not be expensive. In fact, we might be able to make certain advantageous cuts in transportation spending. A few reductions in Amtrak's already minimal maintenance budget would turn the evening Metroliner into a reeling, lurching journey through the pitch dark equal to anything Space Mountain has to offer. And here is a perfect opportunity for public/private partnership. The Disney Co. is looking for new profit centers. The New York subway can become a hair-raising thrill ride by means of a simple return to NYPD 1970s policing practices.

Not all of the new mass transit has to be frenetic. Bringing groceries home on the tilt-o-whirl presents difficulties. We can take a cue from the lucrative cruise ship industry—every commute a mini-luxury vacation. Perhaps this wouldn't be suitable in areas without navigable water. But don't be too sure. Many "riverboat casinos" are completely stationary, and a lot of commuters don't want to go to work anyway. Slot machines could be put on all forms of mass transit. Put slot machines on city buses and people will abandon their cars, or abandon their car payments, which comes to the same thing.

This is a revolutionary approach to mass transit. It can save the planet. And it can save me from taking the kids to Orlando. Now I can stay home in D.C. and send them for a ride on Washington's new, improved Metro of Horrors, where scary things jump out at you from nowhere—things like $52 billion appropriations for mass transit.

PART 3

STYLE AND PRESENTATION IN arguments

12
Style in Arguments

A person you know only slightly objects strenuously to your characterization of her in-class comments as being laced with sarcasm, saying, "Sorry, you're wrong again: sarcasm's not my style." Since you'd meant this as a compliment, you decide to apologize and ask her how *she* would describe her style.

An architectural team working to design a new fast food restaurant studies the most successful franchises of the last twenty-five years. What they find suggests that each franchise has a distinctive architectural style, so they go to work seeking something new and distinctive—and something as *unlike* McDonald's style as possible.

A photographer looking to land the cover photo on *Vogue* takes a tour of college campuses. At each school, he sits patiently in the student union, watching as students pass by. What he's looking for is a face with "fresh new style."

A researcher trying to describe teen style crafted a questionnaire and distributed it to 500 teens in three different cities. Why was she not surprised when the style mentioned most often as being desirable was "hip-hop style"?

• • •

Arguments, of course, have their own styles. One classical orator and statesman outlined three basic styles of communication, identifying them as "high" (formal or even ornate), "middle" (understated and very clear), and "low" (everyday or humorous). Even choice of font can help to convey such a style: think of French Script, for example, as ornate or high, Garamond as understated or middle, and Comic Sans as everyday or low. High style in argument is generally formal, serious, even high-minded—an argument wearing its best tuxedo. Middle style marks most ordinary arguments, from the commonplace to the professional—these arguments have sturdy work clothes on. And low style is informal, colloquial, humorous—an argument with its shoes off and feet propped up.

Such broad characterizations can give only a very general sense of an argument's style, however. To think more carefully about style in argument, consider the relationship among style and word choice, sentence structure, punctuation, and what we'll call special effects.

Using a factual tone with words chosen to draw attention but not alienate or insult the intended audience, the faculty staff and emeriti of Calvin College express their concern, in an open letter to President George W. Bush, over the government's commitments to Christian ideals.

LINK TO P. 876

Style and Word Choice

The vocabulary of an argument helps to create its style; most important, choice of words should match the tone the writer wants to establish as well as the purpose and topic of the argument. For most academic arguments, formal language is appropriate. In an argument urging every member of society to care about energy issues, Chevron CEO Dave

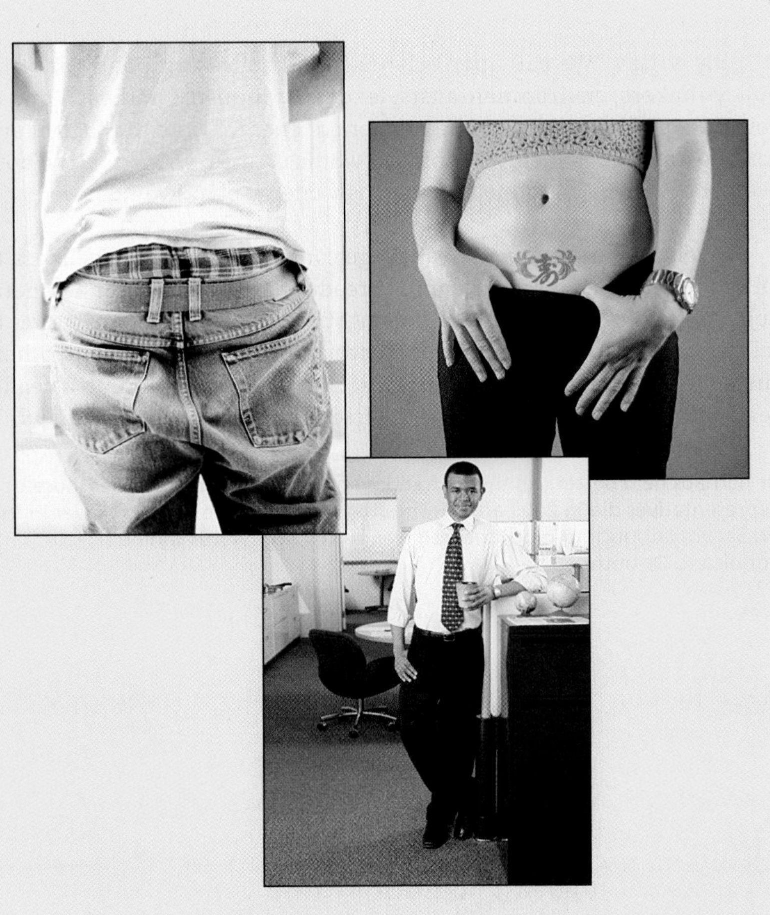

Not Just Words

Choose one of the images above and study it for a few minutes. How would you describe the style of the person depicted—just by thinking about the choice of pants, the stance, and so on? How does the photograph help to convey that style? Consider the composition, the use of color, and so on.

O'Reilly writes, "We call upon scientists and educators, politicians and policy-makers, environmentalists, leaders of industry, and each one of you to be part of reshaping the next era of energy." Note the formal and serious tone that O'Reilly's choice of words creates; writing "How 'bout everybody rallyin' round to mix up a new energy plan" would have had a very different effect.

While slang and colloquial language can sometimes add liveliness to an argument, they also can confuse readers. In an article for a general audience about tense arms-control negotiations, using the term *nukes* to refer to nuclear missiles might confuse some readers and irritate others since the shorthand term could indicate a frivolous reference to a deadly serious subject. Be alert, too, to the use of jargon in arguments: while

Or perhaps he'd better call them "freedom fries," as members of the House of Representatives did in 2003 after France threatened to use its veto power in the UN Security Council to block the Iraq war. A fuss over words can be silly, or significant. Or both.

"Your Honor, please ask the defendant to stop using the word 'fries' where 'French-fried potatoes' is implied."

jargon (the special vocabulary of members of a profession, trade, or field) is very useful for expert or technical audiences, serving as a kind of shorthand, it can also alienate readers who don't understand the terms being used.

Another key to an argument's style is the use of connotation, the associations that accompany many words. Note, for example, the differences in connotation among the following three statements:

> **Students from the Labor Action Committee (LAC) carried out a hunger strike aimed at calling attention to the below-minimum wages being paid to campus temporary workers, saying, "the university must pay a living wage to all its workers."**
>
> **Left-wing agitators and radicals tried to use self-induced starvation to stampede the university into caving in to their demands.**
>
> **Supporters of human rights for all put their bodies on the line to protest the university's thinly veiled racist policies of scandalously low pay for immigrant temporary workers.**

Here the first sentence is the most neutral, presenting the facts and offering a quotation from one of the students. The second sentence uses loaded terms like "agitators" and "radicals" and "stampede" to create a negative image of this event, while the final sentence uses other loaded words to create a positive view. As these examples demonstrate, words matter!

Finally, arguments that use more concrete and specific words rather than more abstract and general ones will make a more vivid impact on readers and listeners. In a review of Steven Bochco's TV series about the Iraq War, *Over There,* the reviewer says:

> **The soldiers are pinned down; with their legs splayed in order to get as close to the ground as possible, they look like frogs in a dissecting tray. There's no cover around them, nowhere to hide, and viewers can feel this, too—a sense of loss of control and of danger everywhere.**
>
> **–Nancy Franklin, "The Yanks Are Coming"**

The reviewer could have been more general, saying, "The soldiers have no hiding places and are completely vulnerable," but the concrete language ("pinned down," "legs splayed," "like frogs in a dissecting tray") makes this depiction much more memorable and hence helps to create an effective style.

Naomi Schaefer Riley utilizes a variety of sentence structures to guide readers through her essay about a new generation of students at religious colleges. Note how the variation, or at times purposeful repetition, draws in the reader.

LINK TO P. 859

Sentence Structure and Argument

Choices about sentence structure also play an important part in establishing the style of an argument. As with most writing, variety may be the key to constructing a strong series of sentences. Writers of effective arguments take this maxim to heart, working to vary such things as sentence pattern and length.

Varying sentence length can be especially effective. Here's George Orwell moving from a long, complicated sentence to a short, punchy one at the end:

> **The fire of, I think, five machine guns was pouring upon us, and there was a series of heavy crashes caused by the Fascists flinging bombs over their parapet in the most idiotic manner. It was intensely dark.**
>
> **–George Orwell, *Homage to Catalonia***

Paying attention to the way sentences begin can also help to build an argument's effectiveness. In the letter from Chevron CEO O'Reilly mentioned on page 372, we find the following paragraph:

> **Demand is soaring like never before. As populations grow and economies take off, millions in the developing world are enjoying the benefits of a lifestyle that requires increasing amounts of energy. In fact, some say that in 20 years the world will consume 40% more oil than it does today. At the same time, many of the world's oil and gas fields are maturing. And new energy discoveries are mainly occurring in places where resources are difficult to extract, physically, economically, and even politically. When growing demand meets tighter supplies, the result is more competition for the same resources.**
>
> **–Dave O'Reilly**

Look at how much less effective this passage becomes when the sentences all begin in the same way—that is, with the subject first:

> **Demand is soaring like never before. Millions in the rapidly developing world are enjoying the benefits of a lifestyle that requires increasing amounts of energy. Some say that in 20 years the world will consume 40% more oil than it does today. Many of the world's oil and gas fields are maturing. New energy discoveries are mainly occurring in places where resources are difficult to extract, physically, economically, and even politically. Growing demand and tighter supplies result in more competition for the same resources.**

In the second version, taking out all the transitions ("In fact," "At the same time,") and the openings that vary the subject-first order ("As populations grow . . . ," "When growing demand meets tighter supplies,") makes the passage much less interesting to read and harder to understand, thus weakening its argument.

Effective arguments can also make good use of parallel structures in sentences. In a review of a new biography of writer Henry Roth, Jonathan Rosen includes the following description:

> **His hands were warped by rheumatoid arthritis; the very touch of his computer keyboard was excruciating. But he still put in five hours a day, helped by Percocet, beer, a ferocious will, and the ministrations of several young assistants.**
>
> **–Jonathan Rosen, "Writer, Interrupted"**

In the first sentence, Rosen chooses a coordinate structure, with the first clause about Roth's arthritic hands perfectly balanced by the following clause describing the results of putting those hands on a keyboard. In the second sentence, Rosen uses a series of parallel nouns and noun phrases ("Percocet," "beer," "the ministrations of . . . ," etc.) to build up a picture of Roth as extremely persistent.

Punctuation and Argument

In a memorable comment, actor and director Clint Eastwood says, "You can show a lot with a look. . . . It's punctuation." Eastwood is right about punctuation's effect, either in acting or in arguing. As you read and write arguments, consider choices of punctuation closely. Here are some ways in which punctuation helps to enhance style.

The semicolon is a handy punctuation mark since it signals a pause stronger than a comma but not as strong as a period. Here is Mary Gordon using a semicolon in an argument about "the ghosts of Ellis Island":

> **Immigration acts were passed; newcomers had to prove, besides moral correctness and financial solvency, their ability to read.**
>
> **–Mary Gordon, "More than Just a Shrine"**

Gordon could have put a period after *passed,* separating this passage into two sentences. But she chooses a semicolon instead, giving the sentence an abrupt rhythm that suits her topic: laws that imposed strict requirements on immigrants. Semicolons can also make passages easier

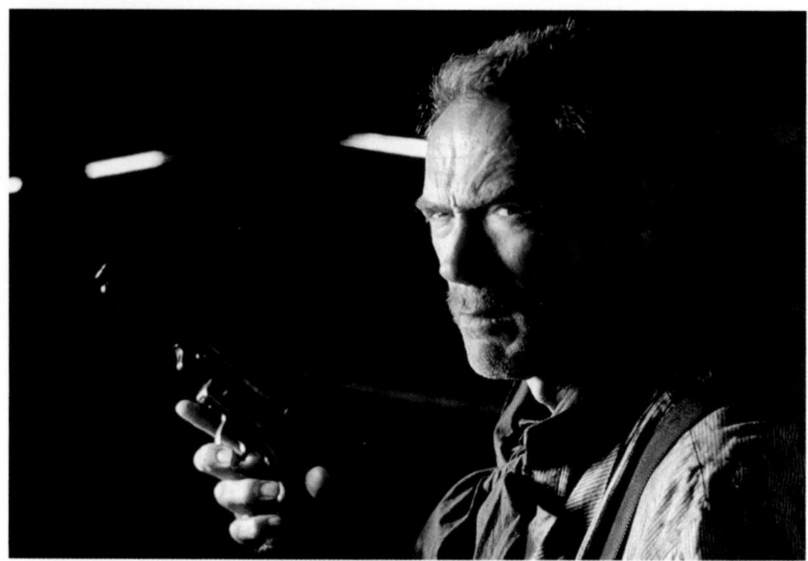

"You can show a lot with a look. . . . It's punctuation."

to read, as in the following example from an argument by William F. Buckley Jr.:

> Every year, whether the Republican or the Democratic party is in office, more and more power drains away from the individual to feed vast reservoirs in far-off places; and we have less and less say about the shape of events which shape our future.
>
> –William F. Buckley Jr., "Why Don't We Complain?"

Writers also use end punctuation to good effect. Though the exclamation point can be distracting and even irritating if overused (think of those email messages you get from friends that fairly bristle with them), it can be very helpful if used infrequently. Exclamation points are especially good for indicating a speaker's tone. For example, in an argument about the treatment of prisoners at Guantánamo, consider how Jane Mayer evokes the sense of desperation in some of the prisoners:

> As we reached the end of the cell-block, hysterical shouts, in broken English, erupted from a caged exercise area nearby. "Come here!" a man screamed. "See here! They are liars! . . . No sleep!" he yelled. "No food! No medicine! No doctor! Everybody sick here!"
>
> –Jane Mayer, "The Experiment"

The question mark is another handy mark of punctuation. In a fairly negative review of Steven Spielberg's *War of the Worlds,* David Denby uses a series of questions to drive home the point he's been making:

> **As the scenes of destruction cease, one has to ponder the oddity of a science-fiction movie without science, or even routine curiosity. Who are the aliens? What is their chemical makeup and how might they be vulnerable? What does the attack mean? Nobody raises any of these issues.**
>
> **–David Denby, "Stayin' Alive"**

Two other punctuation marks are often important in establishing the style of an argument. While sometimes used interchangeably, the colon and the dash have very different effects. The colon introduces explanations or examples and separates elements from one another. Alison Lurie uses a colon in this way:

> **The men may also wear the getup known as Sun Belt Cool: a pale beige suit, open-collared shirt (often in a darker shade than the suit), cream-colored loafers and aviator sunglasses.**
>
> **–Alison Lurie, "The Language of Clothes"**

A dash or a pair of dashes, on the other hand, is most often used to insert comments or highlight material within a sentence. Notice how columnist Maureen Dowd uses dashes to set off an important point she wants to make about the Bush administration's claim that it doesn't need search warrants to spy on individuals:

> **Even when [Vice President Dick Cheney] can easily—and retroactively—get snooping warrants, he doesn't want their stinking warrants. Warrants are for sissies.**
>
> **–Maureen Dowd, "Looking for a Democratic Tough Guy, or Girl"**

In the following example, *New York Times Book Review* critic Joel Conarroe uses dashes to make fun of their overuse by sports writer Roger Angell and to show how they can slow down the pace of the prose:

> **Mr. Angell is addicted to dashes and parentheses—small pauses or digressions in the narrative like those moments when the umpire dusts off home plate or a pitcher rubs up a new ball—that serve to slow an already deliberate movement almost to a standstill.**
>
> **–Joel Conarroe, "Ode on a Rainbow Slider"**

As these examples suggest, punctuation is often key to creating the rhythm of an argument. Take a look at how Maya Angelou uses a dash along with another punctuation mark—ellipsis points—to indicate a pause or hesitation, in this case one that builds anticipation:

> **Then the voice, husky and familiar, came to wash over us—"The winnah, and still heavyweight champeen of the world . . . Joe Louis."**
> **–Maya Angelou, "Champion of the World"**

Creating rhythms can be especially important in online communication, when writers are trying to invest their arguments with emotion or emphasis. Some writers still use asterisks in online communication to convey the sense that italic type creates in print texts: "You *must* respond to this email today!" Others use emoticons or new characters of all kinds (from the ubiquitous smiley face ☺ to combinations like g2g for "got to go") to establish the rhythm, tone, and style they want. The creativity available to writers online allows for great experimentation; but in an argument where the stakes are high, writers are careful not to go too far with such experiments—they don't want to alienate their audiences.

Special Effects: Figurative Language and Argument

Look at any magazine or Web site, and you'll see figurative language working on behalf of arguments. When the writer of a letter to the editor complains that "Donna Haraway's supposition that because we rely on cell phones and laptops we are cyborgs is [like] saying the Plains Indians were centaurs because they relied on horses," he's using an analogy to rebut (and perhaps ridicule) Haraway's claim. When another writer says that "the digital revolution is whipping through our lives like a Bengali typhoon," she's making an implicit argument about the speed and strength of the digital revolution. When still another writer calls Disney World a "smile factory," she begins a stinging critique of the way pleasure is "manufactured" there.

Just what is figurative language? Traditionally, the terms *figurative language* and *figures of speech* refer to language that differs from the ordinary—language that calls up, or "figures," something else. But, in fact, all language could be said to call up something else. The word *table,* for example, isn't itself a table; rather, it calls up a table in our imaginations. Thus just as all language is by nature argumentative, so are all figures of speech. Far from being mere decoration or embellishment (something like icing on the cake of thought), figures of speech are indispensable to language use.

More specifically, figurative language brings two major strengths to arguments. First, it aids understanding by likening something unknown to something known. For example, in arguing for the existence of DNA as they had identified and described it, scientists Watson and Crick used two familiar examples—a helix (spiral) and a zipper—to make their point. Today, arguments about new computer technologies are filled with similar uses of figurative language. Indeed, Microsoft's entire word processing system depends on likening items to those in an office (as in Microsoft Office) to make them more understandable and familiar to users. Second, figurative language is helpful in arguments because it is often extremely memorable. A person arguing that slang should be used in formal writing turns to this memorable definition for support: "Slang is language that takes off its coat, spits on its hands, and gets to work." In a brief poem that carries a powerful argument, Langston Hughes uses figurative language to explore the consequences of unfulfilled dreams:

> What happens to a dream deferred?
>
> Does it dry up
> Like a raisin in the sun?
> Or fester like a sore—
> And then run?
> Does it stink like rotten meat?
> Or crust and sugar over—
> Like a syrupy sweet?
>
> Maybe it just sags
> Like a heavy load.
>
> *Or does it explode?*
>
> –Langston Hughes, "Harlem—A Dream Deferred"

In 1963, Martin Luther King Jr. used figurative language to make his argument for civil rights unmistakably clear as well as memorable:

> In a sense we have come to our nation's capital to cash a check. When the architects of our republic wrote the magnificent words of the Constitution and the Declaration of Independence, they were signing a promissory note to which every American was to fall heir. This note was a promise that all men would be guaranteed the unalienable rights of life, liberty, and the pursuit of happiness.
>
> It is obvious today that America has defaulted on this promissory note insofar as her citizens of color are concerned. Instead of honoring

> **this sacred obligation, America has given the Negro people a bad check; a check which has come back marked "insufficient funds." But we refuse to believe that the bank of justice is bankrupt. We refuse to believe that there are insufficient funds in the great vaults of opportunity in this nation. So we have come to cash this check—a check that will give us upon demand the riches of freedom and the security of justice.**
>
> **–Martin Luther King Jr., "I Have a Dream"**

The figures of the promissory note and the bad check are especially effective here because they suggest financial exploitation, which fits perfectly with the overall theme of King's speech.

You may be surprised to learn that during the European Renaissance, schoolchildren sometimes learned and practiced using as many as 180 figures of speech. Such practice seems more than a little excessive today, especially because figures of speech come so naturally to native speakers of the English language; you hear of "chilling out," "taking flak," "nipping a plot in the bud," "getting our act together," "blowing your cover," "marching to a different drummer," "seeing red," "smelling a rat," "being on cloud nine," "throwing in the towel," "tightening our belts," "rolling in the aisles," "turning the screws"—you get the picture. In fact, you and your friends no doubt have favorite figures of speech, ones you use every day. Why not take a quick inventory during one day—just listen to everything that's said around you, and jot down any figurative language you hear.

We can't aim for a complete catalog of figures of speech here, much less a thorough analysis of the power of the special effects they create. What we can offer, however, is a brief listing—with examples—of some of the most familiar kinds of figures, along with a reminder that they can be used to extremely good effect in the arguments you write.

Figures have traditionally been classified into two main types: *tropes,* which involve a change in the ordinary signification, or meaning, of a word or phrase; and *schemes,* which involve a special arrangement of words. Here are the most frequently used figures in each category, beginning with the familiar tropes of metaphor, simile, and analogy.

Tropes

METAPHOR

One of the most pervasive uses of figurative language, metaphor offers an implied comparison between two things and thereby clarifies and enlivens many arguments. In the following passage, bell hooks uses the metaphor of the hope chest to enhance her argument that autobiography involves a special kind of treasure hunt:

> **Conceptually, the autobiography was framed in the manner of a hope chest. I remembered my mother's hope chest, with its wonderful odor of cedar, and thought about her taking the most precious items and placing them there for safekeeping. Certain memories were for me a similar treasure. I wanted to place them somewhere for safekeeping. An autobiographical narrative seemed an appropriate place.**
>
> **–bell hooks, *Bone Black***

In another example, a profile of conservative activist Grover Norquist quotes him using a metaphor in criticizing Republicans he thinks have gone in the wrong direction:

> **"When you have a brand like Coca-Cola, and you find a rat head in the bottle, you create an outcry. . . . Republicans who raise taxes are rat heads in Coke bottles. They endanger the brand."**
>
> **–John Cassidy, "The Ringleader"**

English language use is so filled with metaphors that these powerful, persuasive tools often zip by unnoticed, so be on the lookout for effective metaphors in everything you read. For example, when a reviewer of new software that promises complete filtering of advertisements on the World Wide Web refers to the product as "a weedwhacker for the Web," he's using a metaphor to advance an argument about the nature and function of that product.

SIMILE

A direct comparison between two things that uses *like* or *as,* simile is pervasive in both written and spoken language. Eminem's song "Like Toy Soldiers," for example, compares human beings to toy soldiers who "all fall down," are "torn apart," and "never win" but fight on anyway; a radio announcer says the UCLA men's basketball team are so eager for the NCAA playoffs that they're "like pit bulls on pork chops." One of our grandmothers used to say "prices are high as a cat's back" or, as a special compliment, "you look as pretty as red shoes." Here's a more formal written example from an article in the *New Yorker* magazine:

> **You can tell the graphic-novels section in a bookstore from afar, by the young bodies sprawled around it like casualties of a localized disaster.**
>
> **–Peter Schjeldahl, "Words and Pictures: Graphic Novels Come of Age"**

Similes play a major part in many arguments, as you can see in this excerpt from a brief *Wired* magazine review of a new magazine for women:

> **Women's magazines occupy a special niche in the cluttered infoscape of modern media. Ask any *Vogue* junkie: no girl-themed Web site or CNN segment on women's health can replace the guilty pleasure of slipping a glossy fashion rag into your shopping cart. Smooth as a pint of chocolate Häagen-Dazs, feckless as a thousand-dollar slip dress, women's magazines wrap culture, trends, health, and trash in a single, decadent package. But like the diet dessert recipes they print, these slick publications can leave a bad taste in your mouth.**
>
> **–Tiffany Lee Brown, "En Vogue"**

Here three similes are in prominent display: "smooth as a pint of chocolate Häagen-Dazs" and "feckless as a thousand-dollar slip dress" in the third sentence, and "like the diet dessert recipes" in the fourth. Together, the similes add to the image the writer is trying to create of mass-market women's magazines as a mishmash of "trash" and "trends."

Lan Cao presents a vivid description of her immersion in the English language by using metaphor and analogy among other tropes.

LINK TO P. 764

ANALOGY

Analogies draw comparisons between two things, often point by point, in order to show similarity in certain respects (as in *Many are tempted to draw an analogy between the computer and the human brain*) or to argue that if two things are alike in one way they are probably alike in other ways as well. Often extended to several sentences, paragraphs, or even whole essays, analogies can clarify and emphasize points of comparison. In considering the movie *Hustle and Flow,* a reviewer draws an analogy between the character DJay and the late, great Duke Ellington:

> **As [actor] Howard develops DJay's frustration and rue, he avoids the obvious, the overemphatic. His self-mocking performance is so ironically refined and allusive that one might think that Duke Ellington himself had slipped into an old undershirt and hit the fetid streets of Memphis.**
>
> **–David Denby, "Stayin' Alive"**

And in an argument about the failures of the aircraft industry, another writer uses an analogy for potent contrast:

> **If the aircraft industry had evolved as spectacularly as the computer industry over the past twenty-five years, a Boeing 767 would cost five hundred dollars today, and it would circle the globe in twenty minutes on five gallons of fuel.**

CULTURAL CONTEXTS FOR ARGUMENT

Formality and Other Style Issues

Style is always affected by language, culture, and rhetorical tradition.

What constitutes effective style, therefore, varies broadly across cultures and depends on the rhetorical situation—purpose, audience, and so on. There's at least one important style question to consider when arguing across cultures: what level of formality is most appropriate? In the United States, a fairly informal style is often acceptable, even appreciated.

Many cultures, however, tend to value formality. If you're in doubt, therefore, it's probably wise to err on the side of formality, especially in communicating with elders or with those in authority:

- Take care to use proper titles as appropriate—*Ms.*, *Mr.*, *Dr.*, and so on.
- Don't use first names unless you've been invited to do so.
- Steer clear of slang. Especially when you're communicating with members of other cultures, slang may not be understood—or it may be seen as disrespectful.

Beyond formality, stylistic preferences vary widely. When arguing across cultures, the most important stylistic issue might be clarity, especially when you're communicating with people whose native languages are different from your own. In such situations, analogies and similes almost always aid in understanding. Likening something unknown to something familiar can help make your argument forceful—and understandable.

Other Tropes

Several other tropes deserve special mention.

One distinctive trope found extensively in African American English is ***signifying,*** in which a speaker cleverly and often humorously needles the listener. In the following passage, two African American men (Grave Digger and Coffin Ed) signify on their white supervisor (Anderson), who has ordered them to discover the originators of a riot:

> **"I take it you've discovered who started the riot," Anderson said.**
> **"We knew who he was all along," Grave Digger said.**

> "It's just nothing we can do to him," Coffin Ed echoed.
> "Why not, for God's sake?"
> "He's dead," Coffin Ed said.
> "Who?"
> "Lincoln," Grave Digger said.
> "He hadn't ought to have freed us if he didn't want to make provisions to feed us," Coffin Ed said. "Anyone could have told him that."
>
> –Chester Himes, *Hot Day, Hot Night*

Coffin Ed and Grave Digger demonstrate the major characteristics of effective signifying: indirection, ironic humor, fluid rhythm—and a surprising twist at the end. Rather than insulting Anderson directly by pointing out that he's asked a dumb question, they criticize the question indirectly by ultimately blaming a white man (and not just any white man, but one they're all supposed to revere). This twist leaves the supervisor speechless, teaching him something and giving Grave Digger and Coffin Ed the last word—and the last laugh.

You'll find examples of signifying in the work of many African American writers. You may also hear signifying in NBA basketball, for it's an important element of trash talking; what Grave Digger and Coffin Ed do to Anderson, Allen Iverson regularly does to his opponents on the court.

Take a look at the example of signifying from a *Boondocks* cartoon (see the figure on p. 385). Note how Huey seems to be sympathizing with Jazmine and then, in not one but two surprising twists, reveals that he has been needling her all along.

Hyperbole is the use of overstatement for special effect, a kind of pyrotechnics in prose. The tabloid papers whose headlines scream at shoppers in the grocery checkout line probably qualify as the all-time champions of hyperbole (journalist Tom Wolfe once wrote a satirical review of a *National Enquirer* writers' convention that he titled "Keeps His Mom-in-Law in Chains Meets Kills Son and Feeds Corpse to Pigs"). Everyone has seen these overstated arguments and, perhaps, marveled at the way they seem to sell.

Hyperbole is also the trademark of more serious writers. In a column arguing that men's magazines fuel the same kind of neurotic anxieties about appearance that have plagued women for so long, Michelle Cottle uses hyperbole and humor to make her point:

> What self-respecting '90s woman could embrace a publication that runs such enlightened articles as "Turn Your Good Girl Bad" and "How to Wake Up Next to a One-Night Stand"? Or maybe you'll smile and

In these *Boondocks* strips, Huey signifies on Jazmine, using indirection, ironic humor, and two surprising twists.

> wink knowingly: What red-blooded hetero chick wouldn't love all those glossy photo spreads of buff young beefcake in various states of undress, ripped abs and glutes flexed so tightly you could bounce a check on them? Either way you've got the wrong idea. My affection for *Men's Health* is driven by pure gender politics. . . . With page after page of bulging biceps and Gillette jaws, robust hairlines and silken skin, *Men's Health* is peddling a standard of male beauty as unforgiving and unrealistic as the female version sold by those dewy-eyed pre-teen waifs draped across covers of *Glamour* and *Elle*.
>
> –Michelle Cottle, "Turning Boys into Girls"

As you can well imagine, hyperbole of this sort can easily backfire, so it pays to use it sparingly and for an audience whose reactions you can predict with confidence. American journalist H. L. Mencken ignored this advice in 1921 when he used relentless hyperbole to savage the literary style of President Warren Harding—and note that in doing so he says that he's offering a "small tribute," making the irony even more notable:

> I rise to pay my small tribute to Dr. Harding. Setting aside a college professor or two and half a dozen dipsomaniacal newspaper reporters, he takes the first place in my Valhalla of literati. That is to say, he writes

> **the worst English that I have ever encountered. It reminds me of a string of wet sponges; it reminds me of tattered washing on the line; it reminds me of stale bean-soup, of college yells, of dogs barking idiotically through endless nights. It is so bad that a sort of grandeur creeps into it. It drags itself out of the dark abysm (I was about to write abcess!) of pish, and crawls insanely up the topmost pinnacle of posh. It is rumble and bumble. It is flap and doodle. It is balder and dash.**
>
> **–H. L. Mencken**

Understatement, on the other hand, requires a quiet, muted message to make its point effectively. In her memoir, Rosa Parks—the civil rights activist who made history in 1955 by refusing to give up her bus seat to a white passenger—uses understatement so often that it might be said to be characteristic of her writing, a mark of her ethos. She refers to Martin Luther King Jr. simply as "a true leader," to Malcolm X as a person of "strong conviction," and to her own lifelong efforts as simply a small way of "carrying on."

Understatement can be particularly effective in arguments that would seem to call for its opposite. When Watson and Crick published their first article on the structure of DNA, they felt that they had done nothing less than discover the secret of life. (Imagine what the *National Enquirer* headlines might have been for this story!) Yet in an atmosphere of extreme scientific competitiveness they chose to close their article with a vast understatement, using it purposely to gain emphasis: "It has not escaped our notice," they wrote, "that the specific pairing we have postulated immediately suggests a possible copying mechanism for the genetic material." A half-century later, considering the profound developments that have taken place in genetics, including the cloning of animals, the power of this understatement resonates even more strongly.

Rhetorical questions don't really require answers. Rather, they help assert or deny something about an argument. Most of us use rhetorical questions frequently; think, for instance, of the times you've said "Who cares?" or "Why me?" or "How should I know?"—rhetorical questions all. Rhetorical questions also show up in written arguments. In a review of a book-length argument about the use and misuse of power in the Disney dynasty, Linda Watts uses a series of rhetorical questions to sketch in part of the book's argument:

> **If you have ever visited one of the Disney theme parks, though, you have likely wondered at the labor—both seen and unseen—necessary to maintain these fanciful environments. How and when are the grounds tended so painstakingly? How are the signs of high traffic**

> **erased from public facilities? What keeps employees so poised, meticulously groomed, and endlessly cheerful?**
>
> **–Linda S. Watts, review of *Inside the Mouse***

And here's Debra Saunders, opening an argument for the legalization of medical marijuana with a rhetorical question:

> **If the federal government were right that medical marijuana has no medicinal value, why have so many doctors risked their practices by recommending its use for patients with cancer or AIDS?**
>
> **–Debra Saunders**

Antonomasia is probably most familiar to you from the sports pages: "His Airness" means Michael Jordan; "The Great One," Wayne Gretzky; "The Sultan of Swat," Babe Ruth; "The Swiss Miss," Martina Hingis. And in the 2006 Winter Olympics, snowboarder Shaun White became "The Flying Tomato." Such shorthand substitutions of a descriptive word or phrase for a proper name can pack arguments into just one phrase. What does calling Jordan "His Airness" argue about him?

Sportscasters who dubbed snowboarder Shaun White "The Flying Tomato" probably didn't realize they were using the trope of antonomasia.

Irony, the use of words to convey a meaning in tension with or opposite to their literal meanings, also works powerfully in arguments. One of the most famous sustained uses of irony in literature occurs in Shakespeare's *Julius Caesar,* as Mark Antony punctuates his condemnation of Brutus with the repeated ironic phrase "But Brutus is an honourable man." You may be a reader of *The Onion,* noted for its ironic treatment of politics. Another journal, the online *Ironic Times,* devotes itself to irony. Take a

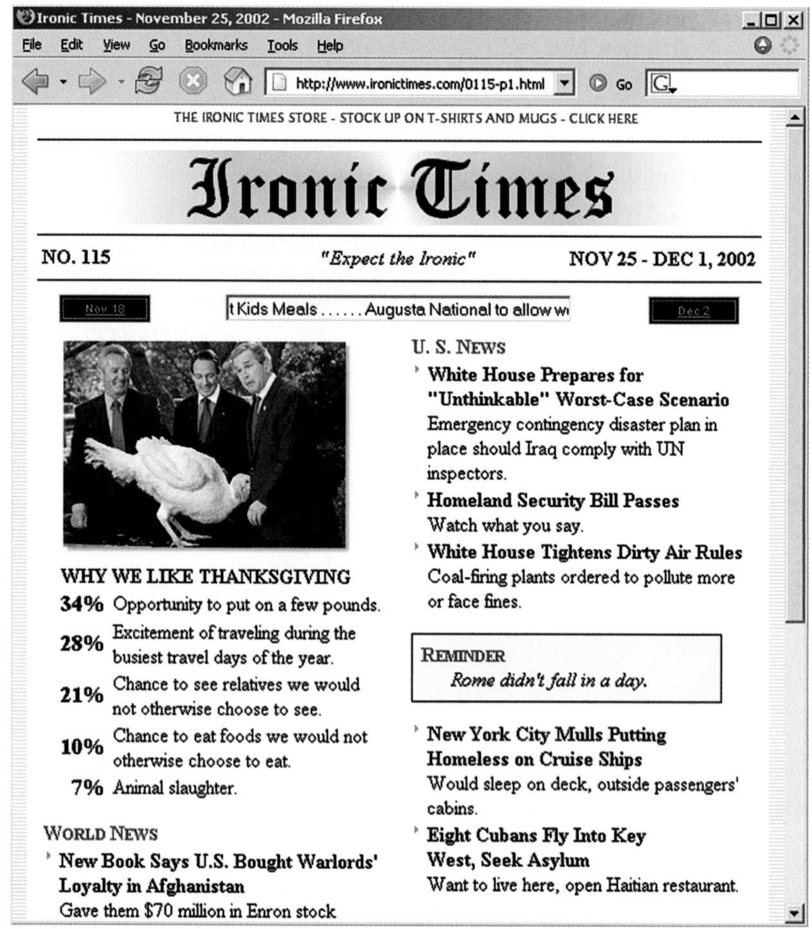

Ironic Times - November 25, 2002 - Mozilla Firefox

File Edit View Go Bookmarks Tools Help

http://www.ironictimes.com/0115-p1.html

THE IRONIC TIMES STORE - STOCK UP ON T-SHIRTS AND MUGS - CLICK HERE

Ironic Times

NO. 115 — *"Expect the Ironic"* — NOV 25 - DEC 1, 2002

Nov 18 | t Kids Meals . . . . . . Augusta National to allow w | Dec 2

WHY WE LIKE THANKSGIVING

34% Opportunity to put on a few pounds.

28% Excitement of traveling during the busiest travel days of the year.

21% Chance to see relatives we would not otherwise choose to see.

10% Chance to eat foods we would not otherwise choose to eat.

7% Animal slaughter.

WORLD NEWS

New Book Says U.S. Bought Warlords' Loyalty in Afghanistan
Gave them $70 million in Enron stock

U. S. NEWS

White House Prepares for "Unthinkable" Worst-Case Scenario
Emergency contingency disaster plan in place should Iraq comply with UN inspectors.

Homeland Security Bill Passes
Watch what you say.

White House Tightens Dirty Air Rules
Coal-firing plants ordered to pollute more or face fines.

REMINDER
Rome didn't fall in a day.

New York City Mulls Putting Homeless on Cruise Ships
Would sleep on deck, outside passengers' cabins.

Eight Cubans Fly Into Key West, Seek Asylum
Want to live here, open Haitian restaurant.

Front page of the *Ironic Times*

look at the front page above, whose lead story has taken on an additional layer of irony since it was published in 2002.

Schemes

Schemes, figures that depend on word order, can add quite a bit of syntactic "zing" to arguments. Here we present the ones you're likely to see most often.

Parallelism involves the use of grammatically similar phrases or clauses for special effect:

> **Those who teach, and who think for a living about American history, need to be told: Keep the text, teach the text, and only then, if you must, deconstruct the text.**
>
> **–Peggy Noonan, "Patriots, Then and Now"**

> **Current government programs don't protect poor people very well against the cost of becoming sick. They do much better at protecting sick people against the risk of becoming poor.**
>
> **–Michael Kinsley, "To Your Health"**

> **The laws of our land are said to be "by the people, of the people, and for the people."**

Antithesis is the use of parallel structures to mark contrast or opposition:

> **That's one small step for a man, one giant leap for mankind.**
>
> **–Neil Armstrong**

> **Marriage has many pains, but celibacy has no pleasures.**
>
> **–Samuel Johnson**

> **Those who kill people are called murderers; those who kill animals, sportsmen.**

Inverted word order, in which the parts of a sentence or clause are not in the usual subject-verb-object order, can help make arguments particularly memorable:

> **Into this grey lake plopped the thought, I know this man, don't I?**
>
> **–Doris Lessing**

> **Hard to see, the dark side is.**
>
> **–Yoda**

> **Good looking he was not; wealthy he was not; but brilliant—he was.**

As with anything else, however, too much of such a figure can quickly become, well, too much.

Anaphora, or effective repetition, can act like a drumbeat in an argument, bringing the point home. In an argument about the future of Chicago, Lerone Bennett Jr. uses repetition to link Chicago to innovation and creativity:

Rob Walker employs an anaphora schema near the end of his essay about Dove's ads using "real women." Consider how his repetition of "enough" strengthens his argument.

LINK TO P. 614

> [Chicago]'s the place where organized Black history was born, where gospel music was born, where jazz and the blues were reborn, where the Beatles and the Rolling Stones went up to the mountaintop to get the new musical commandments from Chuck Berry and the rock'n'roll apostles.
>
> –Lerone Bennett Jr., "Blacks in Chicago"

And speaking of the Rolling Stones, here's Dave Barry using repetition in his comments on their 2002 tour:

> Recently I attended a Rolling Stones concert. This is something I do every two decades. I saw the Stones in the 1960s, and then again in the 1980s. I plan to see them next in the 2020s, then the 2040s, then the 2060s, at their 100th anniversary concert.
>
> –Dave Barry, "OK, What Will Stones Do for 100th Anniversary?"

Reversed structures for special effect have been used widely in political argumentation since President John F. Kennedy's inaugural address in 1961 charged citizens, "Ask not what your country can do for you; ask what you can do for your country." Like the other figures we've listed here, this one can help make arguments memorable:

> The Democrats won't get elected unless things get worse, and things won't get worse until the Democrats get elected.
>
> –Jeane Kirkpatrick

> Your manuscript is both good and original. But the part that is good is not original, and the part that is original is not good.
>
> –Samuel Johnson

> When the going gets tough, the tough get going.

If Everything's an Argument . . .

Choose a passage from this chapter (perhaps the description of high, middle, and low style on p. 370, or the introduction to figurative language on p. 378), and look carefully at the words the authors of this book have chosen to use. What tone do words in these passages create? Do you find the word choice effective—or not?

RESPOND •

1. Turn to something you read frequently—a Web log, a sports or news magazine, a zine—and look closely at the sentences. What seems distinctive about them? Do they vary in terms of their length and the way they begin? If so, how? Do they use parallel structures to good effect? How easy to read are they, and what accounts for that ease?
2. Try your hand at writing a brief movie review for your campus newspaper, experimenting with punctuation as one way to create an effective style. Consider whether a series of questions might have a strong effect, whether exclamation points would add or detract from the message you want to send, and so on. When you've finished the review, compare it to one written by a classmate and look for similarities and differences in your choices of punctuation.
3. In the following advertising slogans, identify the types of figurative language used: metaphor, simile, analogy, hyperbole, understatement, rhetorical question, antonomasia, irony, parallelism, antithesis, inverted word order, anaphora, or reversed structure.

   "Good to the last drop." (Maxwell House coffee)

   "It's the real thing." (Coca-Cola)

   "Melts in your mouth, not in your hands." (M&M's)

   "Be all that you can be." (U.S. Army)

   "Got Milk?" (America's Milk Processors)

   "Breakfast of champions." (Wheaties)

   "Double your pleasure; double your fun." (Doublemint gum)

   "Let your fingers do the walking." (the Yellow Pages)

   "Think small." (Volkswagen)

   "Like a Rock." (Chevy trucks)

   "Real bonding, real popcorn, real butter, real good times." (Pop-Secret Popcorn)
4. Some public speakers are well known for their use of tropes and schemes. (Jesse Jackson comes to mind, as does George W. Bush, who employs folksy sayings to achieve a certain effect.) Using the Internet, find the text of a recent speech by a speaker who uses figures liberally. Pick a paragraph that seems particularly rich in figures and rewrite it, eliminating every trace of figurative language. Then read the two paragraphs—the original and your revised version—aloud to your class. With your classmates' help, try to imagine rhetorical situations in which the figure-free version would be most appropriate.

Now find some prose that seems dry and pretty much nonfigurative. (A technical manual, instructions for operating appliances, or a legal document might serve.) Rewrite a part of the piece in the most figurative language you can muster. Then try to list rhetorical situations in which this newly figured language might be most appropriate.

13
Humor in Arguments

When the city council passes an ordinance requiring bicyclists to wear helmets to protect against head injuries, a cyclist responds by writing a letter to the editors of the local newspaper suggesting other requirements the council might impose to protect citizens—including wearing earplugs in dance clubs, water wings in city pools, and blinders in City Hall.

A distinguished professor at a prestigious school dashes off a column for the campus paper on a controversial issue, perhaps spending a little less time than she should backing up her claims. The op-ed piece gets picked up by a blogger who circulates it nationally, and responses flood in—including one from a student who grades the paper like a freshman essay. The professor doesn't get an "A."

An undergraduate who thinks his school's new sexual harassment policy amounts to Puritanism parodies it for the school humor magazine by describing in a short fictional drama what would happen if Romeo and Juliet strayed onto campus.

Tired of looking at the advertisements that cover every square inch of the campus sports arena walls, a student sends the college newspaper a satirical "news" article entitled "Sports Arena for Sale—to Advertisers!"

• • •

Breathes there a college student who doesn't read *The Onion* in its print or online versions? Sure, its humor can be sophomoric, yet that's just fine with many undergraduates. But it's not just four-letter words and bathroom jokes that make young people fans of *The Onion* today or that made their parents avid readers of *The National Lampoon* or even *Mad Magazine*. Nor has *Saturday Night Live* survived more than thirty years on TV because viewers (again, mainly young) want to hear Madonna sing "Fever" or watch the Rolling Stones creak through "Brown Sugar" one more time. No, we suspect that these productions—print and video—have attracted and held audiences so long because they use humor to argue passionately against all that's pompous, absurd, irritating, irrational, venal, hypocritical, and even evil in the adult world.

By its very nature, humor is risky. Sometimes playing fast and loose with good taste and sound reason, writers using humor turn what's comfortable and familiar inside out and hope readers get the joke. They play with words and situations, manipulating readers' sense of language, propriety, and normalcy until they react with that physiological explosion called laughter (or maybe just a smile or smirk). Here, for example, speaking to a gathering of the Republican Jewish Coalition, President George W. Bush uses a little religious humor to honor a rabbi who had aided victims of Hurricane Katrina:

> **Rabbi Stanton Zamek of the Temple Beth Shalom Synagogue in Baton Rouge, Louisiana, helped an African American couple displaced by the**

storm track down their daughter in Maryland. When Rabbi Zamek called the daughter, he told her, "We have your parents." She screamed out, "Thank you, Jesus!" (Laughter.) He didn't have the heart to tell her she was thanking the wrong rabbi. (Laughter and applause.)

If humorists play it too safe, they lose their audiences; if they step over an unseen line, people groan or hiss or act offended. Humor, especially satire, is a knife's edge that had better cut precisely or not at all.

Understanding Humor as Argument

Humor is the vehicle for expression in the five *New Yorker* cartoons about Gendering Language presented in Chapter 25. How timeless might each of these cartoons be?

LINK TO P. 837

To use humor in arguments, you must first understand the foibles of human nature. That's because humor often works best when it deals with ordinary life and day-to-day events, as well as controversies in the worlds of politics and entertainment. (You might be surprised how many Americans get their daily news from the monologues of late-night comedians or from programs like *The Colbert Report*.) Timeliness, too, makes comedians seem hip and smart: their sharp minds decide what many people will be chuckling and *thinking* about the next day. But for the same reason, a lot of humor doesn't have the shelf life of lettuce. And some humor doesn't easily cross canyons that divide ethnic groups, classes, or generations. Maybe Catholics still laugh hardest at jokes about Catholic schools. But comedians often use humor to demolish societal stereotypes while simultaneously exploring them: Chris Rock can poke fun at African Americans in ways that no white humorist would dare, while Margaret Cho uses her position as a bisexual Korean American to give political focus to her wickedly sharp humor.

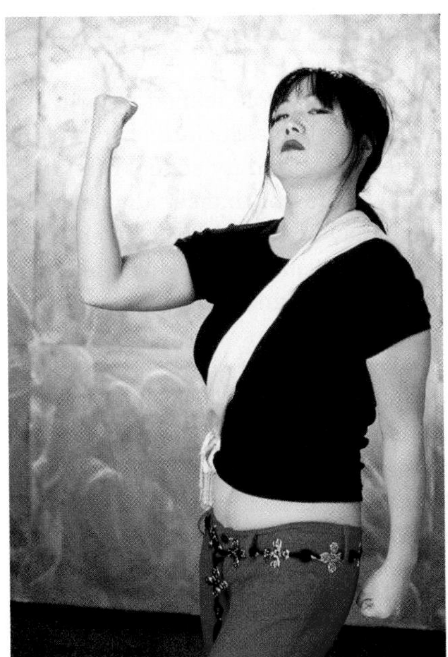

Margaret Cho, a humorist with a political attitude.

Obviously, then, humor isn't simple, nor can it be learned quickly or easily. It often involves subtle strategies of exaggeration, amplification, repetition, understatement, and irony. But it's too powerful a tool to leave solely to comedians. For writers and speakers, humor can sharpen many different kinds of argument by giving heightened presence to logical, emotional, and—especially—ethical appeals. Occasionally, humor even dictates the structure of arguments—when, for example, you choose to make an argumentative point by writing a parody or satire. *The Onion*'s parody of news magazine graphics on p. 397, for example, may not offer an explicit thesis about the way the National Collegiate Athletic Association ranks college football teams, but it makes readers suspect that the current system doesn't work.

Humor can simply make people pay attention or feel good—or make them want to buy stuff or do what others ask. That's the rationale behind many "soft sell" commercials, from classic VW pitches of a generation ago ("Think small") to more recent ads for products such as insurance ("AFLAC!"). Advertisers use humor to capture your interest and make you feel good about their products. Who focused on AFLAC insurance prior to the duck, Geico before the gecko, or Energizer prebunny?

Humor has a darker side, too; it can make people feel superior to its targets of ridicule. And most of us don't want to associate with people who seem ridiculous. Bullies and cliques in secondary school often use humor to torment their innocent victims, behavior that's really nasty. In the political arena, however, politicians may be fairer game, given their resources and ambitions. So when *Saturday Night Live* set out after both George W. Bush and John Kerry during the presidential campaign season of 2004, the parodies of these men rang true. Voters were left to choose between a candidate who was portrayed as a moronic mangler of the English language or a pompous, preening windbag. Does such humor have an effect on voting? Maybe.

Humor plays a large role, too, in arguments of character. If you want audiences to like you, make them laugh. It's no accident that all but the most serious speeches begin with a few jokes or stories. The humor puts listeners at ease and helps them identify with the speaker. In fact, a little self-deprecation can endear writers or speakers to the toughest audiences. You'll listen to people confident enough to make fun of themselves because they seem clever and yet aware of their own limitations.

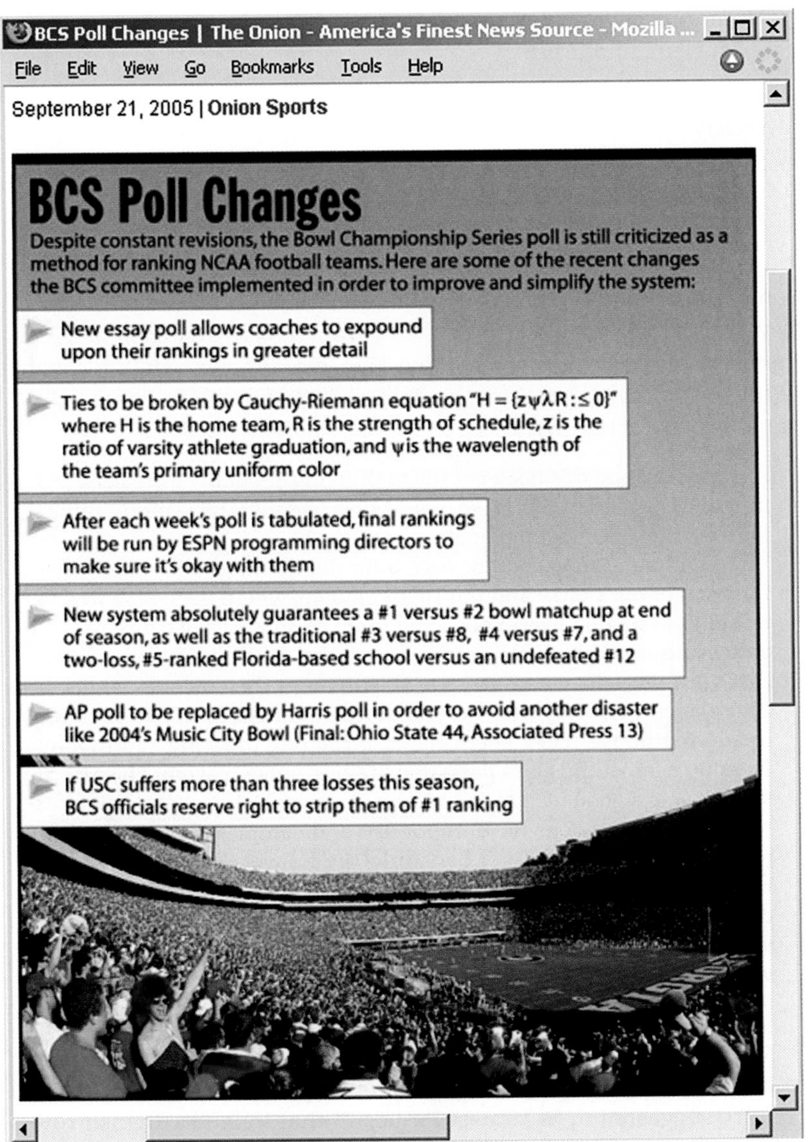

An infographic from *The Onion* takes on the way the NCAA determines its national champions in football.

Humor also works because a funny remark usually contains, at its core, an element of truth:

> Clothes make the man. Naked people have little or no influence in society.
>
> –Samuel Clemens

> Fame changes a lot of things, but it can't change a light bulb.
>
> –Gilda Radner

Some humor may even involve looking at a subject a little too logically. Dave Barry, for example, responds to Elizabeth Marshall Thomas's arguments in *The Hidden Life of Dogs* that Fido is a complex creature capable of highly refined cogitations, by doing a little tongue-in-cheek ethnographic study of his own pets:

> Anyway, reading this book got me to thinking about my own dogs. Did they have a hidden life? If so, could I discover it, and—more important—write a best-selling book?
>
> To find out, I removed my dogs from the confined, controlled environment of our house and put them outside, where they were free to reveal their hidden lives. I observed them closely for the better part of a day, and thus I am able to reveal here, for the first time anywhere, that what dogs do, when they are able to make their own decisions in accordance with their unfettered natural instincts, is: Try to get back inside the house. They spent most of the day pressing sad moony faces up against the glass patio door, taking only occasional breaks to see if it was a good idea to eat worms (Answer: No).
>
> Of course, the dogs have important and complex socio-biological reasons for wanting to get back into the house. For one thing, the house contains the most wondrous thing in the world: the kitchen counter. One time a piece of turkey fell off of it. The dogs still regularly visit the spot where it landed, in case it shows up again. There's an invisible Dog Historic Marker there.
>
> –Dave Barry, "The Hidden Life of Dogs"

Many forms of humor, especially satire and parody, get their power from just such twists of logic. When Jonathan Swift in the eighteenth century suggested in "A Modest Proposal" that Ireland's English rulers consider a diet of fricasseed Irish toddlers, he gambled on readers seeing the parallel between his outrageous proposal and the brutal policies of an oppressive English colonial government. The satire works precisely because it's perfectly logical, given the political facts of Swift's time—though some of his contemporaries missed the joke:

> **I profess, in the sincerity of my heart, that I have not the least personal interest in endeavoring to promote this necessary work, having no other motive but the public good of my country, by advancing our trade, providing for infants, relieving the poor, and giving some pleasure to the rich.**
>
> **–Jonathan Swift, "A Modest Proposal"**

In our own era, columnist Molly Ivins ridicules opponents of gun control by seeming to agree with them and then adding a logical twist that makes her real point:

> **I think that's what we need: more people carrying weapons. I support the [concealed gun] legislation but I'd like to propose one small amendment. Everyone should be able to carry a concealed weapon. But everyone who carries a weapon should be required to wear one of those little beanies on their heads with a little propeller on it so the rest of us can see them coming.**
>
> **–Molly Ivins**

Characterizing Kinds of Humor

It's possible to write whole books about comedy, exploring its many forms such as satire, parody, burlesque, travesty, pastiche, lampoon, caricature, farce, and more. Almost all types of humor involve some kind of argument because laughter can make people think, even while they're having a good time. As we've noted, not all such purposes are praiseworthy; schoolyard bullies and vicious editorial cartoonists may use their humor just to hurt or humiliate their targets. But laughter can also expose hypocrisy or break down barriers of prejudice and thereby help people see their worlds differently. When it's robust and honest, humor is a powerful rhetorical form.

Ellen Goodman deals with such serious topics as eating disorders and school killings yet uses humor to hold readers' attention and goodwill. She opens her deadly serious argument by asking readers to "imagine a place [where] women greet one another at the market with open arms, loving smiles, and a cheerful exchange of ritual compliments: you look wonderful! You've put on weight.'"

LINK TO P. 589

Humor can contribute to almost any argument, but you have to know when to use it—especially in academic writing. You'll catch a reader's attention if you insert a little laughter to lighten the tone of a serious or dry piece. Here, for example, is the African American writer Zora Neale Hurston addressing the very real issue of discrimination, with a nod, a wink, and a rhetorical question:

> **Sometimes I feel discriminated against, but it does not make me angry. It merely astonishes me. How can any deny themselves the pleasure of my company? It's beyond me.**
>
> **–Zora Neale Hurston, "How It Feels to Be Colored Me"**

You might use a whole sequence of comic examples and anecdotes to keep readers interested in a serious point—a rhetorical device called

Not Just Words

Visual arguments that make their case through humor have a way of turning up unexpectedly. Consider the case of U.S. Senator Deborah Stabenow, who took to the floor of the Senate to denounce the Bush administration as "dangerously incompetent"—a theme set by the Democratic Party in spring 2006. Unfortunately, she made the mistake of being photographed next to a large yellow-on-red chart bearing that slogan. Her opponents had a field day, distributing her image across the Internet and even creating a "Dangerous Debbie" Web site. The visual image Stabenow herself had created suddenly became an argument humorously undermining her own competence.

Armed with a digital camera, look for unexpected visual arguments of this kind—preferably humorous ones—in your own environment. Your photograph may make a claim on its own or, if you have the skill, you may want to underscore your point by doctoring the image using PhotoShop or other software, cropping it strategically, or adding a caption. Here, for example, is a photograph taken in Death Valley National Park, which seems to poke fun at the National Park Service, the use of park fees, or perhaps, the competence of government in general.

amplification. How would you, for example, make the rather academic point that nurture and socialization alone can't account for certain differences between girls and boys? Here's how Prudence Mackintosh, mother of three sons, defends that claim:

> **How can I explain why a little girl baby sits on a quilt in the park thoughtfully examining a blade of grass, while my baby William uproots grass by handfuls and eats it? Why does a mother of very bright and active daughters confide that until she went camping with another family of boys, she feared that my sons had a hyperactivity problem? I am sure there are plenty of noisy, rowdy little girls, but I'm not just talking about rowdiness and noise. I'm talking about some sort of primal physicalness that causes the walls of my house to pulsate on rainy days. I'm talking about something inexplicable that makes my sons fall into a mad, scrambling, pull-your-ears-off-kick-your-teeth-in heap just before bedtime, when they're not even mad at each other. I mean something that causes them to climb the doorjamb with honey and peanut butter on their hands while giving me a synopsis of *Star Wars* that contains only five unintelligible words. . . . When Jack and Drew are not kicking a soccer ball or each other, they are kicking the chair legs, the cat, the baby's silver rattle, and inadvertently, Baby William himself, whom they have affectionately dubbed "Tough Eddy."**
>
> **–Prudence Mackintosh, "Masculine/Feminine"**

In reading this cascade of words, you can just about feel the angst of a mother who thought she could raise her boys to be different. Most readers will chuckle at little William eating grass, the house pulsating, doorjambs sticky with peanut butter—and appreciate Mackintosh's point, whether they agree with it or not. Her intention, however, isn't so much to be funny, as to give her opinion presence. And, of course, she exaggerates. But exaggeration is a basic technique of humor. We make a situation bigger than life so we can see it better.

Satire

Most of the humor college students create is either satire or parody, which is discussed in the next section. Type "college humor magazines" into the search engine Google, and you'll find Web sites that list dozens of journals such as the University of Michigan's *Gargoyle*, Penn State's *Phroth*, UC Berkeley's *The Heuristic Squelch*, and Ohio State's *The Shaft*. In these journals you'll find humor of all varieties, some pretty

Digital photography creates new opportunities for college humorists, such as the editors of Penn State's *Phroth*.

raunchy, but much of it aimed at the oddities of college life, ranging from unsympathetic administrations to crummy teachers and courses. There's lots of grousing, too, about women and men and campus parking. Much of this material is satire, a genre of writing that uses humor to unmask problems and then suggest (not always directly) how they might be fixed. The most famous piece of satire in English literature is probably Jonathan Swift's *Gulliver's Travels*, which pokes fun at all human shortcomings, targeting especially politics, religion, science, and sexuality. For page after page, Swift argues for change in human character and institutions. In a much different way, so do campus humor magazines.

You'll find social and political satire in television programs such as *The Simpsons* and *South Park* and movies such as *This Is Spinal Tap*, *Dr. Strangelove*, and *Election*. Most editorial cartoons are also satiric when they highlight a problem in society that the cartoonist feels needs to be both ridiculed *and* remedied (see the figure on p. 403).

Satire often involves a shift in perspective that asks readers to look at a situation in a new way. In *Gulliver's Travels*, for example, we see human society reduced in scale (in Lilliput), exaggerated in size (in Brobdingnag), even viewed through the eyes of a superior race of horses (the Houyhnhnms). In the land of the giants, Gulliver notices that, seen up close on a gargantuan scale, women aren't as alluring as they once seemed to him:

> **Their skins appeared so coarse and uneven, so variously coloured, when I saw them near, with a mole here and there as broad as a trencher, and hairs hanging from it thicker than pack-threads, to say nothing further concerning the rest of their persons.**
>
> **–Jonathan Swift, *Gulliver's Travels***

Was the Supreme Court right to support federal efforts to override state laws supporting the medical use of marijuana? Cartoonists Cox and Forkum don't think so.

So much for human beauty. You'll note that there's nothing especially funny in Gulliver's remarks. That's because satire is sometimes more thought-provoking than funny, the point of some satire being to open readers' eyes rather than to make them laugh out loud.

The key to writing effective satire may be finding a humorous or novel angle on a subject and then following through. In other words, you say "What if?" and then employ a kind of mad logic, outlining in great detail all that follows from the question. For example, to satirize groups that believe homosexuals are using the nation's public schools to recruit children to their lifestyle, *The Onion* asks its readers to consider that the charge might be true. For paragraph after paragraph, the satirists let the idea unfold using all the logic and apparatus of a news story happily reporting on the campaign, complete with a graph. You can see from just a few paragraphs how satire of this kind works by making the implausible seem comically real (see the figure on p. 404).

Cartoonist Mikhaela Blake Reid creates a satire based on the vanity marketing of women's magazines. The humor in the argument is based on taking plastic surgery to a ridiculous degree.

LINK TO P. 630

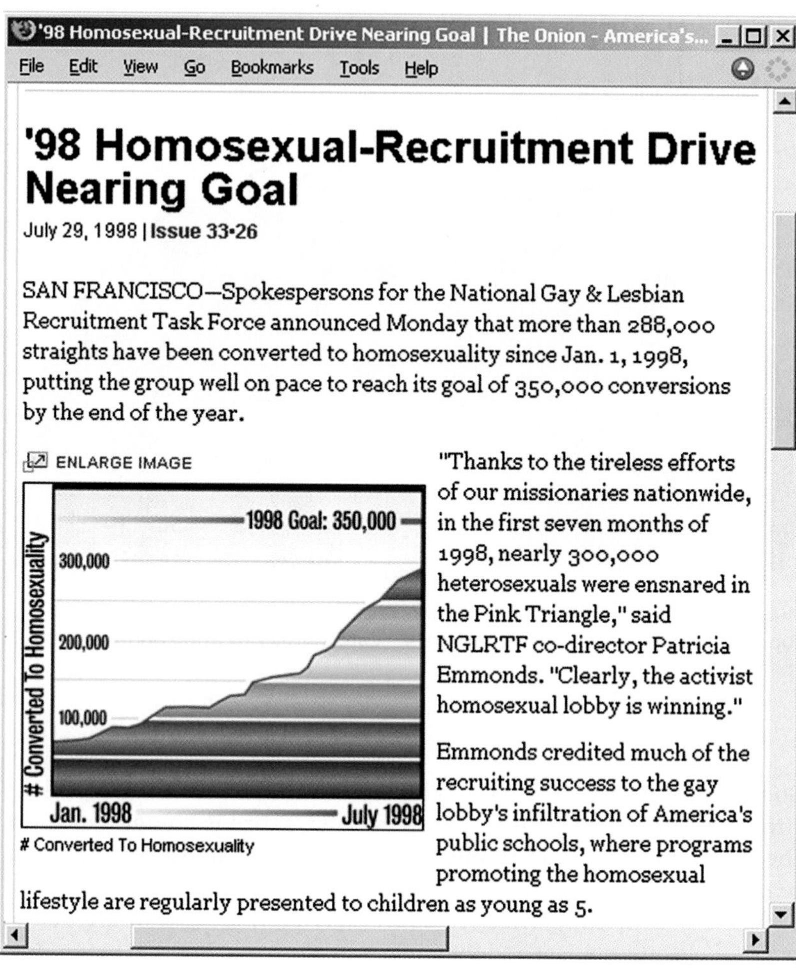
'98 Homosexual-Recruitment Drive Nearing Goal | The Onion - America's...

File Edit View Go Bookmarks Tools Help

'98 Homosexual-Recruitment Drive Nearing Goal

July 29, 1998 | **Issue 33•26**

SAN FRANCISCO—Spokespersons for the National Gay & Lesbian Recruitment Task Force announced Monday that more than 288,000 straights have been converted to homosexuality since Jan. 1, 1998, putting the group well on pace to reach its goal of 350,000 conversions by the end of the year.

ENLARGE IMAGE

Converted To Homosexuality

"Thanks to the tireless efforts of our missionaries nationwide, in the first seven months of 1998, nearly 300,000 heterosexuals were ensnared in the Pink Triangle," said NGLRTF co-director Patricia Emmonds. "Clearly, the activist homosexual lobby is winning."

Emmonds credited much of the recruiting success to the gay lobby's infiltration of America's public schools, where programs promoting the homosexual lifestyle are regularly presented to children as young as 5.

The complete story appears in *The Onion,* July 29, 1998.

In a parody targeting California's Proposition 227, cartoonist Tom Meyer takes aim at the time limit imposed on learners of English in the California public school system. Consider how the different visual and textual arguments work together to create a humorous argument.

LINK TO P. 737

Parody

Like satire, parody also offers an argument. What distinguishes the two forms is that parody makes its case by taking something familiar—be it songs, passages of prose, TV shows, poems, films, even people—and turning it into something new. The argument sparkles in the tension between the original work and its imitation. That's where the humor lies, too. The editors of *The Travesty,* for example, explain exactly how *The Onion* works (see the figure below) in their own parody of that humor publication: "ANYWHERE, US—Normally occurring incidents of everyday life—such as people eating cornflakes, going shopping for new tires and getting bad haircuts—are made humorous when they are written about as if they were serious news." The parody, of course, includes a full mockup of *The Onion*'s distinctive graphics, photographs, and headlines.

Needless to say, parodies work best when audiences make the connection with the object being imitated. For instance, you wouldn't entirely

Home | The Onion - America's Finest News Source - Mozilla Firefox

File Edit View Go Bookmarks Tools Help

http://www.theonion.com/content/index

the ONION

America's Finest News

COMPLETE NEWS ARCI

Now on theonion.com.

HOME
LOCAL
NATIONAL
INTERNATIONAL
POLITICS
SCIENCE & TECHNOLOGY
BUSINESS
ENTERTAINMENT
SPORTS
WORKPLACE
EDUCATION
PEOPLE
OPINION & COLUMNS
ONION RADIO NEWS
NEWS ARCHIVE

Contests
Subscribe

Cover / Texas Travesty - Mozilla Firefox

File Edit View Go Bookmarks Tools Help

NEWS

Woman Opens Door
see LOCAL page 6C

Area Man Can't Find Phone
see FASHION page 8G

God's Last Name Not "Damnit"
see RELIGION page 3H

Hemophiliac Gives Lots Of Blood
see HEALTH page 13F

Skeptic Not So Sure
see ARTS & CRAFTS page 44Q

FACTshot

A look at the numbers that shape your world

What's Up?
13% Chillin' chillin'
22% Fuck off!
17% I got new shoes!
5% Give me your money!
37% Well, I got up this morning at about 6, and then I ate some stuff, and then I saw this guy!

the TRAVESTY

VOLUME 6 ISSUE 3 AMERICA'S FINEST SOURCE FOR NEWS NOV/DEC 2003

Mundane Events Made Humorous, Entertaining By Parody News Format

ANYWHERE, US – Normally occurring incidents of everyday life—such as people eating cornflakes, going shopping for new tires and getting bad haircuts—are made humorous when they are written about as if they were serious news.

In addition to mimicking the dry, just-the-facts tone and style of actual news sources, parody news sources intersperse the text of articles with quotes from several different "area residents" in order to convey the idea of a comprehensive news piece with multiple perspectives.

"I find that reading about almost anything to be at least a little amusing when it's written like it's a real newspaper. Only it's fake," said area man Bob Pilton. "I also like it when there's made-up people in the fake news, and so it's like there's real people being interviewed," he continued. "That makes it seem more like a regular paper to me."

Often, friends or family members of the central character are created in order to present differing viewpoints, explains Rich Waterson, a close friend of Pilton's. "Yeah, sometimes I read that fake news that Bob reads, but I don't like it as much as he does. Sometimes I see some fake paper lying around at his place, and I think it's real at first. But then I realize that it's supposed to be a joke. Some of the stuff is sort of funny, but some of it I just don't get. Like I don't see how a story about someone losing their keys is funny. But Bob thinks all this stuff is brilliant."

"Some people find that parodies of everyday events are inherently quite funny, while others fail to see the humor," said parody expert Joanna Fewell. "Sometimes, people will find a certain parody article funnier overall if quotes from an 'expert' are used. This is imitative of the format of many real newspaper articles. Calling in an 'expert' also gives the story an air of legitimacy, which serves to further enhance the humor."

"I resent that the expert's commentary often comes at the end of a fake news story, however," said Fewell. "Almost nobody ever makes it to the end of those fake news things after they get the main joke and get sick of reading. Stupid, lazy readers."

Headline Catches Reader's Attention

Interest Wanes After Semi-Analysis Of Caption

CAMPUS – Freshman Kyle Smith's interest was briefly seized on Nov. 19 when the reader spotted a punny and mildly-humorous headline in a printed publication on the West Mall. Despite a quick glance at a photograph and caption loosely related to the article, his attention was soon averted to a busty co-ed walking by in a tight jogging suit.

"I liked how the picture probably made sense with the article," said Smith. "And the headline had a smaller one under it that also made me chuckle a little bit under my breath."

Conspirators in the writing and production of the articles—sitting nearby on a wall, smoking and exuding cool—were immediately put off by the rapid pace of reading displayed by the student. In spite of producing a mediocre and overly self-referential publication, the wall-goers stared on, marveling at the speedy pace of informational ingestion.

"I can't believe it," said newly appointed staff member Q.Q. Mercury. "He didn't even make it halfway to the lead. This guy is a total Wolfowitz."

The students watched on as Smith quickly glanced from one catch phrase to another, chuckling at some clever verbiage but not completely absorbing the depth of the humor. Despite a few audible chuckles like "Heh, Bush is stupid" and "Heh, fuzzy gonads," a visage of confusion and disinterest remained.

After floundering on pretentious literary devices, Smith noticed he only had five minutes to get to his class in the UTC, and quickly discarded his copy of the publication in the bushes behind him.

Upon Smith's departure, the wall-sitters focused their attention on another nearby reader, who, upon full completion of an article, winced in disappointment.

The Travesty parodies a parody.

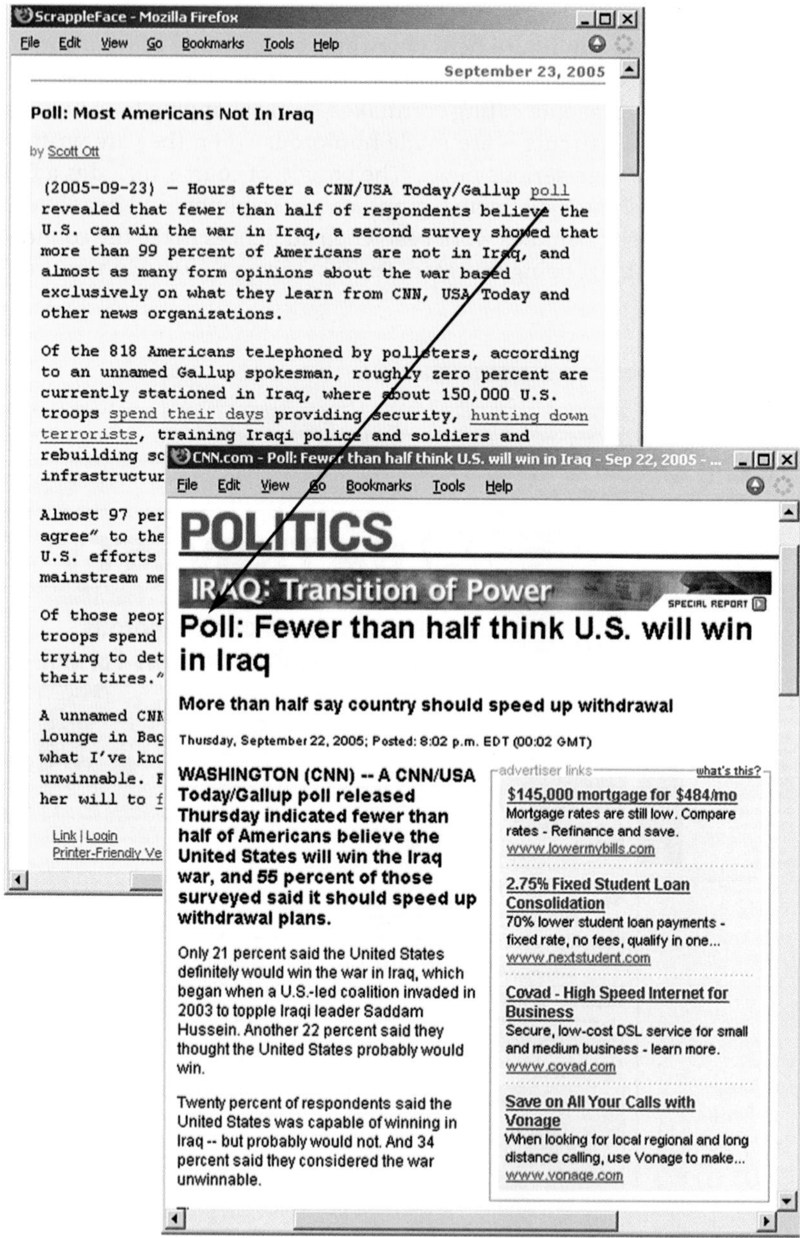

ScrappleFace - Mozilla Firefox

File Edit View Go Bookmarks Tools Help

September 23, 2005

Poll: Most Americans Not In Iraq

by Scott Ott

(2005-09-23) — Hours after a CNN/USA Today/Gallup poll revealed that fewer than half of respondents believe the U.S. can win the war in Iraq, a second survey showed that more than 99 percent of Americans are not in Iraq, and almost as many form opinions about the war based exclusively on what they learn from CNN, USA Today and other news organizations.

Of the 818 Americans telephoned by pollsters, according to an unnamed Gallup spokesman, roughly zero percent are currently stationed in Iraq, where about 150,000 U.S. troops spend their days providing security, hunting down terrorists, training Iraqi police and soldiers and rebuilding sc infrastructur

Almost 97 per agree" to the U.S. efforts mainstream me

Of those peop troops spend trying to det their tires."

A unnamed CNN lounge in Bag what I've knc unwinnable. F her will to f

Link | Login
Printer-Friendly Ve

CNN.com - Poll: Fewer than half think U.S. will win in Iraq - Sep 22, 2005 - ...

File Edit View Go Bookmarks Tools Help

POLITICS

IRAQ: Transition of Power

SPECIAL REPORT

Poll: Fewer than half think U.S. will win in Iraq

More than half say country should speed up withdrawal

Thursday, September 22, 2005; Posted: 8:02 p.m. EDT (00:02 GMT)

WASHINGTON (CNN) -- A CNN/USA Today/Gallup poll released Thursday indicated fewer than half of Americans believe the United States will win the Iraq war, and 55 percent of those surveyed said it should speed up withdrawal plans.

Only 21 percent said the United States definitely would win the war in Iraq, which began when a U.S.-led coalition invaded in 2003 to topple Iraqi leader Saddam Hussein. Another 22 percent said they thought the United States probably would win.

Twenty percent of respondents said the United States was capable of winning in Iraq -- but probably would not. And 34 percent said they considered the war unwinnable.

Clicking on a link in this parody by Scott Ott takes a reader to the source that inspires his humor.

appreciate the film *Galaxy Quest* unless you knew the *Star Trek* series. Blogger and humorist Scott Ott <http://ScrappleFace.com> makes sure his readers know whom he's targeting in his daily parodies simply by providing Web links (see the figure on p. 406). That enables readers to make their own judgments about Ott's criticism and humor.

If you write a parody, you need to be thoroughly knowledgeable about the work on which it's based, particularly its organization and distinctive features. In parodying a song, for example, you've got to be sure listeners recognize familiar lines or choruses. In parodying a longer piece, boil it down to essential elements—the most familiar actions in the plot, the most distinctive characters, the best-known passages of dialogue—and then arrange those elements within a compact and rapidly moving design. When a subject or work becomes the object of a successful parody, it's never seen in quite the same way again.

If Everything's an Argument . . .

Because of its subject matter, this chapter obviously can draw on examples of wit, satire, and parody that lighten the discussion and make it more appealing. But is there any larger and more general role for humor in textbooks? Have you noticed whether humor is used in other chapters of this book? If it's used, how successful did you find it? Why are textbooks generally so free of levity? What are the possible drawbacks of using humor, satire, or parody in such publications? Explore these issues in a brief essay, arguing for or against more humor in college textbooks and drawing on this book for support as appropriate.

Developing Humorous Arguments

It's doubtful anyone can offer a formula for being funny; some would suggest that humor is a gift. But at least the comic perspective is a trait widely distributed among the population. Most people can be funny, given the right circumstances. You can use humor in an argument to:

- point out flaws in a policy, proposal, or other kind of argument
- suggest a policy of your own

- put people in a favorable frame of mind
- acknowledge weaknesses or deflect criticism
- satirize or parody a position, point of view, or style

However, the stars may not always be aligned when you need them in composing an argument. And just working hard may not help: laughter arises from high-spirited, not labored, insights. Yet once you strike the spark, a blaze usually follows.

Look for humor in incongruity or in "What if?" situations, and then imagine the consequences. *What if reading caused flatulence? What if students hired special prosecutors to handle their grade complaints? What if broccoli tasted like chocolate? What if politicians always told the truth? What if the Pope wasn't Catholic?*

Complaining about the proliferation of T-shirts bearing humorous insults, Steve Rushin uses the climate of "clever contempt" in order to argue against it. He suggests that "on our one-dollar bill George Washington ought to smirk like Mona Lisa. On the five, Lincoln's fingers could form a *W*, the international symbol for *whatever.*"

LINK TO P. 828

Don't look for humor in complicated ideas. You're more apt to find it in simple premises, such as a question Dave Barry once asked: "How come guys care so much about sports?" There are, of course, serious answers to the question. But the humor practically bubbles up on its own once you think about men and their favorite games. You can write a piece of your own just by listing details: *ESPN Football, sports bars, beer commercials, sagging couches, fantasy camps, 50-inch plasma-screen TVs, Little League, angry wives.* Push a little further, relate such items to your own personal insights and experiences, and you're likely to discover some of the incongruities and implausibilities at the heart of humor.

Let us stress detail. Abstract humor probably doesn't work for anyone except German philosophers and drunken graduate students. Look for humor in concrete and proper nouns, in people and places readers will recognize but not expect to find in your writing. Consider the technique Dave Barry uses in the following passage defending himself against those who might question his motives for attacking "sports guys":

> **And before you accuse me of being some kind of sherry-sipping ascotwearing ballet-attending MacNeil-Lehrer-NewsHour-watching wussy, please note that I am a sports guy myself, having had a legendary athletic career consisting of nearly a third of the 1965 season on the track team at Pleasantville High School ("Where the Leaders of Tomorrow Are Leaving Wads of Gum on the Auditorium Seats of Today").**
>
> **–Dave Barry, "A Look at Sports Nuts—And We Do Mean Nuts"**

Remove the lively details from the passage, and this is what's left:

And before you accuse me of being some kind of wussy, please note that I am a sports guy myself, having had an athletic career on the track team at Pleasantville High School.

Timeliness is a factor, too; you need to know whom or what your readers will recognize and how they might respond. Seek inspiration for humor in these sources:

- popular magazines, especially weekly journals (for current events)
- TV, including commercials (especially for material about people)
- classic books, music, films, artwork (as inspiration for parodies)
- comedians (to observe how they make a subject funny)

Humorous arguments can be structured exactly like more serious ones—with claims, supporting reasons, warrants, evidence, qualifiers, and rebuttals. In fact, humor has its own relentless logic. Once you set an argument going, you should press it home with the same vigor you apply in serious pieces.

Creating humor is, by nature, a robust, excessive, and egotistical activity. It requires assertiveness, courage, and often a (temporary) suspension of good judgment and taste. Whereas drafting more material than necessary usually makes good sense for writers, you can afford to be downright prodigal with humor. Pile on the examples and illustrations. Take all the risks you can with language. Indulge in puns. Leap into innuendo. Stretch your vocabulary. Play with words and have fun. Be clever, but not immaturely obscene.

Then, when you revise, recall that Polonius in Shakespeare's *Hamlet* is right about one thing: "Brevity is the soul of wit." Once you've written a humorous passage, whether a tooting horn or a full symphonic parody, you must pare your language to the bone. Think: less is more. Cut, then cut again.

That's all there is to it.

RESPOND.

1. For each of the following topics, list particular details that might contribute to a humorous look at the subject:

   overzealous environmentalists

   avaricious builders and developers

aggressive drivers
violent Hollywood films
anti-war or hemp activists
drivers of lumbering recreational vehicles
Britney Spears
high school coaches
college instructors
malls and the people who visit them

2. Spend some time listening to a friend who you think is funny. What kind of humor does he or she use? What sorts of details crop up in it? Once you've put in a few days of careful listening, try to write down some of the jokes and stories just as your friend told them. Writing humor may be excruciating at first, but you might find it easier with practice.

   After you've written a few humorous selections, think about how well they translate from the spoken word to the written. What's different? Do they work better in one medium than in another? Show your written efforts to your funny friend, and ask for comments. How would he or she revise your written efforts?

3. Using Internet search tools, find a transcript of a funny television or radio show. Read the transcript a few times, paying attention to the places where you laugh the most. Then analyze the humor, trying to understand what makes it funny. This chapter suggests several possible avenues for analysis, including normality, incongruity, simplicity, and details. How does the transcript reflect these principles? Or does it operate by a completely different set of principles? (Some of the best humor is funny because it breaks all the rules.)

14
Visual Arguments

You know you shouldn't buy camping gear just because you see it advertised on TV. But what's the harm in imagining yourself in Yosemite with the sun setting, the camp stove open, the tent up and ready? That could be you reminiscing about the rugged eight-mile climb that got you there, just like the tanned campers in the ad. Now what's that brand name again, and what's its URL?

A student government committee is meeting to talk about campus safety. One member has prepared a series of graphs showing the steady increase in the number of on-campus attacks over the last five years, along with several photographs that bring these crimes vividly to life.

It turns out that the governor and now presidential candidate who claims to be against taxes actually raised taxes in his home state—according to his opponent, who's running thirty-second TV spots to make that point. The ads feature a plainly dressed woman who sure looks credible; she's got to be a real person, not an actor, and she says he raised taxes. She wouldn't lie—would she?

You've never heard of the sponsoring time-share firm. But its letter, printed on thick bond with smart color graphics, is impressive—and hey, the company CEO is offering you a free weekend at its Palm Beach resort facility, just to consider investing in a time-share. In addition, the firm's Web site seems quite professional—quick-loading and easy to navigate. Somebody's on the ball. Perhaps you should take the firm up on its offer?

A shiny silver convertible passes you effortlessly on a steep slope along a curving mountain interstate. It's moving too fast for you to read the nameplate, but on the grill you see a three-pointed star. Hmmmm . . . Maybe after you graduate from law school and your student loans are paid off . . .

• • •

The Power of Visual Arguments

We don't need to be reminded that visual images have clout. Just think for a moment of where you were on September 11, 2001, and what you remember of the events of that day: almost everyone we know still reports being able to see the hijacked planes slamming into the World Trade Center Towers as though that image were forever etched in some inner eye.

What other potent images are engraved in your memory? Even in mundane moments, not memorable in the way an event like 9/11 is, visual images still surround us, from T-shirts to billboards to movie and computer screens. It seems everyone's trying to get our attention, and doing it with images as well as words. In fact, several recently published books argue that images today pack more punch than words. As tech-

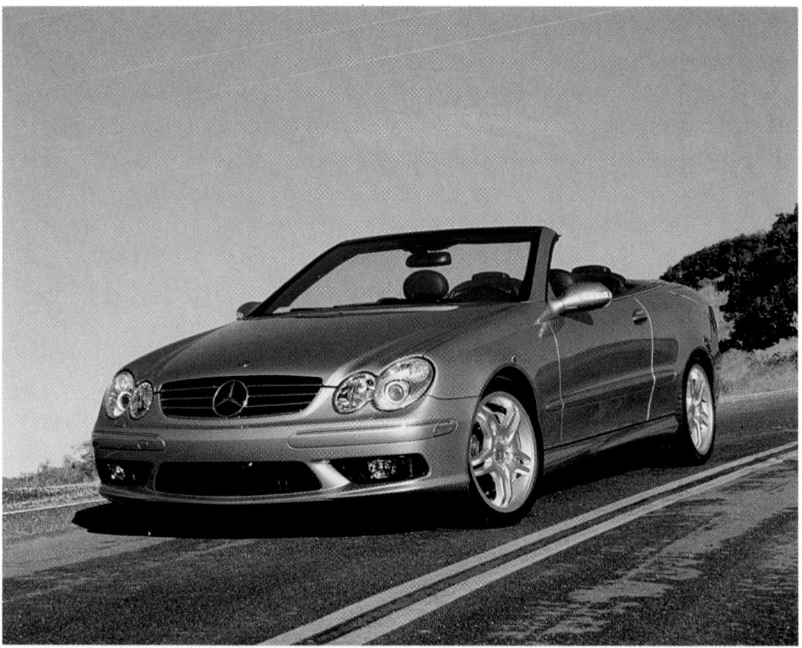

A visual argument on wheels

nology makes it easier for people to create and transmit images, those images are more compelling than ever, brought to us via DVD and HDTV on our cell phones and computers, on our walls, in our pockets, even in our cars.

But let's put this in perspective. Visual arguments weren't invented by Steve Jobs, and they've always had power. The pharaohs of Egypt lined the Nile with statues of themselves to assert their authority, and Roman emperors had their portraits stamped on coins for the same reason. Some thirty thousand years ago people in the south of France created magnificent cave paintings, suggesting that people have indeed always used images to celebrate and to communicate (see the top figure on p. 414).

In our own era (speaking as authors of this book), two events marked turning points in the growing power of media images. The first occurred in 1960, when presidential candidates John F. Kennedy and Richard M. Nixon met in a nationally televised debate. Kennedy, robust and confident in a dark suit, faced a pale and haggard Nixon barely recovered from an illness. Kennedy looked cool and "presidential"; Nixon did not.

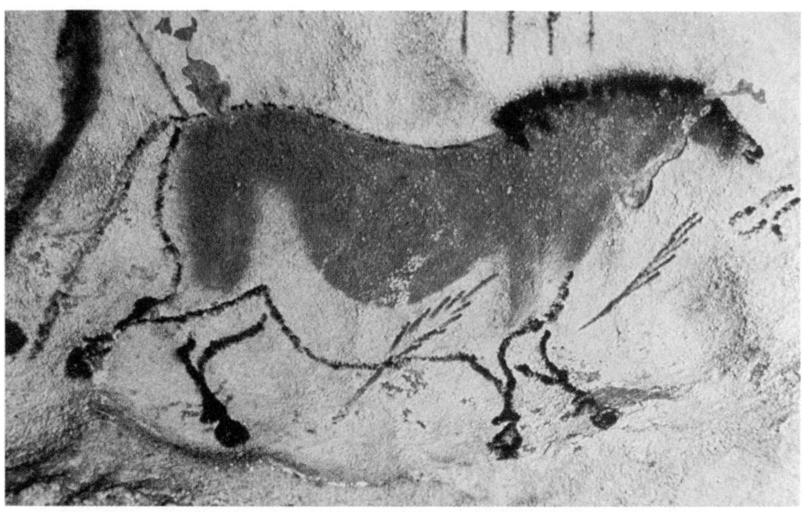

Ceiling of the Lascaux Caves, southern France

Richard Nixon and John Kennedy in a televised debate, 1960

Many viewers believe that the contrasting images Kennedy and Nixon presented on that evening radically changed the direction of the 1960 election campaign, leading to Kennedy's narrow victory. For better or worse, the debate also established television as the chief medium for political communication in the United States.

The second event is more recent—the introduction in the early 1980s of personal computers with graphic interfaces. These machines, which initially seemed strange and toylike, operated with icons and pictures rather than through arcane commands. Subtly at first, and then with the smack of a tsunami, graphic computers (the only kind people use now) moved our society away from an age of print into an era of electronic, image-saturated communications.

So that's where we are in the opening decade of a new millennium. People today are adjusting rapidly to a world of seamless, multichannel, multimedia communications. The prophet of this time is Marshall McLuhan, the guru of *Wired* magazine who proclaimed forty-some years ago that "the medium is the massage," with the play on words (*message/massage*) definitely intentional. Certainly images "massage" us all the time, and anyone reading and writing today has to be prepared to deal with arguments that shuffle more than words.

Shaping the Message

Images make arguments of their own. A photograph, for example, isn't a faithful representation of reality; it's reality shaped by the photographer's point of view. You can see photographic and video arguments at work everywhere, but perhaps particularly so during political campaigns. Staff photographers work to place candidates in settings that show them in the best possible light—shirtsleeves rolled up, surrounded by smiling children and red-white-and-blue bunting—whereas their opponents look for opportunities to present them in a bad light. Closer to home, you may well have chosen photographs that showed you at your best to include on <Myspace.com> or on a Facebook site.

Even if those who produce images shape the messages those images convey, those of us who "read" them are by no means passive. Human vision is selective: to some extent, we actively shape what we see. Much of what we see is laden with cultural meanings, too, and we must have "learned" to see things in certain ways. Consider a photograph of the Statue of Liberty welcoming immigrants to America's shores—and then

Not Just Words

One of the best-loved photographs appearing in the wake of the September 11, 2001, terrorist attacks was shot by Thomas Franklin: it shows three firefighters struggling to hoist the American flag in the wreckage of the World Trade Center as dust settles around them. In 2002, the image was used on a fund-raising "semipostal" stamp that sold for forty-five cents, with proceeds going to the Federal Emergency Management Agency. Part of the picture's appeal was its resemblance to another beloved American image: Joe Rosenthal's photo of U.S. Marines raising the flag on Iwo Jima in 1945. That image was made into a stamp as well, which became the best-selling U.S. stamp for many years. Take a look at the two images and consider how they're composed—what attracts your attention, how your eyes move over the images, what immediate impression they create. Also notice other features of the stamps—tinting, text placement, font, and wording. What argument do these stamps make about America?

In the cultural shorthand of Americans, the Statue of Liberty represents their country's promise of freedom and opportunity. When the Russian art group AES photoshopped Islamic visual elements onto images of the statue and other landmarks of Western countries (such as Big Ben and the Eiffel Tower), they capitalized on such connotations to draw out, in their words, "fears of Western society about Islam."

look at a version that shows her wearing a burka. In this moment, she's a very different kind of statue making a very different statement.

Of course, people don't always see things the same way, which is one reason eyewitnesses to the same event often report it differently. Or why even instant replays don't always solve disputed calls on football fields. Thus the visual images that surround us today—and that argue forcefully for our attention and often for our time and money—are constructed to invite, perhaps even coerce, us into seeing them in just one way. But each of us has our own powers of vision, our own frames of reference that influence how we see. So visual arguments might best be described as a give-and-take, a dialogue, or even a tussle.

The visual accompaniment to Laurie Goodstein's article on modern religion is organized by country, with a photo and data on the number of people in each religion and the growth of the different religions. Note how the information is presented in bar graph form with each bar or group of bars corresponding to a circle representing the relative size of the respective populations.

LINK TO P. 844

Achieving Visual Literacy

Why take images so seriously? Because they matter. Images shape behavior and change lives. When advertisements for sneakers are powerful enough to lead some kids to kill for the coveted footwear, when five- and ten-second images and sound bites are deciding factors in presidential elections, or when a cultural icon like Oprah Winfrey can sell more books in one TV show than a hundred writers might do—or dramatically expose a best-selling author for presenting fiction as fact—it's high time to start paying careful attention to visual elements of argument.

How text is presented affects how it is read—whether it is set in fancy type, plain type, or handwritten; whether it has illustrations or not; whether it looks serious, fanciful, scholarly, or commercial. The figures on pp. 419–420 show information about a peer-tutoring service presented visually in three different ways—as an email message, as a flyer with a table, and as a flyer with a visual (which is how the information was actually presented to its intended audience). Look at the three different versions of this text, and consider in each case how the presentation affects the way you perceive the information. Do the photograph and the play on the movie title *The Usual Suspects,* for example, make you more or less likely to use this tutoring service? The point, of course, is that as you read any text, you need to consider its presentation—a highly crucial element.

Consider the photo of Calista Flockhart that accompanies Ellen Goodman's article about changing notions of body image in Fiji. What does this photo contribute to Goodman's argument and to its persuasiveness?

LINK TO P. 590

Analyzing Visual Elements of Arguments

We've probably said enough to suggest that analyzing the visual elements of argument is a challenge, one that's even greater when you encounter multimedia appeals, especially on the Web. Here are some questions that can help you recognize—and analyze—visual and multimedia arguments. After you've read them, spend some time analyzing the flyer with the visual text on p. 420— in order to assess its effectiveness.

About the Creators/Authors

- Who created this visual text?
- What can you find out about this person(s), and what other work have they done?
- What does the creator's attitude seem to be toward the visual image?
- What does the creator intend its effects to be?

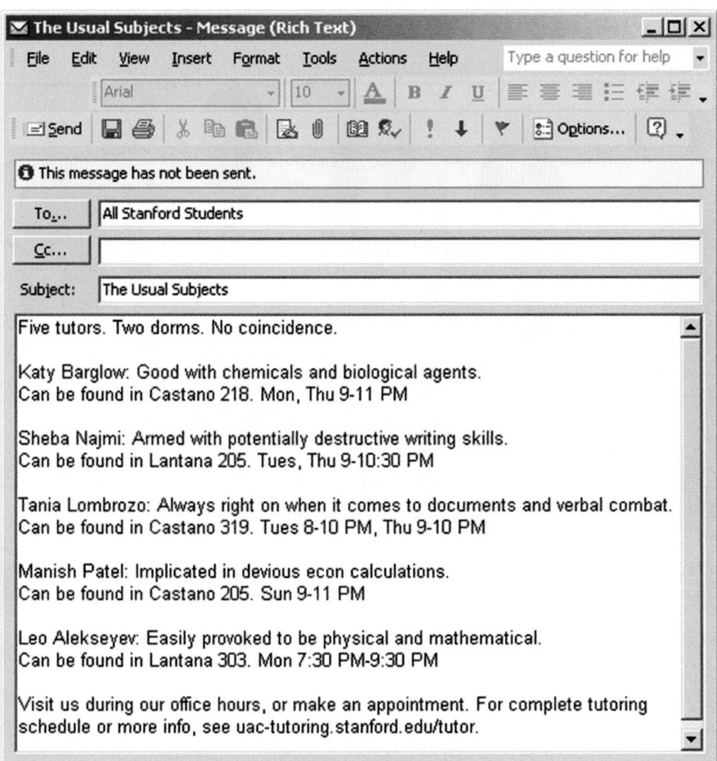

The Usual Subjects - Message (Rich Text)

This message has not been sent.

To... All Stanford Students

Cc...

Subject: The Usual Subjects

Five tutors. Two dorms. No coincidence.

Katy Barglow: Good with chemicals and biological agents.
Can be found in Castano 218. Mon, Thu 9-11 PM

Sheba Najmi: Armed with potentially destructive writing skills.
Can be found in Lantana 205. Tues, Thu 9-10:30 PM

Tania Lombrozo: Always right on when it comes to documents and verbal combat.
Can be found in Castano 319. Tues 8-10 PM, Thu 9-10 PM

Manish Patel: Implicated in devious econ calculations.
Can be found in Castano 205. Sun 9-11 PM

Leo Alekseyev: Easily provoked to be physical and mathematical.
Can be found in Lantana 303. Mon 7:30 PM-9:30 PM

Visit us during our office hours, or make an appointment. For complete tutoring schedule or more info, see uac-tutoring.stanford.edu/tutor.

THE USUAL SUBJECTS

Five tutors. Two dorms. No coincidence.

Katy Barglow	***Sheba Najmi***	***Tania Lombrozo***	***Manish Patel***	***Leo Alekseyev***
Good with chemicals and biological agents.	Armed with potentially destructive writing skills.	Always right on when it comes to documents and verbal combat.	Implicated in devious econ calculations.	Easily provoked to be physical and mathematical.
Can be found in: Castano 218 Mon, Thu 9–11 PM	Can be found in: Lantana 205 Tue, Thu 9–10:30 PM	Can be found in: Castano 319 Tue 8–10 PM Thu 9–10 PM	Can be found in: Castano 205 Sun 9–11 PM	Can be found in: Lantana 303 Mon 7:30–9:30 PM

Visit us during our office hours, or make an appointment. For complete tutoring schedule or more info, see uac-tutoring.stanford.edu/tutor.

Katy Barglow	Sheba Najmi	Tania Lombrozo	Manish Patel	Leo Alekseyev
Good with chemicals and biological agents.	Armed with potentially destructive writing skills.	Always right on when it comes to documents and verbal combat.	Implicated in devious econ calculations.	Easily provoked to be physical and mathematical.
Can be found in:	*Can be found in:*	*Can be found in:*	*Can be found in:*	*Can be found in:*
Castano 218 *Mon, Thu* 9 – 11 PM	Lantana 205 *Tue, Thu* 9 – 10:30 PM	Castano 319 *Tue* 8 – 10 PM *Thu* 9 – 10 PM	Castano 205 *Sun* 9 – 11 PM	Lantana 303 *Mon* 7:30 – 9:30 PM

Visit us during our office hours, or make an appointment.

For complete tutoring schedule or more info, see

uac-tutoring.stanford.edu/tutor

About the Medium

- Which media are used for this visual text? Images only? Words and images? Sound, video, graphs, charts?
- What effect does the choice of medium have on the message of the visual text? How would the message be altered if different media were used?
- What's the role of words that may accompany the visual text? How do they clarify or reinforce (or blur or contradict) the message?

About Viewers/Readers

- What does the visual text assume about its viewers, and about what they know and agree with?
- What overall impression does the visual text create in you?
- What positive—or negative—feelings about individuals, scenes, or ideas does the visual intend to evoke in viewers?

About Content and Purpose

- What argumentative purpose does the visual text convey? What is it designed to convey?
- What cultural values or ideals does the visual evoke or suggest? The good life? Love and harmony? Sex appeal? Youth? Adventure? Economic power or dominance? Freedom? Does the visual reinforce these values or question them? What does the visual do to strengthen the argument?
- What emotions does the visual evoke? Which ones do you think it intends to evoke? Desire? Envy? Empathy? Shame or guilt? Pride? Nostalgia? Something else?

About Design

- How is the visual text composed? What's your eye drawn to first? Why?
- What's in the foreground? In the background? What's in or out of focus? What's moving? What's placed high, and what's placed low? What's to the left, in the center, and to the right? What effect do these placements have on the message?
- Is any particular information (such as a name, face, or scene) highlighted or stressed in some way to attract your attention?
- How are light and color used? What effect(s) are they intended to have on you? What about video? Sound?

- What details are included or emphasized? What details are omitted or deemphasized? To what effect? Is anything downplayed, ambiguous, confusing, distracting, or obviously omitted? To what ends?
- What, if anything, is surprising about the design of the visual text? What do you think is the purpose of that surprise?
- Is anything in the visual repeated, intensified, or exaggerated? Is anything presented as "supernormal" or idealistic? What effects are intended by these strategies, and what effects do they have on you as a viewer? How do they clarify or reinforce (or blur or contradict) the message?
- How are you directed to move within the argument? Are you encouraged to read further? Click on a link? Scroll down? Fill out a form? Provide your email address? Place an order?

Now take a look at the homepage of United Colors of Benetton, <www.http://benetton.com>, a company that sells sportswear, handbags, shoes, and more. You might expect a company that sells eighty million items of clothing and accessories annually to feature garments on its homepage or to make a pitch to sell you something, and indeed the company does all those things. But if you look closer, you'll find a section of the site that features Benetton's well-known campaigns for social and political causes. The 2004 campaign departed from Benetton's usual focus on improving the lives of people to extend its "reflection on diversity as a wealth of our planet, from the human races to our nearest cousins," the great apes.

If you check out this site, you'll find pictures not only of Pumbu (shown on p. 423) but of a number of other orphaned or rescued apes, along with information about them. As the site says, "[photographer] James Mollison has taken close-up pictures of the orphans, who were confiscated from illegal traders and form the population of at least seven sanctuaries in Africa and Asia. Many of them saw their mothers killed before their eyes. Together . . . they testify to the importance of saving the various species of great apes, because even if just one should become extinct, we would lose a significant part of the 'bridge' leading back to the origins of humankind" (see <http://benettongroup.com/apes/pressinfo/press/index.html>). The site goes on to say that this Benetton campaign includes not only the Web-site images and billboard ads (billboards in major cities around the world carried these images during 2004) but also a book, *James and Other Apes*, published in fall 2004. Finally,

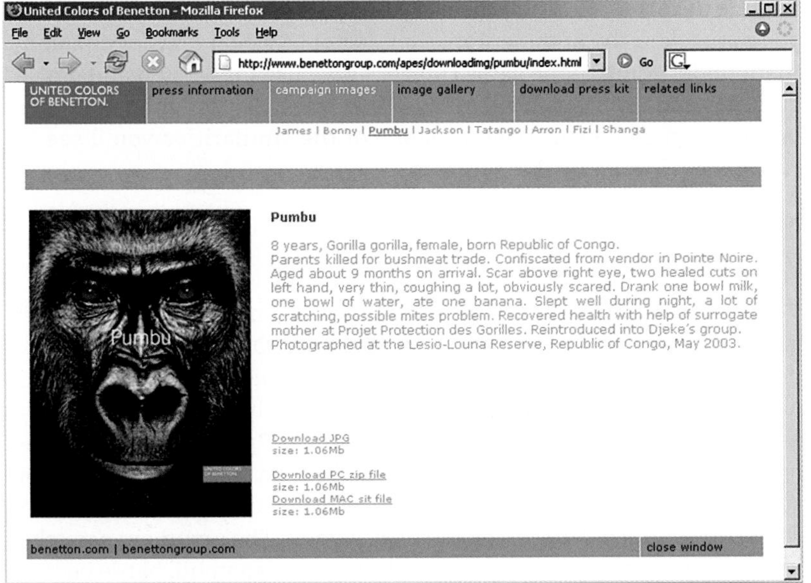

Benetton makes use of design elements like color and composition to draw viewers into "James and Other Apes," one of a number of the company's campaigns for social and political causes.

the Natural History Museum in London hosted an exhibit of the photographs and the entire project in 2005.

Even this brief investigation of the Benetton site reveals that this manufacturer of clothing and accessories promotes its wares through an involvement in social activism. So its images challenge viewers to join in—or at least to consider doing so. What effect does Pumbu's page have on you?

Using Visuals in Your Own Arguments

You too can, and perhaps must, use visuals in your writing. Many college classes now call for projects to be posted on the Web, which almost always involves the use of images. Many courses also invite or require students to make multimedia presentations using software such as PowerPoint, or even good old-fashioned overhead projectors with transparencies.

Here we sketch out some basic principles of visual rhetoric. To help you appreciate the argumentative character of visual texts, we examine them under some of the same categories we use for written and oral arguments earlier in this book (Chapters 2, 3, and 4), though in a different order. You may be surprised by some of the similarities you'll see between visual and verbal arguments.

Visual Arguments Based on Character

What does character have to do with visual argument? Consider two argumentative essays submitted to an instructor. One is scrawled in thick pencil on pages ripped from a spiral notebook, little curls of paper still dangling from the left margin. The other is neatly typed on bond paper and in a form the professor likely regards as "professional." Is there much doubt about which argument will (at least initially) get the more sympathetic reading? You might object that appearances shouldn't count for so much, and you would have a point. The argument scratched in pencil could be the stronger piece, but it faces an uphill battle because its author has sent the wrong signals. Visually, the writer seems to be saying, "I don't much care about this message or the people I'm sending it to." There may be times when you want to send exactly such a signal to an audience, but the point is that the visual rhetoric of any piece you create ought to be a deliberate choice, not an accident. Also keep control of your own visual image. In most cases, when you present an argument, you want to appear authoritative and credible.

LOOK FOR IMAGES THAT REINFORCE YOUR AUTHORITY AND CREDIBILITY

For a brochure about your new small business, for instance, you would need to consider images that prove your company has the resources to do its job. Consumers might feel reassured seeing pictures that show you have an actual office, state-of-the-art equipment, and a competent staff. Similarly, for a Web site about a company or organization you represent, you would consider including its logo or emblem. Such emblems have authority and weight. That's why university Web sites so often include the seal of the institution somewhere on the homepage, or why the president of the United States always travels with a presidential seal to hang upon the speaker's podium. The emblem or logo can convey a wealth of cultural and historical implications.

Three images used to convey authority and credibility: the U.S. presidential seal and corporate logos for McDonald's and Philip Morris

CONSIDER HOW DESIGN REFLECTS YOUR CHARACTER

Almost every design element sends signals about character and ethos, so be sure to think carefully about them. For example, the type fonts you select for a document can mark you as warm and inviting or efficient and contemporary. The warm and inviting fonts often belong to a family called *serif*. The serifs are those little flourishes at the ends of the strokes that make the fonts seem handcrafted and artful:

warm and inviting (Bookman Old Style)

warm and inviting (Times New Roman)

warm and inviting (Bookman)

Cleaner, modern fonts go without those little flourishes and are called *sans serif*. These fonts are cooler and simpler—and, some argue, more readable on a computer screen (depending on screen resolution):

efficient and contemporary (Helvetica)

efficient and contemporary (Arial Black)

efficient and contemporary (Arial)

You may also be able to use decorative fonts. These are appropriate for special uses, but not for extended texts:

decorative and special uses (Zapf Chancery)

decorative and special uses (Goudy Handtooled BT)

Other typographic elements shape your ethos as well. The size of type, for one, can make a difference. If your text or headings are boldfaced and too large, you'll seem to be shouting. Tiny type, on the other hand, might make you seem evasive:

Lose weight! Pay nothing!*

*Excludes the costs of enrollment and required meal purchases. Minimum contract: 12 months.

Similarly, your choice of color—especially for backgrounds—can make a statement about your taste, personality, and common sense. For instance, you'll create a bad impression with a Web page whose background colors or patterns make reading difficult. If you want to be noticed, you might use bright colors—the same sort that would make an impression in clothing or cars. But more subtle shades might be a better choice in most situations.

Don't ignore the impact of illustrations and photographs. Because they reveal what you visualize, images can send powerful signals about your preferences, sensitivities, and inclusiveness—and sending the right ones isn't always easy. Conference planners designing a program,

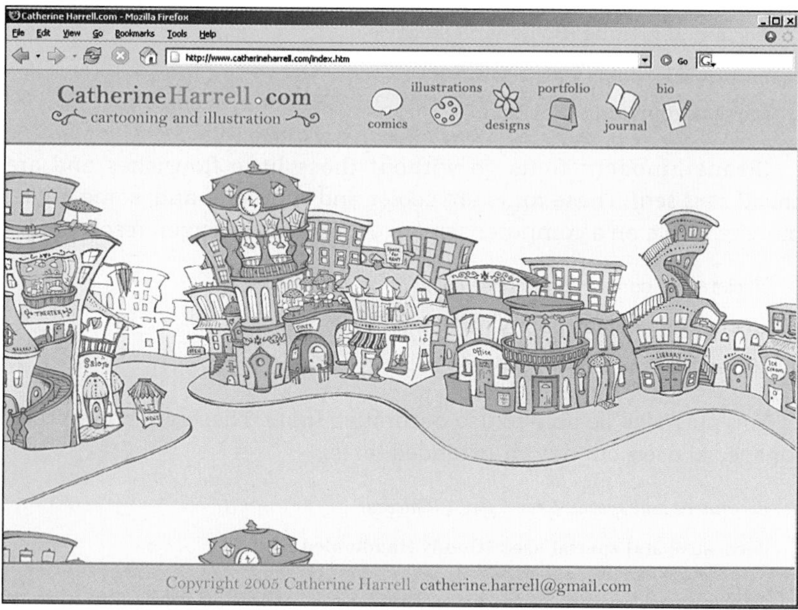

Catherine Harrell's Web site

for example, are careful to include pictures that represent all the participants who'll be attending; as a result, they double-check to make sure that they don't show only women in the program photos, or only men, or only members of one racial or ethnic group.

Even your choice of medium says something important about you. If you decide to make an appeal on a Web site, you send signals about your technical skills and contemporary orientation as well as about your personality. Take a look at the homepage of student Catherine Harrell's Website on p. 426. What can you deduce about her from this page—her personality, her values and interests, and so on?

A presentation that relies on an overhead projector gives a different impression from one presented on an LCD projector with software—or one presented with a poster and handouts. When reporting on a children's story you're writing, the most effective medium of presentation might be old-fashioned cardboard and paper made into an oversized book and illustrated by hand.

Balancing the representation of males and females and different ethnic or racial groups was most likely a goal of the public service campaigns' print advertisements shown in Chapter 26. Each campaign was created to promote religious tolerance and underscore the variety within each of the religious groups profiled.

LINK TO P. 903

FOLLOW REQUIRED DESIGN CONVENTIONS

Many kinds of writing have required design conventions. When that's the case, follow them to the letter. It's no accident that lab reports for science courses are sober and unembellished. Visually, they reinforce the serious character of scientific work. The same is true of a college research paper. You might resent the tediousness of placing page numbers in the right place or aligning long quotations just so, but these visual details help convey your competence. So whether you're composing a term paper, résumé, screenplay, or Web site, look for authoritative models and follow them. Student Erin Krampetz's résumé is shown on p. 428. Note that its look is serious: The type is clear and easy to read; the black on white is simple and no-nonsense; the headings call attention to Krampetz's accomplishments.

Visual Arguments Based on Facts and Reason

People tend to associate facts and reason with verbal arguments, but here too visual elements play an essential role. Indeed, it's hard to imagine a compelling presentation these days that doesn't rely, to some degree, on visual elements to enhance or even make the argument.

Many readers and listeners now expect ideas to be represented graphically. Not long ago, media critics ridiculed the colorful charts and

Erin Krampetz's résumé

ERIN MCCLURE KRAMPETZ
PO Box 12782, Stanford, CA 94309 • (210) 643-7999 Mobile • krampetz@stanford.edu

---

EDUCATION

9/00 – 6/05 **Stanford University,** Stanford, CA
- BA, International Relations (Honors); Minor, Spanish Language and Culture Studies

RESEARCH EXPERIENCE

6/02 – Present **Research Assistant,** Stanford Study of Writing, Stanford, CA
- Contributing author and researcher for study analyzing a large collection of college writing.
- Manage Oracle database; conduct statistical and qualitative analyses of data collected.
- Research presented at Conference on College Composition (2004, 2005).

4/03 – Present **Teaching Assistant/Researcher,** Stanford Program in Writing and Rhetoric, Stanford, CA
- Co-designed, taught, and carried out research new course focusing on multimedia.
- Co-authored multimedia magazine under review: *Computers and Composition: An International Journal.*

7/03 – 9/03 **Researcher,** International Relations Senior Honors Thesis, Ayacucho, Peru
- Completed case study investigating international funding for girls' education.
- Designed and administered surveys to government, teachers, and students in Spanish.
- Presented findings at International Education Society Conference (2005).

BUSINESS/MANAGEMENT EXPERIENCE

9/03 – Present **Development Manager,** MobileMedia, Stanford, CA
- Build relationships with partners IBM, Palm Inc., and the U.S. and Brazilian governments.
- Secured funding from the Kellogg Foundation for pilot project beginning winter 2005.

9/04 – Present **Oral Communication Tutor,** Stanford Center for Teaching and Learning, Stanford, CA

6/04 – 8/04 **Eben Tisdale Fellow,** Hewlett-Packard Company, Washington, DC
- Authored position papers on national e-recycling legislation and state and local procurement reform.
- Collaborated with University Relations team to develop presentation for HP CEO.

6/02 – 9/02 **Program Department Intern,** World Affairs Council, San Francisco, CA
- Compiled outreach database and assisted in speaker selection.

LEADERSHIP EXPERIENCE

9/03 – Present **President,** Future Social Innovators Network (FUSION), Stanford, CA
- Led student group on social entrepreneurship with 350+ members.
- Invited as a guest speaker to the First World Forum on Social Entrepreneurship.

9/03 – Present **Peer Advisor,** Stanford International Relations Department, Stanford, CA
- Oversee program events and provide academic support to current and potential students.

9/03 – Present **Board Member,** Social Entrepreneurship Advisory Board, Stanford, CA
- Developed proposal for minor in Social Innovation.

AWARDS/RECOGNITION

International Relations Summer Research Grant (2003)
Latin American Studies Department Research Fellowship (2003)
Stanford Athletic Director's Scholar Athlete (2001)

graphs in newspapers like *USA Today*. Today, comparable features appear in even the most traditional publications because they work: they convey information efficiently.

ORGANIZE INFORMATION VISUALLY

A design works well when readers can look at an item and understand what it does. A brilliant, much-copied example of such an intuitive design is a seat adjuster invented many years ago by Mercedes-Benz (see below). It's shaped like a tiny seat. Push any element of the control, and the real seat moves the same way—back and forth, up and down. No instructions are necessary.

Good visual design can work the same way in an argument, conveying information without elaborate instructions. Titles, headings, subheadings, blown-up quotations, running heads, boxes, and so on are some common visual signals. When you present parallel headings in a similar type font, size, and color, you make it clear that the information under these headings is in some way related. So in a conventional term paper, you should use headings and subheadings to group information that's connected or parallel. Similarly, on a Web site, you might create two or three types of headings for groups of related information.

Use headings when they'll help guide your readers through the document you're presenting. For more complex and longer pieces, you may choose to use both headings and subheadings.

You should also make comparable inferences about the way text should be arranged on a page: search for relationships among items that should look alike. In this book, for example, bulleted lists are used to offer specific guidelines, while boxes with colored backgrounds mark the sections on visual argument titled "Not Just Words." You might use a list or a box to set off information that should be treated differently from the rest of the presentation, or you might visually mark it in other ways—by shading, color, or typography.

Mercedes-Benz's seat adjuster

An item presented in large type or under a larger headline should be more important than one that gets less visual attention. Place illustrations carefully: what you position front and center will

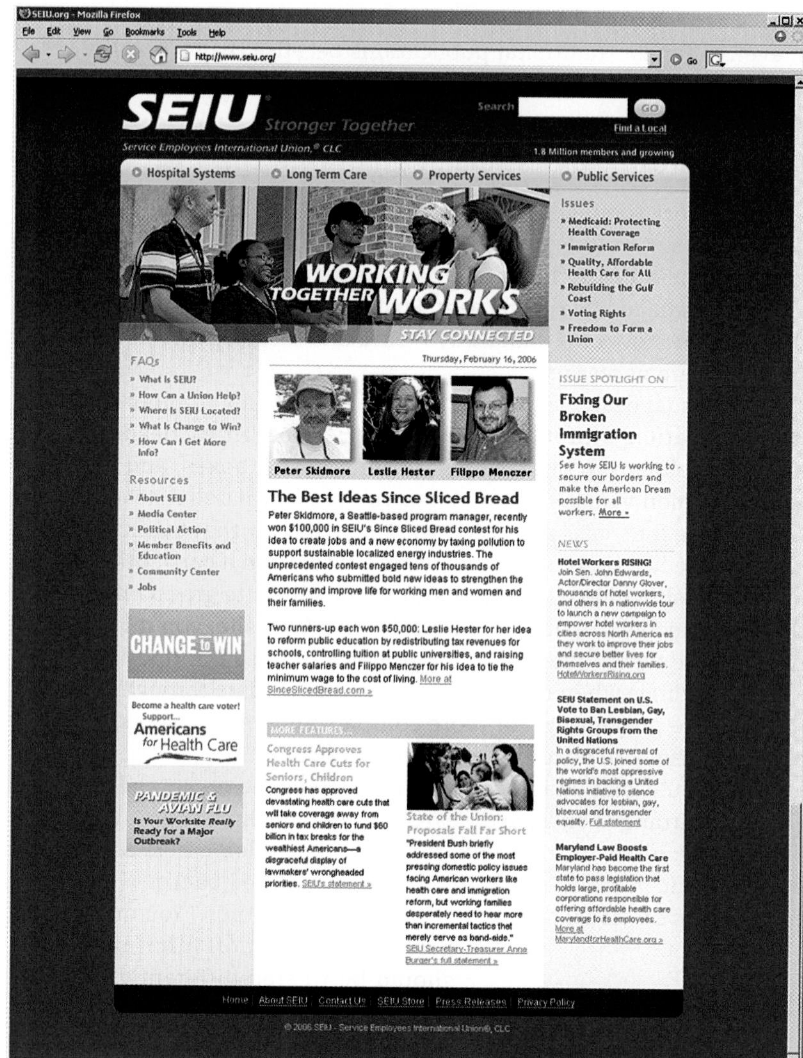

The Service Employees International Union's Web site uses various headings to group different kinds of information.

appear more important than items in less conspicuous places. On a Web site, key headings should usually lead to subsequent pages on the site.

Needless to say, you take a risk if you violate the expectations of your audience or if you present a visual text without coherent signals. Particularly for Web-based materials that may be accessible to people around the world, you can't make many assumptions about what will count as "coherent" across cultures. So you need to think about the roadmap you're giving viewers whenever you present them with a visual text. Remember that design principles evolve and change from medium to medium. A printed text or an overhead slide, for example, ordinarily works best when its elements are easy to read, simply organized, and surrounded by restful white space. But some types of Web pages seem to thrive on visual clutter, attracting and holding audiences' attention through the variety of information they can pack onto a relatively limited screen. Check out the way the opening screens of most search engines assault a viewer with enticements. Yet look closely, and you may find the logic in these designs.

One group that regularly analyzes Web sites, the Stanford Persuasive Technology Lab, recently concluded that Google News may soon become the most credible Web site of all (see the figure on p. 432). Here are just a few of the Lab's points about what makes Google News credible: It's easy to navigate; it provides a diversity of viewpoints; it has a reputation for outstanding performance in other areas; it has no broken links, typos, and so on; it provides clear information about the site; it has an easy-to-understand structure; it discloses information about the organization; and it has no ads. Take a look at Google News yourself. Do you agree that it's a fairly credible site? Beyond the points listed here, what else makes it credible?

USE VISUALS TO CONVEY DATA EFFICIENTLY

Words are immensely powerful and capable of enormous precision and subtlety. But the simple fact is that some information is conveyed more efficiently by charts, graphs, drawings, maps, or photos. When making an argument, especially to a large group, consider what information should be delivered in nonverbal form.

A ***pie chart*** is an effective way of comparing parts to the whole. You might use a pie chart to illustrate the ethnic composition of your school, the percentage of taxes paid by people at different income levels, or the

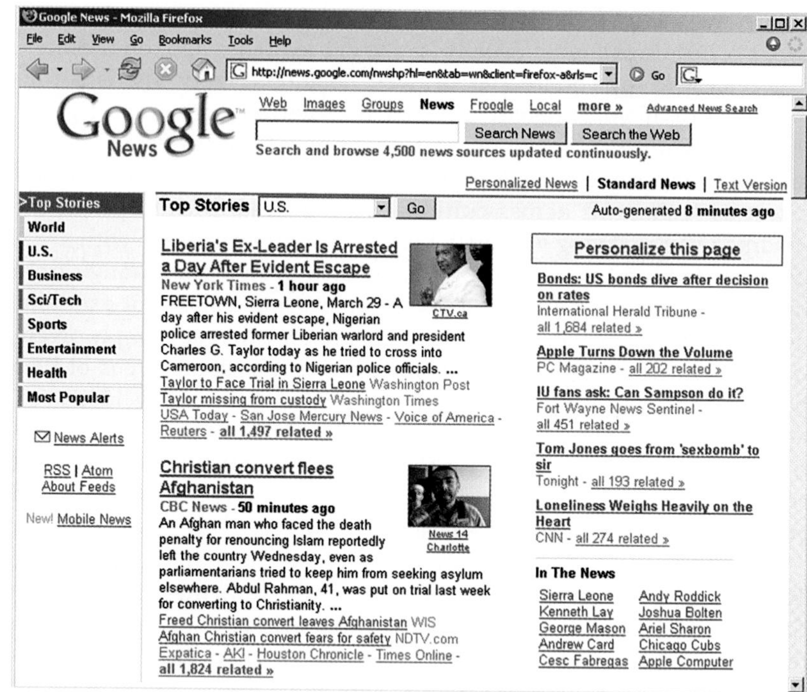

Google News site

consumption of energy by different nations. Pie charts depict such information memorably, as those on p. 433 show.

A ***graph*** is an efficient device for comparing items over time or according to other variables. You could use a graph to trace the rise and fall of test scores over several decades, or to show college enrollment by sex, race, and Hispanic origin, as in the bar graph on p. 433.

Diagrams or drawings are useful for drawing attention to details. You can use drawings to illustrate complex physical processes or designs of all sorts. After the 2001 attack on the World Trade Center, for example, engineers used drawings and diagrams to help citizens understand precisely what led to the total collapse of the buildings.

You can use ***maps*** to illustrate location and spatial relationships—something as simple as the distribution of office space in your student union or as complex as the topography of Utah. Such information would probably be far more difficult to explain using words alone.

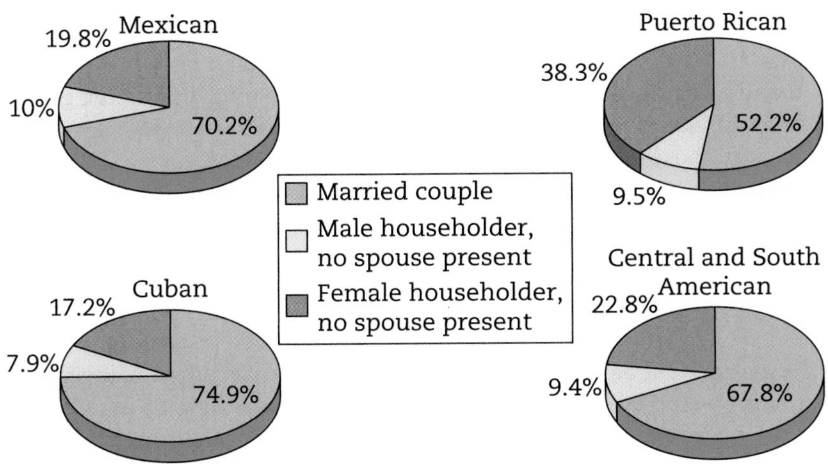

Family households by type and Hispanic origin group: 2002

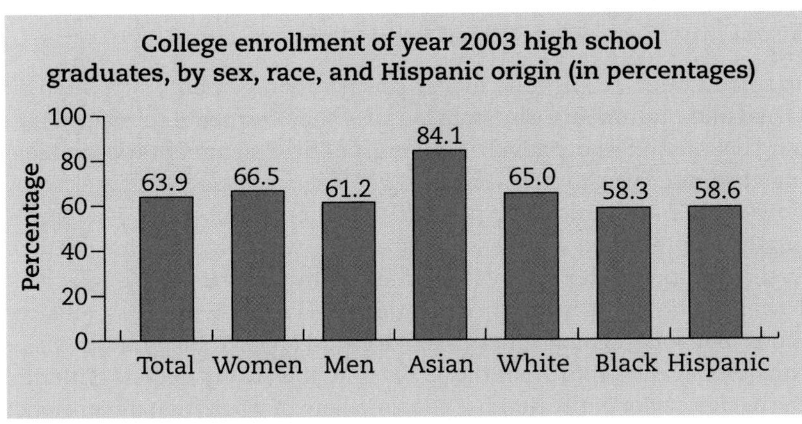

College enrollment 2003, by sex, race, and Hispanic origin

Look at the tables and graphs in a report published by the Pew Global Attitudes Project and the Kaiser Family Foundation. In what cases might one presentation of information be preferable to another?

LINK TO P. 747

FOLLOW PROFESSIONAL GUIDELINES FOR PRESENTING VISUALS

Charts, graphs, tables, and illustrations play such an important role in many fields that professional groups have come up with specific guidelines for labeling and formatting these items. You need to become familiar with those conventions as you advance in a field. A guide such as the *Publication Manual of the American Psychological Association* (5th edition) or the *MLA Handbook for Writers of Research Papers* (6th edition) describes these rules in detail.

REMEMBER TO CHECK FOR COPYRIGHTED MATERIAL

You also must be careful to respect copyright rules when using visual items created by someone else. It's relatively easy these days to download visual texts of all kinds from the Web. Some of these items—such as clip art or government documents—may be in the public domain, meaning that you're free to use them without requesting permission or paying a royalty. But other visual texts may require permission, especially if you intend to publish your work or use the item commercially. And remember: anything you place on a Web site is considered "published." (See Chapter 18 for more on intellectual property.)

Visual Arguments That Appeal to Emotion

To some extent, people tend to be suspicious of arguments supported by visual and multimedia elements because they can seem to manipulate our senses. And many advertisements, political documentaries, rallies, marches, and even church services do in fact use visuals to trigger emotions. Who hasn't teared up at a funeral when members of a veteran's family are presented with the American flag, with a bugler blowing taps in the distance? Who doesn't remember being moved emotionally by a powerful film performance accompanied by a heart-wrenching musical score? But you might also have seen or heard about *Triumph of the Will*, a Nazi propaganda film from the 1930s that powerfully depicts Hitler as the benign savior of the German people, a hero of Wagnerian dimensions. It's a chilling reminder of how images can be manipulated and abused.

Yet you can't flip through a magazine without being cajoled or seduced by images of all kinds—most of them designed in some way to attract your eye and attention. Not all such seductions are illicit, nor should you avoid using them when emotions can support the legitimate claims you hope to advance. Emotions certainly ran high as Lance

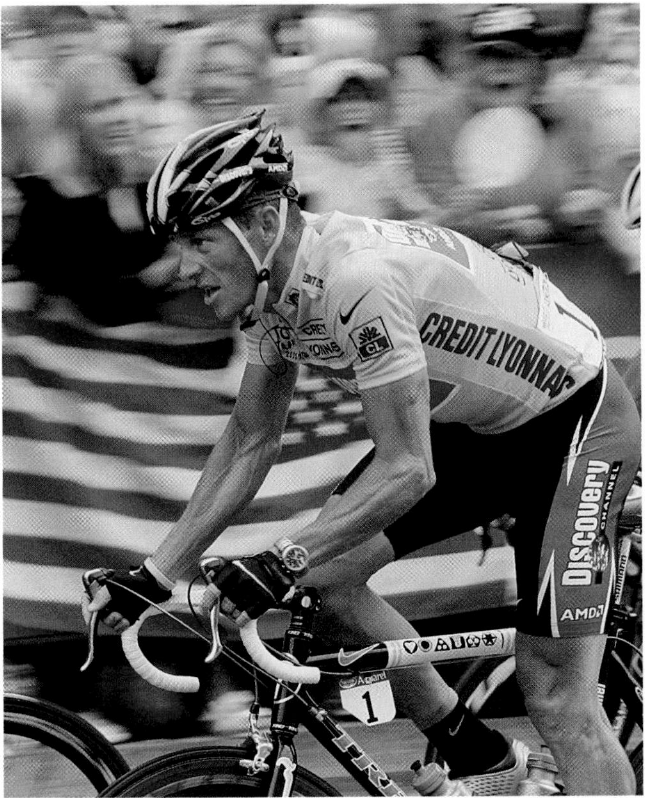

Lance Armstrong wins again.

Armstrong won a record seventh Tour de France: what's the effect of the image presented above?

APPRECIATE THE EMOTIONAL POWER OF IMAGES

Images can bring a text or presentation to life. Sometimes the images have power in and of themselves to persuade. This was the case with images in the 1960s that showed civil rights demonstrators being assaulted by police dogs and water hoses, and with horrifying images in 2005 of victims of Hurricane Katrina, which led many people to contribute to relief campaigns.

Images you select for a presentation may be equally effective if the visual text works well with other components of the argument. Indeed,

Rob Walker explores how the use of "real women" in a Dove ad campaign created a debate across America about women's bodies and advertising. What reaction do you have to the ads included in Walker's article? How does the modified drawing of Venus add to Walker's argument?

LINK TO P. 614

A striking image, like this *Apollo 8* photograph of the earth shining over the moon, can support many different kinds of arguments.

a given image might support many different kinds of arguments. Consider the famous *Apollo 8* photograph of our planet as a big blue marble hanging above the horizon of the moon. You might use this image to introduce an argument about the need for additional investment in the space program. Or it might become part of an argument about the need to preserve our frail natural environment, or part of an argument against nationalism: *From space, we are one world*. You could, of course, make any of these claims without the image. But the photograph—like most images—might touch members of your audience more powerfully than words alone could.

APPRECIATE THE EMOTIONAL POWER OF COLOR

Consider the color red. It attracts hummingbirds—and cops. It excites the human eye in ways that other colors don't. You can make a powerful statement with a red dress or a red car—or red shoes. In short, red evokes emotions. But so do black, green, pink, and even brown. The fact that we respond to color is part of our biological and cultural makeup. So it makes sense to consider carefully what colors are compatible with the kind of argument you're making. You might find that the best choice is black on a white background.

In most situations, you can be guided in your selection of colors by your own good taste (guys—check your ties), by designs you admire, or by the advice of friends or helpful professionals. Some design and presentation software will even help you choose colors by offering dependable "default" shades or an array of preexisting designs and compatible colors—for example, of presentation slides.

The colors you choose for a design should follow certain commonsense principles. If you're using background colors on a poster, Web site, or slide, the contrast between words and background should be vivid enough to make reading easy. For example, white letters on a yellow background will likely prove illegible. Any bright background color should be avoided for a long document. Indeed, reading seems easiest with dark letters against a light or white background. Avoid complex patterns, even though they might look interesting and be easy to create. Quite often, they interfere with other, more important elements of a presentation.

As you use visuals in your college projects, test them on prospective readers. That's what professionals do because they appreciate how delicate the choices about visual and multimedia texts can be. These responses will help you analyze your own arguments as well as improve your success with them.

If Everything's an Argument . . .

Look back through this chapter, paying special attention to visual elements. What part has color played in getting across the message of this chapter—that visual arguments are all around us? What visual example in this chapter do you find most compelling or memorable, and why? Would it be possible to substitute words for that image, and, if so, what would the differences be?

RESPOND •

1. The December 2002 issue of *The Atlantic Monthly* included the following poem, along with the photograph that may have inspired it, shown on the following page. Look carefully at the image and then read the poem several times, at least once aloud. Working with another person in your class, discuss how the words of the poem and the image interact with one another. What difference would it make if the image hadn't accompanied this text? Write a brief report of your findings, and bring it to class for discussion.

   A waterfall of black chains
   looms behind the man in the stovepipe hat.
   Cigar. Wrinkled clothes. This is
   Isambard Kingdom Brunel.
   Who could not stop working. Slept
   and ate at the shipyard.
   The largest ship in the world.
   Driven to outdo himself.
   Fashioned from iron plate and
   powered by three separate means.
   Able to sail to Ceylon and back
   without refueling. Fated
   to lay the Atlantic cable, the India cable.
   Untouched in size for forty years.
   The Great Leviathan. The Little Giant,
   Isambard Kingdom Brunel.
   Builder of tunnels, ships, railroads, bridges.
   Engineer and Genius of England.
   He should have built churches, you know.
   Everything he prayed for came true.

   –John Spaulding, "The Launching Chains of the *Great Eastern*"
   (By Robert Howlett, 1857)

2. Find an advertisement with both verbal and visual elements. Analyze the ad's visual argument by answering some of the questions on pp. 418, 421, and 422, taking care to "reread" its visual elements just as carefully as you would its words. After you've answered each question as thoroughly as possible, switch ads with a classmate and analyze the new argument in the same way. Then compare your own and your classmate's responses to the two advertisements. If they're different—and there's every reason to expect they will be—how do you account for the differences? What's the effect of audience on the argu-

This photograph of Isambard Kingdom Brunel was taken by Robert Howlett and is included in the National Portrait Gallery's collection in London.

ment's reception? What are the differences between your own active reading and your classmate's?

3. You've no doubt noticed the relationships between visual design and textual material on the Web. In the best Web pages, the elements work together rather than simply competing for space. In fact, even if you'd never used the Web, you'd still know a great deal about graphic design: newspapers, magazines, and your own college papers make use of design principles to create effective texts.

   Find three or four Web or magazine pages that you think exemplify good visual design—and then find just as many that don't. When you've picked the good and bad designs, draw a rough sketch of their physical layout. Where are the graphics? Where is the text? What are the size and position of text blocks relative to graphics? How is color used? Can you discern common design principles among the pages, or does each good page work well in its own way? Write a brief explanation of what you find, focusing on the way the visual arguments influence audiences.

4. Go to the Web page for the Pulitzer Prize archives at <http://pulitzer.org>. Pick a year to review, and then study the images of the winners in three categories: editorial cartooning, spot news photography, and feature photography. (Click on "Works" to see the images.) From among the images you review, choose one you believe makes a strong argument. Then, in a paragraph, describe that image and the argument it makes.

15
Presenting Arguments

In the wake of a devastating hurricane, local ministers search for just the right words to offer comfort and inspire hope in their congregations.

At a campus rally, a spoken word poet performs a piece against racism and homophobia.

To raise money for an AIDS awareness campaign, a group of students creates a poster advertising the local AIDS Walk, an informational brochure, and a Web site through which people can learn about the campaign and make a donation.

For a course in psychology, a student creates a multimedia presentation on the work of neuroscientist Constance Pert.

During their wedding, a couple exchanges the special vows they've worked together to create.

Sometimes the choice of how best to deliver an argument to a particular audience is made for you: the boss says "write a report" or an instructor says "build a Web site" or "make a 15-minute presentation that uses slides." But many times, you'll need to think carefully about what form of presentation is most appropriate and effective for your topic, your purpose, and your audience. Providing detailed advice about all available choices for presentation would take a book, not a brief chapter. But we can get you started thinking about issues of presentation in your own work.

• • •

Print Presentations

The Commercial Closet Association has posted to their Web site a guide of best practices for including gay, lesbian, bisexual, and transgender (GLBT) people in advertising. Pay attention to how they present their message with respect to topic organization, bulleted points, bolding, capitalization, and font choice.

LINK TO P. 654

For many arguments you make in college, print is still the best system of delivery. Print texts, after all, are more permanent than most Web-based materials. Moreover, they're relatively cheap and increasingly easy to produce—and they offer an efficient way to convey abstract ideas or to provide complicated chains of reasoning. But in choosing a print presentation, writers face an embarrassment of riches: whereas print arguments used to come in standard formats—black print on 8½ × 11 white paper printed left to right, top to bottom—today's print texts come in a dizzying array of shapes, sizes, colors, and so on. As you think about presenting arguments in print, here are some issues to consider:

- What's the overall tone you want to create in this written argument? What's the purpose of your argument, and to whom is it addressed?
- What format will get your message across most effectively? A triple-fold brochure? A newsletter? A formal report with table of contents, executive summary, and so on?
- What fonts will make your argument most memorable and readable? Will you vary font or type size to guide readers through your text? To get attention or signal what's most important?

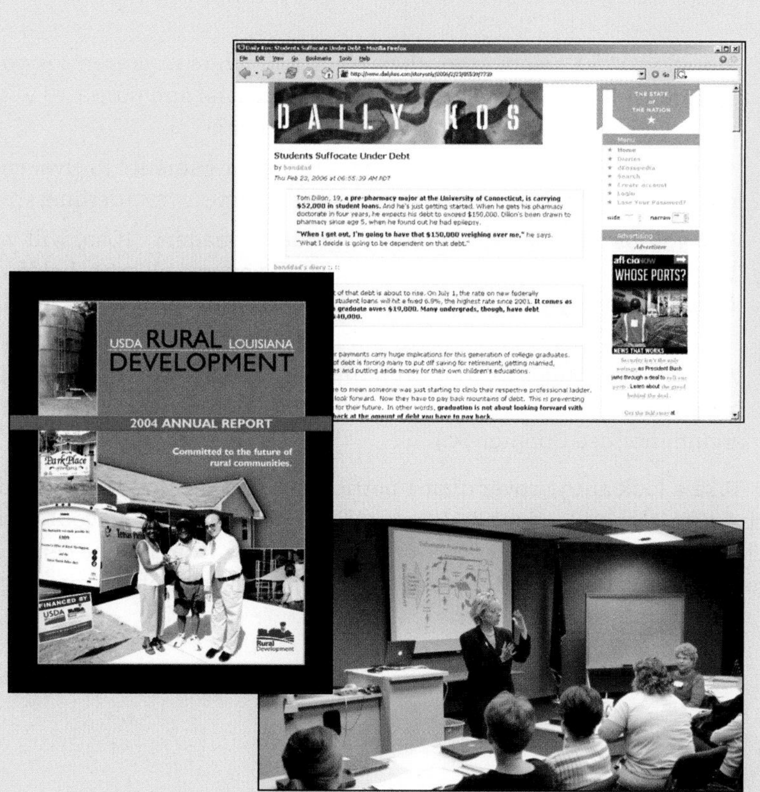

Not Just Words

The figures above illustrate three different modes of presentation—an oral/multimedia presentation for a live audience, a printed report, and an informative blog. Spend some time talking with a classmate about the choices involved in selecting each of these methods of presentation, and then report your findings to the class.

- Should you use colors other than black and white in presenting your argument? If so, what colors best evoke your tone and purpose? What colors will be most appealing to your audience?
- How will you use white or blank space in your argument? To give readers time to pause? To establish a sense of openness or orderliness?
- Will you use subheads as another guide to readers? If so, will you choose a different type size for them? Will you use all caps, boldface, or italics? In any case, be consistent in the type and the structure of subheads (all nouns, for example, or all questions).
- Will you use visuals in your print argument? If so, how will you integrate them smoothly into the text? (For more on the role of visuals in arguments, see Chapter 14.)

Take a look at the cover of one particular print document, the annual report for corporate giant IBM (below). Note the horizontal layout of the report's cover, which draws the reader's eye to the words at the center of the page announcing *IBM Annual Report 2004*. This band of text runs right

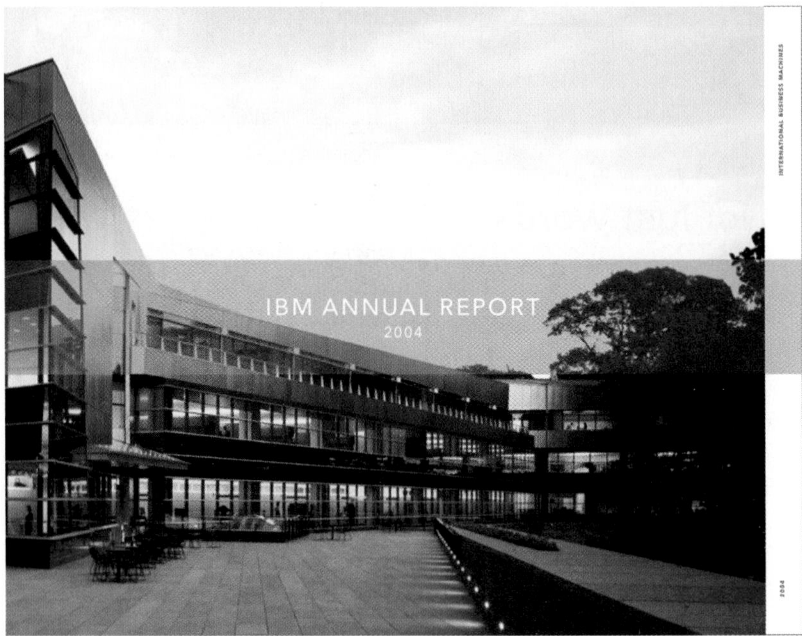

IBM's understated yet stylish design signals seriousness.

across the middle of the cover, within a band of color in a subtly different shade from the photograph of IBM headquarters on which it's superimposed. This superimposition gives the title a three-dimensional quality; the words seem to stand out from the cover. The pale shades of blue and green and grey are very cool and calm, and the building's image is one of light and glass and stability. The "look" of this cover says "I'm important" to its readers.

Oral/Multimedia Presentations

While most students are used to preparing arguments in print forms, you may be less familiar with making effective choices for a live presentation. In fact, students tell us that they're being assigned to make presentations more and more frequently in their classes—but that they're hardly ever given concrete instruction in how to do so. And students coming back from summer internship positions across a range of fields, from engineering to the arts, say that their employers simply expect them to be proficient at delivering arguments orally (and at accompanying such presentations with appropriate illustrative materials).

Consider the *New York Times* report by Janny Scott in which she analyzes data about U.S. foreign–born residents. How might this information be presented differently in an oral presentation? How might Scott have changed her delivery depending on her audience? As a presenter, how would you open a talk on this topic?

LINK TO P. 739

It's hard to generalize here, but we think it's fairly safe to say that successful oral/multimedia presenters credit several crucial elements in their success:

- They have thorough knowledge of their subjects.
- They pay very careful attention to the values, ideas, and needs of their listeners.
- They use structures and styles that make their spoken arguments easy to follow.
- They keep in mind the interactive nature of oral arguments (live audiences can argue back!).
- They realize that most oral presentations involve visuals of some sort, and they plan accordingly for the use of presentation software, illustrations, and so on.
- They practice, practice—and then practice some more.

Oral Arguments and Discussion

It's worth stopping for a moment to remember that the most common context for oral arguments you'll make in college may well take place in ordinary discussions, whether you're trying to persuade your parents that you need a new computer for your coursework, or to explore the meaning of a poem in class, or to argue against a textbook's interpretation of an economic phenomenon. In such everyday contexts, many people automatically choose the tone of voice, kind of evidence, and length of speaking time to suit the situation.

You can improve your own performance in such contexts by observing closely other speakers you find effective and by joining in on conversations whenever you possibly can; after all, the more you participate in lively discussions, the more comfortable you'll be doing so. To make sure your in-class comments count, follow these tips:

- Be well prepared so that your comments will be relevant to the class.
- Listen with a purpose, jotting down important points.
- Ask a key question—or offer a brief analysis or summary of the points that have already been made, to make sure you and other students (and the instructor) are "on the same page."
- Respond to questions or comments by others in specific rather than vague terms.
- Offer a brief analysis of an issue or text that invites others to join in and build on your comments.

Formal Oral/Multimedia Presentations

You've probably already been asked to make a formal presentation in some of your classes or on the job. In such cases, you need to consider the full context carefully. Note how much time you have to prepare and how long the presentation should be. You want to use the allotted time effectively, while not infringing on the time of others. Consider also what visual aids, handouts, or other materials might help make the

CULTURAL CONTEXTS FOR ARGUMENT

Speaking Up in Class

Speaking up in class is viewed as inappropriate or even rude in some cultures. In the United States, however, doing so is expected and encouraged. Some instructors even assign credit for such class participation.

presentation successful. Will you have to use an overhead projector? Can you use PowerPoint or other presentation software? Be aware that a statistical pie chart may carry a lot of weight in one argument, whereas photographs may make your point better in another. (See Chapter 14.)

Think about whether you're to make the presentation alone or as part of a group—and plan and practice accordingly. If you're going to be part of a group, turn-taking will need to be worked out carefully. Check out where your presentation will take place. In a classroom with fixed chairs? A lecture or assembly hall? An informal sitting area? Will you have a lectern? Other equipment? Will you sit or stand? Remain in one place or move around? What will the lighting be, and can you adjust it? Finally, note any criteria for evaluation: how will your live oral argument be assessed?

In addition to these logistical considerations, you need to consider several other key elements whenever you make a formal presentation:

Purpose

- Determine your major argumentative purpose. Is it to inform? To convince or persuade? To explore? To make a decision? To entertain? Something else?

Audience

- Who is your audience? An interested observer? A familiar face? A stranger? What will be the mix of age groups, men and women, and so on? Are you a peer of the audience members? Think carefully about what they'll already know about your topic and what opinions they're likely to hold.

Structure

- Structure your presentation so that it's easy to follow, and take special care to plan an introduction that gets the audience's attention and a conclusion that makes your argument memorable. You'll find more help with structure on p. 449.

Arguments to Be Heard

Even if you work from a print script in delivering a live presentation, that script must be written to be *heard* rather than read. Such a text—whether in the form of an overhead list, note cards, or a fully written-out text—should feature a strong introduction and conclusion, a clear

Azar Nafisi wrote an "aural essay," an essay meant to be heard, for the National Public Radio series *This I Believe*. Read the essay, and then listen to it using the link mentioned in the introduction. Consider her choice of opening and conclusion, signposts, and syntax.

LINK TO P. 909

organization with helpful structures and signposts, concrete diction, and straightforward syntax.

INTRODUCTIONS AND CONCLUSIONS

Like readers, listeners tend to remember beginnings and endings most readily. Work hard, therefore, to make these elements of your spoken argument especially memorable. Consider including a provocative or puzzling statement, opinion, or question; a memorable anecdote; a powerful quotation; or a vivid visual image. If you can refer to the interests or experiences of your listeners in the introduction or conclusion, do so.

Look at the introduction in Toni Morrison's acceptance speech to the Nobel Academy when she won the Nobel Prize for Literature:

> **"Once upon a time there was an old woman. Blind but wise." Or was it an old man? A guru, perhaps. Or a griot soothing restless children. I have heard this story, or one exactly like it, in the lore of several cultures. "Once upon a time there was an old woman. Blind. Wise."**
>
> **– Toni Morrison**

Here Morrison uses a storytelling strategy, calling on the traditional "Once upon a time" to signal to her audience that she's doing so. Note

Toni Morrison accepting the Nobel Prize for Literature in 1993

also the use of repetition and questioning. These strategies raise interest and anticipation in her audience: how will she use this story in accepting the Nobel Prize?

STRUCTURES AND SIGNPOSTS

For a spoken argument, you want your organizational structure to be crystal clear. Offer an overview of your main points toward the beginning of your presentation, and make sure that you have a clearly delineated beginning, middle, and end to the presentation. Throughout, remember to pause between major points and to use helpful signposts to mark your movement from one topic to the next. Such signposts act as explicit transitions in your spoken argument and thus should be clear and concrete: *The second crisis point in the breakup of the Soviet Union occurred hard on the heels of the first,* rather than *The breakup of the Soviet Union came to another crisis.* In addition to such explicit transitions as *next, on the contrary,* or *finally,* you can offer signposts to your listeners by repeating key words and ideas as well as by carefully introducing each new idea with concrete topic sentences.

DICTION AND SYNTAX

Avoid long, complicated sentences, and use straightforward syntax (subject-verb-object, for instance, rather than an inversion of that order) as much as possible. Remember, too, that listeners can hold onto concrete verbs and nouns more easily than they can grasp a steady stream of abstractions. So when you need to deal with abstract ideas, try to illustrate them with concrete examples.

Take a look at the following text that student Ben McCorkle wrote on *The Simpsons,* first as he prepared it for an essay and then as he adapted it for a live oral/multimedia presentation:

Print Version

The Simpson family has occasionally been described as a "nuclear" family, which obviously has a double meaning: first, the family consists of two parents and three children, and, second, Homer works at a nuclear power plant with very relaxed safety codes. The overused label *dysfunctional,* when applied to the Simpsons, suddenly takes on new meaning. Every episode seems to include a scene in which son Bart is being choked by his father, the baby is being neglected, or Homer is sitting in a drunken stupor transfixed by the television

Choose a paragraph from Amy Tan's speech in Chapter 25 and try to deliver it the way you think it might have been done originally. What do you notice about the ways you modify your voice and manner of speaking?

LINK TO P. 804

screen. The comedy in these scenes comes from the exaggeration of commonplace household events (although some talk shows and news programs would have us believe that these exaggerations are not confined to the madcap world of cartoons).

–Ben McCorkle, "The Simpsons: A Mirror of Society"

Oral Version (with a visual illustration)

What does it mean to describe the Simpsons as a *nuclear* family? Clearly, a double meaning is at work. First, the Simpsons fit the dictionary meaning—a family unit consisting of two parents and some children. The second meaning, however, packs more of a punch. You see, Homer works at a nuclear power plant [pause here] with *very* relaxed safety codes!

Homer Simpson in a typical pose

Still another overused family label describes the Simpsons. Did everyone guess I was going to say *dysfunctional?* And like "nuclear," when it comes to the Simpsons, "dysfunctional" takes on a whole new meaning.

Remember the scene when Bart is being choked by his father?

How about the many times the baby is being neglected?

Or the classic view—Homer sitting in a stupor transfixed by the TV screen!

My point here is that the comedy in these scenes often comes from double meanings—and from a lot of exaggeration of everyday household events.

Note that the revised version presents the same information as the original, but this time it's written to be *heard*. The revision uses helpful signposts, some repetition, a list, italicized words to prompt the speaker to give special emphasis, and simple syntax so that it's easy to listen to.

Arguments to Be Remembered

You can probably think of oral/multimedia arguments that still stick in your memory—a song like Bruce Springsteen's "Born in the USA," for instance, or Notorious B.I.G.'s "One More Chance." Such arguments are memorable in part because they call on the power of figures of speech and other devices of language. In addition, careful repetition can make spoken arguments memorable, especially when linked with parallelism and climactic order. (See Chapter 12 for more on using figurative language to make arguments more vivid and memorable.)

REPETITION, PARALLELISM, AND CLIMACTIC ORDER

Whether they're used alone or in combination, repetition, parallelism, and climactic order are especially appropriate for spoken arguments that sound a call to arms or that seek passionate engagement from the audience. Perhaps no person in the twentieth century used them more effectively than Martin Luther King Jr., whose sermons and speeches helped to spearhead the civil rights movement. Standing on the steps of the Lincoln Memorial in Washington, D.C., on August 23, 1963, with hundreds of thousands of marchers before him, King called on the nation to make good on the "promissory note" represented by the Emancipation Proclamation.

Look at the way King uses repetition, parallelism, and climactic order in the following paragraph to invoke a nation to action:

> **It is obvious today that America has defaulted on this promissory note insofar as her citizens of color are concerned. Instead of honoring this sacred obligation, America has given the Negro people a bad check which has come back marked "insufficient funds." But *we refuse* to believe that the bank of justice is bankrupt. *We refuse* to believe that there are insufficient funds in the great vaults of opportunity of this nation. So *we have come* to cash this check—a check that will give us upon demand the riches of freedom and the security of justice. *We have also come* to this hallowed spot to remind America of the fierce urgency of now. This is *no time* to engage in the luxury of cooling off or to take the tranquilizing drug of gradualism. *Now is the time* to rise from the dark and desolate valley of segregation to the sunlit path of racial justice. *Now is the time* to open the doors of opportunity to all of God's children. *Now is the time* to lift our nation from the quicksands of racial injustice to the solid rock of brotherhood.**
>
> **–Martin Luther King Jr., "I Have a Dream" (emphasis added)**

The italicized words highlight the way King uses repetition to drum home his theme. But along with that repetition, he sets up a powerful set of parallel verb phrases, calling on all "to rise" from the "dark and desolate valley of segregation" to the "sunlit path of racial justice" and "to open the doors of opportunity" for all. The final verb phrase ("to lift") leads to a strong climax, as King moves from what each individual should do to what the entire nation should do: "to lift our nation from the quicksands of racial injustice to the solid rock of brotherhood." These stylistic choices, together with the vivid image of the "bad check," help to make King's speech powerful, persuasive—and memorable.

Thank goodness you don't have to be as highly skilled as King to take advantage of the power of repetition and parallelism. Simply repeating a key word in your argument can impress it on your audience, as can arranging parts of sentences or items in a list in parallel order.

The Role of Visuals in Oral/Multimedia Arguments

Visuals often play an important part in oral arguments, and they should be prepared with great care. Don't think of them as add-ons but rather as a major means of getting across your message and supporting the claims you're making. In many cases, a picture can truly be worth a thousand words, helping your audience see examples or illustrations or other data that make your argument compelling.

Whatever visuals you use—charts, graphs, photographs, summary statements, sample quotations, lists—must be large enough to be readily seen by all members of your audience. If you use slides or overhead projections, be sure that the information on each frame is simple, clear, and easy to read and process. In order for audience members to read information on a transparency, this means using 36 point type for major headings, 24 point for subheadings, and at least 18 point for all other text. For slides, use 24 point for major headings, 18 point for subheadings, and at least 14 point for other text.

The same rule of clarity and simplicity holds true for posters, flip charts, or a chalkboard. And remember not to turn your back on your audience while you refer to these visuals. Finally, if you prepare supplementary materials for the audience—bibliographies or other handouts—wait to distribute them until the moment the audience will need them or until the end of the presentation so that they won't distract the audience from your spoken argument.

If you've seen many PowerPoint presentations, you're sure to have seen some really bad ones: the speaker just stands up and reads off what is on each slide. Nothing can be more deadly boring than that. So in your own use of PowerPoint or other presentation slides, make sure that they provide an overview and serve as visual signposts to guide listeners, but *never* read them word for word.

For an oral/multimedia presentation, one student used the PowerPoint slides shown on pp. 454, 456, and 458 to compare Frank Miller's graphic novel *Sin City* and its movie adaptation. Notice that the student uses text throughout, but in moderation. Next take a look at the written script—written to be heard—that the student developed for this presentation. The student does *not* read from the slides; rather, the slides illustrate the points being made. Their text sums up—and, occasionally, supplements—his oral presentation. This careful use of text makes the student's argument clear and easy to follow.

His choices in layout and font size also put a premium on clarity—but without sacrificing visual appeal. The choice of white and red text on a black background is an appropriate one for the topic—a stark black-and-white graphic novel and its shades-of-gray movie version. But be aware that light writing on a dark background can be hard to read. Dark writing on a white or light cream-colored background is a safer choice.

(Note that if your presentation shows or is based on source materials —either text or images—your instructor may want you to include a Works Cited slide listing the sources at the end of the presentation.)

From Frames to Film:
Graphic Novels on the Big Screen

Presentation by Sach Wickramasekara
PWR 2-06, Professor Lunsford
Wallenberg Hall Room 329
March 8, 2006

Introduction

A frame from the *Sin City* graphic novel.

"Instead of trying to make it [*Sin City*] into a movie which would be terrible, I wanted to take cinema and try and make it into this book."

- Robert Rodriguez, DVD Interview

The same scene from the *Sin City* movie.

[Opening Slide: Title]

Hi, my name is Sach.

[Change Slide: Introduction]

Take a look at this pair of scenes. Can you tell which one's from a movie and which one's from a graphic novel? How can two completely different media produce such similar results? Stay tuned; you're about to hear how.

[Pause]

Today I'll be analyzing *Sin City's* transition from a graphic novel to the big screen. The past decade has seen an increasing trend of comic books and graphic novels morphing into big-budget movies, with superhero flicks such as *Spiderman* and *X-men* headlining this list. However, until recently, movies borrowed from their comic book licenses but never stuck fully to their scripts. That all changed with *Sin City,* and I'll show you how dedication to preserving the look and feel of the graphic novel is what makes the screen version of *Sin City* neither a conventional graphic novel nor a conventional movie, but a new, innovative art form that's a combination of the two.

[Body]

[Change Slide—Technology]

Part of what makes *Sin City* so innovative is the technology powering it. The movie captures the look of the graphic novel so

Technology

Right: The original scene from the graphic novel.

Left: The scene is filmed with live actors on a green screen set.

Right: The final version of the scene, after the colors have been changed to shades of black and white. Notice the sapphire shade of the convertible, and how it stands out from the background.

Audio and Voice

"When I read the books, I felt that they were fantastic exactly as they were . . . I loved that the dialogue didn't sound like movie dialogue." - Robert Rodriguez

JUST ONE HOUR TO GO. MY LAST DAY ON THE JOB. EARLY RETIREMENT. NOT MY IDEA. DOCTOR'S ORDERS. HEART CONDITION. *ANGINA*, HE CALLS IT.

"Just one hour to go. My last day on the job. Early retirement. Not my idea. Doctor's orders. Heart condition. Angina, he calls it."

\- *Sin City* movie

well by filming actors on a green screen and using digital imagery to put detailed backdrops behind them. Computer technology also turns the movie's visuals into shades of black and white with rare dashes of color splashed in, reproducing the noir feel of the original novels. Thus, scenes in The *Sin City* have a photorealistic yet stylized quality that differentiates them from both the plain black-and-white images of the comics and the real sets used in other movies.

[Change Slide—Audio and Voice]

Pretty pictures are all well and good, but everyone knows that voice is just as important in a movie, especially because the media of comics and film use words so differently. The *Sin City* movie reproduces many sections of the novel that have a first-person narrator as monologues, and the script is lifted word for word from Miller's originals. This gives the dialogue an exaggerated quality that is more fantastic than realistic, which is exactly what director Robert Rodriguez intended. Here is an example from the film. "*Just one hour to go. My last day on the job. Early retirement. Not my idea. Doctor's orders. Heart condition.* Angina, *he calls it.*" A text box monologue fits perfectly in comics, where you read it and hear the character's voice in your head, but you wouldn't expect to hear it within an actual film. This contrast in narrative styles between the spoken word and how it is used is another factor that makes *Sin City* such an original work.

[Change Slide—Time and Structure]

Films are based on movement and sound, but comics divide movement into a series of "freeze-frame" images and represent

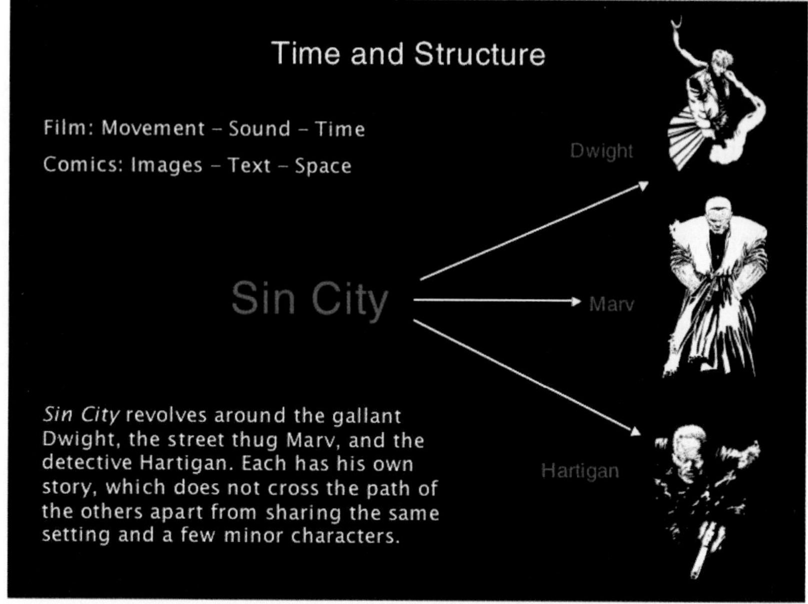

Time and Structure
Film: Movement – Sound – Time
Comics: Images – Text – Space
Dwight
Sin City
Marv
Hartigan
Sin City revolves around the gallant Dwight, the street thug Marv, and the detective Hartigan. Each has his own story, which does not cross the path of the others apart from sharing the same setting and a few minor characters.

Works Consulted

Goldstein, Hillary. "Five Days of Sin." IGN.com. 1 Apr. 2006. IGN Entertainment. 12 Feb. 2006 <http://comics.ign.com/articles/600/600846p1.html>.

"The Making of Sin City." Sin City DVD preview page. Buena Vista Online Entertainment. 4 Feb. 2006 <http://video.movies.go.com/sincity/>.

Miller, Frank. That Yellow Bastard. Milwaukie: Dark Horse Books, 1996.

---. The Big Fat Kill. Milwaukie: Dark Horse Books, 1994.

---. The Hard Goodbye. Milwaukie: Dark Horse Books, 1991.

Otto, Jeff. "Sin City Review." IGN.com: Filmforce. 29 March 2005. IGN Entertainment. 10 Feb 2006 <http://filmforce.ign.com/articles/598/598322p1.html>.

Robertson, Barbara. "The Devil's in the Details." Computer Graphics World Apr. 2005: 18. Expanded Academic ASAP. Gale Group Databases. Stanford U Lib., Palo Alto, CA. 11 Feb. 2006 <http://www.galegroup.com/>.

Sin City. Dir. Robert Rodriguez. Perf. Bruce Willis, Jessica Alba, Mickey Rourke, and Clive Owen. DVD. Dimension, 2005.

sound as text. If you freeze the *Sin City* movie at certain frames, the scene might look identical to what is portrayed in the graphic novel. Press the play button again, and the characters appear to jump to life and begin moving within the frame. Thus, it's easy to view *Sin City* as a beautifully depicted, real-time graphic novel, where time is the factor that makes the story move forward, instead of space separating the different panels of the graphic novel.

[Pause]

Like the graphic novel by Frank Miller that it's based on, the *Sin City* movie is composed of a series of stories with different protagonists such as Marv, Dwight, and the detective Hartigan. These separate tales share only their settings and several secondary characters. Therefore, the movie feels episodic, rather than continuous like a feature-length film. Just as Miller's originals were a compilation of short stories linked by their setting, *Sin City* has the unique feel of being three short films linked by Miller's vision of an alternate universe.

[Change Slide—Works Consulted]

[Pause]

Sin City has opened the doors for future comic adaptations, none more anticipated than *Sin City 2* itself. There hasn't been a lot of info. on this movie, but apparently it'll be based on a brand new story that Frank Miller is writing. It'll be intriguing to see director Rodriguez adapt a graphic novel that hasn't even been written yet, so keep an eye out for this one. Any questions?

The best way to test the effectiveness of all your visuals is to try them out on friends, family members, classmates, or roommates. If they don't get the meaning of the visuals right away, revise and try again.

Finally, remember that visuals can help make your presentation accessible: some members of your audience may not be able to see your presentation or may have trouble hearing it. Here are a few key rules to remember:

- Don't rely on color or graphics alone to get across information; use words along with them.
- Consider providing a written overview of your presentation, or put the text on an overhead projector—for those who learn better by reading *and* listening.
- If you use video, take the time to label sounds that won't be audible to some audience members. (Be sure your equipment is caption capable.)

Some Oral/Multimedia Presentation Strategies

In spite of your best preparation, you may feel some anxiety before a live presentation. This is perfectly natural. (According to one Gallup poll, Americans often identify public speaking as a major fear, scarier than attacks from outer space!) Experienced speakers say they have strategies for dealing with anxiety—and even that a little anxiety (and accompanying adrenaline) can act to a speaker's advantage.

The most effective strategy seems to be knowing your topic and material through and through. Confidence in your own knowledge goes a long way toward making you a confident speaker. In addition to being well prepared, you may want to try some of the following strategies:

- Practice a number of times, and tape yourself (video if at all possible) at least once so that you can listen to your voice. Tone of voice and body language can dispose audiences for—or against—speakers. For most oral arguments, you want to develop a tone that conveys interest in and commitment to your position as well as respect for your audience.
- Time your presentation carefully to make sure you stay within the allotted time.
- Think carefully about how you'll dress for your presentation, remembering that audience members usually take careful note of how a

speaker looks. Dressing for an effective presentation, of course, depends on what's appropriate for your topic, audience, and setting, but most experienced speakers like to wear clothes that are comfortable and that allow for easy movement—but that aren't overly casual. "Dressing up" a little indicates that you take pride in your appearance, that you have confidence in your argument, and that you respect your audience.

- Visualize your presentation. Go over the scene of the presentation in your mind, and think it through completely.
- Get some rest before the presentation, and avoid consuming too much caffeine.
- Concentrate on relaxing. Consider doing some deep-breathing exercises right before you begin.
- Pause before you begin, concentrating on your opening lines.
- Remember that most speakers make a stronger impression standing than sitting. Moving around a bit may help you make good eye contact with members throughout the audience.
- When using presentation slides, remember to stand to the side so that you don't block the view and to look at the audience rather than the slide.
- Remember to interact with the audience whenever possible; doing so will often help you relax and even have some fun.

Finally, remember to allow time for audience members to respond and ask questions. Try to keep your answers brief so that others may get in on the conversation. And at the very end of your presentation, thank the audience for attending so generously to your arguments.

A Note about Webcasts—Live Presentations over the Web

This discussion of live oral/multimedia presentations has assumed that you'll be speaking before an audience that's in the same room with you. Increasingly, though—especially in business, industry, and science—the presentations you make will be live, all right, but you won't actually be in the same physical space as the audience. Instead, you'll be in front of a camera that will capture your voice and image and relay them via the Web to attendees who might be anywhere in the world. Other Webcasts might show only your slides or some software you're demonstrating, using a screen capture relay without cameras. In this second model, you're not visible, but are still speaking live.

In either case, as you learn to adapt to Webcast environments, most of the strategies that work in oral/multimedia presentations for an audience that's actually present will continue to serve you well. But there are some significant differences:

- Practice is even more important in Webcasts, since you need to make sure that you can access everything you need online—a set of slides, for example, or a document or video clip, as well as any names, dates, or sources that you might be called on to provide during the Webcast.
- Because you can't make eye contact with audience members, it's important to remember to look into the camera, if you are using one, at least from time to time. If you're using a stationary Webcam, perhaps one mounted on your computer, practice standing or sitting still enough to stay in the frame without looking stiff.
- Even though your audience may not be visible to you, assume that if you're on camera, the Web-based audience can see you quite well; if you slouch, they'll notice. Also assume that your microphone is always live—don't mutter under your breath, for example, when someone else is speaking or asking a question.

Web-Based Presentations

Even without the interactivity of Webcasts, most students have enough access to the Web to use its powers for effective presentations, especially in Web sites and blogs.

Web Sites

Students we know are increasingly creating Web sites for themselves, working hard at their self-presentation, at showcasing their talents and accomplishments. Other students create Web sites for extracurricular organizations, for work, or for class assignments—or create sites for themselves on <Myspace.com> or as a Facebook.

Chapter 14 includes the homepage of student Catherine Harrell's Web site (see p. 426). Take a look at that example now to see how Harrell works with color and design to create an overall impression of who she is and what she does.

In planning any Web site, you'll need to pay careful attention to your rhetorical situation—to the purpose of your site, the intended audience, and the overall impression you want to make. To get started, you may want to visit several sites you admire, looking for effective design ideas and ways of organizing navigation and information. Creating a map or storyboard for your site will also help you to think through the links from page to page.

Experienced Web designers cite several important principles for Web-based presentations. The first of these is ***contrast,*** achieved through the use of color, icons, boldface, and so on; contrast helps guide readers through the site. The second principle, ***proximity,*** calls on you to keep together the parts of a page that are closely related, again for ease of reading. ***Repetition*** is another important principle: using the same consistent design throughout the site for elements such as headings, links, and so on will help readers move smoothly through the site. Finally, designers caution you to concentrate on ***overall impression,*** or mood, for the site. That means making sure that the colors and visuals you choose help to create that impression rather than challenge or undermine it.

Using the principles and tips for Web site design mentioned in this chapter, evaluate the presentations of one of the sites mentioned in the second half of the book. Some examples of sites are the Christian Alliance for Progress and National Public Radio.

LINK TO PP. 875 AND 909

Here are some additional tips that may help as you design your site:

- The homepage of your site should be eye-catching, inviting, and informative: use titles and illustrations to make clear what the site is about.
- Think carefully about two parts of every page: the navigation area (menus or links) and content areas. You want to make these two areas clearly distinct from one another. And make sure you *have* a navigation area for every page, including links to the key sections of the site and a link back to the homepage. Ease of navigation is one key to a successful Web site.
- Either choose a design template provided by Web-writing tools (like DreamWeaver), or create a template of your own so that the elements of each page will be consistent.
- Remember that some readers may not have the capacity to download heavy visuals or to access elements like Flash. If you want to reach a wide audience, stick with visuals that can be downloaded easily.
- Remember to include your name and contact information on every page.

Below is the homepage for a Web site that's part of a satiric anti-smoking campaign. The site introduces Shards O' Glass Freeze Pops with a straight face, saying that the company's goal is "to be the most responsible, effective, and respected developer of glass shard consumer products intended for adults." This deadpan tone is sustained throughout the site, from the "About Us" page, which informs readers that "We pride ourselves on responsible marketing," to a page on "Health Concerns" that announces, "Those who eat glass freeze pops are far more likely to develop shards-related ailments than those who don't eat them."

Take a close look at the homepage, and assess how well the designers of this site follow the principles of design noted above. How effective do you find the design? What might you suggest to improve it?

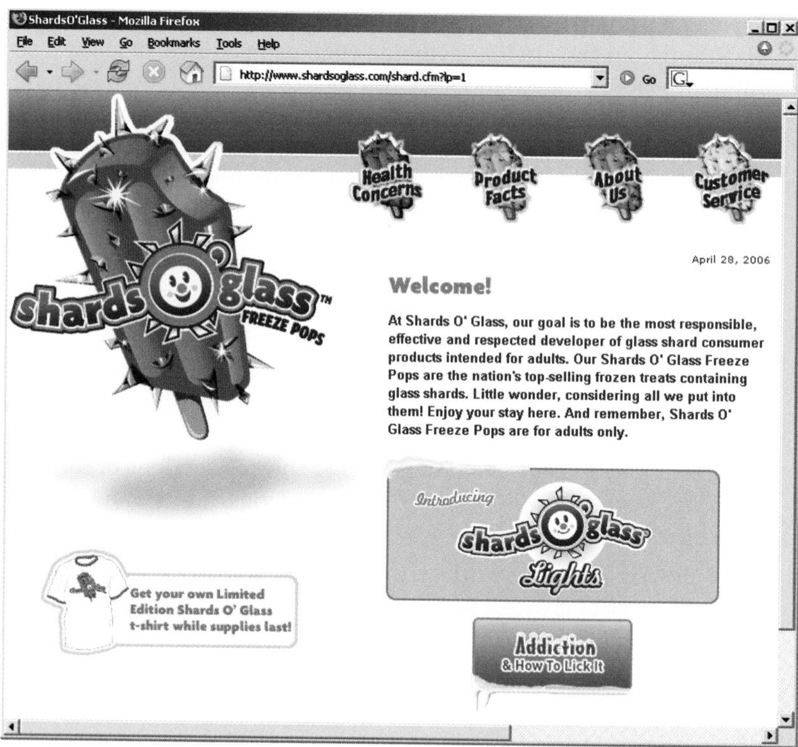

A satirical Web site sponsored by the anti-smoking campaign "The Truth" demonstrates that good design can help sell anything.

Blogs

Of all the kinds of Web texts we know, none has captured the public imagination more swiftly than Web logs, or blogs, which now number, by some estimates, up to 35 million. In essence, blogs take the idea of a personal Web page and give it the interactivity of a listserv, with readers able to make comments and respond both to the blogger and to one another. Many if not most blogs contain nothing more than personal self-expression by the blogger, but others have become prominent sources of news and opinion in politics, entertainment, and other fields.

As such, blogs create an ideal space for building communities, engaging in arguments, and giving voice to views and opinions of ordinary, everyday folks, those we seldom see writing or being written about in major print media (many of which now sponsor blogs themselves as part of their electronic versions). Proponents point to the democratizing function of blogs and to the corrective role they can play as bloggers run efficient and effective fact-checking projects. It was a blog, after all, that identified the many falsehoods disseminated by the Swift Boat Veterans group during the 2004 presidential election campaign, and it was a blog that led to the revelation that Dan Rather used less-than-factual information on a 60 *Minutes* show and that led, eventually, to Rather's withdrawal from that show.

Of course, blogs have a downside (or several): they're idiosyncratic almost by nature and can sometimes be self-indulgent and egoistic. A more serious point is that they can distort issues by spreading misinformation very quickly.

Nevertheless, blogs appear to be changing the ways people communicate and perhaps redistributing power in ways we still don't fully

If Everything's an Argument . . .

Look at the layout and design of the first few pages of any chapter in this book. What choices have the editors and authors made about how to present this print text, and how effective or ineffective do you find those choices? How might this material have been treated differently if it were part of an oral/multimedia presentation or a Web site?

understand. If you're a reader of blogs, be sure to read very carefully indeed, understanding that the information on the blog hasn't been subjected to the rigorous kind of peer review that is expected from traditional print sources. If you're a blogger yourself, you know that the rules of etiquette for blogging and conventions for blogs are still evolving. In the meantime, you'll be wise to join the spirit of any blog you contribute to, to be respectful in your comments—even very critical ones, and to think carefully about the audience you want to reach in every entry you make.

RESPOND •

1. Take a brief passage—three or four paragraphs—from an essay you've recently written. Then, following the guidelines in this chapter, rewrite the passage to be *heard* by a live audience. Finally, make a list of every change you made.
2. Find a print presentation that you find particularly effective. Study it carefully, noting how its format, type sizes, and typefaces, its use of color, white space, and visuals, and its overall layout work to deliver its message. If you find a particularly ineffective print presentation, carry out the same analysis to figure out why it's so bad. Finally, prepare a five-minute presentation of your findings to deliver in class.
3. Attend a lecture or presentation on your campus, and observe the speaker's delivery very carefully. Note what strategies the speaker uses to capture and hold your attention (or not). What signpost language and other guides to listening can you detect? How well are any visuals integrated into the presentation? What aspects of the speaker's tone, dress, eye contact, and movement affect your understanding and appreciation (or lack of it)? What's most memorable about the presentation, and why? Finally, write up an analysis of this presentation's effectiveness.
4. Go to a Web site you admire or consult frequently. Then spend some time answering the following questions: Why is a Web site—a digital presentation—the best way to present this material? What advantages over a print text or a live oral/multimedia presentation does the Web site have? What would you have to do to "translate" the argument(s) of this site into print or live oral format? What might be gained, or lost, in the process?

PART 4

CONVENTIONS OF argument

16
What Counts as Evidence

A downtown office worker who can never find a space in the company lot to park her motorcycle decides to argue for a designated motorcycle parking area. In building her argument, she conducts a survey to find out exactly how many employees drive cars to work and how many ride motorcycles.

A business consultant wants to identify characteristics of effective teamwork so that he can convince his partners to adopt these characteristics as part of their training program. To begin gathering evidence for this argument, the consultant decides to conduct on-site observations of three effective teams, followed by in-depth interviews with each member.

To support his contention that people are basically honest, an economist points to the detailed records kept by a vendor who sells bagels on the honor system in downtown offices. The merchant discovers that only a small percentage of people take advantage of him. The numbers also show that executives cheat more than middle-management employees.

For an argument aimed at showing that occupations are still often unconsciously thought of as either masculine or feminine, a student decides to carry out an experiment: she will ask fifty people chosen at random to draw pictures of a doctor, a police officer, a nurse, a CEO, a lawyer, and a secretary—and see which are depicted as men, which as women. The results of this experiment will become evidence for (or against) the argument.

Trying to convince her younger brother to invest in a PC laptop, a college student mentions her three years of personal experience using a similar computer for her college coursework.

In arguing that virtual reality technology may lead people to ignore or disregard the most serious of "real" world problems, a student writer provides evidence for this claim in part by citing sixteen library sources that review and critique cyberspace and virtual reality.

• • •

Josef Joffe and Michael Medved each discuss the influence of American media on international attitudes toward the United States. Both authors use movies and other media as evidence to support their respective arguments. How is it possible that two authors use similar evidence to arrive at different conclusions about anti-Americanism?

LINK TO PP. 1038 AND 1055

Evidence and the Rhetorical Situation

As the examples above demonstrate, people use all kinds of evidence in making and supporting claims. But this evidence doesn't exist in a vacuum; instead, the quality of evidence—how it was collected, by whom, and for what purposes—may become part of the argument itself. Evidence may be persuasive in one time and place but not in another; it may convince one kind of audience but not another; it may work with one type of argument but not the kind you are writing.

To be most persuasive, then, evidence should match the time and place in which you make your argument. For example, arguing that a Marine general should employ tactics of delay and strategic retreat because that very strategy worked effectively for George Washington is likely to fail if Washington's use of the tactic is the only evidence provided. After all, a military maneuver that was effective in 1776 for an outnumbered band of revolutionaries is more than likely an *irrelevant* one today for a much different fighting force. In the same way, a writer may achieve excellent results by citing her own experience as well as an extensive survey of local teenagers as evidence to support a new teen center for her small-town community, but she may have less success in arguing for the same thing in a distant, large inner-city area, where her personal authority may count for less.

College writers also need to consider in what fields or areas they're working. In disciplines such as experimental psychology or economics, empirical data—the sort that can be observed and counted—may be the best evidence, but the same kind of data may be less appropriate or persuasive, or even impossible to come by, in many historical or literary studies. As you become more familiar with a particular discipline, you'll gain a sense of just what it takes to prove a point or support a claim. The following questions will help you begin to understand the rhetorical situation of a particular discipline:

- How do other writers in the field use precedence—examples of actions or decisions that are very similar—and authority as evidence? What or who counts as an authority in this field? How are the credentials of authorities established?
- What kinds of data are preferred as evidence? How are such data gathered and presented?
- How are statistics or other numerical information used and presented as evidence? Are tables, charts, or graphs commonly used? How much weight do they carry?
- How are definitions, causal analyses, evaluations, analogies, and examples used as evidence?
- How does the field use firsthand and secondhand sources as evidence?
- Is personal experience allowed as evidence?
- How are quotations used as part of evidence?

David Horowitz addresses his audience as a group of politically savvy readers. While presenting his argument for an Academic Bill of Rights, he notes the reservations that some have expressed and discusses the steps he will take to compromise.

LINK TO P. 942

- How are images used as part of evidence, and how closely are they related to the verbal parts of the argument being presented?

As these questions suggest, evidence may not always travel well from one field to another.

Firsthand Evidence and Research

Firsthand evidence comes from research you yourself have carried out or been closely involved with, and much of this kind of research requires you to collect and examine data. Here we'll discuss the kinds of firsthand research most commonly conducted by student writers.

Observations

"What," you may wonder, "could be any easier than observing something?" You just choose a subject, look at it closely, and record what you see and hear. If observing were so easy, eyewitnesses would all provide reliable accounts. Yet experience shows that several people who have observed the same phenomenon generally offer different, sometimes even contradictory, evidence on the basis of those observations. (When TWA Flight 800 exploded off the coast of New Jersey in 1996, eyewitnesses gave various accounts, some even claiming that they saw what might have been a missile streaking toward the passenger jet. The official report found that an internal short likely ignited vapors in a fuel tank.) Trained observers say that getting down a faithful record of an observation requires intense concentration and mental agility.

Before you begin an observation, then, decide exactly what you want to find out and anticipate what you're likely to see. Do you want to observe an action repeated by many people (such as pedestrians crossing a street, in relation to an argument for putting in a new stoplight)? A sequence of actions (such as the stages involved in student registration, which you want to argue is far too complicated)? The interactions of a group (such as meetings of the campus Young Republicans, which you want to see adhere to strict parliamentary procedures)? Once you have a clear sense of what you'll observe and what questions you'll wish to answer through the observation, use the following guidelines to achieve the best results:

- Make sure the observation relates directly to your claim.
- Brainstorm about what you're looking for, but don't be rigidly bound to your expectations.

- Develop an appropriate system for collecting data. Consider using a split notebook or page: on one side, record the minute details of your observations directly; on the other, record your thoughts or impressions.
- Be aware that the way you record data will affect the outcome, if only in respect to what you decide to include in your observational notes and what you leave out.
- Record the precise date, time, and place of the observation.

In the following excerpt, travel writer Pico Iyer uses information drawn from minute and prolonged observation in an argument about what the Los Angeles International Airport (LAX) symbolizes about America:

> **LAX is, in fact, a surprisingly shabby and hollowed-out kind of place, certainly not adorned with the amenities one might expect of the**

The article "Who's a Looter?" by Tania Ralli invites the reader to consider how firsthand observation was interpreted divergently by two different photographers. Some complained that racism was the defining factor while others pointed to personal variation in interpreting "evidence." Do you think that it is a good idea for newspapers to delineate "looting" versus "carrying" for their reporters? What is the burden of evidence for you?

LINK TO P. 640

The LAX Web site offers a more glamorous view of the airport than Pico Iyer does on the basis of his direct observation.

> **world's strongest and richest power. When you come out into the Arrivals area in the International Terminal, you will find exactly one tiny snack bar, which serves nine items; of them, five are identified as Cheese Dog, Chili Dog, Chili Cheese Dog, Nachos with Cheese, and Chili Cheese Nachos. There is a large panel on the wall offering rental car services and hotels, and the newly deplaned American dreamer can choose between the Cadillac Hotel, the Banana Bungalow . . . and the Backpacker's Paradise.**
>
> **–Pico Iyer, "Where Worlds Collide"**

Another observer, however, might see and describe an entirely different LAX.

Interviews

Some evidence is best obtained through direct interviews. If you can talk with an expert—in person, on the phone, or online—you might get information you couldn't have obtained through any other type of research. In addition to getting expert opinion, you might ask for firsthand accounts, biographical information, or suggestions of other places to look or other people to consult. The following guidelines will help you conduct effective interviews:

- Determine the exact purpose of the interview, and be sure it's directly related to your claim.
- Set up the interview well in advance. Specify how long it'll take, and if you wish to tape-record the session, ask permission to do so.
- Prepare a written list of both factual and open-ended questions. (Brainstorming with friends can help you come up with good questions.) Leave plenty of space for notes after each question. If the interview proceeds in a direction that you hadn't expected but that seems promising, don't feel you have to cover every one of your questions.
- Record the subject's full name and title, as well as the date, time, and place of the interview.
- Be sure to thank those you interview, either in person or with a follow-up letter or email message.

In arguing that the Gay Games offer a truly inclusive alternative—rather than a parallel—to the Olympics, Caroline Symons uses data drawn from extensive interviews with organizers and participants in the Gay Games:

> **Out of twenty-four in-depth interviews I conducted with gay men involved in the Gay Games as organizers, over half indicated that they had sufficiently alienating experiences with sport during childhood and adolescence to be put off participating until the advent of gay sports organizations and events. . . . Gay men in particular have found a safe and welcoming environment to engage in sport through the emergence of gay sports organizations and the Gay Games.**
>
> **–Caroline Symons, "Not the Gay Olympic Games"**

Newspapers, too, often use interviews to add perspective to stories or to check the authenticity of claims. Steve Fainuru, a reporter for the *Washington Post,* uses that technique to weigh the validity of an internal army report that found flaws in the Stryker, a military transport vehicle used in Iraq:

> **But in more than a dozen interviews, commanders, soldiers and mechanics who use the Stryker fleet daily in one of Iraq's most dangerous areas unanimously praised the vehicle. The defects outlined in the report were either wrong or relatively minor and did little to hamper the Stryker's effectiveness, they said.**

Do Stryker armored personnel carriers like the one shown here deserve praise or criticism? Ask the man who drives one?

> **"I would tell you that at least 100 soldiers' lives have been saved because of the Stryker," said Col. Robert B. Brown, commander of the 1st Brigade, 25th Infantry Division, Stryker Brigade Combat Team, which uses about 225 Strykers for combat operations throughout northern Iraq. "That's being conservative," he said.**
>
> **–Steve Fainuru, "Soldiers Defend Faulted Strykers"**

Note how the story uses a dramatic quotation to represent the opinion expressed in the interviews. A more academic study, however, might include the full transcript of the interviews to give readers access to more data.

Surveys and Questionnaires

Surveys usually require the use of questionnaires. Any questions posed should be clear, easy to understand, and designed so that respondents' answers can be analyzed readily. Questions that ask respondents to say "yes" or "no" or to rank items on a scale (1 to 5, for example, or "most helpful" to "least helpful") are particularly easy to tabulate. Because tabulation can take time and effort, limit the number of questions you ask. Note also that people often resent being asked to answer more than about twenty questions, especially online.

Here are some other guidelines to help you prepare for and carry out a survey:

- Write out your purpose in conducting the survey, and make sure its results will be directly related to your claim.
- Brainstorm potential questions to include in the survey, and ask how each relates to your purpose and claim.
- Figure out how many people you want to contact, what the demographics of your sample should be (for example, men in their twenties, or an equal number of men and women), and how you plan to reach these people.
- Draft questions as free of bias as possible, making sure that each calls for a short, specific answer.
- Think about possible ways respondents could misunderstand you or your questions, and revise with these points in mind.
- Test the questions on several people, and revise those questions that are ambiguous, hard to answer, or too time-consuming to answer.
- If your questionnaire is to be sent by mail or email or posted on the Web, draft a cover letter explaining your purpose and giving a clear deadline. For mail, provide an addressed, stamped return envelope.

A key requirement of survey questions is that they be easy to understand.

"Next question: I believe that life is a constant striving for balance, requiring frequent tradeoffs between morality and necessity, within a cyclic pattern of joy and sadness, forging a trail of bittersweet memories until one slips, inevitably, into the jaws of death. Agree or disagree?"

- On the final draft of the questionnaire, leave plenty of space for answers.
- Proofread the final draft carefully; typos will make a bad impression on those whose help you're seeking.

After you've done your tabulations, set out your findings in clear and easily readable form, using a chart or spreadsheet if possible.

Hannah Fairfield comments on results from a survey conducted by the Pew Charitable Trust. What can reliably be inferred from these results? How might authors Joffe and Medved have used this information?

LINK TO PP. 985, 1038, AND 1055

In an argument over whether the government should label genetically modified foods, analyst Gary Langer draws on data from an ABC News Poll asking Americans what they thought about such food:

> Nearly everyone—93 percent—says the federal government should require labels on food saying whether it's been genetically modified, or "bio-engineered" (this poll used both phrases). Such near-unanimity in public opinion is rare.
>
> Fifty-seven percent also say they'd be less likely to buy foods labeled as genetically modified. That puts the food industry in a quandary: By meeting consumer demand for labeling, it would be steering business away from its genetically modified products.
>
> –Gary Langer, "Behind the Label: Many Skeptical of Genetically Modified Foods"

Experiments

Some arguments may be supported by evidence gathered through experiments. In the sciences, data from experiments conducted under rigorously controlled conditions are highly valued. For other kinds of writing, "looser" and more informal experiments may be acceptable, especially if they're intended to provide only part of the support for an argument. If you want to argue, for instance, that the recipes in *Gourmet* magazine are impossibly tedious to follow and take far more time than the average person wishes to spend preparing food, you might ask five or six people to conduct a little experiment: following two recipes apiece from a recent issue, and recording and timing every step. The evidence you gather from this informal experiment could provide some concrete support—by way of specific examples—for your contention. But such experiments should be taken with a grain of salt; they may not be effective with certain audiences, and if they can easily be attacked as skewed or sloppily done ("The people you asked to make these recipes couldn't cook a poptart"), then they may do more harm than good.

In an essay about computer hackers and the threats they pose to various individuals and systems, Winn Schwartau reports on an experiment, performed by a former hacker he knows, that was aimed at showing how easy it is to rob a bank. The experiment Schwartau describes makes his claim about bank security more believable:

> Jesse took his audience to a trash bin behind Pacific Bell, the Southern California Baby Bell service provider. Dumpster diving proved to be an effective means of social engineering because within minutes, an internal telephone company employee list was dredged out of the

garbage. On it, predictably, were handwritten notes with computer passwords.

In the neighborhood was a bank, which shall go nameless. After some more dumpster diving, financial and personal profiles of wealthy bank customers surfaced. That was all Jesse said he needed to commit the crime.

At a nearby phone booth, Jesse used a portable computer with an acoustic modem to dial into the telephone company's computer. Jesse knew a lot about the telephone company's computers, so he made a few changes. He gave the pay phone a new number, that of one of the wealthy clients about whom he now knew almost everything. He also turned off the victim's phone with that same number. Jesse then called the bank and identified himself as Mr. Rich, an alias.

"How can we help you, Mr. Rich?"

"I would like to transfer $100,000 to this bank account number."

"I will need certain information."

"Of course."

"What is your balance?"

"About ______," he supplied the number accurately.

"What is your address?"

Jesse gave the address.

"Are you at home, Mr. Rich?"

"Yes."

"We'll need to call you back for positive identification."

"I understand. Thank you for providing such good security."

In less than a minute the phone rang.

"Hello, Rich here."

The money was transferred, then transferred back to Mr. Rich's account again, to the surprise and embarrassment of the bank. The money was returned and the point was made.

–Winn Schwartau, "Hackers: The First Information Warriors"

Personal Experience

Personal experience can serve as powerful evidence when it's appropriate to the subject, to your purpose, and to the audience. If it's your *only* evidence, however, personal experience probably won't be sufficient to carry the argument. Nevertheless, it can be especially effective for drawing in listeners or readers, as Gloria Naylor demonstrates early in an argument about language and racism:

It was Andrea Lo's personal experiences as a child of immigrants that led to her belief in the importance of embracing a bicultural identity. Why might her conversion story be more convincing than the results of a cultural identity survey?

LINK TO P. 771

I remember the first time I heard the word "nigger." In my third-grade class, our math tests were being passed down the rows, and as I handed the papers to a little boy in back of me, I remarked that once

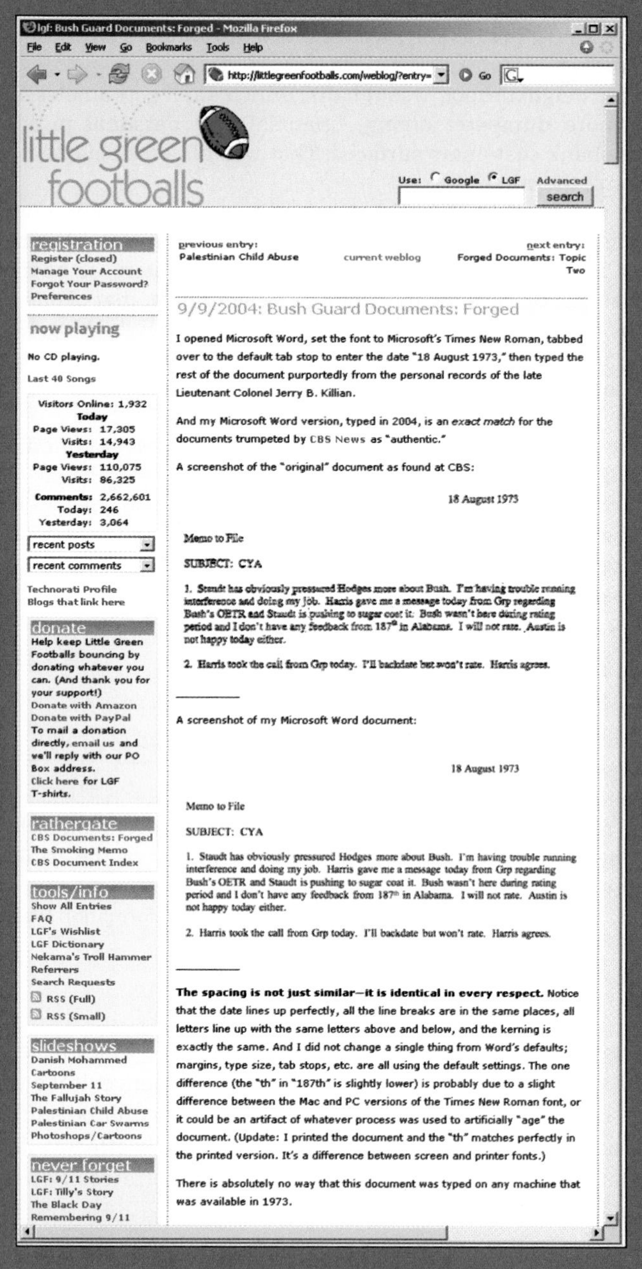

lgf: Bush Guard Documents: Forged - Mozilla Firefox

File Edit View Go Bookmarks Tools Help

http://littlegreenfootballs.com/weblog/?entry=

little green footballs

Use: Google LGF Advanced

search

registration
Register (closed)
Manage Your Account
Forgot Your Password?
Preferences

now playing
No CD playing.
Last 40 Songs

Visitors Online: 1,932
Today
Page Views: 17,305
Visits: 14,943
Yesterday
Page Views: 110,075
Visits: 86,325
Comments: 2,662,601
Today: 246
Yesterday: 3,064

recent posts
recent comments

Technorati Profile
Blogs that link here

donate
Help keep Little Green Footballs bouncing by donating whatever you can. (And thank you for your support!)
Donate with Amazon
Donate with PayPal
To mail a donation directly, email us and we'll reply with our PO Box address.
Click here for LGF T-shirts.

rathergate
CBS Documents: Forged
The Smoking Memo
CBS Document Index

tools/info
Show All Entries
FAQ
LGF's Wishlist
LGF Dictionary
Nekama's Troll Hammer
Referrers
Search Requests
RSS (Full)
RSS (Small)

slideshows
Danish Mohammed Cartoons
September 11
The Fallujah Story
Palestinian Child Abuse
Palestinian Car Swarms
Photoshops/Cartoons

never forget
LGF: 9/11 Stories
LGF: Tilly's Story
The Black Day
Remembering 9/11

previous entry: Palestinian Child Abuse | current weblog | next entry: Forged Documents: Topic Two

9/9/2004: Bush Guard Documents: Forged

I opened Microsoft Word, set the font to Microsoft's Times New Roman, tabbed over to the default tab stop to enter the date "18 August 1973," then typed the rest of the document purportedly from the personal records of the late Lieutenant Colonel Jerry B. Killian.

And my Microsoft Word version, typed in 2004, is an *exact match* for the documents trumpeted by CBS News as "authentic."

A screenshot of the "original" document as found at CBS:

18 August 1973

Memo to File

SUBJECT: CYA

1. Staudt has obviously pressured Hodges more about Bush. I'm having trouble running interference and doing my job. Harris gave me a message today from Grp regarding Bush's OETR and Staudt is pushing to sugar coat it. Bush wasn't here during rating period and I don't have any feedback from 187th in Alabama. I will not rate. Austin is not happy today either.

2. Harris took the call from Grp today. I'll backdate but won't rate. Harris agrees.

A screenshot of my Microsoft Word document:

18 August 1973

Memo to File

SUBJECT: CYA

1. Staudt has obviously pressured Hodges more about Bush. I'm having trouble running interference and doing my job. Harris gave me a message today from Grp regarding Bush's OETR and Staudt is pushing to sugar coat it. Bush wasn't here during rating period and I don't have any feedback from 187th in Alabama. I will not rate. Austin is not happy today either.

2. Harris took the call from Grp today. I'll backdate but won't rate. Harris agrees.

The spacing is not just similar—it is identical in every respect. Notice that the date lines up perfectly, all the line breaks are in the same places, all letters line up with the same letters above and below, and the kerning is exactly the same. And I did not change a single thing from Word's defaults; margins, type size, tab stops, etc. are all using the default settings. The one difference (the "th" in "187th" is slightly lower) is probably due to a slight difference between the Mac and PC versions of the Times New Roman font, or it could be an artifact of whatever process was used to artificially "age" the document. (Update: I printed the document and the "th" matches perfectly in the printed version. It's a difference between screen and printer fonts.)

There is absolutely no way that this document was typed on any machine that was available in 1973.

Not Just Words

Images often play a role in arguments. Charts, tables, and photographs are familiar types of visual evidence, but such arguments can also take unconventional forms. One of the more memorable examples of an argument supported visually occurred during the 2004 presidential election. In a segment aired on September 8, 2004, CBS's *60 Minutes II* claimed that newly discovered documents confirmed that George W. Bush had shirked military duties during his term in the National Guard. The photocopied memos, in official military form, seemed to be the smoking gun in a case that reporters had been pursuing for years. Here's what followed, according to political writer Michael Barone:

> . . . the network posted its 1972-dated documents on the Web. Within four hours, a blogger on freerepublic.com pointed out that they looked as though they had been created in Microsoft Word; the next morning, Scott Johnson of powerlineblog.com relayed the comment and asked for expert views. Charles Johnson oflittlegreenfootballs.com showed that the documents exactly matched one he produced in Word using default settings. CBS defended the documents for 11 days but finally confessed error and eased Rather out as anchor.
>
> –Michael Barone, "Blogosphere Politics"

Details of the documents' style and formatting had been questioned almost as soon as CBS made them available for online scrutiny. But Johnson's discovery brought focus and clarity to the discussion: since Microsoft Word hadn't existed when the CBS documents were supposedly written, documents mirroring its fonts, spacing, and defaults would have been difficult to create.

On the facing page is a screenshot of Johnson's experiment with the text of one of the questionable CBS documents. Examine the screenshot carefully, paying particular attention to the relationship between the two versions of the memo and Johnson's comments on them. Do you find Johnson's analysis convincing? Has he found a smoking gun, or would you want more data before agreeing that the case against the documents has reached a critical mass? Why or why not? What would be lost if Johnson had offered only a verbal description of his comparison of the documents?

again he had received a much lower mark than I did. He snatched his test from me and spit out that word. Had he called me a nymphomaniac or a necrophiliac, I couldn't have been more puzzled. I didn't know what a nigger was, but I knew that whatever it meant, it was something he shouldn't have called me. This was verified when I raised my hand, and in a loud voice repeated what he had said and watched the teacher scold him for using a "bad" word. I was later to go home and ask the inevitable question that every black parent must face—"Mommy, what does 'nigger' mean?"

–Gloria Naylor, "Mommy, What Does 'Nigger' Mean?"

Secondhand Evidence and Research

Secondhand evidence comes from sources beyond yourself—books, articles, films, online documents, photographs, and so on.

Library Sources

Your college library has not only printed materials (books, periodicals, reference works) but also computer terminals that provide access to electronic catalogs and indexes as well as to other libraries' catalogs via the Internet. Although this book isn't designed to give a complete overview of library resources, we can make some important distinctions and pose a few key questions that can help you use the library most efficiently.

CULTURAL CONTEXTS FOR ARGUMENT

Using Personal Experience

Personal experience counts in making academic arguments in some but not all cultures. Showing that you have personal experience with a topic can carry strong persuasive appeal with many English-speaking audiences, however, so it will probably be a useful way to argue a point in the United States. As with all evidence used to make a point, evidence based on your own experience must be pertinent to the topic, understandable to the audience, and clearly related to your purpose and claim.

Two Important Distinctions

- Remember the distinction between the *library databases* and the *Internet/Web*. Your library's computers hold important resources that either aren't available on the Web at all or aren't easily accessible to you except through the library's own system. The most important of these resources is the library's own catalog of its holdings (mostly books), but in addition college libraries usually pay to subscribe to a large number of scholarly databases—guides to journal and magazine articles, the Lexis/Nexis database of news stories and legal cases, and compilations of statistics, for example—that you can use for free. You'll be wise, then, to begin research using the electronic sources available to you through your college library before turning to the Web.
- Remember the distinction between *subject headings* and *keywords*. Library catalogs and databases usually index their contents by author, by title, by publication date, and by subject headings—a standardized set of words and phrases used to classify the subject matter of books and articles. When you do a subject search of the catalog, then, you're searching only one part of the electronic record of the library's books, and you need to use the exact wording of the *Library of Congress Subject Headings* (LCSH) classifications. This reference work is available in your library. On the other hand, searches using keywords make use of the computer's ability to look for any term in any field of the electronic record. So keyword searching is less restrictive than searching by subject headings, but it requires you to think carefully about your search terms in order to get good results. In addition, you need to learn to use the techniques for combining keywords with the terms *and, or,* and *not* and with parentheses and quotation marks (or using similar procedures built into the catalog's or database's search mechanism) to limit (or expand) your search.

Some Questions for Beginning Research

- What kinds of sources do you need to consult? Check your assignment to see whether you're required to consult different kinds of sources. If you'll use print sources, find out whether they're readily available in your library or whether you must make special arrangements (such as an interlibrary loan) to use them. If you need to locate nonprint sources (such as audiotapes or videotapes, artwork, photos), find out where those are kept and whether you need special permission to examine them.

- How current do your sources need to be? If you must investigate the very latest findings about, say, a new treatment for Alzheimer's, you'll probably want to check periodicals, medical journals, or the Web. If you want broader, more detailed coverage and background information, you may need to depend more on books. If your argument deals with a specific time period, you may need to examine newspapers, magazines, or books written during that period.
- How many sources should you consult? Expect to look over many more sources than you'll end up using, and be sure to cover all major perspectives on your subject. The best guideline is to make sure you have enough sources to support your claim.
- Do you know your way around the library? If not, ask a librarian for help in locating the following resources in the library: general and specialized encyclopedias; biographical resources; almanacs, yearbooks, and atlases; book and periodical indexes; specialized indexes and abstracts; the circulation computer or library catalog; special collections; audio, video, and art collections; the interlibrary loan office.

Online Sources

Many important resources for argument are now available in databases, either online or on CD-ROM, and many libraries now share the resources of their electronic catalogs through WorldCat. But the Internet has no overall index quite like the *Library of Congress Subject Headings* yet. However, like library catalogs and databases, the Internet and Web offer two ways to search for sources related to your argument: one using subject categories, and one using keywords.

A subject directory organized by categories—such as you might find at <http://dir.yahoo.com>—allows you to choose a broad category like "Entertainment" or "Science" and then click on increasingly narrow categories like "Movies" or "Astronomy" and then "Thrillers" or "The Solar System" until you reach a point where you're given a list of Web sites or the opportunity to do a keyword search.

With the second kind of Internet search option, a search engine, you start right off with a keyword search—filling in a blank, for example, on the opening page of <http://Google.com>. Because the Internet contains vastly more material than even the largest library catalog or database, exploring it with a search engine requires even more care in the choice and combination of keywords. For an argument about the fate of the hero in contemporary films, for example, you might find that *film* and

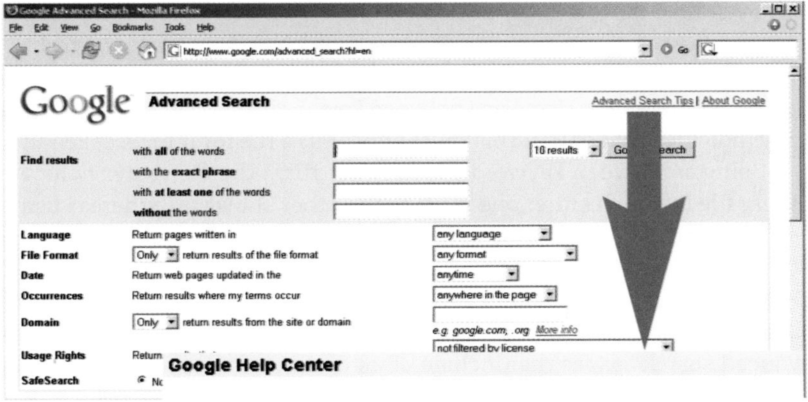

Advanced Search Made Easy

Once you know the basics of Google search, you might want to try Advanced Search, which offers numerous options for making your searches more precise and getting more useful results.

You can reach this page by clicking (no surprise) the "Advanced Search" link on the Google home page.

Here's what the Advanced Search page looks like:

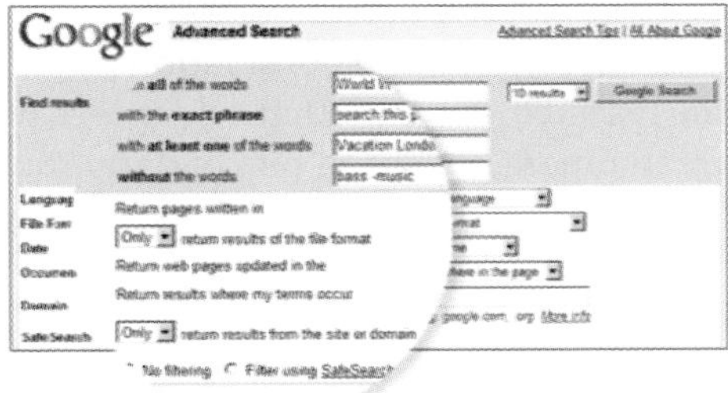

You can do a lot more with Google search than just typing in search terms. With Advanced Search, you can search only for pages:

- that contain ALL the search terms you type in
- that contain the exact phrase you type in
- that contain at least one of the words you type in
- that do NOT contain any of the words you type in
- written in a certain language
- created in a certain file format
- that have been updated within a certain period of time
- that contain numbers within a certain range
- within a certain domain, or website
- that don't contain "adult" material

To refine your online search techniques, use the resources provided by search engines. On Google, clicking on "Advanced Search Tips" takes you to a help center.

hero produce far too many possible matches, or hits. You might further narrow the search by adding a third keyword, say, *American* or *current*.

In doing such searches, you'll need to observe the search logic for a particular database. Using *and* between keywords (*movies and heroes*) usually indicates that both terms must appear in a file for it to be called up.

Using *or* between keywords usually instructs the computer to locate every file in which either one word or the other shows up, whereas using *not* tells the computer to exclude files containing a particular word from the search results (*movies not heroes*).

As you can see, searching has usually become just a matter of typing in a few strategic words. Tools such as Google or Yahoo! incorporate "advanced search" pages that include all of these options in an easy-to-use fill-in-the-blank format, while also allowing you to search for exact phrases or narrow your searches to particular dates, languages, parts of a Web site, domains on the Web (such as .edu, .org, or .gov), and more.

Using Evidence Effectively

You may gather an impressive amount of evidence on your topic—from firsthand interviews, from careful observations, and from intensive library and online research. But until that evidence is woven into the fabric of your own argument, it's just a pile of data. You still have to turn that data into information that will be persuasive to your intended audiences.

Considering Audiences

The ethos you bring to an argument (see Chapter 3) is crucial to your success in connecting with your audience. Of course, you want to present yourself as reliable and credible, but you also need to think carefully about the way your evidence relates to your audience. Is it appropriate to this particular group of readers or listeners? Does it speak to them in ways they'll understand and respond to? Does it acknowledge where they're coming from and speak in terms they'll understand? It's hard to give definite advice for making sure that your evidence fits an audience. But in general, timeliness is important to audiences: the more up-to-date your evidence, the better. In addition, evidence that represents typical rather than extreme circumstances usually is more convincing. For example, in arguing for a campus-wide security escort

Defining Evidence

How do you decide what evidence will best support your claims? The answer depends, in large part, on how you define *evidence*. Differing notions of what counts as evidence can lead to arguments that go nowhere fast. Journalists are often called on to interview those whose view of what constitutes effective evidence differs markedly from their own. For example, when in 1971 Italian journalist Oriana Fallaci interviewed the Ayatollah Khomeini, Iran's supreme leader, she argued in a way that's common in North American and Western European cultures: she presented what she considered to be claims adequately backed up with facts ("Iran denies freedom to people. . . . Many people have been put in prison and even executed, just for speaking out in opposition"). In response, Khomeini relied on very different kinds of evidence: analogies ("Just as a finger with gangrene should be cut off so that it will not destroy the whole body, so should people who corrupt others be pulled out like weeds so they will not infect the whole field") and, above all, the authority of the Qur'an. Partly because of these differing beliefs about what counts as evidence, the interview ended unsuccessfully.

People in Western nations tend to give great weight to factual evidence; but even in those countries, what constitutes evidence can differ radically, as it does, for example, in debates in the United States between proponents of evolutionary theory and supporters of the viewpoint on life's origins termed "intelligent design." In arguing across cultural divides, whether international or otherwise, you need to think carefully about how you're accustomed to using evidence—and to pay attention to what counts as evidence to other people *without simply surrendering your own intellectual principles*. Here are some questions to help you review the types of evidence on which you're building your argument:

- Do you rely on facts? Examples? Firsthand experience?
- Do you include testimony from experts? Which experts are valued most (and why)?
- Do you cite religious or philosophical texts? Proverbs or everyday wisdom?
- Do you use analogies and metaphors as evidence? How much do they count?

Once you've determined what counts as evidence in your own arguments, ask the same questions about the use of evidence by members of other cultures.

service after 10 P.M., a writer who cites actual numbers of students recently threatened or attacked on their way across campus after dark will be in a stronger position than one who cites only one sensational attack that occurred four years ago.

Building a Critical Mass

Throughout this chapter we've stressed the need to discover as much evidence as possible in support of your claim. If you can find only one or two pieces of evidence, only one or two reasons or illustrations to back up your contention, then you may be on weak ground. Although there's no magic quantity, no definite way of saying how much evidence is "enough," you should build toward a critical mass, with a number of pieces of evidence all pulling in the direction of your claim. If your evidence for a claim relies mainly on personal experience or on one major example, you should extend your search for additional sources and good reasons to back up your claim—or modify the claim. Your initial position may have been wrong.

If Everything's an Argument . . .

The authors of this book were trained primarily in the liberal arts. That means that they're more inclined to provide verbal and textual support for the claims they make rather than evidence that's numerical or graphical. Given that this is a textbook on writing, you probably aren't surprised to find many more passages of writing than pie charts, bar graphs, columns of figures, maps, or formulas. Yet how might this book have been different if the authors had backgrounds in, say, business, the natural sciences, the physical sciences, architecture, or some field outside of the traditional humanities (that is, English, philosophy, history, linguistics, foreign languages, and so on)? What if the authors were sports junkies? Do people in different fields instinctively draw upon distinctive kinds of examples or evidence? Explore this topic in a group that includes people with a variety of majors, backgrounds, or interests.

Arranging Evidence

Review your evidence, deciding which pieces support which points in the argument. In general, try to position your strongest pieces of evidence in key places—near the beginning of paragraphs, at the end of the introduction, or where you build toward a powerful conclusion. In addition, try to achieve a balance between, on the one hand, your own argument and your own words, and on the other hand, the sources you use or quote in support of the argument. The sources of evidence are important props in the structure, but they shouldn't overpower the structure (your argument) itself.

RESPOND•

1. What counts as evidence depends in large part on the rhetorical situation. One audience might find personal testimony compelling in a given case, whereas another might require data that only experimental studies can provide.

   Imagine that you want to argue for a national educational campaign promoting the cutting of "pork"—that is, spending projects benefiting a particular state or congressional district that are added to the federal budget mainly to get incumbents reelected. Your campaign will be composed of television ads scheduled to air before and during the Super Bowl—and you want the Democratic and Republican national committees to pay for those ads. Make a list of reasons and evidence to support your claim, aimed simultaneously at political bigwigs *from both parties*. What kind of evidence would be most compelling to that mixed group? How would you rethink your use of evidence if you were writing for the newsletter of a community of retirees or for your student newspaper, urging political activism to cut out-of-control spending by politicians? This isn't an exercise in pulling the wool over anyone's eyes; your goal is simply to anticipate the kind of evidence that different audiences would find persuasive, given the same case.

2. Finding, evaluating, and arranging evidence in an argument is often a *discovery* process: sometimes you're concerned not only with digging up support for an already established claim but also with creating and revising tentative claims. Surveys and interviews can help you figure out what to argue, as well as provide evidence for a claim.

   Interview a classmate with the goal of writing a brief proposal argument about his or her career goals. The claim should be My *classmate should be doing X five years from now.* Limit yourself to ten questions; write them ahead of time, and don't deviate from them. Record the results of the interview (written notes are fine—you don't need a tape recorder).

Then interview another classmate, with the same goal in mind. Ask the same first question, but this time let the answer dictate the rest of the questions. You still get only ten questions.

Which interview gave you more information? Which one helped you learn more about your classmate's goals? Which one better helped you develop claims about his or her future?

3. Imagine that you're trying to decide whether to take a class with a particular professor, but you don't know if he or she is a good teacher. You might already have an opinion, based on some vaguely defined criteria and dormitory gossip, but you're not sure if that evidence is reliable. You decide to observe a class to inform your decision.

   Visit a class in which you aren't currently enrolled, and make notes on your observations following the guidelines in this chapter (p. 472–473). You probably only need a single day's visit to get a sense of the note-taking process, though you would, of course, need much more time to write a thorough evaluation of the professor.

   Write a short evaluation of the professor's teaching abilities on the basis of your observations. Then write an analysis of your evaluation. Is it honest? Fair? What other kinds of evidence might you need if you wanted to make an informed decision about the class and the teacher? What evidence is available to you in terms of local files of teaching evaluations, online teaching evaluation sites, and so on?

17
Fallacies of Argument

"Are you going to agree with what that racist pig is saying?"

"If I don't get an 'A' in this class, I won't get into medical school."

"Ask not what your country can do for you; ask what you can do for your country."

"No blood for oil!"

"All my friends have AOL. I'm the only one who can't get instant messages!"

"9/11 changed everything."

• • •

Certain types of argumentative moves are so controversial they've been traditionally classified as *fallacies*, a term we use in this chapter. But you might find it more interesting to think of them as *flashpoints* or *hotspots* because they instantly raise questions about the ethics of argument—that is, whether a particular strategy of argument is fair, accurate, or principled. Fallacies are arguments supposedly flawed by their very nature or structure; as such, you should avoid them in your own writing and challenge them in arguments you hear or read. That said, it's important to appreciate that one person's fallacy may well be another person's stroke of genius.

Consider, for example, the fallacy termed *ad hominem* argument—"to the man." It describes a strategy of attacking the character of people you disagree with rather than the substance of their arguments: *So you think Eminem is a homophobic racist? Well, you're just a thumb-sucking, white-bread elitist.* Many people have blurted out such insults at some time in their lives and later regretted them. Other *ad hominem* attacks are more consciously produced, such as Edward Klein's book-length attack on Hillary Clinton. Here's just one example of the use of *ad hominem* in that book:

> **Gone was the left-wing Hillary, the gender feminist who sounded to many people like a radical bomb thrower. . . .**
>
> **–Edward Klein, *The Truth about Hillary***

Of course, there are situations when someone's character is central to an argument. If that weren't so, appeals based on character would be pointless. The problem arises in deciding when such arguments are legitimate and when they are flashpoints. You're much more likely to think of attacks on people you admire as *ad hominem* slurs, but personal attacks on those you disagree with as reasonable criticisms. Obviously, debates about character can become quite polarizing. Consider Anita Hill and Clarence Thomas, Eminem and Moby, Barry Bonds and those who accuse him of steroid use. (For more on arguments based on character, see Chapter 3.)

It might be wise to think of fallacies not in terms of errors you can detect and expose in someone else's work, but as strategies that hurt everyone (including the person using them) because they make productive argument more difficult. Fallacies muck up the frank but civil conversations people should be able to have—regardless of their differences.

To help you understand flashpoints of argument, we've classified them according to three rhetorical appeals discussed in earlier chapters: emotional arguments, ethical arguments, and logical arguments (see Chapters 2, 3, and 4).

Flashpoints of Emotional Argument

Emotional arguments can be both powerful and suitable in many circumstances, and most writers use them frequently. However, writers who pull on their readers' heartstrings or raise their blood pressure too often can violate the good faith on which legitimate argument depends. Readers won't trust a writer who can't make a point without frightening someone or provoking tears or stirring up hatred.

Scare Tactics

Corrupters of children, the New Testament warns, would be better off dropped into the sea with millstones around their necks. Would that politicians, advertisers, and public figures who peddle their ideas by scaring people and exaggerating possible dangers well beyond their statistical likelihood face similarly stern warnings. Yet scare tactics are remarkably common in everything ranging from ads for life insurance to threats of audits by the Internal Revenue Service. Such ploys work because it's usually easier to imagine something terrible happening than to appreciate its statistical rarity. That may be why so many people fear flying more than driving. Auto accidents occur much more frequently, but they don't have the same impact on our imaginations as air disasters do.

Scare tactics can also be used to stampede legitimate fears into panic or prejudice. People who genuinely fear losing their jobs can be persuaded, easily enough, to mistrust all immigrants as people who might work for less money; people living on fixed incomes can be convinced that even minor modifications of entitlement programs represent dire threats to their standard of living. Such tactics have the effect of closing off thinking because people who are scared seldom act rationally. Even well-intended fear campaigns—like those directed against the use of illegal drugs or HIV infection—can misfire if their warnings prove too shrill.

Either-Or Choices

A way to simplify arguments and give them power is to reduce the options for action to only two choices. The preferred option or the existing policy might be drawn in the warmest light, whereas the alternative is cast as an ominous shadow. That's the nature of the choices President George W. Bush offered in his August 20, 2005, radio address to the nation:

> **Our troops know that they're fighting in Iraq, Afghanistan, and elsewhere to protect their fellow Americans from a savage enemy. They know that if we do not confront these evil men abroad, we will have to face them one day in our own cities and streets, and they know that the safety and security of every American is at stake in this war, and they know we will prevail.**

Sometimes neither of the alternatives is pleasant: that's the nature of many "ultimatums." For instance, the allies in World War II offered the Axis powers only two choices as the conflict drew to a close: either continued war and destruction, or unconditional surrender. No third option was available.

Either-or arguments can be well-intentioned strategies to get something accomplished. Parents use them all the time, telling children that either they'll eat their broccoli or they won't get dessert. Such arguments become fallacious when they reduce a complicated issue to excessively simple terms or when they're designed to obscure legitimate alternatives.

For instance, to suggest that Social Security must be privatized or the system will go broke may have rhetorical power, but the choice is too simple. The financial problems of Social Security can be fixed in any number of ways, including privatization. But to defend privatization, falsely, as the *only* possible course of action is to risk losing the support of people who know better.

But then *either-or* arguments—like most scare tactics—are often purposefully designed to seduce those who don't know much about a subject. That's another reason the tactic violates principles of civil

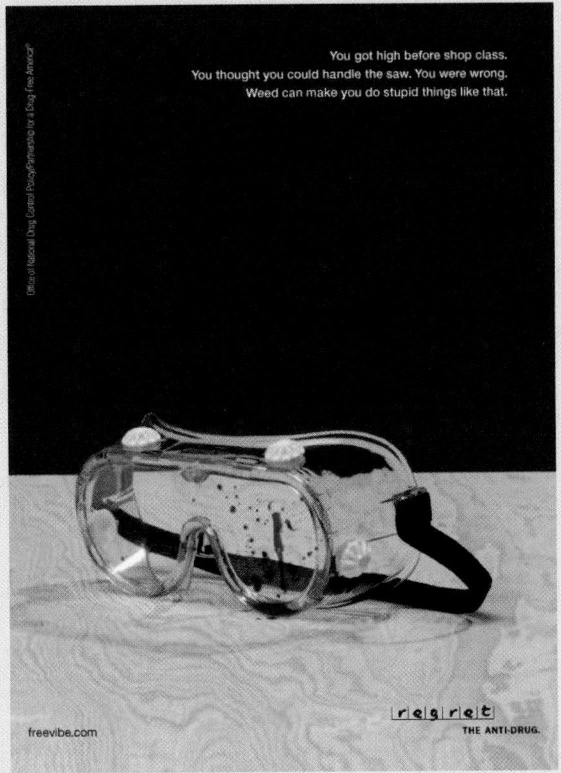

You got high before shop class.
You thought you could handle the saw. You were wrong.
Weed can make you do stupid things like that.
freevibe.com
regret
THE ANTI-DRUG.

Not Just Words

Look at the advertisement above. Is it a scare tactic? A legitimate warning? Something in between? How effective do think this ad would be for college students, or for people you might know who use marijuana or might be tempted to? What effect does the text in the upper right-hand corner have on your answers to these questions? What about the text at the bottom? Do graphic images like this and sponsor labels like "Partnership for a Drug-Free America" make the campaign against marijuana and other illegal drugs more effective—or less so? How does this ad compare with the one about drunk driving on p. 111?

discourse. Argument should enlighten people, making them more knowledgeable and more capable of acting intelligently and independently. Very often, we don't have to choose one side over the other. Here are analysts from the Economic Policy Institute making just that point:

> **The Social Security dilemma is typically framed as a false choice between caring for the nation's elderly at the expense of living standards and fiscal responsibility or reducing our commitment to retirees by cutting back on Social Security and Medicare. The two goals of improving living standards for workers and their families and caring for the elderly do not have to be mutually exclusive. They can be achieved through sensible, equitable economic policies that include productivity-boosting investments, the broad distribution of economic gains, and the fundamental restructuring of the public and private health care systems.**
>
> **–Edith Rasell, Max Sawicky, Dean Baker, "America's Golden Years"**

The parental ultimatum: a classic form of the either-or argument

"They say we can go there for Thanksgiving or they can cut us out of the will. Our choice."

Although the previous discussion focuses on *either-or* arguments as scare tactics to justify proposed or current actions, they can also involve simple lapses of logic, less emotionally charged issues, or matters of fact, definition, evaluation, or causal analysis. For example, in a *New York Times* column about a sociologist's book describing how differently upper-middle-class parents and poor and working-class parents bring up their children, David Brooks concludes that "the core issue is that today's rich don't exploit the poor; they just outcompete them." But these two possibilities aren't mutually exclusive: the rich could be outcompeting the poor *and* exploiting them. (And, in fact, the column mentions the sociologist's finding that the poorer "[c]hildren, like their parents, were easily intimidated and pushed around by verbally dexterous teachers and doctors.") Similarly, a tomato could be considered both a vegetable and a fruit; a novel could be neither a literary masterpiece nor a worthless potboiler but something in between; and current global warming could be the result of both human activity and natural climate cycles.

Slippery Slope

The slippery slope flashpoint is well named, describing an argument that casts today's tiny misstep as tomorrow's slide into disaster. Of course, not all arguments aimed at preventing dire consequences are slippery slope fallacies; for example, the parent who corrects a child for misbehavior now is acting sensibly to prevent more serious problems as the child grows older. A slippery slope argument becomes a flashpoint when a writer exaggerates the likely consequences of an action, usually to frighten readers. As such, slippery slope arguments are also scare tactics. For instance, defenders of free speech often regard even mild attempts to regulate behavior as leading inexorably to Big Brother—charging, for example, that if school officials can require a student to cut his ponytail, they'll eventually be allowed to impose uniforms and crew cuts. Similarly, opponents of gun control warn that any legislation regulating firearms is just a first step toward the government knocking down citizens' doors and seizing weapons.

In recent years, the issue of same-sex marriage has brought out a number of slippery slope arguments:

> **Anyone else bored to tears with the "slippery slope" arguments against gay marriage? Since few opponents of homosexual unions are brave enough to admit that gay weddings just freak them out, they hide behind the claim that it's an inexorable slide from legalizing gay**

> **marriage to having sex with penguins outside JC Penney's. The problem is it's virtually impossible to debate against a slippery slope.**
>
> **–Dahlia Lithwick, "Slippery Slop"**

Of course, ideas and actions do have consequences, but they aren't always as dire as writers fond of slippery slope tactics would have you believe.

Sentimental Appeals

Sentimental appeals are arguments that use tender emotions excessively to distract readers from facts. Quite often, such appeals are highly personal and individual—focusing attention on heart-warming or heart-wrenching situations that make readers feel guilty if they challenge an idea, policy, or proposal. Emotions become an impediment to civil discourse when they keep people from thinking clearly.

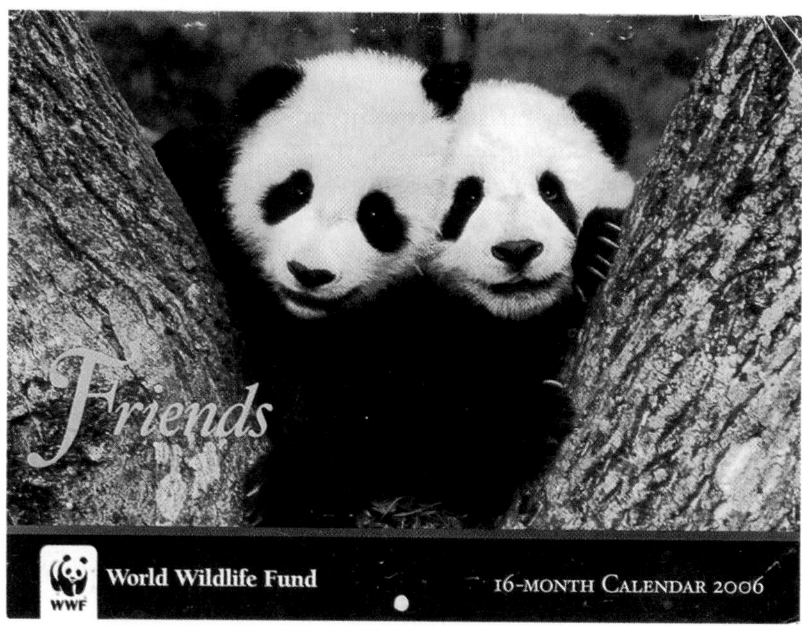

This calendar is designed to elicit sympathy for the giant pandas on its cover and inspire donations for the wildlife organization that protects them. But sentimental images of threatened species are sometimes attached to much less worthy sales pitches—for soda or camping gear, for example.

Yet sentimental appeals are a major vehicle of television news, where it's customary to convey ideas through personal tales that tug at viewers' heartstrings. For example, a camera might document the day-to-day life of a single mother on welfare whose on-screen generosity, kindness, and tears come to represent the spirit of an entire welfare clientele under attack by callous legislators; or the welfare recipient might be shown driving a new pickup and illegally trading food stamps for money while a lower-middle-class family struggles to meet its grocery budget. In either case, the conclusion the reporter wants you to reach is supported by powerful images that evoke emotions in support of that conclusion. But though the individual stories presented may be genuinely moving, they seldom give a complete picture of a complex social or economic issue.

In its "Campaign for America," the Ad Council included a photograph with its short message about religious tolerances. How might a reader's emotion be more stirred by the photograph of three religious leaders walking together than by reading the text of the message alone?

LINK TO P. 901

Bandwagon Appeals

Bandwagon appeals are arguments that urge people to follow the same path everyone else is taking. Curiously, many American parents seem innately endowed with the ability to refute bandwagon appeals. When their kids whine, *Everyone else is going camping overnight without chaperones*, the parents reply instinctively, *And if everyone else jumps off a cliff (or a railroad bridge, or the Empire State Building), you will too?* The children stomp and groan—and then try a different line of argument.

Unfortunately, not all bandwagon approaches are so transparent. Though Americans like to imagine themselves as rugged individualists, they're easily seduced by ideas endorsed by the mass media and popular culture. Such trends are often little more than harmless fashion statements. At other times, however, Americans are encouraged to become obsessed by issues that politicians or the media select for their attention—such as the seemingly endless coverage of the controversy over removing life support systems from Terri Schiavo in 2005. In recent decades, bandwagon issues have included the war on drugs, the nuclear freeze movement, health care reform, AIDS prevention, gun control, drunk driving, tax reform, welfare reform, teen smoking, campaign finance reform, illegal immigration, Social Security reform, and the defense of traditional heterosexual marriage.

In the atmosphere of obsession, there's a feeling that everyone must be concerned by this issue-of-the-day, and something—*anything*—must be done! More often than not, enough people jump on the bandwagon to achieve a measure of change. And when changes occur because people have become sufficiently informed to exercise good judgment, then one can speak of "achieving consensus," a rational goal for civil argument.

But sometimes bandwagons run out of control—as they did in the 1950s when some careers were destroyed by "witch hunts" for suspected communists during the McCarthy era, and in the late 1980s when concerns over child abuse sometimes mushroomed into indiscriminate prosecutions of parents and child care workers. In a democratic society, the bandwagon appeal is among the most potentially serious and permanently damaging flashpoints of argument.

Flashpoints of Ethical Argument

Not surprisingly, readers give their closest attention to authors whom they respect or trust. So, writers usually want to present themselves as honest, well informed, likable, or sympathetic in some way. But *trust me*

When support for a bandwagon cause is just a fashion statement

"Grab some lederhosen, Sutfin. We're about to climb aboard the globalization bandwagon."

is a scary warrant. Not all the devices writers use to gain the attention and confidence of readers are admirable. (For more on appeals based on character, see Chapter 3.)

Appeals to False Authority

One of the effective strategies a writer can use to support an idea is to draw on the authority of widely respected people, institutions, and texts. In fact, many academic research papers are essentially exercises in finding and reflecting on the work of reputable authorities. Writers usually introduce these authorities into their arguments through direct quotations, citations (such as footnotes), or allusions. (For more on assessing the reliability of sources, see Chapter 19.) False authority occurs chiefly when writers offer themselves, or other authorities they cite, as sufficient warrant for believing a claim:

Claim **X is true because I say so.**
Warrant **What I say must be true.**

Claim **X is true because Y says so.**
Warrant **What Y says must be true.**

Rarely will you see authority asserted quite so baldly as in these formulas, because few readers would accept a claim stated in either of these ways. Nonetheless, claims of authority drive many persuasive campaigns. American pundits and politicians are fond of citing the U.S. Constitution or Bill of Rights as ultimate authorities, a reasonable practice when the documents are interpreted respectfully. However, as often as not, the constitutional rights claimed aren't in the texts themselves or don't mean what the speakers think they do. And most constitutional matters are quite debatable—as centuries of court records could prove.

Likewise, religious believers often base arguments on books or traditions that wield great authority within a particular religious community. However, the power of these texts or ways of thinking is usually somewhat limited outside, or even inside, that group and, hence, less capable of persuading others solely on the grounds of their authority alone—though arguments of faith often have power on other grounds.

Institutions can be cited as authorities too. Certainly, serious attention should be paid to claims supported by authorities one respects or recognizes—the Centers for Disease Control, the National Science Foundation, the *New York Times*, the *Wall Street Journal*, and so on. But one ought not to accept information or opinions simply because they have

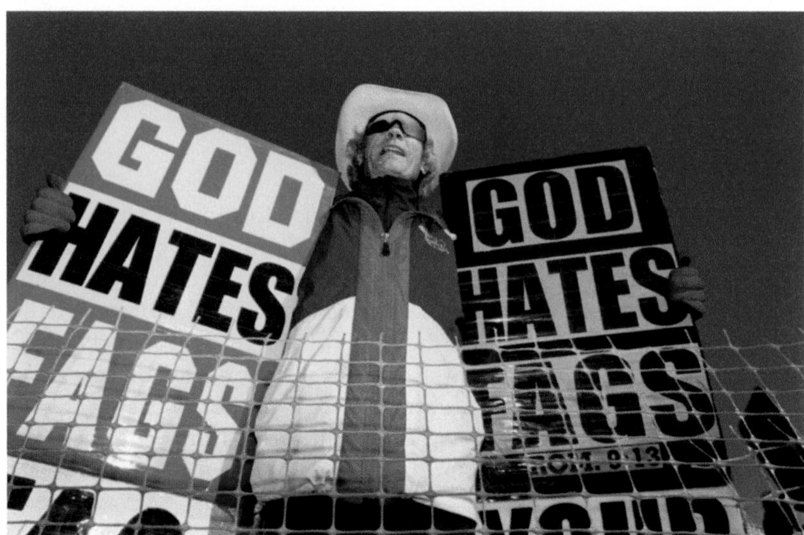

An argument based on the Bible has limited power among nonbelievers. Nor will all believers find such an argument convincing, since there are often many interpretations of a single biblical passage.

the imprimatur of such offices and agencies. To quote a Russian proverb made famous by Ronald Reagan, "Trust, but verify."

The Chicago Women's Club "Pledge for Children" is an example of dogmatism. It's presented as if it is the clear and obvious reason for respecting one's language and one's country.

LINK TO P. 795

Dogmatism

A writer who attempts to persuade by asserting or assuming that a particular position is the only one conceivably acceptable within a community is trying to enforce dogmatism. Indeed, dogmatism is a flashpoint of character because the tactic undermines the trust that must exist between those who make arguments and those to whom they make them. In effect, people who speak or write dogmatically imply that there are no arguments to be made: the truth is self-evident to those who know better. You can usually be sure you're listening to a dogmatic opinion when someone begins a sentence with *No rational person would disagree that . . .* or *It's clear to anyone who has thought about it that . . .*

Of course, there are some arguments beyond the pale of civil discourse—positions and claims so outrageous or absurd that they're unworthy of serious attention. For example, attacks on the historical reality of the Holocaust fall into this category. But relatively few subjects in a free society ought to be off the table from the start—certainly, none that can be defended with facts, testimony, and good reasons. In general, therefore, when someone suggests that merely raising an issue for debate is somehow "unacceptable" or "inappropriate" or "outrageous"—whether on the grounds that it's racist, sexist, unpatriotic, blasphemous, or insensitive or offensive in some other way—you should be suspicious.

Moral Equivalence

A fallacy of argument perhaps more common today than in earlier decades is moral equivalence—that is, suggesting that serious wrongdoings don't differ in kind from minor offenses. A warning sign that this fallacy may be coming into play is the retort of the politician or bureaucrat accused of wrongdoing: *But everyone else does it too!* Richard Nixon insisted that the crimes that led to his resignation were no worse than the actions of previous presidents; Bill Clinton made similar responses to charges about the fund-raising practices of his administration. Regardless of the validity of these particular defenses, there's a point at which such comparisons become highly questionable if not absurd.

For example, political blogger Andrew Sullivan charged that Daniel P. Moloney reached such a point when Moloney suggested in an article in the conservative magazine *National Review* that what he considers inadequate attention to sin by "Western liberal Christians" makes contemporary Western society little better than Nazi Germany:

> **In this regard, the consumerism and relativism of the West can be just as dangerous as the totalitarianism of the East: It's just as easy to forget about God while dancing to an iPod as while marching in a Hitler Youth rally. There's a difference, to be sure, but hardly anyone would contest the observation that in elite Western society, as in totalitarian Germany, the moral vocabulary has been purged of the idea of sin. And if there's no sense of sin, then there's no need for a Redeemer, or for the Church.**
>
> **– Daniel P. Moloney, "Sin's the Thing"**

As this example shows, moral equivalence can work both ways, with relatively innocuous activities or situations raised to the level of major crimes or catastrophes. Some would say that the national campaign against smoking falls into this category—a common and legally sanctioned

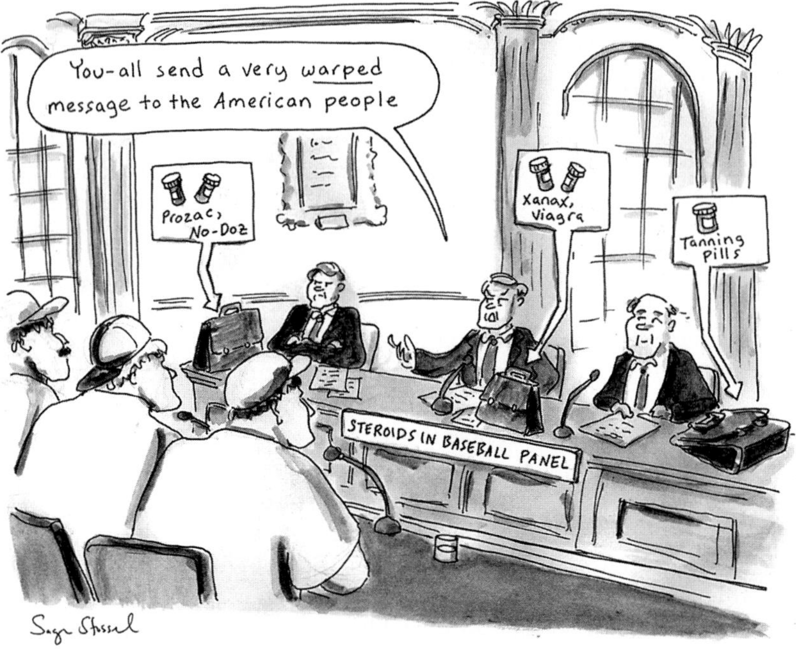

In "American as Apple Pie," cartoonist Sage Stossel equates the common and widely accepted use of prescription drugs with the use of steroids among baseball players.

behavior now given the social stigma of serious drug abuse. And if smoking is almost criminal, shouldn't one be equally concerned with people who use and abuse chocolate—a sweet and fatty food responsible for a host of health problems? You can see how easy it is to make an equivalence argument. Yet suggesting that all behaviors of a particular kind—in this case, abuses of substances—are equally wrong (whether they involve cigarettes, alcohol, drugs, or fatty foods) blurs the distinctions people need to make in weighing claims.

Ad Hominem Arguments

Ad hominem (from the Latin for "to the man") arguments are attacks directed at the character of a person rather than at the claims he or she makes. The theory is simple: Destroy the credibility of your opponents, and either you destroy their ability to present reasonable appeals or you distract from the successful arguments they may be offering. Here, for example, is Christopher Hitchens questioning whether former secretary of state Henry Kissinger should be appointed to head an important government commission in 2002:

> **But can Congress and the media be expected to swallow the appointment of a proven coverup artist, a discredited historian, a busted liar, and a man who is wanted in many jurisdictions for the vilest of offenses?**
>
> **–Christopher Hitchens, "The Case against Henry Kissinger"**

Not much doubt where Hitchens stands. Critics of Rush Limbaugh's conservative politics rarely fail to note his weight (even after he had lost most of it); critics of Michael Brown, former director of the Federal Emergency Management Agency, just as reliably note his earlier job as commissioner of the Arabian Horse Association.

In such cases, *ad hominem* tactics turn arguments into two-sided affairs with good guys and bad guys, and that's unfortunate, since character often does matter in argument. People expect the proponent of peace to be civil, the advocate of ecology to respect the environment, the champion of justice to be fair even in private dealings. But it's fallacious to attack an idea by uncovering the foibles of its advocates or attacking their motives, backgrounds, or unchangeable traits.

Flashpoints of Logical Argument

You'll encounter a flashpoint in any argument when the claims, warrants, and/or evidence in it are invalid, insufficient, or disconnected. In the abstract, such problems seem easy enough to spot; in practice, they can be camouflaged by a skillful use of words or images. Indeed, logical fallacies pose a challenge to civil argument because they often seem quite reasonable and natural, especially when they appeal to people's self-interests. Whole industries (such as phone-in psychic networks) depend on one or more of the logical fallacies for their existence; political campaigns, too, rely on them to prop up that current staple of democratic interchange—the fifteen-second TV spot.

Hasty Generalization

Among logical fallacies, only faulty causality might be able to challenge hasty generalization for the crown of most prevalent. A hasty generalization is an inference drawn from insufficient evidence: *Because my*

Honda broke down, all Hondas must be junk. It also forms the basis for most stereotypes about people or institutions: because a few people in a large group are observed to act in a certain way, one infers that all members of that group will behave similarly. The resulting conclusions are usually sweeping claims of little merit: *Women are bad drivers; men are boors; Scots are stingy; Italians are romantic; English teachers are nit-picking; scientists are nerds*. You could, no doubt, expand this roster of stereotypes by the hundreds.

To draw valid inferences, you must always have sufficient evidence: a random sample of a population, a selection large enough to represent fully the subjects of your study, an objective methodology for sampling the population or evidence, and so on (see Chapter 16). And you must qualify your claims appropriately. After all, people do need generalizations to help make reasonable decisions in life; such claims can be offered legitimately if placed in context and tagged with appropriate qualifiers: *some, a few, many, most, occasionally, rarely, possibly, in some cases, under certain circumstances, in my experience*.

You should be especially alert to the fallacy of hasty generalization when you read reports and studies of any kind, especially case studies based on carefully selected populations. Be alert for the fallacy, too, in the interpretation of poll numbers. Everything from the number of people selected to the time the poll was taken to the exact wording of the questions may affect its outcome.

Faulty Causality

In Latin, the fallacy of faulty causality is described by the expression *post hoc, ergo propter hoc,* which translates word-for-word as "after this, therefore because of this." Odd as the translation may sound, it accurately describes what faulty causality is—the fallacious assumption that because

If Everything's an Argument. . .

Consider the title of this textbook, *Everything's an Argument*. What fallacies could this title carry with it? Take some time to look at the introduction to one of the fallacies in this chapter. Can you detect any fallacious reasoning at work?

one event or action follows another, the first necessarily causes the second. Consider a lawsuit commented on in the *Wall Street Journal* in which a writer sued Coors (unsuccessfully), claiming that drinking copious amounts of the company's beer had kept him from writing a novel.

Some actions, of course, do produce reactions. Step on the brake pedal in your car, and you move hydraulic fluid that pushes calipers against disks to create friction that stops the vehicle. Or, if you happen to be chair of the Federal Reserve Board, you raise interest rates to increase the cost of borrowing to slow the growth of the economy in order to curb inflation—you hope. Causal relationships of this kind are reasonably convincing because one can provide evidence of relationships between the events sufficient to convince most people that an initial action did, indeed, cause subsequent actions.

In other cases, however, a supposed connection between cause and effect turns out to be completely wrong. For example, doctors now believe that when an elderly person falls and is found to have a broken leg or hip, the break usually caused the fall rather than the other way around. And as the Federal Reserve example suggests, causality can be especially difficult to control or determine when economic, political, or social relationships are involved.

Did drinking too much Coors cause a writer's literary paralysis? A court said no.

Jessica Gavora and Ruth Conniff each present arguments about Title IX. While both authors discuss the decline in men's varsity sports and the rising success in women's varsity sports, they each point toward different causes. Who makes the stronger argument?

LINK TO PP. 681 AND 690

That's why suspiciously simple or politically convenient causal claims should always be subject to scrutiny. In the 1990s, for example, crime rates in New York City fell sharply. Then-mayor Rudolph Giuliani and his supporters claimed that the credit was largely due to the Giuliani administration's innovative policing strategies, such as a crack-down on petty crimes to prevent the commission of more serious offenses. But some of these policies had actually begun under Giuliani's predecessor; moreover, during the same period crime fell just as much in many other American cities—including ones whose police operated very differently from New York's. Giuliani's strategies may well have contributed to the drop, but analysts can—and do—disagree strongly about how much.

Begging the Question

There's probably not a teacher in the country who hasn't heard the following argument: *You can't give me a "C" in this course; I'm an "A" student.* For a member of Congress accused of taking bribes, a press secretary makes a version of the same argument: *Congressman X can't be guilty of accepting bribes; he's an honest person.* In both cases, the problem with the claim is that it's made on grounds that cannot be accepted as true because those grounds are in doubt. How can the student claim to be an "A" student when she just earned a "C"? How can the accused bribe-taker defend himself on the grounds of honesty when that honesty is now suspect? Setting such arguments in Toulmin terms helps to expose the fallacy:

Claim + Reason	**You can't give me a "C" in this course because I'm an "A" student.**
Warrant	**An "A" student is someone who can't receive "C"s.**
Claim + Reason	**Congressman X can't be guilty of accepting bribes because he's an honest person.**
Warrant	**An honest person cannot be guilty of accepting bribes.**

With the warrants stated, you can see why begging the question—that is, assuming as true the very claim that's disputed—is a form of circular argument, divorced from reality. If you assume that an "A" student can't receive "C"s, then the first argument stands. But no one is an "A" student *by definition;* that standing has to be earned by performance in individual courses. Likewise, even though someone with a record of honesty is unlikely to accept bribes, a claim of honesty isn't an adequate defense against specific charges. An honest person won't accept bribes, but merely claiming someone is honest doesn't make him so. (For more on Toulmin argument, see Chapter 6.)

Equivocation

Both the finest definition and the most famous literary examples of equivocation come from Shakespeare's tragedy *Macbeth*. In the drama three witches, representing the fates, make prophecies that favor the ambitious Macbeth but that prove disastrous when understood more fully. He's told, for example, that he has nothing to fear from his enemies "till Birnam wood / Do come to Dunsinane" (*Mac.* 5.5.44–45); although it seems impossible that a forest could move, these woods do indeed move when enemy soldiers cut down branches from the forest of Birnam for camouflage and march on Macbeth's fortress. Catching on to the game, Macbeth starts "[t]o doubt the equivocation of the fiend / That *lies like truth*" (5.5.43–44, emphasis added). An equivocation, then, is an argument that gives a lie an honest appearance; it's a half-truth.

Equivocations are usually juvenile tricks of language. Consider the plagiarist who copies a paper word-for-word from a source and then declares—honestly, she thinks—that "I wrote the entire paper myself," meaning that she physically copied the piece on her own. But the plagiarist is using "wrote" equivocally—that is, in a limited sense, knowing that most people would understand "writing" as something more than the mere copying of words. Many public figures are fond of parsing their words carefully so that no certain meaning emerges. In the 1990s, Bill Clinton's "I never had sex with that woman" claim became notorious; in the first decade of the twenty-first century, critics of the Bush administration said its many attempts to deny that "torture" was being used on U.S. prisoners abroad amounted to a long series of equivocations.

Non Sequitur

A *non sequitur* is an argument in which claims, reasons, or warrants fail to connect logically; one point doesn't follow from another. As with other fallacies, children are notably adept at framing *non sequiturs*. Consider this familiar form: *You don't love me or you'd buy me that bicycle!*

Baseball great Barry Bonds admitted to a grand jury that he had taken undetectable steroids during the 2003 season, but claimed he didn't know the substances—a cream and a clear liquid—were steroids. Some observers think that's an equivocation—a dishonest play on the word "know." As Olympic skier Bode Miller opined in a *Rolling Stone* profile, referring to Bonds and other athletes, "Yeah, they're not knowingly taking any substance, they don't . . . ask what it is, but they are sure . . . taking it."

It might be more evident to harassed parents that no connection exists between love and Huffys if they were to consider the implied warrant:

Claim	**You must not love me . . .**
Reason	**. . . because you haven't bought me that bicycle.**
Warrant	**Buying bicycles for children is essential to loving them.**

A five-year-old might endorse that warrant, but no responsible adult would because love doesn't depend on buying things, at least not a particular bicycle. Activities more logically related to love might include feeding and clothing children, taking care of them when they're sick, providing shelter and education, and so on.

In effect, *non sequiturs* occur when writers omit a step in an otherwise logical chain of reasoning, assuming that readers agree with what may be a highly contestable claim. For example, it's a *non sequitur* simply to argue that the comparatively poor performance of American students on international mathematics examinations means the country should spend more money on math education. Such a conclusion might be justified if a correlation were known or found to exist between mathematical ability and money spent on education. But the students' performance might be poor for reasons other than education funding, so a writer should first establish the nature of the problem before offering a solution.

The Straw Man

Those who resort to the "straw man" fallacy attack an argument that isn't really there, one that's much weaker or more extreme than the one the opponent is actually making. By "setting up a straw man" in this way, the speaker or writer has an argument that's easy to knock down and proceeds to do so, then claiming victory over the opponent—whose real argument was quite different.

A lot of "straw man" arguments have been advanced in the recent debate over evolution and intelligent design. Those arguing against intelligent design may say that *intelligent design advocates claim that life was created by some white-haired figure in the sky,* while those arguing against evolution sometimes say that *evolutionists claim that evolution is all random chance, so the human eye just came into existence randomly.* In both instances, these speakers are choosing to refute arguments that go beyond the claims their opponents have actually made. At least in their public political or legal statements, supporters of intelligent design don't make any claims about who or what the "intelligent designer" is. And supporters of evolution contend that the process is random only in the sense that it's driven by random mutations in genes; organisms "evolve" only if such mutations make them better adapted to their environment (such as by increasing their ability to detect light) and thus more likely to reproduce. Both sides are attacking weak arguments their opponents aren't actually making; as a result, both sides are ignoring the tougher issues.

Faulty Analogy

Comparisons give ideas greater presence or help clarify concepts. Consider the comparisons in this comment on Britney Spears's album *In the Zone:*

[R]egardless of how hard she tries, Britney's not Madonna. To be fair, Madonna wasn't Madonna at first either, but emulating someone else—even if they're as successful as Madonna—usually doesn't work in the end.

–Erik J. Barzeski

Consider Barbara Munson's manifesto against the use of Indian mascots. She structures her argument as a series of responses to ignorant and sometimes fallacious statements. Do you recognize any of the flashpoints described in this chapter?

LINK TO P. 702

When comparisons are extended, they become analogies—ways of understanding unfamiliar ideas by comparing them with something that's already known. It's true that people understand the world around them largely through comparisons, metaphors, and analogies. But useful as such comparisons are, they may prove quite false either on their own or when pushed too far or taken too seriously. At this point they become faulty analogies, inaccurate or inconsequential comparisons between objects or concepts. The *Wikipedia* cites the following example of such a questionable analogy:

The universe is like an intricate watch.

A watch must have been designed by a watchmaker.

Therefore, the universe must have been designed by some kind of creator.

RESPOND.

1. Following is a list of political slogans or phrases that may be examples of logical fallacies. Discuss each item to determine what you may know about the slogan; then decide which, if any, fallacy might be used to describe it.

   "Leave no child behind." (George Bush policy and slogan)

   "It's the economy, stupid." (sign on the wall at Bill Clinton's campaign headquarters)

   "Nixon's the one." (campaign slogan)

   "Remember the Alamo."

   "Make love, not war." (antiwar slogan during the Vietnam War)

   "A chicken in every pot."

   "No taxation without representation."

   "There's no free lunch."

   "Loose lips sink ships."

   "Guns don't kill, people do." (NRA slogan)

   "If you can't stand the heat, get out of the kitchen."

2. We don't want you to argue fallaciously, but it's fun and good practice to frame argumentative fallacies in your own language. Pick an argumentative topic—maybe even one that you've used for a paper in this class—and write a few paragraphs making nothing but fallacious arguments in each sentence. Try to include all the fallacies of emotional, ethical, and logical argument that are discussed in this chapter.
3. Choose a paper you've written for this or another class, and analyze it carefully for signs of fallacious reasoning. Once you've tried analyzing your own prose, find an editorial, a syndicated column, and a political speech and look for the fallacies in them. Which fallacies are most common in the four arguments? How do you account for their prevalence? Which are the least common? How do you account for their absence? What seems to be the role of audience in determining what's a fallacy and what isn't?
4. Arguments on the Web are no more likely to contain fallacies than are arguments in any other text, but the fallacies can take on different forms. The hypertextual nature of Web arguments and the ease of including visuals along with text make certain fallacies more likely to occur there. Find a Web site sponsored by an organization (the Future of Music Coalition, perhaps), business (Coca-Cola, perhaps), or other group (the Democratic or Republican National Committee, perhaps), and analyze the site for fallacious reasoning. Among other considerations, look at the relationship between text and graphics, and between individual pages and the pages that surround or are linked to them. How does the technique of separating information into discrete pages affect the argument? Then send an email message to the site's creators, explaining what you found and proposing ways the arguments in the site could be improved.
5. Political blogs such as <wonkette.com>, <andrewsullivan.com>, <DailyKos>, and <InstaPundit.com> typically provide quick responses to daily events and detailed critiques of material in other media sites, including national newspapers. Study one active political blog for a few days to determine whether and how the blogger critiques the material he or she links to. Does the blogger point to flashpoints and fallacies in arguments? If so, does he or she explain them or just assume readers understand them or will figure them out? Summarize your findings in an oral report to your class.

18
Intellectual Property, Academic Integrity, and Avoiding Plagiarism

On a college campus, a student receives a warning: she has been detected using peer-to-peer music file-sharing software. Has she been practicing fair use, or is she guilty of copyright infringement?

A student writing an essay about Title IX's effect on college athletic programs finds some powerful supporting evidence for his argument on a Web site. Can he use this information without gaining permission?

Day care centers around the country receive letters arguing that they'll be liable to lawsuit if they use

Thanks to protests from GM, this car will not be called a "Chery" in the United States.

representations of Disney characters without explicit permission or show Disney films "outside the home."

The importer of a line of low-cost Chinese automobiles agrees not to market the cars under the brand name "Chery" after General Motors threatens to sue, claiming the name looks and sounds too much like "Chevy."

Musicians argue against other musicians, saying that the popular use of "sampling" in songs amounts to a form of musical plagiarism.

In cyberspace, the development of digital "watermarks" and other forms of tracking systems have made it possible to trace not only documents printed out but those read online as well; as a result, some lawyers argue that public access to information is being limited in ways that are unconstitutional.

• • •

In agricultural and industrial eras, products that could provide a livelihood were likely to be concrete things: crops, tools, machines. But in an age of information such as the current one, ideas, which we consider as intellectual property, are arguably society's most important products.

Hence the growing importance of—and growing controversies surrounding—what counts as "property" in an information age.

Perhaps the framers of the Constitution foresaw such a shift in the bases of the nation's economy. At any rate, they expressed in the Constitution a delicate balance between the public's need for information and the incentives necessary to encourage people to produce work —both material and intellectual. Thus the Constitution empowers Congress "[t]o promote the progress of Science and useful Arts, by securing for limited Times to Authors and Inventors the exclusive Right to their respective Writings and Discoveries" (Article 1, Section 8, Clause 8). This passage allows for limited protection (copyright) of the expression of ideas ("Writings and Discoveries"), and through the years that time limit has been extended to up to lifetime plus seventy years.

Why is this historical information important to student writers? First, because writers need to know that ideas themselves cannot be copyrighted—only the expression of those ideas. Second, this information explains why some works fall out of copyright and are available for students to use without paying a fee (as you must for copyright-protected material in a coursepack, for instance). Third, this information is crucial

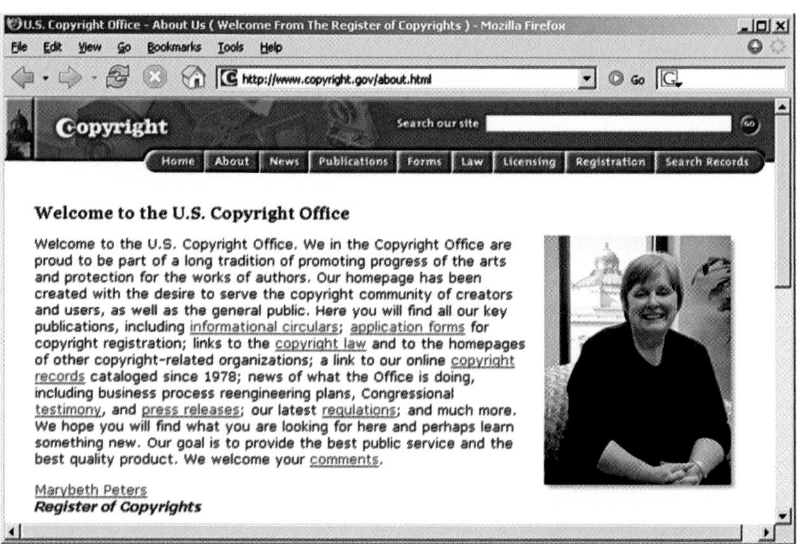

As a unit within the Library of Congress, the U.S. Copyright Office works to uphold copyright laws.

to the current debates over who owns online materials—materials that may never take any form of concrete expression. The debate will certainly be raging during and after the publication of this book—and the way in which it's resolved will have many direct effects on students and teachers. For up-to-date information about copyright law, see the U.S. Copyright Office site at <http://copyright.gov>.

Crediting Sources in Arguments

Acknowledging your sources and giving full credit is especially important in argumentative writing because doing so helps establish your ethos as a writer. In the first place, saying "thank you" to those who've helped you suggests gratitude and openness, qualities that audiences generally respond to well. Second, acknowledging your sources demonstrates that you've "done your homework," that you know the conversation surrounding your topic and understand what others have written about it, and that you want to help readers find other contributions to the conversation and perhaps join it themselves. Finally, acknowledging sources reminds you to think critically about your own stance in an argument and about how well you've used your sources. Are they timely and reliable? Have you used them in a biased or overly selective way? Have you used them accurately, double-checking all quotations and paraphrases? Thinking through these questions will improve your overall argument.

Citing Sources and Recognizing Plagiarism

In many ways, "nothing new under the sun" is more than just a cliché. Most of what you think or write or say draws on what you've previously heard or read or experienced. And trying to recall every influence or source of information you've drawn on, even on just one day, would take so long that you would have little time left to say anything. Luckily, you'll seldom, if ever, be called on to list every single influence on your life. But you do have responsibilities in academic situations to acknowledge the intellectual property you've used to create your own argumentative writing. If you don't, you may be accused of plagiarism—claiming for your own the words or intellectual work of others.

Sarah Karnasiewicz uses quotations from various sources to support her argument about the dearth of men in university-level study. Note how she incorporates sources into prose rather than use parenthetical documentation or footnoting.

LINK TO P. 923

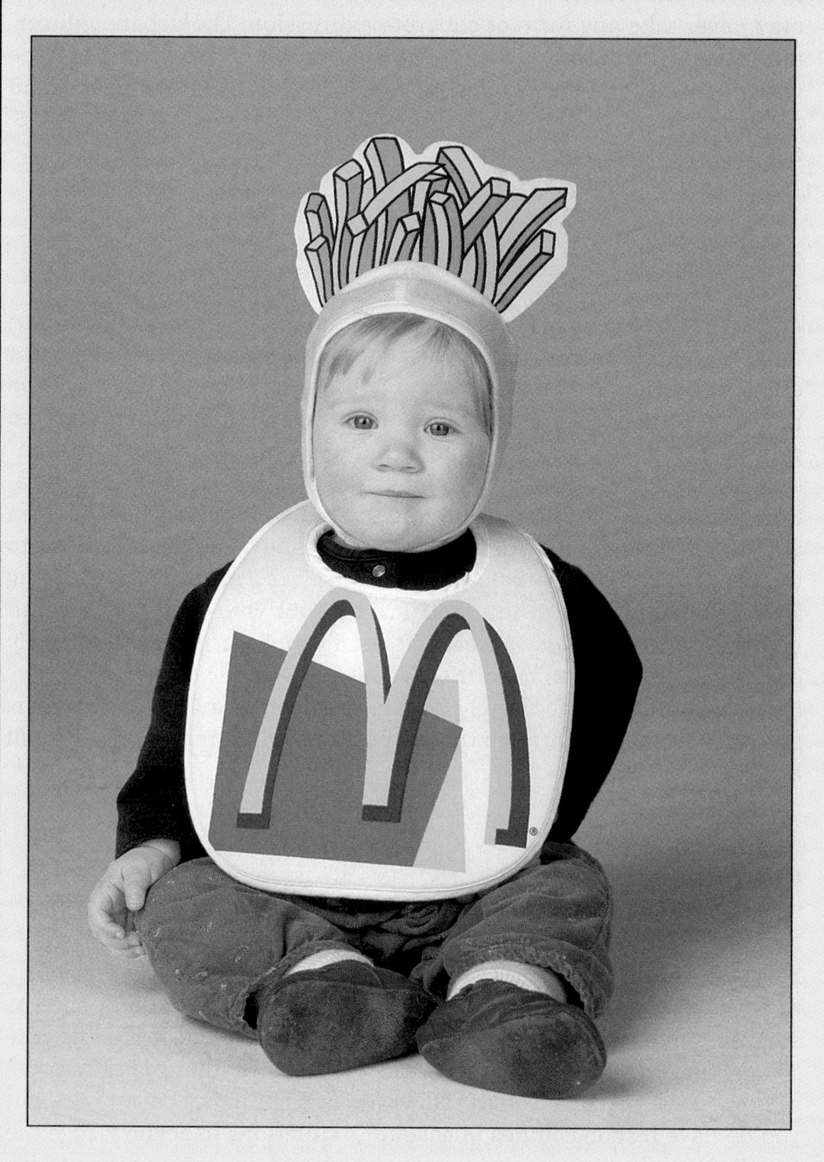

Not Just Words

Like words, images and designs can also be claimed as intellectual property. As we explain in this chapter, you can download a photograph you find on the Web and use it, with appropriate documentation, in an academic paper. But you'd probably need permission from the copyright holder to use it online, even for an academic Web project.

Logos and other visual designs are similarly protected. The T-shirt or ball cap you buy bearing your school's symbol and colors likely has a royalty cost built in, with the money going back to the institution. For commercial and artistic reasons, both institutions and corporations fiercely protect their designs, logos, symbols, and signs.

How then can *The Onion, Saturday Night Live,* or <Adbusters.org> take familiar designs and logos and use them in their publications, shows, or Web sites? For instance, it's unlikely that McDonalds approved a spoof showing a chubby youngster decked out in the company's trademarked golden arches. Yet there it is on <Adbusters.org>, along with dozens of other like-minded parodies.

The answer is in the word *parody:* the Supreme Court has decided that parody falls within fair use provisions of copyright law and that satire is protected by the First Amendment's protection of free speech, at least when such a lampoon targets public figures. You can explore these decisions easily on the Web (by googling "Parody" and "Supreme Court").

Working in a small group, try your hand at creating a parody of some familiar visual item or advertising campaign, perhaps beginning with an image from the Web. Be sure to take advantage of any skills people in your group may have with software such as Photoshop—which will enable you to change or manipulate images. Or use paper: cutting and pasting still works. Design a parody that makes a thoughtful point.

DOONESBURY **BY GARRY TRUDEAU**

A *Doonesbury* cartoon on intellectual property

Avoiding plagiarism is very important, for in Western culture the use of someone else's language and ideas without acknowledgment is an act of dishonesty that can bring devastating results—especially, though not only, in school. Moreover, as we noted above, taking care to cite your sources works to your advantage in an academic setting: it builds your credibility, showing that you've done your homework as a researcher.

Inaccurate or Incomplete Citation of Sources

If you use a paraphrase that's too close to the original wording or sentence structure (even if you cite the source), if you leave out the parenthetical reference for a quotation (even if you include the quotation marks themselves), or if you don't indicate clearly the source of an idea you obviously didn't come up with on your own, you may be accused of plagiarism—even if that wasn't your intent. This kind of inaccurate or incomplete citation of sources often results either from carelessness or from not learning how to use citations accurately and fully.

Here, for example, is the first paragraph from an essay by Russell Platt published in *The Nation* and read in its online version at <http://thenation.com/doc/20051003/platt>:

> **Classical music in America, we are frequently told, is in its death throes: its orchestras bled dry by expensive guest soloists and greedy musicians' unions, its media presence shrinking, its prestige diminished, its educational role ignored, its big record labels dying out or merging into faceless corporate entities. We seem to have too many well-trained musicians in need of work, too many good composers going without commissions, too many concerts to offer an already satiated public.**
>
> **–Russell Platt, "New World Symphony"**

To cite this passage correctly in MLA style, you could quote directly from it, using both quotation marks and some form of attribution. Either of the following versions would be acceptable:

> Russell Platt has doubts about claims that classical music is "in its death throes: its orchestras bled dry by expensive guest soloists and greedy musicians' unions" ("New World").

> But is classical music in the United States really "in its death throes," as some critics of the music scene suggest (Platt)?

You might also paraphrase Platt's paragraph, putting his ideas entirely in your own words but giving him due credit:

> A familiar story told by critics is that classical music faces a bleak future in the United States, with grasping soloists and unions bankrupting orchestras and classical works vanishing from radio and television, school curricula, and the labels of recording conglomerates. The public may not be able or willing to support all the talented musicians and composers we have today (Platt).

All of these sentences with citations would be keyed to a Works Cited entry at the end of the paper that would look like the following in MLA style:

> Platt, Russell. "New World Symphony." The Nation 3 Oct. 2005. 15 Oct. 2005 <http://www.thenation.com/doc/20051003/platt>.

How might a citation go wrong? As we indicated, omitting either the quotation marks around a borrowed passage or the acknowledgment of the source are grounds for complaint. Neither of the following sentences provides enough information for a correct citation:

> But is classical music in the United States really in its death throes, as some critics of the music scene suggest (Platt)?

> But is classical music in the United States really "in its death throes," as some critics of the music scene suggest?

Just as faulty is a paraphrase such as the following, which borrows the words or ideas of the source too closely. It represents plagiarism, though it identifies the source from which almost all the ideas—and a good many words—are borrowed:

> In "New World Symphony," Russell Platt observes that classical music is thought by many to be in bad shape in America. Its orchestras are being sucked dry by costly guest artists and insatiable unionized musicians, its place on TV and radio is shrinking, its stature is diminished, its role in education is largely ignored, and its big record contracts are declining too. The problem may also be that we have too many well-trained musicians who need employment, too many good composers going without jobs, too many concerts for a public that prefers Desperate Housewives.

Even the original observation at the end of the paragraph isn't enough to change the fact that the paraphrase is just Platt's original, lightly stirred.

Precisely because the consequences of even unintentional plagiarism can be severe, it's important to understand how it can happen and how you can guard against it. In a January 2002 article published in *Time* magazine, historian Doris Kearns Goodwin explains how someone else's writing wound up unacknowledged in her book. The book in question, nine hundred pages long and with thirty-five hundred footnotes, took Goodwin ten years to write. During these ten years, she says, she took most of her notes by hand, organized the notes into boxes, and—once the draft was complete—went back to her sources to check that all the material from them was correctly cited. "Somehow in this process," Goodwin claims, "a few books were not fully rechecked," and so she omitted some necessary quotation marks in material she didn't acknowledge. Reflecting back on this experience, Goodwin says that discovering such carelessness in her own work was very troubling—so troubling that in the storm of criticism that ensued over the discovery of these failures to cite properly, she resigned from her position as a member of the Pulitzer Prize Committee.

Acknowledging Your Use of Sources

Mark Hertsgaard uses quotations and footnotes to annotate and strengthen his argument about America's influence in the world. Does it make a writer more credible when he or she cites outside sources?

LINK TO P. 1015

The safest way to avoid charges of plagiarism is to acknowledge as many of your sources as possible, with the following three exceptions:

- common knowledge, a specific piece of information most readers will know (that George W. Bush won the 2004 presidential election, for instance)
- facts available from a wide variety of sources (that the Japanese bombed Pearl Harbor on December 7, 1941, for example)
- your own findings from field research (observations, interviews, experiments, or surveys you have conducted), which should simply be presented as your own.

For all other source material you should give credit as fully as possible, placing quotation marks around any quoted material, citing your sources according to the documentation style you're using, and including them in a list of references or works cited. Material to be credited includes all of the following:

- direct quotations
- facts not widely known or arguable statements
- judgments, opinions, and claims made by others
- images, statistics, charts, tables, graphs, or other illustrations from any source
- collaboration—that is, the help provided by friends, colleagues, instructors, supervisors, or others

For more on using and documenting sources, see Chapters 19 and 20.

Using Copyrighted Internet Sources

If you've done any surfing on the Net, you already know that it opens the doors to worldwide collaborations: as you can contact individuals and groups around the globe and have access to whole libraries of information.

CULTURAL CONTEXTS FOR ARGUMENT

Understanding Plagiarism

Not all cultures accept Western notions of plagiarism, which rest on a belief that language can be owned by writers. Indeed, in many countries, and in some communities within the United States, using the words of others is considered a sign of deep respect and an indication of knowledge—and attribution is not expected or required. In writing arguments in the United States, however, you should credit all materials except those that are common knowledge, that are available in a wide variety of sources, or that are your own findings from field research.

Photos and graphics accompany Laurie Goodstein's *New York Times* article on modern religion. Consider not only what those images add but where they might have come from and how borrowed images are documented.

LINK TO P. 844

As a result, writing (most especially, online writing) seems increasingly to be made up of a huge patchwork of materials that you and many others weave. (For a fascinating discussion of just how complicated charges and countercharges of plagiarism can be on the Internet, see <http://ombuds.org/narrative1.html>, where you can read a description of a mediation involving a Web site that included summaries of other people's work.) But when you use information gathered from Internet sources in your own work, it's subject to the same rules that govern information gathered from other types of sources.

Thus whether or not the material includes a copyright notice or symbol ("© 2007 by John J. Ruszkiewicz and Andrea A. Lunsford," for example), it's more than likely copyrighted—and you may need to request permission to use part or all of it. Although they're currently in danger, "fair use" laws still allow writers to quote brief passages from published works without permission from the copyright holder if the use is for educational or personal, noncommercial reasons and full credit is given to the source. For personal communication such as email or for listserv postings, however, you should ask permission of the writer before you include any of his or her material in your own argument. For graphics, photos, or other images you wish to reproduce in your text, you should also request permission from the creator or owner if the text is going to be disseminated beyond your classroom—especially if it's going to be published online.

Here are some examples of student requests for permission:

To: litman@mindspring.com
CC: lunsford.2@stanford.edu
Subject: Request for permission

Dear Professor Litman:

I am writing to request permission to quote from your essay "Copyright, Owners' Rights and Users' Privileges on the Internet: Implied Licences, Caching, Linking, Fair Use, and Sign-on Licences." I want to quote some of your work as part of an essay I am writing for my composition class at Stanford University to explain the complex debates over ownership on the Internet and to argue that students in my class should be participating in these debates. I will give full credit to you and will cite the URL where I first found your work: <msen.com/~litman/dayton/htm>.

Thank you very much for considering my request.

Raul Sanchez <sanchez.32@stanford.edu>

To: fridanet@aol.com
CC: lunsford.2@stanford.edu
Subject: Request for permission

Dear Kimberley Masters:

I am a student at Stanford University writing to request your permission to download and use a photograph of Frida Kahlo in a three-piece suit <fridanet/suit.htm#top> as an illustration in a project about Kahlo that I and two other students are working on in our composition class. In the report on our project, we will cite <members.aol.com/fridanet/kahlo.htm> as the URL, unless you wish for us to use a different source.

Thank you very much for considering our request.

Jennifer Fox <fox.360@stanford.edu>

Acknowledging Collaboration

We've already noted the importance of acknowledging the inspirations and ideas you derive from talking with others. Such help counts as one form of collaboration, and you may also be involved in more formal kinds

If Everything's an Argument . . .

This chapter concludes with a discussion of how to acknowledge the contributions of various hands when a project is produced collaboratively. *Everything's an Argument* is obviously such a collaboration; like most books, it uses a title page and an acknowledgments section in the Preface to give credit to the authors, editors, designers, reviewers, graduate students, and undergraduates who had a hand in its creation. But who did what exactly? As a reader, would you like to know more specifically who wrote a particular chapter, who edited it, who deserves credit for a particularly good image or bright idea in the book, and so on? When might such information matter to you—if ever?

of collaborative work—preparing for a group presentation to a class, for example, or writing a group report. Writers generally acknowledge all participants in collaborative projects at the beginning of the presentation, report, or essay—in print texts, often in a footnote or brief prefatory note.

Deborah Tannen frequently refers to comments and stories shared by women she interviewed for her book *Are You Wearing That?* Crediting certain insights to one's interviewees sets that information apart from the author's ideas or research conclusions.

LINK TO P. 830

The sixth edition of the *MLA Handbook for Writers of Research Papers* (2003) calls attention to the growing importance of collaborative work and gives the following advice on how to deal with issues of assigning fair credit all around:

> **Joint participation in research and writing is common and, in fact, encouraged in many courses and in many professions. It does not constitute plagiarism provided that credit is given for all contributions. One way to give credit, if roles were clearly demarcated or were unequal, is to state exactly who did what. Another way, especially if roles and contributions were merged and shared, is to acknowledge all concerned equally. Ask your instructor for advice if you are not certain how to acknowledge collaboration.**

RESPOND.

1. Not everyone agrees with the concept of intellectual material as property, as something to be protected. Lately the slogan "information wants to be free" has been showing up in popular magazines and on the Internet, often along with a call to readers to take action against

forms of protection such as data encryption and further extension of copyright.

Using a Web search engine, look for pages where the phrase "free information" appears. Find several sites that make arguments in favor of free information, and analyze them in terms of their rhetorical appeals. What claims do the authors make? How do they appeal to their audience? What's the site's ethos, and how is it created? Once you've read some arguments in favor of free information, return to this chapter's arguments about intellectual property. Which arguments do you find more persuasive? Why?

2. Although this text is principally concerned with ideas and their written expression, there are other forms of protection available for intellectual property. For example, scientific and technological developments are protectable under patent law, which differs in some significant ways from copyright law.

   Find the standards for protection under U.S. copyright law and U.S. patent law. You might begin by visiting the U.S. copyright Web site at <http://copyright.gov>. Then imagine that you're the president of a small, high-tech corporation and are trying to inform your employees of the legal protections available to them and their work. Write a paragraph or two explaining the differences between copyright and patent, and suggesting a policy that balances employees' rights to intellectual property with the business's needs to develop new products.

3. Define plagiarism in your own terms, making your definition as clear and explicit as possible. Then compare your definition with those of two or three other classmates, and write a brief report on the similarities and differences you noted in the definitions. You might research terms such as *plagiarism*, *academic honesty*, and *academic integrity* on the Web.

4. Spend fifteen or twenty minutes jotting down your ideas about intellectual property and plagiarism. Where do you stand, for example, on the issue of music file-sharing? On downloading movies free of charge? Do you think these forms of intellectual property should be protected under copyright law? How do you define your own intellectual property, and in what ways and under what conditions are you willing to share it? Finally, come up with your own definition of *academic integrity*.

19 Evaluating and Using Sources

As many examples in this text have shown, the quality of an argument often depends on the quality of the sources used to support or prove it. As a result, careful evaluation and assessment of all your sources is important, including those you gather in libraries or from other print sources, in online searches, or in field research you conduct yourself. Remember, though, that sources can contribute in different ways to your work. In most cases, you'll be looking for reliable sources that provide accurate and unbiased information or clearly and persuasively expressed opinionsthat might serve as evidence for a case you're making. At other times, you may be looking for material that expresses ideas or attitudes—how people are thinking and feeling at a given time. You might need to use a graphic image, a sample of avant-garde music, or a controversial video clip that won't fit neatly into categories such as reliable, accurate, or unbiased, yet is central to an argument you're making or refuting. With any and all such sources and evidence, you want to be as knowledgeable as possible about them and as responsible in their use as you can be, sharing honestly what you learn about them with readers.

• • •

Indeed, you don't want to be naïve in your use of any source material, even material from influential and well-known sources. The fact is that most of what constitutes the evidence used in arguments on public issues comes with considerable baggage. Scientists and humanists alike have axes to grind, corporations have products to sell, bureaucracies have power to maintain, politicians have policies and candidacies to promote, journalists have reputations to make, media owners and editors have readers, listeners, viewers, and advertisers to attract—and to avoid offending. All of these groups produce and use information to their benefit. It's not (usually) a bad thing that they do so; you just have to be aware that when you take information from a given source, it may carry with it the enthusiasms, assumptions, and biases, conscious or not, of the people who produce and disseminate it. Teachers and librarians are not exempted from this caution.

The way to correct for the biases is always to draw on as many reliable sources as you can manage when you're preparing to write. You shouldn't assume that all arguments are equally good or that all the sides in a controversy can be supported by the same weight of evidence and good reasons. But what you want to avoid is treading so narrowly among sources that you miss essential issues and perspectives. That's especially easy to do when you read only sources that agree with you or when the sources you tend to read all seem to carry the same message. Especially when writing on political subjects, you should be aware that the sources you're reading or viewing will almost always have an agenda to push. That fact has become much more apparent in recent years thanks to the work of a diverse group of bloggers on the Web—from all

CNN's Nancy Grace, a former prosecutor, has been accused of allowing her pro-prosecution bias to influence her commentary.

parts of the political spectrum—who have put the traditional news media under daily scrutiny, exposing stunning errors, biases, and omissions. Of course, political bloggers (mostly amateurs in the realms of journalism, though many are professionals in their own fields) have their own prejudices; but unlike most writers in mainstream news outlets, they admit their biases openly and frankly. How should researchers react when reading the *New York Times*, the *Wall Street Journal*, or the *Washington Post* or watching PBS, NBC, CBS, CNN, or FOX? Trust, but verify.

How would you compare the various comments published about George W. Bush's 2005 commencement speech at Calvin College? In particular consider the *New York Times* report by Elisabeth Bumiller and the commentary released by college president Gaylen J. Byker. How might the authors' affiliations affect their presentations and evaluations of the situation?

LINK TO PP. 872 AND 878

Evaluating Sources

Print Sources

Since you want the information you glean from sources to be reliable and persuasive, it pays to evaluate each potential source thoroughly. The following principles can help you in conducting such an evaluation for print sources:

- *Relevance.* Begin by asking what a particular source will add to your argument and how closely related to your argumentative claim it is. For a book, the table of contents and the index may help you decide. For an article, check to see if there's an abstract that summarizes the contents. And if you can't think of a good reason for using the source, set it aside; you can almost certainly find something better.
- *Credentials of the author.* You may find the author's credentials set forth in an article, book, or Web site, so be sure to look for a description of the author. Is the author an expert on the topic? To find out, you can also go to the Internet to gather information: just open a search tool

such as Yahoo!, and type in the name of the person you're looking for. Still another way to learn about the credibility of an author is to search Google Groups for postings that mention the author or to check the Citation Index to find out how others refer to this author. And if you see your source cited by other sources you're using, look at how they cite it and what they say about it that could provide clues to the author's credibility.

- *Stance of the author.* What's the author's position on the issue(s) involved, and how does this stance influence the information in the source? Does the author's stance support or challenge your own views?
- *Credentials of the publisher or sponsor.* If your source is from a newspaper, is it a major one (such as the *Wall Street Journal* or the *New York Times*) that has historical credentials in reporting, or is it a tabloid? Is it a popular magazine like *People* or a journal sponsored by a professional group, such as the *Journal of the American Medical Association?* If your source is a book, is the publisher one you recognize or can find described on its own Web site?
- *Stance of the publisher or sponsor.* Sometimes this stance will be absolutely obvious: a magazine called *Mother Earth* will clearly take a pro-environmental stance, whereas one called *America First!* will

Note the differences between the *Vanity Fair* cover and that of a literary journal.

Source Map: Evaluating Articles

Determine the relevance of the source.

1 Look for an abstract, which provides a summary of the entire article. Is this source directly related to your research? Does it provide useful information and insights? Will your readers consider it persuasive support for your thesis?

Determine the credibility of the publication.

2 Consider the publication's title. Words in the title such as *Journal, Review,* and *Quarterly* may indicate that the periodical is a scholarly source. Most research essays rely on authorities in a particular field, whose work usually appears in scholarly journals.

3 Try to determine the publisher or sponsor. This journal is published by Johns Hopkins University Press. Academic presses such as this one generally review articles carefully before publishing them and bear the authority of their academic sponsors.

Determine the credibility of the author.

4 Evaluate the author's credentials. In this case, they are given in a note, which indicates that the author is a college professor and has written at least two books on related topics.

Determine the currency of the article.

5 Look at the publication date and think about whether your topic and your credibility depend on your use of very current sources.

Determine the accuracy of the article.

6 Look at the sources cited by the author of the article. Here, they are documented in footnotes. Ask yourself whether the works the author has cited seem credible and current. Are any of these works cited in other articles you've considered?

1

HUMAN RIGHTS QUARTERLY

2

Prisons and Politics in Contemporary Latin America

*Mark Ungar**

ABSTRACT

Despite democratization throughout Latin America, massive human rights abuses continue in the region's prisons. Conditions have become so bad that most governments have begun to enact improvements, including new criminal codes and facility decongestion. However, once in place, these reforms are undermined by chaotic criminal justice systems, poor policy administration, and rising crime rates leading to greater detention powers for the police. After describing current prison conditions in Latin America and the principal reforms to address them, this article explains how political and administrative limitations hinder the range of agencies and officials responsible for implementing those changes.

I. INTRODUCTION

Prison conditions not only constitute some of the worst human rights violations in contemporary Latin American democracies, but also reveal fundamental weaknesses in those democracies. Unlike most other human rights problems, those in the penitentiary system cannot be easily explained with authoritarian legacies or renegade officials. The systemic killing, overcrowding, disease, torture, rape, corruption, and due process abuses all occur under the state's twenty-four hour watch. Since the mid-1990s,

* *Mark Ungar* is Associate Professor of Political Science at Brooklyn College, City University of New York. Recent publications include the books *Elusive Reform: Democracy and the Rule of Law in Latin America* (Lynne Rienner, 2002) and *Violence and Politics: Globalization's Paradox* (Routledge, 2001) as well as articles and book chapters on democratization, policing, and judicial access. He works with Amnesty International USA and local rights groups in Latin America.

4

Human Rights Quarterly 25 (2003) 909–934 © 2003 by The Johns Hopkins University Press

3 The Johns Hopkins University Press

5 2003

915

, the / ed to / cy in / from / mber / form / —with / riots / n in / pread / PCC / ders. / curity / dable / some / irless / ing in / n the / lity of / tra el / lls of / water, / s and / apons / e and / icials, / ard in / ution. / esting / of El

10. Inspector General de Cárceles, Informe Annual (Caracas: Ministerio de Justicia 1994).
11. *Overcrowding Main Cause of Riots in Latin American Prisons*, AFP, 30 Dec. 1997.
12. Interviews with inmates, speaking on condition of anonymity in San Pedro prison (19 July 2000); Interviews with inmates, speaking on condition of anonymity in La Paz FELCN Prison (20 July 2000).
13. Typhus, cholera, tuberculosis, and scabies run rampant and the HIV rate may be as high as 25 percent. The warden of Retén de la Planta, where cells built for one inmate house three or four, says the prisons "are collapsing" because of insufficient budgets to train personnel. "Things fall apart and stay that way." Interview, Luis A. Lara Roche, Warden of Retén de la Planta, Caracas, Venezuela, 19 May 1995. At El Dorado prison in Bolívar state, there is one bed for every four inmates, cells are infested with vermin, and inmates lack clean bathing water and eating utensils.
14. *La Crisis Penitenciaria*, El Nacional (Caracas), 2 Sept. 1988, at D2. On file with author.

6

certainly take a conservative stance. But other times, you need to read carefully between the lines to identify particular positions, so you can see how the stance affects the message the source presents. Start by asking what the source's goals are: what does the publisher or sponsoring group want to make happen?

- *Currency.* Check the date of publication of any book or article. Recent sources are often more useful than older ones, particularly in the sciences. However, in some fields such as history or literature, the most authoritative works are often the older ones.
- *Level of specialization.* General sources can be helpful as you begin your research, but later in the project you may need the authority or currency of more specialized sources. However, keep in mind that extremely specialized works on your topic may be too difficult for your audience to understand easily.
- *Audience.* Was the source written for a general readership? For specialists? For advocates or opponents?
- *Length.* Is the source long enough to provide adequate detail in support of your claim?
- *Availability.* Do you have access to the source? If it isn't readily accessible, your time might be better spent looking elsewhere.
- *Omissions.* What's missing or omitted from the source? Might such exclusions affect whether or how you can use the source as evidence?

If Everything's an Argument . . .

Have you ever checked out the credentials of a textbook publisher or author? Is the publisher of this book, Bedford/St. Martin's, for example, a fly-by-night operation run by the authors using Photoshop in their basements? Or is it a company with real assets and real editors? Spend a few moments on the Web discovering how much you can find out about the company, its reputation, and its track record. You might do the same with one of the authors. They claim to be at Stanford University (Andrea Lunsford) and the University of Texas at Austin (John Ruszkiewicz). How might you quickly and unobtrusively confirm their credentials—and that they do indeed work at the real Stanford and Texas?

Electronic Sources

You'll probably find working on the Internet and the World Wide Web both exciting and frustrating, for even though these tools have great potential, the Web will always contain information of widely varying quality. That's the nature of a source as open and generally unregulated as the Web. As a result, careful researchers look for corroboration before accepting evidence they find online, especially if it comes from a site whose sponsor's identity is less than clear. In such an environment, you must be the judge of how accurate and trustworthy particular electronic sources are. In making these judgments, you should rely on the same kinds of criteria and of careful thinking you would use to assess print sources. In addition, you may find some of the following questions helpful in evaluating online sources:

- Who has posted the document or message or created the site? An individual? An interest group? A company? A government agency? Does the URL offer any clues? Note especially the final suffix in a domain name: .com (commercial); .org (nonprofit organization); .edu (educational institution); .gov (government agency); .mil (military); .net (network)—or the geographical domains that indicate country of origin, as in .ca (Canada) or .ar (Argentina). The homepage or first page of a site should tell you something about the sponsorship of the source, letting you know who can be held accountable for its information. (You may need to click on an "About Us" button.) Finally, links may help you learn how credible and useful the source is. Click on some of them to see if they lead to legitimate and helpful sites.
- What can you determine about the credibility of the author or sponsor? Can the information in the document or site be verified in other sources? How accurate and complete is it? On a blog, for example, look for a link that identifies the creator of the site—some blogs are managed by multiple authors. Also review the links the blog offers; they'll often help you understand both the perspective of the site and its purposes.
- Who can be held accountable for the information in the document or site? How well and thoroughly does it credit its own sources?
- How current is the document or site? Be especially cautious of undated materials. Most reliable will be those that are updated regularly.
- What perspectives are represented? If only one perspective is represented, how can you balance or expand this point of view?

Source Map: Evaluating Web Sources

Determine the credibility of the sponsoring organization.

1 Consider the URL, specifically the top-level domain name. (For example, *.edu* may indicate that the sponsor is an accredited college or university; *.org* may indicate it's a nonprofit organization.) Ask yourself whether such a sponsor might be biased about the topic you're researching.

2 Look for an *About* page or a link to the homepage for background information on the sponsor, including a mission statement. What is the sponsoring organization's stance or point of view? Does the mission statement seem biased or balanced? Does the sponsor seem to take other points of view into account? What is the intended purpose of the site? Is this site meant to inform? Or is it trying to persuade, advertise, or accomplish something else?

Determine the credibility of the author.

3 Evaluate the author's credentials. On this Web page, the authors' professional affiliations are listed, but other information about them isn't provided. You will often have to look elsewhere — such as at other sites on the Web — to find out more about an author. When you do, ask yourself if the author seems qualified to write about the topic.

Determine the currency of the Web source.

4 Look for the date that indicates when the information was posted or last updated. Here, the date is given at the beginning of the press release.

5 Check to see if the sources referred to are also up-to-date. These authors cite sources from September and October 2003. Ask yourself if, given your topic, an older source is acceptable or if only the most recent information will do.

Determine the accuracy of the information.

6 How complete is the information in the source? Examine the works cited by the author. Are sources for statistics included? Do the sources cited seem credible? Is a list of additional resources provided? Here, the authors cite the U.S. Navy and the U.S. Air Force, but they do not give enough information to track down these sources. Ask yourself whether you can find a way to corroborate what a source is saying.

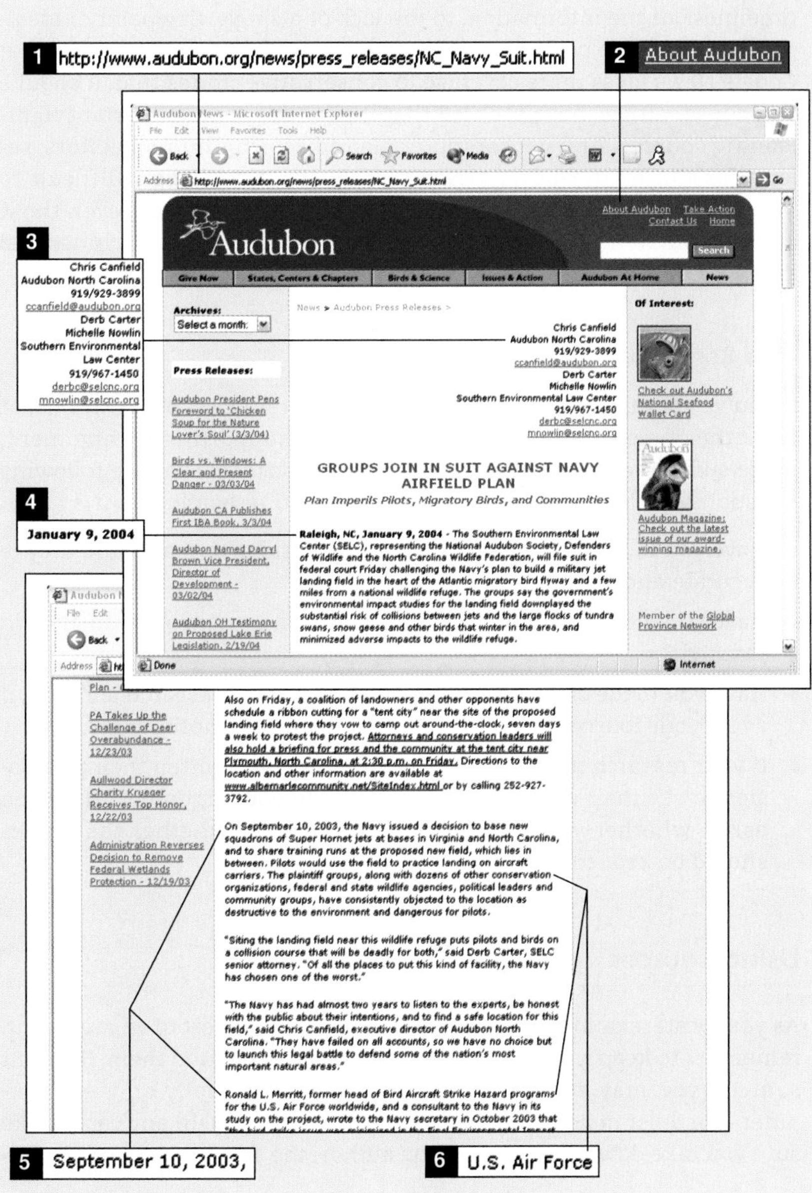

Audubon News - Microsoft Internet Explorer

Address http://www.audubon.org/news/press_releases/NC_Navy_Suit.html

About Audubon Take Action Contact Us Home

Audubon

Give Now | States, Centers & Chapters | Birds & Science | Issues & Action | Audubon At Home | News

Archives: Select a month:

Press Releases:

Audubon President Pens Foreword to 'Chicken Soup for the Nature Lover's Soul' (3/3/04)

Birds vs. Windows: A Clear and Present Danger - 03/03/04

Audubon CA Publishes First IBA Book, 3/3/04

Audubon Named Darryl Brown Vice President, Director of Development - 03/02/04

Audubon OH Testimony on Proposed Lake Erie Legislation, 2/19/04

PA Takes Up the Challenge of Deer Overabundance - 12/23/03

Aullwood Director Charity Krueger Receives Top Honor, 12/22/03

Administration Reverses Decision to Remove Federal Wetlands Protection - 12/19/03

News > Audubon Press Releases >

Chris Canfield
Audubon North Carolina
919/929-3899
ccanfield@audubon.org
Derb Carter
Michelle Nowlin
Southern Environmental Law Center
919/967-1450
derbc@selcnc.org
mnowlin@selcnc.org

GROUPS JOIN IN SUIT AGAINST NAVY AIRFIELD PLAN

Plan Imperils Pilots, Migratory Birds, and Communities

Raleigh, NC, January 9, 2004 - The Southern Environmental Law Center (SELC), representing the National Audubon Society, Defenders of Wildlife and the North Carolina Wildlife Federation, will file suit in federal court Friday challenging the Navy's plan to build a military jet landing field in the heart of the Atlantic migratory bird flyway and a few miles from a national wildlife refuge. The groups say the government's environmental impact studies for the landing field downplayed the substantial risk of collisions between jets and the large flocks of tundra swans, snow geese and other birds that winter in the area, and minimized adverse impacts to the wildlife refuge.

Also on Friday, a coalition of landowners and other opponents have schedule a ribbon cutting for a "tent city" near the site of the proposed landing field where they vow to camp out around-the-clock, seven days a week to protest the project. Attorneys and conservation leaders will also hold a briefing for press and the community at the tent city near Plymouth, North Carolina, at 2:30 p.m. on Friday. Directions to the location and other information are available at www.albemarlecommunity.net/SiteIndex.html or by calling 252-927-3792.

On September 10, 2003, the Navy issued a decision to base new squadrons of Super Hornet jets at bases in Virginia and North Carolina, and to share training runs at the proposed new field, which lies in between. Pilots would use the field to practice landing on aircraft carriers. The plaintiff groups, along with dozens of other conservation organizations, federal and state wildlife agencies, political leaders and community groups, have consistently objected to the location as destructive to the environment and dangerous for pilots.

"Siting the landing field near this wildlife refuge puts pilots and birds on a collision course that will be deadly for both," said Derb Carter, SELC senior attorney. "Of all the places to put this kind of facility, the Navy has chosen one of the worst."

"The Navy has had almost two years to listen to the experts, be honest with the public about their intentions, and to find a safe location for this field," said Chris Canfield, executive director of Audubon North Carolina. "They have failed on all accounts, so we have no choice but to launch this legal battle to defend some of the nation's most important natural areas."

Ronald L. Merritt, former head of Bird Aircraft Strike Hazard programs for the U.S. Air Force worldwide, and a consultant to the Navy in its study on the project, wrote to the Navy secretary in October 2003 that

Of Interest:

Check out Audubon's National Seafood Wallet Card

Audubon Magazine: Check out the latest issue of our award-winning magazine.

Member of the Global Province Network

Done Internet

Several years ago, the Stanford Persuasive Technology Lab argued that Google News might become the "most credible Web site of them all." The Lab listed twenty-five reasons in support of this conclusion, from the timeliness of the information, to the lack of a single viewpoint or ideology, to the ad-free policy. Since then, however, liberals have charged that Google News gives more coverage to conservative stories than it should, and conservatives have claimed that it excludes some important right-leaning sources. And yet computer algorithms, not human editors, select the stories in Google News. Clearly, it's increasingly difficult to satisfy readers sensitive to media perspectives and biases, even those attributable to machines. But, then, humans create the machines and the algorithms.

In his short essay about diversity at the university level, Walter Benn Michaels relies on statistics about race, class, and university attendance to support his argument against racial preferences for university admittance. Where might he have found his statistics? How can you verify the numbers that he presents?

LINK TO P. 976

Field Research

If you've conducted experiments, surveys, interviews, observations, or any other field research in developing and supporting an argument, make sure to review your own results with a critical eye. The following questions can help you evaluate your own field research:

- Have you rechecked all data and all conclusions to make sure they're accurate and warranted?
- Have you identified the exact time, place, and participants in all field research?
- Have you made clear what part you played in the research and how, if at all, your role could have influenced the results or findings?
- If your research involved other people, have you gotten their permission to use their words or other material in your argument? Have you asked whether you could use their names or whether the names should be kept confidential?

Using Sources

As you locate, examine, and evaluate sources in support of an argument, remember to keep a careful record of where you've found them. For print sources, you may want to keep a working bibliography on your computer—or a list in a notebook you can carry with you. In any case, make sure you take down the name of the author; the title of the book or periodical; the title of the article, or the publisher and city of publication of the book; the date of publication; relevant volume, issue, and exact page numbers; and any other information you may later need in preparing a Works Cited list or References list. In addition, for a book, note where you found it—the section of the library, for example, along with the call number for the book.

For electronic sources, keep a careful record of the information you'll need in a Works Cited list or References list—particularly the name of the database or other online site where you found the source; the full electronic address (URL); the date the document was first produced; the date the document was published on the Web or most recently updated; and the date you accessed and examined the document. The simplest way to ensure that you have this information is to get a printout of the source, highlighting source information and writing down any other pertinent information.

Signal Words and Introductions

Because your sources are crucial to the success of your arguments, you need to introduce them carefully to your readers. Doing so usually calls for using a signal phrase of some kind in the sentence to introduce the source. Typically, the signal phrase precedes the quotation, though that's not a hard-and-fast rule by any means:

> According to noted child psychiatrist Robert Coles, children develop complex ethical systems at extremely young ages.

> Children develop complex ethical systems at extremely young ages, according to noted child psychiatrist Robert Coles.

> Most children, observes noted child psychiatrist Robert Coles, develop complex ethical systems at extremely young ages.

In these sentences, the signal phrases all tell readers that you're drawing on the work of a person named Robert Coles and that this person is a "noted child psychiatrist." Now look at an example that uses a quotation from a source in more than one sentence:

> In Job Shift, consultant William Bridges worries about "dejobbing and about what a future shaped by it is going to be like." Even more worrisome, Bridges argues, is the possibility that "the sense of craft and of professional vocation . . . will break down under the need to earn a fee" (228).

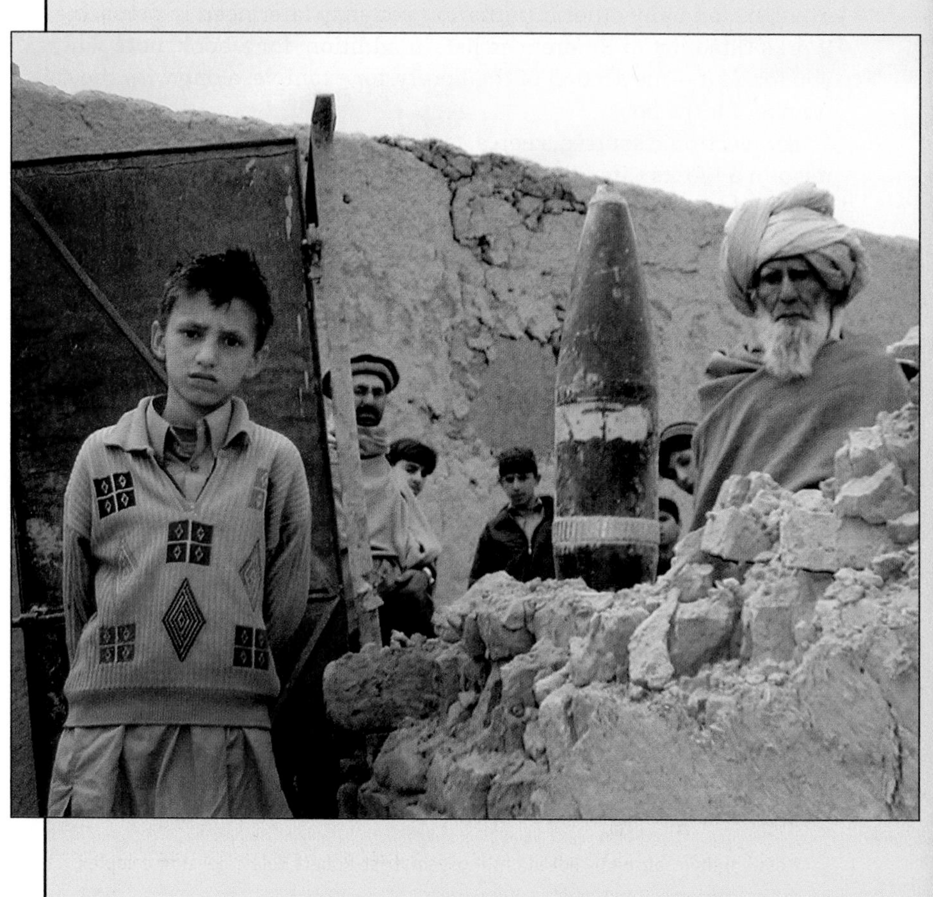

Not Just Words

What's wrong with this picture? the editors of the *New York Times* might have asked before posting it on the paper's Web site following a strike by an American Predator drone on a village in Pakistan. Intelligence had suggested that Al Qaeda's second-in-command, Ayman al-Zawahiri, was in one of the buildings targeted by the missile. But al-Zawahiri was not there, and eighteen villagers died. The compelling photograph purportedly shows the aftermath. Its original caption had read: "Pakistani men with the remains of a missile fired at a house in the Bajaur tribal zone near the Afghan border." But it didn't take long for bloggers to point out that the missile part was actually an artillery shell—and maybe not even of American origin. Here's the correction that the newspaper subsequently ran:

> Correction appended Jan. 17, 2006: A caption Saturday on NYTimes.com with a photograph of damage from a U.S. airstrike in Pakistan misidentified an item in the photograph. Agence France-Presse, the agency that provided the photograph, later changed the caption to report that the item appears to be an unexploded artillery shell, not a piece of a missile from Friday's attack.

What issues do the image, the caption, and the correction raise about evaluating and using sources? For instance, who was responsible for the original photograph? Who was responsible for the error in captioning it? How is your perception of the image (particularly its pose) changed by the correction? Is the correction adequate? What gaps in editorial knowledge does the original caption suggest? To what degree, if any, does such an error undermine the authority of a source?

The signal verbs "worries" and "argues" add a sense of urgency to the message Bridges offers and suggest that the writer either agrees with—or is neutral about—Bridges's points. Other signal verbs have a more negative slant, indicating that the point being introduced in the quotation is open to debate and that others (including the writer) might disagree with it. If the writer of the passage above had said, for instance, that Bridges "unreasonably contends" or that he "fantasizes," these signal verbs would carry quite different connotations from those associated with "argues." In some cases, a signal verb may require more complex phrasing to get the writer's full meaning across:

> Bridges recognizes the dangers of changes in work yet refuses to be overcome by them: "The real issue is not how to stop the change but how to provide the necessary knowledge and skills to equip people to operate successfully in this New World" (229).

As these examples illustrate, the signal verb is important because it allows you to characterize the author's or source's viewpoint as well as your own—so choose these verbs with care.

Some Frequently Used Signal Verbs

acknowledges	claims	emphasizes	remarks
admits	concludes	expresses	replies
advises	concurs	hypothesizes	reports
agrees	confirms	interprets	responds
allows	criticizes	lists	reveals
argues	declares	objects	states
asserts	disagrees	observes	suggests
believes	discusses	offers	thinks
charges	disputes	opposes	writes

In his evaluative essay of the Academic Bill of Rights, Stanley Fish offers various quotes from the bill's author, David Horowitz. Consider not only how Fish signals the quotations, but how including the information creates a well-informed ethos for the author.

LINK TO P. 953

Quotations

For supporting argumentative claims, you'll want to quote—that is, to reproduce an author's precise words—in at least three kinds of situations: when the wording is so memorable or expresses a point so well that you cannot improve it or shorten it without weakening it; when the author is a respected authority whose opinion supports your own ideas particularly well; and when an author challenges or disagrees profoundly with others in the field.

Direct quotations can be effective in capturing your readers' attention—for example, through quoting a memorable phrase in your introduction or quoting an eyewitness account in arresting detail. In an argument, quotations from respected authorities can help build your ethos as someone who has sought out experts in the field. Finally, carefully chosen quotations can broaden the appeal of your argument by drawing on emotion as well as logic, appealing to the reader's mind and heart. A student writing on the ethical issues of bullfighting, for example, might introduce an argument that bullfighting is not a sport by quoting Ernest Hemingway's comment that "the formal bull-fight is a tragedy, not a sport, and the bull is certain to be killed," and might accompany the quotation with an image such as the one below.

The following guidelines can help you make sure that you quote accurately:

- If the quotation extends over more than one page in the original source, note the placement of page breaks in case you decide to use only part of the quotation in your argument.

A tragedy, not a sport?

- Label the quotation with a note that tells you where and/or how you think you'll use it.
- Make sure you have all the information necessary to create an in-text citation as well as an item in your Works Cited list or References list.
- When using a quotation in your argument, make sure you've introduced the author(s) of the quotation and that you follow the quotation with some commentary of your own that points out the significance of the quotation.
- Copy quotations carefully, being sure that punctuation, capitalization, and spelling are exactly as they are in the original.
- Enclose the quotation in quotation marks; don't rely on your memory to distinguish your own words from those of your source. If in doubt, recheck all quotations for accuracy.
- Use square brackets if you introduce words of your own into the quotation or make changes to it. ("And [more] brain research isn't going to define further the matter of 'mind.'")
- Use ellipsis marks if you omit material. ("And brain research isn't going to define . . . the matter of 'mind.'")
- If you're quoting a short passage (four lines or less, MLA style; forty words or less, APA style), it should be worked into your text, enclosed by quotation marks. Longer quotations should be set off from the regular text. Begin such a quotation on a new line, indenting every line one inch or ten spaces (MLA) or five to seven spaces (APA). Set-off quotations do not need to be enclosed in quotation marks.

CULTURAL CONTEXTS FOR ARGUMENT

Identifying Sources

Although some language communities and cultures expect audiences to recognize the sources of important documents and texts, thereby eliminating the need to cite them directly, conventions for writing in North America call for careful attribution of any quoted, paraphrased, or summarized material. When in doubt, explicitly identify your sources.

Paraphrases

Paraphrases involve putting an author's material (including major and minor points, usually in the order they're presented in the original) into your own words and sentence structures. Here are guidelines that can help you paraphrase accurately:

- When using a paraphrase in your argument, make sure that you identify the source of the paraphrase and that you comment on its significance.
- Make sure you have all the information necessary to create an in-text citation as well as an item in your Works Cited list or References list. For online sources without page numbers, record the paragraph, screen, or other section number(s) if indicated.
- If you're paraphrasing material that extends over more than one page in the original source, note the placement of page breaks in case you decide to use only part of the paraphrase in your argument.
- Label the paraphrase with a note suggesting where and/or how you intend to use it in your argument.
- Include all main points and any important details from the original source, in the same order in which the author presents them.
- Leave out your own comments, elaborations, or reactions.
- State the meaning in your own words and sentence structures. If you want to include especially memorable or powerful language from the original source, enclose it in quotation marks.
- Recheck to make sure that the words and sentence structures are your own and that they express the author's meaning accurately.

Summaries

A summary is a significantly shortened version of a passage—or even a whole chapter of a work—that captures the main ideas in your own words. Unlike a paraphrase, a summary uses just enough information to record the points you want to emphasize. Summaries can be extremely valuable in supporting arguments. Here are some guidelines to help you prepare accurate and helpful summaries:

- When using a summary in an argument, be sure to identify the source and add your own comments about why the material in the summary is significant for the argument you're making.

- Make sure you have all the information necessary to create an in-text citation as well as an item in your Works Cited list or References list. For online sources without page numbers, record the paragraph, screen, or other section number(s) if available.
- If you're summarizing material that extends over more than one page, indicate page breaks in case you decide to use only part of the summary in your argument.
- Label the summary with a note that suggests where and/or how you intend to use it in your argument.
- Include just enough information to recount the main points you want to cite. A summary is usually much shorter than the original.
- Use your own words. If you include any language from the original, enclose it in quotation marks.
- Recheck to make sure that you've captured the author's meaning accurately and that the wording is entirely your own.

News stories are often accompanied by a photograph that complements the argument. Richard Bernstein and David Rieff each have a photo accompanying their respective articles about American impact abroad. What do the photos add to the arguments? How are they cited?

LINK TO PP. 987 AND 996

Visuals

If a picture is worth a thousand words, then using pictures calls for caution: one picture might overwhelm or undermine the message you're trying to send in your argument. However, as you've seen in Chapter 14, visuals can have a powerful impact on audiences and can help bring them to understand or accept your arguments. In choosing visuals to include in your argument, make sure that each one makes a strong contribution to your message and that each is appropriate and fair to your subject or topic and your audience.

When you use visuals in your written arguments, treat them as you would any other sources you integrate into your text. Like quotations, paraphrases, and summaries, visuals need to be introduced and commented on in some way. In addition, label (as figures or as tables) and number (Figure 1, Figure 2, and so on) all visuals, provide a caption that includes source information and describes the visual, and cite the source in your bibliography or Works Cited list. Keep in mind that even if you create a visual (such as a bar graph) by using information from a source (the results, say, of a Gallup Poll), you must cite the source. If you use a photograph you took yourself, cite it as a personal photograph.

On the facing page is a visual that accompanied the introduction to an argument about bankruptcy that appeared on the front page of the December 15, 2002, *New York Times* Business section. Note that the source

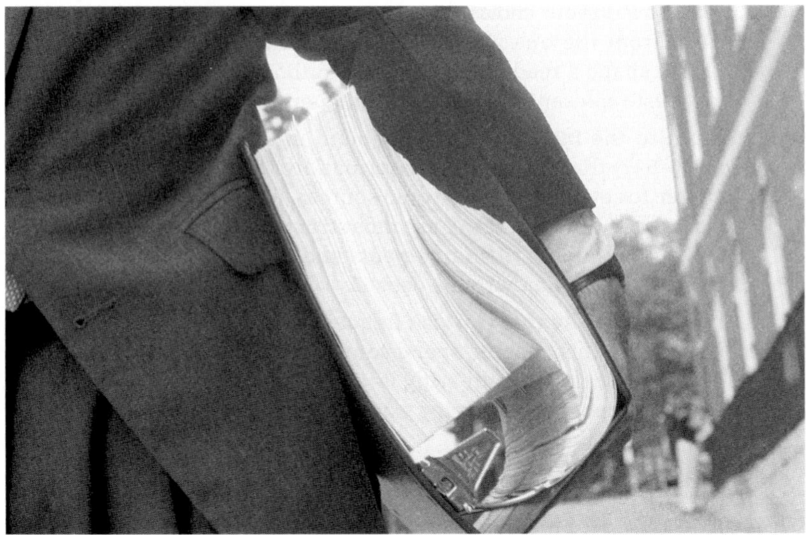

A lawyer with a binder of paperwork involving the US Airways bankruptcy filing. Companies can lose considerable value during the Chapter 11 process. (Source: Bloomberg News)

of the visual is listed (Bloomberg News) and that the caption indicates in what way the visual is related to the argument (in this case, the visual depicts bankruptcy papers). If you were going to use this as the first visual in an essay of your own, you would need to include the source, describe the image in relationship to your topic, and head it Figure 1. As long as this image will appear only in a print text for your instructor and classmates, you're allowed fair use of it. If you intend to post your argument on the Web, however, or otherwise publish it for a wider audience, you would need to request permission from the copyright owner (see Chapter 18, p. 524).

RESPOND.

1. Select one of the essays at the end of Chapters 7 to 11. Write a brief summary of the essay that includes both direct quotations and paraphrases. Be careful to attribute the ideas properly, even when you paraphrase, and to use signal phrases to introduce quotations. Then trade summaries with a partner, comparing the passages you selected to quote and paraphrase, and the signal phrases you used to introduce

them. How do your choices create an ethos for the original author that differs from the one your partner has created? How do the signal phrases shape a reader's sense of the author's position? Which summary best represents the author's argument? Why?

2. Return to the Internet sites you found in exercise 1 of Chapter 18 (p. 526–527) that discuss free information. Using the criteria in this chapter for evaluating electronic sources, judge each of those sites. Select three that you think are most trustworthy, and write a paragraph summarizing their arguments and recommending them to an audience unfamiliar with the debate.
3. Choose a Web site that you visit frequently. Then, using the guidelines discussed in this chapter, spend some time evaluating its credibility. You might begin by comparing it with Google News or another site that has a reputation for being extremely reliable.

20
Documenting Sources

What does documenting sources have to do with argument? First, the sources themselves form part of the argument, showing that a writer has done some homework, knows what others have said about the topic, and understands how to use these sources as support for a claim. The list of works cited or references makes an argument, saying, perhaps, "Look at how thoroughly this essay has been researched" or "Note how up-to-date I am!" Second, even the style of documentation makes an argument, though in a very subtle way. You'll note in the instructions that follow, for example, that for a print source the Modern Language Association (MLA) style requires putting the date of publication at or near the end of an entry, whereas the American Psychological Association (APA) style involves putting the date near the beginning. (An exercise at the end of this chapter asks you to consider what argument this difference represents.) Third, when a documentation style calls for listing only the first author followed by "et al." in citing works by multiple authors, it's subtly arguing that only the first author really matters—or at least that acknowledging the others is less important than keeping citations brief. Pay attention to the fine points of documentation and documentation style, always asking what these elements add (or don't add) to your arguments.

If Everything's an Argument . . .

You may have noticed that this book doesn't document its sources in any formal academic way. Instead, authors, titles, and sometimes information such as magazine names and publication dates are cited informally in the text, and the copyright holders who granted permission for their words or images to be used in the book are acknowledged in a list starting on the copyright page. Why do you think the authors, editors, and publishers of most textbooks don't follow a formal documentation style? What would be gained or lost if they did so?

MLA Style

Documentation styles vary from discipline to discipline, with different formats favored in the social sciences and the natural sciences, for example. Widely used in the humanities, the MLA style is fully described in the *MLA Handbook for Writers of Research Papers* (6th edition, 2003). In this discussion, we provide guidelines drawn from the *MLA Handbook* for in-text citations, notes, and entries in the list of works cited.

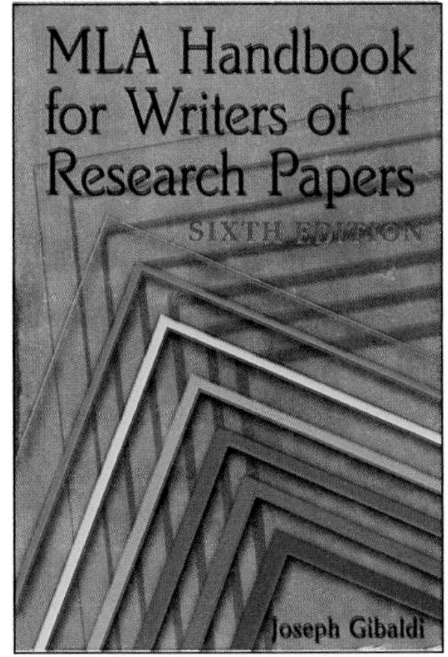

The 6th edition of the *MLA Handbook for Writers of Research Papers*

In-Text Citations

MLA style calls for in-text citations in the body of an argument to document sources of quotations, paraphrases, summaries, and so on. For in-text citations, use a signal phrase to introduce the material, often with the author's name (*As LaDoris Cordell explains . . .*). Keep an in-text citation short, but include enough information for readers to locate the source in the list of works cited. Place the parenthetical citation as near to the relevant material as possible without disrupting the flow of the sentence, as in the following examples. Finally, note that MLA encourages (but does not require) the use of underlining to indicate italics.

1. Author Named in a Signal Phrase

Ordinarily, use the author's name in a signal phrase—to introduce the material—and cite the page number(s) in parentheses.

> Loomba argues that Caliban's "political colour" is black, given his stage representations, which have varied from animalistic to a kind of missing link (143).

2. Author Named in Parentheses

When you don't mention the author in a signal phrase, include the author's last name before the page number(s) in the parentheses.

> Renaissance visions of "other" worlds, particularly in plays and travel narratives, often accentuated the differences of the Other even when striking similarities to the English existed (Bartels 434).

3. Two or Three Authors

Use all authors' last names.

Gortner, Hebrun, and Nicolson maintain that "opinion leaders" influence other people in an organization because they are respected, not because they hold high positions (175).

4. Four or More Authors

The MLA allows you to use all authors' last names, or to use only the first author's name with *et al.* (in regular type, not underlined or italicized). Although either format is acceptable when applied consistently throughout a paper, in an argument it is better to name all authors who contributed to the work.

Similarly, as Goldberger, Tarule, Clinchy, and Belenky note, their new book builds on their collaborative experiences (xii).

5. Organization as Author

Give the full name of a corporate author if it's brief or a shortened form if it's long.

In fact, one of the leading foundations in the field of higher education supports the recent proposals for community-run public schools (Carnegie Corporation 45).

6. Unknown Author

Use the full title of the work if it's brief or a shortened form if it's long.

"Hype," by one analysis, is "an artificially engendered atmosphere of hysteria" ("Today's Marketplace" 51).

7. Author of Two or More Works

When you use two or more works by the same author, include the title of the work or a shortened version of it in the citation.

Gardner presents readers with their own silliness through his description of a "pointless, ridiculous monster, crouched in the shadows, stinking of dead men, murdered children, and martyred cows" (Grendel 2).

8. Authors with the Same Last Name

When you use works by two or more authors with the same last name, include each author's first initial in the in-text citation.

Father Divine's teachings focused on eternal life, salvation, and socioeconomic progress (R. Washington 17).

9. Multivolume Work

Note the volume number first and then the page number(s), with a colon and one space between them.

> Aristotle's "On Plants" is now available in a new translation, edited by Barnes (2: 1252).

10. Literary Work

Because literary works are often available in many different editions, you need to include enough information for readers to locate the passage in any edition. For a prose work such as a novel or play, first cite the page number from the edition you used, followed by a semicolon; then indicate the part or chapter number (114; ch. 3) or act or scene in a play (42; sc. 2).

> In The Madonnas of Leningrad, Marina says "she could see into the future" (7; ch. 1).

For a poem, cite the stanza and line numbers. If the poem has only line numbers, use the word *line(s)* in the first reference (lines 33-34).

> On dying, Whitman speculates "All that goes onward and outward, nothing collapses, / And to die is different from what any one supposed, and luckier" (6.129-30).

For a verse play, omit the page number, and give only the act, scene, and line numbers, separated by periods.

> Before he takes his own life, Othello says he is "one that loved not wisely but too well" (5.2.348).

> As Macbeth begins, the witches greet Banquo as "Lesser than Macbeth, and greater" (1.3.65).

11. Works in an Anthology

For an essay, short story, or other short work within an anthology, use the name of the author of the work, not the editor of the anthology; but use the page number(s) from the anthology.

> In the end, if the black artist accepts any duties at all, that duty is to express the beauty of blackness (Hughes 1271).

12. Sacred Text

To cite a sacred text, such as the Qur'an or the Bible, give the title of the edition you used, the book, and the chapter and verse (or their equivalent), separated by a period. In your text, spell out the names of books. In a parenthetical reference, use an abbreviation for books with names of five or more letters (for example, *Gen.* for Genesis).

> He ignored the admonition "Pride goes before destruction, and a haughty spirit before a fall" (New Oxford Annotated Bible, Prov. 16.18).

13. Indirect Source

Use the abbreviation *qtd. in* to indicate that what you're quoting or paraphrasing is quoted (as part of a conversation, interview, letter, or excerpt) in the source you're using.

> As Catherine Belsey states, "to speak is to have access to the language which defines, delimits and locates power" (qtd. in Bartels 453).

14. Two or More Sources in the Same Citation

Separate the information for each source with a semicolon.

> Adefunmi was able to patch up the subsequent holes left in worship by substituting various Yoruba, Dahomean, or Fon customs made available to him through research (Brandon 115-17; Hunt 27).

15. Entire Work or One-Page Article

Include the citation in the text without any page numbers or parentheses.

> The relationship between revolutionary innocence and the preservation of an oppressive post-revolutionary regime is one theme Milan Kundera explores in The Book of Laughter and Forgetting.

16. Work without Page Numbers

If the work isn't paginated but has another kind of numbered section, such as parts or paragraphs, include the name and number(s) of the section(s) you're citing. (For paragraphs, use the abbreviation *par.* or *pars.*; for section, use *sec.*; for part, use *pt.*)

> Zora Neale Hurston is one of the great anthropologists of the twentieth century, according to Kip Hinton (par. 2).

17. Electronic or Nonprint Source

Give enough information in a signal phrase or parenthetical citation for readers to locate the source in the list of works cited. Usually give the author or title under which you list the source.

> In his film version of Hamlet, Zeffirelli highlights the sexual tension between the prince and his mother.

> Describing children's language acquisition, Pinker explains that "what's innate about language is just a way of paying attention to parental speech" (Johnson, sec. 1).

Explanatory and Bibliographic Notes

The MLA recommends using explanatory notes for information or commentary that doesn't readily fit into your text but is needed for clarification, further explanation, or justification. In addition, the MLA allows bibliographic notes for citing several sources for one point and for offering thanks to, information about, or evaluation of a source. Use superscript numbers in your text at the end of a sentence to refer readers to the notes, which usually appear as endnotes (with the heading *Notes*, not underlined or italicized) on a separate page before the list of works cited. Indent the first line of each note five spaces, and double-space all entries.

TEXT WITH SUPERSCRIPT INDICATING A NOTE

> Stewart emphasizes the existence of social contacts in Hawthorne's life so that the audience will accept a different Hawthorne, one more attuned to modern times than the figure in Woodberry.[3]

NOTE

> [3] Woodberry does, however, show that Hawthorne was often unsociable. He emphasizes the seclusion of Hawthorne's mother, who separated herself from her family after the death of her husband, often even taking meals alone (28). Woodberry seems to imply that Mrs. Hawthorne's isolation rubbed off on her son.

List of Works Cited

A list of works cited is an alphabetical listing of the sources you cite in your essay. The list appears on a separate page at the end of your argument, after any notes, with the heading *Works Cited* centered an inch from the top of the page; don't underline or italicize it or enclose it in quotation marks. Double-space between the heading and the first entry, and double-space the entire list. (If you're asked to list everything you've read as background—not just the sources you cite—call the list *Works Consulted*.) The first line of each entry should align on the left; subsequent lines indent one-half inch or five spaces. See p. 568 for a sample Works Cited page.

BOOKS

The basic information for a book includes three elements, each followed by a period:

- the author's name, last name first
- the title and subtitle, underlined
- the publication information, including the city, a shortened form of the publisher's name (such as Harvard UP), and the date

For a book with multiple authors, only the first author's name is inverted.

1. One Author

Castle, Terry. Boss Ladies, Watch Out: Essays on Women, Sex, and Writing. New York: Routledge, 2002.

2. Two or More Authors

Appleby, Joyce, Lynn Hunt, and Margaret Jacob. Telling the Truth about History. New York: Norton, 1994.

3. Organization as Author

American Horticultural Society. The Fully Illustrated Plant-by-Plant Manual of Practical Techniques. New York: American Horticultural Society and DK Publishing, 1999.

4. Unknown Author

National Geographic Atlas of the World. New York: National Geographic, 1999.

5. Two or More Books by the Same Author

List the works alphabetically by title.

Lorde, Audre. A Burst of Light. Ithaca: Firebrand, 1988.

---. Sister Outsider. Trumansburg: Crossing, 1984.

6. Editor

Rorty, Amelie Oksenberg, ed. Essays on Aristotle's Poetics. Princeton: Princeton UP, 1992.

7. Author and Editor

Shakespeare, William. The Tempest. Ed. Frank Kermode. London: Routledge, 1994.

8. Selection in an Anthology or Chapter in an Edited Book

Brown, Paul. "'This thing of darkness I acknowledge mine': The Tempest and the Discourse of Colonialism." Political Shakespeare: Essays in Cultural Materialism. Ed. Jonathan Dillimore and Alan Sinfield. Ithaca: Cornell UP, 1985. 48-71.

9. Two or More Works from the Same Anthology

Gates, Henry Louis, Jr., and Nellie McKay, eds. The Norton Anthology of African American Literature. New York: Norton, 1997.

Neal, Larry. "The Black Arts Movement." Gates and McKay 1960-72.

Karenga, Maulana. "Black Art: Mute Matter Given Force and Function." Gates and McKay 1973-77.

10. Translation

Hietamies, Laila. Red Moon over White Sea. Trans. Borje Vahamaki. Beaverton, ON: Aspasia, 2000.

11. Edition Other Than the First

Lunsford, Andrea A., John J. Ruszkiewicz, and Keith Walters. Everything's an Argument. 4th ed. Boston: Bedford, 2007.

12. One Volume of a Multivolume Work

Byron, Lord George. Byron's Letters and Journals. Ed. Leslie A. Marchand. Vol. 2. London: J. Murray, 1973-82.

13. Two or More Volumes of a Multivolume Work

Byron, Lord George. Byron's Letters and Journals. Ed. Leslie A. Marchand. 12 vols. London: J. Murray, 1973-82.

14. Preface, Foreword, Introduction, or Afterword

Hymes, Dell. Foreword. Beyond Ebonics: Linguistic Pride and Racial Prejudice. By John Baugh. New York: Oxford, 2000. vii-viii.

15. Article in a Reference Work

Kettering, Alison McNeil. "Art Nouveau." World Book Encyclopedia. 2002 ed.

16. Book That Is Part of a Series

Moss, Beverly J. A Community Text Arises. Language and Social Processes Ser. 8. Cresskill: Hampton, 2003.

17. Republication

Scott, Walter. Kenilworth. 1821. New York: Dodd, 1996.

18. Government Document

United States. Cong. House Committee on the Judiciary. Impeachment of the President. 40th Cong., 1st sess. H. Rept. 7. Washington: GPO, 1867.

19. Pamphlet

An Answer to the President's Message to the Fiftieth Congress. Philadelphia: Manufacturer's Club of Philadelphia, 1887.

20. Published Proceedings of a Conference

Edwards, Ron, ed. Proceedings of the Third National Folklore Conference. Canberra, Austral.: Australian Folk Trust, 1988.

21. Title within a Title

Tauernier-Courbin, Jacqueline. Ernest Hemingway's A Moveable Feast: The Making of a Myth. Boston: Northeastern UP, 1991.

PERIODICALS

The basic entry for a periodical includes the following three elements, separated by periods:

- the author's name, last name first
- the article title, in quotation marks
- the publication information, including the periodical title (underlined), the volume and issue numbers (if any), the date of publication, and the page number(s)

For works with multiple authors, only the first author's name is inverted. Note that the period following the article title goes inside the closing quotation mark. Finally, note that the MLA omits *the* in titles such as *The New Yorker.*

22. Article in a Journal Paginated by Volume

Anderson, Virginia. "'The Perfect Enemy': Clinton, the Contradictions of Capitalism, and Slaying the Sin Within." Rhetoric Review 21 (2002): 384-400.

23. Article in a Journal Paginated by Issue

Radavich, David. "Man among Men: David Mamet's Homosocial Order." American Drama 1.1 (1991): 46-66.

24. Article That Skips Pages

Seabrook, John. "Renaissance Pears." New Yorker 5 Sept. 2005: 102+.

25. Article in a Monthly Magazine

Wallraff, Barbara. "Word Count." Atlantic Nov. 2002: 144-45.

26. Article in a Weekly Magazine

Reed, Julia. "Hope in the Ruins." Newsweek 12 Sept. 2005: 58-59.

27. Article in a Newspaper

Friend, Tim. "Scientists Map the Mouse Genome." USA Today 2 Dec. 2002: A1.

28. Editorial or Letter to Editor

Posner, Alan. "Colin Powell's Regret." Editorial. New York Times 9 Sept. 2005: A20.

29. Unsigned Article

"Court Rejects the Sale of Medical Marijuana." New York Times 26 Feb. 1998, late ed.: A21.

30. Review

Ali, Lorraine. "The Rap on Kanye." Rev. of Late Registration, by Kanye West. Newsweek 5 Sept. 2005: 72-73.

ELECTRONIC SOURCES

Most of the following models are based on the MLA's guidelines for citing electronic sources in the *MLA Handbook* (6th edition, 2003), as well as on up-to-date information available at <http://mla.org/>. The MLA requires that URLs be enclosed in angle brackets. Also, if a URL won't all fit on one line, it should be broken only after a slash. If a particular URL is extremely complicated, you can instead give the URL for the site's search page, if it exists, or for the site's homepage. The basic MLA entry for most electronic sources should include the following elements:

- name of the author, editor, or compiler
- title of the work, document, or posting
- information for print publication, if any
- information for electronic publication
- date of access
- URL in angle brackets

31. CD-ROM, Diskette, or Magnetic Tape, Single Issue

McPherson, James M., ed. The American Heritage New History of the Civil War. CD-ROM. New York: Viking, 1996.

32. Periodically Revised CD-ROM

Include the author's name; publication information for the print version of the text (including its title and date of publication); the title of the database; the medium (CD-ROM); the name of the company producing it; and the electronic publication date (month and year, if possible).

Heyman, Steven. "The Dangerously Exciting Client." Psychotherapy Patient 9.1 (1994): 37-46. PsycLIT. CD-ROM. SilverPlatter. Nov. 2006.

33. Multidisc CD-ROM

The 1998 Grolier Multimedia Encyclopedia. CD-ROM. 2 discs. Danbury: Grolier Interactive, 1998.

34. Article from Online Database or Subscription Service

"Bolivia: Elecciones Presidenciales de 2002." Political Database of the Americas. 1999. Georgetown U and Organization of Amer. States. 12 Nov. 2006 <http://www.georgetown.edu/pdba/Elecdta/Bolivia/pres02B.html>.

35. Document from a Professional Web Site

When possible, include the author's name; title of the document; print publication information; electronic publication information; date of access; and the URL.

"A History of Women's Writing." The Orlando Project: An Integrated History of Women's Writing in the British Isles. 2000. U of Alberta. 14 Mar. 2006 <http://www.ualberta.ca/ORLANDO/>.

36. Entire Web Site

Include the name of the person or group who created the site, if relevant; the title of the site (underlined) or (if there is no title) a description such as *Home page* (neither underlined nor italicized); the electronic publication date or last update, if available; the name of any institution or organization associated with the site; the date of access; and the URL.

Bowman, Laurel. Classical Myth: The Ancient Source. Dept. of Greek and Roman Studies, U of Victoria. 7 Mar. 2006 <http://web.uvic.ca/grs/bowman/myth>.

Mitten, Lisa. The Mascot Issue. 8 Apr. 2006. American Indian Library Assn. 12 Sept. 2002 <http://www.nativeculture.com/lisamitten/mascots.html>.

37. Course, Department, or Personal Web Site

Include the Web site's author; name of the site; description of site (such as *Course home page, Dept. home page,* or *Home page*—neither underlined nor italicized); dates for the course; date of publication or last update; name of academic department, if relevant; date of access; and the URL.

Lunsford, Andrea A. "Memory and Media." Course home page. Sept.-Dec. 2002. Dept. of English, Stanford U. 13 Mar. 2006 <http://www.stanford.edu/class/english12sc>.

Lunsford, Andrea A. Home page. 15 Mar. 2006 <http://www.stanford.edu/~lunsfor1/>.

38. Online Book

Begin with the name of the author—or, if only an editor, a compiler, or a translator is identified, the name of that person followed by *ed.*, *comp.*, or *trans.* (neither underlined nor italicized). Then give the title and the name of any editor, compiler, or translator not listed earlier, preceded by *Ed.*, *Comp.*, or *Trans.* (again, neither underlined nor italicized). If the online version of the text hasn't been published before, give the date of electronic publication and the name of any sponsoring institution or organization. Then give any publication information (city, publisher, and/or year) for the original print version that's given in the source; the date of access; and the URL.

Riis, Jacob A. How the Other Half Lives: Studies among the Tenements of New York. Ed. David Phillips. New York: Scribner's, 1890. 26 Mar. 1998 <http://www.cis.yale.edu/amstud/Inforev/riis/title.html>.

For a poem, essay, or other short work within an online book, include its title after the author's name. Give the URL of the short work, not of the book, if they differ.

Dickinson, Emily. "The Grass." Poems: Emily Dickinson. Boston: Roberts Brothers, 1891. Humanities Text Initiative American Verse Collection. Ed. Nancy Kushigian. 1995. U of Michigan. 9 Oct. 1997 <http://www.planet.net/pkrisxle/emily/poemsOnline.html>.

39. Article in an Online Periodical

Follow the formats for citing articles in print periodicals, but adapt them as necessary to the online medium. Include the page numbers of the article or the total number of pages, paragraphs, parts, or other numbered sections, if any; the date of access; and the URL.

Johnson, Eric. "The 10,000-Word Question: Using Images on the World-Wide Web." Kairos 4.1 (1999). 20 Mar. 2003 <http://english.ttu.edu/kairos/4.1/>.

Walsh, Joan. "The Ugly Truth about Republican Racial Politics." Salon 15 Dec. 2002. 3 Jan. 2003 <http://www.salon.com/politics/feature/2002/12/14/race/index_np.html>.

40. Posting to a Discussion Group

Begin with the author's name, the title of the posting, the description *Online posting* (neither underlined nor italicized), and the date of the posting. For a listserv posting, give the name of the listserv, the date of access, and either the URL of the listserv or (preferably) the URL of an archival version of the posting. If a URL is unavailable, give the email address of the list moderator. For a newsgroup posting, end with the date of access and the name of the newsgroup, in angle brackets.

"Web Publishing and Censorship." Online posting. 2 Feb. 1997. ACW: Alliance for Computers and Writing Discussion List. 10 Oct. 1997 <http://english.ttu.edu/acw-1/archive.htm>.

Martin, Jerry. "The IRA & Sinn Fein." Online posting. 31 Mar. 1998. 31 Mar. 1998 <news:soc.culture.irish>.

41. Work from an Online Subscription Service

For a work from an online service to which your library subscribes, list the information about the work, followed by the name of the service, the library, the date of access, and the URL.

"Breaking the Dieting Habit: Drug Therapy for Eating Disorders." <u>Psychology Today</u> Mar. 1995: 12+. Electric Lib. Green Lib., Stanford, CA. 30 Nov. 2002 <http://www.elibrary.com/>.

If you're citing an article from a subscription service to which you subscribe (such as AOL), use the following model:

Weeks, W. William. "Beyond the Ark." <u>Nature Conservancy</u>. Mar.-Apr. 1999. America Online. 30 Nov. 2002. Keyword: Ecology.

42. Email Message

Include the writer's name, the subject line, the description *E-mail to the author* or *E-mail to [the recipient's name]* (neither underlined nor italicized), and the date of the message.

Moller, Marilyn. "Seeing Crowns." E-mail to Beverly Moss. 3 Jan. 2003.

43. Synchronous Communication (MOO, MUD, or IRC)

Include the name of any specific speaker(s) you're citing; a description of the event; its date; the name of the forum; the date of access; and the URL of the posting (with the prefix *telnet:*) or (preferably) of an archival version.

Patuto, Jeremy, Simon Fennel, and James Goss. The Mytilene debate. 9 May 1996. MiamiMOO. 28 Mar. 1998 <http://moo.cas.muohio.edu>.

44. Online Interview, Work of Art, Radio Program, or Film

Follow the general guidelines for the print version of the source, but also include information on the electronic medium, such as publication information for a CD-ROM or the date of electronic publication, the date of access, and the URL for a Web site.

McGray, Douglas. Interview with Andrew Marshall. Wired. Feb. 2003. 17 Mar. 2003 <http://www.wired.com/wired/archive/11.02/marshall.html>.

Aleni, Giulio. K'un-yu t'u-shu. ca. 1620. Vatican, Rome. 28 Mar. 1998 <http://www.ncsa.uiuc.edu/SDG/Experimental/vatican.exhibit/exhibit/full-images/i-rome-to-china/china02.gif>.

Columbus, Chris, dir. Harry Potter and the Chamber of Secrets. 16 Dec. 2002 <http://movies.go.com/movies/H/harrypotterandthechamberofsecrets_2002/>.

45. FTP (File Transfer Protocol), Telnet, or Gopher Site

Substitute *FTP*, *telnet*, or *gopher* for *http* at the beginning of the URL.

Korn, Peter. "How Much Does Breast Cancer Really Cost?" Self Oct. 1994. 5 May 1997 <gopher://nysernet.org:70/00/BCTC/Sources/SELF/94/how-much>.

46. Computer Software or Video Game

The Sims 2. Redwood City: Electronic Arts, 2004.

Web Cache Illuminator. Vers. 4.02. 12 Nov. 2003 <http://www.tucows.com/adnload/332309_126245.html>.

OTHER SOURCES

47. Unpublished Dissertation

Fishman, Jenn. "'The Active Republic of Literature': Performance and Literary Culture in Britain, 1656-1790." Diss. Stanford U, 2003.

48. Published Dissertation

Baum, Bernard. Decentralization of Authority in a Bureaucracy. Diss. U of Chicago. Englewood Cliffs: Prentice, 1961.

49. Article from a Microform

Sharpe, Lora. "A Quilter's Tribute." Boston Globe 25 Mar. 1989: 13. NewsBank: Social Relations 12 (1989): fiche 6, grids B4-6.

50. Personal and Published Interview

Royster, Jacqueline Jones. Personal interview. 2 Feb. 2003.

Schorr, Daniel. Interview. Weekend Edition. Natl. Public Radio. KQED, San Francisco. 23 Dec. 2002.

51. Letter

Jacobs, Harriet. "Letter to Amy Post." 4 Apr. 1853. Incidents in the Life of a Slave Girl. Ed. Jean Fagan Yellin. Cambridge: Harvard UP, 1987. 234-35.

52. Film

The Lord of the Rings: The Two Towers. Dir. Peter Jackson. Perf. Elijah Wood, Ian McKellen. New Line Cinema, 2002.

53. Television or Radio Program

Box Office Bombshell: Marilyn Monroe. Narr. Peter Graves. Writ. Andy Thomas, Jeff Schefel, and Kevin Burns. Dir. Bill Harris. A&E Biography. Arts and Entertainment Network. 23 Oct. 2002.

54. Sound Recording

Black Rebel Motorcycle Club. "Howl." Red Int / Red Ink. 2005.

Massive Attack. "Future Proof." 100th Window. Virgin, 2003.

55. Work of Art or Photograph

Kahlo, Frida. Self-Portrait with Cropped Hair. 1940. Museum of Modern Art, New York.

56. Lecture or Speech

Steve Jobs. Baccalaureate Address. Stanford University. 18 June 2005.

57. Performance

Anything Goes. By Cole Porter. Perf. Klea Blackhurst. Shubert Theatre, New Haven. 7 Oct. 2003.

58. Map or Chart

The Political and Physical World. Map. Washington: Natl. Geographic, 1975.

59. Cartoon

Brodner, Steve. Cartoon. Nation 31 Mar. 2003: 2.

60. Advertisement

Chevy Avalanche. Advertisement. Time 14 Oct. 2002: 104.

On p. 567, note the formatting of the first page of a sample essay written in MLA style. On p. 568, you'll find a sample Works Cited page written for the same student essay.

Sample First Page for an Essay in MLA Style

Lesk 1

Emily Lesk

Professor Arraéz

Electric Rhetoric

15 November 2005

Red, White, and Everywhere

America, I have a confession to make: I don't drink Coke. But don't call me a hypocrite just because I am still the proud owner of a bright red shirt that advertises it. Just call me an American. Even before setting foot in Israel three years ago, I knew exactly where I could find one. The tiny T-shirt shop in the central block of Jerusalem's Ben Yehuda Street did offer other designs, but the one with a bright white "Drink Coca-Cola Classic" written in Hebrew cursive across the chest was what drew in most of the dollar-carrying tourists. While waiting almost twenty minutes for my shirt (depicted in Fig. 1), I watched nearly every customer ahead of me ask for "the Coke shirt, *todah rabah* [thank you very much]."

Fig. 1. *Hebrew Coca-Cola T-shirt.* Personal photograph. Despite my dislike for the beverage, I bought this Coca-Cola T-shirt in Israel.

At the time, I never thought it strange that I wanted one, too. After having absorbed sixteen years of Coca-Cola propaganda through everything from NBC's Saturday morning cartoon lineup to the concession stand at Camden Yards (the Baltimore Orioles' ballpark), I associated the shirt with singing along to the "Just for the Taste of It" jingle and with America's favorite pastime, not with a brown fizzy beverage I refused to consume. When I later realized the immensity of Coke's

Sample List of Works Cited for an Essay In MLA Style

Lesk 7

Works Cited

Coca-Cola Santa pin. Personal photograph by author. 9 Nov. 2002.

"The Fabulous Fifties." Beverage Industry 87.6 (1996): 16. 2 Nov. 2002 <http://memory.loc/gov.ammem/ccmphtml/indshst.html>.

"Haddon Sundblom." Coca-Cola and Christmas 1999. 2 Nov. 2002 <http://www.coca-cola.com.ar/Coca-colaweb/paginas_ingles/christmas.html>.

Hebrew Coca-Cola T-shirt. Personal photograph by author. 8 Nov. 2002.

Ikuta, Yasutoshi, ed. '50s American Magazine Ads. Tokyo: Graphic-Sha, 1987.

Library of Congress. Motion Picture, Broadcasting and Recorded Sound Division. 5 Nov. 2002 <http://memory.loc.gov/ammem/ccmphtml/index.html>.

Pendergrast, Mark. For God, Country, and Coca-Cola: The Unauthorized History of the Great American Soft Drink and the Company That Makes It. New York: Macmillan, 1993.

http://www.slate.com - Print - Mozilla Firefox

jurisprudence

How Do You Solve the Problem of Scalia?

The razor-thin line between obscenity and bad judgment.

By Dahlia Lithwick

Posted Thursday, March 30, 2006, at 6:21 PM ET

Leave it to Justice Antonin Scalia to trigger a nationwide debate about the hermeneutics of chin flips.

But first, a brief glance at the procedural history: It's undisputed that a newspaper reporter approached Scalia as he left a special Red Mass for lawyers and politicians at Boston's Cathedral of the Holy Cross. It's also not disputed that when the reporter, Laurel Sweet, asked what Scalia had to say to critics who question his impartiality in light of his Roman Catholic beliefs, he offered a familiar hand gesture, adding, "You know what I say to those people?" and, evidently by way of explanation, "That's Sicilian."

Where the parties differ is regarding the meaning of the gesture in question. The *Boston Herald* initially characterized it as "obscene." Supreme Court spokeswoman Kathy Arberg carefully described it, by contrast, as "a hand off the chin gesture that was meant to be dismissive," but not obscene.

The lower courts immediately issued conflicting opinions: Evidently in some jurisdictions, the chin flick "is a gesture of contempt, somewhat less rude than giving a person 'the finger.' When used in the United States, it usually means 'Bug off, I've had enough of you.' Not a polite gesture, but not a particularly hostile one, either," according to one blog. A concurrence by Wonkette (complete with an illustrated appendix) reached a similarly benign conclusion: "Justice Scalia's gesture wasn't a full-fledged flipping of the proverbial bird. But it still wasn't exactly the most polite of actions; in some quarters, it could be interpreted as pretty darn close to giving someone the middle finger." Dissenters disagreed, finding that the gesture, whether chin flip, finger, or otherwise, is improper. The "thought of flipping somebody off in church, minutes after receiving the Eucharist, is just, well, beyond shocking, insulting, infuriating."

Not Just Words

Like the article from *Slate.com* shown above, many online texts acknowledge their sources not with parenthetical citations or lists of references but with direct electronic links to the sources themselves. What are the implications of documenting sources in this nonverbal way? Links obviously make it much easier to check what a source actually says and the context in which it occurs. But is there a downside for the writer or the reader in not having the source's name appear within the text and a list of sources at the end? Might the colors and underlining used to indicate links distract the reader from the writer's point, or give unintended emphasis to the source relative to the writer's own ideas?

APA Style

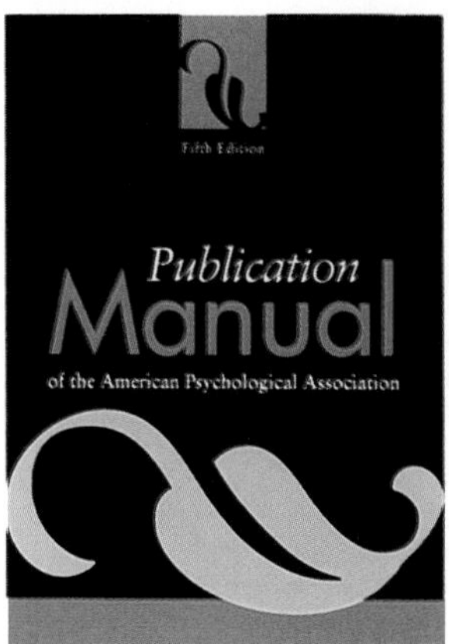

The 5th edition of the *Publication Manual of the American Psychological Association*

The Publication Manual of the American Psychological Association (5th edition, 2001) provides comprehensive advice to student and professional writers in the social sciences. Here we draw on the *Publication Manual*'s guidelines to provide an overview of APA style for in-text citations, content notes, and entries in the list of references.

In-Text Citations

APA style calls for in-text citations in the body of an argument to document sources of quotations, paraphrases, summaries, and so on. These in-text citations correspond to full bibliographic entries in the list of references at the end of the text.

1. Author Named in a Signal Phrase

Generally, use the author's name in a signal phrase to introduce the cited material, and place the date, in parentheses, immediately after the author's name. For a quotation, the page number, preceded by *p.* (neither underlined nor italicized), appears in parentheses after the quotation. For electronic texts or other works without page numbers, paragraph numbers may be used instead, preceded by the ¶ symbol or the abbreviation *para*. For a long, set-off quotation, position the page reference in parentheses two spaces after the punctuation at the end of the quotation.

According to Brandon (1993), Adefunmi opposed all forms of racism and believed that black nationalism should not be a destructive force.

As Toobin (2002) demonstrates, Joseph Lieberman unintentionally aided the Republican cause during most of 2002, playing into the hands of the administration and becoming increasingly unwilling "to question the President's motives, because he doesn't like visceral politics" (p. 43).

2. Author Named in Parentheses

When you don't mention the author in a signal phrase, give the name and the date, separated by a comma, in parentheses at the end of the cited material.

The Sopranos has achieved a much wider viewing audience than ever expected, spawning a cookbook and several serious scholarly studies (Franklin, 2002).

3. Two Authors

Use both names in all citations. Use *and* in a signal phrase, but use an ampersand (&) in parentheses.

Associated with purity and wisdom, Obatala is the creator of human beings, whom he is said to have formed out of clay (Edwards & Mason, 1985).

4. Three to Five Authors

List all the authors' names for the first reference. In subsequent references, use just the first author's name followed by *et al.* (in regular type, not underlined or italicized).

Lenhoff, Wang, Greenberg, and Bellugi (1997) cite tests that indicate that segments of the left brain hemisphere are not affected by Williams syndrome whereas the right hemisphere is significantly affected.

Shackelford (1999) drew on the study by Lenhoff et al. (1997).

5. Six or More Authors

Use only the first author's name and *et al.* (in regular type, not underlined or italicized) in every citation, including the first.

As Flower et al. (2003) demonstrate, reading and writing involve both cognitive and social processes.

6. Organization as Author

If the name of an organization or a corporation is long, spell it out the first time, followed by an abbreviation in brackets. In later citations, use the abbreviation only.

First Citation: (Federal Bureau of Investigation [FBI], 2002)

Subsequent Citations: (FBI, 2002)

7. Unknown Author

Use the title or its first few words in a signal phrase or in parentheses (in the example below, a book's title is italicized).

> The school profiles for the county substantiate this trend (*Guide to secondary schools,* 2003).

8. Authors with the Same Last Name

If your list of references includes works by different authors with the same last name, include the authors' initials in each citation.

> G. Jones (1998) conducted the groundbreaking study of retroviruses, whereas P. Jones (2000) replicated the initial trials two years later.

9. Two or More Sources in the Same Citation

List sources by the same author chronologically by publication year. List sources by different authors in alphabetical order by the authors' last names, separated by semicolons.

> While traditional forms of argument are warlike and agonistic, alternative models do exist (Foss & Foss, 1997; Makau, 1999).

10. Specific Parts of a Source

Use abbreviations (*chap.*, *p.*, and so on) in a parenthetical citation to name the part of a work you're citing.

> Pinker (2003, chap. 6) argued that his research yielded the opposite results.

11. Electronic World Wide Web Document

To cite a source found on the Web, use the author's name and date as you would for a print source, then indicate the chapter or figure of the document, as appropriate. If the source's publication date is unknown, use *n.d.* ("no date"). To document a quotation, include paragraph numbers if page numbers are unavailable. If a Web document has no page numbers, use paragraph numbers and a heading, if available.

> Werbach argued convincingly that "Despite the best efforts of legislators, lawyers, and computer programmers, spam has won. Spam is killing email" (2002, p. 1).

12. Email and Other Personal Communication

Cite any personal letters, email messages, electronic postings, telephone conversations, or personal interviews by giving the person's initial(s) and last name, the identification *personal communication,* and the date.

E. Ashdown (personal communication, March 9, 2003) supported these claims.

Content Notes

The APA recommends using content notes for material that will expand or supplement your argument but otherwise would interrupt the text. Indicate such notes in your text by inserting superscript numerals. Type the notes themselves on a separate page headed *Footnotes* (not underlined or italicized, or in quotation marks), centered at the top of the page. Double-space all entries. Indent the first line of each note five to seven spaces, and begin subsequent lines at the left margin.

TEXT WITH SUPERSCRIPT INDICATING A NOTE

Data related to children's preferences in books were instrumental in designing the questionnaire.[1]

NOTE

[1]Rudine Sims Bishop and members of the Reading Readiness Research Group provided helpful data.

List of References

The alphabetical list of sources cited in your text is called *References*. (If your instructor asks you to list everything you've read as background—not just the sources you cite—call the list *Bibliography*.) The list of references appears on a separate page or pages at the end of your paper, with the heading *References* (not underlined or italicized, or in quotation marks) centered one inch from the top of the page. Double-space after the heading, and begin your first entry. Double-space the entire list. For print sources, APA style specifies the treatment and placement of four basic elements—author, publication date, title, and publication information. Each element is followed by a period.

- *Author:* list all authors with last name first, and use only initials for first and middle names. Separate the names of multiple authors with commas, and use an ampersand (&) before the last author's name.

- *Publication date:* enclose the publication date in parentheses. Use only the year for books and journals; use the year, a comma, and the month or month and day for magazines. Do not abbreviate the month. Put a period after the parentheses.
- *Title:* italicize titles and subtitles of books and periodicals. Do not enclose titles of articles in quotation marks. For books and articles, capitalize only the first word of the title and subtitle and any proper nouns or proper adjectives. Capitalize all major words in a periodical title.
- *Publication information:* for a book, list the city of publication (and the country or postal abbreviation for the state if the city is unfamiliar) and the publisher's name, dropping *Inc.*, *Co.*, or *Publishers*. If the state is already included within the publisher's name, do not include the postal abbreviation for the state. For a periodical, follow the periodical title with a comma, the volume number (italicized), the issue number (if provided) in parentheses and followed by a comma, and the inclusive page numbers of the article. For newspaper articles and for articles or chapters in books, include the abbreviation *p.* ("page") or *pp.* ("pages").

The following APA-style examples appear in a "hanging indent" format, in which the first line aligns on the left and the subsequent lines indent one-half inch or five spaces.

BOOKS

1. One Author

Rheingold, H. (2002). *Smart mobs: The next social revolution.* Cambridge, MA: Perseus.

2. Two or More Authors

Steininger, M., Newell, J. D., & Garcia, L. (1984). *Ethical issues in psychology.* Homewood, IL: Dow Jones-Irwin.

3. Organization as Author

Use the word *Author* (neither underlined nor italicized) as the publisher when the organization is both the author and the publisher.

Linguistics Society of America. (2002). *Guidelines for using sign language interpreters.* Washington, DC: Author.

4. Unknown Author

National Geographic atlas of the world. (1999). Washington, DC: National Geographic Society.

5. Book Prepared by an Editor

Hardy, H. H. (Ed.). (1998). *The proper study of mankind.* New York: Farrar, Straus.

6. Selection in a Book with an Editor

Villanueva, V. (1999). An introduction to social scientific discussions on class. In A. Shepard, J. McMillan, & G. Tate (Eds.), *Coming to class: Pedagogy and the social class of teachers* (pp. 262-277). Portsmouth, NH: Heinemann.

7. Translation

Perez-Reverte, A. (2002). *The nautical chart* (M. S. Peaden, Trans.). New York: Harvest. (Original work published 2000)

8. Edition Other Than the First

Wrightsman, L. (1998). *Psychology and the legal system* (3rd ed.). Newbury Park, CA: Sage.

9. One Volume of a Multivolume Work

Will, J. S. (1921). *Protestantism in France* (Vol. 2). Toronto: University of Toronto Press.

10. Article in a Reference Work

Chernow, B., & Vattasi, G. (Eds.). (1993). Psychomimetic drug. In *The Columbia encyclopedia* (5th ed., p. 2238). New York: Columbia University Press.

If no author is listed, begin with the title.

11. Republication

Sharp, C. (1978). *History of Hartlepool.* Hartlepool, UK: Hartlepool Borough Council. (Original work published 1816)

12. Government Document

U.S. Bureau of the Census. (2001). *Survey of women-owned business enterprises.* Washington, DC: U.S. Government Printing Office.

13. Two or More Works by the Same Author

List the works in chronological order of publication. Repeat the author's name in each entry.

Rose, M. (1984). *Writer's block: The cognitive dimension.* Carbondale: Southern Illinois University Press.

Rose, M. (1995). *Possible lives: The promise of public education in America.* Boston: Houghton Mifflin.

PERIODICALS

14. Article in a Journal Paginated by Volume

Kirsch, G. E. (2002). Toward an engaged rhetoric of professional practice. *Journal of Advanced Composition, 22,* 414-423.

15. Article in a Journal Paginated by Issue

Carr, S. (2002). The circulation of Blair's *Lectures. Rhetoric Society Quarterly, 32*(4), 75-104.

16. Article in a Monthly Magazine

Dallek, R. (2002, December). The medical ordeals of JFK. *The Atlantic Monthly,* 49-64.

17. Article in a Newspaper

Nagourney, A. (2002, December 16). Gore rules out running in '04. *The New York Times,* pp. A1, A8.

18. Editorial or Letter to the Editor

Sonnenklar, M. (2002, January). Gaza revisited [Letter to the editor]. *Harper's,* p. 4.

19. Unsigned Article

Guidelines issued on assisted suicide. (1998, March 4). *The New York Times,* p. A15.

20. Review

Richardson, S. (1998, February). [Review of the book *The secret family*]. *Discover,* 88.

21. Published Interview

Shor, I. (1997). [Interview with A. Greenbaum]. *Writing on the Edge, 8*(2), 7-20.

22. Two or More Works by the Same Author in the Same Year

List two or more works by the same author published in the same year alphabetically by title (excluding *A*, *An*, or *The*), and place lowercase letters (*a*, *b*, etc.) after the dates.

Murray, F. B. (1983a). Equilibration as cognitive conflict. *Developmental Review, 3,* 54-61.

Murray, F. B. (1983b). Learning and development through social interaction. In L. Liben (Ed.), *Piaget and the foundations of knowledge* (pp. 176-201). Hillsdale, NJ: Erlbaum.

ELECTRONIC SOURCES

The following models are based on the APA's updated guidelines for citing electronic sources posted at the APA Web site <http://apa.org> as well as in the APA's *Publication Manual* (5th edition). The basic APA entry for most electronic sources should include the following elements:

- name of the author, editor, or compiler
- date of electronic publication or most recent update
- title of the work, document, or posting
- publication information, including the title, volume or issue number, and page numbers
- a retrieval statement that includes date of access, followed by a comma
- URL, with no angle brackets and no closing punctuation

23. World Wide Web Site

To cite a whole site, give the address in a parenthetical reference. To cite a document from a Web site, include information as you would for a print document, followed by a note on its retrieval.

American Psychological Association. (2000). DotComSense: Commonsense ways to protect your privacy and assess online mental health information. Retrieved January 25, 2002, from http://helping.apa.org/dotcomsense/

Mullins, B. (1995). Introduction to Robert Hass. Readings in contemporary poetry at Dia Center for the Arts. Retrieved April 24, 1999, from http://www.diacenter.org/prg/poetry/95-96/intrhass.html

24. Article from an Online Periodical

If the article also appears in a print journal, you don't need a retrieval statement; instead, include the label *[Electronic version]* after the article title. However, if the online article is a revision of the print document (if the format differs or page numbers aren't indicated), include the date of access and URL.

Steedman, M., & Jones, G. P. (2000). Information structure and the syntaxphonology interface [Electronic version]. *Linguistic Inquiry, 31,* 649-689.

Palmer, K. S. (2000, September 12). In academia, males under a microscope. *The Washington Post.* Retrieved October 23, 2002, from http://www.washingtonpost.com

25. Article or Abstract from a Database (Online or on CD-ROM)

Hayhoe, G. (2001). The long and winding road: Technology's future. *Technical Communication, 48*(2), 133-145. Retrieved September 22, 2002, from ProQuest database.

McCall, R. B. (1998). Science and the press: Like oil and water? *American Psychologist, 43*(2), 87-94. Abstract retrieved August 23, 2002, from PsycINFO database (1988-18263-001).

Pryor, T., & Wiederman, M. W. (1998). Personality features and expressed concerns of adolescents with eating disorders. *Adolescence, 33,* 291-301. Retrieved November 26, 2002, from Electric Library database.

26. Software or Computer Program

McAfee Office 2000. (Version 2.0) [Computer software]. (1999). Santa Clara, CA: Network Associates.

27. Online Government Document

Cite an online government document as you would a printed government work, adding the date of access and the URL. If you don't find a date, use *n.d.*

Finn, J. D. (1998, April). *Class size and students at risk: What is known? What is next?* Retrieved September 25, 2002, from United States Department of Education Web site http://www.ed.gov/pubs/ClassSize/title.html

28. FTP, Telnet, or Gopher Site

After the retrieval statement, give the address (substituting *ftp*, *telnet*, or *gopher* for *http* at the beginning of the URL) or the path followed to access information, with slashes to indicate menu selections.

Korn, P. (1994, October). How much does breast cancer really cost? *Self.* Retrieved May 5, 2002, from gopher://nysernet.org:70/00/BCIC/Sources/SELF/94/how-much

29. Posting to a Discussion Group

Include an online posting in the references list only if you're able to retrieve the message from a mailing list's archive. Provide the author's name; the date of posting, in parentheses; and the subject line from the posting. Include any information that further identifies the message in square brackets. For a listserv message, end with the retrieval statement, including the name of the list and the URL of the archived message.

Troike, R. C. (2001, June 21). Buttercups and primroses [Msg 8]. Message posted to the American Dialect Society's ADS-L electronic mailing list, archived at http://listserv.linguistlist.org/archives/ads-1.html

30. Newsgroup Posting

Include the author's name, the date and subject line of the posting, the access date, and the name of the newsgroup.

Wittenberg, E. (2001, July 11). Gender and the Internet [Msg 4]. Message posted to news://comp.edu.composition

31. Email Message or Synchronous Communication

Because the APA stresses that any sources cited in your list of references must be retrievable by your readers, you shouldn't include entries for email messages or synchronous communications (MOOs, MUDs); instead, cite these sources in your text as forms of personal communication (see p. 572). And remember that you shouldn't quote from other people's email without asking their permission to do so.

OTHER SOURCES

32. Technical or Research Reports and Working Papers

Wilson, K. S. (1986). *Palenque: An interactive multimedia optical disc prototype for children* (Working Paper No. 2). New York: Center for Children and Technology, Bank Street College of Education.

33. Unpublished Paper Presented at a Meeting or Symposium

Welch, K. (2002, March). *Electric rhetoric and screen literacy.* Paper presented at the meeting of the Conference on College Composition and Communication, Chicago.

34. Unpublished Dissertation

Barnett, T. (1997). *Communities in conflict: Composition, racial discourse, and the 60s revolution.* Unpublished doctoral dissertation, Ohio State University, Columbus.

35. Poster Session

Mensching, G. (2002, May). *A simple, effective one-shot for disinterested students.* Poster session presented at the National LOEX Library Instruction Conference, Ann Arbor, MI.

36. Film, Video, or DVD

Jackson, P. (Director). (2002). *The lord of the rings: The two towers.* [Film]. Los Angeles: New Line Cinema.

37. Television Program, Single Episode

Imperioli, M. (Writer), & Buscemi, S. (Director). (2002, October 20). Everybody hurts [Television series episode]. In D. Chase (Executive Producer), *The Sopranos.* New York: Home Box Office.

38. Sound Recording

Begin with the writer's name, followed by the date of copyright. Give the recording date at the end of the entry (in parentheses, after the period) if it's different from the copyright date.

Ivey, A., Jr., & Sall, R. (1995). Rollin' with my homies [Recorded by Coolio]. On *Clueless* [CD]. Hollywood, CA: Capitol Records.

RESPOND •

1. The MLA and APA styles differ in several important ways, both for in-text citations and for lists of sources. You've probably noticed a few: the APA lowercases most words in titles and lists the publication date right after the author's name, whereas the MLA capitalizes most words and puts the publication date at the end of the works cited entry. More interesting than the details, though, is the reasoning behind the differences. Placing the publication date near the front of a citation, for instance, reveals a special concern for that information in the APA style. Similarly, the MLA's decision to capitalize titles isn't arbitrary: that style is preferred in the humanities for a reason. Find as many consistent differences between the MLA and APA styles as you can. Then, for each difference, try to discover the reasons these groups organize or present information in that way. The MLA and APA style manuals themselves may be of help. You might also begin by determining which academic disciplines subscribe to the APA style and which to the MLA.
2. Working with another person in your class, look for examples of the following sources: an article in a journal, a book, a film, a song, and a TV show. Then make a references or works cited entry for each one, using either MLA or APA style.

PART 5

arguments

21
Who's the Fairest of Them All?

In our examination of body image, this chapter begins fittingly with a cartoon of a baby studying its reflection in a mirror as "It begins." Next, an op-ed (opinion-editorial) piece by Ellen Goodman, "The Culture of Thin Bites Fiji," and an excerpt from a research article by medical anthropologist and M.D. Anne E. Becker, "Television, Disordered Eating, and Young Women in Fiji," explore the arrival of American television programs on that island and its consequences for young women and their changing body image. Not only do younger Fijian women want to be thin, a rejection of traditional local notions of beauty, but they also have very specific reasons for wanting to be so. Jane Stern's review of Judith Moore's *Fat Girl: A True Story* and W. Charisse Goodman's essay, "One Picture Is Worth a Thousand Diets," consider how American culture does and does not deal with people, especially women, who are overweight—or "fat," as a growing number of activists among them wish to be called. Two selections examine Dove's "Real Women for Beauty" campaign. Rob Walker's "Social Lubricant: How a Marketing Campaign Became the Catalyst for a Societal Debate" considers arguments sparked by the campaign's choice of models, while Meghan Daum's commentary, "Those Unnerving Ads Using 'Real' Women," raises uncomfortable questions about why people might prefer picture-perfect models in advertisements. An example of the ad from the campaign lets you judge whether or not the women in Dove's ads look like those you encounter in your daily life and whether or not Daum might just be right. A complex graphic from the *New York Times*, "Reshaping America," provides information about the increasing popularity and costs of cosmetic surgical procedures for women *and men*. In "When Did Skivvies Get Rated NC-17?" Guy Trebay examines the eroticization of men's underwear and the male bodies that model, buy, and wear them. The chapter closes with three visual arguments about body image: Toby Old's photograph, "Orchard Beach, NY," Mikhaela Blake Reid's cartoon, "Your Yucky Body: A Repair Manual," and Jason Stirman's flyer for "Reflections: Body Image Seminar," sponsored by Crossroads Baptist Church.

Several decades ago, feminists hoped that our society would change its attitude toward women's bodies and become less obsessed with appearances. American society has indeed changed—as have others, often under the influence of ours. But rather than learning to accept our bodies and ourselves, women and men are encouraged in many ways to gaze into the mirror and be disappointed with what they see. Should we be worried?

This cartoon, by artist P. Byrnes, appeared in a March 2000 issue of the New Yorker. *As you study it, consider the argument we're making by using this cartoon to open the chapter about body image and the media.*

RESPOND.

1. Is the baby in this cartoon male or female? Why do you think so?
2. What is the "it" of "It begins"?
3. Why is this cartoon humorous? What knowledge about American culture does it assume?

▼ *Ellen Goodman, an award-winning columnist, writes regularly for the* Boston Globe, *where this article first appeared in May 1999, a few days after many newspapers had featured a news story about the effects of watching American TV on adolescent Fijian girls' self-image. Goodman's column generally appears on the op-ed pages of newspapers across the country. As you read, consider how she uses a discussion of a scientific study and the evidence it cites to make a claim about what she sees as a larger social problem. Keep in mind that Goodman is writing shortly after the shootings at Columbine High School in Colorado, where two male students killed and wounded a number of other students and teachers.*

The Culture of Thin Bites Fiji

ELLEN GOODMAN

First of all, imagine a place women greet one another at the market with open arms, loving smiles, and a cheerful exchange of ritual compliments:

"You look wonderful! You've put on weight!"

Does that sound like dialogue from Fat Fantasyland? Or a skit from fat-is-a-feminist-issue satire? Well, this Western fantasy was a South Pacific fact of life. In Fiji, before 1995, big was beautiful and bigger was more beautiful—and people really did flatter one another with exclamations about weight gain.

In this island paradise, food was not only love, it was a cultural imperative. Eating and overeating were rites of mutual hospitality. Everyone worried about losing weight—but not the way we do. "Going thin" was considered to be a sign of some social problem, a worrisome indication the person wasn't getting enough to eat.

5 The Fijians were, to be sure, a bit obsessed with food; they prescribed herbs to stimulate the appetite. They were a reverse image of our culture. And that turns out to be the point.

Something happened in 1995. A Western mirror was shoved into the face of the Fijians. Television came to the island. Suddenly, the girls of rural coastal villages were watching the girls of "Melrose Place" and "Beverly Hills 90210," not to mention "Seinfeld" and "E.R."

Within 38 months, the number of teenagers at risk for eating disorders more than doubled to 29 percent. The number of high school girls who vomited for weight control went up five times to 15 percent. Worse yet, 74 percent of the Fiji teens in the study said they felt "too big or fat" at least some of the time and 62 percent said they had dieted in the past month.

This before-and-after television portrait of a body image takeover was drawn by Anne Becker, an anthropologist and psychiatrist who directs research at the Harvard Eating Disorders Center. She presented her research at the American Psychiatric Association last week with all the usual caveats. No, you cannot prove a direct causal link between television and eating disorders. Heather Locklear doesn't cause anorexia. Nor does Tori Spelling cause bulimia.

Fiji is not just a Fat Paradise Lost. It's an economy in transition from subsistence agriculture to tourism and its entry into the global economy has threatened many old values.

10 Nevertheless, you don't get a much better lab experiment than this. In just 38 months, and with only one channel, a television-free culture that defined a fat person as robust has become a television culture that sees robust as, well, repulsive.

All that and these islanders didn't even get "Ally McBeal."

"Going thin" is no longer a social disease but the perceived requirement for getting a good job, nice clothes, and fancy cars. As Becker says carefully, "The acute and constant bombardment of certain images in the media are apparently quite influential in how teens experience their bodies."

Speaking of Fiji teenagers in a way that sounds all too familiar, she adds, "We have a set of vulnerable teens consuming television. There's a huge disparity between what they see on television and what they look like themselves—that goes not only to clothing, hairstyles, and skin color, but size of bodies."

In short, the sum of Western culture, the big success story of our entertainment industry, is our ability to export insecurity: We can make any woman anywhere feel perfectly rotten about her shape. At this rate, we owe the islanders at least one year of the ample lawyer Camryn Manheim in "The Practice" for free.

Calista Flockhart

15 I'm not surprised by research showing that eating disorders are a cultural byproduct. We've watched the female image shrink down to Calista Flockhart at the same time we've seen eating problems grow. But Hollywood hasn't been exactly eager to acknowledge the connection between image and illness.

Over the past few weeks since the Columbine High massacre, we've broken through some denial about violence as a teaching tool. It's pretty clear that boys are literally learning how to hate and harm others.

Maybe we ought to worry a little more about what girls learn: To hate and harm themselves.

Chapter 10 notes that causal arguments are often included as part of other arguments. Goodman's article reports on Anne Becker's research (an excerpt of which is reprinted in the following selection, beginning on page 592) to support a larger argument.

LINK TO P. 288

RESPOND •

1. What is Goodman's argument? How does she build it around Becker's study while not limiting herself to that evidence alone? (Consider, especially, paragraphs 15–17.)
2. What cultural knowledge does Goodman assume her *Boston Globe* audience to have? How does she use allusions to American TV programs to build her argument? Note, for example, that she sometimes uses such allusions as conversational asides—"All that and these islanders didn't even get 'Ally McBeal,' " and "At this rate, we owe the islanders at least one year of the ample lawyer Camryn Manheim in 'The Practice' for free"—to establish her ethos. In what other ways do allusions to TV programs contribute to Goodman's argument?

3. At least by implication, if not in fact, Goodman makes a causal argument about the entertainment industry, women's body image, and the consequences of such an image. What sort of causal argument does she set up? (For a discussion of causal arguments, see Chapter 10.) How effective do you find it? Why?
4. Many professors would find Goodman's conversational style inappropriate for most academic writing assignments. Choose several paragraphs of the text that contain information appropriate for an argumentative academic paper. Then **write a few well-developed paragraphs** on the topic. (Paragraphs 4–8 could be revised in this way, though you would put the information contained in these five paragraphs into only two or three longer paragraphs. Newspaper articles often feature shorter paragraphs, even paragraphs of a single sentence, that are generally inappropriate in academic writing.)

Anne E. Becker currently serves as assistant professor of medical anthropology and of psychiatry in the Department of Social Medicine at the Harvard Medical School, where she received her medical training and a doctorate in anthropology. The excerpts reprinted here, the "Abstract" section from the beginning of the article and the "Discussion" and "Conclusions" sections from the end of her article "Television, Disordered Eating, and Young Women in Fiji," originally appeared in 2004 in a special issue of the academic journal Culture, Medicine and Psychiatry *devoted to global eating disorders, which Dr. Becker edited. As you read, consider how writing for other researchers, as Becker has done, differs from writing about research for a popular audience, as Ellen Goodman did in the previous selection, "The Culture of Thin Bites Fiji."*

Television, Disordered Eating, and Young Women in Fiji: Negotiating Body Image and Identity During Rapid Social Change

ANNE E. BECKER

ABSTRACT. Although the relationship between media exposure and risk behavior among youth is established at a population level, the specific psychological and social mechanisms mediating the adverse effects of media on youth remain poorly understood. This study reports on an investigation of the impact of the introduction of television to a rural community in Western Fiji on adolescent ethnic Fijian girls in a setting of rapid social and economic change. Narrative data were collected from 30 purposively selected ethnic Fijian secondary school girls via semi-structured, open-ended interviews. Interviews were conducted in 1998, 3 years after television was first broadcast to this region of Fiji. Narrative data were analyzed for content relating to response to television and mechanisms that mediate self and body image in Fijian adolescents. Data in this sample suggest that media imagery is used in both creative and destructive ways by adolescent Fijian girls to navigate opportunities and conflicts posed by the rapidly changing social environment. Study respondents indicated their explicit modeling of the perceived positive attributes of characters presented in television dramas, but also the beginnings of weight and body shape preoccupation, purging behavior to control weight, and body disparagement°. Response to television appeared to be shaped by a desire for competitive social positioning during a period of rapid social transition. Understanding vulnerability to images and values imported with media will be critical to preventing disordered eating and, potentially, other youth risk behaviors in this population, as well as other populations at risk.

disparagement: the act of speaking about something in a negative way.

KEY WORDS: body image, eating disorders, Fiji, modernization

DISCUSSION

Minimally, and at the most superficial level, narrative data reflect a shift in fashion among the adolescent ethnic Fijian population studied. A shift in aesthetic ideals is remarkable in and of itself given the numerous social mechanisms that have long supported the preference for large bodies. Moreover, this change reflects a disruption of both apparently stable traditional preference for a robust body shape and the traditional disinterest in reshaping the body (Becker 1995).

Subjects' responses to television in this study also reflect a more complicated reshaping of personal and cultural identities inherent in their endeavors to reshape their bodies. Traditionally for Fijians, identity had been fixed not so much in the body as in family, community, and relationships with others, in contrast to Western-cultural models that firmly fix identity in the body/self. Comparatively speaking, social identity is manipulated and projected through personal, visual props in many Western social contexts, whereas this was less true in Fiji. Instead, Fijians have traditionally invested themselves in nurturing others—efforts that are then concretized in the bodies that one cares for and feeds. Hence, identity is represented (and experienced) individually and collectively through the well-fed bodies of others, not through one's own body (again, comparatively speaking) (Becker 1995). In addition, since Fiji's economy has until recently been based in subsistence agriculture, and since multiple cultural practices encourage distribution of material resources, traditional Fijian identity has also not been represented through the ability to purchase and accumulate material goods.

More broadly than interest in body shape, however, the qualitative data demonstrate a rather concrete identification with television characters as role models of successful engagement in Western, consumeristic lifestyles. Admiration and emulation of television characters appears to stem from recognition that traditional channels are ill-equipped to assist Fijian adolescents in navigating the landscape of rapid social change in Fiji.

syntonic: emotionally responsive to one's environment.

Unfortunately, while affording an opportunity to develop identities syntonic° with the shifting social context, the behavioral modeling on Western appearance and customs appears to have undercut traditional cultural resources for identity-making (Becker et al. 2002). Specifically, narrative data reveal here that traditional sources of information about self-presentation and public comportment have been supplanted by captivating and convincing role models depicted in televised programming and commercials.

5 It is noteworthy that the interest in reshaping the body differs in subtle but important ways from the drive for thinness observed in other social contexts. The discourse on reshaping the body is, indeed, quite explicitly and pragmatically focused on competitive social positioning—for both employment opportunities and peer approval. This discourse on weight and body shape is suffused with moral as well as material associations (i.e., that appear to be commentary on the social body). That is, repeatedly expressed sentiment that excessive weight results in laziness and undermines domestic productivity may reflect a concern about how Fijians will "measure up" in the global economy. The juxtaposition of extreme affluence depicted on most television programs against the materially impoverished Fijians associates the nearly uniformly thin bodies and restrained appetites of television characters with the (illusory) promise of economic opportunity and success. Each child's future, as well as the fitness of the social body, seems to be at stake.

nosologic: relating to diseases.

In this sense, disordered eating among the Fijian schoolgirls in this study appears to be primarily an instrumental means of reshaping body and identity to enhance social and economic opportunities. From this perspective, it may be premature to comment on whether or not disordered eating behaviors share the same meaning as similar behaviors in other cultural contexts. It is also premature to say whether these behaviors correspond well to Western nosologic° categories describing eating disorders. Regardless of any differences in psychological significance of the behaviors, however, physiologic risks will be the same. Quite possibly—and this remains to be studied in further detail—disordered eating may also be a symbolic embodiment of the anxiety and conflict the youth experience on the threshold of rapid social change in Fiji and during their personal and collective navigation through it. Moreover, there is some preliminary evidence that the disordered eating is accompanied by clinical features associated with the illnesses elsewhere and eating disorders may be emerging in this context. Finally, television has certainly imported more than just images associating appearance with material success; it has arguably enhanced reflexivity about the possibility of reshaping one's body and life trajectory and popularized the notion of competitive social positioning.

The impact of imported media in societies undergoing transition on local values has been demonstrated in multiple societies (e.g., Cheung and Chan 1996; Granzberg 1985; Miller 1998; Reis 1998; Tan et al. 1987; Wu 1990). As others have argued in other contexts, ideas from imported media can be used to negotiate "hybrid identities" (Barker 1997) and otherwise incorporated into various strategies for social positioning (Mazzarella 2003) and coping with modernization (Varan 1998). Likewise and ironically, here as elsewhere in the world (see Anderson-Fye 2004), Fijian youth must craft an identity which adopts Western values about productivity and efficiency in the workplace while simultaneously selling their Fijian-ness (an essential asset to their role in the tourist industry). Self-presentation is thus carefully constructed so as to bridge and integrate dual identities. That these identities are not consistently smoothly fused is evidenced in the ambivalence in the narratives about how thin a body is actually ideal.

Becker uses survey and interview data to support her argument about eating disorders in Fiji. Chapter 4 offers other examples of "hard evidence" used in arguments based on fact.

LINK TO PP. 81

The source of the emerging disordered eating among ethnic Fijian girls thus appears multifactorial and multidetermined. Media images that associate thinness with material success and marketing that promotes the possibility of reshaping the body have supported a perceived nexus° between diligence (work on the body), appearance (thinness), and social and material success (material possessions, economic opportunities, and popularity with peers). Fijian self-presentation has absorbed new dimensions related to buying into Western styles of appearance and the ethos of work on the body. A less articulated parallel to admiration for characters, bodies, and lifestyles portrayed on imported television is the demoralizing perception of not comparing favorably as a population. It is as though a mirror was held up to these girls in which they perhaps saw themselves as poor and overweight. The eagerness they express in grooming themselves to be hard workers or perhaps obtain competitive jobs perhaps reflects their collective energy and anxiety about how they, as individuals, and as a Fijian people, are going to fare in a globalizing world. Thus preoccupation with weight loss and the restrictive eating and purging certainly reflect pragmatic strategies to optimize social and economic success. At the same time, they surely contribute to body- and self-disparagement and reflect an embodied distress about the uncertainty of personal future and the social body.

nexus: a point of convergence or intersection.

Epidemiologic data° from other populations confirm an association between social transition (e.g., transnational migration, modernization, urbanization) and disordered eating among vulnerable groups (Anderson-Fye and

epidemiologic data: data, likely quantitative, concerning the cause, spread, and control of diseases.

Becker 2003). In particular, the association between upward mobility and disordered eating across diverse populations has relevance here (Anderson-Fye 2000; Buchan and Gregory 1984; Silber 1986; Soomro et al. 1995; Yates 1989). Exposure to Western media images and ideas may further contribute to disordered eating by first promoting comparisons that result in perceived economic and social disadvantage and then promoting the notion that efforts to reshape the body will enhance social status. It can be argued that girls and young women undergoing social transition may perceive that social status is enhanced by positioning oneself competitively through the informed use of cultural symbols—e.g., by bodily appearance and thinness (Becker and Hamburg 1996). This is comparable to observations that children of immigrants to the U.S. (for whom the usual parental "map of experience" is lacking) substitute alternative "cultural guides" from the media as resources for negotiating successful social strategies (Suarez-Orozco and Suarez-Orozco 2001). In both scenarios, adolescent girls and young women assimilating to new cultural standards encounter a ready cultural script for comportment and appearance in the media.

Conclusions

> "I've wondered how television is made and how the actress and actors, I always wondered how television, how people acted on it, and I'm kind of wondering whether it's true or not." (S-48)

10 The increased prevalence of disordered eating in ethnic Fijian schoolgirls is not the only story—or even the most important one—that can be pieced together from the respondents' narratives on television and its impact.[1] Nor are images and values transmitted through televised media singular forces in the chain of events that has led to an apparent increase in disordered eating attitudes and behaviors. The impact of media coupled with other sweeping economic and social change is likely to affect Fijian youth and adults in many ways. On the other hand, this particular story allows a window into the powerful impact and vulnerability of this adolescent female population. This story also allows a frame for exploring resilience and suggesting interventions for future research.

In some important ways, Fiji is a unique context for investigating the impact of media imagery on adolescents. In Fiji in particular, the evolving and multiple—and potentially overlapping or dissonant—social terrain presents novel challenges and opportunities for adolescents navigating their way in the absence of guidance from "conventional" wisdom and social hierarchies that may have grown obsolete in some respects. Doubtless the profound ways in which adolescent girls are influenced by media imagery extend beyond the borders of Fiji and the ways in which young women in Fiji consume and reflect on televised media may suggest mechanisms for its impact on youth in other social contexts. This study, therefore, allows insight into the ways in which social change intersects with the developmental tasks of adolescence to pose the risk of eating disorders and other youth risk behaviors.

Adolescent girls and young women in this and other indigenous, small-scale societies may also be especially vulnerable to the effects of media exposure for several key reasons. For example, in the context of rapid social change, these girls and young women may lack traditional role models for how to successfully maneuver in a shifting economic and political environment. Moreover, in societies in which status is traditionally ascribed° rather than achieved,° girls and women may feel more compelled to secure their social position through a mastery of self-presentation that draws heavily from imported media. It is a logical and frightening conclusion that vulnerable girls and women across diverse populations who feel marginalized from the locally dominant culture's sources of prestige and status may anchor their identities in widely recognized cultural symbols of prestige popularized by media-imported ideas, values, and images. Further, these girls and women have no reference for comparison of the televised images to the "realities" they portray and thus to critique and deconstruct the images they see compared with girls and women who are "socialized" into a culture of viewership. Without thoughtful interventions[2]—yet to be explored with the affected communities—the unfortunate outcome is likely to be continued increasing rates of disordered eating and other youth risk behaviors in vulnerable populations undergoing rapid modernization and social transition.

ascribed status: status that one is granted by others, often on the basis of external qualities (for example, being a firstborn son in a society that values male children and pays attention to birth order).

achieved status: status that one somehow wins or attains (example, placing first in a competition).

Notes

1. For example, the increased incidence of suicide and other self-injury in Fiji (Pridmore et al. 1995) may index social distress related to rapid social change.
2. Prevention efforts that might be useful include psychoeducational information about the psychological and medical risks associated with bingeing, purging, and self-starvation as well as media literacy programs that assist youth in critical and informed viewing of televised programming and commercials.

References

Anderson-Fye, E.P.
2000 Self-Reported Eating Attitudes Among High School Girls in Belize: A Quantitative Survey. Unpublished Qualifying Paper. Department of Human Development and Psychology, Harvard University, Cambridge, MA.

Anderson-Fye, E.
2004 A "Coca-Cola" Shape: Cultural Change, Body Image, and Eating Disorders in San Andrés, Belize. Culture, Medicine and Society 28: 561–595.

Anderson-Fye, E., and A.E. Becker
2004 Socio-Cultural Aspects of Eating Disorders. *In* Handbook of Eating Disorders and Obesity. J.K. Thompson, ed., pp. 565–589. Wiley.

Barker, C.
1997 Television and the Reflexive Project of the Self: Soaps, Teenage Talk and Hybrid Identities. British Journal of Sociology 48: 611–628.

Becker, A.E.
1995 Body, Self, Society: The View from Fiji. Philadelphia: University of Pennsylvania Press.

Becker, A.E., and P. Hamburg
1996 Culture, the Media, and Eating Disorders. Harvard Review of Psychiatry 4: 163–167.

Becker, A.E., R.A. Burwell, S.E. Gilman, D.B. Herzog, and P. Hamburg
2002 Eating Behaviors and Attitudes Following Prolonged Television Exposure Among Ethnic Fijian Adolescent Girls. The British Journal of Psychiatry 180: 509–514.

Buchan, T., and L.D. Gregory
1984 Anorexia Nervosa in a Black Zimbabwean. British Journal of Psychiatry 145: 326–330.

Cheung, C.K., and C.F. Chan
1996 Television Viewing and Mean World Value in Hong Kong's Adolescents. Social Behavior and Personality 24: 351–364.

Granzberg, G.
1985 Television and Self-Concept Formation in Developing Areas. Journal of Cross-Cultural Psychology 16: 313–328.

Mazzarella, W.
2003 Shoveling Smoke: Advertising and Globalization in Contemporary India. Durham, NC: Duke University Press.

Miller, C.J.
1998 The Social Impacts of Televised Media Among the Yucatec Maya. Human Organization. 57: 307–314.

Pridmore, S., K. Ryan, and L. Blizzard
1995 Victims of Violence in Fiji. Australian and New Zealand Journal of Psychiatry 29: 666–670.

Reis R.
1998 The Impact of Television Viewing in the Brazilian Amazon. Human Organization 57: 300–306.
Silber, T.J.
1986 Anorexia Nervosa in Blacks and Hispanics. International Journal of Eating Disorders 5: 121–128.
Soomro, G.M., A.H. Crisp, D. Lynch, D. Tran, and N. Joughin
1995 Anorexia Nervosa in 'Non-White' Populations. British Journal of Psychiatry 167: 385–389.
Suarez-Orozco, C., and M.M. Suarez-Orozco
2001 Children of Immigration. Cambridge, MA: Harvard University Press.
Tan, A.S., G.K. Tan, and A.S. Tan
1987 American TV in the Philippines: A Test of Cultural Impact. Journalism Quarterly 64: 65–72, 144.
Varan, D.
1998 The Cultural Erosion Metaphor and the Transcultural Impact of Media Systems. Journal of Communication 48: 58–85.
Wu. Y.K.
1990 Television and the Value Systems of Taiwan's Adolescents: A Cultivation Analysis. Dissertation Abstracts International 50: 3783A.
Yates, A.
1989 Current Perspectives on the Eating Disorders: I. History, Psychological and Biological Aspects. Journal of the American Academy of Child and Adolescent Psychiatry 28(6): 813–828.

RESPOND •

1. How does Becker link exposure to Western media to the changing notions young Fijian women have of their own bodies? Why, specifically, does Becker claim these women now want to be thin? How are these changes linked to other social changes occurring in Fiji, to adolescence, and to gender, especially in small-scale societies?
2. As Becker notes, she relies on qualitative data—specifically, interview data—to support her arguments. Why are such data especially appropriate, given her goals of understanding the changing social meanings of body image for young Fijian women as part of other rapid social changes taking place in Fiji? (For a discussion of firsthand evidence, see Chapter 16.)
3. Throughout the Discussion and Conclusions sections, Becker repeatedly qualifies her arguments to discourage readers from extending them further than she believes her data warrant. Find two cases

where she does so, and explain in what specific ways she reminds readers of the limits of her claims. (For a discussion on qualifying claims and arguments, see Chapter 6.)

4. These excerpts from Becker's article obviously represent research writing for an academic audience. What functions does each of the reprinted sections serve for the article's readers, and why is each located where it is? Why, for example, is an abstract placed at the beginning of an article? Why are keywords a valuable part of an abstract?
5. In paragraph 3, in the "Discussion" section of her article, Becker compares and contrasts how Westerners (which would include Americans) and Fijians understand identity, especially as it relates to the body. **Write an essay** in which you evaluate Becker's characterization of Western notions of identity. Unless you have detailed knowledge of a culture very different from Western cultures—Fiji, for example—you may want to begin by trying to demonstrate that Becker's assessment is correct, at least to some degree, rather than claiming that she misunderstands the West. Once you've conceded that there's at least some truth in her assessment, you may be able to cite cases of American subcultures that don't "firmly fix identity in the body/self."

▼ *Jane Stern's review of Judith Moore's autobiographical account,* Fat Girl: A True Story, *appeared in the* New York Times Book Review *in March 2005. The* Review *is a weekly section of the Sunday* New York Times *devoted entirely to book reviews. Stern is the author of* Ambulance Girl *(2003) and, with her husband, Michael, numerous books about American cuisine and culture. She and Michael have won the James Beard Award three times for their column in* Gourmet, "Roadfood," *which provides details about good local food that can be found across America. Their Web site is* <*http:// roadfood.com*>. *As you read, consider how book reviews serve as evaluative arguments.*

Big

Fat Girl: A True Story by Judith Moore

JANE STERN

JUDITH MOORE'S book just might be the Stonewall° for a slew of oversize people who do not fit the template of what every ostensible expert on beauty, health and nutrition tells us we should strive to be. *Fat Girl* is brilliant and angry and unsettling.

Moore is a fat woman who decades ago was a fat girl. This is the story of how throughout her life and to the present day, her weight has made her a large, slow target for other people's prejudices. But Moore is neither a whiner nor a victim. She does not poor-me the reader with weepy confessions or beg for a pat on the head from all the slim, pretty people who have mocked or pitied her.

Moore's welcome to this book acknowledges the pitfalls into which true confessionals all too often fall. As she puts it: "Narrators of first-person claptrap like this often greet the reader at the door with moist hugs and complaisant kisses. I won't. I will not endear myself. I won't put on airs. I am not that pleasant. The older I get the less pleasant I am."

Like most fat people in America, Moore is a veteran of every diet and exercise plan around. "I know so many diets. The pineapple and watermelon diet I stayed on for 10 days. I did the seven-oranges-per-day diet. I did the rice diet. . . . I did canned diet drinks. . . . I did water-packed tuna and asparagus diets. I do three-day juice fasts." She has put in time dancing around her apartment watching the Richard Simmons videotape "Sweatin' to the Oldies." Despite all the calorie counting and exercise, Moore remains a fat person. "My flesh resists loss. My fat holds on for dear life, holds on under my bratwurst arms and between my clabber° thighs."

"My flesh resists loss. My fat holds on for dear life, holds on under my bratwurst arms and between my clabber thighs."

5 *Fat Girl* is not a book about the author trying to get thin. It is the story about a family, a miserable one, that created a hole in Moore's soul that she tried to fill with food. "I will tell the story of my family and the food we ate. We were an unhappy family. . . . Everybody was pretty much in it for themselves. We were hard American isolatos. We were solitaries. Unhappy families, though, still have to eat. For my father and for me, who are this story's primary fatsos, food was the source of some of our greatest pleasure and most terrible pain."

The author's father was a fat man whom everyone called Ham (short for Hamilton). Ham was 6 feet 4 and "at his fattest he must have weighed 300 pounds": "My father could have been mistaken for Charles Laughton° or

Stonewall: a bar in Greenwich Village, New York City, outside which riots occurred in June 1969 following a police raid; these riots are often considered the birth of the gay rights movement in the United States.

clabber: milk that has curdled naturally.

◀ ***Charles Laughton, 1935:*** Academy Award–winning actor (1889–1962).

Whittaker Chambers° or Harold Bloom.° He had the same outsized morose face as those guys and he had the heavy stomach that hung, in rolls, from his breasts."

Food figured into the hellish marriage of Moore's parents from the day she was born: "At the moment I entered the world my father was across the street from the delivery room at a delicatessen run by Germans. He was eating Muenster and headcheese and bratwurst and long pale strands of fresh kraut. When he leaned over to kiss my worn-out, weary mother, she tasted garlic and sour pickle and cabbage on his lips. She would never forget this, never forgive it."

Ham was eventually tossed out of the house by his wife when Moore was nearly 4. Without her father's sturdy presence, Moore was shuttled back and forth between her maternal grandmother, who lived on a farm in Arkansas, and her mother's apartment in Brooklyn. About the time spent with her grandmother there are no comfy memories: "She hated my father. She minced no words. My father was my 'no-good, spoiled, rich-kid father.' I was 'his spitting image.'"

Moore's meals at Grammy's farm were both splendid and lethal: "She fed us bacon and eggs, sausage patties, strawberry jam, butter-soaked hot biscuits, molasses-sopped flapjacks, fried chicken, baked hams, thick pork chops, puffy dumplings, potato pancakes, homemade egg noodles, mashed potatoes, apple and cherry ples and three-layer coconut cakes and huckleberry and peach and boysenberry cobblers, crisp gingerbread cookies, Kadota figs afloat in clotted cream, cows' thick milk and the butter she churned from that milk." Fed like a Strasbourg goose, Moore grew large; and she remembers her grandmother's withering comments about her size. "I grew 'big,' Grammy said, 'as Man Mountain Dean.'" Dean, a popular professional wrestler, was unknown to Moore. "I never knew who Man Mountain Dean was. I assumed that he was a monster who opened his vast gutted mouth so wide that it ached and then ran down mountains, and while he ran he ate every tree, every house, every horse, cow, mother hog and piggies, boar and goat and sheep and bleating lamb that got in his way." In the eyes of her unloving family, Moore was turning into a golem.°

◀ ***Whittaker Chambers, 1950:*** American writer (1901–1969) likely best known for his testimony against Alger Hiss (1904–1996), a U.S. State Department official accused of being a Communist and a spy for the Soviet Union. Chambers was posthumously awarded the Presidential Medal of Freedom in 1984 by then- President Ronald Reagan.

▲ ***Harold Bloom, 2004:*** American literary critic (1930–) who holds chairs at Yale University and New York University.

golem: in Jewish folklore, an artificially fashioned figure from a substance like clay that came to life. In Biblical Hebrew, the term refers to an incomplete or embryonic substance. In Yiddish, it is a slang term for someone who is clumsy.

10 Anyone who grew up fat (and please include your reviewer in this group) will find himself in the chapters that follow. In all the books about weight and the effects it has on the psyche and the impossibility of ridding oneself of it, there has never been a book like *Fat Girl* that lays it all out with such take-no-prisoners prose. Much of it is not pretty. We learn how it feels to wear clothes that don't fit, sweat too much, smell bad, become winded walking up stairs and be unable to do the simple things of childhood, like a somersault. There are so many things that thin children take for granted, such as being lifted up effortlessly on the shoulders of their fathers.

And as Moore grew up, things got even more dire. One man bluntly told her she was too fat to go to bed with. In college a man who Moore thought was sensitive and kind conned her into performing oral sex on him while his friends watched and laughed. A day at the pool turned ugly when a mean boy loudly said, "Old Fatso is going to break the diving board."

Fat Girl is not a litany of complaints. Moore carves out a rather good life for herself. She married (twice), had children and became a writer who was awarded a Guggenheim fellowship. For those of us who have lived this same life to one degree or another, this book should be a rallying cry. We are mad as hell and we are not going to take it anymore. But take it, unfortunately, we do, and we will continue to, as the "obesity epidemic" receives endless press and fat haters coast under the radar as do-gooders.

One last thing I must say about this book. For a writer of Moore's talent, *Fat Girl* has been published to appear second-rate. Its sloppy editing and uninteresting jacket design look like something you would pawn off on a fat girl, no matter what her age. Moore and her audience deserve better.

As a book review, this piece is inherently a rhetorical analysis. Stern evaluates the argument put forth by Moore and recommends it to her audience. Chapter 5 lays out the key elements and considerations involved in reading and writing a rhetorical analysis.

LINK TO P. 102

RESPOND •

1. What functions might you expect a book review like Stern's to serve? How are reviews arguments? What sorts of evaluative criteria does Stern use in reviewing Moore's book? How appropriate are they? Does the accompanying illustration contribute to the review? Why or why not?
2. How effectively does Stern use quotations from Moore's book? How would quotations, especially in a book review, both tell and show something about the book being reviewed? Choose two quotations, and explain how Stern uses them as part of her evaluative argument.
3. How does Stern characterize Moore's ethos? How does Stern create her own ethos as a writer and reviewer? How would you characterize her ethos?
4. Using the information in Chapter 9, **write an essay** in which you evaluate Stern's review of Moore's book. In other words, begin by formulating criteria for evaluating a review and then apply them to this review.

One Picture Is Worth a Thousand Diets

W. CHARISSE GOODMAN

As the title of W. Charisse Goodman's 1995 book, **The Invisible Woman: Confronting Weight Prejudice in America,** *implies, her thesis is that American society tolerates and even encourages prejudice against people, especially women, who are not thin. The chapter excerpted here, "One Picture Is Worth a Thousand Diets," focuses on the ways in which the media render invisible or treat with disdain women whom Goodman refers to as "large."*

> Loyalty to petrified opinions never yet broke a chain or freed a human soul in *this* world—and never *will*. –Mark Twain

In our consumption-addled culture, the mass media encourage us to absorb as many goods as possible far beyond the saturation point. We are urged to buy things we don't really need and luxuries we may not be able to afford. Not only is more better, but we are advised that it will make us sexier or more successful. But this rule has one notable exception; if a woman is perceived as having consumed too much food, she finds she has committed a social crime. By projecting the image of gluttony onto the large woman exclusively, our society can deny and rationalize its colossal overindulgence in the cult of conspicuous consumption. Greed, after all, is hardly restricted to a preoccupation with food. Movies, television, magazines, newspapers, and preachifying self-help books all reinforce and amplify the ignorant stereotypes about fat people that America holds so close and dear; taken together, they constitute a framework of "petrified opinions" which few dare to question.

A survey of merely eleven mainstream magazines, including *Vogue, Redbook, Time, McCall's,* even *Audubon* and *Modern Maturity,* turned up an astounding 645 pictures of thin women as opposed to 11 of heavy women. Scrutinizing the local newspapers over a period of several weeks left me with a body count of 221 thin women as opposed to nine large women; newspaper advertising inserts added another 288 pictures of individual thin women and approximately a dozen heavy women (most of whom were pictured in a single store flyer for large-size clothing). An examination of almost 160 commercials—after that point, it was either stop or incinerate the TV set—contributed 120 ads featuring thin women exclusively, 27 ads depicting heavy males, mostly in a normal or positive light, and all of 12 heavy women, half of whom, interestingly, were either African-American, older, or both. Of ads including fat women, one offered an evil old cartoon witch, another pictured two big women dressed as opera-singer Valkyrie types, and a third depicted *Alice in Wonderland*'s mean-tempered Red Queen. A . . . series of commercials for Snapple soft drinks featured a fairly heavy woman who read complimentary letters from consumers of the product; however, in most of the

Newspaper classified ads or TV commercials can be rich sources of evidence for many kinds of arguments that deal with current cultural or social issues. See Chapter 16 for suggestions about other types of firsthand evidence.

LINK TO P. 472

commercials this woman is visible only from the shoulders up, while the rest of her body is hidden by a very high counter. Ultimately, the burden of proof in this respect was no more than a counting exercise.

After drowning in an ocean of slender female figures everywhere I looked, it was easy to see how women are persuaded that thinness equals happiness and fulfillment. The women of the media are not only overwhelmingly small but also smiling, self-satisfied, exciting, dynamic, romantically involved, and generally having a splendid time. This is sheer marketing fantasy—and yet, as a society, we buy it, we eat it up, we swallow it whole and ask for more.

Television and Movies

The most obvious pattern in television and movies, other than the predominant absence of large women, reflects the unsurprising fact that heavy men, although they suffer from the same general type of discrimination as heavy women, are not as severely censured for being large. Size in a man is often considered either a sign of physical power or a matter of no consequence. In a scene from the movie *Diner,* a large man eats plate after plate of sandwiches in a diner, apparently trying to set a personal record. The main characters, all male, are watching him in awe and cheering him on; no cracks are made about his size or his appetite. It is utterly impossible to imagine a big woman playing the same scene.

In even a cursory review of mass media presentations, one finds many 5
more large men than women. Take, for example, actors John Goodman, the late John Candy (whose death has been attributed not purely to his weight but also to a rapid and substantial weight loss), *Cheers'* George Wendt, Bob Hoskins, the late John Belushi (dead of an overdose of drugs, not food), the late comic Sam Kinison (car accident, not clogged arteries), French actor Gerard Depardieu, and British comic Robbie Coltrane, to name a few. All these men have played characters who, although heavy, are nonetheless portrayed as lovable and appealing enough to attract thin, conventionally attractive women. Can anyone imagine a female version of *Cheers'* Norm—a lazy, workphobic, beer-guzzling woman who assiduously avoids home and husband—being hailed as funny, let alone "beloved," as one news article put it?

John Candy

Of course, we're all well acquainted with that popular movie plot involving the sweet but physically unexceptional male who yearns after the beautiful, thin heroine and eventually, by means of his irresistible personality, wins his true love (*Minnie and Moskowitz* comes immediately to mind). The male-dominated film industry never misses an opportunity to remind us that men should always be loved for themselves. But what about women?

When Hollywood was casting for the 1991 film *Frankie and Johnnie,* a story about an ordinary-looking woman who falls in love with a plain-looking man, Kathy Bates, an Oscar-winning actress who portrayed Frankie on the stage and who just happens to be large, was passed over for the film role. The part went instead to Michelle Pfeiffer, a thin, conventionally glamorous blonde who obviously wanted to prove that she could play a character role. This is typical. If the heavy woman has any consistent role in commercial American films, it is as the peripheral, asexual mother or "buddy," and rarely, if ever, the central, romantic character. Message to all large women: You're not sexy. The only beautiful woman is a thin woman.

Bates herself pointed out in a 1991 interview that when she read for a part in the Sylvester Stallone movie *Paradise Alley,* the character breakdown showed that "after every single female character's name was the adjective 'beautiful,' even if the character was age 82." When Bates questioned the casting director about this, he replied, "Well if you want to make your own female version of *Marty* [a movie about a lonely, aging, unattractive man], be my guest" (Finke, 1991).

Of the approximately 70 movies I randomly surveyed—mostly mainstream commercial American films—only 17 had any large female characters at all in the script, most of whom represented the standard domineering mother figure, the comically unattractive woman, the whore figure, and Bates as her *Misery* psychopath character. Only six of these 17 films presented a big woman as a positive figure, and of these six, only three—*Daddy's Dyin'—Who's Got the Will?* and John Waters' *Hairspray* and *Crybaby*—featured fat women as romantic figures and central characters.

Television shows are not much better, although they occasionally make 10
an effort. Ricki Lake, who has since lost weight, was featured in the defunct series *China Beach;* Delta Burke once co-starred in *Designing Women* and had her own series; and Roseanne's show has long resided among the Top 10 in the Nielsen ratings. Although these women are encouraging examples of talent overcoming prejudice, they are too few and far between. At best, TV shows typically treat large female characters as special cases whose weight is always a matter of comment, rather than integrating women of all sizes and shapes into their programs as a matter of course.

On *L.A. Law,* heavy actress Conchata Ferrell played a new character who was dumped from the program after a relatively short tenure. Her role, that of a tough attorney, was variously described in reviews and on the show as "loud, brash and overbearing," "tubby," "aggressive," "bullying, overpowering," and "a real cash cow." At one point in the series, Ferrell's character marries a handsome, slender man amidst tittering speculation by the firm's slender female attorneys as to the groom's ulterior motive. Naturally, it turns out that he is a foreigner who has married the fat attorney solely to gain citizenship.

WM 46, 5'8" non-smoker looking for woman of my dreams: You are kind, helpful, caring, fun-loving, funny, polite, and smart. You like Sci-fi, comedy, travel, and cats. You're reasonably close to being height/weight proportionate.

NATIVE TEXAN NEW to town interested in SF between 24-34, slim or athletic, attractive, and intelligent. Must love to have fun and be positive about life. Non-smoker, light drinker.

A TALL, THIN woman. Yeah! That's what I want. 5'8" to 6'2", fun, pretty, seeking long-term relationship. I'm 6', muscular, grey and green, 40s, intelligent, V.I.P. businesses. Country life, boating, camping to limousine trips, dinners, tours.

TALL, FIT, HANDSOME, intelligent, emotionally stable, financially secure, laid back professional SWM, mid-40s, looking to fall in love with pretty, fit, SW/HF, 32-45, with varied interests. ☎1301

The Personals: "No Fat Women, Please"

Although it's true the personals are not strictly part of the media establishment, they do constitute a public forum and mass-communication network, and they illustrate in a very raw fashion the reflection of media imagery in the desires of men.

The patterns of the personals reflect the usual stale stereotypes and sexism of weight prejudice. Out of 324 ads by men seeking women in which the men specified body size, 312 requested, or rather demanded, a thin body type, employing [no less than 17] synonyms for "thin." Men have a most creative vocabulary when it comes to describing a woman's body. Indeed, to judge by the phrasing of the ads, "slender" and "attractive" are one word, not two, in the same fashion as "fat" and "ugly."

It is most interesting that male admirers of big women are commonly portrayed as little boys looking for a mother figure; yet here, one finds men who appear to be looking for a very small, dependent, child-woman/daughter figure and status symbol. Could it be that they have their own peculiar incest fantasies? Might one go even further and speculate that the preference for women with androgynous or boyish figures represents a closeted homosexuality in some men, or an unconscious fear of and hostility toward the more powerful femininity of the large woman?

In any case, the overall impression of the personals is that men still care 15 more about a woman's body and looks than her qualities as a human being. An S/B/M (single black male) summed it up perfectly when he wrote, in search of a woman who "weighs no more than 140. Be any race, be yourself, be beautiful." Or else?

Newspapers

The problem with mainstream newspaper journalism is twofold: first, its hearty participation in the national pastime of describing fat people in contemptuous terms; and second, that it purports to be an objective, unbiased observer and reporter of news and culture. But when entertainment journalists describe a large actress as "a blimp on the way to full zeppelin status" (Miller, 1992) or a bone-thin actress as "deliciously gorgeous," the reader can make a pretty good guess as to their personal views as well as their degree of impartiality.

One of the best—or worst—examples of journalistic weight prejudice was the local sports columnist reporting from the 1992 Barcelona Olympics on the Spanish beaches, and his disparaging remarks about local older women possessed of the sheer tasteless gall to walk on said beaches in "nothing but" their swimsuits. This same columnist also deplored women who dared to sunbathe undraped on a topless beach—not because they were naked, but because they lacked the flawless breasts and figures that appeal so to the male eye (Nevius, 1992).

Even in newspaper articles that have nothing to do with diet and weight, women are frequently described in terms of their approximate or specific weight and appearance. Phrases like "tall sexy . . . type," "the mountain of blond hair she balances on 102 pounds," "slender beauty," and "California girl beauty" appear in one article alone about female stand-up comics which includes, interestingly, a graphic description of a man helping himself to generous portions of a buffet while the women sit and drink only water (Kahn, 1991). One newspaper item about singer Ann Peebles refers to her as "the 99-pound vocalist" (Selvin, 1992); another article briefly profiling four blues musicians describes the one woman in the group as "5-foot-3 and 105 pounds" but makes no mention of any of the three men's physical attributes (Orr, 1992).

[M]ost newspaper items omit such detailed descriptions of men's sizes and body parts. One interview of director Robert Altman describes him in terms of his age and hair color, and compares him to a "bemused, slightly grumpy, extremely shrewd owl," but makes no mention of his weight, although the full-body shot accompanying the article reveals a clearly heavyset man (Guthmann, 1992).

As for print advertisements, they lack the dynamics of television ads, and 20
consequently they can come on quite strong in their promotion of thinness as the ultimate aphrodisiac. One diet product ad out of *TV Guide* depicts a thin woman in a leotard examining her hips. Superimposed upon the picture are the words "We'll help you turn on more than your metabolism." Next to the picture, the ad begins, "You're not only dieting for yourself. That's why it's so important to lose those extra pounds. . . ." Another item in a different issue of this magazine hawks an exercise machine, and while the words describing the health benefits are in rather small print, the impossibly slender and leggy female model in the ad is quite noticeable, as are the words, "Hurry! Get that NordicTrack figure you always wanted." Then there are the ubiquitous exercise club advertisements featuring women who are dressed, shaped, and posed more like centerfolds than athletes or average people.

The mass media do not really reflect an idealized reality, as its gurus would like us to think. From the movie studios and directors, to the ad executives and the TV producers and the novelists, rock stars, and music video producers, the media masters have constructed a universe of "petrified opinions" where the only valuable woman is a thin woman, while big women function primarily as shrewish, silly, asexual mommy figures or cheap jokes. Not only is this one-dimensional viewpoint warped and oppressive, it is crashingly dull, redundant, and predictable. Taken as a whole, this so-called creative product conspires to turn impressionable young women into insecure nervous wrecks trying to compete with image upon image of the same tiny-waisted, big-breasted dream girl.

If art really is a reflection of life, and the mass media in turn are a businesslike imitation of art, then when Americans struggle and strive to shape their lives in media's image, they are living life twice removed. The constricted vision of the world fabricated by Hollywood and Madison Avenue compresses the individual and her hopes, needs, and dreams into narrow channels, reducing life to a hopeless pursuit of false perfection in imitation of people who exist primarily for the illusions they can project.

"Be any race, be yourself, but be beautiful." Or else.

Works Cited

Finke, N. "Actress Is Weighed Down by Hollywood Attitudes." *San Francisco Chronicle,* February 17, 1991, Sunday Datebook: 33–34.

Guthmann, E. "Altman's 'Player' for the 90's." *San Francisco Chronicle,* April 23, 1992: E2.

Kahn, A. "The Women of the Night." *San Francisco Chronicle,* June 17, 1991: D3.

Miller, R. "Don't Expect Any Good, Clean Fun from 'Maid.' " *San Jose Mercury News,* January 13, 1992: 10B.

Nevius, C. W. "Life's a Beach—Just Barely." *San Francisco Chronicle,* July 28, 1992: E5.

Orr, J. "Twelve Bars and a Turnaround." *San Jose Mercury News,* July 19, 1992, West Magazine: 18.

Selvin, J. "Ann Peebles Redeems Her Rain Check." *San Francisco Chronicle,* April 16, 1992, Sunday Datebook: 51.

RESPOND.

1. Goodman contends that "[m]ovies, television, magazines, newspapers, and preachifying self-help books all reinforce and amplify the ignorant stereotypes about fat people that America holds so close and dear; taken together, they constitute a framework of 'petrified opinions' which few dare to question" (paragraph 1). What sorts of evidence does she use to support this claim? How is Goodman's evidence similar to and different from the evidence used by Jane Stern in her review of Judith Moore's *Fat Girl* (p. 601)?
2. Examine how Goodman uses quotations as evidence, especially the opening quote about "petrified opinions" from Mark Twain and the one from the personals section of a newspaper ("Be any race, be yourself, but be beautiful") in paragraphs 15 and 23. In what ways do quotations help structure the argument?
3. Personal ads are especially interesting as arguments because of their brevity. Examine some personal ads in a local newspaper, surveying systematically the images that emerge of the ideal male or female partner. What images express the ideals for each group? To what extent are these ideals the ones that occur most frequently in television, movies, and magazines? Are you concerned about the gap between the ideal and the reality of everyday life? Why or why not?
4. Goodman challenges readers to scrutinize the world, looking to see how large women are or are not represented. Part of the persuasiveness of her argument for many readers, especially for readers who aren't large women, likely comes from the volume of evidence she offers. Take the Goodman challenge: choose three familiar magazines or television shows, and survey them as systematically as possible. (For magazines, for example, you will want to distinguish between photographs in advertisements and those in articles.) **Write an essay** arguing for a particular position with regard to the representation of large women in the media.

Reshaping America

POPULAR COSMETIC PROCEDURES, BY SEX

WOMEN

	Botox	Liposuction	Breast enlargement	Eyelid surgery	Breast reduction	Nose reshaping	Fat injections
2003 Procedures	1,963,012	322,975	280,401	216,829	147,173	119,047	83,295
Percentage change since 1997	**+3,177%**	**+117%**	**+177%**	**+60%**	**+207%**	**+29%**	**+141%**

MEN

	Botox	Liposuction	Nose reshaping	Eyelid surgery	Breast reduction	Hair transplant	Fat injections
2003 Procedures	309,063	61,646	53,376	50,798	22,049	14,891	7,017
Percentage change since 1997	**+5,762%**	**+118%**	**+20%**	**+116%**	**+97%**	**–71%**	**+86%**

COSTS OF THE TOP OPERATIONS

National averages in 2003.

Female breast reduction	**$5,351**
Nose reshaping	**3,869**
Breast enlargement	**3,360**
Male breast reduction	**3,124**
Hair transplant	**3,084**
Eyelid surgery	**2,599**
Liposuction	**2,578**

OTHER COSTS

The top five nonsurgical cosmetic procedures in the United States.

Botox injection	**$384**
Laser hair removal	**388**
Microdermabrasion	**161**
Chemical peel	**800**
Collagen injection	**381**

Reshaping America

▲ *This complex graphic appeared in the "Science Times" section of the New York Times on April 27, 2004, as a visual accompanying an article entitled "Plastic Surgery Gets a New Look." As you examine this graphic, consider how it makes an argument and how it can be used to support a variety of arguments.*

RESPOND •

1. How might this graphic have been used to support the argument made by the title of the article it accompanied, "Plastic Surgery Gets a New Look"? (In fact, this graphic appeared not on the first page of the article but on the page where the article was continued and carried the title "Plastic Surgery: Drastic Is Out. Subtle Is In.")
2. One might say that this graphic has three parts. What are they, and how does each contribute to the graphic as a whole?
3. Are you surprised by the information presented in this graphic? Why or why not? How is the visual presentation for women and men especially effective in conveying a great deal of information clearly? The focus of the visual information in this graphic is the number of procedures for women and men. What would we see if the information for "Percentage change since 1997" were presented as bar charts? Compare, for example, the increase in Botox and eyelid surgery for women and men since 1997.
4. You may never have stopped to think about it, but people who are blind or dyslexic often use tape-recorded textbooks to assist them in their studies. One organization, Recording for the Blind & Dyslexic <http://rfbd.org>, uses volunteers to help tape textbooks. Working with a monitor who runs the recording machinery, the reader has to read the entire text, including complex graphics like this one. If you're sighted, imagine that you're the volunteer who's going to read this text; **write a script** that describes the graphic, including all of the information provided, without editorializing. If you're not sighted, work with a sighted classmate, giving her or him feedback on the draft of the script; or, if you prefer, **write an essay** in which you explain your criteria for evaluating a reader's success in reading a graphic like this one.

Rob Walker, a journalist, writes regularly for both the New York Times *and* Slate.com. *He's also the author of* Letters from New Orleans, *published in June 2005, about the three years (2000–2003) he and his girlfriend lived in that city before returning to New York. This essay, "Social Lubricant: How a Marketing Campaign Became the Catalyst for a Societal Debate," appeared in one of his regular "Consumed" columns for the* Times. *Essays featured in the column deal with aspects of American society as a society of consumers. As you read, try to think of other cases where advertisements and ad campaigns became the basis for arguments within American society.*

Social Lubricant

How a Marketing Campaign Became the Catalyst for a Societal Debate

ROB WALKER

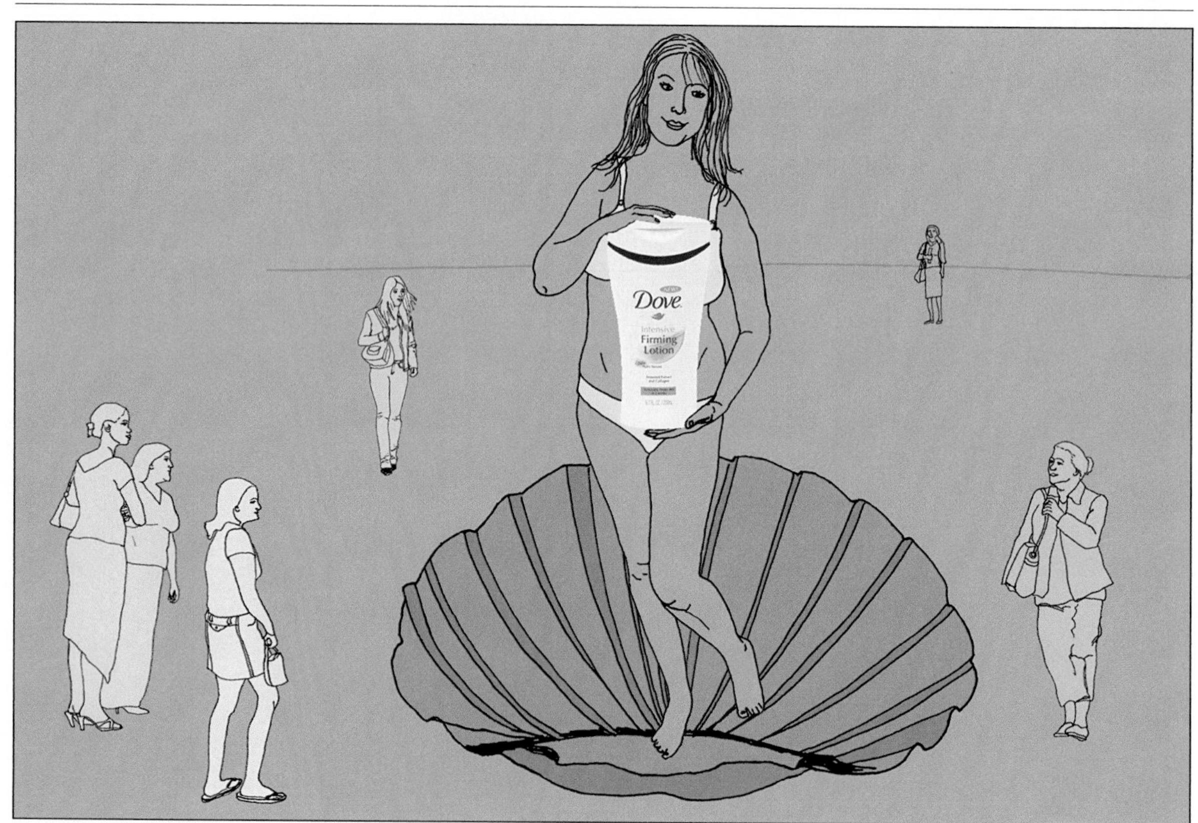

"Fat or Fabulous?" asked a line on the cover of a recent issue of *People* magazine, underneath a small photograph of some of the "Dove Girls." These are the young women appearing on billboards and other advertising on behalf of Dove Body Nourishers Intensive Firming Lotion and related products; they are not the ultrathin fashion-model types common to advertising, and they are dressed only in underwear. They have become a minor sensation, sparking opinion articles in major publications (including a *New York Times* editorial) and showing up as guests on the "Today" show. This is a rare thing and pretty clearly a publicity bonanza for the Dove brand.

The debate over whether these images of women are positive (because they are more "real" than many marketing or media depictions of women) or negative (because they are all well within typical beauty norms, practically naked and pushing a product) has offered few surprises. But lurking behind it is the more intriguing fact that it is a marketing campaign — not a political figure, or a major news organization, or even a film — that "opened a dialogue" (as one of the young women said to *People*). The buzziest pop artifact to dwell on the unthin female form in recent memory was the Showtime series "Fat Actress"; the Dove Girls ads seems almost intellectual in comparison.

Dove's marketing director, Philippe Harousseau, says the campaign has been in the works for a couple of years. It began with a "global study," commissioned by Dove (which is owned by Unilever) that posed questions about beauty to thousands of women in many countries. Among other things, the women tended to agree that "the media and advertising" were pushing "unrealistic" beauty standards. It seems likely that if this same not-so-original conclusion were reached by a university or a think tank, the impact would have been minimal. But a giant corporation with a huge marketing budget is not so easily ignored. Early pieces of the campaign, which actually started last year, included images of older women and women with stretch marks and such. But it was challenging the only-thin-is-beautiful stereotype that "really hit a nerve," Harousseau says. "Women were ready to hear this."

Why they were ready to hear it from marketers is the puzzle. Maybe it is somehow inevitable that marketing, which caused much of the underlying anxiety in the first place, can offer up a point of view that blithely tries to resolve that anxiety. Moreover, as the entertainment side of the media fragments, marketing becomes the one form of communication that permeates everywhere — and is just as effective whether you've actually seen the campaign or you simply have an opinion about it based on what you've heard.

5 Finally, perhaps there is something here that's a backlash against not just the waif-ing of American media culture but also the self-improvement imperative: enough counting carbs, enough lectures from Dr. Phil, enough pressure to learn to dress well enough for the "Queer Eye" crew and achieve Martha-like aesthetic perfection in bathroom décor. The flip side of "Don't you care enough to do better?" could be "Stop telling me how to live."

Unilever will not get specific about the campaign's effect on sales, but ultimately Dove products aren't really the point. The Dove Girls could be selling pretty much anything, since what people are really responding to is the attitude they symbolize: an unapologetic self-confidence so appealing that we're basically willing to overlook the shaky intellectual consistency of linking it to Firming Lotions. In fact, maybe the Dove Girls' next move should be to show up in a Burger King ad, enjoying an Enormous Omelet Sandwich, daring anyone to criticize them for it.

Dove's survey is available on its "Campaign for Real Beauty" Web site, and among its other findings is that the top "attributes of making a woman beautiful" are happiness and kindness. In other words, they had nothing to do with physical appearance at all. But these encouraging insights would not have given Dove much of an opportunity to sell — and would have left everyone else very little to debate and nothing at all to buy. ■

Evaluative essays ask assessment questions like: What makes this marketing campaign successful? Look at Chapter 9 for more examples of criteria for evaluative arguments.

LINK TO P. 256

RESPOND.

1. Whatever else Walker is doing, he's making an argument about advertising, body image, and public debate. How would you characterize this argument? What kind of argument is it? (For a discussion of four kinds of arguments, see Chapter 1.) What evidence can you cite for your claim? Once you have decided what kind of argument Walker is making, evaluate how well he makes it, making explicit your criteria for evaluation.
2. While the Dove survey of women showed that they responded well to efforts to challenge the "only-thin-is-beautiful" stereotype common in American society, it didn't investigate why they might feel this way. Walker seeks to do so in this essay (paragraphs 4–5). How well does he make his case? In other words, do you agree or disagree with his analysis of American women's motivations for rejecting the idea that a woman must be thin to be beautiful? Why or why not? Can you think of reasons he might have included but didn't?

Sandro Botticelli, *The Birth of Venus,* 1485

3. What sort of argument does the visual (p. 614) that accompanied Walker's text make? How does it add to or detract from his argument? How does appreciating its argument depend crucially on the reader's familiarity with Sandro Botticelli's painting from about 1485, *The Birth of Venus*, reproduced at left? Can you give examples of other visual allusions—images whose full interpretation depends on knowledge of other images to which they make reference?
4. Walker's essay refers to Dove's survey of women, available on the Campaign for Beauty's Web site. Visit the Web site at <http://campaignforrealbeauty.com> with an eye toward the topics that are included and excluded as well as the ways in which these arguments are presented. Then **write an essay** evaluating the effectiveness of the kinds of appeals used in one of the links associated with the Web site. (For discussions of kinds of appeals and evaluative essays, respectively, see Chapters 1 and 9.)

▼ *Born in 1970, Meghan Daum is a novelist and essayist; she also contributes a weekly column to the* Los Angeles Times, *where this essay appeared in the summer of 2005. Her books include the collection of essays* My Misspent Youth *(2001) and the novel* The Quality of Life Report *(2003). Her writing is often praised for its use of humor. As you read this essay, consider the ways in which Daum uses humor simultaneously to support and soften an argument that's anything but humorous.*

Those Unnerving Ads Using "Real" Women

MEGHAN DAUM

I realize that as a woman who does not happen to be a supermodel, I'm supposed to appreciate and even feel empowered by Dove's "Real Women for Beauty" ad campaign. You know the one I mean. On billboards and bus stops across the country, six "real" women pose in white bras and panties, their fleshy thighs, generous hips and presumably surgically unaltered breasts on spirited display.

Apparently this is more than just an ad campaign, it's a political movement. "For too long, beauty has been defined by narrow, stifling stereotypes," Dove's Web site explains. "You've told us it's time to change all that."

I don't remember telling Dove anything. But now that they mention it, I actually feel a little sick to my stomach.

Why? It could be the fact that the lead product of this campaign is, ahem, cellulite firming cream. With glorious, backhanded brilliance, Dove is sounding the trumpets of body acceptance while also selling woebegone "real women" a cure for their realness.

5 "Firming the thighs of a size-two supermodel is no challenge," reads the text on the Web site. "Real women have real bodies with real curves."

But that's not really what fazes me. After all, the crazy-making yin and yang of self-love and self-loathe is as old as advertising itself, and Dove is hardly the first company to sell solutions by inventing problems. If anything, this "realness" aesthetic, with its Lifetime Channel aura,

In dowtown Chicago, Gina Crisanti leans against a billboard that features her and five other women posed in their underwear for an ad campaign to sell Dove Beauty products. The ads, featuring "real" women and not models, are a hot topic of conversation.

should seem arcane° and middlebrow.°

Besides, the Machiavellian° irony of employing vaguely feminist rhetoric to sell cellulite cream ought to be more bemusing than offensive. Same goes for the "million faces album" on the Web site, to which thousands of women have submitted their photos along with such phrases as "Beauty is being yourself."

So why am I feeling so uneasy? Is it simply that we're now shocked by any woman in the media who isn't built like a silicon-enhanced greyhound? It's tempting to say that the ads prove how shallow we've all become.

Here we are in 2005—in the same summer that the health manual "Our Bodies, Ourselves,"° the very touchstone of hairy-arm-pitted, bra-burning exuberance, is celebrating its 30th anniversary—and women are clucking their tongues at models who don't meet the preternatural° standards of Tyra Banks and Kate Moss. Has the cultural preoccupation with "narrow, stifling stereotypes" become so ingrained that we're repulsed by our own reflections?

Actually, I think not. In looking at 10
these ads, what's shocking about them has more to do with a curious invasion of privacy than with neuroses surrounding jiggly flesh. Seeing these women blown up to dozens of times their actual size above the thoroughfares of American cities is a bit like seeing an enormous picture of one's own bedroom on display to anyone who drives by.

We love our bedrooms, we're comfortable in them, there's nowhere we'd rather spend our nights. And part of the reason for that is that they're private

---

arcane: hidden from general knowledge or understood only by a few.

middlebrow: of average intellectual or cultural value or interest (always pejorative).

Machiavellian: referring to the Italian political philosopher Niccolò Machiavelli, who, in *The Prince* (1513), argues that rulers (and, by extension, everyone in power) should place personal or political goals over moral or ethical commitments.

Santi di Tito, *Niccolò Machiavelli* (1560–1600)

Our Bodies, Ourselves: best-selling reference book, first commercially published in 1973 by the Boston Women's Health Book Collective, a grass-roots collective that became an important nonprofit organization devoted to women's health issues. Frustrated over an inability to get adequate and accurate information about matters of health and sexuality from the medical establishment, overwhelmingly male dominated at the time, the collective began compiling information to educate women about their bodies. The book has been translated or adapted into nineteen languages. In its most recent edition, it is entitled *Our Bodies, Ourselves: A New Edition for A New Era*. For additional information on the Collective and the book, go to <http://ourbodiesourselves.org>.

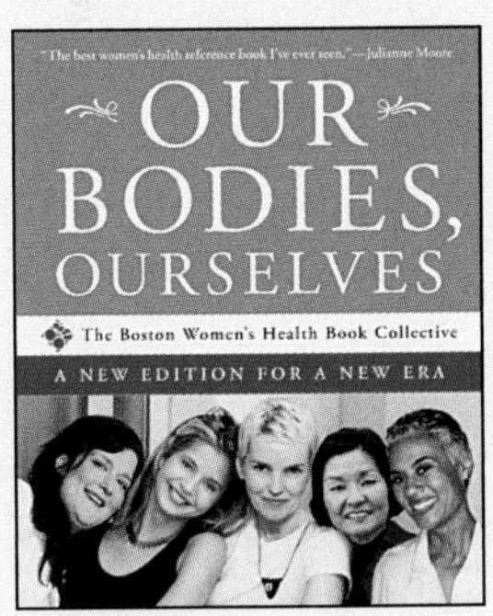

Our Bodies, Ourselves: A New Edition for A New Era

preternatural: extraordinary.

spaces, sanctuaries whose access is limited only to ourselves and the ones we love. The bed may be unmade, clothes may be strewn across the floor, the thread count of the sheets might not meet current bourgeois° standards, but we love this space because of the ineffable, unquantifiable ways that remind us we're at home. These are qualities that don't translate into photographs, let alone enormous billboards.

bourgeois: relating to the middle class, but generally with the pejorative connotations of conformity in matters of taste and values.

Naked bodies—especially, it seems, those of women—work much the same way. Although the visual impact cannot be underestimated, there are hundreds of other sensory expressions—smells, textures, the sound of bare feet walking across the floor—that simply cannot be represented in advertising. That is the reason we have professional models. They show us their bodies without invading our privacy or their own. An underwear model represents intimacy while at the same time protecting us from the rawness of actual intimacy. Her genius lies in her ability to be generic. And this is something Dove's "real women" just can't do.

Can we interpret Daum's article as an argument to explore? See more about the many purposes of argument in Chapter 1.

LINK TO P. 7

That's why so many of us react not with a rallying, "You go, girls!" but with a string of panicked questions. "Who are they?" we ask. "Do I look like that? Should I not look like that? Do I look better than them? Do I look worse?"

The first question can be answered on Dove's Web site, which supplies profiles and journal entries of each of the models (where there's "real" there's always a journal). The other questions reveal an irony far greater than the fact that at the root of all this body acceptance lies a fear of cellulite. These amateur models remind us how much we need professional models, not for their jutting bones and flawless skin but for the way they throw themselves in front of traffic so that we don't have to.

These ads are unnerving because 15
intimacy can be unnerving. Public exposure cancels out intimacy all together, which means that what's shocking about these ads has less to do with body size than the shock of seeing our bedrooms in the harsh midday light. We may gasp, but I suspect what we're saying without realizing it is this: "Leave this work to the pros, girls. Real women have better things to do."

RESPOND •

1. What's Daum's argument? In other words, why does she find the "Real Women" ads disconcerting? What, according to her, is the real reason that all of us want to see "preternatural" (paragraph 9) people as models rather than people who look like us? Do you agree or disagree? Why or why not?
2. What does Daum mean when she contends that actual intimacy has a "rawness" (paragraph 12)? How does her word choice in this case make her argument memorable? How does she support her claim that intimacy is raw? Why is this claim crucial to her argument?
3. In what ways is there "Machiavellian irony" in using "vaguely feminist rhetoric to sell cellulite cream" (paragraph 7)? Where's the irony? Why might Daum label it "Machiavellian"? How does this allusion to Machiavelli represent an argument?
4. Visit the Dove site devoted to the women who appeared in this campaign at <http://www.campaignforrealbeauty.com/flat3.asp?id=2287>. How are these women like and not like the women you see in everyday life? In your opinion, what accounts for the differences? Might these differences have consequences? Of what sort? **Write an essay** in which you define the nature of those consequences, or one in which you propose a serious ad campaign for an actual product using a broader range of "real people" in contrast to those who appear in the Dove ads and elsewhere.

Guy Trebay writes regularly about many aspects of popular culture for several national publications, including the New York Times, *where this article first appeared in the "Sunday Styles" section in August 2004. As you read, think about how you've seen attitudes toward the male body change during your lifetime: consider, for example, the sometimes subtle changes in ads for companies like Abercrombie & Fitch from one season to the next with respect to how male bodies are (or aren't) displayed.*

When Did Skivvies Get Rated NC-17?

GUY TREBAY

Let it be noted that there was a time when buying a pair of men's underpants was a simple matter of grabbing a three-pack of something in one's waist size from a shelf near the hardware department at Sears. What little decision was required involved simple choices between boxers or briefs. In the days before Calvin Klein came along to seduce men into becoming unwitting consumers of personal lingerie, there was little reason to think about stuff like microfibers or combed pima cotton, forget skivvies engineered along the lines of the push-up bra.

That was all a very long time ago. Anybody who hasn't visited the men's underwear section of a department store lately may be in for a shock. Where once there were limited, discreetly shelved selections of what Victorians termed "unmentionables," there is now a welter of choices offered in displays so unabashedly raunchy they practically call out for some form of ratings system or, at the minimum, parental controls.

There are briefs and boxer briefs and "action bikinis" and "athletic strings" and shorts with breathable mesh pouches or waistband condom pockets, and even a new brand called C-IN2 with patented "sling support" designed, in the words of its manufacturer, to "lift, project forward and improve the wearer's profile." And, alas, there are thongs.

That the men who model for the packages containing these garments seem universally blessed with the proportions of pornographic film stars suggests that there may be more customers than one had imagined for those e-mailed spam messages offering "masculine enhancement."

5 "Something it is important to mention with tact," said Claudine Gumbel, a spokeswoman for 2$^{(x)}$ist, one of the more successful recent brands of designer underwear, "is that 2$^{(x)}$ist models are very well endowed." 2$^{(x)}$ist, Ms. Gumbel added, is "a very manly collection of underwear and the director thinks this is an important element."

Indeed it appears to be. What began modestly enough in the early 80's, when Calvin Klein first photographed men in ways that made it acceptable to use sex to sell Y-fronts and incidentally gave Americans permission to ogle the male physique, has expanded to an almost comically lurid degree.

The proliferation of new products not only from upstarts like 2$^{(x)}$ist and Baskit but also more traditional brands like Hanro and Hugo Boss compete furiously to pitch their goods by using voluptuous lighting and moody graphics to delineate men's behinds and other anatomical contours as though they were features in a heroic landscape. It is no exaggeration to say that there are underwear

LIFT AND SUPPORT *A new wave of men's briefs designed to accentuate every contour has made underwear departments, like the one at Macy's, above, resemble sex shops in the old Times Square.*

boxes out there that make a man's crotch look as monumental as an Ansel Adams° picture of El Capitan.

"Sex-oriented underwear is probably a fairly small proportion of the market nationally," said Arnold Karr, the executive editor of the men's wear trade publication DNR, referring to the revealing styles. Their impact on the $13-billion-a-year underwear market is nowhere near as substantial as white cotton basics like Hanes and Fruit of the Loom. Nevertheless, at the department store level their presence is overwhelming and their market share, said Mr. Karr, correspondingly large.

The reasons are simple enough to comprehend. In the decades since the first Calvin Klein ads, men have been substantially feminized and also have genially adapted to their transformation into objects of an erotic gaze.

10 "That early Calvin ad was the first time you really saw that guy in packaging and advertising," said Sam Shahid, the art director responsible for orchestrating Mr. Klein's early campaigns. "That hot, athletic, very physical and sensual man really hadn't been seen before."

Mr. Klein first hired Bruce Weber in 1982 to take the American Olympic pole vaulter Tom Hintnaus to the Greek island of Santorini and photograph him posing in a pair of white briefs against a white wall, his legs spread wide. In doing so, Mr. Klein was marking the beginning of both major changes in the conventions of masculine presentation and an overall democratization of desire.

Some may find it surprising to learn that it was not always commonplace to see buff guys flashing on reality TV or seminaked men with six-pack abs looming above Mid-

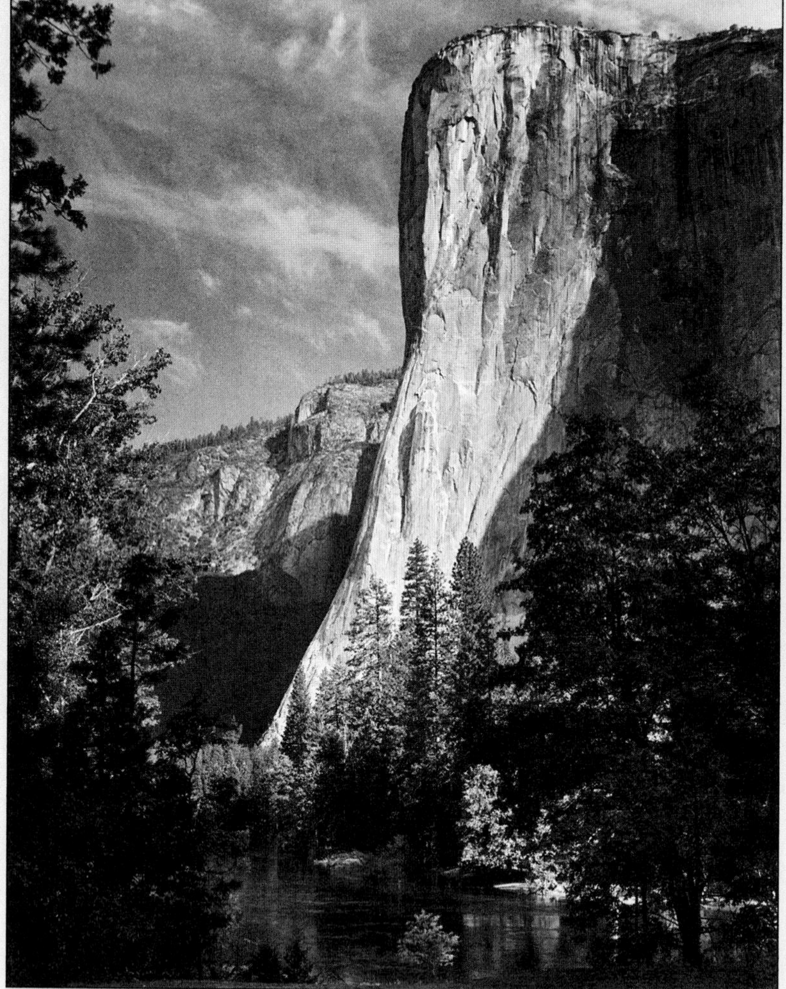

Ansel Adams, *"El Capitan, Sunrise, Yosemite National Park, California,"* 1956

Ansel Adams: American photographer (1902–1984); among his best-known works are nature photographs, including several of El Capitan, a famous peak in Yosemite National Park with a sheer granite face.

town. Such people probably do not remember that before Mark Wahlberg became a mediocre film actor, he was a mediocre crotch-grabbing rapper whose Calvin Klein billboard in Times Square presented him as a himbo° Colossus of Rhodes.°

"Racy packaging for the male underwear Industry's equivalent of the Wonderbra."

Imagery that used to see limited exposure, mainly under brown paper wrappers or in the XXX sex stores that defined Manhattan's tenderloin,° has migrated without any particular fanfare to the main selling floor of department stores. Or at least that is the impression to be gotten from a visit to those stores as they begin stocking their new fall merchandise on the eve of National Underwear Day, which is Aug. 11.

Anniversaries predicated on boosting consumer spending are often occasions to put forward charmingly empty statistics, and the second National Underwear Day shall be no exception. According to a survey conducted by Freshpair.com, an online retailer of undergarments, 82 percent of women have tried on men's underwear, 31 percent of men have tried on women's and married men change theirs twice as often as single guys.

15 There are no statistics, really, to quantify our cultural obsession with male genitalia. But if anything can be extrapolated from the recent Internet frenzy surrounding nude scenes from Colin Farrell's new film, "A Home at the End of the World" — apparently excised because the actor's member distracted from the narrative flow — it is that the percentage of people who dwell on these matters is considerable.

"You know, I don't think any of us ever consciously said, 'We're going to display genitals,'" said Bob Mazzoli, who has been the chief creative director of Calvin Klein underwear since the product's inception. "It just seems right for us."

It seems right, too, for Adam Lippes, the former creative director of Oscar de la Renta, who left the company two years ago to establish a designer underwear start-up called Adam + Eve. It seems right for Melody Fuhr, the former design director of Banana Republic, who left that job last year to take over as creative director at 2(x)ist, a wildly popular underwear brand that started as a gay niche product nearly 15 years ago and has become a mainstream phenomenon, with sales of more than $30 million last year. It seems right for Gregory Sovell, the designer who built 2(x)ist, then sold his stake in the company and recently found himself drawn again by the irresistible lure of sexy underclothes.

"When I started 2(x)ist, the selection of what people were provided was really basic," said Mr. Sovell, whose new company is C-IN2, which sells briefs with extra-low waists, high-cut legs and an adjustable elastic strap in the crotch designed to do for male genitals more or less what the Wonderbra did for breasts.

Mr. Sovell first understood the bar had been raised on male display four years ago on a trip to Barcelona. The peacock habits of young Catalan men caused him to assume, he said, that the entire male population under 30 was gay.

20 "They were taking such chances with fashion, with what they were wearing, with showing off how much they were working out that I just assumed. . . ." the designer said. "But then they all had girlfriends with them."

Like so much else in mainstream culture now, a taste for racy undergarments can probably be traced to a

---

himbo: a male bimbo (a slang combination of *him* + *bimbo*), that is, a handsome, but not very intelligent, male.

Colossus of Rhodes: a huge statue of Helios, the personification of the sun, standing at the port on the Greek island of Rhodes; one of the seven wonders of the ancient world. Although the original statue probably didn't stand astride the port, illustrations from as early as the Renaissance have imagined the statue in this way.

tenderloin: the heart of New York City, which in the late nineteenth century was a seedy, red-light district.

certain segment of the gay population. Thongs, bikinis and those curious experiments in crotch engineering were formerly the stock in trade of catalogs like International Male. But the borders of this territory have blurred a lot in recent years, as anyone who has ever heard the name David Beckham° can attest.

"Sex display is across the board," Mr. Sovell maintained. "Guys have a lot more confidence in what they're wearing, and they don't worry about what people think."

They care less, apparently, about assumptions regarding their sexual orientation than being able to fill out a pair of low-slung jeans from companies like Diesel and G-Star. "You have to give it all to Calvin Klein," said Mr. Lippes of Adam + Eve. "He raised underwear to another level and added sex."

Mr. Lippes left de la Renta to produce designer underclothes at competitive prices ($18 is the average for a pair of designer briefs, but some brands cost as much as $150). Only secondarily did he consider his new brand's sexual component, he said. "I got into it searching for a luxury T-shirt and underwear, meaning beautiful, high-quality construction, not at an insane price point," he said. "Still, today in the underwear market, you have to draw them in and packaging is the first step."

25 So luxuriant and glossy is the packaging for Adam + Eve, which is sold at 60 specialty retailers and at department stores like Saks Fifth Avenue and Bergdorf Goodman, that a consumer might become seduced by the box's unorthodox oblong and fail to notice the cover models are posed, on certain products, wearing no underpants at all. The photographer chosen by Mr. Lippes to define his brand is Matthias Vriens, a former art director and fashion photographer, who is better known these days for his artfully raunchy gallery work: photographs of naked hustlers and porn stars mostly, often tumescent and wearing women's wigs.

If Bruce Weber's was the woozy soft-core aesthetic that once characterized male eroticism in the mainstream marketplace, Mr. Vriens's is the vision likely to define sales-floor Eros today. The Adam + Eve packaging is so ostentatiously tasteful that one almost forgets what's inside. "There's a quality about it, something that turns you on but you can't exactly say what it is," said the former Calvin Klein art director, Mr. Shahid, who also designed the Adam + Eve campaign. "You see these kids on these boxes, and you can't touch them, but you'd die to kiss each one."

Trebay uses a variety of word choices and sentence structures to carry his humorous commentary. Chapter 12 presents guidelines for style and word choice when creating your own essay.

LINK TO P. 370

David Beckham, 2003

◀ ***David Beckham:*** perhaps the world's most famous soccer player (1975–); currently, he plays for *Real Madrid* of Spain and serves as captain of the English national team. Beckham is known to many Americans either as the husband of Victoria Adams of the Spice Girls or as a celebrity endorsing any number of products. Because he has done things like appearing in public with his nails painted bright colors, Beckham is often likewise cited as an example of a metrosexual, an urban heterosexual male concerned about his appearance and not threatened by behaviors and styles traditionally associated with women.

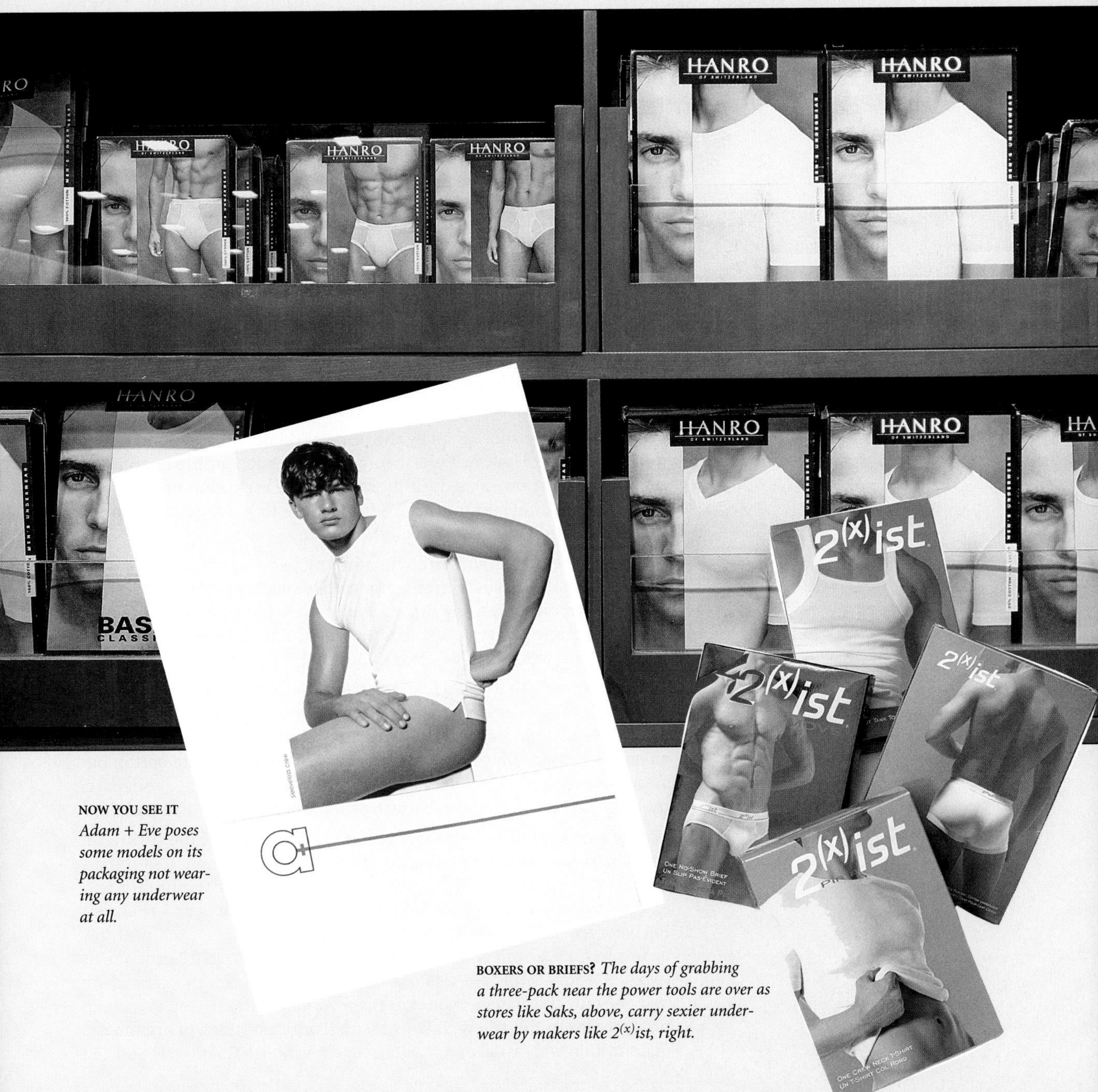

NOW YOU SEE IT *Adam + Eve poses some models on its packaging not wearing any underwear at all.*

BOXERS OR BRIEFS? *The days of grabbing a three-pack near the power tools are over as stores like Saks, above, carry sexier underwear by makers like 2^(x)ist, right.*

RESPOND

1. Although the tone of this piece is often light and even humorous in spots, Trebay makes some very strong claims about changes in American culture's attitudes toward the male body over the past few decades. Among these claims would be statements like the following:

   "In the decades since the first Calvin Klein ads, men have been substantially feminized and also have genially adapted to their transformation into objects of an erotic gaze." (paragraph 9)

   "[Guys] care less, apparently, about assumptions regarding their sexual orientation than being able to fill out a pair of low-slung jeans from companies like Diesel and G-Star." (paragraph 23)

   Do you agree with such claims? Why or why not? Do you believe that young men today face the sorts of pressures with respect to their bodies as "objects of an erotic gaze" that young women have faced for generations? Why or why not?
2. What does the author mean by the phrase "democratization of desire" (paragraph 11)? How, in American culture, is such a phrase an argument of sorts? How does the alliteration—the repetition of the initial consonant sound, *d* in this case—contribute to his argument? Is the democratization of desire a good thing? Why or why not?
3. In light of Trebay's argument, which many people would accept, that the shift in attitudes toward the male body has been encouraged by a certain segment of the gay male population, what sort of argument is the brand name Adam + Eve? To whom might you expect such a name to appeal? To whom might it not appeal? Why?
4. Trebay contends that just a few years ago, the sorts of images one finds on today's men's underwear boxes would have been found only in sex shops. He also notes that the percentage of such men's underwear sales is much smaller than the percentage going to "white cotton basics." Given these two observations, why, in your opinion, are department stores full of displays featuring such underwear and advertising?
5. Trebay's argument is obviously about change across time. **Write an essay** in which you seek to define these changes in more detail than Trebay has. To achieve this goal, you'll need to visit the library and examine popular magazines that feature men's underwear ads at, say, ten-year intervals. Ideally, you'd choose the same issue each year (for example, the December issues from 1955, 1975, and 2005). Select one or two ads from each issue, and use them as the basis for characterizing and defining the changes you note over the years. You'll need to include photocopies of the ads with your essay. (For discussions of arguments of definition and visual arguments, respectively, see Chapters 8 and 14.)

Toby Old, *Orchard Beach, NY,* 2002

Making a Visual Argument: Three Views on Body Image

▲ *Visual arguments that represent the body or use the body as part of argument can be found everywhere in American society. Here, we present three such visual arguments that use bodies in different ways. Consider the arguments each can be said to be making as well as the ways in which, in the latter two cases, images and words work together in complex ways.*

The first is a photograph, "Orchard Beach, NY," taken in 2002 by Toby Old; it was exhibited as part of Waterlog: The Beach Series, *which included forty-six silver gelatin prints of beaches in the United States, France, England, and Cuba. Old was born in 1945 and was drafted into the Army Dental Corps during the Vietnam War. During that period, he discovered photography. Currently, he teaches at the International Center of Photography in New York City.*

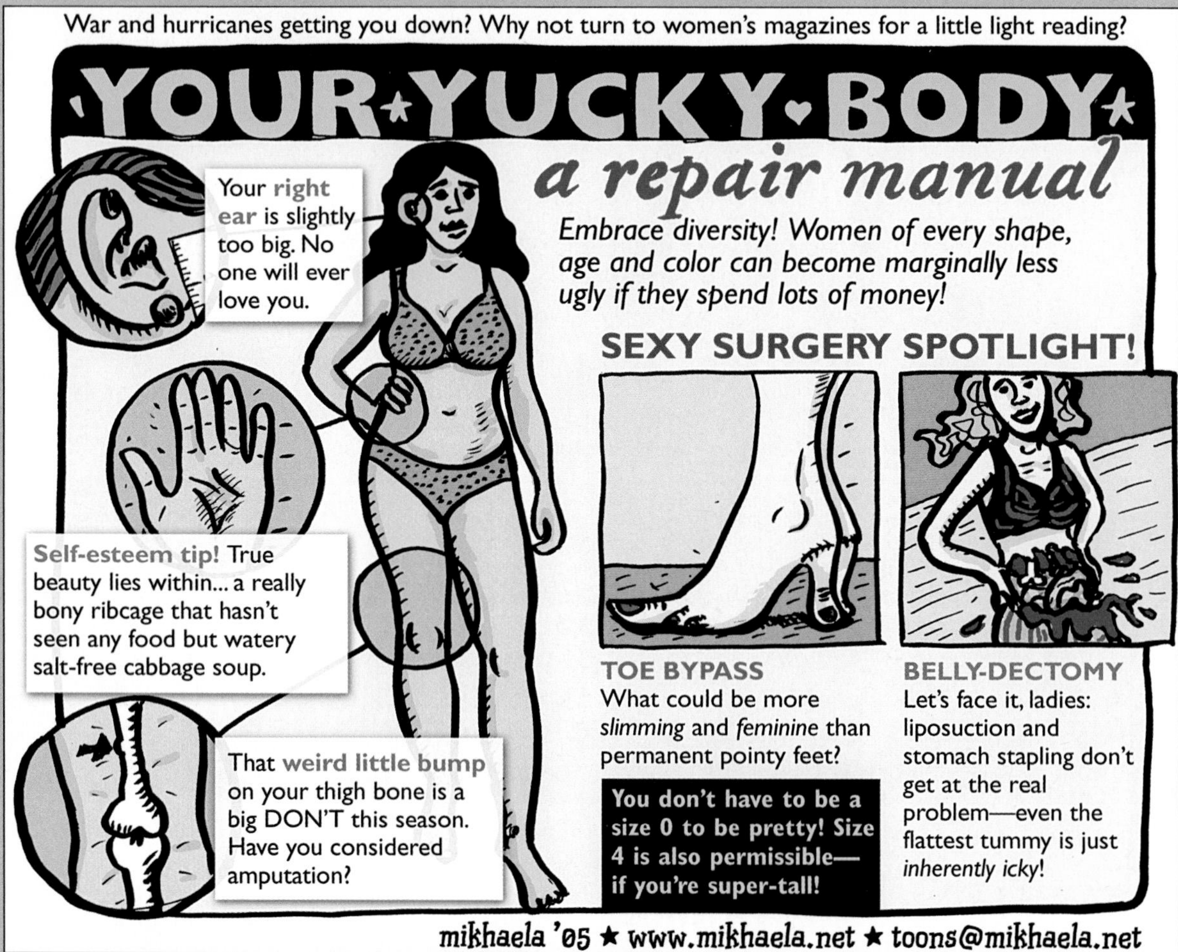

Mikhaela Blake Reid, *Your Yucky Body: A Repair Manual*

▲ *The second, "Your Yucky Body: A Repair Manual," is from the Web site of Mikhaela Blake Reid, a 25-year-old information graphics artist and cartoonist for the* Boston Phoenix *and* Bay Windows. *Her cartoons have appeared in a number of newspapers across the country. While an undergrad, she created weekly cartoons for the* Harvard Crimson. *Her Web site is <http://mikhaela.net>.*

if she were a real woman, barbie would have to walk on all fours due to her proportions.
Crossroads Baptist Church
Saturday April 17th 9am - 5pm
Lunch will not be provided $20 per person
reflections
Body Image Seminar

Jason Stirman, Crossroads Baptist Church, *Reflections: Body Image Seminar*

◀ *The final image is a flyer for a body-image seminar hosted by* Crossroads Baptist Church. *Jason Stirman, a freelance graphic designer currently living and working in The Woodlands, Texas, was given the task of creating a flyer "generating interest in the* Reflections: Body Image Seminar *for mothers and daughters, by exposing a harsh fact regarding women's body image stereotypes" <http://www.stirman.net/portfolio/Barbie.php>. Crossroads Baptist Church was founded in 1992 and serves the wider community of The Woodlands, Texas.*

RESPOND•

1. The people in the photograph by Toby Old are, indeed, "real people," actual people who happened to be at Orchard Beach on the day in 2002 when the photograph was taken. How might you read the photograph as an argument about body image? How would the argument be different if the woman on the right were not holding two Barbie dolls by their hair in her left hand?
2. These selections range from the purely visual (Old's photograph) to the text dominant (Reid's cartoon), with three of the selections including at least some text. What roles does the text play in each of these selections? How do the text and the visual image work together to create the argument? How would the arguments be different if there were no text? If there were no image?
3. How do the selections by Reid and the found-flyer use humor to make their point? Are the two equally effective? What are the strengths of each? (Why, by the way, might a church be sponsoring a seminar on body image? Who might be the audience for such a seminar?)
4. If one of playwright LeBute's goals is to make his audience face uncomfortable truths about American society, how does this poster contribute to his goal?
5. Choose one of these selections, and **write an essay** in which you offer a rhetorical analysis of it. (For a discussion of rhetorical analyses and how to write one, see Chapter 5.)

22
How Does the Media Stereotype *You?*

If you check the dictionary, you'll learn that the term *stereotype* originally referred to a plate for printing that was cast in metal from a mold of a page of set type. English borrowed the word from French, but its parts are ultimately of Greek origin: *stereo,* meaning "solid" or "three-dimensional," and *type,* meaning "model." By extension, a stereotype has come to mean a widely held conception of a group that's fixed and that allows for little individuality among the group's members. Ironic, isn't it, that a term that originally referred to a three-dimensional printing plate has come to refer to one-dimensional representations of groups?

The readings in this chapter focus on issues of stereotypes in media and pop culture, considering what many would regard as unsavory stereotypes of various groups from a range of perspectives. The chapter opens with a group of images involving stereotypes of Japanese women, Hispanic men, and Arabs. In "Who's a Looter?" Tania Ralli explores the politics of photo-captioning in the aftermath of Hurricane Katrina. Chong-suk Han explores the marginal place that gay Asian American men have in both the Asian American and gay communities and the society at large. Writing in the business section of the *New York Times,* David Carr examines the extent to which the covers of women's popular magazines reflect the racial and ethnic diversity of the country—or even the magazines' readership. A Web page from the Commercial Closet Association defines a set of "best practices" for businesses that wish to include lesbians, gays, bisexuals, and transgendered individuals in their ads. Anne-Marie O'Connor investigates why we hear far more news stories about white women who've disappeared than about women of color who've gone missing. David Bositis explores the consequences for our society of failing to poll minority communities in adequate numbers. In his college newspaper, William Sea complains about male gender stereotyping in beer commercials. The chapter closes with a satirical piece from *The Onion* about stereotypes and anthropomorphic recyclables.

Originally, stereotypes were part of a printer's trade, enabling the printer to disseminate information quickly and relatively cheaply. No less a part of popular culture today, stereotypes of a different sort still disseminate information. You'll have to evaluate how much that information is worth.

come as your favorite
stereotype
6540 del playa
april 1st
friday

Geo Vittoratos, *Come as Your Favorite Stereotype*

Making a Visual Argument: Artists and Comics Take On Stereotyping

◀ Come as Your Favorite Stereotype, *a party invitation, was created by Geo Vittoratos, who was born in Canada in 1983 but now lives in California. Her Web site is <http://howtobegeo.com>. As you study it and the other images that open this chapter, consider how each relies crucially on stereotypes in the media and popular culture while simultaneously critiquing them.*

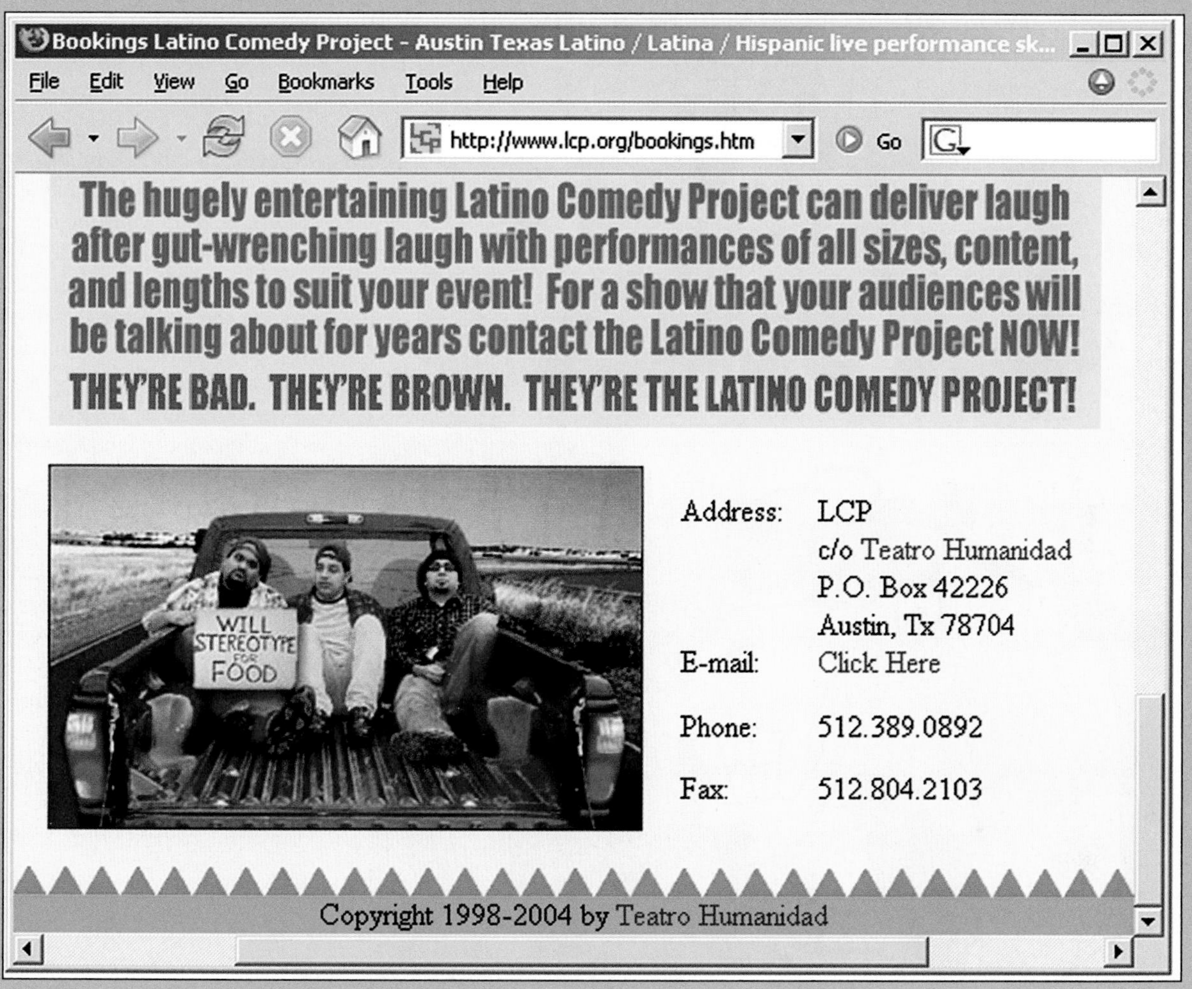
Bookings Latino Comedy Project - Austin Texas Latino / Latina / Hispanic live performance sk...
File Edit View Go Bookmarks Tools Help
http://www.lcp.org/bookings.htm
Go
The hugely entertaining Latino Comedy Project can deliver laugh after gut-wrenching laugh with performances of all sizes, content, and lengths to suit your event! For a show that your audiences will be talking about for years contact the Latino Comedy Project NOW!
THEY'RE BAD. THEY'RE BROWN. THEY'RE THE LATINO COMEDY PROJECT!
WILL STEREOTYPE FOR FOOD
Address: LCP
c/o Teatro Humanidad
P.O. Box 42226
Austin, Tx 78704
E-mail: Click Here
Phone: 512.389.0892
Fax: 512.804.2103
Copyright 1998-2004 by Teatro Humanidad

Latino Comedy Project, *Will Stereotype for Food*

▲ Will Stereotype for Food *is an image of the homepage of the Latino Comedy Project:* <http://lcp.org>*. Since 1998, this award-winning bilingual comedy troupe associated with* Teatro Humanidad *of Austin, Texas, has been entertaining audiences with its social satire and wit. In addition to performing regularly in Austin, the troupe has appeared at a number of festivals, and its videos have been shown on PBS and American Latino TV and featured at the Boston Latino Film Festival.*

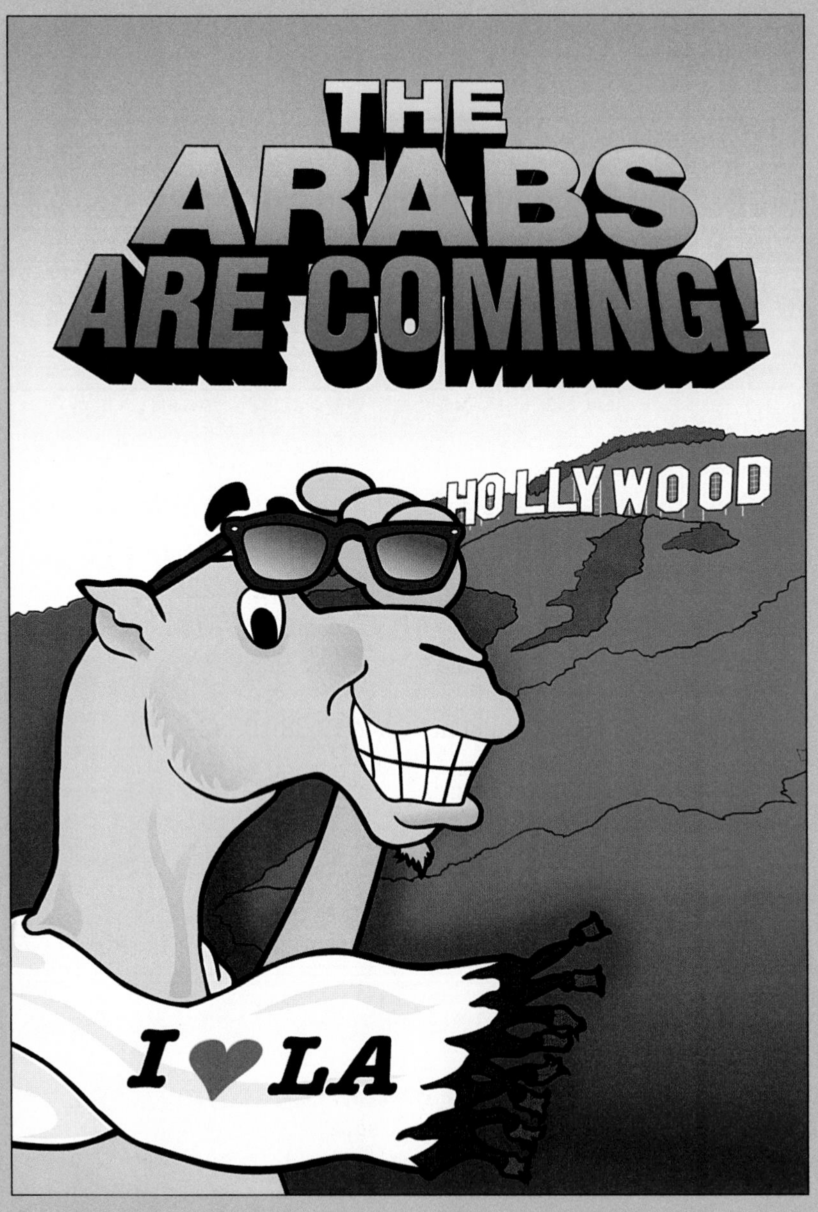

New York Arab-American Comedy Festival, *The Arabs Are Coming!*

The Arabs Are Coming! is *an advertisement for the New York Arab-American Comedy Festival's appearance in Los Angeles, California, in January 2006. The Festival, which was begun in 2003, continues to grow annually. According to the Festival's founders, the goal of the Los Angeles run was to "to create a showcase for the talented Arab-American actors, writers and stand up comics who have appeared in our Festival so that they can be seen by Hollywood casting agents and entertainment executives. We believe that the sooner more Arab-Americans are involved in the entertainment industry, the more effective we can be at encouraging Hollywood to begin portraying us accurately" (see <http://arabcomedy.org/news/article_118.shtml>).*

RESPOND•

1. What arguments are made in each of these images? What sorts of background knowledge must readers bring to the images to fully understand these arguments? (You'll need to check out the Web site for the New York Arab-American Comedy, <http://arabcomedy.org/news/article_118.shtml>, in order to understand some of the poster's humor and its argument.) How does each image represent an argument about stereotypes in the media and popular culture?
2. Choose one of these arguments, and explain how the visual image contributes to the overall argument. Try to comment specifically on the elements of the image that support the argument. If you're having trouble getting started, simply consider the text of any of the arguments without the visual image.
3. Dressing up as a stereotype for a costume party or stereotyping for food (or even laughs) can be risky business. What's at stake if one performs in some way the stereotypes of a group of which he or she is a member? Of a group of which he or she is not a member? Why are the stakes so different? Must such performances always be humorous? Will they necessarily be offensive? Why or why not?
4. Assume that you're going to a Come as Your Favorite Stereotype party. **Write an essay** in which you describe that stereotype, how you would dress in order to represent it, and why. Note that your essay will in many ways be definitional. (For a discussion of arguments of definition, see Chapter 8.) You may wish to consider the preceding question before responding to this assignment.

Journalist Tania Ralli's "Who's a Looter?" appeared in the New York Times early in September 2005, shortly after Hurricane Katrina hit the Gulf coast. This article and related pieces—whether in the print media, on television or radio, or on the Internet on all sorts of Web sites—were the subject of much public discussion following Katrina. The controversy hinged on the captions of two photos—one of an African American, the other of two white Americans—that some people saw as comparable and others claimed were anything but. As you read, consider your initial response to the captions, whether or not it changes as you read the article, and why.

Who's a Looter? In Storm's Aftermath, Pictures Kick Up a Different Kind of Tempest

TANIA RALLI

Two news photographs ricocheted through the Internet last week and set off a debate about race and the news media in the aftermath of Hurricane Katrina.

The first photo, taken by Dave Martin, an Associated Press photographer in New Orleans, shows a young black man wading through water that has risen to his chest. He is clutching a case of soda and pulling a floating bag. The caption provided by The A.P. says he has just been "looting a grocery store."

The second photo, also from New Orleans, was taken by Chris Graythen for Getty Images and distributed by Agence France-Presse. It shows a white couple up to their chests in the same

Information from an A.P. photographer described the young man, left, as looting. In a similar visual circumstance, the white couple was described by a different agency's photographer as finding food.

murky water. The woman is holding some bags of food. This caption says they are shown "after finding bread and soda from a local grocery store."

Both photos turned up Tuesday on Yahoo News, which posts automatic feeds of articles and photos from wire services. Soon after, a user of the photo-sharing site Flickr juxtaposed the images and captions on a single page, which attracted links from many blogs. The left-leaning blog Daily Kos linked to the page with the comment, "It's not looting if you're white."

5 The contrast of the two photo captions, which to many indicated a double standard at work, generated widespread anger toward the news media that quickly spread beyond the Web.

On Friday night, the rapper Kanye West ignored the teleprompter during NBC's live broadcast of "A Concert for Hurricane Relief," using the opportunity to lambaste President Bush and criticize the press. "I hate the way they portray us in the media," he said. "You see a black family, it says they're looting. You see a white family, it says they're looking for food."

Many bloggers were quick to point out that the photos came from two different agencies, and so could not reflect the prejudice of a single media outlet. A writer on the blog BoingBoing wrote: "Perhaps there's more factual substantiation behind each copywriter's choice of words than we know. But to some, the difference in tone suggests racial bias, implicit or otherwise."

According to the agencies, each photographer captioned his own photograph. Jack Stokes, a spokesman for The A.P., said that photographers are told to describe what they have seen when they write a caption.

Mr. Stokes said The A.P. had guidelines in place before Hurricane Katrina struck to distinguish between "looting" and "carrying." If a photographer sees a person enter a business and emerge with goods, it is described as looting. Otherwise The A.P. calls it carrying.

10 Mr. Stokes said that Mr. Martin had seen the man in his photograph wade into a grocery store and come out with the sodas and bag, so by A.P.'s definition, the man had looted.

The photographer for Getty Images, Mr. Graythen, said in an e-mail message that he had also stuck to what he had seen to write his caption, and had actually given the wording a great deal of thought. Mr. Graythen described seeing the couple near a corner store from an elevated expressway. The door to the shop was open, and things had floated out to the street. He was not able to talk to the couple, "so I had to draw my own conclusions," he said.

In the extreme conditions of New Orleans, Mr. Graythen said, taking necessities like food and water to survive could not be considered stealing. He said that had he seen people coming out of stores with computers and DVD players, he would have considered that looting.

"If you're taking something that runs solely from a wall outlet that requires power from the electric company—when we are not going to have power for weeks, even months—that's inexcusable," he said.

Since the photo was published last Tuesday Mr. Graythen has received more than 500 e-mail messages, most of them supportive, he said.

15 Within three hours of the photo's publication online, editors at Agence France-Presse rewrote Mr. Graythen's caption. But the original caption remained online as part of a Yahoo News slide show. Under pressure to keep up with the news, and lacking the time for a discussion about word choice, Olivier Calas, the agency's director of multimedia, asked Yahoo to remove the photo last Thursday.

Now, in its place, when readers seek the picture of the couple, a statement from Neil Budde, the general manager of Yahoo News, appears in its place. The statement emphasizes that Yahoo News did not write the photo captions and that it did not edit the captions, so that the photos can be made available as quickly as possible.

Mr. Calas said Agence France-Presse was bombarded with e-mail messages complaining about the caption. He said the caption was unclear and should have been reworded earlier. "This was a consequence of a series of negligences, not ill intent," he said.

For Mr. Graythen, whose parents and grandparents lost their homes in the disaster, the fate of the survivors was the most important thing. In his e-mail message he wrote: "Now is no time to pass judgment on those trying to stay alive. Now is no time to argue semantics about finding versus looting. Now is no time to argue if this is a white versus black issue."

As a journalist, Ralli presents this news article as an unbiased report of public reaction to photo captions from hurricane Katrina. Chapter 12 offers caveats on avoiding unduly slanted language.

LINK TO P. 370

RESPOND.

1. In what ways does this controversy hinge on a definitional argument? (For a discussion of arguments of definition, see Chapter 8.) What are the relevant terms, and how are they being defined by various parties? Whose definition(s) do you prefer? Why?
2. If the situation Ralli describes is no more than a definitional argument, why was there such controversy? In other words, what, beyond definitions, is or was at stake in this situation? How are these larger issues related to the topic of this chapter? How are they related to differing perceptions of U.S. history and of U.S. society at the present time?
3. As the headnote states, the captions of these two photos were the subject of considerable controversy. Here's a posting by Chris Graythen, who photographed the white couple, on a message board from Sports Shooter, a Web site for sports photographers, <http://sportsshooter.com/message_display.html?tid=17204>. The message was posted on August 31, 2005, at 6:10 P.M. as part of a heated discussion entitled "Finding vs. Looting (word choice in AP caption)." It's reprinted here as it was posted:

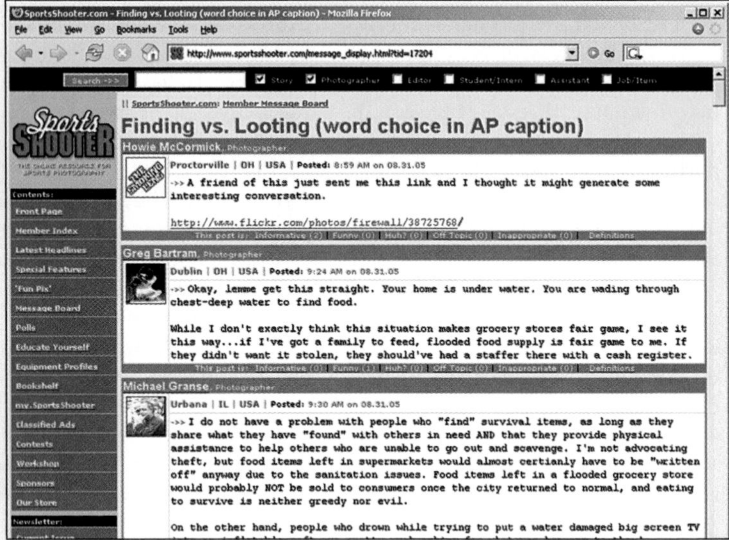

Jeasus, I don't belive how much crap I'm getting from this. First of all, I hope you excuse me, but I'm completely at the end of my rope. You have no Idea how stressful this whole disaster is, espically since I have not seen my wife in 5 days, and my parents and grand parents HAVE LOST THEIR HOMES. As of right now, we have almost NOTHING.

Please stop emailing me on this one.

I wrote the caption about the two people who 'found' the items. I believed in my opinion, that they did simply find them, and not 'looted' them in the definition of the word. The people were swimming in chest deep water, and there were other people in the water, both white and black. I looked for the best picture. there were a million items floating in the water - we were right near a grocery store that had 5+ feet of water in it. it had no doors. the water was moving, and the stuff was floating away. These people were not ducking into a store and busting down windows to get electronics. They picked up bread and cokes that were floating in the water. They would have floated away anyhow. I wouldn't have taken in, because I wouldn't eat anything that's been in that water. But I'm not homeless. (well, technically I am right now.)

I'm not trying to be politically correct. I'm don't care if you are white or black. I spent 4 hours on a boat in my parent's neighborhood shooting, and rescuing people, both black and white, dog and cat. I am a journalist, and a human being - and I see all as such. If you don't belive me, you can look on Getty today and see the images I shot of real looting today, and you will see white and black people, and they were DEFINATELY looting. And I put that in the caption.

Please, please don't argue symantics over this one. This is EXTREMELY serious, and I can't even begin to convey to those not here what it is like. Please, please, be more concerned on how this affects all of us (watch gas prices) and please, please help out if you can.

This is my home, I will hopefully always be here. I know that my friends in this business across the gulf south are going through the exact same thing - and I am with them, and will do whatever I can to help. But please, please don't email me any more about this caption issue.

And please, don't yell at me about spelling and grammar. Im eating my first real meal (a sandwich) right now in 3 days.

When this calms down, I will be more than willing to answer any questions, just ask.

Thank you all -

–Chris Graythen

What sorts of appeals—ethical, logical, and emotional—does Graythen offer his fellow photographers? Do his mistakes in typing and spelling contribute to or detract from his argument and his ethos? Why?

4. **Write an essay** in which you evaluate the claims made by both sides in this controversy, that is, those who argued the captions were racist and those who argued they weren't. (Odds are that you'll be able to find additional information about these photos and the controversies they sparked on the Internet.) Rather than seeking to declare that one side is right while the other is wrong, try to determine what's at stake for people aligning themselves with each side of this controversy.

Chong-suk Han wrote this essay, which appeared in 2005 in the **Gay & Lesbian Review Worldwide,** *while he was a doctoral candidate in the program in social welfare at the University of Washington in Seattle. Prior to enrolling in that program, he was editor of the* **International Examiner: The Journal of the Northwest Asian Pacific American Communities,** *also based in Seattle. In addition to serving as a member of the Seattle Human Rights Commission, he has taught at the University of California—Irvine, where he received his M.A. degree; at Cascadia Community College; and at the University of Washington. His current research focuses on how gay Asian male identities influence sexual behavior. As you read, consider how Han uses a range of kinds of sources, as well as many sorts of examples, to support his claims.*

Han invites the reader to explore the identity plight of gay Asian American men. Chapter 1 outlines what constitutes an argument to explore and what makes it different from other types of arguments.

LINK TO P. 11

Gay Asian-American Male Seeks Home

CHONG-SUK HAN

"The West thinks of itself as masculine—big guns, big industry, big money—so the East is feminine—weak, delicate, poor . . . but good at art, and full of inscrutable wisdom—the feminine mystique . . . I am an Oriental. And being an Oriental, I could never be completely a man."

–Song Linling in *M Butterfly*

In the critically acclaimed play *M Butterfly*, by David Henry Hwang, the main character, Song Linling, explains his ability to fool a French lieutenant into believing that he was a woman for nearly two decades, a feat based not on his mastery of deception but on the lieutenant's inability to see him as anything other than a woman. For decades, the mainstream media have usually portrayed Asian men as meek, asexual houseboy types or as sexual deviants of some kind. When it comes to attitudes about sex, Asian-American men have generally been portrayed as being on the "traditional" or "conservative" side of the spectrum. Recently the magazine *Details*, which caters to "hip, young, urban males," prominently featured an item entitled "Gay or Asian," and challenged its readers to ascertain whether a given man was, in fact, gay or Asian. Interestingly enough, while the broader Asian-American community mounted a protest against the presentation of Asian men as "gay," the larger gay community stood silently by.

"The Orient was almost a European invention," observed Edward Said (1978), "and had been since antiquity a place of romance, exotic beings, haunting memories and landscapes, remarkable experiences." These are all images that happen to be female evocations in the Western mind, and indeed the association between the Orient and the feminine can be traced back to ancient times. The West's view of itself as the embodiment of the male principle was further justified by—and undoubtedly served to justify—Europe's subordination of much of Asia starting in the 18th century: its "masculine thrust" upon the continent, if you will.

This discourse of domination at the level of civilizations has played itself out in countless ways over the centuries. For men of Asian descent who have resided in the United States, this has often meant their exclusion from the labor market of "masculine" jobs and the denial of leadership positions in their communities and even in their families. The cultural emasculation of Asian men in America has produced what Eng (2001) has called "racial castration." This in turn has led to the image of Asian men as largely sexless or undersexed—but this hasn't prevented another stereotype from arising, that of Asian men as sexual deviants, helplessly lusting after white women who don't want them. But more often they fade into the sexual background—even as Asian women are often portrayed as highly desirable, notably to sexually competent white men.

The situation for gay men of Asian descent in the U.S. has been intimately tied to the same processes that led non-gay Asian men to be racialized and marginalized by mainstream society. While straight men have been able to function within the growing Asian-American community, gay Asian men continue to be marginalized both by the dominant society and by the Asian communities. If anything, they've been rendered even more invisible by a new cultural formation that stresses "family values" while it perpetuates the image of Asians as "America's model minority"—an image that denies the very existence of gay Asian-Americans. Studies on gender and sexuality have largely ignored racial minorities in their discussions. Given this invisibility, it is not surprising that so little has been written about the process of identity formation for gay Asian men. What is known about gay Asian-American men has come from the small but growing number of literary and artistic works produced by gay Asian men, as well as the literature on HIV/AIDS in the Asian-American community.

In Chay Yew's acclaimed play *Porcelain*, both the Chinese and the gay com- 5
munities deny "ownership" of John Lee when he's charged with murdering his white lover in a London lavatory. In a particularly trenchant scene, members of the Chinese community exclaim, "He is not one of us!"—a sentiment that's echoed in the gay community as well. Choi et al. (1998) argues that marginalization by both of these communities may lead to low self-esteem among gay Asian men and contribute to the increasing percentage of gay Asian men who engage in unsafe sex and seroconvert.°

seroconvert: to develop antibodies in the blood serum as the result of infection; here, specifically, to become HIV-positive.

In his essay "China Doll," Tony Ayers (1999) discusses his sense of being outside the gay mainstream due to his Chinese ethnicity. In addition to discussing the overt forms of racism—such as gay classified ads that specifically state, "no fats, no femmes, no Asians," and being told by other gay men that they are "not into Asians"—Ayers describes some of the more subtle forms of racism, such as that of "rice queens"° who desire Asian men purely for their exotic eroticism. What rice queens are often attracted to in Asian men is an idealized notion of a passive, docile, submissive—in short, a feminized—lover, eager to please his virile white man.

queen: a slang term, almost always pejorative, for a gay male.

It is indeed striking how the image of gay white men has been transformed from that of "sissy nelly" to "macho stud" over the past few decades, but no such transformation has occurred where gay API (Asian and Pacific Island) men are concerned. Gay white men are often portrayed as rugged, chiseled studs. But the masculinization of gay white men has been coupled with a feminization of gay API men. When a white man and an API man are presented together in a sexual situation, the former is almost always the sexual dominator while the latter is submissive. For better or worse, many gay Asian men seem to have accepted this stereotype, often participating in their own exotification and playing up their "feminine" allure.

What's more, Asian men themselves have also bought into the gay Western notion of what is desirable. Ayers explains that "The sexually marginalized Asian man who has grown up in the West or is Western in his thinking is often invisible in his own fantasies. [Their] sexual daydreams are populated by handsome Caucasian men with lean, hard Caucasian bodies." In a survey of gay Asian men in San Francisco, Choi et al. (1995) found that nearly seventy percent of gay Asian men indicate a preference for white men. More damaging to the gay Asian population is that most of these men seem to be competing for the attention of a limited number of "rice queens." This competition hinders the formation of a unified gay Asian community and further acts to splinter those who should be seen as natural allies.

Not surprisingly, many gay Asian men report feeling inadequate within the larger gay community that stresses a Eurocentric image of physical beauty. Given these feelings of inadequacy, gay Asian men may suffer from low self-esteem and actively pursue the company of white men in order to feel accepted. In addition to seeking the company of white men, the obsession with white beauty leads gay Asian men to reject their cultural roots. For example, Chuang (1999) writes about how he tried desperately to avoid anything related to his Chinese heritage and his attempts to transform his "shamefully slim Oriental frame . . . into a more desirable Western body." Other manifestations of attempting to hide one's heritage may include bleaching one's hair or even the wearing of blue contact lenses.

The fear of rejection from family and friends may be more acute for gay 10
Asians than for other groups. While some have noted the cultural factors associated with Confucianism and the strong family values associated with Asian-Americans, these explanations fall short, given that many Asian-American communities (particularly Filipino and South Asian) are not rooted in a Confucian ethic. Instead, the compounded feeling of fear may have more to do with their status as racial and ethnic minorities within the U.S., which isolates these groups and increases the importance of the family as a nexus

of support. By coming out to their families, Asian-American gays and lesbians risk losing the support of their family and community and facing the sometimes hostile larger society on their own. Unlike gay white men, who can find representation and support in the gay community, gay Asian men often do not have the option of finding a new community outside of the ethnic one they would be leaving behind. In fact, there is some evidence that gay Asian men who are less integrated into the Asian-American community may be at higher risk for HIV/AIDS due to a lack of available support networks. In a study with gay Asian men, Choi et al. (1998) found that gay Asian men often feel that their families would not support their sexual orientation, which leads them to remain closeted until a later age than is typical for white men.

In the absence of a vocabulary to describe their experiences, gay Asian men and women have had to create new words and concepts to define their identity. Within the past few years, a number of gay Asian groups and activists have challenged the Western notions of beauty and questioned the effects of these notions on the gay Asian community. Eric Reyes (1996) asks, "which do you really want—rice queen fantasies at your bookstore or freedom rings° at the checkout stand of your local Asian market?" In posing this question, Reyes asks us where we should begin to build our home in this place we call America, in the "heterosexual male-dominated America, white gay male–centered Queer America, the marginalized People of Color America, or our often-romanticized Asian America?" It is this continuing attempt to find a gay Asian space that lies at the heart of one group's quest for a place in the American sun.

freedom rings: a series of six rings in the colors of the Rainbow Flag, a symbol of the lesbian and gay community, often worn on necklaces or carried on keychains. The stripes of the flag and the colors of the rings are meant to represent the unity and diversity found within the community.

References

Ayers, T. "China Doll: The experience of being a gay Chinese Australian," in *Multicultural Queer: Australian Narratives,* by P. Jackson and G. Sullivan (eds.). Haworth Press, 1999.

Choi K. H., et al. (1998). "HIV prevention among Asian and Pacific Islander American men who have sex with men." *AIDS Education and Prevention,* 1998.

Choi K. H., et al. (1995). "High HIV risk among gay Asian and Pacific Islander men in San Francisco." *AIDS.* 9.

Chuang, K. "Using chopsticks to eat steak," in *Multicultural Queer: Australian Narratives,* by P. Jackson and G. Sullivan (eds.). Haworth Press, 1999.

Eng, D. *Racial Castration: Managing Masculinity in Asian America.* Duke University Press, 2001.

Reyes, Eric E. "Strategies for Queer Asian and Pacific Islander Spaces," in *Asian American Sexualities,* Russell Leong (ed.). Routledge, 1996.

Said, Edward. *Orientalism.* Vintage Books, 1978.

RESPOND•

1. In his essay, Han is making a general argument about stereotypes in the media and popular culture using gay Asian American males as his example. What factors does Han cite that shape the experience of gay Asian American males? How are these men doubly marginalized?
2. Analyze Han's opening paragraph. How does he use the quotation from David Henry Hwang's *M Butterfly* and the description of responses to a then-recent issue of *Details* magazine to set up his argument? What, specifically, is the importance of his characterization of the French lieutenant, who loved Song Linling, in terms of the former's inability to see the latter as "anything other than a woman"? What's the importance of Han's contrast of the responses of the Asian American and gay community to the feature in *Details?*
3. No doubt you rightly assumed that *Gay & Lesbian Review Worldwide* targets lesbians and gay men as its primary audience. In what ways has Han taken that audience into account as he writes? How would you describe his intended audience? His invoked audience? Given Han's claims, how would you expect issues confronting gay Asian American women to be similar to those confronting gay Asian American men? How might they differ? Do these similarities and differences account sufficiently for Han's focus uniquely on the situation of Asian American men?
4. Han contends that the larger gay community's idea of physical beauty is Eurocentric in nature (paragraph 9). What does he see as the consequences of such a situation? In what ways does David Carr's piece, *On Covers of Many Magazines, a Full Racial Palette Is Still Rare* (p. 649), make a similar argument about American society more generally? Do you agree or disagree? Why?
5. Like many people writing on difference, Han contends that if we are to understand how stereotypes work in American culture (or any culture), we must look not only at the stereotypes circulating within the larger society but also at those found within specific minority groups. Likewise, he notes that to be a gay Asian American male, for example, is a more complicated matter than a simple sum of male + gay + Asian American. **In an essay,** evaluate one or both of these claims, drawing on your own experiences, those of people you know, or those of people you've read about. (For a discussion of evaluative arguments, see Chapter 9.)

This news article from the Business Section of the New York Times *in fall 2003 uses many kinds of evidence to examine a situation that many Americans find troubling, namely, the difference between the demographics of the country's population at large and the characteristics of people who end up on the covers of magazines. In so doing, David Carr raises important questions about representation: Who or what do magazine covers represent? Why don't the people on magazine covers look like the population at large? As you read, pay special attention to the kinds of evidence Carr uses, particularly the ways he incorporates statistics and charts based on statistics.*

On Covers of Many Magazines, a Full Racial Palette Is Still Rare

DAVID CARR

Halle Berry, in her role as the sexy superspy Jinx in *Die Another Day,* helps James Bond save the world from certain doom. But Ms. Berry may be performing an even more improbable feat as the cover model of the December issue of *Cosmopolitan* magazine.

Ms. Berry became only the fifth black to appear on the cover of *Cosmopolitan* since the magazine began using cover photographs in 1964, and she is the first since Naomi Campbell in 1990. Ms. Berry is evidently one of a tiny cadre of nonwhite celebrities who are deemed to have enough crossover appeal to appear on the cover of mass consumer magazines.

There are signs that the freeze-out may be beginning to thaw, as the continuing explosion of hip-hop has pushed many black artists into prominence, and as teenagers' magazines that are less anxious about race are bringing more diversity. But in many broad-circulation magazines, the unspoken but routinely observed practice of not using nonwhite cover subjects — for fear they will depress newsstand sales — remains largely in effect.

A survey of 471 covers from 31 magazines published in 2002 — an array of men's and women's magazines, entertainment publications and teenagers' magazines — conducted two weeks ago by the *New York Times* found that about one in five depicted minority members. Five years ago, according to the survey, which examined all the covers of those 31 magazines back through 1998, the figure was only 12.7 percent. And fashion magazines have more than doubled their use of nonwhite cover subjects.

But in a country with a nonwhite 5
population of almost 30 percent, the incremental progress leaves some people unimpressed.

"The magazine industry has been slow and reluctant to embrace the change in our culture," said Roy S. Johnson, editorial director of Vanguarde Media and editor in chief of *Savoy,* a magazine aimed at black men. "The change is broad and profound, and in many ways is now the mainstream."

Carr could have asked almost anybody for his or her opinion, but each of the interviewees here contributes a specific kind of credibility to the piece. Adapt the criteria given in Chapter 19 for evaluating print sources to the task of evaluating Carr's choice of interview subjects with respect to their credentials and relevance.

LINK TO P. 530

The absence of cover-model diversity could reflect the industry's racial homogeneity. Four years ago, the trade publication *Mediaweek* found that only 6.1 percent of the magazine industry's professional staff was nonwhite.

"We do not see ourselves in magazines," said Diane Weathers, editor in chief of *Essence,* a monthly magazine for black women. "Considering what the country we live in looks like today, I think it's appalling."

The women's category has seen the most profound changes, largely as a result of *O, The Oprah Magazine,* whose cover repeatedly hosts Oprah Winfrey and has a large white readership.

10 Both *Cosmo* and *O* are published by Hearst magazines. As a newsstand giant, selling two million copies a month, *Cosmo* uses a near scientific blend of sex and Middle American beauty on its covers—a formula that does not seem to include black women. *O* magazine, in contrast, transcends race with a new, spiritually based female empowerment.

Publishing is a conservative industry, one that has been known to define risk as using a cover model with dark hair instead of blond. But a wave of Latina superstars like Jennifer Lopez, along with genre-breaking athletes like Tiger Woods and the Williams sisters, have redefined what a celebrity looks like. And the audience is changing as well. In the last five years, the nonwhite audience for magazines has increased to 17 percent from 15 percent, according to Mediamark Research Inc.

Yet, even as black and Hispanic women slowly make their way onto the covers of magazines of various genres, black males still find themselves mainly confined to a ghetto of music and sports magazines.

"When it comes to magazine covers, my client, who is one of the busiest guys in Hollywood, can't get arrested," said an agent for an A-list Hollywood actor who declined to give her name or the name of her client for fear of making a bad situation even worse. "Magazines are in trouble and they are fearful of offending their audience of Middle Americans," she said. "But those same people are buying tickets to his movies."

Daniel Peres, editor of *Details,* a men's magazine owned by Fairchild Publications, said there was pressure to stick with outdated conventions because newsstands now display so many more titles competing for the consumer's attention.

"Magazines aimed at teenagers use far more nonwhite cover subjects."

15 "Everyone is terrified of a misstep," he said. "While most people in the business would prefer it go unspoken because they are horrified at being perceived as racist, it is a well-known legend that blacks, especially black males, do not help generate newsstand sales."

Christina Kelly, now editor in chief of *YM,* a teenagers' magazine owned by Gruner & Jahr USA, recalls a struggle with the circulation people when she worked as an editor in 1993 at the now-closed *Sassy* magazine.

"We wanted to put Mecca from the band Digable Planets on the cover because she was huge at the time and gorgeous," she recalled. "The circulation guys hated the idea, but we just went ahead and did it. The magazine was bagged with a separate beauty booklet, which was usually placed in the back, but this time, it was bagged in front. It just happened to have a picture of a blond, blue-eyed woman on it."

Today, magazines like *Teen People* and *YM* feature cover subjects of a variety of hues. In the last year, *YM* has had covers that included nonwhite artists like Ashanti and Enrique Iglesias. And in August, *Teen People* chose Usher, a black R&B singer, as its No. 1 "hot guy" and featured him on the cover.

"Race is a much more fluid concept among teens," said Barbara O'Dair, managing editor of *Teen People.*

20 Magazines for teenagers, because of their reliance on the heavily integrated music industry, use 25 percent nonwhite subjects on their covers. If white teenagers are crossing over to embrace minority artists, many artists are meeting them halfway in terms of style.

Fashion, previously a very segregated world, has become transracial, with young white women adopting street fashion while black artists wear long, flowing tresses. Certain totems of beauty—blond hair, among other things—can now be seamlessly situated on almost anyone regardless of race. The singers Shakira, Beyoncé Knowles, and Christina Aguilera, all nonwhite, have at times worn blond hair that is indiscernible from that of Britney Spears.

"There is virtually no stigma attached to black celebrities changing their hair as there has been in the past," said Leon E. Wynter, author of *American Skin: Pop Culture, Big Business, and the End of White America* (Crown Publishers, 2002). "The hair thing is completely over."

And race itself has become more complicated and less definable, said Mr. Wynter. He suggests that many of the Latin superstars like Jennifer Lopez are often seen not as minorities by young white teenagers, but as a different kind of white person. Very few of the breakout artists featured on covers are dark skinned.

The growing acceptance of nonwhite cover subjects is not restricted to teenaged girls. Men's magazines, for example, are not as racially monolithic as they once were. *GQ,* which has a nonwhite readership of 18 percent, has always had more diverse images by featuring minority athletes and actors.

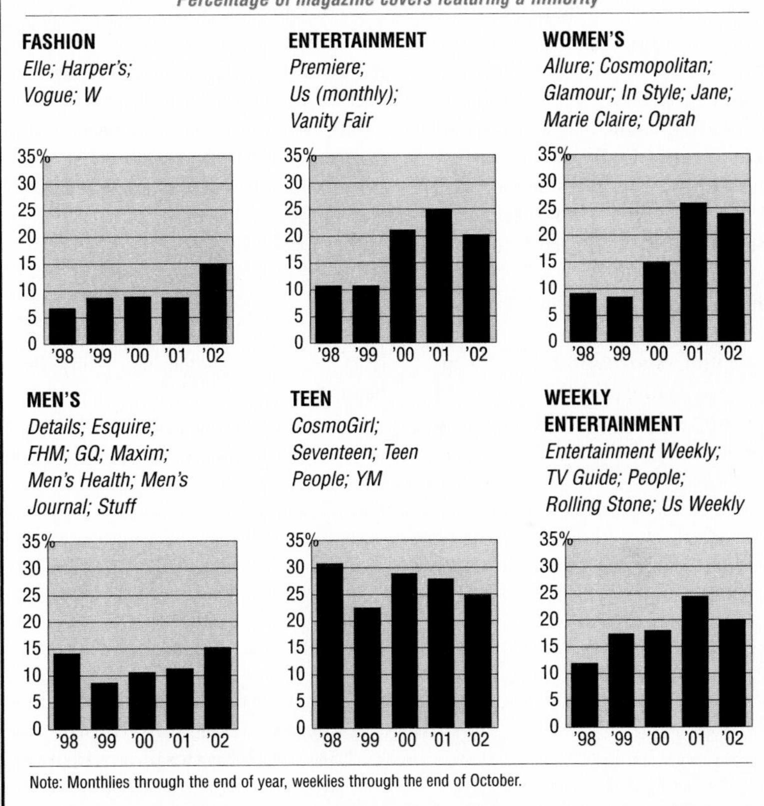
Cover Census
According to the United States Census Bureau, almost 30 percent of America's population belongs to minority groups. Over the last five years, however, the images on the covers of mass-market consumer magazines featured members of a minority less than 25 percent of the time in most categories.
Percentage of magazine covers featuring a minority
FASHION
Elle; Harper's; Vogue; W
ENTERTAINMENT
Premiere; Us (monthly); Vanity Fair
WOMEN'S
Allure; Cosmopolitan; Glamour; In Style; Jane; Marie Claire; Oprah
MEN'S
Details; Esquire; FHM; GQ; Maxim; Men's Health; Men's Journal; Stuff
TEEN
CosmoGirl; Seventeen; Teen People; YM
WEEKLY ENTERTAINMENT
Entertainment Weekly; TV Guide; People; Rolling Stone; Us Weekly
35%
30
25
20
15
10
5
0
'98
'99
'00
'01
'02
Note: Monthlies through the end of year, weeklies through the end of October.

25 But a newer generation of men's magazines seem to find ethnicity sexy. In the last year, 5 of the 12 women featured on the cover of *Maxim,* the spectacularly successful young men's magazine owned by Dennis Publishing USA, were other than white.

"It doesn't stem from any political motivation," said Keith Blanchard, editor in chief of *Maxim.* His readers, mostly white young men, "are listening to Shakira and Beyoncé. They are cheering for Lucy Liu kicking butt in 'Charlie's Angels.' And I think there is a certain attraction to exotic women."

But there are those who would argue that equal opportunity objectification of women does not represent progress. "What is attractive is socially constructed," said Robin D. G. Kelley, a professor of history at New York University who has written extensively about race and black culture. "I think that race still matters, and many times what is happening is that these poly-racial figures are used to fulfill fantasies. It's the Jezebel phenomenon."

As for the December *Cosmopolitan,* Kate White, the magazine's editor in chief, said Ms. Berry was on her cover simply because she meets all the criteria of a typical *Cosmo* girl. "She is beautiful, powerful, successful, and she can open a movie," Ms. White said, suggesting that Ms. Berry has the kind of wattage that can draw people into a movie, or to buy a magazine. Ms. White said the absence of nonwhite women on the cover of *Cosmo* reflected the celebrities that Hollywood produces, not the magazine's preferences.

Still, when the magazine uses a model instead of a celebrity, it almost invariably chooses a white person. "We choose models who have already started to gain critical mass, regardless of hair or eye color," said a Hearst spokeswoman in response. "We want the reader to have a sense of having seen them before."

30 It probably helps, in terms of both newsstand and advertising, that Ms. Berry's face is everywhere now that she has been selected as a spokeswoman for the cosmetics company Revlon. There are important business, as well as cultural reasons, why after so many years that black, at least in some magazines, may be beautiful.

"Part of what is going on is that the beauty industry woke up and realized there was a big market there," said Roberta Myers, editor in chief of *Elle,* a women's fashion magazine that is uncommonly diverse in cover selections. "The old assumptions that there was only one kind of beauty, the typical blond, blue-eyed Christie Brinkley type, are gone."

While editors sweat over the consequences of diversifying their cover mix, they may fall behind a coming generation of young consumers who have decided that race is much less important than how hot a given celebrity's latest record or film is.

"The list of who is acceptable or hot is slowly expanding," said Mr. Wynter. "In the current generation, there is an underlying urge, an aspiration, to assert one's common humanity. You can't see it in the magazines that are on the shelves now, but it is coming to the fore."

RESPOND •

1. What argument is being made in Carr's article? Does it surprise you in any way? Does it matter that the article appeared in the business section of the newspaper rather than, say, on the front page or in the lifestyle section? Why or why not? How might the argument have been framed differently if it had been written for a different section of the newspaper? Why?
2. What sorts of arguments does Carr use to support his thesis? Certainly consider the kinds of evidence discussed in Chapter 16, but don't limit yourself to these sorts of support. For example, how does Carr use figurative language (for example, "a ghetto of music and sports magazines" paragraph 12) to advance his argument?

3. How do you evaluate Carr's discussion of Black males continuing to end up on the covers of sports and music magazines and of the growing number of "exotic" women who appear on the covers of magazines designed for primarily young White men? Do these facts serve as evidence of "progress"? In what sense? Might they be interpreted in other ways?
4. Obviously, magazine covers play a critical role in influencing buyers, especially "impulse" buyers who don't subscribe but purchase the magazine at a newsstand. Thus some might claim that magazine publishers are merely responding to the whims of their buyers. Others will claim that publishers have a hand in creating consumer preferences. **Write an essay** in which you evaluate the situation described by Carr; you may wish to offer a proposal of some sort about this situation, especially if you see it as a problem. (For a discussion of proposal arguments, see Chapter 11.)

Founded in 2001, the Commercial Closet Association seeks to educate advertisers about the gay, lesbian, bisexual, and transgender (GLBT) communities and issues that arise in including them in advertisements so that advertisers can be commercially successful. This selection, "Mainstream/Business-to-Business Advertising Best Practices," represents an increasingly common kind of informative argument—a description and illustration of "best practices," ones that work successfully—directed toward those who need assistance devising policies and, in this case, ad campaigns. You may wish to visit the source for this selection: <http://commercialcloset.org/cgi-bin/iowa/index.html?page=best>. If you do, you'll find the original hypertext document, one with numerous links to sources for factual claims made as well as examples of the ads discussed—the sort of text that wasn't imaginable before the advent of the Internet. As you'll see, the ads come from around the world.

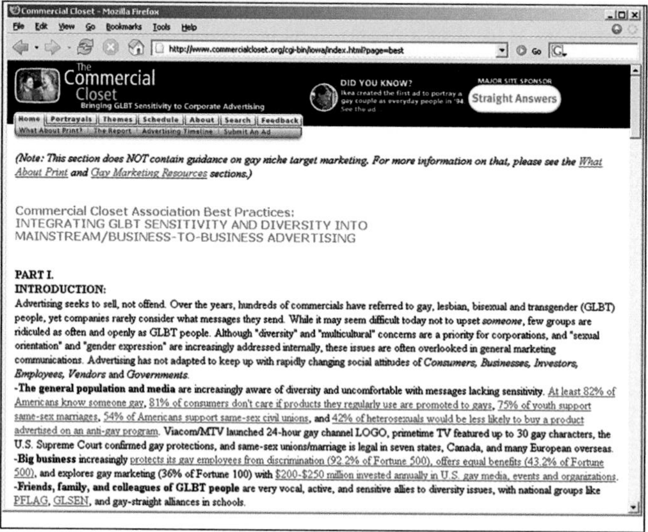
Commercial Closet - Mozilla Firefox

File Edit View Go Bookmarks Tools Help

http://www.commercialcloset.org/cgi-bin/iowa/index.html?page=best

The Commercial Closet

Bringing GLBT Sensitivity to Corporate Advertising

DID YOU KNOW?

Ikea created the first ad to portray a gay couple as everyday people in '94. See the ad

MAJOR SITE SPONSOR

Straight Answers

Home | Portrayals | Themes | Schedule | About | Search | Feedback

What About Print? | The Report | Advertising Timeline | Submit An Ad

(Note: This section does NOT contain guidance on gay niche target marketing. For more information on that, please see the What About Print and Gay Marketing Resources sections.)

Commercial Closet Association Best Practices:
INTEGRATING GLBT SENSITIVITY AND DIVERSITY INTO MAINSTREAM/BUSINESS-TO-BUSINESS ADVERTISING

PART I.
INTRODUCTION:
Advertising seeks to sell, not offend. Over the years, hundreds of commercials have referred to gay, lesbian, bisexual and transgender (GLBT) people, yet companies rarely consider what messages they send. While it may seem difficult today not to upset *someone*, few groups are ridiculed as often and openly as GLBT people. Although "diversity" and "multicultural" concerns are a priority for corporations, and "sexual orientation" and "gender expression" are increasingly addressed internally, these issues are often overlooked in general marketing communications. Advertising has not adapted to keep up with rapidly changing social attitudes of *Consumers, Businesses, Investors, Employees, Vendors* and *Governments*.
-**The general population and media** are increasingly aware of diversity and uncomfortable with messages lacking sensitivity. At least 82% of Americans know someone gay, 81% of consumers don't care if products they regularly use are promoted to gays, 75% of youth support same-sex marriages, 54% of Americans support same-sex civil unions, and 42% of heterosexuals would be less likely to buy a product advertised on an anti-gay program. Viacom/MTV launched 24-hour gay channel LOGO, primetime TV featured up to 30 gay characters, the U.S. Supreme Court confirmed gay protections, and same-sex unions/marriage is legal in seven states, Canada, and many European overseas.
-**Big business** increasingly protects its gay employees from discrimination (92.2% of Fortune 500), offers equal benefits (43.2% of Fortune 500), and explores gay marketing (36% of Fortune 100) with $200-$250 million invested annually in U.S. gay media, events and organizations.
-**Friends, family, and colleagues of GLBT people** are very vocal, active, and sensitive allies to diversity issues, with national groups like PFLAG, GLSEN, and gay-straight alliances in schools.

Mainstream/Business-to-Business Advertising Best Practices

COMMERCIAL CLOSET ASSOCIATION

Part I Introduction:

Advertising seeks to sell, not offend. Over the years, hundreds of commercials have referred to gay, lesbian, bisexual and transgender (GLBT) people, yet companies rarely consider what messages they send. While it may seem difficult today not to upset someone, few groups are ridiculed as often and openly as GLBT people. Today, "diversity" and "multicultural" mean more than just ethnicity and gender—they include "sexual orientation" and "gender expression." But corporations have not adapted to keep general marketing communications in line with rapidly changing social attitudes of *Consumers, Businesses, Investors and Employees.*

- **The general population and media** are increasingly aware of diversity and uncomfortable with messages lacking sensitivity. Over 90% of Americans know someone gay, and 42% of heterosexuals would be less likely to buy a product advertised on an anti-gay program. Viacom/MTV will launch a 24-hour gay channel in 2005, primetime TV has featured up to 30 gay characters, the Supreme Court confirmed gay protections, and same-sex marriage is law in Massachusetts, Canada and overseas.
- **Big business** increasingly protects its gay employees from discrimination (80% of Fortune 500), offers equal benefits (25% of Fortune 500), and explores gay marketing (33% of Fortune 100).
- **Friends, family, and colleagues of GLBT** people are vocal and sensitive to diversity issues.
- **GLBT people** represent 4%-10% of the population (8.4 million to 21 million American adults), and belong to every family and work for every company. Such individuals vary in color, age, religion, national origin, gender expression, ability, politics, profession, and class. About 1.2 million reported to the 2000 U.S. Census they are partnered in rural areas, suburbs and cities, and 1 in 5 have children.

Part II Best Practices:

This document is a tool to assist executives (gay and straight) to create effective, inclusive mainstream and business-to-business advertising that is respectful of gay, lesbian, bisexual and transgender (GLBT) people, while promoting creativity, sales and image goals. Drawing upon reporting observations, trial, and analysis from industry leaders, Commercial Closet Association recommends the following five points:

1. **Be inclusive and diverse.** Whenever people are shown, include GLBT individuals/family members/friends/couples, reflecting varied ages, races, genders, etc. Language references to family, relationships or gender should not be hetero-centric.

This guide to best practices is essentially an argument of proposal about practices. Chapter 11 presents several types of proposal arguments and the essential characteristics of a well-formed argument of this nature.

LINK TO P. 335

2. **Be sensitive to gay, lesbian, bisexual, and transgender stereotypes and avoid positioning homosexuality/transgender as a perceived threat for humor.** Advertising often stereotypes, but beware of complications. Feminine gay men and deceitful/scary transgender people are old ideas that alienate many. Straight-male-fantasy "lipstick lesbians" are narrow clichés.
3. **Do good research.** When conducting general research or forming new mainstream campaigns, GLBT perspectives should be considered and included as often as possible. Don't limit their input only to gay-targeted messages.
4. **Go national.** Consumers outside of major coastal cities are often improperly considered lacking sophistication to handle GLBT themes.
5. **Be consistent and confident.** Modifying or withdrawing ads suggests waffling and creates further trouble. Respond to criticism with business rationales, like diversity and the bottom line. Avoid time-restricted airings of material unless ads legitimately deal with sexual situations inappropriate to youth.

(*View the Best Practices online with links to examples: www.commercialcloset.org/cgi-bin/iowa/index.html?page=best*)

Part III Facing Creative Challenges:

- **Gays & Lesbians:** how do you represent them without stereotypes or clichés? Try using:
  - *a. Real gay or lesbian individuals. Authenticity goes a long way.*
  - *b. Openly gay celebrities or athletes.*
  - *c. Same-sex pairings in everyday situations, such as at home, driving, shopping, eating.*
  - *d. Same-sex pairings with physical affection.*
  - *e. Sexuality can be referenced through verbal, text, graphical, or anthropomorphic mentions.*
  - *f. Unexpected twists, counter time-worn clichés, and add other humor sources.*
  - *g. A mix of masculine/feminine pairings for men or women as couples or friends: butch-femme (men or women), femme-femme (men), butch-butch (women).*

- **Bisexuals** are rarely shown at all, but when they are it is usually as duplicitous cheaters. How do you avoid that problem? Try using:
  a. *Depictions without a defined relationship to another person, keep it ambiguous.*
  b. *References through verbal, text, graphical, or anthropomorphic mentions.*
- **Transgender** is an umbrella term covering a range of identities: male-to-females/M2F, female-to-males/F2M, drag queens, "bad drag," transsexuals and transvestites. Most common in advertising are male-to-females, who typically show up as "deceptive" if they pass as women, or "frightening" if they do not. "Bad drag" refers to intentionally unconvincing straight men half-dressed as women, for example wearing wigs and mustaches simultaneously, as a joke or with a mock-subversive motive like spying. Transvestites are depicted as heterosexual men "caught" cross-dressing in women's undergarments. Drag queens are portrayed as campy men impersonating women. Transsexuals have had a sex-change operation. Female-to-males and androgyny are rarely depicted in advertising. Why not try:
  a. *Incorporating transgender people in everyday situations, not as a punch line, but with acceptance as a twist.*
  b. *Using a real transgender person, or real female impersonator. Seek authenticity.*
  c. *Depicting females-to-males/F2M individuals, masculine/butch women and "drag kings."*

Part IV Execution of Best Practices:

1. Senior executives should visibly endorse and disseminate the Best Practices to all appropriate internal marketing and supporting ad agency staffs.
2. Because of the diversity of the GLBT community, GLBT focus groups are encouraged for guidance—avoid limiting to just one or two GLBT individuals. Gay consultants and agencies are recommended for in-depth feedback and targeted efforts.
3. Prepare consistent responses to media and consumer inquiries about the campaign.
4. Schedule professional, annual sensitivity and awareness training about GLBT issues for general advertising and marketing staffs.

Part V Does It Work?

Specific data is difficult to come by, as companies rarely share proprietary information. But many marketers have repeatedly incorporated GLBT themes into mainstream ads: Viacom (48), Unilever (21), IKEA (14), Levi Strauss (14), Volkswagen (14), Virgin Group (10), Coca-Cola Co. (9), Heineken (8), SABMiller (7), Polaroid (4), Hyundai (3), Hancock (2), Visa (2).

RESPOND.

1. How would you characterize the arguments being made on this Web page? Do any of the suggestions or recommendations surprise you? Why or why not? Do they represent common sense or something more?
2. Visit the Web site for this selection, <http://commercialcloset.org/cgi-bin/iowa/index.html?page=best>. Why is this Web site organized as it is? In other words, why are the parts of the site arranged in the order they are? Why are the sections so labeled? How does each section contribute to the Web page's overall argument? If you take the intended audience to be advertisers seeking advice on how to market to the gay, lesbian, bisexual, or transgender communities or their friends and supporters, how persuasive is the information provided? Why? How effective do you find the layout and navigability of the Web site?
3. Visit the "Best Practices" section of the Web site for this selection, <http://commercialcloset.org/cgi-bin/iowa/index.html?page+best>, which includes links to numerous ads that represent members of the GLBT community. Choose two ads that you think are especially effective, and analyze the kinds of appeals used in these ads. Why do you find that the appeals used are appropriate, given the target audience(s) and the rhetorical goals of the ad?
4. **Write a rhetorical analysis** of this Web page. (For a discussion of how to write a rhetorical analysis, see Chapter 5.) In it, you may wish to evaluate the extent to which one or two of the advertisements given as models in fact follow the best practices described by the Web site. If you choose to make your rhetorical analysis evaluative in nature, you'll need to describe the ad in some detail (and likely include a copy with the essay, perhaps incorporating it into the text) and discuss the specific criteria you believe the ad respects or fails to respect. Finally, you'll need to discuss the ad's overall effectiveness. A boring ad that follows the best practices model isn't likely to be an effective ad.

▼ *Anne-Marie O'Connor is a staff writer for the* Los Angeles Times, *where this article, "Not Only Natalee Is Missing," appeared in the "Style and Culture" section in August 2005. As you read this feature article, note the kinds of evidence O'Connor uses in constructing her argument.*

Not Only Natalee Is Missing

Is the Media Inattention to Missing Women Who Aren't White Due to Deliberate Racism or Unconscious Bias?

ANNE-MARIE O'CONNOR

As one of America's new breed of media critics, Philadelphia blogger Richard Blair watched for weeks as the media devoted intense coverage to the story of the May 30 disappearance of Natalee Holloway while on a high school graduation trip to Aruba.

Then, on July 18, another young woman went missing, this one in his hometown. Photos of LaToyia Figueroa, 24, show the kind of smiling, attractive young woman whose disappearance has become a staple of television news coverage, particularly cable news, in recent years.

Except for one thing, a growing chorus of critics say: Figueroa, five months pregnant and the mother of a 7-year-old, comes from a lower-income black family, while the missing women regularly portrayed on television are overwhelmingly white. Her frustrated family had resorted to picketing on a busy street corner to draw attention to her disappearance when Blair and other Philadelphia bloggers took up Figueroa's case.

"Certainly Natalee Holloway's story is tragic in its own right," Blair said. "But what makes it more newsworthy than a five-month-pregnant mother?"

5 "I think this is part of a larger discussion: Who's news, who's newsworthy, and who's making these decisions," Blair said. "I think race is a factor, as well as economic status."

Criticism of the media disparity has increased with the growth of the news genre focusing on missing women. While the media seem to focus on a parade of attractive disappeared white women — from Laci Peterson and Chandra Levy to "runaway bride" Jennifer Wilbanks — the scores of missing black and Latina women garner little or no national attention, critics say.

The decapitated body of Evelyn Hernandez, 24, who was nine months pregnant, was discovered in the San Francisco Bay a few months before Peterson, but she did not touch off a firestorm of coverage. Nor did the disappearance of Ardena Carter, 23, a pregnant black graduate student who was last seen alive on her way to the library in Georgia in 2003. The remains of Carter and her unborn child turned up in the woods two months later.

"I don't think a media director is sitting around saying, 'Hey, there's this black woman in Philadelphia and she disappeared and we don't care,'" said Todd Boyd, USC° professor of critical studies. "It's an unconscious decision about who matters and who doesn't."

"In general, there is an assumption that crime is such a part of black and Latino culture, that these things happen all the time," Boyd said. "In many people's minds it's regarded as being commonplace and not that big a deal."

USC: because this article originally appeared in the *Los Angeles Times,* USC almost assuredly refers to the University of Southern California. How does the use of the abbreviation here, rather than the school's complete name, signal assumptions about imagined readers?

10 Mark Effron, vice president of MSNBC News Daytime Programming, disagrees. Effron said the stories of missing women typically bubble up from local network affiliates who are covering the stories based on the public outcry they generate in their home communities.

"It's not like there's a kind of cabal° where MSNBC and CNN and Fox get together and say, 'Boy, this is a good one. That's not a good one,' " he said. "Usually, there's an involved family that tends to be sophisticated in how to use the media."

"I'm not disputing numbers. What I'm telling you is that we have never, ever, ever turned down a story based on race or any of those factors."

This week, he said, the network has devoted daily coverage to Figueroa's disappearance.

However, he said, since the controversy began, "we have had discussions with our staff, [saying] 'Let's just make sure. I know we're not doing anything purposely or maliciously or based on any kind of racial or age profiling, but let's just make sure,' " he said.

15 Concern over lack of attention to some cases is not just an issue of fairness. Early coverage of abductions can be crucial to finding the victims alive — a factor that the Philadelphia blogger said promoted his campaign.

"I have a daughter that's not much younger than LaToyia," said Blair, who posted the news on his blog. "In this kind of thing, every minute's crucial."

To some analysts, this gets to the heart of the media's failure to fulfill its public service duty in the case of many missing minority women.

In California, for example, nearly 7,500 Latinas are missing — almost double the number of white women — but they are far less likely to receive attention.

The disparity even extends to abducted children, the critics say. While the sexual assault and murder of JonBenet Ramsey in her Boulder, Colo., home made her a nationally known symbol of a parent's worst fears, no corresponding black girl has become a household name, says author and political analyst Earl Ofari Hutchinson.

20 "When you raise the issue, people say, 'This is a tragedy and we should do more,' " Hutchinson said. "But it only lasts a hot minute. It doesn't leave any lasting imprint in the newsrooms."

One media-savvy relative says her efforts to draw attention to the disappearance of her niece, 24-year-old Tamika Huston, failed to win the attention of local media outlets whose stories might be picked up by national news. The African American woman didn't come home one day in June 2004 in South Carolina. Rebka Howard, her aunt, is a Miami public relations executive, but her media contacts and family news conferences failed to generate the kind of immediate attention they had hoped for.

Controversy over the disparity has grown in recent months as cable news formats seem to have adopted stories of the missing women as a staple news item.

"If there's a void in developing news stories, these things become the fodder for keeping ratings up on cable news networks," said Andrew Kohut, executive director of the Pew Research Center for the People and the Press. "They go for cases that attract tabloid audiences. And tabloid audiences are traditionally more interested in what happens in the lives of rich people than middle-income people and especially poor people."

Kathleen Fitzpatrick, an associate professor of English and media studies at Pomona College, said the issue is more complex. The fact that media icons of missing women tend to be attractive white women is just one manifestation of American cultural myths about race and gender that have created a very specific archetype of the kind of woman who is considered a damsel in distress, she said.

25 "I'm not accusing anybody of conscious racism in telling particular stories," Fitzpatrick said. "If the public were clamoring for stories about the abuse of African American women and how they're damaged by it, probably CNN would be happy to give us that story."

Some analysts also blame a lack of newsroom diversity. Twenty-two percent of the staff of TV newsrooms are minorities, according to the Radio-Television News Directors Assn. An estimated 13 percent of newspaper journalists are minorities, according

---

cabal: a small group of people engaged in some sort of secret intrigue.

to the American Society of Newspaper Editors.

It is simply less likely that a reporter will hear about a story emerging in a community that has less representation in the media, said Maria Len-Rios, an assistant at the Missouri School of Journalism at Columbia and the author of a recent study about the underrepresentation of women in the media.

"I think that when you look at the composition of the newsroom and the people that people in the newsroom know, there aren't many people from underrepresented communities," Len-Rios said. "We don't pay as much attention to someone missing from a community we don't know or are not familiar with."

Erin Bruno, the lead case manager for the National Center for Missing Adults in Phoenix, said her office sends out press releases daily on the 47,828 cases of missing adults they are tracking. They are a diverse pool: 29,553 white or Latino, 13,859 black, 1,199 Asian and 685 American Indian.

30 Yet "what we're seeing in the national media is a lot of young Caucasian females," Bruno said. "I've heard reporters sometimes look for stories that they can identify with, perhaps they themselves are Caucasian . . . or maybe they're looking at who their audience is."

And the reporters' search for the "damsel in distress" leaves another huge group ignored — men, she said. Some 25,447 missing males are being tracked by the Phoenix group, compared with 22,379 females — a gap roughly mirrored by California statistics. Said Bruno: "Women are seen more as victims than men are."

Bruno said the Holloway disappearance has generated a new demand from the media for information on a greater diversity of missing women.

Media criticism over the coverage gap is growing. "When black women disappear, the media silence can be deafening," said a July 2005 article in Essence magazine. In a poll conducted last week by Black Entertainment Television's website, BET.com, 71 percent of respondents said they did not believe that the belated flurry of media attention to Figueroa's disappearance meant that minority women were "finally getting as much attention as whites."

Several media organizations asked for comment on the issue declined. CNN spokeswoman Laurie Goldberg said news executives were unavailable. Barbara Cochran, the president of the Radio-Television News Director's Assn., said in an e-mail she was unavailable. Fox News spokeswoman Dana Klinghoffer said that "a lot of people are out and unavailable. I just think it's one we're going to have to sit out."

35 To Marty Kaplan, the associate dean of the USC Annenberg School for Communication, the silence on the issue "suggests they don't have any good answers and they're a little embarrassed. What are they going to say?"

"It does suggest that it is seeping into their consciousness how blatant it is that only white women are covered. News directors apparently believe the public is interested in every lurid tale about a white woman and not about the bad things happening across the country every day to people who are less photogenic and not Caucasian."

RESPOND.

1. What sorts of analyses (arguments, really) do Richard Blair, Todd Boyd, Mark Effron, Andrew Kohut, Kathleen Fitzpatrick, Maria Len-Rios, Erin Bruno, and Marty Kaplan offer with respect to why women of color are underrepresented in stories of missing women? To what extent do their analyses overlap or complement one another? Are any of the positions they represent as a group contradictory? Which argument(s) do you find most convincing? Why?

O'Connor presents evidence from blogs, interviews, and statistics to support her report about the lack of news coverage on missing minority women. Evaluate the author's argument using the discussion of claims and evidence in Chapter 7.

LINK TO P. 188

2. Andrew Kohut, in particular, focuses on the ways in which cable news networks, borrowing techniques from the tabloid press, go for particular kinds of stories (paragraph 23). Can you give examples of other genres of stories favored by cable networks that have influenced mainstream news programs in your area?
3. Erin Bruno contends that reporters may be choosing stories with their audiences in mind (paragraph 30). If audiences (aside from those of niche channels like Black Entertainment Network or Univision) are majority white, should members of other groups simply accept as fact the idea that their concerns won't be represented in the mainstream media? What are the disadvantages of such a situation for those from minority groups? From the majority group?
4. O'Connor uses several sources of information or kinds of evidence to support her claims. What are they? How effective are they? How would the article be different if she had used far more statistics and far less interview data? Would it be more or less effective? Why? (For a discussion of kinds of evidence, see Chapter 16.)
5. Choose a news source, and track its coverage of majority and minority groups for a week. You may wish to study a newspaper, a television program (for example, the local evening news), or a news Web site. In addition to tracking coverage, try to get information on the news source's target audience. For a newspaper or television program, seek information on the local demographics. (For example, if the population of the town where you watch television is 20 percent Asian American but 30 percent of the local Asian Americans watch the program you're tracking, what percentage of the program's coverage is devoted to Asian Americans?) You may also wish to try to interview people involved in choosing stories or in reporting. Obviously, no one expects a simple or direct correlation between audience demographics and amount of time devoted to specific communities, but patterns that show up may become the basis for recommendations about future action.

   After doing this research, use the information you've collected to **write an essay** in which you evaluate and make recommendations about news sources' coverage of majority and minority groups. (For discussions of evaluative and proposal arguments, respectively, see Chapters 9 and 11.)

   You and your classmates may wish to select a local newspaper and evaluate its coverage over a period of months or even years (for example, by examining the January issues of the paper over the past fifteen years). Such longitudinal data would be especially useful in discerning changes across time.

▼ *David Bositis has been on the staff of the Joint Center for Political and Economic Studies, in Washington, D.C., where he currently serves as senior political associate, since 1992. The Center, founded in 1970, is a nonprofit research and policy institution focusing on public policy issues of interest to African Americans and other communities of color. This article originally appeared in the* Los Angeles Times *in March 2003. As you read, consider how the failure to sample minority populations adequately might encourage stereotypes about and misunderstanding of those groups in society at large.*

Skin-Deep:

What Polls of Minorities Miss

DAVID BOSITIS

The media's knowledge of African Americans, Asians and Latinos is woefully lacking. Opinion polls break out minority-group results from general populations,° but the meaningfulness of the findings is moot at best. Lacking reliable° data on the variable and textured hopes, needs and fears of minority communities, the media instead turn to personal anecdotes and self-appointed spokespeople to gauge community sentiments. That can be terribly misleading—and risky—when reporting on crime, police misconduct and elections. It's no surprise that racial and ethnic tensions and misunderstanding endure in cities such as Los Angeles.

When it comes to polls, news organizations have apparently decided that their typical reader or viewer is most interested in studies of a general population, be it a city, state or the nation. Polling is expensive, of course, and polling subpopulations° even more so.

But there's a price to be paid for not regularly polling minority communities. The quality of the information in minority-group breakouts is inferior because the small sample°

population: all the members of a group that a researcher is interested in studying (for example, adult Americans, Americans who own cars, people who use public transportation in a specific city, college students with tattoos).

reliability (and the related adjective *reliable* and adverb *reliably*): in statistics, the consistency of a measure.

subpopulation: a definable group within a larger population (for example, in relation to the populations given above, adult African Americans, Americans who drive SUVs, riders of buses [as opposed to the subway] in a specific city, fraternity brothers with tattoos).

sample: a subset of the larger population chosen for analysis; in principle, this subset should be representative of the population or subpopulation as a whole.

sizes have large margins of error.° As a result, not much can be reliably said about the differences between black men and women, or Latino young adults and seniors. Such ignorance has serious policy implications.

The standard margin of error in general population surveys is plus or minus 3 percentage points, at a confidence level° of 95%. Media pollsters achieve this low margin of error by randomly interviewing° a sufficient number of respondents.

Consider the *Times*' March 7 poll on the mayor's race. To obtain a 3-percentage-point margin of error, 1,113 Angelenos were polled. The margin of error for the poll's subgroup of 257 African Americans was 6 percentage points. To achieve that, 134 blacks in addition to the 123 in the general sample were interviewed. If the *Times* had not obtained that additional sample, the margin of error for blacks in its survey would have been about plus or minus 9 percentage points.

5 The higher standard was costly. Polling minority communities is more expensive per interview than for the general population, for a number of reasons. Because they make up a smaller proportion of the population, minority group members are harder to reach. Potential interviewees must determine who's suitable for the sample, which adds to the number of calls (a significant cost factor).

When surveying respondents for whom English is not their first lan-

---

margin of error: the range within which researchers expect responses of a subpopulation or population to a survey question to fall, given the responses of the sample. The margin of error is directly related to the size of the sample interviewed. Smaller sample sizes result in higher margins of error. For example, let's assume a survey where 45% of those questioned agree with a particular statement. If the margin of error for the survey is ±3%, one can assume that between 42% (45% −3%) and 48% (45% +3%) of the subpopulation or population from which the sample is drawn would agree with the particular statement. If the margin of error for the survey is ±9%, one can assume only that between 36% (45% − 9%) and 54% (45% + 9%) of the subpopulation or population from which the sample is drawn would agree—a far more tentative finding because of the wider margin of error.

confidence level: the degree to which one can assume a finding is trustworthy and not accidental. For example, a confidence level of 95% with respect to a survey means that if one repeated the survey multiple times with different random samples of the same population or subpopulation, one should get statistically similar results 95% of the time.

random interviewing (more often, *random sampling*): in research, random sampling is the process of selecting a sample such that every member of the population or subpopulation in question has an equal chance of being chosen. In other words, if researchers are sampling the attitudes of adult African Americans across the United States, every adult African American should have an equal chance of being asked to participate in the survey if the sample is to be truly random. Notice that this technical use of *random* differs markedly from the use of the word in everyday conversation, where it might mean "inexplicable" (*That was random*) or "unknown" (*This random guy came up to me*). Students sometimes claim that they've chosen a random sample when they've made a point of asking anyone available to participate in a survey, for example. Such a sample is, for statisticians, a *convenience sample*—one that's convenient. Researchers cannot draw any conclusions about, say, the representativeness of responses from a convenience sample with respect to those they might get from a larger population or subpopulation because they know nothing about the relationship between the sample and the larger group.

guage, interview protocols must be translated, and respondents questioned by interviewers fluent in their language. Also, it's best to match the interviewers' race with that of the polled community.

In the most recent national survey conducted by the Joint Center for Political and Economic Studies, the cost of a completed interview for its black sample was 47% higher than one for the general population.

But polling minority communities is important not only because their views often contrast with those of whites—and one another. It's also important because fundamental demographic° differences frequently mask the significance of divergent attitudes within minority groups. The African American (median° age 31) and Latino (26.7) populations are much younger than their non-Hispanic white counterpart (39.7), which is one reason Republicans have tried to draw young blacks into the Social Security debate.

10 Gender differences between communities are also significant. Black adult women represent 55.8% of all black adults in the nation—outnumbering black men by 2.55 million, or 26%, according to a 2002 census survey. In contrast, there are 4.4% more Hispanic adult men than women, while white adult women outnumber their male counterparts by 8%.

When the *Times* said it had weighted its March 7 poll results according to sex and age, did its samples of blacks and Latinos correspond to these groups' different demographics? Even presuming they did, how many individual respondents represented the views of, say, young unmarried black women?

Although the media have not made much effort to reliably capture the range of views in minority communities, other organizations have filled the vacuum in recent years. These include surveys of minority group opinions by Harvard, the Pew Research Center for the People and the Press, and the Tomas Rivera Institute. The results have not gone unnoticed.

For instance, based on work at the Joint Center for Political and Economic Studies, generational differences in attitudes among African Americans are a hot topic, leading to talk about increased levels of black political independence, black support for education alternatives such as vouchers, partial privatization of Social Security and the significance of Christian conservatism to black politics.

Important as these efforts are, they are national in scope. What's also needed is for other organizations, including news operations, to take this effort to the local level, where people of all racial and ethnic groups live and work in proximity and need to understand the views they do and do not share.

---

demographic (adjective): relating to social groups. Within the past few years, this word has come to be used as a noun meaning the members of a definable demographic group; for example, white males between the ages of eighteen and forty. With this meaning, the word is often shortened to *demo*.

median: in statistics, the middle value in a list of observations, arranged from lowest to highest, in contrast to the mean (or arithmetic average) or mode (or most frequently occuring value).

Bositis presents an argument to convince readers of the importance of including minorities in public polls. Use the descriptions of various arguments in Chapter 1 to compare an "argument to convince" with other types of arguments.

LINK TO P. 10

RESPOND

1. How would you summarize Bositis's argument? In what ways is it an evaluative argument? A proposal argument? What proposal might he be making? Why?
2. What are the challenges of polling minority communities adequately? Paragraphs 6 and 7 give specific problems pollsters face with respect to minority communities. Why do these problems arise? What are the public policy implications of polling minority communities? Of not doing so? How might not doing so contribute to stereotypes of minority communities?
3. Does this essay hold any clues to Bositis's own political beliefs? If so, what are those clues? How would you characterize the ethos Bositis creates for himself?
4. Visit the Web sites of the Pew Research Center for the People and the Press or the Tomas Rivera Policy Institute to find out the sorts of research these institutions support with respect to minority communities in the United States. How does such research support an understanding of the changing nature of American society?
5. Bositis contends that in the absence of reliable information about the opinions of minority communities, the media (and likely others) use "personal anecdotes and self-appointed spokespeople" (paragraph 1). Why might such a move be problematic? What is its impact on the minority community in question? The majority community? In what ways is Bositis's essay an argument about what counts as evidence? (For a discussion of kinds of evidence, see Chapter 16.) **Write an essay** in which you evaluate the advantages and disadvantages of different kinds of evidence in seeking to describe and understand the opinions of minority communities in the United States.

William Sea, a history major, wrote this opinion piece for The Battalion, *the university newspaper at Texas A&M University in College Station, while he was a senior there. It appeared in November 2005. As you read, consider the causal and evaluative arguments he's making.*

Advertising Sets Double Standard for the Male Gender

WILLIAM SEA

As if beer commercials could get any more inane, Miller Brewing Company's latest series of television spots for Milwaukee's Best Light offends good taste while perpetuating gender stereotypes. In each commercial, a group of men notice that one of them is doing something decidedly "unmanly," such as baby-talking to a small dog, swatting effeminately at a fly or dabbing grease off of his pizza. This traitor to manhood receives his recompense: a giant can of beer falling from the sky onto him, followed by the tag line, "Men should act like men, and light beer should taste like beer."

The commercial is no doubt part of the so-called "metrosexual backlash," a return to traditional masculine images in reaction to the recent androgynous° portrayal of the male figure. The metrosexual trend robbed men of their masculinity, while the backlash is forcing it upon them. With fashion advertisements featuring slightly built, effeminate males and truck advertisements featuring quite the opposite, the media creates an ambiguous definition of what it means to be a man. When Milwaukee's Best tells us that "men should act like men," the statement is unclear: How should they act?

This is the problem that popular advertising only complicates. In commercials, men are portrayed in vastly different ways. They are buffoonish father figures, as in a Verizon commercial that features a father attempting vainly to help his annoyed daughter with her homework, as the mother orders him to wash the dog. They are hapless jokers driven to idiocy by women, as in the countless numbers of beer commercials with men making fools of themselves to impress an attractive female. For every advertisement that portrays a woman as a sex object, there is also an offensive portrayal of a man who is unable to do anything but ogle and blunder.

At the same time, the ideal man in advertising is a fearless, muscular, truck-driving hero. And advertisers see no problem with showing women eyeing these Adonis' rear ends.

5 Of course, sexism exists in advertising against both genders. There is no denying that women have been objectified and stereotyped in media for years. However, there is also no denying that a new double standard exists. Imagine the Milwaukee's Best commercial with roles reversed—a woman doing something seen as manly, then being crushed by a bottle of laundry detergent. Or in the Verizon commercial, a woman ordered by her husband to do the dishes after she vainly tries to help her son with homework.

Feminists, then, who point out all the stereotypes of women that advertising offers, would do well to realize that television's portrayal of men does

androgynous: having features associated with males and females; of indeterminate sex.

Sea offers an evaluation of current media portrayals of men and finds them lacking. Turn to Chapter 9 for guidance on preparing your own evaluative argument.

LINK TO P. 262

just as much to hurt their cause. The more that advertising sets the standard for masculinity as macho posturing and the average man as a bumbling fool, the more men are likely to attempt to assert their dominance over women. Advertising says that "men should act like men," and often they show men acting inappropriately.

Advertisers should realize that men will eventually become tired of seeing themselves mocked on television. Perhaps a beer commercial is just the beginning of the metrosexual backlash, but one hopes that men can soon peacefully reconcile their masculinity to an ever-changing society.

RESPOND •

1. How would you summarize Sea's argument? What sorts of causal claims does he make? What sorts of evaluative claims does he make? How well are they supported?
2. The Miller commercial engages in what some researchers term *gender policing,* that is, seeking out and punishing behaviors that don't reflect prescribed gender roles and stereotypes. How does such policing perpetuate stereotypes? Can you think of policing that occurs with other groups—for example, members of ethnic groups, lesbians and gay men, religious believers, and political partisans? What functions does such policing serve? What are its disadvantages?
3. What function does "then" serve in the first sentence of paragraph 6? In what way might Sea be seen as stereotyping feminists and their responses to sexism in advertising? What does this sentence tell you about Sea's invoked readers and their beliefs? (For a discussion of invoked readers, see Chapter 1.)
4. In the closing paragraph of his essay, Sea expresses the hope that men will be able to reconcile their masculinity in the context of an ever-changing society. Is such a wish reasonable? Is it likely to be realized? **Write an essay** in which you propose how women and/or men (or members of some other social group) might think about creating identities in the context of a society that will inevitably be defined by change. (For a discussion of proposal arguments, see Chapter 11.)

Graphic Artist Carefully Assigns Ethnicities to Anthropomorphic° Recyclables

THE ONION

PHILADELPHIA—Freelance graphic artist Chrissie Bellisle carefully delineated the ethnicities, genders, and sexual orientations of the RecyclaBuddies, a group of talking recyclables created for a public-service leaflet she submitted to the Department of Sanitation Monday.

"I assumed the Department of Sanitation would want the recyclables in its new leaflet to represent not only Philadelphia's recycling procedures, but also its diverse ethnic makeup," said Bellisle, flipping through some initial sketches in her studio. "It turned out to be quite a challenge."

As the purpose behind establishing racial and cultural identities for the talking waste was one of celebration, not caricature, Bellisle found herself working within unusual limits.

"For reasons of basic sensitivity, you don't want to make the Chinese take-out container an Asian," Bellisle said, as she flipped past a crossed-out pencil sketch of an Inuit° ice cream carton. "But, if you make the same type of container represent two different races, people notice. It's a delicate balancing act. I discovered that there were negative connotations attached to a surprising number of the things people throw out."

Although she said she is satisfied with her decision to incorporate Asiatic epi- 5
canthic° folds into the eyes of an age-discolored stack of newspapers, Bellisle admitted that infusing everyday household garbage with easily recognizable racial traits—while avoiding demeaning stereotypes—is difficult.

"It took me forever to get this trash can to look like a black guy, especially around the nose," said Bellisle, who noted that she discarded close to 30 preliminary characters, among them a Native American milk carton, a Filipino cereal box, and a stack of East Indian wire-hangers. "I finally made the green recycling drum a woman, which was great, since a garbage can is kind of husky, and I could get around the sexy-garbage/body-image issue."

This article appeared in August 2003 in The Onion, a weekly print and online satirical publication that advertises itself as "America's Finest News Source." All its articles are unsigned. By the way, its Web site contains the disclaimer that it's "not intended for readers under 18 years of age," so if you aren't yet 18, you should stop reading now. (Do you believe this disclaimer discourages or encourages under-age readers to continue reading? Perhaps schools should prohibit students from reading textbooks to encourage disobedience.) As in all Onion articles, all the names are invented except for those of public figures who are the targets of satire. As you read, consider the subtle and not-so-subtle ways in which humor is used to deal with a potentially explosive topic—and no, we don't mean recycling.

anthropomorphic: in the shape (*-morphic*) of humans (*anthropo-*).

Inuit: an alternate name for the Eskimo and the one preferred in Canada.

epicanthic: relating to the skin covering the angle of the eye near the nose.

Added Bellisle: "That brings another problem to light: If you include one woman in the mix, no one cares what race she is. As if one female recycling drum can represent female recycling drums of all races, but male recyclables deserve further distinction."

Drawing friendly, nondescript male characters is not the answer, said Bellisle.

"Look at this grinning soda can giving the thumbs-up here," she said. "Everyone subconsciously assumes it's a Caucasian male."

As of press time, Bellisle was still struggling with drawings for a 10
RecyclaBuddies poster to complement the leaflet.

"I have no idea how to make the plastic milk jug look gay," Bellisle said. "I don't want to make him a bottle of water, for obvious reasons. Maybe I'll use a soy-milk container when I draw the gay jug. Or maybe they'll let me switch him with the Chicano, this tin can here. I wasn't too pleased with the Chicano tin can to begin with, especially because my first instinct was to put tomatoes or beans on the can. Not because he's Chicano, but because he's a can."

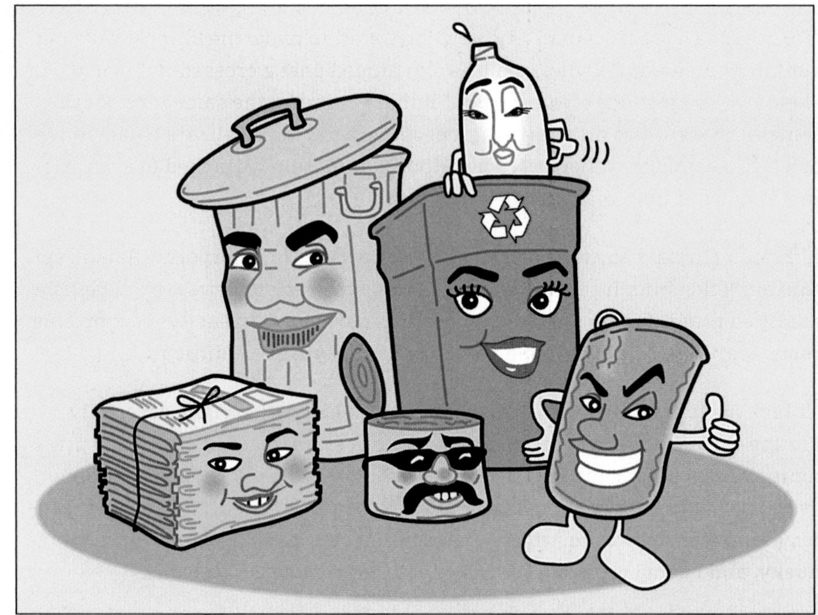

Characters from the culturally sensitive Department of Sanitation leaflet

This article is intended to be satirical in nature. Compare satire with other forms of humorous arguments as discussed in Chapter 13.

LINK TO P. 393

"And I'm *really* not looking forward to doing the page that explains the symbols on the bottom of plastic containers," Bellisle added. "Who am I to determine which RecyclaBuddy of color is a 1 and which is a 5?"

Heather Franks, a public-relations official with Philadelphia's Department of Sanitation, was quick to laud Bellisle's efforts.

"We're very pleased with Chrissie's work on the RecyclaBuddies so far," Franks said. "We haven't given final approval to anything, but we've liked the range and depth of the sketches we've seen. They really provide a sense of the cultural diversity that exists in the Philadelphia trash-collection zone."

Added Franks: "We especially love that soda can giving the thumbs-up. I don't 15
know what it is about that little guy, but we're thinking of making him the boss of the whole crew."

RESPOND •

1. Does *The Onion* live up to its claim? In other words, is this article satirical? If it is, what things are being satirized and how? (For a discussion of satire, see Chapter 13.) The essay likewise employs irony. What, for example, is ironic about Heather Franks's closing remarks about the soda can (paragraph 15)?
2. Do you find this essay amusing? Funny? Did it make you laugh? What might account for your response?
3. A photo of Chrissie Bellisle, the imaginary graphic artist mentioned in the text, appeared with the original article. We did not seek permission to use it but believe it's relevant that Bellisle is white—or appears to be. Why might *The Onion* have included a photo of Chrissie Bellisle? What role would it play for readers? Is it better to be told Bellisle's apparent ethnicity or to be presented with a photo of her? Why?
4. How does a satirical piece like this one contribute to an understanding of stereotypes in the media and popular culture? What does the goal of this argument seem to be?
5. Find a satirical treatment of a stereotype in *The Onion* or elsewhere—a popular song, a comedy routine, a cartoon—and **write a rhetorical analysis** of the argument it makes. Because satire is often subtle, it may be helpful to explain the stereotype being satirized and then illustrate the specific ways in which it's satirized. (For discussions of rhetorical analysis and satire, respectively, see Chapters 5 and 13.)

23
Is Sports Just a Proxy for Politics?

Surely, you've seen word association tests. The examiner gives you a word, and you shout out all the words you can think of that relate to it in one minute. Take the word *sports*, for example, and start shouting. What comes out? *Game? Stadium? Team? Fun? Bar? TV?* How many words would you come up with before you said *politics?* Likely a lot. The readings in this cluster try to persuade you that *politics* is perhaps the first word you should come up with. With respect to several different issues, they all pose a simple question: Is sports just a proxy for politics? Is it ever possible simply to enjoy the game? These readings argue that it's not—and that sports is necessarily about bigger political issues.

The first four readings deal with women in collegiate athletics and the state of affairs brought about by a seemingly clear federal policy enacted in 1972 known as Title IX. The policy states, "No person in the United States shall, on the basis of sex, be excluded from participation in, be denied the benefits of, or be subjected to discrimination under any education program or activity receiving federal financial assistance . . ." and then goes on to list a number of exceptions. Over thirty years later, we continue arguing about the rules, their nature and extent, and even the goals of this game. Juliet Macur's article, "Rowing Scholarships Available. No Experience Necessary." and the accompanying advertisements from a college newspaper demonstrate some of the consequences of Title IX. Jessica Gavora's "Time's Up for Title IX Sports" argues vehemently against the ways in which Title IX has been interpreted and used. Ruth Conniff seeks to defend it, protecting it bravely from the likes of Gavora. Part of the argument is about who supports Title IX: radical feminists, soccer dads, or both? Leslie Heywood's essay, "Despite the Positive Rhetoric about Women's Sports, Female Athletes Face a Culture of Sexual Harassment," argues that sexual harassment is still all too common an experience for women athletes in the United States regardless of Title IX's promises.

The next two articles, along with three cartoons, treat the problematic question of American Indian mascots and imagery in sports. Barbara Munson's "Common Themes and Questions about the Use of 'Indian' Logos" and Jim Shore's "Play with Our Name" present very different perspectives on this topic although both authors are American Indians. The three cartoons by Lucy A. Ganje, Lalo Alcaraz, and Thom Little Moon push the debate further.

In "Bad As They Wanna Be," Thad Williamson raises a different problem as he mourns changes in college basketball, using his beloved Tar Heels as a case study in what he thinks is wrong with collegiate athletics.

Two selections debate the 2005 NBA dress code. We include the NBA dress code itself, which can be read as an interesting definitional argument, and commentary by Tom Sorensen and Larry Stewart, both sports writers. The title of Sorensen's piece, "Dress Code Suitable Only to NBA Suits," makes his perspective clear, while Larry Stewart's feature on the ever-controversial Charles Barkley presents Barkley's arguments for the dress code along with his comments on several other matters.

The chapter closes with Bryan Curtis's query, "Cheerleaders: What to Do about Them?" Analyzing recent efforts by one Lone Star State legislator to tone down what he sees as the lewd performances of high school cheerleaders, Curtis wonders if cheerleaders, especially college cheerleaders, don't ultimately end up having the last laugh—all the way to the bank.

Juliet Macur has written about sports for several major American newspapers. She currently writes for the New York Times, *which sent her to Iraq in the fall of 2005 to report on the war. The article reprinted here, "Rowing Scholarships Available. No Experience Necessary." appeared in the sports section of the* Times *in May 2004. In some editions of the paper, it appeared under the headline "Never Rowed? Take a Free Ride." As you read, consider how Macur presents Title IX and its consequences.*

The ads from The Daily Texan, *the student newspaper at the University of Texas at Austin, appeared on September 2, 2003. There were no comparable ads for men's athletic teams during this period.*

Macur develops a causal argument as she sketches out how female athletes have benefited from Title IX on the university level. Chapter 10 offers a guide to developing and writing your own causal arguments.

LINK TO P. 307

Rowing Scholarships Available. No Experience Necessary.

JULIET MACUR

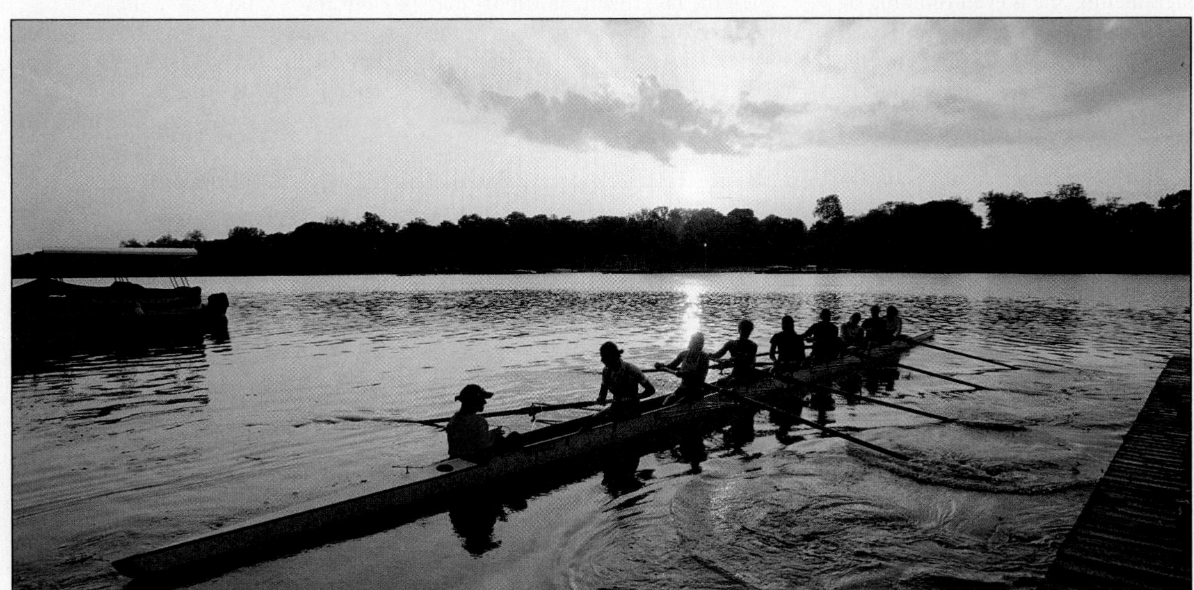

The Ohio State women's eights, leaving the dock at 6:30 for a morning practice.

On the day Ohio State freshmen signed up for extracurricular activities like sororities, paintball and recreational badminton, Amanda Purcell heard a sales pitch. Two women on the university's varsity rowing team begged her to join.

Purcell, a 5-foot-9, 250-pound French horn player and music major who had never played a sport before, said no, but the women persisted. Finally, she decided to give it a try.

Suddenly, she had a new hobby—and a new way to pay her college education.

A junior now, 60 pounds lighter and physically fit, Purcell has been on scholarship for more than a year and is competing in Ohio State's top varsity boat at this weekend's N.C.A.A. women's rowing championships in Sacramento. She is even thinking of the Olympics.

5 "I'm still shocked," Jim Purcell, Amanda's father, said. "She was always afraid to touch any sport, but look at her now."

Purcell and her family quickly learned a fact of life in the 21st century Title IX world: women are getting scholarships in sports they have never tried, perhaps never even heard of.

As an effort to satisfy Title IX legal requirements for gender equity in federally funded institutions, many colleges have added nontraditional sports for women, like rowing. It is a phenomenon particularly true of universities like Ohio State, an institution with a major football program that skews the balance of sports participation and scholarships in the men's favor.

Ohio State elevated its women's rowing program to varsity status nine years ago. Now, as the men's club team runs programs such as Rent-a-Rower ($50 for four hours of chores like raking leaves, cleaning garages or moving furniture to raise money for equipment and travel), the women are fully funded.

"To comply with Title IX, some colleges start women's crew, then start looking for rowers."

The team has an N.C.A.A. maximum 20 scholarships, and 16 women receive full rides. The remaining money is divvied up among other rowers. The team's annual budget is nearly $900,000.

10 "In the fall, rowing is a sport that you carry 70 to 80 people, then in the spring at least 46 kids get out and race," Ohio State's athletic director, Andy Geiger, said. "It's an expensive sport, but it's worth it. It really does help offset football."

Rowing has become a popular way to equalize any imbalance between men's and women's sports because it requires high numbers of athletes. A single varsity eight boat requires nine people: eight rowers and a coxswain,° a small but vocal person who steers the boat and shouts commands.

Most teams have at least two eight-person boats on varsity and two more on the novice team. Many crews also have four-person boats, which carry four rowers and a coxswain.

It isn't easy, however, to keep rowers on the team. Rowing is a year-round activity, with fall and spring seasons, and weekly races from March

The Western Australian coxswain Patrick Riley celebrates winning the Kings Cup during the Australian Rowing Championships in Sydney, Australia, in March 2005.

coxswain: (pronounced as if spelled *coxen* with stress on the first syllable) as noted, the person who steers and shouts commands at rowers in order to help them row more efficiently.

through May. Many women who try the sport don't make it through the winter.

Though the National Collegiate Athletic Association puts limits on the number of practice hours, the time commitment is still daunting. Many teams practice twice a day, with a predawn workout on the water that could last several hours. In the afternoon, rowers head to the gym to lift weights or train on the rowing machine.

15 Blisters form on hands because of friction against oar handles. Pain and soreness develop in nearly every muscle because rowing uses the upper and lower body.

"Sure, you might get a scholarship," Geiger said. "But it's not going to be easy."

Eighty-five Division I colleges this year had women's rowing teams, a 55 percent jump from 1997, the year women's crew became an N.C.A.A. sport. And now the top teams aren't only the traditional rowing powers like the Ivy League universities and, say, the University of Washington.

Michigan, Virginia and Tennessee are all in the top 10. Ohio State is ranked third going into the championships. Cal is ranked No. 1.

"When we beat Princeton and Brown this year at Princeton, the silence was deafening," Ohio State Coach Andy Teitelbaum said. "But these changes haven't happened overnight. It's taken awhile for us to build our programs."

20 With so many programs offering rowing scholarships, recruiting has become instrumental in keeping new programs on top. The problem is that there aren't enough high school rowers to go around.

"We'd be recruiting a kid who'd already have three scholarship offers from Louisville, Texas and Michigan, and we'd be like, 'O.K., this isn't how it used to be,'" said Mike Zimmer, coach of the women's crew at Columbia, which, as an Ivy League

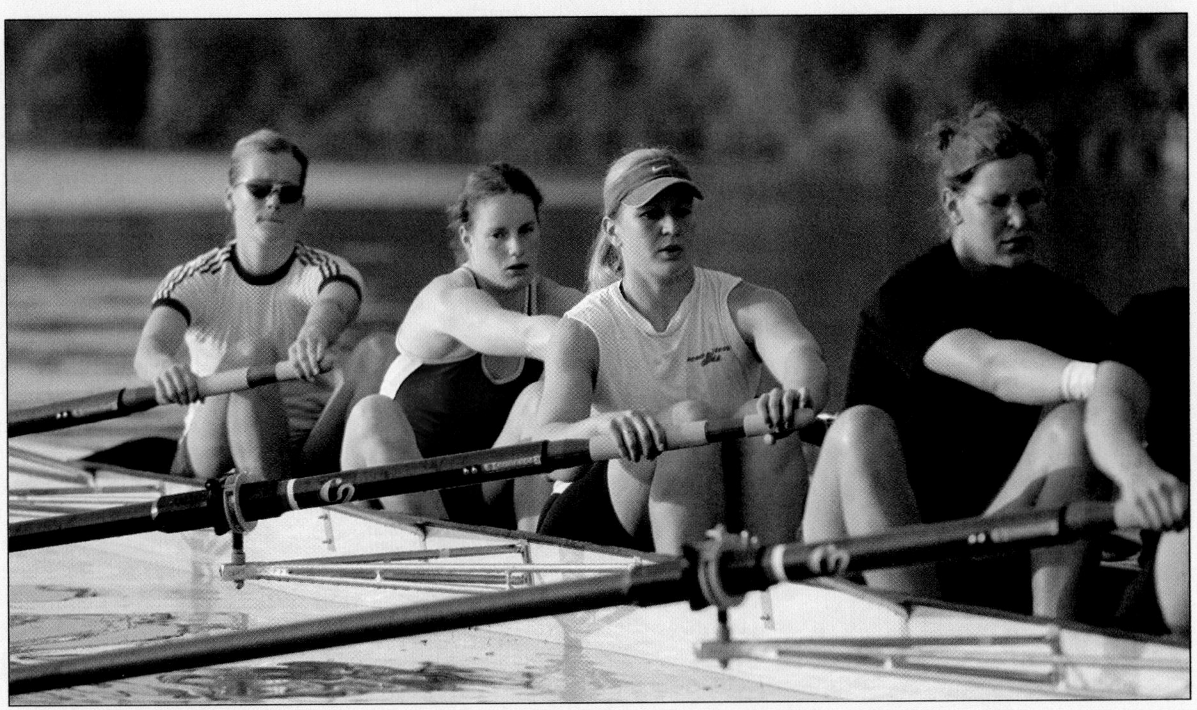

Amanda Purcell, third from left, is on full scholarship at Ohio State and receives a monthly check for room, board and books.

university, does not give athletic scholarships but can offer grants and need-based financial aid.

"Now even the women who are on the middle of our list are being chased by a lot of different schools."

And recruits aren't coming strictly from New England prep schools anymore. They are coming from high schools across the nation, even parts of the country with no history of rowing.

They are also coming from overseas. Ohio State's top varsity boat has rowers from schools called College of Olympic Reserve, Gymnasium Grosse Stadtschule and Red October. Seven of the nine people in the boat are international rowers: five from Germany, one from Russia, one from the Netherlands.

"Rowing has grown so unbelievably fast—it is where soccer was 10 or 15 years ago—so the supply and demand is unbelievably off," Mark Rothstein, coach of Michigan's women's crew, said. "But the idea that there aren't enough rowers to go around is changing pretty quickly."

Still, Rothstein sends a letter to all of Michigan's incoming female freshmen, trying to lure them to the first rowing practice. (He purposely fails to mention that varsity practice begins at 5:45 A.M.)

And at Cal, as at most universities, coaches scour high school rosters for athletes of all kinds who may not want to continue their sport in college. If a woman is tall, aerobically strong and willing to work hard, says Cal Coach Dave O'Neill, chances are she can be a good rower.

"It's not necessarily an easy sport to learn because you have to have certain genetic variables, but it does reward people with a strong work ethic," O'Neill said. "Someone who is a 6-1 swimmer who blew out her shoulder or is sick of being in the pool, now that's the perfect scenario. It's more of a gamble, but it's something that we just have to do."

Heather Mandoli, a 5-foot-10 athlete who played basketball, soccer and rugby in high school, fits into that category. She scarcely had one month's rowing experience when she was flooded with scholarship offers and wound up at Michigan.

"I thought, a scholarship?" she said. "O.K., for basketball, maybe."

As a high school senior in a small town in British Columbia three hours inland from Vancouver, she won a week's worth of rowing lessons at a start-up rowing club. She didn't actually get on the water in a boat, but she learned her technique on a rowing machine. The machine—called an ergometer, or erg—generates a computerized score when set for a specific time or distance.

A few weeks later, Mandoli sent her ergometer score to Canada's national team, and soon she was fielding calls from colleges throughout Canada and the United States, including Michigan, Princeton and Washington.

"After Michigan offered me a scholarship, the first thing I said was, 'You know I can't row, right?'" said Mandoli, who this month was chosen the Big Ten Conference women's rowing athlete of the year. "They just said, 'We're recruiting you on potential.' That was enough for me."

Such stories have been enough to promote the growth of high school and recreational rowing programs. In Oakland, Calif., for example, a local water-sports facility started a rowing program this year strictly for public school girls. None of the 21 who signed up could pass the swimming test, and 16 didn't even have bathing suits. Still, DeDe Birch, executive director of the Jack London Aquatic Center, pushed forward.

"Whatever we can do to get these girls a scholarship, we'll do," she said. "Hey, if colleges gave kayaking scholarships, we'd start that team, too."

None of the talk about scholarship opportunities in rowing had reached Purcell before she signed up for crew that day at Ohio State. She knew nothing about the sport until she showed up for the first practice. But she quickly learned one thing: she was good, particularly on the erg, where her scores were among the best on the team.

But she could not juggle the time commitment with her music studies and her job as a waitress. So she quit the varsity program and joined the club team.

A year later, seeing her potential, her club coach took her to an international rowing machine competition in Boston. Purcell pulled the second-best score of 293 women in the competition and the top collegiate score—6 minutes 48.9 seconds for 2,000 meters.

Later that day, she had voicemails and e-mail messages offering scholarships to Fordham, Michigan and San Diego State. She chose to stay at Ohio State, and now the university not only pays her tuition, but it also sends her a monthly check for about $900 for room, board and books.

Purcell's erg scores were so good that she was invited to a national team training camp last summer. There, she realized how far she could go in rowing. Now she wants to make the 2008 Olympic team.

"In the second grade, I tried the viola, but the teachers said I had no musical talent," Purcell said. "Now look at me. I'm a music major. Rowing has kind of been the same thing. Nobody ever knew I'd be good at it. I guess I can thank Title IX for that."

RESPOND •

1. Macur's piece is clearly intended to be a news article. What sorts of arguments can it be said to make? Why and how?
2. According to Macur, the popularity of rowing as a varsity sport for women has little to do with the appeal of rowing itself. What accounts for its popularity? Why does it appeal to athletic directors at major universities, which generally have large football teams and men's basketball teams? Why does it appeal to collegiate women?
3. Ads like those below from *The Daily Texan* are common in the fall, at least at large universities like those mentioned in question 2. What kinds of arguments do these ads make? What are the advantages of such ads? Are there any disadvantages?

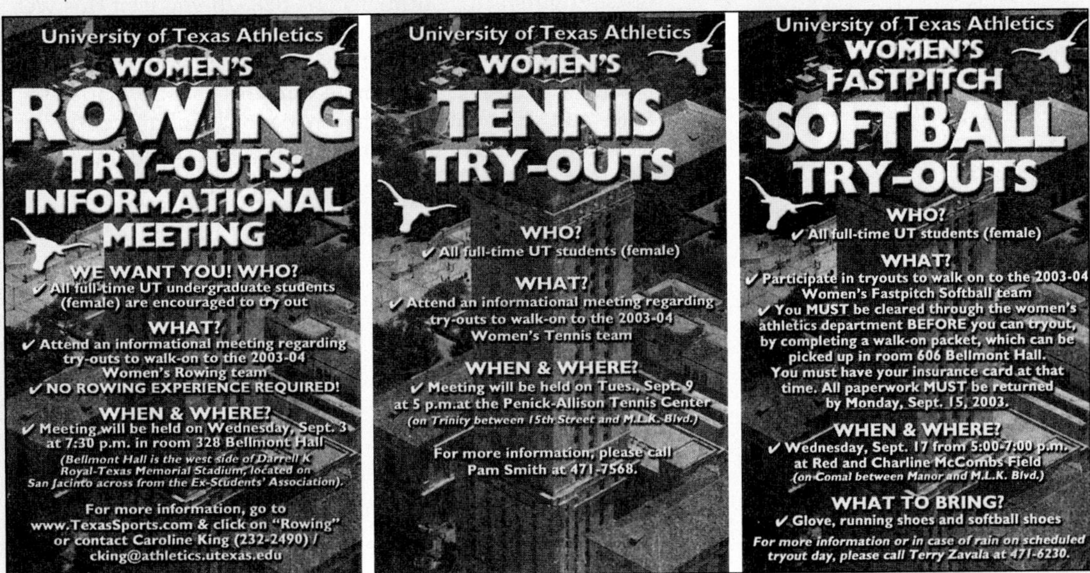

4. As noted in the headnote, Macur's article appeared under two different titles in different editions of the *New York Times*. The titles were "Rowing Scholarships Available. No Experience Necessary." and "Never Rowed? Take a Free Ride." What does the first title remind you of? What sort of word play does the second contain? Which one do you find to be more effective? Why?
5. What might be the benefits of introducing women who haven't previously been involved in team sports to sports like rowing? Are there any disadvantages?
6. Check out the Equity in Athletics reports for your school, a school in your area, or a school you have a particular interest in. (Those for the past several years for the University of Texas at Austin are posted on the Web site mentioned in the ads, under the heading "Equity Reports.") Once you've studied the reports, **write several paragraphs** in which you summarize what you've found as if you were writing an evaluative essay about the extent of the institution's compliance with Title IX. (A description of a school's past behavior would be necessary background to any evaluation of the extent of its compliance with the law.)

   If you aren't already familiar with the details of Title IX or feel you need additional information about its nature, use the Internet to find out about it. In early 2006, when this section of *Everything's an Argument* was written, an easily accessible Web page was "Title IX Q & A," located at <http://womenssportsfoundation.org/cgi-bin/iowa/issues/rights/article.html?record=888>. If you visit this Web page or others on the Women's Sports Foundation Web site, you'll obviously be reading information that's sympathetic to the goals of this organization, which seeks to promote women's participation in college athletics and strict enforcement of Title IX. Such information may prove especially useful in understanding some of the most hotly contested issues about Title IX.

Time's Up for Title IX Sports

JESSICA GAVORA

In the spring of 2001 an ad sponsored by the Independent Women's Forum appeared in UCLA's *Daily Bruin*, offering to expose "the 10 most common feminist myths." Myth number nine—"Gender is a social construction"—was answered thus:

> While environment and socialization do play a significant role in human life, a growing body of research in neuroscience, endocrinology and psychology over the past 40 years suggests there is a biological basis for many sex differences in aptitudes and preferences. Of course, this doesn't mean that women should be prevented from pursuing their goals in any field they choose; what it does suggest is that we should not expect parity in all fields.

The ad's impact on the UCLA campus was immediate and explosive. Rallies were organized. The university women's center demanded that the *Daily Bruin* "retract" the ad. When the paper's editor defended it as an exercise in free speech, Christie Scott, head of the campus feminist "Clothesline Project," dismissed this rationale as "somewhat cowardly."

"Somewhat cowardly" is the wrong term to apply to the editors of the *Daily Bruin*, but the right term for most participants in the discussion of women's role in American life today. Few topics involve more disinformation and shaving of the truth on the one side and political cowardice on the other. Christina Hoff Sommers—the author of the UCLA ad—Judith Kleinfeld, author, and psychiatrist Sally Satel and others have done an excellent job of uncovering the disinformation and false statistics used by women's advocates to advance their agenda. But they are virtually alone. For far too long, a wittingly or unwittingly gullible media has treated even the most outrageous claims of feminists as fact. The effect has been to give artificial life support to the myth that girls and women are an oppressed minority, clinging weakly to their rights only with the assistance of the full weight and authority of government.

Nowhere is the reality gap wider than in women's sports. Congress did a seemingly simple and laudable thing when it passed Title IX of the Educational Amendments in 1972: "No person in the United States shall, on the basis of sex, be excluded from participation in, or denied the benefits of, or be subjected to discrimination under any educational program or activity

This essay, which appeared in the June 2002 issue of The American Spectator, *is an excerpt from* Tilting the Playing Field: Schools, Sports, Sex, and Title IX (2002) *by Jessica Gavora. Gavora served as chief speechwriter for Attorney General John Ashcroft during George W. Bush's first term in office. As you read the essay, pay special attention to the ways in which Gavora seeks to discredit not only Title IX but also its supporters.*

What values does Gavora assume you share with her? How do you know? Chapter 3 discusses how writers establish credibility by highlighting shared values.

LINK TO P. 70

receiving Federal financial assistance." But as applied to organized sports, Title IX has been interpreted and twisted and bent outside the institutions of our electoral democracy, conforming at last to the shape of unintended consequences: A law designed to end discrimination against women is now causing discrimination against men.

And yet Title IX is remarkably entrenched. Before the new Bush adminis- 5
tration even had the chance to appoint a secretary of education, the powerful Women's Sports Foundation fired a shot across the White House bow, vowing to fight "any change that weakens this law and results in unequal treatment of female athletes." And the WSF is just the vanguard of an army of seasoned veterans of the gender wars who stand ready and eager to defend the territory they've gained under Title IX.

To make sure that a risk-averse new Republican president doesn't make the mistake of thinking he can take on the Title IX lobby with impunity, these gender warriors point to the results of a 2000 NBC News/*Wall Street Journal* poll that seems to show widespread public support for Title IX quotas:

Q: Title IX is a federal law that prohibits high schools and colleges that receive federal funds from discriminating on the basis of gender. Title IX is most commonly invoked to ensure equal opportunities for girls and women in high school and college athletics. Do you approve or disapprove of Title IX as it is described here?

Yes, approve of Title IX: 79%

No, do not approve of Title IX: 14%

Do not know enough about it: 4%

Not sure: 3%

But the issue under Title IX isn't the fair and equal division of resources between men and women; it's an attempt to dictate how men and women should behave. Female athletes have more teams to choose from in colleges and universities today than male athletes. They receive more athletic scholarship aid per capita than male athletes. The battle for "gender equity" is not a battle for resources; if it were, women's groups would have declared victory some time ago. The struggle is about power and ideals.

Civil Wrongs

Q: Do you support eliminating men's opportunities to create a 50/50 gender balance in school sports programs?

10 This is not how the pollsters who conducted the survey for NBC News and the *Wall Street Journal* asked the question. Journalists—even ink-stained veterans—routinely describe compliance with Title IX in terms of the equal sharing of resources between men and women in athletics. The result is that it is rare for a citizen who picks up a newspaper or turns on the television to see coverage of the law that is not glowingly positive. And it is a rare politician or government official who will tell the truth about the law's enforcement today. The first step toward re-leveling the playing field between the sexes in our schools, then, is simply beginning to tell the truth about Title IX.

The reality is that the federal government has enforced a quota standard in Title IX athletics for much of the past decade. This enforcement has been opportunistic; not every school has fallen under scrutiny from the Justice Department's Office for Civil Rights and been forced to cut men's teams, add women's teams or do both to achieve "proportionality." But schools don't need to experience a federal investigation or a lawsuit to know that their athletic departments are not under their control. They've read the "policy interpretations"; they've seen how OCR has treated schools like the University of Wisconsin and Boston University; and they've seen how the courts have ruled on the Brown and Cal State Bakersfield cases. American education has received the message loud and clear.

It is a measure of the power of liberal women's rights activists in academia today that universities are unable—or unwilling—to complain as the federal government micromanages more and more of their affairs in the name of "gender equity." When so-called "women's issues" are on the line, defenders of institutional autonomy like Brown's Vartan Gregorian are distressingly rare. Even among students whose lives are most affected by Title IX quotas, there is little questioning of the need or the rationale for federally mandated gender equity. "Nobody questions the underlying assumptions of Title IX, that male and female students will be equally interested in organized sports and that a lack of proportional numbers must indicate something is 'wrong,'" says Robert Geary, professor of English at James Madison University. "Universities are supposed to be places of inquiry, but some subjects appear closed to scrutiny—too sensitive."

Title IX quotas have never been the subject of debate. They were created outside the electoral process by unelected officials working hand in hand with special interest groups. The first step toward ending gender quotas, then, is to demand the truth from those who insist they don't exist.

Here's the reality. In June 1999 the OCR's Northeast regional office sent a letter to the athletic director and administrators of Central Connecticut State University, warning that they must add 20 female athletes to their sports roster to comply with the federal law. CCSU had already brought the percentage of its athletes who are female from 29 to 49 by dropping men's wrestling and adding women's lacrosse. But females made up 51 percent of the students at CCSU, so OCR insisted that 20 more female athletes were needed—the so-called "proportionality" principal.

Then there's the University of Wisconsin at Madison, which received a 15
similar letter in the fall of 2000. Having labored for a decade to attract women to programs, UWM had achieved near-perfect parity in the spring of that year: 429 athletes on campus were men and 425 were women. Not good enough, said Algis Tamosiunas, director of OCR compliance in Chicago. Because females now constituted a majority of students on the Madison campus (53.1 percent), the school would have to add another 25 women.

Letters like these are routinely sent to schools struggling to stay on the right side of the federal authorities. OCR officials such as the Clinton administration's Norma Cantu are being dishonest when they insist that because the regulations don't "require" sex quotas, those who administer the regulations don't work relentlessly to make quotas happen. Proportionality is the threshold test for Title IX compliance in federal regulation. It is the standard adopted by the courts and the only guarantee that a school will not be exposed to a federal investigation or a lawsuit. It is the standard for compliance with Title IX today. To say otherwise is to lie, plain and simple.

Get Smart

The good news is that there are storm clouds gathering on Title IX's horizon.

The past decade of gender-based quota expansion in women's sports has also been a time of relative prosperity for colleges and universities. In some cases, this has meant that schools struggling to meet the gender quota in athletics could do so in relatively painless ways, by adding women's sports and/or limiting men's participation by cutting walk-ons. As long as the funds were there, providing the scholarships and building or upgrading facilities for new women's teams were relatively easy.

A slowing economy combined with escalating expenses in athletic programs, however, threatens to change this. Budgets for women's sports are rising faster than those for men's sports, as is spending on scholarships for women. Another financial strain is accommodating the growing desire among athletic directors and fans alike that teams be competitive on the national level. Less and less are sports treated as another part of a well-rounded educational experience; increasingly teams must justify their existence by winning. This compulsion is helping to fuel an "arms race" in spending, not just on big-time football and basketball programs, but on women's teams and men's "nonrevenue" sports as well. According to the *Chronicle of Higher Education*, "nonrevenue" teams in NCAA Division I cost roughly $220,000 on average in 1999–2000. And at big-time football schools, where more money is available, women's teams and men's nonrevenue squads can cost up to half a million dollars apiece.

These exploding costs have already triggered a fresh round of budget cuts. 20
And because women's sports can't be touched, the sacrifice is borne by men's teams. Iowa State University, the University of Kansas and the University of Nebraska have all recently begun major cuts to their men's athletic programs. The bad news for Title IX quota advocates is that rising budget pressures may finally give schools a real incentive to go to court, to argue that women's programs should be fair game as well.

A school that invites a lawsuit by cutting a women's team or refusing to create a new team to meet the gender quota might very well decide to fight back in court rather than be forced to incur costs it can't afford. Alternately, male athletes whose positions are eliminated might decide to take a cue from Duane Naquin, a Boston College senior who was denied entry on the basis of his sex to a class in feminist ethics taught by theology professor Mary Daly; Naquin sued to win his right to coeducation. As that case showed, if there is one thing university administrators fear more than accusations of gender insensitivity, it's lawsuits. In the Daly case and others to come, public interest law firms like the Center for Individual Rights have been effective in reversing the course of sex discrimination in our schools.

Although Title IX preferences have yet to be struck down in a federal district court—and thus be made a prime target for Supreme Court review—creative legal challenges in the right circuits could yield results for fairness and gender-blind policies. "I have no doubt that the Supreme Court will take the case if and when there is a split in the circuit courts," says Maureen Mahoney, who argued Brown University's case to the Supreme Court. Women's advocates have been careful so far to push for Title IX quotas in liberal district courts that are likely to agree with their version of equity. But according to Mahoney and others, bringing the right challenge in the more conservative Fourth Circuit (which covers Maryland, South Carolina, North Carolina, Virginia and West Virginia) or the Fifth Circuit (including Texas, Louisiana and Mississippi) could bring a judgment that restores the original intent of the law.

The rising cost of fielding intercollegiate athletic teams is also contributing to a reexamination of how sports fit within the mission of the university. All recruited athletes, male or female, receive a preference from college admissions committees. But preferences for female athletes—and arguments for female quotas within athletic programs—are often justified on grounds above and beyond the contribution these women make to sports teams. Make women athletes, we are told, and you make better women. With some justification, women's groups argue that girls who play sports are associated with such positive traits as higher graduation rates, less drug use, higher self-esteem and lower levels of teenage pregnancy.

In *The Game of Life: College Sports and Educational Values,* James Shulman of the Andrew W. Mellon Foundation and former Princeton University president William Bowen examine what kind of students are currently being admitted to schools under athletic preferences. Using the same database that provided the intellectual fodder for Bowen's earlier defense of race-based affirmative action—data on 90,000 students who attended 30 selective colleges and universities in the 1950s, 1970s and 1990s—the authors claim that of all the recipients of affirmative action in colleges and universities today, female athletes are the most preferred. At a representative school in 1999, Shulman and Bowen found that a female who is a member of a minority had a 20 percent admissions advantage, the daughter of an alumnus had a 24 percent advantage, a male athlete had a 48 percent advantage and a female athlete had a 53 percent advantage. That is, a female athlete had a 53 percent better chance of being admitted than a nonathlete with the same SAT score.

25 And what are schools gaining from this admissions preference? *The Game of Life* sets out purposefully to shoot down the various "myths" of intercollegiate athletics, chief among them, in Shulman and Bowen's view, that athletics builds character. Shulman and Bowen argue that athletes today are less academically prepared, less concerned with scholarship and more financially directed than their fellow students. But what is most interesting about their analysis is their finding that these traits are increasing, among female athletes as well as male. And whereas female athletes were once at least as academically qualified as other female students, they now lag behind. Another benefit frequently cited to justify preferences for female athletes under Title IX is racial and ethnic diversity. But Shulman and Bowen found that Title IX produced gains mainly for white girls, not minorities.

The trend in women's athletics, particularly in the most competitive, high-profile sports, is away from the ideal often claimed by Title IX quota ideologues. Instead of representing the female ideal at the start of the twenty-first century—tough, smart, confident and empowered—female athletes are beginning to resemble the dimwitted, half-civilized male athletes of the feminist stereotype. And in such a situation, the rationale that women's preferences under Title IX are justified because they create better students and better citizens becomes hard to sustain.

Less Is Less

As I write this, the University of Kansas has eliminated its men's swimming and tennis teams, citing financial pressures and federal gender equity requirements. Bucknell University has announced it will drop wrestling and men's crew as varsity sports, eliminating 44 men's positions in order to reach male-female proportionality. Seton Hall, Capital University in Columbus, Ohio, and the University of St. Thomas have all dropped their wrestling teams. Iowa State has eliminated baseball and men's swimming. The University of Nebraska has also axed men's swimming and diving, leaving only four of the schools in the Big 12 conference still participating in the sport. The Big 12 is now questioning whether it will continue to stage a men's swimming and diving championship or do away with it altogether, a move that will almost certainly result in the remaining schools eliminating their men's programs.

This denial of opportunity for men is occurring because a group of people with a narrow agenda has worked hard and successfully behind the scenes to make it happen. Driven by the desire to overcome real discrimination against girls and women, activists like Donna Lopiano and Norma Cantu and groups like the Women's Sports Foundation, the National Women's Law Center and the American Association of University Women set out to create preferences for girls and women. They sought out and co-opted friendly government officials. They initiated a shrewd legal strategy when friendly government officials were unavailable. Partly through government fiat, partly through a shared ideology, they built a phalanx of promoters and defenders of "gender equity" on college campuses and in high schools and grade schools across the country. They wooed their allies and cowed their enemies in Congress and insisted that both parrot their message. They conducted a highly effective and sophisticated media campaign. They helped draft regulations and interpretations of regulations and interpretations of interpretations of regulations. At each stage in the legal and bureaucratic evolution of Title IX, they out-thought, out-worked and out-cared the people whose opportunities were being destroyed. The edifice of discrimination these activists built is a testament to their commitment.

In the end, of course, it is up to those charged with enforcing our laws to apply Title IX honestly and forthrightly. This is not, needless to say, a politically painless proposition. After some significant rollback of race-based preferences in the 1990s, elected officials and even conservative activists seem to have lost their appetite for battling identity politics. To stand on principle, many seem to believe, is to risk appearing "mean-spirited" in an age when compassion is the opiate of the electorate.

Writing about the "conundrum of quotas" in the *Wall Street Journal* in the 30
opening months of the Bush administration, Shelby Steele noted that conservatives have a hard time not appearing mean when they stand on principle on the issue of race because they lack moral authority. "Were conservatives of the last generation fastidious about principles when segregation prevailed as a breach of every known democratic principle, including merit?" wrote Steele.

The equation of race preferences with Title IX sex preferences is not perfect. As we have seen, there are real, innate differences between the sexes, of the kind that cannot be shown to exist between people of different races. Even so, Steele's point can easily be applied to conservatives on the issue of sex today. Conservatives of the last generation certainly did not lead the charge for women's rights—properly understood to be the same rights before the law that men historically have enjoyed. It was liberals, of course, who took the battle for women's rights forward. Eventually they corrupted it into a separatist movement in which women's interests are portrayed to be at odds with those of men. Nonetheless, before feminism took that destructive turn, conservatives did not champion the cause of equality for women, and more often than not they resisted it.

Can we now credibly argue that the principle of gender-blindness be upheld in the laws meant to guarantee it? Liberalism has been suborned on the issue of sex quotas. Can a conservative administration challenge quotas for girls and women without appearing "mean" and losing the thin margin of centrist voters who put it in office—voters who would most likely oppose gender preferences if they knew they existed but who nonetheless distrust conservatives on issues involving women? This is a conundrum of sex quotas every bit as difficult as Shelby Steele's conundrum of race quotas.

The way out of this conundrum is the same as it was in the 1920s, when women struggled for the right to vote, and the same as it was in the 1950s, when blacks encountered segregationists at the schoolhouse door. The way out is to defend the principle of nondiscrimination, even when it is hard. Especially when it is hard.

And liberal feminist groups will make it hard to stand on this principle; they will challenge the moral authority of those who seek to restore the original intent of the law. But the principle of nondiscrimination that is embodied in the original intent of Title IX has stood the test of time. It has allowed girls and women to rise from uncomfortable interlopers to become the dominant force in American education. Conservatives can gain new moral authority by insisting on standing by this principle and resisting a distortion of the law that discriminates against a new group of victims and demeans the very achievements of the girls and women it purports to protect.

Re-leveling the playing field in American education will not be easy. But 35
those who go into this battle have at their side two often underrated assets: First, it's the law. And second, it's the right thing to do.

RESPOND•

1. This selection promises "to tell the truth about Title IX" (paragraph 10). What, in Gavora's eyes, is the truth? What specific arguments does she make against Title IX? How persuasive are they?
2. What sorts of evidence does Gavora use in constructing her argument? (For a discussion of what counts as evidence, see Chapter 16.) Unlike the previous reading, which offers an argument in the form of information and facts, Gavora's argument is explicitly combative. Who are the readers that her text invokes (Chapter 1)? What values does she assume they have?
3. What's Gavora's attitude toward feminism? How do you know? How does this attitude manifest itself in this essay? What does she concede about the role that conservatives have traditionally taken toward women's rights (paragraph 31 and following)? Does this concession strengthen or weaken her argument? Why?
4. As mentioned in the headnote, Gavora seeks to discredit not only Title IX but also its supporters. How effective do you find her use of this rhetorical strategy? Why? Why is it a risky strategy?
5. Gavora would surely claim to be a supporter of nondiscrimination. What would she mean by this term? **Write an essay** in which you evaluate the definition of nondiscrimination she assumes. (If you're having trouble figuring out how Gavora's perspective might differ from that of those who support Title IX, visit the Web site discussed in the last question for the previous reading, "Rowing Scholarships Available. No Experience Necessary.") What are the strengths and weaknesses of Gavora's definition? Why?

This essay appeared in the March 24, 2003, issue of The Nation, *a weekly magazine of political analysis and commentary that reflects a liberal point of view. Ruth Conniff is Washington editor of* The Progressive. *Conniff's writing style is rich in descriptive detail. As you read, notice how her word choice enhances her argument.*

Title IX: Political Football

RUTH CONNIFF

Girls in ponytails and soccer jerseys packed the front of a room at the National Press Club in Washington, DC. They elbowed each other and giggled as kids from across the nation spoke lovingly of basketball, pole vaulting and field hockey, and in support of Title IX—the 1972 law that has become synonymous with the rise of women's sports. Since Title IX went into effect thirty-one years ago, girls' athletic participation has skyrocketed. The number of girls' playing varsity sports has gone up from one in twenty-seven in 1972 to almost one in two today.

Despite all the good feeling Title IX has engendered among girls and their parents, the law is currently under attack. The National Wrestling Coaches Association filed a lawsuit against the Education Department claiming that Title IX is decimating men's college sports, forcing colleges to cut hundreds of wrestling programs—along with gymnastics, diving and other teams—in order to meet "quotas" for female athletes. The aggrieved jocks have found an ally in President Bush, who formed the Commission on Opportunity in Athletics last June to re-examine the law.

The high school girls descended on Washington for their press conference–cum–pep rally just as the commission convened its final meeting at the Hotel Washington. Outside the hotel, the Feminist Majority and the conservative Independent Women's Forum held dueling press conferences. Inside the grand ballroom, a wrestling coach wearing a "No Quotas" button cruised the perimeter, handing out literature calling on the commission to "reject the gender politics of the special interest groups."

That would be groups like the Women's Sports Foundation—which helps girls seek equal funding and facilities for their teams—and Dads and Daughters, whose executive director, Joe Kelly, emceed the high school girls' event.

Title IX, said Kelly, "is one of the best things that ever happened to fathers." 5

"Sports is a natural comfort zone for men, and Title IX makes it a bridge to our daughters," he said. He told the story of a friend, Dave, who coached his son and daughter in basketball, and was appalled by the inferior facilities provided to his daughter's team.

"Dads get angry when daughters play on old fields or gyms that are in disrepair," Kelly said. And that's what Title IX was designed to fix. "Guys like Dave are not radical feminists. They simply know sports are good for girls. They also know sports are good for boys. Don't tell me you're going to treat my daughter differently than my son."

High school girls still get about 1.1 million fewer opportunities than boys to play sports, according to the National Coalition for Women and Girls in Education. But Bush's commission finished its work by making a series of recommendations to weaken Title IX. Instead of making girls' sports proportional to the number of female students enrolled, the commission recommended that schools aim for approximately 50/50 boy-girl representation. Schools that don't reach parity would be allowed to use interest surveys to show that girls are getting as much opportunity as they desire. According to the Women's Sports Foundation, the changes could result in the loss of 300,000 participation opportunities and $100 million in scholarships for female athletes.

> **"Sports is a natural comfort zone for men, and Title IX makes it a bridge to our daughters."**
>
> **–Joe Kelly, of Dads and Daughters**

The deck was stacked at the commission from the beginning. High school athletes and coaches who support Title IX didn't get to testify. Title IX opponents like wrestlers' groups and the Independent Women's Forum had disproportionate input. The commission's two strongest Title IX advocates, Julie Foudy, captain of the US National Women's Soccer Team, and Olympic gold medalist Donna de Varona, were treated to eye-rolling by fellow commissioners and outright hostility by wrestlers' groups. In late February, the two refused to sign the final report, charging that the commission failed to acknowledge continuing discrimination against female athletes.

Still, despite the battle-of-the-sexes tone in DC, some sincere anguish is 10
driving the backlash against Title IX.

Doug Klein coaches high school wrestling at the Ida Crown Jewish Academy in Chicago. "I had such a good time when I walked on the team at William and Mary," he recalls. Today his old college team has been cut, and other teams no longer take walk-ons (as opposed to recruits) because, he says, they have to keep their rosters small in order to comply with Title IX genderequity rules. His star wrestler recently visited Lehigh and Cornell, and couldn't even get a coach to talk to him.

"Boys who aren't superstars—nobody is interested in them. And that's really unfair," Klein says. "Somebody made the point on one of these [wrestling] websites: 'I'm 5′5″, 120 pounds, what sport am I going to do?' There are not many opportunities in sports for little boys and little men."

That may be the most painfully honest comment ever made by an opponent of Title IX. Instead of focusing on the big men's sports that suck up all the resources in college athletics, a lot of little guys who are getting crushed blame women. Klein, too, blames Title IX for "gutting wrestling"—though he concedes that Title IX may not be the main problem.

"When you read the wrestling magazines, they're reluctant to point the finger at football," Klein says. "But football is the 800-pound gorilla." Indeed, major teams award up to eighty-five scholarships a year and field rosters of 100 or more players, while top football coaches can earn more than $2 million a year. Schools could easily comply with Title IX by making small cuts in these big-budget programs, instead of cutting men's roster spots. Title IX advocates calculate that just by dropping scholarship spots for football bench-warmers—cutting back from the eighty-five players now allowed by the NCAA to the fifty-three used by the NFL, for example—and by dropping a few of the most ridiculous perks, such as hotel-room stays on home-game nights, schools could add back all those smaller programs they've been eliminating.

There is a myth that spending huge amounts of money on football makes 15
sense because the game will bring in even more. The reality is that in the race to field a winning team, jack up alumni giving and secure lucrative TV contracts, even big-time football schools are losing money. Take the University of Wisconsin. UW lost $286,700 on its Rose Bowl appearance in 1998. Until schools get off the football treadmill, athletic program budgets will feel the squeeze, with or without Title IX.

Donna Shalala, President Clinton's Secretary of Health and Human Services, is one of the nation's biggest boosters of Title IX—and of big-budget football. As UW chancellor, Shalala brought the university's football program into the big time. She hired coach Barry Alvarez and built a giant new sports facility the same year she presided over the elimination of UW's baseball, men's and women's gymnastics, and men's and women's fencing teams. Now president of another football powerhouse, the University of Miami, Shalala is an unabashed proponent of Title IX: "It's had a huge impact on providing opportunities for women's sports." Yet she is also an unabashed proponent of big-time football.

Shalala says it was a budget crisis, not Title IX, that forced the cuts at Wisconsin. "We cannot use Title IX as an excuse for our lack of disciplined management and our financial problems," she says. She argues that it's possible to pay for minor sports and be a football power: "People have to restrain their costs, and they have to be honest about what football costs, and go out and raise more money."

Shalala uses the populist language of Title IX, saying, "The whole point is to provide opportunities for men and women." But in practice, building an athletic department around big-time football has resulted in schools—including UW—killing sports programs that once provided opportunities for regular students. It has also meant that college sports, more and more, are not about promoting amateur participation, sportsmanship or character but rather about raising a school's profile and getting a piece of the sports entertainment action. "This is not," says Shalala, "intramural sports." While Title IX has protected many women from these trends, no structures are in place to save minor men's teams from the football monster.

Talking to university administrators about athletic department budgets is like talking to the Democrats about campaign finance reform. Everyone is in favor of more "opportunity" and "participation," but when it comes to reining in football spending, no one wants to cash out first.

20 According to Cheryl Marra, senior associate director of sports administration at UW, "We don't spend any more here than anywhere else. But who's gonna give first?" UW has to offer its football players chartered jets and posh facilities, says Marra; otherwise, "Ohio and Michigan will say to recruits, 'You know, at Wisconsin they don't treat you right.'" The only way out, according to Marra, is for the NCAA to crack down on excessive football spending. Then no school would be placed at a disadvantage.

The wrestlers' attack on Title IX is based on a gamble: that if the government relaxes Title IX rules, athletic departments will shift money back to their teams. But that's hardly a sure thing. Athletic directors are no more interested in minor men's sports now than they used to be in women's sports. Responding to the complaints of downsized wrestlers, Marra says, dismissively, "Why can't they accept that people don't want to play the same sports they did 100 years ago?"

Ironically, Title IX's very success is being used as an argument for its dismantlement. As with affirmative action, the law's opponents argue that the job is done—women have reached equality and no longer need special attention. This argument resonates with girls of the post–Title IX generation, who feel pangs of guilt when Title IX is blamed for the elimination of minor men's sports. "I'm in favor of Title IX, but not for cutting guys' sports," says Kym Hubing, a sprinter at Wisconsin.

Indeed, many students now take women's athletics for granted. Male and female athletes hang out together and support each other. This is one of the most profound, positive effects of Title IX. "You're friends. You're equals," says Greta Bauer, a UW hurdler. "When you walk into a party, the guys will see you and punch you in the arm and say, 'Hey, how are you doing?' The other girls will look at you like, 'How did you get inside the circle?'"

Being "inside the circle" means that women in Division I sports are envied just like the men. There is an aura of exclusivity about hanging out in the expensive sports facilities, studying in the athletes' study hall, living in jock housing. Like breaking into any formerly segregated club, being part of the sports scene on campus means gaining privilege.

If the Education Department heeds the Commission on Opportunity in 25
Athletics, the march toward equality will stall. High schools and colleges across the nation will stop counting heads and start taking interest surveys. That may sound fair to young athletes like Hubing. But when Title IX started, most girls couldn't imagine themselves as serious athletes. An interest survey at that time would have determined that only a few real tomboys deserved a chance to play. It was the opportunities offered under the law that created such a radical change in the culture. Women now make up 42 percent of college athletes—maybe not equality, but an enormous leap, thanks to the law. Interest surveys would freeze that progress where it is today.

And this would be a loss not only to girl athletes but to the culture of sports as a whole. Title IX has become one of the last bastions of amateur sports. While there are no limits on the amount of money a school can shift from other men's programs to football, Title IX insists they keep open athletic opportunities for women. Women's sports—often praised for their "purity," for the sheer joy of the athletes and for the fact that players get decent grades—have kept alive the ideal of the scholar-athlete.

But maybe not for long.

Consider how Conniff uses arguments from the heart to reach her audience. See Chapter 2 for more uses of emotional appeals.

LINK TO P. 47

RESPOND.

1. What arguments is Conniff putting forth about Title IX? What argument, in particular, is she making in the concluding section of her essay (paragraphs 22–27)? How well do you think she supports her claims? Why?
2. Conniff chooses carefully the sources she cites, especially with regard to quotations likely based on interviews. (For additional information on kinds of evidence such as interviews, see Chapter 16.) In paragraph 5, for example, she quotes Joe Kelly, a father, as claiming that Title IX "is one of the best things that ever happened to fathers." Later, she quotes Kelly as saying that he and other members of Dads and Daughters "are not radical feminists" (paragraph 7). In paragraph 16, she quotes Donna Shalala, "one of the nation's biggest boosters of Title IX—and of big-budget football." Why are such details and characterizations important in the argument Conniff is constructing? In countering arguments put forth by authors like Jessica Gavora in the previous selection?
3. Notice the ways that Conniff's word choice supports her argument. Look back at the text to find several instances of effective word choice, including figurative language, and state why you think they're effective. (For additional information on figurative language, see Chapter 12.) How does word choice contribute to Conniff's ethos as an author? As an authority?
4. **Write a dialogue** between Ruth Conniff and Jessica Gavora about Title IX. You'll likely be most successful if you choose two or three major topics for them to discuss and keep the discussion focused on this text and the previous one. (For example, you may want to use your answer to question 2 above to help you think about relationships between the two texts in this way.)

Leslie Heywood teaches English and cultural studies at the State University of New York at Binghamton. This article appeared in a January 1999 issue of the Chronicle of Higher Education, *a weekly paper covering issues of concern to college and university administrators and faculty. In it she raises difficult questions about women's sports that have received little attention. The* Chronicle *published only one letter—a critical one—in response to Heywood's article. As you read, think about whether—and how—the issues she raises have been addressed at your school.*

Despite the Positive Rhetoric about Women's Sports, Female Athletes Face a Culture of Sexual Harassment

LESLIE HEYWOOD

Last October, Nike and the Partnership for Women's Health at Columbia University announced Helping Girls Become Strong Women, an alliance formed in response to an on-line survey conducted by *Seventeen* and *Ladies' Home Journal.* That survey found that 50 per cent of the 1,100 girls polled reported feeling depressed at least once a week; 29 per cent felt somewhat or very uncomfortable with their bodies; and close to 50 per cent were unhappy with their appearances.

The alliance stresses sports as a major solution to those problems. It echoes a landmark study written under the auspices of the President's Council on Physical Fitness and Sports, which also emphasized the benefits of sports for girls and women. That report cited, for example, the way sports disprove gender stereotypes about female weakness and incompetency, and the ways in which they foster better physical and mental health, self-esteem, and skills such as leadership and cooperation.

Certainly, sports can help with some of the problems faced by young girls and women. And female participation in sports has greatly increased in the years since the 1972 passage of Title IX of the Education Amendments, which barred schools and colleges receiving federal funds from discriminating against women. High-school girls' participation in sports grew from 300,000 in 1972 to 2.25 million in 1995, and today, one in three women in college participates in competitive sports.

But there is another, less-discussed side to the story. A discrepancy exists between the increasing equality and respect for female athletes on the one hand, and, on the other, behavior within the athletics culture that shows profound disrespect for female competitors.

5 For example, old assumptions that women who excel at sports are really more like men (and must, therefore, be lesbians, because they're not conventionally feminine) are rearticulated in the kind of "lesbian baiting" of female coaches and athletes that happens on many campuses.

In her book *Coming on Strong* (Free Press, 1994) the women's-sports historian Susan K. Cahn discusses the recent rumor circulated among coaches that an anonymous list had been mailed to prospective high-school recruits identifying programs as lesbian or straight. "Oddly," Cahn writes, "concerns about lesbianism in sports may even have increased, in inverse relationship to the greater acceptance of women's sports in general." Such concern shows a profound disrespect, because it assumes that good athletes are not "real women," and that lesbianism is something to fear, which undermines the fundamental dignity and worth of all female athletes and fosters a homophobia that may discourage women from participating in sports.

Other denigrating coaching practices—although they are officially discouraged—include mandatory weigh-ins and criticizing athletes about their weight. Many coaches are inordinately preoccupied with what their female athletes eat, and subject them to public ridicule about their diets and bodies. One group of athletes, from an athletically successful university in the South, told me about a coach who dubbed one of his athletes "Janie Snax" because he thought she was overweight (she weighed 125 at 5 feet 8 inches tall), and had the male athletes make fun of her every time she tried to eat anything. I have heard similar tales on many campuses.

Such practices, though disturbing, may stem from assumptions about women's "natures" that are widely accepted. In a recent issue of the *Nation*, in "The Joy of Women's Sports," Ruth Conniff applauds Anson Dorrance, who has coached the women's soccer team at the University of North Carolina at Chapel Hill to 15 national championships, for being responsive to women athletes by making changes in his coaching style. Conniff quotes Dorrance as saying, "You basically have to drive men, but you can lead women. . . . I think women bring something incredibly positive to athletics. They are wonderfully coachable and so appreciative of anything you give them."

Two weeks after the *Nation* article appeared, *The Chronicle* and other news media reported a sexual-harassment lawsuit filed by two of Dorrance's former players, Debbie Keller (now a player on the national women's soccer team) and Melissa Jennings. They charge that he "intentionally and systematically subjected his players to inappropriate conduct and unwelcome harassment and thereby created a hostile environment at U.N.C." The suit alleges that Dorrance made uninvited sexual advances, monitored players' whereabouts outside of practice, and sent them harassing e-mail messages.

10 The idea that women are "wonderfully coachable and so appreciative" has a sinister ring in light of these charges (which Dorrance has denied), and highlights some questionable assumptions underlying the positive rhetoric about women in sports. Gender-based assumptions like Dorrance's, such as the idea that women are more "coachable"—that

Heywood claims that sexual exploitation of female athletes jeopardizes some of the benefits of sports for women. Do you agree that her article could be considered a qualitative evaluation argument? Check out Chapter 9.

LINK TO P. 259

is, open and manipulable—and that they are "appreciative" of whatever attentions the coach chooses to give them, may lead to unethical behavior such as that cited in the charges against Dorrance.

Yet the issue of coaches' behavior toward female athletes—what is acceptable and what is not— has been swept aside, and reports of the lawsuit against Dorrance have had no effect on recruiting for the U.N.C. women's soccer team. One of the nation's top soccer recruits, in a recent article in *College Soccer Weekly,* said that the allegations weren't "an issue"; that the lawsuit, in her opinion, "doesn't exist."

"Creating a climate that fosters open discussion about sexual harassment is crucial, so that athletes feel authorized and safe in speaking out."

That kind of dismissal is a common response when a female athlete comes forward with charges of sexual harassment. As is the case at U.N.C., teams often rally around the coach and ostracize the accuser, creating an environment in which most women are afraid to speak out. In the November 14 issue of *USA Today,* Dorrance noted that there was a "silver lining" to the lawsuit in that it "unified the team very quickly." High-profile cases such as this one, in which the news media seem to stress support for the coach rather than for the athlete, communicate to other athletes that if they speak out, they will be brushed aside and disbelieved.

In fact, sexual harassment and abuse of female athletes are part of the reality of women's sports. The executive director of the Women's Sports Foundation, Donna Lopiano, has written on the foundation's site on the World-Wide Web: "Sexual harassment or even sexual assault is a significant problem in school and open amateur sport settings across the country that often goes unreported."

Michelle Hite, an athlete who competed in track in the mid-'90s at a major Division I university, told me that "one of the reasons I gave up my athletics scholarship was because of the sexual harassment that I felt was as much a part of my athletics routine as practice was." Hite and her teammates cite coaches' preoccupations with their bodies and weight, inappropriate comments about their bodies and their sexuality (and policing of that sexuality, such as forbidding athletes to have romantic relationships), direct sexual come-ons from members of the coaching staff, and romantic relationships between coaches and athletes—which were destructive and disruptive to the athletes involved and to the team as a whole.

15 It wasn't until recently, however, that romantic relationships between coaches and athletes were seen as a problem. When Mariah Burton Nelson wrote *The Stronger Women Get, the More Men Love Football* (Harcourt Brace, 1994), she found that harassment was a part of everyday reality in sports culture. "Some of the 'best' male coaches in the country have seduced a succession of female athletes," she writes. "Like their counterparts in medicine, education, psychotherapy, and the priesthood, coaches are rarely caught or punished."

In a crucial first step, most athletics organizations have drawn a hard line against such behavior. In his 1994 article "Ethics in Coaching: It's Time to Do the Right Thing" in *Olympic Coach* magazine, William V. Nielsens, of the U.S. Olympic Committee, wrote: "One of the most pressing issues today that needs to be addressed concerning coaching ethics is sexual abuse and harassment." The Women's Sports Foundation and WomenSport International have developed extensive anti-harassment and training guidelines for coaches. In Canada, various sports organizations have joined to create the Harassment and Abuse in Sport Collective.

Athletics departments also claim to be sensitive to these issues, but it remains unclear how much action they have taken beyond paying lip service to the problem. Some more-progressive campuses have established preventive measures, such as educational training for coaches and athletes. The University of Arizona, for instance, has implemented an extensive education and support system, which includes seminars prepared for coaches by affirmative-action officers. The seminars specifically deal with the multifaceted nature of sexual harassment, and include case studies and "real-life scenarios" to clarify what exactly constitutes harassment. Freshman orientation for athletes covers "social issues" like harassment, unethical coach/athlete relationships, and eating disorders. This is supplemented by orientation for parents that lets them know about potential problems that may develop in their daughters' athletics careers, and the resources that are available to these young women.

There are several problems, though, with such prevention and treatment strategies at even the most-progressive campuses. The first is that almost all such education programs are initiated by affirmative-action officers, rather than originating in the athletics departments themselves. The Women's Sports Foundation recommends that athletics departments have their own policies and programs, because there is so much more personal contact and interaction in the world of athletics than in ordinary teacher-student relationships.

Furthermore, typical seminars given by affirmative-action offices involve outsiders coming in to lecture individuals who are caught up in an athletics culture that doesn't always take such education seriously. In fact, a conflict exists between athletics, which values winning at all costs, and "sensitivity training," which many athletes see either as distracting or as not applying to them.

20 It is hard to convince coaches and athletes that the problems of female athletes are real and significant: After all, what does the self-esteem of a few girls matter when we've got to go out and win the big game? The women themselves, who may feel that achieving success and respect is bound up with gaining the approval of coaches, view the people who come to talk about harassment as an intrusion or distraction from the larger goal of athletics success.

Many sports administrators also assume that the athlete herself will report any abuses to the proper authorities. But many women rightly believe that doing so would bring about reprisals, such as being ostracized by their teammates and coaches, and being given less playing time.

The problems are complicated, tied up as they are with assumptions inherent in the athletics culture itself. If we really want to create an environment that is supportive to all athletes, we need to change traditional cultural assumptions about which athletes and which sports are most valuable. As continual debates about Title IX reveal, despite the widespread acceptance of female athletes, in many universities male athletes are still seen as "the real thing," the more-valued players. Over all, universities trivialize issues such as harassment, because allegations are perceived as detracting from "business as usual"—that is, producing winning men's teams.

According to the Women's Sports Foundation, every sports organization, from university athletics departments to youth leagues, should have and implement its own code of ethics and conduct for coaches. Creating a climate that fosters open discussion about sexual harassment also is crucial, so that athletes feel authorized and safe in speaking out.

Often, athletes believe that they will be accused of consenting to sexual relations with coaches, or of making up incidents of harassment. Many athletes also feel ashamed to talk about sexual issues publicly. But harassment is an issue of power, not of sex, and college and university policies need to make that distinction clear.

25 Parents and athletes also should look for schools and colleges with education programs that inform coaches clearly about what kinds of behavior won't be tolerated, and that inform athletes of their rights and the recourse available to them if they should encounter harassment. If parents and athletes show a preference for institutions with such programs, others will follow suit. But the programs need to go beyond lip service and show real support for women who file complaints, by showing zero tolerance for harassment and not—as has historically been the case—immediately leaping to the coaches' defense.

Sports are great for women. Some of my best experiences have been, and continue to be, in competitive sports. But for sports to really improve self-esteem and provide character building, camaraderie, and learning, greater attention needs to be paid to coaching, the assumptions that coaches sometimes make about female athletes, and how much control coaches should have over female athletes' lives. If we want women to truly benefit from participation in sports, we need to find ways to prevent their exploitation.

RESPOND •

1. What solutions does Heywood recommend for eliminating the sexual abuse and harassment of female athletes by coaches? Do you think her proposal is viable? Why or why not?
2. The first two paragraphs of Heywood's article don't directly address the main topic. What's Heywood doing in these paragraphs? Why does she open the article in this way? How well does the strategy work?
3. Writing to an audience of educators and policy-making officials of sports organizations such as the NCAA, Heywood uses a combination of personal and statistical evidence to construct her argument. How might she have changed her article for an audience of parents? Of athletes? How might she alter her appeal in a speech to a coaches' conference?

4. In the "Issues and Action" section of the Women's Sports Foundation Web site, <http://womenssportsfoundation.org>, readers can find a document entitled "Addressing the Issue of Verbal, Physical and Psychological Abuse of Athletes: The Foundation Position." Even if this specific document isn't available when you're using this book, there are likely documents on similar topics on the Women's Sports Foundation Web site. Examine the information included in a relevant document, comparing and contrasting it with Heywood's argument. How are they similar? How are they different?
5. Heywood's article uses all four types of argument described in Chapters 2–4 of this book. Choose the type you think is most prominent in her article, and **write an essay** analyzing the rhetorical techniques Heywood uses to construct that type of argument. Give examples from her text, and tell why you think her use of this type of argument is (or isn't) effective.

Barbara Munson is a member of the Oneida Nation, living in Mosinee, Wisconsin. She serves as chair of the Wisconsin Indian Education Association "Indian" Mascot and Logo Taskforce, and she's been active in public service at the state level. We found this selection, "Common Themes and Questions about the Use of 'Indian' Logos," on the Internet, where it's currently posted on several Web sites, including <http://allarm.org> and <http://iwchildren.org>. The former is the site for the organization Alliance Against Racial Mascots; the latter is the site for American Comments: A Web Magazine. Both sites are dedicated to advancing respect for American Indians, the former focusing narrowly on the topic of mascots, team names, and logos, and the latter containing information about negative images of American Indians in popular culture, including sports. The allarm.org site gives a copyright date of 1998 for this selection, so it's the better site to use in bibliographic citations. As you read, consider why Munson may have organized this argument as she did—as a list of everyday statements with commentary.

Common Themes and Questions about the Use of "Indian" Logos

BARBARA MUNSON

"Indian" logos and nicknames create, support and maintain stereotypes of a race of people. When such cultural abuse is supported by one or many of society's institutions, it constitutes institutional racism. **It is not conscionable that public schools be the vehicle of institutional racism.** The logos, along with other societal abuses and stereotypes, separate, marginalize, confuse, intimidate and harm Native American children and create barriers to their learning throughout their school experience. Additionally, the logos teach non-Indian children that it's all right to participate in culturally abusive behavior. Children spend a great deal of their time in school, and schools have a very significant impact on their emotional, spiritual, physical and intellectual development. As long as such logos remain, both Native American and non-Indian children are learning to tolerate racism in our schools. The following illustrate the common questions and statements that I have encountered in trying to provide education about the "Indian" logo issue.

"We have always been proud of our 'Indians'." People are proud of their high school athletic teams, even in communities where the team name and symbolism do not stereotype a race of people. In developing high school athletic traditions, schools have borrowed from Native American cultures the

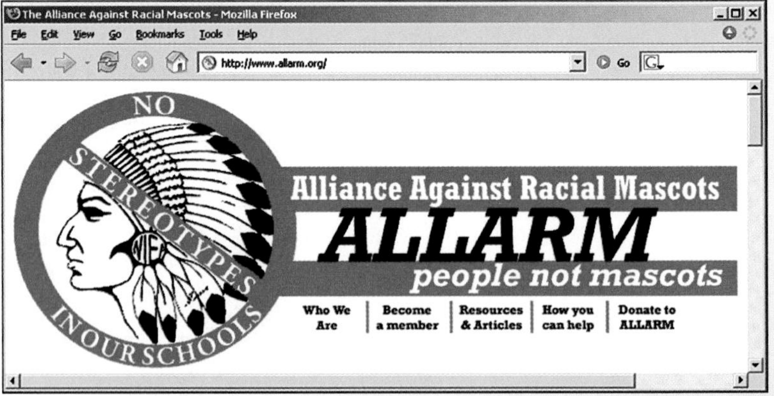

The logo for the Alliance Against Racial Mascots organization

sacred objects, ceremonial traditions and components of traditional dress that were most obvious, without understanding their deep meaning or appropriate use. High school traditions were created without in-depth knowledge of Native traditions; they are replete with inaccurate depictions of Indian people, and promote and maintain stereotypes of rich and varied cultures. High school athletic traditions have taken the trappings of Native cultures onto the playing field where young people have played at being "Indian." Over time, and with practice, generations of children in these schools have come to believe that the pretended "Indian" identity is more than what it is.

Bolded words and sentences lead the reader through this piece. Munson employs these style elements for organization and emphasis. What other characteristics of sentence structure and punctuation add to her argument? Some examples of these style aspects can be found in Chapter 12.

LINK TO P. 374

"We are honoring Indians; you should feel honored." Native people are saying that they don't feel honored by this symbolism. We experience it as no less than a mockery of our cultures. We see objects sacred to us — such as the drum, eagle feathers, face painting and traditional dress — being used, not in sacred ceremony, or in any cultural setting, but in another culture's **game.** We are asking that the public schools stop demeaning, insulting, harassing and misrepresenting Native peoples, their cultures and religions, for the sake of school athletics. Why must some schools insist on using symbols of a **race** of people? Other schools are happy with their logos which offend no human being. Why do some schools insist on categorizing Indian people along with animals and objects? If your team name were the *Pollacks, Niggers, Gooks, Spics, Honkies or Krauts, and someone from the community found the name and symbols associated with it offensive and asked that it be changed, would you not change the name? If not, why not?* I apologize for using this example but have found no way to get this point across without using similar derogatory names for other racial and ethnic groups.

"Why is the term 'Indian' offensive?" The term "Indian" was given to indigenous people on this continent by an explorer who was looking for India, a man who was lost and who subsequently exploited the indigenous people. "Indian" is a designation we have learned to tolerate, it is not the name we call ourselves. We are known by the names of our Nations — Oneida (On ^ yoteaka), Hochunk, Stockbridge-Munsee, Menominee (Omaeqnomenew), Chippewa (Anishanabe), Potawatomi, etc. There are many different nations with different languages and different cultural practices among the Native American peoples — as in Europe there are French, Swiss, Italian, German, Polish, English, Irish, Yugoslavs, Swedes, Portuguese, Latvians etc.

"Why is an attractive depiction of an Indian warrior just as offensive as an ugly caricature?" Both depictions present and maintain stereotypes. 5

Both firmly place Indian people in the past, separate from our contemporary cultural experience. It is difficult, at best, to be heard in the present when someone is always suggesting that your real culture only exists in museums. The logos keep us marginalized and are a barrier to our contributing here and now. Depictions of mighty warriors of the past emphasize a tragic part of our history; focusing on wartime survival, they ignore the strength and beauty of our cultures during times of peace. Many Indian cultures view life as a spiritual journey filled with lessons to be learned from every experience and from every living being. Many cultures put high value on peace, right action and sharing.

Indian men are not limited to the role of warrior; in many of our cultures a good man is learned, gentle, patient, wise and deeply spiritual. In present time as in the past, our men are also sons and brothers, husbands, uncles, fathers and grandfathers. Contemporary Indian men work in a broad spectrum of occupations, wear contemporary clothes and live and love just as men do from other cultural backgrounds.

The depictions of Indian "braves," "warriors" and "chiefs" also ignore the roles of women and children. Although there are patrilineal Native cultures, many Indian nations are both matrilineal and child centered. Indian cultures identify women with the Creator because of their ability to bear children, and with the Earth which is Mother to us all. In most Indian cultures the highest value is given to children; they are closest to the Creator and they embody the future. In many Native traditions, each generation is responsible for the children of the seventh generation in the future.

"We never intended the logo to cause harm." That no harm was intended when the logos were adopted may be true. It is also true that we Indian people are saying that the logos are harmful to our cultures, and especially to our children, in the present. When someone says you are hurting them by your action, if you persist, then the harm becomes intentional.

"We are paying tribute to Indians." Indian people do not pay tribute to one another by the use of logos, portraits or statues. The following are some ways that we exhibit honor:

> In most cultures to receive an eagle feather is a great honor, and often such a feather also carries great responsibility.

> An honor song at a Pow-Wow or other ceremony is a way of honoring a person or a group.
>
> We honor our elders and leaders by asking them to share knowledge and experience with us or to lead us in prayer. We defer to elders. They go first in many ways in our cultures.
>
> We honor our young by not doing things to them that would keep them from becoming who and what they are intended to be.
>
> We honor one another by listening and not interrupting.
>
> We honor those we love by giving them our time and attention.
>
> Sometimes we honor people through gentle joking.
>
> We honor others by giving to them freely what they need or what belongs to them already because they love it more or could use it better than we do.

"Aren't you proud of your warriors?" Yes, we are proud of the warriors who 10
fought to protect our cultures and preserve our lands. We are proud and we don't want them demeaned by being "honored" in a sports activity on a **playing** field. Our people died tragically in wars motivated by greed for our lands. Our peoples have experienced forced removal and systematic genocide. Our warriors gave their sacred lives in often vain attempts to protect the land and preserve the culture for future generations. Football is a game.

"This is not an important issue." If it is not important, then why are school boards willing to tie up their time and risk potential law suits rather than simply change the logos? I, as an Indian person, have never said it is unimportant. Most Indian adults have lived through the pain of prejudice and harassment in schools when they were growing up, and they don't want their children to experience more of the same. The National Council of American Indians, the Great Lakes InterTribal Council, the Oneida Tribe, and the Wisconsin Indian Education Association have all adopted formal position statements because this is a very important issue to Indian people. This issue speaks to our children being able to form a positive Indian identity and to develop appropriate levels of self-esteem. In addition, it has legal ramifications in regard to pupil harassment and equal access to education. If it's not important to people of differing ethnic and racial backgrounds within the community, then change the logos because they are hurting the community's Native American population.

"What if we drop derogatory comments and clip art and adopt pieces of REAL Indian culturally significant ceremony, like Pow-Wows and sacred songs?" Though well intended, these solutions are culturally naive and would exchange one pseudo-culture for another. Pow-Wows are gatherings of Native people which give us the opportunity to express our various cultures and strengthen our sense of Native American community. Pow-Wows have religious, as well as social, significance. To parodize such ceremonial gatherings for the purpose of cheering on the team at homecoming would multiply exponentially the current pseudo-cultural offensiveness. Bringing Native religions onto the playing field through songs of tribute to the "Great Spirit" or Mother Earth would increase the mockery of Native religions even more than the current use of drums and feathers. High school football games are secular; The Creator and Mother Earth are sacred.

"We are helping you preserve your culture." The responsibility for the continuance of our cultures falls to Native people. We accomplish this by surviving, living and thriving; and, in so doing, we pass on to our children our stories, traditions, religions, values, arts and our languages. We sometimes do this important work with people from other cultural backgrounds, but they do not and cannot continue our cultures for us. Our ancestors did this work for us, and we continue to carry the culture for the generations to come. Our cultures are living cultures — they are passed on, not "preserved."

"This logo issue is just about political correctness." Using the term "political correctness" to describe the attempts of concerned Native American parents, educators and leaders to remove stereotypes from the public schools trivializes a survival issue. A history of systematic genocide has decimated over 95% of the indigenous population of the Americas. Today, the average life expectancy of Native American males is age 45. The teen suicide rate among Native people is several times higher than the national average. Stereotypes, ignorance, silent inaction and even naive innocence damage and destroy individual lives and whole cultures. Racism kills.

"What do you mean, there is hypocrisy involved in retaining an 'Indian' 15
logo?" Imagine that you are a child in a society where your people are variously depicted as stoic, brave, honest, a mighty warrior, fierce, savage, stupid, dirty, drunken and only good when dead. Imagine going to a school where many of your classmates refer to your people as "Dirty Squaws" and "Timber Niggers." Imagine hearing your peers freely, loudly and frequently say such

things as "Spear an Indian, Save a Walleye," or more picturesquely proclaim "Spear a Pregnant Squaw, Save a Walleye." Imagine that the teachers and administration do not forbid this kind of behavior. Imagine that this same school holds aloft an attractive depiction of a Plains Indian Chieftain and cheers on its "Indian" team. Imagine that in homecoming displays, cheers and artwork you see your people depicted inaccurately in ways that demean your cultural and religious practices. Imagine that when you bring your experiences to the attention of your school board and request change, they simply ignore you and decide to continue business as usual. Imagine that the same school board states publicly that it opposes discriminatory practices, provides equal educational opportunity and supports respect for cultural differences.

"Why don't community members understand the need to change; isn't it a simple matter of respect?" On one level, yes. But in some communities, people have bought into local myths and folklore presented as accurate historical facts. Sometimes these myths are created or preserved by local industry. Also, over the years, athletic and school traditions grow up around the logos. These athletic traditions can be hard to change when much of a community's ceremonial and ritual life, as well as its pride, becomes tied to high school athletic activities. Finally, many people find it difficult to grasp a different cultural perspective. Not being from an Indian culture, they find it hard to understand that things which are not offensive to themselves might be offensive or even harmful to someone who is from a Native culture. Respecting a culture different from the one you were raised in requires some effort. Even if a person lives in a different culture, insight and understanding of that culture will require interaction, listening, observing and a willingness to learn.

The Native American population, in most school districts displaying "Indian" logos, is proportionally very small. When one of us confronts the logo issue, that person, his or her children and other family members, and anyone else in the district who is Native American become targets of insults and threats; we are shunned and further marginalized — our voices become even harder to hear from behind barriers of fear and anger. We appreciate the courage, support, and sometimes the sacrifice, of all who stand with us by speaking out against the continued use of "Indian" logos. When you advocate for the removal of these logos, you are strengthening the spirit of tolerance and justice in your community; you are modeling for all our children — thoughtfulness, courage and respect for self and others.

RESPOND.

1. What's Munson's argument? Why is it stated where and as it is? How might her purpose in writing have led her to organize her material in this way? Would the selection have been more or less effective if she'd organized her argument as a "regular" essay, consisting of an introduction that leads to her thesis statement, several paragraphs of a body, and a conclusion? Why or why not?
2. Examine the arrangement and organization of the "common questions and statements" to which Munson replies. Why are they arranged in this way? Would her argument be strengthened or weakened if these paragraphs were arranged differently, that is, if they were in a different order? Are there advantages and disadvantages to such implicit organization of an argument?
3. How would you characterize Munson's tone in this selection? Her ethos? What evidence would you cite for your conclusions? How do her tone and ethos contribute to or detract from her argument? Would you characterize this argument as Rogerian? (For a discussion of Rogerian argumentation, see Chapter 1.) Why or why not?
4. One of Munson's concerns is the influence of "Indian" logos on children, both Native American and non-Indian. Do you agree with her argument? Why or why not? How does her mention of children early in the argument add to the weight or gravity of her topic as she defines it?
5. Although American Indian logos, names, mascots, and symbols show up in many places in popular culture, Munson is concerned specifically with athletics and sports events. Why? In what sense does her article demonstrate that these logos, names, mascots, and symbols have become part of larger political debates?
6. One way to understand Munson's argument is to claim that racism of any sort isn't a matter of intention but of effect, and that the effects of racism are pernicious both for those who belong to the group that's the target of the racism and for those who aren't, especially those who perpetrate the racism. Part of her argument is also that members of the targeted group are best positioned to determine whether racism has occurred. **Write an essay** in which you evaluate either or both of these claims, using examples relating to another group.

▼ *Jim Shore, who was blinded in 1970 in an automobile accident, is general counsel of the Seminole Tribe of Florida, which has approximately 3,000 members. He's the first Seminole to become an attorney, having graduated from law school in 1980. "Play with Our Name" originally appeared on the op-ed (opinion-editorial) page of the* New York Times *in August 2005, the same week that the NCAA (National Collegiate Athletic Association) reversed a blanket decision from earlier that month banning the use of Native American mascots and nicknames by all NCAA teams in post-season tournaments. Specifically, after protests from Florida State University (FSU) and an ensuing investigation, the NCAA issued a statement that included the following remarks:*

Statement by NCAA Senior Vice-President for Governance and Membership Bernard Franklin on Florida State University Review

> *The NCAA staff review committee has removed Florida State University from the list of colleges and universities subject to restrictions on the use of Native American mascots, names and imagery at NCAA championships.*
>
> *The NCAA Executive Committee continues to believe the stereotyping of Native Americans is wrong. However, in its review of the particular circumstances regarding Florida State, the staff review committee noted the unique relationship between the university and the Seminole Tribe of Florida as a significant factor. The NCAA recognizes the many different points of view on this matter, particularly within the Native American community. The decision of a namesake sovereign tribe, regarding when and how its name and imagery can be used, must be respected even when others may not agree.*
>
> *The NCAA position on the use of Native American mascots, names and imagery has not changed, and the NCAA remains committed to ensuring an atmosphere of respect and sensitivity for all who participate in and attend our championships. This decision applies to the unique relationship Florida State University has with the Seminole Tribe of Florida. Requests for reviews from other institutions will be handled on a case-by-case basis.*

As you read, consider how Shore seeks to justify the relationship the Tribe has with FSU.

Play with Our Name

JIM SHORE

HOLLYWOOD, FLA—Earlier this week, the National Collegiate Athletic Association reversed its recent decision that would have forced Florida State University to drop the use of the "Seminole" name and related symbols. But it continued to ban the use of Native American mascots and nicknames in post-season N.C.A.A. tournaments, a decision that affects 17 other universities.

As a member of the Seminole Tribe of Florida, I believe the N.C.A.A. should encourage those colleges that have Indian mascots and nicknames to build better relations with the Native American community. Perhaps each university could establish a relationship with a reservation, involving programs like

Much as in the previous text, this article's author is able to create an ethos of authority by sharing his tribe's experience with a university that uses their name as a team mascot. Chapter 3 explores different ways of creating an argument based on character.

LINK TO P. 60

internships, scholarships and tribal history and culture classes.

Here in Florida, the relationship we have with Florida State goes beyond the football field. Florida State

"Indian mascots can be a good thing."

encourages members of the Seminole Tribe to apply for admission and spreads information about Seminole culture and history.

Too many Americans, including Native Americans, get caught up in the debate over the tomahawk chop and miss the opportunity that comes in having a tribe in a close alliance with a major university. While the Seminole Tribe of Florida gets no financial compensation for the university's use of the Seminole name and related symbols, the richness of the relationship brings a variety of social and economic benefits to our tribe.

The Florida State Seminole mascot watches a play during a home game between Florida State and North Carolina on October 2, 2004.

5 The use of Indian nicknames and mascots by colleges and universities started in the early 1900's. Many of these names were generic—Braves, Chiefs and Warriors—but some were the names of tribes like the Chippewas, the Hurons, the Sioux and, of course, the Seminoles. Eventually, there were more than 100 colleges with Indian mascots and some 2,500 high schools. Professional sports teams joined in, too.

In the 60's and 70's, however, activist groups began challenging the use of some of these names, calling them offensive. Around that time, officials from Florida State University approached the Seminole Tribe to make sure their use of certain symbols was accurate and respectful. We requested they stop using the "Sammy the Seminole" caricature, and they did. Sammy was replaced by Chief Osceola, who was a great tribal military leader and a brilliant battlefield tactician. This was long before anyone at the N.C.A.A. even cared about the use of Indian names and symbols.

The university also reached out to the tribe in other ways. For years, Florida State University has invited Seminole Tribe high school students to visit its Tallahassee campus. The university organizes an annual summer trip to encourage young Seminoles to apply for admission. And the program is working. This fall, four new Seminole students will join four already enrolled there.

The school also uses printed materials and statewide television broadcasts to share with the public the history and culture of the Seminole Tribe so that our non-Indian neighbors have a better sense of who we are, where we came from and how deep our historical roots are in Florida.

And then there's the university's impact in Tallahassee. Hundreds of Florida government officials are Florida State graduates and supporters. We deal with these people every day, working with them to clean up the Everglades, to improve the roads that lead to our reservations and to support the public schools that many of our children attend.

10 For all these reasons and more, our five-member Tribal Council voted unanimously to support the university in its efforts to keep the Seminole name. It's a shame that other colleges and tribes aren't finding a way to make similar accommodations.

RESPOND •

1. What's Shore's argument? What evidence does he offer in support of his claim? In what sense might we say that Shore's argument is Rogerian? (For a discussion of Rogerian argumentation, see Chapter 1.)
2. In what senses is Shore's argument a proposal argument? (For a discussion of proposal arguments, see Chapter 11.) Evaluate it as such.
3. Shore concedes that the Seminole Tribe receives no direct financial compensation for use of the Seminole name and related symbols. Should it? What would be the advantages or disadvantages of such an arrangement? For whom?
4. Imagine a dialogue between Barbara Munson, author of the previous selection, "Common Themes and Questions about the Use of 'Indian' Logos," and Jim Shore. What things would they likely agree about? Would there be disagreements? If so, what would be the likely source of those disagreements?
5. As the headnote explains, the NCAA reversed its earlier policy of August 5, 2005, prohibiting the use of Native American mascots and nicknames by all teams in playoffs, because FSU filed a complaint. (In fact, the president of FSU, T. K. Wetherell, wrote to Myles Brand, president of the NCAA, on August 12, 2005, asking that it examine carefully the FSU case.) Using the Internet, investigate the nature of Wetherell's request. You may also wish to locate the original NCAA statement and the revised policy, issued on August 23, 2005, as well as Wetherell's letter. **Write an essay** in which you present a rhetorical analysis of Wetherell's request. (For a discussion of rhetorical analyses and how to write one, see Chapter 5.)

Lucy A. Ganje, *Reality TV*

Making a Visual Argument: Editorial Cartoonists Take On the Use of Native American Mascots and Imagery

▲ *The three cartoons reproduced here are from a gallery of cartoons from the Web site of the American Indian Sports Team Mascots, <http://aistm.org/1indexpage.htm>. The site's purpose is to collect and present information useful in seeking to end the use of American Indian mascots and imagery in athletics in this country. We've chosen these three cartoons because they comment on different aspects of the debate about the ways in which Native American culture is—and isn't—understood in the context of American culture more broadly. As you study each cartoon, consider which audiences would likely be favorably impressed—or offended—by it and why.*

Lucy A. Ganje is an associate professor in the art department of the University of North Dakota. Lalo Alcaraz is a nationally syndicated editorial cartoonist whose biographical comic panel, "La Cucaracha," has been published in the Los Angeles Weekly *since 1992. Thom Little Moon is a former editorial cartoonist for* Indian Country Today, *a national American Indian newspaper.*

BUT I'M **HONORING** YOU, DUDE!
GO WARRIOR SAVAGES
KILL 'EM SAVAGES!
GO SAVAGES KILL EM
INDIANZ .COM
INDI

Thom Little Moon, *Which One Is the Mascot?*

RESPOND •

1. Each cartoon is critical of the ways in which American Indians and their culture are appropriated by the larger culture. What argument does each cartoon make, and how, specifically, does it make it?
2. Which cartoon is most effective with respect to supporting the argument it wishes to make? Why? (Here, you'll need to evaluate the effectiveness of each cartoon in terms of what it seeks to achieve; then, you'll need to compare among the three, choosing the most effective. In other words, you'll be making an evaluative argument, as discussed in Chapter 9.)
3. Cartoons, if effective, are humorous. How does each of these cartoons construct a humorous argument? (For a discussion of how humorous arguments work, see Chapter 13.)
4. Examine the other cartoons in the gallery at the American Indian Sports Team Mascots site, <http://aistm.org/1indexpage.htm>. Choose the one you believe makes the strongest argument. (You may also wish to find a cartoon on this topic that you believe is effective from another source.) **In several paragraphs,** describe the cartoon and its contents as well as the argument it makes, and evaluate it. Write two versions of this assignment. Include the cartoon in one version; in the other, don't include the cartoon but provide a detailed description of it so that the reader can imagine it. After you've finished both versions, write a paragraph in which you describe the challenges of writing about a visual argument like a cartoon when that argument isn't part of the text itself.
5. These cartoons and the Web site from which they come are obviously opposed to the use of American Indian mascots and imagery. In fact, we couldn't locate cartoons—at least not interesting ones—that took a position opposed to the position illustrated here. Is it possible to design such a cartoon? Why or why not? **Design a cartoon** that supports the use of American Indian mascots and imagery. (If you feel you have no artistic abilities, you can write a description of the cartoon you would draw if you could.) If you can't come up with such a cartoon, **write an essay** in which you seek to explain why creating such a cartoon is difficult. In a real sense, your essay will be definitional in that it defines the reasons why it's challenging or perhaps impossible to create a visual argument in support of the use of American Indian mascots and imagery by athletic teams.

▼ *Thad Williamson is an author of books and articles on theology, economic and social policy, and sports. This article was originally published in an August 1998 issue of* The Nation, *a magazine of social and political analysis that takes a liberal viewpoint. Williamson issues a call to action in this proposal argument. As you read, notice how he works to build his credibility and engender his readers' trust before he suggests that they take action on his proposal.*

Bad As They Wanna Be

Loving the Game is Harder As Colleges Sell Out Themselves, the Fans, the Athletes

THAD WILLIAMSON

Growing up in an American college town gives one a better than average chance of being infected with progressive politics, a certain intellectual curiosity and a love for intercollegiate athletics. Growing up in Chapel Hill, North Carolina, makes one susceptible to catching a strong dose of all three.

Such is the case with this writer, who grew up believing that Dean Smith, the legendary coach of the University of North Carolina Tar Heels basketball team (who retired recently after thirty-six years), embodied virtue and goodness as surely as Jesse Helms represented hate and ignorance. A passion for college basketball is *the* tie that binds in "The Triangle," where UNC, North Carolina State and Duke University all play. And if you live in this area, the team you root for inevitably becomes part of your identity. Duke is alternately denounced and adored as the South's answer to the Ivy League; UNC boasts of being the region's premier public university; North Carolina State, a school historically focused on agriculture and engineering, enjoys a large in-state following as the populist alternative to its liberal arts neighbors.

Arguments based on character, such as Williamson's here, can be very effective. See more examples of effective arguments based on character in Chapter 3.

LINK TO P. 60

For decades young Tar Heels fans grew up aware of Dean Smith's unapologetic liberalism: a much-celebrated (albeit modest) role in integrating Chapel Hill in the late fifties and early sixties, opposition to the Vietnam War, support of a nuclear freeze and opposition to the death penalty. Smith's political bent and reputation for treating players like extended family made it possible to imagine that by rooting for UNC, you somehow showed support for doing the right thing.

No one held to that belief more than myself. From age 12 I watched Michael Jordan and others from a courtside perch as an operator of UNC's old manual scoreboard. Now, a decade after leaving Chapel Hill, I remain a devoted follower of Atlantic Coast Conference basketball. Writing a triweekly, inseason column for *InsideCarolina* (northcarolina.com), an independent magazine and Web site devoted to UNC sports, I fancy myself in the rare (but not entirely unknown) position of left-wing sportswriter. Like a Latin American soccer commentator, I strive to keep the game in perspective but still feel elation when the Tar Heels win and supreme dejection when they lose in the Final Four.

5 For the thoughtful fan of college sports, however, it's getting harder to check your critical intelligence at the door and simply enjoy the game. The appeal of college athletics has long rested on their "amateur" status, the notion that the kids play mostly for the love of the game, without the pressures and influences that suffuse professional sports. These days, however, it's increasingly clear that big-time college athletics—in particular, men's basketball and football—are as wrapped in commercial values as the pros, and the system is rapidly spinning out of control.

In college arenas the best seats are now routinely reserved not for students and die-hard fans but for big-money boosters and private donors to the universities. The arenas themselves are being turned into prime advertising venues: Georgia Tech's revamped Alexander Memorial Coliseum, for example, goes so far as to place the McDonald's trademark "M" on the floor. Meanwhile, the NCAA's lucrative television contracts—an eight-year, $1.7 billion deal with CBS for broadcast rights to the Men's Division I basketball tournament and similar deals in football—are changing the fabric of the game, as top competition is slotted for prime-time viewing hours and games are steadily lengthened by TV timeouts.

Even the school I cover, North Carolina, which to this day bans all corporate advertising inside arenas, has largely succumbed to the trend. In the eighties UNC used some $34 million in private funds to build a 21,500-seat basketball arena, in the process setting a precedent of entitlement for major boosters. Not only did they win rights to the best seats in the arena, they are also allowed to pass on those seats to their progeny. More recently, university officials convinced the state highway board to authorize $1.2 million for a special road to allow top-dollar Tar Heels donors a convenient exit from home games.

Highly successful college basketball coach Dean Smith announces a deal between the University of North Carolina and Nike sportswear.

There's more. Last summer the university signed a five-year, $11 million contract to use Nike-provided gear in all practices (for all sports) and to wear the familiar swoosh. No faculty members or students were directly involved in the negotiations, and no serious questions were raised about Nike's notorious labor practices abroad. Subsequently, concerned UNC students and faculty generated considerable public debate about the deal, but UNC plans to remain on the take.

Indeed, shoe companies like Adidas and Nike are now prime players in the college game. Most major Division I football and basketball coaches receive lucrative payments from the companies in exchange for outfitting their teams with the appropriate logo—and in some cases, such as the University of California, Berkeley, for encouraging their players to buy additional Nike gear. The sneaker sellers also operate most of the major summer camps for elite high school athletes, where schoolboy stars show their wares to college coaches (many of whom are themselves on Nike's or Reebok's payroll) in hopes of landing a top-flight scholarship. While the hottest prospects are showered with expenses-paid travel and free athletic gear, the companies develop relationships with future stars that might culminate in endorsement contracts. In his fine book *The Last Shot*, Darcy Frey likened the atmosphere at Nike's annual high school summer camp to a meatmarket, where the mostly black kids are herded around like cattle while the overwhelmingly white coaches and corporate sponsors look on.

Nowhere are the priorities of the new corporate order of college sports clearer 10
than in the treatment of athletes—though you'd never know it from the popular image of those athletes as coddled superstars. In *He Got Game,* Spike Lee depicts the campus as a pleasure dome for young men treated to unlimited cars, women and material perks for four blissfully hedonistic years.

The truth is often far less alluring. "It's not as glamorous as people think," cautions Sheray Gaffney, a former reserve fullback for the football powerhouse Florida State Seminoles. "If you're in the program, it's not glamorous at all."

One reason for this is the so-called grant-in-aid system that characterizes all athletic scholarships in the NCAA. Originally established in 1956, grant-in-aid was intended to level the playing field by providing a fixed set of benefits to college athletes. Schools were allowed to offer scholarships of one to four years and were bound to honor them even if the athlete quit the team altogether. In 1973, however, the NCAA abruptly shifted course and mandated that the grants be limited to a one-year, annually renewable grant. The purpose of this change was to enable schools—in actuality, coaches—to keep tabs on each player's performance from year to year, and to cut off the scholarships of those whom the coach considered dispensable.

"Colleges changed the rule so they could run off the athletes who weren't good enough," explains Walter Byers, who oversaw the growth of college athletics while serving as NCAA executive director from 1951 to 1987. Back in the fifties Byers coined the term "student-athlete," a romantic idea that the NCAA continues to use in its promotional literature. These days, he is one of the NCAA's leading critics. "Once the colleges gave coaches the power to control those grants," he says, "that was a perversion that permanently changed the way things were done. It used to be that at least athletes could get an education if they couldn't play for the team."

Indeed, under the new system athletes do as the coaches say or risk being kicked out. Coach Rick Majerus of Utah, whose team reached the NCAA basketball finals this year, recently "released" Jordie McTavish saying he just wasn't good enough. A year ago, Coach Bobby Cremins of Georgia Tech asked freshman point guard Kevin Morris to leave for the same reason. More often than direct dismissals, coaches pressure players to leave on their own. Indiana's Bobby Knight, seeking to clean house after a disappointing 1996–97 season, drove starting point guard Neil Reed out of town with one year of eligibility remaining. Reed left, but not before accusing Knight of physical and emotional abuse.

15 Given the pressures to stay in the good graces of coaches—players know that missing even one session in the weight room risks incurring the coach's wrath—it's no wonder that graduation rates for Division I football and basketball players in the NCAA hover at roughly 50 percent, a figure that exaggerates the amount of learning that actually takes place. Instead of promoting a balance between sports and academics, the system forces athletes to pour every ounce of energy into the game, with little recognition that the vast majority of players are in a vocational dead end. A sad rite of passage for most college athletes is the existential realization that they will never make it to the pros. "What was astonishing was the number of scars that [the program] left on athletes that came to the surface behind closed doors," recalls Gaffney. "It was painful to see athletes crying in distress because they see their dreams slowly fading away. All of a sudden at age 20, 21, they are required to make a complete transition."

True, college sports still represent a way out for poor or working-class athletes. Some, with the help of coaches like Dean Smith, find jobs in coaching, pro leagues overseas or business. Others succeed in getting an education. But the inequities are glaring. While generating an enormous revenue stream for their universities through ticket sales, merchandising, advertising and TV deals, athletes are forbidden from sharing in any of the gains. "When these commercial activities came along," notes Byers, "the overseers and supervisors made sure that the benefits went to them, not the athletes." College coaches routinely earn six-figure salaries, sign endorsement deals with corporations and jump from school to school for more lucrative contracts. The athletes, meanwhile, are the focus of scandal and media outrage if they so much as accept money for an extra trip home. Under the grant-in-aid rule, athletes may not use their talent or name recognition to earn money while in school except under tightly defined conditions.

In Byers's view, the "gobs of money" now flowing to the universities make a return to the amateur ideal impossible. What is possible, he believes, is scrapping the current grant-in-aid system, which leads not only to the rampant exploitation of athletes but, he argues, violates antitrust laws because colleges essentially operate as a cartel, setting a national limit on what a whole class of students can earn. He would require athletes to apply for financial aid like any other student but would remove all restrictions on how they could earn money while in college.

Rick Telander, a *Sports Illustrated* writer and author of *The Hundred Yard Lie,* an exposé of college football, proposes a more radical solution: namely, severing big-time college football programs from the schools that lend them their name. In Telander's view, an NFL-subsidized "age-group professional league" could be established in which universities would own and operate teams, using university facilities and traditional school colors. Players need not be students but would earn a year of tuition for each year played, redeemable at any time, during or after their playing careers. College basketball would also benefit from the creation of an NBA-backed age-group league. Such leagues could offer gifted players with no interest in academics a credible alternative to college, and a second chance to earn an education should their professional dreams fade.

Of course, given the entrenched institutional support for the status quo, none of this can happen without a sustained demand from the public, including students, coaches not yet corrupted, and athletes themselves. In the meantime, students and faculty can make their voices heard by continuing—and expanding—their campaigns challenging the corporate sponsorship of university athletic departments. Over the past year campus activists at Duke and other universities have successfully pushed administrators to adopt rules requiring that all campus sweatshirts and athletic gear be produced in compliance with labor and human rights standards. These same activists should insist that corporate advertising be banned from all arenas; that universities cap athletic budgets for football and basketball and put an end to the "arms race" for bigger facilities and more amenities; and that the influence of big-money donors be limited so that students and fans can continue to attend athletic events at reasonable prices. Activists might also find unexpected common ground with coaches and fans concerned about how the integrity of the game has been subordinated to television, or how corporations are colonizing and poisoning the high school recruiting scene.

Speaking for myself, probably only death will cure my love affair with 20
North Carolina basketball, and no doubt there are millions of people who feel the same way about their own teams. But loving the game need not mean having a romantic view of how college sports are organized. College sports are far too visible an arena in American society to be simply thrown to the wolves. Ultimately, the only productive route forward is to insist that those who love the game also fight to change it.

RESPOND •

1. What evidence does Williamson provide to support his contention that "the [college athletics] system is rapidly spinning out of control" (paragraph 5)? What kinds of appeals does he use? Arguments from the heart? Arguments of character? Other kinds? (See Chapters 2–4.)

2. Why does Williamson give us so much detailed information about North Carolina coach Dean Smith's political beliefs? Does that information contribute to the argument? How? Why? If not, why not?
3. Williamson's article ends with a strong call to action, yet there's no hint of such an appeal in the title or opening paragraphs of the article. Why do you think Williamson chose this rhetorical strategy?
4. Do you agree with Williamson's suggestion (in paragraph 16) that collegiate sports are "a way out" for poor and working-class students? Do you think that assertion is more (or less) true today than it was in the past? What evidence would you want to present to support or refute Williamson's claim?
5. Walter Byers, NCAA executive director from 1951 to 1987, has proposed removing all restrictions on how student-athletes can earn money while in college. Imagine that your school is considering adopting Byers's proposal. **Write a letter** to your college administrators supporting or rejecting Byers's plan. Provide detailed evidence for your position.

In October 2005, the National Basketball Association (NBA) issued a dress code for players that became the subject of discussion and controversy across sports pages, Web sites, and blogs. Some objected to the idea of a dress code; others objected to the details. Still others thought a dress code was a wonderful idea. In this selection, we present the dress code itself as well as the first of two responses. (We found the dress code at <http://compuserve.nba.com/news/player_dress_code_051017.html>.) *Along with the dress code, you'll find Tom Sorensen's critique of it, "Dress Code Suitable Only to NBA Suits." Sorensen writes about sports for the* Charlotte Observer, *where he's worked for over a quarter century, in Charlotte, North Carolina. This article appeared there in October 2005. As you read, pay careful attention to the style of Sorensen's piece.*

Dress Code Suitable Only to NBA Suits

TOM SORENSEN

Former Carolina Panthers receiver Rae Carruth° was an athlete who liked to dress professionally. I was a regular at his murder trial in 2001, and rarely did I see him wear the same suit twice. Some suits worked well with the leg irons. Others clashed.

Clothes don't make the man. That's the reason the NBA dress code, which is an attempt to sell a sport played primarily by blacks to a ticket-buying audience made up primarily of whites, is unnecessary.

The dress code, which is new this season, dictates that players wear business casual when they are involved in league business. Business casual, as the NBA defines it, means no jewelry, no jerseys and no T-shirts (unless the T-shirt promotes, say, a team basketball clinic and is approved by management).

So if a basketball player wears an outfit approved by the NBA, the PGA,° the Young Republicans and Abercrombie & Fitch, is he less likely to go into the bleachers° after the fans who throw beer at him?

5 Eleven months ago at the Palace in Auburn Hills, Mich., moronic players went after moronic beer-throwing fans, and the ensuing brawl contributed mightily to the thugball reputation the NBA is working to dispel.

The league wants to assure the public that the brawl was an aberration and that its players are professionals. Since it can't prove the players are professionals, it will tell them to dress professionally.

The problem with telling people to dress nicely is that what's nice to some is absurd to others. In Charlotte,

Rae Carruth: former wide receiver for the Carolina Panthers who was convicted of murdering his girlfriend, who was pregnant, in 1999.

PGA: Professional Golfers' Association.

"Go into the bleachers": A reference to a Detroit Pistons/Indiana Pacers game of November 2004 in the Palace in Auburn Hills, Michigan, during which, after Ron Artest was hit by a full drink cup from the stands, he and Stephen Jackson, among others, entered the stands and began fighting with spectators. Officials stopped the game with less than a minute left.

business casual means that you dress as if 18 holes of golf could break out at any moment, and you want to be ready to tee off if they do.

I don't dress that way. I don't understand the safe polo-player-or-emblem-on-the shirt style. Or the dress-the-same-as-everybody-else look.

But it doesn't matter what I like. It's not as if I know the one true way to dress. To be honest with you, I don't devote a lot of attention to the attire of other adult males. That's just me.

10 There is no universal definition of nice. Walk down any street in any city and there will always be somebody to whom you can ask, "Who told you that looked good?"

What counts is what looks good to you, which is why we get to pick our own clothes all by ourselves, provided we don't play in the NBA.

Style changes from generation to generation. When I came of age, it was

Indiana Pacers basketball players Stephen Jackson, Ron Artest, and Jermaine O'Neal attend a pre-trial hearing with their attorneys on September 23, 2005, for the fight that broke out during the Pacers/Pistons game of November 2004.

NBA Player Dress Code

1. General Policy: Business Casual

   Players are required to wear Business Casual attire whenever they are engaged in team or league business.

   "Business Casual" attire means

   - A long- or short-sleeved dress shirt (collared or turtleneck), and/or a sweater.
   - Dress slacks, khaki pants, or dress jeans.
   - Appropriate shoes and socks, including dress shoes, dress boots, or other presentable shoes, but not including sneakers, sandals, flip-flops, or work boots.

2. Exceptions to Business Casual

   There are the following exceptions to the general policy of Business Casual attire:

   a. Players In Attendance At Games But Not In Uniform

      Players who are in attendance at games but not in uniform are required to wear the following additional items when seated on the bench or in the stands during the game:

      - Sport Coat
      - Dress shoes or boots, and socks

   b. Players Leaving the Arena

      Players leaving the arena may wear either Business Casual attire or neat warm-up suits issued by their teams.

   c. Special Events or Appearances

      Teams can make exceptions to the Business Casual policy for special events or player appearances where other attire is appropriate—e.g., participation in a basketball clinic.

3. Excluded Items

   The following is a list of items that players are not allowed to wear at any time while on team or league business:

   - Sleeveless shirts
   - Shorts
   - T-shirts, jerseys, or sports apparel (unless appropriate for the event (e.g., a basketball clinic), team-identified, and approved by the team)
   - Headgear of any kind while a player is sitting on the bench or in the stands at a game, during media interviews, or during a team or league event or appearance (unless appropriate for the event or appearance, team-identified, and approved by the team)
   - Chains, pendants, or medallions worn over the player's clothes
   - Sunglasses while indoors
   - Headphones (other than on the team bus or plane, or in the team locker room)

shoulder length hair and bell-bottoms and a fringed jacket.

When my kids came of age, it was jeans baggy enough to accommodate an offensive lineman and a T-shirt baggy enough to accommodate an offensive line. As silly as I thought they looked, I knew they could find old pictures of me and ask, "Who told you that looked good?"

My favorite all-time NBA players are Earl Monroe° and Magic Johnson.° I liked them so much I would have paid to watch them shoot layups in a gym by themselves. Their moves were amazing.

Yes, but were their clothes amazing? 15

I have no idea.

Earl "The Pearl" Monroe: NBA player (1967–1980) known for his amazing shots. Many compared watching him to listening to great jazz.

Earvin "Magic" Johnson: NBA point guard (1971–1991, 1996) for the Lakers. For many, one of the greatest living basketball players.

Earl Monroe of the New York Knicks drives to the basket during the 1980 NBA game against the Boston Celtics at Madison Square Garden in New York City.

Magic Johnson shoots in the Radio Shack Shooting Stars competition during the NBA All-Star Weekend in Houston, Texas, February 2006.

RESPOND •

1. In what senses is the NBA Player Dress Code a definitional argument? How successful is it as such an argument? Why? (For a discussion of definitional arguments, see Chapter 8.)
2. According to Sorensen, why is the NBA Player Dress Code unnecessary? Which events or circumstances, in particular, does Sorensen see as having led to the creation of a dress code? In what sense can these events be seen as political or as being part of larger political debates in the United States?
3. What functions does the opening example of Rae Carruth serve in Sorensen's argument (paragraph 1)? Is it important that Sorensen is able to use personal experience here (rather than, say, reporting on something he observed on cable television)? Why or why not?
4. One characteristic of much journalistic prose, and especially opinion columns on the sports page like this one, is their style: short sentences, short paragraphs, and a conversational tone. Such characteristics are often evaluated negatively in academic writing. **Rewrite Sorensen's article** using much or all of the content that his column includes, converting it into a form that's more appropriate for academic arguments than the current column is. If you're having trouble getting started, imagine that you're Sorensen and you want to write an essay for the class you're now taking in which you disagree with the NBA Player Dress Code, using the arguments and examples Sorensen uses.

Informal logic is the basis for Sorensen's argument against the NBA's dress code. Use the description of Toulmin argumentation in Chapter 6 to identify the reason, warrant, and claim of this argument.

LINK TO P. 147

▼ *Larry Stewart is a sports writer for the* Los Angeles Times, *where this article appeared in October 2005. In contrast to the previous selection, where Tom Sorensen presents his own opinion about the NBA Player Dress Code, Stewart is writing a news feature focusing on Charles Barkley, who played for the NBA for sixteen years and serves now as a TNT studio commentator on the NBA. Thus it's Barkley's, rather than Stewart's, opinion that we hear. As you read, consider how Stewart uses Barkley's opinions to create an ethos for Barkley and for himself.*

Barkley Fully Supports NBA's New Dress Code

LARRY STEWART

Charles Barkley might not want to be your kids' role model, but he could be a role model for NBA players. And not just because he supports the league's new dress code.

Barkley was in Los Angeles on Wednesday for an appearance on NBC's "Tonight Show With Jay Leno." Years ago, Barkley said that parents, not athletes, should be role models for their kids. But he now at least acknowledges that athletes do influence kids.

"Young black kids dress like NBA players," he said. "Unfortunately, they don't get paid like NBA players. So when they go out in the real world, what they wear is held against them.

"See, these players make $10 million to $15 million a year, so nobody cares how they dress. But regular black kids go out into the real world and how they dress is held against them.

5 "If a well-dressed white kid and a black kid wearing a do-rag and throwback jersey came to me in a job interview, I'd hire the white kid," he said. "That's reality. That's the No. 1 reason I support the dress code.

"From the NBA perspective, they've got a product to sell. They've got to make it as attractive as possible to fans, viewers and corporate sponsors.

"Dr. J [Julius Erving]° told me years ago that we, the players, are the caretakers of the game. I think too many players today have lost sight of that."

Barkley, a TNT network basketball analyst, concedes there are racial overtones to the new dress code but points out there is a dress code in every business in the country. "It's dictated by the boss," he said.

Barkley says young men who are making $10 million a year or more for playing basketball should use their fame and wealth to do some good for society.

10 After the Leno taping, Barkley said, "I wish we would have had time to talk about Katrina."

Barkley explained that he was so moved by the hurricane tragedy and its victims that he visited shelters in Atlanta, Houston and Birmingham, Ala., to see what he might be able to do.

Stewart presents a proposal argument on behalf of Charles Barkley. Barkley is quoted as supporting the action of instating a dress code for the NBA. See Chapter 1 for a comparison of proposal arguments with other types of argumentation.

LINK TO P. 27

Dr. J (Julius Erving) : ABA-NBA player (1972–1987) who's said to have transformed the game with his ability to manipulate the ball and fly through the air. Because of the respect he was accorded, he often served as a spokesman for professional basketball.

"In talking with these people I learned what they needed most was a place to live," he said.

Barkley provided $1 million to pay for houses where Katrina victims can live free for a year.

"I didn't want to just make a donation to the Red Cross," he said. "I wanted to make sure the money would go where it could do the most good."

He has been directly involved in the project. He is in the process of buying five homes in Atlanta, with plans to buy more in other areas.

"Where the Red Cross has helped is in determining what families get these homes," Barkley said. "That's the hard part, picking who gets what."

Such charity is not a first for Barkley. He has given more than $3 million to schools — $1 million to his alma mater, Auburn, $1 million to his high school in Leeds, Ala., and $1 million to other schools in his hometown.

"I've been blessed with a skill, but I don't think God gave me the ability to play basketball just to win a championship — although winning a championship would have been cool," he said. "I think I got this gift so that I could do some good for society and help people. And not just black people. Poor people. That is what is really important."

He hears that Marcus Camby° of the Denver Nuggets wants a stipend to buy clothes to adhere to the dress code, and Barkley cringes.

"Guys like that have lost perspective," he said. "What's he make, $8 million a year? It's like when Latrell Sprewell° said he needed more than $14 million a year so that he could feed his family. Give me a break."

Julius Erving slam dunks during the 1984 All-Star Weekend in Denver, Colorado.

Marcus Camby of the Denver Nuggets looks on during a game against the Philadelphia 76ers on March 9, 2006.

Latrell Sprewell of the Minnesota Timberwolves holds the ball during a game against the Denver Nuggets on April 8, 2005.

Marcus Camby: NBA player since 1997.

Latrell Sprewell: NBA player since 1992–2006; suspended in 1997–1998 for choking his former coach.

RESPOND

1. As noted, Stewart's article focuses on Charles Barkley, but much of the piece is devoted to the NBA Player Dress Code. What's Barkley's opinion of the dress code? Why? How does he support his position?
2. To what extent do Barkley and Tom Sorensen, author of the previous selection, see the NBA Player Dress Code as an effort to respond to similar social forces or issues? To what extent do they see it as an effort to respond to different social forces or issues?
3. What kind of ethos does Barkley create for himself (with the assistance of Stewart)? How does his former career as a professional basketball player contribute to (or perhaps detract from) that ethos?
4. If you examine a number of responses to the NBA Player Dress Code, you'll find that writers seem to agree that a major issue to be considered is the influence of professional basketball players, many of whom are African American, on young African American boys and men. In what ways is this issue a political one?
5. To what extent should public figures—professional athletes, professional musicians, politicians, and television or movie stars—be seen as role models? Should any or all of these groups be expected to behave as role models? For whom? Why or why not? **Write an essay** in which you evaluate the claim that one or more of these groups should (or shouldn't) be taken as role models or be expected to serve as role models.

Cheerleaders: What to Do about Them?

BRYAN CURTIS

The Texas state legislature set aside small matters like the implementation of the death penalty last month to consider a far more arcane ritual: cheerleading. The state's cheerleaders, it seems, have become indistinguishable from exotic dancers—or so says a bill submitted by Al Edwards, a representative from Houston. Edwards' legislation would divert money from high schools that allow cheerleaders to perform overly suggestive lunges and inside-hitch pyramids. "It's just too sexually oriented, you know, the way they're shaking their behinds and going on, breaking it down," Edwards explained.

Fear of cheerleaders has a long and tortured history, stretching back at least to my sophomore year of high school, but rarely does it reach the high offices of state government or incite a reaction as hysterical as Edwards'. The cheerleader doesn't deserve the persecution. While critics like Edwards sneer, she has wrestled with a century-long identity crisis. Is she too sexy or too athletic? Too snobby and remote or too calculatingly ambitious? This is America's cheerleading dilemma.

The cheerleader has grappled with her identity since at least the early 1900s, as Natalie Guice Adams and Pamela J. Bettis explain in their delightful book *Cheerleader!: An American Icon.* Originally, male cheerleaders (or "rooter kings") patrolled the sidelines at college football games, trying to organize the yells of spectators. The male cheerleader was something of a campus eminence, regarded as an up-and-coming entrepreneur and future captain of industry. In 1911, *The Nation* declared that "the reputation of having been a valiant 'cheer-leader' is one of the most valuable things a boy can take away from college. As a title to promotion in professional or public life, it ranks hardly second to that of being a quarterback." (Not everyone saw cheerleading as a benevolent exercise in vocational training. A. Lawrence Lowell, the president of Harvard, called it the "worst means of expressing emotion ever invented.") World War II drained the universities' supply of able-bodied males, and cheerleading became almost exclusively the province of females. A new type of cheerleader emerged: a future housewife—the '50s ideal of womanhood packed into a varsity sweater. The cheerleader dressed as a pillar of moral rectitude: colorful hair bows, an ankle-length skirt, and saddle oxfords. She was, by unanimous acclaim, one of the most popular girls in school and

A native Texan and alumnus of the University of Texas at Austin, Bryan Curtis was serving as the deputy culture editor and as a staff writer for Slate.com *when this selection appeared online in April 2005. He has also written for the* New York Times, New York *magazine, and* The New Republic. *In "Cheerleaders: What to Do about Them?" Curtis focuses on a much-maligned effort by one Texas state representative to pull funds from state high schools that permit "sexually oriented" cheerleading in order to examine how cheerleading plays into changing notions of gender politics in this country.*

Humor can draw an audience into an argument, just as Curtis does throughout his essay on the evolution of cheerleading. Chapter 13 addresses the necessary elements in developing a humorous argument.

LINK TO P. 407

also one of the most beautiful — and her elevation to the squad was usually determined by a schoolwide vote. She wasn't a jock. She demonstrated little athletic ability, rarely performing a move more daring than a modest jump or a split — certainly nothing like the pyramidal artistry that would come later.

The modern cheerleader was forged in 1972 when she was waylaid by two distinct cultural forces. First was the passage of Title IX, which invigorated women's sports programs at colleges and high schools. With more girls drifting toward soccer and volleyball, cheerleading seemed antiquated. Along came Jeff Webb, a former University of Oklahoma cheerleader, who turned his passion into a legitimate athletic pursuit by making it more like gymnastics. Through camps and workshops, Webb taught complicated flips and ditched the sweaters and long skirts for more aerodynamic uniforms. Cheerleading morphed from a purely social enterprise into part of a young woman's athletic regimen: A 2002 survey cited by authors Adams and Bettis showed that more than half of cheerleaders participated in other sports.

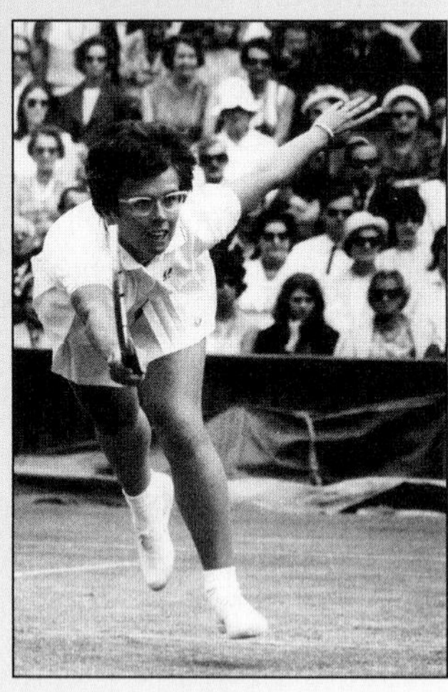

Billie Jean King returns a ball during the June 1967 Wimbledon championships.

The same year Title IX passed, the Dallas Cowboys replaced their high-school 5
cheer squad with seven voluptuous, high-kicking professionals. "A touch of class," the team's general manager declared, before outfitting them in low-cut tops, hot pants, and knee-high white boots. The Dallas Cowboys Cheerleaders — who did not have any vocal cheers — quickly became the favorite "honey shot" of network TV cameras. Their emergence signaled not the sexualization of the cheerleader — she was already plenty sexualized — but her evolution into a sex object that had nothing to do with the sports team. Calling themselves "America's sweethearts," the Cowboys cheerleaders dispensed bosomy good will at children's hospitals and posed for lush swimsuit pictorials. "Most football teams have cheerleaders," a Cowboys player moaned to a Dallas sportswriter. "Our cheerleaders just happen to have a football team."

The following decades marked a crisis of identity for the cheerleader. She found herself at an impasse — stranded between the ideals of vigorous womanhood and carnal objectification; between Billie Jean King° and Ashley Montana.° In 1993, school officials in Hempstead, Texas, discovered that four of the high school's 15 cheerleaders had become pregnant. Two years earlier, again in Texas, a woman named Wanda Holloway hired a hit man to murder her neighbor, whose daughter had aced Holloway's child out of a spot on the cheerleading team. The cheerleader-as-slut myth, which had been around for decades, was given new prominence by movies ranging from *American Beauty* to *Debbie Does Dallas.*

Billie Jean King: professional tennis player, winner of twenty Wimbledon championships, and the first female athlete ever to win over $100,000 prize money in a single season.

Ashley Montana: model who has appeared on the cover of *Sports Illustrated* and in *Sports Illustrated*'s swimsuits videos.

In his remarks to reporters, Al Edwards, the representative from Texas, points out the futility of promoting abstinence curricula when cheerleaders offer a spirited rebuttal to it on Friday nights. He's right that music videos and hip-hop have further sexualized high-school cheerleading routines. But those same music videos have made the cheerleader seem relatively harmless by comparison. And even as cheerleading routines have become more lascivious,° if only to vie for the attention of the crowd, they have also become far more dangerous: From 1982 to 2000, more than half of "direct catastrophic" injuries suffered by collegiate and high-school female athletes came from cheerleading.

lascivious: sexually provocative.

The real news about cheerleading is that the cheerleader may be tilting back toward the captain-of-industry model pioneered by her antecedents. Only it's women instead of men — an intra-gender passing of the torch from George W. Bush (cheerleader at Yale) to Kay Bailey Hutchison° (cheerleader at the University of Texas). Life as a student athlete suits the cheerleader better than the quarterback. While he studies his playbook, she mingles with well-monied alumni on the team airplane. Her grades are higher and she thinks more about life after college. She uses her high kicks and devastatingly sexy outfit to hide Wall Street–style chutzpah. The University of Alabama's cheerleading sponsor tells her charges, "You'll have the interview skills and comfort level others won't. You'll get the job over the one with all A's." What better payback for a century of leering and sexual degradation than career advancement? A message to the representative from Texas: The cheerleader doesn't want to torment you. She wants your job.

Kay Bailey Hutchison: the first woman elected to represent Texas in the U.S. Senate; she has served since 1994.

RESPOND.

1. What, for Curtis, is "America's cheerleading dilemma" (paragraph 2)? Where, for Curtis, are the origins of this dilemma to be found? How does he link the changing nature of this dilemma to shifting gender politics?
2. Most readers would likely characterize Curtis's argument as humorous. What sorts of humor does he employ? Give three examples of different kinds of humor that he uses, explaining how each kind of humor and each example contributes to his goals. (For a discussion of humorous arguments, see Chapter 13.)

3. However misdirected some readers may find Al Edwards's efforts to clean up athletic events at Texas high schools, Edwards has hit upon what he perceives as a contradiction: Texas schools, like many in the country, frame sex education in terms of abstinence-only curricula while female cheerleaders generally wear less and less and behave in ways that increasingly resemble the routines of exotic dancers. Do you think that Edwards is correct in his assessment? Why or why not? If you do agree with him, why do you think the contradiction exists and persists? If you don't see a contradiction, why do you think Edwards does?

4. In what ways do arguments about female cheerleaders, their attire, and their routines demonstrate that arguments about sports are, in the end, often arguments about politics? In other words, how do such arguments relate to debates about a range of topics, many of which are debated among elected officials or various interest groups, in the United States?

5. Cheerleaders are part of American culture; as such, they reflect aspects of American life. Imagine that you're visiting a foreign country where cheerleaders don't exist. (As best we can determine, that will be nearly every other country in the world; every other country seems to have sports teams, but few have anything that corresponds to cheerleaders.) How would you explain who cheerleaders are, what they do, and what functions they serve? **Write a definitional essay** in which you respond to these questions, taking as your audience someone who has never visited the United States and knows little about American culture, except perhaps what she or he has learned from American television shows or movies that are exported—the major source of information many people around the world have about the United States.

24
What's It Like to Be Bilingual in the United States?

This chapter's opening selection, a cartoon captioned "Just 180 Days to Learn Miwok," reminds us that dealing with the existence of more than one language in the place we today call America has been an issue for argument since long before the country itself existed. As Janny Scott's analysis of the 2000 census points out, there are more foreign-born Americans in the United States today than at any time in our country's history. At the same time, the percentage of foreign-born Americans is much lower than it was a century ago. The large growth in the number of foreign-born Americans or native-born Americans of foreign parents means that a growing percentage of the population is bilingual (or even multilingual). What's it like to be bilingual in the United States? The readings in this chapter seek to help you understand that question.

Following Scott's article are excerpts from the 2002 National Survey of Latinos, conducted by the Pew Hispanic Center and the Kaiser Family Foundation, that deal specifically with attitudes among Latinos about Spanish and English. Much of the remainder of the chapter presents personal accounts of bilingualism in this country. Myriam Marquez, a Cuban American columnist, Sandra Cisneros, a Mexican American novelist, and Marjorie Agosín, a professor of Spanish, poet, human rights activist, and refugee from Chile, provide complementary points of view on what it means to speak Spanish and English in our country, whether one is showing respect, making love, or recapturing a lost past. They remind us that languages and their meanings for those who speak them are multiple, overlapping, and often conflicting. Two images, one a painting by Rolando Briseño, and the other an advertisement from the National Institute of Mental Health, illustrate bilingualism in daily life. An excerpt from Lan Cao's novel *Monkey Bridge* describes the situation of another refugee, a Vietnamese adolescent girl who, because she absorbs English and comes to understand American culture quickly, must "parent" her mother, who finds things like supermarkets disorientingly foreign. Thus Cao's excerpt describes a common situation among immigrant children, who become cultural translators and interpreters for their parents, a role reversal that turns traditional notions of parent/child relations on their head. Andrea Lo's essay, "Finding Myself through Language," describes her realization that, like it or not, the Chinese language is an inescapable part of who she is. The last personal account comes from Firoozeh Dumas, an immigrant from Iran who marries someone with a French family name—how American! This account looks at how Americans do and don't deal with foreign names.

The chapter's other two selections, excerpts on language and high school from Mary Pipher's *The Middle of Everywhere: Helping Refugees Enter the American Community* and Samuel G. Freedman's "It's Latino Parents Speaking Out on Bilingual Education Failures," raise questions of how best to educate children growing up in bilingual families. Pipher's passages, based on her work and research in refugee communities, and Freedman's analysis of complaints from Latino parents about New York City's bilingual education program, remind us of the complexity of bilingualism for bilingual speakers and American society.

If you're bilingual (or multilingual), these readings give you a chance to think about how your experiences compare with those of other Americans who speak more than one language. If you don't already speak another language, there's still time: monolingualism isn't a terminal disease, as a favorite bumper sticker argues. Even as English becomes "the" world language, learning another language changes the way you understand yourself and the world. In the meantime, these readings offer you the chance to learn things about the life of a growing number of Americans whom you may otherwise never know.

We open this chapter with a cartoon that rewrites American history in light of recent political debates. The Miwok are an American Indian group that originally lived along much of the coast of California; their language is likewise named Miwok. (In fact, "Miwok" is the name used for seven mutually unintelligible dialects, three of which are completely extinct.) The first documented contact of the Miwok with Europeans occurred in 1579, when Sir Francis Drake's expedition, traveling in the Golden Hind, *landed on the coast of what is today Marin County. The phrase "180 days" is significant because it's the number of days in a school year—the amount of time that Proposition 227, passed in 1998 in California, gives English language learners entering the California schools to learn English. The controversial proposition sought to end bilingual education. Although the proposition passed, it continues to be challenged in court. Tom Meyer, the* San Francisco Chronicle*'s political cartoonist, drew this cartoon. We found it accompanying the article "Students, Parents File Class Action Lawsuit to Block 227" on the news Web site of the ACLU (American Civil Liberties Union) of Northern California, <http://aclunc.org/aclunews/news498/227-lawsuit.html>, dating from July/August 1998.*

Tom Meyer, *Just 180 Days to Learn Miwok*

RESPOND •

1. What is Tom Meyer's argument in this cartoon?
2. Can we state his argument without relating the history of California (and the United States) to current events? Why or why not? What does this fact tell us about Meyer's invoked audience? (For a discussion of invoked audience, see Chapter 1.)
3. Many would claim that Meyer is using irony to make his argument. How does he accomplish this? (For a discussion of the use of irony and other tropes in argumentation, see Chapter 12.)
4. Miwok is a severely endangered, even moribund, language. The remaining varieties of the language are spoken by only a few elders, although some younger Miwok are trying to learn and even revitalize the language. How might American history and the history of indigenous peoples in America be different if these groups had had the power to force European settlers to learn their languages? Why were the settlers not interested in doing so?
5. Although most of the indigenous languages of the United States have become extinct, not all have. Do some research on the language(s) of Native Americans who live in your home state or the state where you attend college or university. Write a summary of the information you find about the status and vitality of one or more of these languages as if you were planning to post the summary in a public forum like Wikipedia. (If you're not familiar with Wikipedia, visit <http://en.wikipedia.org>.)
6. In what ways are the situations of early European settlers to America and recent immigrants to the United States similar with respect to language? **Write an essay** in which you compare and evaluate the similarities and differences of these situations. You'll likely need to do some research on the Internet about several of the following topics: the extent to which recent immigrants are learning English, the pattern of language shift that occurs across three generations in most immigrant families and communities, the motivations that immigrants have to learn English and to ensure that their children do, and the attitudes of early European settlers toward the native peoples and their languages.

This February 2002 news article appeared in the New York Times. *Using data from the 2000 census, its author, Janny Scott, puts recent immigration to the United States in a historical context. In this short piece, she not only provides a great deal of information about recent immigration, using facts and figures, but also explores what the significance of such immigration might be for the country as a whole. As you read, think about the consequences of the situation described for bi- and multilingualism in the United States now, in the past, and in our country's future.*

Foreign Born in U.S. at Record High

Census Puts Number at 56 Million, with Mexico Chief Supplier

JANNY SCOTT

The number of foreign-born residents and children of immigrants in the United States has reached the highest level in history, according to a Census Bureau report released yesterday. It found that the number had leapt to 56 million from 34 million in the last three decades.

Mexico accounted for more than a quarter of all the foreign-born residents, the bureau's analysis of data from its March 2000 Current Population Survey showed. That share is the largest any country has held since the 1890 census, when about 30 percent of the country's foreign-born population was from Germany.

The study found that, on average, foreign-born residents were much more likely than native Americans to live in or around a handful of big cities. They were almost equally likely to be in the labor force. But foreign-born residents earned less and were less likely to have health insurance than native Americans.

While the number of foreign-born residents and their children is higher than ever, their percentage in the population is not. In the 1910 census, that group made up 35 percent of the population, compared with 20 percent in 2000, a spokesman for the Census Bureau said.

5 The report brings together data on the age, sex and birthplaces of the foreign born, their education levels, jobs and earnings. In doing so, it makes clear the near impossibility of generalizing about immigrants and the immigrant experience.

For example, while only 33.8 percent of residents over age 25 and born in Mexico had completed high school, 95 percent of those born in Africa had. While the median household income for those born in Latin America was $29,338, it was $51,363 for those from Asia, well above that of native Americans.

The proportion of married couples with children under 18 ranged from 35 percent for residents born in Europe to 73.4 percent for those from Latin America. The proportion of naturalized citizens varied widely, from 52 percent of those born in Europe to 21.1 percent of those born in Central America.

> **"California leads in foreign-born residents, with New York second."**

"The big question is how the second generation is going to do," said Nancy Foner, a professor of anthropology at the State University of New York at Purchase and the author of *From Ellis Island to JFK: New York's Two Great Waves of Immigration* (Yale,

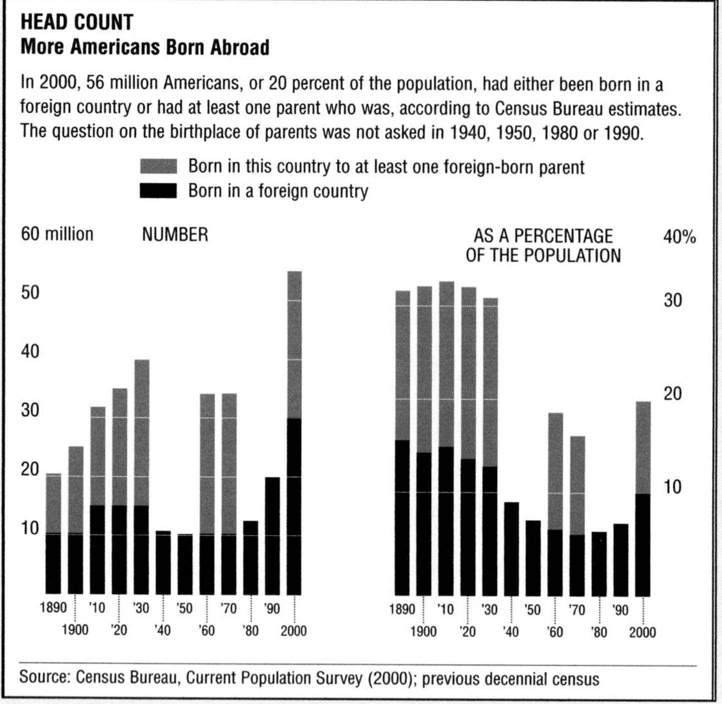
HEAD COUNT
More Americans Born Abroad
In 2000, 56 million Americans, or 20 percent of the population, had either been born in a foreign country or had at least one parent who was, according to Census Bureau estimates. The question on the birthplace of parents was not asked in 1940, 1950, 1980 or 1990.
Born in this country to at least one foreign-born parent
Born in a foreign country
60 million
NUMBER
AS A PERCENTAGE OF THE POPULATION
40%
50
40
30
20
10
30
20
10
1890 '10 '30 '50 '70 '90
1900 '20 '40 '60 '80 2000
1890 '10 '30 '50 '70 '90
1900 '20 '40 '60 '80 2000
Source: Census Bureau, Current Population Survey (2000); previous decennial census

2000). "And how the presence of large proportions of Asians, Latinos and black immigrants are changing Americans' notions of race."

The Census Bureau study found that the foreign-born population was heavily concentrated in California, New York, Florida, Texas, New Jersey and Illinois; those six states accounted for 70.4 percent of the total. Nearly 55 percent lived in the nine metropolitan areas with populations of five million or more.

Does Scott choose appropriate evidence and use it effectively? Use the criteria given in Chapter 16 to determine your answer.

LINK TO P. 471

10 California led the nation with the highest percentage of foreign-born residents with 25.9 percent, followed by New York State with 19.6. The metropolitan areas with the largest percentage of foreign-born populations were Los Angeles with 29.6 percent and New York with 22.8.

In New York City, said John H. Mollenkopf, a demographer at the City University of New York, 43 percent of the residents are foreign born and another 9.2 percent are the children of two foreign-born parents. In 1900, Professor Mollenkopf said, only 23 percent of New Yorkers had native-born parents.

The Census Bureau's report put at 55.9 million the number of people of so-called foreign stock, which includes 28.4 million foreign born, 14.8 million native born with two foreign-born parents, and 12.7 million of mixed parentage. That group is likely to grow, in part because the proportion of births to foreign-born women rose to 20.2 percent in 1999 from 6 percent of all births in 1970, the report said.

While the median ages of the foreign-born and native populations barely differed, foreign-born residents fell disproportionately between the ages of 25 and 54. The percentage of foreign-born residents in that age group was 58.7, compared with 41.7 percent of native Americans.

"In some ways, it has complemented the baby boom," Dianne Schmidley, a Census Bureau statistician and author of the report, said of the rise of the foreign born. "Every discussion you hear about the baby boom and the effect of the baby boom — all that has been made greater by the addition of those young adults."

Flag of faces, Ellis Island

RESPOND •

1. Like many news articles, Scott's argument is informative: her goal is to inform readers of the *Times* about the topic of immigration from several perspectives. Develop a list of the specific generalizations she makes and the sorts of evidence she cites for them. (For a discussion of what counts as evidence, see Chapter 16.) What consequences might these generalizations have for bi- or multilingualism in the United States? Why?
2. A particularly interesting aspect of this article is its use of visual information in the two graphs in "Head Count." As you can see, one bar graph shows (for the past 110 years) the number of people in the United States born in another country or having at least one foreign-born parent, while the other shows the percentage of the total population each group represents for each ten-year cohort. What do we learn from each graph? From the two graphs together? Why is it important to consider both kinds of historical information in understanding immigration? In understanding bi- or multilingualism in the United States?
3. As "Head Count" notes, the Census Bureau didn't ask questions about the birthplace of parents in 1940, 1950, 1980, or 1990. What challenges does this fact present for students of immigration? Of American bi- or multilingualism?

4. Using the Internet, find information from the 2000 census about immigration to your hometown and state (try <http://www.census.gov>). Who moved to your hometown and state in the 1990s? Where did they come from? What consequences might these new arrivals have on bi- or multilingualism there? **Write a short essay** describing the demographic changes to your hometown or state during the 1990s, and speculate on the consequences these changes have had for the linguistic situation there.

This selection offers excerpts from the Pew Hispanic Center/Kaiser Family Foundation's "2002 National Survey of Latinos." (The entire report is available at <http://pewhispanic.org>.) Noting a 142 percent increase in the number of Hispanics between the 1980 and 2002 U.S. censuses, the survey set out "to capture the diversity of the Latino population." To do so, a total of 2,929 adult Latinos from various backgrounds were carefully chosen and sampled, along with 171 African Americans and 1,008 Whites, whose responses were used as a basis for comparison in some questions. The survey uses the phrase "foreign born" to refer to those born outside the fifty states of the Union; hence, those born in Puerto Rico, a U.S. commonwealth, although citizens, are considered foreign born because of the Spanish-dominant nature of Puerto Rican culture. Native-born Latinos are referred to as "U.S.-born Latinos." The survey relies on self-report data about one's ability to speak and read Spanish and/or English.

The excerpts included here, which come from various places in the report, are those that deal most directly with questions of language(s) spoken. First, we present the "Executive Summary," which offers an overview of the results of the study. Next, we present the two primary observations about assimilation and language. Finally, we present a series of more detailed observations, along with data from the survey to support the claims made. As you read, notice how each contributes to the complex picture of language issues among Hispanics.

2002 National Survey of Latinos

PEW HISPANIC CENTER/KAISER FAMILY FOUNDATION

Executive Summary

The Pew Hispanic Center/Kaiser Family Foundation 2002 *National Survey of Latinos* comprehensively explores the attitudes and experiences of Hispanics on a wide variety of topics. This survey was designed to capture the diversity of the Latino population by including almost 3,000 Hispanics from various backgrounds and groups so that in addition to describing Latinos overall, comparisons can be made among key Hispanic subgroups as well.

We find that as a whole, the Hispanic population of the United States holds an array of attitudes, values and beliefs that are distinct from those of non-Hispanic whites and African Americans. Even Latinos who trace their ancestry in the United States back for several generations express views that distinguish them from the non-Hispanic native-born population.

However, there is no single, homogeneous Latino opinion. A diversity of views exists among Latinos, and the differences between the foreign born, regardless of their country of origin, and the native born and those between the English dominant and the Spanish dominant are most notable. In fact, the survey presents a multifaceted representation of a population undergoing rapid change due to immigration that includes individuals at many different stages in the process of assimilation to English and American ways. The survey, however, renders a portrait of a people at a given moment in time — the late spring of 2002 — rather than serving as a prediction for a certain future. Nonetheless, the survey results help resolve a sometimes argumentative though frequently asked question: Are Latino newcomers undergoing the melting pot experience, or are they and their offspring maintaining their native cultures and becoming an ethnic group that is different from the mainstream? The answer is: Both, to some extent.

For example, an examination of Latinos' attitudes on social issues shows that immigrants hold a range of views on matters like gender roles, abortion and homosexuality that are somewhat more conservative than those of most non-Hispanic whites. Meanwhile native-born Latinos, including the children of immigrants, express attitudes that are more squarely within the range of views voiced by non-Hispanics. Nonetheless, some elements of this social conservatism and, in particular, a strong attachment to family is evident among Latinos who predominantly speak English and are generations removed from the immigrant experience.

Immigration is also an important factor in shaping Latinos' sense of their 5
social identity. The survey reveals a robust attachment to countries of origin, and while this attachment is naturally strongest among the foreign born, it also extends to their U.S.-born children and even somewhat among Hispanics whose families are long-time U.S. residents. Social identity for Latinos, however, is much more complex and fluid than simply a connection to an ancestral homeland. Native-born Latinos also use the term "American" to describe themselves more than terms like "Mexican" or "Cuban." Use of the terms "Latino" or "Hispanic," which encompass all national origin groups,

adds another crosscurrent. Respondents use these broader terms to distinguish themselves from non-Hispanics, but in large numbers they also say that Latinos of different countries of origin share no common culture.

The survey also sheds considerable light on the experiences that Latinos have in the United States. Focusing particularly on experiences with discrimination, their economic and financial situations and experiences with the health care system, the survey finds a diversity of experiences largely reflective in differences between native and foreign born and differences between English and Spanish dominant.

Overall, the findings suggest the need for new ways of thinking about the Hispanic population in this country. It is neither monolithic nor a hodgepodge of distinct national origin groups. Rather, Latinos share a range of attitudes and experiences that set them apart from the non-Hispanic population. Yet this common culture embraces a diversity of views that is most evident in the contrasts between immigrants and the native born. The survey argues for a more dynamic approach in regard to Latinos because this is a population undergoing constant change due to immigration. Regardless of nativity or country of origin, Hispanics who reside in the United States are engaging the English language and American ways to various degrees. Yet, simultaneously, newly arrived immigrants are bringing new energy to Spanish and to attitudes shaped in Latin America. In interpreting the survey results it is important to keep in mind that these two processes — assimilation and immigration — are taking place side-by-side in Latino communities, often within a single family.

Survey Highlights

- Hispanics, particularly those who are Spanish speakers, feel very strongly that Hispanics must learn English in order to be successful in the United States.
- Spanish remains the dominant language in the adult Hispanic population. English, however, clearly gains ground even within immigrant households. The second generation — the U.S.-born children of immigrants — predominantly speak English or are bilingual. Indeed, Hispanic parents, even those who are immigrants, report that English is the language their children generally use when speaking to their friends.

Additional Key Demographic Differences

Primary Language

As might be expected, native-born Latinos are much more likely than foreign- 10
born Latinos to speak English as their primary language (61% vs. 4%) or to be bilingual (35% vs. 24%), while foreign-born Latinos are much more likely than native-born Latinos to be Spanish dominant (72% vs. 4%). (Table 1.1)

Age at Immigration

Definition

Respondents who were born outside of the United States were asked their age at the time they immigrated to the United States (Puerto Ricans born on the island were not asked this question and are not included in these groups). Based on their responses they were categorized into four groups: those who arrived when they were age 10 or younger, ages 11–17, ages 18–25, and those who arrived when they were age 26 or older.

Foreign-born Latinos are more likely to report having immigrated to the United States at an older age.

Additional Key Demographic Differences

Primary Language

Those who arrived when they were very young, in this case age 10 or younger, may have experiences more similar to Hispanics who were born in the United States than to others who are foreign-born. In particular, foreign-born Hispanics who arrive at a young age are much more likely to speak English as adults and will have received a majority of their education from American schools. In contrast, foreign-born Hispanics who arrived when they were older, particularly those who arrived when they are already into adulthood, in this case age 26 and older, are more likely to be Spanish dominant than those who arrived when they were younger. (Table 1.2)

As noted above, a large majority (72%) of first generation or foreign-born Latinos are Spanish dominant; about one in four (24%) is bilingual while only 4% are English dominant. In contrast, second generation Latinos are mostly divided between those who are English dominant (46%) and those who are bilingual (47%). Third generation or higher Hispanics are largely English dominant (78%). While a few Hispanics whose families have been in the United States for multiple generations are bilingual (22%), none indicate that they are Spanish dominant. (Table 1.3)

Primary Language

Definition

Respondents were asked a series of four questions about their language ability. They were asked about their ability to carry on a conversation in Spanish and to carry on a conversation in English ("Would you say you can carry on a conversation in Spanish/English, both understanding and speaking—very well, pretty well, just a little, or not at all?") and questions about their ability to read in English and in Spanish ("Would you say you can read a newspaper or book in Spanish/English—very well, pretty well, just a little, or not at all?"). Based on their answers to these four questions, respondents were divided into three language groups: English dominant, bilingual, and Spanish dominant. Using these divisions, almost half (47%) of Hispanics are categorized as "Spanish dominant." The remaining half of Latinos split between those who are English dominant (25%) and those who are bilingual (28%). (Table 1.4)

Table 1.1 Primary Language, by Foreign/Native-Born Latinos

	Foreign-Born Latinos	*Native-Born Latinos*
English-Dominant	4%	61%
Bilingual	24	35
Spanish-Dominant	72	4

Table 1.3 Primary Language among Latinos, by Generation in the United States

	Generation in the United States		
	1st Generation	*2nd Generation*	*3rd Generation and Higher*
English-Dominant	4%	46%	78%
Bilingual	24	47	22
Spanish-Dominant	72	7	–

Table 1.2 Primary Language among Foreign-Born Latinos, by Age at Immigration to the United States

	Age at Immigration to the United States among Foreign-Born Latinos			
	10 years or younger	*Ages 11–17*	*Ages 18–25*	*Ages 26+*
English-Dominant	18%	4%	1%	2%
Bilingual	70	31	15	10
Spanish-Dominant	11	66	84	89

Table 1.4 Primary Language among Latinos

	Percentage of Latino Adults
English-Dominant	25%
Bilingual	28
Spanish-Dominant	47

Throughout the report English-dominant Latinos are also referred to as those "who predominantly speak English" and Spanish-dominant Latinos are also referred to as those "who predominantly speak Spanish." This wording is used for brevity. Please note, however, that the variables used to establish language dominance included both reading and speaking ability.

Primary Language

Hispanics associated with different countries of origin have differences in the primary language they speak. Hispanics from "other" countries are much more likely than other groups to be English dominant. Puerto Ricans also stand out as being much more likely than other groups to speak English predominantly or to be bilingual.

In contrast, Latinos from Central America, El Salvador, and the Dominican Republic are more likely than Puerto Ricans, Mexicans and Hispanics from "other" countries to be Spanish dominant. (Table 1.5)

Assimilating to the United States
Language Assimilation

Hispanics, whites, and African Americans all agree that adult Hispanic immigrants need to learn to speak English to succeed in the United States. Hispanics who speak Spanish primarily and those born outside of the United States are particularly likely to hold this view. (Chart 1.1)

- About nine in ten (89%) Latinos indicate that they believe immigrants need 20
  to learn to speak English to succeed in the United States. Similar numbers of whites (86%) and African Americans (86%) agree. Far fewer (10%) Latinos believe immigrants can succeed if they only speak Spanish.

Table 1.5 Dominant Language among Latinos, by Country of Origin

	Country of Origin								
	Mexican	*Puerto Rican*	*Cuban*	*Total Central American*	*Total South American*	*Salvadoran*	*Dominican*	*Colombian*	*All Other*
English-Dominant	23%	39%	17%	10%	12%	12%	6%	12%	70%
Bilingual	26	40	30	25	34	25	34	30	27
Spanish-Dominant	51	21	53	65	54	63	61	58	3

- Slightly more Spanish-dominant (92%) compared to bilingual (88%) or English-dominant (86%) Latinos believe immigrants need to learn to speak English to succeed in the United States. Similarly, foreign-born Latinos are slightly more likely than U.S.-born Latinos to feel English language skills are necessary for success (91% vs. 86%).

In many ways, Spanish remains the dominant language among adult Hispanics. Not only do more Latinos speak and read Spanish than English, but also it is spoken more in the home and used a great deal at work. In addition, Spanish language media are important sources of news for many. (Chart 1.2)

- Overall, a very large majority (86%) of Hispanics report that they can carry on a conversation in Spanish both understanding and speaking "very" (74%) or "pretty" (12%) well, while a significant minority (40%) speaks and understands "just a little" (29%) or no (11%) English.
- Similarly, Latinos are more likely to say they can read a newspaper or book at least pretty well in Spanish than in English (74% vs. 58%). A significant number (42%) indicate that they read "just a little" or no English.
- In addition, a slight majority (53%) of Hispanics report they predominantly 25
speak Spanish at home. About one in five (19%) says Spanish and English are spoken equally in their homes, while 28% say they predominantly speak English at home.

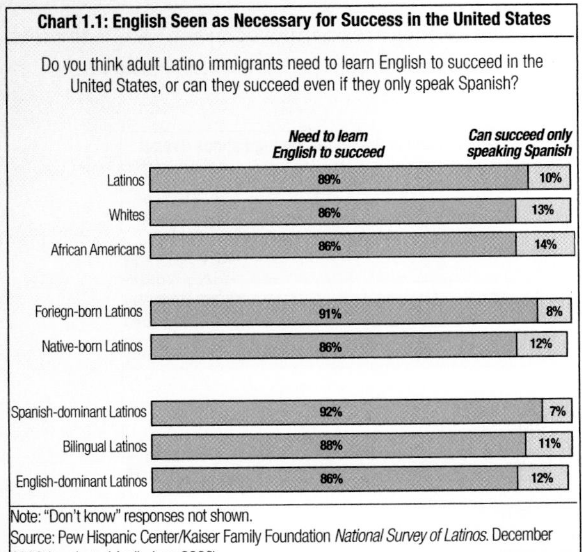

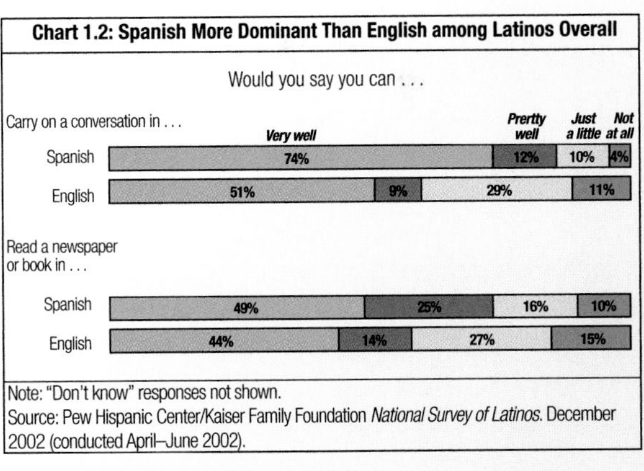

- While almost half (48%) of Latinos who are employed say they predominantly speak English at work, Spanish is also used a great deal in the workplace. More than half (52%) of employed Hispanics report that they speak Spanish at work at least some of the time. This includes about one in four (26%) Hispanics who report speaking predominantly Spanish at work, including 14% who report that they *only* speak Spanish at work. About one in four (26%) say they speak both Spanish and English equally.
- Spanish language media are an important source of broadcast news for a majority of Latinos: 38% of Latinos report that they usually listen to and predominantly watch Spanish language news programs, including one in four who *only* tune in to Spanish language broadcasts. An additional 26% report that they get their news from both Spanish and English news sources equally. Older Latinos rely on the Spanish language media most heavily while younger, those who are better-educated and those who are more affluent are more likely to get their broadcast news in English.

While Spanish remains the dominant language in the adult Hispanic population, English gains ground even within immigrant households. The second generation — the U.S.-born children of immigrants — is either bilingual or predominantly speaks English. Indeed, Hispanic parents, even those who are immigrants, report that English is the language their children generally use when their children are speaking to their friends. (Chart 1.3)

- Only 7% of second generation Latinos are Spanish dominant, while the rest are divided between those who are bilingual (47%) and those who are

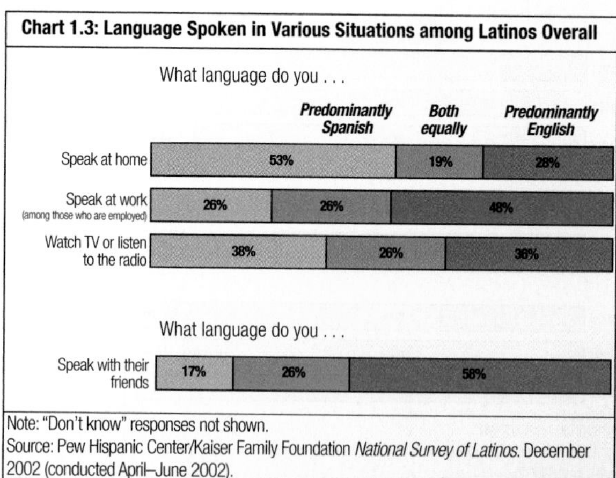

English dominant (46%). Those whose parents were born in the United States (third generation and higher) are much more likely to speak English predominantly (78%), while about one in five (22%) are bilingual.

- 30 Over half (58%) of Latinos with children say their children usually speak English with their friends, including 36% who only speak English. About one in four (26%) says their children speak both Spanish and English equally with their friends, while 17% report their children speak predominantly Spanish, including 13% who *only* speak Spanish.
- English is making inroads among immigrant households. Among foreign-born parents, 45% say their children communicate with their friends predominantly in English and another 32% say their children use both English and Spanish equally. Just 18% of immigrant parents say that their children *only* speak Spanish with their friends.

How do the authors of this study use evidence to make an argument? See Chapter 19 for more on summarizing and other ways of using sources to bolster an argument.

LINK TO PP. 530 AND 545

RESPOND •

1. What's your response to this information? Were you already aware of the situation described in the report, or did this selection present you with information or perspectives that were new? How? Why?
2. This report from the Pew Hispanic Center/Kaiser Family Foundation represents an increasingly common genre of writing: the presentation of quantitative information in summary form so that it can be used by many sorts of researchers for many purposes. How have the creators of this report written it with the users in mind? In other words, what features of the text help readers with respect to understanding and using the data? How?
3. What does this report teach us about language among Americans who identify as Latino or Hispanic? About bilingualism? About identity?
4. **Write a summary** of the information presented in this selection that you might use in a research paper on language in the Hispanic community. Specifically, you'll need to choose two or three main points that you believe are most relevant, state them and the relationships among them clearly, and provide data from the report to support your claim. You'll also need to use the proper documentation. (For questions on documentation, see Chapter 20.) Obviously, one can use the facts and observations presented in the report to support many different sorts of arguments. At the same time, the facts and observations made in the report cannot be used as evidence for just any claim about language in the Hispanic community.

Rolando Briseño, *Bicultural Tablesetting*

▲ *Rolando Briseño lives and paints in San Antonio, Texas.* Bicultural Tablesetting *is part of a series of images,* Tablescapes, *that has been shown across the United States. Briseño's art is widely collected by many institutions, including the Museum of South Texas, Corpus Christi; the Contemporary Art Museum, San Juan, Puerto Rico; the Brooklyn Museum; and the Corcoran Gallery of Art, Washington, D.C. Food and tables are central metaphors in Briseño's work; in fact, he sees the motif of the table "as a life source, a symbol for communication, and a locus of community" (from the Web site* <http:// latinoartcommunity .org/community/Gallery/Prints/Briseno/Rolando.html>*).*

RESPOND •

1. The title of Rolando Briseño's painting, *Bicultural Tablesetting*, can be read as an argument of several sorts. In what ways might it be seen as an argument of definition? Of evaluation? (Which items in the painting are associated with Spanish-language or Mexican culture? Which are associated with English-language or American culture? Are these two groups of associations valued differently? By whom and why?)
2. How can we interpret Briseño's painting as an argument about tradition and innovation? About separation, segregation, and difference? About the nature of bilingual and bicultural life? About *mestizaje*, the Spanish word used to refer to "cultural mixing," specifically the contact between Europeans and indigenous peoples in the Americas?
3. In what ways might we see Briseño's painting as an argument from the heart? One based on Briseño's ethos? One based on facts or reason?
4. We might argue that there are three major parts of Briseño's painting—the left half, the right half, and the center, which comprises the plate, its design, and its contents. (By the way, in writing about the painting, Briseño reminds us that tomatoes are a pre-Columbian food, and he compares the tomatoes on the plate to quarks positioned in a proton.) How might we describe each part and the complex relationships among them? **Write an essay** in which you explicate the painting's argument(s), using a description of the parts of the painting to support your claims. Your essay could take the form of a definitional essay in which you seek to define the painting's arguments.

▼ *Myriam Marquez writes regularly for the* Orlando Sentinel, *and her columns are syndicated nationally. (We ran across this one in July 1999 in the* Austin American Statesman.*) In this op-ed piece, Marquez explains why she, a Cuban American who grew up in Miami, and her family use Spanish in public within the earshot of people who don't speak Spanish. As you read, consider the ways in which Marquez relies on arguments based on values, arguments from the heart, arguments based on character, and arguments based on reason to make her point.*

Why and When We Speak Spanish in Public

MYRIAM MARQUEZ

When I'm shopping with my mother or standing in line with my stepdad to order fast food or anywhere else we might be together, we're going to speak to one another in Spanish.

That may appear rude to those who don't understand Spanish and overhear us in public places.

Those around us may get the impression that we're talking about them. They may wonder why we would insist on speaking in a foreign tongue, especially if they knew that my family has lived in the United States for 40 years and that my parents do understand English and speak it, albeit with difficulty and a heavy accent.

Let me explain why we haven't adopted English as our official family language. For me and most of the bilingual people I know, it's a matter of respect for our parents and comfort in our cultural roots.

It's not meant to be rude to others. 5
It's not meant to alienate anyone or to Balkanize° America.

It's certainly not meant to be un-American — what constitutes an "American" being defined by English speakers from North America.

Being an American has very little to do with what language we use during our free time in a free country. From its inception, this country was careful not to promote a government-mandated official language.

We understand that English is the common language of this country and the one most often heard in international-business circles from Peru to Norway. We know that, to get ahead here, one must learn English.

But that ought not mean that somehow we must stop speaking in our native tongue whenever we're in a public area, as if we were ashamed of who we are, where we're from. As if talking in Spanish — or any other language, for that matter — is some sort of litmus test used to gauge American patriotism.

Throughout this nation's history, 10
most immigrants — whether from Poland or Finland or Italy or wherever else — kept their language through the first generation and, often, the second. I suspect that they spoke among themselves in their native tongue — in public. Pennsylvania even provided voting ballots written in German during much of the 1800s for those who weren't fluent in English.

In this century, Latin American immigrants and others have fought for this country in U.S.-led wars. They have participated fully in this nation's democracy by voting, holding political office and paying taxes. And they have watched their children and grandchildren become so "American" that they resist speaking in Spanish.

Balkanize: to divide a country or people into smaller, generally mutually hostile groups or areas, as occurred a century ago in the Balkan Peninsula.

You know what's rude?

When there are two or more people who are bilingual and another person who speaks only English and the bilingual folks all of a sudden start speaking Spanish, which effectively leaves out the English-only speaker. I don't tolerate that.

One thing's for sure. If I'm ever in a public place with my mom or dad and bump into an acquaintance who doesn't speak Spanish, I will switch to English and introduce that person to my parents. They will respond in English, and do so with respect.

RESPOND •

1. How does Marquez explain and justify her behavior and that of many immigrants, including Spanish-speaking immigrants? What fear does she acknowledge on the part of those who don't speak Spanish? How does she seek to respond to it?
2. What are the specific ways in which Marquez relies on arguments based on values, arguments from the heart, arguments based on character, and arguments based on reason to make her point? What values does Marquez appeal to when she explains why bilinguals like her speak Spanish in public?
3. The last three paragraphs of this essay represent a clear shift in tone and emphasis from the rest of this selection, especially the previous few paragraphs. What's their purpose? Do you find that they contribute to or detract from the overall effect of the selection? Why?
4. **Write an essay** in which you define and evaluate the notion of public space with respect to speaking languages other than English as presented by Marquez. As Marquez notes, for her and many Americans, the public space is not a space where only English can be spoken. At the same time, there are limits to what's permissible. Thus you'll need to define the public space with respect to language in the terms Marquez uses and then evaluate her definition or characterization of that space, depending on your own values and experiences.

Who are Marquez's intended readers? Who are her invoked readers? Her real readers? See Chapter 1 for more on how writers address audiences.

LINK TO P. 32

Sandra Cisneros is a Mexican American writer who lives and writes in a much-discussed violet house in San Antonio, Texas. The author of several books about the Mexican American experience, she has most recently published the 2002 novel* Caramelo*. Born in Chicago in 1954, she's the recipient of a number of important awards, including a MacArthur Foundation fellowship. In this short excerpt from the short story "Bien Pretty," which appeared in* Woman Hollering Creek and Other Stories *(1991), Cisneros helps readers understand how bilinguals experience the languages they know. As you read, note how Cisneros uses careful description to make her argument.

From "Bien Pretty"

SANDRA CISNEROS

I'd never made love in Spanish before. I mean not with anyone whose *first* language was Spanish. There was crazy Graham, the anarchist labor organizer who'd taught me to eat jalapeños and swear like a truck mechanic, but he was Welsh and had learned his Spanish running guns to Bolivia.

And Eddie, sure. But Eddie and I were products of our American education. Anything tender always came off sounding like the subtitles to a Buñuel° film.

But Flavio. When Flavio accidentally hammered his thumb, he never yelled "Ouch!" he said "*¡Ay!*" The true test of a native Spanish speaker.

¡Ay! To make love in Spanish, in a manner as intricate and devout as la Alhambra.° To have a lover sigh *mi vida, mi preciosa, mi chiquitita,* and whisper things in that language crooned to babies, that language murmured by grandmothers, those words that smelled like your house, like flour tortillas, and the inside of your daddy's hat, like everyone talking in the kitchen at the same time, or sleeping with the windows open, like sneaking cashews from the crumpled quarter-pound bag Mama always hid in her lingerie drawer after she went shopping with Daddy at the Sears.

That language. That sweep of palm leaves and fringed shawls. That 5
startled fluttering, like the heart of a goldfinch or a fan. Nothing sounded dirty or hurtful or corny. How could I think of making love in English again? English with its starched *r*'s and *g*'s. English with its crisp linen syllables. English crunchy as apples, resilient and stiff as sailcloth.

But Spanish whirred like silk, rolled and puckered and hissed. I held Flavio close to me, in the mouth of my heart, inside my wrists.

Incredible happiness. A sigh unfurled of its own accord, a groan heaved out from my chest so rusty and full of dust it frightened me. I was crying. It surprised us both.

"My soul, did I hurt you?" Flavio said in that other language.

I managed to bunch my mouth into a knot and shake my head "no" just as the next wave of sobs began. Flavio rocked me, and cooed, and rocked me. *Ya, ya, ya.* There, there, there.

I wanted to say so many things, but all I could think of was a line I'd read 10
in the letters of Georgia O'Keeffe years ago and had forgotten until then. Flavio . . . did you ever feel like flowers?

Buñuel: Spanish filmmaker (1900–1983), famous for his Surrealist images and groundbreaking, often bizarre, visual imagery.

la Alhambra: from an Arabic phrase meaning "the red palace"; la Alhambra was the palace, citadel, gardens, fortress, and home of the Nasrid sultans in the thirteenth and fourteenth centuries in Grenada in the south of Spain.

RESPOND •

1. For Cisneros—and one can likely claim it for all bilinguals—the languages she knows aren't equal in some sense. Rather, each language is associated with different worlds of experience. What does Spanish connote for the narrator in Cisneros's text? What does English connote? Where would such connotations come from?
2. Whereas Myriam Marquez writes about the use of Spanish in public, Cisneros writes about the use of Spanish in the most private of contexts. Are there things Marquez and Cisneros (or at least her narrator) would agree about? What might they be? Why?
3. One resource bilingual writers have is codeswitching: switching between the languages they know. In this excerpt, we see the simple noun phrase "la Alhambra" (paragraph 4) from Spanish, which we can correctly understand even if we know no Spanish. We also see the phrase "*Ya, ya, ya*" (paragraph 9), which is followed immediately by the English equivalent, "There, there, there." Yet we also find the phrases "*mi vida, mi preciosa, mi chiquitita*" (paragraph 4), which we may not be able to figure out the meanings of. (In fact, the phrases translate literally as "my life, my precious [one], my dearest little [one]"—things native speakers of English wouldn't normally say to one another, even when being intimate. Such phrases are perfectly normal among speakers of Spanish.) Why might writers purposely create texts that include parts readers may not be able to understand? Why would such a strategy be especially effective when talking about intimacies like making love?
4. Likely all humans have an affective or emotional attachment to one or more languages or language varieties, most often one associated with childhood. **Create a text** in which you explore and define the meaning of some language or language variety—a regional, social, or ethnic variety of English, for example—for you. Your text can take the form of an essay, or you may wish to create a sketch more like Cisneros's (though you needn't write about anything so intimate as love making!). In it, seek to help readers—both those who know that language variety and those who don't—understand its meanings and significance for you.

Which tropes does Cisneros use in her essay? See descriptions of the different types of figurative language in Chapter 12 to help you figure out your answer.

LINK TO P. 378

Marjorie Agosín is a professor of Spanish at Wellesley College in Massachusetts and an award-winning writer and human rights activist. She was reared in Chile, the country to which her grandparents had moved early in the twentieth century at a time when Jews faced persecution in parts of Europe. Her family moved to the United States in the 1970s, when Augusto Pinochet took over the Chilean government. In this essay, which originally appeared in Poets & Writers *in 1999 and was translated by Celeste Kostopulos-Cooperman, Agosín explains why she, as a political exile, "writes only in Spanish and lives in translation." In the poem that follows, "English," translated by Monica Bruno, Agosín compares and contrasts English and Spanish.*

Always Living in Spanish

MARJORIE AGOSÍN

Yiddish: Germanic language, much influenced by Hebrew and Aramaic, spoken by Ashkenazi Jews in Central and Eastern Europe and their descendents. In the nineteenth century, it was found in most of the world's countries with an Ashkenazi population, including the United States. Yiddish is written in the Hebrew alphabet.

Agosín uses her personal experiences as an exile in the United States to argue about her reasons for continuing to write in Spanish. Check out what Chapter 16 has to say about using personal experience in your writing.

LINK TO P. 479

Recovering the Familiar, Through Language

In the evenings in the northern hemisphere, I repeat the ancient ritual that I observed as a child in the southern hemisphere: going out while the night is still warm and trying to recognize the stars as it begins to grow dark silently. In the sky of my country, Chile, that long and wide stretch of land that the poets blessed and dictators abused, I could easily name the stars: the three Marias, the Southern Cross, and the three Lilies, names of beloved and courageous women.

But here in the United States, where I have lived since I was a young girl, the solitude of exile makes me feel that so little is mine, that not even the sky has the same constellations, the trees and the fauna the same names or sounds, or the rubbish the same smell. How does one recover the familiar? How does one name the unfamiliar? How can one be another or live in a foreign language? These are the dilemmas of one who writes in Spanish and lives in translation.

Since my earliest childhood in Chile I lived with the tempos and the melodies of a multiplicity of tongues: German, Yiddish,° Russian, Turkish, and many Latin songs. Because everyone was from somewhere else, my relatives laughed, sang, and fought in a Babylon of languages. Spanish was reserved for matters of extreme seriousness, for commercial transactions, or for illnesses, but everyone's mother tongue was always associated with the memory of spaces inhabited in the past: the shtetl,° the flowering and vast Vienna avenues, the minarets of Turkey, and the Ladino° whispers of Toledo. When my paternal grandmother sang old songs in Turkish, her voice and body assumed the passion of one who was there in the city of Istanbul, gazing by turns toward the west and the east.

shtetl: a small Jewish village or town in Eastern Europe (originally, a Yiddish word meaning "little town").

Ladino: a nearly extinct Romance language, based on archaic Castilian Spanish, spoken by Sephardic Jews in the Balkans, North Africa and the Middle East, Turkey, and Greece. It originated in Spain and was carried elsewhere by the descendents of Jews exiled from there during the Inquisition.

Destiny and the always ambiguous nature of history continued my family's enforced migration, and because of it I, too, became one who had to live and speak in translation. The disappearances, torture, and clandestine deaths in my country in the early seventies drove us to the United States, that other America that looked with suspicion at those who did not speak English and especially those who came from the supposedly uncivilized regions of Latin America. I had left a dangerous place that was my home, only to arrive in a dangerous place that was not: a high school in the small town of Athens, Georgia, where my poor English and my accent were the cause of ridicule and insult. The only way I could recover my usurped country and my Chilean childhood was by continuing to write in Spanish, the same way my grandparents had sung in their own tongues in diasporic° sites.

diasporic: relating to a diaspora, or dispersion of a group of people across a large geographic area to which they aren't native.

5 The new and learned English language did not fit with the visceral emotions and themes that my poetry contained, but by writing in Spanish I could recover fragrances, spoken rhythms, and the passion of my own identity. Daily I felt the need to translate myself for the strangers living all around me, to tell them why we were in Georgia, why we ate differently, why we had fled, why my accent was so thick, and why I did not look Hispanic. Only at night, writing poems in Spanish, could I return to my senses, and soothe my own sorrow over what I had left behind.

This is how I became a Chilean poet who wrote in Spanish and lived in the southern United States. And then, one day, a poem of mine was translated and published in the English language. Finally, for the first time since I had left Chile, I felt I didn't have to explain myself. My poem, expressed in another language, spoke for itself . . . and for me.

Sometimes the austere sounds of English help me bear the solitude of knowing that I am foreign and so far away from those about whom I write. I must admit I would like more opportunities to read in Spanish to people whose language and culture is also mine, to join in our common heritage and in the feast of our sounds. I would also like readers of English to understand the beauty of the spoken word in Spanish, that constant flow of oxytonic° and

oxytonic: with main stress on the final or single syllable of a word.

paraoxytonic° syllables (*Verde que te quiero verde*°), the joy of writing—of dancing—in another language. I believe that many exiles share the unresolvable torment of not being able to live in the language of their childhood.

I miss that undulating and sensuous language of mine, those baroque descriptions, the sense of being and feeling that Spanish gives me. It is perhaps for this reason that I have chosen and will always choose to write in Spanish. Nothing else from my childhood world remains. My country seems to be frozen in gestures of silence and oblivion. My relatives have died, and I have grown up not knowing a young generation of cousins and nieces and nephews. Many of my friends were disappeared,° others were tortured, and the most fortunate, like me, became guardians of memory. For us, to write in Spanish is to always be in active pursuit of memory. I seek to recapture a world lost to me on that sorrowful afternoon when the blue electric sky and the Andean cordillera° bade me farewell. On that, my last Chilean day, I carried under my arm my innocence recorded in a little blue notebook I kept even then. Gradually that diary filled with memoranda, poems written in free verse, descriptions of dreams and of the thresholds of my house surrounded by cherry trees and gardenias. To write in Spanish is for me a gesture of survival. And because of translation, my memory has now become a part of the memory of many others.

Translators are not traitors, as the proverb says, but rather splendid friends in this great human community of language.

paraoxytonic: with main stress on the next-to-last syllable of a word.

Vérde qué té quiéro vérde: (translation [stressed syllables marked]: "Green. How I want you green," the opening line of a famous poem by Federico García Lorca), an illustration of stress falling on oxytonic and paraoxytonic syllables.

were disappeared: although *disappear* is generally an intransitive verb that cannot take a direct object and cannot be used in the passive voice, Chileans and Spanish speakers from other countries with repressive political regimes began using this "incorrect" grammatical construction to refer to individuals who disappeared and were presumed dead after being taken into custody by the authorities, often for no valid reason. The expression is now used in many languages, including English.

cordillera: mountain ranges consisting of more or less parallel chains of peaks.

English

MARJORIE AGOSÍN Translated by Monica Bruno

I discovered that English
is too skinny,
functional,
precise,
too correct,
meaning
only one thing.
Too much wrath,
too many lawyers and sinister policemen,
too many deans at schools for small females,
in the Anglo-Saxon language.

II

In contrast Spanish
has so many words to say come with me friend,
make love to me on
the *césped,* the *grama,* the *pasto.*[1]
Let's go party,[2]
at dusk, at night, at sunset.
Spanish
loves
the unpredictable, it is
dementia,
all windmills° and velvet.

III

Spanish
is simple and baroque,

Torres del Paine National Park, Chile

windmills: an allusion to Don Quixote, who tilted at windmills on his old nag, imagining them to be giants.

[1]All three words mean "grass" in English.

[2]The Spanish version of this poem uses two phrases that mean "to party": *de juerga* and *de fiesta.*

(Pablo) Neruda: pen name of the Nobel prize–winning Chilean poet, politician, and diplomat (1904–1973), considered by many to be the finest Latin American poet of the twentieth century.

Federico García Lorca: Spanish poet and playwright (1898–1936); a sympathizer with leftist causes and a homosexual, Lorca was executed by a Nationalist firing squad early on in the Spanish Civil War under mysterious circumstances. Lorca penned "Verde, que te quiero verde," cited by Agosín in her essay.

Don Quixote: (also spelled Quijote) the hero of Miguel de Cervantes's comic and satiric novel of the same name, originally published in two volumes in 1605 and 1615. It concerns Quixote, who, having read too many courtly romances, goes off to find adventure. Quixote's name and the adjective *quixotic* are often applied to someone who, inspired by high (but often false) ideals, pursues an impossible project or task.

Violeta Parra: Chilean folksinger (1917–1967) most often associated with "La Nueva Canción," a new style of Chilean and Latin American popular music, much influenced by folk traditions. Her best-known work is perhaps "Gracias à la vida," "Thanks to Life."

a palace of nobles and beggars,
it fills itself with silences and the breaths of dragonflies.
Neruda's° verses
saying "I could write the saddest verses
tonight,"
or Federico° swimming underwater through the greenest of greens.

IV

Spanish
is Don Quijote° maneuvering,
Violeta Parra° grateful
spicy, tasty, fragrant
the rumba, the salsa, the cha-cha.
There are so many words
to say
naive dreamers
and impostors.
There are so many languages in our
language: Quechua,° Aymará,° Rosas chilensis,° Spanglish.°

V

I love the imperfections of
Spanish,
the language takes shape in my hand:
the sound of drums and waves,
the Caribbean in the radiant foam of the sun,
are delirious upon my lips.
English has fallen short for me,
it signifies business,
law
and inhibition,
never the crazy, clandestine,
clairvoyance of
love.

RESPOND •

1. Why does Agosín write only in Spanish? How do her reasons for using Spanish compare with those of Marquez and Cisneros? How does she regard using Spanish as relating to her ancestry as a Jew?
2. What sort of experiences did Agosín have while trying to learn English? How typical do you think her experiences were? In other words, how do Americans who are native speakers of English treat nonnative speakers of English? How did Spanish represent a source of strength and consolation to Agosín during the period when she was learning English?
3. What does Spanish represent for Agosín? Why would it represent these things for her?
4. As the selections by Marquez, Cisneros, and Agosín make clear, even though Spanish doesn't mean the same thing to everyone who speaks it, its various meanings remain significant to many Americans whose ancestors can be traced somehow to the Spanish-speaking world. The selections by these writers, along with the survey data from the Pew Hispanic Center/Kaiser Family Foundation (p. 743), also make clear that for many Hispanics, to lose Spanish would be to lose a fundamental part of their identity as individuals and as members of larger groups. Using these texts, perhaps personal experience, and perhaps discussions you have with people who claim to be bilingual or bidialectal (that is, to speak a dialect of English other than Standard English, the variety expected and rewarded at school), **write an essay** in which you seek to define the role of language(s) in the creation of individual and group identity.

Quechua: the language of the former Inca empire and the major indigenous language of the central Andes today.

Aymará: one of the major indigenous languages of Bolivia.

Rosas chilensis: Latin species name for a rose indigenous to Chile.

Spanglish: popular label for the practice of switching between Spanish and English within a conversation or sentence, as many bilingual Hispanics do when they speak with other bilinguals.

Lan Cao is currently Boyd Fellow and Professor of Law at the Marshall-Wythe School of Law at the College of William and Mary. She's the author of Monkey Bridge *(1997), the novel from which this excerpt comes. (A monkey bridge is a spindly bamboo bridge used by Vietnamese peasants.) The novel recounts the experiences of a young woman who, like Lan Cao, came to the United States fleeing the Vietnam War. Cao herself arrived here in 1975.*

At this point in the novel the narrator, an adolescent girl, and her mother have moved to the States, having had to leave behind the girl's maternal grandfather—their only other living relative. The girl had arrived before the mother and had stayed with an American colonel her family had befriended while he was in Vietnam. He and his wife are the Uncle Michael and Aunt Mary referred to in the text. This excerpt begins with a comparison of American and Asian markets but quickly moves to more complex topics. As you read, try to put yourself in Lan Cao's position. For some readers, it will be an all too familiar one; for others, it may be an almost unimaginable one.

The Gift of Language

LAN CAO

I discovered soon after my arrival in Falls Church that everything, even the simple business of shopping the American way, unsettled my mother's nerves. From the outside, it had been an ordinary building that held no promises or threats beyond four walls anchored to a concrete parking lot. But inside, the A & P brimmed with unexpected abundance. Built-in metal stands overflowed with giant oranges and grapefruits meticulously arranged into a pyramid. Columns of canned vegetables and fruits stood among multiple shelves as people well rehearsed to the demands of modern shopping meandered through the fluorescent aisles. I remembered the sharp chilled air against my face, the way the hydraulic door made a sucking sound as it closed behind.

My first week in Connecticut with Uncle Michael and Aunt Mary, I thought Aunt Mary was a genius shopper. She appeared to have the sixth sense of a bat and could identify, record, and register every item on sale. She was skilled in the art of coupon shopping—in the American version of Vietnamese haggling, the civil and acceptable mode of getting the customers to think they had gotten a good deal.

The day after I arrived in Farmington, Aunt Mary navigated the cart—and me—through aisles, numbered and categorized, crammed with jars and cardboard boxes, and plucked from them the precise product to match the coupons she carried. I had been astonished that day that the wide range of choices did not disrupt her plan. We had a schedule, I discovered, which Aunt Mary mapped out on a yellow pad, and which we followed, checking off item after item. She called it the science of shopping, the ability to resist the temptations of dazzling packaging. By the time we were through, our cart would be filled to the rim with cans of Coke, the kinds with flip-up caps that made can openers obsolete, in family-size cartons. We had chicken and meat sealed in tight, odorless packages, priced and weighed. We had fruits so beautifully polished and waxed they looked artificial. And for me, we had mangoes and papayas that were still hard and green but which Aunt Mary had handed to me like rare jewels from a now extinct land.

But my mother did not appreciate the exacting orderliness of the A & P. She could not give in to the precision of previously weighed and packaged

Bilingual outreach worker helping Vietnamese shoppers in the United States

Cao uses a variety of metaphors in describing her early years in the United States. This trope adds to her style as an author. Consider the points of style and delivery presented in Chapter 12.

LINK TO P. 369

food, the bloodlessness of beef slabs in translucent wrappers, the absence of carcasses and pigs' heads. In Saigon, we had only outdoor markets. "Sky markets," they were called, vast, prosperous expanses in the middle of the city where barrels of live crabs and yellow carps and booths of ducks and geese would be stacked side by side with cardboard stands of expensive silk fabric from Hong Kong. It was always noisy there—a voluptuous mix of animal and human sounds that the air itself had assimilated and held. The sharp acrid smell of gutters choked by the monsoon rain. The unambiguous odor of dried horse dung that lingered in the atmosphere, partially camouflaged by the fat, heavy scent of guavas and bananas.

My mother knew the vendors and even the shoppers by name and would 5
take me from stall to stall to expose me to her skills. They were all addicted to each other's oddities. My mother would feign indifference and they would inevitably call out to her. She would heed their call and they would immediately retreat into sudden apathy. They knew my mother's slick bargaining skills, and she, in turn, knew how to navigate with grace through their extravagant prices and rehearsed huffiness. Theirs had been a mating dance, a match of wills.

Toward the center of the market, a man with a spotted boa constrictor coiled around his neck stood and watched day after day over an unruly hodgepodge of hand-dyed cotton shirts, handkerchiefs, and swatches of white muslin; funerals were big business in Vietnam. To the side, in giant paper bags slit with round openings, were canaries and hummingbirds which my mother bought, one hundred at a time, and freed, one by one, into our garden; it was a good deed designed to generate positive karma for the family. My mother, like the country itself, was obsessed with karma. In fact, the Vietnamese word for "please," as in "could you please," means literally "to make good karma." "Could you please pass the butter" becomes "Please make good karma and pass me the butter." My mother would cup each bird in her hand and set it on my head. It was her way of immersing me in a wellspring of karmic charm, and in that swift moment of delight when the bird's wings spread over my head as it contemplated flight, I believed life itself was utterly beautiful and blessed.

Every morning, we drifted from stack to stack, vendor to vendor. There were no road maps to follow—tables full of black market Prell and Colgate were pocketed among vegetable stands one day and jars of medicinal herbs the next. The market was randomly organized, and only the mighty and experienced like my mother could navigate its patternless paths.

But with a sense of neither drama nor calamity, my mother's ability to navigate and decipher simply became undone in our new life. She preferred the improvisation of haggling to the conventional certainty of discount coupons, the primordial messiness and fishmongers' stink of the open-air market to the aroma-free order of individually wrapped fillets.

Now, a mere three and a half years or so after her last call to the sky market, the dreadful truth was simply this: we were going through life in reverse, and I was the one who would help my mother through the hard scrutiny of ordinary suburban life. I would have to forgo the luxury of adolescent experiments and temper tantrums, so that I could scoop my mother out of harm's way and give her sanctuary. Now, when we stepped into the exterior world, I was the one who told my mother what was acceptable or unacceptable behavior.

All children of immigrant parents have experienced these moments. 10
When it first occurs, when the parent first reveals the behavior of a child, is a defining moment. Of course, all children eventually watch their parents' astonishing return to the vulnerability of childhood, but for us the process begins much earlier than expected.

"We don't have to pay the moment we decide to buy the pork. We can put as much as we want in the cart and pay only once, at the checkout counter."

It took a few moments' hesitation for my mother to succumb to the peculiarity of my explanation.

And even though I hesitated to take on the responsibility, I had no other choice. It was not a simple process, the manner in which my mother relinquished motherhood. The shift in status occurred not just in the world but in the safety of our home as well, and it became most obvious when we entered the realm of language. I was like Kiki, my pet bird in Saigon, tongue untwisted and sloughed of its rough and thick exterior. According to my mother, feeding the bird crushed red peppers had caused it to shed its tongue in successive layers and allowed it to speak the language of humans.

Every morning during that month of February 1975, while my mother paced the streets of Saigon and witnessed the country's preparation for imminent defeat, I followed Aunt Mary around the house, collecting words like a beggar gathering rain with an earthen pan. She opened her mouth, and out came a constellation of gorgeous sounds. Each word she uttered was a round stone, with the smoothness of something that had been rubbed and polished by the waves of a warm summer beach. She could swim straight through her syllables. On days when we studied together, I almost convinced myself that we would continue that way forever, playing with the movement of sound itself. I would listen as she tried to inspire me into replicating the "th" sound with the seductive powers of her voice. "Slip the tip of your tongue between your front teeth and pull it back real quick," she would coax and coax. Together, she and I sketched the English language, its curious cadence and rhythm, into the receptive Farmington landscape. Only with Aunt Mary and Uncle Michael could I give myself an inheritance my parents never gave me: the gift of language. The story of English was nothing less than the poetry of sound and motion. To this day, Aunt Mary's voice remains my standard for perfection.

My superior English meant that, unlike my mother and Mrs. Bay, I knew the difference between "cough" and "enough," "bough" and "through," "trough" and "thorough," "dough" and "fought." Once I made it past the fourth or fifth week in Connecticut, the new language Uncle Michael and Aunt Mary were teaching me began gathering momentum, like tumbleweed in a storm. This was my realization: we have only to let one thing go—the language we think in, or the composition of our dream, the grass roots clinging underneath its rocks—and all at once everything goes. It had astonished me, the ease with which continents shift and planets change course, the casual way in which the earth goes about shedding the laborious folds of its memories. Suddenly, out of that difficult space between here and there, English revealed itself to me with the ease of thread unspooled. I began to understand the levity and weight of its sentences. First base, second base, home run. New terminologies were not difficult to master, and gradually the possibility of perfection began edging its way into my life. How did those numerous Chinatowns and Little Italys sustain the will to maintain a distance, the desire to inhabit the edge and margin of American life? A mere eight weeks into Farmington, and the American Dream was exerting a sly but seductive pull.

15 By the time I left Farmington to be with my mother, I had already created for myself a different, more sacred tongue. Khe Sanh,° the Tet Offensive,° the Ho Chi Minh Trail°—a history as imperfect as my once obviously imperfect English—these were things that had rushed me into the American melting pot. And when I saw my mother again, I was no longer the same person she used to know. Inside my new tongue, my real tongue, was an astonishing new power. For my mother and her Vietnamese neighbors, I became the keeper of the word, the only one with access to the light-world. Like Adam, I had the God-given right to name all the fowls of the air and all the beasts of the field.

The right to name, I quickly discovered, also meant the right to stand guard over language and the right to claim unadulterated authority. Here was a language with an ocean's quiet mystery, and it would be up to me to render its vastness comprehensible to the newcomers around me. My language skill, my ability to decipher the nuances of American life, was what held us firmly in place, night after night, in our Falls Church living room. The ease with which I could fabricate wholly new plot lines from TV made the temptation to invent especially difficult to resist.

And since my mother couldn't understand half of what anyone was saying, television watching, for me, was translating and more. This, roughly, was how things went in our living room:

The Bionic Woman had just finished rescuing a young girl, approximately my age, from drowning in a lake where she'd gone swimming against her mother's wishes. Once out of harm's way, Jaime made the girl promise she'd be more careful next time and listen to her mother.

Translation: the Bionic Woman rescued the girl from drowning in the lake, but commended her for her magnificent deeds, since the girl had heroically jumped into the water to rescue a prized police dog.

20 "Where's the dog?" my mother would ask. "I don't see him."

"He's not there anymore, they took him to the vet right away. Remember?" I sighed deeply.

"Oh," my mother said. "It's strange. Strong girl, Bionic Woman."

The dog that I convinced her existed on the television screen was no more confusing than the many small reversals in logic and the new identities we experienced her first few months in America.

Khe Sanh: a remote U.S. Marine base in Vietnam. On January 21, 1968, troops from the North Vietnamese Army launched an attack on the base, starting a seventy-seven day-battle that's often considered one of the most brutal of the entire Vietnam War.

Tet Offensive: a surprise attack launched on over a hundred South Vietnamese cities and towns by 70,000 North Vietnamese Army troops during the truce declared to celebrate Tet, the Vietnamese New Year. While it cost the lives of many North Vietnamese troops and left their military unstable, the Offensive is often considered a public relations defeat for the United States, as it made North Vietnam's military seem stronger than many believed and reduced the American public's drive to continue fighting the war.

Ho Chi Minh Trail: a complex network of paths, roads, and jungle trails leading from the panhandle of northern Vietnam through Laos and Cambodia and into southern Vietnam. The Trail was used throughout the Vietnam War to resupply the North Vietnamese military with food and weaponry, to transport soldiers into South Vietnam, and as a base to launch close-range attacks on South Vietnam.

"I can take you in this aisle," a store clerk offered as she unlocked a new register to accommodate the long line of customers. She gestured us to "come over here" with an upturned index finger, a disdainful hook we Vietnamese use to summon dogs and other domestic creatures. My mother did not understand the ambiguity of American hand gestures. In Vietnam, we said "Come here" to humans differently, with our palm up and all four fingers waved in unison—the way people over here waved goodbye. A typical Vietnamese signal beckoning someone to "come here" would prompt, in the United States, a "goodbye," a response completely opposite from the one desired.

"Even the store clerks look down on us," my mother grumbled as we 25
walked home. This was a truth I was only beginning to realize: it was not the enormous or momentous event, but the gradual suggestion of irrevocable and protracted change that threw us off balance and made us know in no uncertain terms that we would not be returning to the familiarity of our former lives.

It was, in many ways, a lesson in what was required to sustain a new identity: it all had to do with being able to adopt a different posture, to reach deep enough into the folds of the earth to relocate one's roots and bend one's body in a new direction, pretending at the same time that the world was the same now as it had been the day before. I strove for the ability to realign my eyes, to shift with a shifting world and convince both myself and the rest of the world into thinking that, if the earth moved and I moved along with it, that motion, however agitated, would be undetectable. The process, which was as surprising as a river reversing course and flowing upstream, was easier said than done.

RESPOND •

1. What's your initial response to this excerpt from Cao's novel? Given the mother's cultural expectations, which she has brought from Vietnam, is it logical for her to respond as she does? In what senses is Cao forced to parent her mother?
2. How does Cao construct the argument she makes here? What sorts of evidence does she rely on? How does she use language effectively to convey her ideas? (Chapters 6, 16, and 12, respectively, will help you answer these questions.)
3. The tale that Cao tells has been told many times in the writings of immigrants, especially those who arrive in the United States as children

with parents who speak little or no English. What are the consequences for family life? How does language become a source of power for the child? How does this power disrupt traditional patterns of family life?

4. Cao, like many immigrant children, lost much of her native language—Vietnamese—as well as French, another language widely spoken by educated Vietnamese at that time. (France had colonized Vietnam for many years prior to the war.) The decline in her ability to use these languages had negative repercussions for her relationship with her parents. As she commented in an interview given while she was a visiting law professor at Duke University, "The more educated I became, the more separate I was from my parents. I think that is a very immigrant story." Even native speakers of English who aren't from middle-class backgrounds often report similar situations in their own lives. Should such separation from one's home community be a necessary consequence of education for native or nonnative speakers of English in the United States? Why or why not? Might there be ways to prevent it? Are there benefits to preventing it? Should such efforts be made? Why? **Write an essay** in which you tackle these questions. Your essay will likely include features of evaluative, causal, and proposal arguments. If the situation described is unfamiliar to you, you might make a point of interviewing people who know about it firsthand.

Finding Myself through Language

ANDREA LO

Andrea Lo graduated from the Plan II Honors Program at the University of Texas at Austin in 2004 with a major in mathematics. She wrote this essay in a course entitled "Arguing about Language," which used an earlier edition of this textbook supplemented with additional readings focusing on popular debates about language and language issues, some of which appear in this chapter. Following graduation, Andrea took a position as a technical writer for National Instruments (NI) in Austin. In January 2006, she moved to Shanghai to supervise NI's growing team of technical writers there. One of her major goals while in Shanghai is to become fluent in Chinese. As you read, notice how Lo uses language—or the lack of it—to define who she is and isn't.

"Wo men dou shi zhong guo ren." *We are all Chinese.* These were the lyrics to the first song I learned at Chinese Sunday school. It's a song that brings a sense of national and cultural pride to millions of Chinese around the world. But for me, it was a song that represented a national and cultural identity of which I didn't want to be—and indeed of which I *wasn't*—a part. I was not Chinese. Growing up in the American school system, I recited the Pledge of Allegiance each day and sang the American national anthem every Monday morning. I was born of Chinese blood, but I was born and raised in the USA. I was Chinese-*American,* and I was adamant in making that distinction.

Of course I couldn't drop the "Chinese" altogether. People always questioned my nationality based on my appearance, which was something I could never change. Even if I dyed my hair blonde and wore blue contact lenses, nobody would believe I was anything but Asian. So I settled for "Chinese-American," using the word "Chinese" as if it was simply a qualifier to account for my physical appearance. "I'm American even though I look Chinese." If it had been grammatically acceptable, I probably even would have said I was "chinese-American"—with a lowercase "c"—after all my efforts to minimize that portion of my identity that fell before the hyphen. And, indeed, I expended a great deal of energy on this project.

I rejected numerous aspects of Chinese culture. I refused to watch the Chinese soap operas and Hong Kong dramas that my parents and grandparents loved. I grew to dislike Chinese furniture and Chinese art, and I dreaded learning about any era in China's expansive history. I even began to feel uncomfortable around my group of friends, who were often peers from Chinese school or children of my parents' close friends and therefore of Asian descent like me. Terms like "Asian pride" were popular with my Asian friends, who scrawled it across their notebooks and shouted it out in the hallways, but those words made me cringe. I didn't want to get "stuck" in the Asian crowd and be stigmatized or stereotyped because of them.

Most importantly, however, I rejected the Chinese language. As is the experience for many American children of non-English-speaking parents, I was ashamed of my parents' native tongue. I clearly remember the day in elementary school when I had to present my family tree to the class. All of the other children were talking about Adams and Walkers and Johnsons. One boy could

Closed sign (in Chinese and English)

even trace his lineage back to Johnny Appleseed. But my family tree was full of strange names like Sau Kam Siu and Wing Wa Lo that nobody—except me—could pronounce properly or gracefully, let alone recognize. I could feel my ears burning as I read out the names of my family members and heard the snickers of my classmates. They were laughing because my family's names were Chinese. Perhaps this is understandable. People tend to laugh at things that sound odd to them, and surely a foreign language can sound strange to one's ears. But for me at the time, my classmates' laughter was a signal of exclusion. If Chinese names were "different," then, by extension, so was I.

This experience and others, like the time a boy shouted "Ching chang 5
chong" when he passed me on the track during gym, made me embarrassed about the Chinese language. I made the conscious effort to *avoid* learning it with the hope that I would never be associated with it or humiliated by it again. When my parents spoke to me at home in Cantonese, I would no longer respond to them in the same language. Instead, I would insist on speaking in English. In Chinese Sunday school—which I was forced to attend—I exerted effort only to get a good grade but not to learn the language. My grades were a quantitative measure that my parents could manipulate by praising or punishing me. My actual retention of the language was something over which they had no control. Therefore, I would memorize Chinese

characters on Saturday night, regurgitate them the following morning, and promptly forget about them for the rest of the week. In this way, then, I tried to distance myself from the language that had been the source of so much humiliation. I threw away Chinese and embraced English, hoping that in doing so I could erase all my Chinese connections.

Soon, my knowledge of Mandarin consisted only of those words that I had involuntarily retained from Chinese school lessons. My spoken Cantonese was so poor that I could no longer hold an extended conversation with my own grandparents, who speak only Cantonese. My rejection of the Chinese language had thus severed my ties to members of my own family. However, it never succeeded in guaranteeing my acceptance as an American. For example, my elementary and middle-school classmates could observe that I couldn't converse in Chinese with new students who came from Taiwan or Hong Kong. Yet in the ninth grade, when I told them about my upcoming move to China for my father's job, few could understand my fear of going to this new country. They assumed that for me it would be like "going home."

Moving to Beijing made my struggle to establish an American identity even more difficult. There, despite the fact that, for once, I looked like the millions of people around me, I felt like I was in a sea of foreigners. I felt like I was the American in a crowd of Chinese faces. But the Chinese in Beijing didn't consider me to be American. For them, anybody of Chinese blood was a Chinese person. I just didn't make a very "good" Chinese person because I didn't know how to speak "my" language. I was reprimanded by everybody from my parents' coworkers to our telephone repairman for not knowing how to speak my "native" tongue. Many white Americans or other Caucasian foreigners in Beijing didn't see me as an American, either. I was just one of the many indistinguishable faces in the vast Chinese sea.

In Asia, then, as in the United States, cultivating an ignorance of the Chinese language was not sufficient for me to reject my Chinese identity or to establish an American one. I, therefore, placed more emphasis on my knowledge of and fluency in English in order to justify my claim to being American. I attended international schools with students from all around the world, yet I gravitated towards the native English speakers when building my social networks. I volunteered to teach conversational English in local Hong Kong schools, making sure to tell my students from the first day that I didn't speak Cantonese, that I was a native speaker of English, and that I wasn't from Hong Kong. I was American.

I wasn't the only one in my family to use English in this way. Walking through the street markets in China, I noticed my brother would always make a comment in English about a piece of clothing or an interesting piece of art each time a Caucasian person would pass by. More often than not, my brother's comment would cause the Caucasian person to look our way in surprise. It didn't matter if the person was American or not. My brother's intention was solely to differentiate himself from the rest of the Chinese around him. He wanted people to know he was American, and he demonstrated this fact by speaking fluent English with a clearly American accent.

I returned to the U.S. after three-and-a-half years in Asia. After learning of 10
my experiences, people would often ask me if I were fluent in Chinese. Before my trip to China, I was often expected to speak Chinese simply because I looked Chinese. Now, people expected me to speak Chinese because I had spent a significant amount of time in China. I used to have a reason for my ignorance, but now I no longer did. I had no excuse for spending more than three years in a foreign country and never learning its language.

I realized that in my determination to reject learning about Chinese culture as *my* culture, I had also rejected learning about it as a *new* culture. I had buried myself in the international communities, emphasizing each of my ties to American culture. Meanwhile, I had failed to explore the local communities that were just around the corner. I had been so caught up in using language to create my own identity that I had ignored its utility in learning about others. Knowing how to speak Chinese, regardless of my ethnic background, could have enabled me to speak with people of the local culture, to learn from them about their beliefs, their values, and their way of life. It could have helped me to learn about their history and their politics and to develop meaningful relationships with them on a more personal level. I denied myself of all these opportunities simply by rejecting the language.

I also realize now that the culture I failed to learn about while living in China is an inseparable part of my own heritage. The Chinese names on my family tree aren't just names—they are my family and my history. They are indeed "different" from typically Caucasian names, and I am indeed "different" from Caucasians, but this fact should not be the source of shame. Adopting a family with names that are easier to pronounce or changing the history of which my family was a part will not make me feel any more accepted in this predominantly Caucasian society. I was born in America to Chinese parents. Because of that, both the American and Chinese cultures have helped to shape who I am. Growing up, I used language in an attempt to reject one and adopt the other. But I understand now that renouncing the Chinese language can never erase my Chinese heritage, nor can embracing the English language uniquely write me a new personal history.

I still choose to make the distinction that I'm not Chinese but Chinese-American. The "Chinese," however, is no longer a qualifier to account for my appearance. Instead, it's a part of me that is equal in importance to the "American" that follows. Of course, I still have much to learn about Chinese culture and about my own family's Chinese background in order to discover how these cultural influences have shaped my own behavior and identity. But now I know exactly where to begin in this exploration. I should begin with the part of the culture that I once tried the hardest to reject. The place for me to begin is in the language. I may not be able to become literate in Chinese quickly or easily, but I hope to at least regain my fluency in the language. Learning to speak Cantonese will allow me to rebuild connections with my family members. It will give me a greater understanding of Hong Kong life and culture—the life and culture that my own parents and grandparents experienced before coming to America. If nothing else, learning to speak Cantonese will be a constant reminder of that part of my identity that I was once so keen to ignore and that I am now so lucky to still have the opportunity to embrace.

Among the elements in Lo's finely crafted essay are definition arguments exploring what it means to be labeled *Chinese* and *American*. See Chapter 8 for more on making definition arguments.

LINK TO P. 232

RESPOND •

1. How does this essay recount Lo's changing understanding of her own identity and the roles that language and labels have played in it? In what ways has she let Chinese define her identity, even as (or perhaps because) she struggled against it?
2. What might Lo's comment in paragraph 2 that " 'I'm American even though I look Chinese' " mean? After all, she was born in the United States. What does an American look like? What does it mean when Americans say "You don't look American" to someone like Lo?
3. One memorable aspect of this essay is its use of crisp detail. Choose three specific examples of detail that Lo uses, explaining how each contributes to her point, both in the paragraph in which the detail occurs and in the essay overall.
4. Lo's essay focuses on the knowledge and use of a language other than English—perhaps one of the most salient examples of negotiating an identity through language in the United States, where the majority of citizens seem to take pride in being monolingual. Yet all Americans must, in some sense, find themselves through language. **Write an essay** in which you recount your own efforts to do so—to understand the varieties of language or the languages you've had access to in your life as well as, perhaps, your efforts to change them. There will likely be aspects of definitional, evaluative, and causal argumentation in your essay—and perhaps a proposal about the future, as there is for Lo.

Mary Pipher, who has received the American Psychological Association's Presidential Citation for her research, writing, and other professional work, is the author of several books, including Reviving Ophelia: Saving the Selves of Adolescent Girls *(1995),* The Shelter of Each Other: Rebuilding American Families *(2003), and* The Middle of Everywhere: Helping Refugees Enter the American Community *(2002), from which these selections come. Her newest book,* Writing to Change the World *(2006), should have appeared by the time you're reading this textbook. Pipher's work combines her training in anthropology and clinical psychology as she examines the complex links between mental health and culture.*

In The Middle of Everywhere, *Pipher seeks to document and analyze the experiences of refugees, those who come to the United States in order to escape oppressive political regimes, as they become part of American society. In preparing to write this book, Pipher worked for several years with various refugee communities, conducting research among them, in Lincoln, Nebraska, where she lives. In these two passages, "Language" and "High School," Pipher explains why language itself represents a barrier for refugees—and, indeed, all immigrants—and why the experience of going to an American high school is especially challenging for them. As you read, note how Pipher tries to explain to a general audience why adolescent refugees, in particular, find it challenging to fit into American culture while still being part of their families—all without forgetting the past that brought them and their families here.*

From *The Middle of Everywhere*

Helping Refugees Enter the American Community

MARY PIPHER

LANGUAGE

How does Pipher make refugees more real to the reader? Chapter 2 addresses how to use arguments from the heart to build a bridge between the author and reader.

LINK TO P. 51

It takes most people from one to three years to learn social English and five to seven years to learn academic English. At first, refugees feel like children: vulnerable, dependent, and unable to express themselves. An educated man communicates only via hand signals and a few simple phrases. A doctor cannot ask for a glass of water. A teacher cannot understand her first-grade son's homework. Simple tasks, such as exchanging a pair of shoes or making a dental appointment, are complex without language. The intelligence, personality, and energy of new arrivals are submerged by their lack of English. We Americans just see the tip of the iceberg.

Language is connected to both good judgment and to forming relationships. Humans trust or mistrust others on the basis of nuances, tonal variations, and small contradictions. Without language, we miss metaphors and subtleties. We cannot read between the lines or sense what is not being said. We can't convey character or style. Imagine yourself applying for jobs, negotiating bureaucracies, and making friends with a working vocabulary of one hundred words. "Hi." "Thank you." "Where is the bathroom?" "Good morning." "You're welcome."

English isn't phonetic° and has an amazing number of irregular verbs and plural nouns. It's filled with slang, academic jargon, and technical terms. Rules for prepositions and punctuation seem arbitrary. Many words sound alike, such as *writing* and *riding, a basement* and *abasement,* or *aunt* and *ant.*

phonetic: here, pronounced as written or written as pronounced. While in some languages, like Italian and Spanish, the links between sounds and letters are fairly unambiguous, they aren't in English, where we find many silent letters and many ways to spell a single sound.

And learning the language isn't enough. Certain people may speak Spanish but have limited understanding of the culture of Cuba. Likewise, one may know about the customs of a culture without being able to speak its language. To really become American, refugees must become both bilingual and bicultural.

HIGH SCHOOL

5 Refugees are allowed to attend our high schools until they are twenty-one. Many have to drop out and work, but those who can stay feel lucky to be in high school. Many of the students work after school, both part-time and full-time jobs. Others go home to clean, cook, and care for younger siblings while their parents work. One Guatemalan student, who was in Nebraska without parents, worked all night at a factory. A Croatian student supported her family by working in housekeeping at a downtown hotel.

The teachers' biggest challenge is helping students with English vocabularies of two-year-olds to feel respected as adults. These students can express so little of what they are thinking and feeling. Mainstream classes are hard. Often students don't have prerequisites. Some teachers talk too fast and won't repeat.

The students make small but significant mistakes. A Bosnian girl, assigned a report on Stokely Carmichael,° misunderstood and researched

Stokely Carmichael (1941–1998): Trinidadian-born U.S. civil rights activist, generally associated with the Black Power movement and the use of the phrase "Black is Beautiful." In 1978, he adopted the name Kwame Ture in honor of two of sub-Saharan Africa's best-known socialist leaders, Kwame Nkrumah of Ghana and Ahmed Sekou Toure of Guinea. Carmichael spent most of the last three decades of his life in Guinea, advocating Pan-African socialism.

Hoagy Carmichael° for her political science class. One Kurdish girl liked the flower-covered packaging of a box of raspberry douche. She thought it was perfume or lotion and bought it for the school gift exchange. Fortunately a teacher intercepted this gift and found something less personal for her to give her seat mate.

ELL° students are often smart and eager. They speak several languages and possess many life skills. However, because of language problems, many have low ACT° scores. The older students are at the time they start American schools, the more difficult it is for them to catch up. Sometimes students surmount all the academic hurdles and are accepted to college, but then they do not have the right INS° paperwork to qualify for loans or grants.

Many of the students feel tremendous pressure to succeed. Their parents have literally risked their lives so that they can go to school. And yet some start from far behind their American peers—some students don't know that the earth revolves around the sun. They've never heard of gravity, of germs, or of fractions.

Between past traumas and present stresses, students are often upset. 10
Many report headaches, stomachaches, tiredness, or dizziness. During class, students periodically "check out." Their teachers touch them gently and say their names to bring them back to the classroom. Other times, students are so anxious they run out of the room or burst into tears. Small changes in the classroom trigger anxiety. A loud noise or a chair falling can make them jump. The regular Wednesday 10:15 A.M. civil defense siren upsets students. Many are fearful of thunderstorms and tornadoes.

These students are expected to have a lot of emotional stretch. A Bosnian student whose father was killed two weeks earlier came to his first day of school. He had no friends and spoke no English. At the same time he was grieving his father's death, he was learning the states and capitals and how to work American machine tools.

Some students express their emotional difficulties with cruel practical jokes, bullying, and harsh teasing. Many come from places where homosexuals are feared, reviled, and even killed, and hence many are homophobic. Once some ELL students made fun of a special education student who couldn't talk. Their teacher dealt with that by teaching them about mental handicaps. She encouraged students to befriend handicapped students and learn more about their experiences. Some refugees come from places where handicapped people are not respected. Their teacher said, "We are in America now. At school everyone deserves respect for trying to learn."

Refugee students in high school seem more affected by poverty than do younger kids. They are more sensitive about class and status differences. Except for the gang kids, the ELL students can't afford the designer clothes

Hoagy Carmichael (1899–1981): Indiana-born white jazz musician, songwriter, singer, actor, radio star, and author. He's the composer of "Heart and Soul," a piano duet known to all Americans who have studied piano and many who haven't.

ELL: English Language Learners, the term educators use for students who are learning English while they're also learning academic subjects.

ACT: a standardized test required by some schools for college admission. The name of the test derives from the name of the company that developed it, ACT (pronounced A-C-T), which was originally American College Testing.

INS: Immigration and Naturalization Service, the branch of the U.S. government that formerly dealt with matters relating to immigration and naturalization (that is, becoming a U.S. citizen). In 2002, the INS was reorganized and divided into Citizenship and Immigration Services, Immigration and Customs Enforcement, and Border and Customs Protection, all of which are part of the Office of Homeland Security.

many American kids wear. Most wear Goodwill clothes, although some kids do amazingly well with what they pull from used clothing boxes. Other kids have parents who spend their meager salaries buying them a pair of designer jeans or Doc Martins. One particularly cold year a teacher bought all the ELL kids hats and gloves for the holidays. Several marveled that they had something actually new to wear.

Some teens learn all the wrong things about America. Instead of listening to their teachers, they listen to their peers, the media, and ads. Sometimes when parents realize they have lost control and that their children are in trouble, they return to their old countries to save the teenager from American problems.

Boys, especially, are trapped in a weird bind. Their peers teach them that 15
"to act white" is to be disloyal to their ethnic group. Studying, making good grades, being polite, or joining school clubs are all defined as "acting white." So the boys must choose between social acceptance by peers and meeting parental expectations. Many conform their way into being rebellious at school. They learn not to learn.

The Vietnamese gang boys are a good example of the perils and complexity of cultural switching. They are an odd combination of playful and tough. They often take on a "tough guise" in class. But they don't date and many work after school and hand their mothers their checks. When a community celebration occurs, they show up with their families and act like good sons, but some are dealing drugs, stealing cars, and robbing their own people.

There are Bosnian gangs, Kurdish gangs, and Latino gangs as well. The gangs meet two legitimate needs—the need for a peer community and the need for power. Gangs are default communities that exist because there is nothing better.

However, in spite of some sad stories, results from the National Longitudinal Study of Adolescent Health show a remarkably high level of general adjustment in refugee kids. They tend to make grades that are equal to or better than those of American kids and they are less likely to drop out of school. They are physically and mentally healthier. As teens they are less likely than American kids to use drugs and alcohol, to be obese, or to have asthma. This study found a high level of self-esteem compared to native-born kids. In fact, with acculturation, the well-being of refugee students actually decreases. The longer kids are in America, the less time they spend on homework and the more likely they are to be sexually active.

On the surface, it seems as if American teens would be happier than refugee teens. They generally have more money and fewer obstacles in their paths. However, American kids have much more exposure to a toxic media culture than do most of the refugee kids. They don't necessarily have the newcomer zest of refugee kids. Also, being useful gives humans great pride and satisfaction. Overcoming obstacles and transcending difficulties builds self-regard. Refugee students know they are vital to their family's functioning. American kids sometimes feel like they are a drain on family resources.

RESPOND •

1. Pipher clearly believes that language presents a great challenge for refugees. How does she characterize the nature of this challenge? How persuasive is she? Why?
2. In the excerpt on language, Pipher notes that "It takes most people from one to three years to learn social English and five to seven years to learn academic English" (paragraph 1), a claim that much research supports. How is this claim in conflict with movements like California's Proposition 227, discussed in the opening selection of this chapter, "Just 180 Days to Learn Miwok"? Why, in your opinion, might some Americans want to assume that schoolchildren coming from homes where a language other than English is used can master English sufficiently within a school year?
3. What challenges in particular do high-school-aged refugees face at school? As Pipher describes American high schools, only a small part of what occurs there involves the mastery of information learned in classes. What other developmental tasks are high-school-aged students engaging in? (Here, *developmental task* means any task related to growing up or to becoming an adult member of American culture.) Given the background and life experience of refugees, why are these tasks particularly difficult for them?
4. As noted, Pipher's book grew out of her work with and research on refugees in her city of Lincoln, Nebraska. Investigate refugees in your hometown or area or in the town, city, or area where you're attending school or college. (If you have trouble finding or getting information about refugees, you may wish to investigate the much broader category of immigrants.) **Write an essay** about your findings. You may wish to describe and define some of the characteristics of that population, evaluate some aspect of their needs and the extent to which the local community is meeting those needs, or propose how the community might do a better job of understanding and meeting those needs. If you live in an area where there are refugees (or immigrants) from many areas, you may wish to focus on a single group or even a subgroup—for example, the situation of Sudanese Christian adolescent girls.

"En la comunidad latina tenemos una cultura de silencio".
—Rodolfo Palma-Lulión, Estudiante Universitario
Real Men. Real Depression.
Estos hombres son reales.
La depresión también.
"Nadie tiene depresión en la comunidad latina. En la comunidad latina tenemos una cultura de silencio en ciertos aspectos de nuestra vida. Especialmente como inmigrantes trabajamos duro. Eso es lo que se espera. Y decir que uno tiene depresión es como dejar que la vida te gane". La depresión es una enfermedad real que se puede tratar con éxito. Para más información, llame al 1-866-227-6464, visite www.nimh.nih.gov, o contacte a su médico.
Hay que tener valor para solicitar ayuda. Rodolfo lo hizo.
NIMH
National Institute of Mental Health
National Institutes of Health

Idiomatic translation for the NIMH poster:

"In the Latino community, we have a culture of silence."

–Rodolfo Palma-Lulión, University Student

These men are real.
So is depression.

"No one in the Latino community suffers from depression. In the Latino community, we have a culture of silence about certain aspects of our life. Especially, as immigrants, we work hard. That's what's expected. And to say that you're depressed is like letting life defeat you." Depression is a real illness that can be treated successfully. For more information, call 1-866-227-6464, visit www.nimh.nih.gov, or contact your doctor.

You have to be brave to ask for help. Rodolfo did it.

National Institute of Mental Health, *En la comunidad latina tenemos una cultura de silencio.*

▲ *Here we present a bilingual advertisement from the National Institutes of Health that represents and, in some real sense, comments on bilingualism in America. The National Institute of Mental Health (NIMH), which is a part of the U.S. Department of Health and Human Services, is devoted to awareness, advocacy, and research for mental and behavioral disorders. This poster is part of a campaign to raise awareness about depression in men, with outreach that includes public service announcements, publications, and a Web site (at <http://nimh.nih.gov>).*

If the text of this poster were reprinted without the photo of the young man, it would probably have much less impact on its intended audience. Chapter 14 highlights the importance of visuals in argumentation.

LINK TO P. 412

RESPOND •

1. The advertisement for the National Institute of Mental Health (NIMH) is primarily in Spanish. Why? How do language choice and targeted audience interact in this advertisement? Why might the designers have included the phrase "Real Men. Real Depression." in English?
2. Evaluate this advertisement as an argument. What roles does the personal testimony of Rodolfo Palma-Lulión play in the advertisement? Does it matter that Palma-Lulión is a university student? Why or why not? Are the design and layout of the advertisement effective and appropriate? Why or why not?
3. Some Americans might criticize NIMH for producing advertisements or running programs in any language other than English. What arguments might they use for such criticisms? What costs might there be if NIMH doesn't produce advertisements or design programs in languages other than English?
4. Bilingualism is part of daily life in a growing number of places in the United States. Find two advertisements that include a language other than English, and then **write an evaluative essay** in which you compare them and evaluate which is likely more effective as an argument in reaching the targeted audience, which you'll have to define. (After all, billboard advertisements in Spanish for Mexican beer near a major university in Central Texas may be targeted as much at students who know no Spanish other than *cerveza* as at those native or nonnative speakers who are fluent in the language.) Billboards in many cities, signs and flyers in certain neighborhoods, and advertisements in certain magazines are sometimes in a language other than English or are bilingual in some way. Be sure to include copies of the advertisements you analyze in or with your evaluative essay. (For discussions of rhetorical analysis and evaluative arguments, respectively, see Chapters 5 and 9.)

▼ *We began this chapter with a cartoon about bilingualism, specifically bilingual education; here we present a news article on the same topics from the* New York Times *regular column "On Education." The article, part news, part feature, was written by Samuel G. Freedman, an education columnist for the* Times, *where this article first appeared in July 2004. Freedman is also an award-winning author and award-winning professor of journalism at Columbia University. His books include* Letters to a Young Journalist *(2006);* Who She Was: My Search for My Mother's Life *(2005);* Jew vs. Jew: The Struggle for the Soul of American Jewry *(2000);* The Inheritance: How Three Families and America Moved from Roosevelt to Reagan and Beyond *(1996);* Upon This Rock: The Miracles of a Black Church *(1993); and* Small Victories: The Real World of a Teacher, Her Students and Their High School *(1990). As you read Freedman's comments, consider why Latino parents from different countries might have different responses to the idea of bilingual education.*

On Education

It's Latino Parents Speaking Out on Bilingual Education Failures

SAMUEL G. FREEDMAN

On a sultry night in late June, when the school term was nearly over, two dozen parents gathered in a church basement in Brooklyn to talk about what a waste the year had been. Immigrants from Mexico and the Dominican Republic, raising their children in the battered neighborhood of Bushwick, they were the people bilingual education supposedly serves. Instead, one after the other, they condemned a system that consigned their children to a linguistic ghetto, cut off from the United States of integration and upward mobility.

These parents were not gadflies and chronic complainers. Patient and quiet, the women clad in faded shifts, the men shod in oil-stained work boots, they exuded the aura of people reluctant to challenge authority, perhaps because they ascribed wisdom to people with titles, or perhaps because they feared retribution.

With the ballast of one another's company, however, they spoke. Gregorio Ortega spoke about how his son Geraldo, born right here in New York, had been abruptly transferred into a bilingual class at P.S. 123 after spending his first four school years learning in English. Irene De Leon spoke of her daughter being placed in a bilingual section at P.S. 123 despite having done her first year and a half of school in English when the family lived in Queens. Benerita Salsedo wondered aloud why, after four years in the bilingual track at P.S. 145 in Bushwick, her son Alberto still had not moved into English classes. Her two other children were also stuck in bilingual limbo.

Freedman's article is a proposal argument for English immersion classes in the public school system. Does his presentation of bilingual versus English immersion programs approach the fallacy of "either-or choices"? Read about different emotional argument fallacies in Chapter 17.

LINK TO P. 493

"I'm very angry," Ms. Salsedo said in Spanish through an interpreter. "The school is supposed to do what's best for the kids. The school puts my kids' education in danger, because everything is in English here."

5 And the children had no trouble expressing their own frustration lucidly enough in English. "I ask the teacher all the time if I can be in English class," said Alberto, a 9-year-old who will enter sixth grade in the fall. "The teacher just says no." For the time being, Alberto added, he learns English by watching the Cartoon Network.

Listening to this litany, I experienced the sensation that Yogi Berra memorably called "déjà vu° all over again." Five years earlier, in the rectory of another church only a few blocks away, another group of immigrant parents voiced the identical complaints about bilingual education—that the public schools shunted Latino children into it even if those pupils had been born in the United States and previously educated in English, and that once the child was in the bilingual track it was almost impossible to get out. An association of Bushwick parents, virtually all of them Hispanic immigrants, had gone as far as suing in State Supreme Court in a futile attempt to reform the bilingual program in local schools.

Back then, the school system's many critics ascribed the bilingual fiasco in Bushwick largely to the failed policy of decentralization. What "community control" meant then in Bushwick was a school district dominated by the neighborhood's City Council member, Victor Robles (now the city clerk). School jobs, including those in bilingual education, were patronage plums.

For years, bilingual education coasted along on its perception as a virtual civil right for Hispanics. Maybe such a reputation was deserved 30 years ago, when the Puerto Rican Legal Defense Fund sued and won a consent decree° requiring that New York City offer bilingual education. But as the innovation hardened into an orthodoxy, and as a sort of employment niche grew for bilingual educators and bureaucrats, the idealistic veneer began to wear away.

The grievances of Bushwick's parents point at an overlooked truth. The foes of bilingual education, at least as practiced in New York, are not Eurocentric nativists but Spanish-speaking immigrants who struggled to reach the United States and struggle still at low-wage jobs to stay here so that their children can acquire and rise with an American education, very much including fluency in English.

10 As a candidate for mayor, Michael R. Bloomberg assailed the status quo in bilingual education and called for its replacement with English-immersion classes. His pledge rested on firm ground. Reports commissioned by Chancellor Ramon Cortines in 1994 and Mayor Rudolph W. Giuliani in 2000 concluded that children qualified for mainstream classes more rapidly coming from English as a Second Language programs than from bilingual ones. E.S.L. classes take place largely in English; bilingual education in the students' native language.

déjà vu: a French expression meaning "the experience of having already seen something in another context"; hence Berra's phrase "*déjà vu* all over again," while redundant on one level, is frequently used to refer to situations, usually unfortunate, that recur.

consent decree: a judicial decision, often one in which the accused agrees to cease the activities that the plaintiff claims are illegal without having to acknowledge any guilt.

With decentralization dismantled in 2002 and a hand-picked school chancellor installed the next year, Mayor Bloomberg seemingly backed away. Diana Lam, the top aide to Chancellor Joel I. Klein until her ouster, was both a product and proponent of traditional bilingualism. The mayor now emphasizes improving the existing bilingual program, despite its demonstrable shortcomings.

With Ms. Lam gone, perhaps the mayor and Mr. Klein can fulfill their erstwhile pledges. Carmen Fariña, the new deputy chancellor, yesterday promised large-scale reforms beginning next September. What she means by that is not junking bilingual education or even curtailing its use as much as improving teacher training and incorporating clear performance standards and oversight. Yet the Department of Education already has a highly successful model of E.S.L. instruction in two existing high schools, Bronx International and La Guardia International.

"Bushwick is a test case of how bilingual programs are actually being implemented," said Michael Gecan, a national organizer for the Industrial Areas Foundation, which has worked closely with parents there for more than a decade. "We have great confidence in Klein. We've found him to be very responsive and very aggressive. But we've been concerned about the bilingual effort. This is a large vestige of the old school culture. It remains in the system. And it's intensively guarded by the local politicians and the teachers' union."

In one respect, though, the bilingual program in Bushwick did subscribe to the English-immersion approach. Parent after parent in the church basement last month remembered receiving, and then naively signing, a letter from school that apparently constituted their agreement to having a child put into bilingual classes. The letter, recalled these Spanish-speaking parents, was written only in English.

RESPOND •

1. As in most newspaper arguments, and especially in columns that comment on contemporary issues while including quotations from various parties, this article includes several simultaneous arguments. What argument(s) are the Latino parents from Mexico and the Dominican Republic making? What argument is the mayor's office making? What argument is the Industrial Areas Foundation making? Finally, what argument is Freedman making?
2. As Freedman notes, bilingual education remains a very controversial topic in New York City. Why do recent Latino immigrants—Mexicans and Dominicans—oppose the idea of bilingual education? Freedman also refers to a lawsuit filed by the Puerto Rican Legal Defense Fund, dating from 1973, that mandated bilingual education in New York City. In this case, *Aspira vs. Board of Education of the City of New York*, Aspira, a group of middle-class Puerto Rican professionals, successfully filed suit against the city's Board of Education, arguing that the school board's programs didn't meet the needs of Puerto Rican students, especially those who didn't speak English well. Why might Puerto Ricans, in particular, have been and remain supportive of bilingual education? (Freedman doesn't discuss this issue. If you don't know the answer, you'll need to do some research to get information about the

linguistic situation on Puerto Rico, a self-governing commonwealth of the United States. Although Puerto Ricans are U.S. citizens, they can't vote in federal elections, nor do they pay taxes.)

3. How does Freedman use the trope of irony in this article, especially in its ending? (For a discussion of irony, see Chapter 12.)
4. Freedman's article points to several issues that are often overlooked in discussions of bilingual education, including diversity within the Latino community with respect to the need for or value of bilingual education and the issue of the existence of bilingual education programs versus their implementation. Research one of these topics, and then **write an essay** in which you evaluate the range of attitudes you find. In presenting your findings, rather than focusing on whose view is correct and whose is incorrect, seek to demonstrate the internal logic of each position, given the assumptions made by those who hold that opinion and the evidence they attend to or fail to attend to.

This selection, an excerpt from Funny in Farsi: A Memoir of Growing Up Iranian in America *(2003), is Firoozeh Dumas' often hilarious account of what happens when language and cultures come in contact and often collide as they inevitably do in the children of immigrants. (By the way, Farsi is another name for the Persian language, which is the most widely spoken language in Iran.) In "The 'F Word,'" Dumas describes how Americans in general deal (or fail to deal) with names from languages unfamiliar to them. Dumas explains how dealing with this situation is part of the immigrant experience for those from many language backgrounds. As you read, note how she employs humor and figurative language, using the latter even as a structural device.*

The "F Word"

FIROOZEH DUMAS

My cousin's name, Farbod, means "Greatness." When he moved to America, all the kids called him "Farthead." My brother Farshid ("He Who Enlightens") became "Fartshit." The name of my friend Neggar means "Beloved," although it can be more accurately translated as "She Whose Name Almost Incites Riots." Her brother Arash ("Giver") initially couldn't understand why every time he'd say his name, people would laugh and ask him if it itched.

Humor is the underlying thread in this book excerpt. Does Dumas' humor increase the interest and appeal of her argument? Chapter 13 offers a guide to developing your own humorous arguments.

LINK TO P. 407

All of us immigrants knew that moving to America would be fraught with challenges, but none of us thought that our names would be such an obstacle. How could our parents have ever imagined that someday we would end up in a country where monosyllabic names reign supreme, a land where "William" is shortened to "Bill," where "Susan" becomes "Sue," and "Richard" somehow evolves into "Dick"? America is a great country, but nobody without a mask and a cape has a z in his name. And have Americans ever realized the great scope of the guttural sounds they're missing? Okay, so it has to do with linguistic roots, but I do believe this would be a richer country if all Americans could do a little tongue aerobics and learn to pronounce "kh," a sound more commonly associated in this culture with phlegm, or "gh," the sound usually made by actors in the final moments of a choking scene. It's like adding a few new spices to the kitchen pantry. Move over, cinnamon and nutmeg, make way for cardamom° and sumac.°

cardamom: a spice commonly used in the Middle East, South Asia, and East Asia.

sumac: a dark red, sour-tasting spice used in many Middle Eastern cuisines.

Exotic analogies aside, having a foreign name in this land of Joes and Marys is a pain in the spice cabinet. When I was twelve, I decided to simplify my life by adding an American middle name. This decision serves as proof that sometimes simplifying one's life in the short run only complicates it in the long run.

My name, Firoozeh, chosen by my mother, means "Turquoise" in Farsi. In America, it means "Unpronounceable" or "I'm Not Going to Talk to You Because I Cannot Possibly Learn Your Name and I Just Don't Want to Have to Ask You Again and Again Because You'll Think I'm Dumb or You Might Get Upset or Something." My father, incidentally, had wanted to name me Sara. I do wish he had won that argument.

To strengthen my decision to add an American name, I had just finished 5
fifth grade in Whittier, where all the kids incessantly called me "Ferocious." That summer, my family moved to Newport Beach, where I looked forward to starting a new life. I wanted to be a kid with a name that didn't draw so much attention, a name that didn't come with a built-in inquisition as to when and why I had moved to America and how was it that I spoke English without an accent and was I planning on going back and what did I think of America?

My last name didn't help any. I can't mention my maiden name, because:

"Dad, I'm writing a memoir."

"Great! Just don't mention our name."

Suffice it to say that, with eight letters, including a z, and four syllables, my last name is as difficult and foreign as my first. My first and last name together generally served the same purpose as a high brick wall. There was one exception to this rule. In Berkeley, and only in Berkeley, my name drew people like flies to baklava. These were usually people named Amaryllis or Chrysanthemum, types who vacationed in Costa Rica and to whom lentils described a type of burger. These folks were probably not the pride of Poughkeepsie, but they were refreshingly nonjudgmental.

When I announced to my family that I wanted to add an American name, 10
they reacted with their usual laughter. Never one to let mockery or good judgment stand in my way, I proceeded to ask for suggestions. My father suggested "Fifi." Had I had a special affinity for French poodles or been considering a career in prostitution, I would've gone with that one. My mom suggested "Farah," a name easier than "Firoozeh" yet still Iranian. Her reasoning made sense, except that Farrah Fawcett was at the height of her popularity and I didn't want to be associated with somebody whose poster hung in every postpubescent boy's bedroom. We couldn't think of any American

names beginning with F, so we moved on to *J*, the first letter of our last name. I don't know why we limited ourselves to names beginning with my initials, but it made sense at that moment, perhaps by the logic employed moments before bungee jumping. I finally chose the name "Julie" mainly for its simplicity. My brothers, Farid and Farshid, thought that adding an American name was totally stupid. They later became Fred and Sean.

That same afternoon, our doorbell rang. It was our new next-door neighbor, a friendly girl my age named Julie. She asked me my name and after a moment of hesitation, I introduced myself as Julie. "What a coincidence!" she said. I didn't mention that I had been Julie for only half an hour.

Thus I started sixth grade with my new, easy name and life became infinitely simpler. People actually remembered my name, which was an entirely refreshing new sensation. All was well until the Iranian Revolution,° when I found myself with a new set of problems. Because I spoke English without an accent and was known as Julie, people assumed I was American. This meant that I was often privy to their real feelings about those "damn I-raynians." It was like having those X-ray glasses that let you see people undressed, except that what I was seeing was far uglier than people's underwear. It dawned on me that these people would have probably never invited me to their house had they known me as Firoozeh. I felt like a fake.

Iranian Revolution: the series of events, beginning in 1979, that transformed Iran from a constitutional monarchy to a populist Islamic theocracy, first ruled by Ayatollah Khomeini. Americans associate the Revolution with the holding of 66 American hostages for a period of 444 days (1979–1981).

When I went to college, I eventually went back to using my real name. All was well until I graduated and started looking for a job. Even though I had graduated with honors from UC–Berkeley, I couldn't get a single interview. I was guilty of being a humanities major, but I began to suspect that there was more to my problems. After three months of rejections, I added "Julie" to my résumé. Call it coincidence, but the job offers started coming in. Perhaps it's the same kind of coincidence that keeps African Americans from getting cabs in New York.

Once I got married, my name became Julie Dumas. I went from having an identifiably "ethnic" name to having ancestors who wore clogs. My family and non-American friends continued calling me Firoozeh, while my coworkers and American friends called me Julie. My life became one big knot, especially when friends who knew me as Julie met friends who knew me as Firoozeh. I felt like those characters in soap operas who have an evil twin. The two, of course, can never be in the same room, since they're played by the same person, a struggling actress who wears a wig to play one of the twins and dreams of moving on to bigger and better roles. I couldn't blame my mess on a screenwriter; it was my own doing.

I decided to untangle the knot once and for all by going back to my real 15
name. By then, I was a stay-at-home mom, so I really didn't care whether people remembered my name or gave me job interviews. Besides, most of the people I dealt with were in diapers and were in no position to judge. I was also living in Silicon Valley, an area filled with people named Rajeev, Avishai, and Insook.

Every once in a while, though, somebody comes up with a new permutation and I am once again reminded that I am an immigrant with a foreign name. I recently went to have blood drawn for a physical exam. The waiting room for blood work at our local medical clinic is in the basement of the building, and no matter how early one arrives for an appointment, forty coughing, wheezing people have gotten there first. Apart from reading *Golf Digest* and *Popular Mechanics,* there isn't much to do except guess the number of contagious diseases represented in the windowless room. Every ten minutes, a name is called and everyone looks to see which cough matches that name. As I waited patiently, the receptionist called out, "Fritzy, Fritzy!" Everyone looked around, but no one stood up. Usually, if I'm waiting to be called by someone who doesn't know me, I will respond to just about any name starting with an F. Having been called Froozy, Frizzy, Fiorucci, and Frooz and just plain "Uhhhh . . . ," I am highly accommodating. I did not, however, respond to "Fritzy" because there is, as far as I know, no *t* in my name. The receptionist tried again, "Fritzy, Fritzy DumbAss." As I stood up to this most linguistically original version of my name, I could feel all eyes upon me. The room was momentarily silent as all of these sick people sat united in a moment of gratitude for their own names.

Despite a few exceptions, I have found that Americans are now far more willing to learn new names, just as they're far more willing to try new ethnic foods. Of course, some people just don't like to learn. One mom at my children's school adamantly refused to learn my "impossible" name and instead settled on calling me "F Word." She was recently transferred to New York where, from what I've heard, she might meet an immigrant or two and, who knows, she just might have to make some room in her spice cabinet.

RESPOND •

1. How might you summarize Firoozeh Dumas' argument? What's its exact subject—the importance of names, the ways in which Americans have traditionally responded to unfamiliar names, the immigrant experience, all of these?
2. Carefully reread paragraph 12, in which Dumas explains how having an "American" name and speaking English without a foreign accent was like having "X-ray glasses." Is Dumas' portrayal of Americans in this passage and in the entire essay more broadly flattering? Humorous? Honest? In this passage, Dumas notes that "people assumed I was American." What definition of "American" must she (and those she writes about) be assuming? Is such a definition valid, given evidence she presents elsewhere in the essay and the fact that the United States likes to think of itself as a nation of immigrants? At what point does an immigrant become an American?
3. How would you describe Dumas' use of humor? Find three examples that you especially like, and explain how the humor helps the author achieve her goals. In what ways does Dumas' argument represent satire, with the simultaneous goals of ridiculing and remedying a problematic situation? (For a discussion of the uses of humor, including satire, in argumentation, see Chapter 13.)
4. How does Dumas use the repeated metaphor of the spice cabinet to help structure her argument? Why is this metaphor an appropriate one, given her topic? How does the metaphor permit her to critique the mother who called her "F Word" (paragraph 17)?
5. Chapter 5 explains how to write a rhetorical analysis of an argument, and Chapter 13 provides information on the uses of humor in argument. **Write a rhetorical analysis** of Dumas' argument with a focus on evaluating the contribution of humor to the overall effect. (One way to think about the contribution of humor to this argument is to imagine what the essay might have been like had Dumas tried to treat her subject in a more straightforward, serious manner.)

25
What Does Your Language Say about Your Identity?

Language isn't just a tool for communicating information. It also works as a symbol, a powerful one, that we use to create identities for ourselves as individuals and as members of myriad social groups. How we use language (whether spoken, signed, or written) tells others who we are or want to be—and whom we don't want to be mistaken for. Take a moment to list ten groups you belong to. Odds are that all these groups are defined in some way by the language they use or don't use.

The arguments in this chapter examine the topic of languages and identities from several perspectives. The questions raised here ask you to consider the roles that language in general and specific varieties of language in particular play in telling the world who you are and how you wish to be perceived. The chapter begins with a pledge distributed by the Chicago Women's Club about ninety years ago; its argument assumes there's a link between patriotism and the way someone speaks English. Do you agree? Should bilingualism be encouraged or discouraged? In what form? How should bilinguals be accommodated in American society? Essays by two successful writers, Ariel Dorfman and Chang-rae Lee, both born outside the United States, treat this complex topic. Amy Tan's much anthologized "Mother Tongue" adds to the discussion of language in immigrant households and American society. John Rickford's "Suite for Ebony *and* Phonics" and David D. Troutt's "Defining Who We Are in Society" treat a very contentious issue, Ebonics, a variety of American English spoken by many African Americans and some Americans of other ethnic backgrounds. Rickford and Troutt bring their expertise as a sociolinguist and a law professor, respectively, to bear on this topic. Next, a portfolio of advertisements aimed at encouraging young people not to get involved in illegal drugs illustrates how the ads' creators sought to use language that would speak to the intended audience. You get to decide whether or not they succeed. Steve Rushin's "Hip Unchecked" critiques language use in sports and television and a particular image such usage seeks to create. A selection from Deborah Tannen's latest book, *You're Wearing That? Understanding Mothers and Daughters in Conversation*, reminds us that identity categories include roles like parent and child, which are no less created and shaped by language use than are categories like ethnicity or social class. The chapter ends with a series of cartoons from the *New Yorker* about women's and men's efforts to communicate with one another despite the language they share.

"Don't believe everything you think"—or so states one of our favorite bumper-sticker arguments. The arguments in this chapter should challenge you to recognize and reexamine some of your assumptions about language and identity—your own and everyone else's.

This pledge was distributed by the Chicago Women's Club American Speech Committee to the schoolchildren of the city in 1918.

Pledge for Children

CHICAGO WOMEN'S CLUB

I love the United States of America. I love my country's flag.
I love my country's language. I promise:

1. That I will not dishonor my country's speech by leaving off the last syllables of words.
2. That I will say a good American "yes" and "no" in place of an Indian grunt "um-hum" and "nup-um" or a foreign "ya" or "yeh" and "nope."
3. That I will do my best to improve American speech by avoiding loud, rough tones, by enunciating clearly, and by speaking pleasantly, clearly, and sincerely.
4. That I will learn to articulate correctly as many words as possible during the year.

Not all proposal arguments about practices are as overt as this one. See examples of more subtle proposal arguments in Chapter 11.

LINK TO P. 352

RESPOND •

1. What sorts of arguments are being made by this pledge? In other words, how is Americanness defined in general? With respect to language use in particular? According to the pledge, how does the "ideal American," or the American who loves his or her country, speak?
2. According to the criteria of the pledge, do you qualify as an "ideal American"? Does that trouble you in any way? Why or why not? How do you think you'd respond if you'd been given such a pledge as, say, an eighth-grader? Why?
3. Consider the table on p. 796, which presents statistics about immigrants in Chicago in 1900, 1910, 1920, and 1990. At the time the pledge was issued, many of the immigrants living in Chicago had come from

Germany, Austria, Poland, and Russia and, to a far lesser extent, Ireland, Sweden, and Italy. Upon arrival, they were generally poor and uneducated. How do these figures, along with the 1918 pledge, construct an argument? What, specifically, is the argument?

Immigrants in Chicago

Year	*Population*	*Foreign Born*	*Foreign-born Stock**
1900	1,698,575	35%	77%
1910	2,185,283	36%	78%
1920	2,701,705	30%	72%
1990	2,783,726	17%	Not Available

*Foreign-born stock = Immigrants from other countries and their U.S.-born children.

4. You're certainly aware that immigration and immigrants continue to be hot topics in American public discourse, the subject of much debate. Does language become part of these debates? If so, how? For example, do people comment on the presence of other languages in public space (as discussed by Myriam Marquez, "Why and When We Speak Spanish in Public," p. 754), bilingual media or media in languages other than English, or the way English is spoken by immigrants or their descendants? What specific forms do these comments take? What do they tell us about language and identity among some Americans?

5. **Write an essay** analyzing the goals of the pledge in the historical context of the census data presented in question 3. Is the pledge, for example, a case of forensic, epideictic, or deliberative rhetoric? Why? (For a discussion of kinds of rhetoric, see Chapter 1.)

▼ *Ariel Dorfman teaches literature and Latin American studies at Duke University. One of his books,* Heading South, Looking North: A Bilingual Journey *(1998), which appeared in both English and Spanish, expands on issues raised in this piece. The essay reprinted here originally appeared in the* New York Times *in June 1998.*

If Only We All Spoke Two Languages

ARIEL DORFMAN

DURHAM, N.C. — Ever since I came to settle in the United States 18 years ago, I have hoped that this nation might someday become truly multilingual, with everyone here speaking at least two languages.

I am aware, of course, that my dream is not shared by most Americans: if the outcome of California's referendum on bilingual education earlier this month is any indication, the nation will continue to stubbornly prefer a monolingual country. California voters rejected the bilingual approach — teaching subjects like math and science in the student's native language and gradually introducing English. Instead, they approved what is known as the immersion method, which would give youngsters a year of intensive English, then put them in regular classrooms.

The referendum was ostensibly about education, but the deeper and perhaps subconscious choice was about the future of America. Will this country speak two languages or merely one?

The bilingual method, in spite of what its detractors claim, does not imprison a child in his or her original language. Rather, it keeps it alive in order to build bridges to English. The immersion method, on the other hand, wants youngsters to cut their ties to the syllables of their past culture.

5 Both methods can work. I should know. I have endured them both. But my experience was unquestionably better with bilingual education.

I first suffered the immersion method in 1945 when I was 2½ years old. My family had recently moved to New York from my native Argentina, and when I caught pneumonia, I was interned in the isolation ward of a Manhattan hospital. I emerged three weeks later, in shock from having the doctors and nurses speak to me only in English, and didn't utter another word in Spanish for 10 years.

That experience turned me into a savagely monolingual child, a xenophobic all-American kid, desperate to differentiate himself from Ricky Ricardo°

Ricky Ricardo: the husband of Lucy in *I Love Lucy,* a TV series in the 1950s. In real life, Lucille Ball (1911–1989), who played Lucy, and Desi Arnaz (1917–1986), who played Ricky, were married from 1940 to 1960. Arnaz had immigrated to the United States at age 16 from Cuba.

and Chiquita Banana.° But when my family moved to Chile in 1954, I could not continue to deny my heritage. I learned Spanish again in a British school in Santiago that used the gradualist method. Thus I became a bilingual adolescent.

Later, during the ideologically charged 1960's, I foolishly willed myself to become monolingual again, branding English as the language of an imperial power out to subjugate Latin America. I swore never to speak or write in English again. The 1973 military coup in Chile against the democratically elected government of Salvador Allende Gossens sent me into exile—and back into the arms of English, making me into this hybrid creature who now uses both languages and writes a memoir in English and a play in Spanish as if it were the most ordinary thing to do.

I have developed a linguistic ambidexterity that I will be the first to admit is not at all typical. Even so, it is within reach of others if they start early enough, this thrilling experience of being dual, of taking from one linguistic river and then dipping into the other, until the confluence of the two vocabularies connects distant communities. This is an experience I wish all Americans could share.

10 Or maybe I would be satisfied if voters in this country could understand that by introducing children from other lands to the wonders of English while leaving all the variety and marvels of their native languages intact, the American experience and idiom are fertilized and fortified.

"Bilingualism as a bridge to other cultures."

If people could realize that immigrant children are better off, and less scarred, by holding on to their first languages as they learn a second one, then perhaps Americans could accept a more drastic change. What if every English-speaking toddler were to start learning a foreign language at an early age, maybe in kindergarten? What if these children were to learn Spanish, for instance, the language already spoken by millions of American citizens, but also by so many neighbors to the South?

Most Americans would respond by asking why it is necessary at all to learn another language, given that the rest of the planet is rapidly turning English into the lingua franca of our time. Isn't it easier, most Americans would say, to have others speak to us in our words and with our grammar? Let them make the mistakes and miss the nuances and subtleties while we occupy the more powerful and secure linguistic ground in any exchange.

But that is a shortsighted strategy. If America doesn't change, it will find itself, let's say in a few hundred years, to be a monolingual nation in a world that has become gloriously multilingual. It will discover that acquiring a second language not only gives people an economic and political edge, but is also the best way to understand someone else's culture, the most stimulating way to open your life and transform yourself into a more complete member of the species.

No tengan miedo. Don't be afraid.

15 Your children won't be losing Shakespeare. They'll just be gaining Cervantes.

Chiquita Banana: a brand of banana; the reference here is to commercials from the 1950s that included a dancing banana and/or a woman, both wearing large-brimmed hats full of fruit. See and hear them at <http://chiquita.com/discover/ media/origjingle.wav>.

Dorfman is making a proposal argument, but how good is its proposal? Use the criteria under "Developing Proposals" in Chapter 11 to decide.

LINK TO P. 335

RESPOND •

1. What event motivated Dorfman to write this essay? What seems to be his ultimate argument: that the United States should be multilingual (or encourage multilingualism), that it should be bilingual (or encourage bilingualism), or that it should become bilingual in English and Spanish (or encourage such bilingualism)? What evidence can you provide for your position?
2. What experiences led to Dorfman's bilingualism? How are his experiences similar to or different from those of the typical immigrant to the United States? Why is this question in particular important when thinking about generalizing Dorfman's experiences to other situations?
3. Supporters of the California referendum on bilingual education would likely argue that immigrants are free to speak, use, and pass on to their children any languages other than English that they might speak but that they shouldn't expect publicly funded schools to teach their children these languages. Does Dorfman anticipate or respond in any way to this criticism? If he doesn't, why not? Can an argument that doesn't address the concerns of those taking an opposing view still be effective? Give reasons for your answer.
4. Those who write about bilingual education distinguish among three types of programs: *transitional programs*, which seek to help children make the transition from the home language to the school language as quickly as possible; *maintenance programs,* which seek to produce bilinguals able to speak and write both the language of the school and that of the home community; and *enrichment programs,* which enable students who already speak the language of the school to learn a second language that they (or their parents) believe will be of use to them. (Legally mandated bilingual programs in the United States are transitional programs.) **Write an essay** evaluating the advantages and disadvantages of each of the three kinds of programs for the individual, the community, and the society. (Note that you're not being asked to support bilingual education for this or any other country; rather, you're being asked to evaluate objectively the different kinds of bilingual programs.)

Chang-rae Lee is author of Native Speaker *(1995), a powerful novel about language as a locus of identity, especially for immigrants and their children, in which the protagonist, a Korean American, tries to make sense of who he is—and isn't. In "Mute in an English-Only World," which was published on the op-ed page of the* New York Times *in 1996, Lee writes of his mother's experience as a nonnative speaker of English, using her situation to offer an unexpected perspective on a Palisades Park law requiring that commercial signs be written at least half in English.*

Mute in an English-Only World

CHANG-RAE LEE

When I read of the troubles in Palisades Park, N.J., over the proliferation of Korean-language signs along its main commercial strip, I unexpectedly sympathized with the frustrations, resentments and fears of the longtime residents. They clearly felt alienated and even unwelcome in a vital part of their community. The town, like seven others in New Jersey, has passed laws requiring that half of any commercial sign in a foreign language be in English.

Now I certainly would never tolerate any exclusionary ideas about who could rightfully settle and belong in the town. But having been raised in a Korean immigrant family, I saw every day the exacting price and power of language, especially with my mother, who was an outsider in an English-only world.

In the first years we lived in America, my mother could speak only the most basic English, and she often encountered great difficulty whenever she went out.

We lived in New Rochelle, N.Y., in the early 70's, and most of the local businesses were run by the descendants of immigrants who, generations ago, had come to the suburbs from New York City. Proudly dotting Main Street and North Avenue were Italian pastry and cheese shops, Jewish tailors and cleaners and Polish and German butchers and bakers. If my mother's marketing couldn't wait until the weekend, when my father had free time, she would often hold off until I came home from school to buy the groceries.

5 Though I was only 6 or 7 years old, she insisted that I go out shopping with her and my younger sister. I mostly loathed the task, partly because it meant I couldn't spend the afternoon playing catch with my friends but also because I knew our errands would inevitably lead to an awkward scene, and that I would have to speak up to help my mother.

I was just learning the language myself, but I was a quick study, as children are with new tongues. I had spent kindergarten in almost complete silence, hearing only the high nasality of my teacher and comprehending little but the cranky wails and cries of my classmates. But soon, seemingly mere months later, I had already become a terrible ham and mimic, and I would crack up my father with impressions of teachers, his friends and even himself. My mother scolded me for aping his speech, and the one time I attempted to make light of hers I rated a roundhouse smack on my bottom.

For her, the English language was not very funny. It usually meant

Do you think Lee's article is an example of an argument from the heart? Check out Chapter 2 to find out exactly what such arguments are—and aren't.

LINK TO P. 47

Tim Bower

trouble and a good dose of shame, and sometimes real hurt. Although she had a good reading knowledge of the language from university classes in South Korea, she had never practiced actual conversation. So in America, she used English flashcards and phrase books and watched television with us kids. And she faithfully carried a pocket workbook illustrated with stick-figure people and compound sentences to be filled in.

But none of it seemed to do her much good. Staying mostly at home to care for us, she didn't have many chances to try out sundry words and phrases. When she did, say, at the window of the post office, her readied speech would stall, freeze, sometimes altogether collapse.

One day was unusually harrowing. We ventured downtown in the new Ford Country Squire my father had bought her, an enormous station wagon that seemed as long—and deft—as an ocean liner. We were shopping for a special meal for guests visiting that weekend, and my mother had heard that a particular butcher carried fresh oxtails—which she needed for a traditional soup.

We'd never been inside the shop, 10
but my mother would pause before its window, which was always lined with whole hams, crown roasts and ropes of plump handmade sausages. She greatly esteemed the bounty with her eyes, and my sister and I did also, but despite our desirous cries she'd turn us away and instead buy the packaged links at the Finast supermarket, where she felt comfortable looking them over and could easily spot the price. And, of course, not have to talk.

But that day she was resolved. The butcher store was crowded, and as we stepped inside the door jingled a welcome. No one seemed to notice. We waited for some time, and people who entered after us were now being served. Finally, an old woman nudged my mother and waved a little ticket, which we hadn't taken. We patiently waited again, until one of the beefy men behind the glass display hollered our number.

My mother pulled us forward and began searching the cases, but the oxtails were nowhere to be found. The man, his big arms crossed, sharply said, "Come on, lady, whaddya want?" This unnerved her, and she somehow blurted the Korean word for oxtail, *soggori.*

The butcher looked as if my mother had put something sour in his mouth, and he glanced back at the lighted board and called the next number.

Before I knew it, she had rushed us outside and back in the wagon, which she had double-parked because of the crowd. She was furious, almost vibrating with fear and grief, and I could see she was about to cry.

15 She wanted to go back inside, but now the driver of the car we were blocking wanted to pull out. She was shooing us away. My mother, who had just earned her driver's license, started furiously working the pedals. But in her haste she must have flooded the engine, for it wouldn't turn over. The driver started honking and then another car began honking as well, and soon it seemed the entire street was shrieking at us.

In the following years, my mother grew steadily more comfortable with English. In Korean, she could be fiery, stern, deeply funny and ironic; in English, just slightly less so. If she was never quite fluent, she gained enough confidence to make herself clearly known to anyone, and particularly to me.

Five years ago, she died of cancer, and some months after we buried her I found myself in the driveway of my father's house, washing her sedan. I liked taking care of her things; it made me feel close to her. While I was cleaning out the glove compartment, I found her pocket English workbook, the one with the silly illustrations. I hadn't seen it in nearly 20 years. The yellowed pages were brittle and dog-eared. She had fashioned a plain-paper wrapping for it, and I wondered whether she meant to protect the book or hide it.

I don't doubt that she would have appreciated doing the family shopping on the new Broad Avenue of Palisades Park. But I like to think, too, that she would have understood those who now complain about the Korean-only signs.

I wonder what these same people would have done if they had seen my mother studying her English workbook—or lost in a store. Would they have nodded gently at her? Would they have lent a kind word?

RESPOND •

1. Throughout the piece, Lee offers numerous insights into the strategies those who don't speak English well use to negotiate American society. List some of these strategies along with their consequences for people like Lee's mother and their loved ones.
2. One of the interesting things about this essay from a rhetorical perspective is the way in which Lee bucks reader expectations. Many readers would assume that the son of an immigrant, writing about his mother's struggles with English, would oppose a law mandating the use of English in signs. How and why does Lee challenge reader expectations? How does this use of his mother's experiences contribute to his ethos and authority?

3. Read Ariel Dorfman's essay, "If Only We All Spoke Two Languages" (p. 797), which also discusses bilingualism in American society. Then, **write a dialogue** representing the conversation Lee and Dorfman might have about bilingualism in the United States. Lee became bilingual because he grew up in an immigrant household, while Dorfman learned English under different circumstances. What, if anything, might the authors share in terms of experience or stance? How and why might they differ? The conversation you construct should take the form of an argument—perhaps exploratory, perhaps antagonistic.
4. Lee's essay describes a series of events relating to language that were embarrassing for his mother (and, one imagines, sometimes for the author himself). **Write an essay** about an experience in your life when you were embarrassed by someone's use or misuse of a particular language. Reflecting on the experience, discuss what you learned from the experience about yourself and about language and identity.

Amy Tan, best known for her novels The Joy Luck Club *(1989) and* The Kitchen God's Wife *(1991), writes most often about relationships between Chinese American daughters and their mothers and about each group's struggles with generational and cultural differences. Her work is often praised for its sensitive and realistic rendering of dialogue. During her adolescence, Tan lost her father and her brother to brain tumors. As she recounts, she went on to study English at San Jose State University rather than becoming a neurosurgeon, as her mother had hoped. Tan began as a technical writer but started writing fiction after reading a novel by Louise Erdrich, a Native American writer. This text is a talk Tan gave as part of a panel entitled "Englishes: Whose English Is It Anyway?" at a language symposium in San Francisco in 1989. As you read, try to imagine hearing Tan deliver this speech.*

Tan's open, informal style may make you feel as if you're part of a conversation among friends, but her speech is carefully prepared in ways that casual conversation rarely is. See Chapter 15 to learn some of the techniques that Tan uses so effectively.

LINK TO P. 445

Mother Tongue

AMY TAN

I am not a scholar of English or literature. I cannot give you much more than personal opinions on the English language and its variations in this country or others.

I am a writer. And by that definition, I am someone who has always loved language. I am fascinated by language in daily life. I spend a great deal of my time thinking about the power of language—the way it can evoke an emotion, a visual image, a complex idea, or a simple truth. Language is the tool of my trade. And I use them all—all the Englishes I grew up with.

Recently, I was made keenly aware of the different Englishes I do use. I was giving a talk to a large group of people, the same talk I had already given to half a dozen other groups. The nature of the talk was about my writing, my life, and my book, *The Joy Luck Club*. The talk was going along well enough, until I remembered one major difference that made the whole talk sound wrong. My mother was in the room. And it was perhaps the first time she had heard me give a lengthy speech—using the kind of English I have never used with her. I was saying things like, "The intersection of memory upon imagination" and "There is an aspect of my fiction that relates to thus-and-thus"—a speech filled with carefully wrought grammatical phrases, burdened, it suddenly seemed to me, with nominalized forms, past perfect tenses, conditional phrases—all the forms of standard English that I had learned in school and through books, the forms of English I did not use at home with my mother.

Just last week, I was walking down the street with my mother, and I again found myself conscious of the English I was using, the English I do use with her. We were talking about the price of new and used furniture and I heard myself saying this: "Not waste money that way." My husband was with us as well, and he didn't notice any switch in my English. And then I realized why. It's because over the twenty years we've been together I've often used that same kind of English with him, and sometimes he even uses it with me. It has become our language of intimacy, a different sort of English that relates to family talk, the language I grew up with.

So you'll have some idea of what this family talk I heard sounds like, I'll 5
quote what my mother said during a recent conversation which I videotaped and then transcribed. During this conversation, my mother was talking about

a political gangster in Shanghai who had the same last name as her family's, Du, and how the gangster in his early years wanted to be adopted by her family which was rich by comparison. Later, the gangster became more powerful, far richer than my mother's family, and one day showed up at my mother's wedding to pay his respects. Here's what she said in part:

"Du Yusong having business like fruit stand. Like off the street kind. He is Du like Du Zong—but not Tsung-ming Island people. The local people call putong, the river east side, he belong to that side local people. That man want to ask Du Zong father take him in like become own family. Du Zong father wasn't look down on him, but didn't take seriously, until that man big like become mafia. Now important person, very hard to inviting him. Chinese way, came only to show respect, don't stay for dinner. Respect for making big celebration, he shows up. Mean gives lots of respect. Chinese custom. Chinese social life that way. If too important won't have to stay too long. He come to my wedding. I didn't see, I heard it. I gone to boy's side, they have YMCA dinner. Chinese age I was 19."

You should know that my mother's expressive command of English belies how much she actually understands. She reads the Forbes report, listens to Wall Street Week, converses daily with her stockbroker, reads all of Shirley MacLaine's books with ease—all kinds of things I can't begin to understand. Yet some of my friends tell me they understand fifty percent of what my mother says. Some say they understand eighty to ninety percent. Some say they understand none of it, as if she were speaking pure Chinese. But to me, my mother's English is perfectly clear, perfectly natural. It's my mother tongue. Her language, as I hear it, is vivid, direct, full of observation and imagery. That was the language that helped shape the way I saw things, expressed things, made sense of the world.

Lately, I've been giving more thought to the kind of English my mother speaks. Like others, I have described it to people as "broken" or "fractured" English. But I wince when I say that. It has always bothered me that I can think of no way to describe it other than "broken," as if it were damaged and needed to be fixed, as if it lacked a certain wholeness and soundness. I've heard other terms used, "limited English," for example. But they seem just as bad, as if everything is limited, including people's perception of the limited English speaker.

I know this for a fact, because when I was growing up, my mother's "limited" English limited my perception of her. I was ashamed of her English. I believed that her English reflected the quality of what she had to say. That is, because she expressed them imperfectly her thoughts were imperfect. And I had plenty of empirical evidence to support me: the fact that people in department stores, at banks, and at restaurants did not take her seriously, did not give her good service, pretended not to understand her, or even acted as if they did not hear her.

10 My mother has long realized the limitations of her English as well. When I was fifteen, she used to have me call people on the phone to pretend I was she. In this guise, I was forced to ask for information or even to complain and yell at people who had been rude to her. One time it was a call to her stockbroker in New York. She had cashed out her small portfolio and it just so happened we were going to go to New York the next week, our very first trip outside California. I had to get on the phone and say in an adolescent voice that was not very convincing, "This is Mrs. Tan."

And my mother was standing in the back whispering loudly, "Why he don't send me check, already two weeks late. So mad he lie to me, losing me money."

And then I said in perfect English, "Yes, I'm getting rather concerned. You had agreed to send the check two weeks ago, but it hasn't arrived."

Then she began to talk more loudly, "What he want, I come to New York tell him front of his boss, you cheating me?" And I was trying to calm her down, make her be quiet, while telling the stockbroker, "I can't tolerate any more excuses. If I don't receive the check immediately, I am going to have to speak to your manager when I'm in New York next week." And sure enough, the following week there we were in front of this astonished stockbroker, and I was sitting there redfaced and quiet, and my mother, the real Mrs. Tan, was shouting at his boss in her impeccable broken English.

We used a similar routine just five days ago, for a situation that was far less humorous. My mother had gone to the hospital for an appointment, to find out about a benign brain tumor a CAT scan had revealed a month ago. She said she had spoken very good English, her best English, no mistakes. Still, she said, the hospital did not apologize when they said they had lost the CAT scan and she had come for nothing. She said they did not seem to have any sympathy when she told them she was anxious to know the exact diagnosis since her husband and son had both died of brain tumors. She said they would not give her any more information until the next time and she would have to make another appointment for that. So she said she would not leave until the doctor called her daughter. She wouldn't budge. And when the doctor finally called her daughter, me, who spoke in perfect English—lo and behold—we had assurances the CAT scan would be found, promises that a conference call on Monday would be held, and apologies for any suffering my mother had gone through for a most regrettable mistake.

15 I think my mother's English almost had an effect on limiting my possibilities in life as well. Sociologists and linguists probably will tell you that a per-

son's developing language skills are more influenced by peers. But I do think that the language spoken in the family, especially in immigrant families which are more insular, plays a large role in shaping the language of the child. And I believe that it affected my results on achievement tests, IQ tests, and the SAT. While my English skills were never judged as poor, compared to math, English could not be considered my strong suit. In grade school, I did moderately well, getting perhaps Bs, sometimes B+s in English, and scoring perhaps in the sixtieth or seventieth percentile on achievement tests. But those scores were not good enough to override the opinion that my true abilities lay in math and science, because in those areas I achieved As and scored in the ninetieth percentile or higher.

This was understandable. Math is precise; there is only one correct answer. Whereas, for me at least, the answers on English tests were always a judgment call, a matter of opinion and personal experience. Those tests were constructed around items like fill-in-the blank sentence completion, such as "Even though Tom was ________, Mary thought he was ________." And the correct answer always seemed to be the most bland combinations of thoughts, for example, "Even though Tom was shy, Mary thought he was charming," with the grammatical structure "even though" limiting the correct answer to some sort of semantic opposites, so you wouldn't get answers like "Even though Tom was foolish, Mary thought he was ridiculous." Well, according to my mother, there were very few limitations as to what Tom could have been, and what Mary might have thought of him. So I never did well on tests like that.

The same was true with word analogies, pairs of words, in which you were supposed to find some sort of logical, semantic relationship—for example, "sunset" is to "nightfall" as ________ is to ________. And here, you would be presented with a list of four possible pairs, one of which showed the same kind of relationship: "red" is to "stoplight," "bus" is to "arrival," "chills" is to "fever," "yawn" is to "boring." Well, I could never think that way. I knew what the tests were asking, but I could not block out of my mind the images already created by the first pair, "sunset is to nightfall"—and I would see a burst of colors against a darkening sky, the moon rising, the lowering of a curtain of stars. And all the other pairs of words—red, bus, stoplight, boring—just threw up a mass of confusing images, making it impossible for me to sort out something as logical as saying: "A sunset precedes nightfall" is the same as "a chill precedes a fever." The only way I would have gotten that answer right would have been to imagine an associative situation, for example, my being disobedient and staying out past sunset, catching a chill at night, which turns into feverish pneumonia as punishment, which indeed did happen to me.

I have been thinking about all this lately, about my mother's English, about achievement tests. Because lately I've been asked, as a writer, why there are not more Asian-Americans represented in American literature. Why are there few Asian-Americans enrolled in creative writing programs? Why do so many Chinese students go into engineering? Well, these are broad sociological questions I can't begin to answer. But I have noticed in surveys—in fact, just last week—that Asian students, as a whole, always do significantly better on math achievement tests than in English. And this makes me think that there are other Asian-American students whose English spoken in the home might also be described as "broken" or "limited." And perhaps they also have teachers who are steering them away from writing and into math and science, which is what happened to me.

Fortunately, I happen to be rebellious in nature, and enjoy the challenge of disproving assumptions made about me. I became an English major my first year in college after being enrolled as pre-med. I started writing non-fiction as a freelancer the week after I was told by my former boss that writing was my worst skill and I should hone my talents toward account management.

20 But it wasn't until 1985 that I finally began to write fiction. And at first I wrote using what I thought to be wittily crafted sentences, sentences that would finally prove I had mastery over the English language. Here's an example from the first draft of a story that later made its way into *The Joy Luck Club,* but without this line: "That was my mental quandary in its nascent state." A terrible line, which I can barely pronounce.

Fortunately, for reasons I won't get into today, I later decided I should envision a reader for the stories I would write. And the reader I decided upon was my mother, because these were stories about mothers. So with this reader in mind—and in fact, she did read my early drafts—I began to write stories using all the Englishes I grew up with: the English I spoke to my mother, which for lack of a better term, might be described as "simple"; the English she used with me, which for lack of a better term might be described as "broken"; my translation of her Chinese, which could certainly be described as "watered down"; and what I imagined to be her translation of her Chinese if she could speak in perfect English, her internal language, and for that I sought to preserve the essence, but not either an English or a Chinese structure. I wanted to capture what language ability tests can never reveal: her intent, her passion, her imagery, the rhythms of her speech and the nature of her thoughts.

Apart from what any critic had to say about my writing, I knew I had succeeded where it counted when my mother finished reading my book, and gave me her verdict: "So easy to read."

RESPOND •

1. How have Tan's attitudes toward her mother's English changed over the years? Why? Have you had similar experiences with your parents or other older relatives?
2. Why, ultimately, is Tan suspicious of language ability tests? What are her complaints? What sorts of evidence does she offer? Do you agree or disagree with her argument? Why?
3. Tan's text was written to be read aloud by the author herself. In what ways might this fact be important? (For a discussion of the features of spoken arguments, see Chapter 15.) What would it be like, for example, to have heard Tan deliver this text? How would such an experience have been different from reading it on the page? Had Tan written the piece to be read silently by strangers—as her novels are, for example—how might she have altered it? Why?
4. What does Tan mean when she claims that she uses "all the Englishes [she] grew up with" (paragraph 2)? What are these Englishes? What are her problems in giving them labels? Do you agree with Tan's implied argument that we should use all our Englishes and use them proudly? Why or why not? Are there any limits to this position? If so, what are they? **Write an essay** evaluating Tan's position. (In preparing for this assignment, you might think about the Englishes that you know and use. Do they all have recognizable names or convenient labels? Do you associate them with certain people or places or activities? What does each represent to you? About you? Do you have ambivalent feelings about any of them? Why?)

John Rickford teaches linguistics and directs the Center for African American Studies at Stanford University. A native speaker of Guyanese Creole, Rickford has devoted much research to documenting the links among various Caribbean creoles and their links to the language used by African Americans. In this essay, which originally appeared in Discover *in 1997, he explains how linguists look at Ebonics and why.*

Suite for Ebony *and* Phonics

JOHN RICKFORD

To James Baldwin, writing in 1979, it was "this passion, this skill . . . this incredible music." Toni Morrison, two years later, was impressed by its "five present tenses" and felt that "the worst of all possible things that could happen would be to lose that language." What these novelists were talking about was Ebonics, the informal speech of many African Americans, which rocketed to public attention a year ago this month after the Oakland School Board approved a resolution recognizing it as the primary language of African American students.

The reaction of most people across the country—in the media, at holiday gatherings, and on electronic bulletin boards—was overwhelmingly negative. In the flash flood of e-mail on America Online, Ebonics was described as "lazy English," "bastardized English," "poor grammar," and "fractured slang." Oakland's decision to recognize Ebonics and use it to facilitate mastery of Standard English also elicited superlatives of negativity: "ridiculous, ludicrous," "VERY, VERY STUPID," "a terrible mistake."

However, linguists—who study the sounds, words, and grammars of languages and dialects—though less rhapsodic about Ebonics than the novelists, were much more positive than the general public. Last January, at the annual meeting of the Linguistic Society of America, my colleagues and I unanimously approved a resolution describing Ebonics as "systematic and rule-governed like all natural speech varieties." Moreover, we agreed that the Oakland resolution was "linguistically and pedagogically sound."

Why do we linguists see the issue so differently from most other people? A founding principle of our science is that we describe *how* people talk; we don't judge how language should or should not be used. A second principle is that all languages, if they have enough speakers, have dialects—regional or social varieties that develop when people are separated by geographic or social barriers. And a third principle, vital for understanding linguists' reactions to the Ebonics controversy, is that all languages and dialects are systematic and rule-governed. Every human language and dialect that we have studied to date—and we have studied thousands—obeys distinct rules of grammar and pronunciation.

What this means, first of all, is that Ebonics is not 5
slang. Slang refers just to a small set of new and usually short-lived words in the vocabulary of a dialect or language. Although Ebonics certainly has slang words—such as *chillin* ("relaxing") or *homey* ("close friend"), to pick two that have found wide

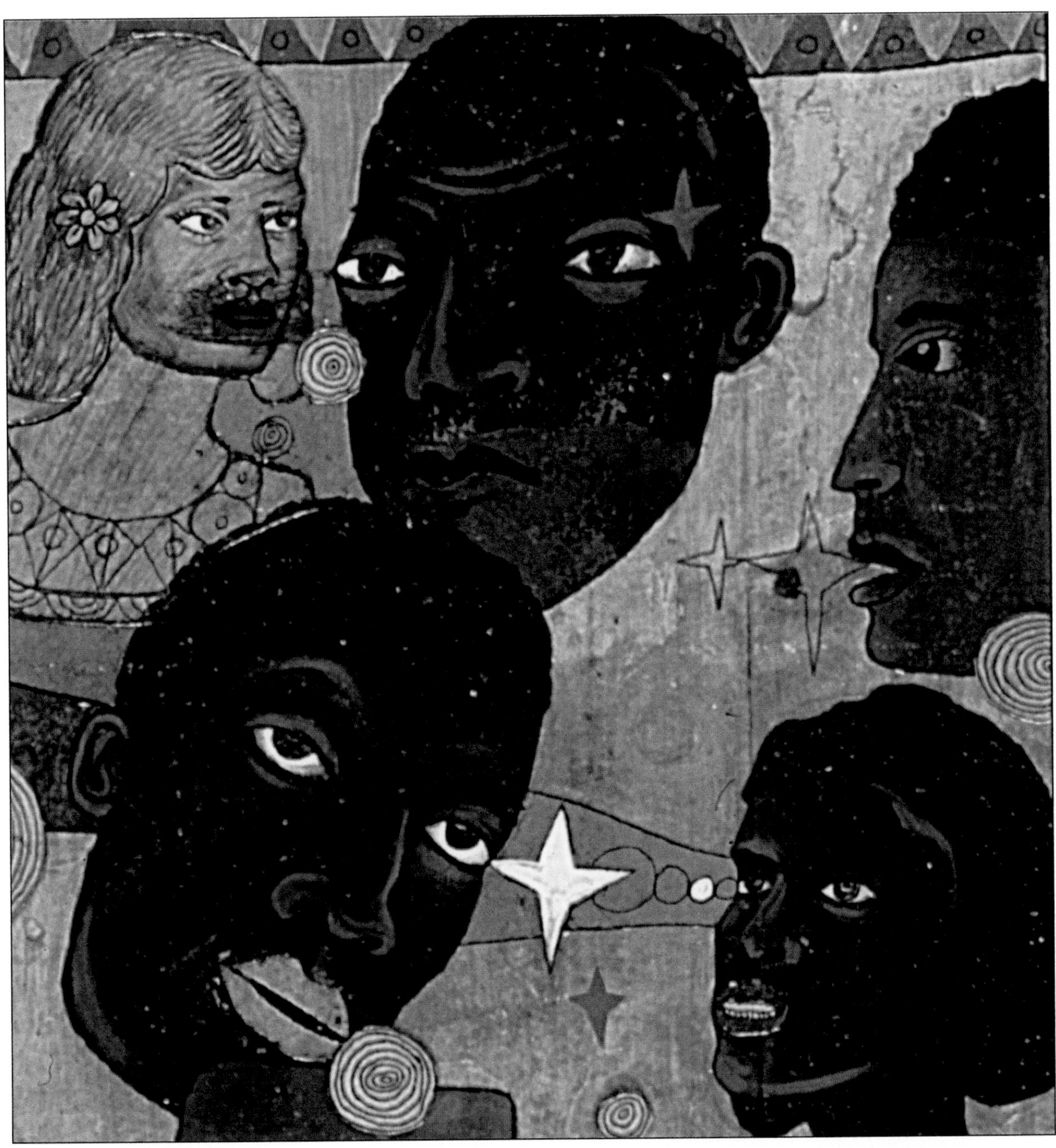

dissemination by the media—its linguistic identity is described by distinctive patterns of pronunciation and grammar.

But is Ebonics a different language from English or a different dialect of English? Linguists tend to sidestep such questions, noting that the answers can depend on historical and political considerations. For instance, spoken Cantonese and Mandarin are mutually unintelligible, but they are usually regarded as "dialects" of Chinese because their speakers use the same writing system and see themselves as part of a common Chinese tradition. By contrast, although Norwegian and Swedish are so similar that their speakers can generally understand each other, they are usually regarded as different languages because their speakers are citizens of different countries. As for Ebonics, most linguists agree that Ebonics is more of a dialect of English than a separate language, because it shares many words and other features with other informal varieties of American English. And its speakers can easily communicate with speakers of other American English dialects.

Yet Ebonics is one of the most distinctive varieties of American English, differing from Standard English—the educated standard—in several ways. Consider, for instance, its verb tenses and aspects. ("Tense" refers to *when* an event occurs, "aspect" to *how* it occurs, whether habitual or ongoing.) When Toni Morrison referred to the "five present tenses" of Ebonics, she probably had usages like these—each one different from Standard English—in mind:

1. He runnin. ("He is running.")
2. He be runnin. ("He is usually running.")
3. He be steady runnin. ("He is usually running in an intensive, sustained manner.")
4. He bin runnin. ("He has been running.")
5. He BIN runnin. ("He has been running for a long time and still is.")

In Standard English, the distinction between habitual or nonhabitual events can be expressed only with adverbs like "usually." Of course, there are also simple present tense forms, such as "he runs," for habitual events, but they do not carry the meaning of an ongoing action, because they lack the "-ing" suffix. Note too that "bin" in example 4 is unstressed, while "BIN" in example 5 is stressed. The former can usually be understood by non-Ebonics speakers as equivalent to "has been" with the "has" deleted, but the stressed BIN form can be badly misunderstood. Years ago, I presented the Ebonics sentence "She BIN married" to 25 whites and 25 African Americans from various parts of the United States and asked them if they understood the speaker to be still married or not. While 23 of the African Americans said yes, only 8 of the whites gave the correct answer. (In real life a misunderstanding like this could be disastrous!)

Word pronunciation is another distinctive aspect of dialects, and the regularity of these differences can be very subtle. Most of the "rules" we follow when speaking Standard English are obeyed unconsciously. Take for instance English plurals. Although grammar books tell us that we add "s" to a word to form a regular English plural, as in "cats" and "dogs," that's true only for writing. In speech, what we actually add in the case of "cat" is an *s* sound; in the case of "dog" we add *z*. The difference is that *s* is voiceless, with the vocal cords spread apart, while *z* is voiced, with the vocal cords held closely together and noisily vibrating.

Now, how do you know whether to add *s* or *z* to 10
form a plural when you're speaking? Easy. If the word ends in a voiceless consonant, like "t," add voiceless *s*. If the word ends in a voiced consonant, like "g," add voiced *z*. Since all vowels are voiced, if the word ends in a vowel, like "tree," add *z*. Because we spell both plural endings with "s," we're not aware that English speakers make this systematic difference every day, and I'll bet your English teacher never told you about

voiced and voiceless plurals. But you follow the "rules" for using them anyway, and anyone who doesn't—for instance, someone who says "bookz"—strikes an English speaker as sounding funny.

One reason people might regard Ebonics as "lazy English" is its tendency to omit consonants at the ends of words—especially if they come after another consonant, as in "tes(t)" and "han(d)." But if one were just being lazy or cussed or both, why not also leave out the final consonant in a word like "pant"? This is not permitted in Ebonics; the "rules" of the dialect do not allow the deletion of the second consonant at the end of a word unless both consonants are either voiceless, as with "st," or voiced, as with "nd." In the case of "pant," the final "t" is voiceless, but the preceding "n" is voiced, so the consonants are both spoken. In short, the manner in which Ebonics differs from Standard English is highly ordered; it is no more lazy English than Italian is lazy Latin. Only by carefully analyzing each dialect can we appreciate the complex rules that native speakers follow effortlessly and unconsciously in their daily lives.

Who speaks Ebonics? If we made a list of all the ways in which the pronunciation and grammar of Ebonics differ from Standard English, we probably couldn't find anyone who always uses all of them. While its features are found most commonly among African Americans (*Ebonics* is itself derived from "ebony" and "phonics," meaning "black sounds"), not all African Americans speak it. The features of Ebonics, especially the distinctive tenses, are more common among working-class than among middle-class speakers, among adolescents than among the middle-aged, and informal contexts (a conversation on the street) rather than formal ones (a sermon at church) or writing.

The genesis of Ebonics lies in the distinctive cultural background and relative isolation of African Americans, which originated in the slaveholding South. But contemporary social networks, too, influence who uses Ebonics. For example, lawyers and doctors and their families are more likely to have more contact with Standard English speakers—in schools, work, and neighborhoods—than do blue-collar workers and the unemployed. Language can also be used to reinforce a sense of community. Working-class speakers, and adolescents in particular, often embrace Ebonics features as markers of African American identity, while middle-class speakers (in public at least) tend to eschew them.

Some Ebonics features are shared with other vernacular varieties of English, especially Southern white dialects, many of which have been influenced by the heavy concentration of African Americans in the South. And a lot of African American slang has "crossed over" to white and other ethnic groups. Expressions like "givin five" (slapping palms in agreement or congratulation) and "Whassup?" are so widespread in American culture that many people don't realize they originated in the African American community. Older, nonslang words have also originated in imported African words. *Tote,* for example, comes from the Kikongo word for "carry," *tota,* and *hip* comes from the Wolof word *hipi,* to "be aware." However, some of the distinctive verb forms in Ebonics—he run, he be runnin, he BIN runnin—are rarer or nonexistent in white vernaculars.

How did Ebonics arise? The Oakland School 15
Board's proposal alluded to the Niger-Congo roots of Ebonics, but the extent of that contribution is not at all clear. What we do know is that the ancestors of most African Americans came to this country as slaves. They first arrived in Jamestown in 1619, and a steady stream continued to arrive until at least 1808, when the slave trade ended, at least officially. Like the forebears of many other Americans, these waves of African "immigrants" spoke languages other than

English. Their languages were from the Niger-Congo language family, especially the West Atlantic, Mande, and Kwa subgroups spoken from Senegal and Gambia to the Cameroons, and the Bantu subgroup spoken farther south. Arriving in an American milieu in which English was dominant, the slaves learned English. But how quickly and completely they did so and with how much influence from their African languages are matters of dispute among linguists.

The Afrocentric view is that most of the distinctive features of Ebonics represent imports from Africa. As West African slaves acquired English, they restructured it according to the patterns of Niger-Congo languages. In this view, Ebonics simplifies consonant clusters at the ends of words and doesn't use linking verbs like "is" and "are"—as in, for example, "he happy"—because these features are generally absent from Niger-Congo languages. Verbal forms like habitual "be" and BIN, referring to a remote past, it is argued, crop up in Ebonics because these kinds of tenses occur in Niger-Congo languages.

"Media uproar over Ebonics missed the point. What's really important is not what kind of language Ebonics isn't, but what kind it is."

Most Afrocentrists, however, don't cite a particular West African language source. Languages in the Niger-Congo family vary enormously, and some historically significant Niger-Congo languages don't show these forms. For instance, while Yoruba, a major language for many West Africans sold into slavery, does indeed lack a linking verb like "is" for some adjectival constructions, it has another linking verb for other adjectives. And it has *six* other linking verbs for nonadjectival constructions, where English would use "is" or "are." Moreover, features like dropping final consonants can be found in some vernaculars in England that had little or no West African influence. Although many linguists acknowledge continuing African influences in some Ebonics and American English words, they want more proof of its influence on Ebonics pronunciation and grammar.

A second view, the Eurocentric—or dialectologist—view, is that African slaves learned English from white settlers, and that they did so relatively quickly and successfully, retaining little trace of their African linguistic heritage. Vernacular, or non-Standard features of Ebonics, including omitting final consonants and habitual "be," are seen as imports from dialects spoken by colonial English, Irish, or Scotch-Irish settlers, many of whom were indentured servants. Or they may be features that emerged in the twentieth century, after African Americans became more isolated in urban ghettos. (Use of habitual "be," for example, is more common in urban than in rural areas.) However, as with Afrocentric arguments, we still don't have enough historical details to settle the question. Crucial Ebonics features, such as the absence of linking "is," appear to be rare or nonexistent in these early settler dialects, so they're unlikely to have been the source. Furthermore, although the scenario posited by this view is possible, it seems unlikely. Yes, African American slaves and whites sometimes worked alongside each other in households and fields. And yes, the number of African slaves was so low, especially in the early colonial period, that distinctive African American dialects may not have formed. But the assumption that slaves rapidly and successfully acquired the dialects of the whites around them requires a rosier view of their relationship than the historical record and contemporary evidence suggest.

A third view, the creolist view, is that many African slaves, in acquiring English, developed a pidgin language—a simplified fusion of English and African languages—from which Ebonics evolved. Native to none of its speakers, a pidgin is a mixed language, incorporating elements of its users' native languages but with less complex grammar and fewer words than either parent language. A pidgin language emerges to facilitate communication between speakers who do not share a language; it becomes a creole language when it takes root and becomes the primary tongue among its users. This often occurs among the children of pidgin speakers—the vocabulary of the language expands, and the simple grammar is fleshed out. But the creole still remains simpler in some aspects than the original languages. Most creoles, for instance, don't use suffixes to mark tense ("he walk*ed*"), plurals ("boy*s*"), or possession ("John'*s* house").

20 Creole languages are particularly common on the islands of the Caribbean and the Pacific, where large plantations brought together huge groups of slaves or indentured laborers. The native languages of these workers were radically different from the native tongues of the small groups of European colonizers and settlers, and under such conditions, with minimal access to European speakers, new, restructured varieties like Haitian Creole French and Jamaican Creole English arose. These languages do show African influence, as the Afrocentric theory would predict, but their speakers may have simplified existing patterns in African languages by eliminating more complex alternatives, like the seven linking verbs of Yoruba I mentioned earlier.

Within the United States African Americans speak one well-established English creole, Gullah. It is spoken on the Sea Islands off the coast of South Carolina and Georgia, where African Americans at one time constituted 80 to 90 percent of the local population in places. When I researched one of the South Carolina Sea Islands some years ago, I recorded the following creole sentences. They sound much like Caribbean Creole English today:

1. E. M. run an gone to Suzie house. ("E. M. went running to Suzie's house.")
2. But I does go to see people when they sick. ("But I usually go to see people when they are sick.")
3. De mill bin to Bluffton dem time. ("The mill was in Bluffton in those days.")

Note the creole traits: the first sentence lacks the past tense and the possessive form; the second sentence lacks the linking verb "are" and includes the habitual "does"; the last sentence uses unstressed "bin" for past tense and "dem time" to refer to a plural without using an *s*.

What about creole origins for Ebonics? Creole speech might have been introduced to the American colonies through the large numbers of slaves imported from the colonies of Jamaica and Barbados, where creoles were common. In these regions the percentage of Africans ran from 65 to 90 percent. And some slaves who came directly from Africa may have brought with them pidgins or creoles that developed around West African trading forts. It's also possible that some creole varieties—apart from well-known cases like Gullah—might have developed on American soil.

This would have been less likely in the northern colonies, where blacks were a very small percentage of the population. But blacks were much more concentrated in the South, making up 61 percent of the population in South Carolina and 40 percent overall in the South. Observations by travelers and commentators in the eighteenth and nineteenth centuries record creole-like features in African American speech. Even today, certain features of Ebonics, like the absence of the linking verbs "is" and "are," are widespread in Gullah and Caribbean English creoles but rare or nonexistent in British dialects.

My own view is that the creolist hypothesis incorporates the strengths of the other hypotheses and avoids their weaknesses. But we linguists may never be able to settle that particular issue one way or another. What we can settle on is the unique identity of Ebonics as an English dialect.

So what does all this scholarship have to do with the Oakland School Board's proposal? Some readers might be fuming that it's one thing to identify Ebonics as a dialect and quite another to promote its usage. Don't linguists realize that nonstandard dialects are stigmatized in the larger society, and that Ebonics speakers who cannot shift to Standard English are less likely to do well in school and on the job front? Well, yes. The resolution we put forward last January in fact stated that "there are benefits in acquiring Standard English." But there is experimental evidence both from the United States and Europe that mastering the standard language might be easier if the differences in the student vernacular and Standard English were made explicit rather than entirely ignored.

25 To give only one example: At Aurora University, outside Chicago, inner-city African American students were taught by an approach that contrasted Standard English and Ebonics features through explicit instruction and drills. After eleven weeks, this group showed a 59 percent reduction in their use of Ebonics features in their Standard English writing. But a control group taught by conventional methods showed an 8.5 percent increase in such features.

This is the technique the Oakland School Board was promoting in its resolution last December. The approach is not new; it is part of the 16-year-old Standard English Proficiency Program, which is being used in some 300 California schools. Since the media uproar over its original proposal, the Oakland School Board has clarified its intent: the point is not to teach Ebonics as a distinct language but to use it as a tool to increase mastery of Standard English among Ebonics speakers. The support of linguists for this approach may strike nonlinguists as unorthodox, but that is where our principles—and the evidence—lead us. ■

Rickford constructs his argument on a very emotionally loaded subject using evidence based on fact and reason—historical fact, statistics, and studies. Find out about other kinds of fact- and reason-based evidence in Chapter 4.

LINK TO P. 81

RESPOND •

1. In light of Rickford's argument, what do the following sentences from p. 814 mean: "Media uproar over Ebonics missed the point. What's really important is not what kind of language Ebonics isn't, but what kind it is"?
2. What are the three theories of the origins of Ebonics that Rickford discusses? How effectively does he summarize each theory? (In other words, how clear an idea do you have of what each theory argues?) What does he say are the strengths and weaknesses of each? How persuasive is he in arguing for the creolist view, given the evidence he offers? Do you think Rickford assumes you'll agree with him? Why or why not?

3. As Rickford notes, linguists contend that they study language scientifically. Assuming they do, how much knowledge about language or linguistics do you find in the other piece about Ebonics in this chapter? What, in your opinion, accounts for the fact that the knowledge claimed by linguists, as scientists, is generally absent from public debates about language?
4. What does Rickford's final sentence mean? How does it support his own position and that of other linguists? How does it indirectly criticize the negative responses to the Ebonics resolution summarized in paragraph 2 of the essay? **Write an essay** evaluating the evidence Rickford provides for taking a linguistically informed stance on Ebonics.

David D. Troutt is a professor at the Rutgers School of Law at Newark and also author of a collection of short stories, The Monkey Suit *(1998), based on famous legal cases involving African Americans. In this essay, he seeks to analyze why the actions of the Oakland school board regarding Ebonics caused such an uproar in Black and non-Black communities. This article originally appeared in January 1997 in* the Los Angeles Times.

Defining Who We Are in Society

DAVID D. TROUTT

When passing a controversial resolution to help black schoolchildren learn standard English through Ebonics, the speech patterns many use at home, the Oakland School District reminded the nation of what language means to us. It is our very beginning. Once we as toddlers are given the gift of the communicating self, we can forever discover, learn and expand in a world of common symbols.

Perhaps nothing defines us more than our linguistic skills; nothing determines as much about where we can and cannot go. How we talk may be the first—and last—clue about our intelligence and whether we're trusted or feared, heard or ignored, admitted or excluded.

But we treat our fluency like property. Depending where we are, our ability to speak in certain ways entitles us to access, membership and social riches, such as employment or popularity. As a culture, the greatest benefits go to those who write and speak in standard English, ways identified by most of us as "white," specifically middle-class white.

But participating in the benefits of communication doesn't require being white. It only requires that people around us—wherever we are—understand what we're saying. Ebonics merely validates the distinctive talk among people on a margin far from the majority's view of competence and invites them in. It recognizes that a voice developed amid inequality does not bespeak inferiority.

The problem with Ebonics is not that it will teach children what they al- 5
ready know, which, as critics point out, would be silly. The problem is that its public acceptance might throw into question claims of ownership to intelligence and belonging. After all, Ebonics is not as much the language of blackness as it is the only dialect of persistently poor, racially segregated people—the so-called black underclass. It is the dumbness against which all smartness is measured. But if we reached consensus that Ebonics is a real linguistic system born of difference whose use in schools may facilitate inclusion for children of the excluded, we must deal frankly with the exclusion itself.

Ebonics therefore becomes a troubling measure of separation. For many whites, it measures the contradictions of colorblind convictions. For many blacks, Ebonics measures the complications of assimilation and the resiliency of shame.

The ridicule and disparagement on talk radio confirm why an Ebonics program makes sense. Many whites have used the issue as an opportunity to vent racist jokes ordinarily kept underground or in sports bars. Others invoke it in order to restrict black cultural influences, such as banning rap music or canceling TV shows in which black characters use slang.

Meanwhile, more serious mainstream criticism sees the colorblind vision of the republic at stake. Suddenly interested in the achievement of poor black schoolchildren, pundits, federal officials and policy-makers unanimously condemn Ebonics for lowering standards. Inadvertently echoing English-only advocacy, they argue that Oakland's resolution would replace children's individuality with militant group identification and promote black "separatism." The Standard English language, they say, belongs to all of us.

Such hypocrisy is hard to beat. Of course, language, like intelligence, is no group's personal property. But despite the well-meaning ring of colorblind ideals, you cannot demand sameness of language while perpetuating segregated education. Privately, any master of the language will admit, the best thing you can do for your kids is get them into schools with the tiniest percentage of (poor) blacks. Thus, it is no coincidence that the public school districts experimenting with Ebonics have long been abandoned by white parents. In fact, many public schools are funded by property taxes, making direct the connection between residential and education segregation. This separatism is quite normal. It is how social advantages are reproduced. But you can't enjoy them at a distance and demand conformity, too.

10 Since the Supreme Court declared separate-but-equal school facilities unconstitutional in Brown vs. Board of Education,° most urban school districts have become more, not less, segregated. Moreover, as wealth and resources develop the suburbs, the residential segregation that accompanies separate schooling has produced a degree of racial isolation among inner-city blacks that approaches complete homogeneity.

Brown v. Board of Education: landmark 1954 U.S. Supreme Court decision that declared segregated schooling unconstitutional and put an end to the doctrine of "separate but equal."

To be sure, the Oakland resolution's description of Ebonics as a "primary" language was unfortunate. Such a language would not be English, and non-English cannot be criticized for being "bad English." It is enough that Ebonics has a distinct lexicon and grammatical rules that are spoken exclusively by some blacks. It then qualifies as a reliable measurement of the gulf between many poor blacks and the middle-class world where Standard English is spoken.

Notice how Troutt makes values-based arguments by invoking the authority of respected Black writers. Arguments based on values often work in combination with arguments based on character; see Chapter 3 for more on arguments based on character.

LINK TO P. 65

Recognition of this fact by sociolinguists and its application in school settings are at least three decades old. In addition to Los Angeles and Oakland, schools in Michigan, Texas and New York use what scholars call Black English

Vernacular (BEV) as a teaching tool. The principle is hardly new: Begin teaching from where students are and bridge the familiar with the untried.

Another principle at work, however, is assimilation. If Ebonics measures distance, it also measures a closeness more successful blacks have to mainstream culture. Formally educated blacks who use both Standard English and Ebonics depending on social context, or "code switching," remain close to two worlds that seem at odds with each other. For white co-workers, they may introduce black English idioms into common parlance. Among less-assimilated family and friends, they may be ostracized for "talking white." As a result, they often both bemoan and boast of their bidialectalism. It is a mark of cross-cultural identification, involving a complicated mix of pride, achievement and lingering shame.

Jesse Jackson illustrated this when he immediately denounced the Oakland resolution as an "unacceptable surrender," then, soon after, changed his mind. His first reaction honored a long, revolutionary tradition of black educators teaching Standard English to children at a time when white institutions and hate groups forcibly and deliberately denied us the written and spoken language. Much of the NAACP's legacy—including the Brown decision—was built on such demands for access. It is not surprising, then, that its current director, Kweisi Mfume, denounced Ebonics by resurrecting the memory of Frederick Douglass,° the freed slave who taught himself to read five languages.

Frederick Douglass: African American orator, autobiographer, and journalist (1818–1895), much involved in the abolitionist movement and considered by many to have been the most significant Black American writer and speaker of the nineteenth century.

15 Jackson inherits that tradition of civil-rights leadership. He understands how the social benefits of assimilation come primarily through language acquisition. Surely, he also recognizes a deep-seated shame many blacks feel at the persistent inability of less-advantaged blacks to cross over and speak both tongues. The public and institutional denigration of black speech patterns for so long contributes to an undeniable sense of stigma against which blacks from a variety of class backgrounds still struggle.

But in his second reaction, Jackson must have resolved that Ebonics does not dignify some shameful difference. If done right, it should validate, then transcend difference. This reaction also enjoys a long tradition in black culture, as illustrated by the diverse work of writers such as Zora Neale Hurston° and Amiri Baraka.° Many wrote powerfully in Standard English, only to return at times to black dialect and write just as beautifully there.

Although Ebonics may prove valuable in teaching underperforming black children Standard English, implementing Ebonics programs probably shouldn't be confused with bilingualism. This would create potential competition for scarce funds between blacks and students for whom English is not a primary language. Hopefully, we will find a better way than pitting outsiders against outsiders. There are important differences in the experience of a Guatemalan or Vietnamese third-grader, who returns from school to immigrant parents. The stigma may not result from associating her language with ignorance, but the unkindness is just as real.

Instead, the Ebonics debate should heighten our appreciation of differences among us, as well as the special difficulties faced by students on the margins, who, along with their families, are trying, against long odds, to belong.

Zora Neale Hurston: African American writer (1891–1960) who wrote novels and short stories as well as book-length folklore and anthropological studies of African American, Haitian, and Jamaican culture.

Amiri Baraka: African American writer, political activist, and theatrical director (1934–) especially known for his influence on Black American writers of the last third of the twentieth century who, following his example, proudly drew on their own cultural heritage.

RESPOND •

1. Troutt begins with the assertion that "[p]erhaps nothing defines us more than our linguistic skills" (paragraph 2). Throughout the rest of the essay, what evidence does he offer for such a strong assertion?
2. According to Troutt, how did the responses of Blacks and Whites to the Ebonics controversy differ? What were the origins and consequences of these differences? Again, what sorts of evidence does Troutt offer to support his position? How, specifically, does he use the example of Jesse Jackson to demonstrate the ambivalence of most African Americans toward Ebonics?
3. Troutt argues that American society isn't exactly honest about Standard English. "As a culture, the greatest benefits go to those who write and speak in Standard English," but, according to Troutt, these "ways [of using language are] identified by most of us as 'white,' specifically middle-class white" (paragraph 3). At the same time, "[t]he Standard English language, they say, belongs to all of us" (paragraph 8). Does Standard English indeed belong to everyone? To what extent is it linked implicitly or explicitly to issues of class and ethnicity (and perhaps to other axes of social difference such as gender or region)? **Write an essay** in which you explore the ownership of Standard English.

This portfolio of public service advertisements as well as an advertisement reproduced on p. 495 of Chapter 17 are all part of "The Anti-Drug" Campaign created by the National Youth Anti-Drug Media Campaign, which is funded by the Office of National Drug Control Policy, a component of the Executive Office of the President. In other words, these advertisements are part of the federal government's initiative to control illegal drugs in the United States. As you study these visual arguments, pay special attention to the language they use. Ask yourself how "real" this language is and evaluate how appropriate it is, given the advertisements' intended audiences.

He might dump me.
He'll think I'm judging him.
But I care about him.
SPECIAL
2 SLICE
$3.00
Office of National Drug Control Policy
www.freevibe.com
Give him a call. Send an email. Catch him after school. It doesn't matter how you do it. As long as you do it. If a friend has a problem with drugs or drinking, talk to them. It could make all the difference.
courage
THE ANTI-DRUG.

Give him a call. Send an email. Catch him after school. It doesn't matter how you do it. As long as you do it. If a friend has a problem with drugs or drinking, talk to them. **It could make all the difference.**

National Youth Anti-Drug Media Campaign, *He might dump me . . .*

Making a Visual Argument: Public Service Campaigns Use Language to Send a Message

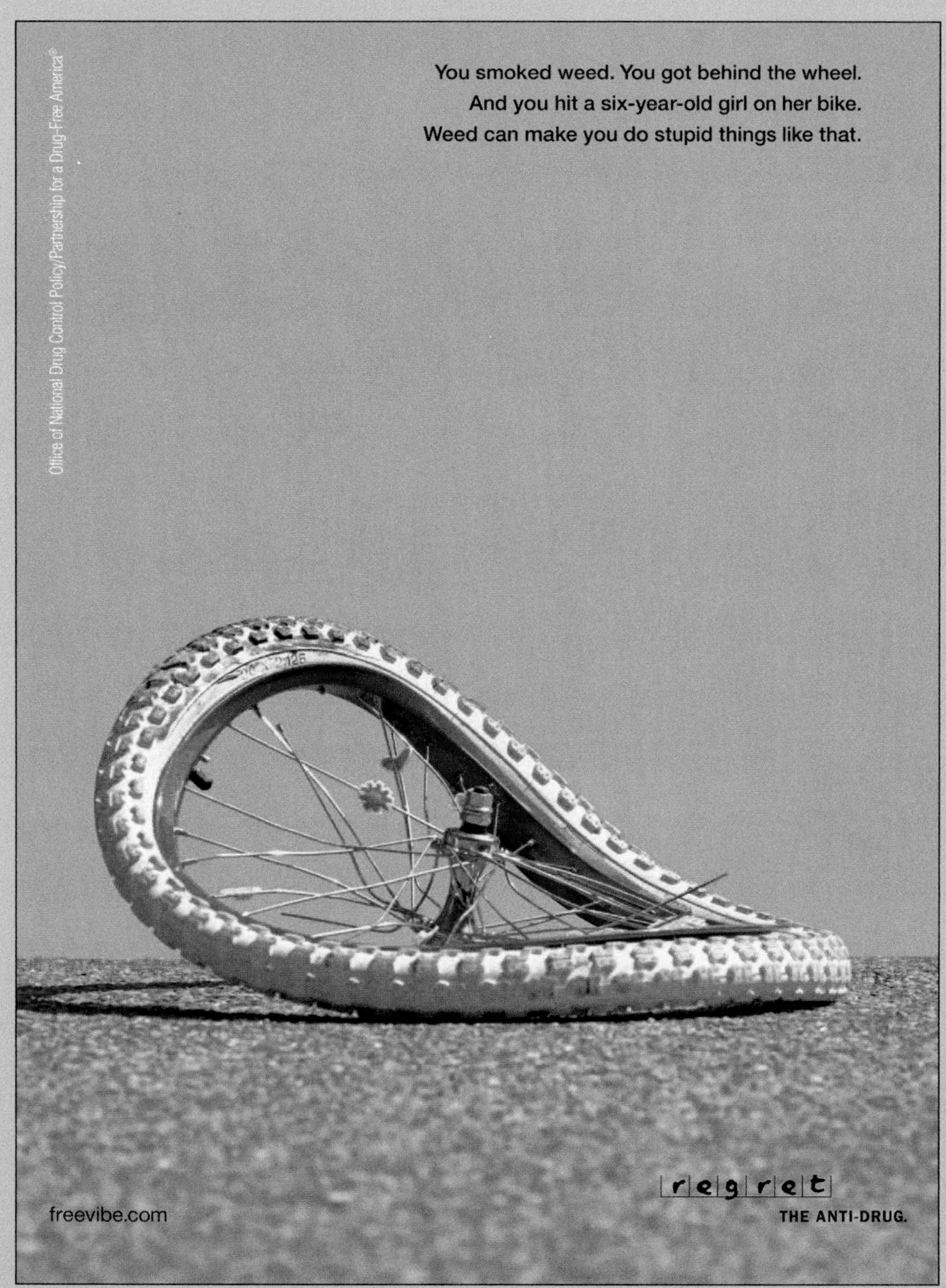

You smoked weed. You got behind the wheel.
And you hit a six-year-old girl on her bike.
Weed can make you do stupid things like that.
Office of National Drug Control Policy/Partnership for a Drug-Free America®
freevibe.com
regret
THE ANTI-DRUG.

National Youth Anti-Drug Media Campaign, *You smoked weed* . . .

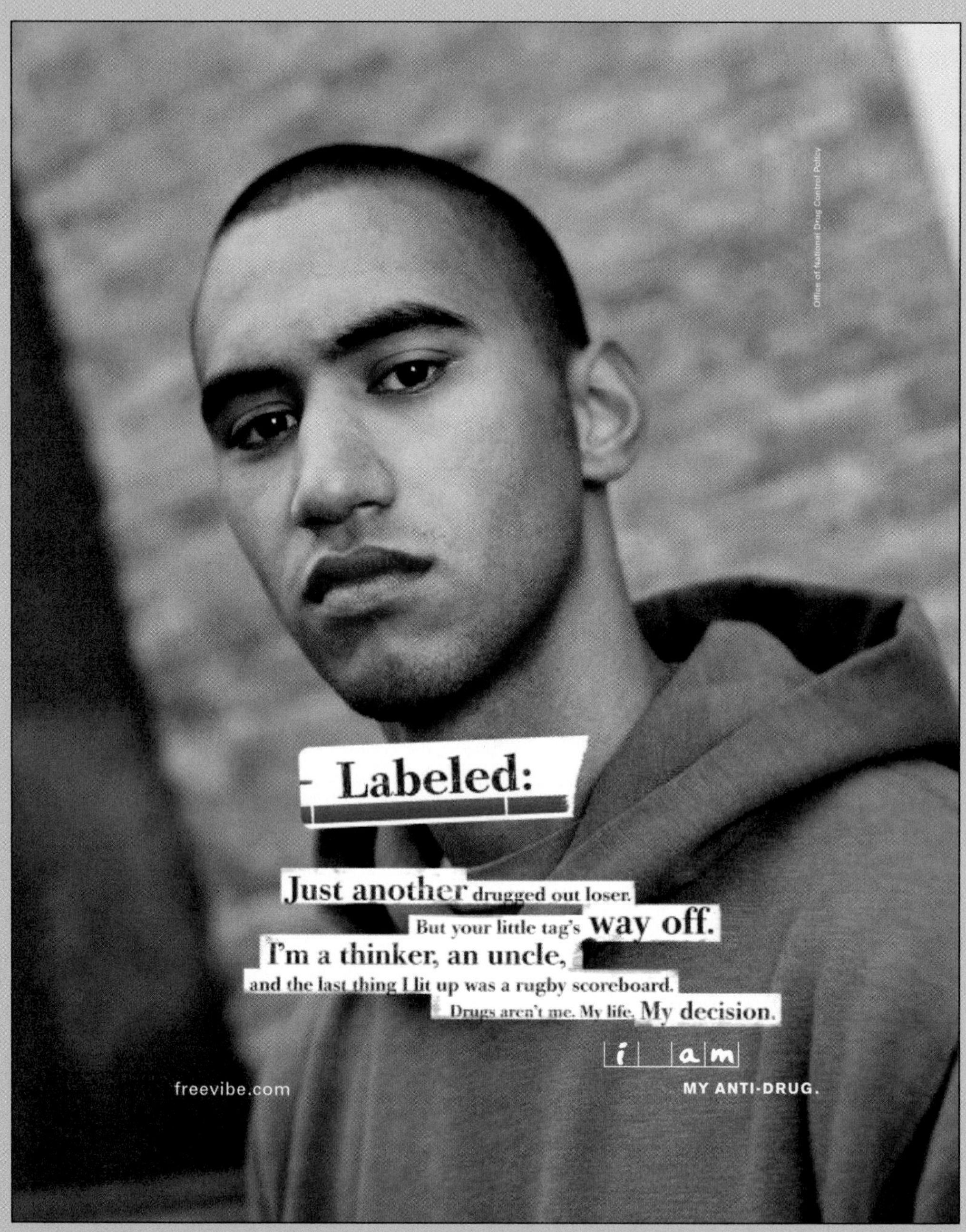

National Youth Anti-Drug Media Campaign, *Labeled* . . .

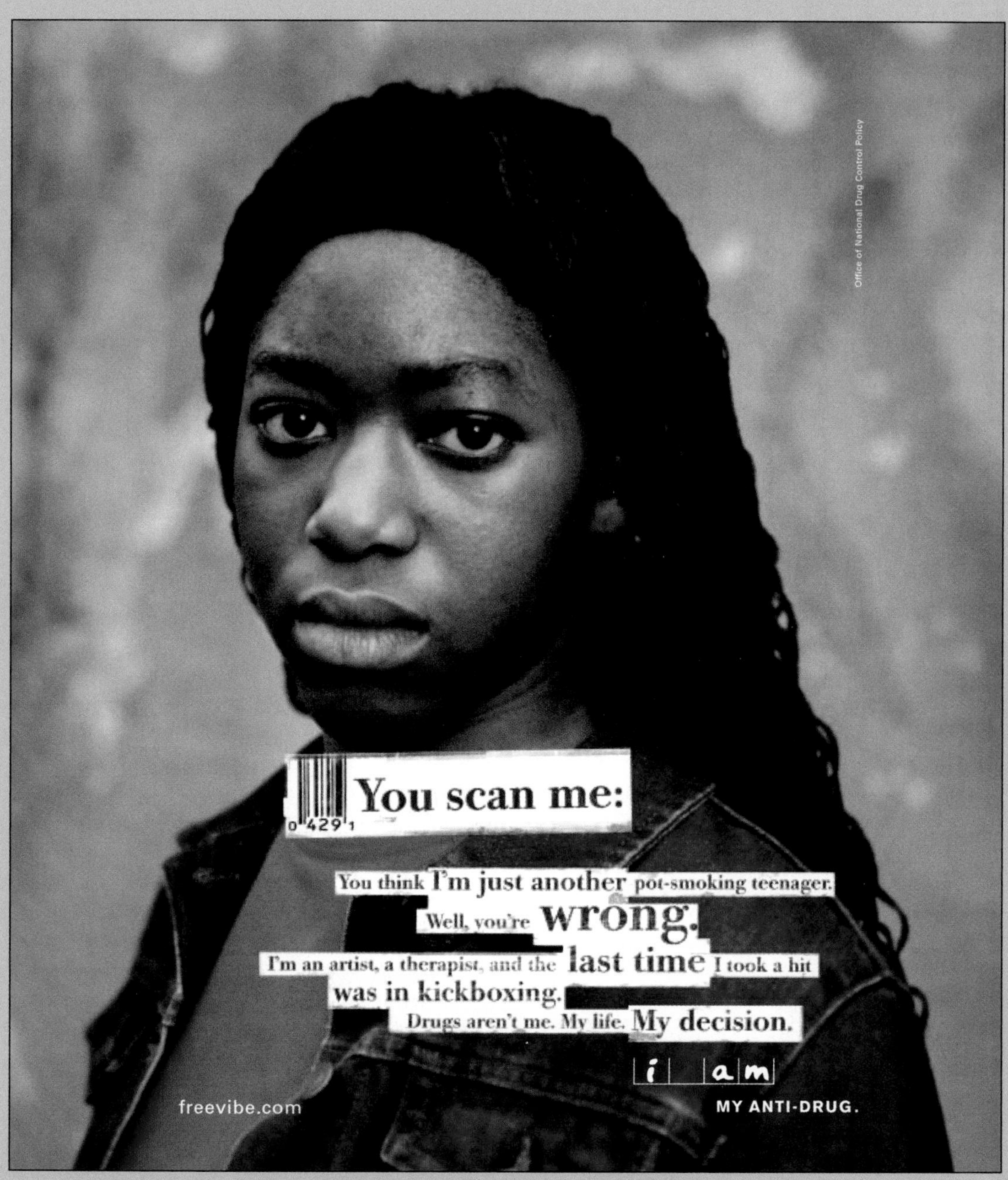

National Youth Anti-Drug Media Campaign, *You scan me . . .*

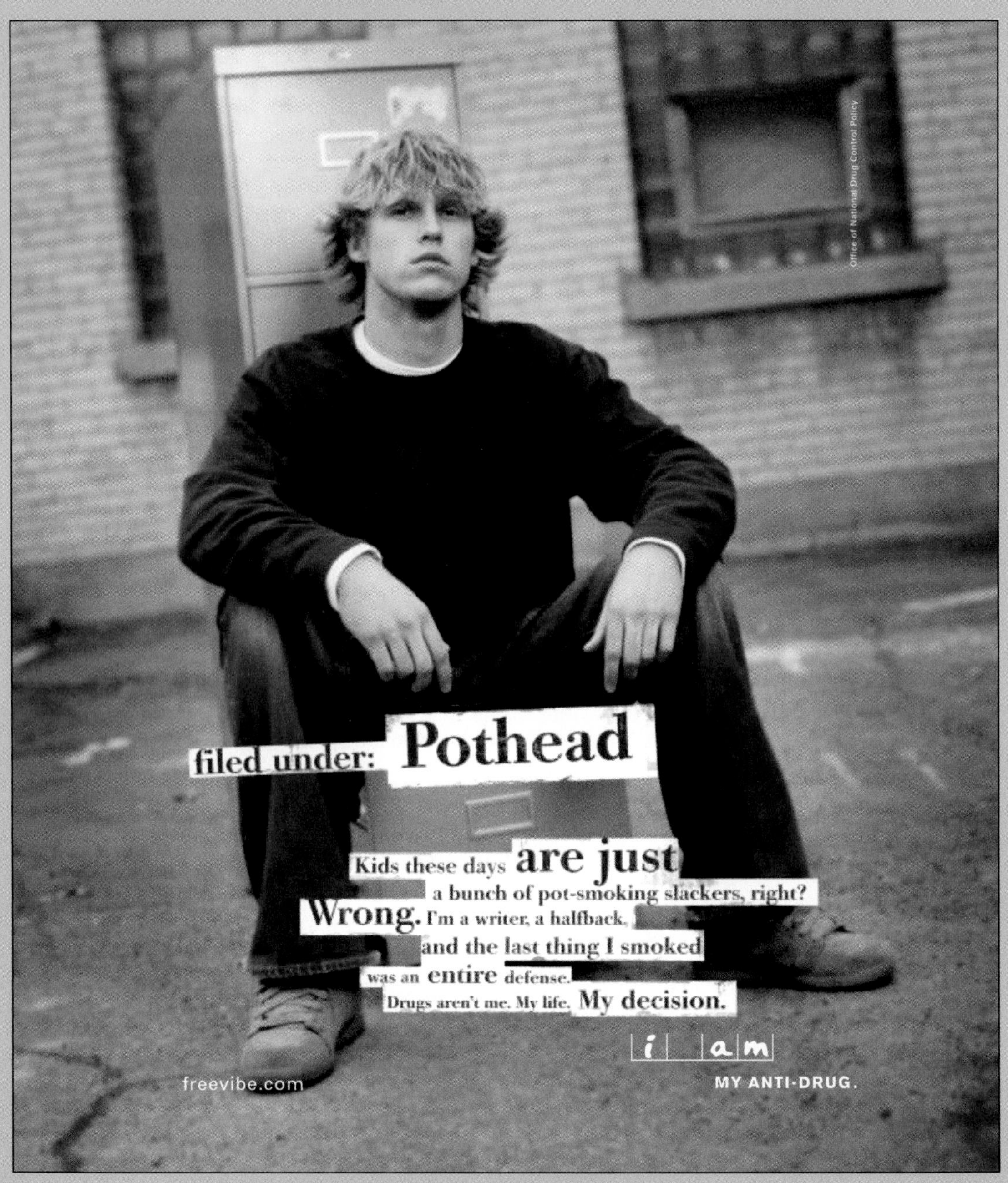

Office of National Drug Control Policy
filed under: Pothead
Kids these days are just
a bunch of pot-smoking slackers, right?
Wrong. I'm a writer, a halfback,
and the last thing I smoked
was an entire defense.
Drugs aren't me. My life. My decision.
i am
MY ANTI-DRUG.
freevibe.com

National Youth Anti-Drug Media Campaign, *filed under: Pothead* . . .

RESPOND.

1. Obviously, each of these advertisements is meant to discourage the use of illegal drugs. However, they represent different ways of doing so. In the lower right-hand corner of each advertisement, you'll find one of three different labels: "courage: the anti-drug," "regret: the anti-drug," and "i am my anti-drug." What sorts of appeals are each of these ad categories making? How are those appeals linked to the content of each of the visual arguments—its subject, its image, and its text?
2. In what ways is the advertisement in the "courage: the anti-drug" campaign a proposal argument? In what way(s) are all of these advertisements proposal arguments? (For a discussion of proposal arguments, see Chapter 11.)
3. In what ways is the advertisement in the "regret: the anti-drug" campaign a causal argument? In what way(s) are all of these advertisements causal arguments? (For a discussion of causal arguments, see Chapter 10.)
4. Who are the multiple audiences for the "i am my anti-drug" campaign? Whom are the advertisements addressing directly? Who are the invoked audiences? Compare and contrast the three ads in this series. Which is most effective? Why? Do you contend this sort of argument in general is effective with the target audience? Why or why not?
5. **Write an essay** in which you evaluate the language used in one or more of these ads, focusing on the degree to which and ways in which it matches the expectations or practices of the audiences the ads target. As part of your essay, you may wish to comment on the appropriateness of the language in context—that is, the language itself, how it's used, and how it's presented visually.

In this column from the June 1999 issue of *Sports Illustrated*, Steve Rushin describes and critiques one aspect of what we might term "the American character." Crucially, the patterns of behavior he criticizes are linguistic in nature, involving ways we use language to create our identities. As you read, pay special attention to the sorts of examples Rushin uses to support his claim that the United States has become "Wise Guy Nation."

Hip Unchecked

In Sports and on TV, Sarcasm and Cynicism Are Drowning Out Sincerity and Compassion

STEVE RUSHIN

LAST WEEK, at an amusement park in middle America, I saw a seven-year-old boy in a basketball-themed T-shirt that read KNOW YOUR ROLE — SHUT YOUR MOUTH. Within minutes came another kid, maybe 12, in a trash-talking T-shirt that said YOU SHOULD BE IN A MUSEUM — YOU'RE GETTIN' WAXED. Moments later, yet another child walked world-wearily by in a T-shirt that commanded SPEAK TO MY AGENT. He was, at most, five years old.

All day these pip-squeaks passed, like the little boy in a T-shirt manufactured by the No Fear, Inc. apparel company, one that declared IF YOU CAN'T WIN, DON'T PLAY. (He was holding his father's hand.) Retreating to my hotel, I switched on ESPN2 in time to see a commercial in which a man dressed as a giant Slim Jim was yelling, "Eat me!" Flipping to *The Late Late Show* on CBS, I watched former ESPN anchor Craig Kilborn read a phony news item about drug agents seizing several tons of cocaine before it reached its intended destination of — smirk, leer, arched eyebrow — "Darryl Strawberry's left nostril." So ended an unremarkable day in the life of America, where every citizen is a snarky, cynical, hipper-than-thou, irony-dripping icon of comedy and cool.

I don't know when, exactly, everyone became a smart-ass, only that it has happened. "Everybody I know is sarcastic all the time, in everything they say," a guy named Scott Dikkers recently told *The New Yorker*. Dikkers is editor-in-chief of — what else? — a satirical newspaper called *The Onion*, and he and I seem to know all the same people. In sports the smart-aleck attitude is inescapable, be it on *SportsCenter*, in ads for EA Sports, or wherever two sportswriters gather — invariably to make fun of everyone, including each other.

It is exhausting, all this clever contempt for everything. I have seen major league baseball trainers wearing T-shirts bearing the slogan I WILL GIVE TREATMENT, NOT SYMPATHY. On such seemingly minor everyday messages — call them incidental incivilities — a popular culture has been built.

5 So remind me: Why is it wrong to give sympathy to someone who might need it? What is uncool about occasional earnestness, sincerity or genuine human emotion? Does every TV commercial have to be a winking, we-know-that-you-know-that-this-is-a-cheesy-commercial commercial? With the spoofed-up news on *The Daily Show with Jon Stewart,* and "Headlines" on *The Tonight Show,* and the mock newscast on *The Late Late Show,* and the mock newscast on *Dennis Miller Live,* and the mock newscast on *Saturday Night Live,* television now broadcasts more news parodies than actual news programs. We have become Wise Guy Nation. On our one-dollar bill George Washington ought to smirk like Mona Lisa. On the five, Lincoln's fingers could form a *W,* the international symbol for *whatever.*

In an interview broadcast during halftime of the Knicks-Pacers playoff game on NBC last Friday night, Indiana guard Mark Jackson spoke movingly about the recent death of his father. It was telling that Jackson felt it necessary to point out, "There's no shame in crying and saying 'I love him to death.'"

You wouldn't think so. But people now feel shame for their virtues (e.g., loving one's parents) and no shame for their sins (e.g., loving one's White House intern). Losers—socially or athletically—deserve ridicule. As I left the amusement park last week, I saw an adult in a T-shirt that bore the image of a high school wrestler and the following slogan across the chest: WIN WITH HUMILITY, LOSE WITH DIGNITY.

The earnest and simple sentiment gave me hope, so I nodded solemnly as the man passed. Only then did I see the back of his shirt. It read BUT DON'T LOSE! ■

Rushin's article is about values, but is his appeal based on values? Emotion? A combination? Check out Chapters 2 and 3 to help you decide.

LINK TO PP. 45 AND 60

RESPOND •

1. How well does the article's subtitle—"In Sports and on TV, Sarcasm and Cynicism Are Drowning Out Sincerity and Compassion"—summarize Rushin's argument? Why do you think that Rushin doesn't include an explicit thesis in his essay? How might doing so have altered the tone of the piece?
2. How would you describe the tone of Rushin's essay? To what extent does his tone enact the very attitudes and behaviors he's criticizing? Do you think the tone contributes to or detracts from his argument? Why or why not?
3. Nearly all of Rushin's examples involve males. Is the pattern of behavior Rushin describes and criticizes "a guy thing" or "an American thing"? Why?
4. Rushin claims in paragraph 7 that "people now feel shame for their virtues . . . and no shame for their sins. . . ." **Write an essay** supporting or rejecting this claim.

Deborah Tannen, a sociolinguist who teaches at Georgetown University, is the author of numerous scholarly works and several popular books on language, including the best-selling You Just Don't Understand: Women and Men in Conversation *(1990),* Talking from 9 to 5: Women and Men at Work *(1994), and* The Argument Culture: Stopping America's War of Words *(1998). "Can We Talk?" is an excerpt from the opening chapter of her most recent book,* You're Wearing That? Understanding Mothers and Daughters in Conversation *(2006). As the book's title states, in this work Tannen seeks to describe and analyze mother/daughter interactions. As you read, notice the kinds of evidence Tannen uses to illustrate and support her claims.*

Can We Talk?

DEBORAH TANNEN

"My daughters can turn my day black in a millisecond," says a woman whose two daughters are in their thirties.

Another woman tells me, "Sometimes I'll be talking on the phone to my mom, and everything's going fine, then all of a sudden she'll say something that makes me so mad, I just hang up. Later I can't believe I did that. I would never hang up on anyone else."

But I also hear comments like these: "No one supports me and makes me feel good like my mother. She's always on my side." And from the mother of a grown daughter: "I feel very lucky and close with my daughter, and particularly since I didn't have a close relationship with my mother, it's very validating for me and healing."

Mothers and daughters find in each other the source of great comfort but also of great pain. We talk to each other in better and worse ways than we talk to anyone else. And these extremes can coexist within the same daughter-mother pairs. Two sisters were in an elevator in the hospital where their mother was nearing the end of her life. "How will you feel when she's gone?" one asked. Her sister replied, "One part of me feels, How will I survive? The other part feels, Ding-dong, the witch is dead."

The part of a daughter that feels "How will I survive?" reflects passionate 5
connection: Wanting to talk to your mother can be a visceral, almost physical longing, whether she lives next door, in a distant state, in another country—or if she is no longer living on this earth. But the part that sees your mother as a wicked witch—a malevolent woman with magical power—reflects the way your anger can flare when a rejection, a disapproving word, or the sense that she's still treating you like a child causes visceral pain. American popular culture, like individuals in daily life, tends to either romanticize or demonize mothers. We ricochet between "Everything I ever accomplished I owe to my mother" and "Every problem I have in my life is my mother's fault." Both convictions come laden with powerful emotions. I was amazed by how many women, in the midst of e-mails telling me about their mothers, wrote, "I am crying as I write this."

Women as mothers grapple with corresponding contradictions. The adoration they feel for their grown daughters, mixed with the sense of responsibility for their well-being, can be overwhelming, matched only by the hurt

Throughout her argument, Tannen uses colons to set off quotations and break up sentences. This use of punctuation and longer sentences defines the style of the author and the piece. See Chapter 12 for an in-depth discussion of writing style.

LINK TO P. 375

they feel when their attempts to help or just stay connected are rebuffed or even excoriated° as criticism or devilish interference. And the fact that these pushes and pulls continue after their daughters are grown is itself a surprise, and not a pleasant one. A woman in her sixties expressed this: "I always assumed that once my daughter became an adult, the problems would be over," she said. "We'd be friends; we'd just enjoy each other. But you find yourself getting older, things start to hurt, and on top of that, there are all these complications with your daughter. It's a big disappointment."

excoriated: strongly criticized or denounced; its original meaning was "to tear off the skin of a human or animal."

Small Spark, Big Flare-up

Especially disappointing—and puzzling—is that hurt feelings and even arguments can be sparked by the smallest, seemingly insignificant remarks. Here's an example that comes from a student in one of my classes named Kathryn Ann Harrison.

"Are you going to quarter those tomatoes?" Kathryn heard her mother's voice as she was preparing a salad. Kathryn stiffened, and her pulse quickened. "Well, I was," she answered. Her mother responded, "Oh, okay," but the tone of her voice and the look on her face prompted Kathryn to ask, "Is that wrong?"

"No, no," her mother replied. "It's just that personally, I would slice them."

Kathryn's response was terse: "Fine." But as she cut the tomatoes—in 10
slices—she thought, Can't I do anything without my mother letting me know she thinks I should do it some other way?

I am willing to wager that Kathryn's mother thought she had asked a question about cutting a tomato. What could be more trivial than that? But her daughter bristled because she heard the implication "You don't know what you're doing. I know better."

When daughters react with annoyance or even anger at the smallest, seemingly innocent remarks, mothers get the feeling that talking to their daughters can be like walking on eggshells: They have to watch every word.

A mother's questions and comments which seem to imply that a daughter should do things another way can spark disproportionate responses because they bring into focus one of the central conundrums of mother-daughter relationships: the double meaning of connection and control. Many mothers and daughters are as close as any two people can be, but closeness always carries with it the need, indeed the desire, to consider how your actions will affect the other person, and this can make you feel that you are no longer in control of your own life. Any word or action intended in the spirit of connection can be interpreted as a sign that the other person is trying to control you. This double meaning was crystallized in a comment that one woman made: "My daughter used to call me every day," she said. "I loved it. But then she stopped. I understand. She got married, she's busy, she felt she had to loosen the bonds. I understand, but I still miss those calls." In the phrase "loosen the bonds" lies the double meaning of connection and control. The word "bonds" evokes the connection of "a close bond" but also the control of "bondage": being tied up, not free.

There is yet another reason that a small comment or suggestion can grate: It can come across as a vote of no confidence. This is annoying coming from anyone, but it's especially hurtful when it comes from the person whose opinion counts most—your mother. Unaccountable as this may seem to mothers, the smallest remark can bring into focus the biggest question that hovers over nearly all conversations between mothers and daughters: Do you see me for who I am? And is who I am okay? When mothers' comments to daughters (or, for that matter, daughters' comments to mothers) seem to answer that question in the affirmative, it's deeply reassuring: All's right with the world. But when their words seem to imply that the answer is No, there's something wrong with what you're doing, then daughters (and, later in life, mothers) can feel the ground on which they stand begin to tremble: They start to doubt whether how they do things, and therefore who they are, really is okay.

You're Not Going to Wear That, Are You?

Loraine was spending a week visiting her mother, who lived in a senior living 15
complex. One evening they were about to go down to dinner in the dining room. As Loraine headed for the door, her mother hesitated. Scanning her daughter from head to toe, she asked, "You're not going to wear that, are you?"

"Why not?" Loraine asked, her blood pressure rising. "What's wrong with it?"

"Well, people tend to dress nicely for dinner here, that's all," her mother explained, further offending her daughter by implying that she was not dressed nicely.

Her mother's negative questions always rubbed Loraine the wrong way, because they so obviously weren't questions at all. "Why do you always disapprove of my clothes?" she asked.

Now her mother got that hurt look which implied it was Loraine who was being a cad. "I don't disapprove," she protested. "I just thought you might want to wear something else."

A way to understand the difference between what Loraine heard and 20
what her mother said she meant is the distinction between message and metamessage.° When she said "I don't disapprove," Loraine's mother was referring to the message: the literal meaning of the words she spoke. The disapproval Loraine heard was the metamessage—that is, the implications of her mother's words. Everything we say has meaning on these two levels. The message is the meaning that resides in the dictionary definitions of words. Everyone usually agrees on this. But people frequently differ on how to interpret the words, because interpretations depend on metamessages—the meaning gleaned from how something is said, or from the fact that it is said at all. Emotional responses are often triggered by metamessages.

metamessage: here, the Greek prefix *meta* means "beyond" or "about"; in a sense, a *metamessage* is a(n additional) message about how to understand the message itself—much like when a smiley face tells you to take whatever precedes it humorously or someone's tone of voice lets you know that a comment is to be taken sarcastically rather than literally.

When Loraine's mother said "I don't disapprove," she was doing what I call "crying literal meaning": She could take cover in the message and claim responsibility only for the literal meaning of her words. When someone cries literal meaning, it is hard to resolve disputes, because you end up talking about the meaning of the message when it was the meaning of the metamessage that got your goat. It's not that some utterances have metamessages, or hidden meanings, while others don't. Everything we say has metamessages indicating how our words are to be interpreted: Is this a serious statement or a joke? Does it show annoyance or goodwill? Most of the time, metamessages are communicated and interpreted without notice because, as far as anyone can tell, the speaker and the hearer agree on their meaning. It's only when the metamessage the speaker intends—or acknowledges—doesn't match the one the hearer perceives that we notice and pay attention to them.

In interpreting her mother's question as a sign of disapproval, Loraine was also drawing on past conversations. She couldn't count the times her mother had commented, on this visit and on all the previous ones, "You're wearing that?" And therein lies another reason that anything said between mothers and daughters can either warm our hearts or raise our hackles: Their conversations have a long history, going back literally to the start of the daughter's life. So anything either one says at a given moment takes meaning not only from the words spoken at that moment but from all the conversations they have had in the past. This works in both positive and negative ways. We come to expect certain kinds of comments from each other, and are primed to interpret what we hear in that familiar spirit.

Even a gift, a gesture whose message is clearly for connection, can carry a metamessage of criticism in the context of conversations that took place in the past. If a daughter gives her artist mother a gift certificate to an upscale clothing store, it may be resented if her daughter has told her again and again, "You're too old to keep dressing like a hippie, Mom." And criticism may be the impression if a mother who has made clear she can't stand her daughter's messy kitchen gives her as a gift an expensive organizer for kitchen utensils. The gift giver may be incensed that her generosity has been underappreciated, but the lack of gratitude has less to do with the message of the gift than with the metamessage it implies, which came from past conversations.

The long history of conversations that family members share contributes not only to how listeners interpret words but also to how speakers choose them. One woman I talked to put it this way: "Words are like touch. They can caress or they can scratch. When I talk to my children, my words often end up scratching. I don't want to use words that way, but I can't help it. I know their sensitivities, so I know what will have an effect on them. And if I'm feeling hurt by something they said or did, I say things that I know will scratch. It happens somewhere in a zone between instinct and intention." This observation articulates the power of language to convey meanings that are not found in the literal definitions of words. It highlights how we use past conversations as a resource for meaning in present ones. At the same time, it describes the distinction between message and metamessage, a distinction that will be important in all the conversations examined in this book.

Who Cares?

While talking casually to her husband, Joanna absentmindedly tugs at a 25
hangnail until the skin tears and a tiny droplet of blood appears. Unthinking, she holds it out before her husband's eyes. "Put on a Band-Aid," he says flatly. Her husband's non-reaction makes Joanna wonder why she showed him so insignificant an injury. And then she realizes: She developed the habit of displaying her wounds, no matter how small, to her mother. Had she shown the ever so slightly broken skin to her, her mother would have reached out, taken Joanna's finger in her hand, and examined it with a soothing grimace. Joanna was looking for that glance of sympathy, that fleeting reminder that someone else shares her universe. Who but her mother would regard so small an injury as worthy of attention? No one—because her mother would be responding not to the wound but to Joanna's gesture in showing it to her. It isn't only, isn't really, concern for the torn hangnail that her mother shares but a subtle language of connection: The tiny drop of blood is an excuse for Joanna to remind her mother "I'm here" and for her mother to reassure her daughter "I care."

Many women develop the habit of telling their mothers about minor misfortunes because they treasure the metamessage of caring they know they will hear in response, though, like Joanna, they may not notice until they get a different response from someone else. This also happened to a student in one of my classes, Carrie, when she was sick with the flu and called home. Carrie usually talked to her mother when she called, but this time her mother was out of the country, so she spoke to her father instead. This is how Carrie recounted the conversation in a class assignment:

CARRIE: Hey, Daddy. I'm sick with the flu. It's absolutely awful.

DAD: Well, take some medicine.

CARRIE: I already did, but I still feel terrible.

DAD: Well then, go to the doctor.

CARRIE: But everyone else at school is sick too. I couldn't get an appointment for today.

DAD: Well then, I'm sorry. I can't help you there.

In commenting on this conversation, Carrie explained that she knows perfectly well to take medicine and go to the doctor when she's sick. What she had been looking for when she called home was a metamessage of caring. In her words: "I am used to talking to my mother and having her fuss and worry over the smallest of my problems." In contrast to her mother's characteristic response, her father's pragmatic° approach came across as indifference and left her feeling dissatisfied, even slightly hurt.

pragmatic: here, concerned with practical solutions to a situation or problem.

RESPOND •

1. How would you summarize Tannen's account of why mother/daughter communication is necessarily difficult? Do you agree? Why or why not? Is mother/son communication less complex? Why or why not?
2. In the section "You're Not Going to Wear That, Are You?" Tannen distinguishes between the notions of *message* and *metamessage* (paragraph 20) and then continues by distinguishing between focusing on the message itself and "crying literal meaning" (paragraph 21), and focusing on the metamessage and the history of past conversations. In what ways is this section of her chapter a definitional argument? (For a discussion of definitional arguments, see Chapter 8.) Why is it important to the remainder of her analysis?

3. Although Tannen's focus in her book is mother/daughter communication, this excerpt includes another of her favorite topics—male and female interactional styles. How does she characterize prototypical female and male interactional styles in the section "Who Cares?" Why is the notion of metamessage crucial in understanding such a characterization? To what extent do you agree with her assessment of mothers' and fathers' (hence female and male) ways of showing concern or interacting? Why?
4. What sorts of evidence does Tannen use to support her claims? (For a discussion of what counts as evidence, see Chapter 16.) Given that her goal is to understand and explicate the nature of interaction, how appropriate are the kinds of evidence she uses? What's the likelihood that other kinds of evidence would have been effective?
5. Tannen's analysis of mother/daughter interaction reminds us that in addition to categories like age, social class, ethnicity, religion, gender, and sexuality, certain role relationships like parent/child (and, more specifically, mother/daughter) are part of our identity. What other role relationships inside and outside the family shape your identity and influence the way you use language? **Write an essay** in which you describe—and hence define—the social categories and role relationships that most influence your own use of language.

Women and Men Speaking in *New Yorker* Cartoons

Do men and women speak differently? If so, how and why? This is the subject of many talk shows and self-help books (generally directed at women, by the way) and much academic research. People often talk as if women and men spoke completely different languages—as if neither could understand a word the other said. More nuanced approaches focus on how and why women and men might use language differently, generally without realizing it. Perhaps the best exemplar of research in this framework is the work of Deborah Tannen, a sociolinguist at Georgetown University, who in numerous scholarly books and papers and in her best-selling popular book, You Just Don't Understand: Women and Men in Conversation *(1990), argues that men and women often have different goals in conversation and interaction more generally, a fact that she attributes to differences in male and female socialization. (Tannen is also the author of the selection "Can We Talk?"—an excerpt from* You're Wearing That? Understanding Mothers and Daughters in Conversation*—which appears on p. 830.) There have been many popularizers of this perspective, including John Gray's* Men Are from Mars, Women Are from Venus: A Practical Guide for Improving Communication and Getting What You Want in Your Relationships *(1993). Other schools of research contend that there are few, if any, significant differences in how men and women, as groups, use language, focusing instead on women and men of particular backgrounds in specific situations. All researchers agree, however, that everyone expects men and women to use language differently and that expectations greatly influence how women and men understand (and misunderstand) one another.*

The cartoons in this portfolio originally appeared in the New Yorker*, a magazine that focuses on, well, New York. It's read, however, by fans across the United States. The cartoonists represented here are all familiar to regular readers of the magazine; indeed, each has a very identifiable style. As you'd likely guess, Mick Stevens, Leo Cullum, William Hamilton, and Peter Steiner are all men, and Roz Chast is a woman. As you read, think about the assumptions being made about how women and men speak. As you*

"Talk to me, Alice. I speak woman."

Mick Stevens, *Talk to me, Alice. I speak woman.*

The Emergence of Language

"Look, all I'm saying is, why don't we just stop the car for a minute and ask for some directions?"

Roz Chast, An excerpt from *Men Are from Belgium, Women Are from New Brunswick*

"And do you, Deborah Tannen, think they know what they're talking about?"

Peter Steiner, *And do you, Deborah Tannen, think they know what they're talking about?*

RESPOND •

1. What differences and similarities do you find among these cartoonists with respect to the way they represent the problems women and men often have in communicating? What different behaviors do men and women appear to engage in, based on these cartoons?
2. With the exception of the cartoon by William Hamilton, "Look, all I'm saying is . . .," the cartoons all focus on heterosexual couples in interaction. What are the advantages and disadvantages of taking (adult) heterosexual couples as the best or only example of how men and women talk or interact?
3. Which cartoon do you find most successful? Why? Which do you find least successful? Why?
4. Much humor, especially in cartoons, depends on intertextuality—that is, shared references to other texts or, by extension, other things, like cultures or events, that can be "read" as texts. How does intertextuality play an important role in the cartoons by Roz Chast and Peter Steiner? (By the way, why do you suppose John Gray chose the title that he did for his book about communication between members of a heterosexual couple?)
5. Using these cartoons as evidence, describe the kinds of people who are the intended audience of the *New Yorker*. What are their lives like? What values do they hold? What concerns do they have? What sorts of things are they expected to know about?
6. The most complex and multilayered of these visual arguments is Roz Chast's cartoon, "An excerpt from *Men Are from Belgium, Women Are from New Brunswick*," largely because of her combination of text and images. What argument(s) is she making about the way women and men communicate? How do the images contribute to her argument? How does her argument rely on knowledge of stereotypes about how men and women in a relationship generally interact? **Write an essay** in which you explain to someone who isn't from the United States why many Americans would find this cartoon humorous and what it reveals about the way Americans understand the relationships between language and gendered identity. (For a discussion of humorous arguments, see Chapter 13.)

speaking in tongues and miracle healing. Brazil, where American missionaries planted Pentecostalism in the early 20th century, now has a congregation with its own TV station, soccer team and political party.

Most scholars of Christianity believe that the world's largest church is a Pentecostal one — the Yoido Full Gospel Church in Seoul, South Korea, which was founded in 1958 by a converted Buddhist who held a prayer meeting in a tent he set up in a slum. More than 250,000 people show up for worship on a typical Sunday.

"If I were to buy stock in global Christianity, I would buy it in Pentecostalism," said Martin E. Marty, professor emeritus of the history of Christianity at the University of Chicago Divinity School and a coauthor of a study of fundamentalist movements. "I would not buy it in fundamentalism."

After the American presidential election in November, some liberal commentators warned that the nation was on the verge of a takeover by Christian "fundamentalists."

But in the United States today, most of the Protestants who make up what some call the Christian right are not fundamentalists, who are more prone to create separatist enclaves, but evangelicals, who engage the culture and share their faith. Professor Marty defines fundamentalism as essentially a backlash against secularism and modernity.

10 For example, at the fundamentalist Bob Jones University, in Greenville, S.C., students are not allowed to listen to contemporary music of any kind, even Christian rock or rap. But at Wheaton College in Illinois, a leading evangelical school, contemporary Christian music is regular fare for many students.

Christian fundamentalism emerged in the United States in the 1920's, but was already in decline by the 1960's. By then, it had been superceded by evangelicalism, with its Billy Graham°-style revival meetings, radio stations and seminaries.

The word "fundamentalist" itself has fallen out of favor among conservative Christians in the United states, not least because it has come to be associated with extremism and violence overseas.

Fundamentalism in non-Christian faiths became a phenomenon in the rest of the world in the 1970's with "the failure and the bankruptcy of secular, nationalistic liberal creeds around the world," said Philip Jenkins, a professor of history and religious studies at Pennsylvania State University. Among the "creeds cracking up" were nationalism,° Marxism,° socialism,° pan-Arabism° and pan-Africanism.°

Billy Graham, 1918–   : born William Franklin Graham Jr., a Protestant Evangelical minister best known for his Crusades, or public revivals.

nationalism: the belief that nations (composed of ethnically or culturally defined groups of people) are the most appropriate unit for organizing political life and that one's loyalty to her or his nation should preempt or be more important than all others.

Marxism: the school of thought associated with Karl Marx (1818–1883), a philosopher, political theorist, and economist who focused on class-based struggle as the major force in history.

socialism: an economic, political, and social system in which ownership of the means of production (industry, natural resources, etc.) lies in the hands of the government with the stated goal of minimizing social inequality by distributing wealth equitably; it's usually contrasted with capitalism.

pan Arabism: various twentieth-century political movements focused on uniting all Arab countries in a single cultural or even political entity.

pan-Africanism: various twentieth-century political movements focused on uniting all African nations, especially those south of the Sahara, by ending all forms of colonialism and external domination, especially that of European countries.

"From the 1970's on, you get the growth of not just more conservative religion, but religion with a political bent," said Professor Jenkins, the author of *The Next Christendom: The Coming of Global Christianity.*

15 Now, the future of fundamentalism is murky, with several contradictory trends at work simultaneously.

There is little doubt that one fundamentalism can feed another, spurring recruitment and escalating into a sort of religious arms race. In Nigeria's central Plateau State, Muslim and Christian gangs have razed one another's villages in the last few years, leaving tens of thousands of dead and displaced. In rioting in India in 2002, more than 1,000 people, most of them Muslims, were killed by Hindus in Gujarat state—retaliation for a Muslim attack a day earlier on a train full of Hindus, which killed 59.

Husain Haqqani, a Pakistani political commentator and visiting scholar at the Carnegie Endowment for International Peace in Washington, said that insurgents in Falluja, Iraq, recruited fighters with the false rumor that Christian crusaders with the Rev. Franklin Graham's° aid organization, Samaritan's Purse, were on the way over to convert Muslims. (Mr. Graham is known throughout the Muslim world for his statement that Islam is a "very evil and wicked religion.") Fundamentalism does not necessarily lead to intolerance, said Professor Jenkins of Pennsylvania State. "People with very convinced, traditional views can get along together for a very long time," he said. "But sometimes we get into cycles where they can't, and we seem to be in one of those cycles right now."

Analysts are also seeing signs of a backlash as religious believers grow disenchanted with movements that have produced little but bloodshed, economic stagnation and social repression.

In last year's elections in India, voters repudiated the ruling Bharatiya Janata Party,° a Hindu nationalist group whose cadres had helped stir up violence in some Indian states against Muslims and others.

20 And in Indonesia, the world's largest Muslim country, mainstream Islamic groups in September helped elect as president a secular general who had been relatively outspoken about the threat posed by the radical group Jemaah Islamiyah,° which is responsible for several acts of terrorism, including the bombing in Bali in 2002.

Fundamentalist movements also stumble because they plan for the overthrow, but not for the governing. Half the Muslim world is illiterate, Mr. Haqqani said, but the Taliban didn't make a dent in improving literacy when it ruled in Afghanistan. If Iran had a free and fair plebiscite° today, Professor Marty said, "the ayatollahs would be dumped."

For reasons like this, said R. Scott Appleby, a history professor at the University of Notre Dame and director of the Joan B. Kroc Institute for International Peace Studies, "it would be misleading to say fundamentalism is on the rise now." He added: "I would say we're just more aware of it because these people are better organized, more mobile and more vocal than ever before."

In 2003, Professor Appleby and two other scholars, Gabriel A. Almond

---

Franklin Graham, 1952– : born William Franklin Graham III, a Protestant Evangelical minister; he now serves as president of a mission organization, Samaritan's Purse, and is chief executive officer of his father's organization, the Billy Graham Evangelical Organization.

Bharatiya Janata Party: Indian People's Party, one of the largest political parties in India, seen by some as representing Hindu fundamentalism.

Jemaah Islamiyah: Islamic Community, a militant Islamic terrorist organization found in certain southeast Asian countries and committed to establishing a theocracy, or state ruled according to religion or by religious leaders. It is assumed to be responsible for bombings in Manila, Philippines; Jakarta, Indonesia; and Bali, Indonesia.

plebescite: a direct vote of the people to decide an important matter.

and Emmanuel Sivan, published "Strong Religion," a book based on research done with Professor Marty for the Fundamentalism Project. The book's subtitle was the "The Rise of Fundamentalisms Around the World."

Now, Mr. Appleby said, "There is some evidence, some literature that says fundamentalism is on the decline, that it has peaked or is peaking precisely because it has a tendency toward violence and intolerance, and those ultimately don't work. They lead to bloodshed, loss of life, and no recognizable economic upturn, and there is an exhaustion with it."

25 That is not to say that he does not foresee more bitter, sometimes violent religious clashes. By their very nature, fundamentalists endure because they are motivated by transcendant° ideas like salvation or, in some places, martyrdom. Mr. Appleby said he did not expect to see growth, but a persistence of "deadly pockets of would-be revolutionaries who are empowered to a greater degree than ever by a little technological savvy and organizational ability."

The American government is poorly prepared to make the necessary distinctions between what is merely religious fervor and what is potentially dangerous fundamentalism, said Thomas F. Farr, who left his post as director of the office of international religious freedom in the State Department about a year ago.

"Most of my foreign service friends would rather have root canal than talk to a Muslim imam about religion," said Mr. Farr, who now works with the Institute for Global Engagement, a Washington-based group working on international religious freedom.

What they need to ask, he said, is: "Do these religions have within them exclusivist tendencies in an absolutist sense, or can they be open to other human beings outside their circle? These are inevitably theological questions."

RESPOND •

1. How would you characterize Laurie Goodstein's argument in this selection? Why might it be important to contextualize her subject—religion as a "rising force"—globally? How would you characterize the ethos Goodstein creates in discussing this topic? Why might she do so? (For a discussion of how writers create their ethos and why it's important, see Chapter 3.)
2. Like many complex arguments, this selection contains arguments of several kinds, including definitional arguments. Based on the information given in the article, how would you define and distinguish among the categories "fundamentalists," "evangelicals," and "Pentecostals"? Are these definitions adequate for this context—that is, for understanding the information presented in this selection? Why or why not? (For a discussion of definitional arguments, see Chapter 8.)
3. This selection also offers a number of causal claims. List three. What sorts of causal claims are they? Who makes the claims you've listed—the author or the sources she cites? Is the origin of the causal claims important in how you or other readers might evaluate the strength or

transcendant: beyond the limits of human thought or understanding.

validity of the selection's arguments? Why or why not? How do these causal claims advance its argument(s)? (For a discussion of causal arguments, see Chapter 10.)

4. This selection contains a visual argument—a complex set of "country profiles" that provides several kinds of information about Nigeria, India, Indonesia, and Brazil—reproduced from the original version of the article. What do the profiles contribute to the selection? (In other words, do you think you would have read or understood the selection differently had this visual argument not been included? How so?) Study the information given in the country profiles. Make a list of the kinds of information each profile gives. Why is this information useful and appropriate, given the focus of the selection? What functions do the circles of different sizes play in communicating information? How do the illustrations contribute to this visual argument?
5. Create a country profile like the ones given here for the United States and one other country of your choosing (other than the four given here). Be sure to include the sources of your information. When you've completed this assignment, compare your profile for the United States with those created by two classmates. If there are differences, seek to locate the cause(s) of those differences: for example, did you rely on different sources for the basic information you used, or did you classify, combine, or represent the information you found in different ways?
6. The closing paragraphs of this selection juxtapose Thomas F. Farr's contrast between "merely religious fervor" and "potentially dangerous fundamentalism" (paragraph 26), on the one hand, and religions that are "open to other human beings outside their circle" and those having "within them exclusivist tendencies in an absolutist sense" (paragraph 28). Farr argues that the former contrast has political implications for the U.S. government, while the latter involves "theological questions." Are these two dichotomies equivalent? **Write an essay** in which you define the terms of each dichotomy and evaluate the relationships among them.

▼ *The two-year Pew Global Attitudes Project, sponsored by the Pew Charitable Trust with additional funding from the William and Flora Hewlett Foundation, represents "a series of worldwide public-opinion surveys that will measure the impact of globalization, modernization, rapid technological and cultural change and the September 11 terrorist events on the values and attitudes of more than 38,000 people in 44 countries worldwide." Here, we present the opening pages of a December 2002 report on attitudes toward religion and its importance in people's lives around the world. As the text and accompanying charts—a defining characteristic of social science writing—clearly illustrate, the United States is unique among wealthy nations in the high percentage of people reporting that religion is very important in their life. Should we be surprised that religious beliefs play a significant role in public life in our country?*

This report offers an evaluative argument that compares the importance of religion in the lives of people in the United States and in those from other nations. For more about constructing evaluative arguments, see Chapter 9.

LINK TO P. 262

Among Wealthy Nations . . . , U.S. Stands Alone in Its Embrace of Religion

PEW GLOBAL ATTITUDES PROJECT

Religion is much more important to Americans than to people living in other wealthy nations. Six-in-ten (59%) people in the U.S. say religion plays a *very* important role in their lives. This is roughly twice the percentage of self-avowed religious people in Canada (30%), and an even higher proportion when compared with Japan and Western Europe. Americans' views are closer to people in developing nations than to the publics of developed nations.

The 44-nation survey of the *Pew Global Attitudes Project* shows stark global regional divides over the personal importance of religion.[1] In Africa, no fewer than eight-in-ten in any country see religion as very important personally. Majorities in every Latin American country also subscribe to that view, with the exception of Argentina. More than nine-in-ten respondents in the predominantly Muslim nations of Indonesia, Pakistan, Mali and Senegal rate religion as personally very important. In Turkey and Uzbekistan, however, people are more divided over religion's importance.

Secularism is particularly prevalent throughout Europe. Even in heavily Catholic Italy fewer than three-in-ten (27%) people say religion is very important personally, a lack of intensity in belief that is consistent with opinion in other Western European nations. Attitudes are comparable in former Soviet bloc countries. In the Czech Republic, fully 71% say religion has little or no importance in their lives—more than any nation surveyed—while barely one-in-ten (11%) say it is very important. And in Poland, the birthplace of the Pope and where the Catholic Church

[1]Question wording: How important is religion in your life—very important, somewhat important, not too important, or not at all important?

played a pivotal role during the communist era, just 36% say religion is very important.

The Global Attitudes study correlated views on religion with annual per capita income and found that wealthier nations tend to place less importance on religion—with the exception of the United States. This is seen most clearly in Asia, where publics in the two wealthiest nations surveyed—Japan and South Korea—are far less likely to cite religion as personally important than those in poorer nations of the region. The lone exception is Vietnam, however, where just 24% of the public view religion as very important. (Questions on the personal importance of religion were not permitted in China, and were deemed too sensitive to ask in Egypt, Jordan and Lebanon.) ■

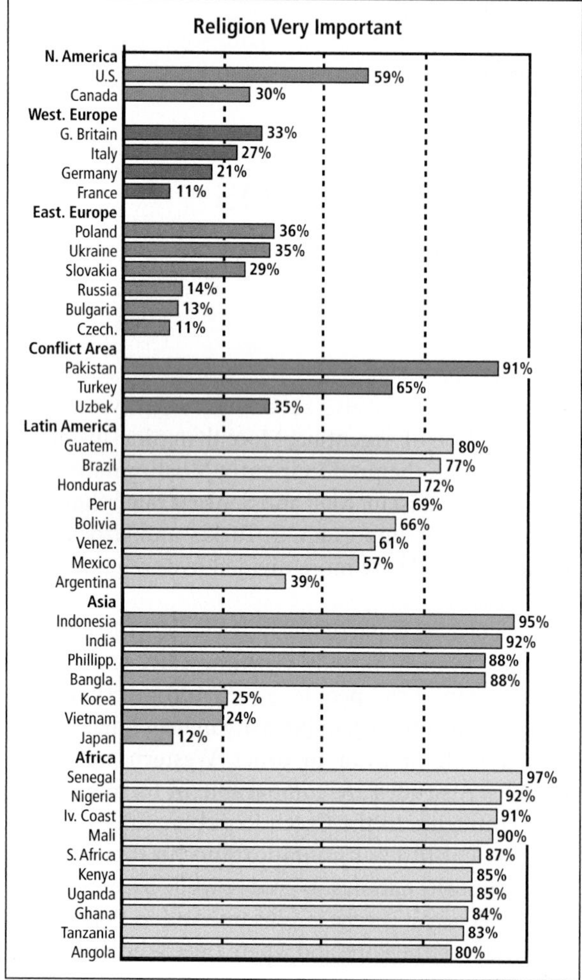

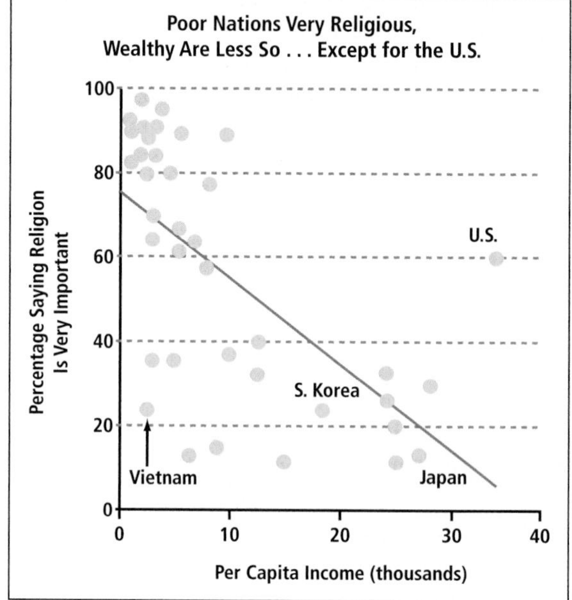

RESPOND •

1. Does the information contained in this brief introductory section to the Pew Global Attitudes Project surprise you in any way? Why or why not? In your opinion, what might account for the unusual attitudes and behavior of Americans in comparison to citizens of other wealthy nations that the United States often sees as its peers and allies?
2. What do you learn about China, Egypt, Jordan, and Lebanon in this text? Why might these governments not want their citizens discussing religion? (You may need to do some research to find out something about these countries, their demographic makeup, and their history.)
3. As mentioned in the headnote, social scientists often rely on charts, tables, figures, and diagrams to do much of their work for them. Not only do such visuals generally contain a great deal of information that's never discussed explicitly in the text, but they also permit the reader to check conclusions drawn in the text against the visual display, whether it's a chart (like the ones used in this excerpt) or a table, figure, or diagram. What sorts of additional observations not already mentioned in the text can you make on the basis of information included in the two charts?

   (The second chart, "Poor Nations Very Religious, Wealthy Are Less So . . . Except for the U.S.," may be difficult for you to read at first. It represents the results of the correlation, or statistical relationship, between wealth, as measured by annual per capita income, and importance reportedly placed on religion, as measured in terms of percentage of answers of "very important" to the question given in footnote 1. The horizontal sloping line in the chart, the regression line, represents a perfect negative correlation: if greater wealth in a country always meant comparably less importance reportedly attached to religion, all the dots or data points, each representing a country, would fall along this line. The closer the data point representing a country is to the line, the tighter the negative relationship between the wealth and importance of religion. Outliers, those data points farthest from the regression line, represent exceptions—for example, Vietnam and the United States in this case.)
4. **Write an essay** in which you evaluate your own responses to this text. Following question 1, you may discuss your surprise (or lack of it) or some other emotional response that you had: chagrin, dismay, happiness. As Chapter 9 reminds us, good evaluative arguments are based on explicit criteria. Hence you'll need to examine your own assumptions about the United States and the larger world and about religion in public life.

In "Selling Safe Sex in Public Schools," Michelle Bryant, formerly of the Office of Public Affairs at the University of Texas at Austin, interviews Shelby Knox, then a government major at UT–Austin and the subject of an award-winning documentary. Bryant wrote this selection for the fall 2005 issue of Life & Letters: A Publication of the College of Liberal Arts of the University of Texas at Austin. As you read, consider why someone like Knox is an appropriate subject for such a publication.

Selling Safe Sex in Public Schools

MICHELLE BRYANT

Teenagers are viewing sexual content in music videos, movies, and, thanks to Paris Hilton,° even hamburger commercials. But what do they really know or need to know about sex? Some people feel schools need to teach teenagers about abstinence only. Opponents say that withholding information about condom use and birth control will only lead to unwanted pregnancies and sexually transmitted diseases (STDs).°

The debate over sex education has intensified in recent years because of substantial increases in federal funding for abstinence-only programs. In 2005, $167 million was appropriated, up from $80 million in 2001. President George W. Bush's proposed 2006 budget includes $206 million for such programs. Schools that choose comprehensive or abstinence-plus curricula don't qualify for this funding and must pay for the programs out of their general budget, provided by local and state governments.

On the frontline of the heated sex education debate stands Shelby Knox, currently a government major at The University of Texas at Austin. Although her hometown's high schools teach abstinence as the only safe alternative, Knox was shocked to learn that Lubbock, Texas, has some of the highest rates of teen pregnancy and STDs in the nation.

At age 15, Knox, a budding opera singer and a devout Christian who has pledged abstinence until marriage, became an unlikely advocate for comprehensive sex education, attracting the attention of documentary filmmakers Rose Rosenblatt and Marion Lipschutz. They documented her efforts in the

Bryant's interview with Shelby Knox provides nearly all of the information and evidence to support her argument. See the guidelines in Chapter 16 to help you plan and conduct your own interviews.

LINK TO P. 474

Paris Hilton, 1981– : American celebrity, heiress, socialite, model, actress, and entrepreneur. Here, she attends the Weinstein Co. Golden Globe after-party on January 16, 2006, in Beverly Hills, California.

STDs: sexually transmitted diseases, that is, diseases that can be transmitted during sexual activity or intercourse, including chlamydia, crabs, gonorrhea, hepatitis, herpes, HIV, HPV, scabies, and syphilis.

Shelby Knox

film "The Education of Shelby Knox" which has been broadcast nationally on the P.O.V. series on PBS and won the Excellence in Cinematography Award in the documentary category at the 2005 Sundance Film Festival.

Through her work with the Lubbock Youth Commission, a group of high 5
school students empowered by the mayor to give Lubbock's youth a voice in city government, Knox began her fight for comprehensive sex education in public schools.

"We decided sex education was going to be our issue because we all knew someone who had been touched by the high rates of STDs and teen pregnancy," Knox said.

The youth commission received extensive media coverage, but little attention from school officials. After repeated requests, the school board finally allowed them to present their recommendations, but to no avail. However, Knox refused to give up, despite being repeatedly discouraged by the pastor of her church and the conservative Southern Baptist culture of the town. She was even told that she was "going to hell," literally.

"I felt like it was my responsibility as a student to use my voice and speak out," Knox said. "I was surprised when we did that the school board didn't recognize us. They didn't say 'You're students. Maybe you know what's going on.' They were really blasé about the whole thing and that was a little disconcerting.

"That's why I got certified to teach at the local health department," she added. "I became a peer educator in my high school because once I learned that the school board wasn't going to do anything I felt like I should.

"Most students were very supportive of sex education," she said. "They re- 10
alized that the fact that we didn't have sex education was a big problem. Once students realized that I had the information they were looking for, they would ask me questions about where they could get tested for STDs and how they could get condoms.

"If a student asks a teacher about sex," she added, "the teacher is required to answer with 'Abstinence is the only way to prevent STDs and teen pregnancy.' If they don't, they're in danger of losing their job."

During the time the youth commission led the comprehensive sex education campaign, STDs and teen pregnancy rates in Lubbock dropped. The Texas Health Department attributed this to a "rise in responsibility" because of the youth commission's advocating condom use.

By her senior year, Knox committed to working with a group of gay teens who decided to sue the Lubbock School Board because they were denied the right to form a gay-straight alliance in school. This was not a fight the other members of the youth commission, afraid of adding more controversy to their already contentious agenda, wanted to join. Soon after, the mayor of Lubbock announced that he was considering doing away with the youth commission because of a city budget shortfall. The youth commission agreed to operate without funding and, in the process, abandoned the sex education campaign. Since that time, the rates of STDs and teen pregnancy in Lubbock have gone back up. An infuriated Knox resigned from the youth commission, but continued fighting for what she felt was right.

When an organization came to Lubbock to protest the gay teenagers' lawsuit, Knox, along with her mother, joined a counter protest, carrying a sign that read "God Loves Everybody," an affirming belief that has guided Knox into adulthood.

"I think that God wants you to question," Knox said. "To do more than just 15
blindly be a follower, because he can't use blind followers. He can use people like me who realize there's more in the world that can be done."

During the Spring 2006 semester, Knox will participate in the UT in D.C. program, which offers qualified students the opportunity to study and intern in Washington, D.C. She hopes to do an internship with Advocates for Youth or the Sexuality Information and Education Council of the United States. She

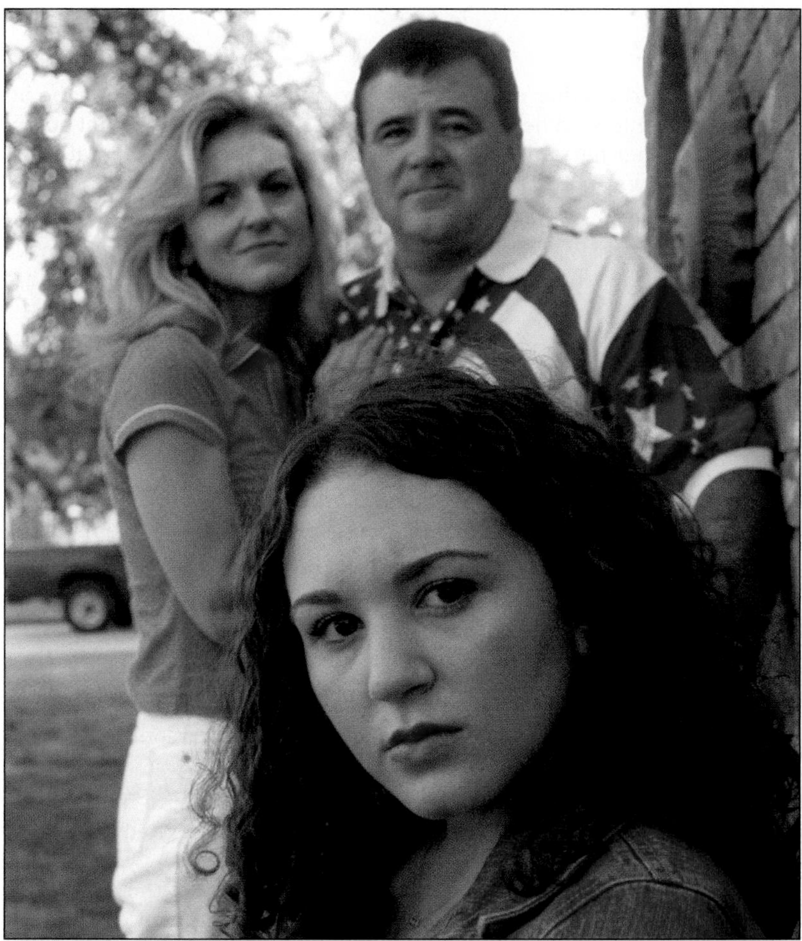

Shelby Knox at home in Lubbock, Texas, with her parents, Danny and Paula Knox

is also a member of the Student Senate, University Democrats and Madrigal Choir. She continues to be an advocate for comprehensive sex education and has spoken with teen activists across the nation in conjunction with the film.

"Getting to connect with teens who can make a difference in their communities is the best part of this," Knox said. "I wish that I would have known of other teens that were doing this. When I speak I give them my e-mail and tell them we can talk because I know how hard it is to be a teenager in high school who is doing something controversial."

RESPOND.

1. What sort of ethos does Shelby Knox create for herself during the interview reported here? What role(s) does her faith play in that ethos? Would her narrative or ethos be different if Knox were an atheist? Why or why not? (For a discussion of ethos, see Chapter 3.)
2. What causal arguments do you find in the narrative of Shelby Knox's experiences? Why are these arguments crucial to the argument made by the selection? (For a discussion of causal arguments, see Chapter 10.)
3. In paragraph 15, Knox contends, "I think that God wants you to question." What does Knox want people of faith to question? Why? Why do you imagine Knox believes "he [God] can't use blind followers"? (Obviously, Knox is using "blind" metaphorically in this case.)
4. This article appeared in *Life & Letters: A Publication of the College of Liberal Arts of the University of Texas at Austin,* a magazine that highlights the research and achievements of faculty and students in the college. It's distributed within the college and to its friends and supporters, including donors, many of whom would be politically conservative and would identify as evangelical Christians. How can you see awareness of the magazine's intended audience in the selection of Shelby Knox as the topic of an article? In the way her story is presented? How might the selection challenge readers holding various political or religious beliefs? How do the illustrations contribute to the article's argument?
5. This selection represents an especially popular genre in American culture, a narrative about an individual who, motivated by a set of principled beliefs—whether sacred, secular, or both—was moved to action in the public arena. Find another example of this genre that you believe to be especially effective, and **write a rhetorical analysis** of it. (For information about writing a rhetorical analysis, see Chapter 5.) In your analysis, be sure to include information about why you find the narrative you've chosen effective and perhaps moving. Be sure to include a copy of the text you analyze when you turn in your rhetorical analysis.

▼ *Naomi Schaefer Riley graduated from Harvard in 1998. She's the recipient of numerous fellowships, and she has worked in various capacities for several national publications, including* The American Enterprise, Commentary, *the* Wall Street Journal, *and the* National Review. *She edits* In Character, *a journal from the John Templeton Foundation that focuses on "the nature and power of the everyday virtues." Riley currently also serves as deputy editor of the journal's "Taste" page. This selection is the introduction to her 2005 book,* God on the Quad: How Religious Colleges and the Missionary Generation Are Changing America. *In conducting research for this book, Riley visited twenty religious colleges during 2001 and 2002, including two Mormon schools, seven Catholic schools, five nondenominational evangelical Protestant schools, two denominational Protestant evangelical schools, one fundamentalist Protestant school, one Buddhist school, and two Jewish schools. As you read, consider how Riley sets up a contrast between religious schools and those whose mission isn't religious, and how she encourages us to think in deliberative terms: how might the "missionary generation" change the nature of American public life?*

Introduction to *God on the Quad:*° *How Religious Colleges and the Missionary Generation Are Changing America*

quad (shortened form of **quadrangle):** a square or rectangular courtyard or space around which the buildings of a college stand.

NAOMI SCHAEFER RILEY

In February 1988, with his novel *The Bonfire of the Vanities* on the best-seller list, social satirist Tom Wolfe gave a Class Day address at Harvard in which he described ours as the era of the "fifth freedom"—freedom from religion. "After you've had every other freedom—the four that Roosevelt enunciated," Wolfe observed in an interview with *Time* a few months later, "the last hobble on your freedom is religion. We saw it in the '60s in the hippie movement, when tens of thousands of young people quite purposely emancipated themselves from ordinary rules."

Interviews and participant observation are the basis for Riley's argument about the missionary generation. Data collected from testimony, narrative, and interview are considered hard evidence just like facts and statistics. Review Chapter 4 for a discussion of factual evidence.

LINK TO P. 81

Today, the legacy of that emancipation is most viscerally felt in the nation's universities. College faculties, which are now demographically dominated by baby boomers, continue their generation's endeavor to "liberate" others from the strictures of orthodox religion and traditional morality. Students who do arrive on campus their freshman year with some traditional religious identity quickly find themselves a beleaguered minority both in the classroom, where their beliefs are derided as contrary to the principles of tolerance and "diversity" (since they are not accepting of every lifestyle and don't believe that every viewpoint deserves equal consideration), and in their extracurricular lives, where their sensibilities are consistently offended by what they regard as the amoral behavior of their peers and its tacit approval by college officials.

In April 2001, for example, the student judiciary at Tufts University voted to withdraw recognition from the Tufts Christian Fellowship for refusing to let a "practicing" lesbian run for one of the group's offices, holding that the exclusion violated the school's nondiscrimination policy. Similar controversies have since arisen for Christian groups at more than a dozen schools, including Williams and Middlebury colleges and Ball State University. In 1995, a Muslim student group at the University of North Carolina at Chapel Hill was denied recognition because it would not allow non-Muslims to hold office. In 2003, a Christian women's residence at Purdue University was told it could not consider gender in choosing its membership or it would risk losing recognition as a campus group and its building.[1]

In other respects as well, religious students regularly confront a hostile environment on today's college campuses. A Harvard student running for president of the undergraduate council a few years ago was vilified by the campus newspaper for his religious beliefs. He never mentioned them on the campaign trail, but a young woman on the election commission, unbeknownst to him, had e-mailed some friends asking them to pray for the candidate. That was enough for the editorial board of the Harvard *Crimson* to warn that the candidate's "ties to religious groups have raised concerns among many students." In an earlier, more widely publicized case, a group of Orthodox Jewish students at Yale sought to live off campus because the coed dormitories forced them routinely to encounter half-naked members of the opposite sex in the hallways. The students were denounced for being "judgmental" about their classmates' behavior, and told that if they did leave campus, they would still have to pay the seven thousand dollar dorm fee. As a Yale spokesman explained, coed dorms are just one "aspect of the Yale educational experience."

5 While some students are able to find religious fulfillment in off-campus churches and other religious organizations, both formal religious practice and adherence to traditional moral codes drop off among undergraduates. Among the relatively few students who are actually involved in faith groups on campus, many describe themselves as "spiritual, not religious." A recent book entitled *Religion on Campus* offers a clear picture of what this means. At a weekly meeting of the Wesley Foundation (a United Methodist group) on a large western university's campus, for instance, the leaders asked, "How can

we keep the spark of God burning inside us this week?" The responses included, "I'm a vegetarian, and that's religious to me," "Smile," and "Take time to be quiet and alone." Another student, who is active in the (Catholic) Newman Center, calls herself a "spiritual junkie," citing as an example her experience of turning out the lights in the room with a male friend and listening to the Indigo Girls.

Feel-good spirituality turns out to be a sorry substitute for the real thing. Academic insiders and outsiders alike have often described a certain malaise among today's college students. For example, a 2002 *New York Times* story profiled Jeffrey Lorch, a sophomore at Columbia, whom the reporter found typical of the more than 2,600 students who had sought help at Columbia's counseling center the previous year. Jeffrey apparently has no real problems, but it takes him three quadruple espressos and an unknown quantity of Prozac to get through the day. Looking at his college experience, Jeffrey notes, "There have been times when I've felt like every conversation [I've had at school] was a sham."

"Souls without longing." That's what Robert Bartlett, a professor of political science at Emory University, calls the dozens, if not hundreds, of Jeffreys he has encountered in the classroom. In a striking essay in *The Public Interest,* Bartlett argues that this malaise is evident in the "narrowness of students' frame of reference or field of vision; in the pettiness of their daily concerns; in the tepid character of their admiration and contempt, their likes and dislikes; in the mediocrity of their ambitions. . . . The world could be their oyster, but they tend to stare back at it, pearls and all—and yawn."

Bartlett argues that one "cause of students' ennui is the absence of religion in their lives," a problem articulated by the seventeenth-century theologian and scientist Blaise Pascal. As Bartlett summarizes Pascal's view, "Without knowledge of or concern for God, human beings vacillate between fits of diversion, which keep them from thinking of their fundamental condition, and enervating boredom which reminds them of it."

But to say these students are "without longing" is to miss the point. Obviously they long for something. Otherwise, why all the caffeine, alcohol, and psychotropic medications? Indeed, a recent UCLA survey on spirituality in higher education found 75 percent of undergraduates were "searching for meaning or purpose in life," while 78 percent discuss religion and spirituality with their friends.

Of course, alcohol, caffeine, and late-night bull sessions are long-standing 10
aspects of American college life. What has changed, however, is that the spiritual longings of these students are less likely than their predecessors' to be fulfilled in today's universities.[2] Only 8 percent of the students in the same

survey reported that their professors frequently encourage classroom discussion of religious or spiritual matters or provide opportunities to discuss the purpose or meaning of life. Most faculty, of course, would not be surprised by those numbers. They would say that it is not part of their job description to host such discussions, and, given the current legal climate in which educational institutions—both public and private—are brought to court for allegedly using public money to advance religious causes, many professors would rightly worry that talking about God in class, not necessarily promoting a religious worldview, would provoke loud complaints from some corners, if not lawsuits.

Sociologists and pundits from David Brooks and Gertrude Himmelfarb on the right to E. J. Dionne and Michael Lind on the left agree that, more than ever before, Americans are living in a nation divided between a religious and a secular culture. In addition to the generational divide, there is also a geographical one. Those who consider traditional religion a small and sometimes backward part of American life, best confined to the private sphere, are part of Blue° America, while those who find faith governs their attitudes and behavior both publicly and privately are part of Red° America. What started out as a political formulation—the states colored red on television newsroom maps, inland and largely more rural areas, voted for Bush in the 2000 presidential election, while the blue-colored states, more urban and coastal, went for Gore—is also a cultural one, with religious practice being the most reliable indicator of which side of the divide people fall on.

red/blue: over the past few years in the United States, the color red has become associated with the Republican Party and the color blue with the Democratic Party, such that one now speaks of "red states" and "blue states."

The crudest formulation of the difference came from political strategist Paul Begala, who infamously wrote:

> Tens of millions of good people in Middle America voted Republican. But if you look closely at the map, you see a more complex picture. You see the state where James Byrd was lynch-dragged behind a pickup truck until his body came apart—it's red. You see the state where Matthew Shepard was crucified on a split-rail fence for the crime of being gay—it's red. You see the state where right-wing extremists blew up a federal office building and murdered scores of federal employees. The state where an Army private who was thought to be gay was bludgeoned to death with a baseball bat, and the state where neo-Nazi skinheads murdered two African-Americans because of their skin color, and the state where Bob Jones University spews its anti-Catholic bigotry: they're all red, too.

Red America sympathizers fired back, referring to the Blue side as "the Porn Belt"—that part of the country in which sex videos constitute the largest share of the home-video market. Mark Steyn, writing in *National Review,* described Blue America as constituting people who had been rushed through the immigration process without sufficient background checks, along with "Al Sharpton's entourage, gay scoutmasters, partial-birth abortion fetishists, [and] Hollywood airheads."

Four years later, that divide has not changed. According to a recent poll by the Pew Research Center for the People and the Press, voters who frequently attend religious services favor President Bush by a margin of 63 percent to 37 percent, while those who never attend lean Democratic by 62 percent to 38 percent. And the fires are continually being reignited. Evolutionary biologist Richard Dawkins and philosopher Daniel Dennett, in an attempt to give non-believers a sort of rallying cry, recently urged that atheists henceforth be referred to as "brights." Dawkins coyly leaves it to others to find a name for religious people.

Most representatives of Blue America, though, are not interested in the 15
goings-on in Red America—they refer to that area between the coasts as "flyover country"—but a group of Red Americans is determined to change the culture of Blue America from the inside out.

Call them the "missionary generation." The 1.3 million graduates of the nation's more than seven hundred religious colleges are quite distinctive from their secular counterparts. And the stronger the religious affiliation of the school, the more distinctive they are. The young men and women attending the twenty religious colleges I visited in 2001 and 2002 are red through and through. (Though the schools are sometimes located in blue states, the majority of their students hail from red states and their attitude toward faith is all red-state.) They reject the spiritually empty education of secular schools. They refuse to accept the sophisticated ennui of their contemporaries. They snub the "spiritual but not religious" answers to life's most difficult questions. They rebuff the intellectual relativism of professors and the moral relativism of their peers. They refuse to accept their "fifth freedom."

In practical terms, these students challenge what has become, since the sixties, the typical model of college-student behavior. They don't spend their college years experimenting with sex or drugs. They marry early and plan ahead for family life. Indeed, they oppose sex outside of marriage and homosexual relationships. Most dress modestly and don't drink, use drugs, or smoke. They study hard, leaving little time for sitting in or walking out. Most vote, and a good number join the army. They are also becoming lawyers, doctors, politicians, college professors, businessmen, psychologists, accountants, and philanthropists in the cultural and political centers of the country.

While they would disagree among themselves about what it means to be a religious person, it is assumed that trying to live by a set of rules, generally ones laid down in scripture, is the prerequisite for a healthy, productive, and moral life.

Administrators and faculty of many seriously religious colleges of all different denominations believe they can produce young professionals who will transform the broader secular culture from within. If they're right, the implications are enormous. Advocates of religious higher education argue: CEOs won't need to scramble to send their employees to business ethics classes when they can hire college graduates who already know them; the armed forces may find it less difficult to recruit from the educated classes than they have in fifty years; faith in our elected leaders may override the cynical attitudes that have characterized American politics for the last half century; instead of appointing special committees, hospitals may be able to hire entire staffs of doctors with backgrounds in bioethics; and secular universities may be overrun by professors studying the interaction of religion with philosophy, science, mathematics, or literature. Is this vision of the future realistic? Can these young men and women become pioneers, bringing an ethical perspective back into their professions, their schools, their communities, and their government institutions?

The initial signs of this cultural shift are everywhere. A Brigham Young graduate was just elected governor of Massachusetts, one of the most liberal states in the Union. Indeed, the number of BYU grads living in New England went from 100 to 3,000 in the last ten years. House Speaker Dennis Hastert, an alumnus of the evangelical Wheaton College, has become one of the most effective occupants of that position in recent years, according to a recent profile in the *New Yorker*. Wheaton also ranks eleventh in the nation in the percentage of graduates who go on to receive PhDs. It was two women who had attended the Baptist Baylor University who were captured by the Taliban while they were doing missionary work in Afghanistan. Yeshiva University, which is ranked by *U.S. News & World Report* as one of the top fifty research universities in America, recently graduated its first Rhodes Scholar. The Ave Maria School of Law just had a higher percentage of its graduates pass the bar than any school in Michigan. Although Ave Maria, a conservative Catholic school, is too new to have received full accreditation from the American Bar Association, its students (whose average LSATs would make it the twenty-fifth ranked law school in the country) are being sought after by leading law firms, justice department offices, prosecutors, and federal judges. Probably less surprisingly, more students at Bob Jones University dropped out to join the army after September 11 than did students at Harvard.

Religious higher education is on the rise in America. The numbers back 20
up the anecdotal evidence here: Colleges and universities with strong faith identities, which enforce strict rules on alcohol, relations with the opposite sex, and attendance at religious services, and offer classes from a religious perspective, are becoming more popular, even while their academic standards have risen. For instance, enrollment at the over one hundred member institutions of the Council for Christian Colleges & Universities (four-year liberal arts colleges committed to teaching Christian doctrine, hiring only professors who share the faith, and providing a Christian atmosphere outside the classroom) jumped a remarkable 60 percent between 1990 and 2002, while the number of students at public and private schools barely fluctuated. As a percentage of total enrollment in institutions of higher education, the number of students at colleges with religious affiliations has not changed much over the last twenty years (8.34 percent in 1984 and 8.07 percent today), but schools with the strongest religious identities have been steadily gaining.

While evangelical schools like the members of the CCCU are at the heart of this new strength in religious higher education, they are hardly alone. Schools affiliated with the Church of Jesus Christ of Latter Day Saints have been expanding, in part because of the fast-growing Mormon population. Not only has BYU added an Idaho campus to its Utah and Hawaii ones, but a new Mormon college (not officially affiliated with the church) was recently established in Virginia. It has grown to a student body of five hundred in six years and is already looking to expand its campus. Populations at Catholic colleges and universities have seen a dramatic rise as well. Applications to Notre Dame, for example, have risen steadily in the last decade—a rise of 23 percent last year broke the 1994 record of 20 percent. And numerous smaller Catholic schools have opened across the country to cater to a more strictly religious population. In California, Thomas Aquinas College, a small Catholic "Great Books" school at the forefront of this movement, is operating at capacity, and its administrators are considering opening another branch on the East Coast. Yeshiva University, the country's flagship Orthodox Jewish college, has many more qualified applicants than it can take, and the more recently established Touro College has stepped in to cater to more traditionally Orthodox students. The trend toward religious higher education extends from the fundamentalist Bob Jones University to the newly established Buddhist college, Soka University.

These developments, of course, did not occur in a vacuum. The number of students attending nondenominational Christian elementary and high schools (usually evangelical) and Jewish day schools has climbed significantly in the last decade. Homeschooling, meanwhile, has experienced a much more dramatic rise in popularity, growing annually at a rate of 15 to 20 percent, to approximately 1.5 million families, according to the Census Bureau. A nationwide survey by the National Center for Education Statistics reports that 38 percent of homeschooling parents cite religion as the main reason for their decision.

Looking at the larger context, the growth in religious education is not surprising. During the 1990s, the churches that grew the fastest demanded the highest commitment from their members, including regular attendance at worship services, strict behavioral codes, tithing, and public confessions of faith. While mainline Protestant churches° continued to lose members, the Mormon Church, for instance, grew by about 19 percent, and the evangelical Churches of Christ and the Roman Catholic Church recorded increases of 18.6 and 16.2 percent respectively. Over the last twenty-five years, Gallup polls have consistently shown that American teens are slightly more likely to attend worship services than adults. Much of the energy driving the current "great awakening" in organized religion is coming from the most traditional corners, and young people are the ones demanding stricter rules and more tradition.

Both a Gallup poll and a University of Pennsylvania study recently noted a positive correlation between teen church attendance and parents' level of education. Richard Gelles, coauthor of the Penn survey, noted: "Karl Marx would say religion was the way lower classes delude themselves into thinking that life is fair. Marx was wrong. Faith is embraced as part of a commitment to traditional values—hard work, education, religion." Plenty of Americans assume that education is some kind of substitute for religion—that only people ignorant of modern science or philosophy would believe in God as the creator or rely on him for moral guidance. But the facts do not bear that assumption out.

The attitude that faith and intellect are incompatible has a long history in 25
America. In 1932, a few years after the Scopes trial,° Philip E. Wentworth, then a recent Harvard graduate, wrote an article for the *Atlantic Monthly* entitled "What College Did to My Religion." Having grown up in a strict Presbyterian household in the Midwest, Wentworth was discouraged from attending Harvard by his local pastor, who feared he would lose his faith, and told instead to try a denominational college nearby. Sure enough, Wentworth writes of his career at Harvard (with the zeal of a convert to secularism), "In the course of time the impact of new knowledge and especially knowledge of science and the scientific method wrought great havoc with my original ideas. All things, it seemed, were subject to the laws of nature. This concept

mainline Protestant churches: in the United States, those denominations or churches that are seen as theologically moderate or progressive, adjusting their understanding of traditional Christian faith to the conditions of the contemporary world. They're contrasted with conservative or fundamentalist denominations, on the one hand, and liberal denominations like the Unitarian Universalists, on the other. Examples would include most churches affiliated with the United Church of Christ, the Disciples of Christ, the American Baptists, the Presbyterians, and the Evangelical Lutherans.

Scopes trial, 1925: the Tennessee trial of John T. Scopes, a teacher charged with violating the Butler Act, a state law forbidding the teaching of "any theory that denies the story of the Divine Creation of man as taught in the Bible, and to teach instead that man has descended from a lower order of animals" in a state-funded institution. The case, which is popularly understood to outlaw the teaching of any form of evolution, drew attention not only for its subject—still controversial—but also because it was argued by two of America's finest attorneys and public speakers, William Jennings Bryan and Clarence Darrow.

supplied my mind with a wholly new pattern into which my religious beliefs refused to fit. In such an orderly universe, there seemed to be no place for a wonder-working God."

The stinging reply to Wentworth came three months later in an article in the same magazine by Columbia religion professor Bernard Iddings Bell. "[Mr. Wentworth] seems to be reasonably intelligent, not at all incapable of understanding religion. The trouble is that he apparently has no knowledge of what religion is. He has outgrown a crude and semi-magical concept of God, such as a child may properly hold, with no realization that grown men mean by religion something both more delicate and more complex." Bell goes on to blame Harvard for the deficiency.

Seventy years later, Josh Jalinski, a senior at a public school in New Jersey, was faced with the same choice as Phillip Wentworth. Having excelled in his academic and extracurricular pursuits, Josh was admitted to Harvard. But Josh, an evangelical Christian, keeping in mind his ambitions to go to seminary, get a PhD in history, and then to become mayor of Asbury Park, work as a minister there, and start his own Christian school, chose to attend Bob Jones University instead. It's unlikely that Josh or his fellow religious college students will experience the sort of spiritual crisis that Wentworth did. Strongly religious colleges aim to give their students (perhaps now more than in the 1930s) the tools to succeed in the secular world and the strength to do so without compromising their faith.

Though it is important to understand the mission that religious colleges see for themselves, my ultimate concerns in this book are not the same as those of the members of the religious communities that sponsor them. I am not simply trying to determine whether religious colleges and universities will keep their distinctive identity over time, or whether they will be successful in propagating their particular faith.

The most important question about the recent growth of religious higher education for observers of American civic and political life is whether this movement tends to make religious communities more insular; whether this missionary generation, as its leaders hope, will transform the broader, secular culture from within; or whether those hopes are bound to be dashed by the influence of secularism on these young men and women. While I can offer no definitive answer to this question, I hope to illuminate it in this book by providing extensive profiles of six of the most significant schools I visited, and then, in subsequent chapters, considering some of the most salient issues affecting the identity of religious colleges and the interactions of their graduates with the outside world.

I must readily acknowledge that the schools I visited were chosen some- 30
what haphazardly. First, the schools I discuss constitute a tiny fraction of the religiously affiliated colleges out there, and for each school I stopped at, I heard about another four or five that I should also have visited. I tried to visit schools of a variety of denominations, but the number of each kind of school does not correspond with the population they represent. In some cases, I visited a few from one religious group to see if my observations were true across institutional lines. For the most part, I focused on undergraduate programs, but there are a few graduate schools I visited as well, which I think display characteristics similar to the colleges'. I picked some well-known schools of which many readers are likely already to have at least some impressions, and others that are quite obscure to the general public.

I tried to spend time mostly at schools that have strong religious affiliations, but that judgment is inevitably subjective. As indicators of the strength of a school's religious affiliation I considered such factors as whether the majority of a school's students were religious, whether professors had to sign a statement of faith, whether they had to be of the same denomination as the school, whether the school had mandatory chapel attendance, and how strict the behavior codes were. The schools described here nonetheless represent various levels of religiosity; in a couple of cases, the schools turned out to be hardly religious at all.

On the basis of interviews I conducted with students, administrators, faculty, and alumni at each school, this book addresses four sets of questions:

1. *Why have students chosen the school?* Answers to this question were often far-ranging, and included factors such as the students' family life, their religious practices growing up, and what kind of primary and secondary schools they had attended, as well as their families' financial situations. Of course, their academic performance in high school was also an issue. I tried to interview some students at each school who had transferred there from secular colleges, since they were in a position to provide useful comparative judgments. I also asked students what their friends and family at home thought of their decision to attend that school.
2. *How is the curriculum different from that of secular schools?* In my interviews with professors and administrators, I asked how the mission of each school is evident in its curriculum. I sat in on both secular and religious classes to assess the academic caliber of students and professors. I tried to determine how much religion entered into secular classes, and how much freedom of debate there was in religious classes. I also examined how each school dealt with the issue of academic freedom for both students and professors.

3. *What is the life outside the classroom like?* This was the most enjoyable part of the project. I spent time visiting dorms, hanging out with students on weekends, approaching them in student centers or on quads. I spoke to students both individually and in groups, to see how they interacted with each other. I asked about dating and drinking and dress codes. Having made inquiries about the official rules, I tried to learn from students about the extent to which they were actually followed. I asked about recent controversies: Which students or faculty had been dismissed, and why? I sat in on meetings of clubs, from Bible study groups to newspaper editorial meetings. I attended musical performances and intramural games. I asked about race relations on campus. I tried to interview students who were religious minorities at the school to find out how they felt about their status there. I went to religious services with students, both on campus and off.
4. *How will these colleges affect students' post-graduation choices?* Finally, I wanted to know what students planned to do after they graduated. Of course, most couldn't tell me exactly how their choices would have been different if they had attended a secular school, but I asked them to explain what parts of their religious education had significantly shaped their plans. I asked them to speculate about whether their religious beliefs would affect the way they practiced their various professions. I asked about whether they intended to have families, and when. I asked both women and men their thoughts on balancing family and career. I asked them where they wanted to live—in what area of the country, and in what type of community. Did they need to be surrounded by coreligionists or were they satisfied being in a minority? What did they think of the secular world? Did they intend to proselytize? If so, how would they do it? And generally, I asked how they envisioned their future roles in the community and in the country.

Readers of *God on the Quad,* I should note, will not find interviews with graduates of these schools who have since left the faith or decided that their education was a failure. It is not because such people aren't out there—they are, and they're easy to find; just type "Bob Jones" or "ex-Mormon" into Google—but rather because such graduates are unlikely to have an effect on the culture that is different from graduates of secular schools. Moreover, I assume that readers of this book can come up on their own with dozens of reasons why they would not want to attend a school like Bob Jones University or Brigham Young (though the freshman retention rates at these schools are very similar to those of secular schools at the same academic level). My interviews with the members of these religious college communities will, I hope, provide answers as to why young men and women *do* choose to attend these schools and what they are learning that is different.

I began the first formal interviews for this book on September 10, 2001. The next day, two thousand miles from home, I sat on the edge of my hotel bed, looking out over the strip malls to the treeless mountains beyond, wondering more than anything else about how to get home. Home for me is Blue America. I have lived in four states, all in the Northeast. I attended two secular colleges and grew up with a sense that religion, while socially beneficial (in that it provided people with a moral compass they might not otherwise have), was not true. In other words, I had already expected to feel distinctly out of place on these campuses. And the events of that Tuesday morning only intensified the feeling.

Over the next week, the students at Brigham Young tried to welcome me 35
into their lives. While national tragedies tend to bring out the best in many people, the first representatives of the "missionary generation" I encountered could not have made a greater impression upon me. Their kindness and compassion, their civic-mindedness, their understanding and interest in national and international affairs, the quiet comfort they were able to find in their faith, and their ability to relate to this stranger in their midst gave me cause for optimism.

At the end of his Class Day address, Tom Wolfe worried that the "religious self-discipline that ran through the American people from one side to the other" and held this country together through the nineteenth and twentieth centuries has now disappeared. Wolfe predicted that the twenty-first century would be a period of "revaluation," in which we will have to "create an entirely new ethical and moral framework." Searching for a person who "has a higher synthesis on the order of Rousseau or Jefferson that will light up the sky and lead mankind into a new era," Wolfe asked his audience, "Where else should we find such a person but at Harvard?" Where else, indeed?

Notes

1. For more examples of the type of problems that traditionally religious students have experienced at secular colleges, please see the Web site of the Foundation for Individual Rights in Education: www.thefire.org.
2. A hundred years ago, for instance, most of the nation's most prominent universities were religious themselves, and so discussions of religion in class and chapel attendance were a staple of university education.

RESPOND •

1. In this selection, Riley tells readers a great deal about the methodology she used in conducting her study with respect to selecting both categories of schools and kinds of schools. She also gives readers a list of the specific questions she sought to answer. How is this information helpful and even necessary to the reader of her research?
2. What does Riley reveal about her identity, including her own religious and political beliefs? (In interviews about her work, she has identified herself as a Conservative Jew.) Is this information useful or necessary for the reader? Why might she have included this information near the end of the "Introduction" rather than elsewhere in the piece? Are there strategic advantages to her choice? Potential disadvantages?
3. In what historical, social, and political contexts does Riley place her research? How is her research an outgrowth of or a response to these contexts?
4. Riley makes much of the contrast between the terms *spiritual* and *religious*. What definitions does she and those she studied provide for each? Might her argument have been different if she had acknowledged that many who prefer the term *spiritual* to *religious* do so because of the negative connotations of the latter, which are linked to its association with fundamentalists of an especially narrow-minded sort?
5. Early in this selection, Riley contends that whether schools are public or private, "religious students regularly confront a hostile environment on today's college campuses" (paragraph 4), and she provides evidence for her claim. She later makes clear that at some of the schools she visited, all of which were private institutions, students would have little, if any, tolerance for those who didn't share their religious beliefs. Should Americans find either or both of these situations troubling? Why or why not? **Write an essay** in which you evaluate the similarities and differences between the two situations. You'll want to do research on several schools, likely a range of them, by visiting their Web sites to learn about their mission statements as you prepare for this assignment. (Every college has a mission statement, a short description of what it understands its mission, or goals, to be. The mission statement can generally be found on the "About [name of institution]" page, which you can reach with a link from the institution's homepage.)

This selection, "Preaching to the Choir? Not This Time," and the three that follow—an open letter from concerned faculty, staff, and emeriti of Calvin College; Gaylen J. Byker's "Reflections on the 2005 Commencement"; and John Zwier's "An Opportunity for Intelligent Debate"—examine how Calvin College sought to deal with campus disagreement regarding President Bush's invitation to be the commencement speaker in May 2005. (Calvin College is a Christian school in the Reformed Evangelical tradition located in Grand Rapids, Michigan, and one of the schools Naomi Schaefer Riley visited for her study God on the Quad.*) Thus these arguments represent a case study of sorts of religious beliefs in the public arena and demonstrate the ways in which members of a single faith tradition may disagree as well as how they handle those disagreements.*

In "Preaching to the Choir? Not this Time," Elisabeth Bumiller, who writes for the New York Times, *provides necessary background information to understand what occurred at Calvin College in May 2005 and why. As you read, consider what sorts of arguments she might understand herself to be constructing and why.*

Preaching to the Choir? Not This Time

ELISABETH BUMILLER

It's that time of year again when President Bush turns up around the country in sumptuous commencement robes, assures thousands of college graduates that a C average does not preclude the presidency and urges them to go forth and do good.

Calvin College, a small evangelical school in the strategic Republican stronghold of Grand Rapids, Mich., seemed a perfect stop on Saturday for the president's message. Or so thought Karl Rove, the White House political chief, who two months ago effectively bumped Calvin's scheduled commencement speaker when he asked that Mr. Bush be invited instead.

In her report on the controversy over Bush speaking at Calvin College, Bumiller creates a causal argument by outlining how each detail of the presidential invitation and the prevailing politics of the college played into the very public debate on campus. Chapter 10 lays out the key features of a causal argument along with a writing guide.

LINK TO P. 307

But events at Calvin did not happen as smoothly as Mr. Rove might have liked. A number of students, faculty members and alumni objected so strongly to the president's visit that by last Friday nearly 800 of them had signed a letter of protest that appeared as a full-page advertisement in *The Grand Rapids Press*. The letter said, in part, "Your deeds, Mr. President—neglecting the needy to coddle the rich, desecrating the environment and misleading the country into war—do not exemplify the faith we live by."

The next day, Mr. Bush was greeted by another letter in *The Press* signed by some 100 of 300 faculty members that objected to "an unjust and unjustified war in Iraq" and policies "that favor the wealthy of our society and burden the poor."

5 At first glance, it seemed as if a mainstay of Mr. Bush's base, the Christian right, had risen up against him. At second glance, the reality was more complex. The protests at Calvin showed that Mr. Bush's evangelical base was not monolithic and underscored the small but growing voice of the Christian left.

That movement, loosely defined as no more than several million of some 50 million white evangelicals, opposes abortion and generally supports traditional marriage. But as a group it is against the Iraq war, the administration's tax cuts, Mr. Bush's environmental policies and, not least, the close identification of evangelicals with the current White House.

A leader of the Christian left is Jim Wallis, the editor and founder of the Christian political magazine *Sojourners* and the author of *God's Politics: Why the Right Gets It Wrong and the Left Doesn't Get It*. Mr. Wallis, whose book has been on the *New York Times* best-seller list for the past 15 weeks, appeared at Calvin College on May 5 and is advising Democrats on how to appeal to religious voters.

"The monologue of the religious right is over," Mr. Wallis said in an interview before Mr. Bush's appearance. "There is a progressive, moderate evangelical constituency that is huge."

Others see the group as a far less powerful force, but they acknowledge that the Christian left cannot be a cheery development for Mr. Rove. "Were this movement to continue to grow, it could create some problems, probably not for President Bush but for future Republican candidates," said John C. Green, the director of the Ray Bliss Institute of Applied Politics at the University of Akron and an expert on the voting patterns of religious groups. In short, Mr. Green said, "Democrats have an opportunity to get some votes."

10 One question is whether Mr. Rove knew what he was getting into when he asked that Mr. Bush be invited to Calvin, a theologically conservative college in the tradition of the Christian Reformed Church that is politically more progressive than other evangelical colleges. (Faculty members estimate that about 20 percent of students opposed Mr. Bush in 2004.)

Mr. Rove secured the invitation through Representative Vernon J. Ehlers, the Republican who represents Grand Rapids and who attended Calvin.

"I think they understood the nature of Calvin," said Jon Brandt, Mr. Ehlers's press secretary, who also attended Calvin. "The White House isn't stupid."

That would be the view of Corwin Smidt, a political science professor at Calvin and the director of the Henry Institute for the Study of Christianity and Politics. Mr. Bush's visit, he said, was both "rewarding the faithful" who voted for him in 2004 and a strategic positioning for 2006.

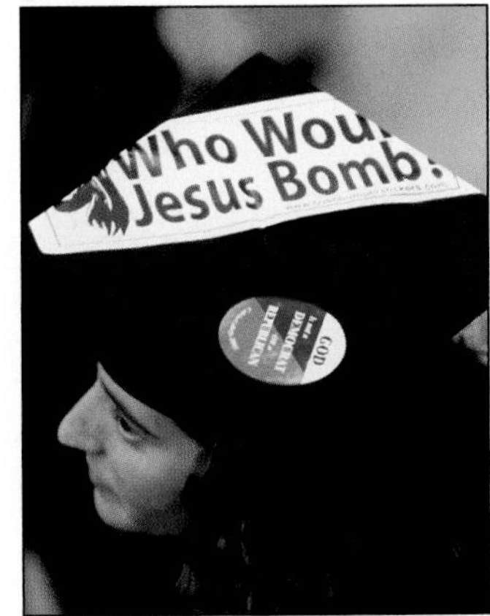

A Calvin College student wore her feelings on her mortarboard during President Bush's speech.

That is when Dick De Vos, an heir to the Amway fortune and a member of a Michigan family that has been a major contributor to the Republican Party and Calvin College, may challenge Gov. Jennifer M. Granholm, a Democrat. Republicans will also try next year to unseat another Democrat, Senator Debbie Stabenow.

As for Mr. Bush, his commencement address on Saturday drew no 15
protests in the Calvin field house other than from students who wore buttons that proclaimed "God is not a Democrat or a Republican."

One other small objection came from the bumped commencement speaker, Nicholas Wolterstorff, a Democrat, a former Calvin academic and a recently retired philosophy of religion professor at Yale. Dr. Wolterstorff said in an interview last week, "Here's a Yale professor being bumped by a Yale graduate with a very average college record." He said he planned to stay home and garden in Grand Rapids instead of attending the president's speech.

Dr. Smidt, a Republican, had a different view of the presidential visit. "I do think it's an honor for the college," he said. "Even if Bill Clinton had come at the height of Monica Lewinsky, I don't think I would have objected then, either."

RESPOND•

1. What are Elisabeth Bumiller's goals in writing this text? How would you characterize her arguments in terms of stasis theory? (For a discussion of stasis theory, see Chapter 1.)
2. Bumiller's subject is the controversy surrounding a college commencement address. First, why are such addresses called "commencement addresses"? Should we expect such speeches to represent forensic, epideictic, or deliberative occasions for argument? (For a discussion of these categories of occasions for argument, see Chapter 1.) Why? Based on this article, how do politicians and political strategists see such events? University administrators? Graduate students and their families? Why?
3. Bumiller contends that Christians, even evangelical Christians, aren't monolithic. How and why is such a claim contrary to popular discourse about religion and politics in American life?
4. Bumiller reports that many students wore buttons proclaiming, "God is not a Democrat or a Republican." What argument do such buttons make? How is their meaning linked to the immediate context at Calvin College? To the larger context of American political and public life in 2005?

5. In this article, Bumiller refers to the Christian left. An organization that represents this perspective on Christian faith is Christian Alliance for Progress, which claims to be "the movement to reclaim Christianity and transform American politics." Thus it's an organization committed to being sure its religious beliefs are in the public arena. Visit this organization's Web site, <http://christianalliance.org>. Choose one of the arguments you find there and **write a rhetorical analysis** of it, seeking to demonstrate how its argument is structured and why it's structured in that particular way. (For a discussion of rhetorical analyses, see Chapter 5.)

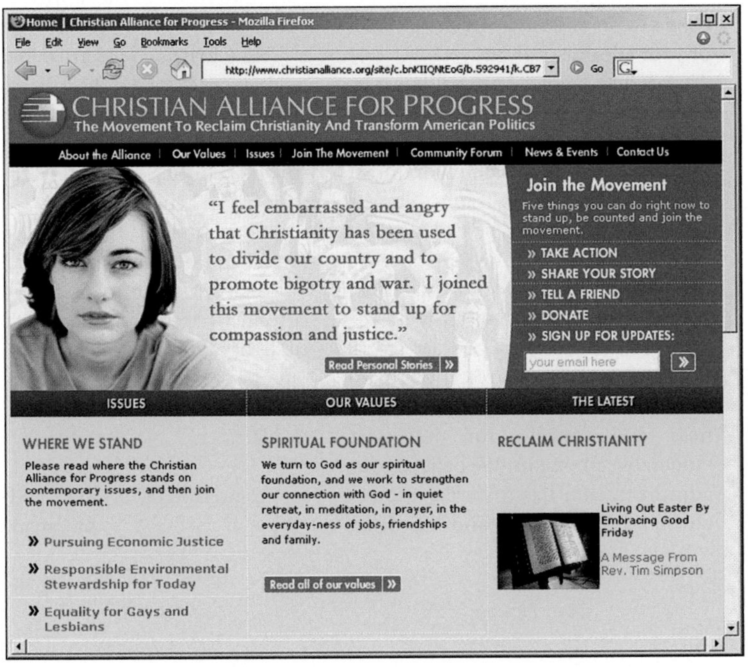

As Elisabeth Bumiller's article, "Preaching to the Choir? Not This Time," notes, the Grand Rapids Press in the city where Calvin College is located ran different letters on two consecutive days in May 2005 about President Bush's visit. Below, you will find the second one, referred to in paragraph 4 of Bumiller's article. As you read it, pay careful attention to the ethos the letter's authors create for themselves and the audience they invoke.

An Open Letter to the President of the United States of America, George W. Bush

On May 21, 2005, you will give the commencement address at Calvin College. We, the undersigned, respect your office, and we join the college in welcoming you to our campus. Like you, we recognize the importance of religious commitment in American political life.

We seek open and honest dialogue about the Christian faith and how it is best expressed in the political sphere. While recognizing God as sovereign over individuals and institutions alike, we understand that no single political position should be identified with God's will, and we are conscious that this applies to our own views as well as those of others. At the same time we see conflicts between our understanding of what Christians are called to do and many of the policies of your administration.

As Christians we are called to be peacemakers and to initiate war only as a last resort. We believe your administration has launched an unjust and unjustified war in Iraq.

As Christians we are called to lift up the hungry and impoverished. We believe your administration has taken actions that favor the wealthy of our society and burden the poor.

As Christians we are called to actions characterized by love, gentleness, and concern for the most vulnerable among us. We believe your administration has fostered intolerance and divisiveness and has often failed to listen to those with whom it disagrees.

As Christians we are called to be caretakers of God's good creation. We believe your environmental policies have harmed creation and have not promoted long-term stewardship of our natural environment.

Our passion for these matters arises out of the Christian faith that we share with you. We ask you, Mr. President, to reexamine your policies in light of our God-given duty to pursue justice with mercy, and we pray for wisdom for you and all world leaders.

–Concerned faculty, staff, and emeriti of Calvin College

Who are the intended readers of this open letter in a widely read publication? Who are the invoked readers? The real readers? See Chapter 1 for more on how writers address audiences.

LINK TO P. 32

RESPOND •

1. What argument(s) does this letter make?
2. You can analyze this letter as an example of Rogerian argumentation, which seeks to acknowledge and build on common ground (in contrast, say, to highlighting or exacerbating differences between parties). Where in the text do you find efforts to acknowledge and build on shared assumptions, beliefs, or premises?
3. At the same time, it's clear that those who signed this letter disagree profoundly with President Bush and invoke their religious beliefs as justifications—or even warrants—for those disagreements. We can therefore characterize the letter as an argument of definition, one that contrasts competing understandings of Christian belief. What specific definitional criteria are enumerated in the letter? (For a discussion of arguments of definition, see Chapter 8.)
4. How might Christians who support President Bush respond to this letter? You may wish to offer responses (or even rebuttals) to the criteria listed or offer additional criteria not mentioned here. If you feel that you're not familiar enough with the tenets of Christianity or with liberal and conservative approaches to Christianity, work with classmates who are answering this question or use the Internet to research this topic.
5. Using your responses to questions 3 and 4, **write an essay** in which you define the competing understandings—definitions, really—of the Christian faith and of religious belief represented in this letter and in possible responses to it. Rather than a definitional essay, you may wish to write an evaluative essay in which you argue for the value of one characterization of Christianity or religious belief over the other. (For a discussion of arguments of definition, see Chapter 8. For a discussion of evaluations, see Chapter 9.)

Gaylen J. Byker, a Calvin alum (1973), is currently president of the college. He received his MA and JD from the University of Michigan and his PhD from the University of Pennsylvania. A Vietnam veteran, Byker worked in international banking and energy before becoming president of Calvin in 1995. "Reflections on the 2005 Commencement" originally appeared on the Calvin College Web site at <http://calvin.edu/commencement/2005/reflections.htm>. As with much institutional discourse, we cannot be sure who actually wrote or edited the text. It's likely the result of a group of people working together; the opinions expressed, however, are taken to represent those of the institution (in this case, Calvin College) and the person to whom it's attributed (in this case, Gaylen J. Byker, the college's president).

As the president of the university, Dr. Byker has a vested interest in his school's reputation. To what extent can the reader take this report at face value? Chapter 3 explores authors' motives.

LINK TO P. 73

Reflections on the 2005 Commencement

GAYLEN J. BYKER, PRESIDENT OF CALVIN COLLEGE

Calvin College was pleased to host President George W. Bush as our 2005 Commencement speaker on Saturday, May 21.

We consider it a singular honor to host the sitting President of the United States and to have our country's leader address our graduates; that is why the decision was made to send an invitation at the suggestion of the White House. In his message, President Bush charged our graduates to live lives of commitment and service, a theme that resonates with Calvin's mission statement and our call "to engage in vigorous liberal arts education that promotes lifelong Christian service."

In short, it was an overwhelmingly positive Commencement occasion that those present will never forget.

But many are unable to acknowledge the spirit and mood that prevailed on Commencement Day because of the events that led up to that day.

For in the weeks prior to Commencement we had spirited yet civil discussions 5
on our campus about faith, politics, social policies and more, the exact sort of discussions one might expect to find at a place that takes so seriously the life of the mind as well as matters of the heart.

Yet while there was some *disagreement* within our Calvin community concerning certain policies of the President's administration, there was no *protest* over his participation in Commencement—as inaccurately reported in some media accounts.

A Celebratory Commencement

Hosting the President of the United States at Commencement does not imply that the college embraces a particular party, policy or action. President Bush was greeted warmly at the ceremony. Indeed, he received standing ovations and thunderous applause. Those who differed expressed their differences quietly and respectfully. We were fully confident that the Calvin community would treat the President hospitably, demonstrating Christian civility and the respect due the office of the President — and that is how it was.

Here is an email I received after the event from Calvin parents John and Marilyn Wiesehan of St. Louis, Mo., who witnessed the graduation of their son, Chris:

"John and I just wanted to let you know how impressed we were with the 2005 Commencement at Calvin.

"Despite all the rumors and some dissent, President Bush was welcomed 10
enthusiastically by the Calvin community. The students and guests were clearly thrilled to have their country's President speak at Calvin. There was no booing, and not one disruption during his speech. My 82-year-old mother-in-law was so impressed, she lamented that her granddaughter had not given Calvin a look. Most of all, Chris was ecstatic.

"With the complex world situation, it is only natural that there would be some faculty and student dissent. We did not want to send our sons to a monastery to escape the outside world. We wanted to send our sons to a place where world problems could be discussed and examined in the light of Holy Scriptures. We found that Calvin not only met our expectations, but far exceeded them. Although only God truly knows the heart, Chris appears to have grown quite a bit in his Christian faith and credits his Calvin professors and Calvin friends."

Disagreement, Not Protest

Some have expressed concerns to the college about either the choice of President Bush as speaker or about those in the Calvin community who have publicly voiced differences with President Bush or policies of his administration. Some tell us that simply inviting President Bush politicized our commencement and diminished the send-off for our graduates — and that hosting the President implies that Calvin fully embraces everything that President Bush endorses. Still others think that any articulated dissent indicates a lack of respect for our Christian brother in the White House. Critics on either side of this argument have been equally vehement in their protestations, and some cite Scripture to fortify their statements.

Calvin College respectfully states that neither view is accurate.

People who are reacting to second-hand accounts of what transpired here over the last few weeks do not have the benefit of living and working within this Christian academic community. They read about the invitation to President Bush and hear about faculty and students worried that Calvin will be identified with President Bush on various issues—and some aspect of this offends them. But that kind of event and dialogue is *exactly* what an engaged Christian college should be doing—challenging one another to think carefully and Biblically about important issues, rather than simply making quick judgments based on information gleaned from general sources (and for most Americans today that means television, radio, newspaper stories and the internet). And it is clear at Calvin College that well-meaning believers who agree on the essentials of the faith and that affirm the mission of our institution can disagree, not only on matters of politics and public policy, but in all academic areas from economics to philosophy and from the sciences to social work.

Calvin is an institution of higher learning that takes its faith and learning 15
seriously. Our faculty and students have had the advantage of participating in intense discussion for many weeks now so that, by the time Commencement Day arrived, most of the strong feelings and emotions found civil avenues for expression, disagreements notwithstanding.

However, some faculty members chose to express their dissent in an open letter placed in the *Grand Rapids Press* on Commencement Day. The letter's intent was to articulate their convictions and urge President Bush to reconsider several policy matters on the basis of a shared Christian faith. The open letter was itself the center of campus debate. While some felt strongly that making these statements was a matter of Christian conscience, a majority of the Calvin community feared that the media and media audiences would construe the statement as disrespectful protest and a challenge of the President's Christian faith. Yet, about 120 of the nearly 700 people who work at Calvin (along with a few emeriti) signed the letter. (Before the statement was even in print, two professors appeared on a confrontational political television show, which many also saw as sure to be interpreted as merely about protest and disrespect.)

In the same May 21 edition of the *Press*, an opinion piece written by Calvin communications professor Randall Bytwerk also appeared, articulating his view that President Bush should be welcomed without dissent—and his confidence that despite the debate, the Calvin community would put its differences aside and welcome the President with enthusiasm. Yet another column was printed that same morning, penned by the religion editor of the *Grand Rapids Press,* which praised Calvin for being a college "that likes to mix it up on a firm platform of faith."

Complicating the picture further, a full-page ad appeared on Friday, May 20, in the *Grand Rapids Press.* On this page, 823 Calvin alumni and others expressed their views, without the benefit of the weeks of campus discussion that preceded the faculty statement. Calvin College had no part in that more harshly worded ad. Unfortunately, media reports confused the alumni ad with the faculty statement, fueling the charges of campus disrespect.

In fairness to the entire Calvin community, perhaps we should put those numbers in context. There are 53,600 members of the Calvin Alumni Association. Of those members, less than 700 participated in the "alumni and friends" letter—and, on the other side of the spectrum, it should be known that a "calvin4bush" website collected 1,754 alumni and friends names for a supportive statement in a matter of a few days.

"Convicted Civility"

It is not surprising that some do not understand that a college can be deeply 20
Christian and engage in intense dialogue about the world and society—even venturing into areas of great contention in the public square. It is not surprising because, in this day and age of polarized public debate (even in Christian circles), there seems little room for any middle ground or for civility. To best describe the nature of the conversation among Calvin College community members concerning President's Bush's visit, consider these excerpts from the work of my good friend and former Calvin professor (and now Fuller Theological Seminary president) Richard Mouw in his call for "convicted civility." Mouw, in his excellent book *Uncommon Decency,* quotes theologian Martin Marty: "One of the real problems in modern life is that the people who are good at being civil often lack strong convictions and people who have strong convictions often lack civility." Mouw says we need both a civil outlook and a "passionate intensity" about our convictions; thus, a "convicted civility."

Mouw bemoans the fact that today "civility" is equated with being a pushover. "But," writes Mouw, "in the past civility was understood in much richer terms.

To be civil was to genuinely care about the larger society. It required a heartfelt commitment to your fellow-citizens. It was a willingness to promote the well-being of people who were very different, including people who seriously disagreed with you on important matters. Civility wasn't merely an external show of politeness. It included an inner politeness as well" (pp. 12–13). Mouw calls for Christians to lead the way in modeling this virtue to a skeptical world.

Calvin College professors and students have engaged in spirited conversation and debate during these final weeks of school. And while no one at Calvin claims perfection or a sinless heart, pondering the meaning of the President's appearance here on Commencement Day has been an exercise in "convicted civility"—with many earnest calls to examine speech and motives as followers of Jesus Christ.

On May 21, Calvin faculty, staff and students displayed that "convicted civility" with "inner politeness." Commencement 2005 at Calvin College was first and foremost a time when our community gathered to praise God for His faithfulness and to commission 875 Calvin graduates to bring hope and healing to the corner of God's Kingdom where they are sent. This year President George W. Bush was a part of that ceremony, singing and praying with us and charging the graduates to "embrace this tradition of service and help set an example for all Americans."

At my inauguration as Calvin's eighth president in 1995, my first address to the Calvin community had to do with acknowledging and embracing the tensions inherent in being a college that does not sacrifice faith *or* learning. These events underscore the difficulty—and necessity—of taking such a path. We promise to respond to our critics with humility and grace. We also reassert Calvin's mission to be agents of renewal in the academy, church and society, pledging fidelity to Jesus Christ and offering our hearts and lives to do God's work in God's world.

RESPOND.

1. How does Gaylen J. Byker construct and evaluate President Bush's visit to his campus? What arguments is he making? In what ways do they reflect and result from his role as president of the college?
2. What sort of evidence does Byker use as he develops his argument? How does he rely on personal testimony in particular? Why is personal testimony especially effective in contexts like this one? (For a discussion of kinds of evidence, see Chapter 16.)
3. How does Byker define and characterize "convicted civility"? How does he use this concept to build his argument? How does "convicted civility" relate to Rogerian argumentation, discussed in Chapter 1 and in question 2 on p. 874.
4. In explaining her research, Naomi Schaefer Riley, author of *God on the Quad*, notes that one of her goals is to understand the political impact of what she terms the "missionary generation" on the future of American life. If graduates of Calvin College and some of the other colleges Riley investigated take convicted civility or something like it as the basis for argumentation into the workplace, into their participation in their communities, and into civic and political life, how might American society be different? Would such a change be for better or for worse? Why? **Write an essay** in which you evaluate convicted civility as a method of argumentation for dealing with differences in society. (For a discussion of evaluative arguments, see Chapter 9.)

Zwier uses his personal experience as a graduating senior to reflect on the campus debate. See Chapter 16 for ideas about how to evaluate the use of personal experience as evidence.

LINK TO P. 479

▼ *John Zwier was a graduating senior at Calvin College in May 2005 when he wrote this piece, "An Opportunity for Intelligent Debate," for the student newspaper,* Chimes. *As you read this selection, pay special attention to the way Zwier frames not only the issue of President Bush's visit but also discussion of it by Calvin students.*

An Opportunity for Intelligent Debate

JOHN ZWIER

Hiemenga Hall: a classroom building on the Calvin College campus.

Nicholas (Nick) Wolterstorff: Calvin alum (1953) who, after receiving a PhD in philosophy at Harvard and teaching two years at Yale, returned to Calvin to teach for thirty years. He then was named Noah Porter Professor of Philosophical Theology in the Philosophy Department at Yale. Wolterstorff is the author of eight books, the co-author of another, and the co-editor of a collection of essays. He's a former president of the Society of Christian Philosophers.

I arrived at school around noon on Thursday, April 21, feeling late for class and overly tired from writing a paper all night. One could say I was not in the mood. As I hustled down the hallway of Hiemenga,° I nodded to a friend, intending to do the "Wazzup?" acknowledgement and pass on by. He had a grin painted on his face, "What do you think? President Bush is speaking at commencement."

A minute later, I ran into another friend, shaking his head with a bemused, "I don't know how to respond, but I'm not happy" demeanor. I feigned ignorance when he mentioned the news. It allowed me to escape again with a promise to talk to him later.

Class was no refuge. "Political Philosophy in Historical Perspective" with Professor Goi does not give one the opportunity to avoid current political events. She asked us what we thought. Being argumentative, my reaction was, "It is the President of the United States, and the college cannot turn this opportunity down." I leaned on justifications: President Bush will put my college on the map; the school can only benefit in enrollment and donations; and finally, this gives the Calvin community an opportunity to put away communal apathy and discuss how our community interacts with the country. I left class feeling content with my conclusions.

Over the next few hours I noticed conservatives alternating between vocal elation and quiet, excited glee. Liberals cursed and thought of protest. Two discussions later and my contentment felt less universal. I had missed two implications of the president's visit, which were extremely important. First, the seniors would miss the chance to hear Nick Wolterstorff° speak to us; this was a greater loss than I had first suspected, as I learned from multiple people how much they were looking forward to his thoughtful, intellectual style. Second, and I think more importantly, the college risked associating itself indelibly with politics. That is, Calvin College risked lending its name and its reputation to the Republican bully-pulpit.° Americans are increasingly associating Christianity with the Republican Party, and I worried that allowing the president to speak at Calvin College aided the administration in making this point, whether it's justified or not.

bully-pulpit: a position (for example, a job or elected office) that enables its holder to speak publicly about any topic or issue.

I realize now that my main concern with President George W. Bush speak- 5
ing at Calvin is this association, this one-to-one ratio of president-to-Christianity. I want Americans to realize that Christians, and Calvin College in particular, do not recognize this one-to-one ratio without reservations.

For this reason, I have talked with the leadership of the College Republicans and the Social Justice Coalition as well as Calvin College's administration, including Vice President for Student Life Shirley Hoogstra. We would like to offer Calvin students and faculty the opportunity to express their hope that President George W. Bush does not politicize religion during the Commencement ceremony of 2005.

Our aim is to offer students and faculty a respectful, non-intrusive way to be seen, in lieu of boycotting graduation, protesting vocally or disrupting the celebration. The idea is to give buttons to willing participants, inscribed with the words, "God is not a Democrat or a Republican."

We believe that Calvin College students are intelligent, critical thinkers who wish to give a fair hearing to President Bush's oration; but, we want to make it clear that students at Calvin College do not sanction the joining of Christianity with the Republican platform or the administration's policies.

This visual statement is not divisive but encourages the type of intellectual debate for which Calvin College should be known: open dialogue about Christianity's role in the world.

Regardless of the reader's personal view, President Bush should recognize 10
that Calvin does not have a monolithic response to his attendance at our Commencement celebration.

A mixed crowd will welcome him. I hope that we may welcome him respectfully, but I also hope that speaking at a Christian college, Calvin College especially, makes him nervous. Calvin College is not a tame, adoring town hall meeting. Our students and faculty will listen carefully to what he says and will judge the content of the speech by its merits.

I, as a graduating senior, hope that President Bush reflects on the educational experience, on youth and on the great possibilities which our future offers us.

RESPOND.

1. In what ways is John Zwier's argument a proposal argument? What is his specific proposal? What steps led him to make that proposal? In other words, in what ways has he considered questions of definition, cause, and evaluation before offering his proposal? (For a discussion of proposal arguments, see Chapter 11.)
2. Zwier comments that the button's statement—a visual argument—isn't divisive (paragraph 9). Do you agree or disagree? Why? How would wearing such a button compare with boycotting graduation as a form of argument?
3. Clearly, one of Zwier's concerns is the association of "Christianity with the Republican Party . . . whether it's justified or not" (paragraph 4). Zwier later explains that wearing the button provides students and faculty "the opportunity to express their hope that President George W. Bush does not politicize religion during the Commencement ceremony of 2005" (paragraph 6). What does it mean to "politicize religion"? Did those who signed "An Open Letter to the President . . ." (p. 876) likely believe they were politicizing religion? Why or why not? Is it possible or beneficial *not* to politicize religion in American society or any society? Why or why not?
4. In what ways does Zwier's proposal offer "an opportunity for intelligent debate," as promised by the selection's title? **Write a letter** responding to Zwier's proposal as if you were writing a letter to *Chimes*, the newspaper of Calvin College. Obviously, you shouldn't pretend to be a student at Calvin if you aren't. In your letter, be sure your evaluation of this proposal is clear. (For a discussion of evaluative arguments, see Chapter 9.)

God's Justice and Ours

ANTONIN SCALIA

Justice Antonin Scalia has served as a member of the U.S. Supreme Court since 1986. This article, which originally appeared in First Things: The Journal of Religion and Public Life *in May 2002, is based on earlier remarks Justice Scalia had made at a forum on religion and public life at the University of Chicago's Divinity School. In it, Scalia distinguishes between two fundamentally different ways of interpreting the U.S. Constitution, discusses the changing attitude of democratic societies to the death penalty (that is, capital punishment), and ends by disagreeing with the papal encyclical* Evangelium Vitae *and the most recent version of the Catholic catechism. As you read, note the care with which Scalia defines and illustrates the terms he uses; also, consider the ways in which these comments were written to be read aloud.*

Before proceeding to discuss the morality of capital punishment, I want to make clear that my views on the subject have nothing to do with how I vote in capital cases that come before the Supreme Court. That statement would not be true if I subscribed to the conventional fallacy that the Constitution is a "living document"—that is, a text that means from age to age whatever the society (or perhaps the Court) thinks it ought to mean.

In recent years, that philosophy has been particularly well enshrined in our Eighth Amendment° jurisprudence, our case law dealing with the prohibition of "cruel and unusual punishments." Several of our opinions have said that what falls within this prohibition is not static, but changes from generation to generation, to comport with "the evolving standards of decency that mark the progress of a maturing society." Applying that principle, the Court came close, in 1972, to abolishing the death penalty entirely. It ultimately did not do so, but it has imposed, under color of the Constitution, procedural and substantive limitations that did not exist when the Eighth Amendment was adopted—and some of which had not even been adopted by a majority of the states at the time they were judicially decreed. For example, the Court has prohibited the death penalty for all crimes except murder, and indeed even for what might be called run-of-the-mill murders, as opposed to those that are somehow characterized by a high degree of brutality or depravity. It has prohibited the mandatory imposition of the death penalty for any crime, insisting that in all cases the jury be permitted to consider all mitigating factors and to impose, if it wishes, a lesser sentence. And it has imposed an age limit at the time of the offense (it is currently seventeen) that is well above what existed at common law.

If I subscribed to the proposition that I am authorized (indeed, I suppose compelled) to intuit and impose our "maturing" society's "evolving standards of decency," this essay would be a preview of my next vote in a death penalty case. As it is, however, the Constitution that I interpret and apply is not living but dead—or, as I prefer to put it, enduring. It means today not what current society (much less the Court) thinks it ought to mean, but what it meant when it was adopted. For me, therefore, the constitutionality of the death penalty is not a difficult, soul-wrenching question. It was clearly permitted when the Eighth Amendment was adopted (not merely for murder, by the

Eighth Amendment: "Excessive bail shall not be required, nor excessive fines imposed, nor cruel and unusual punishments inflicted."

way, but for all felonies—including, for example, horse-thieving, as anyone can verify by watching a western movie). And so it is clearly permitted today. There is plenty of room within this system for "evolving standards of decency," but the instrument of evolution (or, if you are more tolerant of the Court's approach, the herald that evolution has occurred) is not the nine lawyers who sit on the Supreme Court of the United States, but the Congress of the United States and the legislatures of the fifty states, who may, within their own jurisdictions, restrict or abolish the death penalty as they wish.

But while my views on the morality of the death penalty have nothing to do with how I vote as a judge, they have a lot to do with whether I can or should be a judge at all. To put the point in the blunt terms employed by Justice Harold Blackmun towards the end of his career on the bench, when he announced that he would henceforth vote (as Justices William Brennan and Thurgood Marshall had previously done) to overturn all death sentences, when I sit on a Court that reviews and affirms capital convictions, I am part of "the machinery of death." My vote, when joined with at least four others, is, in most cases, the last step that permits an execution to proceed. I could not take part in that process if I believed what was being done to be immoral.

Capital cases are much different from the other life-and-death issues that 5
my Court sometimes faces: abortion, for example, or legalized suicide. There it is not the state (of which I am in a sense the last instrument) that is decreeing death, but rather private individuals whom the state has decided not to restrain. One may argue (as many do) that the society has a moral obligation to restrain. That moral obligation may weigh heavily upon the voter, and upon the legislator who enacts the laws; but a judge, I think, bears no moral guilt for the laws society has failed to enact. Thus, my difficulty with Roe v. Wade is a legal rather than a moral one: I do not believe (and, for two hundred years, no one believed) that the Constitution contains a right to abortion. And if a state were to permit abortion on demand, I would—and could in good conscience—vote against an attempt to invalidate that law for the same reason that I vote against the invalidation of laws that forbid abortion on demand: because the Constitution gives the federal government (and hence me) no power over the matter.

With the death penalty, on the other hand, I am part of the criminal-law machinery that imposes death—which extends from the indictment, to the jury conviction, to rejection of the last appeal. I am aware of the ethical principle that one can give "material cooperation" to the immoral act of another when the evil that would attend failure to cooperate is even greater (for example, helping a burglar tie up a householder where the alternative is that the burglar would kill the householder). I doubt whether that doctrine is even applicable to the trial judges and jurors who must themselves determine that the death sentence will be imposed. It seems to me these individuals are not merely engaged in "material cooperation" with someone else's action, but are themselves decreeing death on behalf of the state.

The same is true of appellate judges in those states where they are charged with "reweighing" the mitigating and aggravating factors and determining de novo° whether the death penalty should be imposed: they are themselves decreeing death. Where (as is the case in the federal system) the appellate judge merely determines that the sentence pronounced by the trial court is in accordance with law, perhaps the principle of material cooperation could be applied. But as I have said, that principle demands that the good deriving from the cooperation exceed the evil which is assisted. I find it hard to see how any appellate judge could find this condition to be met, unless he believes retaining his seat on the bench (rather than resigning) is somehow essential to preservation of the society—which is of course absurd. (As Charles de Gaulle is reputed to have remarked when his aides told him he could not resign as President of France because he was the indispensable man: "Mon ami, the cemeteries are full of indispensable men.")

de novo: Latin phrase meaning "anew, afresh"; considering the matter anew; with regard to law, the same as if a case had not been heard before and as if no decision previously had been rendered.

I pause here to emphasize the point that in my view the choice for the judge who believes the death penalty to be immoral is resignation, rather than simply ignoring duly enacted, constitutional laws and sabotaging death penalty cases. He has, after all, taken an oath to apply the laws and has been given no power to supplant them with rules of his own. Of course if he feels strongly enough he can go beyond mere resignation and lead a political campaign to abolish the death penalty—and if that fails, lead a revolution. But rewrite the laws he cannot do. This dilemma, of course, need not be confronted by a proponent of the "living Constitution," who believes that it means what it ought to mean. If the death penalty is (in his view) immoral, then it is (hey, presto!) automatically unconstitutional, and he can continue to sit while nullifying a sanction that has been imposed, with no suggestion of its unconstitutionality, since the beginning of the Republic. (You can see why the "living Constitution" has such attraction for us judges.)

It is a matter of great consequence to me, therefore, whether the death penalty is morally acceptable. As a Roman Catholic—and being unable to jump out of my skin—I cannot discuss that issue without reference to Christian tradition and the Church's Magisterium.°

Magisterium: in Catholic theology, the divinely appointed authority given to the pope and bishops of the Catholic Church to teach the truths of religion.

The death penalty is undoubtedly wrong unless one accords to the state a 10
scope of moral action that goes beyond what is permitted to the individual. In my view, the major impetus behind modern aversion to the death penalty is the equation of private morality with governmental morality. This is a

predictable (though I believe erroneous and regrettable) reaction to modern, democratic self-government.

Few doubted the morality of the death penalty in the age that believed in the divine right of kings. Or even in earlier times. St. Paul had this to say (I am quoting, as you might expect, the King James version):

> Let every soul be subject unto the higher powers. For there is no power but of God: the powers that be are ordained of God. Whosoever therefore resisteth the power, resisteth the ordinance of God: and they that resist shall receive to themselves damnation. For rulers are not a terror to good works, but to the evil. Wilt thou then not be afraid of the power? Do that which is good, and thou shalt have praise of the same: for he is the minister of God to thee for good. But if thou do that which is evil, be afraid; for he beareth not the sword in vain: for he is the minister of God, a revenger to execute wrath upon him that doeth evil. Wherefore ye must needs be subject, not only for wrath, but also for conscience sake. (Romans 13:1–5)

This is not the Old Testament, I emphasize, but St. Paul. One can understand his words as referring only to lawfully constituted authority, or even only to lawfully constituted authority that rules justly. But the core of his message is that government—however you want to limit that concept—derives its moral authority from God. It is the "minister of God" with powers to "revenge," to "execute wrath," including even wrath by the sword (which is unmistakably a reference to the death penalty). Paul of course did not believe that the individual possessed any such powers. Only a few lines before this passage, he wrote, "Dearly beloved, avenge not yourselves, but rather give place unto wrath: for it is written, Vengeance is mine; I will repay, saith the Lord." And in this world the Lord repaid—did justice—through His minister, the state.

These passages from Romans represent the consensus of Western thought until very recent times. Not just of Christian or religious thought, but of secular thought regarding the powers of the state. That consensus has been upset, I think, by the emergence of democracy. It is easy to see the hand of the Almighty behind rulers whose forebears, in the dim mists of history, were supposedly anointed by God, or who at least obtained their thrones in awful and unpredictable battles whose outcome was determined by the Lord of Hosts, that is, the Lord of Armies. It is much more difficult to see the hand of God—or any higher moral authority—behind the fools and rogues (as the losers would have it) whom we ourselves elect to do our own will. How can their power to avenge—to vindicate the "public order"—be any greater than our own?

So it is no accident, I think, that the modern view that the death penalty is immoral is centered in the West. That has little to do with the fact that the West has a Christian tradition, and everything to do with the fact that the West is the home of democracy. Indeed, it seems to me that the more Christian a country is, the less likely it is to regard the death penalty as immoral. Abolition has taken its firmest hold in post-Christian Europe, and has least support in the church-going United States. I attribute that to the fact that, for the believing Christian, death is no big deal. Intentionally killing an innocent person is a big deal: it is a grave sin, which causes one to lose his soul. But losing this life, in exchange for the next? The Christian attitude is reflected in the words Robert Bolt's play has Thomas More° saying to the headsman: "Friend, be not afraid of your office. You send me to God." And when Cranmer asks whether he is sure of that, More replies, "He will not refuse one who is so blithe to go to Him." For the nonbeliever, on the other hand, to deprive a man of his life is to end his existence. What a horrible act!

Thomas More: beheaded in 1535 for refusing to take the oath of the Act of Succession, which would have passed the British throne to Elizabeth, a Protestant, rather than the Catholic Princess Mary. His final words were "the king's good servant, but God's first."

15 Besides being less likely to regard death as an utterly cataclysmic punishment, the Christian is also more likely to regard punishment in general as deserved. The doctrine of free will—the ability of man to resist temptations to evil, which God will not permit beyond man's capacity to resist—is central to the Christian doctrine of salvation and damnation, heaven and hell. The post-Freudian secularist, on the other hand, is more inclined to think that people are what their history and circumstances have made them, and there is little sense in assigning blame.

Of course those who deny the authority of a government to exact vengeance are not entirely logical. Many crimes—for example, domestic murder in the heat of passion—are neither deterred by punishment meted out to others nor likely to be committed a second time by the same offender. Yet opponents of capital punishment do not object to sending such an offender to prison, perhaps for life. Because he deserves punishment. Because it is just.

The mistaken tendency to believe that a democratic government, being nothing more than the composite will of its individual citizens, has no more moral power or authority than they do as individuals has adverse effects in other areas as well. It fosters civil disobedience, for example, which proceeds on the assumption that what the individual citizen considers an unjust law—even if it does not compel him to act unjustly—need not be obeyed. St. Paul would not agree. "Ye must needs be subject," he said, "not only for wrath, but also for conscience sake." For conscience sake. The reaction of people of faith to this tendency of democracy to obscure the divine authority behind government should not be resignation to it, but the resolution to combat it as effectively as possible. We have done that in this country (and continental Europe has not) by preserving in our public life many visible reminders that—in the words of a Supreme Court opinion from the 1940s—"we are a religious people, whose institutions pre-suppose a Supreme Being." These reminders include: "In God we trust" on our coins, "one nation, under God" in our Pledge of Allegiance, the opening of sessions of our legislatures with a prayer, the opening of sessions of my Court with "God save the United States and this Honorable Court," annual Thanksgiving proclamations issued by our President at the direction of Congress, and constant invocations of divine support in the speeches of our political leaders, which often conclude, "God bless America." All this, as I say, is most un-European, and helps explain why our people are more inclined to understand, as St. Paul did, that government carries the sword as "the minister of God," to "execute wrath" upon the evildoer.

A brief story about the aftermath of September 11 nicely illustrates how different things are in secularized Europe. I was at a conference of European and American lawyers and jurists in Rome when the planes struck the twin towers. All in attendance were transfixed by the horror of the event, and listened with rapt attention to the President's ensuing address to the nation. When the speech had concluded, one of the European conferees—a religious man—confided in me how jealous he was that the leader of my nation could conclude his address with the words "God bless the United States." Such invocation of the deity, he assured me, was absolutely unthinkable in his country, with its Napoleonic tradition° of extirpating religion from public life.

It will come as no surprise from what I have said that I do not agree with the encyclical Evangelium Vitae° and the new Catholic catechism (or the very latest version of the new Catholic catechism), according to which the death penalty can only be imposed to protect rather than avenge, and that since it is (in most modern societies) not necessary for the former purpose, it is wrong.

I have given this new position thoughtful and careful consideration—and 20
I disagree. That is not to say I favor the death penalty (I am judicially and judiciously neutral on that point); it is only to say that I do not find the death penalty immoral. I am happy to have reached that conclusion, because I like my job, and would rather not resign. And I am happy because I do not think it would be a good thing if American Catholics running for legislative office had to oppose the death penalty (most of them would not be elected); if American Catholics running for Governor had to promise commutation of all death sentences (most of them would never reach the Governor's mansion); if American Catholics were ineligible to go on the bench in all jurisdictions imposing the death penalty; or if American Catholics were subject to recusal° when called for jury duty in capital cases.

Napoleonic tradition: during his coronation as Emperor of France in 1804, Napoleon Bonaparte (1769–1821) famously took the crown out of the hands of the Pope and crowned himself, a symbolic demonstration that power in his empire stemmed from the state and not the church.

Evangelium Vitae: Latin title, meaning "The Gospel of Life," of a 1995 encyclical, or papal letter, defining the Church's teachings on the value and sacredness of all stages of human life, from conception to death. Papal encyclicals are always written in Latin, and their titles are the opening words of the document. They are not considered to be infallible.

recusal: a judge's voluntarily removing himself or herself from hearing a specific case because of conflict of interest, bias, or other reasons.

RESPOND •

1. Justice Scalia devotes the first part of this article to distinguishing between those who read the Constitution as a "living document," the meaning of which changes as society "matures," and those who see it as "enduring," with a focus on its meaning at the time it was drafted. What, for Scalia, are the characteristics and consequences of each view? Which of the two views do you prefer? Why? Does either one leave you uncomfortable? Why or why not?
2. Throughout the article, Scalia makes other important distinctions: cases in which the state (that is, the government) decrees death versus those where it does not restrain death from occurring (paragraph 5), private morality versus governmental morality (paragraph 10), European versus American attitudes toward religion in public life (paragraph 14), legal versus moral matters (paragraph 17), and Christian versus post-Freudian secularist perspectives on death (paragraph 15), among others. Choose two such distinctions, and specify the basis of the distinction (in each case, a kind of definition—see Chapter 8).
3. Scalia concludes by claiming that it's a good thing for American Catholics (and, by extension, people of any faith in America) to be involved in aspects of public and political life in the United States. Do you agree or disagree? Why?
4. Scalia argues that a justice who finds the death penalty immoral should resign from the bench (paragraph 8). Do you agree or disagree? Why? Whatever your stance, you'll need to do your best to anticipate and acknowledge potential rebuttals against your position.
5. Scalia claims that the state should be accorded "a scope of moral action that goes beyond what is permitted to the individual" (paragraph 10); in other words, he believes that it's a grave mistake to assume that "a democratic government, being nothing more than the composite will of its individual citizens, has no more moral power or authority than they do as individuals" (paragraph 17). **Write an essay** in the form of a proposal argument in which you propose and evaluate the consequences of each of these positions, arguing ultimately for the position you find more justifiable.

Justice Scalia embeds a definition argument in his article as evidence for his principal argument. See Chapter 8 for more about definition arguments and how to use them effectively.

LINK TO P. 218

In "The Ethicist," a weekly advice column in the New York Times *that's also syndicated nationally, Randy Cohen helps readers make sense of dilemmas they encounter in their daily lives. Since the late nineteenth century, Americans have turned to newspaper columnists for advice; from the perspective of argumentation, columnists evaluate situations (Chapter 9) and offer readers proposals about potential courses of action they might take—or should have taken (Chapter 11). In this specific case, a New Yorker asked how she might balance her opposition to what she perceived as an act of sexism committed in the name of religion with her commitment to others' right to religious expression.*

Read the query, read Cohen's response, and decide whether you agree or disagree with Cohen's analysis. Then, read on to see what readers of the Times *had to say about Cohen's analysis and advice. The letters to the editor about this specific column spanned several weeks, with readers ultimately responding to other readers' letters. The first three letters appeared three weeks after the initial column with the editorial comment, "The Ethicist was reprimanded by hundreds of Orthodox Jews, outraged at criticism of a religious rule banning a handshake between the sexes." (Interestingly, among the published letter writers criticizing Cohen, several have last names that are traditionally Jewish, but none identifies him- or herself as Orthodox. One wonders if the editors of the* Times *had sufficient evidence for their claim.) The last three letters appeared two weeks after the initial letters were printed.*

Between the Sexes

THE ETHICIST
RANDY COHEN

The courteous and competent real-estate agent I'd just hired to rent my house shocked and offended me when, after we signed our contract, he refused to shake my hand, saying that as an Orthodox Jew he did not touch women. As a feminist, I oppose sex discrimination of all sorts. However, I also support freedom of religious expression. How do I balance these conflicting values? Should I tear up our contract?

–J. L., New York

This culture clash may not allow you to reconcile the values you esteem. Though the agent dealt you only a petty slight, without ill intent, you're entitled to work with someone who will treat you with the dignity and respect he shows his male clients. If this involved only his own person—adherence to laws concerning diet or dress, for example—you should of course be tolerant. But his actions directly affect you. And sexism is sexism, even when motivated by religious convictions. I believe you should tear up your contract.

Had he declined to shake hands with everyone, there would be no problem. What he may not do, however, is render a class of people untouchable. Were he, say, an airline ticket clerk who refused to touch Asian-Americans, he would find himself in hot water and rightly so. Bias on the basis of sex is equally discreditable.

Some religions (and some civil societies) that assign men and women distinct spheres argue that while those two spheres are different, neither is inferior to the other. This sort of reasoning was rejected in 1954 in the great school desegregation case, Brown v. Board of Education, when the Supreme Court declared that separate is by its very nature unequal. That's a pretty good ethical guideline for ordinary life.

There's a terrific moment in "Cool Hand Luke," when a prison guard about to put Paul Newman in the sweatbox says—I quote from memory—"Sorry, Luke, just doing my job." Newman replies, "Calling it your job don't make it right, boss." Religion, same deal. Calling an offensive action religious doesn't make it right.

Letters in Response to Cohen's Advice

As a Jew, a feminist and a future rabbi, I share the Ethicist's contempt for discriminatory religious norms and practices (Oct. 27). However, the practice of "shomer negiah" — of refraining from engaging in any physical contact with members of the opposite sex who are not family — does not fall into this category. Had the Ethicist done his research, he would have known that the laws of negiah apply equally to both sexes and do not render either women or men peculiarly "untouchable." These laws are based on the belief that platonic male-female contact can easily degenerate into sexual impropriety.

Whether or not one agrees with this logic, it does not lend itself to an accusation of sexism. The real disgrace is that the Ethicist answered this query without educating himself about the religious practice upon which it is based and without consulting Jewish authorities who could assist him in this endeavor.

– Cara Weinstein Rosenthal
South Orange, N.J.

The Orthodox Jew who refused to shake a woman's hand after signing a real-estate contract was wrongfully accused of sexism and of acting without the "dignity and respect he shows his male clients." Rather, it was out of respect to his own wife and to other women that the man did not extend his hand; his intent was to elevate and sanctify the relationship between men and women, which is all too often trivialized.

– Helen Pogrin
New York

A real-estate agent is hired to rent a house, and the woman who hires him wants to tear up the contract because his religious beliefs prevent him from shaking hands? The agent was courteous and competent. What more did she want? The prohibition of physical contact between unrelated men and women has nothing to do with sexism. Religious freedom is a constitutional and moral right. No one should understand that more than the Ethicist.

– Robert M. Gottesman
Englewood, N.J.

Randy Cohen sure unleashed the Furies (Letters, Nov. 17, responding to the Ethicist from Oct. 27). Actually, Cohen has a good point, and his critics protest too much. Orthodox Judaism hardly treats women as equal to men. Orthodox men regularly express in prayer their gratitude to God for not having made them women. I suspect that the prohibition against touch isn't all that egalitarian either. After all, it is women who are viewed as impure for large segments of their lives.

– Eva Landy
Barrington, R.I.

Our rabbi — who is modern and egalitarian — gave a sermon on the Ethicist column, and he carefully drew the distinction between a religious belief and a discriminatory act. One question I have heard frequently: had the religion in question been one less familiar to the writer — say, Islam — would Cohen have given such a glib response without checking with religious experts and without considering both parties' sensitivities?

– Paul Berman
Edison, N.J.

As a Jewish woman, respectful but nonobservant, I can understand the discomfort of the woman who was offended. As a lawyer, however, I know that discomfort is never cause for breaking a contract.

– Margaret R. Loss
New York

In order for his readers to trust his advice, Cohen must first convince them of his credibility as "The Ethicist." See Chapter 3 for more on how authors establish credibility with their audiences.

LINK TO P. 69

RESPOND •

1. Do you agree or disagree with Randy Cohen's analysis of the situation J. L. describes? In other words, did the Orthodox Jew's refusal to shake hands with a woman who wasn't a relative by blood or marriage constitute an act of sexism in terms of the intentions of the real estate agent or its effect upon his client? Should J. L., as Cohen suggests, have torn up the contract? Why or why not?
2. Evaluate the responses to Cohen's column. What sorts of arguments—those from the heart, those based on character, or those based on fact and reason—do the letter writers use? Which specific arguments do you find most persuasive? Why?
3. How should a pluralistic society like ours accommodate religious expression when that expression violates—or appears to violate, in the eyes of some—other principles that are important, such as gender equality? **Write a proposal argument** (Chapter 11) in which you offer criteria for balancing these two when they're in conflict. Note that the case described here involves an individual's providing a contractual service to another; the range of such conflicts is, in fact, much broader. Thus you may wish to write about the case Cohen describes, or you may prefer to research other cases, which may have involved, for example, such issues as the right of parents who are Christian Scientists to deny or limit medical care for their children and the display of religious symbols such as menorahs or Christmas trees in various public places. The most effective proposals will be those that demonstrate they've dealt with the case they examine in its complexity.

▼ *"Wearing a Head Scarf Is My Choice as a Muslim; Please Respect It," by Mariam Rahmani, originally appeared in July 2005 in the* Austin American Statesman. *During that summer, Rahmani, a rising high-school senior from Theodore Roosevelt High School in Kent, Ohio, was participating in the 2005 Telluride Association Summer Program at the University of Texas at Austin. (The Telluride Association sponsors several such programs for high school juniors annually at institutions around the country. The six-week programs, which focus on various topics, are seminars much like upper-division college courses.) As you read, consider how Rahmani's proposal for dealing with differences of religion and culture in the public space anticipates and responds to potential counterarguments.*

Wearing a Head Scarf Is My Choice as a Muslim; Please Respect It

MARIAM RAHMANI

Among the elements in Rahmani's article are definition arguments exploring the meanings of the *hijab* and gender oppression. See Chapter 8 for more on making definition arguments.

LINK TO P. 218

This fall, French public school students will experience their second year under a law that bans the display of all religious symbols in schools. The law has aroused immense controversy because it forbids female Muslims to wear *hijab*°—hence its nickname, "the veil law."°

hijab: the head covering worn by some Muslim women; it usually covers the hair and neck, but not the face. A woman's wearing the *hijab* is generally taken by Muslims to signify modesty.

"the veil law": a French law passed in March 2004 that outlaws the wearing of "conspicuous religious symbols" in public schools. Although the law named no specific articles of clothing or jewelry, it was understood as outlawing the *hijab* (or even headscarves), yarmulkes (worn by some Jewish boys), turbans (as worn by Sikh boys), and large crosses (as some Christians might wear). "Discreet symbols of faith," such as hands of Fatima (worn by some Muslims), Stars of David (a symbol of Judaism), and small crosses (associated with Christianity), were permitted. To understand the law, one must appreciate that the separation of church and state has been much stronger in France than in the United States for quite some time. In general, the French assume that religion is a private matter and shouldn't be part of the public arena. Those supporting the law contend that it ensures that schools will be places where ethnic or religious identities don't become more important than the values all French people share.

In December 2003, about 3,000 people attended a demonstration in Paris to protest a law forbidding Islamic veils in French schools.

In passing it, the French government argued that its public school system should be an open arena encouraging students to engage in independent thought. This is a worthy aim for any educational system. Here in the United States, we have generally kept religion out of public schools for similar reasons. The trouble is not the French law's goal, but rather the Western perception that the Islamic *hijab* can't exist in a system allowing free inquiry.

I will soon begin my senior year of high school in Kent, Ohio, and am spending my summer here in Austin. Seven years ago, I made a personal decision to begin wearing *hijab*. You might wonder why.

At the root of *hijab* is the philosophy that a woman should be regarded for her personality, mind and abilities rather than her physicality. Wearing *hijab* reminds me not to focus on the superficial and instead to channel my energies toward developing my character and intellect. To me, this encapsulates the spirit of independent thought.

5 Ironically, much of the Western world views the Islamic *hijab* as a symbol of male oppression. But every day in the West, we are inundated with images that reduce women to sex symbols. Why do people think that my choosing to act on my own will—and without the pressure of having to physically impress the opposite sex—is "oppressive"?

Are advertisements that use scantily clothed women merely to sell a product, or that present women as mindless individuals valued only for their beauty, really "liberating"?

Hijab enables a woman to maintain her dignity. It helps her demand respect as an equal of any man rather than as an object for his pleasure.

The negative association Westerners have of *hijab* is that weak or brainwashed Muslim girls are forced by their families to wear it. The French law supposedly will liberate these girls.

My experience shows the opposite: a number of Muslim girls with *hijab* have passed through Kent's school system as dedicated and involved students who have become a part of the school community's fabric. Most females who are found with *hijab* in the Western world are strong, independently minded women who consciously and voluntarily resolve to wear it because it makes sense to them. I suspect this is why some people have grown afraid: they are intimidated by the prospect of capable young women choosing to live lives different than their own.

10 The issue is not oppression of women. It is about the unwillingness of two ideologies to coexist in mutual respect and understanding. A female with *hijab* registers as an unknown in the common Western mind, and humans are naturally wary of the unknown. Legislation inspired by such fear only succeeds in ostracizing these women.

It's pointless to debate whether young women with *hijab* have excluded themselves from society or vice versa. A barrier now separates the two, making impossible the very kind of open, cooperative intellectual understanding that the French law was meant to foster.

Mainstream societies have often rejected the customs and beliefs of immigrant communities. These communities then isolate themselves to preserve their customs. No one benefits.

In an increasingly interdependent world, we must tolerate one another even when our attitudes diverge. On the issue of *hijab* in the West, both parties must first agree to disagree. Muslim women with *hijab* are not asking Western women to do the same, and likewise, Western society should respect our decisions. Furthermore, people who are ignorant of the principles behind *hijab* should seek to inform themselves, and Muslims should be patient to provide answers.

As human beings, we must realize that we all share the same basic desires for happiness and meaning in our lives. No one should suffer discrimination because we choose different paths to achieve these common goals.

RESPOND •

1. What is Mariam Rahmani's argument? How does she define the meaning of wearing the *hijab* and justify it? How effectively does she anticipate and respond to potential counterarguments?
2. How does Rahmani call into question Western notions of "liberation" for women?
3. If women of any faith or no faith at all believe that they're regarded by men or society at large for their "physicality," should they have to take action, or should men or society change? Why? How?
4. Rahmani sets up a strong contrast between the West and Islam, yet she is, based on available evidence, a Muslim in and of the West. If we assume this statement is true, has Rahmani contradicted herself or weakened her argument? In other words, must there be a strong contrast between Islam and the West? Why or why not?
5. In paragraph 13, Rahmani contends that we must "agree to disagree." Do you agree with her position, or are there alternatives she hasn't mentioned? What might they be?
6. In the same paragraph, Rahmani issues a challenge both to those who "are ignorant of the principles behind *hijab*" and to Muslims. Whatever your background, do some research on the topic, seeking to

understand why some Muslim women wear the *hijab* and why others, including many who are very devout, choose not to. As you'll soon discover, differences are linked in complex ways to a woman's understanding of Islam and, especially for recent immigrants or their children or grandchildren, the country or region from which they've come. You'll easily be able to find information on this topic on the Web, but you may also want to try to interview several Muslim women to obtain their views on this complex topic. **Write a definitional essay** in which you seek to make explicit the principles that various women attend to in their decision to wear or not wear the *hijab* or to cover their hair in some other way.

A PRIEST, *a* RABBI *and an* IMAM ARE WALKING DOWN THE STREET.

(There's no punch line.)

What do you get when you mix Christianity, Judaism and Islam? In many parts of the world, it's a recipe for disaster. Yet in America, it's a formula that has peacefully endured for over 200 years. In fact, not only has it endured, it's flourished.

The pundits may say that the ability for different faiths to coexist here comes from a lack of intensity and passion for any religion in America. But nothing could be further from the truth. Because we are free to choose which religion, if any, we'd like to follow, it enables us to have a deeper, more personal relationship with our faith than would otherwise be possible.

And because no one religion needs to feel threatened by another, we can look to the similarities that unite us, instead of focusing on the differences. Two hundred million Christians, Jews, Muslims, Buddhists and Hindus agree. To learn more about freedom of religion, visit rememberfreedom.org. Or, feel free to ask the spiritual leader of your choice.

FREEDOM. APPRECIATE IT. CHERISH IT. PROTECT IT.

This ad, "A Priest, a Rabbi, and an Imam Are Walking down the Street," was part of the Ad Council's "Campaign for America," launched in September 2003 to mark the second anniversary of the events of September 11, 2001. The Ad Council is a private, nonprofit organization that seeks to use the talents and resources of those in communications and advertising to create public service advertisements for radio, television, and print media. As you study the ad, consider the ways in which it's a response to September 11 even though the events of that day are never explicitly mentioned.

RESPOND •

1. How would you summarize the argument(s) made by this advertisement? Imagine trying to explain the argument(s) to someone from another country—France, for example. (See the previous selection, Mariam Rahmani's "Wearing a Head Scarf Is My Choice . . . ," for information on how France deals with religious differences among its citizens.) How would you describe what's distinctly American about the argument(s) being made here?
2. The advertisement begins, "A priest, a rabbi, and an imam are walking down the street. (There's no punch line.)" What sorts of cultural knowledge do the ad's creators expect the reader to bring to the text? How does the sentence "There's no punch line" disrupt expectations readers might have? Which genre is associated with such an opening? How does the ad's beginning in this way contribute to its message?
3. This advertisement goes on to claim, "Because we [Americans] are free to choose which religion, if any, we'd like to follow, it enables us to have a deeper, more personal relationship with our faith than would otherwise be possible." Do you agree or disagree? Why? How would America likely be different if it did have a state religion or if, as in some countries, only a single religion could be practiced?
4. In what ways is this advertisement a proposal argument? In what ways are all advertisements proposal arguments? (For a discussion of proposal arguments, see Chapter 11.)
5. You can find more recent advertisements by the Ad Council at <http://adcouncil.org/>. Choose one of the ads currently featured that you find especially effective, and **write a rhetorical analysis** of it, explaining why, given its goals, it is effective. Even if you're able to include a copy of the advertisement in your analysis, remember to describe it in order to orient the reader. (For a discussion of rhetorical analyses, see Chapter 5.)

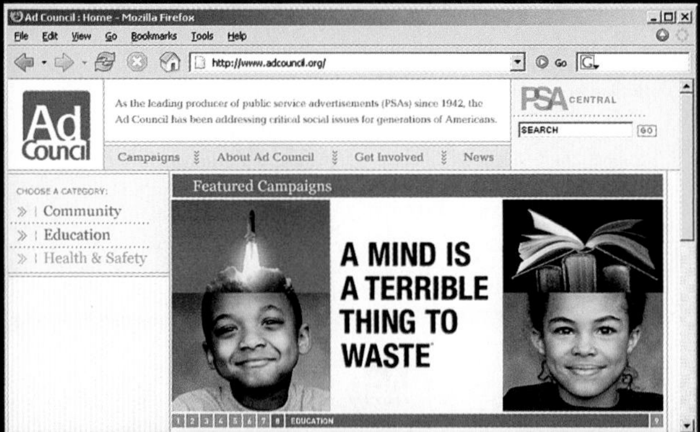

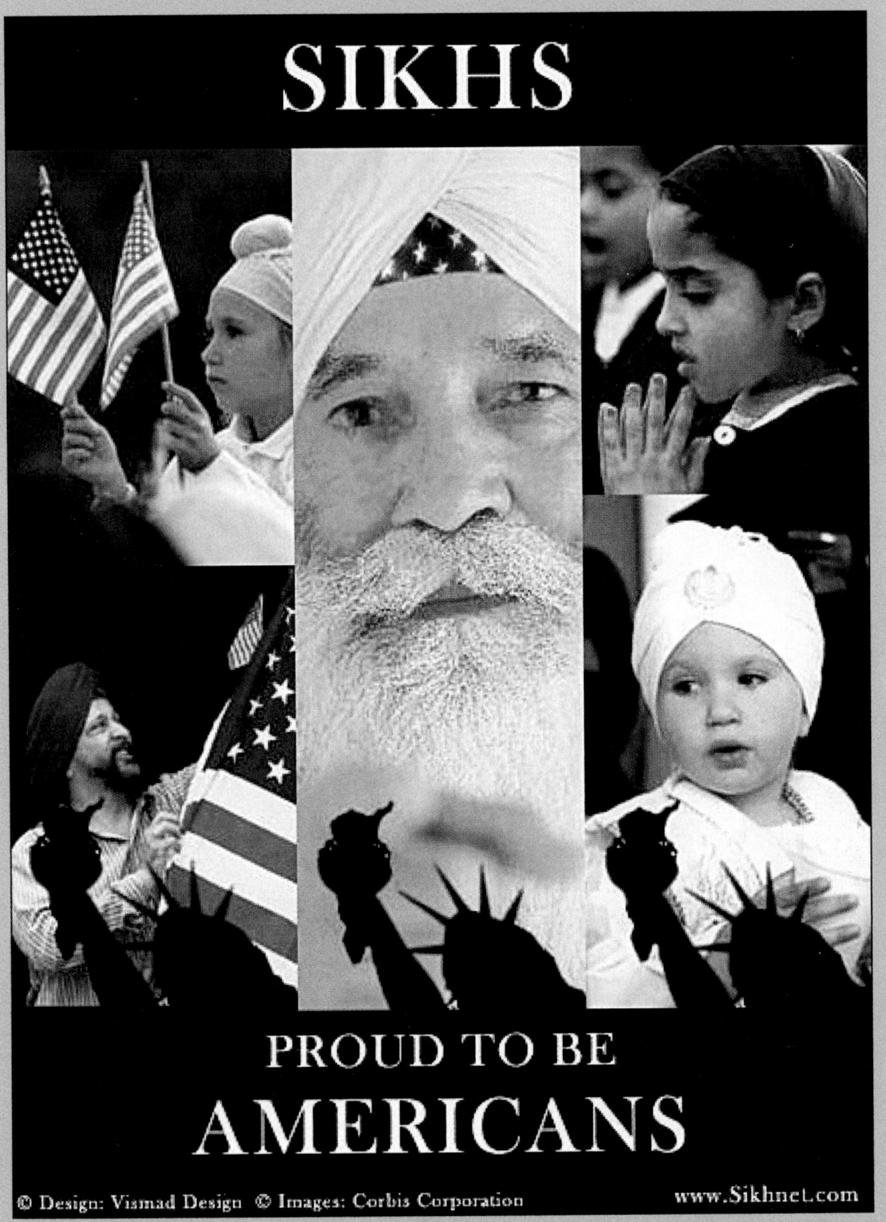

The SikhNetwork, *Sikhs: Proud to Be Americans*

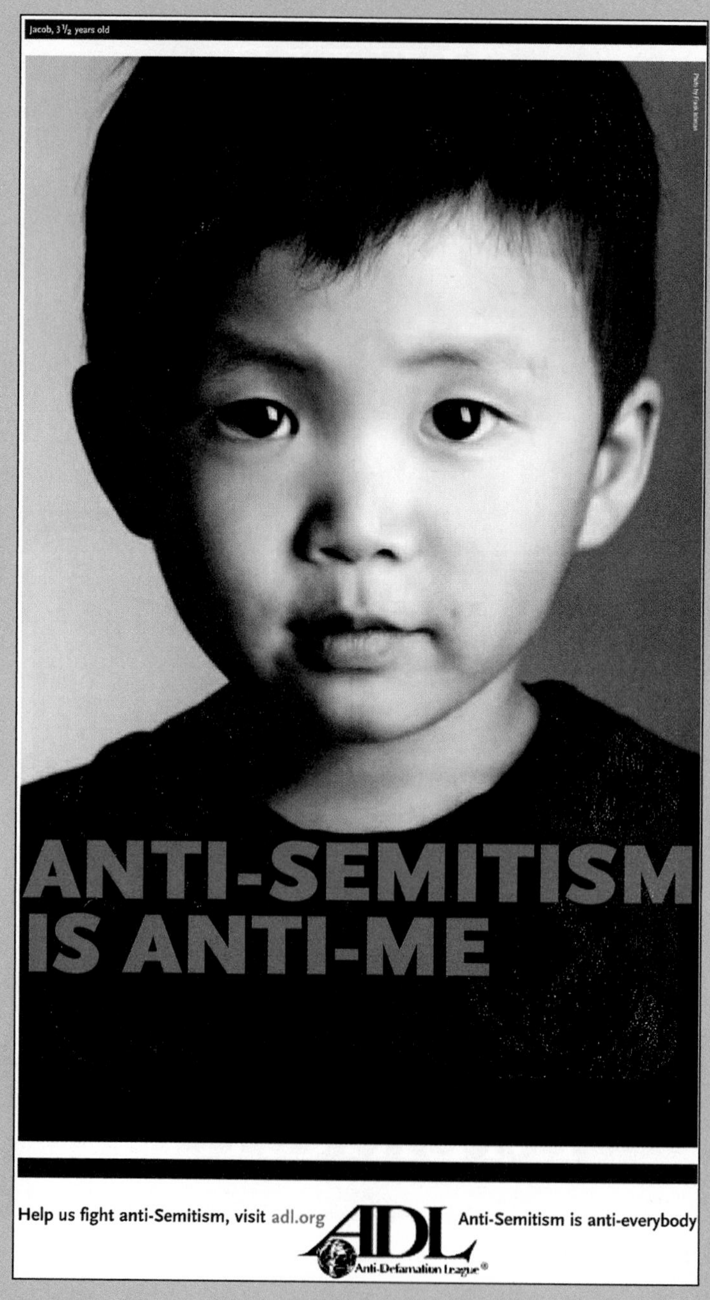

Anti-Defamation League, *Anti-Semitism Is Anti-Me*

Azar Nafisi was born in Iran but now lives in Washington, D.C., where she teaches at Johns Hopkins School of Advanced International Studies. She's the author of the best-selling Reading Lolita in Tehran: A Memoir in Books *(2003), which recounts her experiences teaching English and American literature in Tehran, both at universities there and secretly in her home. The book is especially interesting not only because of the interpretations of English-language works of literature offered by Nafisi and her students but also because of the information it offers on daily life in Iran during a time of social and political upheaval. "Mysterious Connections That Link Us Together" was one of a series of aural essays in the* This I Believe *series on National Public Radio, and it first aired in July 2005. (You can listen to Nafisi deliver these remarks at <http://npr.org/templates/story/story.php?storyId=4753976>.) As you read, consider how she uses Huckleberry Finn's struggle with the religion of his childhood to address far broader questions in today's world.*

Mysterious Connections That Link Us Together

AZAR NAFISI

Nafisi returns to the example of Huckleberry Finn several times throughout her essay. How does this strategy organize and strengthen her argument? Review Chapter 12 for examples of different styles of argument and help with developing your own style and delivery in arguments.

LINK TO P. 370

I believe in empathy. I believe in the kind of empathy that is created through imagination and through intimate, personal relationships. I am a writer and a teacher, so much of my time is spent interpreting stories and connecting to other individuals. It is the urge to know more about ourselves and others that creates empathy. Through imagination and our desire for rapport, we transcend our limitations, freshen our eyes, and are able to look at ourselves and the world through a new and alternative lens.

Whenever I think of the word empathy, I think of a small boy named Huckleberry Finn° contemplating his friend and runaway slave, Jim. Huck asks himself whether he should give Jim up or not. Huck was told in Sunday school that people who let slaves go free go to "everlasting fire." But then, Huck says he imagines he and Jim in "the day and nighttime, sometimes moonlight, sometimes storms, and we a-floating along, talking and singing and laughing." Huck remembers Jim and their friendship and warmth. He imagines Jim not as a slave but as a human being, and he decides that, "alright, then, I'll go to hell."

Huckleberry Finn: the hero of Mark Twain's 1884 novel of the same name; the novel is considered by many to be one of the finest works of American literature.

What Huck rejects is not religion but an attitude of self-righteousness and inflexibility. I remember this particular scene out of *Huck Finn* so vividly today, because I associate it with a difficult time in my own life. In the early

1980s when I taught at the University of Tehran, I, like many others, was expelled. I was very surprised to discover that my staunchest allies were two students who were very active at the University's powerful Muslim Students' Association. These young men and I had engaged in very passionate and heated arguments. I had fiercely opposed their ideological stances. But that didn't stop them from defending me. When I ran into one of them after my expulsion, I thanked him for his support. "We are not as rigid as you imagine us to be, Professor Nafisi," he responded. "Remember your own lectures on Huck Finn? Let's just say, he is not the only one who can risk going to hell!"

This experience in my life reinforces my belief in the mysterious connections that link individuals to each other despite their vast differences. No amount of political correctness can make us empathize with a child left orphaned in Darfur° or a woman taken to a football stadium in Kabul° and shot to death because she is improperly dressed. Only curiosity about the fate of others, the ability to put ourselves in their shoes, and the will to enter their world through the magic of imagination, creates this shock of recognition. Without this empathy there can be no genuine dialogue, and we as individuals and nations will remain isolated and alien, segregated and fragmented.

I believe that it is only through empathy, that the pain experienced by an 5
Algerian woman, a North Korean dissident, a Rwandan child or an Iraqi prisoner, becomes real to me and not just passing news. And it is at times like this when I ask myself, am I prepared—like Huck Finn—to give up Sunday school heaven for the kind of hell that Huck chose?

Darfur: provinces of western Sudan, where since 2003 the Janjaweed, a militia made up of ethnic Arabs, who've been in the region for the past several centuries, has been seeking to displace non-Arab groups that are indigenous to the region. Western media have generally referred to the conflict as genocide or ethnic cleansing. By summer 2006, likely over 2 million people had been displaced and as many as 300,000 killed in the region.

Kabul: the capital city of Afghanistan; here Nafisi is referring to the sort of event common under the Taliban and even more recently in which women's lives are taken because they violate cultural norms enforced by the Taliban and their supporters.

RESPOND •

1. What arguments is Azar Nafisi making in this commentary? How would you characterize them—as arguments based on reason and facts? Emotions? Character and values? (For a discussion of kinds of arguments, see Chapters 2–4.)
2. In this commentary, Nafisi combines a literary example, personal experience, and current events to make her argument(s). How does she weave these together? What are the relationships among them?
3. What's the significance of Nafisi's title? What sorts of "mysterious connections" linking people together do you see evidence of in her essay?
4. Imagine a conversation among Nafisi, Mariam Rahmani (author of "Wearing a Head Scarf Is My Choice . . ."), and Shelby Knox, who's featured in Michelle Bryant's "Selling Safe Sex in Public Schools" earlier

in this chapter. How might religion and religious beliefs figure into that conversation? What might these women agree on? Would there be things they might agree to disagree about?

5. As noted, this selection originally aired as a contribution to the *This I Believe* series on National Public Radio (NPR), based on a series by the same name that had broadcast in 1950. (The URL for the NPR series is <http://npr.org/templates/story/story.php?storyId=4538138>.) As the link for essay-writing instructions noted, submitted essays should be 350 to 500 words in length and discuss a value you believe in—and, obviously, they should be written to be read aloud because they're radio essays. Following the instructions and advice given on the *This I Believe* Web site, **write an essay** for the series, one that in many ways will define and explain a belief you hold. You may want to listen to earlier contributions to the series. If the series is still continuing, we'd encourage you to consider submitting your essay to the program once you've written and revised it with feedback from your classmates and teacher. Instructions for submitting your essay can be found on the series' Web site.

27
What Should "Diversity on Campus" Mean?

Visit your school's homepage, and odds are that you won't have to look very far or google very long to find links about diversity. The Web site for the home institution of one of this book's co-authors features a "Diversity" banner in the lower-right corner. Run your mouse over it, and you see "Diverse People and Ideas." Click on it, and you're carried to a page with links to statements on diversity and statistics of various sorts. If you study the individuals and groups featured in the statements, in particular, you might deduce that "diversity" has a rather specific meaning, one far narrower than the

Oxford English Dictionary's definition of the term as "the condition or quality of being diverse, different, or varied; difference, unlikeness." (Linguists are interested in such cases of semantic narrowing because they often are evidence of social change of one sort or another in the community where the narrowing occurs.) The arguments in this chapter challenge you to think about the meaning of diversity on your own campus, what it might mean, and what it should mean—if it's a relevant notion at all.

The chapter opens with a portfolio of visual arguments, award-winning posters in an annual campus-wide competition with the theme of diversity at Western Washington University. Each of these posters is a definitional argument of sorts. Next, Sarah Karnasiewicz's "The Campus Crusade for Guys" documents how many campuses are struggling to attract and keep male students as the percentage of males attending college continues to drop. Katherine S. Mangan's "Bar Association Moves to Strengthen Diversity Requirements for Accreditation of Law Schools" reports on a proposal by the American Bar Association, which accredits law schools across the country, to require clear evidence of efforts to attract and keep an ethnically and racially diverse student body, faculty, and staff. Mangan's discussion of this proposal is followed by a visual portfolio of cartoons about the 2003 Supreme Court case that permitted the University of Michigan

Law School to continue using particular forms of affirmative action in admissions. In "Schools of Reeducation?" Frederick M. Hess roundly criticizes many teacher education programs for punishing students who hold certain views. The number of seats on any campus is limited. The question is: who is going to get to occupy them and why?

The next eight selections deal not with students but with faculty, by examining what's currently an extremely controversial notion on campuses—intellectual diversity, the brainchild of David Horowitz. He defends this notion in his essay "In Defense of Intellectual Diversity" and defines it in the following selection, "Academic Bill of Rights." Stanley Fish criticizes the idea of intellectual diversity in his essay, "'Intellectual Diversity': The Trojan Horse of a Dark Design." Writing for *The Dartmouth Review*, student Michael J. Ellis explains his points of agreement and disagreement with Horowitz in "Once More unto the Breach." Ann Marie B. Bahr, a professor who identifies herself as a conservative in at least certain ways, expresses her concern with intellectual diversity in "The Right to Tell the Truth," an essay based on her experiences teaching courses in religion. *New York Times* columnist John Tierney aligns himself with many of Horowitz's claims and values as he criticizes schools of journalism and law in particular. Seven writers of letters to the editor of the *Times* respond to Tierney's claims in a range of ways.

Walter Benn Michael's "Diversity's False Solace" contends that all the discussions of diversity, especially when they're focused on ethnic or racial diversity, are simply on the wrong track. While such discussions may keep us occupied, he says, they conveniently prevent us from dealing with what he contends are deeper, more serious issues that no one really wants to talk about. In a sense, all these selections challenge you to do the sort of thinking required of a good writer in order to produce an evaluative essay examining competing answers to a single question: what should "diversity on campus" mean?

a universe within

UNIVERSITY RESIDENCES

WESTERN
WASHINGTON UNIVERSITY

James Sanders, *A Universe Within*, 2006

Making a Visual Argument: Student-Made Diversity Posters

From the Western Washington University homepage <http://wwu.edu> click on "Diversity" and you'll find this quote from the university president, Karen W. Morse: "Diversity is central to Western's mission and strategic action plan and is considered to be an integral component of a quality education. Our goals recognize the changing composition of society as a whole, and its impact on the world for which students are educated." The posters that follow were designed to promote the residence halls for Western Washington University in Bellingham, Washington. Called Residence Life, the student-run organization that oversees the on-campus dormitories holds a poster contest each year to showcase Western Washington's overall commitment to diversity.

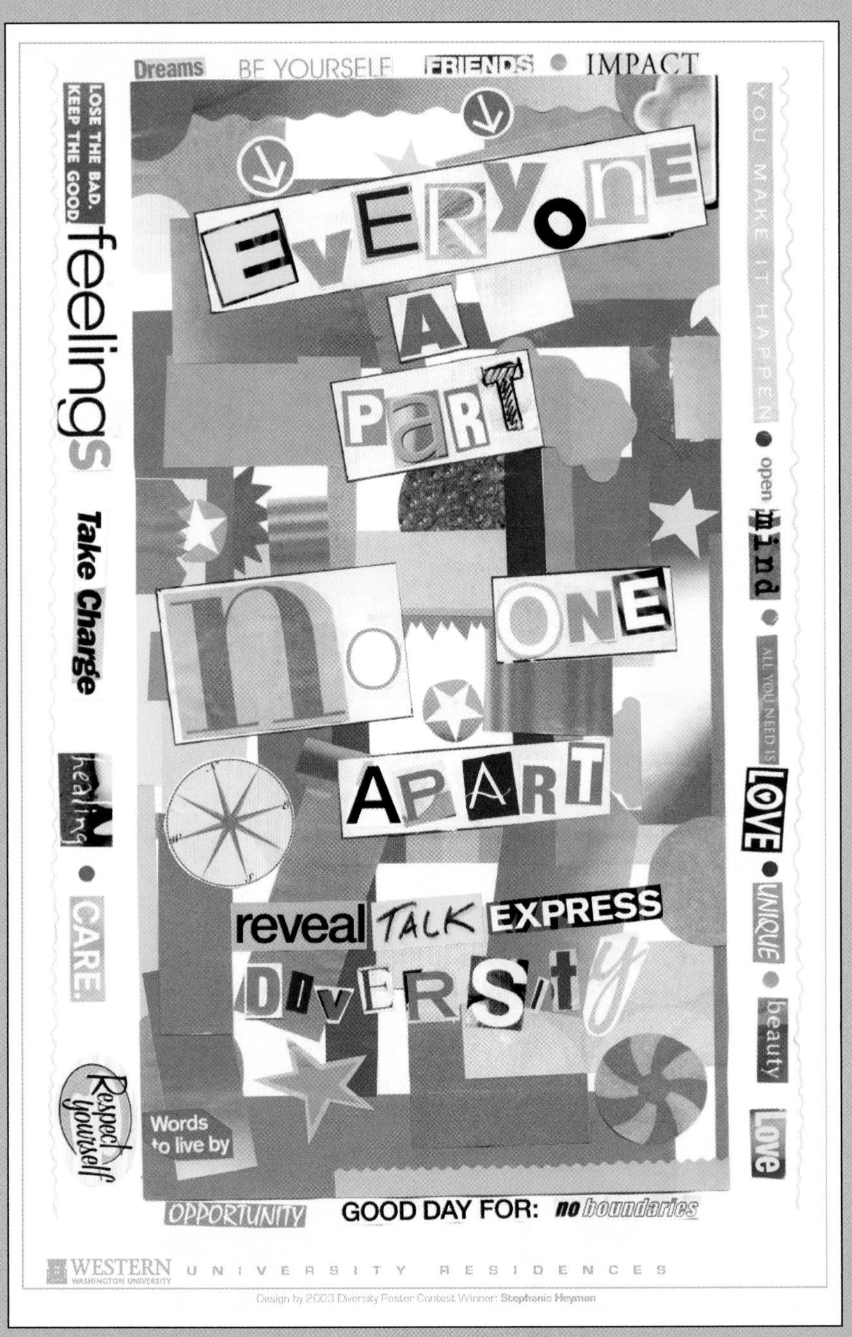

Stephanie Heyman, *Everyone A Part, No One Apart*, 2003

Heidi Small, *Lives Woven Together*, 2000

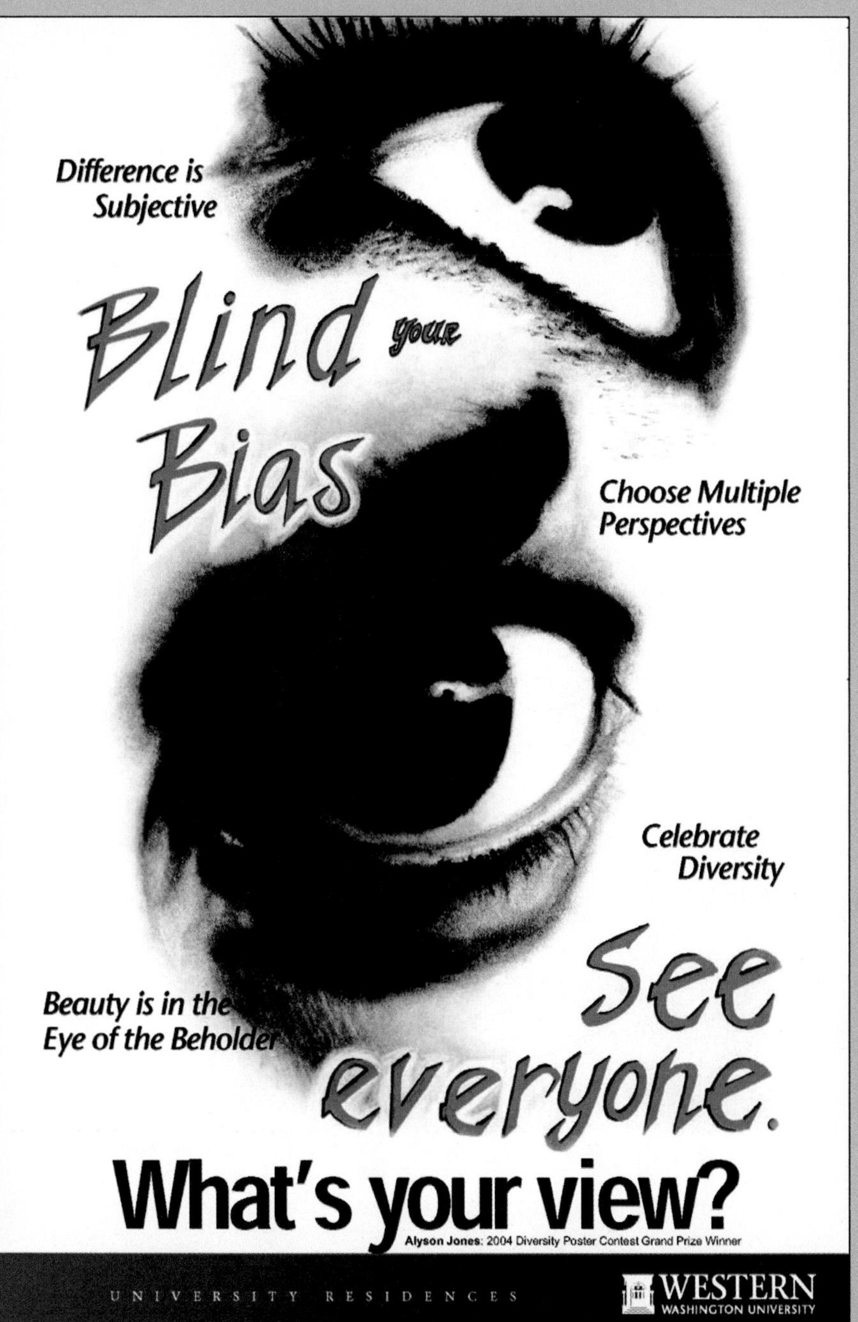

Alyson Jones, *What's Your View?*, 2004

Megan Stampfli, *Embrace Diversity*, 2004

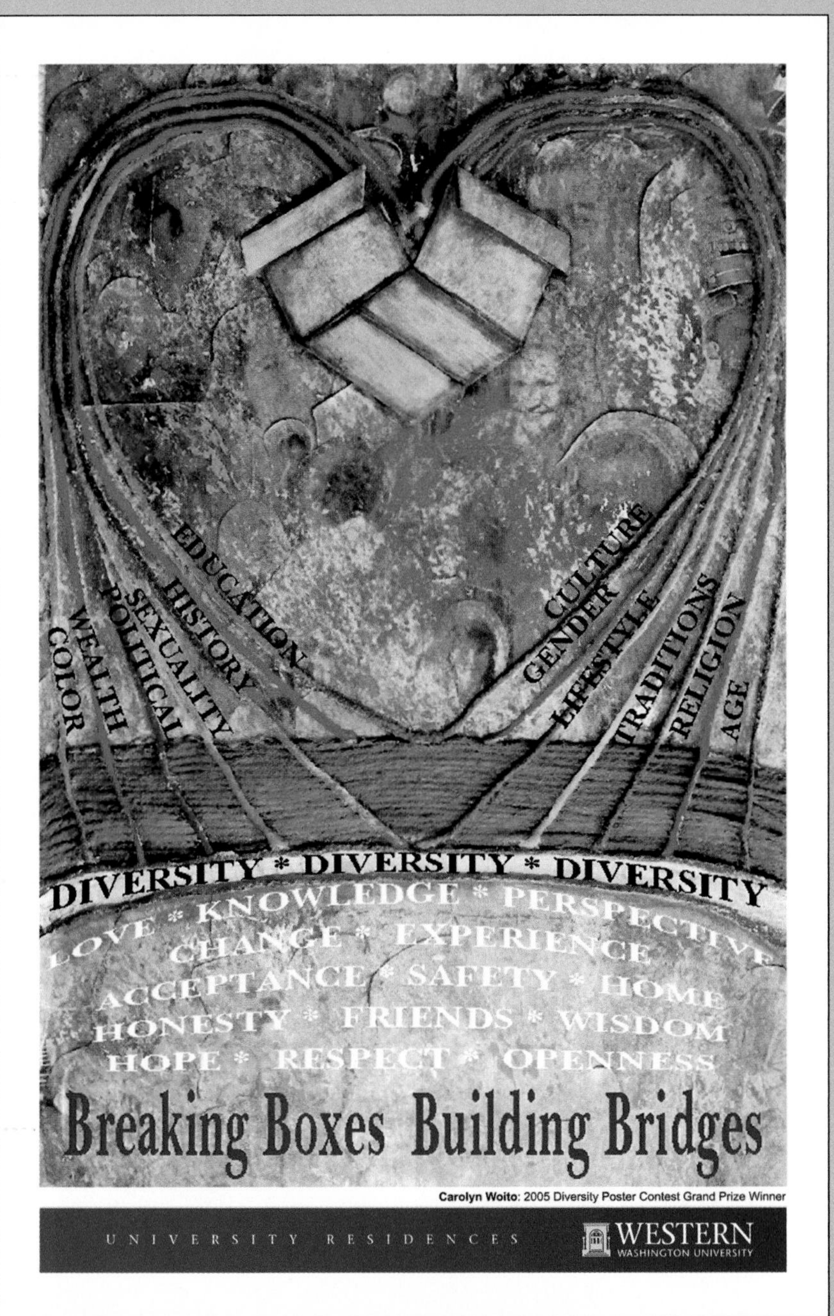

Carolyn Woito, *Breaking Boxes, Building Bridges*, 2005

RESPOND •

1. Which of these visual arguments do you find most appealing? Least appealing? Why?
2. Analyze the relationship between text—the words used—and the visual images and layout in each of the posters. What's the interaction between the text, on the one hand, and the visual images and layout, on the other, in each one? Which poster is most effective in this regard? Why?
3. If you take each of these posters to be a definitional argument, defining diversity in some way, what arguments is each making? In other words, how does each poster define diversity? (For a discussion of definitional arguments, see Chapter 8.)
4. In defining and commenting on the notion of diversity, these posters range from approaching the topic in a didactic fashion (that is, seeking to teach a moral lesson) to approaching it much more vaguely. (Note the evaluative—and potentially negative—connotations the labels "didactic" and "vague" carry.) Choose the posters that you find most explicitly didactic and those that you find most vague in their approach to the topic. Justify your choices. Which approach do you prefer? Why? Which do you believe is more effective in situations like this one? Why?
5. **Write an essay** in which you evaluate two of these posters, commenting on the definition of diversity presented or assumed (question 3); the relationship between text, on the one hand, and visual images and layout, on the other (question 2); and the artists' approach to the subject (question 4). (For a discussion of evaluative arguments, see Chapter 9.)
6. **Write a definitional essay** in which you define the notion of diversity as it might or should be understood on American college campuses today or your campus specifically. (For a discussion of definitional arguments, see Chapter 8.)

The Campus Crusade for Guys

SARAH KARNASIEWICZ

Sarah Karnasiewicz, writer, editor, and photographer, is currently an associate editor of Salon.com's Life section. She has degrees in journalism, children's literature, and fine art. Much of her work focuses on the topics of education, youth culture, food, and family. In "The Campus Crusade for Guys," which originally appeared in February 2005 on Salon.com, Karnasiewicz examines the growing practice of what seems to be affirmative action for male applicants to many of the country's colleges and universities. As you read, consider the gender balance on your campus and how it, along with your own biological sex, might influence your response to this selection.

Child psychologist Michael Thompson has devoted his professional life to advocating for America's boys. As the bestselling author of "Raising Cain," he's logged thousands of hours as an educational speaker and makes frequent appearances on national television as an authority on troubled young men. But Thompson is also the father of a 20-year-old daughter. And when asked if, given their much-maligned status in schools these days, boys ought to be given a leg up in college admissions, his answer is blunt: "I'd be horrified if some lunkhead boy got accepted to a school instead of my very talented and prepared daughter," he says, "just because he happened to be a guy."

But that may be just what is happening. Amid national panic over a growing academic gender gap, educators have begun to ask, might it be time to adopt affirmative action for boys?

The statistics are revealing: Fewer men apply to colleges every year and those who do disproportionately occupy the lowest quarter of the applicant pool. Thirty-five years ago, in the early days of widespread coeducation, the gender ratio on campuses averaged 43-57, female to male. Now, uniformly, the old ratios have been inverted. Across races and classes — and to some extent, around the Western world — women are more likely to apply to college and, once enrolled, more likely to stick around through graduation.

Even in a vacuum, discussions of gender-based affirmative action would be deeply political. But the possibility of a full-fledged battle appears especially likely these days, as we find ourselves in the middle of what's popularly known as the "war on boys." If you watch the news or read the papers, you know the soldiers: Last year, Laura Bush launched a federal initiative focused on boys who have been neglected by their schools and communities; Christina Hoff Sommers, George Gilder and Michael Gurian have swarmed the talk show circuit and editorial pages, bemoaning the lack of male role models in American schools and accusing educators of alienating boys by prizing passive, "feminized" behavior such as sitting quietly, reading independently, and focusing on sedentary rather than dynamic projects. (Though Thompson, for the record, says "education has actually become more dynamic and teaching gotten better for boys" — and, I quote, "We used to have to hit them to keep

Karnasiewicz presents convincing statistics in support of her argument that the college male population is waning. Explore other aspects of arguments of fact in Chapter 7.

LINK TO P. 175

them still.") *New York Times* Op-Ed writer John Tierney made waves in January with an essay warning that educational success will come back to haunt women as a dearth of educated, eligible husbands turns them into miserable spinsters—and in a rebuttal, *Nation* columnist Katha Pollitt asked why, years ago when she was in school and men made up the majority, no one was worrying about whether they'd find wives. Finally, a few weeks ago, *Newsweek* joined the fray with an eight-page cover story by Peg Tyre, breathlessly captioned "The Boy Crisis," and laden with oversize color photos of doleful white boys, seemingly adrift in a sea of competent, well-adjusted girls.

5 With all this coverage, you'd be excused for thinking the debate is a recent development. But the truth is that affirmative action for men, like the gender gap itself, is simply not news. Back in 1999, a young woman filed a federal civil rights lawsuit against the University of Georgia in Athens, after it was revealed that the school had attempted to balance gender on campus by awarding preference to male applicants, much the way it might build racial diversity by assigning extra admissions "points" to minority students. At the time, the school, in its defense, told the *Christian Science Monitor* that it was trying to reverse male flight from campus (at the time the ratio was 45-55) before it "became something bad." Unfortunately for the university, the district court judge assigned to the case wasn't convinced, ruling instead that "the desire to 'help out' men who are not earning baccalaureate degrees in the same numbers as women . . . [was] far from persuasive."

Talk to admissions insiders today, though, and they'll tell you that the University of Georgia case did not so much end affirmative action for men as drive it underground. "My belief is that there are already many informal affirmative action policies," says Thompson. "It is entirely possible that a better qualified girl has not gotten into a school because admissions officers were trying to create a more even ratio." Tom Mortenson, senior policy analyst at the Pell Institute for Opportunity in Higher Education and creator of the *Postsecondary Education Opportunity Newsletter*, who in the mid-'90s was one of the first scholars to draw attention to the gender gap, agrees. "I know [affirmative action for boys] is being practiced, especially on liberal arts campuses where the gap is biggest," he explains, "because I've had administrators tell me so."

Last fall, their interest piqued by the flurry of news stories describing the growing chasm between boys and girls in higher education, Sandy Baum and Eban Goodstein, economics professors at Skidmore College and Lewis and Clark College, respectively, embarked on a close study of admissions data from 13 liberal arts schools, hunting for an unacknowledged preference for men in the admissions process. "I'd just read so many stories about the declining number of men applying to colleges," says Baum, "that it seemed inevitable that the disparity would or already had launched a campaign of affirmative action."

Baum and Goodstein's findings, while not conclusive, did carry weighty implications for the future of college admissions. At the time of their research, explains Baum, the incoming class at every school they studied was still composed of more than 50 percent girls, which made sweeping pronouncements about the prevalence of affirmative action difficult to support. And their profiles of male and female applicants were based primarily on statistical data—a standardized test score or GPA—thereby preventing them from taking into account many of the murky intangibles, like extracurricular activities, recommendations and personal essays, on which many admissions officers rely.

Still, in the case of schools where the gender imbalance was most acute—at colleges that were once single-sex, for instance—and where women consistently accounted for more than 60 percent of applicants, Baum and Goodstein *did* find compelling evidence that male students had a statistically greater probability of being accepted than female students of comparable qualifications. Their conclusion? "There seems to be a kind of affirmative action tipping point that occurs when an application pool becomes too heavily weighted toward women. But the interesting thing is that that point is by no means the 50-50 mark—it's likely closer to 40-60," explains Baum. "So while we did not find widespread gender preferencing, given the trends on campuses, with more and more schools approaching that tipping point, we could certainly see a big change."

And it's not just former women's colleges facing a 40-60 divide anymore. 10
A quick survey of colleges and universities around the nation found that Kalamazoo College in Michigan comes in at 45-55, the University of New Mexico at 43-57, New York University at 40-60, and Howard University at 34-66 (low-income, minority men and women are most affected by the educational gender gap). Michael Barron, director of admissions at the University of Iowa, has watched his school's 44-56 ratio hold steady throughout his nearly two-decade tenure at the university. "We just have consistently had more women than men, and I know there's a lot of schools—like the University of North Carolina, Chapel Hill, for example—that have been even closer to 40-60 for quite some time," he says. As a state-supported institution that, according

to Barron, "has a stewardship responsibility to accept students regardless of issues of gender or race," Iowa maintains that it has no intention of "either consciously or subconsciously" differentiating between men and women in the admissions process. But, Barron admits, "I wouldn't want it said that we are unconcerned. We are watchful and mindful and will be looking to see what happens . . . and whether there is a role for colleges and universities to play as part of the solution."

Karen Parker, director of admissions at Hampshire College in Amherst, Mass., reports that for the past three years her entering classes have had an average ratio of 41-59, and that men only account for 38 percent of applicants. "I don't believe that the school needs to be exactly 50-50, but from a cultural standpoint, I do think it's important that we have men engaged," she says. "Hampshire doesn't practice affirmative action right now—but I certainly can't say we won't in the future. It's a really perplexing problem and just not a good sign of things to come."

But schools that have not gone so far as to accept male students over more qualified women are still finding ways to shift their admissions agenda toward young men. "There are things schools can and do do," says Christina Hoff Sommers, resident scholar at the American Enterprise Institute for Public Policy Research and author of "Who Stole Feminism?" and "The War Against Boys." "Strengthening their engineering departments, getting a hockey team. Some schools are changing admission documents to appeal to male minds—and I know we're supposed to pretend there's no difference [between male and female minds], but anyone in advertising will tell you there is."

And for sure, many colleges are banking on these differences. "At our national conference each year we invariably have a speaker devoted specifically to recruiting boys," explains David Hawkins, the director of public policy at the National Association of College Admission Counseling. "Now most four-year colleges work with their own internal marketing department or contract out to an independent agency that tailors their marketing to young men—and they are very, very aggressive."

Since teenage boys are often crazy about technology, a number of universities, including Case Western Reserve, Seton Hill and MIT (which, admittedly, at 57-43, doesn't seem to have a problem attracting men), have launched admission-oriented blogs designed to offer an intimate, uncensored look at college life. Other schools take a more subliminal approach, by packing their catalogs with pictures of smiling, confident young men and playing up dark, "masculine" color schemes in mailings.

"There is no doubt that schools are trying to market themselves to boys now, 15
just the way they did to women 30 years ago," says Joseph Tweed, president-elect of the New York State Association of College Counselors and director of college counseling at the Trinity-Pawling School, a private all-boys school in upstate New York. "Everyone is asking, 'How do we do this? Do we change the structure of classes? Do we send out glossier materials?' But I think what worries educators the most is that boys don't seem as focused on the process as girls. [Boys] seem to feel they'll be OK, whereas with girls there's still a sense that if they don't do well, don't go to college, there'll be a consequence that will be negative."

Tweed's point raises a controversial question that most crusaders in the "war on boys" would rather dismiss. Despite their flagging performance in elementary and high school, men have hardly abdicated their power to women. While women may have held the majority in higher education for more than a decade, men still earn more than women, still hold the vast number of tenure-track university positions. Women possess executive positions at less than 2 percent of Fortune 500 companies. Could it be that men aren't going to college because they don't *have* to?

According to Laura Perna, assistant professor of educational policy and leadership at the University of Maryland, the gender gap is all about economics. Last fall, Perna published a paper in the *Review of Higher Education* in which she determined that young women might be more motivated to pursue higher education because, consciously or unconsciously, they sense that there are real economic advantages at stake. Her examination of a Department of Education sample of more than 9,000 high school students, interviewed over a period of eight years, revealed that women with bachelor's degrees earn 24 percent more than women without, while young men with bachelor's degrees experience no significant economic gains. For practical proof of her hypothesis, one need only consider that most well-paid, skilled, blue-collar professions continue to be dominated by men — while minimum-wage jobs in hospitality and service remain the province of women.

Tom Mortenson, of Opportunity, remains skeptical. "I've heard that story, but think of it this way — men have had a 3,000-year head start, while everything women have accomplished has largely been in the last 30 years," he says. "So yes, if you're a big, strong guy, there are jobs out there. But the fields that are growing fastest are in healthcare, education, leisure and travel, and the services—all areas that women are better at than we are. So if guys want access to that world, they'd better get an education that qualifies them. Because they won't be big and strong forever." In the future Mortenson imagines, America's changing economy leaves generations of unprepared, aimless, undereducated and emasculated men wasting away, taking the health and happiness of their wives and families with them. But as with Tierney and some of the other boy crusaders, some of Mortenson's greatest fears aren't focused on the perils facing men who lose course in school, but on the freedoms of women who don't. "On the one hand, you want to embrace the success of women," he tells me. "Yet, as more and more women substitute careers for having babies, I've come to see that we're looking at a population crisis. The most educated women have the fewest children—this is not rocket science, it's just the way things work. We need women to have 2.1 children [in order to maintain the U.S. population], but the recent Census Bureau reports show that American women with bachelor's degrees average only 1.7. You can do the math—if we continue this way the white population is headed for extinction."

Having worked for decades to increase educational opportunities across class, race and gender lines, Mortenson knows his talk about women's responsibility to preserve the species will get him in trouble—indeed, it already has. He says his daughter, age 29 and childless (but equipped with a master's degree), won't speak to him on the subject. But even his fatherly concern ("I want my daughter to have it all, but I worry that in old age she'll be lonely") can't disguise some of the insidious implications underneath those concerns: that educated white women might single-handedly be responsible for the decline of Western civilization.

In the fall 2005 issue of *Ms.* magazine, Phyllis Rosser wrote that rather than 20
being "celebrated for [our] landmark achievements, [women] have engendered fear," and offers up this fact, conspicuously absent from most media coverage of the gender gap: "There has been no decline in bachelor's degrees awarded to men," she writes. "The numbers awarded to women have simply increased." Put simply, in the words of Jacqueline King, director of the Center of Policy Analysis at the American Council of Education, who is quoted in Rosser's piece, "The [real news] story is not one of male failure, or even lack of opportunity—but rather one of increased academic success among females and minorities."

The boy crusaders believe that the seeds of academic failure are planted in primary school, which raises the question: Why are we waiting until college to redress the problem? "I've read many reports that male middle-school students are lagging behind their female counterparts," says Michael Barron. "So it seems to me that that's where we need to look. Because the fact is, all we have available to us, once people begin applying to college, is a product of what they've done before. Our reaction has to come sooner."

Until that happens, however, and should current enrollment trends continue, it's reasonable to assume that creative forms of admissions preferencing will continue to stir debate. As our phone conversation ends, Michael Thompson's voice turns grave. "I want to make very clear that I do not subscribe to this notion of a 'war' on boys," he says. "I think we have been living in a very exciting time when we have taken the shackles off of girls in education. I loved what feminism did for girls — we got inside them and understood them. My personal mission just happens to be to get people to think about boys with the same depth."

RESPOND •

1. What argument(s) is Karnasiewicz making with respect to the nature of diversity on campus? How persuasive do you find them? Why? Should there be affirmative action for men? Why or why not? In what ways does the visual argument accompanying the article support its claims? How effective do you find it? Why?
2. Although this article is about gender, it's also about issues of race or ethnicity and class as well as the intersection of these social variables. What sorts of observations or claims are made about each of these variables in the article? Do you agree or disagree? Do you find any of the claims made about these topics troubling? Why or why not?
3. How and why are females and males stigmatized by a lack of education or by the kind of job they might hold? Although it isn't mentioned, in what ways might the marriage market encourage young women to attend college (or even to succeed academically, more broadly)?
4. What's the allusion in Karnasiewicz's title? (If you need a hint, check out <http://ccci.org/>.) How and why is it appropriate, given the subject matter of the article? Is the allusion risky in any way? Why or why not?

5. Among the kinds of evidence that Karnasiewicz uses effectively is statistics. Where and how does she and those she cites use statistics advantageously? In what ways does she qualify claims made on the basis of statistical data? How does qualifying arguments in this way contribute to Karnasiewicz's ethos? (For a discussion of using facts like statistics, see Chapter 4; for a discussion of ethos, see Chapter 3.)
6. Investigate gender and admissions at the college or university you attend, and **write an essay** in which you treat this topic in some way. Ideas might include an analysis of statistics on the sex of applicants, those accepted, and those who enroll over some period of time; an analysis of your institution's efforts to attract females, males, or males and females; or interviews with students over whether the school should strive to ensure that a certain percentage of students is male (or female). If you attend a college that is or was single sex, you may wish to investigate debates about admitting students of the other sex. Your essay may define something, analyze a causal relationship, evaluate something, or make a proposal.

Katherine S. Mangan is correspondent for the Chronicle of Higher Education, *which is the major source of news and information about colleges and universities. It was originally a weekly publication but now also appears in a daily online version. Mangan writes regularly about topics relating to professional schools for two sections of the paper, "The Faculty" and "Students." In "Bar Association Moves to Strengthen Diversity Requirements for Accreditation of Law Schools," which originally appeared in February 2006, she reports on a proposal by the American Bar Association (ABA), the professional association that accredits law schools, to require law schools to demonstrate that they're taking "concrete steps" to ensure a racially and ethnically diverse student body, faculty, and staff. As you read, consider how accrediting organizations like the ABA have a role in shaping social policy with regard to our understanding of notions like diversity.*

Bar Association Moves to Strengthen Diversity Requirements for Accreditation of Law Schools

KATHERINE S. MANGAN

Law schools would be required to demonstrate the concrete steps they are taking to ensure that their student bodies, faculties, and staffs are racially and ethnically diverse under a revised standard approved on Saturday by the accrediting arm of the American Bar Association.

The revision requires a stronger and clearer commitment to diversity even from law schools in states, like California and Washington, that ban the consideration of race in admissions.

The standard was approved by the bar association's Section of Legal Education and Admissions to the Bar. In order to take effect, it must also be approved by the ABA's House of Delegates, which is scheduled to meet in August.

The change had been discussed earlier in the meeting, which ended Monday in Chicago, and drew immediate fire from lawyers opposed to affirmative action. In an op-ed commentary published in *The Wall Street Journal* on Saturday, David E. Bernstein, a professor of law at George Mason University, accused the bar association of using blackmail to force law schools to violate the law by instituting racial preferences.

5 "If passed, the new written standards will only embolden the accreditation bureaucracy, composed mainly of far-left law professors, to demand explicit racial preferences and implicit racial quotas—all in brazen defiance of the law," he wrote.

Mr. Bernstein, who is spending this year as a visiting professor at the University of Michigan Law School, is the author of *You Can't Say That! The Growing Threat to Civil Liberties from Antidiscrimination Law* (Cato Institute, 2003).

In his *Journal* commentary, he cited a controversial study by Richard H. Sander, a professor of law at the University of California at Los Angeles,

As a reporter, Mangan is describing the controversy caused by a diversity requirement. Her factual argument is based on quotations and reputable secondhand sources. Read about secondhand evidence like libraries and Internet resources in Chapter 16.

LINK TO P. 482

that concluded that affirmative action hurts black law students by admitting them to law schools where they will be in over their heads academically and be more likely to drop out and fail their states' bar examinations (*The Chronicle,* November 12, 2004).

A top bar-association official accused Mr. Bernstein of misrepresenting both the intent and the effect of the revised standard.

"He got it completely wrong," said John A. Sebert, the association's consultant on legal education. The revised standard clarifies that law schools *may* consider race and ethnicity in admissions, Mr. Sebert said on Monday, but does not require them to take that approach.

10 If they do not, however, they must demonstrate specific steps they are taking to achieve the goal of diversity, such as recruiting at historically black colleges, offering scholarships to minority or disadvantaged students, or holding summer programs to help potential applicants prepare for law school.

Mr. Sebert said that the standard, which has not been revised in 15 years, needed to be updated in light of the U.S. Supreme Court's 2003 decision upholding the Michigan law school's use of race-conscious admissions (*The Chronicle,* July 4, 2003).

The title of the revised policy, Standard 211, would be changed from "Equal Opportunity" to "Equal Opportunity and Diversity." It would apply to admitting students, appointing faculty members, and hiring other staffers.

The policy says that law schools must demonstrate, "by concrete action, a commitment to providing full opportunities for the study of law and entry into the profession by members of underrepresented groups, particularly racial and ethnic minorities," and that the schools must commit "to having a student body that is diverse with respect to gender, race, and ethnicity."

It also says: "Consistent with sound educational policy and the standards, a law school shall demonstrate by concrete action a commitment to having a faculty and staff that are diverse with respect to gender, race, and ethnicity."

15 The revised standard also clarifies that "the mere fact that you may be in a state that has a statutorial provision prohibiting the consideration of race in the admissions process does not relieve you" of that obligation, Mr. Sebert said.

RESPOND●

1. According to Mangan, what specific proposal did the ABA make? What details of the proposal are presented here? How does the proposal define the sorts of "concrete steps" that a law school might take to demonstrate its commitment to the requirement? (If you're interested in seeing the actual document that sparked this debate, a version of it is available at <http://abanet.org/legaled/standards/adoptedstandards2006/standards210_212.pdf>.) Why is this proposal controversial?
2. What objections does Professor David E. Bernstein raise to the ABA proposal? How does John A. Sebert, the Association's consultant on legal education, seek to rebut these criticisms? Based on the information given in this article, do Bernstein's criticisms seem well founded? Why or why not? How effective do you find Sebert's replies?

3. What arguments might be made in favor of requiring law schools (or professional schools like business schools, engineering schools, or medical schools) to demonstrate that they've taken explicit and concrete steps to achieve an ethnically diverse student body? What arguments might be made against such a requirement?
4. One way to analyze debates about any sort of affirmative action is to see them as an effort to balance two competing forces. On the one hand, there's the reality of a limited number of places; programs and schools can accommodate only a certain number of students, and for each student who's admitted, some other won't be. On the other hand, there's often a desire to achieve a certain social goal, whether it's ensuring a certain percentage of students from a particular group (for example, males in contrast to females, as detailed in the previous selection) or correcting past injustices (because members of certain groups weren't permitted to enroll, or weren't permitted to enroll in large numbers, or because of something about their life history—or the experience of a group of which they're members—has made it difficult for them or members of the group to be admitted). Which aspects of such arguments are definitional? Causal? Evaluative? Geared to making proposals?
5. Are there situations that merit affirmative action of some sort? What are they? Why do they merit special consideration? **Write a proposal argument** in which you offer criteria for responding to these questions. (For a discussion of proposal arguments, see Chapter 11.)

Making a Visual Argument: Cartoonists Take On Affirmative Action

The most recent Supreme Court decision about affirmative action having a direct impact on higher education is Grutter v. Bollinger *(2003). In this decision, the Court declared that the University of Michigan Law School had "a compelling interest in achieving a diverse student body" and could use considerations of race and ethnicity in questions of admissions within certain bounds. The decision was criticized by many, not least of all because it didn't draw what lawyers term "a bright line" delimiting the situations when considerations of race or ethnicity are permissible and when they aren't.*

Here, we present five cartoonists' response to this decision and issues related to affirmative action more broadly. Mike Lester is a cartoonist for the Rome News-Tribune *in Rome, Georgia; "It's GOT to Be the Shoes" appeared in June 2003. Dennis Draughon's "Supreme Irony" appeared in April 2003 in the* Scranton Times *of Scranton, Pennsylvania. "Daniel Lives on Detroit's Eastside . . . ," by Mike Thompson, originally appeared in the* Detroit Free Press *in June 2003. Signe Wilkinson's "Admissions" was first published in January 2003 in the* Philadelphia Daily News *in Philadelphia, Pennsylvania. Finally, "Pricey" first appeared in November 2003 in* The Breeze, *the student newspaper of James Madison University in Harrisonburg, Virginia; it was drawn by Dean Camp, who was a cartoonist for the paper during academic year 2003–2004.*

As you study these cartoons, consider the range of ways in which the artists wed words and illustrations to create humorous arguments about a not-so-humorous issue.

Mike Lester, ***It's GOT to Be the Shoes***

Dennis Draughon, *Supreme Irony*

Mike Thompson, *Daniel Lives on Detroit's Eastside . . .*

Signe Wilkinson, *Admissions*

Dean Camp, *Pricey*

RESPOND •

1. Briefly summarize the argument being made by each cartoon. Which do you find most effective? Least effective? Why?
2. In what ways do the cartoons by Mike Lester and Dennis Draughon mock the Supreme Court? How does Lester's cartoon use gender and gender stereotypes humorously? How might Sarah Karnasiewicz, author of "The Campus Crusade for Guys," respond to this cartoon? How does each of these cartoons use irony?
3. In what ways do the cartoons by Mike Thompson and Signe Wilkinson make similar arguments? How do their arguments differ?
4. How can the cartoon by Dean Camp be read as relevant to debates about affirmative action?
5. Investigate the admissions practices at your college or university to see if you can discover the percentage of students who were admitted on the basis of so-called objective criteria like scores alone and the number who weren't. Dig a bit deeper to see whether you can get information about the cases of "discretionary admission," that is, students who are "legacy admits" as the children of alumni, the children of donors or well-known personalities, athletes, those from out of state, and those who aren't members of the dominant ethnic group(s) on your campus. How do you evaluate what you discover? If you're unable to gather such information, why do you suppose it isn't readily available? **Write an essay** in which you make a proposal about how your school might (or should) deal with managing the competing demands for seats in the entering class. What sorts of demands are there? From whom? What are the consequences of heeding some of these demands but not others?

▼ *Frederick M. Hess is Resident Scholar and Director of Education Policy Studies at the American Enterprise Institute for Public Policy Research, a Washington think-tank whose purposes are "to defend the principles and improve the institutions of American freedom and democratic capitalism—limited government, private enterprise, individual liberty and responsibility, vigilant and effective defense and foreign policies, political accountability, and open debate." Hess is also the author of a number of influential books, including, most recently,* No Child Left Behind Primer *(2006) with Michael J. Petrilli, and* Tough Love for Schools: Essays on Competition, Accountability, and Excellence *(2006). In "Schools of Reeducation?" (which appeared in the* Washington Post *in February 2006), Hess criticizes what he sees as a troublesome practice in some programs in teacher education. As you read, notice how he offers a negative assessment of such practices while doing so in a fairly measured way.*

Schools of Reeducation?

FREDERICK M. HESS

For those who have been troubled by the tendency of universities to adopt campus speech codes, a worrisome new fad is rearing its head in the nation's schools of education. Stirred by professional opinion and accreditation pressures, teachers colleges have begun to regulate the dispositions and beliefs of those who would teach in our nation's classrooms.

At the University of Alabama, the College of Education explains that it is "committed to preparing individuals to promote social justice, to be change agents, and to recognize individual and institutionalized racism, sexism, homophobia, and classism." To promote its agenda, part of the program's self-proclaimed mission is to train teachers to "develop anti-racist, anti-homophobic, anti-sexist . . . alliances."

The University of Alaska at Fairbanks School of Education declares on its Web site: "Teachers often profess 'colorblindness' . . . which is at worst patronizing and at best naïve, because race and culture profoundly affect what is known and how it is known." Consequently, the program emphasizes "the interrelatedness of race, identity, and the curriculum, especially the role of white privilege."

Professors at Washington State University's College of Education evaluate candidates to ensure they exhibit "an understanding of the complexities of race, power, gender, class, sexual orientation, and privilege in American society." The relevance of these skills to teaching algebra or the second grade is, at a minimum, debatable.

Brooklyn College's School of 5
Education announces: "We educate teacher candidates and other school personnel about issues of social injustice such as institutionalized racism, sexism, classism, and heterosexism; and invite them to develop strategies and practices that challenge [such] biases."

One can sympathize with the sentiments at work. Moreover, in theory, academics can argue that merely addressing these issues implies no

Before offering his own opinion on free speech in academia, Hess cites various sources and offers a few examples to bolster his point. Read Chapter 19 for ideas on how to evaluate sources.

LINK TO P. 530

ideological bias. But in practice, education courses addressing "white privilege" and the "language of oppression" typically endorse particular views on issues such as affirmative action and student discipline. These codes have real consequences.

Ed Swan is pursuing a degree in teacher education at Washington State. The *Chronicle of Higher Education* reports that he flunked an evaluation of dispositions° last year. The teacher who failed him explained that Swan, a conservative Christian and father of four Mexican American children, had "revealed opinions that have caused me great concern in the areas of race, gender, sexual orientation and privilege." Washington State insisted that Swan agree to attend sensitivity training before being allowed to do his student teaching—where observers could observe his classroom performance.

In 2005 Scott McConnell was informed by LeMoyne College's Graduate Program in Education that he was not welcome to return and complete his degree. His offense? He wrote a paper advocating the use of corporal punishment that was given a grade of A-minus. The department chairwoman's letter to McConnell cited the "mismatch between [his] personal beliefs . . . and the LeMoyne College program goals."

The conviction that teachers should hold certain views regarding sexuality or social class is rooted in a commendable impulse to ensure that they teach all students. But even if scientific evidence established that certain beliefs or dispositions improved teacher effectiveness, colleges should hesitate to engage in this kind of exercise. The truth, of course, is that no such body of rigorous, empirical evidence does exist.

10 In any event, there's good reason to be skeptical of claims that to be effective, teachers must have certain views or attitudes. Given that both kind-hearted and callous doctors may be effective professionals, it's not clear why we should expect good teachers to be uniform in disposition. In fact, with the array of students that schools serve, it may be useful to hire teachers with diverse views and values. Ultimately, screening on "dispositions" serves primarily to cloak academia's biases in the garb of professional necessity.

Schools of education are not merely private entities. Rather, in each state, they are deputized by licensure systems to serve as gatekeepers into the teaching profession. Even the vast majority of "alternative" training programs are sponsored by a school of education.

The National Council for the Accreditation of Teacher Education—which established requirements that would-be teachers embrace "multicultural and global perspectives" and develop "dispositions that respect and value differences"—has tried to backpedal recently by protesting that it didn't "expect or require institutions to attend to any particular political or social ideologies." Much more is needed. The cultivation of right-thinking cadres has no place in America's colleges and universities.

dispositions: here, feelings or attitudes toward specific groups or topics; being favorably or unfavorably disposed toward a group or idea.

RESPOND •

1. What is Frederick Hess's argument in this essay? What practices is he critiquing? How does he do so? Why? In what ways is this essay an argument about diversity?
2. How would you characterize the tone of Hess's argument? What evidence can you give to show that he wishes to be critical? What evidence can you give to show that he simultaneously wishes to be reasonable?
3. In paragraph 4, Hess claims, "[t]he relevance of these skills [namely, an understanding of the complexities of race, power, gender, class, sexual orientation, and privilege in American society] to teaching algebra or the second grade is, at minimum, debatable." If you accept Hess's position, what arguments might each side give for the relevance or irrelevance of such skills in teaching? Which set of arguments do you find more persuasive? Why?
4. Hess chooses his examples effectively. Choose two of his examples, explaining why they're ideally suited to support his claims.
5. Two often-opposed philosophies of teaching (and teacher training) might be characterized as student centered and knowledge or skill centered. In student-centered teaching, a teacher seeks to be mindful of his or her audience, the students, and seeks to present the material to them at their own level, often paying attention to their background. (Thus a teacher whose students lived on farms would discuss topics related to agriculture differently than one who had taught students living in a city.) In knowledge- or skill-centered teaching, a teacher focuses primarily on the material, whether knowledge or skills, assuming that if one teaches the material clearly, any student, regardless of background, can understand it. Most classrooms and most teacher education programs represent some combination of these two approaches to teaching. What should the proper balance between the two be? Is one correct and the other incorrect? Should one be favored? Which one? Why? **Write an essay** in which you evaluate these approaches to teaching and teacher training and make a proposal about the proper relationship between the two. (If you're having difficulty with this assignment, begin by locating Hess with regard to these two approaches to teaching; based on his comments, you can easily place him in one of the two camps. With that information, you should be able to find examples of other thinkers or teachers who are closer to the other approach.)

David Horowitz is founder of the Center for the Study of Popular Culture, a nonprofit organization in Los Angeles, California, and editor of the popular conservative Web site <http://FrontPageMag.com>. A frequent commentator on Fox News network, he's affiliated with Students for Academic Freedom, <http://studentsforacademicfreedom.org/> (see the following selection, "Academic Bill of Rights"), and Campus Watch, <http://campus-watch.org/>. Always a social activist, Horowitz identified earlier in his life as a leftist and even as a Marxist but later became a conservative. He's the author of numerous books, including Uncivil Wars: The Controversy over Reparations for Slavery *(2002),* Left Illusions: An Intellectual Odyssey *(2003), and* The Professors: The 101 Most Dangerous Academics in America *(2006). (One source reports that the decision to use* Dangerous *in the last title was his publisher's, not his.) As you read, consider how Horowitz seeks to acknowledge and rebut possible critiques of his arguments.*

In Defense of Intellectual Diversity

DAVID HOROWITZ

I am the author of the Academic Bill of Rights, which many student governments, colleges and universities, education commissions, and legislatures are considering adopting. Already, the U.S. House of Representatives has introduced a version as legislation, and the Senate should soon follow suit.

State governments are also starting to rally around efforts to protect student rights and intellectual diversity on campuses: In Colorado, the State Senate president, John K. Andrews Jr., has been very concerned about the issue, and State Rep. Shawn Mitchell has just introduced legislation requiring public institutions to create and publicize processes for protecting students against political bias. Lawmakers in four other states have also expressed a strong interest in legislation of their own, based on some version of the Academic Bill of Rights. Students for Academic Freedom is working to secure the measure's adoption by student governments and university administrations on 105 member campuses across the country (http://www.studentsforacademicfreedom.org).

The Academic Bill of Rights is based squarely on the almost 100-year-old tradition of academic freedom that the American Association of University Professors° has established. The bill's purposes are to codify that tradition; to emphasize the value of "intellectual diversity," already implicit in the concept of academic freedom; and, most important, to enumerate the rights of students to not be indoctrinated or otherwise assaulted by political propagandists in the classroom or any educational setting.

American Association of University Professors (AAUP): an organization created in 1915 "to advance academic freedom and shared governance, to define fundamental professional values and standards for higher education, and to ensure higher education's contribution to the common good." Its motto is "Academic Freedom for a Free Society," and its "Statement of Principles on Academic Freedom and Tenure" (1940, 1970) is the basis for employment practices, including the granting of tenure (the right not to be dismissed after some initial probationary period without cause), at many colleges and universities across the country.

Although the AAUP has recognized student rights since its inception, however, most campuses have rarely given them the attention or support they deserve. In fact, it is safe to say that no college or university now adequately defends them. Especially recently, with the growing partisan activities of some faculty members and the consequent politicization of some aspects of the curriculum, that lack of support has become one of the most pressing issues in the academy.

5 Moreover, because I am a well-known conservative and have published studies of political bias in the hiring of college and university professors, critics have suggested that the Academic Bill of Rights is really a "right-wing plot" to stack faculties with political conservatives by imposing hiring quotas. Indeed, opponents of legislation in Colorado have exploited that fear, writing numerous op-ed pieces about alleged right-wing plans to create affirmative-action programs for conservative professors.

Is it wise for Horowitz to remind his readers that he's "a well-known conservative" and to point out that he's accused of pushing a "right-wing plot"? How might his frankness affect his argument? For some ideas, read the sections of Chapter 3 that deal with establishing credibility and presenting motives.

LINK TO P. 69

Nothing could be further from the truth. The actual intent of the Academic Bill of Rights is to remove partisan politics from the classroom. The bill that I'm proposing explicitly forbids political hiring or firing: "No faculty shall be hired or fired or denied promotion or tenure on the basis of his or her political or religious beliefs." The bill thus protects all faculty members—left-leaning critics of the war in Iraq as well as right-leaning proponents of it, for example—from being penalized for their political beliefs. Academic liberals should be as eager to support that principle as conservatives.

Some liberal faculty members have expressed concern about a phrase in the bill of rights that singles out the social sciences and humanities and says hiring in those areas should be based on competence and expertise and with a view toward "fostering a plurality of methodologies and perspectives." In fact, the view that there should be a diversity of methodologies is already accepted practice. Considering that truth is unsettled in these discipline areas, why should there not be an attempt to nurture a diversity of perspectives as well?

Perhaps the concern is that "fostering" would be equivalent to "mandating." The Academic Bill of Rights contains no intention, implicit or otherwise, to mandate or produce an artificial "balance" of intellectual perspectives. That would be impossible to achieve and would create more mischief than it would remedy. On the other hand, a lack of diversity is not all that difficult to detect or correct.

By adopting the Academic Bill of Rights, an institution would recognize scholarship rather than ideology as an appropriate academic enterprise. It would strengthen educational values that have been eroded by the unwarranted intrusion of faculty members' political views into the classroom. That corrosive trend has caused some academics to focus merely on their own partisan agendas and to abandon their responsibilities as professional educators with obligations to students of all political persuasions. Such professors have lost sight of the vital distinction between education and indoctrination, which—as the AAUP recognized in its first report on academic freedom, in 1915—is not a legitimate educational function.

10 Because the intent of the Academic Bill of Rights is to restore academic values, I deliberately submitted it in draft form to potential critics who did not share my political views. They included Stanley Fish, dean of the College of Liberal Arts and Sciences at the University of Illinois at Chicago; Michael Bérubé, a professor of English at Pennsylvania State University at University Park; Todd Gitlin, a professor of journalism and sociology at Columbia University; and Philip Klinkner, a professor of government at Hamilton College. While their responses differed, I tried to accommodate the criticisms I got, for example, deleting a clause in the original that would have required the deliberations of all committees in charge of hiring and promotion to be recorded and made available to a "duly constituted authority."

I even lifted wholesale one of the bill's chief tenets—that colleges and professional academic associations should remain institutionally neutral on controversial political issues—from an article that Dean Fish wrote for *The Chronicle* ("Save the World on Your Own Time," January 23, 2003). He has also written an admirable book, *Professional Correctness* (Clarendon Press, 1995), which explores the inherent conflict between ideological thinking and scholarship.

Since the Academic Bill of Rights is designed to clarify and extend existing principles of academic freedom, its opponents have generally been unable to identify specific provisions that they find objectionable. Instead, they have tried to distort the plain meaning of the text. The AAUP itself has been part of that effort, suggesting in a formal statement that the bill's intent is to introduce political criteria for judging intellectual diversity and, thus, to subvert scholarly standards. It contends that the bill of rights "proclaims that all opinions are equally valid," which "negates an essential function of university education." The AAUP singles out for attack a phrase that refers to "the uncertainty and unsettled character of all human knowledge" as the rationale for respecting diverse viewpoints in curricula and reading lists in the humanities and social sciences. The AAUP claims that "this premise . . . is anti-thetical to the basic scholarly enterprise of the university, which is to establish and transmit knowledge."

The association's statements are incomprehensible. After all, major schools of thought in the contemporary academy — pragmatism,° postmodernism,° and deconstructionism,° to name three — operate on the premise that knowledge is uncertain and, at times, relative. Even the hard sciences, which do not share such relativistic assumptions, are inspired to continue their research efforts by the incomplete state of received knowledge. The university's mission is not only to transmit knowledge but to pursue it — and from all vantage points. What could be controversial about acknowledging that? Further, the AAUP's contention that the Academic Bill of Rights threatens true academic standards by suggesting that all opinions are equally valid is a red herring,° as the bill's statement on intellectual diversity makes clear: "Exposing students to the *spectrum of significant scholarly viewpoints* on the subjects examined in their courses is a major responsibility of faculty." (Emphasis added.)

As the Academic Bill of Rights states, "Academic disciplines should welcome a diversity of approaches to unsettled questions." That is common sense. Why not make it university policy?

The only serious opposition to the Academic Bill of Rights is raised by those 15
who claim that, although its principles are valid, it duplicates academic-freedom guidelines that already exist. Elizabeth Hoffman, president of the University of Colorado System, for example, has personally told me that she takes that position.

But with all due respect, such critics are also mistaken. Most universities' academic-freedom policies generally fail to make explicit, let alone codify, the institutions' commitment to intellectual diversity or the academic rights of students. The institutions also do not make their policies readily available to students — who, therefore, are generally not even aware that such policies exist.

For example, when I met with Elizabeth Hoffman, she directed me to the University of Colorado's Web site, where its academic-freedom guidelines are posted. Even if those guidelines were adequate, posting them on an Internet

pragmatism: an American philosophical school dating from the later 1800s; among its concerns — and the concerns of those who would use this label today — are the relationships among meaning, reality, and truth. Its early practitioners included Charles Sanders Peirce, William James, John Dewey, and George Herbert Mead.

postmodernism: an intellectual movement during the last quarter of the twentieth century representing a reaction to and rejection of the tenets of modernism, which was often characterized as emphasizing reason and rationality and "grand narratives" of progress and the harnessing of nature through science. In contrast, discussions of postmodernism often emphasize the jarring juxtaposition of things that seem not to go together in some sense — for example, wearing a very expensive piece of clothing with something from a thrift store, or a contemporary building that combines design features from several periods of architectural history. Postmodernists are quick to point out that things that are, in fact, unreal — Disneyland, Las Vegas, television crime shows, *American Idol* or *Survivor* — often seem more real to many people than

(*continued*)

actual everyday reality, whether the existence of poverty across town or violence around the world committed in the name of doing good. One finds talk of postmodernism in disciplines as varied as literature, architecture, anthropology, philosophy, and film.

deconstructionism: a way of reading texts of all kinds—whether philosophical, literary, or everyday—that was extremely influential in academic circles in the last quarter of the twentieth century. Drawing its inspiration from the French philosopher Jacques Derrida, deconstruction focused on the ways in which all texts contain contradictions of various sorts. Hence, there can be no single, correct interpretation of a text; instead, there will always be competing interpretations—a position misinterpreted by some of deconstruction's critics as arguing that all interpretations are equally valid.

red herring: a logical fallacy that introduces an irrelevant topic, thereby shifting focus from the topic at hand. The label is said to come from an early practice of using a strongly scented smoked herring to distract a dog following the scent of something else.

site does not provide sufficient protection for students, who are unlikely to visit it. Contrast the way that institutions aggressively promote other types of diversity guidelines—often establishing special offices to organize and enforce all sorts of special diversity-related programs—to such a passive approach to intellectual diversity.

At Colorado's Web site, for example, one can read the following: "Sections of the AAUP's 1940 Statement of Principles on Academic Freedom and Tenure have been adopted as a statement of policy by the Board of Regents." Few people reading that article or visiting the site would suspect that the following protection for students is contained in the AAUP's 1940 statement: "Teachers are entitled to freedom in the classroom in discussing their subject, but they should be careful not to introduce into their teaching controversial matter which has no relation to their subject."

Is there a college or university in America—including the University of Colorado—where at least one professor has not introduced controversial matter on the war in Iraq or the Bush White House in a class whose subject matter is not the war in Iraq, or international relations, or presidential administrations? Yet intrusion of such subject matter, in which the professor has no academic expertise, is a breach of professional responsibility and a violation of a student's academic rights.

We do not go to our doctors' offices and expect to see partisan propaganda 20
posted on the doors, or go to hospital operating rooms and expect to hear political lectures from our surgeons. The same should be true of our classrooms and professors, yet it is not. When I visited the political-science department at the University of Colorado at Denver this year, the office doors and bulletin boards were plastered with cartoons and statements ridiculing Republicans, and only Republicans. When I asked President Hoffman about that, she assured me that she would request that such partisan materials be removed and an appropriate educational environment restored. To the best of my knowledge, that has yet to happen.

Not everyone would agree about the need for such restraint, and it should be said that the Academic Bill of Rights makes no mention of postings and cartoons—although that does not mean that they are appropriate. I refer to them only to illustrate the problem that exists in the academic culture when it comes to fulfilling professional obligations that professors owe to all students. I would ask liberal professors who are comfortable with such partisan expressions how they would have felt as students seeking guidance from their own professors if they had to walk a gantlet of cartoons portraying Bill Clinton as a lecher, or attacking antiwar protesters as traitors.

The politicized culture of the university is the heart of the problem. At Duke University this year, a history professor welcomed his class with the warning that he had strong "liberal" opinions, and that Republican students should probably drop his course. One student did. Aided by Duke Students for Academic Freedom, the young man then complained. To his credit, the professor apologized. Although some people on the campus said the professor had been joking, the student clearly felt he faced a hostile environment. Why should the professor have thought that partisanship in the classroom was professionally acceptable in the first place?

At the University of North Carolina at Chapel Hill, a required summer-reading program for entering freshmen stirred a controversy in the state legislature last fall. The required text was Barbara Ehrenreich's socialist tract on poverty in America, *Nickel and Dimed: On (Not) Getting By in America* (Metropolitan Books, 2001). Other universities have required the identical text in similar programs, and several have invited Ehrenreich to campus to present her views under the imprimatur of the institution and without rebuttal.

That reflects an academic culture unhinged. When a university requires a single partisan text of all its students, it is a form of indoctrination, entirely inappropriate for an academic institution. If many universities had required Dinesh D'Souza's *Illiberal Education: The Politics of Race and Sex on Campus* (Vintage Books, 1992) or Ann Coulter's *Treason: Liberal Treachery from the Cold War to the War on Terrorism* (Crown Forum, 2003) as their lone freshman-reading text, there would have been a collective howl from liberal faculties, who would have immediately recognized the inappropriateness of such institutional endorsement of controversial views. Why not require two texts, or four? (My stepson, who is a high-school senior, was required to read seven texts during his summer vacation.)

25 The remedy is so simple. Requiring readings on more than one side of a political controversy would be appropriate educational policy and would strengthen, not weaken, the democracy that supports our educational system. Why is that not obvious to the administrators at Chapel Hill and the other universities that have instituted such required-reading programs? It's the academic culture, stupid.°

"It's the academic culture, stupid": allusion to the phrase "It's the economy, stupid," used by Bill Clinton's strategists during the 1992 election to keep him focused on his message.

RESPOND.

1. What argument(s) is David Horowitz making? How valid do you find them? Why?
2. How does Horowitz characterize the recent history of higher education in America in paragraphs 4–5 and 10? Pay special attention to his word choices, for example, "restore academic values" in paragraph 10. How do they give you insight into his understanding of the history of higher education and the readers he's invoking? What evidence does he provide for his claims?
3. Horowtiz is critical of professors who discuss "controversial matter on the war in Iraq or the Bush White House in a class whose subject matter is not the war in Iraq, or international relations, or presidential administrations," arguing that the "intrusion of such subject matter, in which the professor has no academic expertise, is a breach of professional responsibility and a violation of a student's academic rights" (paragraph 19). From Horowitz's perspective, should the arguments in Chapters 21 through 28 of this textbook be seen as breaches of the authors' professional responsibility or a violation of your academic rights? Why or why not? By what criteria can such decisions be made?
4. In paragraph 8, Howowitz distinguishes between "fostering" and "mandating." Is the distinction a valid one? How does the dispute he describes here compare with the dispute over the American Bar Association's proposal to strengthen diversity requirements for accreditation? (See the news article by Katherine S. Mangan on p. 931.)
5. In his closing paragraphs, Horowitz contends that "the remedy is so simple." Do you agree or disagree? Do you feel the "problem," as he has formulated it, is a fair or correct assessment of the situation, or does it need to be defined in other terms—perhaps not as a "problem," for example? **Write an evaluative essay** in which you assess Horowitz's definition of the situation as a problem, his characterization of that problem, and his favored solution.

In the previous selection, "In Defense of Intellectual Diversity," David Horowitz argues for the principles enshrined in a document he authored, "Academic Bill of Rights." Here, we present the document in its entirety. (For more information on Horowitz, see the headnote to the previous selection.) The text of the "Academic Bill of Rights" is posted at <http://studentsforacademicfreedom.org/>, the Web site of the Students for Academic Freedom. Much of the document is devoted to a discussion of the nature of academic freedom—an argument of definition. For an interesting discussion of how this notion differs in the United States, Germany, and France, check out Wikipedia's entry on "academic freedom" at <http://en.wikipedia.org/wiki/Academic_freedom>. (That entry also contains a discussion of this document.) As you read this selection, think about how such statements of principle function as arguments, that is, the way they're proposals about how the world should be.

Academic Bill of Rights

DAVID HOROWITZ

I. The Mission of the University

The central purposes of a University are the pursuit of truth, the discovery of new knowledge through scholarship and research, the study and reasoned criticism of intellectual and cultural traditions, the teaching and general development of students to help them become creative individuals and productive citizens of a pluralistic democracy, and the transmission of knowledge and learning to a society at large. Free inquiry and free speech within the academic community are indispensable to the achievement of these goals. The freedom to teach and to learn depend upon the creation of appropriate conditions and opportunities on the campus as a whole as well as in the classrooms and lecture halls. These purposes reflect the values—pluralism, diversity, opportunity, critical intelligence, openness and fairness—that are the cornerstones of American society.

The Academic Bill of Rights is a highly organized document in which word choice, order, and punctuation are carefully presented. More information about formality of argument and appropriate styles can be found in Chapter 12.

LINK TO P. 370

II. Academic Freedom

1. The Concept. Academic freedom and intellectual diversity are values indispensable to the American university. From its first formulation in the General Report of the Committee on Academic Freedom and Tenure of the American Association of University Professors, the concept of academic freedom has been premised on the idea that human knowledge is a never-ending pursuit of the truth, that there is no humanly accessible truth that is not in principle open to challenge, and that no party or intellectual faction has a monopoly on wisdom. Therefore, academic freedom is most likely to thrive in an environment of intellectual diversity that protects and fosters independence of

thought and speech. In the words of the General Report, it is vital to protect "as the first condition of progress, [a] complete and unlimited freedom to pursue inquiry and publish its results."

Because free inquiry and its fruits are crucial to the democratic enterprise itself, academic freedom is a national value as well. In a historic 1967 decision (*Keyishian v. Board of Regents of the University of the State of New York*) the Supreme Court of the United States overturned a New York State loyalty provision for teachers with these words: "Our Nation is deeply committed to safeguarding academic freedom, [a] transcendent value to all of us and not merely to the teachers concerned." In *Sweezy v. New Hampshire* (1957) the Court observed that the "essentiality of freedom in the community of American universities [was] almost self-evident."

2. The Practice. Academic freedom consists in protecting the intellectual independence of professors, researchers and students in the pursuit of knowledge and the expression of ideas from interference by legislators or authorities within the institution itself. This means that no political, ideological or religious orthodoxy will be imposed on professors and researchers through the hiring or tenure or termination process, or through any other administrative means by the academic institution. Nor shall legislatures impose any such orthodoxy through their control of the university budget.

This protection includes students. From the first statement on academic 5
freedom, it has been recognized that intellectual independence means the protection of students—as well as faculty—from the imposition of any orthodoxy of a political, religious or ideological nature. The 1915 General Report admonished faculty to avoid "taking unfair advantage of the student's immaturity by indoctrinating him with the teacher's own opinions before the student has had an opportunity fairly to examine other opinions upon the matters in question, and before he has sufficient knowledge and ripeness of judgment to be entitled to form any definitive opinion of his own." In 1967, the AAUP's Joint Statement on Rights and Freedoms of Students reinforced and amplified this injunction by affirming the inseparability of "the freedom to teach and freedom to learn." In the words of the report, "Students should be free to take reasoned exception to the data or views offered in any course of study and to reserve judgment about matters of opinion."

Therefore, to secure the intellectual independence of faculty and students and to protect the principle of intellectual diversity, the following principles and procedures shall be observed.

These principles fully apply only to public universities and to private universities that present themselves as bound by the canons of academic freedom. Private institutions choosing to restrict academic freedom on the basis of creed have an obligation to be as explicit as is possible about the scope and nature of these restrictions.

1. All faculty shall be hired, fired, promoted and granted tenure on the basis of their competence and appropriate knowledge in the field of their expertise and, in the humanities, the social sciences, and the arts, with a view toward fostering a plurality of methodologies and perspectives. No faculty shall be hired or fired or denied promotion or tenure on the basis of his or her political or religious beliefs.
2. No faculty member will be excluded from tenure, search and hiring committees on the basis of their political or religious beliefs.
3. Students will be graded solely on the basis of their reasoned answers and appropriate knowledge of the subjects and disciplines they study, not on the basis of their political or religious beliefs.
4. Curricula and reading lists in the humanities and social sciences should reflect the uncertainty and unsettled character of all human knowledge in these areas by providing students with dissenting sources and viewpoints where appropriate. While teachers are and should be free to pursue their own findings and perspectives in presenting their views, they should consider and make their students aware of other viewpoints. Academic disciplines should welcome a diversity of approaches to unsettled questions.
5. Exposing students to the spectrum of significant scholarly viewpoints on the subjects examined in their courses is a major responsibility of faculty. Faculty will not use their courses for the purpose of political, ideological, religious or anti-religious indoctrination.
6. Selection of speakers, allocation of funds for speakers programs and other student activities will observe the principles of academic freedom and promote intellectual pluralism.
7. An environment conducive to the civil exchange of ideas being an essential component of a free university, the obstruction of invited campus speakers, destruction of campus literature or other effort to obstruct this exchange will not be tolerated.
8. Knowledge advances when individual scholars are left free to reach their own conclusions about which methods, facts and theories have been validated by research. Academic institutions and profes-

sional societies formed to advance knowledge within an area of research, maintain the integrity of the research process and organize the professional lives of related researchers serve as indispensable venues within which scholars circulate research findings and debate their interpretation. To perform these functions adequately, academic institutions and professional societies should maintain a posture of organizational neutrality with respect to the substantive disagreements that divide researchers on questions within, or outside, their fields of inquiry.

RESPOND •

1. The eight points listed at the end of this document are said to define the principles in question. Why might there be such a focus on "political or religious beliefs"? How would the document be different if only one of these categories were listed? Why or why not?
2. How and why are such statements of principle implicitly and explicitly simultaneously definition arguments and proposal arguments? (For a discussion of arguments of definition and proposal arguments, see Chapters 8 and 11, respectively.)
3. In the eight points, the humanities and social sciences are treated differently from other branches of intellectual endeavor. Why? Could similar arguments be made for the sciences, for example, in light of recent discussion of Intelligent Design? Why or why not?
4. This document leaves certain key notions unspecified or undefined—for example, "where appropriate" in principle 4, "indoctrination" in principle 5, and "intellectual pluralism" in principle 6. Are there advantages to this situation? Disadvantages? What might they be? Why?
5. Principle 7 contends that "an environment conducive to the civil exchange of ideas" is "essential . . . [to] a free university." To what extent does the previous selection by Horowitz and the Web site of the Students for Academic Freedom embody "the civil exchange of ideas"? **Write an essay** in which you define this phrase or one of the phrases listed in question 4. (If you choose to define the notion of the civil exchange of ideas, you may wish to consider the selections in Chapter 26 that deal with the controversy over President Bush's May 2005 visit to Calvin College—selections 5 through 8—as a model of the civil exchange of ideas that you accept, modify, or reject.)

Since 2005, Stanley Fish has served as Davidson-Kahn Distinguished University Professor of Humanities and Law at Florida International University, teaching in the College of Law there. At the time he wrote "'Intellectual Diversity': The Trojan Horse of a Dark Design," which first appeared in the Chronicle of Higher Education *in February 2004, he was dean of the College of Liberal Arts and Sciences at the University of Illinois at Chicago. Fish made his reputation as one of the most important literary theorists of this era with his work on the poet John Milton, the notion of interpretive communities, and issues of legal and literary texts and interpretation. He's the author of many books, including* Is There a Text in This Class? The Authority of Interpretive Communities *(1980),* Doing What Comes Naturally: Change, Rhetoric, and the Practice of Theory in Literary and Legal Studies *(1989), and* There's No Such Thing As Free Speech, and It Is a Good Thing, Too *(1994).*

"Intellectual Diversity": The Trojan Horse° of a Dark Design°

STANLEY FISH

Whenever I've been asked who won (or is winning) the culture wars in the academy, I say it depends on what you mean by winning.

If victory for the right meant turning back or retarding the growth of programs like women's studies, African-American studies, Chicano studies,

A scene with the Trojan horse in the 2004 movie Troy, *directed by Wolfgang Petersen*

Trojan horse: According to Virgil's *The Aeneid,* ten years into the Trojan War the Greeks hit upon a strategy that might break the stalemate. They decided to give the Trojans a gift of a large hollow wooden horse that would, unbeknownst to them, be full of Greek soldiers; the soldiers would descend from inside the horse once the Trojans, convinced the Greeks had given up and gone home, got drunk in celebration. The Trojans fell for the ruse, the Greeks descended from inside the horse, they opened the gates of the city to let in the other Greek soldiers who had hidden themselves, and the Greek army destroyed the city, murdering the men and taking the women and children as slaves.

Dark Design: possibly an allusion to *The Dark Design,* a science-fiction novel by American novelist Philip José Farmer.

Latino studies, cultural studies, gay and lesbian (and now transgender) studies, postmodern studies, and poststructuralist theory, then the left won big time, for these programs flourish (especially among the young) and are the source of much of the intellectual energy in the liberal arts.

But if the palm is to be awarded to the party that persuaded the American public to adopt its characterization of the academy, the right wins hands down, for it is now generally believed that our colleges and universities are hotbeds (what is a "hotbed" anyway?) of radicalism and pedagogical irresponsibility where dollars are wasted, nonsense is propagated, students are indoctrinated, religion is disrespected, and patriotism is scorned.

The left may have won the curricular battle, but the right won the public-relations war. The right did this in the old-fashioned way, by mastering the ancient art of rhetoric and spinning a vocabulary that, once established in the public mind, performed the work of argument all by itself. The master stroke, of course, was the appropriation from the left (where it had been used with a certain self-directed irony) of the phrase "political correctness," which in fairly short order became capitalized and transformed from an accusation to the name of a program supposedly being carried out by the very persons who were the accusation's object. That is, those who cried "political correctness" hypostatized° an entity about which they could then immediately complain. This was genius.

hypostatize: to make into a substance; that is, in this case, by creating the label, the right had created something they could complain about.

5 Now they're doing it again, this time by taking a phrase that seems positively benign and even progressive (in a fuzzy-left way) and employing it as the Trojan horse of a dark design. That phrase is "intellectual diversity," and the vehicle that is bringing it to the streets and coffee shops of your hometown is David Horowitz's Academic Bill of Rights, which has been the basis of legislation introduced in Congress, has stirred some interest in a number of states, and has been the subject of editorials (both pro and con) in leading newspapers.

Opponents of the Academic Bill of Rights contend that despite disclaimers of any political intention and an explicit rejection of quotas, the underlying agenda is the decidedly political one of forcing colleges and universities to hire conservative professors in order to assure ideological balance.

Horowitz replies (in print and conversation) that he has no desire to impose ideological criteria on the operations of the academy; he does not favor, he tells me, legislation that would have political bodies taking over the responsibility of making curricular and hiring decisions. His hope, he insists, is that colleges and universities will reform themselves, and he offers the Academic Bill of Rights (which is the product of consultation with academics of various persuasions) as a convenient base-line template to which they might refer for guidance.

For the record, and as one of those with whom he has consulted, I believe him, and I believe him, in part, because much of the Academic Bill of Rights is as apolitical and principled as he says it is. It begins by announcing that "the central purposes of a University are the pursuit of truth, the discovery of new knowledge through scholarship and research, the study and reasoned criticism of intellectual and cultural traditions . . . and the transmission of knowledge and learning to a society at large." (I shall return to the clause deleted by my ellipsis.)

The bill goes on to define academic freedom as the policy of "protecting the intellectual independence of professors, researchers and students in the pursuit of knowledge and the expression of ideas from interference by legislators or authorities within the institution itself."

In short, "no political, ideological or religious orthodoxy will be imposed 10
on professors." Nor shall a legislature "impose any orthodoxy through its control of the university budget," and "no faculty shall be hired or fired or denied promotion or tenure on the basis of his or her political or religious beliefs." The document ends by declaring that academic institutions "should maintain a posture of organizational neutrality with respect to the substantive disagreements that divide researchers on questions within, or outside, their fields of inquiry."

It's hard to see how anyone who believes (as I do) that academic work is distinctive in its aims and goals and that its distinctiveness must be protected from political pressures (either external or internal) could find anything to disagree with here. Everything follows from the statement that the pursuit of truth is a—I would say the—central purpose of the university. For the serious embrace of that purpose precludes deciding what the truth is in advance, or ruling out certain accounts of the truth before they have been given a hearing, or making evaluations of those accounts turn on the known or suspected political affiliations of those who present them.

While it may be, as some have said, that the line between the political and the academic is at times difficult to discern—political issues are legitimately the subject of academic analysis; the trick is to keep analysis from sliding into advocacy—it is nevertheless a line that can and must be drawn, and I would go so far as to agree with Horowitz when he criticizes professors who put posters of partisan identification on their office doors and thus announce to the students who come for advice and consultation that they have entered a political space.

But it is precisely because the pursuit of truth is the cardinal value of the academy that the value (if it is one) of intellectual diversity should be rejected.

The notion first turns up, though not by name, in the clause I elided where Horowitz lists among the purposes of a university "the teaching and general development of students to help them become creative individuals and productive citizens of a pluralistic society."

Teaching, yes—it is my job to introduce students to new materials and 15
equip them with new skills; but I haven't the slightest idea of how to help students become creative individuals. And it is decidedly not my job to produce citizens for a pluralistic society or for any other. Citizen building is a legitimate democratic activity, but it is not an academic activity. To be sure, some of what happens in the classroom may play a part in the fashioning of a citizen, but that is neither something you can count on—there is no accounting for what a student will make of something you say or assign—nor something you should aim for. As admirable a goal as it may be, fashioning citizens for a pluralistic society has nothing to do with the pursuit of truth.

For Horowitz, the link between the two is to be found in the idea of pluralism: Given the "unsettled character of all human knowledge" and the fact (which is a fact) "that there is no humanly accessible truth that is not in principle open to challenge," it follows, he thinks, that students being prepared to live in a pluralistic society should receive an education in pluralism; and it follows further, he says, that it is the obligation of teachers and administrators "to promote intellectual pluralism" and thereby "protect the principle of intellectual diversity."

But it is a mistake to go from the general assertion that no humanly accessible truth is invulnerable to challenge to the conclusion that therefore challenges must always be provided. That is to confuse a theory of truth with its pursuit and to exchange the goal of reaching it for a resolution to keep the question of it always open.

While questions of truth may be generally open, the truth of academic matters is not general but local; questions are posed and often they do have answers that can be established with certainty; and even if that certainty can theoretically be upset—one cannot rule out the future emergence of new evidence—that theoretical possibility carries with it no methodological obligation. That is, it does not mandate intellectual diversity, a condition that may attend some moments in the pursuit of truth when there is as yet no clear path, but not a condition one must actively seek or protect.

To put it simply, intellectual diversity is not a stand-alone academic value, no more than is free speech; either can be a help in the pursuit of truth, but neither should be identified with it; the (occasional) means should not be confused with the end.

Now if intellectual diversity is not an academic value, adherence to it as 20
an end in itself will not further an academic goal; but it will further some goal, and that goal will be political. It will be part of an effort to alter the academy so that it becomes an extension of some partisan vision of the way the world should be.

Such an effort will not be a perversion of intellectual diversity; intellectual diversity as a prime academic goal is already a perversion and its transformation into a political agenda, despite Horowitz's protestations and wishes to the contrary, is inevitable and assured. It is just a matter of which party seizes it and makes it its own.

For a while (ever since the Bakke decision°), it was the left that flew the diversity banner and put it to work in the service of affirmative action, speech codes, hostile-environment regulations, minority hiring, and more. Now it is the right's turn, and Horowitz himself has mapped out the strategy and laid bare the motives:

Bakke decision: reference to the 1978 Supreme Court case *University of California Regents v. Bakke,* which outlawed quotas but reaffirmed the legality of affirmative action.

> "I encourage [students] to use the language that the left has deployed so effectively on behalf of its own agendas. Radical professors have created a 'hostile learning' environment for conservative students. There is a lack of 'intellectual diversity' on college faculties and in academic classrooms. The conservative viewpoint is 'under-represented' in the curriculum and on its reading lists. The university should be an 'inclusive' and intellectually 'diverse' community" ("The Campus Blacklist," April 2003).

It is obvious that for Horowitz these are debating points designed to hoist the left by its own petard;° but the trouble with debating points is that they can't be kept in bounds. Someone is going to take them seriously and advocate actions that Horowitz would probably not endorse.

hoist . . . by its own petard: an allusion to a line from Shakespeare's *Hamlet;* it means literally to be blown into the air by one's own bomb, that is, to be injured figuratively by something one had planned to use to injure others.

Someone is going to say, let's monitor those lefty professors and keep tabs on what they're saying; and while we're at it, let's withhold federal funds from programs that do not display "ideological balance" ("balance" is also an unworthy academic goal); and let's demand that academic institutions demonstrate a commitment to hiring conservatives; and let's make sure that the material our students read is pro-American and free of the taint of relativism; and let's publish the names of those who do not comply.

This is not a hypothetical list; it is a list of actions already being taken. In 25
fact, it is a list one could pretty much glean from the Web site of State Senator John K. Andrews Jr., president of the Colorado Senate (http://www.andrewsamerica.com/), a site on which the Academic Bill of Rights is invoked frequently.

Lynne Cheney campaigning with her husband, Vice President Dick Cheney, in Philadelphia in August 2000

Lynne Cheney: public servant who holds or has held important positions in the American Enterprise Institute for Public Policy Research, the American Council of Trustees and Alumni, and the Reader's Digest Association, all considered conservative organizations. Trained as a scholar of nineteenth-century British literature, she's the author of numerous books, including *American Memory: A Report on the Humanities in the Nation's Public Schools* (1987), *Academic Freedom* (1992), *America: A Patriotic Primer* (2002), *A Is for Abigail: An Almanac of Amazing American Women* (2003), *When Washington Crossed the Delaware: A Wintertime Story for Young Patriots* (2004), and *A Time for Freedom: What Happened When in America* (2005). She's also the wife of Vice President Dick Cheney.

Andrews, like everyone else doing the intellectual diversity dance, insists that he opposes "any sort of quotas, mandated hiring or litmus test"; but then he turns around and sends a letter to Colorado's universities asking them to explain how they promote "intellectual diversity."

Anne D. Neal, of the Lynne Cheney°-inspired American Council of Trustees and Alumni, plays the same double game in a piece entitled "Intellectual Diversity Endangered" (http://www.cfif.org/htdocs/freedomline/current/guest_commentary/student_right_to_learn.htm). First she stands up for the value of academic freedom ("no more important value to the life of the mind"), but then she urges university trustees to see to it "that all faculty . . . present points of view other than their own in a balanced way" (something you might want to do but shouldn't have to do) and to "insist that their institutions offer broad-based survey courses," and "to monitor tenure decisions" for instances of "political discrimination," and to "conduct intellectual diversity reviews and to make the results public."

These are only two examples of what the mantra of "intellectual diversity" gets you. And to make the point again, these are not examples of a good idea taken too far, but of a bad idea taken in the only direction—a political direction—it is capable of going. As a genuine academic value, intellectual diversity is a nonstarter. As an imposed imperative, it is a disaster.

RESPOND•

1. What is Stanley Fish's attitude toward the Academic Bill of Rights and the notion of intellectual diversity? Which issues do Fish and David Horowitz, author of the Academic Bill of Rights, agree about? Which issues do they disagree about? Why?
2. Fish argues that if one agrees that "the pursuit of truth is the cardinal value of the academy," then one must reject the notion of intellectual diversity (paragraph 13). What arguments does he offer for this position? Do you agree or disagree? Why?
3. Fish likewise rejects the idea that the job of higher education is to produce "creative individuals" and help students become "productive citizens." What are his arguments for this position? Do you agree or disagree? Why?
4. In paragraphs 16–23, Fish contends that despite Horowitz's claims to the contrary, his goal is to "hoist the left by its own petard." What evidence does Fish provide for his claims? How do these claims compare

with Horowitz's comments in his essay, "In Defense of Intellectual Diversity" (p. 942)?

5. In paragraph 24, Fish argues that the notion of balance is an unworthy academic goal. What does he mean here? Should the idea of balance mean that all possible positions are represented as being of equal value? Should it have some other meaning? Is it, as Fish contends, in contrast to Horowitz, not a useful goal in the pursuit of knowledge or truth? (In answering these questions, you'll likely want to consider several topics from different disciplines, using them as examples.)

Fish takes apart two major aspects of Horowitz's bill of rights, essentially claiming that they are undermined by their own fallacious logic. Do you agree? Use the descriptions of fallacies in Chapter 17 to support your answer.

LINK TO P. 493

6. Throughout this book, we've argued that images are arguments. Let's consider specifically the photo of Dr. Lynne Cheney that appears near the end of this selection. As the caption notes, it shows Cheney campaigning with her husband, the vice president. We can imagine some readers criticizing us for using a photo of Cheney in which she is represented as acting on behalf of her husband rather than being represented in terms of her own professional achievements. Why might such readers be critical? Others might praise us for using this photo. What might their reasoning be? What is your opinion about the choice of this photo? What values lead you to your conclusions?

7. Reread this selection and the previous two selections by David Horowitz, all of which constitute arguments for and against the notion of intellectual diversity, with the Academic Bill of Rights being the document most discussed in this debate. **Write an evaluative essay** in which you consider the strengths and weaknesses of each side. You may choose either to take a strong stance or to be as objective as possible so that the reader won't know where you locate yourself in this debate. (To consider: should we expect those who align themselves with Horowitz to choose the latter alternative, working hard to demonstrate complete balance in the everyday sense of the term, while expecting those who align themselves with Fish to choose the former alternative, taking a strong stance—or vice versa? Why?)

▼ *Michael J. Ellis wrote "Once More unto the Breach" for* The Dartmouth Review, *the college's "only independent newspaper," which was founded by students unhappy with the campus newspaper in 1980. The essay appeared in April 2005. The title is part of a line from scene 3 of the final act of Shakespeare's* Henry V:

Once more unto the breach, dear friends, once more,
Or close the wall up with our English dead!
In peace there's nothing so becomes a man
As modest stillness and humility;
But when the blast of war blows in our ears,
Then imitate the action of the tiger:
Stiffen the sinews, summon up the blood.

The line is, thus, a call to arms. As you read, consider which battle Ellis is encouraging his readers to fight and which battle or battles he's encouraging them to avoid.

Once More unto the Breach

MICHAEL J. ELLIS

It goes almost without saying that the student bodies, faculties, and administrations of the nation's colleges and universities lean heavily to the left. Since the tumultuous decade of the 1960s, the intellectual atmosphere of the academy has become increasingly ideologically charged, with liberals decisively in the majority. Nevertheless, those who point out this self-evident fact are often met derisively and treated as if they were reporting on the proverbial dog biting a man.

Recent events, however, have made it necessary to revisit the impact of ideology in academia. Most notably, perhaps, long-haired and pseudo-Indian University of Colorado professor Ward Churchill° derided the victims of the

Ward Churchill: a long-controversial political activist and academic, much of whose work has focused on America's treatment of political dissenters and the nation's indigenous peoples. In 2005, Churchill found himself at the center of a heated controversy over comments he'd made after September 11, 2001, when he wrote that the attacks were a direct result of U.S. foreign policy and claimed that those killed at the World Trade Center were "technocrats" and "little Eichmanns"—a reference to Adolf Eichmann, who managed many of the logistics of the Holocaust. As we go to press, this controversy continues.

9/11 attacks as "little Eichmanns." More recently, Harvard President Larry Summers° faced a media maelstrom after he had the gall to suggest that perhaps the sexes' brains may function in different ways. Here at Dartmouth, Todd Zywicki° '88 and Peter Robinson° '79 have faced an establishment backlash, in the form [of] a dubious and malicious website against their petition-driven attempts to become Trustees.

A number of recent studies, moreover, have offered quantitative evidence to back up the anecdotes of liberal bias. A team of professors from George Mason University, Smith College, and the University of Toronto found that 72 percent of those teaching at American universities and colleges identify themselves as liberal, while just 15 percent call themselves conservatives. Given that the general population has roughly twice as many conservatives as it does liberals, something is wrong with this picture. Daniel Klein, a professor of economics at Santa Clara University who spoke on campus on Wednesday, has found similar results at Stanford and UC-Berkeley. Speaking of Berkeley, research after the 2004 election found that employees of the Cal system and Harvard were the top two contributors to John Kerry's campaign, more than any Hollywood studio or personal injury law firm. [. . .] *The Review*'s own research of professors here shows that the Hanover Plain is no exception to the rule.

Is this a problem? There are certainly many who think so, including David Horowitz, founder of the ambitiously named Center for the Study of Popular Culture. Barnstorming across the nation's campuses and occasionally its legislatures, Horowitz and others trumpet these statistics as if they were proof that the liberal academy is brainwashing America's youth, as if, when Angela Lansbury° flips over a Queen of Hearts, students across the country will simultaneously recite Marx and switch their majors to Queer Studies.

Larry Summers: economist and former president of Harvard. He resigned in 2006 after a series of controversies on topics as diverse as the World Bank's policies on pollution in developing nations, the scholarship and teaching of now former Harvard professor Cornell West, the possible role of biological differences as an explanation for why fewer women than men become scientists, and his support for a colleague who settled with the government over a conflict-of-interest case, as well as a vote of no-confidence from the Harvard faculty.

Todd Zywicki and Peter Robinson: a George Mason law professor and a Hoover Institution fellow, respectively, who were elected to Dartmouth College's Board of Trustees, which oversees college policy, in 2005 after a contentious campaign; they were opposed by Dartmouth's current president. Issues in the campaign included class size, free speech, and a strong athletics program.

Angela Lansbury: award-winning actress who portrayed the evil, manipulative mother of Laurence Harvey in John Frankenheimer's film *The Manchurian Candidate*. A famous scene in the film involves the use of the card game Solitaire for purposes of brainwashing.

5 The situation, however, is not so clear-cut. Some of the most unabashedly liberal professors at Dartmouth are also some of its best, and some professors who might be more doctrinally acceptable to Mr. Horowitz are some of the worst teachers. One of the chief missions of the university (or the College, as the case may be) is to challenge its students intellectually, to make them reconsider their long-held assumptions, and to create stronger thinkers from the process. Professors have a duty to inject some degree of controversy into the classroom, if for no other reason but to stimulate a healthy intellectual debate. If I wanted to be surrounded by those who agreed with me I would have attended a college like Hillsdale,° Hampden-Sydney,° or, were I of different faith, Grove City.° Or, as Mark Bauerlein argued in the *Chronicle of Higher Education*, "being the lone dissenter in a colloquy, one learns to acquire sure facts, crisp arguments, and a thick skin."

If Horowitz were to have his way, conservatives would be the next group to join the list of those victimized and oppressed by the campus status quo, the very type of fragmentation and fractionalizing that destroys a common experience. This "solution," while appealing on its face, would set us on the road towards admissions preferences for students from Utah, a special major in conservative studies, and, to ensure that we never have to leave our comfort zones, separate conservative housing (no doubt strewn with *National Reviews*° and empty bourbon bottles).

Ellis agrees with Horowitz that there is a dearth of conservative presence in academia, but he proposes an alternative to treating conservatives as a protected class. What is his proposal? For a guide to writing your own proposal argument, turn to Chapter 11.

LINK TO P. 344

What is truly concerning is that the disproportionate percentage of professors who subscribe to liberal or "progressive" ideologies leaves many students comfortably complacent about their views. [. . .] [I]t is liberal students who are unwittingly injured the most by faculty homogeneity. Your average freshman, the scion° of upper-middle-class parents, hails from a socially acceptable blue area (Manhattan or the right suburb of Boston is preferable, but New Jersey or Long Island will do in a pinch), and will likely never encounter a conservative professor throughout their Dartmouth career. Such was the experience of Dan Knecht '05, who wrote in a recent *Daily Dartmouth* edito-

---

Hillsdale (College): "A selective, coeducational college of liberal arts" in Hillsdale, Michigan. Founded in 1854 by the Freewill Baptists, it was "the first American college to prohibit in its charter all discrimination based on race, religion, or sex."

Hampden-Sydney (College): "A selective private four-year liberal arts college for men" in Hampton-Sydney, Virginia.

Grove City (College): a Christian college in Grove City, Pennsylvania.

National Review: an influential bi-weekly conservative/libertarian magazine founded in 1955 by William F. Buckley Jr. and Revilo P. Oliver.

scion: a descendent.

rial that "I am sure they roam the halls of Silsby and Carpenter, but they either remain shamefully quiet or teeter on the verge of extinction" (1/26/05). While fellow students (and, hopefully, *The Review* itself) may take on the faculty's proper role by challenging the long-held assumptions of Knecht and his peers, the College is failing in its mission.

If Horowitz's call to the barricades is the wrong approach to fight the problem of liberal bias, what is correct? Let me suggest as a parallel the growth of the conservative movement itself in the lonely days after 1964's electoral debacle. Funding by philanthropic foundations spurred the emergence of a number of think-tanks, including the Heritage Foundation° (founded 1973) and the Cato Institute° (founded 1977). Instead of merely lamenting the lack of conservative policy initiatives at the highest levels, the think-tanks provided the apparatus necessary to create original ideas and research. Only recently have left-leaning groups caught up and started to build their own infrastructure of think-tanks to complement academia, the more traditional liberal bastion. Here at Dartmouth, they have awarded thousands of dollars to a leftist rag. Now is the time for conservatives to fight back, by adding our voices to the fray in academia just as we did in the public sector a generation ago.

Yes, there are countless stories of promising conservative doctoral candidates driven away by the Shelby Granthams° and Marysa Navarros° of the

---

Heritage Foundation: according to its Web site, "Founded in 1973, The Heritage Foundation is a research and educational institute—a think tank—whose mission is to formulate and promote conservative public policies based on the principles of free enterprise, limited government, individual freedom, traditional American values, and a strong national defense."

Cato Institute: Of its work, supported by the Cato Foundation, the Institute notes: "The Jeffersonian philosophy that animates Cato's work has increasingly come to be called 'libertarianism' or 'market liberalism.' It combines an appreciation for entrepreneurship, the market process, and lower taxes with strict respect for civil liberties and skepticism about the benefits of both the welfare state and foreign military adventurism. . . . Market liberals have a cosmopolitan, inclusive vision for society. We reject the bashing of gays, Japan, rich people, and immigrants that contemporary liberals and conservatives seem to think addresses society's problems. We applaud the liberation of blacks and women from the statist restrictions that for so long kept them out of the economic mainstream. Our greatest challenge today is to extend the promise of political freedom and economic opportunity to those who are still denied it, in our own country and around the world."

Shelby Grantham and Marysa Navarro: Grantham is a senior lecturer who teaches writing at Dartmouth; in one *Dartmouth Review* article, she's labeled "Dartmouth's worst prof" at least partly because of her liberal convictions. Marysa Navarro is the Charles Collis Professor of History at Dartmouth, where she teaches courses in Latin American history.

world. But to restore an intellectual atmosphere where different viewpoints are encouraged rather than stifled, where Larry Summers and Todd Zywicki are free to speak their minds without retribution, it will be necessary for more conservatives to enter academia. Fields like economics and engineering have always been more hospitable towards conservatives, but more are needed in biology to teach the ethics that must accompany scientific research, more are needed in English classes to teach the great books, and more are needed in history to teach the roots of Western civilization. It will only be after conservatives are no longer bizarre oddities on campuses that stories on ideological bias in academia can become as newsworthy as the man biting the dog.

RESPOND •

1. What position does Michael J. Ellis take with respect to "intellectual diversity"? What upsets him most about "the disproportionate percentage of professors who subscribe to liberal or 'progressive' ideologies" (paragraph 7)? In contrast to Horowitz, what suggestion does he offer to fellow conservatives who might be concerned about the alleged liberal bias of professors?
2. How does Ellis use humor throughout his argument? How does humor contribute to his ethos as a writer?
3. What sorts of knowledge does Ellis expect his readers to have? What sorts of values? In other words, who are his invoked readers?
4. What sorts of evidence does Ellis use in the opening paragraphs to support his argument that liberal faculty have undue influence on campuses? Why might he have arranged his argument as he did? For example, if he had reordered the information, would his argument have been more or less effective? Why? (For a discussion of kinds of evidence, see Chapter 16.)
5. In the closing paragraphs of his argument, Ellis observes that some disciplines are likely more hospitable to conservatives than others. **Write an essay** in which you evaluate this claim by examining several specific cases, seeking to understand why they might or might not be welcoming of conservatives or liberals (or people with other political commitments, or none at all). Likewise, consider the possible influence that someone's political commitments might have on her or his research or teaching.

▼ *Ann Marie B. Bahr teaches courses about world religions, Old Testament, New Testament, and religion in America at South Dakota State University in Brookings, South Dakota. She edits a series on World Religions for Chelsea House, which has published two books by her,* Indigenous Religion *(2002) and* Christianity *(2005). Like several other pieces in this chapter, "The Right to Tell the Truth" first appeared in the* Chronicle of Higher Education, *which is the major source of news and information about colleges and universities; Bahr's piece was published in May 2005. As you read, consider how she creates an argument for specific intended readers—professors and administrators at colleges and universities.*

The Right to Tell the Truth

ANN MARIE B. BAHR

I did not know about David Horowitz's "academic bill of rights" when I began teaching my courses last fall, but even if I had, I would not have thought that I had anything to fear from it.

I teach religious studies at a public university in a conservative part of the nation—not too different from the traditionally Republican state where I grew up. When I arrived here 16 years ago, I had no trouble adapting to the conservative religious background of many of my students. In graduate school I was more religiously and socially conservative than most of my fellow students. But although I have had my differences with liberals, I never felt that they forbade me to express an informed professional opinion. The chilling effect of today's conservative watchdogs is a much more serious matter.

Last semester I had my first significant falling-out with students, inspired—I have no doubt—by David Horowitz and his crusade against liberal bias in academe. Some of the students in my course on "Religion in American Culture" were upset that George M. Marsden's *Religion and American Culture* (2nd ed., Harcourt, 2001) and Randall Balmer's *Mine Eyes Have Seen the Glory: A Journey Into the Evangelical Subculture in America* (3rd ed., Oxford University Press, 2000) were on the reading list. They felt that those two books were biased against evangelicals.

Marsden is a highly respected evangelical scholar, and Balmer's work on evangelicals has also been highly acclaimed. Although his religious affiliation is not as clear as Marsden's, I had never before heard complaints that he has been unfair to the evangelicals about whom he writes. I would have thought that the two scholars had impeccable credentials for inclusion in my course, but I now suspect that the objective, scholarly tone of the books upset my students.

5 I had also assigned some online readings about Christian Identity, a white-supremacist movement that considers Jews and anyone who is not white to belong to inferior races; believes that anything—e.g., feminism and homosexuality—not in accordance with traditional gender roles is sinful; and claims to be based on the Bible. Those readings were part of a series of items about Protestant, Catholic, Nation of Islam, American Indian, and other visions of America.

In the session that I had set aside for discussion of the Christian Identity readings, a student asked me if I would have included them had I known how many students believed in the movement. I had not expected many, if any, of my students to be affiliated with Christian Identity, so I had not prepared a response to that question. I think I said something to the effect that I did not fear for my life from the group because I was a white person who was neither a feminist nor a lesbian. (There have been reports of violence associated with Christian Identity.)

About two-thirds of my students did not return to class after that day, which was around the midpoint of the semester, except to take exams. Because I never had an opportunity to discuss the matter with the students who left, I don't know if they were members of Christian Identity, or if they simply believed that a movement that claimed to be based on the Bible could not be wrong. I had never had a large-scale problem with attendance before.

I had another problem with my course on the New Testament in the fall, also unprecedented in my teaching career. I had not included any discussion of homosexuality and the Bible in the syllabus, which was already crowded thanks to the requirements placed on general-education courses by the state Board of Regents, piled on top of the disciplinary imperative of explaining academic methods of studying the Bible and applying them to the New Testament. But when students requested that we take up homosexuality, I did what I normally do when students show a particular interest in something: I modified the syllabus to include it.

We read a Jewish scholar's interpretation of several passages in the Bible for a Jewish view on the subject. I invited a Reformed Church minister to speak to the students, and he explained why there is plenty of room for debate on the question of how Christians should respond to their homosexual brethren. It turned out, however, that at least one student had a specific book in mind for us to discuss: *The Bible and Homosexual Practice* (Abingdon Press, 2001), by Robert A. J. Gagnon.

10 Although the students realized they were not academically advanced enough to read the book on their own, they wanted to know what I thought about it. The semester was rapidly drawing to a close. Not having time to read the entire book, I promised to take a look at Gagnon's discussion of Romans 1:24–27, the most explicit and substantial discussion of homosexual behavior in the New Testament.

After I read that part of the book, I told the students that I thought the linguistic work was excellent, and that the linkage of Paul's views on homosexual behavior to his remarks on idolatry was brilliant. However, I did not think that Gagnon's argument would stand up for long.

I was about to explain why when I saw anger flash across several of the students' faces, and I realized that they thought my explanation was going to echo the beliefs of the minister they had already heard, whom they considered a liberal. So I simply said that anyone who wanted to know what flaws I saw in Gagnon's argument would have to come talk to me about that outside of class. No one did.

For the first time in my life, I felt as if I had to leave my commitment to the truth (which is what scholarship is all about!) at the door of the classroom. I didn't feel that I could tell my students they were wrong to avoid hearing my explanation—in the current political climate, that would have been considered both anti-Republican and insulting to their conservative religious beliefs.

I have to believe that my students' behavior is a direct result of the new political climate on the campus that has been nurtured by the Horowitz "academic bill of rights," in cooperation with conservative media. I do not think that Horowitz intended those results. The problem is that students do not have the academic maturity to know how to use his document.

15 Nor do I see how they could have that maturity before completing a liberal-arts program of studies. Taking a smattering of liberal-arts courses, which is all that most students are required to do, does not give students the ability to detect bias in their professors or in what they read. Furthermore, many students take their definition of bias from conservative talk-radio shows and Fox News—even people considered to be moderates from a liberal viewpoint seem biased from such conservative perspectives.

It seems that I must now bow to political or popular pressure because the ultimate judges of my professional expertise will not be my scholarly peers, but the public. And while members of the public and students may be able to judge many aspects of my teaching (that is why we have student evaluations of professors), they cannot judge whether I am teaching according to the best standards of the discipline.

Politics has always played a role on our campuses, but we are now experiencing a new form of political intrusion in academic life, and it is extremely dangerous. It has a direct impact on academic freedom because it threatens professors—with the loss of the usual presumption that they are experts in their subject matter, or even with the loss of employment, if they do not agree with popular opinions.

That is too high a price for me to pay to keep my job, and I have resolved never again to bow to religious or political pressure in the classroom. In the future I will send students to the Internet to view authors' credentials. When I next teach the New Testament, I will use the disagreement between Gagnon and myself to demonstrate that scholarly debate—unlike political debate, in which each side is expected to be partisan—is a way of systematically testing the beliefs of both sides, and that my job is to critically assess all the arguments, from within my area of expertise.

Like many other academics, I have dedicated my life to the faithful transmission of the truth as best I can discern it. It makes me sick to my stomach to think of falsifying the truth, or even sacrificing my right to have an informed professional opinion.

How does Bahr create a causal argument within her essay? Chapter 10 offers an overview of the key features of such an argument.

LINK TO P. 305

RESPOND •

1. What is Ann Marie B. Bahr's position on intellectual diversity? How does she use her own experience to support her position? How effectively does she do so?
2. How does Bahr characterize herself? In other words, what do you, as a reader, know about her values and commitments? How does this knowledge influence the ethos Bahr is able to create?
3. What might Bahr mean when she writes, "I now suspect that the objective, scholarly tone of the books upset my students" (paragraph 4)? What specifically might she mean by "objective" and "scholarly"? Why might her students have wanted or expected some other sort of book?
4. What should our response be when works accepted as sound scholarship of the sort mentioned in paragraph 3 of this essay present a less-than-flattering picture of a group of which we are a member or one for which we have some empathy?
5. Because this essay appeared in the *Chronicle of Higher Education*, we can assume that Bahr's intended readers are professors and administrators at colleges and universities. Thus, throughout the essay, Bahr is talking about—not to—students when she makes such claims as "[t]he problem is that students do not have the academic maturity to know how to use [Horowitz's "Academic Bill of Rights"]" (paragraph 14) and "members of the public and students . . . cannot judge whether I am teaching according to the best standards of the discipline" (para-

graph 16). How do you respond to such claims? Why? What sorts of things are students capable of judging? With respect to the sorts of topics covered in college and university courses, is Bahr correct in claiming that there are certain things students (and the general public) are incapable of judging? If so, what would those things be?

6. Bahr frames the potential controversy about intellectual diversity as one of "popular opinions" (that is, public attitudes, especially the attitudes of students, toward certain information or knowledge they may dislike) versus "informed professional opinion" (paragraphs 17 and 19). Using your response to question 4 and discussions with classmates and others, **write an essay** in which you seek to define the limits of student opinion and professional opinion with regard to the subject matter taught in college and university classrooms.

▼ *John Tierney is a columnist for the* New York Times *(where this selection first appeared); his comments appear twice a week on the Op-Ed page. He's known for his conservative viewpoints and humorous approach. For the* New York Times *he has written extensively about science, technology, economics, and the environment. With Christopher Buckley, he co-authored* The Best Case Scenario Handbook: A Parody *(2002), which includes chapters on "How to manage tensions when you are promoted over the head of your insufferable boss" and "What to do when a drunken Bill Gates rear-ends your car and mumbles 'isn't there some way we can work this out without the police?'" The essay below was written in response to the controversies around David Horowitz's Academic Bill of Rights (see p. 949). See the next selection for letters to the editor that were published in the* New York Times *after Tierney's column appeared.*

Where Cronies Dwell

JOHN TIERNEY

The left has a lock on journalism and law schools.

Journalists and legal scholars have been decrying "cronyism" and calling for "mainstream" values when picking a Supreme Court justice. But how do they go about picking the professors to train the next generation of journalists and lawyers?

David Horowitz, the conservative who is president of the Center for the Study of Popular Culture, analyzed the political affiliations of the faculty at 18 elite journalism and law schools. By checking all the party registrations he could find, he found that Democrats outnumber Republicans by 8 to 1 at the law schools, with the ratio ranging from 3 to 1 at Penn to 28 to 1 at Stanford.

Only one journalism school, the University of Kansas, had a preponderance of Republicans (by 10 to 8). At the rest of the schools, there was a 6-to-1 ratio of Democrats to Republicans. The ratio was 4 to 1 at Northwestern and New York University, 13 to 1 at the University of Southern California, 15 to 1 at Columbia. Horowitz didn't find any Republicans at Berkeley.

5 Some academics try to argue that their political ideologies don't affect the way they teach, which to me is proof of how detached they've become from reality in their monocultures. This claim is especially dubious if you're training lawyers and journalists to deal with controversial public policies.

I realize, from experience at six newspapers, that most journalists try not to impose their prejudices on their work. When I did stories whose facts challenged liberal orthodoxies, editors were glad to run them. When liberal reporters wrote stories, they tried to present the conservative perspective.

The problem isn't so much the stories that appear as the ones that no one thinks to do. Journalists naturally tend to pursue questions that interest them. So when you have a press corps that's heavily Democratic — more than 80 percent, according to some surveys of D.C. journalists — they tend to do stories that reflect Democrats' interests.

When they see a problem, their instinct is to ask what the government can do to solve it. I once sat in on a newspaper story conference the day after an armored-car company was robbed of millions of dollars bound for banks. The first idea that came up for a follow-up story was: Does this robbery show the need for stricter regulation of armored-car companies?

We kicked this idea around until I suggested that companies in the business of transporting cash already had a fairly strong incentive not to lose it — presumably an even stronger incentive than any government official regulating their security arrangements. That story idea died, but not the mind-set that produced it.

10 The surest way to impress the judges for a journalism prize is to write articles that spur a legislature to right some evil, particularly if it was committed by a corporation. When journalists do expose government malfeasance, they usually focus on the need for more regulations and bigger budgets, not on whether the government should be doing the job in the first place.

To some extent, this is a problem of self-selection. Journalism attracts people who want to right wrongs, and the generation that's been running journalism schools and media businesses came of age when government, especially the federal government, was seen as the solution to most wrongs. These executives, like the tenured radicals in law schools and the rest of academia, hired ideological cronies and shaped their institutions to reflect their views.

But those views are no longer dominant outside newsrooms and academia. A lot of young conservatives and libertarians have simply given up on the traditional media, either as a source of news or as a place to work. Instead, they post on blogs and start careers at magazines like *The Weekly Standard*° and *Reason*,° knowing these credentials will hurt their chances of becoming reporters for "mainstream" publications — whereas a job at *The New Republic*° or *The Washington Monthly*° wouldn't be a disqualifying credential.

I'm not suggesting that journalism or law schools should be forced to have ideological balance on their faculties — this is one of those many problems that doesn't require a solution by government. But it's curious how little the institutions care about it.

They keep meticulous tabs on the race and gender and ethnic background of their students and faculty. But the lack of political diversity is taken as a matter of course. As long as the professors look different, why worry if they all think the same?

The Weekly Standard: a magazine founded in 1995 by William Kristol and Fred Barnes and noted for its neoconservative views, which include interventionist foreign policy and, in general, a lack of opposition to "big government."

Reason: a monthly print magazine that, in its own words, "provides a refreshing alternative to right-wing and left-wing opinion magazines by making a principled case for liberty and individual choice in all areas of human activity."

The New Republic: a weekly magazine of opinion generally associated with liberal positions and particularly "business-friendly" Democrats like Bill Clinton and Joseph Lieberman.

The Washington Monthly: a magazine founded in 1969 that treats issues relating to government and culture; its politics can be characterized as moderately but firmly left of center.

Tierney's argument is one of definition. He speaks to what he sees as the nature of liberal academia. Consider Chapter 8's discussion of different types of definitional arguments.

LINK TO P. 223

RESPOND.

1. Tierney discusses another aspect of the intellectual diversity controversy—"the stories that . . . no one thinks to do" (paragraph 7). Why does he feel this issue is a matter of some importance? Do you agree or disagree? Why?
2. Tierney contends there's bias in hiring in what he terms the "mainstream" publications (paragraphs 11–12). What's the nature of this bias? How is it perpetuated, according to Tierney?
3. In paragraph 13, Tierney offers a qualification to his argument: "I'm not suggesting that journalism or law schools should be forced to have ideological balance on their faculties—this is one of those many problems that doesn't require a solution by government." How does qualifying his position strengthen Tierney's argument? Why is it important for him to mention this situation as a problem government doesn't need to help solve, given the ethos he creates for himself and the position he has taken on this issue?
4. As do all the writers in this chapter, Tierney makes causal claims, among others. What's the exact nature of his causal argument(s)? In other words, for Tierney, what specific causes yield which specific results? (For a discussion of causal arguments, see Chapter 10.)
5. Tierney cites David Horowitz's studies of the political affiliation of professors in journalism and law schools, and Tierney, like many, finds these results troubling. Why, in your opinion, is the focus on these fields, rather than, say, engineering or biology?
6. **Write a rhetorical analysis** of this column, paying special attention to the ways in which Tierney qualifies certain claims and provides evidence for his own claims. Part of your analysis may be an evaluation of Tierney's position itself.

The New York Times, a daily newspaper published in New York with a national audience, covers national and international issues and has won 116 Pulitzer Prizes for its reporting—more than any other news organization. The Letters to the Editor page offers readers a chance to "talk back" to the paper's writers and editors; those printed here were published in response to John Tierney's opinion editorial, "Where Cronies Dwell" (p. 969). As you read, notice the format and style of the letters, and think about the range of opinions they offer on Tierney's column.

Through the Prism of Left and Right: Responses to John Tierney's "Where Cronies Dwell"

To the Editor:

Re "Where Cronies Dwell," by John Tierney (column, Oct. 11):

The liberal nature of journalism and academia (including law schools) is not so much the result of cronyism as of self-selection. The universities aren't hiring conservatives because conservatives aren't applying for the jobs.

People who choose those professions tend to be liberal because that is what those professions require.

Both journalism and academia attract people who have made it their business to observe human society, and both careers usually involve travel and exposure to a wide variety of individuals and viewpoints.

This travel and exposure teach important lessons: a variety of different government styles can work well; societies have destroyed themselves by consuming all environmental resources too fast; individual prosperity is as much a matter of lucky birth as of personal merit.

If you want to debate genuine political issues like the role of government in providing social services, the pros and cons of labor unions or the wisdom of imposing American values on foreign countries, you can find plenty of university and law school faculty members who would be willing to argue these points from a traditionally conservative viewpoint.

–Amy Hackney Blackwell
Greenville, S.C., Oct. 11, 2005

As you read the letters to the editor, pay attention to the ethos that the authors create for themselves. Does character carry much weight in such communications? Review the discussion of arguments based on character in Chapter 3.

LINK TO P. 65

To the Editor:

Is John Tierney concerned about monocultures or just liberal monocultures?

When I changed careers three years ago, I traded one monoculture (a corporate management team) for another (an independent high school faculty).

A more interesting question might be, "Why was I in the minority in my last career, and why am I in the majority now?"

If Mr. Tierney can shed light on that question, perhaps we will understand the clustering of common political and societal outlooks (and the effects of this clustering) a little better.

–Mark Hammond
Middletown, Del., Oct. 11, 2005

To the Editor:

When John Tierney complains about the number of liberals in academia and suggests that this is somehow comparable to President Bush's hiring friends for important government jobs, he misses the point.

Academics aren't hired because they are loyal to a department chairman. Instead, they are hired because they fulfill certain needs and because—get this—they are extremely qualified.

Mr. Tierney hints that self-selection may play a role in the more liberal bent of academia. Would he expect anything different? Republicans and conservatives routinely disparage anything in academia that has no money-making application.

(*continued*)

Government money spent on the humanities is anathema to the far right. Is it any wonder that people interested in advancing the understanding of the human condition might lean toward a political ideology that embraces their efforts?

–Lance Allred
Baltimore, Oct. 11, 2005

To the Editor:

John Tierney tries to equate a preponderance of Democrats in academia with cronyism. If we take cronyism to mean favoritism shown to friends without regard to qualifications, it is obvious that preponderance does not logically imply the presence of cronyism.

There is a preponderance of right-handedness in academia, too.

Moreover, Mr. Tierney provides no evidence for his claim that "tenured radicals" have preferred to hire "ideological cronies" in academia. This may happen anecdotally, but it strains credulity to suggest that top universities, in their constant struggle for higher rankings, would not simply try to hire the best candidates.

Perhaps the more useful question to ask is why the products of top law schools and journalism schools who are interested in teaching future generations are disproportionately Democrats. Do Republicans simply value teaching less?

–Maurits van der Veen
Athens, Ga., Oct. 11, 2005
The writer is an assistant professor in the department of international affairs, University of Georgia.

Lars Leetaru

To the Editor:

As a graduate of both law school and journalism school, I find it hard to argue with John Tierney's premise that law professors and especially journalism professors tend toward liberalism. But it's harder to argue that either profession favors liberals outside the academy.

Indeed, conservative lawyers, if they are a minority, have a much better shot at judgeships or high-level government positions since it's conservatives who are doing the appointing more often than not.

More broadly, if liberals are channeling their own most brilliant acolytes into law and journalism, that just leaves more space in business schools, banks and corporations for young conservatives. Thus, the conservatives wind up wielding greater power, lacking only vague cultural influence.

If conservatives had concocted this arrangement deliberately, they could have hardly done better for themselves.

–Daniel L. Ackman
Jersey City, Oct. 11, 2005

To the Editor:

If Democrats outnumber Republicans in elite university faculties by up to 8 to 1, as John Tierney writes, then academia indeed has a problem. But the culprit is not necessarily how universities "go about picking the professors to train the next generation."

Rather, Republicans themselves may choose to forgo academic penury for more lucrative careers in keeping with their party's self-help doctrine.

As a registered independent who stresses the teaching of diverse perspectives, I am troubled if students are hearing mainly from one side of the aisle. But let's not rush to blame demand when the culprit may be supply.

–Alan J. Kuperman
Austin, Tex., Oct. 11, 2005
The writer is an assistant professor at the L.B.J. School of Public Affairs, University of Texas.

To the Editor:

There is an easy solution to John Tierney's concern about lack of ideological balance among journalism and law professors: Raise their pay enough to make them Republicans.

If those who go into professions "to right wrongs" did not have to take vows of poverty, some of them might show more interest in tax cuts for the rich and other acute conservative concerns.

–Robert Stein
Weston, Conn., Oct. 11, 2005
The writer is the author of a new book about the media.

RESPOND •

1. Briefly, summarize the argument each of these letters to the editor makes. Which letter do you find most effective in making its point and doing so memorably? Why? Which do you find least effective in doing so?
2. Which letter is most in line with your own response to Tierney's column "Where Cronies Dwell"? Which is least in line? To what extent does your reply to this question correspond to your reply to question 1? Should you be concerned if it does? If it doesn't? Is it possible to separate one's own commitments to or stance about an issue from one's evaluations of arguments about that issue?
3. Which letters present actual criticism of the arguments Tierney made, and which are more general critiques of the broader position he takes? Focusing on those that criticize specific arguments made by Tierney, make a list of the aspects of his column these letter writers objected to.
4. If you take these letters to be successful—they did manage to get published, after all—what are the criteria for a successful letter to the editor of the *New York Times?*
5. The *Times*, like many newspapers, sometimes provides one sentence of information about who a letter writer is. How does such information—or its absence—likely influence readers' evaluations of the letter? Of the letter writer?
6. On the next page, we present two cartoons about the controversy over intellectual diversity, each by a cartoonist known for his or her political slant on contemporary events. The first, a strip from *Mallard Fillmore* by Bruce Tinsley, might have been drawn to accompany Tierney's column. The second, by Signe Wilkinson, appeared in April 2005 and examines another side of this debate. Each raises a different question about the constellation of issues that has been labeled intellectual diversity. How would you summarize the argument each cartoon makes? **Write an essay** in which you evaluate each cartoon in terms of its effectiveness at conveying its point and doing so visually.

Bruce Tinsley, *Mallard Fillmore*

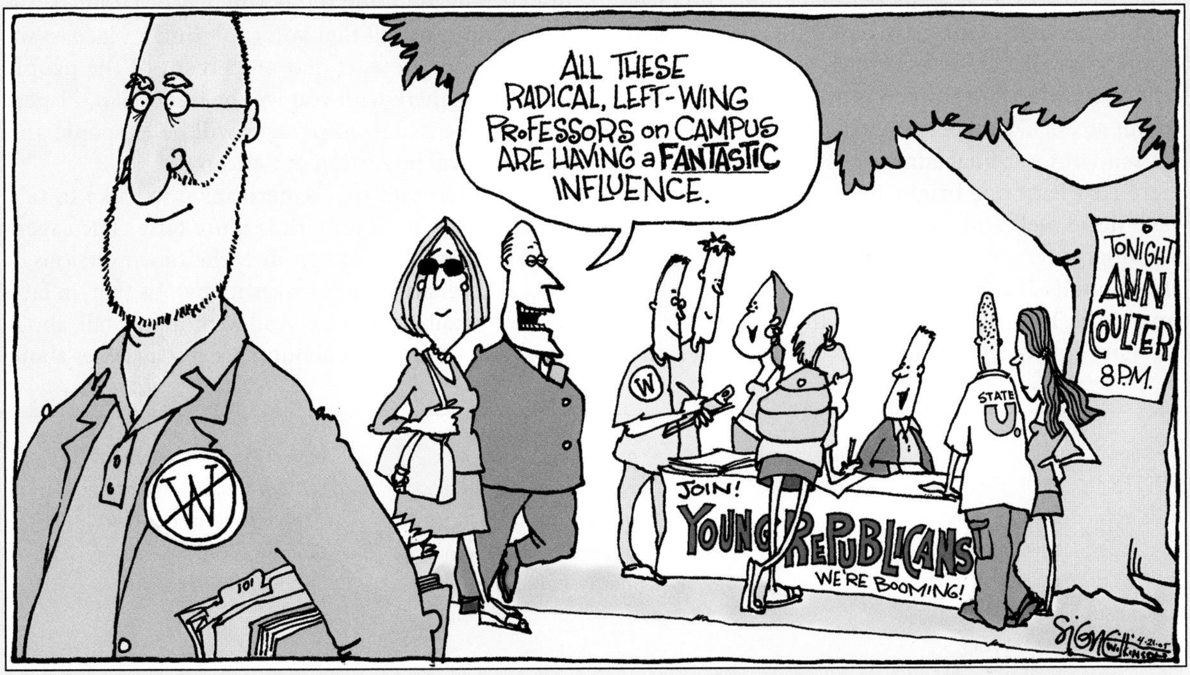

Signe Wilkinson, *Young Republicans*

▼ *Walter Benn Michaels is the chair of the Department of English at the University of Illinois at Chicago, where he teaches literary theory and American literature. His influential essay "Against Theory" was published in 1982, and his most recent book,* The Shape of the Signifier: 1967 to the End of History, *was published in 2004. He wrote this essay for the* New York Times *Sunday magazine. While you read, think about why this book's editors chose to end the chapter with this selection.*

Diversity's False Solace°

WALTER BENN MICHAELS

The university where I have taught for the last three years — the University of Illinois, Chicago — is a large, increasingly underfinanced public university. Our classrooms are overcrowded. Our physical plant is deteriorating. Many departments cannot afford to hire any new professors.

But as we, like other universities around the country, send out our final admissions letters this month, there is at least one bright spot, one area where we have done well and are poised to do even better. Seemingly every piece of literature that U.I.C. distributes about itself announces that we have been "ranked among the Top 10 universities in the country for the diversity" of "our student body." And that diversity, the literature goes on to point out, "is one of the greatest aspects of our campus." The bad news about our current condition is that you may be jammed into a classroom so full that you can't find a place to sit. But the good news is that 46 percent of the people jammed in there with you will be Caucasian, 21 percent will be Asian, 13 percent will be Hispanic and 9 percent will be African-American.

It is often said that Americans don't like to talk about race, but no remark is more false. The eagerness of other schools to produce their own versions of U.I.C.'s diversity figures makes it obvious that, in fact, we love to talk about race. And we not only talk about it, we also write books about it, we teach classes about

---

Michaels builds his argument using facts in the form of numbers and statistics about race and economics. Do you think he draws logical conclusions from his data? Why or why not? For help, review the section in Chapter 7 on developing a factual argument.

LINK TO P. 184

solace: comfort or consolation.

meritocracy: a society where those holding power of various kinds do so because of their proven merit or ability, often demonstrated through educational achievement rather than, say, the social class of their birth, their bloodline, or some other defining characteristic.

it and we arrange our admissions policies to take it into account.

It is true, however, that we don't so much like to call it race. Students, faculty members and administrators often prefer to speak of their cultural identities. Unimpressed by the objection that—speaking the same language, wearing the same clothes, reading the same books—they all seem to me to belong to the same culture, my students speak proudly of their own cultures and respectfully of others'. Some might be taller than others, some might be smarter than others, some might be better-looking than others, but all belong to cultures, and all the cultures are worthy of respect. And that's the advantage of the idea of culture: it gives us a world of differences without inequality.

5 And the enthusiasm for such differences is widespread. When I asked a group of Harvard literature students about what distinguished them from a parallel group of literature students at U.I.C., they were prepared to acknowledge that the U.I.C. students might be even more diverse than they were, but they were unable to see the relevance of the fact that the U.I.C. group was also less wealthy. And this is equally true of the students at U.I.C. who identify themselves as black, white, Arab, Asian and Hispanic and not as poor or working class. After all, your ethnicity is something you can be proud of in a way that your poverty or even your wealth (since it's your parents' wealth) is not.

But the real value of diversity is not primarily in the contribution it makes to students' self-esteem. Its real value is in the contribution it makes to the collective fantasy that institutions ranging from U.I.C. to Harvard are meritocracies° that reward individuals for their own efforts and abilities—as opposed to rewarding them for the advantages of their birth. For if we find that the students at an elite university like Harvard or Yale are almost as diverse as the students at U.I.C., then we know that no student is being kept from a Harvard because of his or her culture. And white students can understand themselves to be there on merit because they didn't get there at the expense of black people.

We are often reminded of how white our classrooms would look if we did away with affirmative action. But imagine what Harvard would look like if instead we replaced race-based affirmative action with a strong dose of class-based affirmative action. Ninety percent of the undergraduates come from families earning more than $42,000 a year (the median household income in the U.S.)—and some 77 percent come from families with incomes of more than $80,000, although only about 20 percent of American households have incomes that high. If the income distribution at Harvard were made to look like the income distribution of the United States, some 57 percent of the displaced students would be rich, and most of them would be white. It's no wonder that many rich white kids and their parents seem to like diversity. Race-based affirmative action, from this standpoint, is a kind of collective bribe rich people pay themselves for ignoring economic inequality. The fact (and it is a fact) that it doesn't help to be white to get into Harvard replaces the much more fundamental fact that it does help to be rich and that it's virtually essential not to be poor.

Hence the irrelevance of Harvard's recent announcement that it won't ask parents who earn less than $40,000 a year to help pay for their children's education. While this is no doubt great news to those financially pressed students who have gone to great schools, taken college-prep courses and scored well on their SAT's, it's bound to seem a little beside the point to the great majority of the poor, since what's keeping them out of elite universities is not their inability to pay the bill but their inability to qualify for admission in the first place.

In the end, we like policies like affirmative action not so much because they solve the problem of racism but because they tell us that racism is the problem we need to solve. And the reason we like the problem of racism is that solving it just requires us to give up our prejudices, whereas solving the problem of economic inequality might require something more—it might require us to give up our money. It's not surprising that universities of the upper middle class should want their students to feel comfortable. What is surprising is that diversity should have become the hallmark of liberalism.

10 This, if you're on the right, is the gratifying thing about campus radicalism. When student and faculty activists struggle for cultural diversity, they are in large part battling over what skin color the rich kids should have. Diversity, like gout,° is a rich people's problem. And it is also a rich people's solution. For as long as we're committed to thinking of difference as something that should be respected, we don't have to worry about it as something that should be eliminated. As long as we think that our best universities are fair if they are appropriately diverse, we don't have to worry that most people can't go to them, while others get to do so because they've had the good luck to be born into relatively wealthy families. In other words, as long as the left continues to worry about diversity, the right won't have to worry about inequality. ■

---

gout: a disease most often associated with painful swelling of the big toe, resulting from a build-up of uric acid. Because alcohol and a rich diet aggravate the condition, it's often associated with the wealthy, although nearly one-fifth of those who develop the disease have a family history of it.

RESPOND •

1. Why does Walter Benn Michaels contend that diversity offers a "false solace" at best? What, in his opinion, is the real issue American society needs to confront? How, for him, does arguing about ethnic diversity simultaneously insulate Americans from seeing the real issue while preventing them from dealing with it?
2. For what reasons does Michaels argue that the notions of culture and cultural difference are comforting ones? And why, in his opinion, is race such an unpleasant one for Americans?
3. How does Michaels fit his observations about diversity into the American political landscape, recasting it in terms of the liberal left and the conservative right?
4. What sort of ethos does Michaels create for himself in this essay? What sorts of appeals does he use—ethical appeals, emotional appeals, logical appeals? How do they contribute to the tone of the essay and the ethos Michaels creates for himself?
5. This chapter has provided many perspectives on a hotly debated issue on American college and university campuses: diversity. What should a diverse campus look like, and why? Should diversity be something schools strive for or not? What kinds of diversity? Why? **Write a proposal essay** in which you define and justify the sort(s) of diversity, if any, your school should aim for. Seek to draw widely on the perspectives you've been exposed to in reading this chapter.

28
Why Do They Love Us? Why Do They Hate Us?

Within days of the events of September 11, 2001, people across America found themselves asking, “Why do they hate us?” In some cases, the referent for “they” was quite clear; in others, it seemed to refer to anyone who wasn’t American—and even to some Americans, especially those who were from the Middle East, were Muslim, or held certain political beliefs. A profitable way to reframe this question might be “How is it that Americans came to see themselves so differently than citizens of other countries see them?” From this perspective, the question becomes one of what

Americans don't seem to know or understand about how others perceive their country or why.

At the same time, then and even now, it's clear that people risk their lives daily to come to America, and there's ample evidence of many kinds that American music, movies, and television — not to mention food and drinks, clothing, and technology — are much appreciated around the globe. "Why do they love us?" we might ask.

The readings in this chapter challenge you to think about why people from outside the United States might claim to have ample reason to love and hate America and Americans. (The people of some countries and cultures seem to have no trouble distinguishing between a country and its citizens; others are less charitable or rigorous in their thinking. Where do Americans fit?) The first five selections focus in some way on how America and Americans are viewed by those outside the country. Hannah Fairfield's "America: Not Their First Choice" presents a visual argument displaying the findings of a survey showing that people from many countries don't believe the United States is the best place to find a good life. In the wake of Hurricane Katrina, Richard Bernstein explains to American readers how Europeans did and didn't make sense of the disaster in his essay, "The Days After: The View from Abroad." Waleed Ziad's essay, "Jihad's Fresh Face," argues that what he terms Islamic neo-fundamentalism grows out of very specific social and historical circumstances the United States plays a role in and can help change. Similarly, David Rieff in "Their Hearts and Minds?" examines how challenges currently facing the U.S. government differ from those it faced during the Cold War. "How Others See Us" presents a visual portfolio of works by several artists responding to America and its place in the world.

The next three readings seek to help explain why other countries see America as they do. Dinesh D'Souza's "America the Beautiful: What We're Fighting For" is in many ways an effort to define what America stands for and why it is and should be loved by other governments and the citizens of other countries even as it encourages Americans to stay the course by accepting what he sees as its destiny. Mark Hertsgaard's "The Oblivious Empire" presents America and Americans in a very different light, detailing the reasons others often have little patience with Americans. In "Revolution Is U.S.," Thomas L. Friedman explains why many people around the world find America's "global arrogance"—a term he borrows from Iranian mullahs—insufferable while also explaining why, in some sense, what's going on in the world today is in many ways not an American conspiracy but the way globalization works.

Next come four selections that tackle the question of soft power—the influence America has or that's attributed to America because of the popularity of things

American around the world. Josef Joffe, a German journalist, writes of "the perils of soft power" associated with the export of American culture. Historian Richard Pells questions whether American culture is, in fact, American, contending that the strength of American culture is its cosmopolitanism and ability to meld cultures. Michael Medved's "That's Entertainment?" argues that American movies are one of the causes of anti-Americanism abroad. "Exporting America," a visual portfolio, provides clear evidence of the familiarity and ubiquity of aspects of American culture around the world.

The chapter closes with two very personal responses to America and its role in the world. One is by the daughter of an immigrant to the United States; the other is by an immigrant. In "My Suspicious Last Name," Diana Abu-Jaber is critical of Americans' responses—and especially the American government's response—since September 2001 to the complexity of the world inside and outside America's borders. In "Passing Through," Yiyun Li reminds readers of some of the reasons that America remains a beacon on a hill for many.

To the extent we've succeeded, these readings will encourage—and perhaps even force—you to think about America and its place in the world in new ways. Why do they love us? Why do they hate us? Are those the most relevant questions to ask? You decide the answer.

▼ *"America: Not Their First Choice" appeared in "The Basics," a column in the Week in Review section of the Sunday New York Times early in July 2005. As Hannah Fairfield notes, the data come from the 2005 Pew Global Attitudes Survey, a project of the Pew Charitable Trust, which surveyed people from sixteen countries about their attitudes toward the United States with the goal of understanding anti-Americanism. For more information about this study, visit <http://pewglobal.org/reports/display.php?ReportID= 247>. For more information about the Global Attitudes Survey, visit <http://pewglobal.org/about/>. As you study this selection, consider the many kinds of information this visual argument conveys simultaneously because of its design.*

America: Not Their First Choice

HANNAH FAIRFIELD

Where's the love?

The Pew Research Center recently asked nearly 17,000 people from 16 countries: "Suppose a young person who wanted to leave this country asked you to recommend where to go to lead a good life—what country would you recommend?" Only India rated America as its top pick.

Except for respondents in India, Poland and Canada, no more than 1 in 10 people in the other nations said they would recommend the United States.

Canada and Australia won the popularity contest, selected as first choice by several other countries.

The question was posed in April and May, the first time it was asked in the Pew Global Attitudes Survey, which has tracked sentiments toward the United States, among many issues, since 2002. The survey has a margin of error ranging from plus or minus 2 percentage points to plus or minus 4 percentage points.

Percentage of people from these countries . . . ↓

. . . who said they would recommend these destinations for "a good life."
Blue circles indicate each country's top choice.

		United States	Canada	Australia	Britain	Germany	Other top choices	
India		38%	6	13	6	3		
Poland		19	9	8	21	10		
Canada		13		18	7	3		
Germany	*Tie for first*	10	11	11	3			
China		10	12	10	4	4		
Russia		8	6	9	4	22		
Turkey		8	7	12	5	18		
Lebanon		8	17	18	6	6	France	19
Jordan		8	9	8	9	2	United Arab Emirates	17
Spain		7	2	9	14	6		
Britain		6	9	31		2		
France		5	14	7	4	7		
Pakistan		5	3	1	6	1	China	18
Netherlands	*Tie for first*	3	16	16	3	3		
Indonesia		2	2	8	5	4	Japan	24

Fairfield's article is short; the majority of the data on which she draws is presented in a large table accompanying the text. How do the various circles add to the clarity of the argument? Chapter 14 offers a guide to using visuals in your own arguments.

LINK TO P. 423

RESPOND.

1. What's your response to this selection? Surprise? Amazement? Anger? Agreement? Why? How do you think most Americans would respond to these data? Why?
2. Evaluate this selection as a visual argument. How clear and easy to follow is it? What principle, if any, accounts for the ordering of countries in the column on the left? In the rows across the top? What principle, if any, accounts for the relative size of the circles representing responses? The shading of circles?
3. Try to divide the countries in the left column into subgroups based on some characteristic they share; for example, Northern European countries, countries with large Muslim populations, traditional friends or allies of the United States, countries that have opposed the United States and that the United States has opposed at some time since World War II, and so on. Do any patterns in responses begin to emerge once you examine these subgroups?
4. Choose two countries and look for information necessary to help account for those countries' responses. (Choose at least one country that isn't part of Europe and that's neither Canada nor Australia.) **Write an analysis** of the factors that might account for the responses. Here's an example of a possible analysis of the responses of French people to the question. (By the way, since we used France as an example, you shouldn't choose France, either!)

   The French respondents replied Canada (14%), Australia (7%), Germany (7%), United States (5%), and Great Britain (4%). Among the options, it isn't surprising that the French might choose Canada as their first choice. Canada is officially bilingual, with French being one of its official languages; hence, if speakers of French move to Canada, they aren't faced with being forced to use another language, especially if they move to the French-speaking regions of the country. Similarly, it's likewise not surprising that Britain comes in last because the French and the British have long perceived themselves to be in direct competition as powers in Europe and, formerly, as colonial powers. The United States and France often clash in the international arena over any number of political issues, and across the twentieth century, as France saw its international power decline, the power of the United States increased. The French often complain that their language is under threat because of the growing use of the English language, and it's the uses of English associated with American popular culture and the globalization of American culture and capitalism — for example, McDonalds and American movies and music — that the French complain most often about. The French see the spread of these things as threats to their culture and way of life. In contrast, Germany is France's neighbor, and despite their differences and the competition between the two countries, both have aligned themselves squarely with the idea of the European Union to a degree Britain has refused to. Perhaps the responses favoring Australia result from the fact that it's neither Britain nor the United States but still an English-speaking country, and more French speak English than German.

5. Where's the love? **Write an essay** in which you explain your understanding of why people from various countries might not recommend the United States to a young person as a place to go in order to "lead a good life." Your essay will surely be a causal essay because you're analyzing the reasons or causes people wouldn't make a specific recommendation.

Currently the Berlin Bureau Chief for the New York Times, *Richard Bernstein has been associated with the paper for over twenty years. Before moving to Germany, Bernstein served in a range of positions: book critic, bureau chief at the United Nations, bureau chief in Paris, and national cultural reporter. He's author or co-author of several books, including* Out of the Blue: A Narrative of September 11, 2001, From Jihad to Ground Zero *(2002, with the staff of the* Times), Ultimate Journey: Retracing the Path of an Ancient Buddhist Monk Who Crossed Asia in Search of Enlightenment *(2002),* The Coming Conflict with China *(1998, with* Ross H. Munro), Dictatorship of Virtue: How the Battle over Multiculturalism Is Reshaping Our Schools, Our Country, and Our Lives *(1995), and* Fragile Glory: A Portrait of France and the French *(1991). This essay, "The View from Abroad," was part of the* Times*'s coverage of Hurricane Katrina and appeared under the heading "The Days After." As you read, try to put yourself in the place of people around the world who watch tragedies of any sort unfold in America. How might you respond?*

The Days After: The View from Abroad

RICHARD BERNSTEIN

BERLIN — They were perhaps a bit slow, but the expressions of sympathy and offers of aid in the wake of Hurricane Katrina did materialize in Europe through the week.

Chancellor Gerhard Schröder of Germany declared, "Our American friends should know that we are standing by them." The French prime minister, Dominique de Villepin, offered to send supplies, two airplanes, 35 members of civil security rescue teams, and other equipment and personnel.

Still, Europe's response so far to the calamity of Katrina has been complicated, even ambivalent. There was plenty of sympathy and willingness to help, but there was also, as with Mr. de Villepin's offer, a rather formulaic quality and an absence of any powerful, spontaneous surge of empathy and affection for the afflicted nation.

Why?

5 It is hard to measure this, but judging from the commentary and the blogs, the collective European response to the victims of the tsunami or the famine in Niger, to the killings in Darfur or the deaths of Shiite pilgrims in Baghdad seems to have been more immediate and deeply felt than for the victims of Katrina. And one reason for this relative coolness may be that these other disasters took place in poor, troubled nations, not in the most powerful and richest country on earth.

In fact, the spectacle of the hurricane causing a disaster of third-world° proportions in the United States seems to have provoked a sort of dismay among Europeans, mingling with the sorrow. As a reporter on BBC Television argued on Friday, not able to

third world: refers to countries that receive low scores on the United Nations Human Development Index, which seeks to measure a country's degree of development in several domains. Such countries are generally less technologically advanced or industrialized than other countries. Originally, the term referred to countries that weren't aligned with the West (the first world) or with the Soviet Bloc (the second world) during the Cold War, hence the name *third world.*

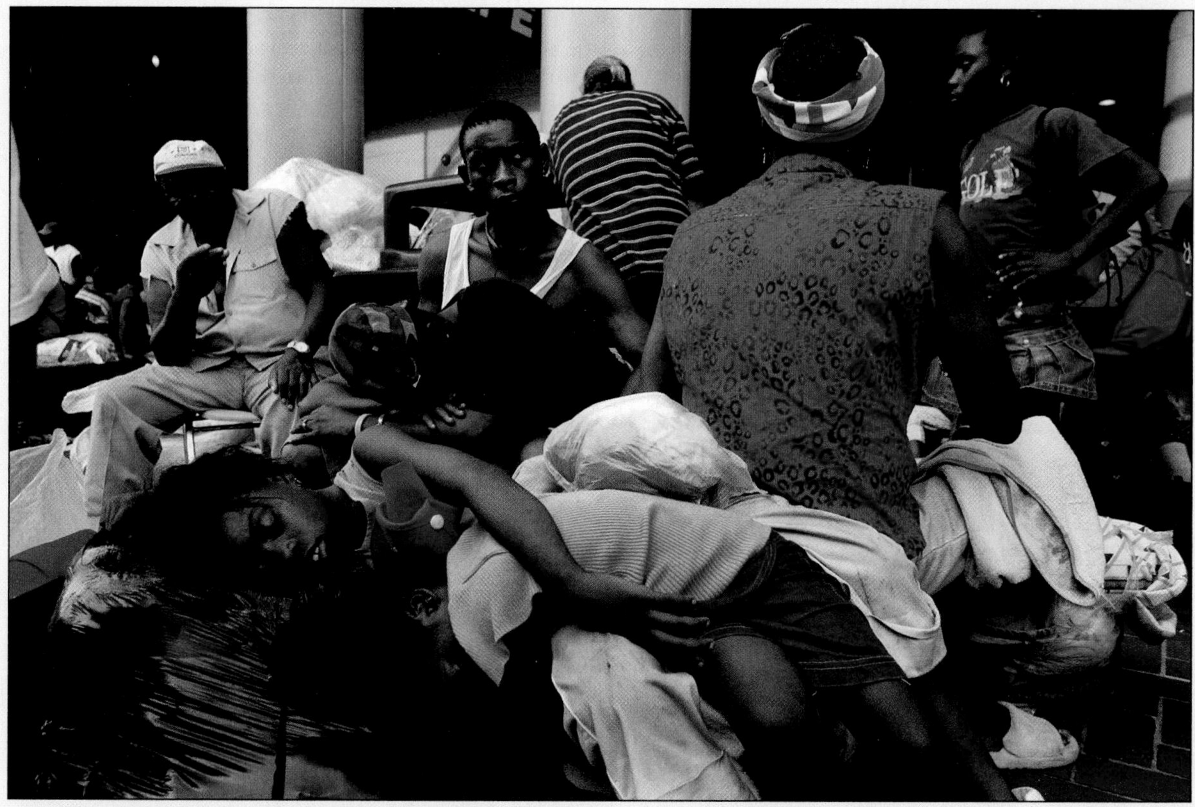

HARD TIMES *The plight of New Orleans's evacuees has aroused wonder and indignation in Europe.*

keep the anger from his voice, the looting, the armed gangs, the gunplay and, especially, the arrogance, in his view, that the mostly white police displayed toward mostly black residents represented "the dark underbelly of life in this country." There was something shameful, he said, about the way a natural disaster has produced behavior that, for example, the tsunami didn't produce in the third-world countries it hit. And it is painful to be a witness to somebody else's shame.

"Why should hundreds die, mostly African-Americans, in a predicted disaster in the richest nation on earth" was one expression of a widespread feeling in Europe, this one appearing Friday in a letter in the British newspaper the *Guardian*.

There were many comments to the effect that earlier predictions of the

Bernstein builds a causal argument as he outlines the various reactions from abroad to the Hurricane Katrina disaster. What, according to Bernstein, is the root of slow "expressions of sympathy"? Do you find his argument convincing? Use the key features of causal arguments as described in Chapter 10 to evaluate this article.

LINK TO P. 305

disaster did not lead public officials to make sure the levees would withstand any possible onslaught, and there was the unspoken opinion that such would not have been the case, say, with the dikes of the Netherlands, or in any of the rich European countries.

"These are incredible scenes from the richest and the biggest country in the world," Jean-Pierre Pernaud, the anchorman on one of the main mid-day French news programs, said on Friday. A program on the competing channel ran an interview with a specialist on the United States, Nicole Bacharan, who said, "These images reveal to the world the reality in the Southern states: the poverty of 37 million Americans."

10 A few environmentalists in Europe seized on the situation to express one of their greatest irritations: the unwillingness of the Bush administration to sign the Kyoto Protocol° on global warming. Jürgen Trittin, minister of the environment in Germany, was the most prominent among these, though others in Europe echoed this sentiment.

"The American president has closed his eyes to the economic and human damage that natural catastrophes such as Katrina—in other words, disasters caused by a lack of climate protection measures—can visit on his country," Mr. Trittin said.

But Mr. Trittin's comment, which made headlines in Germany, provoked as much outrage as approval. "Instead of standing by the Americans as they try to come to grips with the hurricane catastrophe, our environment minister Trittin shows the world the face of the ugly German," the mass circulation *Bild Zeitung* wrote Friday. A British commentator, Gerard Baker, called comments like those of Mr. Trittin and a few others examples of "intellectual looting." It was, he said, "the predictable exploitation of tragedy for political purposes."

Still, Mr. Baker also went on to make the point that the real problem was the inherent inequality of suffering. "The tragedy has been visited disproportionately, indeed almost exclusively, on the city's African-Americans," he wrote.

There is no doubt most Europeans feel sorrow over the scenes of devastation they see on television, and many will no doubt contribute to funds set up to help the victims. At the same time, however, the particular circumstances of New Orleans and Biloxi, Miss., have tended to confirm the worst image of America that prevails in Europe, the vision of a country of staggering inequalities, indifference to the general welfare (especially during the Bush administration), and lacking in what Europeans call "solidarity."

15 As that BBC reporter put it, there were no scenes of armed gangs of looters in gun battles with the police in Sri Lanka after the tsunami.

That things have gone so badly so quickly after the storm in New Orleans has produced, beyond sympathy, feelings in Europe of disappointment, distress and even fear that a major city in the world's superpower could have fallen into something that looks, from this side of the Atlantic, like anarchy.°

Kyoto Protocol: 1997 United Nations–brokered agreement on climate change. Ratifying countries agree to reduce their emissions of greenhouse gases or otherwise engage in emissions trading. In emissions trading, a country that exceeds the agreed-upon limits buys sufficient emissions credits from countries that remain below their limits to compensate for the excess. Although the United States signed the protocol, its refusal to ratify it for domestic economic reasons is often cited as evidence of the country's contempt for international agreements and other countries in general, especially since the United States emits more of these gases per person than any other country.

anarchy: here, chaos and confusion, implying the absence of political authority or a system of law.

RESPOND •

1. What is Richard Bernstein's argument? What causes does he give in response to his short question "Why?" (paragraph 4)?
2. According to Bernstein, what vision of Americans did Europeans have at the time he wrote the column? What might Europeans mean by "solidarity" (paragraph 14)?
3. How does Bernstein see the responses of Europeans to Hurricane Katrina as evidence that a people's responses to others' tragedies say much about how they see themselves? (Examine paragraphs 6 and 8, for example.) Were the Europeans merely being smug, or might other things have been going on? In other words, what might Europeans' response to Katrina tell us about their own worst fears?
4. What's your response to this "view from abroad?" How often are you exposed to views from abroad, that is, to responses to events in the United States or to reactions to the behavior of the United States as reported by foreign news media rather than American media? Are there disadvantages to the fact that few Americans seem to be exposed to such views? Many Web sites created in other countries and languages are available in English-language versions. Will this fact likely increase Americans' exposure to views from abroad? Should it? What might the consequences of such exposure be?
5. Noted anthropologist Clifford Geertz has written, "To see ourselves as others see us can be eye opening. To see others as sharing a nature with ourselves is the nearest decency. But it is a far more difficult achievement of seeing ourselves among others as a local example of the forms human life has locally taken, a case among cases, a world among worlds, that the largeness of mind without which objectivity is self congratulation and tolerance a sham, comes." How might we apply Geertz's claims to an understanding of how Americans do or don't see themselves among others? As a case of how other countries see the United States? **Write an essay** in which you respond to these questions. In preparing to write this essay, you may want to reflect on your own ideas about these issues and those you think most Americans have. You may also want to visit <http://nettizen.com/newspaper/> or some other Internet directory that provides links to newspapers from around the world in order to sample views toward the United States that you find there. Doing so may help you focus your comments.

Waleed Ziad, who received his B.A. from Yale in Near Eastern Studies and Economics, is a specialist in international development and the roots of Islamic fundamentalism. In addition to contributing to a newspaper in Pakistan, he's a principal with the Truman National Security Project, a group of Democrats who favor a strong national security policy and progressive values. He wrote "Jihad's Fresh Face" for the New York Times, *where it first appeared in September 2005. As you read, ask yourself how much you know about the historical roots of Islamic fundamentalism and consider why.*

Jihad's Fresh Face

WALEED ZIAD

Of the many questions surrounding Egypt's presidential elections last week—Were opposition candidates unfairly removed from the ballot? Did the ruling party of President Hosni Mubarak cheat at the polls?—a more general query has gone largely unmentioned: Did this election, or the other recent democratic experiments in Saudi Arabia and elsewhere, really further American aims in the Muslim world?

The answer is troubling. The post-9/11 prevailing wisdom has held that military force and exporting democracy are the West's twin weapons against terrorism. Islamic fundamentalism is the product of a "medieval" mindset, we are told, and if we can deliver elections to the Arab world, our enemies will cower before the spirit of the Enlightenment.

Yet the establishment of the first popularly elected governments in Iraqi and Afghan history has been followed by more suicide bombings and unabated violence. And nobody expects real change, in terms of political freedoms or human rights, any time soon in Saudi Arabia or Egypt. What are we missing?

While there is no doubt that elections are a worthy goal, we will not be able to change the Muslim world or dislodge the militancy until we gain a better understanding of the roots of the problem. While these conflicts are often painted as millennium-old, they are essentially modern phenomena, bred of postcolonial° politics, social upheavals and territorial struggles.

5 And as we look at the causes of anti-Western jihadism, we tend to overlook one major contributing factor: the absence not just of democracy but also of grass-roots representative institutions like a free press and independent political, cultural and social-welfare institutions.

Today's jihadists°—I call them "neo-fundamentalists," because they are a world apart from earlier fundamentalists—are not throwbacks to the crusades, nor are they, as President Bush unfortunately put it, just "a group of folks." They are a singular and recent byproduct of decades of oppressive rule.

---

postcolonial: following the period of colonial rule. Many countries in the Arab and Islamic worlds were colonized and controlled by a European power during the nineteenth and twentieth centuries. The postcolonial period began between the end of World War II and the 1960s, depending on the specific country.

jihadists: those engaged in *jihad,* which they see as "holy war" against nonbelievers, although the term can have a much broader meaning in Arabic and in Islamic thought.

Yes, the Muslim world had an unfortunate introduction to post-Enlightenment ideals,° which came in the context of invasion, colonialism and exploitation. But the Arab philosophical and political movement that came out of that experience was not inherently anti-Western. In fact, in traditional Islamic thought the concept of violent resistance against an unjust ruler was virtually unheard of; for classical jurists,° tyranny was preferable to the anarchy that accompanies revolt.

The first wave of modern Islamic fundamentalists, which crested primarily in Egypt in the late 19th century and included such figures as the Iranian-born reformer Jamal al-Din al-Afghani° and his Egyptian disciple, Muhammad Abduh,° opposed colonialism but saw no incompatibility between Islamic and Western philosophy, law or scientific method. These men called for political reform and the revival of free inquiry.

The big change did not occur until the middle of the 20th century. In states like Egypt, Iraq and Syria, colonial governments were replaced by

Enlightenment ideals: reference to the ideals developed in Europe during the eighteenth century; specifically, a belief in the value and power of reason, rationality, and progress. These ideals became the basis of the French and American revolutions, among others.

classical jurists: here, Islamic jurists (that is, students of Islamic law) during earlier periods.

Jamal al-Din al-Afghani: nineteenth-century Muslim political activist. Opposed to foreign colonization of Muslim countries, he argued for Muslim unity and constitutional systems of government and the rule of law. Al- Afghani was from Afghanistan, as his name implies.

Muhammad Abduh: nineteenth-century Egyptian religious scholar, jurist, and reformer. A student of Al-Afghani, he is known as the founder of Islamic Modernism, which emphasized adapting Islamic principles to modern conditions, partly as a way of staving off European control of the Muslim world.

The data that Ziad presents is factual. We aren't told what his exact sources are, but we do know that he is a specialist in the area under discussion. Read the section in Chapter 7 that address refining a claim and presenting factual evidence, and then evaluate Ziad's argument.

LINK TO P. 188

military, Arab-nationalist,° royalist or Soviet-sponsored socialist regimes. All deteriorated quickly into dictatorships, embracing the institutions of colonial subjugation.°

10 A host of political parties and civic institutions were founded to challenge the autocrats;° many, combined Enlightenment concepts like public participation with Islamic ideals of popular consent and justice. Even Egypt's Muslim Brotherhood° (founded in 1928) was not a militant revolutionary group; instead it promoted social-welfare programs, democracy and land reform on the Western model. When the mass movements became influential, however, they were answered not by reform but by persecution, ranging from the violent crackdown against the Muslim Brotherhood in Egypt in the 1950's to the massacre of more than 10,000 dissidents by the dictator Hafez al-Assad in Hama, Syria, in 1982.

The story of Sayyid Qutb, the father of neo-fundamentalism, exemplifies what happened next. Qutb was an Egyptian teacher trained in the Western system. Contrary to the conventional wisdom, it was not his trip to America in 1948 that radicalized him. While he was shocked by some aspects of American culture, like women dancing in public, he returned to write about the importance of emulating the educational, economic and scientific achievements of the West.

But in the 1950's, he was jailed and tortured for speaking out against Gamal Abdel Nasser's° autocracy, while scores of dissidents were executed. Only then did he decide that violence could be used against an unjust government. He spoke as a Muslim, but his rhetoric was grounded in Western-nationalist and leftist revolutionary principles. His call had great resonance, and thus was neo-fundamentalism born.

As persecution continued across the Arab world, the neo-fundamentalist rhetoric became more Manichean° and xenophobic.° With mainstream opponents silenced, ultraradicals be-

Arab nationalism: a form of nationalism that encouraged Arabs from all countries to think of themselves as belonging to a single Arab nation and to treat this loyalty as greater than any loyalty to the nation-state or country in which they happened to live. Often referred to as "pan-Arabism."

subjugation: imposing the rule of a conquering power.

autocrat: a leader who imposes absolute rule.

Muslim Brotherhood: an Egyptian Islamist religious, social, and political movement of Sunni Muslims founded by Hassan al-Banna, now globalized. The movement's motto is "God is our objective; the Qur'an is our constitution; the Prophet is our leader; struggle is our way; and death for the sake of God is the highest of our aspirations." Like most fundamentalist movements, it calls for a return to the original form of the faith, which is understood in very conservative terms. This populist movement was founded partly in response to what it saw as foreign domination of Egypt by Europeans early in the twentieth century.

Gamal Abdel Nasser: leader of Egypt from 1952 until his death in 1970; he was a strong supporter of Arab nationalism and foreign policies that didn't favor the former colonial powers of Europe. Like many Arab leaders, he ruled autocratically.

Manichean: dualist in thinking; here, the mentality that one is either "with us or against us."

xenophobic: fearing or disliking foreigners and, by extension, anyone or anything unfamiliar.

came the loudest voices of dissent. In Egypt, for example, those who emerged from prison in the 1970's formed militant organizations, including Al Jihad, led by Ayman al-Zawahiri, who is now chief lieutenant for Osama bin Laden. These men were not thinkers or theologians; rather, many were disillusioned Westernized professionals, former leftists and nationalists.

> **"The terrorists are not 'medieval,' and they can be stopped."**

This new wave of fundamentalism, unlike all the others before it in the Islamic tradition, is inherently anti-intellectual and reactive; it is more reminiscent of the anarchical movements of 19th-century Russia. This "Islamism" is nihilistic,° expressing a lack of faith in all political systems, in history, and in all past social developments. The jihadists justify their actions by claiming that they are returning to "pure" Islamic sources to establish a "government of God." Of course, the paradox here is that the Koran does not lay down a mode of governance. What perhaps we in the United States do not understand is that in rejecting the status quo, these groups demonize not just the West, but mainstream Islamic culture and philosophy as well; they pose perhaps the greatest existential° threat to 1,400 years of Islamic tradition.

15 So how does this history help us reverse the trend? It requires that we look at the jihadists not as an ancient foe, but as yet another contemporary terrorist group. Recent history — in northern India, Sri Lanka, Kurdish Turkey° — has taught us that grassroots democracy and allowing the aggrieved group a public voice can be effective weapons against terrorism. A good strategy would be to support groups across the Muslim world, both secular and religious, that provide social services where the government falls short; they range from women's rights organizations like the Union for Feminine Action in Morocco to trade groups like the Lebanese Businessmen Association.

We must foster these organizations — along with a free press and educational and cultural institutions. At the same time, our corporations should guide local entrepreneurs to promote a free market, the backbone of democracy. If anything is going to come of the neoconservative° hope of making Iraq into a beacon of our values, it will be along these lines.

It is vital, however, that we not be put off from helping organizations tied to Islam — faith-based parties calling for peaceful democratic reforms are emerging across the Muslim world as the main political opposition. They are the necessary counterweights to central governments, and without them, autocratic rule, and the neo-fundamentalism that it breeds, will remain the norm.

nihilistic: rejecting prevailing beliefs, often seeking to overthrow all systems of order and government, by terrorism if necessary.

existential: having implications for the existence of something.

northern India, Sri Lanka, Kurdish Turkey: areas in which, at the time of the article, progress had been made toward defusing long-simmering ethnic tensions by granting the minorities some recognition. In all cases, the minorities had previously responded to the situation with what the majority labeled terrorist acts.

neoconservative (or more popularly ***neocon***): an American political movement or ideology that generally supports a strong, often interventionist foreign policy stance usually justified on moral grounds, less interest in social conservatism (for example, issues like abortion, divorce, or homosexuality), and little commitment to limited government.

RESPOND.

1. What are Waleed Ziad's proposals for dealing with "jihad's fresh face," or what he terms neo-fundamentalism? What particular problems do his proposals seek to redress? What caused these problems in the first place?

2. Ziad's selection represents a complete proposal argument. It contains definitional arguments, causal arguments, and evaluative arguments, and, based on these elements, it offers a proposal. Find the relevant sections of the selection that represent each kind of argument.

3. Why does Ziad include the historical information included in paragraphs 7–14? Is such information new to you? Given the discussion of Islamic neo-fundamentalism since the events of September 11, 2001, why, in your opinion, has historical information like that given here generally been absent from public discussion? How does this absence encourage Americans and Westerners more generally to believe that Islam and Muslim societies are frozen in time, somewhere in the distant past?

4. As noted in a marginal gloss, the neoconservatives argue that perhaps America's greatest imperative is to spread American-style democracy around the world, replacing repressive rulers, if necessary, with democratically elected governments. According to Ziad, what else should the United States be doing if it has such goals?

5. Ziad's comments assume that Americans, including American policymakers, generally distrust anyone or anything associated with Islam. How does he reply to this tendency? Why is his use of the phrase "faith-based" in the article's final paragraph important in this regard?

6. What do you understand the argument of the hand-drawn illustration that accompanies this selection to be?

7. Research one of the countries of the Middle East or the Muslim world where there have been neo-fundamentalists threats or actions. (This article mentions several—Egypt, Iraq, Saudi Arabia, and Afghanistan—though there are others.) In your research, seek to discover whether Ziad's claims in paragraph 4 that the conflicts in which such groups are engaged result from "postcolonial politics, social upheavals and territorial struggles" and in paragraph 5 that the conflicts are fueled by the absence of key institutions: "not just . . . democracy but also . . . grass-roots representative institutions like a free press and independent political, cultural and social-welfare institutions." **Write an essay** in which you evaluate Ziad's claims with respect to the country you research. You will, of course, need to document the sources you use. (For a discussion of evaluative essays, see Chapter 9; for a discussion of documenting sources, see Chapter 20.)

▼ *A former literary editor at Farrar, Straus and Giroux, David Rieff has been a policy analyst and freelance writer for nearly two decades. In addition to writing essays that appear in a range of publications, he's the author of over a half-dozen books, including* The Exile: Cuba in the Heart of Miami *(1993),* Slaughterhouse: Bosnia and the Failure of the West *(1995),* A Bed for the Night: Humanitarianism in Crisis *(2003), and* At the Point of a Gun: Democratic Dreams and Armed Intervention *(2005). Rieff is a Fellow at New York University's Institute for the Humanities, a Senior Fellow at the New School's World Policy Institute, and a board member of both the Arms Division of Human Rights Watch and the Open Society Institute's Central Eurasia Project. This essay, "Their Hearts and Minds?" originally appeared in the Sunday magazine of the* New York Times *in September 2005 in the series "The Way We Live Now." As you read this selection, pay special attention to the criteria Rieff uses in constructing his evaluative argument.*

Their Hearts and Minds?

Why the Ideological Battle against Islamists Is Nothing Like the Struggle against Communism

DAVID RIEFF

With its bitter echoes of Vietnam, the expression "hearts and minds"° is one that many Americans understandably use ironically rather than seriously. But if the last three years have demonstrated anything, it is that hearts and minds are essential to defeating the insurgencies that United States forces face in Iraq and, increasingly, again in Afghanistan. Whatever you think about the Iraq war, or the fight against Islamic terrorism more broadly, the move among American policymakers away from military solutions and toward political ones can only be a good thing.

President Bush's appointment of his longtime confidante Karen Hughes as under secretary of state for public diplomacy and public affairs, and of Dina Powell, an Egyptian-American Washington highflier, as her deputy, is perhaps the clearest sign that the administration is finally getting serious about beliefs as well as bullets. Certainly, the agenda Hughes outlined during her Senate confirmation hearings in July was ambitious. "We're involved," she told the Foreign Relations

"hearts and minds": originally, a euphemistic name for a pro-war propaganda campaign run by the U.S. military in Vietnam during the war there. (The phrase is from speeches by then president Lyndon B. Johnson.) Since that time, the phrase has come to refer to efforts by an occupying force to encourage or force those whose land is being occupied to accept the occupation and to act, in some ways, like the occupiers.

Committee, "in a generational and global struggle of ideas." She added: "I recognize the job ahead will be difficult. Perceptions do not change easily or quickly."

Refreshing though it was for its candor, Hughes's statement neglected the larger question: Is hostility toward the United States based largely on misperceptions of America's actions and intentions or on a genuine dislike of the power America wields around the world?

Foreign Opinions: Percentage of population in selected countries that holds a "favorable opinion" of the United States

	2004	*2005*
Jordan	5%	21%
Turkey	30	23
Pakistan	21	23
Morocco	27	–
Indonesia	–	38
Lebanon	–	42
India	–	71

Source: Pew Global Attitudes Project, 2005

It would be wonderful, of course, if the bin Ladens and al-Zarqawis drew their support primarily from the miseducation of young people in radical madrasas° and the misinformation that the administration believes to be dished out on Al Jazeera.° But in their equa-

madrasa: a Muslim school devoted to the teaching of Islamic law and theology; the term has come to be associated with schools in parts of the Islamic world that spread a particularly anti-Western form of Islam.

Al Jazeera: an Arabic-language television channel based in Qatar; the station is widely watched across the Arab world as an alternative to state-controlled media. In the United States, Al Jazeera is best known as the station to which Osama bin Laden and others associated with Al Qaeda send videotaped statements that the station broadcasts.

tion of hatred with ignorance, Hughes, and the rest of the Bush administration, including the president himself, may be falling into a determinist trap. Their profound belief that American ideals *should* prevail leads them to assume that these ideals *must* prevail if only they are communicated well enough.

To believe this, however, you must believe that there is an inevitable progress to history—a progress toward freedom. The president said as much in his second Inaugural Address, arguing that it was the United States' mission to spread such freedom throughout the world. His view is shared by many Americans. But non-Americans have become increasingly wary of this mission. Is it possible to persuade them that, as Hughes put it in her Senate testimony, the United States is "a tremendous force for good"?

5 Between the end of World War II and the fall of the Berlin Wall, a large number of people in Western Europe, the Soviet empire and elsewhere did believe this. (Latin America was, of course, the great exception.) The Bush administration has often expressed its confidence that the American mission in Iraq will eventually succeed, just as the occupations of Germany and Japan and the struggle with Soviet communism succeeded. The problem is that despite the old cliché about history repeating itself, history rarely repeats itself.

Able officials like Karen Hughes do not seem to have come to grips with the difficulties of waging a war of ideas against the exponents° of a radically unfamiliar worldview. The administration is doubtless right to insist that, like the communists before them, the Islamists are marked by their contempt for individual liberty and by their willingness to commit mass murder in the name of some radiant future. But there is an essential distinction—one that may make the strategy that worked against the Soviet empire impotent with regard to the jihadists. Communism was a version of modernity. It valued education—above all, scientific education—and it insisted on gender equality. The United States was also committed to modernity. The conflict was thus a clash between two systems that shared certain fundamental presuppositions. And given the rank inferiority of the communist version, the belief that democracy and capitalism could and would prevail made sense.

But the conflict with jihadism is a contest between modernity and antimodernity, and, as we are discovering to our cost, obscurantism° has a far larger constituency and a far more powerful hold on the popular imagination, certainly in the Islamic world, than most people imagined a generation ago. Jihadists have the advantage of speaking to a Muslim population that already shares many of their beliefs, whereas communists had to indoctrinate many of their constituents from scratch. Add to this the fact that, in countries like Egypt, a version of modernity has largely failed to provide ordinary people with a decent life, and the appeal of the fundamentalists is neither so difficult to explain nor so irrational as it sometimes appears.

Restating America's case more eloquently would certainly be a good thing. But the assumption that everyone in the world will gravitate toward a variation on American democracy if given half a chance is more likely based on wishful thinking (and, doubtless, good

---

exponent: a person who sets forth or expounds a certain position.

obscurantism: opposition to the questioning of dogma and the spreading of knowledge beyond set limits.

Rieff presents an argument grounded in the present, a contemporary argument. Review the occasions for argument discussed in Chapter 1.

LINK TO P. 15

intentions) than on a sound and sober reading of history. In her Senate testimony, Karen Hughes said that "people will choose freedom over tyranny and tolerance over extremism every time." Would that it were true. Of course people crave freedom, but Karen Hughes's idea of it and the Ayatollah al-Sistani's° idea of it are very different. As for people unfailingly choosing tolerance, the historical perspective suggests that this has been the exception rather than the rule. An American public diplomacy that convinces itself otherwise has little chance of success, no matter how influential the person at its helm and how many resources she has at her disposal. ■

RESPOND •

1. David Rieff's argument is evaluative in several regards. What assumptions held by many Americans and President George W. Bush's administration is Rieff questioning? What evidence does he provide for the need to question these assumptions? What is Rieff's evaluation of them? What is yours? Why? Why is questioning someone's assumptions often a useful strategy in constructing an argument?
2. Rieff compares and contrasts the United States' "war of ideas" against communism and what he terms "jihadism" (paragraphs 5–7). (Comparison — discussing similarities — and contrast — discussing differences — often form parts of an evaluative argument.) What similarities does he see? What differences? How does this section of his argument contribute to his overall argument?
3. Examine the visual argument "Foreign Opinions," based on data from the 2005 Pew Global Attitudes Project, which was discussed in the first selection in this chapter. What percentage of the population of each country is Muslim? What's the number of Muslims living in each of the countries listed? (You'll likely need to use the Internet to answer these questions.) Why is this information useful — or even necessary — in understanding these data? Does this visual argument work to support or contextualize Rieff's claims? Why or why not? How does the photograph of Muslim men prostrating themselves as they participate in Friday communal prayers in Iraq contribute to his argument?
4. In paragraph 8, Rieff contends, "Of course people crave freedom, but Karen Hughes's idea of it and the Ayatollah al-Sistani's idea of it are very different." In what ways does this claim represent a definitional argument? **Write a definitional essay** in which you define "freedom" for Karen Hughes and the Ayatollah al-Sistani. While you may be able to define "freedom" for Karen Hughes based on your experience and your knowledge of the Bush administration policies, you'll almost assuredly need to research the views of Ayatollah al-Sistani and perhaps Shi'ite Muslims more broadly.

Ayatollah al-Sistani: Grand Ayatollah Sayyid Ali Husaini al-Sistani, the most senior cleric in Shi'a Islam and an important political force in Iraq, where he lives. (Shi'ites give the title "Ayatollah" to their highest-ranking clerics; only a few of these become Grand Ayatollahs.)

Making a Visual Argument: How Others See Us

The paintings by Anipas P. Delotavo Jr., Zaid Omar, and Jibby Yunibandhu all appeared in a 2004–2005 exhibit, Identities and Globalisation, *sponsored by the Heinrich Böll Foundation, which is headquartered in Germany but has twenty-five offices worldwide. The exhibit was shown in Chiang Mai and Bangkok in Thailand and in Berlin, Germany. The exhibit contained works by sixty artists from the ASEAN (Association of Southeast Asian Nations) countries—Brunei, Cambodia, Indonesia, Laos, Malaysia, Myanmar, Philippines, Singapore, Thailand, and Vietnam. We include three here that comment directly on the United States in some way. Anipas P. Delotavo Jr. is from the Philippines, and his painting,* Europe Gave Us Shakespeare and Beethoven; America Gave Us Jesse James and John Wayne, *reminds us how American popular culture—and its metaphors—are viewed by many.*

Anipas P. Delotavo Jr., *Europe Gave Us Shakespeare and Beethoven; America Gave Us Jesse James and John Wayne*, 2003

▶ Malaysian Zaid Omar's Misconception *takes a* kaffiyeh, *a headscarf traditionally worn by Arab men, and transforms its pattern in a way that shows two conflicting views of the Arab world—and perhaps, by extension, Islam. Finally, Jibby Yunibandhu's* At Home with the Braves *represents her reflection on the nine years she spent in the United States receiving an education and the ambivalence she, as a Thai citizen, has because of her strong feelings of affection and compassion toward Americans and America—where her heart is, especially in the wake of the events of September 11. As you study these paintings, think about the challenge that America, its culture, and its power might present to people and nations in an increasingly globalized world as they seek to maintain a sense of identity.*

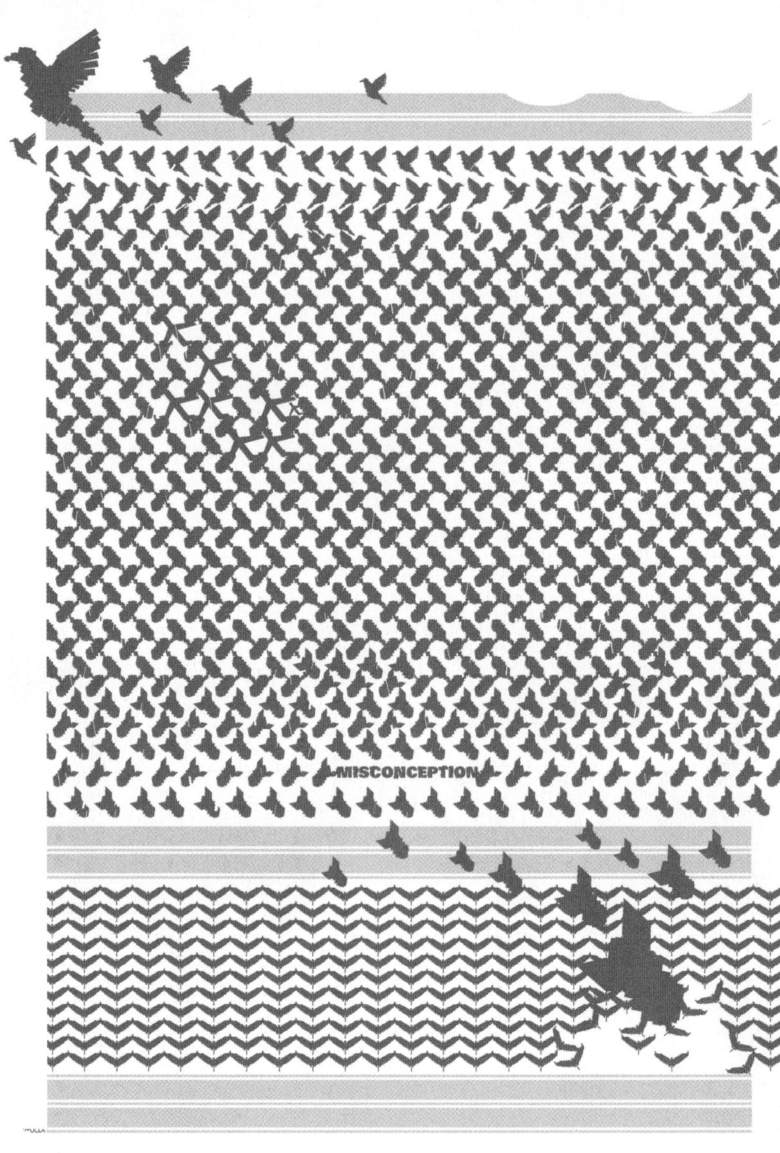

Zaid Omar, *Misconception,* 2002

Jibby Yunibandhu, *At Home with the Braves,* 2003. Photograph by Prach Kongsubto Rohitchan.

1. What's your response to each of these paintings? Is it primarily visceral—a feeling in the gut, emotional, intellectual, or some combination of these? Why, in your opinion? Is one of these categories of response more important? Why or why not?

2. Examine the imagery and title of each of the three paintings. How has the artist used them to support his or her argument? With respect to Delotavo's painting, *Europe Gave Us Shakespeare and Beethoven; America Gave Us Jesse James and John Wayne*, pay special attention to the spots on the horse. How do the images of Jesse James and John Wayne relate to contemporary political debates around the world about America's proper role? With respect to Omar's *Misconception*, what conflicting images does he offer of Arabs (and, perhaps, Islam)? What does his work remind us about the importance of perspective? With respect to Jibby Yunibandhu's *At Home with the Braves*, what historical and visual allusion does she employ to make her argument? What must one know about American history in order to appreciate this painting? What must one know about American culture to appreciate its title?

3. What might Americans learn from these visual arguments about how they're seen around the world? What challenges and resources do America, its culture, and its power present to people and nations in an increasingly globalized world as they seek to maintain a sense of identity?

4. Which of the three visual arguments is most effective, in your opinion? Why? (Obviously, you'll be relying on an implicit or explicit definition of effectiveness in answering these questions. Be sure to make your criteria for effectiveness explicit.) **Write a short essay** in which you describe the painting you find most effective and explain your criteria for evaluating its effectiveness. (For a discussion of evaluative essays, see Chapter 9.)

America the Beautiful: What We're Fighting For

DINESH D'SOUZA

Born in India into a Luso-Goan family, Dinesh D'Souza was educated at Dartmouth; he became an American citizen in 1990. He was a senior domestic policy analyst in the Reagan White House and is currently a Robert and Karen Rishwain Fellow at the Hoover Institution on War, Revolution, and Peace, a libertarian and conservative public policy think tank at Stanford University. D'Souza is the author of numerous best-selling books. Among them are Illiberal Education: The Politics of Race and Sex on Campus *(1991),* The End of Racism: Principles for a Multiracial Society *(1995),* Ronald Reagan: How an Ordinary Man Became an Extraordinary Leader *(1997),* The Virtue of Prosperity *(2000), and* Letters to a Young Conservative *(2002). This selection, "America the Beautiful: What We're Fighting For," is from* What's So Great About America? *(2002). As you read, notice D'Souza's analysis of why people from many countries don't like the United States.*

> We have it in our power to begin the world all over again.
>
> –Thomas Paine

America represents a new way of being human and thus presents a radical challenge to the world. On the one hand, Americans have throughout their history held that they are special: that their country has been blessed by God, that the American system is unique, that Americans are not like people everywhere else. This set of beliefs is called "American exceptionalism." At the same time, Americans have also traditionally insisted that they provide a model for the world, that theirs is a formula that others can follow, and that there is no better life available elsewhere. Paradoxically enough, American exceptionalism leads to American universalism.

Both American exceptionalism and American universalism have come under fierce attack from the enemies of America, both at home and abroad. The critics of America deny that there is anything unique about America, and they ridicule the notion that the American model is one that others should seek to follow. Indeed, by chronicling the past and present crimes of America, they hope to extract apologies and financial reparations out of Americans. Some even seek to justify murderous attacks against America on the grounds that what America does, and what she stands for, invites such attacks.

These critics are aiming their assault on America's greatest weakness: her lack of moral self-confidence. Americans cannot effectively fight a war without believing that it is a just war. That's why America has only lost once, in Vietnam, and that was because most Americans did not know what they were fighting for. The enemies of America understand this vulnerability. At the deepest level their assault is moral: they seek to destroy America's belief in herself, knowing that if this happens, America is finished. By the same token, when Americans rally behind a good cause, as in World War II, they are invincible. The outcome of America's engagements abroad is usually determined by a single factor: America's will to prevail. In order to win, Americans need to believe that they are on the side of the angels. The good news is that they usually are.

The triumph of American ideas and culture in the global marketplace, and the fact that most immigrants from around the world choose to come to the United States, would seem to be sufficient grounds for establishing the superiority of American civilization. But this is not entirely so, because we have not shown that the people of the world are *justified* in preferring the American way of life to any other. We must contend with the Islamic fundamentalists' argument that their societies are based on high principles while America is based on low principles. The Islamic critics are happy to concede the attractions of America, but they insist that these attractions are base. America, they say, appeals to what is most degraded about human nature; by contrast, Islamic societies may be poor and "backward," but they at least aspire to virtue. Even if they fall short, they are trying to live by God's law.

5 Americans usually have a hard time answering this argument, in part because they are bewildered by its theological cadences. The usual tendency is to lapse into a kind of unwitting relativism. "You are following what you believe is right, and we are living by the values that we think are best." This pious buncombe° usually concludes with a Rodney King°–style plea for tolerance, "So why don't we learn to appreciate our differences? Why don't we just get along?" To see why this argument fails completely, imagine that you are living during the time of the Spanish Inquisition.° The Grand Inquisitor is just starting to pull out your fingernails. You make the Rodney King move on him. "Torquemada,° please stop pulling out my fingernails. Why don't we learn to appreciate our differences?" Most of us probably realize that Torquemada would not find this persuasive. But it is less obvious why he would not. Let me paraphrase Torquemada's argument: "You think I am taking away your freedom, but I am concerned with your immortal soul. Ultimately virtue is far more important than freedom. Our lives last for a mere second in the long expanse of eternity. What measure of pleasure or pain we experience in our short life is trivial compared to our fate in the never ending life to come. I am trying to save your soul from damnation. Who cares if you have to let out a few screams in the process? My actions are entirely for your own benefit. You should be *thanking me* for pulling out your fingernails."

I have recalled the Spanish Inquisition to make the point that the Islamic argument is one that we have heard before. We should not find it so strange that people think this way; it is the way that many in our own civilization used to think not so very long ago. The reason that most of us do not think this way now is that Western history has taught us a hard lesson. That lesson is that when the institutions of religion and government are one, and the secular authority is given the power to be the interpreter and enforcer of God's law, then horrible abuses of power are perpetrated in God's name. This

buncombe: political rhetoric produced for show, rather than something growing out of conviction.

Rodney King: African American resident of Los Angeles whose 1991 confrontation with the police, videotaped by chance by a bystander, made his a household name. When the police involved in the arrest were acquitted of charges of police brutality the following year, riots ensued in L.A. and elsewhere. After the riots, King appeared on television and asked, "People, I just want to say, you know, can('t) we all get along?"

Spanish Inquisition: court set up by the Catholic Church in the Spain of Ferdinand and Isabella from 1478 to 1510 that targeted Jewish and Muslim converts to Christianity, often using torture to extract confessions of supposed guilt for heresy of some sort. Punishment was often burning at the stake.

Torquemada: fifteenth-century Dominican priest whose role in the Inquisition has made his name a symbol for fanaticism in the service of one's beliefs, especially religious beliefs, and a willingness to use torture in the name of serving one's cause.

is just what we saw in Afghanistan with the Taliban,° and what we see now in places like Iran. This is not to suggest that Islam's historical abuses are worse than those of the West. But the West, as a consequence of its experience, learned to disentangle the institutions of religion and government—a separation that was most completely achieved in the United States. As we have seen, the West also devised a new way of organizing society around the institutions of science, democracy, and capitalism. The Renaissance, the Reformation, the Enlightenment, and the Scientific Revolution were some of the major signposts on Western civilization's road to modernity.

By contrast, the Islamic world did not have a Renaissance or a Reformation. No Enlightenment or Scientific Revolution either. Incredible though it may seem to many in the West, Islamic societies today are in some respects not very different from how they were a thousand years ago. Islam has been around for a long time. This brings us to a critical question: why are we seeing this upsurge of Islamic fundamentalism and Islamic fanaticism now?

To answer this question, we should recall that Islam was once one of the greatest and most powerful civilizations in the world. Indeed, there was a time when it seemed as if the whole world would fall under Islamic rule. Within a century of the prophet Muhammad's° death, his converts had overthrown the Sassanid dynasty in Iran and conquered large tracts of territory from the Byzantine dynasty.° Soon the Muslims had established an empire greater than that of Rome at its zenith. Over the next several centuries, Islam made deep inroads into Africa, Southeast Asia, and southern Europe. The crusades were launched to repel the forces of Islam, but the crusades ended in failure. By the sixteenth century, there were no fewer than five Islamic empires, unified by political ties, a common religion, and a common culture: the Mamluk sultans in Egypt, the Safavid dynasty in Iran, the Mughal empire in India, the empire of the Great Khans in Russia and Central Asia, and the Ottoman Empire based in Turkey. Of these, the Ottomans were by far the most formidable. They ruled most of North Africa, and threatened Mediterranean Europe and Austria. Europe was terrified that they might take over all the lands of Christendom. In all of history, Islam is the only non-Western civilization to pose a mortal threat to the West.

Then it all went wrong. Starting in the late seventeenth century, when the West was able to repel the Ottoman siege of Vienna, the power of Islam began a slow but steady decline. By the nineteenth century the Ottoman Empire was known as the "sick man of Europe," and it collapsed completely after World War I, when the victorious European powers carved it up and parceled out the pieces. Not only did the Muslims lose most of the territory they had conquered, but they also found themselves being ruled, either directly or

Taliban: a Sunni Islamist movement that ruled Afghanistan from 1996 to 2001, when it was bombed by the United States and a coalition of countries in the wake of the events of September 11, 2001, because of the Taliban's support for Al Qaeda, the movement directly associated with those events. The Taliban imposed a particularly strict and severe reading of Islamic law, or Shari'ah, as the basis of its rule.

Muhammad: the Prophet of Islam, seen by Muslims as the last or "seal" of the prophets in a line stretching back to the prophets of the Old Testament and including Jesus. He died in 632 C.E.

Byzantine dynasty: During the period 632–718 C.E., Islam spread from Saudi Arabia to many areas, including what are today Syria, Armenia, Egypt, and North Africa; these areas were at that time under the control of the Byzantine Empire, the Greek-speaking Roman Empire centered in Constantinople, which is today Istanbul, Turkey.

indirectly, by the West. Today, even though colonialism has ended, the Islamic world is in a miserable state. Basically all that it has to offer is oil, and as technology opens up alternative sources of energy, even that will not amount to much. Without its oil revenues, the Islamic world will find itself in the position of sub-Saharan Africa: it will cease to matter. Even now it does not matter very much. The only reason it makes the news is by killing people. When is the last time you opened the newspaper to read about a great Islamic discovery or invention? While China and India, two other empires that were eclipsed by the West, have embraced Western technology and even assumed a leadership role in some areas, Islam's contribution to modern science and technology is negligible.

10 In addition to these embarrassments, the Islamic world faces a formidable threat from the United States. This is not the threat of American force or of American support for Israel. Israel is an irritant, but it does not threaten the existence of Islamic society. By contrast, America stands for an idea that is fully capable of transforming the Islamic world by winning the hearts of Muslims. The subversive American idea is one of shaping your own life, of making your own destiny, of following a path illumined not by external authorities but by your inner self. This American idea endangers the sanctity of the Muslim home, as well as the authority of Islamic society. It empowers women and children to assert their prerogatives against the male head of the household. It also undermines political and religious hierarchies. Of all American ideas, the "inner voice" is the most dangerous because it rivals the voice of Allah as a source of moral allegiance. So Islam is indeed, as bin Laden° warned, facing the greatest threat to its survival since the days of Muhammad.

In recent decades, a great debate has broken out in the Muslim world to account for Islamic decline and to formulate a response to it. One response—let us call it the reformist or classical liberal response—is to acknowledge that the Islamic world has been left behind by modernity. The reformers' solution is to embrace science, democracy, and capitalism. This would mean adaptation—at least selective adaptation—to the ways of the West. The liberal reformers have an honorable intellectual tradition, associated with such names as Muhammad Abduh,° Jamal al-Afghani,° Muhammad Iqbal,° and Taha Husayn.° This group also enjoys a fairly strong base of support in the Muslim middle class. In the past two decades, however, the reformers have been losing the argument in the Islamic world to their rival group, the fundamentalists.

Here, in short, is the fundamentalist argument. The Koran promises that if Muslims are faithful to Allah, they will enjoy prosperity in this life and par-

[Osama] bin Laden: An Islamic fundamentalist and founder of Al Qaeda, an Islamic organization committed to establishing an Islamic government around the world, bin Laden is a member of an especially wealthy Saudi Arabian family. Bin Laden and Al Qaeda are considered responsible for the September 11, 2001, attacks as well as over a dozen bombings elsewhere in the world.

Muhammad Abduh: nineteenth-century Egyptian religious scholar, jurist, and reformer. He's known as the founder of Islamic Modernism, which emphasized adapting Islamic principles to modern conditions, partly as a way of staving off European control of the Muslim world.

Jamal al-Afghani: nineteenth-century Muslim political activist. Opposed to foreign colonization of Muslim countries, he argued for Muslim unity and constitutional systems of government and the rule of law. He was a teacher of Muhammad Abduh. Al-Afghani was from Afghanistan, as his name implies.

Muhammad Iqbal: early twentieth-century Indian Muslim reformer, politician, and scholar whose philosophical and poetic works remain important. Considered the spiritual founder of Pakistan, he worked for Muslim unity and

(continued)

adise in the next life. According to the fundamentalists, the Muslims were doing this for centuries, and they were invincible. But now, the fundamentalists point out, Islam is not winning any more; in fact, it is losing. What could be the reason for this? From the fundamentalist point of view, the answer is obvious: Muslims are not following the true teaching of Allah! The fundamentalists allege that Muslims have fallen away from the true faith and are mindlessly pursuing the ways of the infidel. The fundamentalists also charge that Islamic countries are now ruled by self-serving despots who serve as puppets for America and the West. The solution, the fundamentalists say, is to purge American troops and Western influence from the Middle East; to overthrow corrupt, pro-Western regimes like ones in Pakistan, Egypt, and Saudi Arabia; and to return to the pure, original teachings of the Koran. Only then, the fundamentalists insist, can Islam recover its lost glory.

One can see, from this portrait, that the fundamentalists are a humiliated people who are seeking to recover ancestral greatness. They are not complete "losers": they are driven by an awareness of moral superiority, combined with political, economic, and military inferiority. Their argument has a powerful appeal to proud Muslims who find it hard to come to terms with their contemporary irrelevance. And so the desert wind of fundamentalism has spread throughout the Middle East. It has replaced Arab nationalism° as the most powerful political force in the region.

The success of the fundamentalists in the Muslim world should not blind us from recognizing that their counterattack against America and the West is fundamentally defensive. The fundamentalists know that their civilization does not have the appeal to expand outside its precinct. It's not as if the Muslims were plotting to take, say, Australia. It is the West that is making incursions into Islamic territory, winning converts, and threatening to subvert ancient loyalties and transform a very old way of life. So the fundamentalists are lashing out against this new, largely secular, Western "crusade." Terrorism, their weapon of counterinsurgency, is the weapon of the weak. Terrorism is the international equivalent of that domestic weapon of discontent: the riot. Political scientist Edward Banfield once observed that a riot is a failed revolution. People who know how to take over the government don't throw stones at a bus. Similarly terrorism of the bin Laden variety is a desperate strike against a civilization that the fundamentalists know they have no power to conquer.

But they do have the power to disrupt and terrify the people of America 15
and the West. This is one of their goals, and their attack on September 11, 2001, was quite successful in this regard. But there is a second goal: to unify the Muslim world behind the fundamentalist banner and to foment

sought to help Muslims rethink Islamic philosophy in response to the intellectual challenges presented by Western philosophy.

Taha Husayn: much-loved twentieth-century Egyptian literary scholar and reformer. Although of very modest means and blind from childhood, Husayn gained entry to the newly opened secular Cairo University; he was awarded its first doctoral degree. He's responsible for free public education in Egypt.

Arab nationalism: a form of nationalism that encouraged Arabs from all countries to think of themselves as belonging to a single Arab nation and to treat this loyalty as greater than any loyalty to the nation-state or country in which they happened to have been born or live. Often referred to as "pan-Arabism."

uprisings against pro-Western regimes. Thus the bin Ladens of the world are waging a two-front war: against Western influence in the Middle East and against pro-Western governments and liberal influences within the Islamic world. So the West is not faced with a pure "clash of civilizations."° It is not "the West" against "Islam." It is a clash of civilizations within the Muslim world. One side or the other will prevail.

clash of civilizations: a perspective on the relationship of Western and non-Western cultures represented by Samuel P. Huntington's 1996 book of the same name (although the phrase was first used by Bernard Lewis). Contending that differences in societies' cultural and religious identity will be the source of conflicts in the twenty-first century, Huntington argues that the culture of "Western Christendom" is essentially different from that of other "civilizations" and will inevitably end up in conflict with them.

So what should American policy be toward the region? It is a great mistake for Americans to believe that their country is hated because it is misunderstood. It is hated because it is understood only too well. Sometimes people say to me, "But the mullahs have a point about American culture. They are right about Jerry Springer."° Yes, they are right about Springer. If we could get them to agree to stop bombing our facilities in return for us shipping them Jerry Springer to do with as they like, we should make the deal tomorrow, and throw in some of Springer's guests. But the Islamic fundamentalists don't just object to the excesses of American liberty: they object to liberty itself. Nor can we appease them by staying out of their world. We live in an age in which the flow of information is virtually unstoppable. We do not have the power to keep our ideals and our culture out of their lives.

Jerry Springer: a former politician, now a television and radio talk-show host best known for his television program *The Jerry Springer Show,* which first aired in 1991. The show is often used as an example of the talk-show genre at its most outrageous because of the program's tawdry and sexually explicit themes, including the results of paternity tests and confessions by adulterous partners.

Thus there is no alternative to facing their hostility. First, we need to destroy their terrorist training camps and networks. This is not easy to do, because some of these facilities are in countries like Iraq, Iran, Libya, and the Sudan. The U.S. should demand that those countries dismantle their terror networks and stop being incubators of terrorism. If they do not, we should work to get rid of their governments. How this is done is a matter of prudence. In some cases, such as Iraq, the direct use of force might be the answer. In others, such as Iran, the U.S. can capitalize on widespread popular dissatisfaction with the government.[1] Iran has a large middle class, with strong democratic and pro-American elements. But the dissenters are sorely in need of leadership, resources, and an effective strategy to defeat the ruling theocracy.

The U.S. also has to confront the fact that regimes allied with America, such as Pakistan, Egypt, and Saudi Arabia, are undemocratic, corrupt, and repressive. Indeed, the misdoings and tyranny of these regimes strengthen the cause of the fundamentalists, who are able to tap deep veins of popular discontent. How do the regimes deal with this fundamentalist resistance? They subsidize various religious and educational programs administered by the fundamentalists that teach terrorism and hatred of America. By focusing the people's discontent against a foreign target, the United States, the regimes of Saudi Arabia, Egypt, and Pakistan hope to divert attention from their own failings. The United States must make it clear to its Muslim allies that this "solution" is unacceptable. If they want American aid and American support, they must stop funding mosques and schools that promote terrorism and anti-Americanism. Moreover, they must take steps to reduce corruption, expand civil liberties, and enfranchise their people.

In the long term, America's goal is a large and difficult one: to turn Muslim fundamentalists into classical liberals. This does not mean that we want them to stop being Muslims. It does mean, however, that we want them to practice their religion *in the liberal way*. Go to a Promise Keepers meeting in Washington, D.C., or another of America's big cities. You will see tens of thousands of men singing, praying, hugging, and pledging chastity to their wives. A remarkable sight. These people are mostly evangelical and fundamentalist Christians. They are apt to approach you with the greeting, "Let me tell you what Jesus Christ has meant to my life." They want you to accept Christ, but their appeal is not to force but to consent. They do not say, "Accept Christ or I am going to plunge a dagger into your chest." Even the fundamentalist Christians in the West are liberals: they are practicing Christianity "in the liberal way."

The task of transforming Muslim fundamentalists into classical liberals 20
will not be an easy one to perform in the Islamic world, where there is no tradition of separating religion and government. We need not require that Islamic countries adopt America's strict form of separation, which prohibits any government involvement in religion. But it is indispensable that Muslim fundamentalists relinquish the use of force for the purpose of spreading Islam. They, too, should appeal to consent. If this seems like a ridiculous thing to ask of Muslims, let us remember that millions of Muslims are already living this way. These are, of course, the Muslim immigrants to Europe and the United States. They are following the teachings of their faith, but most of them understand that they must respect the equal rights of others. They have renounced the *jihad*° of the sword and confine themselves to the *jihad* of the pen and the *jihad* of the heart. In general, the immigrants are showing the way for Islam to change in the same way that Christianity changed in order to survive and flourish in the modern world.

jihad: an Arabic noun derived from the verb meaning "to endeavor or strive, to fight, or to engage in holy war against infidels, or nonbelievers."

Whether America can succeed in the mammoth enterprises of stopping terrorism and liberalizing the Islamic world depends a good deal on the people in the Middle East and a great deal on us. Fundamentalist Islam has now succeeded Soviet communism as the organizing theme of American foreign policy. Thus our newest challenge comes from a very old adversary. The West has been battling Islam for more than a thousand years. It is possible that this great battle has now been resumed, and that over time we will come to see the seventy-year battle against communism as a short detour.

But are we up to the challenge? There are some who think we are not. They believe that Americans are a divided people: not even a nation, but a collection of separate tribes. The multiculturalists actually proclaim this to be a good thing, and they strive to encourage people to affirm their differences. If, however, the multiculturalists are right in saying that "all we have in common is our diversity," then it follows that we have *nothing* in common. This does not bode well for the national unity that is a prerequisite to fighting against a determined foe. If the ethnic group is the primary unit of allegiance, why should we make sacrifices for people who come from ethnic groups other than our own? Doesn't a nation require a loyalty that transcends ethnic particularity?

Of course it does. And fortunately America does command such a loyalty. The multiculturalists are simply wrong about America, and despite their best efforts to promote a politics of difference, Americans remain a united people with shared values and a common way of life. There are numerous surveys of national attitudes that confirm this,[2] but it is most easily seen when Americans are abroad. Hang out at a Parisian café, for instance, and you can easily pick out the Americans: they dress the same way, eat the same food, listen to the same music, and laugh at the same jokes. However different their personalities, Americans who run into each other in remote places always become fast friends. And even the most jaded Americans who spend time in other countries typically return home with an intense feeling of relief and a newfound appreciation for the routine satisfactions of American life.

It is easy to forget the cohesiveness of a free people in times of peace and prosperity. New York is an extreme example of the great pandemonium that results when countless individuals and groups pursue their diverse interests in the normal course of life. In a crisis, however, the national tribe comes together, and this is exactly what happened in New York and the rest of America following the terrorist attack. Suddenly political, regional, and racial differences evaporated; suddenly Americans stood as one. This surprised many people, including many Americans, who did not realize that, despite the centrifugal° forces that pull us in different directions, there is a deep national unity that holds us together.

centrifugal: flying out or off from the center of a revolving body.

25 Unity, however, is not sufficient for the challenges ahead. America also needs the moral self-confidence to meet its adversary. This is the true lesson of Vietnam: Americans cannot succeed unless they are convinced that they are fighting on behalf of the good. There are some, as we have seen, who fear that America no longer stands for what is good. They allege that American freedom produces a licentious, degenerate society that is scarcely worth defending. We return, therefore, to the question of what America is all about,

and whether this country, in its dedication to the principle of freedom, subverts the higher principle of virtue.

So what about virtue? The fundamental difference between the society that the Islamic fundamentalists want and the society that Americans have is that the Islamic activists seek a country where the life of the citizens is *directed by others,* while Americans live in a nation where the life of the citizens is largely *self-directed*. The central goal of American freedom is self-reliance: the individual is placed in the driver's seat of his own life. The Islamic fundamentalists presume the moral superiority of the externally directed life on the grounds that it is aimed at virtue. The self-directed life, however, also seeks virtue—virtue realized not through external command but, as it were, "from within." The real question is: which type of society is more successful in achieving the goal of virtue?

Let us concede at the outset that, in a free society, freedom will frequently be used badly. Freedom, by definition, includes freedom to do good or evil, to act nobly or basely. Thus we should not be surprised that there is a considerable amount of vice, licentiousness, and vulgarity in a free society. Given the warped timber of humanity, freedom is simply an expression of human flaws and weaknesses. But if freedom brings out the worst in people, it also brings out the best. The millions of Americans who live decent, praiseworthy lives deserve our highest admiration because they have opted for the good when the good is not the only available option. Even amidst the temptations that a rich and free society offers, they have remained on the straight path. Their virtue has special luster because it is freely chosen. The free society does not guarantee virtue any more than it guarantees happiness. But it allows for the pursuit of both, a pursuit rendered all the more meaningful and profound because success is not guaranteed: it has to be won through personal striving.

By contrast, the externally directed life that Islamic fundamentalists seek undermines the possibility of virtue. If the supply of virtue is insufficient in self-directed societies, it is almost nonexistent in externally directed societies because coerced virtues are not virtues at all. Consider the woman who is required to wear a veil. There is no modesty in this, because the woman is being compelled. Compulsion cannot produce virtue: it can only produce the outward semblance of virtue. And once the reins of coercion are released, as they were for the terrorists who lived in the United States, the worst impulses of human nature break loose. Sure enough, the deeply religious terrorists spent their last days in gambling dens, bars, and strip clubs, sampling the licentious lifestyle they were about to strike out against.[3] In this respect they were like the Spartans,° who—Plutarch° tells us—were abstemious in public but privately coveted wealth and luxury. In externally directed societies, the absence

Spartans: the inhabitants of Sparta and the enemies of the Athenians in ancient Greece; as an adjective, *spartan* means "simple," "unadorned," "frugal," or "courageous."

Plutarch: early Greek historian, biographer, and essayist.

of freedom signals the absence of virtue. Thus the free society is not simply richer, more varied, and more fun: it is also morally superior to the externally directed society. There is no reason for anyone, least of all the cultural conservatives, to feel hesitant about rising to the defense of our free society.

Even if Americans possess the necessary unity and self-confidence, there is also the question of nerve. Some people, at home and abroad, are skeptical that America can endure a long war against Islamic fundamentalism because they consider Americans to be, well, a little bit soft. As one of bin Laden's lieutenants put it, "Americans love life, and we love death." His implication was that Americans do not have the stomach for the kind of deadly, drawn-out battle that the militant Muslims are ready to fight. This was also the attitude of the Taliban. "Come and get us," they taunted America. "We are ready for *jihad*. Come on, you bunch of weenies." And then the Taliban was hit by a juggernaut° of American firepower that caused their regime to disintegrate within a couple of weeks. Soon the Taliban leadership had headed for the caves, or for Pakistan, leaving their captured soldiers to beg for their lives. Even the call of *jihad* and the promise of martyrdom could not stop these hard men from—in the words of Mullah Omar° himself—"running like chickens with their heads cut off." This is not to say that Americans should expect all its battles against terrorism and Islamic fundamentalism to be so short and so conclusive. But neither should America's enemies expect Americans to show any less firmness or fierceness than they themselves possess.

juggernaut: here, an object or force crushing everything in its path.

Mullah Omar: Pashtun leader of the Taliban who controlled Afghanistan between 1996 and 2001; currently, a collaborator with Osama bin Laden.

. . . The firefighters and policemen who raced into the burning towers of 30
the World Trade Center showed that their lives were dedicated to something higher than "self-fulfillment." The same can be said of Todd Beamer° and his fellow passengers who forced the terrorists to crash United Airlines Flight 93 in the woods of western Pennyslvania rather than flying on to Camp David or the White House. . . . The military has its own culture, which is closer to that of the firefighters and policemen, and also bears an affinity with the culture of the "greatest generation." Only now are those Americans who grew up during the 1960s coming to appreciate the virtues—indeed the indispensability—of this older, sturdier culture of courage, nobility, and sacrifice. It is this culture that will protect the liberties of all Americans. . . .

Todd Beamer: a passenger on United Airlines Flight 93 on September 11, 2001. His last known words were "Let's roll."

As the American founders knew, America is a new kind of society that produces a new kind of human being. That human being—confident, self-reliant, tolerant, generous, future oriented—is a vast improvement over the wretched, servile, fatalistic, and intolerant human being that traditional societies have always produced, and that Islamic societies produce now. In America, the life we are given is not as important as the life we make.

Ultimately, America is worthy of our love and sacrifice because, more than any other society, it makes possible the good life, and the life that is good.

America is the greatest, freest, and most decent society in existence. It is an oasis of goodness in a desert of cynicism and barbarism. This country, once an experiment unique in the world, is now the last best hope for the world. By making sacrifices for America, and by our willingness to die for her, we bind ourselves by invisible cords to those great patriots who fought at Yorktown,° Gettysburg,° and Iwo Jima,° and we prove ourselves worthy of the blessings of freedom. By defeating the terrorist threat posed by Islamic fundamentalism, we can protect the American way of life while once again redeeming humanity from a global menace. History will view America as a great gift to the world, a gift that Americans today must preserve and cherish.

Yorktown, VA: site of the 1781 battle that ended the Revolutionary War when General Cornwallis surrendered to George Washington.

Gettysburg, PA: site of the 1863 Civil War battle, the bloodiest of the war and seen by many as the war's turning point.

Iwo Jima, Japan: site of the 1945 Battle of Iwo Jima, which gave the United States control of the strategically important island. The United States lost close to 7,000 soldiers while the Japanese lost over 20,000. Most Americans know of this battle because of the famous photo of American soldiers raising the U.S. flag on Mount Suribachi on the island during the battle.

Notes

1. See, for example, Amy Waldman, "In Iran, an Angry Generation Longs for Jobs, More Freedom, and Power," *New York Times,* 7 December 2001.
2. See, for example, John Fetto and Rebecca Gardyn, "An All-American Melting Pot," *American Demographics,* July 2001, 8. The survey was conducted by Maritz Marketing Research.
3. Diane McWhorter, "Terrorists Tasted Lusty Lifestyle They So Despised," *USA Today,* 26 September 2001, 11-A.

RESPOND •

1. What does Dinesh D'Souza contend America and Americans are "fighting for"? Why, for D'Souza, are these things worth the fight? To what extent do you agree with his reasons for fighting and his assessment of the value of these reasons?
2. Throughout his essay, D'Souza uses definitions as part of his argument; for example, he defines the terms "American exceptionalism" (paragraph 1), "American universalism" (paragraph 1), "the reformist or classical liberal response" (paragraph 11), "the fundamentalist argument" (paragraph 12), "Promise Keepers" (paragraph 19), and "multiculturalists" (paragraph 22). What kind of definitions does he offer for each of these terms? (For a discussion of kinds of definitions, see Chapter 8.) How do these definitional arguments contribute to the essay's major argument?

Chapter 6 explains how to perform a Toulmin analysis of an argument, identifying such elements as enthymemes, warrants, and backing. What's D'Souza's enthymeme? What would be the warrant for that enthymeme? Refer to Chapter 6 for help in answering the question.

LINK TO P. 147

3. After distinguishing between societies that are "self-directed" and those that are "directed by others" (paragraph 26), D'Souza argues in paragraph 28: "the externally directed life that Islamic fundamentalists seek undermines the possibility of virtue." Do you agree or disagree? Why? Although D'Souza is making a specific claim about Islamic fundamentalists, to what extent does his claim apply to all religious fundamentalists who long for a society in which their understanding of God's truth plays a defining role in determining the country's laws and shaping its culture?
4. Like David Rieff in "Their Hearts and Minds?" D'Souza refers to Vietnam (for example, paragraphs 3 and 25) although he doesn't mention it when he lists specific battles in three wars in the essay's closing paragraph. Why is Vietnam relevant to discussions of the War on Terror? How does D'Souza use his discussion of Vietnam to help support his claim and structure his argument?
5. Although D'Souza makes very strong claims, he frequently qualifies them and anticipates or acknowledges potential counterarguments to his own. For example, in paragraph 6, D'Souza writes, "The reason that most of us do not think this way now" and "This is not to suggest that Islam's historical abuses are worse than those of the West." In what ways do these rhetorical practices strengthen D'Souza's argument? Find other examples of these strategies elsewhere in his essay.
6. Near the beginning and end of his essay, in paragraphs 2 and 32, respectively, D'Souza uses personification, a kind of figurative language, when he writes about America: "what America does, and what *she* stands for" and "our willingness to die for *her*" (emphases added). He doesn't refer to other countries, empires, or cultures as persons, for example, "Israel . . . it" (paragraph 10). Whereas in the past it was quite common to refer to countries, automobiles, and ships in writing by using feminine pronouns, thus personifying them, the practice may strike some readers as quaint and others as sexist today. (For a discussion of biased or slanted language, see Chapter 17.) How does D'Souza's use of personification constitute an emotional appeal? Do you find it effective? Why or why not?
7. The arguments by D'Souza and two authors earlier in this chapter, Waleed Ziad ("Jihad's Fresh Face") and David Rieff ("Their Hearts and Minds?"), treat similar issues. Although there's much about which they disagree, there's also much about which they agree. **Write an essay** in which you describe and evaluate the topics and issues about which D'Souza and either Ziad or Rieff agree. (For a discussion of evaluative arguments, see Chapter 9.)

The Oblivious Empire

MARK HERTSGAARD

Based in San Francisco, Mark Hertsgaard is an independent author and journalist. His most recent book, **The Eagle's Shadow: Why America Fascinates and Infuriates the World** *(2005), is the source of this selection, "The Oblivious Empire." His other books include* **Earth Odyssey: Around the World in Search of Our Environmental Future** *(1998),* **A Day in the Life: The Music and Artistry of the Beatles** *(1995), and* **On Bended Knee: The Press and the Reagan Presidency** *(1988). Hertsgaard also writes regularly for the* **San Francisco Chronicle,** *the* **Los Angeles Times,** *and* **The Nation** *and hosts an investigative news program,* **Spotlight,** *that's broadcast weekly on the satellite network LinkTV. As you read this selection, reflect on whether and why the information he discusses might be new to you and how, to the extent it is new, Hertsgaard's thesis is supported.*

"Texans are the worst," said the London cabbie. It was a fine late summer morning and we were waiting for the light to change so we could cross the Thames.° "I had one in the cab a few weeks ago, must have been in his thirties. We were driving past the London Eye° and he says, 'What's 'at?' I tell him it's the London Eye, the tallest Ferris wheel in the world. He says, 'We got one bigger than that.' I thought, 'Uh-oh, one of those.' I mean, I don't care if the Eye is the tallest in the world or not, maybe there is a bigger one in Texas for all I know. It's the bragging and the arrogance that put me off. No matter what he saw, Texas had more. I forget what we passed next, a double-decker bus,° maybe, or Big Ben—something totally unique to London. He says, 'What's 'at?' I tell him. He says, 'We got one bigger than that.' After that I couldn't be bothered."

The light went green, the cabbie hit the accelerator. "I like most Americans," he added, "but it is quite amazing how they don't know anything about other places in the world"—he shot me a sly glance through the rearview mirror—"unless they're invading them."

The cabbie delivered that little jab on September 10, 2001, but I doubt he would have repeated it two days later. In the immediate aftermath of September 11, the mood in Europe was one of shock and deep sympathy for Americans. "We are very sorry," friends in Paris told me, as if I myself had been attacked. A couple of days later, in Prague, I happened to walk by the United States embassy one night on the way to dinner. The entire block was softly lit by candles well-wishers had left, along with hundreds of flowers and notes of condolence and encouragement. I found more flowers and notes at one of Prague's most revered public places: the monument on Wenceslas Square where the student Jan Palach set himself on fire to protest

Thames: river that flows through London.

London Eye: the world's largest Ferris wheel, built on the southern bank of the Thames as part of the 2002 Millennium celebration.

double-decker bus: one of the red two-level city buses associated with London.

Hertsgaard presents an argument of fact as he chronicles evidence of what characterizes America as oblivious. Read more on developing a factual argument in Chapter 7.

LINK TO P. 184

the Soviet crackdown of 1968. "No Terrorism" read one message spray-painted onto the concrete. Newspapers across the Continent ran articles reporting similar acts of solidarity in Japan, Russia, and elsewhere, as well as commentaries declaring, "We are all Americans now."

The sympathy was genuine and genuinely touching, but as I continued in the following weeks to talk with people across Europe and to survey the local media, it was also clear that the terror attacks had not caused Europeans to forget whatever they had once believed about the United States. Good manners might have restrained the London cabbie from repeating his remark, but it didn't mean he'd stopped thinking Americans were arrogant know-nothings. History did not begin on September 11.

5 Horrified as they were by the tragedy in the United States, many foreigners were not exactly surprised. Most of them knew the reasons why the United States was resented, even hated, in parts of the world, and they usually had complaints of their own. A high school teacher in Spain offered condolences for the September 11 victims and their families, but he told me he hoped Americans would recognize that the tragedy was "a consequence of U.S. foreign policy," especially its one-sided approach to the Israeli-Palestinian conflict. Some Europeans went so far as to cite America's conduct overseas as a virtual justification for the attacks. Even those who rejected the argument that the United States had brought September 11 on itself admitted that America could be infuriating at times.

Perhaps nothing irritates foreigners more than America's habit of thinking it has all the answers, and the right to impose them on everyone else. An outstanding example was President Bush's first major speech after the terror attacks. Speaking before Congress on September 20, Bush declared that foreign nations had to understand that, in the impending U.S.-led war against terrorism, "either you are with us, or you are with the terrorists." Like Bush's declaration that he wanted bin Laden "dead or alive," this was more cowboy talk, the Wild West sheriff warning, "Do as I say or get out of town"—the very attitude that had irritated America's friends and enemies alike for decades. Never mind that many nations already had their own painful experiences with terrorism; they would follow Washington's orders or else.

The United States would never accept such ultimatums itself, yet the arrogance of Bush's remark went unnoticed by America's political and journalistic elite. The *International Herald Tribune*, the overseas daily published by the *New York Times* and the *Washington Post*, did not even mention Bush's statement until the twentieth paragraph of its story, deep inside the paper. By contrast, the French daily *Le Monde* highlighted it three times on its front page, including in the headline and first paragraph. If opinion polls can be trusted, ordinary Americans also saw nothing wrong with their president's stance toward the rest of the world. Throughout the autumn of 2001, Bush's approval rating remained at above 75 percent.[1]

But I would plead ignorance rather than venality° on behalf of my fellow Americans. The embarrassing truth is that most of us know little about the outside world, and we are particularly ill-informed about what our government is doing in our name overseas. For example, Americans are ceaselessly, and accurately, reminded that Saddam Hussein is an evil man, but not that American-enforced economic sanctions have, since 1991, caused the deaths of at least 350,000[2] Iraqi children and impoverished a once prosperous Iraqi middle class. The bloody violence between Israelis and Palestinians that raged throughout March and April of 2002 got plenty of media coverage in the United States. Nevertheless, many Americans remained uninformed about basic aspects of the conflict. A poll conducted in early May by the University of Maryland's Program on International Policy Attitudes revealed, for example, that only 32 percent of Americans were aware that more Palestinians than Israelis had died in the fighting; only 43 percent knew that most other countries in the world disapproved of America's Middle East policies; and a mere 27 percent knew that most countries were more sympathetic to the Palestinian than to the Israeli side of the dispute.[3]

venality: a willingness to offer support in exchange for reward or to be bribed.

In the wake of September 11, the question obsessing Americans about the Muslim world was "Why do they hate us?" But Muslims had long wondered the same about Americans. In a sparkling exception to most American news coverage, Sandy Tolan reported on National Public Radio in January 2002 that nearly everyone he had interviewed during six weeks of recent travel through the Middle East resented the negative stereotypes attached to Muslims and Arabs by American movies, television, and news coverage. In Europe, stretching back to the novels of Goethe° and the operas of Mozart,° there had long been respect for the great achievements of Islamic civilization in culture, astronomy, architecture, and more. America, by contrast, regarded Muslims as primitive, untrustworthy fanatics, worth dealing with only because they had oil.

Johann Wolfgang von Goethe: German writer, philosopher, and politician of the late eighteenth and early nineteenth centuries; he's the author of *Faust*.

Wolfgang Amadeus Mozart: eighteenth-century Austrian musician and composer whose music is often taken as the best representative of the classical era.

"You are dealing here with people who are almost childlike in their un- 10
derstanding of what is going on in the world," Gerald Celente, director of the Trends Research Institute in Rhinebeck, New York, told the *Financial Times* shortly after September 11.[4] "It's all: 'We never did anything to anybody, so why are they doing this to us?'"

Some Americans have taken refuge in the obvious answer: they envy our wealth and resent our power. There is truth in this, as I'll discuss, but it barely scratches the surface. The reason many foreigners don't share Americans' high opinion of themselves is simple: they dislike both how America behaves overseas and its attitude about that behavior.

America, foreigners say, is a trigger-happy bully that is both out for itself and full of itself. It feels no obligation to obey international law; it often pushes other countries around, forcing on them policies and sometimes tyrannical leaders that serve only American interests, and then, if they resist too much, it may bomb obedience into them with cruise missiles. Only an American would blink to hear the United States called the most bellicose° major power in the world; to foreigners, the observation is obvious to the point of banality. America's high-handed behavior puzzles admirers of its domestic freedoms: how to explain the inconsistency? Less sentimental observers point out that this is how the strong have treated the weak throughout history. But, they add, what makes the United States uniquely annoying is its self-righteous insistence that it does nothing of the kind, that it is the epitome of evenhanded virtue and selfless generosity—the Beacon of Democracy that other nations should thank and emulate.

On November 10, 2001, President Bush made his first appearance before the United Nations General Assembly and, in a speech praised by the *New York Times* for its "plain-spoken eloquence,"[5] told the rest of the world it wasn't doing enough to help the United States fight terrorism. "Every nation in the world has a stake in this cause," declared Bush before lecturing his audience that the responsibility to fight terrorism was "binding on every nation with a place in this chamber." Yet on the same day—indeed, at the very moment—that Bush was admonishing others about their international responsibilities, his own administration was shunning negotiations in Morocco to finalize the Kyoto protocol° on global warming. Talk about an issue that every nation has a stake in! Already the earth's glaciers are melting, sea levels are rising, and catastrophic storms are becoming more severe and frequent—this after a mere 1 degree Fahrenheit increase in temperatures over the past century. The scientific consensus predicts 3 to 10.5 degrees of additional warming by 2100, bringing more violent weather, flooded coastlines, and social havoc. Yet the Bush administration insists on doing nothing to lower U.S. greenhouse gas emissions. No wonder foreigners resent us.

American elites sometimes talk of our nation's isolationist° tendencies, but the correct adjective is unilateralist.° The United States has hardly shunned overseas involvement over the years; we simply insist on setting our own terms. This tendency has become especially pronounced since victory in the Cold War left us the only remaining superpower. Determined to keep it that way, senior officials in the first Bush administration drafted a grand strategy for the new era (which got leaked to the *New York Times*):[6]

bellicose: hostile or warlike.

Kyoto Protocol: a 1997 United Nations–brokered agreement on climate change. Ratifying countries agree to reduce their emissions of greenhouse gases or otherwise to engage in emissions trading. In emissions trading, a country that exceeds the agreed-upon limits buys sufficient emissions credits from countries that remain below their limits to compensate for the excess. Although the United States signed the protocol, its refusal to ratify it for domestic economic reasons is often cited as evidence of the country's contempt for international agreements and other countries in general, especially since the United States emits more of these gases per person than any other country.

isolationist: favoring a foreign policy in which the country isolates itself rather than intervening in the affairs of other countries.

unilateralist: favoring a foreign policy in which the country acts alone.

henceforth the goal of American foreign policy would be to prevent any other nation or alliance from becoming a superpower; the United States would rule supreme. This strategy lives on under George W. Bush—which is no surprise, since Vice President Dick Cheney and other key advisers were the ones who devised the strategy for Bush's father. Shortly after taking office, the administration of Bush II announced it was going to withdraw from the Anti-Ballistic Missile Treaty, a cornerstone of nuclear arms control for the past thirty years, in an assertion of unilateralism that evoked dismay not just from treaty partner Russia but from the entire global community. Bush's oddest rejection of global cooperation was his refusal to join, even retroactively, the accord against bioterrorism reached in July 2001 that could hinder future anthrax attacks. The United States delegation walked out of the negotiations because the Bush administration refused to accept the same rules it demands for Iraq and other "rogue states": international inspections of potential weapons production sites.[7]

I don't mean to pick on Mr. Bush. Double standards have a long bipartisan 15
pedigree in American foreign policy. Bush's father uttered one of the most feverish declarations of American prerogative in 1988, while serving as Ronald Reagan's vice president. Five years earlier, when the Soviet Union shot down a Korean Airlines passenger jet over the Pacific, killing all 276 people on board, the United States had condemned the attack as further evidence of the "evil empire's" true nature, rejecting the Soviet explanation that the jet was acting like a military aircraft. Now the tables were turned: the United States had shot down an Iranian civilian jet it mistakenly believed was a military craft. All 290 passengers died. When Bush senior was asked if an apology was in order, he replied, "I will never apologize for the United States. I don't care what the facts are."

Democrats have been just as bad about this kind of thing. In 1998 critics at home and abroad were condemning the Clinton administration's launch of cruise missiles against Iraq as at best unnecessary and at worst a self-serving ploy to weaken impeachment proceedings against the president. But no, Secretary of State Madeleine Albright modestly explained, "if we have to use force, it is because we are America. We are the indispensable nation. . . . We see farther into the future." As Rupert Cornwell, the Washington correspondent for the British newspaper *The Independent*, observed on another occasion, "No one wraps self-interest in moral superiority quite like the Americans do."[8]

Americans are a fair-minded people, however, and I doubt that a majority of us would support such hypocrisy if we were truly aware of it. I believe most of us would instead urge that the United States bring its global behavior into accord with its domestic principles. But that might threaten what Washington considers vital national interests, so the powers that be resist. Since America is the land of both Hollywood and Madison Avenue,° our official response has instead been to hire public relations experts to do a better job of "getting our message out" overseas. Brilliant touch, no? After all, the problem couldn't possibly be our policies themselves.

Americans will continue to misunderstand the world, and our place within it, until we face the full truth of how our government has acted overseas—a fact made powerfully clear to me in South Africa, where . . . enthusiasm for America . . . is balanced by the anger of those who recall that the United States was a firm, long-standing supporter of apartheid.°

Why Don't They Love Us?

The ferry from Cape Town° takes forty minutes to reach Robben Island, the notorious prison where Nelson Mandela° and other South African freedom fighters were jailed during their struggle for freedom. The ferry lands at a jetty two hundred yards from a complex of low buildings with corrugated tin roofs that is the prison proper. A sign retained from apartheid days reads, in English and Afrikaans,° "Robben Island. Welcome. We Serve with Pride."

There are now guided tours of the island, and what makes them especially 20
compelling is that they are conducted by a thin man in a white windbreaker
named Siphiwo Sobuwa. Speaking in a flat, deliberate tone, Sobuwa said he

Madison Avenue: a reference to Madison Avenue in New York City; figuratively, advertising.

apartheid: the South African system of race-based segregation that was in effect from 1984 to 1992. White, Black, Indian, and Coloured groups were confined by and large to separate institutions and homelands. (The term *Coloured* referred generally to people of mixed ethnic heritage.)

Cape Town: the third largest city in South Africa; as its name implies, it's on the coast.

Nelson Mandela: following the end of apartheid, the first president of South Africa elected in democratic elections where all could vote. He was imprisoned for twenty-seven years because of his anti-apartheid activism.

Nelson Mandela in 1991, one year after his release from prison

had been imprisoned at age seventeen after being captured smuggling arms for the ANC's° military wing. Interrogated, beaten, denied a lawyer, he was sentenced to forty-eight years in jail. He served fifteen years, all on Robben Island, before the crumbling of apartheid enabled his release in 1991.

As he ushered us into the prison's entry hall, Sobuwa recalled how he spent his first two years in solitary confinement because he didn't speak Afrikaans. A warden told his group of arriving prisoners that no talking was allowed, but since Sobuwa didn't understand Afrikaans, he asked another inmate what was going on. The warden decided to make an example of Sobuwa. "I was sent to A section, the torture section," he told us. "I could not write or receive letters. I could not speak, sing, or whistle. Food was slipped underneath the grille of my cell. Those two years were the hardest."

We pushed through a door into an open-air courtyard, where we listened to Sobuwa recount other punishments common on Robben Island. Most humiliating was the guards' game of ordering an inmate buried in the ground up to his neck and then leaving him there all day to roast in the sun while guards took turns urinating on him. More gruesome was the practice of hanging a prisoner upside down from a tree and waiting as the hours passed for him to pass out and, in one case, to perish as the body's blood supply gradually accumulated in the brain, starving it of oxygen. But of all the deprivations—punishing physical labor, numbing boredom, inedible food, lack of heat—Sobuwa said the blackout on news was the hardest to bear. Inmates did their best to compensate. "The guard towers had no toilets," he explained, "so guards would relieve themselves in newspapers, then throw the papers down to the ground. We would retrieve those papers, scrape them off, and read the news they contained. We didn't care what kind of mess was inside, we wanted that news."

Afrikaans: a language that developed out of the contact between Dutch speaking Protestant settlers in South Africa and those who worked as their slaves or indentured workers; the latter group included people indigenous to South Africa as well as South Indians, Malays, and Malagasies. Early in the twentieth century, Afrikaans replaced Dutch as one of the two official languages (with English being the other) of South Africa. Today it's one of the eleven official languages of post-apartheid South Africa.

ANC (African National Congress): an anti-apartheid movement founded in 1912 under a different name to defend the legal rights of South Africa's black majority. Its struggle continued until apartheid ended in 1992; in 1994, it became the ruling party in elections and remains so.

Hearing about such abominations firsthand makes visiting Robben Island as unforgettable as a pilgrimage to Dachau° or Hiroshima.° And talking with a man like Sobuwa rescues foreign policy from its usual abstractions, making concrete the implications of such diplomatic double-talk as "constructive engagement,"° the Reagan administration's justification for its unswerving support for apartheid. When I interviewed Sobuwa at his cinder-block house in a Cape Town township, he said his work had taught him to distinguish between Americans as people and the American government. He had little good to say about the latter. Washington, he pointed out, as well as Israel, had supported apartheid—and thus the oppression on Robben Island—until the very end. Furthermore, he said, "it is a trend among United States presidents that so-called Third World° countries must be destabilized. America believes in solving problems not by negotiations but through military pressure."

But his tour guide conversations had made Sobuwa realize that not all Americans supported their government's policy. He was grateful for those who had joined the protests that eventually forced Western governments, including that of the United States, to endorse apartheid's demise. He was unaware that America's new vice president had, as a U.S. congressman in 1985, voted against urging Mandela's release from jail,[9] but then neither were most Americans aware of this aspect of Dick Cheney's past. What Sobuwa did know was that Bill Clinton had a lot of nerve. "He came here a couple years ago to visit Mandela and speak to our Parliament, and he told us South Africa should cut its ties to Cuba because Cuba was a bad government. Well, when we needed help during our liberation struggle, Cuba gave it. When we needed food, Cuba provided it. For someone who did not help our struggle to come now and ask us to distance ourselves from someone who did, that is very arrogant behavior."

Arrogant but, alas, not atypical. The United States has long pressed South 25
American nations to cut ties with the Castro government. Likewise, in June 2002 George W. Bush announced that Yasir Arafat had to go as the Palestinian leader. Free elections had to be held, said Bush, but Washington would push for a Palestinian state only if those "free" elections got rid of Arafat.

Washington's might-makes-right view of such matters was succinctly expressed by Henry Kissinger when, as President Richard Nixon's national security adviser, he privately defended overthrowing the elected government of Chile by saying he saw no reason why the United States had to allow Chile to "go Marxist" simply because "its people are irresponsible."[10] Testifying before the U.S. Senate on the day of the coup, Kissinger claimed the United States had played no role in the 1973 coup that toppled Allende. But voluminous government documents show that Kissinger, as head of the so-called Forty Committee that supervised U.S. covert actions between 1969 and 1976,

Dachau, Germany: the first German concentration camp and the prototype for later camps, in use from 1933 to 1945. Some 30,000 were killed there beginning in 1941 in addition to the many thousands who perished because of mistreatment and malnourishment.

Hiroshima, Japan: The city where one of two atomic bombs was dropped by the U.S. Army in 1945; an estimated 80,000 were killed.

constructive engagement: the Reagan administration's failed policy in the early 1980s of seeking change in apartheid through private conversations with the leaders of South Africa, all of whom were white.

Third World: term used to refer to countries that receive low scores on the United Nations Human Development Index, which seeks to measure a country's degree of development in several domains. Such countries are generally less technologically advanced or industrialized than other countries. Originally, the term referred to countries that weren't aligned with the West (the first world) or with the Soviet Bloc (the second world) during the Cold War; hence, the name "third world."

was well-informed about how the CIA° had ordered a coup in 1970 that had failed to thwart Allende and, in 1973, had at least condoned if not actively aided the Chilean military men who, under future dictator General Augusto Pinochet, imposed martial law and eventually killed 3,197 Chilean citizens.[11]

CIA (Central Intelligence Agency): U.S. government agency organized in 1947 and set up to collect and analyze information about foreign entities—individuals, companies, or governments—and pass that information on to the relevant parts of the national government. Most controversially, the CIA engages in covert operations at the president's behest.

Note the date of the U.S.-sponsored assault on democratic government in Chile: September 11, 1973. Note the estimated Chilean death toll—executions plus military casualties—of 3,197 people. Is not the congruence between that coup and the World Trade Center attack striking? True, one was authored by religious fanatics and the other by a state, and the events were separated in time by twenty-eight years, yet both took place on the same date and caused comparable numbers of deaths. Nevertheless, this eerie coincidence passed virtually unremarked in the United States.

This is self-defeating. It's no secret to Chileans that the United States helped bring to power the dictatorship that ruled them for seventeen years. Nor are the people of El Salvador and Guatemala unaware that the United States gave money, weapons, and training to the military governments that killed so many of their fellow citizens in recent decades. In Guatemala, a truth commission sponsored by the United Nations concluded in 1999 that "American training of the officer corps in counterinsurgency techniques" was a "key factor" in a "genocide" that included the killing of 200,000 peasants.

Switch to Asia[12] or the Middle East and the same point applies. Virtually every one of Washington's allies in the Middle East is an absolute monarchy where democracy and human rights are foreign concepts and women in particular are second-class citizens. But they have oil, so all is forgiven. Likewise, in South Korea everyone knows that the United States chose the generals that ruled their country from the end of World War II until 1993; the facts came out during a trial that found two of the surviving dictators guilty of state terrorism. Ferdinand Marcos of the Philippines, General Suharto of Indonesia, General Lon Nol of Cambodia—the list of tyrants that Washington has supported in Asia is widely known, except in the United States.

Again, what offends is not simply the ruthlessness of American policies 30
but their hypocrisy. The United States insists on the sanctity of United Nations resolutions when they punish enemies like Iraq with arms inspections, but not when they oblige its number-one foreign aid recipient, Israel, to withdraw from occupation of Palestinian territories in the West Bank and Gaza. On trade policy, Washington demands that poor countries honor World Trade Organization rules against subsidizing° domestic farmers or industries because these rules enable U.S.-based multinational firms to invade those countries' economies. Without blushing, Washington then lavishes billions of dollars in subsidies on our own agriculture sector (dominated, by the way, by those same multinationals) and imposes tariffs° against foreign steel imports.

subsidize: of a government, to pay the producers of certain goods or products to continue producing them.

tariffs: taxes imposed by a government on imported goods.

Why do we violate fair play so brazenly? Because we can. "The United States can hurt us a lot worse than we can hurt them," grumbled one Canadian trade official.

Then there is our self-serving definition of "terrorism," a concept America's political and media elites never apply to the United States or its allies, only to enemies or third parties. No one disputes that the September 11 attacks against the United States were acts of terrorism; that is, they targeted innocent civilians to advance a political or military agenda. When the Irish Republican Army exploded bombs inside London subway stations and department stores in the mid-1990s, that, too, was terrorism. So were the Palestinian suicide bombings in Israel in early 2002, and Saddam Hussein's use of poison gas against Kurds° in Iraq in 1988. But when Israel attacked Palestinian refugee camps in April 2002, demolishing buildings and killing or wounding many civilians, was that not also terrorism? When the United States lobbed Volkswagen-sized shells into Lebanese villages in 1983 and dropped "smart bombs" on Baghdad in 1991, many innocent civilians perished while Washington sent its geopolitical message. The napalm° dropped during the Vietnam War, the bombing of Dresden,° and the annihilation of Hiroshima and Nagasaki in World War II—these acts all pursued military or political objectives by killing vast numbers of civilians, just as the September 11 attacks did. Yet in mainstream American discourse, the United States is never the perpetrator of terrorism, only its victim and implacable foe.

These and other unsavory aspects of America's overseas dealings are not completely unknown in the United states. Academic specialists, human rights activists, and partisans of the political left are familiar with this history. Glimpses of the truth appear (very) occasionally in mainstream press coverage, and the CIA's role in subverting democracies and overthrowing governments was documented by congressional investigations in 1975. In 2002 Samantha Powers published a book, *A Problem from Hell,* that meticulously documented how Washington deliberately chose not to intervene against some of the worst acts of genocide in the twentieth century, including Pol Pot's° rampages in Cambodia, ethnic cleansing in Bosnia,° and tribal slaughter in Rwanda.° The book received considerable attention within media circles; its message got out. But in general, critical perspectives on American actions are given nowhere near the same prominence or repetition in government, media, and public discussion as is the conventional view of the United States as an evenhanded champion of democracy and freedom. Thus the basic direction of American foreign policy rarely shifts, and Washington creates for itself what the late *Wall Street Journal* reporter Jonathan Kwitny called "endless enemies"[13] around the world. Worse, aver-

Kurds: ethnic group of some 30 million with members in Iraq, Turkey, Iran, and Syria, a region often referred to as Kurdistan.

napalm: in common usage, a category of flammable liquids used in warfare.

Dresden: the capital of the German state of Saxony. Prior to its bombing in 1945 by the Allied Forces, it was among the world's most beautiful cities. In the bombing, 25,000–35,000 were likely killed and 24,886 of the city's 28,410 houses in the inner city were destroyed. Historians continue to debate the bombing and its effects, some claiming it was a war crime.

Pol Pot: ruler of the Khmer Rouge and, later, Cambodia's prime minister in the 1970s; his government may have been responsible for the death of as many as 5 million Cambodians.

ethnic cleansing in Bosnia: Following the breakup of Yugoslavia in the early 1990s, Serbian and Croatian Christians in Bosnia sought to exterminate the local Muslim population that constituted the region's majority.

Rwanda: In the mid-1990s, the Hutus, in collaboration with the Rwandan government forces, sought to commit the genocide of the Tutsis, their rivals, resulting in over half a million deaths.

age Americans are left unaware that this is happening, and so are shocked when foreigners don't love us as much as we think they should.

Ignorance is an excuse, but it is no shield. "Although most Americans may be largely ignorant of what was, and still is, being done in their names, all are likely to pay a steep price . . . for their nation's continued efforts to dominate the global scene," veteran Asian affairs analyst Chalmers Johnson wrote in his fierce book, *Blowback*. America's tendency to bully, warns Johnson, will "build up reservoirs of resentment against all Americans—tourists, students, and businessmen, as well as members of the armed forces—that can have lethal results."

"Blowback" is a CIA term for how foreign policy can come back to haunt a country years later in unforeseen ways, especially after cases of secret operations. Thus Johnson quotes a 1997 report by the Pentagon's Defense Science Board: "Historical data show a strong correlation between U.S. involvement in international situations and an increase in terrorist attacks against the United States." A glaring example is the Iranian hostage crisis of 1979. To protect American oil interests, the CIA in 1953 overthrew the elected government of Iran and installed Shah Reza Pahlavi (an act a subsequent CIA director, William Colby, described as the CIA's "proudest moment").[14] The shah ruled with an iron hand, murdered thousands, duly became widely hated, and was forced from power in 1979. Residual Iranian anger led to an attack on the United States embassy in Tehran and seizure of fifty-four hostages, a crisis that doomed Jimmy Carter's presidency.[15]

Because Johnson's book was published in 2000, it was unable to address the most spectacular of all cases of blowback: the September 11 terror attacks. But in the October 15 and December 10, 2001, issues of *The Nation*, Johnson explained how the CIA supported Osama bin Laden° from at least 1984 as part of its funding of the mujahideen,° the Islamic resistance to the Soviet Union's occupation of Afghanistan. The CIA funneled its support for bin Laden and other mujahideen, including building the complex where bin Laden trained some thirty-five thousand followers, through Pakistan's intelligence service. But bin Laden turned against the United States after the 1991 Persian Gulf War, when "infidel"° American troops were stationed on the Islamic holy ground of Saudi Arabia° to prop up its authoritarian regime. The September 11 attacks, Johnson concludes, were the blowback from America's covert action in Afghanistan in the 1970s, and the cycle is probably not over: "The Pentagon's current response of 'bouncing the rubble' in Afghanistan [is] setting the stage for more rounds to come."

Osama bin Laden: An Islamic fundamentalist and founder of Al Qaeda, an Islamic organization committed to establishing an Islamic government around the world, bin Laden is a member of an especially wealthy Saudi Arabian family. Bin Laden and Al Qaeda are considered responsible for the September 11, 2001, attacks as well as over a dozen bombings elsewhere in the world.

mujahideen: Arabic plural noun meaning "strugglers" but more often "those engaged in *jihad*, or holy war." The reference here is to the Afghani "freedom fighters" who were financed, armed, and trained by the Carter and Reagan administrations and other countries to defeat the Soviet presence in Afghanistan during the 1980s. The movie *Rambo III* portrayed these fighters as heroic.

infidel: someone who doesn't follow the tenets of Islam.

holy ground of Saudi Arabia: Because Saudi Arabia is home to Mecca and Medina, the two cities associated with the founding of Islam and the holiest of Muslim sites, which Muslims visit when making the *hajj* of pilgrimage, it's considered "sacred ground" by many Muslims. No alcohol may be sold or consumed in Saudi airspace, for example, and until recently tourist visas to visit the country weren't issued to non-Muslims.

Notes

1. Bush's 77 percent approval rating was reported in *Time,* February 4, 2002.
2. The justification for the 350,000 figure, which is considerably lower than some frequently cited estimates, is discussed in "A Hard Look at Iraq Sanctions," by David Cortright, *The Nation,* December 3, 2001.
3. Americans' views of the Middle East conflict were examined in a poll conducted by the Program on International Policy Attitudes of the University of Maryland, released to the media on May 8, 2002, and available via the program's Web site at www.pipa.org.
4. Gerald Celente's quote appeared in the *Financial Times* of September 29–30, 2001.
5. Bush's speech was reported, and praised, in the November 11 edition of the *New York Times.*
6. The first Bush administration's grand strategy is described in *The New Yorker* of April 1, 2002.
7. Bush's rejection of the verification protocol for biological weapons was analyzed by Milton Leitenberg in the *Los Angeles Times Book Review,* October 28, 2001.
8. Rupert Cornwell's remark appeared in *The Independent* on July 27, 2001.
9. Dick Cheney was one of only eight members of Congress who voted against the resolution urging the government of South Africa to release Mandela from jail and initiate negotiations with the African National Congress. See Joe Conason's story in Salon.com, August 1, 2000.
10. Kissinger's quote about Chile and his activities with the Forty Committee are described in "The Case Against Henry Kissinger," by Christopher Hitchens, in *Harper's Magazine,* February and March 2001.
11. The death toll resulting from the 1973 coup in Chile is documented by John Dinges in *The Condor Years: How Pinochet and His Allies Brought Terrorism to Three Continents* (New York: New Press, 2003), Chapter 1.
12. The findings of the United Nations–sponsored Commission for Historical Clarification, as well as American support for Asian dictators, were summarized in *Blowback: The Costs and Consequences of American Empire,* by Chalmers Johnson (New York: Henry Holt, Owl Books, 2001), pages 14 and 25–27, respectively.
13. Kwitny's phrase was the title of his illuminating and comprehensive book *Endless Enemies: The Making of an Unfriendly World* (New York: Congdon & Weed, 1984).
14. The quotes from Johnson, *Blowback,* are from pages 33 and 4, respectively.
15. The definitive account of America's actions in Iran, including the help that the local *New York Times* correspondent gave to the coup plotters, is found in Kwitny, *Endless Enemies,* pages 161–78.

RESPOND

1. What's the meaning of Mark Hertsgaard's title, "The Oblivious Empire"? How does it summarize his argument? Do you agree with his claim that Americans are generally unaware of the role their government's actions have played in world politics? Why or why not? To what extent were you aware of the historical evidence he details in the second section of the essay, "Why Don't They Love Us?"? Does it matter if you were? If you weren't? Why or why not?
2. According to Hertsgaard, people from other countries "dislike both how America behaves overseas and its attitude about that behavior" (paragraph 11). How does he and those he cites characterize America's behavior? Its attitude about those actions? In the context of the information Hertsgaard provides, do such assessments seem justified or rational? Why or why not?
3. In criticizing the actions of the U.S. government, Hertsgaard cites cases involving both Democratic and Republican administrations. Is he even-handed in his treatment of both parties, that is, is he equally critical (or laudatory) of the behavior of both parties? Why or why not?
4. What kinds of evidence does Hertsgaard rely on in constructing his argument? How does he use evidence effectively? How successful is his opening narrative based on personal experience? Why?
5. We can safely predict that Hertsgaard and Dinesh D'Souza, author of the previous selection, "America the Beautiful: What We're Fighting For," would find much to disagree about. Based on their texts, would you claim that one cares more passionately about America or its place in the world than the other, or is it that they express their commitments differently? Imagine and **write a dialogue** between the two authors about America's place in the world and why Americans generally see themselves so differently from the way they're seen by others.

▼ *Associated with the* New York Times *since 1981, Thomas Friedman has won the Pulitzer Prize three times: twice for international reporting (1983 from Lebanon and 1988 from Israel) and once for commentary (2002). He's currently the paper's foreign-affairs columnist. He's generally considered a political centrist who supports neoliberal ideas on globalization; he writes frequently about the Middle East. Friedman is the author of several award-winning books, including* From Beirut to Jerusalem *(1989),* The Lexus and the Olive Tree *(1999),* Longitudes and Attitudes: Exploring the World after September 11 *(2002), and* The World Is Flat: A Brief History of the Twenty-first Century *(2005).*

This selection, "Revolution Is U.S.," comes from The Lexus and the Olive Tree, *an extended study of globalization. The book's title grew out of an experience Friedman had in 1992 while reading yet another story in the* International Herald Tribune *about controversy between Israelis and Arabs over land and the olive trees that grow on it while he was riding a bullet train in Japan at 180 miles per hour as he returned from touring a Lexus factory populated by robots. Of this experience, he writes, "It struck me then that the Lexus and the olive tree were actually pretty good symbols of this post–Cold War era; half the world seemed to be emerging from the Cold War intent on building a better Lexus, dedicated to modernizing, streamlining and privatizing their economies in order to thrive in the system of globalization. And half the world—sometimes half the same country, sometimes half the same person—was still caught up in the fight over who owns which olive tree."*

As you read this selection, look for evidence of longing for the bright, shiny promises of globalization—the Lexus—and the desire for rootedness and adhering to one's own way of life—the olive tree—as Friedman discusses how and why other countries see the United States as they do.

Revolution Is U.S.

THOMAS L. FRIEDMAN

I saw the sign above the front door as soon as I walked into the lobby of the Homa Hotel in downtown Teheran in September 1996. Written there were the words "Down with USA." It wasn't a banner. It wasn't graffiti. It was *tiled* into the wall.

"Jeez," I thought to myself. "That's tiled into the wall! These people really have a problem with America."

A short time later I noticed that the Iranian mullahs,° who have always been more sensitive to the ups and downs of American cultural and military power than anyone else, had started calling the United States something other than just the "Great Satan" and the bastion of "imperialism and Zionism."° The Iranians had started to call America "the capital of global arrogance." I found that a subtle but revealing shift. The Iranian leadership seemed to understand that "global arrogance" was different from imperial-

mullah: an Islamic clergyman who has studied the Qur'an, the Islamic traditions, and Islamic law; generally, he has memorized the entire Qur'an. The term is most often applied to Shi'a clerics; however, in the Indian subcontinent it's used for both Sunni and Shi'a clerics.

Zionism: a political ideology and movement supporting a homeland for the Jewish people in *Eretz Yisrael,* The Land of Israel, which was home to the Jews of the Old Testament. Modern political Zionism began in the late 1800s; since the founding of the state of Israel in 1948, the term is often used to mean support for the Israeli state.

ism. Imperialism is when you physically occupy another people and force your ways upon them. Global arrogance is when your culture and economic clout are so powerful and widely diffused that you know that you don't need to occupy other people to influence their lives. As India's Finance Minister, Shri Yashwant Sinha, once said to me about America's relations with the rest of the world today: "There is no balance, no counterpoise.° Whatever you say is law."

And that is what makes today's combination of Americanization and globalization so powerful. What bothers so many people about America today is not that we send our troops everywhere, but that we send our culture, values, economics, technologies and lifestyles everywhere — whether or not we want to or others want them. "America is different," German foreign policy expert Josef Joffe noted in a September 1997 essay in *Foreign Affairs*. "It irks and domineers, but it does not conquer. It tries to call the shots and bend the rules, but it does not go to war for land and glory. . . . The United States has the most sophisticated, not the largest, military establishment in the world. But it is definitely in a class of its own in the soft-power° game. On that table, China, Russia and Japan, and even Western Europe cannot hope to match the pile of chips the United States holds. People are risking death on the high seas to get into the United States, not China. There are not too many who want to go for an M.B.A. at Moscow University, or dress and dance like the Japanese. Sadly, fewer and fewer students want to learn French or German. English, the American-accented version, has become the world's language. This type of power — a culture that radiates outward and a market that draws inward — rests on pull not push; on acceptance not on conquest. Worse, this kind of power cannot be aggregated,° nor can it be balanced. In this arena, all of them together — Europe, Japan, China, and Russia — cannot gang up on the United States as in an alliance of yesteryear. All their movie studios together could not break the hold of Hollywood. Nor could a consortium of their universities dethrone Harvard. . . . This is why the 'strategic partnership' forged by Russia and China appears so anachronistic°

---

counterpoise: one weight balancing another, thereby creating a state of equilibrium or balance.

soft-power: As Josef Joffe explains in the following selection, soft power is "the contagious appeal of [America's] ideas, its culture and its way of life"; it contrasts with "hard power," or military force.

aggregated: gathered or assembled into a whole.

anachronistic: out of its appropriate time period or era; here, used to imply that the partnership was of no use or value because the era during which such partnerships might have been valuable is long past.

Redefining what it means to be a world power, Friedman crafts an argument that explains why other countries resent the United States. Chapter 8 describes the key features of a definitional argument and offers a guide to writing your own such argument.

LINK TO P. 232

in 1997. What are they going to do about America? Boris Yeltsin° will hardly want to shop for know-how and computers in Beijing. And China will not want to risk its most important export market."

No wonder then as I traveled around the world at the end of the 1990s, I 5
found that not only the Iranians were calling America "the capital of global arrogance," but, behind our backs, so too were the French, the Malaysians, the Russians, the Canadians, the Chinese, the Indians, the Pakistanis, the Egyptians, the Japanese, the Mexicans, the South Koreans, the Germans—and just about everybody else. Iraqi President Saddam Hussein, who, like the Iranians, is ever sensitive to even subtle changes in America's international standing, shrewdly tried to tap into this newfound resentment by changing his propaganda line. In the first Gulf War° crisis in the early 1990s, Saddam depicted himself as the Arab Robin Hood, come to steal from the Arab rich to give to the Arab poor. In the second Gulf War crisis,° in the late 1990s, Saddam depicted himself as Luke Skywalker,° standing up to the American Evil Empire. Every time he was interviewed on television, Saddam's Foreign Minister complained that America behaved like "the last days of the Roman Empire." This became Iraq's new propaganda line, from the top of the regime right down to the street. I was watching CNN one day and heard them do an interview with "a man in the street in Baghdad," who just happened to refer to America as an "international Dracula that sucks the blood of people around the world."

O.K., O.K., so the rest of the world thinks we're obnoxious bullies and is envious of us. So what? What impact does this really have on relations between the United States and other governments? The short answer is that it makes America's relations with every country a little more complicated today. Some countries now go out of their way just to tweak America's beak; others sit back and enjoy the role of the "free rider"—they let America be the global

---

President Yeltsin after his election in 1991

Boris Yeltsin: president of Russia from 1991 to 1999.

first Gulf War (also called the Persian Gulf War or Operation Desert Storm): a 1991 United Nations–sanctioned initiative led by the United States to free Kuwait, which had been invaded by Iraq during the previous fall.

second Gulf War crisis: crisis during the late 1990s during which Iraq generally refused to cooperate with the United Nations Special Commission monitoring the country's weapons; in 1997, all American members of the inspection team were expelled from Iraq.

Luke Skywalker: a Jedi Knight in the *Star Wars* films.

sheriff, pay all the costs of confronting the Saddam Husseins and other rogues, and enjoy the benefits, while all the time complaining about America; others stew with resentment at American domination; others just quietly fall into line.

In fact, America's relationship to the rest of the world today is a lot like Michael Jordan's° relationship was—in his heyday—with the rest of the NBA.° Every other player and team wanted to beat Michael Jordan; every other player and team hated him for the way he could expose all their weaknesses; every other player and team measured themselves against Michael Jordan, and to some extent modeled their moves after him; every other player and team constantly complained that the referees let Michael Jordan get away with all sorts of fouls that no one else could. But despite all of that, none of the other teams really wanted to see Michael Jordan injured or retire, because anytime he came into town every seat was sold. He was the straw that stirred the drink for them all.

Consider just a few examples of this phenomenon: When Anatoly Chubais, one of the original architects of Russia's privatization program, was negotiating yet another Russian bailout by the IMF° in the summer of 1998, the IMF was demanding more stringent terms than ever, and Chubais had little choice but to give in. At the height of the negotiations, the Russian television show *Kukli*, which features puppets dressed up as various Russian leaders, did a takeoff on "Little Red Riding Hood." Boris Yeltsin was Grandmother and then Prime Minister Kiryenko was Little Red Riding Hood, trying to get to Yeltsin to influence the latest Russian bailout plan before anyone else. When Kiryenko arrived at Grandmother's house, though, he found Chubais already sitting next to Yeltsin. Chubais was dressed in a space suit and moon helmet. On the front of the suit were the Russian letters for "IMF" and an American flag. Chubais was literally depicted as an agent from planet

---

Michael Jordan ("Air Jordan," "His Airness"): Considered by many to be the greatest basketball player of all time, Jordan also helped market the NBA internationally.

NBA: National Basketball Association.

IMF: International Monetary Fund; in its own words, "an organization of 184 countries, working to foster global monetary cooperation, secure financial stability, facilitate international trade, promote high employment and sustainable economic growth, and reduce poverty." When the IMF agrees to help a country in financial difficulty, it often sets conditions on its assistance, sometimes requiring profound changes in how the country's economy is organized.

Davos World Economic Forum: annual meeting of high-ranking national political leaders, business leaders, journalists, and academics to encourage discussion and debate of economic and social challenges worldwide; sponsored by a Swiss foundation, it is generally held in Davos, Switzerland.

hubris: excessive pride or confidence; originally, among the ancient Greeks, the term was used of mortals like Oedipus who acted presumptively toward the gods.

Kyoto Conference: meeting that gave rise to the Kyoto Protocol, a 1997 United Nations–brokered agreement on climate change. Ratifying countries agree to reducing their emissions of greenhouse gases or otherwise to engage in emissions trading. In emissions trading, a country that exceeds the agreed-upon limits buys sufficient emissions credits from countries that remain below their limits to compensate for the excess. Although the United States signed the protocol, its refusal to ratify it for domestic economic reasons is often cited as evidence of the country's contempt for international agreements and other countries more generally, especially since the United States emits more of these gases per person than any other country.

America, there to tell the Russians what to do. When Kiryenko saw him sitting next to Yeltsin he said to the audience, "I guess I arrived too late."

At the 1999 Davos World Economic Forum,° Minoru Murofushi, chairman of Japan's giant trading company the Itochu Corporation, was on a panel with Russian Prime Minister Yevgeny Primakov. Murofushi was commenting on Primakov's efforts to negotiate an end to Russia's economic crisis when, in something of a Freudian slip, the Japanese businessman said, "I know Mr. Primakov is meeting tomorrow with Mr. Fischer from IBM—I mean from the IMF." Oh well, IBM, IMF, what's the difference—they're both controlled by the Americans!

10 Yuan Ming, a professor of international relations at Beijing University, is one of China's leading experts on America. She once told me a story that indicated that China thought the only way to react to American global arrogance was with some arrogance of its own: "Our political leaders in their public speeches don't use the term 'globalization.' They use the term 'modernization.' There is a cultural reason for this. The historical lesson is still fresh in Chinese people's minds that China was forced into the international community in the last century by gun-boats—so globalization represents something that China doesn't pursue but rather something that the West or America is imposing. Modernization, on the other hand, is something we can control. There is an annual New Year's television program that is shown on the main national television channel. It is one of the biggest TV events of the year in China. Almost a billion people watch it. Usually it is just singers and comedians. Three years ago, though, [in 1995] the show had a skit about two parents in a rural area calling their son who was studying in the United States. They ask him, 'How are you on this New Year's Day?' He says he's fine and that he plans to return home after finishing his Ph.D. in the United States. The parents are pleased to hear this. The line I remember most, though, is the parents telling the son that China is getting as good as America at many things. They say: 'You did some dishwashing for the Americans. Now we have to have some Americans come and do some dishwashing for us.'"

I was flying home from Japan on December 14, 1997, and was reading the letters to the editor in that day's *Japan Times*. I like to read them in whatever country I am in, because I always find interesting nuggets there. This letter was entitled "American Hubris,"° and it spoke for a lot of people. It said: "I am at (another) loss for words over the continuing bullying tactics of the United States. This time, I read that the U.S. refuses to sign any agreement [at the Kyoto Conference° on climate change] unless three of its 'demands' are met. . . . I would never belittle the U.S. history of 'helping' where it can—but the 'world's greatest country' (its claim, not mine) *must* learn humility. Its recent return to glory has been equally due to the failure of its competitors' political and economic systems. Pride comes before a fall. The U.S. government would do well to remember that." Signed: Andrew Ogge. Tokyo.

I visited India following its 1998 nuclear tests, and Indian Lieutenant General (retired) V. R. Raghavan, the former chief of operations of the Indian Army and now an analyst at the Delhi Policy Group, told me he had just taken part in an international seminar on the nuclear issue. The participants included British, American, Chinese and Indian experts, among others. "During one of the breaks we went out to tour a tiny Indian village and I showed them the shops and homes and the cow dung being used as an energy source," said General Raghavan. "But most fascinating was a visit we made to a middle school in the village. There were about thirty children in their early teens, and some teachers, and members of our group wanted to talk to them. So they set out some benches and had a chat. There was a lawyer from New York in the group and he asked the kids what they thought of China and the United States. Without any prompting these kids said that China is our biggest neighbor, we had a war with China, but China stands up for weaker nations and we have no problems with China. 'How about the United States?' he asked them. They said the United States is 'a bully, it elbows everybody and thinks only of itself.' People in the group couldn't believe it."

In 1997, I attended an academic conference in Morocco entitled "Globalization and the Arab World." Most of the Arab participants were French-educated Arabs from North Africa and France. (To be a French-educated Arab intellectual is the worst combination possible for understanding globalization. It is like being twice handicapped, since both of these cultures are intuitively hostile to the whole phenomenon.) I was asked to give a brief introductory talk on globalization, which I did. When I was done, a former Algerian Prime Minister, who was living in exile and attending the conference, asked to respond to my remarks. Speaking in French, he denounced everything I had to say. He argued that "this globalization you speak about is just another American conspiracy to keep the Arab world down, just like Zionism and imperialism."

I listened politely to his remarks, which went on in this vein at great length, and then I decided to respond in a deliberately provocative manner, in hopes of bursting through his fixed mind-set. I said roughly the following (with my profanities edited out): "Mr. Prime Minister, you spoke of globalization as just another American conspiracy to keep you down. Well, I have to tell you something—it's much worse than you think. Much worse. You see, you think we are back there in Washington thinking about you and plotting how to keep you down, and turning all the dials and pulling all the levers to do just that. I wish we were. God, I wish we were. Because I like you, and I would turn the dials the other way to let you up. But the truth is, *we aren't thinking about you at all!* Not for a second. We don't give a flying petunia about you. And it's not out of malice. It's because we're trapped under the same pressures as you are, and we're trying to keep one step ahead of the competition just like you are, and we're worried about what the bond market° is going to do next, just like you are. So I wish I could confirm for you that there is a conspiracy to keep you down, but I can't. . . . Now if you want to build an Islamic bridge to this globalization train, build an Islamic bridge. If you want to build a Maoist° bridge to this train, build a Maoist bridge. If you want to build a Jeffersonian° bridge to this train, build a Jeffersonian bridge. But promise me one thing—that you will build a bridge. Because this train will leave without you."

But for every North African who is reacting to Americanization- 15
globalization by shaking his fist at it, another is simply falling into line and trying to get the best out of it. While I was visiting Casablanca° in 1997, the guided missile frigate USS *Carr* pulled into the port for a call. The U.S. consulate in Casablanca held a reception for local officials and guests on the deck of the *Carr* and invited me to attend. While some young Moroccan girls elbowed each other to get pictures with the U.S. sailors in their dress uniforms and guests dined on chicken fingers and Budweiser on tap from a big steel keg, I fell into conversation with the governor of the Casablanca district. Sporting a tailored suit, the Moroccan official proudly explained to me in perfect French why he was sending his two children to the American school in Casablanca, and not to the French schools where he was educated.

"Two reasons," he offered. "First, in the world we are going into, if you don't speak English, you're illiterate. Second, the French system teaches you how to be an administrator. The American system teaches you how to survive on your own. That's what I want my kids to know."

Although French culture and education have been embedded in Morocco's major cities since 1912,° there are now three American schools there, and they are in such demand they each have waiting lists for the waiting list. In fact, there is a real cultural competition now between America and France for the hearts and minds of the new generation in traditionally French-dominated North and West Africa, and it is a competition that America is in-

bond market: Bonds are a kind of investment, like loans in certain ways; because the value of bonds is linked to interest rates, the term "bond market" is often used to refer to shifts in interest rates, which have a great influence on investment.

Maoist: associated with Mao Zedong, who ruled the People's Republic of China from 1949 until his death in 1976. He was responsible for the Cultural Revolution and other events that, in the eyes of many, have left China ill equipped to modernize. "Maoist" thought usually refers to Mao's particular development of earlier Marxist-Leninist socialism.

Jeffersonian: associated with Thomas Jefferson, Founding Father and third president of the United States. The reference here is to an American-style democracy.

Casablanca: the largest city in Morocco.

1912: the year that Morocco became a French protectorate; it gained its independence in 1956.

creasingly winning—without even trying. It's all demand-driven. "The French higher education system has not adapted to this revolutionary period," remarked Dominique Moisi, who used to teach at France's renowned ENA, the National School of Administration, and is one of his country's leading experts on international affairs. "The French system rewards people for their capacity to follow the path that is open to them. It does not encourage people to rebel or to develop their character. The mood out there is that if things are changing now in the 1990s, it is not because of France. America has become a mirror of our own doubts. We look at you and see what's missing."

Another popular reaction to Americanization-globalization today is the tendency of some countries to complain bitterly about America throwing its weight around, while they sit back and reap the fruits of American power. The Japanese will tell us privately that we are "dead right" in demanding that China live up to international copyright laws. And they will tell us that Japanese companies, such as Sony and Nintendo, suffer every bit as much from Chinese pirates as Disney and Microsoft. But Japan is not going to butt heads with Beijing on this issue. It will let Washington, the world's only superpower, do this while Japan holds America's coat and goes on doing as much business with China as it can—even taking advantage of whatever markets the United States loses in its confrontation with Beijing. At the end of the day, if the Americans are successful at winning new copyright concessions from China, Japan will enjoy this as well. How do you say "free rider" in Japanese?

Finally, there is a trend of countries looking for opportunities to complicate American diplomacy and check American power, both for traditional geopolitical reasons and for the sheer feel-good sport of it. Take Russia or France, for example: the more they are unable to achieve honor and dignity in the Fast World,° the more they look to achieve it in all the wrong places instead—by challenging American diplomacy in Bosnia, Kosovo, the UN or Iraq. In fact, the weaker Russia gets, the more it is tempted to magnify even its small differences with the United States and the more some Russians try to stick a finger in America's eye to feel better about themselves—to feel that somehow they are still America's equal.

Fast World: Friedman's characterization of the world in an era of globalization. As he notes in "A Manifesto for the Fast World": "If globalization were a sport, it would be the 100-yard dash, over and over and over. And no matter how many times you win, you have to race again the next day. And if you lose by just a hundredth of a second it can be as if you lost by an hour."

As Russian commentator Aleksei Pushkov once said to me: "The prevail- 20
ing attitude here now is that Russia should be a balancing force to correct situations where America gets infatuated with its own power." I would put it a little differently. The unspoken motto of Russia and many others today is: "If you can't have a good war anymore to change the subject from your domestic troubles, at least have a good argument with the Americans."

Being the world's sole superpower doesn't guarantee that America will get its way everywhere, but it does guarantee that America will be criticized everywhere. Again, think of the NBA. Gary Payton is the all-star guard for the Seattle SuperSonics. He's a great player, but he's not Michael Jordan and he makes up for some of his shortage in skills by talking trash to his opponents, particularly to Michael Jordan before he retired. To my mind, France and Russia today are the Gary Paytons of geopolitics—the biggest trash talkers in the world, always trying to make up for their weaknesses by giving everybody a lot of lip—especially Washington.

RESPOND

1. How does Thomas Friedman use his contrasting definitions of "imperialism" and "global arrogance" to help structure his argument? Writing in 1999, Friedman contends that people around the world are more concerned about our nation's global arrogance than its imperialism. How might America's military presence in Afghanistan and, even more so in Iraq subsequent to the events of September 11, 2001, complicate the feelings of citizens of other countries toward the United States, exacerbating already existing anti-Americanism?
2. Friedman might argue that the question "Why do they hate us?" isn't the question Americans should be asking because it misconstrues the situation. Instead, he argues that globalization, a force much larger than anything America controls, is in the driver's seat (for example, in paragraph 14). From this perspective, every country has to struggle to survive, and some countries are better equipped to do so than others. For Friedman, what do Americans need to understand about America in the world and why?
3. Friedman lists a range of possible responses countries can have to the United States and illustrates them. What possible responses does he discuss? Which countries illustrate each? Which example(s) do you find most memorable? Why? How can this rhetorical strategy be seen as constructing a definitional argument based on examples? (For a discussion of examples and definitional arguments, see Chapter 8.)
4. Friedman cites a conversation with Yuan Ming, one of China's leading experts on the United States, during which she explained why the Chinese government always speaks of "modernization" but never "globalization" (paragraph 10). What does this example reveal about the challenges of cross-cultural communication, even when everyone is speaking the same language?

5. Friedman likewise reports a conversation with Dominique Moisi, a leading French expert on international affairs, during which she commented that "America has become a mirror of our own doubts. We look at you and see what's missing" (paragraph 17). Moisi was speaking of France when she used "our," but her observation could be shared by thinkers in many other countries. What burden does such a situation place on the United States?
6. In the closing paragraph of this selection, Friedman writes, "Being the world's sole superpower doesn't guarantee that America will get its way everywhere, but it does guarantee that America will be criticized everywhere" (paragraph 21), a claim many who study globalization would fully concur with. What should America's response to this situation be? Should Americans use this situation as an excuse to remain ignorant of or ignore how other countries view them? Should this situation influence how they choose to deal with other countries and the citizens of other countries they encounter? How? **Write a proposal argument** in which you analyze this situation and offer suggestions about how Americans might or perhaps should deal with it.

▼ *Josef Joffe is publisher/editor of* Die Zeit, *a German news weekly; he's also known as a scholar, having been a fellow at the Hoover Institution on War, Revolution and Peace at Stanford University and having taught at various universities in the United States and Europe. Joffe is known for his research on American foreign policy, international security policy, America's relations with Europe, and the Middle East. He's the author or co-author of several books in German and English; his English titles include* The Limited Partnership: Europe, the United States, and the Burden of Alliance *(1987),* The Future of the Great Powers: Predictions *(1999), and* Überpower: The Imperial Temptation of America *(2006), from which this selection, "The Perils of Soft Power," is adapted. It first appeared in "The Way We Live Now," a weekly column in the* New York Times Sunday Magazine *in May 2006. As you read, consider how Joffe's status as a German might in some senses grant him the right to criticize his home country as he does; in other words, think about how who you are influences the ethos you're sometimes permitted to create for yourself.*

The Perils of Soft Power

JOSEF JOFFE

In recent years, a number of American thinkers, led by Joseph S. Nye Jr. of Harvard, have argued that the United States should rely more on what he calls its "soft power"—the contagious appeal of its ideas, its culture and its way of life—and so rely less on the "hard power" of its stealth bombers and aircraft carriers. There is one problem with this argument: soft power does not necessarily increase the world's love for America. It is still power, and it can still make enemies.

America's soft power isn't just pop and schlock; its cultural clout is both high and low. It is grunge and Google, Madonna and MoMA,° Hollywood and Harvard. If two-thirds of the movie marquees carry an American title in Europe (even in France), dominance is even greater when it comes to translated

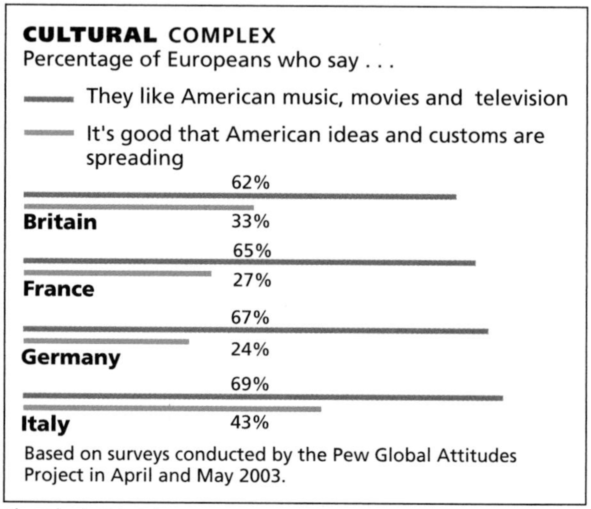

Alteration adds to the style of the second paragraph of Joffe's essay. What other tropes or schemes can you find in this piece? Use Chapter 12 to look for examples.

LINK TO P. 380

MoMA: Museum of Modern Art in New York City.

CULTURAL COMPLEX
Percentage of Europeans who say . . .

	They like American music, movies and television	It's good that American ideas and customs are spreading
Britain	62%	33%
France	65%	27%
Germany	67%	24%
Italy	69%	43%

Based on surveys conducted by the Pew Global Attitudes Project in April and May 2003.

Chart by L. Eckstein

books. The figure for Germany in 2003 was 419 versus 3,732; that is, for every German book translated into English, nine English-language books were translated into German. It used to be the other way around. A hundred years ago, Humboldt University in Berlin was the model for the rest of the world. Tokyo, Johns Hopkins, Stanford and the University of Chicago were founded in conscious imitation of the German university and its novel fusion of teaching and research. Today Europe's universities have lost their luster, and as they talk reform, they talk American. Indeed, America is one huge global "demonstration effect,°" as the sociologists call it. The Soviet Union's cultural presence in Prague, Budapest

demonstration effect: a term used by sociologists and political scientists to refer to the results that can be triggered when individuals or groups observe the consequences of the behavior of others. For example, some supporters of the War in Iraq claim that the creation of a democratic Iraq will spur citizens in other Middle Eastern countries to demand similar changes in their own countries. Should this occur, supporters of the war could claim that a demonstration effect had occurred.

and Warsaw vanished into thin air the moment the last Russian soldier departed. American culture, however, needs no gun to travel.

There may be little or no relationship between America's ubiquity and its actual influence. Hundreds of millions of people around the world wear, listen, eat, drink, watch and dance American, but they do not identify these accouterments of their daily lives with America. A Yankees cap is the epitome of things American, but it hardly signifies knowledge of, let alone affection for, the team from New York or America as such.

The same is true for American films, foods or songs. Of the 250 top-grossing movies around the world, only four are foreign-made: *The Full Monty* (U.K.), *Life Is Beautiful* (Italy) and *Spirited Away* and *Howl's Moving Castle* (Japan); the rest are American, including a number of co-productions. But these American products shape images, not sympathies, and there is little, if any, relationship between artifact° and affection.

5 If the relationship is not neutral, it is one of repulsion rather than attraction—the dark side of the "soft power" coin. The European student movement° of the late 1960's took its cue from the Berkeley free-speech movement° of 1964, the inspiration for all post-1964 Western student revolts. But it quickly turned anti-American; America was reviled while it was copied.

Now shift forward to the Cannes Film Festival of 2004, where hundreds of protesters denounced America's intervention in Iraq until the police dispersed them. The makers of the movie *Shrek 2* had placed large bags of green Shrek ears along the Croisette, the main drag along the beach. As the demonstrators scattered, many of them put on free Shrek ears. "They were attracted," noted an observer in this magazine, "by the ears' goofiness and sheer recognizability." And so the enormous pull of American imagery went hand in hand with the country's, or at least its government's, condemnation.

Between Vietnam and Iraq, America's cultural presence has expanded into ubiquity,° and so has the resentment of America's soft power. In some cases, like the French one, these feelings harden into governmental policy. And so the French have passed the Toubon law, which prohibits on pain of penalty the use of English words—make that D.J. into a disque-tourneur.° In 1993, the French coaxed the European Union into adding a "cultural exception" clause to its commercial treaties exempting cultural products, high or low, from normal free-trade rules. Other European nations impose informal quotas on American TV fare.

artifact: here, objects made by humans.

European student movement: a series of student demonstrations in various European countries beginning in the mid-1960s calling for "revolution" or drastic social change. Riots beginning in 1967 in Germany gave rise to the Baader-Meinhoff terrorist gang, glossed later in this selection. In France in 1968, in particular, these demonstrations nearly toppled the government.

Berkeley free-speech movement: a series of demonstrations, beginning in 1964 at Berkeley, calling for greater academic freedom and students' right to free speech. The movement is seen as the origin of protest movements on campuses across the United States during the 1960s.

ubiquity: the condition of being in all places at once.

disque-tourneur (French): "a record turner," that is, someone who "turns" or plays record albums.

Nor is America's high culture more easily accepted than its pop — at least not by the cultural elites. A fine example is how the art critics of two distinguished German newspapers, *Suddeutsche Zeitung* (leftish) and *Frankfurter Allgemeine Zeitung* (centrist), dealt with an exhibit of 200 pieces from the Museum of Modern Art in Berlin in 2004. More than a million visitors stood in line, many for up to nine hours, to view the objets° from across the Atlantic. Yet the fervor of the hoi polloi° mattered little to their betters, whose comments ran the gamut from contempt to conspiracy.

The opening shots were fired by the *Suddeutsche Zeitung* of Munich. Without having seen the collection, its critic aimed his volley straight against imperial America. Regurgitating a standard piece of European ressentiment,° the author insinuated that what America has in the way of culture is not haute,° and what is haute is not American. (Or as Adolf Hitler is said to have declared, "A single Beethoven symphony contains more culture than all that America has ever created.")

10 After World War II, the critic contended, America had wrested "artistic hegemony"° from Europe in two sleazy ways. One culprit was "a new abstract school of painting" — Abstract Expressionism° — "that had hyped itself into high heaven." The other was American mammon:° "Everything still available in old Europe was bought up." And this "stolen idea of modern art will now be presented in Berlin." Thus were pilferage and grand theft added to the oldest of indictments: America's cultural inferiority.

The critic of *Frankfurter Allgemeine* went one worse. If his colleague claimed that America's art was either hyped or heisted, the man from Frankfurt thundered that MoMA's Berlin show was a mendacious° ploy, indeed, an imperialist conspiracy. It was done by "concealment" and "censorship" in a game full of "marked cards," and its aim was not only to

---

objets (French): "objects," likely an allusion to the French expression *objets d'art,* or art objects.

hoi polloi: the masses, or the majority.

ressentiment (French): "resentment."

haute (French): "high," in the sense of "high culture," in contrast to popular culture; or "high fashion," in contrast to ready-to-wear or manufactured clothing.

hegemony: the dominance of one group over others, even without force, such that the dominated come to accept their domination as "natural" and "the way things must be," when in fact that may not be the case.

Abstract Expressionism: a movement in American painting in the middle of the twentieth century; the movement helped make New York City, rather than Paris, the center of the art world.

mammon: desire for riches or possessions, often seen as something evil. The word came into English from Aramaic: "No man can serve two masters: for either he will hate the one, and love the other; or else he will hold to the one, and despise the other. Ye cannot serve God and mammon" (Matthew 6:24, KJV).

mendacious: false or insincere, as if lying.

blank out Europe's greats but also to suppress their magnificent contribution to American art in the second half of the 20th century. This was an instance of the selective perception that suffuses anti-Americanism or any other "anti-ism," for the exhibit contained an impressive number of European works: Matisse,° Picasso,° Manet,° Rousseau,° Brancusi° and Mondrian,° plus assorted Expressionists° and Surrealists.°

That did not count. What about contemporary Germans like Beuys,° Baselitz° and Kiefer?° the critic huffed. But even here, MoMA had done its duty, cap-

---

Henri Matisse: twentieth-century French artist known for his draftsmanship and use of color. In his paintings, he often combined multiple patterns—on wallpaper, rugs, upholstery, and clothing—to great effect; late in life, because of illness he was no longer able to paint but devoted himself to creating a series of cut paper collages.

Pablo Picasso: twentieth-century Spanish painter and sculptor and one of the founders of Cubism. Many consider him the most important twentieth-century artist because of his insistence on pushing whatever boundaries existed at any given time and his openness to new influences.

Édouard Manet: nineteenth-century French painter whose works represent the shift from Realism to Impressionism in French art.

Henri Rousseau: a self-taught nineteenth- and early twentieth-century post-Impressionist French painter. Although he never left France, his best-known paintings are of jungles.

Constantin Brancusi: twentieth-century Romanian abstract sculptor. The 1923 *Bird in Space* series, which tries to capture the sensation of a bird flying, is among his best-known works.

Piet Mondrian: twentieth-century Dutch painter involved in the De Stijl movement. His geometric nonrepresentational canvases often consist of primary colors separated by heavy black lines.

Expressionists: those artists who distort representations of reality in some way to achieve an affective, or emotional, response. Although not a movement per se, Expressionism is associated with artists as varied as Edvard Munch, Wassily Kandinsky, and Franz Marc.

Surrealists: members of an artistic and intellectual movement that emerged in Europe in the 1920s; its goal was to liberate the unconscious and to create art that's "surreal," that is, more than real. It's associated with names like André Breton, René Magritte, Salvador Dalí, Alberto Giacometti, and Giorgio de Chirico.

Joseph Beuys: German Conceptual artist active in the third quarter of the twentieth century; he worked in sculpture, installations, video art, and performance art. Many consider him one of the most influential European artists of the century.

Georg Baselitz: German Expressionist painter active in the second half of the twentieth century.

Anselm Kiefer: late twentieth-century German painter who incorporates ash, clay, and straw into his paintings, many of which explore the Holocaust and German history.

Baader-Meinhoff terrorist gang: also known as the Red Army Faction, the most active left-wing terrorist group in Germany since World War II. The anarchist group came together in 1967 following the shooting by police of a student demonstrator, and its members continued to commit acts of terrorism, killing at least thirty-four, until the 1990s.

ping the progression with Gerhard Richter's "18 October 1977" cycle, which depicts dead members of the Baader-Meinhof terrorist gang.° That MoMA would display these German works enraged the feuilletoniste° from Frankfurt even more. That particular choice, he fumed, was the final proof of American perfidy.° The terrorist motif was insidiously selected to finger Europe as a "creepy" place, as a messenger of "bad news."

There is a moral in this tale of two critics: the curse of soft power. In the affairs of nations, too much hard power ends up breeding not submission but resistance. Likewise, great soft power does not bend hearts; it twists minds in resentment and rage. And the target of Europe's cultural guardians is not just America, the Great Seductress. It is also all those "little people," a million in all, many of whom showed up in the wee hours to snag an admissions ticket to MoMA's Berlin exhibit. By yielding to America-the-beguiling,° they committed cultural treason — and worse: they ignored the stern verdict of their own priesthood. So America's soft power is not only seductive but also subversive.

Hard power can be defanged by coalitions and alliances. But how do you balance against soft power? No confederation of European universities can dethrone Harvard and Stanford. Neither can all the subsidies fielded by European governments crack the hegemony of Hollywood. To breach the bastions of American soft power, the Europeans will first have to imitate, then improve on, the American model. Imitation and leapfrogging is the oldest game in the history of nations.

15 But competition has barely begun to drive the cultural contest. Europe, mourning the loss of its centuries-old supremacy, either resorts to insulation (by quotas and "cultural exception" clauses) or seeks solace in the disparagement of American culture as vulgar,° inauthentic or stolen. If we could consult Dr. Freud,° he would take a deep drag on his cigar and pontificate about inferiority feelings being compensated by hauteur° and denigration. ■

---

feuilletoniste (French): a writer of *feuilletons,* articles appearing in French newspapers in the section devoted to literature or criticism.

perfidy: treachery, untrustworthiness.

beguiling: involved in the action of deceiving or deluding.

vulgar: here, the earlier meaning of "common" or "unrefined" because it's "of the people," rather than the elite.

Dr. Freud: Sigmund Freud (1856–1939), Austrian doctor who was the founder of psychoanalysis, which sought to understand the influence of the unconscious on human actions.

A portrait of Sigmund Freud from the early twentieth century

hauteur (borrowed from French): "haughtiness," behaving as if one is of great importance.

RESPOND.

1. Josef Joffe's argument begins by offering definitions for soft power and hard power and critiquing soft power and its uses. How persuasive do you find his analysis of the situation he describes? Why?
2. Joffe has much to say about the cultural elite in European countries—those who care about "high culture" and especially the classical music, painting, and literature of their own countries' traditions—in contrast to those interested in popular culture, which appeals to the majority of the people, or folk culture, which represents traditional, often rural, crafts. Part of his argument is that the European cultural elite dislike American culture and its popularity for several reasons. What are they? Does Joffe believe that the majority of Europeans share the opinions of the cultural elite? Why or why not?
3. What proposal does Joffe make to Europeans, including the cultural elite, with respect to "the cultural contest" (paragraph 15)? How would Thomas Friedman, author of "Revolution Is U.S.," respond to such a proposal? Why? What's your response? Why?
4. As is very evident from the glosses for this selection, Joffe's style is laced with allusions to high culture and French words (though he's German). In fact, many of the English words we've glossed were borrowed into English from French or Latin, via French. How do you respond to Joffe's writing style? Is it effective, given his argument? His audience in the *New York Times Sunday Magazine?* Do you think you were among Joffe's intended or invoked readers? Why or why not? Would you expect writing styles—even if one is writing in English—to vary across cultures and countries? Why or why not?
5. Although Joffe doesn't mention the data included in the chart "**Cultural** Complex" and they were no doubt added by the editors of the *Times,* they support his argument. How? How does the photograph of a movie marquee in Paris add credibility to his claims?
6. Are you surprised to learn that the spread of American popular culture simultaneously encourages the spread of resentment of various kinds? **Write an essay** in which you analyze the causes of this resentment and the causes of your responses to this situation.

Is American Culture "American"?

RICHARD PELLS

Historian Richard Pells, who teaches at the University of Texas at Austin, specializes in twentieth-century cultural and intellectual history. He has taught in the Netherlands, Denmark, Germany, Austria, Finland, Brazil, Australia, and Indonesia. His books include Radical Visions and American Dreams: Culture and Social Thought in the Depression Years *(1973),* The Liberal Mind in a Conservative Age: American Intellectuals in the 1940s and 1950s *(1985), and* Not Like Us: How Europeans Have Loved, Hated, and Transformed American Culture since World War II *(1997). He's currently at work on a book entitled* From Modernism to the Movies: The Globalization of American Culture in the Twentieth Century, *a topic directly relevant to this selection. As you read, consider whether and how America might be different from other countries in terms of the culture it has created and shared with (and some would claim imposed on) the world.*

From the beginning of the 20th century, people abroad have been uncomfortable with the global impact of American culture. In 1901, the British writer William Stead published a book called, ominously, *The Americanization of the World*. The title captured a set of apprehensions—about the disappearance of national languages and traditions, and the obliteration of a country's unique "identity" under the weight of American habits and states of mind—that persists until today.

More recently, globalization has been the main enemy for academics, journalists, and political activists who loathe what they see as the trend toward cultural uniformity. Still, they usually regard global culture and American culture as synonymous. And they continue to insist that Hollywood, McDonald's, and Disneyland are eradicating regional and local eccentricities—disseminating images and subliminal messages so beguiling° as to drown out competing voices in other lands.

Despite those allegations, the cultural relationship between the United States and the rest of the world over the past 100 years has never been one-sided. On the contrary, the United States was, and continues to be, as much a consumer of foreign intellectual and artistic influences as it has been a shaper of the world's entertainment and tastes.

In fact, as a nation of immigrants from the 19th to the 21st century, the United States has been a recipient as much as an exporter of global culture. Indeed, the influence of immigrants on the United States explains why its culture has been so popular for so long in so many places. American culture has spread throughout the world because it has incorporated foreign styles and ideas. What Americans have done more brilliantly than their competitors overseas is repackage the cultural products we receive from abroad and then retransmit them to the rest of the planet. That is why a global mass culture has come to be identified, however simplistically, with the United States.

Americans, after all, did not invent fast food, amusement parks, or the 5
movies. Before the Big Mac, there were fish and chips. Before Disneyland, there was Copenhagen's Tivoli Gardens° (which Walt Disney used as a proto-

beguiling: involved in the action of deceiving or deluding.

Tivoli Gardens: an amusement park in Copenhagen, Denmark, dating from 1843; it contains the world's largest carousel, or merry-go-round.

Pells uses headings to organize his article into sections. What is the overall structure of his argument? Chapter 6 presents several organizational choices.

LINK TO P. 147

type for his first theme park in Anaheim, California, a model later re-exported to Tokyo and Paris). And in the first two decades of the 20th century, the two largest exporters of movies around the world were France and Italy.

THE INFLUENCE OF MODERNISM

So, the origins of today's international entertainment cannot be traced only to P. T. Barnum's circuses° or Buffalo Bill's Wild West Show.° The roots of the new global culture lie as well in the European modernist assault, in the early 20th century, on 19th-century literature, music, painting, and architecture—particularly in the modernist refusal to honor the traditional boundaries between high and low culture. Modernism° in the arts was improvisational, eclectic, and irreverent. Those traits have also been characteristic of American popular culture.

The artists of the early 20th century also challenged the notion that culture was a means of intellectual or moral improvement. They did so by emphasizing style and craftsmanship at the expense of philosophy, religion, or ideology. They deliberately called attention to language in their novels, to optics in their paintings, to the materials in and function of their architecture, to the structure of music instead of its melodies.

Although modernism was mainly a European affair, it inadvertently accelerated the growth of mass culture in the United States. Surrealism,° with

---

P.T. Barnum: nineteenth-century American showman whose "Grand Traveling Museum, Menagerie, Caravan, and Circus," which he billed as "The Greatest Show on Earth," later became Ringling Brothers and Barnum and Bailey Circus.

Buffalo Bill's Wild West: the name of a circus-like touring show created in 1883 by William F. Cody, better known as "Buffalo Bill." At times, the show included as many as 1,200 performers.

Modernism: a cultural movement that emerged in Europe in the period before World War I. Its supporters rejected the values of the nineteenth century as old-fashioned, preferring instead to look to the future. Modernism generally placed a high value on technology, whether the trains that began to appear in French painting early in the twentieth century (in contrast to classical scenes, religious scenes, or portraits of the wealthy in their homes) or architectural achievements like the Eiffel Tower, built in 1889, and notions like progress. It likewise focused on how people—of various classes—perceived daily life, as seen in the Impressionist paintings of Claude Monet, who sought to paint light on objects, or the stream-of-consciousness novels of Virginia Woolf.

Surrealism: an artistic and intellectual movement that emerged in Europe in the 1920s; its goal was to liberate the unconscious and to create art that's "surreal," that is, more than real. It's associated with names like André Breton, René Magritte, Salvador Dalí, Alberto Giacometti, and Giorgio de Chirico.

its dreamlike associations, easily lent itself to the wordplay and psychological symbolism of advertising, cartoons, and theme parks. Dadaism° ridiculed the snobbery of elite cultural institutions and reinforced an already-existing appetite (especially among the immigrant audiences in the United States) for "low-class," disreputable nickelodeons and vaudeville shows. Stravinsky's° experiments with unorthodox, atonal music validated the rhythmic innovations of American jazz.

Modernism provided the foundations for a genuinely new culture. But the new culture turned out to be neither modernist nor European. Instead, American artists transformed an avant-garde° project into a global phenomenon.

Pop Culture Potpourri

It is in popular culture that the reciprocal relationship between America and 10
the rest of the world can best be seen. There are many reasons for the ascendancy of American mass culture. Certainly, the ability of American-based media conglomerates to control the production and distribution of their products has been a major stimulus for the worldwide spread of American entertainment. But the power of American capitalism is not the only, or even the most important, explanation for the global popularity of America's movies and television shows. . . .

Another factor is the international complexion of the American audience. The heterogeneity of America's population—its regional, ethnic, religious, and racial diversity—forced the media, from the early years of the 20th century, to experiment with messages, images, and story lines that had a broad multicultural appeal. The Hollywood studios, mass-circulation magazines, and the television networks have had to learn how to speak to a variety of

---

Dadaism: a cultural and artistic movement that began in Switzerland around 1915. Critical of what it saw as the hold of bourgeois values on art generally, Dadaism, which claimed to be "anti-art," rejected traditional aesthetic values, often praising the absurd, the irrational, and the random. A number of influential European artists influenced by Dadaism came to New York fleeing World War II and brought some of its ideas with them.

Igor Stravinsky: twentieth-century Russian composer of classical music influenced by folk music and jazz as well as innovations in classical music itself. Much as contemporary vocal artists often sample others' work, Stravinsky quoted from others' compositions in his own work. His music for the 1913 ballet *Le Sacré du Printemps* (The Rite of Spring), staged by the Russian Ballet in Paris, and the ballet itself were so controversial that a riot broke out in the theater on opening night.

avant-garde (French): "vanguard"; often used to describe artists who are "ahead of the rest," in that their work breaks new ground because of its experimental nature.

groups and classes at home. This has given them the techniques to appeal to an equally diverse audience abroad.

One important way that the American media have succeeded in transcending internal social divisions, national borders, and language barriers is by mixing up cultural styles. American musicians and composers have followed the example of modernist artists like Picasso° and Braque° in drawing on elements from high and low culture. Aaron Copland,° George Gershwin,° and Leonard Bernstein° incorporated folk melodies, religious hymns, blues and gospel songs, and jazz into their symphonies, concertos, operas, and ballets. Indeed, an art form as quintessentially American as jazz evolved during the 20th century into an amalgam of African, Caribbean, Latin American, and modernist European music. This blending of forms in America's mass culture has enhanced its appeal to multiethnic domestic and international audiences by capturing their different experiences and tastes.

European Influences on Hollywood

Nowhere are foreign influences more unmistakable than in the American movie industry. For better or worse, Hollywood became, in the 20th century, the

---

Pablo Picasso: twentieth-century Spanish painter and sculptor and, with Georges Braque, founder of Cubism. Many consider him the most important twentieth-century artist because of his insistence on pushing whatever boundaries existed at any given time and his openness to new influences.

Georges Braque: twentieth-century French painter and sculptor and, with Pablo Picasso, founder of Cubism, which sought to reduce the objects painted to the flat planes that composed them and represent multiple perspectives on objects in a single painting. Braque also experimented with media, using collage, for example.

Aaron Copland: twentieth-century American composer who created music for films as well as the concert hall. His music is seen as central to creating an American style of classical music, taking influences from many popular American musical traditions as well as modern classical music. Much of his work has overtly American themes, including the ballets *Billy the Kid* (1938), *Rodeo* (1942), and *Appalachian Spring* (1944); film music, including *Our Town* (1940), *Music for the Movies* (1942), and *The Red Pony* (1948); orchestral works like *Fanfare for the Common Man* (1942) and *Lincoln Portrait* (1942); an opera, *The Tender Land* (1954); and song cycles, *Twelve Poems of Emily Dickinson* (1950) and *Old American Songs* (1952).

George Gershwin: twentieth-century American composer who wrote many classic jazz compositions, including songs that are still frequently covered by jazz singers, as well as classical music, including the symphonic piece *Rhapsody in Blue* (1924) and the opera *Porgy and Bess* (1935), and Broadway show tunes.

Leonard Bernstein: twentieth-century American composer, conductor, and pianist. In addition to orchestral, choral, chamber, and vocal works, he composed the musical *West Side Story* (1957) and wrote for film and theater, often bridging the gap between high and low cultural traditions.

cultural capital of the modern world. But it was never an exclusively American capital. Like past cultural centers—Florence, Paris, Vienna—Hollywood has functioned as an international community, built by immigrant entrepreneurs and drawing on the talents of actors, directors, writers, cinematographers, editors, composers, and costume and set designers from all over the world.

Moreover, during much of the 20th century, American moviemakers thought of themselves as acolytes, entranced by the superior works of foreign directors. From the 1940s to the mid-1960s, for example, Americans revered auteurs° like Ingmar Bergman,° Federico Fellini,° Michelangelo Antonioni,° François Truffaut,° Jean-Luc Godard,° Akira Kurosawa,° and Satyajit Ray.°

---

auteur (French): "author"; or a film director, one whose influential body of works stands as a unified whole in terms of themes and techniques.

Ingmar Bergman: Swedish film director and screenwriter who was among the most important influences on movie making in the world during the latter half of the twentieth century. His films are known for their emotional power on the viewer. His best-known films include *Smiles of a Summer Night* (1955), *The Seventh Seal* (1957), *Wild Strawberries* (1957), *The Virgin Spring* (1960), *Through a Glass Darkly* (1961), *Persona* (1966), *Cries and Whispers* (1973), *Scenes from a Marriage* (1973), *Face to Face* (1975), *Autumn Sonata* (1978), and *Fanny and Alexander* (1982); three of these films received the Academy Award for Best Foreign Language Film.

Federico Fellini: Italian film director considered one of the most important filmmakers of the twentieth century. Four of his films won the Academy Award for Best Foreign Film. Among his best-known movies are *La Strada* (1954), *Le Notti di Cabiria* (1957, Nights of Cabiria), *La Dolce Vita* (1960), *8 ½* (1963), *Giulietta degli Spiriti* (1965, Juliet of the Spririts), *Satyricon* (1969), *Amarcord* (1973), and *Il Casanova di Federico Fellini* (1976, Fellini's Casanova). His themes include desire, fantasy, and memory.

Michelangelo Antonioni: Italian film director active in the second half of the twentieth century whose work often focuses on themes of alienation. He's likely best known to Americans for his 1966 film *Blowup,* his first film in English, which was considered sexually explicit by then-current standards.

François Truffaut: French film director most active in the third quarter of the twentieth century. Associated with the New Wave, (see p. 1050), he was much influenced by Hollywood, Alfred Hitchcock in particular. His films, which often explore the dynamics of human relationships, include *The 400 Blows* (1959), *Jules and Jim* (1962), *Fahrenheit 451* (1966), and *Day for Night* (1973), which won the Academy Award for Best Foreign Language Film.

Jean-Luc Godard: French-Swiss film director active in the second half of the twentieth century; he's also associated with the New Wave, of which he's often considered the most radical member with respect to cinematic innovation. Committed to making films with political and philosophical messages, his films include *Breathless* (1959) and *My Life to Live* (1962).

Akira Kurosawa: Japanese filmmaker, producer, and screenwriter who worked in the second half of the twentieth century. His films include *Rashomon* (1950), *The Seven Samurai* (1954), and *Ran* (1985), an adaptation of *King Lear* set in medieval Japan. Techniques he used are now part of the vocabulary of filmmaking around the world.

Satyajit Ray: twentieth-century Indian film director

(*continued*)

15 Nevertheless, it is one of the paradoxes of the European and Asian cinema that its greatest success was in spawning American imitations. By the 1970s, the newest geniuses—Francis Ford Coppola,° Martin Scorsese,° Robert Altman,° Steven Spielberg,° Woody Allen°—were American. The Americans owed their improvisational methods and autobiographical preoccupations to Italian neo-Realism° and the French New Wave.° But the use of these techniques revolutionized the American cinema, making it even harder for

---

whose movies focused on various aspects of life in Bengal. Many consider his trilogy *Pather Panchali* (1955, Song of the Little Road), *Aparajito* (1957, The Unvanquished), and *Apur Sansar* (1959, The World of Apu) to be his masterpiece. In addition to influencing Bengali and Indian filmmakers more broadly, his stylistic innovations have influenced filmmakers around the world.

Francis Ford Coppola: American director and screenwriter active in the second half of the twentieth-century. He is likely best known for *Apocalypse Now* (1979), a film about the Vietnam War, and the *Godfather* trilogy (1972, 1974, and 1990).

Martin Scorsese: American director known for such films as *Taxi Driver* (1976), *The Last Temptation of Christ* (1988), *Goodfellas* (1990), *Gangs of New York* (2002), and *The Aviator* (2004). His films are much influenced by his working-class Italian American Catholic upbringing.

Robert Altman: American film director whose films include *The James Dean Story* (1957), *M*A*S*H* (1970), *Nashville* (1972), *3 Women* (1977), *Come Back to the Five and Dime, Jimmy Dean, Jimmy Dean* (1982), *Gosford Park* (2003), and *A Prairie Home Companion* (2006).

Steven Spielberg: Master of the Hollywood blockbuster but increasingly willing to tackle emotionally laden topics, Spielberg has directed *Jaws* (1975), *Close Encounters of the Third Kind* (1977), the *Raiders of the Lost Ark* series (1981, 1984, and 1989, with another in the works), *E.T.* (1982), the *Jurassic Park* films (1993 and 1997), *Amistad* (1997), *Schindler's List* (1998), and *Munich* (2005), among other films. He has been more successful financially than any other film director.

Woody Allen: American author, director, and actor who often writes, directs, and acts in his own movies. A native New Yorker, he sets many of his films there. His first screenplay was *What's New Pussycat?* (1965), while his directorial debut came in *What's Up, Tiger Lily?* (1965). Among the best known of his films are *Everything You Always Wanted to Know about Sex (But Were Afraid to Ask)* (1972), *Annie Hall* (1977), *Manhattan* (1979), *Stardust Memories* (1980), *The Purple Rose of Cairo* (1985), *Hannah and Her Sisters* (1986), *Crimes and Misdemeanors* (1989), and *Match Point* (2005).

Italian Neo-Realism: a movement in Italian cinema during the decade 1943–1952, marked by the films *Obsession* and *Umberto D.* A response to Italy's defeat in World War II, Neo-Realist films had plots about the working class or the poor with themes of desperation and poverty; even films that dealt with the wealthy showed the banality and emptiness of their lives. Films were often shot on location and used nonprofessional actors for some roles. Michelangelo Antonioni, glossed earlier, and Luchino Visconti are among the names associated with this movement.

French New Wave: (French, Nouvelle Vague), a group of French filmmakers in the late 1950s and the 1960s who rebelled against an earlier style of French filmmaking. Influenced by Italian Neo-Realism, they experimented with cinematic and narrative techniques.

(continued)

any other continent's film industry to match the worldwide popularity of American movies.

Still, American directors in every era have emulated foreign artists and filmmakers by paying close attention to the style and formal qualities of a movie, and to the need to tell a story visually. Early 20th-century European painters wanted viewers to recognize that they were looking at lines and color on a canvas rather than at a reproduction of the natural world. Similarly, many American films—from the multiple narrators in *Citizen Kane,*° to the split-screen portrait of how two lovers imagine their relationship in *Annie Hall,*° to the flashbacks and flash-forwards in *Pulp Fiction*°—deliberately remind the audience that it is watching a movie instead of a photographed version of reality. American filmmakers (not only in the movies but on MTV) have been willing to use the most sophisticated techniques of editing and camera work, much of it inspired by foreign directors, to create a modernist collage of images that captures the speed and seductiveness of life in the contemporary world.

Hollywood's addiction to modernist visual pyrotechnics is especially evident in the largely nonverbal style of many of its contemporary performers. After Marlon Brando's° revolutionary performance in *A Streetcar Named Desire,*° on stage in 1947 and in the 1951 screen version, the model of American acting became inarticulateness—a brooding introspection that one doesn't find in the glib and fast-talking heroes or heroines of the screwball comedies and gangster films of the 1930s.

Vivien Leigh and Marlon Brando in the 1951 film

Truffaut and Godard, glossed earlier, are among the best-known New Wave directors.

Citizen Kane: 1941 drama directed by Orson Welles; it was Welles's first feature film and is considered one of the most innovative movies ever made. Technical innovations included the use of light, dark, and shadow as well as jump cuts and deep focus.

Annie Hall: 1977 romantic comedy directed by Woody Allen. The film used several innovative cinematic techniques.

Pulp Fiction: 1994 film directed by Quentin Tarantino, which was seen as establishing independent moviemaking. The film is important in film history because of the cinematic techniques such as a fragmented storyline that it used.

Marlon Brando: Among the greatest American actors of the twentieth century, Brando used techniques associated with Method acting that influenced later actors, including James Dean, Paul Newman, Jack Nicholson, and Johnny Depp. Brando starred in *A Streetcar Named Desire* (1951), *On the Waterfront* (1954), *The Godfather* (1972), and *Last Tango in Paris* (1972).

A Streetcar Named Desire: 1951 movie based on Tennessee Williams's Pulitzer Prize–winning play of the same name. Although Vivien Leigh won an Academy Award for Best Actress as Blanche DuBois, an alcoholic, nymphomaniac southern belle, Marlon Brando's electrifying performance as Stan Kowalski, Blanche's brother-in-law, marked the beginning of a new period in acting in America.

Brando was trained in the Method, an acting technique originally developed in Stanislavsky's° Moscow Art Theater in pre-Revolutionary Russia. The Method encouraged actors to improvise, to summon up childhood memories and inner feelings, often at the expense of what a playwright or screenwriter intended. Thus, the emotional power of American acting—as exemplified by Brando and his successors—often lay more in what was not said, in the exploration of passions that could not be communicated in words.

The influence of the Method, not only in the United States but also abroad where it was reflected in the acting styles of Jean-Paul Belmondo° and Marcello Mastroianni,° is a classic example of how a foreign idea, originally meant for the stage, was adapted in postwar America to the movies, and then conveyed to the rest of the world as a paradigm for both cinematic and social behavior. More important, the Method actor's disregard for language, the reliance on physical mannerisms and even on silence in interpreting a role, has permitted global audiences—even those not well versed in English—to understand and appreciate what they are watching in American films.

Human Relationships

Finally, American culture has imitated not only the modernists' visual flam- 20
boyance, but also their tendency to be apolitical and anti-ideological. The refusal to browbeat an audience with a social message has accounted, more than any other factor, for the worldwide popularity of American entertainment. American movies, in particular, have customarily focused on human relationships and private feelings, not on the problems of a particular time and place. They tell tales about romance, intrigue, success, failure, moral conflicts, and survival. The most memorable movies of the 1930s (with the excep-

---

Konstantin Stanislavsky: Russian theater director who created "The System," which is associated in English with what's known as Method acting, whereby the focus is on understanding the inner life of the character being portrayed and her or his motivations, translating those into the performance. This way of concep- tualizing acting was widely adopted in the United States.

Jean-Paul Belmondo: French actor popular during the last forty years of the twentieth century after his role in *Breathless* (1960); he's associated with the French New Wave, a school of cinema glossed earlier.

Marcello Mastroianni: twentieth-century Italian actor who starred as the romantic lead in such films as *La Dolce Vita* (1960) and *8 ½* (1963) during the third quarter of the century.

tion of *The Grapes of Wrath*°) were comedies and musicals about mismatched people falling in love, not socially conscious films dealing with issues of poverty and unemployment. Similarly, the finest movies about World War II (like *Casablanca*°) or the Vietnam War (like *The Deer Hunter*°) linger in the mind long after those conflicts have ended because they explore their characters' most intimate emotions rather than dwelling on headline events.

Such intensely personal dilemmas are what people everywhere wrestle with. So Europeans, Asians, and Latin Americans flocked to *Titanic,*° as they once did to *Gone with the Wind,*° not because those films celebrated American values, but because people all over the world could see some part of their own lives reflected in the stories of love and loss.

America's mass culture has often been crude and intrusive, as its critics have always complained. But American culture has never felt all that foreign to foreigners. And, at its best, it has transformed what it received from others into a culture everyone, everywhere, could embrace—a culture that is both emotionally and, on occasion, artistically compelling for millions of people throughout the world.

So, despite the current resurgence of anti-Americanism—not only in the Middle East but in Europe and Latin America—it is important to recognize that America's movies, television shows, and theme parks have been less

---

The Grapes of Wrath: 1940 film based on John Steinbeck's 1939 dark novel of the same name. The film starred Henry Fonda. It traces the Joad family as they move from Oklahoma, where the Dust Bowl had made the survival of farmers impossible, to California, where life was little better.

Casablanca: 1942 World War II film that's set in Casablanca, Morocco, which was under the control of the French Vichy government, a puppet regime of the Nazi state. It stars Ingrid Bergman as Ilsa Lund and Humphrey Bogart as Rick Blaine. Winner of three Academy Awards, it's one of the best-loved films of all time.

The Deer Hunter: 1978 film that portrays the devastating consequences of the Vietnam War for an industrial town in Pennsylvania. The film won five Academy Awards; it starred Robert De Niro as Mike Vronsky, Christopher Walken as Nick Chevotarevich, and Meryl Streep as Linda Venkarvaatar.

Titanic: 1997 film and winner of eleven Academy Awards and the third-highest grossing film, once returns are adjusted for inflation. Its plot was inspired by the sinking of the *Titanic* on its maiden voyage in 1912 after striking an iceberg. It starred Leonardo DiCaprio as Jack Dawson and Kate Winslet as Rose DeWitt Bukater.

Gone with the Wind: 1939 film based on Margaret Mitchell's novel of the same name, starring Vivien Leigh as Scarlett O'Hara and Clark Gable as Rhett Butler. The winner of eight Academy Awards, it has grossed more than any other film, once returns are adjusted for inflation.

"imperialistic"° than cosmopolitan.° In the end, American mass culture has not transformed the world into a replica of the United States. Instead, America's dependence on foreign cultures has made the United States a replica of the world.

RESPOND •

1. What is Richard Pells's argument about the sources, nature, and uniqueness of American culture? What reasons and evidence does he give for his claims? Why, for him, is American culture cosmopolitan, rather than imperialistic?
2. Although the Web site we found this essay on carries the disclaimer, "The opinions expressed in this article do not necessarily reflect the views or policies of the U.S. government," why might the U.S. Department of State have chosen to include it there? What sort of argument does this essay make to the world about American culture? Why is the disclaimer significant? How is it American?
3. To the extent that Pells's claims are correct, especially his contention that "the influence of immigrants on the United States explains why its culture has been so popular for so long in so many places" (paragraph 4), what implications might his argument have for debates about immigration policies in the United States?
4. Pells relies heavily on examples, mentioning the names of painters, art movements, musicians, actors, directors, and films. In so doing, he includes examples from high culture and popular culture. We predict that few readers will have the background knowledge to appreciate and evaluate all of his examples, a fact Pells is surely aware of. What purposes do these examples serve, then? How do they help him turn real readers into invoked readers—perhaps the ultimate task of all writers?
5. **Write a rhetorical analysis** of Pells's discussion of American culture, which is, in many ways, a definitional argument. As you write, pay special attention to his treatment of the factors that make American or American-inspired cultural artifacts as appealing as they are around the world. (For information about rhetorical analyses, see Chapter 5.)

imperialistic: of a country, wishing to spread its own power or system of government in an imperial or despotic fashion.

cosmopolitan: not limited to any specific part of the world but having the features of many different parts; the word's Greek roots mean "citizen of the world," while the Latin suffix *-an* means "belonging to."

That's Entertainment? Hollywood's Contribution to Anti-Americanism Abroad

MICHAEL MEDVED

Michael Medved is a nationally syndicated radio talk-show host, an author, and a film critic. He's especially interested in popular culture and politics. His books include What Really Happened to the Class of '65 *(1976 with David Wallechinsky),* The Shadow Presidents: The Secret History of the Chief Executives and Their Top Aides *(1979),* Hollywood vs. America: Popular Culture and the War on Traditional Values *(1992),* Saving Childhood: Protecting Our Children from the National Assault on Innocence *(1999 with Diane Medved), and* Right Turns: From Liberal Activist to Conservative Champion in 35 Unconventional Lessons *(2005). "That's Entertainment? Hollywood's Contribution to Anti-Americanism Abroad" originally appeared in summer 2002 in* The National Interest, *a journal founded by Irving Kristol and devoted to international affairs. As you read, try to determine what sorts of movies Medved wishes Hollywood made, whether you'd like them, and whether you think they'd be as popular abroad as American movies currently are.*

"THINK AMERICA: WHY THE HOLE WORLD HATES YOU?"

This message, proudly proclaimed in a hand-lettered sign held aloft by a scowling, bearded Pakistani protestor during one of the angry demonstrations that followed September 11, continues to challenge the world's dominant power. In responding to such disturbing questions about the origins of anti-Americanism, glib commentators may cite the imperial reach of U.S. corporations, or Washington's support for Israel, or sheer envy for the freedom and prosperity of American life. But they must also contend with the profound impact of the lurid Hollywood visions that penetrate every society on earth. The vast majority of people in Pakistan or Peru, Poland or Papua New Guinea, may never visit the United States or ever meet an American face to face, but they inevitably encounter images of L.A. and New York in the movies, television programs, and popular songs exported everywhere by the American entertainment industry.

Those images inevitably exert a more powerful influence on overseas consumers than they do on the American domestic audience. If you live in Seattle or Cincinnati, you understand that the feverish media fantasies provided by a DMX music video or a *Dark Angel* TV episode do not represent everyday reality for you or your neighbors. If you live in Indonesia or Nigeria, however, you will have little or no first-hand experience to balance the negative impressions provided by American pop culture, with its intense emphasis on violence, sexual adventurism, and every inventive variety of anti-social behavior that the most overheated imagination could concoct. No wonder so many Islamic extremists (and so many others) look upon America as a cruel, Godless, vulgar society—a "Great Satan," indeed.

During violent anti-American riots in October 2001, mobs in Quetta, Pakistan, specifically targeted five movie theaters showing U.S. imports and offered their negative review of this cinematic fare by burning each of those theaters to the ground. "Look what they did!" wailed Chaudary Umedali amid the smoking ruins of his cinema. He said that a thousand rioters smashed the doors of his theater and threw firebombs inside because "they didn't like our showing American films." Ironically, the last movie he had offered his

Quetta customers was *Desperado*—a hyper-violent, R-rated 1995 shoot-em-up with Antonio Banderas° and Salma Hayek,° specifically designed by its Texas-born director Robert Rodriguez for export outside the United States (in this case, to worldwide Hispanic audiences).

Even the President of the United States worries publicly about the distorted view of this embattled nation that Hollywood conveys to the rest of the world. In his eloquent but uncelebrated address to students at Beijing's Tsinghua University on February 22, George W. Bush declared: "As America learns more about China, I am concerned that the Chinese people do not always see a clear picture of my country. This happens for many reasons, and some of them of our own making. Our movies and television shows often do not portray the values of the real America I know."

5 Ironically, the President assumed in his remarks that the Beijing students he addressed felt repulsed by the messages they received from American entertainment—despite abundant evidence that hundreds of millions of Chinese, and in particular the nation's most ambitious young people, enthusiastically embrace our pop culture. During the tragic Tiananmen Square° rebellion more than a decade ago, pro-democracy reformers not only seized on the Statue of Liberty as a symbol of their movement, but indulged their taste for the music and fashions identified everywhere as part of American youth culture. American conservatives may abhor the redoubtable Madonna and all her works, but the youthful activists who brought about the Velvet Revolution° in Prague reveled in her cultural contributions.

Antonio Banderas: likely the best Spanish actor working in America; he has appeared in *Women on the Verge of a Nervous Breakdown* (1988), *Philadelphia* (1993), *The Mask of Zorro* (1998), and *The Legend of Zorro* (2005) as well as the voiceover for Puss in Boots in *Shrek 2* (2004).

Salma Hayek: Mexican actress who has enjoyed great success in Hollywood movies as well as Mexican *telenovelas* and films. Her films include *Mi Vida Loca* (1993), *Desperado* (1995), *Frida* (2002), and *Once upon a Time in Mexico* (2003).

Tiananmen Square: large public plaza in Beijing where Chinese students, intellectuals, and labor activists demonstrated in 1989; the protests, which lasted for several weeks, were brutally crushed by the Chinese army. Official estimates claim 400–800 people were killed and 7,000–10,000 were wounded. Unofficial estimates put the number killed at about 2,000.

Velvet Revolution: a series of peaceful demonstrations during the last six weeks of 1989 in what was then Czechoslovakia that led to the bloodless overthrow of Communism there.

This contradiction highlights the major dispute over the worldwide influence of Hollywood entertainment. Do the spectacularly successful exports from the big show business conglomerates inspire hatred and resentment of the United States, or do they advance the inevitable, End-of-History triumph of American values? Does the near-universal popularity of national icons from Mickey Mouse to Michael Jackson represent the power of our ideals of free expression and free markets, or do the dark and decadent images we broadcast to the rest of the world hand a potent weapon to American-haters everywhere?

Telling It Like It Isn't

Of course, apologists° for the entertainment industry decry all attempts to blame Hollywood for anti-Americanism, insisting that American pop culture merely reports reality, accurately reflecting the promise and problems of the United States, and allowing the worldwide audience to respond as they may to the best and worst aspects of our society. During a forum on movie violence sponsored by a group of leading liberal activists, movie director Paul Verhoeven (author of such worthy ornaments to our civilization as *Robocop* and *Basic Instinct*) insisted: "Art is a reflection of the world. If the world is horrible, the reflection in the mirror is horrible." In other words, if people in developing countries feel disgusted by the Hollywood imagery so aggressively marketed in their homelands, then the problem cannot be pinned on the shapers of show business but rather arises from the authentic excesses of American life.

apologist: defender, champion, one who presents arguments in favor of a cause.

This argument runs counter to every statistical analysis of the past twenty years on the distorted imagery of American society purveyed by the entertainment industry. All serious evaluations of movie and television versions of American life suggest that the pop culture portrays a world that is far more violent, dangerous, sexually indulgent (and, of course, dramatic) than everyday American reality. George Gerbner, a leading analyst of media violence at the Annenberg School of Communications at the University of Pennsylvania, concluded after thirty years of research that characters on network television fall victim to acts of violence *at least fifty times more frequently* than citizens of the real America.

If anything, the disproportionate emphasis on violent behavior only intensifies with the export of American entertainment. For many years, so-called action movies have traveled more effectively than other genres, since explosions and car crashes do not require translation. This leads to the widespread assumption abroad that the United States, despite the dramatically declining crime rate of the last decade, remains a dangerous and insecure society. On a recent trip to England, I encountered sophisticated and thoughtful Londoners who refused to travel across the Atlantic because of their wildly exaggerated fear of American street crime—ignoring recent statistics showing unequivocally that muggings and assaults are now more common in London than in New York. On a similar note, a recent traveler in rural Indonesia met a ten-year-old boy who, discovering the American origins of the visitor, asked to see her gun. When she insisted that she didn't carry any firearms, the child refused to believe her: he knew that all Americans carried guns because he had seen them perpetually armed on TV and at the movies.

10 The misleading media treatment of sexuality has proven similarly unreliable in its oddly altered version of American life. Analysis by Robert and Linda Lichter at the Center for Media and Public Affairs in Washington, DC reveals that on television, depictions of sex outside of marriage are nine to fourteen times more common than dramatizations of marital sex. This odd emphasis on non-marital intercourse leads to the conclusion that the only sort of sexual expression frowned upon by Hollywood involves physical affection between husband and wife. In reality, all surveys of intimate behavior (including the famous, sweeping 1994 national study by the University of Chicago) suggest that among the more than two-thirds of American adults who are currently married, sex is not only more satisfying, but significantly more frequent, than it is among their single counterparts. One of pop culture's most celebrated representatives of the "swinging singles" lifestyle today, Kim Cattrall° of *Sex and the City,* recently published a best-selling book full of revealing confessions. In *Satisfaction: The Art of the Female Orgasm,* Cattrall describes a life dramatically different from the voracious and promiscuous escapades of the character she portrays on television. In the intimate arena, she felt frustrated and unfulfilled—as do nearly half of American females, she maintains—until the loving ministrations of her husband, Mark Levinson, finally enabled her to experience gratification and joy.

Kim Cattrall: Anglo-Canadian actress who played Samantha Jones in the HBO series *Sex and the City.* Mark Levinson was her third husband.

Even without Cattrall's revelations, anyone acquainted with actual unattached individuals could confirm that *Friends* and *Ally McBeal* hardly represent the common lot of American singles. On television and at the movies, the major challenge confronted by most unmarried characters is trying to decide among a superficially dazzling array of sexual alternatives. The entertainments in question may suggest that these explorations will prove less than wholly satisfying, but to most American viewers, single or married, they still look mightily intriguing. To most viewers in more traditional societies, by contrast, they look mightily decadent and disrespectful.

Consider, too, the emphasis on homosexuality in contemporary television and movies. In less than a year between 2001 and 2002, three major networks

(NBC, HBO, MTV) offered different, competing dramatizations of the murder of Matthew Shepard — the gay Wyoming college student beaten to death by two thugs. No other crime in memory — not even the murder of Nicole Brown Simpson° — has received comparable attention by major entertainment companies. The message to the world at large not only calls attention to homosexual alternatives in American life, but focuses on our brutal and criminal underclass.

The Gay and Lesbian Alliance Against Defamation (GLAAD) publishes an annual scorecard in which it celebrates the number of openly gay characters who appear regularly on national television series, and recently counted more than thirty. This trendy fascination with homosexuality (as illustrated by the worshipful attention given to Rosie O'Donnell's° hugely publicized "coming out") obviously overstates the incidence of out-of-the-closet gay identity; all scientific studies suggest that less than 3 percent of adults unequivocally see themselves as gay.

For purposes of perspective, it is useful to contrast the pop culture focus on gay orientation with media indifference to religious commitment. A handful of successful television shows such as *Touched by an Angel* and *Seventh Heaven* may invoke elements of conventional faith, if often in simplistic, childlike form, but ardent and mature believers remain rare on television and at the movies. The Gallup Poll and other surveys suggest that some 40 percent of Americans attend religious services on a weekly basis — more than four times the percentage who go to the movies in any given week. Church or synagogue attendance, however, hardly ever appears in Hollywood or television portrayals of contemporary American society, while mass media feature gay references far more frequently than religious ones. This is hardly an accurate representation of mainstream America, and the distortion plays directly into the hands of some of our most deadly enemies. In October 2001, an "official" press spokesman for Osama bin Laden's° al-Qaeda terror network summarized the struggle between Islamic fanatics and the United States as part of the eternal battle "between faith and atheism." Since the United States represents by far the most religiously committed, church-going nation in the Western world, this reference to the nation's godlessness gains credibility abroad only because of Hollywood's habitual denial or downplaying of the faith-based nature of our civilization.

15 The ugly media emphasis on the dysfunctional nature of our national life transcends examples of widely decried, tacky and exploitative entertainment, and pointedly includes the most prodigiously praised products of the popular culture. In recent years, some 1.5 billion people around the world watch at least part of Hollywood's annual Oscar extravaganza, and in April 2000 they

Nicole Brown Simpson: ex-wife of professional football player O. J. Simpson; she, along with her friend, Ronald Goldman, was found brutally murdered at her condominium in 1994. Simpson was charged with the murders. He was acquitted in the criminal trial but found liable for the deaths in a civil trial and ordered to pay the families of Brown and Goldman $33,500,000 in damages.

Rosie O'Donnell: American comedian, actress, and talk-show host. In 2002, she publicly acknowledged that she's a lesbian. An adoptive mother, she made the decision to make the announcement at a time when some adoption agencies were refusing to assist lesbian and gay male couples wishing to adopt.

Osama bin Laden: An Islamic fundamentalist and founder of Al Qaeda, an Islamic organization committed to establishing an Islamic government around the world, bin Laden is a member of an especially wealthy Saudi Arabian family. Bin Laden and Al Qaeda are considered responsible for the September 11, 2001, attacks as well as over a dozen bombings worldwide.

puerile: childlike, childish (the word always carries negative connotations).

pastiche: a creative technique that can take two very different forms: one is imitation, often playful or affectionate in nature, while the other is a juxtaposition of several kinds of styles in a kind of hodge-podge. One can understand the *Star Wars* movies as a pastiche in both senses: they represent an imitation of earlier sci-fi television or radio serials and a juxtaposition of influences from several of these as well as other sources.

harridan: like a scolding woman; a very formal way of saying "bitchy."

saw the Motion Picture Academy confer all of its most prestigious awards (Best Picture, Best Actor, Best Director, Best Screenplay) on a puerile° pastiche° called *American Beauty*. This embittered assault on suburban family life shows a frustrated father (Kevin Spacey) who achieves redemption only through quitting his job, lusting after a teenaged cheerleader, insulting his harridan° wife, compulsively exercising, and smoking marijuana. The only visibly loving and wholesome relationship in this surreal middle class nightmare flourishes between two clean-cut gay male neighbors. The very title, *American Beauty*, ironically invokes the name of an especially cherished flower to suggest that all is not, well, rosy with the American dream. If the entertainment establishment chooses to honor this cinematic effort above all others, then viewers in Kenya or Kuala Lumpur might understandably assume that it offers a mordantly accurate assessment of the emptiness and corruption of American society.

Explaining Media Masochism

This prominent example of overpraised artistic ambition suggests that the persistent problems in Hollywood's view of America go far beyond the normal pursuit of profit. While *American Beauty* director Sam Mendes and screenwriter Alan Ball might well aspire to critical acclaim, the movie's producers always understood that this tale of suburban dysfunction probably would not be a slam-dunk box office blockbuster (though the Oscars ensured that it did quite well commercially). The most common excuse for the ferocious focus on violence and bizarre behavior—the argument that the "market made me do it" and that public demands leave entertainment executives no choice—falls apart in the face of the most rudimentary analysis.

Every year, the American movie industry releases more than 300 films, with a recent average of 65 percent of those titles rated "R"—or adults only—by the Motion Picture Association of America. Conventional wisdom holds that the big studios emphasize such disturbing, edgy R-rated releases precisely because they perform best at the box office, but an abundance of recent studies proves that the public prefers feel-good, family fare. A recent comprehensive analysis confirms the conclusions on this point in my 1992 book, *Hollywood Vs. America*. Two economists, Arthur DeVany of the University of California at Irvine and W. David Walls of the University of Hong Kong, summarized their research: "This paper shows that Medved is right: there are too many R-rated movies in Hollywood's portfolio. . . . We show that, as Medved claimed, R-rated movies are dominated by G, PG, and PG-13 movies in all three dimensions of revenues, costs, return on production cost, and profits."

The other argument in defense of the entertainment emphasis on troubled aspects of American life involves the inherently dramatic nature of social dysfunction. According to the celebrated Tolstoyan° aphorism, "All happy families are the same; every unhappy family is unhappy in its own way." This logic suggests an inevitable tendency to highlight the same sort of unpleasant but gripping situations so memorably brought to life by eminent pre-cinematic screenwriters like Sophocles° and Shakespeare. Divorce and adultery offer more obvious entertainment value than marital bliss; criminality proves more instantly compelling than good citizenship. In an intensely competitive international marketplace, the dark—even deviant—obsessions of the present potentates of pop culture may seem to make a crude sort of sense.

This approach, however, ignores the striking lessons of Hollywood's own heritage and the wholesome basis on which our star-spangled entertainment industry came to conquer the world. In the 1920s and 1930s, the American movie business faced formidable competition from well-developed production centers in Italy, France, Germany, England, and even Russia. Obvious political disruptions (including the brutal intrusion of fascist and communist tyranny) helped U.S. corporations triumph over their European rivals, and drove many of the most talented individuals to seek refuge across the Atlantic. But even more than the historic circumstances that undermined America's competitors, Hollywood managed to dominate international markets because of a worldwide infatuation with the America it both exploited and promoted. Without question, iconic homegrown figures such as Jimmy Stewart,° Mae West,°

Leo Tolstoy: nineteenth-century novelist, author of *War and Peace* (1865–1869) and *Anna Karenina* (1875–1877), of which the quotation about families is the opening line.

Sophocles: Greek tragic playwright from the fifth century B.C.E. He is best known for the Theban plays, *Œdipus Rex, Œdipus at Colonus,* and *Antigone.*

James Stewart: American actor who worked on Broadway, in Hollywood, and on television in a range of genres. His films include *Mr. Smith Goes to Washington* (1939), *The Philadelphia Story* (1940), *It's a Wonderful Life* (1946), *Harvey* (1950), *Rear Window* (1954), *Vertigo* (1958), *How the West Was Won* (1962), and *The Magic of Lassie* (1978).

Mae West: American actress, screenwriter, and sex symbol famous for her bawdy comments delivered as double entendres, or statements that can be interpreted in two different ways, one of which is vulgar or off-color. Her films include *She Done Him Wrong* (1933), *I'm No Angel* (1933), *Klondike Annie* (1936), *My Little Chickadee* (1940), *The Heat's On* (1943), and *Myra Breckinridge* (1970).

Mae West in a scene from My Little Chickadee *in 1940*

Henry Fonda,° Shirley Temple,° Clark Gable,° Jimmy Cagney,° and John Wayne,° in addition to charismatic imports like Charlie Chaplin,° Cary Grant,° and Greta Garbo,° projected qualities on screen that came to seem quintessentially, irresistibly American. As film critic Richard Grenier aptly commented during a March 1992 symposium:

> Aside from the country's prominence, there seems to have been an irresistible magnetism about a whole assemblage of American attitudes—

Henry Fonda: American actor who was successful on the stage, in films, and on television. His films include *The Grapes of Wrath* (1940), *The Ox-Bow Incident* (1943), *12 Angry Men* (1957), and *On Golden Pond* (1981). He's the father of actors Peter Fonda and Jane Fonda.

Shirley Temple, later Shirley Temple Black: Likely the greatest child film actor of all time and the youngest person ever to receive an Academy Award, she was appointed as a diplomat in the 1970s. Her films continue to appeal to young children. Her films include *Stand Up and Cheer!* (1934), *The Little Colonel* (1935), *Rebecca of Sunnybrook Farm* (1938), *Since You Went Away* (1944), *The Bachelor and the Bobby-Soxer* (1947), and *Fort Apache* (1948).

Clark Gable: American actor who was the biggest star of the early talking movies. His films include *The Painted Desert* (1931), *It Happened One Night* (1934), *The Call of the Wild* (1935), *Mutiny on the Bounty* (1935), *Gone with the Wind* (1939), and *Soldier of Fortune* (1955).

Jimmy Cagney: American actor who worked in vaudeville, on Broadway, in Hollywood, and on television, often in the role of a tough guy. His films include *The Public Enemy* (1931), *Smart Money* (1931), *Hard to Handle* (1933), *Yankee Doodle Dandy* (1942), *White Heat* (1949), *The West Point Story* (1950), *What Price Glory?* (1952), *Mister Roberts* (1955), and *Ragtime* (1981).

John Wayne: American actor whose career spanned fifty years. His roles are often seen as embodying quintessential American heterosexual masculinity, the cowboy or the soldier. His films include *The Forward Pass* (1929), *Sagebrush Trail* (1933), *Westward Ho* (1935), *Stagecoach* (1939), *Red River* (1948), *Sands of Iwo Jima* (1949), *The Alamo* (1960), *North to Alaska* (1960), *How the West Was Won* (1962), *The Green Berets* (1968), and *True Grit* (1969).

Charlie Chaplin: British-born actor who became one of Hollywood's most famous actors (especially during the silent era) and directors. He's perhaps best known for his role as the Tramp.

Cary Grant: British-born actor who came to personify the notion of a suave and debonair gentleman in American films. He starred in such films as *Bringing Up Baby* (1938), *Gunga Din* (1939), *His Girl Friday* (1940), *The Philadelphia Story* (1940), *The Talk of the Town* (1942), *Arsenic and Old Lace* (1944), *To Catch a Thief* (1955), *North by Northwest* (1959), and *Charade* (1963). He was married four times; his sexuality continues to be debated by film scholars.

Greta Garbo: Swedish-born actress. Although she was very much the recluse, she became one of Hollywood's greatest and most glamorous stars in both silent movies and later "talkies." Her films include *The Temptress* (1926), *Flesh and the Devil* (1926), *Mata Hari* (1931), *Grand Hotel* (1932), *Anna Karenina* (1935), *Camille* (1936), and *Ninotchka* (1939). Her sexuality has been the subject of much discussion.

> optimism, hope, belief in progress, profound assumptions of human equality, informality—often more apparent to foreigners than to Americans themselves, that the outside world has found compelling. Over many decades these attitudes became so entrenched in world opinion as "American" that in recent times, when certain Hollywood films have taken on a distinctly negative tone, America has still retained its dramatic power, Hollywood, as it were, living on its spiritual capital.

In other words, in its so-called Golden Age, the entertainment industry 20
found a way to make heroism look riveting, even fashionable, and to make decency dramatic. In contrast to the present day, when most of the world watches American pop culture with the sort of guilty fascination we might lavish on a particularly bloody car crash, people in every corner of the globe once looked to our entertainment exports as a source of inspiration, even enlightenment. As the English producer David Puttnam revealed in an eloquent 1989 interview with Bill Moyers, he cherished the days of his childhood when

> the image that was being projected overseas was of a society of which I wanted to be a member. Now cut to twenty years later—the image that America began projecting in the 1970s, of a self-loathing, very violent society, antagonistic within itself—that patently isn't a society that any thinking person in the Third World° or Western Europe or Eastern Europe would wish to have anything to do with. America has for some years been exporting an extremely negative notion of itself.

The change came about in part because of a change in the people running the major studios and television networks. As movie historian Neal Gabler perceptively observed in his influential book, *An Empire of Their Own*, Hollywood's founding generation consisted almost entirely of East European immigrant Jews who craved American acceptance so powerfully that they used celluloid fantasies to express their ongoing adoration for their adopted country. Their successors, on the other hand, came from far more "respectable" backgrounds—in some cases as the privileged children and grandchildren of the founders themselves. In the 1960s and 1970s, they sought to establish their independence and artistic integrity by burnishing their countercultural° credentials. To illustrate the magnitude and speed of the change, the 1965 Academy Award for Best Picture went to the delightful and traditionally romantic musical, *The Sound of Music*. A mere four years later, that same coveted Oscar went to *Midnight Cowboy*—the gritty story of a down-and-out male hustler in New York City, and the only X-rated feature ever to win Best Picture.

Third World: term used to refer to countries that receive low scores on the United Nations Human Development Index, which seeks to measure a country's degree of development in several domains. Such countries are generally less technologically advanced or industrialized than other countries. Originally, the term referred to countries that weren't aligned with the West (the first world) or with the Soviet Bloc (the second world) during the Cold War, hence, the name "third world."

counterculture: a culture that's against ("counter to") the dominant or mainstream one; often used in reference to that part of American culture in the 1960s and 1970s that was associated with protests against the Vietnam War and America's role in Latin America, support for civil rights and feminism, and a rejection of the cultural and social values that had dominated the country since the end of World War II.

From the beginning and through to the present day, the leaders of the entertainment community have felt a powerful need to be taken seriously. The creators of the industry were born outsiders who earned that respect by expressing affection for America; the moguls of the later generations have been for the most part born insiders who earned their respect by expressing their alienation. This negativity naturally found an eager international audience during the Vietnam War era and in the waning years of the Cold War with the widespread dismissal of the "cowboy culture" of Reaganism. Even after the collapse of the Soviet Empire, anti-Americanism remained fashionable among taste-setting elites in much of the world, appealing with equal fervor to critics from the Right and the Left. In Afghanistan in the 1980s, for example, the beleaguered Russian Communists and the indefatigable *mujaheddin*° might agree on very little—but they both felt powerful contempt for the freewheeling and self-destructive mores° of American culture as promoted everywhere by the Hollywood entertainment machine.

Even as post–Cold War globalization enhanced the economic power and political influence of the United States, it helped the entertainment industry sustain its anti-American attitudes. With the removal of the Iron Curtain, vast new markets opened up for Hollywood entertainment, with developing economies in Asia and Latin America, too, providing hundreds of millions of additional customers. Between 1985 and 1990, inflation-adjusted revenues from overseas markets for U.S. feature films rose 124 percent at a time when domestic proceeds remained relatively flat. As a result, the portion of all movie income derived from foreign distribution rose from 30 percent in 1980 to more than 50 percent in 2000. James G. Robinson, influential chairman of Morgan Creek Productions, was right to have predicted to the *Los Angeles Times* in March 1992: "All of the real growth in the coming years will be overseas."

The fulfillment of his forecast has served to further detach today's producers from any sense of patriotic or parochial° identification, encouraging their pose as Americans who have nobly transcended their own Americanism. A current captain of the entertainment industry need not ask whether a putative project will "play in Peoria"°—so long as it plays in Paris, St. Petersburg, and Panama City. As I argued in the pages of *Hollywood Vs. America* in 1992: "While the populist products of Hollywood's Golden Age most certainly encouraged the world's love affair with America, today's nihilistic° and degrading attempts at entertainment may, in the long run, produce the opposite effect, helping to isolate this country as a symbol of diseased decadence."

mujaheddin: Arabic plural noun meaning "strugglers" but more often "those engaged in *jihad,* or holy war." The reference here is to the Afghani "freedom fighters" who were financed, armed, and trained by the Carter and Reagan administrations and other countries to defeat the Soviet presence in Afghanistan during the 1980s. Many mujaheddin later supported the Taliban and Al Qaeda.

mores (pronounced as *more-A's;* always used in the plural): a people's or society's customs and practices, particularly those linked to ethical or moral codes.

parochial: here, focusing on narrow loyalties or concerns rather than broader or more general ones.

play in Peoria: an allusion to the question, reputedly coined by Groucho Marx and used when creating a new show, "Will it play in Peoria?"—a town in Illinois that was often used as a test market for new products because it was seen as representing mainstream American values and culture.

nihilistic: rejecting prevailing beliefs, often seeking to overthrow all systems of order and government, by terrorism if necessary.

Why Do They Watch It?

With that isolation increasingly apparent after the unprecedented assault of 25
9/11, the question remains: Why does so much of the world still seem so single-mindedly obsessed with American entertainment, for all its chaotic and unrepresentative elements?

The most likely answer involves what might be descried as the "*National Enquirer*° appeal" of Hollywood's vision of life in the United States. While waiting in the supermarket checkout lines, we turn to the scandal-ridden tabloids not because of our admiration for the celebrities they expose, but because of our uncomfortable combination of envy and resentment toward them. The tabloids compel our attention because they allow us to feel superior to the rich and famous. For all their wealth and glamour and power, they cannot stay faithful to their spouses, avoid drug addiction, or cover up some other guilty secret. We may privately yearn to change places with some star of the moment, but the weekly revelations of the *National Enquirer* actually work best to reassure us that we are better off as we are.

National Enquirer: best known of the American supermarket tabloid newspapers featuring stories about celebrities. Although often criticized as sensationalist, it has been the source of some of the most detailed reporting of various scandals involving public figures. Its focus on the private lives of celebrities and public figures has, in the eyes of many, contributed to the role that these subjects play in contemporary American news coverage.

In much the same way, Hollywood's unpleasant images of America enable the rest of the world to temper inevitable envy with a sense of their own superiority. The United States may be rich in material terms (and movies and television systematically overstate that wealth), but the violence, cruelty, injustice, corruption, arrogance, and degeneracy so regularly included in depictions of American life allow viewers abroad to feel fortunate by comparison. Like the *Enquirer* approach to the private peccadilloes° of world-striding celebrities, you are supposed to feel fascinated by their profligate° squandering of opportunity and power.

peccadillo: a minor fault or offense; originally, "a little sin."

profligate: wildly wasteful or extravagant, often with the implication of being immorally so.

In this sense, American pop culture is not so much liberating as it is anarchic° and even nihilistic. Our entertainment offerings do not honor our freedom and liberty as political or cultural values so much as they undermine all restraints and guidelines, both the tyrannical and the traditional. As Dwight Macdonald wrote in his celebrated 1953 essay, "A Theory of Mass Culture": "Like 19th century capitalism, Mass Culture is a dynamic, revolutionary force, breaking down the old barriers of class, tradition, taste, and dissolving all cultural distinctions." Amplifying Macdonald's work, Edward Rothstein of the *New York Times* wrote in March 2002: "There is something inherently disruptive about popular culture. It undermines the elite values of aristocratic art, displaces the customs of folk culture, and opposes any limitation on art's audiences or subjects. It asserts egalitarian tastes, encourages dissent, and does not shun desire." It should come as no surprise, then, that even those who embrace the symbols and themes of American entertainment may feel little

anarchic: here, characterized by a lack or complete absence of authority, order, common purpose, or hierarchy.

gratitude toward a force that casts them loose from all traditional moorings, but offers no organized system of ideas or values by way of replacement.

Patriotism and Profit

In 1994, I participated in an international conference on the family in Warsaw and listened to the plaintive recollections of a troubled Polish priest. He recalled the days of the Cold War, "when we listened in basements to illegal radios to Radio Free Europe° so we could get a little bit of hope, a little bit of truth, from the magical land of America." After the collapse of Communism, however, America's message seemed dangerous and decadent rather than hopeful. "All of a sudden, we're struggling against drugs and free sex and AIDS and crime—and all of that seems to be an import from America. It's like the message of freedom that we heard before was only the freedom to destroy ourselves."

On a similar note, an American businessman of my acquaintance travel- 30
ing in Beirut struck up a conversation with the proprietor of a falafel stand who announced himself an enthusiastic supporter of the radical, pro-Iranian terrorist group, Hizballah. Ironically, his small business featured a faded poster showing a bare-chested, machine-gun toting Sylvester Stallone as Rambo. My friend asked about the place of honor provided to an American movie hero. "We all like Rambo," the Hizballah supporter unblushingly declared. "He is a fighter's fighter." But wouldn't that make the Lebanese dissident more favorably inclined toward the United States, the visitor inquired. "Not at all," was the response. "We will use Rambo's methods to destroy the evil America."

This love-hate relationship with Hollywood's twisted imagery also characterized the 19 conspirators who made such a notable attempt to "destroy evil America" with their September 11 atrocities. During their months and years in the United States, Mohammed Atta and his colleagues savored the popular culture—renting action videos and visiting bars, peep shows, lap dancing parlors, and Las Vegas—immersing themselves in Western degradation to stiffen their own hatred (and self-hatred?) of it.

In response to the terrorist attacks and to the onset of the war that followed, leaders of the Hollywood community expressed some dawning awareness that they may have indeed contributed to some of the hatred of America expressed around the world. Beyond a brief flurry of flag-waving, and the generous contributions to the 9/11 fund by leading celebrities from Julia Roberts° to Jim Carrey,° members of the entertainment elite showed a new willingness to cooperate with the defense establishment. Working through the Institute

Radio Free Europe: congressionally funded radio station that broadcast to countries under Soviet control from 1950 to 1975. From 1950 to 1971, the CIA oversaw the organization as part of its campaign to destabilize the Soviet Bloc; in 1971, Radio Free Europe was put under the control of a nonprofit corporation, the International Broadcasting Bureau, which also oversees the Voice of America. Radio Free Europe's mission was to "to promote democratic values and institutions by disseminating factual information and ideas." In 1975, Radio Free Europe was merged with another anti-communist radio program under a new name.

Julia Roberts: American actress whose films include *Pretty Woman* (1990), *Notting Hill* (1999), and *Erin Brockovich* (2000).

Jim Carrey: Canadian/American actor and comedian. His films include *Dumb and Dumber* (1994), *The Truman Show* (1998), and *Bruce Almighty* (2003).

for Creative Technologies at USC (originally created to enlist Hollywood talent for shaping virtual reality simulators for military training), creators of movies like *Die Hard, Fight Club,* and even *Being John Malkovich* brainstormed with Pentagon brass. Their purpose, according to several press reports, involved an attempt to concoct the next possible plot that might be launched against the United States, and then to devise strategies to counteract it.

In a sense, this unconventional program acknowledged the fact that violent, demented, anti-social, and conspiratorial thinking has come to characterize a major segment of the entertainment establishment. How else could an objective observer interpret the idea that the military turned first to millionaire screenwriters in order to understand the thought processes of mass-murdering terrorists?

Beyond this strange collaboration, top show business executives met with Karl Rove, political representative of President Bush, in an attempt to mobilize Hollywood creativity to serve America in the war against terror. The well-publicized "summit" discussed public service ads to discourage bigotry against Muslims in America and additional productions to give the United States a more benign image in the Islamic world. A handful of top directors, including William Friedkin (*The French Connection, The Exorcist,* and the excellent *Rules of Engagement*) expressed their willingness to drop all their pressing projects and enlist full-time to help the American war effort. In this determination, these pop culture patriots hoped to follow the example of the great Golden Age director Frank Capra, who served his country during World War II through the creation of the epic *Why We Fight*° series.

Why We Fight: a series of seven government-commissioned newsreels to educate American soldiers and the general public about the need for American intervention in World War II. They were a direct response to Leni Riefenstahl's propaganda films for the Nazi cause. (*Why We Fight* is generally considered propaganda as well. The word's earlier meaning was "a message seeking to influence opinion directly, instead of providing information in an impartial manner." Over time, *propaganda* has come to have a negative connotation because in many cases, propaganda not only seeks to persuade but also omits crucial information to such an extent that it can be labeled misleading. Such an assessment often depends on the perspective and value commitments of the reader or viewer.)

Alas, the White House and the Pentagon failed to take advantage of the 35
self-sacrificing spirit of the moment, or to pursue the entertainment industry opportunities that presented themselves after September 11. As the trauma of terrorist attacks gradually recedes into memory and the nation loses focus on its sense of patriotic purpose, the popular culture is displaying few long-term changes. Perhaps a more positive attitude toward the military may be the chief legacy of the deadly attacks—an attitude publicly celebrated so far in a handful of movies (*Behind Enemy Lines, Black Hawk Down, We Were Soldiers*), incidentally, all produced before the September 11 catastrophe. More significant changes, involving a new sense of responsibility for the images of America that pop culture transmits around the world, never even merited serious discussion in Hollywood. For the top entertainment conglomerates, this may count as an unseized opportunity for public service, but also a missed chance for corporate profit.

In his February speech in Beijing, President Bush held the Chinese students transfixed with a picture of America that departed dramatically from

How appealing and effective do you find Medved's article? Turn to Chapter 5 for some guidelines on examining arguments based on fact.

LINK TO P. 113

the visions they had received from made-in-USA music, movies, and television. "America is a nation guided by faith," the President declared. "Someone once called us 'a nation with the soul of a church.' This may interest you—95 percent of Americans say they believe in God, and I'm one of them." Bush went on to appeal to the family priorities that have characterized Chinese culture for more than 3,000 years: "Many of the values that guide our life in America are first shaped in our families, just as they are in your country. American moms and dads love their children and work hard and sacrifice for them because we believe life can always be better for the next generation. In our families, we find love and learn responsibility and character."

If Hollywood's leaders placed themselves within the context of the wider American family, they might also learn responsibility and character—and discover that a more wholesome, loving, and balanced portrayal of the nation they serve could enhance rather than undermine their worldwide popularity.

RESPOND •

1. Why, in the opinion of Michael Medved, do people from other countries misunderstand the United States and American culture? Why do they find American cinema appealing? Why do they dislike it?
2. Medved's essay is a proposal argument. What proposals is he making? To whom? How might Thomas Friedman, author of "Revolution Is U.S.," and Richard Pells, author of "Is American Culture 'American'?" evaluate them? Why? What's your evaluation of them?
3. Medved closes his argument by referring to values Americans learn in their families, noting "In our families, we find love and learn responsibility and character" (paragraph 36). Do you think he would number among American families the "loving and wholesome relationship . . . between two clean-cut gay male neighbors" mentioned in his discussion of *American Beauty* (paragraph 15)? Why or why not? Should he? Why or why not? Would you? Why or why not?
4. If all you knew about American women came from American movies or television programs that you had watched, what view would you have of them? How does such a view contrast with the view you in fact have? How does such a contrast support Medved's point? Might it help account for why American women who travel abroad often complain bitterly of being harassed?
5. In paragraph 17, Medved employs an interesting rhetorical strategy when he cites research to support claims he made in an earlier book he had written. How do you respond to such a strategy and Medved's

use of it? Does it contribute to his ethos in a positive or negative way? Why? Why might it be risky to cite research in support of one's own earlier claims?

6. Medved uses 1965, the year that *The Sound of Music* won the Academy Award for Best Picture, as marking the end of an era in American movies. Those critical of Medved's position in this essay might claim that he expresses a particular nostalgia for movies made before this period. Why does he find these earlier films appealing and compelling? Did the films of that era represent American life in its complexity, or did they choose to represent only part of it? Using the Internet, research American movies before 1965 and analyses of them. **Write an essay** in which you analyze the themes of the cinema of the earlier period, evaluating the view of America and American life that it presented.
7. The selections by Thomas Friedman ("Revolution Is U.S."), Josef Joffe ("The Perils of Soft Power"), Richard Pells ("Is American Culture 'American'?"), and Medved treat the subject of how America's widely exported popular culture is perceived abroad and why, as well as some of the potential consequences of that situation for America and Americans. **Write an essay** in which you present your evaluation of this situation, focusing on its causes and consequences. In addition to using the ideas found in these selections, you may wish to use the Internet to find opinions about this topic by writers from other countries and cultures. Discussions of American-made movies may be a productive place to start.

Making a Visual Argument: Exporting America

The images in this visual portfolio all provide evidence that all things American—or nearly all things—have been exported around the world. In some cases, translation seems simple: Snoopy speaks Mandarin, the Titanic is subtitled, and the golden arches are called Mài dāng láo *in an effort to string together Chinese characters that sound like "McDonald's." What's more difficult to gauge is the meanings people around the world attach to these goods and the way of life they represent. (To use an extreme example, several years ago the trendiest place to be in Tokyo on New Year's Eve was the Kentucky Fried Chicken restaurant, which took reservations!) As you study these images, consider how you might respond if artifacts of the culture of China or Russia or Egypt or India began to take over the American landscape.*

Les Stone, *Advertisement for Metropolitan Life Insurance in Taipei,* 1996

China Features/Corbis Sygma, *Poster for the film* Titanic *in Peking,* 1998

Tatiana Markow, *McDonald's in Shanghai,* 1996

Koren Ziv, *Nike in Jerusalem,* 2000

Haruyoshi Yamaguchi, ***Mother and Children at DisneySea, the Disney Theme Park in Japan,*** **2001**

John Van Hasselt, *Advertising Budweiser as Capitalism Comes to China* (no date)

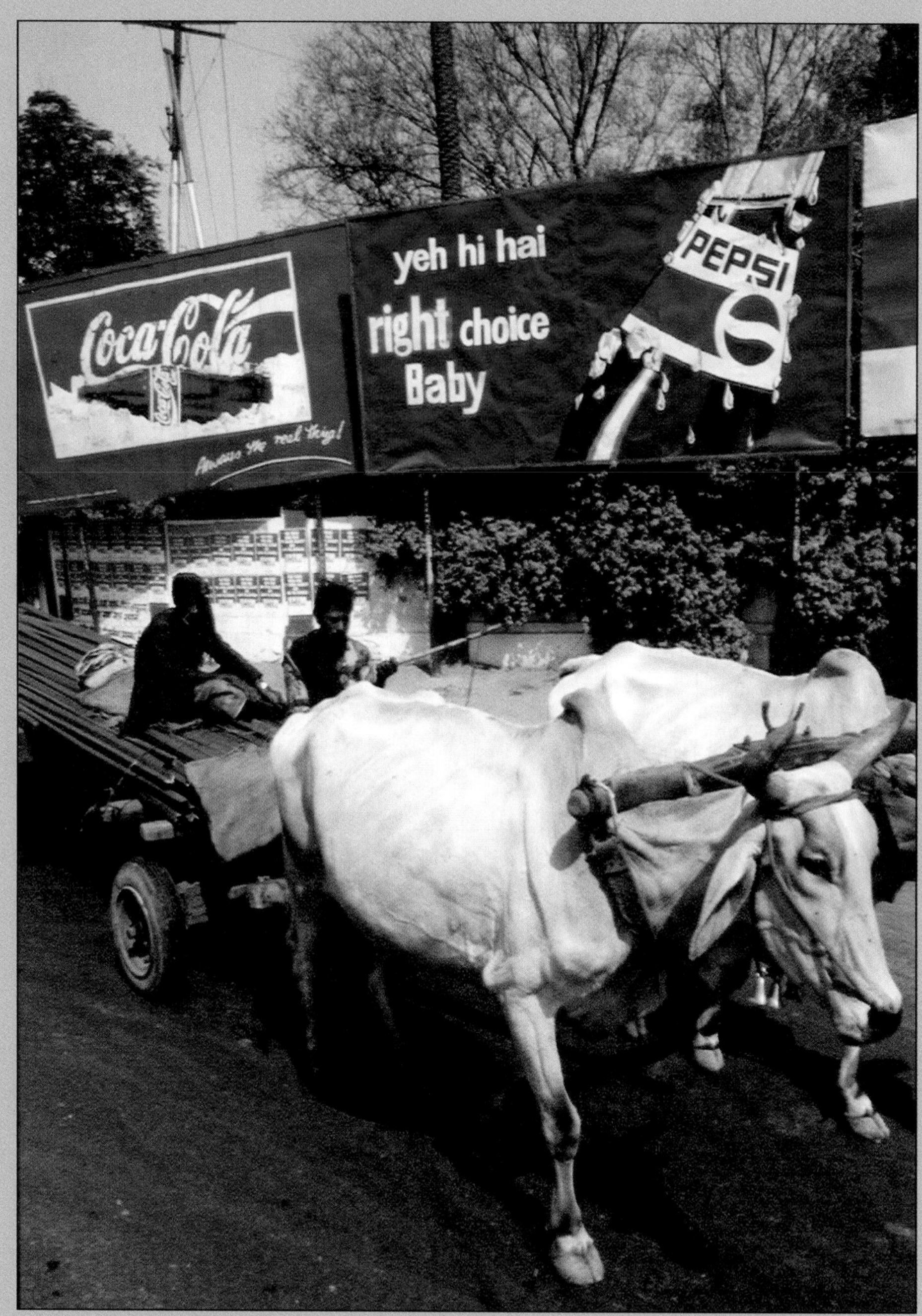

John Van Hasselt, *Selling Coke and Pepsi in India,* 1995

Mohsen Shandiz, *Coca-Cola and Marlboro in Iran,* 1993

RESPOND

1. Based on these photographs, which aspects of American culture have been exported around the world, especially to developing nations? Are these aspects of American culture you're proud of? Why or why not?
2. How might the authors whose work is represented in this chapter respond to these photos? Would they be encouraged, discouraged, or both? Why?
3. Can the artifacts represented here symbolize the spread of American democracy, of consumer capitalism, or both? Do they symbolize and give evidence of other things?
4. Do these photos give you insight into why people from some countries might resent American culture and, by extension, America? Why? Do they give you insight into the comments and examples made by the authors of selections included in this chapter? How?
5. Are these photographs merely documentation of reality somewhere around the globe, or do they make a stronger and more pointed argument? Can they? Does the argument they make depend on the context in which they're viewed? Why or why not?
6. Choose the photograph that you find the most interesting or appealing, and **write an essay** in which you analyze it as a visual argument. What argument is being made? How do the design features contribute to the photograph's effectiveness? (For a discussion of visual arguments, see Chapter 14.) Be sure to include a thorough description of the photo you're analyzing in your essay.

▼ *Diana Abu-Jaber is currently writer-in-residence and associate professor of English at Portland State University in Portland, Oregon. She's the author of two novels,* Arabian Jazz *(1993) and* Crescent *(2003), and a memoir,* The Language of Baklava *(2005). In her work, Abu-Jaber often explores questions of identity through the kinds of stories that people tell. "My Suspicious Last Name" was originally published in the* Washington Post, *although we read it in the* Austin American Statesman *in August 2005; it recounts a post-9/11 experience that's common for some and one that occurred to Abu-Jaber. As you read this essay, imagine how a foreigner coming to the United States from abroad might feel if she or he received a welcome like the one Abu-Jaber received on returning to the country of her birth.*

My Suspicious Last Name

DIANA ABU-JABER

My heart plummeted when the man at the immigration counter gestured to the back room. I'm an American born and raised, and this was Miami, where I live, but they weren't quite ready to let me in yet.

"Please wait in here, Ms. Abu-Jaber," the immigration officer said. My husband, with his very American last name, accompanied me. He was getting used to this. The same thing had happened recently in Canada when I'd flown to Montreal to speak at a book event. That time they held me for 45 minutes. Today we were returning from a literary festival in Jamaica, and I was startled that I was being sent "in back" once again.

The officer behind the counter called me up and said, "Miss, your name looks like the name of someone who's on our wanted list. We're going to have to check you out with Washington."

"How long will it take?"

5 "Hard to say . . . a few minutes," he said. After an hour, Washington still hadn't decided anything about me. "Isn't this computerized?" I asked at the counter. "Can't you just look me up?"

Just a few more minutes, they assured me. After an hour and a half, I pulled my cell phone out to call the friends I was supposed to meet that evening. An officer rushed over. "No phones!" he said. "For all we know you could be calling a terrorist cell and giving them information."

"I'm just a university professor," I said. My voice came out in a squeak. "Of course you are. And we take people like you out of here in leg irons every day." I put my phone away.

My husband and I were getting hungry and tired. Whole families had been brought into the waiting room, and the place was packed with hyper children, exhausted parents, even a flight attendant. Scanning the room, I realized that the place resembled a modern Ellis Island.° But when my father immigrated to this country from Jordan more than 45 years ago, he didn't have any trouble. "They let me right in," he said.

Forty-five years later, I was stuck on the border. Something in me snapped. "There isn't any legitimate reason that

Ellis Island: island in the New York Harbor that was home to the United States' main immigration port from 1892 to 1954. Some 12 million immigrants, most of European origin, were processed there.

you've sent me here—it's just because of my name! You just grab anyone named Abu-Jaber or Abdul-Rahman or Al-Hussain! Isn't that right?" The man smiled blankly. "I'm not at liberty to discuss this case," he said.

10 After two hours in detention, an officer approached. "You're free to go," he said. No explanations or apologies. For a moment, neither of us moved, we were still in shock. Then we leaped to our feet.

"Oh, one more thing." He handed me a paper with an address on it. "If you weren't happy with your treatment, you can write to this agency." "Will they respond?" I asked.

"I don't know—I don't know of anyone who's ever written to them before." Then he added, "By the way, this will probably keep happening each time you travel internationally."

"What can I do to keep it from happening again?"

He smiled the empty smile we'd seen all day. "Absolutely nothing."

15 After telling several friends about our ordeal, probably the most frequent advice I've heard in response is to change my name. Twenty years ago, my own graduate school writing professor advised me to write under a nom de plume° so that publishers wouldn't stick me in what he called "the ethnic ghetto"—a separate, secondary shelf in the bookstore. But a name is an integral part of anyone's personal and professional identity—just like the town you're born in and the place you're raised.

Like my father, I'll keep the name, but my airport experience has given me a whole new perspective on what diversity and tolerance are supposed to mean. We're told that these heightened security measures are intended to keep us safe. Instead, what seems to be happening is that we're kept in a state of heightened anxiety, trying desperately to separate "us" from "them," when in fact, there can be no separation. The world is a place of nuance, flux, hardship and complexity: We all live together in it. The real safety will come from learning how to live together better, not from trying to push others out.

I had no idea that being an American would ever be this hard.

nom de plume: pseudonym used by an author, a French expression meaning "pen name."

Why might this first-person narrative be more effective in communicating Abu-Jaber's argument than observation or secondhand evidence? Chapter 16 discusses different types of evidence and when each is most appropriate.

LINK TO P. 470

RESPOND •

1. What might Abu-Jaber mean by her closing comment, "I had no idea that being an American would ever be this hard"? Why, in your opinion, might she have written this essay? What might it teach you about America? About the situation of some Americans? About the situation of some who might try to come to America?
2. Part of the power of Abu-Jaber's narrative of her experience results from her descriptions of the responses she received from the various immigration officers she dealt with. How would you characterize their responses to her? How might they justify their behavior if asked to do so? What's your evaluation of the situation?
3. For Abu-Jaber, what sort of argument is one's name? What decisions has she faced and does she continue to face with respect to her name? Why?

4. One of the tropes, or kinds of figurative language, that Abu-Jaber uses in this essay is one that students of rhetoric, following Aristotle, often call "the greater and the less." If you assume that Abu-Jaber is "the greater," who (or what categories of people) might be "the less," and what are you, as a reader, supposed to take from Abu-Jaber's use of this trope?
5. Let's imagine that you take the role of Abu-Jaber and decide to write to the relevant government agency about what happened. You might choose, of course, to vent and rant. You might also wish to make proposals about such situations—how the agency might deal with them in a more humane way or how the agency might seek to change its policies or procedures would represent two possibilities. **Write the body of such a letter** along with a paragraph or two explaining your motivations for using the rhetorical strategies that you've chosen.

▼ *Yiyun Li came to America in 1996, having grown up in Beijing, China. Her first book,* A Thousand Years of Good Prayers *(2005), won that year's Frank O'Connor International Short Story Award, among the most prestigious short story prizes, as well as several other awards. She teaches in the MFA program in creative writing at Mills College in Oakland, California. This essay, "Passing Through," appeared in the "Lives" column on the last page of the* New York Times Magazine *in September 2005, the week that* A Thousand Years of Good Prayers *was published. As you read it, consider what it reminds us about why many people around the world cherish America.*

Passing Through

I was privileged to glimpse another world in a candy wrapper. But in the remote mountains of China, the view was different.

YIYUN LI

After the Tiananmen Square° massacre in 1989, the Chinese Ministry of Education began sending future students of Beijing University, a hotbed of pro-democratic protest, into the military for a year. So in 1991, at the age of 18, instead of beginning studies, I entered the army. There, along with 1,500 other students, I spent hours in formation training and even more time being lectured on the inevitable demise of capitalism and the victory of Communism.

The next spring, the army sent us on a march through Mount Dabie° to get to know our "revolutionary heritage"; the mountain area served, between the 1920's and 1930's, as a base for the Communist Party. Hard as the marching was, with no bath for weeks and blisters on our feet, the mountain air and spring fields made the trip into a kind of sightseeing adventure. That was why we entered a village one particular evening smiling and holding our hands up to the sky.

We were the only girls' company, and we marched behind a battalion of boys; the road across the village was shrouded by dust. A water buffalo, used to the tramping, grazed undisturbed. A villager saw us and called out, "Girl-soldiers this time." The villagers appeared in every door, bowls of rice in their hands, pointing at us with their chopsticks. "Girl-soldiers," young children echoed, running along beside us. We smiled, waved and kept walking. An old woman was pounding dried peppers in a huge stone mortar.° The breeze spread the fine powders, and many of us sneezed; the villagers laughed.

Tiananmen Square: large public plaza in Beijing where Chinese students, intellectuals, and labor activists demonstrated in 1989; the protests, which lasted for several weeks, were brutally crushed by the Chinese army. Official estimates claim 400–800 people were killed and 7,000–10,000 were wounded. Unofficial estimates put the number killed at about 2,000.

Mount Dabie: Dabie Shan, a major mountain range in central China.

mortar: a cup-shaped receptacle of some hard material like wood, brass, or stone in which foodstuffs or ingredients used in pharmacy are pounded with a pestle, or club-shaped instrument.

Outside the village, we were ordered to take a break. The dust settled, and hundreds of green-uniformed figures sat single-file by the winding road. The scene was soon disrupted by the village children, all holding out their hands, begging for candies and refusing to leave when they got their share. Even the most charitable soldiers among us started to shoo away the children like flies. When yet another girl stood in front of me, I said, "How many do you have to have before you go home?"

5 "Can I just have a candy wrapper?" she asked. I looked at the girl, too small for her passed-down blouse. "Do you collect candy wrappers?" I said. She nodded and showed me a dogeared book. Between the pages were mostly cheap wrappers, red and green with plain characters, *tang guo* (candy) printed on them diagonally.

"How old are you?" I asked. "Eight," she said. "Are you in school?" She shrugged. Not many girls in the mountains would receive much education. They worked hard for their parents until they were old enough to work for their husbands. Today, I suppose, if girls from this region manage to leave their villages, they might try to participate in the Chinese economic boom by becoming laborers in a factory.

I handed her a candy. She unfolded the wrapper and returned the chocolate to me. I watched her flatten it between her palms. It had snowy mountains and blue sky in the background, with a small white flower blooming in the center.

At her age, I collected candy wrappers, too, and I understood the joy of having a prize wrapper in your collection. I had one that was given to me by a Westerner in the late 1970's, when foreign faces were still rare in Beijing. It was made of cellophane with transparent gold and silver stripes, and if you looked through it, you would see a gilded° world, much fancier than our everyday, dull life.

By the time I turned 10, I was working at the goal set by my parents: to excel in schoolwork so that one day I could go to the United States. I attended a high school in Beijing that admitted only the students with the best scores in the entrance exam. Financed by UNESCO,° it had an indoor swimming pool, color TV's and a science building.

10 I did not change my life because of a candy wrapper, but it was the seed of a dream that came true: I left China for an American graduate school in 1996 and have lived here since.

The girl studied the wrapper before putting it in her book. I wondered if it would nourish thoughts about other worlds. But I did not tell her about my collection. I did not tell her that the candy had come all the way from Switzerland. I could not explain that the flower on the wrapper was edelweiss or that it was featured in a song in the American movie *The Sound of Music*—I had watched it many times at my school so that we could perform the songs when Western delegates visited.

Even at 18, despite my forced re-education in the army, I knew I was luckier than she was, a passer-by on this mountain and bound for a better destination. I knew that she would never see a blooming edelweiss anywhere but on a wrapper. ■

gilded: made golden.

UNESCO: United Nations Educational, Scientific, and Cultural Organization.

This essay takes the form of an argument from the heart because it makes an emotional appeal to the reader. Read Chapter 2 for more examples of the different kinds of arguments that fall into this category.

LINK TO P. 47

RESPOND •

1. In what sense is Yiyun Li "passing through"? What argument is she making about the power of dreams? About the importance of America in the dreams of many?
2. Why is the setting of this essay important? Why is it ironic that the events occurred in Communist China? How have recent changes in the Chinese economy—especially the growth of capitalism there and the meteoric rise of a small but powerful, very well-to-do professional class—made the setting even more ironic?
3. What was Li's initial encounter with the West? What role did her parents play in her dreams and achievements—a recurring theme among Chinese people wherever they might be around the globe?
4. What sort of ethos does Li create for herself in this essay?
5. This selection was written by an immigrant to the United States. The previous one was written by the daughter of an immigrant. What do these stories teach us about why some people from other countries consider America a place they want to come to? Do they give you insights into why some people might not want to come to America? How do these personal narratives complement the more analytic essays in this chapter?
6. This chapter began by posing three questions. One of them was frequently asked after September 11, 2001: "Why do they hate us?" A potentially useful reframing of this question is "Why do we as a country see ourselves so differently than those in other countries see us?" To these questions, we've added a third: "Why do they love us?" We've added this last one because we know that American culture and, in many ways, America remain popular around the world. Reflecting on what you have learned from the readings in this chapter, **write an essay** in which you seek to respond to at least one of these questions. If you choose to respond to only one, write in such a way that you demonstrate that you're aware of the other questions. In other words, essays that do nothing more than lavishly praise or bitterly damn America will fail to fulfill this assignment. Obviously, you'll be writing an essay that analyzes causes and evaluates them.

GLOSSARY

accidental condition in a definition, an element that helps to explain what's being defined but isn't essential to it. An accidental condition in defining a bird might be "ability to fly" because most, but not all, birds can fly. (See also *essential condition* and *sufficient condition*.)

***ad hominem* argument** a fallacy of argument in which a writer's claim is answered by irrelevant attacks on his or her character.

analogy an extended comparison between something unfamiliar and something more familiar for the purpose of illuminating or dramatizing the unfamiliar. An analogy might, say, compare nuclear fission (less familiar) to a pool player's opening break (more familiar).

anaphora a figure of speech involving repetition, particularly of the same word at the beginning of several clauses.

antithesis the use of parallel structures to call attention to contrasts or opposites, as in *Some like it hot; some like it cold.*

antonomasia use of a title, epithet, or description in place of a name, as in *Your Honor* for *Judge*.

argument (1) a spoken, written, or visual text that expresses a point of view; (2) the use of evidence and reason to discover some version of the truth, as distinct from *persuasion*, the attempt to change someone else's point of view.

artistic appeal support for an argument that a writer creates based on principles of reason and shared knowledge rather than on facts and evidence. (See also *inartistic appeal*.)

assumption a belief regarded as true, upon which other claims are based.

assumption, cultural a belief regarded as true or commonsensical within a particular culture, such as the belief in individual freedom in American culture.

audience the person or persons to whom an argument is directed.

authority the quality conveyed by a writer who is knowledgeable about his or her subject and confident in that knowledge.

background the information a writer provides to create the context for an argument.

backing in Toulmin argument, the evidence provided to support a *warrant*.

bandwagon appeal a fallacy of argument in which a course of action is recommended on the grounds that everyone else is following it.

begging the question a fallacy of argument in which a claim is based on the very grounds that are in doubt or dispute: *Rita can't be the bicycle thief; she's never stolen anything.*

causal argument an argument that seeks to explain the effect(s) of a cause, the cause(s) of an effect, or a causal chain in which A causes B, B causes C, C causes D, and so on.

ceremonial argument an argument that deals with current values and addresses questions of praise and blame. Also called *epideictic*, ceremonial arguments include eulogies and graduation speeches.

character, appeal based on a strategy in which a writer presents an authoritative or credible self-image to dispose an audience to accept a claim.

claim a statement that asserts a belief or truth. In arguments, most claims require supporting evidence. The claim is a key component in *Toulmin argument*.

connotation the suggestions or associations that surround most words and extend beyond their literal meaning, creating associational effects. *Slender* and *skinny* have similar meanings, for example, but carry different connotations, the former more positive than the latter.

context the entire situation in which a piece of writing takes place, including the writer's purpose(s) for writing; the intended audience; the time and place of writing; the institutional, social, personal, and other influences on the piece of writing; the material conditions of writing (whether it's, for instance, online or on paper, in handwriting or print); and the writer's attitude toward the subject and the audience.

conviction the belief that a claim or course of action is true or reasonable. In a proposal argument, a writer must move an audience beyond conviction to action.

credibility an impression of integrity, honesty, and trustworthiness conveyed by a writer in an argument.

criterion in evaluative arguments, the standard by which something is measured to determine its quality or value.

definition, argument of an argument in which the claim specifies that something does or doesn't meet the conditions or features set forth in a definition: *Pluto is not a major planet.*

deliberative argument an argument that deals with action to be taken in the future, focusing on matters of policy. Deliberative arguments include parliamentary debates and campaign platforms.

delivery the presentation of a spoken argument.

dogmatism a fallacy of argument in which a claim is supported on the grounds that it's the only conclusion acceptable within a given community.

either-or choice a fallacy of argument in which a complicated issue is misrepresented as offering only two possible alternatives, one of which is often made to seem vastly preferable to the other.

emotional appeal a strategy in which a writer tries to generate specific emotions (such as fear, envy, anger, or pity) in an audience to dispose it to accept a claim.

enthymeme in Toulmin argument, a statement that links a claim to a supporting reason: *The bank will fail* (claim) *because it has lost the support of its largest investors* (reason). In classical rhetoric, an enthymeme is a *syllogism* with one term understood but not stated: *Socrates is mortal because he is a human being.* (The understood term is: *All human beings are mortal.*)

epideictic argument see *ceremonial argument.*

equivocation a fallacy of argument in which a lie is given the appearance of truth, or in which the truth is misrepresented in deceptive language.

essential condition in a definition, an element that must be part of the definition but, by itself, isn't enough to define the term. An essential condition in defining a bird might be "winged": all birds have wings, yet wings alone don't define a bird since some insects and mammals also have wings. (See also *accidental condition* and *sufficient condition.*)

ethical appeal see *character, appeal based on*, and *ethos.*

ethnographic observation a form of field research involving close and extended observation of a group, event, or phenomenon; careful and detailed note-taking during the observation; analysis of the notes; and interpretation of that analysis.

ethos the self-image a writer creates to define a relationship with readers. In arguments, most writers try to establish an ethos that suggests authority and credibility.

evaluation, argument of an argument in which the claim specifies that something does or doesn't meet established criteria: *The Nikon F5 is the most sophisticated 35mm camera currently available.*

evidence material offered to support an argument. See *artistic appeal* and *inartistic appeal.*

example, definition by a definition that operates by identifying individual examples of what's being defined: *sports car—Corvette, Viper, Miata, Boxster.*

experimental evidence evidence gathered through experimentation; often evidence that can be quantified (for example, a survey of students before and after an election might yield statistical evidence about changes in their attitudes toward the candidates). Experimental evidence is frequently crucial to scientific arguments.

fact, argument of an argument in which the claim can be proved or disproved with specific evidence or testimony: *The winter of 1998 was the warmest on record for the United States.*

fallacy of argument a flaw in the structure of an argument that renders its conclusion invalid or suspect. See *ad hominem argument, bandwagon appeal, begging the question, dogmatism, either-or choice, equivocation, false authority, faulty analogy, faulty causality, hasty generalization, moral equivalence, non sequitur, scare tactic, sentimental appeal, slippery slope*, and *straw man.*

false authority a fallacy of argument in which a claim is based on the expertise of someone who lacks appropriate credentials.

faulty analogy a fallacy of argument in which a comparison between two objects or concepts is inaccurate or inconsequential.

faulty causality a fallacy of argument making the unwarranted assumption that because one event follows another, the first event causes the second. Also called *post hoc, ergo propter hoc*, faulty causality forms the basis of many superstitions.

firsthand evidence data—including surveys, observation, personal interviews, etc.—collected and personally examined by the writer. (See also *secondhand evidence.*)

fisking a term invented by Glenn Reynolds to describe a point-by-point refutation, usually online, of an argument that the writer finds inaccurate or rhetorically suspect.

flashpoint see *fallacy of argument.*

forensic argument an argument that deals with actions that have occurred in the past. Sometimes called judicial arguments, forensic arguments include legal cases involving judgments of guilt or innocence.

formal definition a definition that identifies something first by the general class to which it belongs *(genus)* and then by the characteristics that distinguish it from other members of that class *(species)*: *Baseball is a game* (genus) *played on a diamond by opposing teams of nine players who score runs by circling bases after striking a ball with a bat* (species).

genus in a definition, the general class to which an object or concept belongs: *baseball is a* sport; *green is a* color.

grounds in Toulmin argument, the evidence provided to support a claim or reason, or *enthymeme*.

hard evidence support for an argument using facts, statistics, testimony, or other evidence the writer finds.

hasty generalization a fallacy of argument in which an inference is drawn from insufficient data.

hyperbole use of overstatement for special effect.

hypothesis an expectation for the findings of one's research or the conclusion to one's argument. Hypotheses must be tested against evidence, opposing arguments, and so on.

immediate reason the cause that leads directly to an effect, such as an automobile accident that results in an injury to the driver. (See also *necessary reason* and *sufficient reason*.)

inartistic appeal support for an argument using facts, statistics, eyewitness testimony, or other evidence the writer finds. (See also *artistic appeal*.)

intended readers the actual, real-life people whom a writer consciously wants to address in a piece of writing.

invention the process of finding and creating arguments to support a claim.

inverted word order moving grammatical elements of a sentence out of their usual order (subject-verb-object/complement) for special effect, as in *Tired I was; sleepy I was not*.

invitational argument a term used by Sonja Foss to describe arguments that are aimed not at vanquishing an opponent but at inviting others to collaborate in exploring mutually satisfying ways to solve problems.

invoked readers the readers directly addressed or implied in a text, which may include some that the writer didn't consciously intend to reach. An argument that refers to *those who have experienced a major trauma*, for example, invokes all readers who have undergone this experience.

irony use of language that suggests a meaning in contrast to the literal meaning of the words.

line of argument a strategy or approach used in an argument. Argumentative strategies include appeals to the heart (emotional appeals), to character (ethical appeals), and to facts and reason (logical appeals).

logical appeal a strategy in which a writer uses facts, evidence, and reason to make audience members accept a claim.

metaphor a figure of speech that makes a comparison, as in *The ship was a beacon of hope*.

moral equivalence a fallacy of argument in which no distinction is made between serious issues, problems, or failings and much less important ones.

necessary reason a cause that must be present for an effect to occur; for example, infection with a particular virus is a necessary reason for the development of AIDS. (See also *immediate reason* and *sufficient reason.*)

non sequitur a fallacy of argument in which claims, reasons, or warrants fail to connect logically; one point doesn't follow from another. *If you're really my friend, you'll lend me five hundred dollars.*

operational definition a definition that identifies an object by what it does or by the conditions that create it: *A line is the shortest distance between two points.*

parallelism use of similar grammatical structures or forms for pleasing effect: *in the classroom, on the playground, and at the mall.*

parody a form of humor in which a writer transforms something familiar into a different form to make a comic point.

pathos, appeal to see *emotional appeal.*

persuasion the act of seeking to change someone else's point of view.

precedents actions or decisions in the past that have established a pattern or model for subsequent actions. Precedents are particularly important in legal cases.

premise a statement or position regarded as true and upon which other claims are based.

propaganda an argument advancing a point of view without regard to reason, fairness, or truth.

proposal argument an argument in which a claim is made in favor of or opposing a specific course of action: *Sport utility vehicles should have to meet the same fuel economy standards as passenger cars.*

purpose the goal of an argument. Purposes include entertaining, informing, convincing, exploring, and deciding, among others.

qualifiers words or phrases that limit the scope of a claim: *usually*; *in a few cases*; *under these circumstances.*

qualitative argument an argument of evaluation that relies on nonnumerical criteria supported by reason, tradition, precedent, or logic.

quantitative argument an argument of evaluation that relies on criteria that can be measured, counted, or demonstrated objectively.

reason in writing, a statement that expands a claim by offering evidence to support it. The reason may be a statement of fact or another claim. In *Toulmin argument*, a *reason* is attached to a *claim* by a *warrant*, a statement that establishes the logical connection between claim and supporting reason.

rebuttal an answer that challenges or refutes a specific claim or charge. Rebuttals may also be offered by writers who anticipate objections to the claims or evidence they offer.

rebuttal, conditions of in Toulmin argument, potential objections to an argument. Writers need to anticipate such conditions in shaping their arguments.

reversed structures a figure of speech that involves the inversion of clauses: *What is good in your writing is not original; what is original is not good.*

rhetoric the art of persuasion. Western rhetoric originated in ancient Greece as a discipline to prepare citizens for arguing cases in court.

rhetorical analysis an examination of how well the components of an argument work together to persuade or move an audience.

rhetorical questions questions posed to raise an issue or create an effect rather than to get a response: *You may well wonder, "What's in a name?"*

Rogerian argument an approach to argumentation that's based on the principle, articulated by psychotherapist Carl Rogers, that audiences respond best when they don't feel threatened.

Rogerian argument stresses trust and urges those who disagree to find common ground.

satire a form of humor in which a writer uses wit to expose—and possibly correct—human failings.

scare tactic a fallacy of argument presenting an issue in terms of exaggerated threats or dangers.

scheme a figure of speech that involves a special arrangement of words, such as inversion.

secondhand evidence any information taken from outside sources, including library research and online sources. (See also *firsthand evidence*.)

sentimental appeal a fallacy of argument in which an appeal is based on excessive emotion.

simile a comparison that uses *like* or *as*: *My love is like a red, red rose* or *I wandered lonely as a cloud*.

slippery slope a fallacy of argument exaggerating the possibility that a relatively inconsequential action or choice today will have serious adverse consequences in the future.

species in a definition, the particular features that distinguish one member of a *genus* from another: *Baseball is a sport* (genus) *played on a diamond by teams of nine players* (species).

spin a kind of political advocacy that makes any fact or event, however unfavorable, serve a political purpose.

stance the writer's attitude toward the topic and the audience.

stasis theory in classical rhetoric, a method for coming up with appropriate arguments by determining the nature of a given situation: *a question of fact*; *of definition*; *of quality*; or *of policy*.

straw man a fallacy of argument in which an opponent's position is misrepresented as being more extreme than it actually is, so that it's easier to refute.

sufficient condition in a definition, an element or set of elements adequate to define a term. A sufficient condition in defining God, for example, might be "supreme being" or "first cause." No other conditions are necessary, though many might be made. (See also *accidental condition* and *essential condition*.)

sufficient reason a cause that alone is enough to produce a particular effect; for example, a particular level of smoke in the air will set off a smoke alarm. (See also *immediate reason* and *necessary reason*.)

syllogism in formal logic, a structure of deductive logic in which correctly formed major and minor premises lead to a necessary conclusion:

Major premise	All human beings are mortal.
Minor premise	Socrates is a human being.
Conclusion	Socrates is mortal.

testimony a personal experience or observation used to support an argument.

thesis a sentence that succinctly states a writer's main point.

Toulmin argument a method of informal logic first described by Stephen Toulmin in *The Uses of Argument* (1958). Toulmin argument describes the key components of an argument as the *claim*, *reason*, *warrant*, *backing*, and *grounds*.

trope a figure of speech that involves a change in the usual meaning or signification of words, such as *metaphor*, *simile*, and *analogy*.

understatement a figure of speech that makes a weaker statement than a situation seems to call for. It can lead to powerful or to humorous effects.

values, appeal to a strategy in which a writer invokes shared principles and traditions of a society as a reason for accepting a claim.

warrant in *Toulmin argument*, the statement (expressed or implied) that establishes the logical connection between a claim and its supporting reason.

Claim	Don't eat that mushroom;
Reason	it's poisonous.
Warrant	What is poisonous should not be eaten.

ACKNOWLEDGMENTS

Chapter-Opening Art

Part 1 (left to right): Courtesy <www.adbusters.org>; Copyright © Brian Snyder/Reuters/Corbis; Copyright © Kelly Owen/ZUMA/Corbis; Copyright © Nicholas Kristof; Copyright © Warner Brothers Entertainment, Inc.

Part 2 (left to right): (foreground) Courtesy General Electric; (background) John Ruszkiewicz; Copyright © Bettmann/Corbis; Copyright © Robin Raffer.

Part 3 (left to right): Lionel Cironneau/AP/Wide World Photos; Art Resource, NY; The Granger Collection, Office of the Counsel to the President at the White House, D.C.; Warner Brothers/Photofest; Mick Roessler/Index Stock Imagery; Courtesy McDonald's.

Part 4 (left to right): Jay Berkowitz-L.A.W.A.; Juan Castillo/AFP/Getty Images; Courtesy <www.adbusters.org>; Bill Aron/PhotoEdit, Inc.; Courtesy World Wildlife Fund.

Part 5 (left to right): Scott Halleran/Getty Images; (foreground) Dita Alangkora/AP/Wide World Photos; (background) Copyright © Clementine Hope/nb illustration; Jacob Silberberg/Getty Images; Copyright © Les Stone/Sygma/Corbis; Courtesy Western Washington University.

Texts

Diana Abu-Jaber. "My Suspicious Last Name" from *The Washington Post.* Reprinted with the permission of the author.

Marjorie Agosín. "Always Living in Spanish" translated by Celeste Kostopulos-Cooperman, from *Poets and Writers* 27.2 (1999). "English," translated by Monica Bruno. Both reprinted with the permission of the author.

Ann Marie B. Bahr. "The Right to Tell the Truth" from *The Chronicle Review* 51, Issue 35. Reprinted with the permission of the author.

Dave Barry. Excerpt from "Introduction" and cover photo from *Dave Barry Hits below the Beltway.* Copyright © 2000 by Dave Barry. Reprinted with the permission of Ballantine Books, a division of Random House, Inc. Excerpt from "Step No. 1: Bang Head against Wall" from *The Miami Herald* (June 30, 2002). Copyright © 2002 by Dave Barry and *The Miami Herald.* Excerpt from "How to Vote in 1 Easy Step" from *The Miami Herald* (September 13, 2002). Copyright © 2002 by Dave Barry and *The Miami Herald.* Excerpt from "The Hidden Life of Dogs" from *The Miami Herald* (December 12, 1993). Copyright © 1993 by Dave Barry and *The Miami Herald.* Reprinted with the permission of the author.

Anne E. Becker. "Abstract," "Discussion," "Conclusions," and selected "References" from "Television, Disordered Eating, and Young Women in Fiji: Negotiating Body Image and Identity During Rapid Social Change" from *Culture, Medicine and Psychiatry* 28 (2004). Copyright © 2004 by Springer Science and Business Media, Inc. Reprinted with kind permission from Springer Science and Business Media.

Richard Bernstein. "The Days After: The View from Abroad" from *The New York Times*, September 4, 2005. Includes photograph by Tyler Hicks. Copyright © 2005 by The New York Times Company. Reprinted with permission.

Derek Bok. "Protecting Freedom of Expression at Harvard" from *The Boston Globe* (May 25, 1991). Reprinted with the permission of the author.

David Bositis. "Skin-Deep: What Polls of Minorities Miss." Originally published in *The Los Angeles Times*, March 13, 2005. Reprinted with the permission of the author.

David Brower. Excerpts from "Let the River Run through It" from *Sierra Magazine* (March/April 1997). Copyright © 1997 by David Brower. Reprinted with the permission of the Estate of David Brower.

Michelle Bryant. "Selling Safe Sex in Public Schools" from *Life & Letters: A Publication of the College of Liberal Arts of the University of Texas at Austin* 4, Issue 2, Fall 2005. Reprinted with the permission of *Life & Letters*.

Elisabeth Bumiller. "Preaching to the Choir? Not This Time" from *The New York Times*, May 23, 2005. Copyright © 2005 by The New York Times Company. Reprinted with permission.

Gaylen J. Byker. "Reflections on the 2005 Commencement." Reprinted with the permission of Gaylen J. Byker, Office of the President, Calvin College.

David Carr. "On Covers of Many Magazines, a Full Racial Palette Is Still Rare" from *The New York Times*, November 18, 2002. Copyright © 2002 by The New York Times Company. Reprinted with permission.

Sandra Cisneros. Excerpt from "Bien Pretty" from *Woman Hollering Creek and Other Stories*. Copyright © 1991 by Sandra Cisneros. Reprinted with the permission of Susan Bergholz Literary Services, New York.

Randy Cohen. "Between the Sexes" from *The New York Times*, October 27, 2002. Copyright © 2002 by Randy Cohen. Reprinted with the permission of the author. Letters to the Editor in response to this piece are all reprinted by permission of the authors.

Commercial Closet Association. "Mainstream/Business-to-Business Advertising Best Practices" from <www.commercialcloset.org>. Reprinted with the permission of The Commercial Closet Association.

Concerned Faculty, Staff, and Emeriti of Calvin College. "An Open Letter to the President of the United States of America, George W. Bush" from *Grand Rapids (Michigan) Press*, May 21, 2005. Reprinted by permission.

Ruth Conniff. "Title IX: Political Football" from *The Nation*, March 24, 2003. Reprinted with the permission of *The Nation*. For subscription information, call 1-800-333-8536. Portions of each week's *Nation* magazine can be accessed at <http://www.thenation.com>.

Bryan Curtis. "Cheerleaders: What to Do about Them?" from *Slate*, April 1, 2005. Copyright © 2005 by Washington Post.Newsweek Interactive Co. LLC. Reprinted with the permission of United Media.

Meghan Daum. "Those Unnerving Ads Using 'Real' Women" from *The Los Angeles Times*, August 2, 2005. Reprinted with the permission of the author.

Craig R. Dean. Excerpt from "Legalize Gay Marriage" from *The New York Times* (1991). Copyright © 1991 by The New York Times Company. Reprinted with permission.

Alan M. Dershowitz. "Testing Speech Codes" from *The Boston Globe Index* (2002). Reprinted with permission of the author.

Gregory Dicum. Excerpt from "GREEN Flaming SUVs: A Conversation with Convicted Ecoterrorist Jeff Luers" from *The San Francisco Chronicle* (June 22, 2005). Reprinted with the permission of Gregory Dicum.

Ariel Dorfman. "If Only We All Spoke Two Languages" from *The New York Times*, June 24, 1998. Copyright © 1998 by The New York Times Company. Reprinted with permission.

Dinesh D'Souza. "America the Beautiful: What We're Fighting For" from *What's So Great About America*. Copyright © 2002 by Dinesh D'Souza. Reprinted with the permission of Regnery Publishing, Inc.

Firoozeh Dumas. "The 'F Word'" from *Funny in Farsi: A Memoir of Growing Up Iranian in America*. Copyright © 2003 by Firoozeh Dumas. Used by permission of Villard Books, a division of Random House, Inc.

Michael J. Ellis. "Once More unto the Breach" from *The Dartmouth Review*, April 8, 2005. Reprinted with permission.

Jennifer L. Ernst and Matthew Barge. "Abortion Distortions: Senators from Both Sides Make False Claims about *Roe v. Wade*" from <FactCheck.org>. Copyright © 2005 by the Annenberg Public Policy Center of the University of Pennsylvania. Reprinted with the permission of <FactCheck.org>.

Hannah Fairfield. "America: Not Their First Choice" from *The New York Times*, July 3, 2005. Copyright © 2005 by The New York Times Company. Reprinted with permission.

Peter Ferrara. Excerpt from "What Is an American?" from *National Review Online* (September 25, 2001). Copyright © 2001 by *National Review*, <www.nationalreview.com>. Reprinted by permission.

Stanley Fish. "'Intellectual Diversity': The Trojan Horse of a Dark Design" from *The Chronicle Review*, February 13, 2004. Reprinted with the permission of the author.

Samuel G. Freedman. "It's Latino Parents Speaking Out on Bilingual Education Failures" from *The New York Times*, July 14, 2004. Copyright © 2004 by The New York Times Company. Reprinted with permission.

Thomas L. Friedman. Excerpt from "Revolution Is U.S." from *The Lexus and the Olive Tree: Understanding Globalization*. Copyright © 1999 by Thomas L. Friedman. Reprinted with the permission of Farrar, Straus & Giroux, LLC.

Jessica Gavora. "Tilt! Time's Up for Title IX Sports" from *The American Spectator*, May/June 2002. Reprinted with permission.

Nick Gillespie. Excerpt from "Star Wars, Nothing But Star Wars" (May 19, 2005) from ReasonOnline, <www.reason.com/hod/ng051905.shtml>. Copyright © 2005 by *Reason* Magazine, <www.reason.com>. Reprinted with permission.

Dana Gioia. "Why Literature Matters" from *The Boston Globe* (April 10, 2005). Copyright © 2005 by Dana Gioia. Reprinted with permission.

Ellen Goodman. "The Culture of Thin Bites Fiji" from *The Boston Globe*, May 1999. Copyright © 1999 by The Boston Globe Newspaper Co./Washington Post Writers Group. Reprinted with the permission of The Washington Post Writers Group.

W. Charisse Goodman. "One Picture Is Worth a Thousand Diets" from *The Invisible Woman: Confronting Weight Prejudice in America*. Copyright © 1995 by W. Charisse Goodman. Reprinted with the permission of Gurze Books.

Laurie Goodstein. "More Religion, but Not the Old-Time Kind" from *The New York Times*, January 9, 2005. Copyright © 2005 by The New York Times Company. Reprinted with permission.

William M. Gray and Philip J. Klotzback. Excerpt from "Forecast of Atlantic Hurricane Activity for September and October 2005 and Seasonal Update through August" (September 2, 2005), <http://hurricane.atmos.colostate.edu/

forecasts/2005/sep2005/>. Reprinted with the permission of Dr. William M. Gray, Department of Atmospheric Science, Colorado State University.

Chong-suk Han. "Gay Asian-American Male Seeks Home" from *The Gay and Lesbian Review*, September–October 2005. Reprinted with permission.

Mark Hertsgaard. "The Oblivious Empire" from *The Eagle's Shadow: Why America Fascinates and Infuriates the World*. Copyright © 2002 by Mark Hertsgaard. Reprinted with the permission of Farrar, Straus & Giroux, LLC.

Frederick M. Hess. "Schools of Reeducation?" from *The Washington Post* (February 5, 2006). Reprinted with the permission of the author.

Leslie Heywood. "Despite the Positive Rhetoric about Women's Sports, Female Athletes Face a Culture of Sexual Harassment" from *The Chronicle of Higher Education*, January 1999. Copyright © 1999 by Leslie Heywood. Reprinted with the permission of the author.

David Horowitz. "In Defense of Intellectual Diversity" from *The Chronicle Review*, February 13, 2004. Copyright © 2004 by David Horowitz. Reprinted with the permission of the author. "Academic Bill of Rights." Reprinted with the permission of the Students for Academic Freedom.

Langston Hughes. "Harlem—A Dream Deferred" from *Collected Poems of Langston Hughes*. Copyright © 1994 by the Estate of Langston Hughes. Used by permission of Alfred A. Knopf, a division of Random House, Inc.

Josef Joffe. "The Perils of Soft Power" from *Überpower: The Imperial Temptation of America*. Copyright © 2006 by Josef Joffe. Used by permission of W. W. Norton & Company, Inc. Accompanying photograph by Patrick Tourneboeuf/Tendance Floue. Reprinted by permission.

Sarah Karnasiewicz. "The Campus Crusade for Guys" from <Salon.com> (2/15/06). Copyright © 2006. Reprinted with permission.

Armen Keteyian. Excerpt from "Bats Should Crack, Not Skulls" from *The Sporting News* (June 24, 2002). Copyright © 2002 by Armen Keteyian. Reprinted with the permission of the author.

Lan Cao. "The Gift of Language" excerpt from *Monkey Bridge*. Copyright © 1997 by Lan Cao. Used by the permission of Viking Penguin, a division of Penguin Group (USA) Inc.

Michael Lassell. Excerpt from "How to Watch Your Brother Die." Copyright © 1985 by Michael Lassell. Reprinted with the permission of the author.

Chang-rae Lee. "Mute in an English-Only World" from *The New York Times* (April 18, 1996), Op-Ed. Copyright © 1996 by The New York Times Company. Reprinted with permission.

Yiyun Li. "Passing Through" from *The New York Times Magazine*, September 25, 2005. Reprinted with the permission of the author.

James Lindgren. Excerpt from a review of Michael Bellesiles, *Arming America* from *Yale Law Review* 111 (2002). Reprinted with permission.

Dahlia Lithwick. "How Do You Solve the Problem of Scalia?" from *Slate* (March 30, 2006). Copyright © 2006 by Washington Post.Newsweek Interactive Co. LLC. Reprinted by permission of United Media.

Juliet Macur. "Rowing Scholarships Available. No Experience Necessary" from *The New York Times*, May 28, 2004. Copyright © 2004 by The New York Times Company. Reprinted with permission.

Katherine S. Mangan. "Association Moves to Strengthen Diversity Requirements for Accreditation of Law Schools" from *The Chronicle of Higher Education*,

February 14, 2006. Copyright © 2006 by The Chronicle of Higher Education. Reprinted with permission.

Myriam Marquez. "Why and When We Speak Spanish in Public" from *The Orlando Sentinel* June 28, 1999. Copyright © 1999 by The Orlando Sentinel. Reprinted with permission.

Michael Medved. "That's Entertainment? Hollywood's Contribution to Anti-Americanism Abroad" from *The National Interest* (Summer 2002). Reprinted with the permission of the author.

Walter Benn Michaels. "Diversity's False Solace" from *The New York Times*, April 11, 2004. Copyright © 2004 by Walter Benn Michaels. Reprinted with permission.

Barbara Munson. "Common Themes and Questions about the Use of 'Indian' Logos." Copyright © 1998 by Barbara Munson. Reprinted with the permission of the author.

Azar Nafisi. "Mysterious Connections That Link Us Together" from *This I Believe*. Copyright © 2006 by This I Believe, Inc. Reprinted with the permission of Henry Holt and Company, LLC.

Peggy Noonan. Excerpt from "Stand Up and Take It Like an American" from *Opinion Journal* (November 29, 2002). Copyright © 2002 by Peggy Noonan and *The Wall Street Journal*. Reprinted with the permission of William Morris Agency, LLC on behalf of the author.

Kathleen Norris. Excerpt from "Little Girls in Church" from *Little Girls in Church*. Copyright © 1995 by Kathleen Norris. Reprinted with the permission of University of Pittsburgh Press.

Anne-Marie O'Connor. "Not Only Natalee Is Missing" from *The Los Angeles Times*, August 5, 2005. Copyright © 2005 by *The Los Angeles Times*. Reprinted with permission.

The Onion. "Graphic Artist Carefully Assigns Ethnicities to Anthropomorphic Recyclables" from *The Onion*, August 27, 2003. Copyright © 2003 by The Onion, Inc. Reprinted with permission. <www.theonion.com>.

P. J. O'Rourke. "Mass Transit Hysteria" from *Opinion Journal* (March 16, 2005). Copyright © 2005 by Dow Jones & Company, Inc. All rights reserved.

Michael Osofsky. "The Psychological Experience of Security Officers Who Work with Executions" from *Stanford Undergraduate Research Journal* (May 2002). Reprinted with the permission of the author.

Scott Ott. "Poll: Most Americans Not in Iraq" from <www.ScrappleFace.com> (September 23, 2005). Reprinted with the permission of the author, editor/anchor, <ScrappleFace.com>, daily news satire site.

Jon Pareles. "The Case against Coldplay" from *The New York Times* (June 5, 2005). Copyright © 2005 by The New York Times Company. Reprinted with permission.

Lynn Peril. Excerpt from "Introduction" from *Pink Think: Becoming a Woman in Many Easy Lessons*. Copyright © 2002 by Lynn Peril. Reprinted with the permission of W. W. Norton & Company, Inc.

Pew Global Attitudes Project. "Among Wealthy Nations . . . U.S. Stands Alone in Its Embrace of Religion" (Pew Research Center, December 2002). Copyright © 2002 by The Pew Research Center. Reprinted with the permission of the Pew Global Attitudes Project.

Pew Hispanic Center/Kaiser Family Foundation. Excerpts [approximately 1820 words] from "2002 National Survey of Latinos" from <www.pewhispanic.org>.

Copyright © 2002 by The Pew Hispanic Center, a Pew Research Center project, <www.pewhispanic.org>. Reprinted with permission.

Mary Pipher. "Language" and "High School" from *The Middle of Everywhere: Helping Refugees Enter the American Community*. Copyright © 2002 by Mary Pipher. Reprinted with the permission of Harcourt, Inc.

Mariam Rahmani. "Wearing a Head Scarf Is My Choice as a Muslim: Please Respect It" from *Austin American-Statesman*, July 16, 2005. Copyright © 2005 by Mariam Rahmani. Reprinted with the permission of the author.

Tania Ralli. "Who's a Looter? In Storm's Aftermath, Pictures Kick Up a Different Kind of Tempest" from *The New York Times*, September 5, 2005. Copyright © 2005 by The New York Times Company. Reprinted with permission.

John Rickford. "Suite for Ebony *and* Phonics" from *Discover*, December 1997. Copyright © 1997. Reprinted with the permission of *Discover*.

David Rieff. "Their Hearts and Minds?" from *The New York Times*, September 4, 2005. Copyright © 2005 by David Rieff. Reprinted with the permission of The Wylie Agency, Inc. Accompanying photograph copyright © Ashley Gilbertson/AURORA. Accompanying table copyright © 2005 by Pew Research Center. Reprinted with permission.

Naomi Schaefer Riley. "Introduction" to *God on the Quad: How Religious Colleges and the Missionary Generation Are Changing America*. Copyright © 2005 by Naomi Schaefer Riley. Reprinted with the permission of St. Martin's Press, LLC.

Steve Rushin. "Hip Unchecked" from *Sports Illustrated*, June 21, 1999. Copyright © 1999 by Time, Inc. Courtesy of *Sports Illustrated*. All Rights Reserved.

Antonin Scalia. "God's Justice and Ours" from *First Things: The Journal of Religion and Public Life*, May 2002. Reprinted with permission.

Janny Scott. "Foreign Born in U.S. at Record High" from *The New York Times*, February 7, 2002. Copyright © 2002 by The New York Times Company. Reprinted with permission.

William Sea. "Advertising Sets Double Standard for the Male Gender" from *The Battalion* November 2005. Copyright © 2005 by *The Battalion*. Reprinted with the permission of Texas A & M University Press.

Jim Shore. "Play with Our Name" from *The New York Times*, August 27, 2005. Copyright © 2005 by The New York Times Company. Reprinted with permission.

Tom Sorensen. "Dress Code Suitable Only to NBA Suits" from *The Charlotte Observer*, October 26, 2005. Reprinted with the permission of *The Charlotte Observer*.

Jane Stern. Review of Judith Moore's *Fat Girl: A True Story* from *The New York Times Book Review*, March 27, 2005. Copyright © 2005 by The New York Times Company. Reprinted with permission.

Seth Stevenson. Excerpt from "Tangled Up in Boobs" from *Slate* (April 12, 2004), <www.slate.com>. Copyright © 2004 by Slate. Reprinted with the permission of United Media.

Larry Stewart. "Barkley Fully Supports NBA's New Dress Code" from *The Los Angeles Times* October 21, 2005. Copyright © 2005 by The Los Angeles Times. Reprinted with permission. Reprinted with the permission of Tribune Media Services.

Margaret Talbot. Excerpt from "Men Behaving Badly" from *The New York Times Magazine*, October 13, 2002. Copyright © 2002 by The New York Times Company. Reprinted with permission.

Amy Tan. "Mother Tongue" copyright © 1990 by Amy Tan. First appeared in *The Threepenny Review.* Reprinted with the permission of the author and the Sandra Dijkstra Literary Agency.

Deborah Tannen. "Can We Talk?" from *You're Wearing That? Understanding Mothers and Daughters in Conversation.* Copyright © 2006 by Deborah Tannen. Used by permission of Random House, Inc.

John Tierney. "Where Cronies Dwell" [original title "Where Cronies on the Left Can Be Found"] from *The New York Times*, October 12, 2005. Copyright © 2005 by The New York Times Company. Reprinted with permission. Letters to the Editor in response to this article are all reprinted by permission of the authors.

The Travesty. "Mundane Events Made Humorous, Entertaining by Parody News Format" and "Headline Catches Reader's Attention; Interest Wanes after Semi-Analysis of Caption" from *Texas Travesty* (November/December 2003). Copyright © 2003. Reprinted with permission.

Guy Trebay. "When Did Skivvies Get Rated NC-17?" from *The New York Times,* August 1, 2004. Copyright © 2004 by The New York Times. Reprinted with permission.

David D. Troutt. "Defining Who We Are in Society" from *The Los Angeles Times*, January 1997. Copyright © 1997 by David D. Troutt. Reprinted with the permission of the author.

Rob Walker. "Social Lubricant: How a Marketing Campaign Became the Catalyst for a Societal Debate" from *The New York Times*, September 4, 2005. Copyright © 2005 by The New York Times Company. Reprinted with permission.

Thad Williamson. "Bad as They Wanna Be" from *The Nation,* August 1998. Reprinted with the permission of *The Nation.* For subscription information, call 1-800-333-8536. Portions of each week's *Nation* magazine can be accessed at <http://www.thenation.com>.

Waleed Ziad. "Jihad's Fresh Face" from *The New York Times,* September 16, 2005. Copyright © 2005 by The New York Times Company. Reprinted with permission.

John Zwier. "An Opportunity for Intelligent Debate" from *Chimes: The Newspaper of Calvin College* 99, Issue 28 (May 6, 2005). Reprinted with permission.

Illustrations

p. i: (clockwise from top left) Copyright © Royalty-Free/Corbis; Copyright © Andersen Ross/Jupiter Images; Copyright © Bob Sacha/Corbis; Copyright © Ryan Red Corn from Red Hand Media; Copyright © Webstream/Alamy; Copyright © StockTrek/Getty Images; Copyright © Joseph Sohm, ChromoSohm, Inc./Corbis; p. iv: (l–r) Courtesy <www.adbusters.org>; Kevin Daley/Ellis Island Immigration Museum, National Park Service; (foreground) Copyright © Jerome Sessini/In Visu/Corbis; (background) Office of National Drug Control Policy/Partnership for a Drug-Free America; (foreground) Dave Martin/AP/Wide World Photos; (background) Courtesy The Ad Council; (l–r) Copyright © Clementine Hope/nb illustration; Anti-Defamation League, photo by Frank Ishman; Jeff Kowalsky/European Pressphoto Agency/Corbis; p. 5: cover, *Dave Barry Hits below the Beltway*, by Dave Barry, Copyright © 2001, used by permission of Random House, Inc.; p. 6: (b) Copyright © Linda Eddy; pp. 9 and xvii 1st: Copyright © Kelly Owen/ZUMA/Corbis; p. 10: Georgia O'Keeffe, *Rust Red Hills,* 1930. Oil on canvas, 16 x 30 inches. Sloan

Fund Purchase, 62.02, Valparaiso University. Copyright © Brauer Museum of Art. Permission granted by the Artists Rights Society; pp.11 and xvii 2nd: Stephen Jaffe/AFP/Getty Images; p. 13: Copyright © Lower Manhattan Development Corporation, 2004; p. 14: Copyright © *The New Yorker* Collection 1999 Donald Reilly from <cartoonbank.com>. All Rights Reserved; p. 16: Scala, Art Resource, NY; p. 18: Copyright © Stapleton Collection/Corbis; pp. 22 and xvii 3rd: Copyright © Branson Reynolds/Index Stock Imagery; p. 25: Alexander Tamargo/Getty Images; p. 26: Copyright © Bettmann/Corbis; p. 28: Copyright © Viviane Moos/Corbis; p. 30: Copyright © Alexei Kalmykov/Reuters/Corbis; p. 31: Copyright © *The New Yorker* Collection 1999 Mick Stevens from <cartoonbank.com>. All Rights Reserved; p. 34: Courtesy, *Soul Sistah*; p. 37: Courtesy Sharon Clahchischilliage; p. 38: Evelyn Hockstein/Polaris Images; p. 40: EPA; p. 41: Courtesy *Atlantic Monthly*; p. 43: Copyright © Sean John. Reprinted with permission; p. 44: BumperArt; pp. 46, 48 and xviii 2nd: Courtesy <www.adbusters.org>; p. 50: Advertising created by PlowShare Group for Save the Children; p. 53: Copyright © *The New Yorker* Collection 1992 Robert Mankoff from <cartoonbank.com>. All Rights Reserved; pp. 54 and xviii 1st: Copyright © Nicholas Kristof; pp. 55 and xviii 3rd: Copyright © Carlos Barria/Reuters/Corbis; p. 58: (l) <StampandShout.com>; (r) Copyright © <BumperTalk.com>; pp. 61 and xviii 4th: Copyright © Brian Snyder/Reuters/Corbis; p. 64: Copyright © 2004 Reprise Records; p. 66: (l) Frank Capri/Getty Images; (r) Evelyn Floret/TimeLife Pictures/Getty Images; p. 72: The Advertising Archives; p. 77: (l–r) Copyright © Kimberly White/Reuters/Corbis; Jay Laprete/AP/Wide World Photos; Kathy Willens/AP/Wide World Photos; Yves Logghe/AP/Wide World Photos; pp. 79 and xix 1st: Copyright © Bettmann/Corbis; p. 80:<www.protestwarrior.com>; pp. 87 and xix 2nd: Cindy Clark and Alejandro Gonzalez/*USA Today* Copyright © 2006. Reprinted with permission; p. 89: Copyright © 2002 The Friedman Foundation; pp. 103 and xix 3rd: (l) Dave Hogan/Getty Images; (r) Chris Farina/Getty Images; p. 107: Courtesy Jo-Ann Mort; p. 111: Texas Dept. of Transportation/Sherry Matthews Advocacy Marketing; p. 114: <caglecartoons.com/español>; p. 116: Shelley Eades/*San Francisco Chronicle*; pp. 117–18: Copyright © zombie; p. 122: (l) Copyright © Lionsgate Films; (r, p. xvii l, and p. xix 4th) Copyright © Warner Brothers Entertainment, Inc.; p. 126: Courtesy Milena Ateya; p. 140 and p. xx 1st, 2nd, and r: The Advertising Archives; p. 143: Manuscripts and Special Collections, New York State Library; p. 145: National Archives; p. 146: AP/Wide World Photos; p. 151: Copyright © Charles Barsotti from <cartoonbank.com>. All Rights Reserved; p. 154: *Mushrooms: An Introduction to Familiar North American Species*, text by James Kavanagh, illustrations by Raymond Leung. Used by permission of Waterford Press; pp. 173 and xx 3rd: Courtesy General Electric; p. 176: (t and p. xxi 2nd) Collection of The New-York Historical Society; (b) Copyright © David Luneau; p. 177: Cornell Lab of Ornithology; p. 180: Copyright © Robin Raffer; p. 181: National Hurricane Center; p. 183: Michael Newman/PhotoEdit, Inc.; pp. 189 and xx 4th: Copyright © Bettmann/Corbis; pp. 191 and xxi 1st: cover, *Epileptic*, by David B., used by permission, Pantheon Books/Random House, Inc.; p. 192: National Endowment for the Arts; p. 193: National Archives; p. 201: Mel Evans/AP/Wide World Photos; p. 203: US-Ireland Alliance; p. 220: Copyright © 2002 Brad Roberts <www .lowdiameter.com>; p. 221: (t) Copyright © Khalil Bendib/The Muslim Observer; (b) Copyright © Robin Nelson/PhotoEdit, Inc.; p. 224: Courtesy Ford; p. 225: Copyright © 2006 FOX News Network; pp. 227 and xxi 3rd: Copyright © Robin Raffer; pp. 243

and xxi 4th: Fox Searchlight Pictures/Photofest; p. 252: Kristin Cole; pp. 253 and xxii 1st: Frazer Harrison/Getty Images; p. 256: Copyright © Ron Kimball Stock; p. 260: Lucasfilm, Ltd./Twentieth Century Fox Film Corp./Photofest; pp. 263 and xxii 2nd: Bud Freund/Index Stock Imagery; p. 264: Courtesy UTStarcom; p. 267: (l and p. xxii 3rd) Chris Weeks/AP Wide World Photos; (r) Copyright © Bettmann/Corbis; p. 276: Courtesy Nisey Williams; p. 281: Scott Gries/Getty Images; pp. 287 and xxii 4th: Karen Kasmauski/*National Geographic*; p. 290: Mark Alan Stamaty/<slate.com> Copyright © 2006 Washington Post.Newsweek Interactive Co. LLC; pp. 294–96: <http://fightingmalaria.org>; p. 297: J Griffis Smith/TxDot; pp. 299 and xxiii 1st: Continental Distributing, Inc./Photofest; p. 304: <http:// news.bbc.co.uk>; p. 305: Cox & Forkum; p. 329: (t and p. xxiii 2nd) John Ruszkiewicz; (b and p. xxiii 3rd) Glen Canyon Institute; p. 333: Courtesy, Americans for the Arts; p. 334: Copyright © Yvonne Baron Estes, *Gardening Among Deer Without Hiring a Mountain Lion*, Ponyfoot Press; pp. 337 and xxiii 4th: Mary Godleski/AP/Wide World Photos; p. 342: Courtesy San Diego Chargers; p. 343: <http://www.sierralarana.com>; p. 344: NASA; p. 352: Photographer: Christina S. Murrey, University of Texas at Austin; p. 371: (tl and p. xxiv 2nd) DesignPics Inc./Index Stock Imagery; (tr) ThinkStock LLC/Index Stock Imagery; (b) The Image Bank/Index Stock Imagery; p. 372: Copyright © *The New Yorker* Collection 1987 Al Ross from <cartoonbank.com>. All Rights Reserved; pp. 376 and xxiv 3rd: Warner Brothers/Photofest; p. 385: *The Boondocks* Copyright © 2006 Aaron McGruder. Dist. by Universal Press Syndicate. Reprinted with permission. All Rights Reserved; pp. 387 and xxiv 1st: Lionel Cironneau/AP/Wide World Photos; p. 388: Reprinted by permission of *Ironic Times*; pp. 395 and xxiv 4th: David Kramer/<www.margaretcho.com>; p. 397: Reprinted with permission of *The Onion* Copyright © 2005; p. 400: John Ruszkiewicz; p. 402: Courtesy *Phroth*, Penn State; p. 403: Cox & Forkum; p. 404: Reprinted with permission of *The Onion* Copyright © 1998 by Onion, Inc.; p. 405: *Texas Travesty*, The University of Texas at Austin; p. 406: (back) Courtesy Scott Ott; (front) Courtesy <CNN.com>; p. 413: Copyright © Ron Kimball Stock; p. 414: (t and p. xxv 1st) Art Resource, NY; (b) Copyright © Bettmann/Corbis; p. 416: (both) National Postal Museum; p. 417: (l, p. xxiv r, and p. xxv 2nd) Mick Roessler/Index Stock Imagery; (r) AES Group. *New Liberty*, 1996, from the series *AES-Witnesses of the Future. Islamic Project* (1996–2006), digital collage, variable dimensions, variable media. Courtesy M. Guelman Gallery, Moscow, and artists. Permission granted by the Artists Rights Society; pp. 419–20: <uac -tutoring.stanford.edu/tutor>; p. 423: <www.benettongroup.com>. Reprinted with permission; p. 425: (l–r) The Granger Collection, Office of the Counsel to the President at the White House, D.C.; Courtesy McDonald's; Courtesy Philip Morris; p. 426: Copyright © 2005 Catherine Harrell; p. 429: Copyright © Ron Kimball Stock; p. 430: Copyright © 2006 SEIU, Service Employees International Union ® CTW, CLC; p. 432: Copyright © 2006 Google; pp. 435 and xxv 3rd: Franck Fife/AFP/Getty Images; p. 436: NASA; p. 439: National Portrait Gallery, London; p. 443: (t–b and p. xxv 4th): Copyright © Daily Kos. Reprinted with permission; USDA Rural Development; Dennis MacDonald/ PhotoEdit Inc.; p. 444: Courtesy IBM; p. 448: AP/Wide World Photos; p. 450: TM Copyright © 2001 FOX; pp. 454, 456, 458: Copyright © Frank Miller; p. 464: Courtesy American Legacy Foundation; pp. 473 and xxvi 1st: Jay Berkowitz-L.A.W.A.; pp. 475 and xxvi 2nd: Jim MacMillan/AP/Wide World Photos; p. 477: Copyright © *The New Yorker* Collection 1989 George Price from <cartoonbank.com>. All Rights Reserved; p. 480: Copyright ©

<littlegreenfootballs.com>. Reprinted with permission; p. 485: Copyright © 2006 Google; pp. 495 and xxvii 3rd: Office of National Drug Control Policy/Partnership for a Drug-Free America; p. 496: Copyright © *The New Yorker* Collection 2001 David Sipress from <cartoonbank.com>. All Rights Reserved; pp. 498 and xxvi 3rd: Courtesy World Wildlife Fund; p. 500: Copyright © *The New Yorker* Collection 2001 Robert Weber from <cartoonbank .com>. All Rights Reserved; pp. 502 and xxvi 4th: Mike Stewart/Corbis Sygma; p. 504: Sage Stossel, *The Atlantic* Online; pp. 507, xxvi r, and xxvii 1st: Bill Aron/PhotoEdit, Inc.; pp. 510 and xxvii 2nd: Eric Risberg/AP/Wide World Photos; p. 515: Courtesy The Lexicomm Group; p. 516: U.S. Copyright Office; pp. 518 and xxvii 4th: Courtesy <www.adbusters.org>; p. 520: *Doonesbury* Copyright © 2002 G. B. Trudeau. Reprinted with permission of Universal Press Syndicate. All Rights Reserved; pp. 530 and xxviii 1st: Reed Saxon/AP/Wide World Photos; p. 531: (l) Courtesy *Vanity Fair*; (r) Courtesy *Tin House*; p. 537: Copyright © National Audubon Society. Reprinted with permission; pp. 540 and xxviii 2nd: Thir Khan/AFP/Getty Images; pp. 543 and xxviii 3rd: Juan Castillo/AFP/Getty Images; p. 547: Bloomberg News; pp. 551 and xxviii 4th: Copyright © MLA; p. 567: Copyright © Emily Lesk; p. 570: Copyright © American Psychological Association; p. 588: Copyright © *The New Yorker* Collection 2000 Pat Byrnes from <cartoonbank.com>. All Rights Reserved; p. 590: Reed Saxon/AP/Wide World Photos; pp. 601 and xxix 3rd: Matthew Bandsuch; p. 602: The Kobal Collection/Picture-Desk; p. 603: (l) Copyright © Bettmann/Corbis; (r) Copyright © Nancy Kaszerman/ZUMA/Corbis; p. 606: Archive Photos/Getty Images; p. 612: Courtesy, *The New York Times*; p. 614: Copyright © Clementine Hope/nb illustration; p. 616: Scala/Art Resource, NY; pp. 618 and xxix 4th: Nam Y Huh/AP/Wide World Photos; p. 619: (l) Erich Lessing/Art Resource, N.Y.; (r and xxix 1st): Boston Women's Health Book Collective, Inc.; p. 623: Norman Y. Lono/*The New York Times*; pp. 626 and xxix 2nd: Copyright © Fatih Saribas/Reuters/Corbis; p. 627: Tony Cenicola/*The New York Times*; p. 629: Copyright © Toby Old; p. 630: Mikhaela Reid; p. 631: Jason Stirman; pp. 636 and xxx 2nd: Geo Vittoratos; p. 637: Latino Comedy Project/Teatro Humanidad. Reprinted with permission; p. 638: Copyright © 2005, Michael Kabbash, <www.graphix4change.com>; p. 640: (l) Dave Martin/AP/Wide World Photos; (r and p. xxx 1st) Chris Graythen/Getty Images; p. 642: <www.sharpshooter .com>. Reprinted with permission; p. 654: <www.commercialcloset.com>. Reprinted with permission; pp. 670 and xxix l: Reprinted with permission of *The Onion* Copyright © 2003; p. 675: Kevin Fitzsimmons/*The New York Times*; pp. 676 and xxxi 2nd: Matt King/Getty Images; pp. 677 and xxx 3rd: Kevin Fitzsimmons/*The New York Times*; p. 679: *The Daily Texan*. Reprinted with permission; p. 690: Illustration by Robert Grossman; pp. 696, 699: Illustrations by Julie Delton; p. 702: Copyright © ALLARM; pp. 710 and xxx 4th: Scott Halleran/Getty Images; p. 712: Lucy A. Ganje; p. 713: Copyright © Lalo Alcaraz; p. 714: Copyright © Thom Little Moon; p. 718: Copyright © Jim McDonald/Corbis; p. 723: Elsa Hasch/Allsport/Getty Images; p. 724: Copyright © Jeff Kowalsky/epa/Corbis; p. 725: (t) Jim Cummins/NBAE/Getty Images; (b) Lisa Blumenfeld/Getty Images; p. 727: (l) Andrew D. Bernstein/NBAE/ Getty Images; (m) Jesse D. Garrabrant/NBAE/Getty Images; (r and p. xxxi 1st) David Sherman/NBAE/Getty Images; p. 730: AFP/AFP/Getty Images; p. 731: Richard Ellis/Getty Images; p. 737: Copyright © Tom Meyer/*San Francisco Chronicle*; p. 740: Courtesy of the Ellis Island Immigration Museum, National Park Service/USDI; pp. 741 and xxxi 3rd: Kevin Daley/Ellis Island Immigration Museum, National Park

Service; pp. 752 and xxxii 1st: Rolando Briseño; pp. 761 and xxxi 4th: Copyright © B. Martinez Roger-Viollet/The Image Works; p. 765: Copyright © David Wells/The Image Works; p. 772: Joel Gordon; p. 777: Copyright © Bettmann/Corbis; p. 781: National Institute of Mental Health; p. 797: Photofest; p. 798: Ed Bailey/AP/Wide World Photos; p. 801: Illustration by Tim Bower; p. 811: Illustration by Christian Clayton, <www.claytonbrothers.com>; p. 820: Library of Congress; pp. 821 and xxxii 4th: Photo by Carl Van Vechten reprinted with permission of his estate; photo courtesy of the James Weldon Johnson Memorial Collection, Beinecke Library, Yale University; pp. 822–826, p. xxxii 2nd and 3rd, and p. xxxiii 1st and 2nd: Office of National Drug Control Policy/Partnership for a Drug-Free America; p. 828: Illustration by Dan Picasso; p. 838: (t) Copyright © *The New Yorker* Collection 1992 Mick Stevens from <cartoonbank.com>. All Rights Reserved; (bl) Copyright © *The New Yorker* Collection 1995 Leo Cullum from <cartoonbank.com>. All Rights Reserved; (br) Copyright © William Hamilton from <cartoonbank.com>. All Rights Reserved; p. 839: (l) Copyright © *The New Yorker* Collection 1997 Roz Chast from <cartoonbank .com>. All Rights Reserved; (r) Copyright © *The New Yorker* Collection 1995 Peter Steiner from <cartoonbank.com>. All Rights Reserved; p. 845 (t and p. xxxiv 2nd): Jacob Silberberg/Getty Images; (b and p. xxxiii 3rd) Punit Paranjpe/Reuters/Corbis; p. 846: (t) Dita Alangkora/AP/Wide World Photos; (b and p. xxxiii 4th) Paolo Fridman; pp. 854 and xxxiv 1st: David Livingston/Getty Images; pp. 855, 857: Robert Maas; p. 873: Jeff Kowalsky/European Pressphoto Agency/Corbis; p. 875: Christian Alliance for Progress. Reprinted with permission; p. 898: Copyright © Jerome Sessini/In Visu/Corbis; pp. 901, 902: Courtesy The Ad Council; p. 904: U.S. Department of Justice, Civil Rights Division, 2004; p. 905: Sikhnet.com; pp. 906–907: Anti-Defamation League, photos by Frank Ishman; pp. 916–921, p. xxxiv 4th, and p. xxxv 1st: All, Courtesy Western Washington University; p. 923: Copyright © <salon.com>; p. 934: Mike Lester/Rome News Tribune/Cagle Cartoons, Inc.; p. 935: Dennis Draughon; p. 936: Mike Thompson/Detroit Free Press/Copley News Service; p. 937: (t) Signe Wilkinson/The Cartoonist Group; (b) Dean Camp; pp. 953 and xxxv 2nd: Warner Brothers/The Kobal Collection/Alex Bailey; p. 958: Copyright © Reuters/Corbis; pp. 973 and xxxv 3rd: Lars Leetaru; p. 975: (t) Copyright © King Features Syndicate; (b) Signe Wilkinson/The Cartoonist Group; pp. 987 and xxxv 4th: Tyler Hicks/*The New York Times*; p. 991: Copyright © David Suter; pp. 996 and xxxvi 1st: Ashley Gilbertson/Aurora; p. 999: Courtesy Anipas P. Delotavo Jr.; p. 1000: Courtesy Zaid Omar; p. 1001: Courtesy Jibby Yunibandhu; photograph by Prach Kongsubto Rohitchan; pp. 1020, xxxvi 2nd, and 1030: Copyright © Reuters/Corbis; pp. 1039 and xxxvi 3rd: Patrick Tourneboeuf/Tendance Floue; p. 1043: Copyright © Corbis; pp. 1051 and xxxvi 4th: Copyright © Bettmann/Corbis; p. 1061: Universal/ The Kobal Collection; p. 1070: Copyright © Les Stone/Sygma/Corbis; p. 1071: Copyright © China Features/Corbis Sygma; p. 1072: Copyright © Tatiana Markow/ Sygma/Corbis; p. 1073: Copyright © Koren Ziv/Corbis Sygma; p. 1074: Copyright © Haruyoshi Yamaguchi/Corbis Sygma; pp. 1075–1076: Copyright © John Van Hasselt/ Corbis Sygma; p. 1077: Copyright © Mohsen Shandiz/Sygma/Corbis.

INDEX